Curtin's California Land Use & Planning Law

PUBLISHER'S NOTE

Before you rely on the information in this book, be sure you are aware that some changes in the statutes or case law may have gone into effect since the date of publication. The book, moreover, provides general information about the law. Readers should consult their own attorneys before relying on the representations found herein.

THIRTY-FOURTH EDITION
2014

Curtin's California Land Use & Planning Law

CECILY TALBERT BARCLAY

MATTHEW S. GRAY

Copyright © 2014 by Perkins Coie LLP
All rights reserved.
Printed in the United States of America.

No part of this publication may be reproduced, stored in a retrieval system, or transmitted, in any form or by any means, electronic, mechanical, photocopied, recorded, or otherwise, without the prior written approval of the authors and the publisher.

Solano Press Books
Post Office Box 773
Point Arena, California 95468
tel: 800 931-9373
fax: 707 884-4109
email: spbooks@solano.com

Cover design: Catherine Courtenaye
Interior design and production: Catherine Courtenaye
Cover photographs: Jon E. Handel, RHAA, Solano Press Books

Index: Galen Schroeder

ISBN 978-1-938166-06-8

This book may be cited as follows:
Cecily Talbert Barclay and Matthew S. Gray
Curtin's California Land Use and Planning Law
(Solano Press, 34th ed. 2014)

Notice
This book is designed to assist you in understanding land use and planning law. It is necessarily general in nature and does not discuss all exceptions and variations to general rules. Also, it may not reflect the latest changes in the law. It is not intended as legal advice and should not be relied on to address legal problems. You should always consult an attorney for advice regarding your specific factual situation.

IN MEMORIAM
Daniel J. Curtin, Jr.
(1933–2006)

In the fall of 2006, Daniel J. Curtin, Jr., passed away unexpectedly from natural causes after seventy-three years of living a wonderful life, full of family and friends. Dan's professional life can be described as a never-ending passion to improve our understanding of the land use laws and regulations which govern our lives.

This year's edition is again dedicated to Dan's memory and spirit. Widely regarded as the "Dean" of land use and local government law, Dan received countless honors and awards for his leadership and service, including the Jefferson Fordham Lifetime Achievement Award from the State and Local Government Law Section of the American Bar Association; the International Municipal Lawyers Association Charles S. Rhyne Award for Lifetime Achievement in Municipal Law; the American Planning Association's Distinguished Leadership Award, recognizing more than two decades of writing and teaching and his support for planning ideas and education; and was named Honorary Life Member of the California Park and Recreation Society for his contributions to parklands.

He served as Chair of the State and Local Government Law Section of the American Bar Association in 2001–2002, and was past Chair of the Land Development, Planning and Zoning Section of the International Municipal Lawyers Association. Also, he was past Vice-Chair of the Executive Committee of the Real Property Law Section of the State Bar of California. He served as President of the City Attorneys' Department of the League of California Cities, as a member of the Board of Directors of the League, and as Regional Vice President of the International Municipal Lawyers Association. He was recognized on numerous "Best Lawyers" lists for the state and nation.

During his legal career, Dan shaped the general plan as the center point for land use decisionmaking. In *Lesher Communications v. City of Walnut Creek*, 52 Cal. 3d 551 (1990), the California Supreme Court adopted Dan's description of the general plan as the "constitution for all future development." Later, in *DeVita v. County of Napa*, 9 Cal. 5th 763 (1995), the court accepted the notion of "vertical consistency" that Dan had been teaching for years: that all key development decisions must be consistent with the general plan. Other notable decisions involving Dan include *Associated Home Builders, Inc. v. City of Walnut Creek*, 4 Cal. 3d 633 (1971), wherein the court upheld a city's police power to require developers to dedicate land or pay fees for park and recreation purposes.

Along with this text, Dan authored the *Subdivision Map Act Manual*, published by Solano Press, the *Subdivision Map Act and the Development Process*, published by California Continuing Education of the Bar, as well as hundreds of articles. He was a frequent lecturer for University of California Extension and Continuing Education of the Bar (CEB) and was an adjunct professor for the University of San Francisco Law School teaching Land Use Law. He also traveled extensively to provide land use expertise to the international community and to several developing nations.

A native San Franciscan, Dan was raised by Irish-immigrant parents. He earned his A.B. and J.D. from the University of San Francisco. After serving as an officer in the U.S. Army for eight years, Dan worked as Assistant Secretary for the California State Senate, as Counsel to the Assembly Committee on Local Government, and Deputy City Attorney for Richmond. From 1965 to 1982, Dan served as City Attorney of Walnut Creek. Dan then entered private practice and, in 1984, joined Van Voorhis & Skaggs, which later became part of Bingham McCutchen, LLP, where he continued to practice until his death. Dan visited over sixty-five countries, including several trips to his beloved Ireland, and voyaged on thirty-nine cruises, typically with many family members in tow.

While Dan's accolades and accomplishments are long, the list of planners and land use practitioners he guided and befriended is even longer. His skills as a mentor were legendary and Dan counted as friends virtually every planning director and city attorney in the state, as well as planning experts around the country and the world. He had an exceptional memory, often surprising people who had not seen him for many years by asking about their close relatives or children by name. Anyone involved in local government or land use in California knew of Dan or had been influenced by his work and teachings.

In a fitting tribute, the California League of Cities described Dan's most important contribution to the land use field:

> Dan's lasting professional legacy truly rests with his peers who loved and respected him. Dan was a mentor and a friend to two generations of land use professionals. He reveled in mentoring young attorneys and planners and making them feel part of his circle. He would take an interest in their careers and go out of his way to cite their work. Dan made his numerous friends feel like they were the most important person in his life. He loved hosting dinners at conferences and hearing about everyone's practices and his invitees relished the heady conversations and the wisdom he could share. His gracious, old-school style of lawyering and living—always courteous, respectful, and inquiring about family—will be enormously missed.

> The state of California is fortunate that Dan Curtin was so generous with his talent and shared his knowledge so freely. He trained countless lawyers, planners, commissioners, and elected officials. Many have asked, "who will replace him?" The answer is that this responsibility falls upon us all. He was a moral compass for the legal and planning profession. And now we must make our way without him.

Dan is survived by his younger sister, Kathleen Curtin, and his five children and eight grandchildren. Myrtle Rose, his wife of forty-six years, passed away in 2005. Dan is deeply missed by the legion of colleagues for whom he was such a valued inspiration, resource, and most of all, friend.

Chapters at a Glance

1	Local Land Use Authority	1
2	General Plan	9
3	Specific Plan	35
4	Zoning	39
5	Subdivisions	71
6	California Environmental Quality Act (CEQA)	139
7	Federal and State Wetland Regulation	179
8	Endangered Species Protections	217
9	Design Review, Historic Preservation, Williamson Act, Coastal Development, Stormwater, Prevailing Wage and Public Bidding	249
10	Vested Rights and Ability to Bind City by Contract	273
11	Regulatory Takings	287
12	Exactions: Dedications and Development Fees	319
13	Initiative and Referendum	357
14	Local Agency Formation Commissions (LAFCOs): Local Agency Boundary Changes	387
15	Affordable Housing	409
16	Sustainable Development	447
17	Rights of the Regulated	477
18	Enforcement of Land Use Laws	495
19	Land Use Litigation	503

Contents

Preface	xvii
Conventions in This Book	xx

CHAPTER 1
Local Land Use Authority — 1
- Police Power — 1
- Legislative Preemption — 5
- State Statutory Framework for Land Use Decisions — 6
- City Council — 6
- Planning Commission — 7
- Planning Staff — 8
- Public Meetings — 8

CHAPTER 2
General Plan — 9
- From Advisory Status to Constitution for Development — 9
- General Plan—The Constitution — 10
  - General Plan—Purposes and Contents; General Plan Guidelines
  - Legal Adequacy of the General Plan
    - Description of the mandatory elements • Optional (permissive) elements • Organization
  - Legal Implications of a Legally Inadequate General Plan
    - California Environmental Quality Act • Charter cities
  - Internal (Horizontal) Consistency
  - Consistency Between General Plan and Other Land Use and Development Actions (Vertical Consistency)
  - Consistency with Airport Land Use Plan
  - Procedure for Adoption and Amendment
  - Implementation and Annual Report
  - Checklist for General Plan Adequacy
    - Is it complete? • Is it informational, readable, and available to the public? • Is it internally consistent? • Is it consistent with state policy? • Does it cover all territory within its boundaries and outside its boundaries that relate to its planning? • Is it long-term in perspective? • Does it address all locally relevant issues? • Is it current? • Does it contain the statutory criteria required by state law as interpreted by the courts? • Are the diagrams or maps adequate? • Does it serve as a yardstick? • Does it contain an action plan or implementation plan? • Is it horizontally consistent? • Was it adopted correctly?
- Adoption of General Plans by New Cities, Revisions of Existing General Plans, and Related Approvals
- The General Plan as a Source of Dedications and Development Fees
- The General Plan as a Tool in Growth Management and Other Innovative Land Use Controls
- Judicial Review of the Adequacy of the General Plan

CHAPTER 3
Specific Plan — 35
- Introduction — 35
- Contents of a Specific Plan — 35
- Adoption — 36
- Interplay with CEQA — 36
- Judicial Review — 37

CHAPTER 4
Zoning — 39
- Zoning Defined — 39
- Application to Charter Cities — 39
- Judicial Review — 39
  - Presumption of Validity
  - Limited Role of Court Review—Policy Issue
- Enactment of Zoning Regulations — 41
  - In General
  - The Ordinance Must Be Reasonably Related to the Public Welfare
  - Zoning Must Be Consistent with the General Plan
  - Zoning Must Be Consistent with Airport Land Use Plan
  - Due Process Requirements
  - Sufficiency of Standards—Vagueness and Uncertainty
  - Adoption of a Zoning Ordinance
  - Motives
  - Zoning by Initiative and/or Referendum
  - No Formal Rules of Evidence; Effect of Procedural Errors
- Zoning and the First Amendment — 49
  - Regulation of Adult Businesses
  - Protection of Religious Exercise
- Administrative Zoning Relief—Variances—Conditional Use Permits — 54

In General
Variances
Conditional Use Permit
Nonconforming Uses
Voluntary and Required Repairs of Nonconforming Uses
Structural Alterations of Nonconforming Uses
Destruction of a Nonconforming Use by Fire or Other Catastrophic Events

Amortization   60

Other Types of Zoning   61
Form-Based Zoning
Prezoning
Interim Ordinance
Conditional Zoning
Specific Plan as Zoning
Planned-Unit Development

Inclusionary Zoning/Housing Programs   64

Applicability of Zoning to the Federal and State Governments   65
Federal Government
State Government

Applicability of Zoning to Joint Powers Agencies, School Districts, and County and Other Local Districts   66

Applicability of Zoning to Indian Lands   68

CHAPTER 5
Subdivisions   71

Introduction   71
Subdivision Map Act
Need for a local ordinance; applicable to charter cities • Preemption

Subdivisions Covered by the Map Act   73
What Is a Subdivision?

What Type of Map Is Required?   76
General Rule: Tentative and Final Map or Parcel Map?
Counting Parcels
Successive subdivisions • Remainder parcels • Conveyances to or from public entities and public utilities

Important Exemptions to Mapping Requirements   79
Lot Line Adjustments
"Second" Units
Conveyances to or from Public Entities and Public Utilities
Financing and Leasing of Certain Units
Condominium, Stock Cooperatives, and Community Apartment Projects
Conversions • Three-dimensional divisions
Agricultural Leases and Agricultural Labor Housing
Other Exemptions
Map Waivers
Condominium projects • Mobile home park conversions • Other parcel map waivers

Tentative Map Processing   84
Tentative Maps
Necessity for tentative maps • Local ordinances • Other regulations • Applicable time periods to act upon the tentative map
Time Limits Imposed by the Permit Streamlining Act
Notice and hearing; processing
Life of tentative maps
Initial life • Multiple final maps • Development agreements • Discretionary extensions • Statutory extensions • Moratoria • Litigation stays • Summary • Conditions imposed on extensions • Expiration of other permits issued in conjunction with a tentative map
Effect of Approval of Map on the Right to Develop—Vested Rights
Vesting Tentative Map
Background • Procedures
Effect of Annexation to City Upon Maps
Effect of Incorporation into a Newly Incorporated City

Conditions to Map Approval   100
In General
Conditions Imposed through the Subdivision Process
Specific Conditions Allowed by the Map Act and Local Ordinance
Parkland dedication • Adequate water supply • School site dedication • Reservations • Street and bicycle path dedications • Dedication for local transit facilities • Fees for drainage and sewer facilities • Fees for bridges and major thoroughfares • Groundwater recharge • Fees for transportation facilities • Supplemental improvements—reimbursement agreements • Soils investigations and reports • Setting of monuments • Grading and erosion control requirements • Public access to public resources and dedication of public easements along banks of rivers and streams • Energy conservation • Dedication for solar access easements • Indemnification • Off-site improvements • Standards and criteria for public improvements: residential subdivisions
Conditions Imposed Under City's Authority to Regulate "Design" and "Improvement" and Ensure General and Specific Plan Consistency
Map Act Requirements vs. General Plan Standards
Conditions That May Be Imposed Through the CEQA Process
Condominium, Stock Cooperative, and Community Apartment Project Conversions
Timing of Conditions and Subsequent Conditions
Refunds
Reconveyances

Grounds for Map Approval or Denial   112
Grounds for Approval
Grounds for Denial
Findings for Approval or Denial

Appeals and Judicial Review   115
Appeals
Judicial Review
Exhaustion of administrative remedies • Statute of limitations

Final Maps and Parcel Maps — 118

Final Maps
Form and filing of final maps • Procedures for approval

Final Map Is Deemed Valid When Recorded
Filing of certificates and security for tax liens • Subdivider to provide evidence of consent of record title holders • Recorder has 10 days to accept or reject map for filing • Condominium, stock cooperatives, and community apartment project conversions • Dedications of streets, utilities, and other property • Improvement agreements

Improvement Security
Types of security • How much security is required? • Rights and requirements • Releasing security • Remedies

Parcel Maps
Local ordinance requirements • Parcel map requirements • Special case: four or fewer parcels and no dedications or improvements

Correction and Amendment of Maps

Grounds
Errors and omissions • Changed circumstances

Amendment Procedure

Changes Affecting Property Rights

Enforcement — 129

Prohibition

Remedies of Private Persons

Remedies of a City

Certificates of Compliance

Exclusions and Reversions — 131

Antiquated Subdivisions — 133

Antiquated Subdivisions—Legally Created Parcels?

Maps Before 1929

Maps After 1893 Generally

U.S. Survey Maps and Federal Patents

Merger and Unmerger
Merging parcels under one ownership • Unmerger or deemed not to have merged

Presumption of Legal Parcels

CHAPTER 6
California Environmental Quality Act (CEQA) — 139

Introduction — 140

Definition of a Project under CEQA — 140

Approval

Environmental Change

Process — 143

Determining if the Activity Is Exempt from CEQA

Preparation of an Initial Study

Adoption of a Negative Declaration

Preparation of an Environmental Impact Report

EIR Procedure
Scoping • Draft EIR • Final EIR

Contents of an Environmental Impact Report
Project description • Environmental setting/baseline • Evaluation of environmental impacts • Thresholds of significance • Water supply • Climate change • Cumulative impacts • Mitigation • Project alternatives • Range of alternatives • Extent of discussion • Growth inducement

Responses to Comments

Recirculation of an EIR

Project Approval and Findings

Mitigation Monitoring and Reporting Programs

Supplemental and Subsequent EIRs and Negative Declarations

Use of an Addendum

EIR Deadlines and Required Notices

Judicial Challenges to Agency Action — 176

Time Limits for Judicial Challenges

Judicial Review

CHAPTER 7
Federal and State Wetland Regulation — 179

Introduction — 179

A Brief History of the Federal Program — 180

How "Wetlands" and Other "Waters of the United States" Are Defined Under the CWA — 181

Legal Definitions of Wetlands and Other "Waters of the United States" — 182

The Narrowing of Federal Jurisdiction — 183

Continued Uncertainty Over the Boundaries of Federal Jurisdiction — 186

California Response to Reduced Federal Wetlands Jurisdiction — 187

The Scientific/Technical Definition of Wetlands — 188

Wetland Hydrology

Hydric Soils

Wetland Vegetation

California's State Law Definition of Wetlands

Procedural Issues in Delineating Wetlands

Activities Regulated by the Corps — 191

Statutory Exemptions — 192

The Corps' Permitting Process — 193

Nationwide Permits

The Corps' Individual Permitting Process — 194

Regulatory Guidance Letters — 198

Scope of Environmental Analysis Under NEPA — 198

Alternatives Analysis Under EPA's 404(b)(1) Guidelines — 200

Project Purpose and Wetlands Avoidance (Sequencing) — 201

Practicability

Availability

Mitigation

The EPA's Role in the Permit Process — 206

Other Federal Statutes — 207
Section 401 of the Clean Water Act • National Environmental Policy Act • Endangered Species Act • Fish and Wildlife Coordination Act • Section 302 of the Marine Protection, Research and Sanctuaries Act of 1972 • National Historic

Preservation Act of 1966 • Land Sales Full Disclosure Act • Coastal Zone Management Act of 1972 • Food Security Act of 1985

State Statutory Authority   209
Porter-Cologne Water Quality Control Act • Streambed Alteration Agreement • Navigation Dredging Permit • Coastal Zone Management

Enforcement   211
Citizen Suits
Standing to Sue
Investigations and Compliance Orders
Criminal, Civil, and Administrative Penalties

Practical Considerations   215

CHAPTER 8
Endangered Species Protections   217

Introduction   217

Listing Process   218
Listing of a Species as Threatened or Endangered
Listing of a "Distinct Population Segment"
"Significant Portion of Its Range"
Listing Procedures and Requirements
Five-Year Review and Delisting
Emergency Listings
Designation of "Critical Habitat"

Consultation Process   228
Components of the Consultation Process
Agency action • The "Action Agency," "Action Area," and "Effects of the Action" • "Informal" vs. "formal" consultation • Duty to use best available science • Climate change impacts • Biological opinion • Incidental take statement • Reinitiation of consultation

Exemptions from the Endangered Species Act Requirements   236

Prohibitions Against Takings   237
Fish and Wildlife
Plants
Definition of Take
No Exceptions for Religious Practices or the Protection of Private Property

Habitat Conservation Plans and Incidental Take Permits   241

Safe Harbor and Candidate Conservation Agreements   242

Judicial Review and Enforcement   242
Citizen Suits
Suits Under the Administrative Procedure Act
Judicial Remedies and Penalties

California Endangered Species Act   244
The CESA Listing Process
"Take" Under the CESA
Incidental Take Permits Under the CESA

CHAPTER 9
Design Review, Historic Preservation, Williamson Act, Coastal Development, Stormwater, Prevailing Wage and Public Bidding   249

Introduction   249

Design Review   249

Historic Preservation   252
Federal Level
State Level
Local Level

Preservation of Agricultural Lands by Williamson Act Contract   255
California Coastal Commission
Composition • Constitutionality
California Coastal Act of 1976
Coastal Zone
Development and Permitting
Local Coastal Programs
Appeals
Judicial Review of Commission Decisions
Other Coastal Commission Responsibilities
San Francisco Bay Conservation and Development Commission
Composition • Jurisdiction • Permitting Authority

Storm Water Quality Requirements   265
Regulatory Background
The Statewide Construction General Permit
The Statewide Industrial General Permit
Municipal Separate Storm Sewer System (MS4) Permits

Prevailing Wage Concerns on Private Development Projects   269

Public Bidding Concerns on Private Development Projects   266

CHAPTER 10
Vested Rights and Ability to Bind City by Contract   273

Vested Rights   273
The *Avco* Rule
Refinements of the *Avco* Rule

Development Agreements   277

Vesting Tentative Maps   283

Vesting Tentative Maps vs. Development Agreements   284

CHAPTER 11
Regulatory Takings   287

Introduction   287
The Four Types of Regulatory Takings
Regulation that effects a physical taking (*Loretto*) • Regulation that denies all economic use (*Lucas*) • Regulation that goes too far (*Penn Central*) • Exactions (*Nollan/Dolan*)
Temporary Takings
Federal decisions • California decisions • Measure of compensation for a temporary taking

Segmentation—the Relevant Parcel Issue

Grounds for Denial of a Takings Claim
The ripeness requirement • Ripeness and the requirement for a final determination of the agency • Ripeness and the requirement to seek compensation through state procedures • The requirement to challenge an unconstitutional condition in court before seeking compensation • The requirement of a unique injury • The role of California constitutional expenditure limitations • Nuisance defense

Takings in the Flood Control Context 310

Civil Rights Action Under Section 1983 311
Procedural issues arising in Section 1983 Cases • Substantive claims under Section 1983—equal protection and due process

Substantive Due Process and Rent Control 314

Interplay Between Takings Claims and Substantive Due Process Claims 315

Legislative Acts Given More Deference Than Adjudicatory Acts 316

CHAPTER 12
Exactions: Dedications and Development Fees ... 319

Introduction 319

Proper Exercise of Police Power 320

Development: Privilege or Right? 320

Test of Reasonableness/Nexus Requirement 322
In General

The *Nollan* and *Dolan* Decisions
Nollan v. California Coastal Commission • *Dolan v. City of Tigard* • What does *Dolan* mean in California?

Applicability of the *Nollan/Dolan* Test to Impact Fees and Exactions: *Koontz v. St. Johns River Water Management District* and *Ehrlich v. Culver City*
Koontz v. St. Johns River Water Management District: expansion of *Nollan* and *Dolan* • *Ehrlich v. City of Culver City*: legislatively formulated vs. ad hoc development fees

California's "Nexus Legislation"—The Mitigation Fee Act ... 333
Documenting the Nexus

Double Taxation 336

Equal Protection 336

Opportunities for Dedications or Fees 337
In General
The General Plan
Subdivision Process
Building Permits
Processing Fees—Land Use and Building Permit Fees
School District Facilities Fee
Nonprofit private university is not exempt from school fees • Redevelopment construction is not exempt from school fees
Habitat Conservation Plans and Natural Communities Conservation Plans
CEQA

Special Requirements Relating to Imposition of Fees ... 343
Waiting Period Before Fees Become Effective; Public Hearing Required
When Fees Are Required to Be Paid
Reasonableness of Development Fee Amount
Fees Cannot Be Levied for Maintenance and Operation

Dedication of Land—Reconveyance to Subdivider ... 345

Judicial Review 346

Development Fee or a Tax? 346
Historical Background
Effect of Jarvis Initiatives—Prop. 13 (1978), Prop. 62 (1986), and Prop. 218 (1996)
Proposition 218 • Impacts on local general taxes • Impacts on local special taxes • Impacts on special assessments • Impacts on fees and charges • Possible impacts on new development fees • Impacts on standby charges • Use of initiatives

Conditions Attached to Land Use Approvals for Financing and Maintaining Public Facilities
GHADs in particular

CHAPTER 13
Initiative and Referendum ... 357

Introduction 357

The Initiative 358

The Referendum 358
Procedural Requirements for Placing an Initiative or Referendum Measure on the Ballot
Initiatives proposed by council or board • Voter-sponsored initiatives and referenda

Form of Petition

Notice of Intention to Circulate; Ballot Title and Summary

Publication and Posting

Circulation; Signature

Filing; Examination of Signatures

Actions by Local Legislative Bodies on Initiatives and Referenda 365
Initiatives
Referenda

Limitations on the Use of Initiative and Referendum ... 368
Cannot be unconstitutional • Cannot conflict with state law • Vertical consistency • Horizontal or internal consistency • Cannot invade a duty delegated exclusively to the council or board or imposed on an agent of the state • Cannot adopt non-legislative measures • Cannot impair an essential governmental function • Must address a single subject • Cannot be used to reject urgency measures

Initiatives and Referenda Are Not Subject to the Same Procedural Requirements as City Council Measures ... 375

Pre-Election Challenges to Initiatives and Referenda ... 376

Initiatives Limiting Housing: Burden of Proof ... 379

Conflicting Initiatives on the Same Ballot ... 379

Restrictions on a City's Role in Campaigns ... 382

Conclusion 383

CHAPTER 14
Local Agency Formation Commissions (LAFCOs): Local Agency Boundary Changes — 387

- Introduction — 387
- History of LAFCO Law — 387
- Composition and Function of LAFCOs — 389
- Spheres of Influence — 390
  - Municipal Service Review Requirement
- LAFCOs' Jurisdiction Over Changes of Organization and Reorganizations — 392
  - Authority to Make Determinations Regarding Changes of Organization or Reorganizations
  - Agencies Over Which LAFCOs Have Jurisdiction
  - Procedures for Changes of Organization or Reorganizations
- Factors LAFCOs Must Consider When Reviewing a Boundary Change Proposal — 397
  - General Factors
  - Additional Factors That LAFCO Must Consider in Certain Proceedings
  - Additional Factors That LAFCO May Consider
  - LAFCOs' Consideration of Boundary Change Proposals
  - Reconsideration Hearing
  - Protest Proceedings
  - Final Actions, Filings, and Notifications
  - Processing Multi-County Changes of Organization or Reorganization
  - Environmental Review

CHAPTER 15
Affordable Housing — 409

- Introduction: The Affordable Housing Crisis in California — 409
- State Housing Element Law — 410
  - Purpose of the Mandated Housing Element
  - Required Contents of the Housing Element
  - Regional Housing Needs Allocation Process
  - Preparing the Land Inventory and Identifying Adequate Sites
  - Analysis of Governmental and Non-Governmental Constraints
  - Consistency with General Plan, Preparation of Annual Report, and Notification Requirements
  - Special Provisions Regarding Housing Needs within the Coastal Zone
  - Review, Certification, and Legal Adequacy of Housing Elements
- Restrictions on the Disapproval of Certain Housing Projects — 418
  - Disapproval Restrictions on Affordable Housing Projects
  - Disapproval of Housing Development Projects Generally
  - Prioritization of Services to Certain Affordable Housing Projects
  - Certain Multifamily Housing Projects May Be a Permitted Use
- Other State Laws Designed to Facilitate Housing Production — 423
  - Least Cost Zoning Law
  - Density Bonuses
  - Second Units
- Growth Management and Affordable Housing — 427
- Inclusionary Housing — 429
  - Introduction
  - Judicial Treatment of Inclusionary Housing
  - History of Inclusionary Housing—The Pre-*Nollan* and *Dolan* Era
  - Inclusionary Housing in California in the Post-*Nollan* and *Dolan* Era
  - Legal Issues to Consider When Adopting and Implementing an Inclusionary Housing Program
  - Method of Enactment
  - Factual Record to Support Enactment and Application
  - Inclusion of "Safety Valve" Provisions
  - Provision of Incentives and Concessions to Developers
  - Relationship to the Costa-Hawkins (Anti-Rent Control) Act
  - Policy Issues to Consider When Crafting an Inclusionary Housing Program
  - Nature of the Program—Mandatory or Voluntary?
  - Determining the Classes and Size of Development That Will Be Subject to the Inclusionary Housing Program
  - Required Amount and Affordability Levels of Inclusionary Units
  - Timing Issues and Design Standards for Inclusionary Units
  - Preserving Affordability of Inclusionary Units
  - Sales Price Limitations
  - Qualification of Applicants
  - Length of Time That Inclusionary Units Must Remain Affordable
  - Enforcement and Monitoring Mechanisms

CHAPTER 16
Sustainable Development — 447

- Introduction — 447
- Growth Management Measures — 448
- "Smart Growth" — 449
- Sustainable Development and Transportation Policy — 451
  - Congestion Management Planning
  - Relationship Between CMPs and Regional Transportation Plans
  - "Complete Streets"
- Water Supply Planning and Conservation — 453
  - Senate Bills 610 and 221
  - Senate Bill X7-7
  - Graywater Systems
- Assembly Bill 32: The California Global Warming Solutions Act of 2006 — 460

Senate Bill 375: The Sustainable Communities and 458
Climate Protection Act of 2008
   Sustainable Communities Strategies
   Traffic Model Guidance
   Affordable Housing

Accounting for Climate Change Impacts in CEQA 462
Documents: Guidance from CEQA Guidelines,
Regional Air Quality Management Districts, and the Courts
   2010 CEQA Guidelines Changes
   CEQA Streamlining for Sustainable Development

Green Building 467
   State Green Building Standards
      Energy Code, Title 24, Part 6 • Green Building Code, Title 24, Part 11
   Local Green Building Standards
   Potential Issues Arising from a City's Use of Rating Systems
   State Preemption and Required Findings
   Federal Preemption of State and Local Green Building Codes

Development of Renewable Energy 471
   Required Renewable Procurement
   Lowering Barriers to Development and Permitting of Renewable Energy
      Subdivision Map Act exemptions for solar projects • Permitting process for wind systems outside urbanized areas • Williamson Act express inclusion of biofuels and probable inclusion of wind • Public interest cancellation of Williamson Act contract to allow solar facility • Minimizing private entity restrictions on solar energy systems • Minimizing public entity restrictions on solar energy systems • Minimizing public entity restrictions on solar energy systems • Solar panels as a standard option on new homes • Geothermal heat pump and geothermal ground loop technologies

Adaptation to Effects of Climate Change 474

CHAPTER 17
Rights of the Regulated 477
In General 477
Notice and Hearing 477
The One Who Decides Must Review Evidence 479
Findings 481
   When Are Findings Required?
   Legislative Acts
   Adjudicative Acts Under 1094.5
      Findings can take many forms • The record must contain evidence supporting the findings

Maintaining Separation Between Prosecutorial 483
and Adjudicatory Function
Ralph M. Brown Act 484
Ex Parte Contacts 487
Permit Streamlining Act 488
Other Procedural Requirements 492
Developer Misrepresentations 493

CHAPTER 18
Enforcement of Land Use Laws 495
Introduction 495
Administrative and Criminal Sanctions 495
   Misdemeanor
   Infraction
   Administrative Penalties
   Warrant
   Enforcement under the Revenue and Taxation Code
   Enforcement under the Subdivision Map Act
   Enforcement under CEQA
   Enforcement under the Business and Professions Code

Possible Defenses to a City's Enforcement Action 498
   Denial of Due Process or Equal Protection
   Estoppel

CHAPTER 19
Land Use Litigation 503
Introduction 503
Overview and Terminology 503
Types of Mandate Proceedings 504
   Traditional Mandate Proceedings under Section 1085 Challenge Legislative and Ministerial Acts
      Legislative acts • Ministerial acts
   Administrative Mandate Proceedings under Section 1094.5 Challenge Administrative and Quasi-Judicial Decisions
   Administrative Mandate Is the Exclusive Procedure for Challenging Administrative Decisions

Standards Courts Apply in Reviewing 509
and Use Decisions
   Standard of Judicial Review of Legislative Decisions
      The "arbitrary-and-capricious" standard of review • Individual legislator's motives are irrelevant • The intent and purpose of the legislative body is relevant • Due process and fair hearing requirements
   Standard of Judicial Review of Administrative Decisions
      "Excess of jurisdiction" • "Fair hearing" • "Proceeding in the manner required by law" • "Supported by the findings and evidence"
   Standard of Judicial Review of Agency Decisions with Both Legislative and Administrative Aspects
   Standard of Judicial Review of an Aspect of an Agency Decision That Interprets or Applies Law

Deadlines for Bringing Actions 516
   Actions Subject to More Than One Statute
   How to Find the Applicable Statute of Limitations

Process of a Mandate Proceeding 524
   Prerequisite to Litigation: Exhaustion of Administrative Remedies
      The common law exhaustion doctrine • The exhaustion requirement has two components • Issue exhaustion • Appeal exhaustion • Rehearing/reconsideration • Exceptions to the exhaustion requirement • Codification of the exhaustion requirement

Ripeness and Finality
Identifying the Proper Parties
Petitioner standing • Beneficial interest • Associational standing • Public interest standing • Taxpayer suits • Respondent • Real party in interest
Joining Other Causes of Action with a Writ Claim
Early Mediation
Preparation of the Record
Discovery and Evidence Outside the Record
Evidence outside the record generally is inadmissible and undiscoverable to determine whether a local agency's decision is valid • Evidence outside the record regarding issues other than the validity of a local agency's decision generally is admissible and discoverable • Evidence outside the record may be admissible in traditional mandate proceedings that challenge ministerial acts • Decisionmaker's thought processes • Attorney-client privilege and work product doctrine • Judicial notice
Setting a Briefing and Hearing Schedule
Alternative writ • Noticed motion • Informal means of obtaining hearing date
Summary Judgment
Preparing the Briefs
A Stay or Preliminary Injunction May Issue Pending a Final Decision on the Writ Petition
Stays • TROs and preliminary injunctions
Issuance of the Writ
Appeal in a Writ of Mandate Case
Time to appeal • Effect of appeal on judgment • Administrative mandate • Traditional mandate • Injunction

Litigation under CEQA 546
Special Procedures for CEQA Actions
Contents of a CEQA Record
Web-based materials • Documents for which a general website address is provided • Documents for which a specific web address is provided • Documents for which no website address is provided • Documents in consultant and subconsultant files • Responsibility of preparation of the record
CEQA Exhaustion and Standing Rules
Standard of Judicial Review of CEQA Decisions
Remedies in a CEQA Case

Litigation Under the Mitigation Fee Act 554
As Applied Challenges to Development Fees • Facial Challenges To Sewer and Water Fees, Capacity Charges and Processing Fees
Challenge to Imposition of Fees on a Development Project (Gov't Code § 66020)
Challenge to Enactment or Increase of Water, Sewer, Capacity or Processing Fees (Gov't Code § 66022)
Remedy

Anti-SLAPP Statute 560
Application of the Anti-SLAPP Statute to the Land Use Context

Attorneys' Fees in Land Use Cases 562
Legal Liability of Local Agencies and Personnel 564
California Tort Claims Act
Liability of Public Employees and Entities
Employees • Entities
Immunity of Public Employees and Entities
Federal Civil Rights Act
Color of Law
Treatment of Persons and Public Entities Under Section 1983: Municipal Liability and Legislative Immunity

Short Articles
Calculating the Life of a Tentative Map 88
Map Act Definitions of "Design and Improvement" 108
Nationwide Permits 195

List of Figures
Figure A: Certificate of Compliance Flow Chart 131
Figure B: CEQA Flow Chart for Local Agencies 148
Figure C: Lead Agency Decision to Prepare an EIR 149
Figure D: Time Periods for Review of Environmental Documents 177
Figure E: U.S. Army Corps of Engineers Permitting Process 197
Figure F: LAFCO Proceedings 398

List of Tables
Table 1: A Comparison of California's Vested Rights Statutes 284
Table 2: LAFCO Protest Proceedings—Effect of Protests 406
Table 3: Comparison of SB 610 and SB 221 454
Table 4: Summary of CEQA Streamlining Provisions for Sustainable Development 465
Table 5: Statutes Applicable to Common Land Use Decisions 520
Table 6: Summary of Government Code 66022 and Related Provisions 558

Glossary 569
List of Acronyms 578
Suggested Reading 579
Table of Authorities 581
Index 611

Preface

For twenty-seven years, Dan Curtin authored this book as a desk reference for those interested in California land use and planning law. Cecily joined Dan as a co-author in 2000 and worked with him to continually update the book based on their own and their partners' decades of experience representing both public agencies and private developers. Following Dan's passing in November 2006, Matt joined Cecily—first as Managing Editor and later as co-author—in preserving and expanding upon the legacy Dan started with this book. Like all editions published since his passing, this book is again dedicated to Dan.

This thirty-fourth edition contains new, expanded discussions of several topics, including:

- Analysis of new California Supreme Court case law on the proper identification of an environmental baseline under the California Environmental Quality Act (CEQA) (chapter 6)
- New and expanded analysis of the legal standards relating to an agency's establishment of significance thresholds under CEQA (chapter 6)
- Discussion of the United States Supreme Court's decision in *Koontz v. St. Johns River Water Management District*, which expands application of the "nexus" and "rough proportionality" standards the Court previously established in *Nollan* and *Dolan* (chapter 12)
- New discussion of recent judicial guidance on the handling of climate change impacts in CEQA documents (chapter 16)
- Treatment of several new decisions affecting affordable housing programs, including application of the Density Bonus Law and the procedure for bringing a legal challenge to inclusionary programs (chapter 15)
- Expanded discussion of state and federal endangered species protection, including new regulation governing how agencies consider economic effects when designating critical habitat and new law on federal agency consultation with the United States Fish and Wildlife Service (chapter 8)

This 2014 edition has benefited from the contributions made by attorneys in Perkins Coie's California Land Use and Development Practice.

Barbara Schussman authored chapter 6 (CEQA). Barbara litigates land use and environmental cases on behalf of public agencies and private entities, and provides comprehensive CEQA compliance advice. Her recent engagements include representing Stanford University, Stanford Hospital, and Lucile Packard Children's Hospital in securing land use approvals for major campus and hospital expansion projects in Santa Clara County and Redwood City; representing the Port of Stockton as special counsel in litigation challenging the EIR prepared for reuse of a 1,500-acre former Navy facility as expanded port maritime and industrial facilities; representing American

President Lines in securing approvals for expansion of its shipping terminal at the Port of Los Angeles; and representing Contra Costa Water District in expansion of the Los Vaqueros Reservoir. Barbara received her law degree from the University of California, Berkeley School of Law (Boalt Hall), where she was elected to the Order of the Coif. She graduated *magna cum laude* from the University of California, Los Angeles, where she was elected to Phi Beta Kappa.

Marc Bruner, co-author of chapters 7 (Federal and State Wetland Regulation) and 8 (Endangered Species Protections) represents governmental entities and private companies in a wide variety of environmental and land use matters. Marc's work involves federal laws and regulations, including the National Environmental Policy Act (NEPA); the Clean Air Act; the Clean Water Act; and the Endangered Species Act. He also focuses his practice on numerous California laws and regulations such as: CEQA; the Porter-Cologne Water Quality Control Act; the California Endangered Species Act; the Integrated Waste Management Act; the Subdivision Map Act; the Planning and Zoning Law; the Building Code; and California laws and regulations governing water supply, green buildings, recycled water, coastal development, state lands and the public trust, conversion of agricultural lands, historic resources, hazardous materials and wastes, and flood protection and safety. After Marc graduated from Yale Law School, where he was Managing Editor of the Yale Journal of Law and the Humanities, he clerked for the Honorable José A. Cabranes, Chief Judge of the U.S. District Court for the District of Connecticut. Marc received his bachelor's degree, *magna cum laude*, from Harvard College.

Julie Jones, co-author of chapters 7 and 8 and author of chapter 16 (Sustainable Development), is an experienced litigator in trial and appellate advocacy in both state and federal courts. Julie's counseling experience includes providing CEQA, NEPA, and other environmental and land use advice in the permitting of major solar energy, reservoir, and port expansion projects. She works extensively with universities to obtain approvals for their large projects by addressing CEQA, historic resources, wetlands, and local permitting issues. Julie has assisted developers of thermal and wind energy projects, regional distribution centers, and residential projects in securing land use entitlements. Julie regularly defends projects against CEQA and other claims and has helped clients overcome challenges to a university/county agreement for trails, a city annexation process, a transportation sales tax ballot measure, a city/county agreement for provision of urban services, a light rail project, and a university development and roadway project. Julie also successfully defended major expansion and dredging projects against NEPA and Endangered Species Act claims. Julie received her law degree from the University of California, Berkeley School of Law (Boalt Hall), where she was Executive Editor of the Ecology Law Quarterly. She graduated from Stanford University with distinction and was elected to Phi Beta Kappa.

Geoff Robinson, co-author of chapter 19 (Land Use Litigation), focuses his practice on land use, development, and real estate litigation. He represents clients in civil and administrative proceedings involving planning and zoning laws, CEQA, development fees and exactions, and public facilities financing. He is an authority on writs of mandate in the trial court and is co-author of the treatise *California Administrative Mandamus* (CEB, 3rd ed. 2012) and other publications on civil writ practice. He also has substantial experience in the area of development mitigation and has litigated numerous cases involving challenges to development exactions, mitigation requirements, and public financing districts. Geoff has also handled a broad range of water law matters, including a ground water basin rights adjudication, and appellate litigation involving the validity of a water supply assessment and an Urban Water Management Plan.

Geoff has been an active participant in pro bono efforts, representing individuals, nonprofits and public agencies before state and federal courts, including several matters in the California Supreme Court. He is the recipient of the California State Bar President's Pro Bono Award. Geoff served as law clerk to the Honorable Thomas J. MacBride of the United States District Court for the Eastern District of California and as extern to the Honorable Joseph T. Sneed of the United States Court of Appeals for the Ninth Circuit. Geoff attended law school at the University of Virginia and Hastings College of the Law, from which he received his law degree with honors. He graduated with distinction from the University of California, Berkeley.

Marie Cooper, co-author of chapter 19, focuses her practice on land use and development, entitlement processing, and land use litigation at the trial and appellate court levels. Marie is experienced in addressing issues arising under the Planning and Zoning laws, CEQA, NEPA, the Religious Land Use and Institutionalized Persons Act (RLUIPA), water supply bills, water rights law, election laws pertaining to initiatives and referenda, and annexation-related laws. Marie is also skilled in handling Williamson Act matters, having represented the developer in the first easement exchange project processed through the Department of Conservation. Marie has substantial litigation experience in challenging and defending land use entitlements, general planning and zoning enactments, development fees and dedications, annexation proceedings, and initiatives and referenda. Her land use litigation practice focuses on writ of mandate proceedings, validation actions, and inverse condemnation. She is adept at navigating the peculiar procedures applicable to land use cases and focusing on rational solutions that fit the client's particular circumstances. Marie served as an extern to the Honorable Otto Kaus of the California Supreme Court. She graduated from the University of California, Berkeley School of Law (Boalt Hall), where she was elected to the Order of the Coif. Marie graduated with high honors from the University of California, Santa Barbara.

We also wish to thank the following individuals in the San Francisco office of Perkins Coie for their contributions to this 2014 edition: Alan Murphy and Christopher Tom, associate attorneys, for their review, writing, and editing of portions of this edition; and Shari Harewood and Michelle Rodriguez, administrative assistants, for reviewing and preparing numerous draft revisions of each chapter.

This book is not a substitute for the guidance and advice of an attorney, especially in complex matters in which refinements and interpretations of the law are essential before final conclusions are drawn about planning and development processes, property rights, due process, and procedural matters.

In addition, although legal reference points are essential, in matters pertaining to local public planning and the development process, there is no substitute for an understanding of how the planning process works at the city and county levels. Much of the process is delineated by California law and indeed most of the process is mandated. The law does not say a great deal, however, about what local planning policies should be or how a city or county should organize its land uses. That is a local task. But the law does require cities and counties to prepare, adopt, and update general plans before making land use and land use-related decisions, and it requires that certain procedures be followed to carry out public policies, protect private rights, and ensure due process prior to making decisions. We hope you find this book a helpful guide to better understanding how those mandates and procedures may be applied at the local level. For regular insights into legal issues relating to development and use of land and federal, state, and local permitting and approval processes, subscribe to Perkins Coie's California Land Use and Development Law Report at www.californialandusedevelopmentlaw.com.

Cecily Talbert Barclay
Matthew S. Gray

January 2014

CONVENTIONS IN THIS BOOK

For brevity and readability, this text uses the following conventions:
- When the word "city" is used, it also means "county"; "city council" also means "county board of supervisors." The text will note instances where there is a substantive distinction between how land use and planning law affects cities and counties.
- All references to the Legislature are to the California State Legislature, unless otherwise indicated.

Code references are to the California Code, unless otherwise indicated.

CHAPTER 1

Local Land Use Authority

POLICE POWER

The legal basis for all land use regulation is the police power of the city to protect the public health, safety, and welfare of its residents. *See Berman v. Parker*, 348 U.S. 26, 32–33 (1954). A land use regulation lies within the city's police power if it is reasonably related to the public welfare. *See Associated Home Builders, Inc. v. City of Livermore*, 18 Cal. 3d 582, 600–601 (1976).

> The legal basis for all land use regulation is the police power of the city to protect the public health, safety, and welfare of its residents.

As Justice William O. Douglas, speaking for the United States Supreme Court, stated about the police power:

> An attempt to define its reach or trace its outer limits is fruitless, for each case must turn on its own facts. The definition is essentially the product of legislative determinations addressed to the purposes of government, purposes neither abstractly nor historically capable of complete definition....
>
> Public safety, public health, morality, peace and quiet, law and order—these are some of the more conspicuous examples of the traditional application of the police power to municipal affairs. Yet they merely illustrate the scope of the power and do not delimit it. The concept of the public welfare is broad and inclusive.... The values it represents are spiritual as well as physical, aesthetic as well as monetary. It is within the power of the legislature to determine that the community should be beautiful as well as healthy, spacious as well as clean, well balanced as well as carefully patrolled.

Berman, 348 U.S. at 32–33 (citations omitted)

This statement is recognized by California courts as "a correct description of the authority of a state or city to enact legislation under the police power." *Metromedia, Inc. v. City of San Diego*, 26 Cal. 3d 848, 861 (1980).

The police power, even though recognized by common law, is set forth in the California Constitution, which confers on cities the power to "make and enforce within [their] limits all local police, sanitary and other ordinances and regulations not in conflict with general laws." Cal. Const. Art. XI, § 7.

The California Supreme Court has stated:

> Under the police power granted by the Constitution, counties and cities have plenary authority to govern, subject only to the limitation that they exercise this power within their territorial limits and subordinate to state law. Apart

from this limitation, the "police power [of a county or city] under this provision...is as broad as the police power exercisable by the Legislature itself."

Candid Enters., Inc. v. Grossmont Union High Sch. Dist., 39 Cal. 3d 878, 885 (1985) (citation omitted)

Land use regulations are a manifestation of the local police powers conferred by the California Constitution, not an exercise of authority delegated by statute. *See Scrutton v. County of Sacramento*, 275 Cal. App. 2d 412, 417 (1969). As stated by the California Supreme Court:

> We have recognized that a city's or county's power to control its own land use decisions derives from this inherent police power, not from the delegation of authority by the state. *See, e.g., Candid Enters., Inc. v. Grossmont Union High Sch. Dist.*, 39 Cal. 3d 878, 885–86 (1985) (upholding a school facilities impact fee imposed by a county without statutory authorization); *Birkenfeld v. City of Berkeley*, 17 Cal. 3d 129, 140–42 (1976) (upholding city rent control initiative despite lack of express statutory authority).

DeVita v. County of Napa, 9 Cal. 4th 763, 782 (1995); *see also Big Creek Lumber Co. v. City of Santa Cruz*, 38 Cal. 4th 1139, 1151 (2006) (land use regulation in California historically a function of local government under the grant of police power contained in the California Constitution)

> **State zoning laws pertaining to the adoption of local zoning regulations are not intended as specific grants of authority, but as minimum standards to be observed in local zoning practices.**

As such, state zoning laws pertaining to the adoption of local zoning regulations are not intended as specific grants of authority, but as minimum standards to be observed in local zoning practices.

The police power is an elastic power. It allows cities to tailor regulations to suit the interests and needs of a "modern, enlightened and progressive community" even as those interests and needs change. *Rancho La Costa v. County of San Diego*, 111 Cal. App. 3d 54, 60 (1980). Regulations are sustained under current complex conditions that but a short time ago might have been condemned as arbitrary and unreasonable. *See Village of Euclid v. Ambler Realty Co.*, 272 U.S. 365, 387 (1926).

In the 1970s, Justice Douglas, speaking for the United States Supreme Court, upheld a village's zoning ordinance relating to land use restrictions on single-family dwelling units. His opinion identified the interests that supported the village's exercise of its police power at the time:

> A quiet place where yards are wide, people few, and motor vehicles restricted are legitimate guidelines in a land use project addressed to family needs. This goal is a permissible one within *Berman v. Parker, supra*. The police power is not confined to elimination of filth, stench, and unhealthy places. It is ample to lay out zones where family values, youth values, and the blessings of quiet seclusion and clean air make the area a sanctuary for people.

Village of Belle Terre v. Boraas, 416 U.S. 1, 9 (1974)

Today, many cities face needs and interests different than those identified in *Village of Belle Terre*. Regulations permitting smaller yards, denser housing, and narrower streets, so as to provide more housing within already-developed areas, now address some cities' changing needs. Such regulations are as proper an exercise of a city's police power as were those in *Village of Belle Terre*, thanks to the elasticity of that power.

California courts have upheld the premise that an expansive range of interests can support a city's exercise of its police power. For example, the California Supreme Court has held that aesthetic reasons alone can justify the exercise of the police power. *See, e.g., Ehrlich v. City of Culver City,* 12 Cal. 4th 854, 881–82 (1996) (upholding a city's public art fee ordinance); *Metromedia,* 26 Cal. 3d at 858–59 (upholding in part a city's total ban of offsite advertising signs); *Disney v. City of Concord,* 194 Cal. App. 4th 1410 (2011) (upholding a city ordinance regulating the storage of recreational vehicles on residential property as a proper use of police power to regulate based on aesthetic concerns).

The United States Supreme Court held similarly in *City Council v. Taxpayers for Vincent,* 466 U.S. 789, 805 (1984) (upholding a local ordinance prohibiting the posting of signs on public property), and *Penn Central Transportation Company v. City of New York,* 438 U.S. 104, 129 (1978) (upholding New York City's landmark preservation law as proper regulation of "desirable aesthetic features of a city").

A city's ability to limit big-box retail stores was upheld on police power grounds in *Wal-Mart Stores, Inc. v. City of Turlock,* 138 Cal. App. 4th 273, 303 (2006). There, Wal-Mart challenged a city zoning ordinance prohibiting the development of discount superstores as exceeding the police power. The court held the police power empowers cities to "control and organize development within their boundaries as a means of serving the general welfare." *Id.*

Courts have held that regulations affecting economic interests in real property also are an appropriate exercise of the police power. *See, e.g., Birkenfeld v. City of Berkeley,* 17 Cal. 3d 129, 158 (1976) (regulations implementing local rent control laws are valid); *Griffin Dev. Co. v. City of Oxnard,* 39 Cal. 3d 256, 261–62 (1985) (regulations relating to condominium conversions are proper). Although it did not directly address the police power, the United States Supreme Court, in *Kelo v. City of New London,* demonstrated the breadth of this power in holding a city may condemn land for the purpose of economic development. 545 U.S. 469 (2005).

> Courts have held that regulations affecting economic interests in real property also are an appropriate exercise of the police power.

Protection of a city's "character," "stability," and "soul" has served to justify invocation of the police power. In *Ewing v. City of Carmel-by-the-Sea,* homeowners challenged the constitutionality of a zoning ordinance prohibiting commercial use of residential property for remuneration for less than thirty consecutive days. 234 Cal. App. 3d 1579 (1991). The homeowners claimed the ordinance was a taking, was void as arbitrary and vague, and violated their right of privacy. In ruling for the city, the court held that the ordinance was a proper exercise of the city's land use authority under its police power "to enhance and maintain the residential character of the city." *Id.* at 1590. The court stated that this is a wholly proper purpose of zoning:

> It stands to reason that the "residential character" of a neighborhood is threatened when a significant number of homes—at least twelve percent in this case, according to the record—are occupied not by permanent residents but by a stream of tenants staying a weekend, a week, or even twenty-nine days.... [Transient] rentals undoubtedly affect the essential character of a neighborhood and the stability of a community. Short-term tenants have little interest in public agencies or in the welfare of the citizenry. They do not participate in local government, coach little league, or join the hospital guild. They do not lead a Scout troop, volunteer at the library, or keep an eye on an elderly neighbor. Literally, they are here today and gone tomorrow without engaging in the sort of activities that weld and strengthen a community.

Id. at 1591

In holding that the ordinance was related to a legitimate governmental goal, the court continued:

Blessed with unparalleled geography, climate, beauty, and charm, Carmel naturally attracts numerous short-term visitors. Again, it stands to reason that Carmel would wish to preserve an enclave of single-family homes as the heart and soul of the city. We believe that this reason alone is "sufficiently cogent to preclude us from saying, as it must be said before the ordinance can be declared unconstitutional, that such provisions are clearly arbitrary and unreasonable, having no substantial relation to the public health, safety, morals or general welfare."

Id. at 1591–92 (internal citation omitted)

Judicial review of a city's exercise of its police power is closely circumscribed. The California Supreme Court established the following rule:

It is a well settled rule that determination of the necessity and form of regulations enacted pursuant to the police power "is primarily a legislative and not a judicial function, and is to be tested in the courts not by what the judges individually or collectively may think of the wisdom or necessity of a particular regulation, but solely by the answer to the question is there any reasonable basis in fact to support the legislative determination of the regulation's wisdom and necessity?"

Consolidated Rock Prods. Co. v. City of Los Angeles, 57 Cal. 2d 515, 522–23 (1962)

Predictably, this test has resulted in substantial judicial deference when reviewing a city's decision to exercise the police power. *See Remmenga v. California Coastal Comm'n*, 163 Cal. App. 3d 623, 629 (1985); *Santa Monica Beach, Ltd. v. Superior Court*, 19 Cal. 4th 952, 962–63 (1999) (advocating a hands-off policy for reviewing local legislative acts). Indeed, so long as "it is fairly debatable that the restriction in fact bears a reasonable relation to the general welfare," a land use regulation should withstand constitutional attack. *Associated Home Builders, Inc. v. City of Livermore*, 18 Cal. 3d 582, 601 (1976).

The United States Supreme Court, federal courts, and California courts generally uphold a city's action so long as it is not arbitrary or capricious, substantially advances a legitimate governmental interest, and does not deny an owner economically viable use of its land. In the last 30 years, only a handful of court decisions have struck down a city's land use ordinance or decision because it went beyond the bounds of its police power.

Indeed, in a unanimous decision, the California Supreme Court held that a city's police power is as broad as the police power of the Legislature itself. *See Candid Enters.*, 39 Cal. 3d at 885. However, if the power is not exercised within constitutional mandates or statutory provisions set forth by the Legislature, the decision or regulation may be set aside. Thus, a city must respect constitutional and statutory mandates, such as adopting a valid general plan, conducting the required hearings, making the necessary findings, and following the California Environmental Quality Act. Also, a city's police powers may be limited by the California State Legislature. *See Legislative Preemption*, in this chapter.

A city must act within all applicable statutory provisions so there will be no "conflict with general laws." A city's actions also must meet constitutional principles of due process: they must be reasonable and nondiscriminatory, and not arbitrary or capricious. *See, e.g., G & D Holland Constr. Co. v. City of Marysville*, 12 Cal. App. 3d 989, 994 (1970).

A city's reservation of the police power is implicit in all land use regulations. In *Richeson v. Helal,* the court determined that where there was ambiguity on the face of a written agreement between the city and a landowner as to whether a conditional use permit for property could be extended beyond the original expiration date set forth in the agreement, the agreement could not be read to contract away a city's future exercise of the police power. 158 Cal. App. 4th 268, 278 (2007). Thus, the court narrowly interpreted the contracted provisions of the agreement and allowed the city to extend expiration of the conditional use permit. *Id.* at 280–281.

LEGISLATIVE PREEMPTION

Despite the breadth of its police power, a city cannot act where the California State Legislature has enacted laws which completely occupy the field. *See, e.g., Morehart v. County of Santa Barbara,* 7 Cal. 4th 725, 747 (1994); *People ex rel. Deukmejian v. County of Mendocino,* 36 Cal. 3d 476, 483–85 (1984). Under the California Constitution, a city's ordinance cannot conflict with the state's general laws that preempt the subject matter. A conflict exists if the ordinance "duplicates, contradicts or enters an area fully occupied by general law, either expressly or by legislative implication." *Viacom Outdoor, Inc. v. City of Arcata,* 140 Cal. App. 4th 230, 236 (2006). For example, the Housing Accountability Act preempts a city's discretion to deny certain types of affordable housing projects. Gov't Code § 65589.5. Another example is Government Code section 65858, which preempts the field of "moratorium" ordinances. *See Bank of the Orient v. Town of Tiburon,* 220 Cal. App. 3d 992, 1001 (1990) (city's interim moratorium ordinance may not exceed the two-year maximum prescribed in state law). The Subdivision Map Act also preempts a city's police power in certain areas. *See, e.g., Sequoia Park Associates v. County of Sonoma,* 176 Cal. App. 4th 1270, 1296-97 (2009) (Subdivision Map Act's provisions for mobile home park conversion preempt local authorities' power to inject other factors while considering conversion application); *Morehart,* 7 Cal. 4th at 761 (county's zoning ordinances relating to merger of antiquated lots were impliedly preempted by the merger provisions of the Subdivision Map Act).

> Despite the breadth of its police power, a city cannot act where the California State Legislature has enacted laws which completely occupy the field.

The scope of the state's preemption can be broad. For example, the Legislature has adopted health and safety policies and criteria for the establishment of certain residential uses that preempt local zoning. See Health & Safety Code § 1597.40(a) (preempting local zoning and other regulations regarding family day care homes); Health & Safety Code § 1566.3 (preempting local zoning with respect to residential facilities serving six or fewer mentally disabled or handicapped persons). However, preemption may not be found where the Legislature has not fully occupied a subject matter. For example, in *Viacom Outdoor, Inc. v. City of Arcata,* the city's demand that the owner obtain a permit to rebuild storm-damaged billboards pursuant to its building and sign codes was not preempted by state law because the state law (the California Outdoor Advertising Act) did not categorically prohibit local legislation and explicitly invited augmentation from local authorities. 140 Cal. App. 4th at 246. Moreover, local legislation is preempted by virtue of its contradiction with state law when it is "inimical" thereto, meaning that "the ordinance directly requires what the state statute forbids or prohibits what the state enactment demands." *City of Riverside v. Inland Empire Patients Health & Wellness Center, Inc.,* 56 Cal. 4th 729, 743 (2013) (local ordinance classifying medical marijuana dispensaries as prohibited use within city not preempted by California's medical marijuana statutes).

Under the Supremacy Clause of the United States Constitution, Congress may preempt both state and local law through federal regulation. For example, the Federal Telecommunications Act (47 U.S.C. § 253) precludes states and cities from passing laws that would prohibit any entity from providing telecommunications services. In *Qwest Communications, Inc. v. City of Berkeley*, the city's telecommunications ordinance was pre-empted by section 253 because it burdened city service providers with regulations and requirements that prohibited companies from providing telecommunication services in the city. 433 F. 3d 1253, 1257-58 (9th Cir. 2006).

STATE STATUTORY FRAMEWORK FOR LAND USE DECISIONS

The following state laws provide most of the legal framework for a city's exercise of its police power in the context of land use regulation:

- Establishment of local planning agencies, commissions, and departments. Gov't Code § 65100 *et seq.*
- General and specific plans. Gov't Code § 65300 *et seq.*
- Zoning regulations. Gov't Code § 65800 *et seq.*
- Subdivision Map Act. Gov't Code § 66410 *et seq.*
- Development agreements. Gov't Code § 65864 *et seq.*
- California Environmental Quality Act. Pub. Res. Code § 21000 *et seq.*; Cal. Code Regs. tit. 14, §§ 15000-15387 (also known as the CEQA Guidelines)
- Ralph M. Brown Act. Gov't Code § 54950 *et seq.* (also known as the Open Meeting Act or the Brown Act)
- Permit Streamlining Act. Gov't Code § 65920 *et seq.*
- Mitigation Fee Act. Gov't Code § 66000 *et seq.*

CITY COUNCIL

The city council of a general law city is made up of five council members, one of whom is the mayor.[1] Gov't Code §§ 36501, 34900, 36801. The mayor has the duty of presiding at all city council meetings. Gov't code § 36802. In a chartered city, organization and power of the city's government is subject to control by the city's charter, which may provide for a different number of council members. Cal. Const. Art. XI § 5(a); *Socialist Party v. Uhl*, 155 Cal. 776, 788 (1909).

The city council makes three types of decisions: legislative, quasi-judicial, and ministerial. Legislative acts are general policy decisions, such as general plan revisions (*see* chapter 2) and zoning ordinances (*see* chapter 4). Legislative acts are binding only when approved by the city council. Quasi-judicial acts are decisions that apply legislative policy to individual development projects. These decisions are generally made by the city council or the planning commission. Ministerial acts are those acts in which the city has no discretion, such as the mandatory issuance of a permit if certain conditions are met. Because they involve no discretion, ministerial decisions often are delegated to city staff. However, the mayor and city council may not delegate any portion of their discretionary powers unless authorized by statute. *See City of Los Angeles v. Superior Court*, 193 Cal. App. 4th 1159, 1173 (2011) ("As a general rule, powers conferred upon public agencies and officers which involve the exercise of judgment or discretion are in nature of public trusts and cannot be surrendered or delegated to subordinates in the absence of statutory authorization.") (citations omitted).

---

1 The governing body of a county is generally the board of supervisors. Cal. Const. Art. XI § 1(b); Gov't Code § 23005.

PLANNING COMMISSION

The planning commission is a permanent committee of five or more citizens appointed by the city council or the mayor to review and act on planning and development matters. A city need not create a planning commission. Gov't Code § 65101. In some jurisdictions, especially smaller ones, there is no planning commission and the city council serves in that capacity. Gov't Code §§ 65100, 65101.

The planning commission holds regularly scheduled public hearings to consider land use matters, such as the general plan, specific plans, zoning and rezoning, use permits, and subdivisions. In some cities, a subset of these matters also may be considered by a zoning administrator or a design or architectural review board. Depending upon a city's local ordinance, planning commission membership may change at the pleasure of the mayor or council, or at the expiration of fixed terms.[2] In general law cities with an elected mayor, the mayor appoints the commissioners, but the appointments must be approved by the council. Gov't Code § 40605; 89 Ops. Cal. Atty. Gen. 178 (2006).

A city council may assign any or all of the following tasks to its planning commission:

- Assist in writing the general plan and community or specific plans, hold public hearings, and recommend action on proposed amendments to such plans. Gov't Code §§ 65103, 65353
- Investigate and make recommendations to the city council regarding reasonable and practical means for implementing the general plan or elements of the general plan, so that it will serve as an effective guide for orderly growth and development, preservation and conservation of open space and natural resources, and the efficient expenditure of public funds relating to the subjects addressed in the general plan. Gov't Code § 65400
- Provide an annual report to the city council on the status of the general plan and progress in its implementation, including meeting the city's share of regional housing needs, local efforts to remove governmental constraints on housing, and compliance of the general plan with Government Code guidelines. Gov't Code §§ 65584, 65583(c)(3), 65040.2
- Hold hearings and make recommendations on proposed changes to the city's zoning ordinances and zoning maps. Gov't Code § 65854
- Hold hearings and act on subdivision maps. Gov't Code § 66452.1
- Annually review the city's capital improvement program and the public works projects of other local agencies for consistency with the general plan. Gov't Code §§ 65401, 65403
- Promote public interest in the general plan and consult with and advise public officials and agencies, utilities, organizations, and citizens regarding its implementation. Gov't Code § 65351
- Coordinate local plans and programs with other public agencies. Gov't Code § 65352
- Report to the city council on the conformity of proposed public land acquisition or disposal with the adopted general plan. Gov't Code § 65402
- Undertake special planning studies as needed. Gov't Code § 65101

> The planning commission holds regularly scheduled public hearings to consider land use matters, such as the general plan, specific plans, zoning and rezoning, use permits, and subdivisions.

---

2 Suggested reading material for planning commissioners includes:
- *The Planning Commissioner's Book* (Governor's Office of Planning and Research, 1998)
- *Planning Commissioner's Handbook* (League of California Cities, 2004)
- William Fulton and Paul Shigley, *Guide to California Planning* (Solano Press, 4th ed. 2012)

Most often, the commission acts in an advisory capacity to the city council on land use matters. In some instances, the commission's decision on a project is referred to the city council as a recommendation for action (e.g., general plan amendments and rezonings). In other instances, depending on state law and local ordinances, it is considered a final action unless appealed to the council (e.g., subdivisions, variances, and use permits). If a matter has been referred or appealed to the council, it may choose to follow the commission's recommendation, reverse or modify the commission's action, or send the project back to the commission for further review.

PLANNING STAFF

A city's community development or planning department is the commission's and city council's staff. These city planners advise the commission or council on the city's general plan, specific plans, zoning ordinance, subdivision ordinance, and other land use regulations. In addition, they provide background information and recommendations on the proposals under consideration, answer technical questions, and ensure meetings have been properly noticed. The city attorney's office and the public works department also advise the commission and the council.

PUBLIC MEETINGS

The planning commission and city council hold regular meetings and special meetings as needed. Although usually held separately, such hearings may be jointly noticed and held, if both bodies agree to a joint hearing process. For the most part, state law requires public hearings before planning actions are taken. At its meetings, the planning commission weighs all city and planning proposals in light of federal, state, and local regulations and potential environmental effects; it also listens to testimony from citizens and other interested parties. If necessary, the commission or council generally may continue a hearing to allow more information to be gathered or to take additional testimony. The commission and council usually consider several items at each hearing, considering each item separately and taking action on one before moving on to the next agenda item.

Pursuant to the Brown Act, all meetings, including study sessions and workshops, must be open and public. Gov't Code § 54950 *et seq*. This means a quorum of commissioners can discuss commission business only in a public meeting. For a more thorough discussion of the Brown Act and its restrictions on communications between members of the public and members of the commission or council, see chapter 17 (Rights of the Regulated).

CHAPTER 2

General Plan

FROM ADVISORY STATUS[1] TO CONSTITUTION FOR DEVELOPMENT

The general plan is a city's basic planning document. It provides the blueprint for development throughout the community, and is the vehicle through which competing interests and the needs of the citizenry are balanced. The general plan addresses all aspects of development, including housing, traffic, natural resources, open space, safety, land use, and public facilities.

Before 1971, the general plan was considered to be an advisory document. Government Code section 65860 then read, "No county or city shall be required to adopt a general plan prior to the adoption of a zoning ordinance." Although originally discretionary, general plans were eventually made "mandatory" for all cities and counties. *DeVita v. County of Napa*, 9 Cal. 4th 763, 812 n. 8 (1995) (citing this book).

In 1971, the Government Code was expanded to require that a city's zoning and subdivision approvals must be consistent with a city's general plan. *Id.* at 772. This requirement is known as the "consistency doctrine." Perhaps the most significant change in California planning law and practice in the past four decades is the key role played by a city's general plan.

> Perhaps the most significant change in California planning law and practice in the past four decades is the key role played by a city's general plan.

The initial 1971 legislation[2] and subsequent amendments require cities to "engage in the discipline of setting forth their development policies, objectives and standards in a general plan composed of various elements of land use." 58 Ops. Cal. Atty. Gen. 21, 23 (1975). The general plan thus was transformed from an "interesting study" to the basic land use charter that embodies fundamental land use and planning decisions and governs the direction of future land use in a city's jurisdiction. *See City of Santa Ana v. City of Garden Grove*, 100 Cal. App. 3d 521, 532 (1979); *see also DeVita*, 9 Cal. 4th at 763. Today, general plan requirements are set forth in Government Code section 65300 *et seq.*

---

1 For a good history of planning law in California, starting with the adoption of the first planning law in 1927 by the Legislature, see the dissent by J. Arabian in *DeVita v. County of Napa*, 9 Cal. 4th 763, 808–13 (1995); see also William Fulton and Paul Shigley, *Guide to California Planning* (Solano Press, 4th ed. 2012) for an excellent discussion of how planning works in California.

2 1971 Cal. Stat. ch. 1446 (McCarthy legislation).

GENERAL PLAN—THE CONSTITUTION

Although the consistency doctrine has been in effect since 1971, it was not until 1990 that the California Supreme Court finally held that the general plan was the "constitution for all future development." *Lesher Communications, Inc. v. City of Walnut Creek*, 52 Cal. 3d 531, 540 (1990). The Court confirmed the general plan as the single most important planning document. *See Citizens of Goleta Valley v. Board of Supervisors*, 52 Cal. 3d 553, 570-71 (1990).

In *Lesher*, the California Supreme Court struck down a growth management initiative that conflicted with the City of Walnut Creek's general plan. 52 Cal. 3d at 544. *Lesher* thus marked the first occasion where the Court squarely addressed the general plan's position in the planning hierarchy, and especially its interplay with the initiative process.

Lesher arose from a challenge to Measure H, a traffic-based growth management initiative adopted by Walnut Creek voters in 1985. The trial court had determined that Measure H was not a general plan amendment but rather a zoning ordinance or other land use regulation. As a mere regulation, Measure H was required to be consistent with the city's general plan and, because it was not consistent, the trial court declared it invalid. This holding was overturned on appeal. The Court of Appeal agreed that Measure H was inconsistent with the city's general plan, but interpreted it as a general plan amendment in order to give the greatest possible protection to the initiative process. The California Supreme Court rejected this interpretation and struck down the initiative, thereby upholding the trial court's decision.

The Court emphasized that all laws are subject to the same constitutional and statutory limitations and rules of construction, whether enacted by the local legislative body or the electorate. Focusing on the absence of any ballot materials that labeled Measure H a general plan amendment, as well as the detailed scope and self-executing nature of its text (resembling a zoning ordinance), the Court ruled that Measure H was a land use regulation subordinate to the city's general plan and therefore invalid under the consistency doctrine. "The tail does not wag the dog," pronounced the Court. *Lesher*, 52 Cal. 3d at 541.

Under *Lesher*, any subordinate land use action, such as a zoning ordinance, tentative map, or development agreement that is not consistent with a city's current general plan is "invalid at the time it is passed." *Id.* at 544. The supremacy of the general plan has been reinforced by many courts since *Lesher*. *Goleta Valley*, 52 Cal. 3d at 570-571 (affirming that general plan is the "constitution for all future developments within the city or county" to which local land use decisions must conform); *Mira Mar Mobile Community v. City of Oceanside*, 119 Cal. App. 4th 477, 494 (2004) (local coastal program had become part of city's general plan and therefore part of the "constitution" for future development in that community); *Friends of Lagoon Valley v. City of Vacaville*, 154 Cal. App. 4th 807, 815 (2007) (general plan provides "charter for future development" and sets forth "a city or county's fundamental policy decisions about such development") (citing *Federation of Hillside & Canyon Assns. v. City of Los Angeles*, 126 Cal. App. 4th 1180, 1194 (2004)).

GENERAL PLAN—PURPOSES AND CONTENTS; GENERAL PLAN GUIDELINES

A city's general plan must include a comprehensive, long-term plan for the physical development of both the city and any land outside the city's boundaries that the city determines is related to its planning. Gov't Code § 65300. The general plan shall consist of a "statement of development policies," and must include diagrams and text setting forth "objectives, principles, standards, and plan proposals." Gov't Code § 65302. The general plan consists of seven mandatory elements—land use, circulation, housing, conservation, open space, noise, and safety—and any optional element that a city chooses to adopt. Gov't Code § 65302.

The Governor's Office of Planning and Research (OPR) must develop and adopt guidelines for the preparation and content of the seven mandatory elements. Gov't Code § 65040.2. These general plan guidelines must include guidelines for associated environmental justice matters, and advice for collaborative land use planning of adjacent civilian and military lands and facilities, as well as advice for addressing the effects of civilian development on military readiness activities. In 2003, OPR issued a revised edition of the General Plan Guidelines, which added the following:

- Guidance for addressing environmental justice in the general plan
- Guidance on developing optional water and energy elements
- Expanded guidance on public participation in the development of the general plan
- Revised and expanded housing element guidelines
- Expanded guidance on consolidation of individual general plan elements
- Suggested reporting formats for the annual general plan progress report[3]

In 2004, the Legislature added a requirement that the Guidelines also contain advice for consulting with California Native American tribes for preservation of Native American places, features, and objects. Gov't Code § 65040.2(g). While courts have held the guidelines are merely advisory and not mandatory, they may assist in determining compliance with the general plan laws. *See Twain Harte Homeowners Ass'n v. County of Tuolumne*, 138 Cal. App. 3d 664, 702 (1982).

Responding to strong public interest in environmental sustainability, the Legislature created the Strategic Growth Council in 2008. The Council oversees grants and loans to support planning and development of sustainable communities, including grants to cities for preparing, adopting, and implementing a general plan or general plan element consistent with the goals of the state's climate change legislation (AB 32, The California Global Warming Solutions Act of 2006). For further discussion of sustainable development in general, please see chapter 16 (Sustainable Development).

Except for mandating development and adoption of a general plan, specifying the elements to be included, and imposing on cities the general requirement that land use decisions be guided by that plan, the Legislature has not preempted the decisionmaking power of local legislative bodies as to the specific contours of the general plan or actions taken under it. *See DeVita*, 9 Cal. 4th at 783.

In sum, the preparation, adoption, and implementation of a general plan serve to:
- Identify the community's circulation, housing, environmental, economic and social goals and policies as they relate to land use and development
- Provide a basis for local government decisionmaking, including decisions on development approvals and exactions
- Provide citizens with opportunities to participate in the planning and decisionmaking processes of their community
- Inform citizens, developers, decisionmakers, and other cities of the ground rules that guide development within the community

> The Governor's Office of Planning and Research (OPR) must develop and adopt guidelines for the preparation and content of the seven mandatory elements.

---

3 For further discussion of these and other changes, see the Introduction in OPR's *General Plan Guidelines* (2003), page 8 *et seq.*, available at http://opr.ca.gov/docs/General_Plan_Guidelines_2003.pdf.

Thus, the general plan bridges the gap between community values, visions, and objectives on the one hand, and physical decisions such as subdivisions and public works projects on the other.

LEGAL ADEQUACY OF THE GENERAL PLAN

> The key to the validity of a general plan is its legal adequacy.

The key to the validity of a general plan is its legal adequacy. To be legally adequate, a plan must show "substantial compliance with the statutory requirements" for general plans. *See Camp v. Board of Supervisors*, 123 Cal. App. 3d 334, 348 (1981). The court in *Garat v. City of Riverside* stated:

> [T]he following statutory requirements...are necessary for an adequate general plan:
>
> a. A general plan must be "comprehensive" and "long-term." (Gov't Code § 65300)
>
> b. The plan and its elements and parts must comprise "an integrated, internally consistent and compatible statement of policies...." (Gov't Code § 65300.5)
>
> c. The plan must address all the elements specified in section 65302, i.e., land use, circulation, housing, conservation, open space, noise, and safety. (Gov't Code §§ 65301, 65302). The degree of specificity and level of detail shall reflect local conditions and circumstances (Gov't Code § 65301)
>
> d. The required elements must meet the criteria, if any, set out in section 65302; for example, the components of the circulation element must be correlated with the land use element (Gov't Code § 65302(b))
>
> It follows that even though a plan or its parts may not, from a court's subjective point of view, be "satisfactory" or "suitable," unless there is a statutory requirement on point, such unsatisfactoriness or unsuitability may not form a basis for concluding that the plan is legally inadequate.

2 Cal. App. 4th 259, 293 (1991) (overruled on other grounds in *Morehart v. County of Santa Barbara*, 7 Cal. 4th 725, 743 n.11 (1994))

There is a presumption that a city's general plan is valid and that official duties have been regularly performed. Therefore, the burden is on those challenging the plan to demonstrate the plan is inadequate, except in the case of growth management provisions, where the burden of proof is shifted to the city. *See Hernandez v. City of Encinitas*, 28 Cal. App. 4th 1048, 1072 (1994). The challenger also must demonstrate the existence of a nexus between any plan inadequacies and the project or action being challenged. *See Garat*, 2 Cal. App. 4th at 293.

Description of the mandatory elements. A general plan contains seven mandatory elements: land use, circulation, housing, conservation, open space, noise, and safety.[4]

Land use element. The land use element of a general plan must identify the proposed general distribution and intensity of uses of the land for housing, business, industry, open space, natural resources, public facilities, waste disposal sites, and other categories of public and private uses. This element serves as the central framework for the entire plan and is intended to correlate all land use issues into a set of coherent development

---

[4] *See* Government Code section 65302; *see also* chapter 4 of OPR's General Plan Guidelines (2003) for a detailed discussion of the seven mandatory elements of the general plan.

policies. Its goals, objectives, policies, programs, diagrams, and maps relate directly to the other elements. *See* Gov't Code § 65302(a).

While all general plan elements generally carry equal weight legally, in practice the land use element is the most visible and frequently used. *See Sierra Club v. Board of Supervisors*, 126 Cal. App. 3d 698, 708 (1981).

The land use element must include standards of population density (measured in numbers of persons) and building intensity (using measures such as site coverage, floor-to-area ratio, building type and size, or units per acre). *See Twain Harte Homeowners Ass'n*, 138 Cal. App. 3d at 696–97; *Camp*, 123 Cal. App. 3d at 349. The land use element also must identify parcels designated for timberland production and areas subject to flooding, as identified by flood plain maps prepared by the Federal Emergency Management Agency or the State Department of Water Resources. Gov't Code § 65302(a). In addition, the law requires general plans to account for growth of military activities at bases, ports, airports, or other training installations. Gov't Code § 65302(a)(2). The text and diagrams in the land use element also may express community intentions regarding urban form and design. Gov't Code § 65302.4.[5] For a discussion of form-based zoning, see chapter 4 (Zoning).

Circulation element. The circulation element must identify the general location and extent of existing and proposed major thoroughfares, transportation routes, terminals, and other local public utilities and facilities. It serves as an infrastructure plan and must correlate with the remaining elements of the plan, including the land use element. *See Concerned Citizens of Calaveras County v. Board of Supervisors*, 166 Cal. App. 3d 90, 94 (1985).

The circulation element both determines and constrains the pattern and extent of development. Generally, this element contains detailed maps, standards for operation (e.g., traffic level of service), policies (e.g., promoting disabled accessibility), and financing plans. Specific circulation components addressed by this element may include, among many others, public transit, bicycle facilities, parking, truck routes, sewage transport and treatment, electric and gas transmission lines, drainage facilities, and waterways. Gov't Code § 65302(b). Legislation enacted in 2008 requires legislative bodies revising their circulation elements after January 1, 2011 to plan for a transportation network that meets the needs of all types of users, including bicyclists, children, persons with disabilities, pedestrians, public transit users, and seniors. The legislation also requires the Office of Planning and Research to develop guidelines to help cities and counties comply with this mandate prior to the OPR's next revision to its general plan guidelines, which must occur no later than January 1, 2014. Gov't Code § 65040.2.

OPR = Office of Planning and Research

Housing element. While cities generally have considerable flexibility in drafting the elements of the general plan, the housing element must comply with the elaborate statutory provisions of article 10.6 of the Government Code (Gov't Code § 65580 *et seq.*). Government Code section 65583 establishes the required contents of a housing element. In adopting a housing element, a city must consider economic environmental, and fiscal factors, as well as community goals set forth in the general plan. Gov't Code § 65580(e).

---

5 *See* Rebecca Retzlaff, *California Enacts Form-Based Zoning Legislation*, Zoning Practice, pages 10–11 (APA, January 2005) (discussing California's form-based zoning law which seeks to integrate streets, open space, housing, commercial development, and neighborhoods, rather than grouping similar and related land uses); *see also* Carla M. Moynihan, *Implementing Form-Based Zoning in Your Municipality*, 47 Mun. Lawyer 15 (2006); Robert J. Sitkowski & Brian W. Ohm, *Form-Based Land Development Regulations*, 38 The Urban Lawyer 163 (2006); Michael Moore, *Form-Based Zoning Is Not the (Whole) Answer*, APA Northern News, page 1 (May/June 2006); William Fulton, *Transition Away from Suburbia Bolsters Form-Based Zoning Movement*, 21 Cal. Plan. & Dev. Rep. 1 (April 2006).

Among other things, the housing element must contain an assessment of the jurisdiction's existing and projected housing needs that includes the jurisdiction's "fair share" of regional housing needs in accordance with Government Code section 65584. Gov't Code § 65583(a). It must also contain a land inventory (Gov't Code § 65583(a)(3)), and identify adequate sites to provide for the needs of households at all income levels. The element must contain a statement of the community's goals, policies, quantified objectives, financial resources, and scheduled programs for the preservation, improvement, and development of housing. (Gov't Code § 65583(b)(1)) and shall address and remove—where appropriate and possible—governmental constraints to the development of housing for all income levels. Gov't Code § 65583(c)(3). When the inventory of sites does not identify adequate sites to accommodate the need for all household income groups, rezoning of the identified sites is required to be completed within specified timelines, with extensions of time allowed for only limited circumstances. Gov't Code §§ 65583(c)(1)(A), 65583(f). Where a city fails to complete rezoning with the time required, its ability to disapprove a housing development project or to require a local discretionary permit for such development may be limited. Gov't Code § 65583(g). An applicant for a housing development project or any other interested party may bring an action to enforce these rezoning requirements. Gov't Code § 65583(g)(3).

In evaluating the adequacy of a housing element, a court will limit its review to determining whether a city has "substantially complied" with the statutory requirements, and will not engage in an examination of the merits. *Hernandez*, 28 Cal. App. 4th at 1059 (a city's housing element withstood attack by low-income and homeless petitioners since it complied with statutory requirements); *but see Hoffmaster v. City of San Diego*, 55 Cal. App. 4th 1098, 1111 (1997) (providing guidance regarding what constitutes "substantial compliance").

In enacting these requirements, the Legislature declared that the availability of housing is a matter of "vital statewide importance," and "the early attainment of decent housing and a suitable living environment for every Californian, including farmworkers, is a priority of the highest order." Gov't Code § 65580(a). The housing "goal requires cooperative participation between government and the private sector," and the use of state and local governmental power "to facilitate the improvement and development of housing…[for] all economic segments of the community." Gov't Code §§ 65580(b)-(d).

At least one court has discussed the Legislature's intent to ensure that cities recognize their responsibility to adopt housing elements that contribute to the attainment of state housing goals. *See Committee for Responsible Planning v. City of Indian Wells*, 209 Cal. App. 3d 1005, 1013 (1989).

In some respects, the housing element has been elevated above other required elements of the general plan. Under Government Code section 65589.5(d), a city may not deny specific types of affordable housing projects or condition approval of such a project in a manner that makes the project infeasible unless certain findings are made, such as the project would have a specific adverse impact upon the public health and safety that cannot be satisfactorily mitigated without rendering it unaffordable. In addition, the Housing Accountability Act, also known as the "Anti-NIMBY" law, prohibits denial of a housing project that "complies with applicable, objective general plan and zoning standards and criteria, including [applicable] design review standards," without making specific findings based on substantial evidence, even if the project does not include any affordable units. *Honchariw v. County of Stanislaus*, 200 Cal. App. 4th 1066, 1068 (2011).

The housing element shall be reviewed "as frequently as appropriate" in order to evaluate progress made and any changes in conditions affecting a city's housing needs. It must be revised as necessary, though depending on jurisdiction and other factors, a minimum four-year, five-year, or eight-year cycle may apply. Gov't Code § 65588. For example, a housing element revision is due every eight years where (1) the jurisdiction at issue lies within a "non-attainment" region under the federal Clean Air Act (42 U.S.C. § 7506); or (2) the local government has elected to opt into an eight-year cycle pursuant to Government Code section 65080(b)(2)(L). Gov't Code § 65588(a), (b), (e). More specific provisions regarding the timetables by which cities must revise their housing elements are set forth in Government Code sections 65588 and 65588.1.

Generally, the schedule for housing element revisions is dependent on the adoption of regional transportation plans; anti-sprawl legislation passed in 2008 (SB 375) established this link in an effort to tie land use development to transportation planning. For more discussion, see chapter 16 (Sustainable Development). Nevertheless, failure to comply with the timetable will not automatically invalidate a general plan or its housing element. *See San Mateo County Coastal Landowners' Ass'n v. County of San Mateo*, 38 Cal. App. 4th 523, 544 (1995) (to invalidate a housing element on the basis that it has not been timely revised, plaintiff must show how the failure to timely revise is connected to a substantive deficiency in the general plan or the housing element). This revision schedule is unique to the housing element; the remainder of the general plan must be reviewed only periodically and updated only when warranted by changing circumstances. Gov't Code § 65103(a); *see also Citizens of Goleta Valley*, 52 Cal. 3d at 572; *Garat*, 2 Cal. App. 4th at 298; *Friends of Aviara v. City of Carlsbad*, 210 Cal. App. 4th 1103, 1112–13 (2012) (delay in amending land use element to ensure consistency with updated housing element does not render housing element invalid provided city adopts a timeline for amending land use element).

Special attention is given to housing needs within the state's coastal zone, and detailed provisions apply. Gov't Code §§ 65588(d), 65590, 65590.1.

Conservation element. While there may be some overlap with the open space and safety elements, the conservation element's primary focus is on natural resources. The conservation element of the general plan must address the identification, conservation, development, and use of natural resources including water, forests, soils, waterways, wildlife, and mineral deposits. Gov't Code § 65302(d). This element may consider issues such as flood control, water and air pollution, erosion, conversion of farmland, endangered species, and the timing and impact of mining and logging activities. Moreover, under flood control legislation enacted in 2007, any revision to this element must identify rivers, creeks, streams, flood corridors, riparian habitat, and land that may accommodate floodwater for purposes of groundwater recharge and storm water management. Gov't Code § 65302(d). The portion of the conservation element addressing water issues must be developed in coordination with all local agencies that deal with water.

Regarding geologic resources, the conservation element must include mineral resource management policies to address the conservation and development of identified mineral deposits designated by the state geologist as being of statewide or regional significance. The goal is to balance the value of those deposits against competing land uses that may prevent future access to the minerals, and to minimize the impact of mining activities. Pub. Res. Code § 2761 *et seq.*

Open space element. The primary purpose of the open space element is "[t]o assure that cities and counties recognize that open space land is a limited and valuable resource which must be conserved wherever possible," and to discourage "premature and unnecessary conversion of open space land to urban uses...and non-contiguous development patterns...." Gov't Code §§ 65561(a), (b). To this end, state law specifically forbids building permits, subdivision maps, and open space zoning ordinances that are inconsistent with the local open space plan. Gov't Code § 65567.

The open space element is the plan for the "comprehensive and long-range preservation and conservation of open space land." Gov't Code § 65563. Under the Government Code, "open space" includes open space for the preservation of natural resources, for the managed production of resources, for outdoor recreation, for public health and safety, and in support of military installations. Gov't Code § 65560(b).

State law also requires that an open space plan account for the preservation of Native American artifacts, sites, and remains. Gov't Code § 65560(b)(6) (citing Pub. Res. Code §§ 5097.9, 5097.993). Where land designated or proposed to be designated as open space contains such sites, the city must consult with the tribe regarding the level of confidentiality required to protect the site and the treatment of the site in any management plan. Gov't Code § 65562.5.

State law mandates an ambitious and detailed planning effort for open space. The open space element "shall contain an action program consisting of specific programs which the legislative body intends to pursue." Gov't Code § 65564. That action program must include the adoption of an open space zoning ordinance consistent with the element (Gov't Code § 65910) that, among other things, designates exclusive agricultural zones, large-lot zones, and special overlay requirements for hazard areas, and avoids taking or damaging private property without compensation. Gov't Code §§ 65910, 65912. The open space element also must contain goals and policies for preserving and managing open space and an inventory of all open space property, whether privately or publicly owned. Gov't Code §§ 65560, 65563, 65564; *see also Save El Toro Ass'n v. Days*, 74 Cal. App. 3d 64, 72 (1977).[6]

Noise element. The noise element must identify and appraise noise problems in the community. To the extent practicable, current and projected noise levels are calculated and mapped for roadways, railroads, airports, industrial plants, and other major noise sources. Gov't Code § 65302(f). In addition to identifying problems, noise measurements are used as a guide for establishing a pattern of land uses in the land use element that minimizes the exposure of community residents to excessive noise. Implementation measures and possible solutions to existing and foreseeable noise problems must be included in the noise element. Gov't Code § 65302(f)(4); *see Camp*, 123 Cal. App. 3d at 352. These measures may involve sound barriers to shield noise-sensitive land uses (i.e., hospitals, schools, and housing), restricted operating hours for stationary noise generators, protective building design, and location of new roadways. Noise element guidelines issued by the State Office of Noise Control, as well as the state's noise insulation standards, must be considered and applied during preparation of the noise element. Gov't Code § 65302(f).

Safety element. The safety element must establish policies and programs to protect the community from risks associated with seismic, geologic, flood, and wildfire hazards. Known seismic and other geologic hazards must be mapped, and issues such

---

[6] For a discussion of fees in the context of open space programs, see *Funding Open Space Acquisition Programs: A Guide for Local Agencies in California* (Institute for Local Government, League of California Cities, 2005), available at http://www.cailg.org/sites/ilgbackup.org/files/2005-Open_Space-w.pdf.

as emergency evacuation routes and water supply for firefighting must be addressed. Gov't Code § 65302(g).

The safety element is the major tool for identifying hazards that should be considered in preparing the land use element and other elements of the general plan, and should be consulted before making land use decisions. The policies and programs in the safety element usually are supported by detailed maps of fault zones, mudslides, watercourse and oceanside flooding, dam collapse inundation areas, ground subsidence, vegetation density/slope combinations for fire risk, and other safety-related concerns. Some cities include a broad range of safety-related issues that may be locally relevant, such as the use, transport, and disposal of hazardous materials, power failure, and vehicle accidents.

Consistent with the goals of the safety element, a statewide program has been established to identify and work to mitigate potentially hazardous buildings located within dangerous seismic areas. Gov't Code §§ 8875, 8876. The program requires local building departments to identify potentially hazardous buildings within their jurisdictions, including the current building use and daily occupancy load. It also requires that building owners be notified that the building is considered to be at risk in an earthquake. Building departments must establish mitigation programs for identified buildings, which may include measures to strengthen buildings and incentives such as low-cost seismic rehabilitation loans. Gov't Code § 8875.2. The program does not require the state or any local government to assume the cost associated with compliance. It also gives such governments immunity from liability for action or inaction under the program. Gov't Code § 8875.3.

Each city is also required to consult with the Division of Mines and Geology of the Department of Conservation and to include in the safety element information available from both the Division and the Office of Emergency Services. Gov't Code § 65302(g). A city must submit a copy of the draft element or amendment to the Division for its review and comment at least 45 days prior to the adoption of or amendment to the safety element. Gov't Code § 65302.5. The Division is authorized to report its findings to the city's planning commission for its consideration within 30 days of receipt of the draft element or amendment. *Id.*

The Division's findings must be considered by a city prior to final adoption of the element or amendment, unless such comments are not available within the 45-day period, or where the Division has indicated it will not review the element. After the safety element is adopted, a copy of the adopted element or amendment must be submitted to the Division.

In addition, any county containing a "state responsibility area" and any city or county containing a "very high fire hazard severity zone" must submit its safety element for review and comment by the State Board of Forestry and Fire Protection and any local agencies that provide fire protection to the city or county. Gov't Code §§ 65302.5(a)(1), (a)(2). The city or county must submit its existing safety element for such review by dates established in Government Code section 65302.5(a)(2). Where a city or county proposes to adopt a new safety element or amend its safety element, it shall submit the draft element or proposed amendment to the reviewing Board and local fire agencies at least 90 days prior to adoption or amendment. Gov't Code §§ 65302.5(a) (1), (a)(2). The Board shall, and the local agency may, report recommendations to the city's planning commission or the county's board of supervisors within 60 days of receipt of the existing or draft safety element. Gov't Code § 65302.5(a)(3).

Prior to its adoption of a draft safety element or draft amendment, the city or county must consider the Board's and the local agency's recommendations. If the city or county declines to accept some or all of the recommendations, it must communicate its reasons in writing to the Board or the local agency. Gov't Code § 65302.5(b). If the Board's or local agency's recommendations are not available within the above timeframes, the city or county may act without them. Gov't Code § 65302.5(c).

Concern about vulnerabilities in the Sacramento-San Joaquin Valley region triggered a spate of flood legislation in 2007, adding a number of requirements, including a consultation requirement. Gov't Code § 65302(g)(2). In addition to identifying various hazards, the safety element now must establish a set of comprehensive goals, policies, and objectives that would protect a given community from the unreasonable risks of flooding. *Id.* Each city and county located within the boundaries of the Sacramento and San Joaquin Drainage District must also submit a draft of the safety element to the newly created Central Valley Flood Protection Board (formerly the Reclamation Board, but with new powers and a new governance structure), as well as to every local agency that provides flood protection to territory in the city or county. *Id.*; *see* Gov't Code § 65302.9(a) (requiring flood protection amendments to the general plan within 24 months after the Central Valley Protection Board's adoption of a specified flood protection plan under Water Code section 9612. Note this draft must be submitted to the Central Valley Flood Protection Board and local agencies at least 90 days prior to the adoption of, or amendment to, the safety element. Gov't Code § 65302.7. Written recommendations by the Board and local agencies are due within 60 days. *Id.* Once the required flood protection amendments are effective, cities within the Sacramento-San Joaquin Valley shall not approve discretionary permits, ministerial permits for new residences, or tentative or parcel maps, for projects within a flood hazard zone unless the city makes certain findings based on substantial evidence. Gov't Code §§ 65962, 66474.5.

Statutory criteria for mandatory elements. To be legally adequate, the mandatory elements of the general plan must meet the minimum requirements contained in state law. *See Hernandez,* 28 Cal. App. 4th at 1070; *Buena Vista Gardens Apartments Ass'n v. City of San Diego,* 175 Cal. App. 3d 289, 298 (1985); *Concerned Citizens of Calaveras County,* 166 Cal. App. 3d at 95; *Twain Harte Homeowners Ass'n,* 138 Cal. App. 3d at 696; *Camp,* 123 Cal. App. 3d at 352.

> To be legally adequate, the mandatory elements of the general plan must meet the minimum requirements contained in state law.

In *Camp,* the court addressed the fatal inadequacies of the county's noise element:

> The so-called "noise element" of the Mendocino County General Plan is set out in a separate pamphlet which shows that it was adopted by the Board in 1976.... It includes no "noise exposure information...presented" in the technical nomenclature ("CNEL" and "Ldn") required...[and] shows nothing "determined by monitoring" with regard to "areas deemed noise sensitive" as required by the next paragraph of the statute.... For these reasons and others, it does not substantially comply with the requirements of section 65302, subdivision (g).

> The County asserts that it is "certainly adequate for [a] quiet rural county such as Mendocino," but the test is neither geographical nor subjective: it is purely statutory, and the County has failed it.

123 Cal. App. 3d at 352

In *Twain Harte,* the court found the county's general plan legally inadequate because it lacked an "appropriate statement of standards" for population density based on numbers of people, and no standards for building intensity for the nonresidential areas of the county. 138 Cal. App. 3d at 699. The land use element, moreover, failed to include standards of population density and building intensity as required by Government Code section 65302(a), and the circulation element was fatally flawed because it was not correlated with the land use element, as required by Government Code section 65302(b). *Id.* at 700–02.

In *Concerned Citizens*, the court stated that the correlation between the land use and circulation elements required by Government Code section 65302(b) could not be achieved if the general plan called for solving traffic deficiencies simply by asking other governmental agencies for money. 166 Cal. App. 3d at 99.

In *Buena Vista Gardens*, the court held that a permit for a planned residential development could not be approved until the city demonstrated that its plan included housing development programs to "conserve and improve the condition of existing affordable housing stock" as required by Government Code section 65583(c)(4). 175 Cal. App. 3d at 303.

As the examples illustrate, it is imperative that a city ensure that all of the statutory criteria are contained in the mandatory elements of its general plan.

Optional (permissive) elements. In addition to the seven mandatory elements, the general plan may include any other elements or address any other subjects that, in the judgment of a city, relate to the physical development of the city. Gov't Code § 65303.[7]

Once an optional element has been adopted, it becomes a full-fledged part of the general plan, with the same legal force and effect as the mandatory elements. The requirements of internal consistency among all general plan elements, and of consistency between the general plan and other land use decisions, apply equally to optional elements. *See* 58 Ops. Cal. Atty. Gen. 21, 25 (1975).

Optional general plan elements have been adopted by cities on a wide variety of topics. Any subject is appropriate when there is a concern in the community to study and plan regarding an issue not addressed in sufficient detail in the mandatory elements. Some of the more common areas of concern have been air quality, recreation, design, economic development, infrastructure, energy, historic preservation, and redevelopment. Elements addressing more unique subjects also have been adopted, such as tourism, urban forest, law enforcement, quality of life, arts, and agriculture.[8]

It is possible for a city to expand its authority by adopting an element to its general plan. For example, if a city adopts a certified geothermal element, state agencies then may delegate their responsibility for environmental review of exploratory wells to the city as lead agency. Pub. Res. Code § 3715.5. Similarly, primary permitting powers for large geothermal plants may be delegated to the city upon its request. Pub. Res. Code § 25540.5.

Organization. All elements of the general plan have equal legal status. In *Sierra Club*, the court declared void a precedence clause giving one element priority over another. 126 Cal. App. 3d at 704. This general rule is subject to limits on a city's discretion to deny certain affordable housing projects, resulting in an elevation of the housing element over the other elements of a general plan. Even if an affordable housing project is inconsistent with a city's zoning ordinance and general plan land use designation, such inconsistency may not be the basis for denying the project if it is proposed on a site that is identified for very low-, low-, or moderate-income households in the city's housing elements, and is consistent with the density specified in the housing element.

> Optional general plan elements have been adopted by cities on a wide variety of topics. Any subject is appropriate when there is a concern in the community to study and plan regarding an issue not addressed in sufficient detail in the mandatory elements.

---

7   See chapter 6 of OPR's General Plan Guidelines (2003) for a detailed discussion of optional elements.

8   For examples of optional elements, see Governor's Office of Planning and Research, *California Planners' 2011 Book of Lists (2012)*, pages 83–98, available at http://opr.ca.gov/docs/2011.bol.pdf

Gov't Code § 65589.5(d)(5). *See also* chapter 15 (Affordable Housing). Otherwise, each city is accorded great flexibility in designing the general plan's structure, as long as it satisfies the minimum requirements as to content, format, and procedure. Gov't Code §§ 65300.7, 65300.9; *see also Camp*, 123 Cal. App. 3d at 348.

Two or more state-mandated elements may be combined in a single element. Gov't Code § 65301(a). A combined element should explicitly set forth the relationship between its contents and planning requirements.

In addition to the text, the general plan "shall include a diagram or diagrams." Gov't Code § 65302. This requirement suggests that specificity as to individual parcels is not required because a "map" is considered to represent precision, whereas "diagram" represents approximation. *See* 67 Ops. Cal. Atty. Gen. 75 (1984). In one case, for example, the California Supreme Court noted the distinction between a circle drawn on a general plan, designating an area for potential commercial development, and the more precise location of a commercial "zone." *United Outdoor Adver. Co. v. Business, Transp. and Hous. Agency*, 44 Cal. 3d 242 (1988). The Court held:

> Unlike a zone, which delimits a well defined geographic area, the circle on the General Plan no more represents the precise boundary of a present or future commercial area than the dot or square on a map of California represents the exact size and shape of Baker or any other community.

Id. at 250

While some cities adopt their elements individually, this practice may create a number of problems, particularly if the elements have been prepared and adopted over many years without any correlation. Individual adoption makes internal consistency difficult to maintain, results in duplication, and usually results in a plan that is difficult to use and review.

LEGAL IMPLICATIONS OF A LEGALLY INADEQUATE GENERAL PLAN

Where a city's general plan is found to be inadequate, a land use approval is vulnerable whenever the inadequacy is relevant to the challenged approval. If a challenger can establish a nexus between the claimed deficiency or inadequacy and the approval being challenged, the approval may be set aside. *See Flavell v. City of Albany*, 19 Cal. App. 4th 1846 (1993); *Garat*, 2 Cal. App. 4th at 292-93; *Neighborhood Action Group v. County of Calaveras*, 156 Cal. App. 3d 1176, 1187 (1984). For example, if the defects in the general plan are related to a proposed land use action, such as a rezoning, the city cannot find that the new zoning is consistent with the general plan. Therefore, the rezoning could be declared invalid when passed—*void ab initio*—if successfully challenged in court. *See Lesher*, 52 Cal. 3d at 541 (citing *Sierra Club*, 126 Cal. App. 3d at 704); 73 Ops. Cal. Atty. Gen. 78 (1990).

The requirement that a city's general plan be adequate as a prerequisite to undertaking any land use approval has been emphasized repeatedly by the courts. *See Resource Defense Fund v. County of Santa Cruz*, 133 Cal. App. 3d 800, 806 (1982) ("Since consistency with the general plan is required, absence of a valid general plan, or valid relevant elements or components thereof, precludes any enactment of zoning ordinances and the like."); *see also Kings County Farm Bureau v. City of Hanford*, 221 Cal. App. 3d 692, 744-745 (1990) (project approval overturned based on the inadequacy of general plan elements related to the project); *Neighborhood Action Group*, 156 Cal. App. 3d at 1188 (issuance of a conditional use permit authorizing a project which would create noise impacts was beyond the county's authority if the noise element of the county's general plan does not conform to the statutory criteria); *City of Carmel-by-the-Sea v. Board of Supervisors*, 137 Cal. App. 3d 964, 974 (1982) (due to the inadequacy of the general plan, a use permit to constrict a resort hotel was necessarily void).

In 1991, however, one court upheld a land use initiative against a challenge based on an allegedly inadequate general plan. *See Garat*, 2 Cal. App. 4th at 298. The court held there were no statutory requirements that the general plan be updated at any particular time, except for the housing element, or that it be organized or kept in any particular format or location. In addition, the court held that since the petitioner did not prove a nexus between other alleged inadequacies in the general plan and the initiative, the challenge failed. *Id.*; *see also Flavell*, 19 Cal. App. 4th at 1853 (1993) (claim failed since the challenger did not prove a nexus between the alleged inadequacy of the housing element (not timely revised), and the adoption of a zoning ordinance relating to residential off-street parking requirements); *but see* Gov't Code § 65103(a) (city shall periodically revise its general plan) and *Garat*, 2 Cal. App. 4th at 296 n.28 (failure to update the general plan may cause it to be not in compliance with statutory requirements).

Subdivision approvals also must be consistent with an adequate general plan. Gov't Code § 66473.5. If one of the mandatory elements is missing, or if a relevant element is inadequate, a city cannot legally find the subdivision to be consistent with the general plan; thus, no valid subdivision approval will occur. For example, in *Camp v. Board of Supervisors*, the court said the county could not approve subdivisions because some of its general plan elements were inadequate under state law. 123 Cal. App. 3d at 349; *see also Friends of "B" St. v. City of Hayward*, 106 Cal. App. 3d 988, 999 (1980) (city could not proceed with a public works project because it was missing its noise element, and the project therefore could not conform to an officially adopted general plan); *Save El Toro Ass'n v. Days*, 74 Cal. App. 3d 64, 74 (1977) (city could not approve any subdivisions as its ordinances were not sufficient to constitute a comprehensive and long-range open space plan—as required by Government Code section 65563—due to its failure to prepare maps to be used in conducting an inventory of the open space resources available).

California Environmental Quality Act. Environmental review of a land use proposal also may be hampered by the legal inadequacy of a general plan. If a general plan lacks a mandatory element, an environmental impact report (EIR) on a project is "prepared in a vacuum." One court stated, "[t]he lack of a noise element in the general plan resulted in a subversion of CEQA, because a necessary foundation as to the level of acceptable noise made the EIR deficient." *Guardians of Turlock's Integrity v. City Council*, 149 Cal. App. 3d 584, 593 (1983).

EIR = environmental impact report

CEQA = California Environmental Quality Act

Environmental review also can flounder where actions taken under CEQA are inconsistent with a general plan provision. While the standard of review is highly deferential, "deference is not abdication," and a court will not sustain a city's interpretation of its general plan where the reading is unreasonable. *California Native Plant Society v. City of Rancho Cordova*, 172 Cal. App. 4th 603, 642 (2009) (quoting *People v. McDonald*, 37 Cal. 3d 351, 377 (1984)). In *California Native Plant Society*, the court invalidated a project approval where the city's general plan required the city to design mitigation measures "in coordination with" various federal and state agencies, but the city instead merely solicited and rejected advice from the agencies. *Id.* at 641. Turning to the dictionary, the court held the definition of "coordination" meant more than "*trying* to work together with someone else," and was not synonymous with "consultation." *Id.*

(emphasis in original) The court also looked at the procedural context at issue, and noted at least one of the agencies would be issuing a later permit, thus reinforcing the idea that "coordination" required a higher level of reciprocation among the parties. *Id.* at 641–42. The city's interpretation to the contrary therefore was rejected, and the resulting project approval was found to have violated the city's general plan. *Id.* at 642. For a further discussion of the requirements of CEQA, see chapter 6 (CEQA).

Charter cities. Charter cities have considerable autonomy regarding certain types of land use regulation. Where a regulation relates to a municipal affair, a charter city's own charter provisions or ordinances are controlling even where there is conflict with state law. Only where regulation is a matter of statewide concern must the charter city follow state law.

Much of the State Planning and Zoning Law does not apply to charter cities unless either a specific section provides otherwise or the charter city has expressly adopted the Planning and Zoning Law through its charter or an ordinance. Gov't Code § 65700. State law does require, however, that even a charter city adopt a general plan that includes all of the mandatory elements. Gov't Code §§ 65700, 65300.

With the exception of Los Angeles, charter cities are exempt from the requirement that zoning be consistent with the general plan, unless the charter city requires such consistency by its charter or by local ordinance. Gov't Code §§ 65803, 65860(d); *see also Garat*, 2 Cal. App. 4th at 281; *City of Irvine v. Irvine Citizens Against Overdevelopment*, 25 Cal. App. 4th 868, 874 (1994) (Irvine, a charter city, was subject to the consistency requirement because it had adopted a consistency rule). Almost 25 percent of charter cities have adopted a consistency rule. Notwithstanding the consistency exemption for charter cities, flood protection legislation requires all cities in the Sacramento-San Joaquin Valley, including charter cities, to make their zoning ordinances consistent with the flood protection goals and policies of each city's respective general plan. Gov't Code § 65860.1. Additionally, all subdivisions and all public works projects within a city, whether or not the city is a charter city, must be consistent with the general plan, or they will be subject to legal attack. *See Friends of "B" St.*, 106 Cal. App. 3d at 999.

INTERNAL (HORIZONTAL) CONSISTENCY

In general, a general plan must be integrated and internally consistent, both among the elements and within each element. Gov't Code § 65300.5; *see also Concerned Citizens of Calaveras County*, 166 Cal. App. 3d at 97-98 (general plan found to be internally inconsistent where one portion of the circulation element indicated that roads were sufficient for projected traffic increases, while another section of the same element described increased traffic congestion as a result of continued subdivision development). This rule applies to both optional elements and mandatory elements. If there is internal inconsistency, the general plan is legally inadequate and the required finding of consistency for land use approvals cannot be made. This section also applies to charter cities. *See Garat*, 2 Cal. App. 4th 259 at 286.

As discussed earlier in the chapter, the general rule requiring internal consistency may be trumped by state affordable housing law, which may limit a city's power to disapprove certain affordable housing projects even where the projects are inconsistent with a city's zoning ordinance and general plan designation. Gov't Code 65589.5(d)(5).

Because the adoption or amendment of a general plan is a legislative act presumed to be valid, cities need not make explicit findings to support their actions. A court therefore cannot find a general plan to be internally inconsistent unless, based on the evidence before the city council, a reasonable person could not conclude that the plan was internally consistent. *Federation of Hillside & Canyon Ass'ns v. City of Los Angeles*, 126 Cal. App. 4th 1180 (2004).

Internal consistency requires that diagrams in the land use, circulation, open space, and natural resource elements reflect the written policies and programs of those elements. *See generally Citizens Ass'n for Sensible Dev. of Bishop Area v. County of Inyo*, 172 Cal. App. 3d 151 (1985); *Environmental Council v. Board of Supervisors*, 135 Cal. App. 3d 428 (1982); *Karlson v. City of Camarillo*, 100 Cal. App. 3d 789 (1980). The internal consistency requirement may not be evaded by incorporating a subordination or precedence clause, such as "in the event of a conflict, the land use element controls." *See Sierra Club*, 126 Cal. App. 3d at 708 (expressly rejecting use of a precedence clause, where the county general plan's land use and open space elements designated conflicting land uses for the same property). However, where a delay in amending the land use element to make it consistent with an updated housing element causes a temporary internal inconsistency, the adopted housing element is not invalid provided the city adopts a timeline for amending the land use element to eliminate the inconsistency. *Friends of Aviara v. City of Carlsbad*, 210 Cal. App. 4th 1103, 1112–13 (2012)

CONSISTENCY BETWEEN GENERAL PLAN AND OTHER LAND USE AND DEVELOPMENT ACTIONS (VERTICAL CONSISTENCY)

Since the general plan is the constitution for all future development, any decision by a city affecting land use and development must be consistent with the general plan. *See Friends of Lagoon Valley*, 154 Cal. App. 4th at 815; *Citizens of Goleta Valley*, 52 Cal. 3d at 570.

"An action, program or project is consistent with the general plan if, considering all its aspects, it will further the objectives and policies of the general plan and not obstruct their attainment." Governor's Office of Planning and Research, *General Plan Guidelines* (2003), page 164; *see Corona-Norco Unified Sch. Dist. v. City of Corona*, 13 Cal. App. 4th 1577 (1993); *Irvine Citizens Against Overdevelopment*, 25 Cal. App. 4th at 879 (1994). To be consistent, an action, program, or project must be "in agreement or harmony" with the general plan. *Friends of Lagoon Valley*, 154 Cal. App. 4th at 817 (upholding the City's approval of the Lower Lagoon Valley Policy Plan Implementation Project and the City's finding that the Project was consistent with its general plan).

As discussed above, charter cities are exempt from the mandate that zoning be consistent with the general plan, unless the city's charter provides otherwise. Gov't Code § 65803. *See Garat*, 2 Cal. App. 4th at 282 (where city regulations did not provide for consistency); *Irvine Citizens Against Overdevelopment*, 25 Cal. App. 4th at 868 (where city ordinance did require consistency). However, this exemption applies only to zoning and not to consistency requirements for subdivision map approval, public works construction, or for other subordinate land use or development approvals. *See Friends of "B" St.*, 106 Cal. App. 3d at 999; *but see* Gov't Code § 65860.1 (charter cities, as well as general law cities, within Sacramento-San Joaquin Valley must ensure zoning is consistent with flood protection goals and polices of general plan).

Reviewing courts generally defer to cities' superior abilities to interpret and apply the general plan policies they have authored. "When we review an agency's decision for consistency with its own general plan, we accord great deference to the agency's determination. This is because the body which adopted the general plan policies in its legislative capacity has unique competence to interpret those policies when applying them in its adjudicatory capacity." *Save Our Peninsula Comm. v. County of Monterey*, 87 Cal.

> Reviewing courts generally defer to cities' superior abilities to interpret and apply the general plan policies they have authored.

App. 4th 99, 142 (2001) (citing *City of Walnut Creek v. County of Contra Costa*, 101 Cal. App. 3d 1012, 1021 (1980)). The court's review is highly deferential because "policies in a general plan reflect a range of competing interests" and the city "must be allowed to weigh and balance the plan's policies when applying them, and it has broad discretion to construe its policies in light of the plan's purpose." *Friends of Lagoon Valley*, 154 Cal. App. 4th at 816; *see Anderson First Coalition v. City of Anderson*, 130 Cal. App. 4th 1173, 1192 (2005); *San Franciscans Upholding the Downtown Plan v. City and County of San Francisco*, 102 Cal. App. 4th 656, 668 (2002).

It is the city's responsibility to determine whether proposed land use development approvals are consistent with the general plan. A determination regarding such consistency is a legislative decision and will not be set aside by a court unless the city has acted arbitrarily, capriciously, or without evidentiary support, or has failed to follow proper procedures, such as failing to give notice as required by law. *See San Franciscans Upholding the Downtown Plan*, 102 Cal. App. 4th at 668 (claim that redevelopment plan amendments were inconsistent with the general plan reviewed under arbitrary and capricious standard); *No Oil, Inc. v. City of Los Angeles*, 196 Cal. App. 3d 223, 233 (1987) (judicial review of a zoning ordinance's consistency with the general plan is limited to a determination of whether the agency's action was arbitrary, capricious, or entirely without evidentiary support); *Mitchell v. County of Orange*, 165 Cal. App. 3d 1185, 1191–92 (1985) (county's determination that a specific plan is consistent with its general plan is legislative, and the reviewing court is limited to an examination of whether the action was arbitrary and capricious); *Ideal Boat & Camper Storage v. County of Alameda*, 208 Cal. App. 4th 301, 320 (2012) (county's denial of discretionary site development permit as inconsistent with general plan policies held not to be arbitrary, capricious, or without evidentiary support).

Although a city's decision regarding consistency of an action with the general plan is legislative, the decision necessitates some factual determinations. *See Building Indus. Ass'n v. City of Oceanside*, 27 Cal. App. 4th 744, 761 (1994); *Building Indus. Ass'n v. Superior Court*, 211 Cal. App. 3d 277, 291 (1989). A court will defer to a city's interpretation of its own general plan and factual findings unless "based on the evidence before [the] city council, a reasonable person could not have reached the same conclusion." *No Oil*, 196 Cal. App. 3d at 243 (applying the "arbitrary and capricious" standard of review and upholding the city's specific finding of consistency between the general plan and an ordinance establishing oil drilling zones). In *Endangered Habitats League, Inc. v. County of Orange*, the court overturned a set of project approvals due to their inconsistency with mandatory requirements of the general plan and the specific plan. 131 Cal. App. 4th 777, 788, 785-86 (2005); *see also California Native Plant Society*, 172 Cal. App. 4th at 642 (city could not reasonably have determined mitigation was designed "in coordination" with federal agency, as the general plan required).

Notwithstanding such purported judicial deference, some appellate courts have overturned a city or county's finding that a land use approval was consistent with the agency's general plan. In *Families Unafraid to Uphold Rural El Dorado County v. County of El Dorado*, the court overturned the county's finding that a planned development was consistent with the general plan, stating it was "readily apparent that the [Low Density Residential] designation for [the development] is inconsistent with the Draft General Plan." 62 Cal. App. 4th 1332, 1341 (1998). Despite the usual deference of courts to consistency determinations, the county was unable to overcome the "specific, mandatory and fundamental inconsistencies" of the project with the land use policies of the general plan. *Id.* at 1342.

Even where there was no direct conflict, at least one appellate court found a land use approval inconsistent where it did not implement or advance the goals of the general plan.

In *Napa Citizens For Honest Government v. County of Napa Board of Supervisors*, the court overturned the county's determination that an updated specific plan was consistent with the general plan. 91 Cal. App. 4th 342 (2001). While the specific plan did not directly conflict with any stated goals or policies of the general plan, it did not actually implement general plan goals and policies, nor did it require any specific action that would further such goals and policies. The specific plan included a circulation element that contained no specific highway improvements, nor any detailed statement of goals or policies, even though the general plan explicitly stated an increase in traffic would cause unacceptable congestion, and even though the project was found to increase traffic. In addition, the specific plan contained no specific action for providing housing even though the general plan stated it was the county's goal to meet the housing needs of persons living in the area, and it was found the approved project would increase the need for housing. *Id.* at 379-81. The court found the specific plan would improperly "frustrate" the general plan. *Id.* at 379.

In the subdivision context, Government Code section 66473.5 requires that approvals of tentative maps be consistent with a city's general plan. However, the Subdivision Map Act (Gov't Code § 66410 *et seq.*) does not require an exact match between the tentative map and the general plan or specific plan. The tentative map only need be in agreement or harmony with the general or specific plan. *See Sequoyah Hills Homeowners Ass'n v. City of Oakland*, 23 Cal. App. 4th 704, 717-18 (1993) (city's determination that the map was consistent with 14 of 17 general plan policies was held legally adequate); *Greenebaum v. City of Los Angeles*, 153 Cal. App. 3d 391, 408 (1984). As to consistency, the court in *Sequoyah Hills* held that a given project including a map need not be in perfect conformity with each and every general plan policy.

> Indeed, it is beyond cavil that no project could completely satisfy every policy stated in the [Oakland Comprehensive Plan], and that state law does not impose such a requirement (*Greenebaum v. City of Los Angeles*, 153 Cal. App. 3d at 406-07; 59 Ops. Cal. Atty. Gen. 129, 131 (1976)). A general plan must try to accommodate a wide range of competing interests—including those of developers, neighboring homeowners, prospective homebuyers, environmentalists, current and prospective business owners, jobseekers, taxpayers, and providers and recipients of all types of city-provided services—and to present a clear and comprehensive set of principles to guide development decisions. Once a general plan is in place, it is the province of elected city officials to examine the specifics of a proposed project to determine whether it would be "in harmony" with the policies stated in the plan. It is, emphatically, not the role of the courts to micromanage these development decisions. Our function is simply to decide whether the city officials considered the applicable policies and the extent to which the proposed project conforms with those policies, whether the city officials made appropriate findings on this issue, and whether those findings are supported by substantial evidence. (Code Civ. Proc. § 1094.5(c); *Youngblood v. Board of Supervisors*, 22 Cal. 3d 644, 651 (1978)).

Sequoyah Hills, 23 Cal. App. 4th at 719-20 (internal citation omitted); *but see Families Unafraid to Uphold Rural El Dorado County*, 62 Cal. App. 4th at 1332 (holding the county's findings of consistency between a proposed residential subdivision and the draft general plan were not supported by substantial evidence).

There are several exceptions to the Subdivision Map Act's consistency requirement. In *Corona-Norco Unified School District v. City of Corona*, the court held that Government Code section 65996 creates an express exception to the general requirement of

> The tentative map only need be in agreement or harmony with the general or specific plan.

consistency by precluding a city from denying approval of a development project under the Map Act based on inadequate school facilities. 13 Cal. App. 4th at 1584. Although the court stated that it did not "mean to diminish the importance of the consistency doctrine in the planning process," the Legislature made clear "that development takes precedence to the adequacy of school facilities." Id. at 1585.

In addition, under Government Code section 65589.5(d), a city may not disapprove a housing development on the basis that such development is inconsistent with the city's general plan and zoning designation so long as the proposed project is on a site identified for very low-, low-, or moderate-income households in the city's housing element, and is consistent with the density specified in the housing element, even if the project is inconsistent with the city's general plan and zoning designation.

Finally, consistency is required only in the context of approvals for future development. For example, as to public works projects, a city is not required to bring existing public works projects, including neighborhoods and streets, into compliance with the general plan. See *Friends of H Street v. City of Sacramento*, 20 Cal. App. 4th 152, 169 (1993) (requirements of general plan compliance were not applicable to the maintenance and operation of an existing street completed before the consistency mandate came into effect).

CONSISTENCY WITH AIRPORT LAND USE PLAN

ALUP = Airport Land Use Plan

General plans must be consistent with any Airport Land Use Plan (ALUP) adopted by a county airport land use commission pursuant to Public Utilities Code section 21675, unless the city overrules the commission and makes certain findings. Gov't Code § 65302.3(a); *Muzzy Ranch Co. v. Solano County Airport Land Use Comm'n*, 41 Cal. 4th 372, 384 (2007). If a city does not concur with any aspect of the ALUP, it may overrule the commission's ALUP by a two-thirds vote if it makes specific findings that the decision to overrule the ALUP is consistent with the purposes of protecting public health, safety, and welfare, minimizing the public's exposure to excessive noise, and minimizing safety hazards within areas around the public airport. See Pub. Util. Code §§ 21670, 21676. At least 45 days prior to such decision, the city shall provide a copy of the proposed decision and findings to the commission and the Division of Aeronautics of the State Department of Transportation. The commission and the Division may provide comments to the local agency governing body within 30 days of receiving the proposed decision and findings. If the commission's or Division's comments are not available within this time limit, the city may overrule the ALUP without receiving them. These comments are merely advisory to the city; however, the city must include them in the final record of any final decision to overrule the ALUP. See *California Aviation Council v. City of Ceres*, 9 Cal. App. 4th 1384, 1395 (1992) (a city's ordinance approving a portion of a specific plan that was inconsistent with the local ALUP was invalid because the city did not make the specific findings required by Public Utilities Code section 21676(b)). The general plan must be amended as necessary within 180 days of any amendment to the ALUP. Gov't Code § 65302.3(b).

A county airport land use commission may not "exempt" a general or specific plan from this consistency requirement where a conflict otherwise exists. The California Attorney General has opined that to allow a city's or county's plan to simply be "exempted" from consistency with the more stringent requirements of an ALUP would undermine the legislative intent behind the detailed procedure provided in the Public Resources Code for resolving conflicts between a city or county's plan and an ALUP. 87 Ops. Cal. Atty. Gen. 102 (2004).

PROCEDURE FOR ADOPTION AND AMENDMENT[9]

When adopting or amending a general plan, a city must follow the procedures set forth in Government Code section 65350 *et seq.* The planning commission must hold a public hearing on the adoption or amendment and make a written recommendation to the city council. Gov't Code §§ 65353(a), 65354. The commission's recommendation for approval must be made by an affirmative vote of not less than a majority of its total membership; thus, if a planning commission consists of seven members, there must be four affirmative votes to recommend approval to the city council. Gov't Code § 65354. Unless an applicant appeals a planning commission's denial of a request for a general plan amendment, the request will not be automatically heard by the council. Accordingly, a city with a planning commission that has the authority to consider and recommend approval or disapproval of a general plan amendment must provide a procedure to appeal the action of the planning commission to the city council. Gov't Code § 65354.5.

Once it receives the recommendation of the planning commission, and prior to adopting or amending the general plan, the city council must hold at least one public hearing. The city council may approve, modify, or disapprove the recommendation of the planning commission, but any substantial modification made to the proposed plan or amendment that was not previously considered by the commission must be referred back for its recommendation. Gov't Code § 65356.

A general plan is adopted or amended by resolution. Gov't Code § 65356. Because the nature of the resolution is legislative, it does not take effect until the 30-day period for referendum has elapsed. *See Midway Orchards v. County of Butte*, 220 Cal. App. 3d 765, 780 (1990). For a detailed discussion of the referendum process, see chapter 13 (Initiative and Referendum).

For a discussion of the additional requirements that apply when adopting or amending a general plan's housing element, see the earlier discussion in this chapter on the housing element and the discussion in chapter 15 (Affordable Housing). For a thorough discussion of the environmental review process required by CEQA and applicable to all discretionary land use actions, including adoption and amendment of general plans, see chapter 6 (CEQA).

A mandatory element of the general plan may be amended only four times during any calendar year. Gov't Code § 65358(b). However, more than one change can be made at a time and will be considered a single general plan amendment. *Id.*; *see also* 66 Ops. Cal. Atty. Gen. 258 (1983). Amendments for affordable housing projects are exempt from this restriction. Gov't Code § 65358(c).

Prior to legislative approval, a city shall refer a proposal to adopt or substantially amend a general plan to the following agencies:

- Any county and city within or abutting the area covered by the proposal
- Any special district that may be significantly affected by the proposed action as determined by the planning agency
- Any elementary, high school, or unified school district within the area covered by the proposed action
- The local agency formation commission

---

[9] For a good history of planning law in California, starting with the adoption of the first planning law in 1927 by the Legislature, see the dissent by J. Arabian in *DeVita v. County of Napa*, 9 Cal. 4th 763, 808–13 (1995); see also William Fulton and Paul Shigley, *Guide to California Planning* (Solano Press, 4th ed. 2012) for an excellent discussion of how planning works in California.

- Any area-wide planning agency whose operations may be significantly affected by the proposed action
- Any federal agency if lands within its jurisdiction may be significantly affected by the proposed action
- Any public water system with 3,000 or more service connections that serves customers within the area covered by the proposal
- The Bay Area Air Quality Management District for a proposed action within its boundaries
- Any branch of the military with installations within 1,000 feet of the proposed action or if the action is within special use airspace or beneath a low-level flight path
- Any Native American tribe with traditional lands located within the city or county's jurisdiction
- The Central Valley Flood Protection Board for a proposed action within the boundaries of the Sacramento and San Joaquin Drainage District

Gov't Code § 65352

Generally, these agencies have 45 days to comment. Although the provision uses the word "shall," this section is directory, not mandatory (Gov't Code § 65352(c)(1)) and failure to comply does not invalidate the adoption or amendment of the plan.

Cities and counties also must refer a "proposed action" (general plan, specific plan, or zoning) to one another pursuant to Government Code section 65919 et seq. Thus, before acting on the proposed action, a county must refer it to the affected cities for comment and vice-versa. Gov't Code § 65919.3. If a housing element or an amendment to it is proposed for adoption, the draft first must be referred to the Department of Housing and Community Development (HCD) for its review and comment. Gov't Code § 65585(b). A 90-day review period is provided for an element; for an amendment, the review period is 60 days.

HCD = Department of Housing and Community Development

Copies of the general plan and amendments shall be made available for inspection by the public one working day following adoption. Within two working days after a request, copies shall be furnished to those so requesting. Gov't Code § 65357(b)(2); see *City of Poway v. City of San Diego*, 229 Cal. App. 3d 847, 862 (1991) (a general plan amendment was ineffective because it was not timely made available to the public).

IMPLEMENTATION AND ANNUAL REPORT

The planning agency must investigate and make recommendations to the city regarding reasonable and practical means for implementing the general plan or one of its elements so that the plan will serve as an effective guide for orderly growth and development, preservation and conservation of open space and natural resources, and the efficient expenditure of public funds relating to the subjects addressed in the general plan. The planning agency must render an annual report by April 1 of each year to the city council, OPR, and HCD, through the use of forms and definitions adopted by HCD, on the status of the plan and the progress in its implementation. Specifically, the report must include the progress in meeting its share of regional housing needs as determined by Government Code section 65584.01; the progress on local efforts to remove governmental constraints to the maintenance, improvement, and development of housing pursuant to Government Code section 65583(c)(3); the degree to which its approved general plan complies with the guidelines developed and adopted pursuant to Government Code section 65040.2; and the date of the last revision to the general plan. Gov't Code § 65400.

A general plan may be amended by initiative. *See DeVita*, 9 Cal. 4th at 777 (upholding a land use element amendment by initiative). However, the Court in *DeVita* said it was not determining whether an initiative that later amends or conflicts with the housing element is valid. *Id.* at 793 n.11. A general plan adoption or amendment also is subject to the referendum process. *See Yost v. Thomas*, 36 Cal. 3d 561, 570 (1984).

CHECKLIST FOR GENERAL PLAN ADEQUACY

The brief questionnaire that follows highlights various issues that may be raised in a challenge to the legal adequacy of a general plan. For a more detailed discussion of judicial review of general plans, see chapter 19 (Land Use Litigation).

Is it complete? The seven mandatory elements must be addressed. Gov't Code § 65302; *see Camp*, 123 Cal. App. 3d at 349.

Is it informational, readable, and available to the public? The courts have suggested that a general plan must set forth the required elements in a logical, understandable manner in order to be in substantial compliance. *See Kings County Farm Bureau*, 221 Cal. App. 3d at 743-44 (citing *Camp*, 123 Cal. App. 3d at 334). However, there is no requirement that a general plan be organized or kept in any particular format or location. *See Garat*, 2 Cal. App. 4th at 296.

The courts appear to be concerned with public availability of general plans and their amendments, which is required by Government Code section 65357. A general plan amendment that was not contained in a city's public version of its general plan was held to be ineffective. *See City of Poway*, 229 Cal. App. 3d at 861. A deficient element cannot be saved by consideration of documents that are not relied upon in the discussion of that element. *See Kings County Farm Bureau*, 221 Cal. App. 3d at 744.

Is it internally consistent? The data, assumptions, and projections (e.g., for population, housing, jobs) used in various parts of the plan must be consistent with one another. Gov't Code § 65300.5; *see Concerned Citizens of Calaveras County*, 166 Cal. App. 3d at 96-97; *Sierra Club*, 126 Cal. App. 3d at 704.

Is it consistent with state policy? The plan must comport with legislative policies relating to:
- California Coastal Act. Pub. Res. Code § 30000 *et seq.*
- Open space. Gov't Code § 65561
- Housing. Gov't Code § 65580. *See* HCD's "Housing Element Review Worksheet," 2009
- Surface mining—Surface Mining and Reclamation Act (SMARA). Pub. Res. Code § 2712
- Airport land use plans adopted pursuant to Public Utilities Code § 21675. Gov't Code § 65302.3[10]

See OPR's General Plan Guidelines, chapter 10 (Special General Plan Considerations) (2003).

Does it cover all territory within its boundaries and outside its boundaries that relate to its planning? For purposes of determining the adequacy of a general plan, "territory" covers "any land outside its boundaries that in the planning agency's judgment bears relation to its planning." Gov't Code § 65300.

> The courts have suggested that a general plan must set forth the required elements in a logical, understandable manner in order to be in substantial compliance.

---

[10] For exceptions to this consistency requirement, see Consistency with Airport Land Use Plan earlier in this chapter.

Is it long-term in perspective? The plan must be long-term. Gov't Code § 65300. However, at least one court has emphasized that, with the exception of the housing element, there is no statutory requirement that a general plan be updated at any given interval or in connection with a specific event. See *Garat*, 2 Cal. App. 4th at 296.

Does it address all locally relevant issues? The degree of detail in the discussion must reflect local conditions and circumstances. Gov't Code § 65301(c).

Is it current? Each city shall "periodically review, and revise, as necessary, the general plan." Gov't Code § 65103(a); see *Citizens of Goleta Valley*, 52 Cal. 3d at 572. The California Supreme Court stated that there is an implied duty to keep the general plan current. See *DeVita*, 9 Cal. 4th at 792 (citing *Garat*). While the appellate court confirmed in *Garat* there is no statutory requirement that a general plan be updated at any given interval or in connection with a specific event (except for the housing element, which must be updated according to statutory timelines, this statement was qualified in footnote 28 of the opinion:

> This conclusion does not preclude a court from looking at the results of a public entity's failure to update its entire plan or any parts thereof, *i.e.*, the failure to update a plan and/or its parts may cause a general plan or mandatory element to not be in compliance with the statutory requirements ("legally inadequate") which, in turn, if properly challenged in a timely manner, may subject the entity to an attack on its validity pursuant to those proceedings provided in section 65750 *et seq.*

2 Cal. App. 4th at 296 n.28

Other elements must be updated to reflect changed circumstances. The OPR must notify a city that its general plan has not been revised within eight years and must notify the Attorney General if a city has not revised its general plan within ten years. Gov't Code § 65040.5.

Does it contain the statutory criteria required by state law as interpreted by the courts? For example:

- Does the land use element identify areas that are subject to flooding? Gov't Code § 65302(a)
- Are noise contours shown for all of the listed sources? See *Camp*, 123 Cal. App. 3d at 351–52
- Does it contain adequate standards of population density and building intensity for the various districts? See *Twain Harte Homeowners Ass'n*, 138 Cal. App. 3d at 699
- Is the circulation element fiscally responsible? See *Concerned Citizens of Calaveras County*, 166 Cal. App. 3d at 101–03
- Is the circulation element correlated with the land use element? Gov't Code § 65302(b)
- Does the general plan clearly specify allowable uses for each land use district? Gov't Code § 65302(a)
- Are the density ranges specific enough to provide guidelines in making consistency findings where necessary, e.g., regarding zoning, use permits, and subdivisions? Gov't Code § 65302(a)
- Does the housing element contain a program to conserve and improve the condition of the existing affordable housing stock? See *Hernandez*, 28 Cal. App. 4th at 1069; *Buena Vista Gardens Apartments Ass'n*, 175 Cal. App. 3d at 303

- Has the city adopted an analysis and program for preserving assisted housing developments as part of its housing element? Gov't Code § 65583(a)(8)
- Does the housing element comply with the statutory mandate to, among other things: i) identify adequate sites that will be available to accommodate the city's share of regional housing needs; ii) identify a timeline for implementation of programs within the planning period; and iii) provide for rezonings within certain timeframes where the inventory of sites does not identify adequate sites to accommodate the needs for groups of all household income levels? Gov't Code § 65583

Are the diagrams or maps adequate?
- Do the diagrams or maps show proposed land uses for the entire planning area? Gov't Code § 65302
- Is the land use map linked directly to the text of the general plan?
- Are the maps and text consistent? Gov't Code § 65300.5

Does it serve as a yardstick? Can one take an individual parcel and check it against the plan and then know which uses would be permissible?

Does it contain an action plan or implementation plan? For example: "Every local open space plan shall contain an action program consisting of specific programs that the legislative body intends to pursue in implementing its open space plan." Gov't Code § 65564

Is it horizontally consistent? Is it integrated and internally consistent among the elements and within each element? Gov't Code § 65300.5

Was it adopted correctly?
- Did it receive proper environmental review? Pub. Res. Code § 21000 *et seq.*
- Was the draft housing element or amendment thereto sent to HCD for its review before adoption? Gov't Code § 65585(b)
- Was there consultation with Native American tribes for the preservation of Native American features, places, or objects within the city's jurisdiction? Gov't Code § 65352.3; *see also* Gov't Code § 65562.5
- Was there consultation on the safety element with the Division of Mines and Geology, the State Board of Forestry and Fire Protection, the Central Valley Flood Protection Board, and local agencies, if required? Gov't Code §§ 65302(g)

ADOPTION OF GENERAL PLANS BY NEW CITIES, REVISIONS OF EXISTING GENERAL PLANS, AND RELATED APPROVALS

A newly incorporated city must adopt a general plan within 30 months following its incorporation. During that time, the city is not subject to the requirement that it have an adopted general plan or that its land use approvals be consistent with the general plan so long as it is proceeding in a timely fashion with preparation of the general plan, and the planning agency makes certain findings when approving projects and taking other actions. Gov't Code § 65360.

A new city in the process of preparing a general plan, or an existing city that must update its general plan, may apply to the Director of OPR for an extension of time of up to two years. Gov't Code § 65361(a), (c); *see* Gov't Code § 65103(a); *see also Harroman Co. v. Town of Tiburon*, 235 Cal. App. 3d 388, 395 (1991); *Garat*, 2 Cal. App. 4th at 296 n. 28. OPR will grant an extension if the city makes certain findings explaining why the general plan was not previously adopted or updated (e.g., coordination problems with

A newly incorporated city must adopt a general plan within 30 months following its incorporation.

another agency, natural disaster, difficulty recruiting staff, extensive public review). Gov't Code § 65361(a). One additional extension, which shall not exceed one year, may be granted upon a showing of substantial progress. Gov't Code § 65361(f).

OPR may not grant an extension for the preparation or adoption of a housing element except in the case of a new city. Gov't Code §§ 65361(b), 65587(a). Projects approved during the extension period must still be consistent with the adopted general plan and those portions of the general plan for which the extension was granted, except as provided by the conditions imposed by the OPR director. Gov't Code §§ 65361(d), (e).

Land use approvals that predate the extension are not immune from a consistency challenge vis-à-vis a newly adopted general plan, as the extension is not retroactive. An approval granted before the extension can be attacked only based on the general plan in effect at the time of the approval. See *Neighborhood Action Group*, 156 Cal. App. 3d at 1191; *Resource Defense Fund*, 133 Cal. App. 3d at 812.

The extension can serve to prevent a court-ordered, citywide moratorium on project approvals resulting extension that might restrict a city's ability to approve development during the extension period. For example, OPR could require that any development be consistent with the general plan proposal being considered or studied. In *Harroman Co.*, the court held that a tentative subdivision map must be evaluated against a draft general plan being prepared under an OPR extension, rather than against the existing general plan. 235 Cal. App. 3d at 395-96; *see also Families Unafraid to Uphold Rural El Dorado County*, 62 Cal. App. 4th at 1336. Under a law passed in 1996, during the extension period, development approvals generally must be consistent with those portions of the general plan for which an extension has been granted. Gov't Code § 65361(e). Moreover, OPR could bar approvals that vest development rights or limit individual general plan amendments.

THE GENERAL PLAN AS A SOURCE OF DEDICATIONS AND DEVELOPMENT FEES

Each city, under the umbrella of its police power, can look to its zoning ordinance, subdivision ordinance, and use permit regulations for many of the standard types of dedications or development fees. However, more cities now are relying on the general plan or applicable specific plan to support such requirements. The goals and policies contained in general plans have been upheld as a basis for dedication requirements. See *J.W. Jones Cos. v. City of San Diego*, 157 Cal. App. 3d 745, 757-58 (1984).

The general plan is the most comprehensive statement of a city's interest and welfare. Thus, the plan can assist in defending a condition judicially attacked as beyond the city's police power. If the condition is mandated by the plan, that mandate evinces that the condition substantially advances a legitimate state interest. See Edward J. Sullivan and Isa Lester, *The Role of the Comprehensive Plan in Infrastructure Financing*, 37 Urb. Law. 53 (2005) (arguing that by incorporating a comprehensive financing scheme into its comprehensive plan, a local government will reduce its exposure to Takings Clause challenges); *see also* Daniel J. Curtin, Jr., and Jonathan D. Witten, "Windfalls, Wipeouts, Givings, and Takings in Dramatic Redevelopment Projects: Bargaining for Better Zoning on Density, Views, and Public Access," 32 B.C. Envtl. Aff. L. Rev. 325 (2005).

The power to impose a condition of approval need not be expressed by the specific enactment of an ordinance or regulation. Thus, a city's requirement that smoke detectors be installed in all units in a condominium conversion was upheld based on the objectives of the city's general plan to "promote safe housing for all." *Soderling v. City of*

Santa Monica, 142 Cal. App. 3d 501, 506 (1983). The court said such a condition was valid to achieve the goals of the city's general plan. *Id.; see also J.W. Jones Cos.*, 157 Cal. App. 3d at 757-58.

Cities have amended their general plans to adopt goals and policies relating to the need for fire stations, police stations, libraries, and child day care centers, for example, in order to support subsequent ordinances requiring developers to pay a fee for those purposes. These requirements are valid if they are reasonably related to the burden created by the proposed development. *See Dolan v. City of Tigard*, 512 U.S. 374, 390-91 (1994). For a thorough discussion of exactions and fees, *see* chapter 12 (Exactions).

THE GENERAL PLAN AS A TOOL IN GROWTH MANAGEMENT AND OTHER INNOVATIVE LAND USE CONTROLS

Growth management refers to the variety of measures cities implement to improve population growth patterns and build viable communities. There are practical as well as legal reasons for growth management measures to be tied directly to the general plan. A growth management program will be more effective, and perhaps subject to fewer legal challenges, if it is linked directly to the general plan rather than adopted independently.

Growth management regulations based on the police power must promote the general welfare of the community. The general plan represents the most comprehensive statement of the community's welfare relative to environmental and land use matters. Thus, the data and policies in the general plan supporting the growth management objectives can provide a rationale upon which the regulations rest.

> Growth management refers to the variety of measures cities implement to improve population growth patterns and build viable communities.

The general plan contains projections of future population that form the basis for proposed land uses and facilities. Population projections set forth in the general plan can give legitimacy to specific measures that regulate population growth by either an absolute growth limit or an annual growth rate.

The general plan also is a forum for balancing competing interests and objectives in deciding the future of the city. The city's desire to regulate growth may conflict with its obligation to provide adequate housing opportunities. The general plan is the most appropriate mechanism for making the necessary tradeoffs between these two competing objectives.

JUDICIAL REVIEW OF THE ADEQUACY OF THE GENERAL PLAN

Since they are legislative acts, general plans are subject to judicial review in an action for ordinary mandate. See chapter 19 (Land Use Litigation) for a detailed discussion of this topic. The court generally considers whether the adoption or amendment of the general plan was arbitrary, capricious, or entirely lacking in evidentiary support. *See Environmental Council*, 135 Cal. App. 3d at 436. The court determines whether the plan substantially complies with the statutory criteria. Substantial compliance is achieved when there is actual compliance with the "'substance essential to every reasonable objective of the statute', as distinguished from 'mere technical imperfections of form.'" *Camp*, 123 Cal. App. 3d at 348; *Hernandez*, 28 Cal. App. 4th at 1058 (citing Gov't Code § 65587(b) and uncodified section 44 of Chapter 1009 of the 1984 statutes).

However, the housing element, because it is subject to more detailed requirements, faces closer judicial scrutiny. *See Hernandez*, 28 Cal. App. 4th at 1059.

Actions and remedies relating to general plan adequacy generally are governed by Government Code sections 65750-65763. *See Garat*, 2 Cal. App. 4th at 303. Housing element challenges also are subject to Government Code sections 65587(b) and (c). The action must be brought pursuant to Code of Civil Procedure section 1085 (traditional mandamus) generally within 90 days after the adoption or amendment of the general plan. Gov't Code § 65009(c); *see also A Local & Reg'l Monitor (ALARM) v. City of Los Angeles*, 16 Cal. App. 4th 630, 649 (1993). There are exceptions related to the development of low- or moderate-income housing, and a unique set of timelines applies to challenges to a city's adoption or revision of a housing element. Gov't Code § 65009. Challenges also may be brought after the 90-day period when a project approval is claimed to be inconsistent with relevant portions of the general plan because those portions are inadequate. *See Garat*, 2 Cal. App. 4th at 289.

In the event of a judicial determination that the plan is inadequate, the Government Code specifies the types of municipal actions (e.g., rezonings, subdivision approvals) that may be suspended, and specifies time limits to be imposed on the preparation of an adequate plan. Gov't Code §§ 65755, 65754. The law also details other relief the court may grant during the life of the suit. Gov't Code § 65753.

In *Committee for Responsible Planning v. City of Indian Wells*, a court enunciated the circumstances under which development may be allowed to proceed after a judicial determination of general plan inadequacy. 209 Cal. App. 3d 1005, 1013 (1989). After finding the city's general plan inadequate, the court issued a writ of mandate prohibiting the issuance of building permits and discretionary land use approvals until the city brought its general plan into compliance with state law.

After judgment, a developer intervened, and moved for an order allowing approval of its 29-unit subdivision on the basis that under Government Code section 65755, a project approval could still be granted so long as it did not "significantly impair" a city's ability to adopt or amend its general plan. The developer argued that in order to significantly impair adoption or amendment of a special plan, a project must be of such size or nature that it would necessarily and significantly reduce the city's options in drafting a general plan. The court rejected this argument, and, noting the special importance of the housing element, deferred to the trial court's determination that the moratorium was necessary to prevent development that might frustrate the ability to implement a new housing element, because of the limited area available for new housing. *Id.* at 1013-14. The court compared the Legislature's emphasis on the need for an adequate general plan to its intent that CEQA be applied to afford the fullest possible protection to the environment, and held that the definition of "significant" in CEQA should apply to Government Code section 65755 as well. Based on this analogy, the court adopted CEQA's "significant effect" definition as being "a substantial, or potentially substantial, adverse change in the environment." Pub. Res. Code § 21068. Of key importance in the *Indian Wells* case was the city's recent approval of a resort containing 4,500 hotel rooms, which would generate a substantial need for affordable housing for the resort's employees.

CHAPTER 3

Specific Plan

INTRODUCTION

The specific plan is just a step below the general plan in the land use approval hierarchy, and is used to systematically implement the general plan in particular geographical areas. Gov't Code § 65450. Zoning ordinances, subdivisions, public works projects, and development agreements all must be consistent with an applicable adopted specific plan. Gov't Code §§ 65455, 65867.5. Thus, it is important for a property owner or developer to check with the city planning or community development department to determine whether the city has adopted a specific plan covering the property.

> A property owner or developer should always check with the local planning department to see if a specific plan covers the property since that plan will govern the property's future development and use.

CONTENTS OF A SPECIFIC PLAN

State law requires that a specific plan include text and a diagram or diagrams that specify all of the following in detail:

- Distribution, location, and extent of the uses of land, including open space, within the area covered by the plan
- Proposed distribution, location, extent and intensity of major components of public and private transportation, sewage, water, drainage, solid waste disposal, energy, and other essential facilities proposed to be located within the area covered by the plan and needed to support the land uses described in the plan
- Standards and criteria by which development will proceed and, where applicable, standards for conservation, development, and utilization of natural resources
- A program of implementation measures including regulations, programs, public works projects, and financing measures necessary to carry out the matters listed above

Gov't Code § 65451(a)

The specific plan also must include a statement of the relationship between the specific plan and the general plan. Gov't Code § 65451(b). In *Napa Citizens for Honest Government v. County of Napa Board of Supervisors*, the court reviewed a specific plan for consistency with the county's general plan. 91 Cal. App. 4th 342, 377-81 (2001). The specific plan in question did not directly conflict with the general plan, but nevertheless was determined by the court to be incompatible with certain goals and policies of the general plan. The court acknowledged that a county's conclusion that a specific plan is consistent with its general plan "carries a strong presumption of regularity that can be overcome only by a showing of abuse of discretion." *Id.* at 357. Despite this stated deference, the court invalidated the specific plan. In declaring the specific plan inconsistent with the general plan, the court noted the specific plan frustrated the general plan's goals and policies by failing to include definite affirmative commitments to mitigate the specific plan's adverse effects. *Id.* at 379. The court stated that the consistency doctrine requires that a specific plan do more than simply recite goals and policies that are consistent with those set forth in the county general plan, making clear that an outright conflict is not required for a finding of inconsistency. *Id.* In fact, a project is consistent with the general plan if, considering all its aspects, it will further the objectives and policies of the general plan and not obstruct their attainment. *Id.* at 378.

The specific plan also may address any other subjects that, in the judgment of the city, are necessary or desirable for implementation of the general plan. Gov't Code § 65452. Additionally, cities are increasingly adopting more comprehensive and detailed specific plans by ordinances and declaring such plans to constitute the zoning for areas. See chapter 4 (Zoning).

ADOPTION

The procedures for adopting and amending a specific plan are essentially the same as for a general plan, except that it may be amended as often as necessary, and may be adopted by ordinance or resolution. The adoption or amendment of a specific plan, like a general plan, is a legislative act. *See Yost v. Thomas*, 36 Cal. 3d 561, 570 (1984). To defray the cost of preparation of the specific plan, cities may impose a specific plan fee upon persons seeking governmental approvals that are required to be consistent with the specific plan. Gov't Code § 65456(a).

ALUP = Airport Land Use Plan

Specific plans, like general plans, must be consistent with any applicable county Airport Land Use Plans (ALUPs) adopted pursuant to Public Utilities Code section 21675, unless the city overrules the airport land use commission and makes certain findings. The Attorney General has opined that allowing a specific plan to be exempted from compliance with more stringent land use compatibility standards in a local ALUP would undermine the legislative intent behind the detailed procedure in the Public Resources Code for resolution of inconsistencies; while the city may overrule the commission under section 21675, it cannot otherwise grant an exemption from the consistency requirement. 87 Ops. Cal. Atty. Gen. 102 (2004); *see Citizens for Planning Responsibly v. County of San Luis Obispo*, 176 Cal. App. 4th 357, 376 (2009) (where initiative is concerned, electorate need not make findings under section 21675). For a discussion of how to address conflicts between a specific plan and an ALUP, see chapter 2 (General Plan).

INTERPLAY WITH CEQA

CEQA = California Environmental Quality Act

To assist and encourage cities and developers to use specific plans for development of housing, state law exempts certain residential development projects from further CEQA requirements if they are undertaken to implement and are consistent with a specific plan for which an EIR has been certified. Gov't Code § 65457; Pub. Res. Code §§ 21156–21159.9 (use of Master Environmental Impact Report process applicable to specific plan adoptions); Stephen L. Kostka and Michael H. Zischke, *Practice Under the*

California Environmental Quality Act, chapter 5 (Cal. CEB 2013). For a more thorough discussion of the requirements of CEQA, see chapter 6 (CEQA).

For a more detailed discussion of specific plans, *see* Governor's Office of Planning and Research, *The Planner's Guide to Specific Plans*, January 2001.[1]

JUDICIAL REVIEW

Because the adoption of a specific plan is a legislative act, it is reviewed by the courts in traditional mandate proceedings. Judicial review is generally limited to an examination of the proceedings before the city to determine whether its adoption of the specific plan was arbitrary or capricious, entirely lacking in evidentiary support, or whether it failed to follow the procedures and give the notices required by law. *See* Code Civ. Proc. § 1085; *Mitchell v. County of Orange*, 165 Cal. App. 3d 1185, 1191-92 (1985). This "arbitrary and capricious" test also applies to challenges to a specific plan's conformance with a general plan. *Id.*; *see Kawaoka v. City of Arroyo Grande*, 17 F. 3d 1227, 1238 (9th Cir. 1994) (applying the arbitrary and capricious test and holding that a general plan's requirement that specific plan be prepared before land was converted to residential use was not arbitrary; nor was requiring payment of a fee for preparation of a specific plan unconstitutional). Any lawsuit challenging the adoption or amendment of a specific plan must be brought within ninety days after the city council's decision. Gov't Code § 65009.

Once a specific plan is adopted, courts give substantial deference to a city's determination of whether a particular project is consistent with that specific plan. *Sierra Club v. County of Napa*, 121 Cal. App. 4th 1490, 1497 (2004). In *Sierra Club*, the petitioners challenged the county's issuance of a use permit for development of a winery. The EIR for the project concluded that the project would result in the loss of some seasonal wetlands. Petitioners claimed the project was inconsistent with a policy in an applicable specific plan providing that wetlands shall be protected in their natural state unless shown to be infeasible. *Id.* at 1506. In upholding the county's approval of the use permit, the court deferred to the county's conclusion that preservation of the wetlands was not "feasible," finding there was substantial evidence in the record to support that conclusion. It also noted that the "agency had discretion to approve a plan even though the plan is not consistent with all of the specific plan's policies. It is enough that the proposed project will be compatible with the objectives, policies, general land uses and programs specified in the applicable plan." *Id.* at 1511-12.

For a more thorough discussion of judicial review, see chapter 19 (Land Use Litigation).

> Because the adoption of a specific plan is a legislative act, it is reviewed by the courts in traditional mandate proceedings.

---

1 *Available at* http://opr.ca.gov/docs/specific_plans.pdf.

CHAPTER 4

Zoning

ZONING DEFINED

In general terms, zoning is the division of a city into districts and the application of different regulations in each district. Zoning regulations are generally divided into two classes: (1) those that regulate the height or bulk of physical structures within certain designated districts—in other words, regulations that have to do with structural and architectural design of the buildings; and (2) those that prescribe the use to which buildings within certain designated districts may be put. "[Z]oning is a separation of the municipality into districts, and the regulation of buildings and structures, according to their construction, and the nature and extent of their use, and the nature and extent of the uses of land." *O'Loane v. O'Rourke*, 231 Cal. App. 2d 774, 780 (1965).

The Legislature has given cities maximum control over zoning matters while ensuring uniformity of, and public access to, zoning and planning hearings. *See Beck Dev. Co. v. Southern Pac. Transp. Co.*, 44 Cal. App. 4th 1160, 1187–88 (1996).

APPLICATION TO CHARTER CITIES

The State Zoning Law (Gov't Code § 65800 *et seq*.) applies to general law cities and all counties. The State Zoning Law does not apply to a charter city, however, except to the extent a city adopts it by charter or ordinance, or the Legislature has specifically required its application. Gov't Code § 65803. For example, Government Code section 65804, requiring cities to implement minimum procedural standards for the conduct of zoning hearings, is specifically applicable to charter cities. *See also* Gov't Code § 65589.5 (restricting a city's power to disapprove affordable housing).

JUDICIAL REVIEW[1]

PRESUMPTION OF VALIDITY

A zoning ordinance is a legislative act and, unlike administrative decisions, does not require explicit findings. A zoning ordinance is valid if it is reasonably related to the public welfare. *See Arnel Dev. Co. v. City of Costa Mesa*, 28 Cal. 3d 511, 522 (1980). Such an ordinance comes before the court with every presumption in its

> A zoning ordinance is a legislative act and, unlike administrative decisions, does not require explicit findings.

---

1 For a detailed discussion of judicial review, see chapter 19 (Land Use Litigation).

favor, including a presumption of constitutionality. *See Lockard v. City of Los Angeles*, 33 Cal. 2d 453, 460 (1949).

Because zoning is legislative, it is reviewed in ordinary mandate proceedings. Generally, the burden rests with the party challenging the constitutionality of an ordinance to present the evidence and documentation that a court will require in undertaking a constitutional analysis. *See Associated Home Builders, Inc. v. City of Livermore*, 18 Cal. 3d 582, 601 (1976). There is an exception, however. When a city adopts an ordinance directly limiting the number of dwelling units, the burden of proof reverts to the city to justify its action. Evid. Code § 669.5. This applies to ordinances adopted by the city council or the voters through the initiative process. *See Lee v. City of Monterey Park*, 173 Cal. App. 3d 798, 806-07 (1985); *Bldg. Indus. Ass'n v. City of Camarillo*, 41 Cal. 3d 810, 818 (1986); *but see Hernandez v. City of Encinitas*, 28 Cal. App. 4th 1048, 1074-75 (1994) (Evidence Code section 669.5 did not apply to challenges to a city's housing element and its implementing regulations).

LIMITED ROLE OF COURT REVIEW—POLICY ISSUE

Because of the broad construction of the police power as it relates to land use regulations, including zoning, the courts have consistently taken a "hands off" approach when reviewing the validity of such regulations. The courts have recognized the separation of powers between the legislative and judicial branches, and as long as the ordinance bears a reasonable relationship to the public welfare, courts have consistently refused to substitute judicial judgment for the legislative decisions made by a city. As the United States Supreme Court stated:

> It is not our function to appraise the wisdom of its decision.... In either event, the city's interest in attempting to preserve the quality of urban life is one that must be accorded high respect. Moreover, the city must be allowed a reasonable opportunity to experiment with solutions to admittedly serious problems.

Young v. Am. Mini Theatres, Inc., 427 U.S. 50, 71 (1976)

A California court described the judiciary's role in considering the validity of zoning regulations as follows:

> [a.] The wisdom of the [zoning regulation] is a matter for legislative determination, and even though a court may not agree with that determination, it will not substitute its judgment for that of the zoning authorities if there is any reasonable justification for their action.

> [b.] In passing upon the validity of legislation,...the rule is well settled that the legislative determination that the facts exist which make the law necessary, must not be set aside by the courts, unless the legislative decision is clearly and palpably wrong and the error appears beyond reasonable doubt from facts or evidence which cannot be controverted....

> [c.] In considering the scope...of appellate review,...[it] must be kept in mind that the courts are examining the act of a coordinate branch of the government—the legislative—in a field in which it has paramount authority and, are not reviewing the decision of a lower tribunal or a fact-finding body.

> [d.] Courts have nothing to do with the wisdom of laws and regulations, and the legislative power must be upheld unless manifestly abused so as to infringe on constitutional guaranties....

[e.] The only function of the courts is to determine whether the exercise of legislative power has exceeded constitutional limitations....

[f.] [T]he function of this court is to determine whether the record shows a reasonable basis for the action of the zoning authorities, and, if the reasonableness of the ordinance is fairly debatable, the legislative determination will not be disturbed.

Carty v. City of Ojai, 77 Cal. App. 3d 329, 333 (1978)

ENACTMENT OF ZONING REGULATIONS

IN GENERAL

Every city in California has an existing zoning ordinance. The effect of that zoning ordinance on real property can be changed by a city's adoption of an amending ordinance.

There are two basic types of substantive amendments to zoning ordinances: (1) reclassification of the zoning applicable to a specific property, designating a change from one district to another district, commonly called "rezoning"; and (2) changes in the permitted uses or regulations on property within particular zones or citywide, commonly called "text amendments." The first type of amendment usually involves a change in the zoning map, without any change in the text of the basic zoning ordinance. The second type of amendment usually involves amending the text of the zoning ordinance, but not the zoning map.

THE ORDINANCE MUST BE REASONABLY RELATED TO THE PUBLIC WELFARE

Zoning ordinances, as with other land use regulations, must be reasonably related to the public welfare. *See Associated Home Builders, Inc.*, 18 Cal. 3d at 604; *City of Del Mar v. City of San Diego*, 133 Cal. App. 3d 401, 409 (1982); *Arnel Dev. Co.*, 126 Cal. App. 3d at 336. See Chapter 1 (Local Land Use Authority) for examples of the broad range of ordinances upheld under a city's police powers. Consistently, courts have construed broadly what constitutes a reasonable relationship. For example, maintaining the character of residential neighborhoods is a proper purpose. In *Ewing v. City of Carmel-by-the-Sea*, an ordinance prohibiting transient commercial use of single-family homes was upheld based on the existence of a reasonable relationship to the public welfare. 234 Cal. App. 3d 1579, 1592 (1991).

> Zoning ordinances, as with other land use regulations, must be reasonably related to the public welfare.

The courts have interpreted the relationship to the public welfare to include not only the public welfare of the citizens of the city but also of the affected region, if necessary. In *Associated Home Builders, Inc. v. City of Livermore*, the California Supreme Court set forth the *"Livermore* test:" a three-step analysis for determining whether a land use regulation bears a reasonable relationship to the regional welfare. 18 Cal. 3d at 604. First, the court must forecast the probable effect and duration of the restriction. Second, the court must identify the competing interests affected by the restriction, e.g., open space versus affordable housing. Finally, the court must determine whether the regulation, in light of its probable effect, represents a reasonable accommodation of the competing interests. In all cases, the regulation must have a "real and substantial" relationship to the public welfare.

Numerous courts have applied the *Livermore* test to determine whether a zoning ordinance is valid, reaching varied results. For example, in *Arnel*, the court struck down a rezoning initiative aimed at defeating a multifamily housing project as an improper exercise of the police power. 126 Cal. App. 3d 330, 337-38 (1981). The record demonstrated that the initiative discriminated against a particular piece of property, and failed to consider the competing interest of the community in the development of affordable housing. *Id.* Conversely, in *Del Mar*, the court upheld the San Diego North City West Housing Development Plan, concluding that the regulation bore a substantial and reasonable relationship to the public welfare. 133 Cal. App. 3d at 415.

The California Supreme Court upheld the City of Santa Monica's anti-demolition ordinance against an attack that it operated to deprive a landowner of property without due process of law by restricting his right to go out of the rental business. *See Nash v. City of Santa Monica*, 37 Cal. 3d 97 (1984). The Court stated that the applicable legal test "requires the regulation be 'procedurally fair and reasonably related to a proper legislative goal. The wisdom of the legislation is not at issue in analyzing its constitutionality....'" *Id.* at 108–09. The Court stated that the city's ordinance met the *Livermore* test. *Id.* at 109.

In *Hernandez v. City of Hanford*, the California Supreme Court upheld a city ordinance that prohibited the sale of furniture in a planned commercial district, with a limited exception for large department stores. 41 Cal. 4th 279 (2007). The Court held that the ordinance was adopted to promote the legitimate public purpose of preserving the economic viability of the Hanford downtown business district. *Id.* at 298.

ZONING MUST BE CONSISTENT WITH THE GENERAL PLAN[2]

Zoning ordinances must be consistent with the general plan and any applicable specific plan. Gov't Code § 65860(a). This provision does not apply to charter cities, with the exception of Los Angeles. Gov't Code §§ 65803, 65860(d). However, a charter city can, on its own, require consistency by charter or by ordinance. *See Verdugo Woodlands Homeowners Ass'n v. City of Glendale*, 179 Cal. App. 3d 696 (1986); *City of Irvine v. Irvine Citizens Against Overdevelopment*, 25 Cal. App. 4th 868 (1994) (where the charter city of Irvine required consistency); *Garat v. City of Riverside*, 2 Cal. App. 4th 259 (1991) (the charter of the City of Riverside did not require consistency) (overruled on other grounds in *Morehart v. County of Santa Barbara*, 7 Cal. 4th 725, 743 & n.11 (1994)).

A zoning ordinance is consistent with a city's general plan only if:
- The city has officially adopted such a plan; and
- The various land uses authorized by the ordinance are compatible with the objectives, policies, general land uses, and programs specified in such a plan

Gov't Code § 65860(a)

Applying the consistency test set forth in the Governor's Office of Planning and Research, *General Plan Guidelines* (2003), page 166, a zoning ordinance is consistent with a city's general plan where, considering all of its aspects, the ordinance furthers the objectives and policies of the general plan and does not obstruct their attainment. *See City of Irvine*, 25 Cal. App. 4th at 879.

Any resident or property owner within a city may bring an action in superior court to enforce compliance with the consistency requirement. Such actions or proceedings are governed by Code of Civil Procedure section 1084 *et seq.* Except for certain exceptions in Government Code section 65009(d) expressly relating to housing projects for low-income persons and families, any actions or proceedings must be taken within 90

---

[2] For further discussion of general plan consistency, see chapter 2 (General Plan).

days of the enactment of any new zoning ordinance or the amendment of any existing zoning ordinance, and any such action also must be served on a city within this 90-day period. Gov't Code § 65860(b). The purpose of this remedy is to "compel amendment of a nonconforming zoning ordinance to bring it into compliance with the general plan." *Gonzalez v. County of Tulare*, 65 Cal. App. 4th 777, 785 (1998). Also, a city can avail itself of this statute of limitations period in a pre-election challenge to an initiative or referendum related to zoning. *See City of Irvine*, 25 Cal. App. 4th at 879.

A city's findings that the zoning ordinance is consistent with its general plan can be reversed only if it is based on evidence from which no reasonable person could have reached the same conclusion. *See A Local & Reg'l Monitor v. City of Los Angeles*, 16 Cal. App. 4th 630, 648 (1993).

The courts have stated that a zoning ordinance inconsistent with the general plan at the time of enactment is "void *ab initio*," meaning invalid when passed. *See Lesher Communications, Inc. v. City of Walnut Creek*, 52 Cal. 3d 531, 541 (1990); *City of Irvine*, 25 Cal. App. 4th at 879; *Bldg. Indus. Ass'n v. City of Oceanside*, 27 Cal. App. 4th 744, 762 (1994); *deBottari v. City Council*, 171 Cal. App. 3d 1204, 1212 (1985). However, while an inconsistent ordinance is void when adopted, its invalidity still must be determined judicially in an appropriate legal action, and any such action is governed by the appropriate statute of limitations. *See Gonzalez*, 65 Cal. App. 4th at 785-91. If a zoning ordinance becomes inconsistent with a general plan by reason of an amendment to the plan, or to any element of the plan, the ordinance must be amended within a reasonable time so that it is consistent with the amended general plan. Gov't Code § 65860(c).

Pursuant to legislation adopted in 2007, each city located within the Sacramento-San Joaquin Valley is required to amend its zoning ordinances so that they are consistent with the flood protection goals and policies of the city's general plan. Gov't Code §§ 65302.9(a), 65860.1.

Since general plan consistency is required, the absence of a valid general plan, or the failure of any relevant elements thereof to meet statutory criteria, precludes the enactment of zoning ordinances and the like. *See Res. Def. Fund v. County of Santa Cruz*, 133 Cal. App. 3d 800, 806 (1982).[3]

ZONING MUST BE CONSISTENT WITH AIRPORT LAND USE PLAN

Just as a city's general plan must be consistent with any Airport Land Use Plan (ALUP) that overlaps with the city's planning area, so too must a city's zoning be consistent with any applicable ALUP, unless the city overrules the local Airport Land Use Commission and makes certain findings. Pub. Util. Code § 21676(b). Prior to adoption or approval of a zoning ordinance or building regulation within the planning boundary established by the ALUP, a city must first refer the proposed action to the commission that adopted the relevant ALUP. Pub. Util. Code § 21676(b). In the event the commission finds the zoning regulation to be inconsistent with its ALUP, and upon making specific findings, the city may overrule the commission by a two-thirds vote. Pub. Util. Code § 21676(b). The timeframes, procedures, and findings requirements for overruling a commission's findings of inconsistency in order to approve a zoning regulation are the same as those for overruling an ALUP to amend a general plan and are explained in

ALUP = Airport Land Use Plan

---

[3] The Attorney General opined that a county may incorporate land use designations and other provisions of its zoning ordinances into its general plan and then repeal its zoning ordinances and replace them with a single ordinance that requires all land use activity to conform to the general plan. *See* 81 Ops. Cal. Atty. Gen. 57 (1998).

chapter 2 (General Plan). *See also* Pub. Util. Code § 21676(b). For a comprehensive discussion of Airport Land Use Commissions, how they devise Airport Land Use Plans, and how they determine consistency with local agencies' proposed general plans and zoning regulations, see *The California Airport Land Use Planning Handbook*, California Department of Transportation, Division of Aeronautics, January 2002 (available at www.dot.ca.gov/hp/planning/aeronaut/documents/ALUPHComplete-7-02rev.pdf).

DUE PROCESS REQUIREMENTS

Rezonings, no matter how small the parcel, and zoning text amendments are legislative acts and are not administrative or quasi-judicial in nature. *See Arnel Dev. Co. v. City of Costa Mesa*, 28 Cal. 3d 511, 514 (1980). As a general rule, procedural due process requirements of notice and hearing to nearby property owners only apply in quasi-judicial or adjudicatory hearings and not in the adoption of general legislation. *See Horn v. County of Ventura*, 24 Cal. 3d 605, 612 (1979). However, notice and hearing are statutorily required where zoning ordinance amendments change property from one zone to another, or impose or delete certain regulations listed in Government Code section 65850.

For more detail, see the requirements set forth in Government Code section 65854 *et seq.* Any other amendment to a zoning ordinance may be adopted as other ordinances are adopted (Gov't Code § 65853), although special provision is made for notice and hearing on interim ordinances, such as urgency measures. Gov't Code § 65858.

Although the State Zoning Law requires both a hearing before the planning commission, if there is one, and a hearing before the city council prior to the enactment of certain amendments to zoning ordinances, it requires only that minimum due process standards be observed in conducting those hearings. Gov't Code § 65804. This applies to all zoning authorities, including charter cities.

Government Code section 65804 requires that every city:
- Develop and publish procedural rules governing the conduct of hearings so that all interested parties shall have advance knowledge of the procedures to be followed
- Keep and provide a record of the hearings when a matter is contested and a request is made in writing prior to the date of hearing
- Make public any planning commission's staff report prior to a hearing, and
- Prepare a staff report with recommendations and the basis for the recommendations, which shall be included in the record of the hearing, when a hearing is held on an application for a change of zone for parcels of at least ten acres

Proposed zoning amendments must be submitted to the planning commission and given a noticed public hearing. Gov't Code § 65854. After the hearing, the planning commission must render its decision in the form of a written recommendation to the city council that includes the reasons for the recommendation and the relationship of the proposed amendment to applicable general and specific plans. Gov't Code § 65855.

Except in limited circumstances, upon receipt of the recommendation of the planning commission, the city council must hold a public hearing on the proposed amendment. Gov't Code § 65856. Following a noticed hearing, the city council may approve, modify, or disapprove the planning commission's recommendation. A zoning ordinance adopted without the required notice and hearing will be void. *See Sounhein v. City of San Dimas*, 11 Cal. App. 4th 1255, 1260 (1992).

In *Environmental Defense Project of Sierra County v. County of Sierra*, the court held that the notice of the legislative body's hearing on a zoning ordinance was required to be given *after* the planning commission's recommendation had been received by the legislative body. 158 Cal. App. 4th 877, 888 (2008). The court also held that the recommendation must be included in the notice, although it did not indicate how a recommendation—which may be voluminous and may include numerous detailed conditions—should be reflected in the notice.

If the city council wants to modify a recommendation not previously considered by the planning commission, it is required to refer the modification back to the planning commission for a report and recommendation. However, the planning commission is not required to hold a public hearing regarding the modification under consideration. Failure of the planning commission to report within 40 days after the referral was made shall be considered an approval of the proposed modification. Gov't Code § 65857.

SUFFICIENCY OF STANDARDS—VAGUENESS AND UNCERTAINTY

A land use ordinance, including a zoning ordinance, cannot be so vague or uncertain that a person of common intelligence and understanding must guess as to its meaning. If this occurs, due process of law could be violated. *See People v. Gates*, 41 Cal. App. 3d 590, 601–02 (1974); *see also Associated Home Builders, Inc.*, 18 Cal. 3d at 596 (upholding the general terms of a growth management initiative against a vagueness challenge). However, the California courts have stated that a substantial amount of vagueness is permitted in land use ordinances.

> A land use ordinance, including a zoning ordinance, cannot be so vague or uncertain that a person of common intelligence and understanding must guess as to its meaning.

In *Novi v. City of Pacifica*, the court held that a city's land use ordinance, which precluded uses that were detrimental to the "general welfare" as well as developments that were "monotonous" in design and external appearance, was not unconstitutionally vague, either facially or as applied. 169 Cal. App. 3d 678 (1985). Novi was a developer who sought to construct a 48-unit condominium project. The project was turned down because it would have violated the city's anti-monotony ordinance. Novi argued that the city's ordinance lacked objective criteria for reviewing the element of monotony, and that such criteria are required for aesthetic land use regulations. The court disagreed, however, stating:

> In fact, a substantial amount of vagueness is permitted in California zoning ordinances: "[I]n California, the most general zoning standards are usually deemed sufficient. 'The standard is sufficient if the administrative body is required to make its decision in accord with the general health, safety, and welfare standard.... California courts permit vague standards because they are sensitive to the need of government in large urban areas to delegate broad discretionary power to administrative bodies if the community's zoning business is to be done without paralyzing the legislative process.'" (alteration in original) (citations omitted).
>
> Here, subdivision (g) of section 9-4.3204 requires "variety in the design of the structure and grounds to avoid monotony in the external appearance." The legislative intent is obvious: the Pacifica city council wishes to avoid "ticky-tacky"

development of the sort described by songwriter Malvina Reynolds in the song, "Little Boxes." No further objective criteria are required, just as none are required under the general welfare ordinance. Subdivision (g) is sufficiently specific under the California rule permitting local legislative bodies to adopt ordinances delegating broad discretionary power to administrative bodies.

Id. at 682

Relying on *Novi*, another court held that a view protection ordinance was not unconstitutionally vague, finding that such an ordinance supported a building permit denial. *See Ross v. City of Rolling Hills Estates*, 192 Cal. App. 3d 370, 376 (1987); *see also Hotel & Motel Ass'n of Oakland v. City of Oakland*, 344 F. 3d 959 (9th Cir. 2003) (an ordinance improving conditions in and around hotels was not vague; a party challenging the facial validity of an ordinance on vagueness grounds outside the domain of the First Amendment must demonstrate that the "enactment is impermissibly vague in all of its applications"); *Personal Watercraft Coalition v. Marin County Board of Supervisors*, 100 Cal. App. 4th 129, 140 (2002) (prohibition of personal watercraft in specific area was not unconstitutionally vague); *Briggs v. City of Rolling Hills Estates*, 40 Cal. App. 4th 637, 643 (1995) (a "neighborhood compatibility" ordinance protecting privacy was not unconstitutionally vague); *City of Los Altos v. Barnes*, 3 Cal. App. 4th 1193, 1203 (1992) (specific land use ordinances were not unconstitutionally vague); *Ewing v. City of Carmel-by-the-Sea*, 234 Cal. App. 3d at 1595 (ordinance that prohibited rental of residential property for fewer than 30 days was not unconstitutionally vague).

ADOPTION OF A ZONING ORDINANCE

If the city council approves, or approves as modified, a proposed zoning amendment, the council must introduce it at a regular or adjourned regular meeting and then adopt the amendment by ordinance at a subsequent meeting. Gov't Code §§ 36934, 65850. In contrast, county boards of supervisors are authorized to adopt a rezoning ordinance with only one reading after a noticed public hearing. Gov't Code § 25131.

The amendment of a zoning ordinance is a legislative rather than a quasi-judicial function; therefore, findings are not required unless state law or local ordinance so provides. *See Arnel Dev. Co. v. City of Costa Mesa*, 28 Cal. 3d 511, 514 (1980). For example, state law requires findings when a city limits the number of housing units through general plan or zoning adoption—both of which are legislative acts. Gov't Code §§ 65302.8, 65863.6.

A California court held that Government Code section 65030.2, which contains a policy statement that land use decisions be made with "full knowledge of their economic and fiscal implications," creates no duty to prepare a financing plan for a public facility prior to approving a rezoning. *See Towards Responsibility in Planning v. City Council*, 200 Cal. App. 3d 671, 677–78 (1988). The court declined the plaintiffs' request to treat the policy statement as a substantive requirement. Instead, the court concluded that rezoning is a legislative act, and that review of such acts is limited to a determination of whether it was arbitrary and capricious or without any evidentiary basis. *Id.*

MOTIVES

As a general rule, motives of the city council or local officials in amending or declining to amend a zoning ordinance are irrelevant to any inquiry concerning its reasonableness.

See Cormier v. County of San Luis Obispo, 161 Cal. App. 3d 850, 858 (1984). For further discussion of this principle, see chapter 19 (Land Use Litigation).

The issue of motives of an individual member of a board of supervisors was discussed in *County of Butte v. Bach*:

> The Bachs suggest that, by advancing the interests of the neighbors who opposed commercial use of the corner lots, Supervisor Wheeler, and by attribution the County of Butte, acted improperly. The implication is that Wheeler's affiliation with the cause of those constituents who opposed the commercial use is an illicit motivation for her official acts in the course of the controversy. With few exceptions, *e.g.*, racially discriminatory animus, none of which are made out in this case, the motive of officials enacting a zoning ordinance is immaterial. Absent such an unconstitutional motivation, we discern no legal impropriety in an elected official siding with one faction in what is, so long as the alternative chosen is not unreasonable, ultimately a political contest. (citation omitted.)

172 Cal. App. 3d 848 (1985) at 862 n.1

Motives also are irrelevant to an inquiry concerning other land use decisions, including nonlegislative ones; the subjective motives or mental processes of city council members are subject to the legislative privilege. *See Kleitman v. Superior Court*, 74 Cal. App. 4th 324, 335-36 (1999). Thus, a showing of individual bias or prejudice based upon prior statements of an individual legislator is irrelevant. *See City of Fairfield v. Superior Court*, 14 Cal. 3d 768, 773 (1975). Discovery to learn whether local legislators arrived at their position before the hearing also is barred as irrelevant. Such positions do not disqualify one from voting or invalidate the decision. *Id.* at 780. Discovery into council members' legislative motives or mental processes to support a claim of a general plan's invalidity is not permitted. *See City of Santa Cruz v. Superior Court*, 40 Cal. App. 4th 1146, 1148 (1995).

Further, acquisition of information outside the hearing does not disqualify or invalidate the actions in the hearing. *See Board of Supervisors v. Superior Court*, 32 Cal. App. 4th 1616, 1627 (1995) (citing *City of Fairfield v. Superior Court*, 14 Cal. 3d 768, 779-80, 782 (1975). The Attorney General opined that a city council member who signed a petition opposing a land use project is not disqualified from participating in the council proceeding during which the application for a conditional use permit for the project is considered. *See* 78 Ops. Cal. Atty. Gen. 77 (1995) (citing *City of Fairfield*, 14 Cal. 3d at 780-81).

Subject to the limited exceptions discussed below, a government official's motive for voting on a land use issue is irrelevant to assessing the validity of the action. For example, in *Breneric Assocs. v. City of Del Mar*, the court rejected allegations of hostile feelings of design review board members and the city council in denying a design review permit. 69 Cal. App. 4th 166, 184 (1998). In another case, a court said that nothing illegal transpired when one city council member did everything he could to delay a project and then have it denied. *See Stubblefield Constr. Co. v. City of San Bernardino*, 32 Cal. App. 4th 687, 710-11 (1995).

A limited exception to the general rule has been recognized when the facts reveal that a zoning action was taken for an unlawful purpose. For example, when the police power has been exercised in such a manner as to oppress or discriminate against an individual or individuals or against a particular parcel of land, it will be overturned. *See, e.g., Pacific Shores Properties v. City of Newport Beach*, 730 F.3d 1142, 1162-63 (2013)

> Motives are irrelevant to an inquiry concerning other land use decisions, including nonlegislative ones; the subjective motives or mental processes of city council members are subject to the legislative privilege.

(evidence indicating that ordinance restricting group living arrangements was intended to discriminate against protected class of recovering alcohol and drug abusers should be considered by trial court); *G & D Holland Constr. Co. v. City of Marysville*, 12 Cal. App. 3d 989, 994 (1970); *Kissinger v. City of Los Angeles*, 161 Cal. App. 2d 454 (1958).

In order to successfully claim a due process violation due to bias or improper motives, there must be a sufficient showing that a party's rights were prejudiced by the bias. *See Sladovich v. County of Fresno*, 158 Cal. App. 2d 230, 239-40 (1958). For instance, in *Arnel Development Company v. City of Costa Mesa*, the court held an initiative rezoning ordinance to be invalid as discriminatory, stating that motives and legislative purpose are factors to be considered in determining whether a zoning ordinance is invalid as discriminatory. 126 Cal. App. 3d at 337. The court looked at the ballot arguments, in part, to determine that the initiative ordinance discriminated against a particular parcel of land.

In *Nasha v. City of Los Angeles*, the court set aside the decision of the planning commission and ordered a new hearing after it was disclosed that one of the commissioners wrote an unsigned article in a newsletter that was hostile to the project. 125 Cal. App. 4th 470 (2004). The court held that authorship of such an article while the matter was pending before the commission showed an unacceptable probability of actual bias and was sufficient to preclude the Commissioner from serving as a "reasonably impartial, noninvolved reviewer." *Id.* at 484.

For a discussion of the admissibility of such evidence in court proceedings and discovery regarding a legislator's motives, see chapter 19 (Land Use Litigation).

ZONING BY INITIATIVE AND/OR REFERENDUM

Under California law, all zoning ordinances are subject to initiative and referendum. *See Arnel Dev. Co.*, 126 Cal. App. 3d at 336. While an initiative ordinance must comply with the substantive law, it need not comply with procedural requirements such as findings, notice, and hearing. *See Building Indus. Ass'n v. City of Camarillo*, 41 Cal. 3d 810, 815 (1986). However, when a referendum petition on a zoning ordinance will cause an inconsistency with the general plan, it cannot be processed. *See deBottari*, 171 Cal. App. 3d at 1213; *City of Irvine v. Irvine Citizens Against Overdevelopment*, 25 Cal. App. 4th 868, 879 (1994); *Lesher Communications, Inc. v. City of Walnut Creek*, 52 Cal. 3d 531, 541 (1990). For further discussion of this subject, see chapter 13 (Initiative and Referendum).

NO FORMAL RULES OF EVIDENCE; EFFECT OF PROCEDURAL ERRORS

Under Government Code section 65010(a), formal rules of evidence and procedure applicable in judicial actions and proceedings do not apply to any proceedings under the Planning and Zoning Law (Gov't Code § 65000 *et seq.*), except to the extent a city provides otherwise by charter, ordinance, resolution, or rule of procedure.

Government Code section 65010 is the "curative" statute for procedural errors in any action under the Planning and Zoning Law. Section 65010 applies to cure procedural errors so long as there has been no denial of due process. *See Mack v. Ironside*, 35 Cal. App. 3d 127, 130 (1973); *City of Sausalito v. County of Marin*, 12 Cal. App. 3d 550, 557 (1970). This statute makes it extremely difficult to invalidate land use decisions based upon mere procedural errors. It provides that no action regarding any planning or zoning matter by a city may be held void or invalid, or be set aside by any court, on grounds of improper admission or rejection of evidence or by reason of any error in matters pertaining to petitions, applications, notices, findings, records, hearings, reports, recommendations, appeal, or any other matters of procedure.

The court may invalidate a decision, however, when after an examination of the entire case including the evidence, it determines (1) that the error was prejudicial; (2) that the complaining party suffered substantial injury as a result of the error; and (3) that a different result would have been probable if such error had not occurred. Gov't Code § 65010(b).

ZONING AND THE FIRST AMENDMENT

REGULATION OF ADULT BUSINESSES[4]

Zoning ordinances regulating adult businesses, such as adult motion picture theaters and adult bookstores and arcades, will be upheld as not violating the First Amendment Freedom of Speech Clause of the United States Constitution if the ordinance is a content-neutral "time, place, and manner" regulation designed to serve a substantial governmental interest, and if it allows for reasonable alternative avenues of communication. *See City of Renton v. Playtime Theatres, Inc.*, 475 U.S. 41 (1986); *Young v. American Mini Theatres, Inc.*, 427 U.S. 50, 58 (1976).

In 1992, the California Supreme Court upheld such a zoning ordinance where a city sought to close an adult bookstore and arcade. *See City of National City v. Wiener*, 3 Cal. 4th 832, 843 (1992). That ordinance prohibited any adult business from locating within 1,500 feet of another adult business, 1,500 feet of a school or public park, or 1,000 feet of any residentially zoned property. There was no limit on the total number of adult businesses that could locate in National City, nor on the hours they could operate. The ordinance also provided that adult businesses were not subject to the distance requirements and could locate anywhere within the city's 572 acres of commercially zoned property if the business was located in a retail shopping center. The Court concluded that the ordinance was content-neutral because it was not aimed at the content of materials sold. In addition, the "substantial government interest" requirement was satisfied based on adult businesses being a source of urban decay. Moreover, reasonable alternative avenues of communication were provided. The argument that current sites were not available for rent did not establish constitutional infirmity. "The inquiry for First Amendment purposes is not concerned with economic impact." *Id.* at 847.

> The Court concluded that the ordinance was content-neutral because it was not aimed at the content of materials sold.

An ordinance that keeps adult businesses a reasonable distance from residential areas may be a constitutional time, place, and manner restriction that does not violate the First Amendment. However, such a restriction is not per se constitutional, and can be enforced only if the restriction is reasonably related to preventing undesirable secondary effects, such as neighborhood blight or crime. For example, in *Gammoh v. City of Anaheim*, a court found the denial of a permit unconstitutional after finding that the applicant adult business could not create any secondary effects upon a single undeveloped residential parcel located within an industrial zone. 73 Cal. App. 4th 186, 191 (1999).

However, while a city must demonstrate that there is a reasonable relationship between the restriction and the purported secondary effects, in *City of Los Angeles v. Alameda Books, Inc.*, the United States Supreme Court made it clear that this burden

---

4 *See* Daniel R. Mandelker and Rebecca Rubin, eds., *Protecting Free Speech and Expression: The First Amendment and Land Use Law* (Sect. of State and Local Gov't Law, ABA, 2001).

is not a heavy one. 535 U.S. 425 (2002). In 1977, the City of Los Angeles conducted a study concluding that concentration of adult entertainment establishments was associated with higher crime rates. In response, in 1983, the city enacted a zoning ordinance prohibiting more than one adult operation from occupying a single structure. Alameda Books, Inc., which shared building space with another adult entertainment business, sued to have the ordinance declared unconstitutional. The Ninth Circuit affirmed the grant of summary judgment in favor of Alameda Books by the trial court. Specifically, the Ninth Circuit found that the city could not reasonably rely on the 1977 study to show that the ordinance was designed to reduce crime.

The United States Supreme Court, in ruling for the city, reversed and remanded. The Court found that it was reasonable for the city to conclude from the 1977 report that the reduction of adult businesses in a single locale would help reduce crime. The city could have rationally concluded that a number of adult operations in one single establishment drew the same dense foot traffic as would separate establishments in close proximity. This is a reasonable conclusion drawn from the 1977 report, although other conclusions were also possible. The Ninth Circuit imposed too high a burden by requiring the city to prove that its conclusion was the only one to be drawn from the 1977 study. Alameda Books failed to provide evidence that refuted the city's interpretation of the study. Therefore, the city had satisfied the evidentiary requirement to survive summary judgment.

In arriving at its decision, the Court relied on its earlier decision in *Renton v. Playtime Theatres, Inc.*, wherein it upheld the validity of a municipal zoning ordinance prohibiting any adult movie theater from locating within 1,000 feet of any residential zone, family dwelling, church, park, or school. 475 U.S. 41 (1986).

The Court stated that in *Renton*, it specifically refused to set such a high bar for municipalities that want to address merely the secondary effects of protected speech. It held that a municipality may rely on any evidence that is "reasonably believed to be relevant" for demonstrating a connection between speech and a substantial, independent government interest. *Id.* at 51. A city may not rely on shoddy data or reasoning, and its evidence must fairly support its rationale for its ordinance. However, if the plaintiffs fail either to demonstrate that the city's evidence does not support its rationale or furnish evidence that disputes the city's factual findings, the city meets the standard set forth in *Renton*. If the plaintiffs succeed in casting doubt on a city's rationale in either manner, the burden shifts back to the city to supplement the record with evidence renewing support for a theory that justifies its ordinance. The Court then stated that this case was at a very early stage in this process, noting that it arrived on a summary judgment motion by the respondents defended only by complaints that the 1977 study failed to prove that the city's justification for its ordinance was necessarily correct. Therefore, the Court concluded that the city, at this stage of the litigation, had complied with the evidentiary requirement in *Renton*. *Id.* at 54.

In *Isbell v. City of San Diego*, the plaintiff adult business owner claimed that the city's zoning ordinance, which prohibited adult businesses within 1,000 feet of each other or any residential zone, school, church, public park, or social welfare institution, failed to offer reasonable alternative avenues of expression. 258 F. 3d 1108 (9th Cir. 2001). The Ninth Circuit first found that the methods used by both parties to compute the number of available alternative sites within the city were fatally flawed, and calculated a number of sites based on evidence in the record. It then held that the city's failure to analyze the supply and demand of adult businesses and to conduct other inquiries pursuant to a comprehensive and collective analysis failed to establish that reasonable alternative avenues of communication existed in the city under the ordinance. *Id.* at 1114.

The plaintiff next argued that because the freeway running between his property and the residential neighborhood 900 feet away would alleviate any secondary effects of his business, the 1,000-foot rule served no valid purpose in his case and thus violated the First Amendment. The Ninth Circuit rejected this contention. Noting that any application of the 1,000-foot rule would have varying effects in each situation, it held that if each situation must be examined and exceptions tailored, there would be nothing left of the 1,000-foot rule approved by the United States Supreme Court in *American Mini Theatres*. Thus, the city could apply the rule without exception.

Finally, the plaintiff contended that the ordinance violated the Equal Protection Clause by applying variance standards more stringent for adult entertainment businesses than for non-adult businesses, since the city could take into account the mitigating effect that barriers such as freeways have on the secondary effects of a non-adult business, but could not do so with respect to an adult entertainment business. The court concluded that since the regulation of adult businesses is not a regulation of content and therefore may survive an equal protection challenge if it has a rational basis, the fact that the secondary effects of adult businesses are arguably more extreme than those of other businesses was enough to justify the more stringent review of variance applications for adult businesses.

In *City of Littleton, Colorado v. Z.J. Gifts D-4, LLC*, the owner of an adult business attacked a city's licensing requirement for adult business as unconstitutional on its face, claiming that the city's ordinance did not provide sufficiently prompt judicial review of license denials. 541 U.S. 774, 776–77 (2004). The Littleton ordinance called for applicants to take claims of improperly denied licenses to the Colorado state courts. The Tenth Circuit Court of Appeals agreed with the business owner, holding that Colorado law did not "assure that [the city's] license decisions will be given expedited [judicial] review" and hence, did not assure the prompt judicial decision that is required when First Amendment expression is implicated. *Id.* at 777.

On appeal to the United States Supreme Court, the city made two arguments in defense of its ordinance. First, it claimed that the First Amendment requires only prompt access to judicial review of adult-oriented business license denials or zoning decisions, not a prompt final judicial determination. The city noted that nothing stopped business owners from going to court immediately to seek review of license denials. Second, the city claimed that, even with a requirement of prompt judicial determination, Colorado law satisfied that requirement.

The Supreme Court reversed the Tenth Circuit and upheld the city's ordinance. The Court, however, rejected the city's argument that a requirement for prompt judicial review somehow did not include a prompt judicial determination. "A delay in issuing a judicial decision, no less than a delay in obtaining access to a court, can prevent a license from being 'issued within a reasonable period of time.'" *Id.* at 781. But the Court agreed with the city that Colorado's ordinary "judicial review" rules were adequate to satisfy this "prompt judicial determination" requirement in any event. It reasoned that state courts have great flexibility in accelerating procedures and are presumed to know when they must exercise such power to protect against "unconstitutional suppression of protected speech." *Id.* at 782. The Court also noted that Littleton's ordinance imposed objective, nondiscretionary licensing criteria unrelated to the content of the expressive materials in the adult business. The use of such objective criteria meant there was not

> The Court rejected the city's argument that a requirement for prompt judicial review somehow did not include a prompt judicial determination.

grave danger of suppression of any type of adult material. These circumstances indicated that Colorado's ordinary rules of judicial review were adequate to protect First Amendment interests. *Id.* at 784.

For further discussion of the intersection between adult entertainment zoning ordinances and the First Amendment, see Jules B. Gerard, *Local Regulation of Adult Businesses* (West, 2005) and Gov't Code § 65850.4 (regarding adoption of zoning ordinances to regulate sexually oriented businesses; authorizing cities to consider secondary effects of adult businesses on adjacent cities and to enter into joint powers authority and other cooperative agreements with adjacent cities for the purpose of regulating such effects).

PROTECTION OF RELIGIOUS EXERCISE

Courts have grappled with what constitutes the proper standard of review in cases involving claims of infringement on the free exercise of religion. Prior to 1990, courts generally reviewed government actions that imposed burdens on the exercise of religion under the strict scrutiny test (i.e., a regulation must be the least restrictive means of furthering a compelling governmental interest). In 1990, the United States Supreme Court eliminated in large part this heightened scrutiny for cases involving the free exercise of religion. In *Employment Division v. Smith*, the Court upheld a state law of general applicability criminalizing the use of peyote, which was used to deny unemployment benefits to Native American church members who lost their jobs for using peyote. 494 U.S. 872 (1990). There, the Court declined to apply a balancing test that would have asked whether the law substantially burdened the religious use of peyote and, if so, whether that burden was justified by a compelling government interest. *Id.* at 885.

RFRA = Religious Freedom and Restoration Act

In response to the Court's decision, Congress enacted the Religious Freedom and Restoration Act of 1993 (RFRA). RFRA prohibited the government from imposing a substantial burden on a person's free exercise of religion unless the government could demonstrate that the burden furthered a compelling governmental interest and used the least restrictive means in doing so.

The Catholic Archbishop of San Antonio, Texas, invoked RFRA in *City of Boerne v. Flores*, 521 U.S. 507 (1997). The Archbishop applied for a building permit to enlarge a church to accommodate its growing parish. The city denied the application based on a local preservation ordinance that required the city's landmark commission to preapprove construction affecting historic landmarks, such as the church. The Archbishop argued the preservation ordinance constituted a substantial burden under RFRA. In ruling RFRA unconstitutional, the Court held RFRA's coverage of state and local governments exceeded Congressional authority and "contradict[ed] vital principles necessary to maintain separation of powers and the federal balance." *Id.* at 536.

RLUIPA = Religious Land Use and Institutionalized Persons Act

In 2000, Congress passed the Religious Land Use and Institutionalized Persons Act (RLUIPA), 42 U.S.C. § 2000cc et seq. Under RLUIPA, a government may not "impose or implement a land use regulation in a manner that imposes a substantial burden" on religious exercise unless the government demonstrates the burden imposed is "in furtherance of a compelling governmental interest" and is the "least restrictive means of furthering" that interest. *Id.* at § 2000cc. RLUIPA's definition of "exercise of religion" includes "any exercise of religion, whether or not compelled by, or central to, a system of religious belief." *Id.* at § 2000cc-5(7)(A).

While RLUIPA does not itself define "substantial burden," the Ninth Circuit Court of Appeals clarified what must be shown to demonstrate a "substantial burden" on religious exercise under RLUIPA. *See San Jose Christian College v. City of Morgan Hill*, 360 F. 3d 1024, 1035 (9th Cir. 2004). The Ninth Circuit held that for a land use regulation to "impose a 'substantial burden,' it must be 'oppressive' to a 'significantly great' extent" and must impose a "significantly great restriction or onus upon religious exercise." *Id.* at 1034. The court held that the ordinance at issue merely required the college to submit a *complete* application for rezoning, as it required of all applicants, imposed no restriction whatsoever on the college's exercise of religion. *Id.* at 1035. Because the college was not precluded from using other sites within the city and the city would have imposed the same application requirements on any other applicant similarly seeking approval of a rezone, the court found no "substantial burden." *Id.*; *see also County of Los Angeles v. Sahag-Mesrob Armenian Christian School*, 188 Cal. App. 4th 851 (2010) (requiring religious schools to secure a conditional use permit and comply with CEQA does not constitute a substantial burden on the exercise of religious freedom). The Ninth Circuit did find a county's denial of a conditional use permit for construction of a temple constituted a substantial burden under RLUIPA in *Guru Nanak Sikh Society of Yuba City v. County of Sutter*, 456 F. 3d 978 (9th Cir. 2006). In *Guru Nanak*, the county twice denied the group's use permit application: once due to noise and traffic concerns, when the temple was proposed as an infill project on a residentially-zoned site, and later, due to concerns of leapfrog development when proposed on a larger, agriculturally-zoned site. The court found that denial of the second application lessened to a significantly great extent the possibility the group ever would be permitted to construct a temple, and that the county had not asserted any compelling interest for its action. *Id.* at 992. The court explained that unlike *San Jose Christian*, where there was no evidence that the desired permit could not be obtained merely by submitting a complete application, the applicant in *Guru Nanak* had no reason to believe that a further application would be accepted. *Id.*

If a claimant demonstrates that a regulation constitutes a substantial burden on its religious exercise, the burden shifts to the government to prove that the burden is the least restrictive means of furthering a compelling governmental interest. Courts will "examine the particular burden imposed by the implementation of the relevant zoning code on the claimant's religious exercise and determine, on the facts of each case, whether that burden is 'substantial.'" *International Church of the Foursquare Gospel v. City of San Leandro*, 634 F.3d 1037, 1044 (9th Cir. 2011). Where a city denied both a church's rezoning application and application for a conditional use permit to operate a church, the Ninth Circuit held the church offered sufficient evidence that the city imposed a substantial burden on its religious exercise and the city failed as a matter of law to prove a compelling interest for its actions. *Id.* at 1049. The court reasoned the preservation of industrial lands does not by itself constitute a "compelling interest" and even if the county had a compelling interest, the City presented no evidence it could not achieve its stated goals by using other property within its jurisdiction for that purpose. *Id.*

RLUIPA also includes a nondiscrimination provision that renders a city strictly liable for implementing a land use regulation that discriminates against religious uses regardless of the justifications offered by the city. *See Midrash Sephardi, Inc. v. Town of Surfside*, 366 F. 3d 1214, 1229 (11th Cir. 2004). This provision operates independently from the "substantial burden" provision of RLUIPA. In *Midrash*, the nondiscrimination provision of RLUIPA was violated where the Town of Surfside imposed certain zoning restrictions on synagogues and churches but not on similar nonreligious assemblies or institutions like private clubs and lodges. *Id.* at 1231.

> If a claimant demonstrates that a regulation constitutes a substantial burden on its religious exercise, the burden shifts to the government to prove that the burden is the least restrictive means of furthering a compelling governmental interest.

In California, Government Code sections 25373 and 37361 provide statutory exemptions from local landmark preservation laws for noncommercial property owned by religious organizations. These exemptions were upheld following a challenge by the City and County of San Francisco and several organizations concerned with landmark preservation under the state and federal constitutions. *See East Bay Asian Local Dev. Corp. v. State of California*, 24 Cal. 4th 693 (2000). The California Supreme Court, in finding the exemptions did not constitute an endorsement of religion, held it is lawful for a state to act to reduce a burden on the religious freedom of those within its jurisdiction, particularly when the state itself is imposing the burden. *Id.*

Note the exemption applies even where property is no longer used or capable of being used for a religious purpose, and even where a religious institution intends to sell it for development as a non-religious, commercial venture. *California-Nevada Annual Conference of the United Methodist Church v. City and County of San Francisco*, 173 Cal. App. 4th 1559, 1565–66 (2009) (holding *East Bay Asian Local Development Corporation* makes unmistakably clear the statute permits a religiously affiliated nonprofit entity to sell a place of worship for profit).

RLUIPA has forced cities to walk the fine line between the Free Exercise Clause and the Establishment Clause of the First Amendment. RLUIPA provides religious groups with a powerful weapon with which to challenge zoning ordinances, requiring cities to be more flexible when responding to zoning applications from religious groups. Given this reality, many cities have or should revise their ordinances to avoid lengthy and expensive lawsuits. However, cities must also be careful not to favor religious groups too much, or they may face lawsuits alleging the endorsement of religion in violation of the Establishment Clause. Cities should develop a detailed record in administrative actions involving religious institutions, both to detail findings of "substantial burden" and "compelling government interest," as well as to include evidence of steps taken to explore alternative means of solving the problems that the proposed religious activity may pose. Local governments also may want to develop a more detailed record in cases not involving religious groups, to assist them in fighting claims of discrimination in cases that do involve religious organizations.[5]

ADMINISTRATIVE ZONING RELIEF—VARIANCES—CONDITIONAL USE PERMITS

IN GENERAL

CUP = conditional use permit

Variances and conditional use permits (CUPs) are methods by which a property owner may seek relief from the strict terms of a comprehensive zoning ordinance. While the amendment of a zoning regulation is a legislative function, the granting of variances and use permits are quasi-judicial, administrative functions. Variances

---

5 For good overviews of RLUIPA and recommendations on how to successfully navigate its provisions, see Alan C. Weinstein, *Recent Developments Concerning RLUIPA* in Current Trends and Practical Strategies in Land Use Law and Zoning 1 (Patricia E. Salkin ed., 2004); Alan C. Weinstein, *RLUIPA: Where are we now? Where are we heading?*, 56 Planning & Environmental Law, no. 2, page 3 (2004); Robert B. Hall, Zen and the Art of Zoning—Constitutional Challenge to RLUIPA, 13 California Land Use Law & Policy Reporter, no. 6 (March 2004); Helene Leichter, Zoning Churches: An Update on Religious Land Use Litigation, Western City, page 27 (July 2004); Anthony R. Picarello, Jr., *RLUIPA Is Constitutional*, Marci A. Hamilton, *RLUIPA Is Unfair, Unwise, and Unconstitutional*, and Lora Lucero, *Where Does APA Stand on RLUIPA?*, point/counterpoint commentaries in 56 Planning and Environmental Law, no. 4, pages 3–14 (APA, April 2004); Sara Smolik, The Utility and Efficacy of the RLUIPA: Was It a Waste?, 31 Boston Col. Env'tl Aff. L. Rev., no. 3, page 723 (2004) (analyzing the constitutionality of RLUIPA and discussing whether RLUIPA serves the purpose for which it was designed).

and use permits run with the land. *See County of Imperial v. McDougal*, 19 Cal. 3d 505, 510 (1977). Therefore, a city cannot condition a use permit on its nontransferability. *See Anza Parking Corp. v. City of Burlingame*, 195 Cal. App. 3d 855, 860 (1987). In addition, variances and conditional use permits must be consistent with a city's general plan. *See Neighborhood Action Group v. County of Calaveras*, 156 Cal. App. 3d 1176, 1187 (1984); *City of Carmel-by-the-Sea v. Board of Supervisors*, 137 Cal. App. 3d 964, 997 (1982).

In *Neighbors in Support of Appropriate Land Use v. County of Tuolumne*, the court held that the county violated the "uniformity requirement" by granting an *ad hoc* exception to the county's zoning ordinance without properly granting either a conditional use permit or a variance. 157 Cal. App. 4th 997, 1007–08 (2007). The "uniformity requirement" embodied in Government Code section 65852 provides: "All such [zoning] regulations shall be uniform for each class or kind of building or use of land throughout each zone, but the regulation in one type of zone may differ from those in other types of zones."

The Government Code provides that any restriction imposed by a municipal entity on an owner's ability to convey real property or a leasehold interest in real property shall be set forth in a recorded document in order to impart notice of the restriction. Gov't Code § 27281.5. This provision has been held to require recordation of a conditional use permit that placed restrictions on the occupancy of units in a particular apartment building. *1119 Delaware v. Continental Land Title Co.*, 16 Cal. App. 4th 992, 999–1000 (1993) (CUP required that at least one occupant of each unit be at least 62 years of age or physically handicapped). A zoning ordinance of general application, however, is considered to impart constructive notice of its terms to the public and need not be recorded against an owner's title to be enforceable. *Id.* at 1002; *see City of W. Hollywood v. Beverly Towers, Inc.*, 52 Cal. 3d 1184, 1194 (1991).

VARIANCES[6]

A variance is a permit issued to a landowner by an administrative agency (e.g., zoning administrator, board of zoning adjustment, planning commission, or the city council acting as an administrative agency) to build a structure or engage in some action not otherwise permitted under the current zoning regulations. The statutory justification for a variance is that the owner otherwise would suffer unique hardship under the general zoning regulations because a particular parcel is different from the others to which the regulation applies due to its size, shape, topography, location, or surroundings. Gov't Code § 65906. This section is applicable to all cities and counties except charter cities, and can be supplemented by harmonious local legislation. *See Topanga Ass'n for a Scenic Community v. County of Los Angeles*, 11 Cal. 3d 506, 511 (1974).

Variances may not be granted to authorize a use that is not otherwise authorized by the zoning regulations. Rather, variances allow deviations from regulations on physical standards such as lot sizes, floor area ratios for buildings, and off-street parking requirements. Variances are, in effect, constitutional safety valves to permit administrative adjustments when application of a general regulation would be confiscatory or produce unique hardship.

> Variances are, in effect, constitutional safety valves to permit administrative adjustments when application of a general regulation would be confiscatory or produce unique hardship.

Some basic principles that must be applied in the consideration of an application for a variance are:

---

[6] *See The Variance* (Governor's Office of Planning and Research, July 1997) *available at* ceres.ca.gov/planning/var/variance.htm.

- A variance must be consistent with the objectives of the general plan and the zoning ordinance
- A variance may not be granted if it will adversely affect the interests of the public or the interests of other residents and property owners within the vicinity of the premises in question.
- To justify the authorization of a variance, the applicant's unique circumstances must cause the property owner unique hardship and create disparities between the applicant's property and other neighboring properties. While such circumstances are generally limited to physical conditions of the property, in *Craik v. County of Santa Cruz*, the court held a grant of variance did not require a showing of physical disparity. 81 Cal. App. 4th 880, 890 (2000), stating there was no authority to support that a physical disparity is a precondition for a variance.
- The mere existence of a peculiar situation that will result in unnecessary hardship to the applicant if the ordinance is enforced does not necessarily require the granting of a variance.
- A variance must not grant a "special privilege" inconsistent with the limitations on other nearby properties.

The variance criteria contained in Government Code section 65906 prevail over any inconsistent requirements in local ordinances. A variance can be sustained only if all applicable legislative requirements of Government Code section 65906 are met. *See Topanga*, 11 Cal. 3d 506, 518 (1974).

In *Orinda Association v. Board of Supervisors*, the court invalidated a height variance as a kind of special privilege explicitly prohibited by Government Code section 65906. 182 Cal. App. 3d 1145 (1986). The court held there were no facts sufficient to justify a variance, and there was no affirmative showing that the subject property differed substantially and in relevant aspects from other parcels in the applicable zones. *Id.* at 1167.

CONDITIONAL USE PERMIT

The second administrative method of providing relief from the strict terms of a comprehensive zoning ordinance is a conditional use permit. Unlike the variance procedure, the Planning and Zoning Law is silent with respect to the proper criteria to evaluate whether a CUP should be issued. Rather, this is determined by local ordinance. Gov't Code § 65901. Typically, following a list of permitted uses in each zone, a local zoning ordinance will provide for other uses that are not permitted as a matter or right, but for which a CUP must be obtained. The CUP is well recognized by zoning administrators and the courts as a necessary and proper method to provide flexibility and alleviate hardship. *See Groch v. City of Berkeley*, 118 Cal. App. 3d 518 (1981); *Upton v. Gray*, 269 Cal. App. 2d 352 (1969). However, it must be issued pursuant to proper procedures. In *League of Residential Neighborhood Advocates v. City of Los Angeles*, a settlement agreement granting a CUP for a synagogue in an area zoned residential was held invalid because it did not provide for the required public hearing and it permitted the city to disregard its own zoning ordinance. 498 F. 3d 1052, 1057 (9th Cir. 2007).

A CUP or other similar permit does not expire automatically even when a condition to the CUP provides for such expiration or the local code provides for an automatic expiration. For instance, in *Cmty. Dev. Comm'n v. City of Fort Bragg*, the court held that a CUP cannot be revoked without notice and hearing despite an automatic expiration condition, and that such revocation must be reasonable. 204 Cal. App. 3d 1124, 1131–32 (1988).

> The CUP is well recognized by zoning administrators and the courts as a necessary and proper method to provide flexibility and alleviate hardship.

Until a CUP is issued and relied upon, no right has vested. Therefore, the initial denial of an application for a CUP is subject to judicial review under the substantial evidence test. However, the grant of a CUP with subsequent reliance on the permit by the permit holder creates a fundamental vested property right that subjects a CUP revocation to judicial review under the independent judgment test. *See Malibu Mountains Recreation, Inc. v. County of Los Angeles*, 67 Cal. App. 4th 359, 367 (1998); *see also Bauer v. City of San Diego*, 75 Cal. App. 4th 1281, 1294 (1999) (once a right to a CUP vests, the permittee is entitled to all the protections of due process before the permit may be revoked). For a more detailed discussion of the proper standard of judicial review of agency decisions, see chapter 19 (Land Use Litigation).

The types of uses subject to obtaining a CUP are quite varied. The courts generally have upheld the issuance of a CUP by a city if all applicable laws are followed. Examples of CUPs that have been upheld include the following:

- Planned residential development. *Concerned Citizens of Palm Desert, Inc. v. Board of Supervisors*, 38 Cal. App. 3d 257 (1974)
- Airplane hangar in residential zone. *Mitcheltree v. City of Los Angeles*, 17 Cal. App. 3d 791 (1971)
- Mobile home park in residential-agricultural (R-A) zone. *Jones v. City Council*, 17 Cal. App. 3d 724 (1971)
- Synagogue in residential zone. *Stoddard v. Edelman*, 4 Cal. App. 3d 544 (1970)
- Farm equipment repair shop. *Upton v. Gray*, 269 Cal. App. 2d 352 (1969)
- Extraction of minerals (sand and gravel quarry). *Rapp v. County of Napa Planning Comm'n*, 204 Cal. App. 2d 695 (1962)
- Erection of a radio tower. *McManus v. KPAL Broad. Corp.*, 182 Cal. App. 2d 558 (1960)
- Cemetery [in "Family Zone"], *Essick v. City of Los Angeles*, 34 Cal. 2d 614 (1950)

The following cases have upheld the denial of CUPs for the following proposed uses:

- Three-story home in a single-family zone, because of view impairment and towering effect. *Saad v. City of Berkeley*, 24 Cal. App. 4th 1206 (1994)
- Automobile service station. *Van Sicklen v. Browne*, 15 Cal. App. 3d 122 (1971)
- Use of a bus for a restaurant. *Melton v. City of San Pablo*, 252 Cal. App. 2d 794 (1967)
- Storage yard for houses. *Snow v. City of Garden Grove*, 188 Cal. App. 2d 496 (1961)
- Used car business. *Felice v. City of Inglewood*, 84 Cal. App. 2d 263 (1948)

In granting a new CUP, a city need not consider evidence of purported violations of an original CUP. Instead, a city can revoke the original CUP if there were violations, but such violations are not relevant to the application for a new CUP. *See Baird v. County of Contra Costa*, 32 Cal. App. 4th 1464, 1470 (1995) (upholding grant of an additional CUP to expand an addiction treatment facility despite evidence of prior permit violations).

Where a city's CUP requirement implicates speech rights, it must also circumscribe the zoning administrator's discretion in deciding whether to grant or deny the CUP. *Vo v. City of Garden Grove*, 115 Cal. App. 4th 425 (2004). The plaintiffs in *Vo* sought to enjoin preliminarily the city's ordinance requiring that they obtain CUPs to continue operating cyber-cafes. Plaintiffs claimed the CUP requirement violated the First Amendment.

Agreeing with plaintiffs that First Amendment activity was implicated by the regulation of cybercafes, the court upheld an injunction against the CUP requirement. The court noted that the city's code, which would allow the zoning administrator to deny the CUPs based on such ambiguous criteria as the "general welfare" of the community, gave the zoning administrator unfettered discretion to make decisions on any basis and left open the possibility that the city could require installation of content-filtering software to advance the "general welfare." Id. at 438. The potential for an impact upon First Amendment expression required "precise standards capable of objective measurement" missing in the city's CUP requirement. Id. at 437.

A requirement that a CUP be obtained may raise takings concerns. However, in *Allegretti & Co. v. County of Imperial*, a landowner's claim that the county's CUP requirement constituted inverse condemnation was rejected. 138 Cal. App. 4th 1261 (2006). Allegretti filed for a CUP to re-drill an inoperable well and the county approved the CUP but limited the draw of groundwater. Allegretti argued the limitation constituted a taking, however the court concluded the CUP was not a physical taking since the county did not divert any water or invade the property. Id. at 1273. Further, the CUP did not unreasonably impair the value or use of the property but merely resulted in a reduction in profit. Id. at 1278-79. For more discussion on takings, see chapter 11 (Takings).

NONCONFORMING USES

A nonconforming use describes a lawful use existing on the effective date of a new zoning restriction that has continued since that time without conformance to the ordinance. While the policy of the law is for elimination of nonconforming uses to effectuate change or to accommodate changed circumstances, as a general rule, a new zoning ordinance may not operate constitutionally to compel immediate discontinuance of an otherwise lawfully established use or business. See *City of Los Angeles v. Wolfe*, 6 Cal. 3d 326, 337 (1971); *Livingston Rock & Gravel Co. v. County of Los Angeles*, 43 Cal. 2d 121, 127 (1954). However, if an activity constitutes a public nuisance, it can be removed immediately as long as due process protections are provided. Id.; see also *City of Bakersfield v. Miller*, 64 Cal. 2d 93, 103 (1966).

The legal means of terminating a nonconforming use is a prime concern of zoning law, and a city can provide a period of time to eliminate nonconforming uses. See *Nat'l Adver. Co. v. County of Monterey*, 1 Cal. 3d 875, 880 (1970). Given the objective of zoning, courts generally follow a strict policy against the extension or enlargement of nonconforming uses. See *County of San Diego v. McClurken*, 37 Cal. 2d 683, 686-87 (1951). "The ultimate purpose of zoning is to confine certain classes of buildings and uses to particular localities and to reduce all nonconforming uses with the zone to conformity as speedily as is consistent with proper safeguards for the interests of those affected. *Dienelt v. County of Monterey*, 113 Cal. App. 2d 128, 131 (1952). Intensification or expansion of an existing nonconforming use, or moving the use to another location on the property, is not permitted. For a general discussion of intensification of a nonconforming use, see *Hansen Bros. Enterprises, Inc. v. Board of Supervisors*, 12 Cal. 4th 533 (1996).

VOLUNTARY AND REQUIRED REPAIRS OF NONCONFORMING USES

Most nonconforming use provisions of local zoning ordinances expressly permit repairs of nonconforming buildings. Usually extensive repairs are not allowed, but repairs that are part of normal annual maintenance and preserve the owner's right to continue the nonconforming use often are permitted. *Ricciardi v. County of Los Angeles,* 115 Cal. App. 2d 569, 576-577 (1953).

Determination of whether an alteration or improvement would be considered an extensive repair or, alternatively, a substantial alteration, enlargement, or expansion, is fact-specific. Restoration of an oil terminal berth which had been 75 percent destroyed constituted a "repair" and was not an enlargement or expansion under Public Resources Code section 30610(c) because the restoration essentially reflected the facility's original specifications, and wherever possible undamaged or salvageable portions were utilized or retained. *Union Oil Co. v. South Coast Regional Com.,* 92 Cal. App. 3d 327, 331 (1979). Some local ordinances set limits for repair based upon the percentage of the structure's value to insure such that repairs will not constitute substantial alterations.

Many local ordinances make an exception for alterations required by law. *See, e.g., City of Fontana v. Atkinson,* 212 Cal. App. 2d 499 (1963).

STRUCTURAL ALTERATIONS OF NONCONFORMING USES

Local zoning ordinances often prohibit structural alterations that would expand a nonconforming use, better accommodate it, make it more permanent, or create a new use. *Dienelt,* 113 Cal. App. 2d at 130-131 (holding replacement of a patio that was a nonconforming structure and devoted to a nonconforming use with a larger concrete patio constituted a structural alteration in violation of the local ordinance because the change tended to make the structure more permanent); *Hopkins v. MacCulloch,* 35 Cal. App. 2d 442, 452 (1939) (remodeling grocery store and lunchroom was a structural alteration constituting discontinuance of the nonconforming use; any future use of the building was required to conform to existing standards).

DESTRUCTION OF A NONCONFORMING USE BY FIRE OR OTHER CATASTROPHIC EVENTS

Under many local ordinances, if fire or other catastrophic events destroy a certain percentage (often between 25 and 75 percent) of a building's value, the owner may not rebuild and resume a nonconforming use. "[W]here a nonconforming use has been carried on in a building which has been accidently destroyed in large measure, it is not unreasonable to compel the owner to conform to zoning requirements thereafter. The investment in an improvement that may not be readily adaptable to a conforming use has been taken away from him by the accident and not by the ordinance." *O'Mara v. Council of City of Newark,* 238 Cal. App. 2d 836, 838 (1965). Generally, the value of the destroyed building is determined to be the fair market value of the structure at the time of the fire or other catastrophic event, unless the applicable ordinance explicitly gives another definition. *Manhattan Sepulveda v. City of Manhattan Beach,* 22 Cal. App. 4th 865 (1994).

To partially compensate an owner for termination of the nonconforming use by destruction, Government Code section 43007 allows for property tax relief for owners of property that is destroyed and cannot be rebuilt because of zoning prohibitions. Additionally, section 65852.25(a) requires local agencies not to prohibit reconstruction of a multifamily dwelling destroyed by fire. Section 65863.4(a) addresses the situation in which a local agency wants to reduce the density of property on which one or more multifamily dwellings exist. Prior to noticing a public hearing on a proposed

> Under many local ordinances, if fire or other catastrophic events destroy a certain percentage of a building's value, the owner may not rebuild and resume a nonconforming use.

zoning ordinance or amendment that sets the density, the local agency is required to approve a nonconforming use ordinance for multifamily dwellings that are involuntarily damaged or destroyed on such property. Gov't Code § 65863.4(a).

AMORTIZATION

California courts have relied upon a case-by-case balancing approach to determine when a city can properly terminate a nonconforming use. The courts have upheld termination provisions where a reasonable period of time to recover the permit holder's investment is allowed. *See Livingston Rock & Gravel Co. v. County of Los Angeles*, 43 Cal. 2d at 127 (upholding a period commensurate with the investment involved); *Sabek, Inc. v. County of Sonoma*, 190 Cal. App. 3d 163, 168 (1987) (upholding loss of nonconforming status when remodeling costs were more than 15 percent of a structure's appraised value); *City of Los Angeles v. Gage*, 127 Cal. App. 2d 442, 460 (1954) (constitutionality of a termination period depends upon the relative importance to be given to the public gain and the private loss).

The leading case discussing elimination of nonconforming uses with a proper amortization period is *Metromedia, Inc. v. City of San Diego*, 26 Cal. 3d 848 (1980), void on other grounds, 453 U.S. 490 (1981). This case involved an action by owners of billboards to enjoin the enforcement of a city ordinance banning all off-site advertising billboards, and requiring the removal of existing billboards following expiration of an amortization period. The California Supreme Court stated that the amortization period, which ranged from one to four years depending on the depreciated value of the sign, was not unreasonable on its face. Moreover, the owners had the burden of proving the invalidity of the amortization period as it applied to each structure. The Court laid down the following rule:

> Zoning legislation may validly provide for the eventual termination of nonconforming uses without compensation if it provides a reasonable amortization period commensurate with the investment involved.

Id. at 882

This rule was not changed by the United States Supreme Court decisions in *First English Evangelical Lutheran Church v. County of Los Angeles*, 482 U.S. 304 (1987), and *Nollan v. California Coastal Commission*, 483 U.S. 825 (1987). *See also Tahoe Reg'l Planning Agency v. King*, 233 Cal. App. 3d 1365, 1393-1400 (1991).

In terms of defining what constitutes a "reasonable" amortization period, the court in *City of Salinas v. Ryan Outdoor Adver., Inc.* stated that the reasonableness of the amortization period depends on the interplay of many factors, including the depreciated value of the structures to be removed, their remaining useful life, and the harm to the public if they are left standing. 189 Cal. App. 3d 416, 424 (1987).

With respect to "on-premises signs," the Legislature has provided, with some exceptions, that cities cannot terminate nonconforming signs without payment. Bus. & Prof. Code § 5490 *et seq.* In *Denny's Inc. v. City of Agoura Hills*, 56 Cal. App. 4th 1312 (1997), the court held that Business and Professions Code section 5499 bars local ordinances that proscribe on-premises signs or advertising displays based on their height or size if "nontemporary" topographic features, including natural or man-made features, would cause a sign or display that conformed to the ordinance to be less visible or less effective in communicating to the public. *Id.* at 1323.

OTHER TYPES OF ZONING

FORM-BASED ZONING

Increasingly, cities are adopting form-based zoning principles. Form-based codes place primary emphasis on the design and physical form of buildings, streetscapes, and public places, with less emphasis than conventional land use regulations on allowed uses inside the buildings. In contrast to traditional zoning, form-based zoning regulates building types, dimensions, parking locations, and design features. Often, form-based codes are applied through regulating plans that map a community with geographic designations based on scale, character, intensity, and form of development instead of differences in land uses. Form-based development regulations commonly include a regulating plan (showing sites for buildings, street types, and possibly design features), urban regulations (addressing height, bulk, area coverage, and use standards), street regulations (including street and sidewalk dimensions), landscape regulations and architectural regulations (concerning building styles and materials).[7] Many form-based regulations are presented in or illustrated by graphical diagrams and drawings.

Advocates of form-based zoning believe that this approach makes sense where one key planning task is managing the transition from suburban to urban development.[8] Further, technological advances that minimize certain environmental effects may help alleviate what were formerly considered incompatible uses. California cities such as Petaluma, Hercules, and Azusa, as well as Contra Costa County[9] have adopted or incorporated form-based zoning.

PREZONING

A city may prezone unincorporated territory outside its limits for the purpose of determining zoning that will apply to such property in the event of subsequent annexation to the city. Gov't Code § 65859. In fact, pursuant to the Cortese-Knox-Hertzberg Local Government Reorganization Act of 2000, a local agency formation commission (LAFCO) shall require as a condition of annexation that a city prezone the territory to be annexed. Gov't Code §§ 56375; 56375(a). For a detailed discussion of LAFCOs, see chapter 14 (LAFCOs). Prezoning becomes effective at the same time the annexation becomes effective. Prezoning must also be consistent with the city's general plan. *See City of Irvine v. Irvine Citizens Against Overdevelopment*, 25 Cal. App. 4th 868, 879 (1994).

LAFCO = local agency formation commission

INTERIM ORDINANCE

There are times when a property owner will submit a land use proposal or request a building permit for use of property that may be in conflict with a contemplated general plan, specific plan, or zoning proposal that the city is considering, studying, or

---

7 For an excellent discussion of form-based regulations, see Robert J. Sitkowski and Brian W. Ohm, *Form-Based Land Development Regulations*, 38 The Urban Lawyer 163 (Winter 2006).

8 *See* William Fulton, *Transition Away from Suburbia Bolsters Form-Based Zoning Movement*, 21 Cal. Plng. & Dev. Rep. 1 (April 2006).

9 *See* Rebecca Retzlaff, *California Enacts Form-Based Zoning Legislation*, Zoning Practice, pages 10–11 (APA, January 2005) (discussing California's form-based zoning law which seeks to integrate streets, open space, housing, commercial development, and neighborhoods, rather than grouping similar and related land uses). *See also* Carla M. Moynihan, *Implementing Form-Based Zoning in Your Municipality*, 47 Municipal Lawyer 15 (IMLA July/August 2006); Michael Moore, *Form-Based Zoning Is Not the (Whole) Answer*, APA Northern News, page 1 (May/June 2006).

intending to study within a reasonable period of time. In such situations, Government Code section 65858 authorizes a city to adopt, as an urgency measure, an interim ordinance prohibiting such uses that may conflict with a general plan, specific plan, or zoning proposal that the city is considering, without following the procedures otherwise required for the adoption of a zoning ordinance. However, such an urgency measure requires a four-fifths vote of the city council for adoption. No notice or hearing is required for the first adoption of an interim ordinance. *See Beck Dev. Co. v. Southern Pac. Transp. Co.*, 44 Cal. App. 4th 1160 (1996).

> No notice or hearing is required for the first adoption of an interim ordinance.

Interim urgency ordinances have statutory time limitations. Gov't Code § 65858. If an interim ordinance is initially adopted without notice and hearing, it is effective for only 45 days from the date of adoption. However, after notice and hearing, the city council may extend such interim ordinance for 10 months and 15 days and subsequently extend the interim ordinance for an additional one year. However, like the ordinance itself, extensions require a four-fifths vote for adoption. Additionally, not more than two extensions may be adopted for a total extension of two years. Alternatively, an interim ordinance may be adopted initially by a four-fifths vote following notice and hearing, in which case it is effective for 45 days and can be extended, after notice and hearing, by a four-fifths vote for 22 months and 15 days. Gov't Code § 65858(b). Under either approach, interim "urgency" ordinances are limited by statute to a two-year period.

However, upon termination of a prior interim ordinance, the city council may adopt another interim ordinance if the new interim ordinance arises from an event, occurrence, or set of circumstances different from that which led to the adoption of the prior interim ordinance. Gov't Code § 65858(f).

Before adopting or extending an interim ordinance, the city council must make a finding that there is a current and immediate threat to the public health, safety, or welfare, or that the approval of additional subdivisions, use permits, variances, building permits, or the like would result in such a threat. The proper findings must be contained in the ordinance. *See 216 Sutter Bay Assocs. v. County of Sutter*, 58 Cal. App. 4th 860, 868 (1997) (upholding interim ordinance that recited facts that "may reasonably be held to constitute" an urgency). Ten days prior to the expiration of the ordinance, the city council must issue a written report describing the measures taken to alleviate the condition that led to the adoption of the ordinance. Gov't Code § 65858(d).

Extensions of an interim ordinance beyond 45 days that have the effect of denying approvals needed for the development of projects with a "significant component" (at least one-third of the total project square footage) of multifamily housing are prohibited unless specific findings are made and supported by substantial evidence. Those findings include a conclusion that continued approval of multifamily housing projects would have a specific, adverse impact on public health or safety, that the interim ordinance is necessary to avoid that impact, and that there is no feasible alternative to satisfactorily avoid or mitigate such impact. The ban on extensions does not, however, apply to demolition, conversion, redevelopment, or rehabilitation of lower income multifamily housing. Gov't Code § 65858(e), (g), (h).

Since the purpose of an interim ordinance is to preserve the status quo by prohibiting a use of land that may be inconsistent with a contemplated general plan, specific plan, or zoning proposal currently under consideration, an interim ordinance cannot be used to authorize construction. This authorization can only be accomplished after notice and hearing under the State Zoning Law. *See Silvera v. City of S. Lake Tahoe*, 3 Cal. App. 3d 554, 558 (1970). Nor can an interim ordinance be used to halt a use already in existence. *See Kieffer v. Spencer*, 153 Cal. App. 3d 954, 963 (1984). However, a court has held that an interim ordinance may be used to cancel a development agreement prior to the expiration of the 30-day period between approval of the agreement and its effective date. *See 216 Sutter Bay Assocs.*, 58 Cal. App. 4th at 870–871.

Although Government Code section 65858 provides that an interim ordinance can be used to prohibit uses of property, it cannot be used to prohibit the processing of a development application. *See Building Indus. Legal Defense Found. v. Superior Court*, 72 Cal. App. 4th 1410, 1420 (1999) (city's interim ordinance was invalid to the extent that it applied to processing a development application).

The United States Supreme Court's decision in *Tahoe-Sierra Preservation Council, Inc. v. Tahoe Regional Planning Agency* reaffirmed the ability of cities to use temporary development moratoria as a planning tool without necessarily compensating property owners for the time period during which development is banned. 535 U.S. 302 (2002). The Court noted California and other states had enacted statutory provisions for interim ordinances, including moratoria, with specific time limits. *Id.*

Although *Tahoe-Sierra* reaffirmed a city's ability to impose a temporary moratorium, a slight risk remains that a moratorium that constitutes an improper land use regulation may effect a temporary taking, and that money damages for such taking might have to be paid. *See First English Evangelical Lutheran Church v. County of Los Angeles*, 482 U.S. 304, 321 (1987).

Tahoe-Sierra makes clear unless the regulation eliminates *all* economically beneficial uses of the land, the more flexible ad hoc analysis enunciated in *Penn Central* applies. 535 U.S. at 321. Therefore, it is good practice to allow some use of the property while the interim period is in effect and to insert a "safety valve" provision to allow the owner to apply for an exception. For a detailed discussion of takings jurisprudence, see chapter 11 (Takings).

Government Code section 65858 preempts the entire field of interim zoning moratoria. *See Bank of the Orient v. Town of Tiburon*, 220 Cal. App. 3d 992, 1004 (1990) (the people, via an initiative, could not add an additional year to the two-year moratorium the town council had earlier imposed).

CONDITIONAL ZONING

"Conditional zoning" describes a zoning change that permits use of a particular property subject to conditions not generally applicable to land similarly zoned. *See Scrutton v. County of Sacramento*, 275 Cal. App. 2d 412, 417 (1969). Although the term "contract zoning" has been used synonymously with "conditional zoning" the *Scrutton* court stated the phrase "contract zoning" has no legal significance and simply refers to a reclassification of land use in which the landowner agrees to perform conditions not imposed on other landowners. *Id.* at 419.

In *Scrutton*, a landowner filed an application to have property rezoned from agricultural to multiple-family residential to permit development of residential apartments. The planning commission recommended approval of the application subject to certain conditions, which included dedication and improvement of certain streets adjacent to the parcel. The board of supervisors, after a hearing, approved the planning commission's recommendation. Before adopting a rezoning ordinance, however, the board tendered a deed and contract for the owner's signature and would not formally adopt the rezoning ordinance until the owner returned the executed deed and contract. The owner refused to sign, and filed an action for declaratory

> "Conditional zoning" describes a zoning change that permits use of a particular property subject to conditions not generally applicable to land similarly zoned.

relief against the county on the theory that the imposition of such conditions to a rezoning was improper.

The court upheld both the county's action and the conditional rezoning as a proper exercise of the same police power that supports the imposition of conditions on approval of subdivisions, building permits, and zoning variances. *Id.* at 418. However, the court also found that the conditions cannot require an automatic reversion of the land to its former zoning if the conditions are not met. Such a reversion would be a zoning amendment invalid for failure to comply with the State Zoning Law notice and hearing procedures. *Id.* at 420.

SPECIFIC PLAN AS ZONING

A specific plan, provided it is sufficiently comprehensive and detailed as to regulations of the use of property within the plan area, may be adopted by ordinance as zoning for the plan area. A specific plan can create new zoning regulations for unique areas and developments, such as mixed use districts and master planned communities, where other conventional zoning districts are too restrictive to achieve the desired planning results. Some local ordinances mandate that specific plans be adopted into the zoning code by ordinance to become either the base zone or an overlay zone for the specific plan area.

PLANNED-UNIT DEVELOPMENT

PUD or PD = planned-unit development

The planned-unit development (PUD or PD) concept is simultaneously a type or method of development and a zoning classification. As a method of development, it normally consists of individually owned lots with common areas (e.g., open space, recreation, and street improvements) owned in common by the lot owners. As a zoning classification, it allows a single zoning district to combine a variety of uses (residential, commercial, and industrial) that are otherwise generally not permitted within the same zoning district. The term "planned-unit development" is often synonymous with such terms as "cluster development," "planned development," and "master-planned community." The planned-unit development concept has been approved by the California courts. *See Orinda Homeowners Comm. v. Board of Supervisors*, 11 Cal. App. 3d 768, 773 (1970).

Depending upon the local ordinance, the plan of development (either the general or precise development plan) for a PUD may constitute the zoning restrictions for the property after the plan has been approved by a city. Thus, any substantial change or alteration in the property's physical configuration may amount to a rezoning that must be accomplished pursuant to state statutes governing local zoning ordinances, such as notice and public hearing. However, certain local ordinances require that the plan is adopted through a quasi-judicial permit process and cannot be amended by ordinance. Instead, the plan and its conditions can be amended only by the method prescribed in the enabling PUD ordinance or set forth in the conditions of approval. *See W.W. Dean & Assoc. v. City of South San Francisco*, 190 Cal. App. 3d 1368, 1374, 1380 (1987); *Lincoln Property Co. No. 41 v. Law, Inc.* 45 Cal. App. 3d 230 (1975).

INCLUSIONARY ZONING/HOUSING PROGRAMS

Inclusionary housing programs provide mechanisms for cities to ensure that new development creates affordable housing options. Inclusionary housing programs have been in effect since the early 1970s and have grown in popularity as more jurisdictions view them as innovative ways to increase the supply of affordable housing and combat exclusionary zoning practices. In general, an "inclusionary" housing program is one that requires a residential developer to set aside a specified percentage of new units (often 10 to 15 percent) for very low-, low-, or moderate-income households alongside the development of market-rate units.[10] Cities enact such programs and pursuant to their local police power and effectuate them through inclusionary housing ordinances, zoning codes, policy statements, or a city's housing element.

As of 2006, nearly one-third of California jurisdictions had adopted inclusionary housing programs and 80,000 Californians have housing through inclusionary programs.[11] Examples of creative inclusionary housing programs also can be found across the nation in Colorado, Florida, Maryland, Massachusetts, Minnesota, New Jersey, New Mexico, and Virginia. For further discussion of inclusionary zoning, see chapter 15 (Affordable Housing).

APPLICABILITY OF ZONING TO THE FEDERAL AND STATE GOVERNMENTS

FEDERAL GOVERNMENT

Under the Supremacy Clause (Art. vi, § 2) and the Property Clause (Art. iv, § 3) of the United States Constitution, Congress has preemptive power over state and local control of federal lands. *See Mayo v. United States*, 319 U.S. 441, 445 (1943). Even a federal government lessee, such as an oil company, is not required to obtain a permit from a city in compliance with zoning ordinances governing oil explorations and extraction activities. *See Ventura County v. Gulf Oil Corp.*, 601 F. 2d 1080, 1085 (9th Cir. 1979). The United States Postal Service need not comply with local zoning regulations in constructing a post office on land owned or leased by the United States. *See* 68 Ops. Cal. Atty. Gen. 310 (1985).

However, reference should be made to the National Environmental Policy Act (NEPA) (42 U.S.C. § 4321 *et seq.*), the Intergovernmental Coordination Act of 1968 (31 U.S.C. § 6506), and the Intergovernmental Coordination Executive Order (Exec. Order No. 12,372, reprinted in 31 U.S.C. § 6506). Both NEPA and the intergovernmental coordination statute and order require federal agencies to solicit and consider local views on their projects.

NEPA = National Environmental Policy Act

A county can apply its building codes to construction of an office building to be leased by the federal government, and the builder cannot share in the sovereign immunity of the United States. *See Smith v. County of Santa Barbara*, 203 Cal. App. 3d 1415, 1419 (1988). The *Smith* court also noted the Intergovernmental Coordination Act does not preempt land use regulations but, in fact, encourages cooperation with local zoning and land use practice. *Id.* at 1424; *see also Maryland-Nat'l Capital Park Planning Comm'n v. U.S. Postal Serv.*, 487 F. 2d 1029, 1037 (D.C. Cir. 1973) (NEPA requires close scrutiny of federal projects deviating from local land use regulations); *Town of Groton v. Laird*, 353

---

10 However, the term "inclusionary housing" or "inclusionary zoning" can include a variety of methods designed to create more affordable housing. Some examples include density bonuses, reduced development standards, and imposition of fees on developers to fund affordable housing projects.

11 *See* David L. Callies, Leigh Anne King, James C. Nicholas, and Cecily Talbert Barclay, *Workforce and Affordable Housing: Local Government Inclusionary Housing Programs and the Courts*, 63 Plan. & Envtl. Law no. 10, page 8 (2011); Cal. Coal. for Rural Hous. & Non-Profit Hous. Ass'n of N. Cal., *Affordable by Choice: Trends in California Inclusionary Housing Programs* (2006), *available at* http://www.nonprofithousing.org/pdf_attachments/IHIReport.pdf.

F. Supp. 344, 351 (D. Conn. 1972) (NEPA should not be used to shore up exclusionary zoning in a Navy housing program).

The United States Supreme Court ruled states may, however, impose environmental controls on activities occurring on federal lands. *See California Coastal Comm'n v. Granite Rock Co.*, 480 U.S. 572 (1987). In *Granite Rock*, the Court held the California Coastal Commission could require a private company to obtain a permit for its limestone mining operations in the Big Sur region of the federally owned Los Padres National Forest. *Id.* at 588–89. The decision represented a victory for states, particularly western states with substantial acreage owned by the federal government, by allowing them to subject private mining operations conducted on federal lands to environmental regulations.

For an interesting discussion on the intersection between federal law and a city's power to regulate telecommunications services and facilities, see Paul Valle-Riestra, *Telecommunications: The Local Government Role in Managing the Connected Community* (Solano Press 2002).

STATE GOVERNMENT

In general, the state is exempt from a city's zoning regulations. *See Hall v. City of Taft*, 47 Cal. 2d 177, 184 (1956). For example, the Regents of the University of California, a state agency, in constructing improvements solely for educational purposes, is exempt from local building codes and zoning regulations, and is exempt from local permit and inspection fees. *Regents of Univ. of Cal. v. City of Santa Monica*, 77 Cal. App. 3d 130, 136–37 (1978). It is not relevant that the affected city is a charter city, nor does it matter whether the property involved is owned or leased by the Regents. *Id.* at 138.

However, the same general rule does not apply to a city's subdivision powers. Gov't Code § 66428. The Attorney General determined that a city's subdivision ordinance applied to the California Department of Transportation (Caltrans) when it desired to dispose of real property. It can be stated as a general rule that a city's subdivision regulations apply so long as they do not affect the fundamental purposes and functions of the state. *See* 62 Ops. Cal. Atty. Gen. 410 (1979); *see also* 75 Ops. Cal. Atty. Gen. 984, (1992).

Cities may assess only certain capital facilities fees on the state. Government Code section 54999.1(d) limits the imposition of such fees to facilities that provide water, light, heat, communications, power, or garbage service for flood control, drainage or sanitary purposes, or for sewage collection, treatment, or disposal.

APPLICABILITY OF ZONING TO JOINT POWERS AGENCIES, SCHOOL DISTRICTS, AND COUNTY AND OTHER LOCAL DISTRICTS

All local agencies, except the state, a city or a county, and other specifically named agencies such as the San Francisco Bay Area Rapid Transit District, must comply with local zoning ordinances. Gov't Code § 53090 *et seq.* Government Code section 53091 does not mandate compliance with applicable general plans but does contemplate compliance with building and zoning ordinances. *Friends of the Eel River v. Sonoma County Water Agency*, 108 Cal. App. 4th 859 (2003). Zoning ordinances do not apply, however, to the location or construction of facilities for the production, generation, storage, or transmission of water, or facilities for the production or generation of electricity. Gov't Code § 53091. Moreover, the governing board of a local agency (such as a water district) can override otherwise applicable zoning ordinances by a four-fifths vote if it determines by resolution that there is no feasible alternative to a project for facilities not related to the storage or transmission of water or electricity, such as warehouses, administrative buildings, or automotive storage and repair buildings. Gov't Code § 53096(a); *Delta Wetlands Props. v. County of San Joaquin*, 121 Cal. App. 4th 128 (2004) (clarifying that exemptions allowed by §§ 53091 and 53096 extend only to local agencies and not to private parties); *see also City of Lafayette v. East Bay Mun. Util. Dist.*, 16 Cal. App. 4th 1005, 1014–16 (1993) (absolute and qualified exemptions from local zoning regulations inapplicable to a water district's proposed facility for a maintenance storage center); 78 Ops. Cal. Atty. Gen. 31 (1995) (a water district must comply with building and zoning ordinances, with certain exceptions).

A joint powers agency (JPA) may be exempt from local land use regulation, depending upon its membership and which constituent member is designated by the JPA to supply the JPA's procedural restrictions. *Zack v. Marin Emergency Radio Auth.*, 118 Cal. App. 4th 617, 628 (2004). The JPA at issue in *Zack* was the Marin Emergency Radio Authority (MERA), which included over two dozen cities and districts within Marin County as well as the county itself. MERA sought to place an emergency radio antenna in the Town of Tiburon, and the trial court halted the project, concluding that it first had to comply with the town's land use ordinances.

JPA = joint powers agency

The appellate court reversed. It noted that under the Joint Exercise of Powers Act, the exercise of "common power" specified in a JPA "is subject to the restrictions upon the manner of exercising the power of one of the contracting parties, which party shall be designated in the agreement." *Id.* at 628 (citing Gov't Code § 6509). The plaintiffs had not shown that any member of MERA lacked the implied power to construct an emergency radio system. MERA was therefore exercising a "common power" in executing the project. *Id.* at 637. MERA had designated Marin County as the member agency whose procedures would govern the exercise of common power under the JPA. Because the county is not subject to the town's land use regulation, neither was MERA. *Id.* at 638.

Government Code section 53094 allows a school district, by a two-thirds vote, to render a city zoning ordinance inapplicable to classroom facilities, except when the proposed use of the property by the school district is for non-classroom facilities. Gov't Code § 53094. Before a school district can override a local zoning ordinance, it must first comply with expanded coordination and communication requirements. When a city notifies a school district of a proposed general plan adoption or amendment, the revised law allows the district to request a meeting with the planning agency. Conversely, when a school district is preparing a facility needs analysis, master plan, or other long-range plan for school siting, it must notify the appropriate planning agencies, which may then request a meeting with the district. If either agency requests a meeting, the parties must meet within 45 days to discuss school siting-related issues. The district also must comply with pre-existing CEQA requirements regarding school site review before overriding local zoning. Gov't Code §§ 53094, 65352.2. In *City of Santa Cruz v. Santa Cruz Bd. of Educ.*, the court held that a school athletic field was a "classroom facility" for the purpose of exemption from a city's zoning ordinance and, therefore, the installation of new lights was exempt pursuant to a two-thirds vote by the school board. 210 Cal. App. 3d 1, 9 (1989).

CEQA = California Environmental Quality Act

Cities are exempt from zoning regulations with respect to property that one such entity may own within the territory of the other. Gov't Code §§ 53090– 53091; 40 Ops. Cal. Atty. Gen. 243 (1962). Note also that a city is not bound by its own zoning ordinance. *See Sunny Slope Water Co. v. City of Pasadena*, 1 Cal. 2d 87, 98 (1934). Moreover, the court held that nonconformance with a county's general plan did not prevent a city from constructing a public project, because Government Code section 65402(b) requires only that the county where the project is located have an opportunity to review and report on whether the location, purpose, and extent of the acquisition or disposition of a public structure is in conformity with the general plan. *See Lawler v. City of Redding*, 7 Cal. App. 4th 778, 783 (1992). The court further held that, under a fair reading of Government Code sections 53090–53091, there is intergovernmental immunity from building and zoning regulations, including compliance with county general plans. *Id.* at 783–84.

APPLICABILITY OF ZONING TO INDIAN LANDS

Indian tribes enjoy attributes of sovereignty over both their members and their territory. That sovereignty "is dependent on, and subordinate to, only the Federal government, not the States." *California v. Cabazon Band of Mission Indians*, 480 U.S. 202, 207 (1987). As a general rule, state laws cannot be applied to tribal Indians on Indian lands except where Congress has expressly provided such laws shall apply. *See Gobin v. Snohomish County*, 304 F. 3d 909, 914 (9th Cir. 2002).

In the area of land use regulation, it has long been recognized that "any concurrent jurisdiction the states might inherently have possessed to regulate Indian use of reservation lands has long ago been preempted by extensive Federal policy and legislation." *Santa Rosa Band of Indians v. Kings County*, 532 F. 2d 655, 658 (9th Cir. 1975). Federal law, with its power to regulate Indian affairs, has not given cities or counties any general authority to enforce local land use regulation on Indian lands. Courts have interpreted federal laws relating to Indian lands as making "tribal government over the reservation more or less the *equivalent* of a county or local government in other areas within the state, empowered...to regulate matters of local concern within the area of its jurisdiction." *Id.* at 661 (emphasis added). Thus, tribes have been held to have power to impose their own building, health, and safety regulations on reservation lands, *see Cardin v. De La Cruz*, 671 F. 2d 363, 366 (9th Cir. 1982), and county building codes and ordinances have been held not to apply on those lands. *Santa Rosa Band of Indians*, 532 F. 2d at 661 (zoning ordinance and building code held not to apply); *see also Segundo v. City of Rancho Mirage*, 813 F. 2d 1387, 1393–94 (9th Cir. 1987).

Mere ownership of land by an Indian tribe, however, is not sufficient to insulate it from local land use regulation. The California Attorney General opined that local ordinances pertaining to land use and planning, building standards, and health and sanitation regulations applied to a low-income housing project owned by an Indian tribe and occupied by Native Americans but located outside of the tribe's reservation and on land not held in trust for the tribe by the United States. 83 Ops. Cal. Atty. Gen. 190, 193–94 (2000). For an explanation of the various classification of Indian lands, *see* Conference of Western Attorneys General, *American Indian Law Deskbook*, chapters 2–3 (2nd ed., 1998).

The issue of the role, if any, state and local governments should play with respect to Indian lands has become a particularly charged topic in light of the growth in Indian gaming in California.

The regulatory framework for Indian gaming was established by the Indian Gaming Regulatory Act (IGRA), passed by Congress in 1988. 25 U.S.C. § 2701 *et seq.*

IGRA = Indian Gaming Regulatory Act

The IGRA divides gaming into three classes. 25 U.S.C. § 2710. Class I gaming consists of social games for prizes of minimal value or traditional Indian games in connection with a tribal ceremony or celebration, and is not regulated by the IGRA. 25 U.S.C. §§ 2703(6), 2710. Class II gaming includes bingo and certain card games, and while subject to the IGRA, remains within the jurisdiction of individual Indian tribes for regulatory purposes. 25 U.S.C. §§ 2703(7), 2710. Class III gaming, which includes casino-style games like slot machines, blackjack, craps, and roulette, is allowed: (a) to the extent such games are allowed by the state where the Indian land is located;[12] (b) is on land within a reservation or land that is either held in trust for an Indian tribe by the United States or held by a tribe or individual subject to restrictions by the United States upon alienation and over which the tribe exercises governmental power; and (c) is subject to a compact to be negotiated between the tribe and the state and then approved by the Secretary of the Interior. 25 U.S.C. § 2710(d)(1)(B).

The IGRA requires states to negotiate with Indian tribes in good faith to enter into tribal-state compacts to allow gaming. 25 U.S.C. § 2710(d)(3). If the state fails to negotiate in good faith, a tribe may after 180 days bring an action in federal district court. 25 U.S.C. § 2710(d)(7). If the court finds that the state has failed to negotiate in good faith, it shall order the state and the tribe to conclude a compact within a 60-day period. 25 U.S.C. § 2710(d)(7)(B)(iii).

The California Legislature has ratified scores of tribal-state compacts allowing Class III gaming on Indian lands within the state pursuant to the IGRA. *See* Ratified Tribal-State Compacts, California Gambling Control Commission, *available at* http://www.cgcc.ca.gov/?pageID=compacts.

Under many tribal compacts, tribes pay the state substantial casino revenues and agree to address the effects of their gaming operations as described below:

- A tribe must prepare a Tribal Environmental Impact Report (TEIR) before commencing a new project, defined as any activity occurring on Indian Lands to serve the tribe's gaming activities that may cause a direct or indirect physical change in the off-reservation environment[13]
- The TEIR must include detailed information about the significant effects, mitigation, and alternatives to the project
- Failure to prepare a TEIR could result in the state obtaining an injunction to stop the project
- Tribes must meet and negotiate with local governments and adopt an enforceable written agreement that addresses off-reservation impacts, including public safety, gambling addiction, and environmental impacts

See, e.g., Tribal-State Gaming Compact Between the Coyote Valley Band of Pomo Indians and the State of California, §§ 11.1, 11.2, *available at* www.governor.ca.gov; *see also* California State Ass'n of Counties, CSAC Comparison of the Five Tribal-State Compacts (Aug. 23, 2004), *available at* www.csac.counties.org/legislation/Indian_gaming/compacts_summary.pdf.

TEIR = Tribal Environmental Impact Report

---

12 Although casino-style gaming is generally prohibited under the California Constitution, state voters in 2000 passed Proposition 1A, which expressly allowed gaming by Indian tribes on Indian lands in accordance with federal law. Cal. Const., Art. IV, § 19(f).

13 However, in deference to tribal sovereignty, none of the following shall be deemed a project for purposes of CEQA: execution of the compacts, execution of the required agreements between tribes and local governments, on-reservation impacts resulting from the compacts, and the sale of any compact assets. *See* Gov't Code §§ 12012.40, 12012.45. Therefore, while the language of certain compacts may impose requirements for environmental study, CEQA itself cannot ensure the disclosure, avoidance, or mitigation of impacts associated with Indian gaming.

MOU = memorandum of understanding

Cities also negotiate memoranda of understanding (MOUs) with local tribes to address anticipated impacts from casinos. Negotiation and execution of these MOUs has been held to be an administrative act by cities and not subject to referendum, given that only the federal and state governments have legislative power over Indian affairs. *Worthington v. City Council of the City of Rohnert Park*, 130 Cal. App. 4th 1132, 1139-40 (2005); *see also Citizens to Enforce CEQA v. City of Rohnert Park*, 131 Cal. App. 4th 1594 (2005) (holding an MOU such as the one in *Worthington* did not trigger environmental review under CEQA).

CHAPTER 5

Subdivisions

Matthew Gray

INTRODUCTION

SUBDIVISION MAP ACT[1]

The Map Act vests in a city the power to regulate and control the design and improvement of subdivisions within its boundaries. Gov't Code § 66411. Each city must adopt an ordinance regulating and controlling subdivisions for which the Map Act requires a tentative and final or parcel map. Gov't Code § 66411. The authority for a city to regulate land use, including subdivisions, flows from the general police power. Cal. Const. Art. XI, § 7. However, the Map Act sets forth certain mandates that must be followed for subdivision processing. A city can impose conditions on the subdivision process when the Map Act is silent. *Soderling v. City of Santa Monica*, 142 Cal. App. 3d 501, 506–07 (1983) (holding that smoke detectors can be required in a condominium conversion map process); *see also Ayres v. City Council of Los Angeles*, 34 Cal. 2d 31, 37 (1949) (finding that certain street improvement conditions could be imposed even though they were not expressly provided for in the Map Act and local city ordinances). However, a city cannot regulate contrary to specific provisions contained in the Map Act. *Shelter Creek Dev. Corp. v. City of Oxnard*, 34 Cal. 3d 733, 735–36 (1983) (holding that a city cannot override a specific provision in the Map Act grandfathering certain stock cooperative conversions).

> The Map Act vests in a city the power to regulate and control the design and improvement of subdivisions within its boundaries.

The Map Act's primary goals are:
- To encourage orderly community development by providing for the regulation and control of the design and improvement of the subdivision, with a proper consideration of its relation to adjoining areas
- To ensure that the areas within the subdivision that are dedicated for public purposes will be properly improved by the subdivider so that they will not become an undue burden on the community
- To protect the public and individual transferees from fraud and exploitation

61 Ops. Cal. Atty. Gen. 299, 301 (1978); 77 Ops. Cal. Atty. Gen. 185 (1994)

The Map Act is applied in conjunction with other state land use laws, such as the general plan and the specific plan provisions (Gov't Code § 65300 *et seq.*), zoning

---

[1] *See also* Daniel J. Curtin, Jr., and Robert E. Merritt, *California Subdivision Map Act and the Development Process* (Cal. CEB, 2d ed. 2001) (2012 Update).

CEQA = California Environmental Quality Act

(Gov't Code § 65800 et seq.), the California Environmental Quality Act (CEQA) (Pub. Res. Code § 21000 et seq.), and the Permit Streamlining Act (Gov't Code § 65920 et seq.).

The Map Act must be distinguished from the Subdivided Lands Act. Bus. & Prof. Code § 11000 et seq. The Map Act provides for regulation of land divisions by a city and is interpreted and enforced by the city. The Subdivided Lands Act,[2] on the other hand, is a consumer protection statute primarily intended to ensure that adequate disclosures are made. It regulates public offerings of land in subdivisions for sale or lease, and is interpreted and enforced by the California Bureau of Real Estate. An excellent discussion on the differences between the two acts is found in both *Daro v. Superior Court*, 151 Cal. App. 4th 1079, 1093-94 (2007) and *California Coastal Commission v. Quanta Inv. Corp.*, 113 Cal. App. 3d 579, 588 (1980).

Need for a local ordinance; applicable to charter cities. Each city must, by ordinance, regulate and control subdivisions for which the Map Act requires a tentative and final map or a parcel map. In addition, a city may, by ordinance, regulate other subdivisions, provided that such regulations are not more restrictive than the regulations for those subdivisions for which a tentative and final or parcel map are required by the Map Act, with certain exceptions related to short-term leases for railroads. Gov't Code § 66411. *See also City of Tiburon v. Northwestern Pac. R.R. Co.*, 4 Cal. App. 3d 160 (1970). The Map Act applies to charter cities. *Santa Clara County Contractors and Homebuilders Ass'n v. City of Santa Clara*, 232 Cal. App. 2d 564 (1965).

Preemption. The courts have been reluctant to hold that local subdivision ordinances are preempted by the Map Act. *See Griffin Dev. Co. v. City of Oxnard*, 39 Cal. 3d 256, 261-62 (1985) (the Map Act does not preempt a city's condominium conversion ordinance); *Santa Monica Pines, Ltd. v. Rent Control Bd.*, 35 Cal. 3d 858 (1984) (a city has independent authority from the police power to regulate subdivisions); *The Pines v. City of Santa Monica*, 29 Cal. 3d 656, 659-60 (1981) (the Map Act does not preempt local revenue taxes); *Benny v. City of Alameda*, 105 Cal. App. 3d 1006, 1010-11 (1980) (a tentative subdivision map application can be conditioned on receiving prior land use approval, including zoning). For instance, one court upheld a "removal permit" requirement that was imposed by the voters after the plaintiff's map had been approved. *McMullan v. Santa Monica Rent Control Bd.*, 168 Cal. App. 3d 960, 963 (1985). "While the [Map] act may be the final word respecting the subdivision process, it does not purport and may not be understood to be preemptive of all land use regulation." *Id.*

However, a city cannot regulate contrary to specific Map Act provisions. *Shelter Creek*, 34 Cal. 3d at 738. For example, in *Griffis v. County of Mono*, the court held that a local ordinance that limited the maximum duration of a discretionary map extension to one year was not valid since the Map Act allows discretionary extensions for more than one year. 163 Cal. App. 3d 414, 420 (1985). Another court found an implied preemption based on the merger provision of the Map Act, and held invalid local zoning ordinances requiring merger under certain circumstances upon application of a development permit. *Morehart v. County of Santa Barbara*, 7 Cal. 4th 725, 748 (1994).

With regard to imposing conditions on mobile home park conversions from rental to residential ownership, local ordinances are preempted by Government Code section 66427.5. *Sequoia Park Associates v. County of Sonoma*, 176 Cal. App. 4th 1270, 1297 (2009). In *Sequoia Park*, the county adopted a mobile home park conversion ordinance

---

[2] See *Forming California Common Interest Development*, chapter 3 (Cal. CEB 2013 Update) for a discussion of the Subdivided Lands Act.

that required compliance with section 64427.5 and imposed additional requirements, such as consistency with the county's general plan. In holding that section 66427.5 preempted the county's ordinance, the court noted the Legislature's dominant presence in mobile home-related laws and the Legislature's express intent to ensure mobile home conversions are "bona fide resident conversions." *Id.*; *see also Colony Cove Properties LLC v. City of Carson*, 187 Cal. App. 4th 1487, 1507–08 (2010) (city's ordinance that effectively gave residents veto power over mobile home park conversion—a right not afforded by section 64427.5 at the time—was preempted); *Chino MHC, LP v. City of Chino*, 210 Cal. App. 4th 1049, 1069 (2012) (city may delay a mobile home conversion on the basis of a statutorily required survey of residents where survey results show such conversion is a scam). While Government Code section 66427.5 preempts local ordinances on mobile home conversion, it does not exempt such conversion from the requirements of the Coastal Act and the Mello Act where those statutes apply. *Pacific Palisades Bowl Mobile Estates, LLC v. City of Los Angeles*, 55 Cal. 4th 703 (2012); *Dunex v. City of Oceanside*, 218 Cal. App. 4th 1158, 1170 (2013) (city properly denies subdivision map application for inconsistency with adopted local coastal program).

SUBDIVISIONS COVERED BY THE MAP ACT

WHAT IS A SUBDIVISION?

A subdivision is defined in the statute as:

> [T]he division, by any subdivider, of any unit or units of improved or unimproved land, or any portion thereof, shown on the latest equalized county assessment roll as a unit or as contiguous units, for the purpose of sale, lease, or financing, whether immediate or future.

Gov't Code § 66424

The Map Act distinguishes between a subdivision consisting of five or more parcels and one consisting of four or fewer parcels. In general, a subdivision of five or more parcels requires a tentative and a final map; a subdivision of four or fewer requires just a parcel map.

"the division..." In order to achieve the purposes of the Map Act, the courts have broadly defined what is covered under this definition. Several Attorney General opinions have attached importance to divisions that award the right to exclusive occupancy in determining a subdivision under the Map Act. *See* 39 Ops. Cal. Atty. Gen. 82 (1962); 17 Ops. Cal. Atty. Gen. 79 (1951).

Divisions created by deeds, leases, and deeds of trust are clearly ones that fall under Government Code section 66424. Other divisions are less certain. For example, do easements create divisions? It can be argued that a non-exclusive easement is not a division because of the lack of any right to exclusive occupancy. However, an exclusive easement may be subject to the Map Act because it gives the right of exclusive occupancy similar to a fee interest. *But see Robinson v. City of Alameda*, 194 Cal. App. 3d 1286 (1987) (holding that an agreement allowing exclusive use of a portion of land for an indefinite term after sale was not subject to the Map Act). Divisions also can be created via an agency's exercise of eminent domain under certain conditions. *See* 86 Ops. Cal. Atty. Gen. 70 (2003) (opining that a public agency which condemned and acquired most of a 640-acre parcel to create a reservoir, leaving the parcel's two remaining areas divided by water, lawfully created two parcels because the division met the conclusive presumption of legality under Government Code section 66412.6).

> In general, a subdivision of five or more parcels requires a tentative and a final map; a subdivision of four or fewer requires just a parcel map.

"*...by any subdivider...*" The term "subdivider" is defined broadly by the Map Act. Any person, firm, corporation, partnership, or association (but not their consultants or employees) who will divide land for itself or others is a subdivider. Gov't Code § 66423. Governmental agencies such as the Department of Transportation (Caltrans) and public agencies such as agricultural associations are also considered subdividers and subject to the provisions of the Map Act in certain situations. 62 Ops. Cal. Atty. Gen. 136 (1979); 62 Ops. Cal. Atty. Gen. 140 (1979). However, the Attorney General has said a tax collector is not a subdivider. Thus, the Map Act does not apply to a sale of a portion of a tax-deeded parcel conducted by the tax collector. 64 Ops. Cal. Atty. Gen. 814 (1981).

"*...of any unit or units of improved or unimproved land, or any portion thereof...*" The Map Act does not make a distinction between improved and unimproved land. Land as defined by Civil Code section 659 includes free or occupied space for an indefinite distance upwards as well as downwards. Thus a division of airspace, such as the sale of a floor in a high rise building, would be subject to the Map Act.[3]

"*...shown on the latest equalized county assessment roll as a unit...*" Reference to the assessor's roll provides a convenient method of identifying the property being divided and its ownership during a given period of time. 59 Ops. Cal. Atty. Gen. 581 (1976). It often is misunderstood as permitting the owner to convey assessor's parcels without first obtaining a subdivision map. The assessor's parcel designations have no effect on application of the Map Act, and owners may not divide land along the lines of the assessor's parcels for the purpose of sale, lease, or financing without obtaining a subdivision map. The function and purpose of the assessor is to raise revenue, not to regulate the division of land. 62 Ops. Cal. Atty. Gen. 147 (1979) (a property owner may not rely on county assessor's assignment of two separate parcel numbers as compliance with Map Act in proposed sale of one of the areas given a separate parcel number); 59 Ops. Cal. Atty. Gen. 581 (1976) (when three legally subdivided lots are subsequently combined as one assessment parcel, no new parcel map need be processed before conveyance of the lots).

> The purchaser of a unit of land created under the Map Act may divide the property one or more times before completion of the equalized assessment roll for that unit, and may not be prevented by local ordinance from making consecutive subdivisions of the unit.

When property is subdivided, the new parcels do not appear on the latest equalized assessment roll until the roll comes into existence on August 20 of that year. Rev. & Tax. Code §§ 2050, 2052; 55 Ops. Cal. Atty. Gen. 414 (1972). The purchaser of a unit of land created under the Map Act may divide the property one or more times before completion of the equalized assessment roll for that unit, and may not be prevented by local ordinance from making consecutive subdivisions of the unit. Gov't Code § 66424.1.

An assessor may not assign parcel numbers until the required map has been recorded. If the requirement for a parcel map is waived, the assessor may not assign parcel numbers until the applicant provides a copy of the finding required to justify such waiver. Rev. & Tax. Code § 327.5.

"*...or as contiguous units...*" Property that will be divided must be contiguous as shown on the assessor's roll. The Map Act expressly provides that property is contiguous even though separated by roads, streets, utility easements, or railroad rights-of-way. Gov't Code § 66424. Note that the list in Government Code section 66424 might not be exclusive, but merely illustrative. For example, the Attorney General has stated that parcels on two sides of a canal owned in fee by the Federal Bureau of Reclamation are considered to be contiguous. 61 Ops. Cal. Atty. Gen. 299 (1978).

---

[3] The Map Act does not apply to the leasing or financing of apartments, offices, stores, or similar space within buildings. Gov't Code § 66412(a).

"*...for the purpose of sale, lease, or financing, whether immediate or future.*" The division must be for the purpose of sale, lease, or financing, whether immediate or future. According to the Attorney General, partitions are considered a division for the purpose of sale and thus governed by the Map Act. *See* 64 Ops. Cal. Atty. Gen. 762 (1981); Code Civ. Proc. § 872.040; *Pratt v. Adams*, 229 Cal. App. 2d 602, 605 (1964).

> The conversion and exchange of property interest in a partition action may be considered a "sale" in the broad sense of the term.... [O]wnership and title to partitioned property is changed and transferred among the owners in consideration for each's mutual undertaking. Accordingly, a division under the partition action statutory scheme may be said to be "for the purpose of sale" and thus constitute a "subdivision" for purposes of section 66424 and the requirements of the Act.

64 Ops. Cal. Atty. Gen. 762, 766–67 (1981)

Gifts also can fall under the definition of subdivision. For instance, in *Pescosolido v. Smith*, the court held that bona fide gifts of distinct, independently developable and salable parcels are encompassed under Government Code section 66424. 142 Cal. App. 3d 964, 972 (1983). The Pescosolidos conveyed parcels of land to their children for estate planning, tax, and college financing purposes. Although they testified that it was not their intent to sell the property given to their children, the evidence showed an intent by some of the children to sell parcels. The court held that the transfer was a "sale" for purposes of the Map Act because the court found that the ultimate purpose of the gift was to sell the property in the future and "it was the intent of the Pescosolidos to circumvent the map filing and approval provisions required under the Subdivision Map Act...." *Id.* at 970.

However, an agreement allowing use of a portion of land after sale for an indefinite term was found not to be subject to the Map Act. *Robinson v. City of Alameda*, 194 Cal. App. 3d 1286, 1288–89 (1987). In that case, the Robinsons owned two parcels of land, Parcel A and Parcel B. They sold Parcel B, but reserved the exclusive right to use a portion of Parcel B until they sold Parcel A or until both of them died. The court held that the Robinsons' interest in Parcel B was not a sale because they had no ownership interest in the portion of Parcel B. Additionally, it was not a lease because a lease by definition must be for a definite period of time, and the term of "until the Robinsons sold Parcel A or died" was not a definite period of time. *Id.*

The *Robinson* decision appears inconsistent with the *Pescosolido* decision in that neither the Robinsons nor the Pescosolidos had any immediate intention to sell, lease, or finance their respective properties. Yet, the gift in *Pescosolido* was held to be subject to the Map Act because of future purpose of sale, while the court in *Robinson* failed to look at the purpose of conveyance. This is the result of the *Robinson* court taking a narrow view of what constituted a "sale" or "lease," and basing its holding on the ground that the interest reserved was neither.

A deed approving a non-exclusive easement authorizing construction of a garage for the easement-holder's use on a portion of the burdened property has been held not to require compliance with the Map Act. *Blackmore v. Powell*, 150 Cal. App. 4th 1593, 1603–04 (2007). Although it found that exclusive use of the garage (which occupied approximately ten percent of the otherwise non-exclusive easement area) was a necessary incident of the easement, the court nonetheless held that the easement was "merely the right to use a portion of appellant's property in a restricted manner, and [did] not divide or sever the property into distinguishable possessory estates or

> The *Robinson* court took a narrow view of what constituted a "sale" or "lease," and based its holding on the ground that the interest reserved was neither.

interests." *Id.* at 1599, 1604. The easement was "too restricted in scope to constitute a subdivision under the Act." *Id.* at 1605.

Leases are subdivisions under Government Code section 66424. However, it is not always easy to spot a lease. In making this assessment, the focus should be more on the substance rather than the form of the instrument. For example, the Attorney General opined that an agreement called a "permit" authorizing the construction and use of a house, mobile home, or camping facilities on lots owned by a fraternal organization was subject to the Map Act because the permit was actually a lease. 57 Ops. Cal. Atty. Gen. 556 (1974). Even though the instrument stated "THIS IS A PERMIT AND NOT A LEASE" on its face, the Attorney General found:

> The contents and the effect of said conveyance will prove its legal nature. No particular or set language such as "let" or "demise" or the usual words of hiring is necessary to constitute a given writing as a lease. Any words sufficient to express the intent of the parties that one party shall divest himself of the possession, and the other come into possession for a determinate time...will, by construction of law, amount to a lease.

Id. at 558

While there are no published cases involving financing, it seems clear that divisions are created by the execution and recording of mortgages, deeds of trust, and land installment contracts. *See* 58 Ops. Cal. Atty. Gen. 408 (1975). This makes sense given that if the financing instrument is foreclosed, a division in ownership will result. There has been a question whether release provisions in a deed of trust by which the lender agrees to reconvey portions of the land as payments create subdivisions. While no court has considered this question, the better view is that these agreements, alone, do not create subdivisions; however, a subdivision will happen upon actual reconveyance of one or more parcels, and a map must be processed before this occurs. To address this concern, as a practical matter, release agreements should be drafted to condition reconveyance on compliance with the Map Act and local subdivision ordinances.

Whether a devise of property, alone, will constitute a division is another unresolved question. However, in *Wells Fargo Bank v. Town of Woodside*, the court held that a local subdivision ordinance cannot require the filing of a map for a parcel created as a probate homestead by the probate court. The court based its holding on preemption—that the Probate Law superseded the local subdivision ordinance. 33 Cal. 3d 379, 391 (1983).

The Attorney General has opined that the creation of a conservation easement pursuant to Civil Code section 815 *et seq.* in which the owner maintains ownership and possession of the land does not, in itself, constitute a subdivision requiring compliance with the Subdivision Map Act. 90 Ops. Cal. Atty. Gen. 69 (2007). While the grant of a conservation easement may involve identifying a portion of a larger tract of land upon which enforceable use restrictions will be placed, the grant does not constitute a division of the land within the meaning of the Act, according to the Attorney General. The mere granting of a conservation easement neither conveys the land subject to the easement, nor expresses any future intent to convey it, as a separate unit.

WHAT TYPE OF MAP IS REQUIRED?

GENERAL RULE: TENTATIVE AND FINAL MAP OR PARCEL MAP?

The general rule is that a tentative and final map are required for all subdivisions creating five or more parcels, five or more condominiums, a community apartment project containing five or more parcels, or the conversion of a dwelling to a stock cooperative containing five or more dwelling units, unless specifically excepted. Gov't Code § 66426. However, there are five exceptions that allow a parcel map instead of a tentative and final map regardless of the number of parcels created. These are:

- Divisions of less than five acres where each parcel abuts upon a maintained public street and no dedications or improvements are required by the local agency
- Twenty-acre-plus parcels with approved access to a maintained public street
- Industrial and commercial developments with approved access to public streets, where the street alignment and width have been approved by the local agency
- Parcels that consist of not less than 40 acres or not less than a quarter of a quarter-section
- A division solely for the creation of an environmental subdivision pursuant to Government Code section 66418.2 (an environmental subdivision allows a landowner to sell property for off-site mitigation based on defined criteria such as a subdivision for biotic and wildlife purposes; the division must be at least 20 acres, or less than 20 acres but contiguous to other property also qualifying as an environmental subdivision with a total of at least 20 acres)

Gov't Code § 66426

COUNTING PARCELS

Successive subdivisions. When counting parcels to determine whether a final map or a parcel map is required, all previous subdivisions by the same subdivider are included. *Bright v. Board of Supervisors*, 66 Cal. App. 3d 191 (1977). In 1966, Bright acquired title to one parcel, Parcel A, which he held as separate property. An adjoining parcel, Parcel B, was acquired in 1968 by Bright and his wife as joint tenants. In 1973, Bright transferred a portion of Parcel B to his wife as her separate property, thereby creating a new parcel, Parcel C. He then applied for a tentative parcel map to divide Parcel A into four lots. *Id.* at 193. The county refused to process the parcel map, stating a final map instead was required. On appeal, the court agreed. Since Bright was the owner of two contiguous lots, Parcels A and B, the division of Parcel B into Parcel C must be taken into account when dividing Parcel A. Thus, six parcels were created by this division. *Id.* at 195.

> When counting parcels to determine whether a final map or a parcel map is required, all previous subdivisions by the same subdivider are included.

The subdivider may not avoid the tentative and final map requirements by subdividing one parcel four times using a parcel map and then, through agents, repeating the process over and over again. This practice, known as "quartering" or "4 x 4" is illegal. If discovered, it will be prosecuted by cities because it can result in a subdivision of numerous lots without compliance with the more stringent requirements applicable to final maps.

A form of quartering was attempted in *Pratt v. Adams*, 229 Cal. App. 2d 602 (1964). The plaintiffs tried to circumvent the requirement of a final map by partitioning land held in joint tenancy into 12 parcels, and then dividing each parcel four or fewer times resulting in 38 parcels. The court held that the division of the land into 38 parcels was part of a general scheme to multiply the number of parcels, and required a tentative and final map:

> [This] is a case where the permit is sought as the culmination of a plan to circumvent the law by one of the planners. The courts will not assist, by equitable process, the fulfillment of this plan.

Id. at 606

The action by a subdivider in creating divisions also includes divisions by its agent. The Attorney General has indicated that an agency relationship will be found in cases where the parties may not be dealing at "arm's length":

> If there is evidence that the transfer is not an "arm's length transaction," for example, a sale for inadequate consideration, a transfer to a close relative or business associate, retention of control or financial interest, or generally a transfer which is part of a conspiracy to evade the Subdivision Map Act, the total number of lots should be treated as a subdivision.

55 Ops. Cal. Atty. Gen. 414, 417–18 (1972)

Quartering may be tempting for subdividers, but it can result in a criminal prosecution under the Map Act. Gov't Code § 66499.31. It may also result in severe penalties under the Subdivided Lands Act, which governs the offering of subdivided lands for sale or lease and is administered by the California Bureau of Real Estate. *See* Bus. and Prof. Code § 11000 *et seq.*

Remainder parcels. When a subdivider only divides a portion of a parcel of land, the Map Act allows the subdivider to designate the undivided portion as a "remainder" parcel so long as that portion is not divided for the purpose of sale, lease, or financing immediately or in the future. If the gross area of the remainder parcel is five acres or more, the subdivider may omit from the map the portion of land that is not divided for the purpose of sale, lease, or financing. In that case, the location need only be indicated by deed reference to the existing boundaries of the remainder parcel. Gov't Code §§ 66424.6(a), 66434(e) (final maps), 66445(d) (parcel maps). A parcel designated as "not a part" is considered to be a remainder parcel. Gov't Code §§ 66434(e), 66445(d)(3). If the subdivider elects to designate a remainder:

- The designated remainder shall not be counted as a parcel when determining whether a final map or parcel map is required
- A city may not require construction of improvements or payment of fees associated with improvements on the remainder parcel until a permit or other approval for development of the remainder parcel is issued
- If a city has an ordinance that authorizes agreements between the subdivider and the local agency, the construction of the improvements will be done pursuant to the terms of the agreement
- If there is no agreement, a city may require construction of improvements or payment of fees within a reasonable time after final map approval and prior to the issuance of a permit if the improvements are necessary for the public health and safety or necessary for the orderly development of the surrounding area

Gov't Code § 66424.6(a)

A subdivider must not designate a remainder parcel with the present intent to sell that remainder parcel. As the court in *Pescosolido v. Smith* stated:

> [T]he phrase "for the purpose of sale...whether immediate or future" in the definition provided by Government Code section 66424 must encompass the ultimate purpose for which the particular land division is done.

142 Cal. App. 3d 964, 972 (1983)

The Attorney General issued an opinion stating that two or more remainder parcels may not be designated when a developer subdivides portions of more than one parcel with the intention of further dividing the remainder parcels in a subsequent phase. Only one remainder parcel may result from the division of each unit of land when a subdivider creates a subdivision. 77 Ops. Cal. Atty. Gen. 185 (1994).

The remainder parcel may eventually be sold without any subsequent filing of a parcel map or a final map. However, a city may require a certificate or conditional certificate of compliance. Gov't Code § 66424.6(d).[4]

Conveyances to or from public entities and public utilities. Conveyance of a parcel of land to or from a governmental agency, public entity, or public utility is not counted when counting parcels and determining which type of map to file. Gov't Code § 66426.5. A "conveyance" includes a fee interest, a leasehold interest, an easement, or a license. For example, if the division results in five parcels, but one parcel will be conveyed to a public utility, the subdivider will only be required to file a parcel map.

IMPORTANT EXEMPTIONS TO MAPPING REQUIREMENTS

All divisions of property that fall under the definition of subdivision in Government Code section 66424 are covered under the Map Act, unless specifically exempted by statute. The following exemptions are most commonly utilized.

LOT LINE ADJUSTMENTS

Lot line adjustments are exempt from the Map Act.[5] Gov't Code § 66412(d).

There are limits on the circumstances under which the lot line adjustment procedure can be used. For example:

- A lot line adjustment can only be between four or fewer parcels
- The parcels must be adjoining
- The new parcels must conform to the local general plan, applicable specific plan, any applicable coastal plan, and zoning and building ordinances

A city is prohibited from requiring a tentative, final, or parcel map as a condition of approval of a lot line adjustment. The city may only require conditions (1) to conform to the local general plan, applicable specific plan, applicable coastal plan, and zoning and building ordinances, (2) to require the prepayment of real property taxes, and (3) to facilitate the relocation of existing utilities, infrastructure, or easements. The lot line adjustment process under Government Code section 66412(d) has been characterized as a ministerial one. *Sierra Club v. Napa County Board of Supervisors*, 205 Cal. App. 4th 162, 179 (2012).

> A city is prohibited from requiring a tentative, final, or parcel map as a condition of approval of a lot line adjustment.

The lot line adjustment must be reflected in a recorded deed in which the owner is both the grantor and the grantee to show the lot line adjustment in the chain of title. No record of survey can be required unless required by Business and Professions Code section 8762. Gov't Code § 66412(d); 77 Ops. Cal. Atty. Gen. 231 (1994).

A local ordinance permitting multiple, sequential lot line adjustments under certain circumstances does not violate Government Code section 66412(d). *Sierra Club*, 205 Cal. App. 4th at 179. The sequential lot line adjustment ordinance upheld in *Sierra Club* allowed sequential adjustments only where a prior adjustment involving four or

---

[4] For a practical discussion of how and why certificates of compliance may be used by land owners, buyers, and public agencies, see Robert E. Merritt and Tedra E. Fox, *Using Certificates of Compliance to Help Clients Under the Subdivision Map Act*, 26 Real Property Law Reporter (Cal. CEB, July 2003).

[5] However, lot line adjustments are not exempt from the requirements of the California Coastal Act (Pub. Res. Code § 30000 et seq.) because the Coastal Act defines "development" more broadly than the Map Act. *La Fe, Inc. v. County of Los Angeles*, 73 Cal. App. 4th 231, 239 (1999).

fewer adjoining parcels had been approved and deeds recorded before any sequential lot line adjustment application was filed. It also did not permit lot line adjustments to convert otherwise nonbuildable parcels into buildable ones. *Id.* at 174.

If one or more of the parcels affected by a lot line adjustment is encumbered by a deed of trust, a mortgage, or a lien for a special assessment imposed by a special district, the instrument should be amended to reflect the new lot lines. Otherwise, an illegal lot may be created if the lender forecloses. One court has held that language in a deed of trust encumbering "all the improvements now or hereafter erected on the property, and all easements, rights, appurtenances...and all fixtures now or hereafter a part of the property," was sufficient to automatically add property acquired in a lot line adjustment to the encumbered parcel. *Hellweg v. Cassidy*, 61 Cal. App. 4th 806, 809 (1998). However, this kind of language should not be relied upon to protect against the creation of an illegal lot. The better practice is to amend the financing instrument so the encumbered property conforms to the new parcels created by the lot line adjustment.

Many cities require recording of a drawing or plat showing the lot line adjustment and a certificate of compliance to finalize the lot line adjustment. The local subdivision ordinance should be consulted to determine whether this is required.

"SECOND" UNITS

The Map Act exempts the construction, financing, or leasing of "second" units.[6] However, if the unit is sold or transferred, the Map Act applies. Gov't Code § 66412.2. A "second" unit is defined as an attached or detached residential dwelling providing complete independent living facilities for one or more persons. Gov't Code § 65852.2(i)(4). It must contain permanent provisions for living, sleeping, eating, cooking, and sanitation on the same parcel as the main residential unit is located. A "second" unit also is an efficiency unit as defined by Health and Safety Code section 17958.1, and a manufactured home as defined by Health and Safety Code section 18007. Gov't Code § 65852.2(i)(4). Legislation passed in 2007 repealed provisions concerning so-called "granny" units, but specified that units approved pursuant to the law prior to 2007 are valid. Gov't Code § 65852.1.

CONVEYANCES TO OR FROM PUBLIC ENTITIES AND PUBLIC UTILITIES

The Map Act exempts from the requirement of a parcel map land conveyed to or from a governmental agency, public entity, public utility, or land conveyed to a subsidiary of a public utility for conveyance to the public utility for rights-of-way unless a showing is made in individual cases, upon substantial evidence, that public policy necessitates a parcel map. Gov't Code § 66428(a)(2). The conveyance may be for a fee interest, easement, leasehold interest, or license.

This exemption, however, is only from a parcel map requirement. Divisions requiring final maps are not exempted. However, parcels conveyed to or from governmental agencies, public entities, and public utilities are not counted under Government Code section 66426.5 for purposes of determining whether a final map is required.

The Attorney General has opined that the Map Act will not apply if the public agency is engaged in performing its official functions. For example, the University of California was not bound by the Map Act when it was constructing for-sale

---

6 *See* California State Department of Housing and Community Development, Division of Housing Policy Development, Report on Second Units (Dec. 1990) and Second-Unit Legislation (Aug. 2003).

on-campus homes as part of its program to provide faculty housing since such a program helped fulfill the university's educational mission and purpose. 75 Ops. Cal. Atty. Gen. 98 (1992).

Even though a map may not be required, dedications and improvements may still be required. The legislative history of the Map Act makes clear that the intent was only to exempt the mapping requirement and not place the transfer outside the Map Act entirely. *See* 1977 Cal. Stat. ch. 234, § 19 (uncodified); 62 Ops. Cal. Atty. Gen. 140 (1979) (determining that local merger ordinance, authorized by Government Code section 66424.2–later repealed, *see* Gov't Code § 66451.10 *et seq.*—applies to California Department of Transportation); 62 Ops. Cal. Atty. Gen. 136 (1979) (finding District Agricultural Association subject to provisions of Map Act in subdivision and sale of its property).

FINANCING AND LEASING OF CERTAIN UNITS

Financing and leasing of apartments, offices, stores, or similar space within apartment buildings, industrial buildings, commercial buildings, mobile home parks, or trailer parks are expressly exempt from the Map Act. Gov't Code § 66412(a).

The financing or leasing of (1) existing separate commercial or industrial buildings on a single parcel or (2) any parcel of land in conjunction with the construction of commercial or industrial buildings on a single parcel is exempt, unless the project is not subject to review under other city ordinances regulating design and improvement. Gov't Code § 66412.1. It is uncertain what types of local ordinances would qualify as regulating design and improvement. A building permit probably would not suffice because it is a ministerial permit that only requires compliance with the relevant building code. However, regulations that involve exercise of discretion by a city (e.g., design review) would probably qualify. The exemptions under Government Code section 66412.1 apply only to "leasing" and "financing," not to sale.

CONDOMINIUM, STOCK COOPERATIVES, AND COMMUNITY APARTMENT PROJECTS

Conversions. Conversions of a community apartment to a condominium are exempt from the Map Act under limited circumstances.[7] All of the following conditions must be met for the exemption to apply:
- The property was subdivided before January 1, 1992, as evidenced by a recorded deed creating the community apartment project
- Subject to compliance with Civil Code §§ 4290 and 4295, all conveyances and other documents necessary to effectuate the conversion shall be executed by the number of owners specified in the organization documents or, if no number is specified, by a majority of owners
- If subdivision occurred after January 1, 1964, a final or parcel map was approved and recorded with all conditions of the map remaining in effect after the conversion and no more than forty-nine percent of the units were owned by one person on January 1, 1982
- The local agency certifies that the above requirements were satisfied if the local agency provides, by ordinance, for such certification

Gov't Code § 66412(g)

---

[7] *See* F. Scott Jackson, *Forming California Common Interest Developments,* "Condominium Conversions," chapter 4 (Cal. CEB 2013 Update).

Likewise, conversions of a stock cooperative into a condominium are exempt if certain conditions are met:
- The property was subdivided before January 1, 1982, as evidenced by a recorded deed creating the stock cooperative, an assignment of lease, or issuance of shares to a stockholder
- A person renting a unit in a cooperative shall be entitled at the time of conversion to all tenant rights in state or local law, including first refusal, notice, and displacement and relocation benefits
- Subject to compliance with Civil Code §§ 4290 and 4295 or §§ 6626 and 6628, all conveyances and other documents necessary to effectuate the conversion shall be executed by the number of owners specified in the organization documents or, if no number is specified, by a majority of owners
- If subdivision occurred after January 1, 1980, a final or parcel map was approved and recorded with all conditions of the map remaining in effect after the conversion and no more than forty-nine percent of the shares in the project were owned by any one person on January 1, 1982
- The local agency certifies that the above requirements were satisfied if the local agency provides, by ordinance, for such certification

Gov't Code § 66412(h)

Because of the occupancy requirements dating back to 1981 and 1982, these exemptions are of limited applicability today. Also, a city may regulate condominium conversions by adopting other ordinances under its police power, such as zoning and rent control ordinances, or by taxing them under its taxing power. *See, e.g., Santa Monica Pines, Ltd. v. Rent Control Board*, 35 Cal. 3d 858 (1984) (Map Act did not preempt a city's right to regulate conversion in connection with its rent control law); *see also The Pines v. City of Santa Monica*, 29 Cal. 3d 656, 664 (1981) (upholding a city's revenue tax). However, a city cannot enforce condominium conversion regulations enacted after a developer secures final Map Act approval and permission from the Bureau of Real Estate to sell. *City of West Hollywood v. Beverly Towers, Inc.*, 52 Cal. 3d 1184, 1191 (1991).

Three-dimensional divisions. A final or parcel map is required for a condominium project depending on the number of units created, although the division of air space need not be shown on the map. Gov't Code §§ 66426, 66427. However, another map is not required in a division of a condominium project into three-dimensional units if there was a previously approved parcel or final map and the following requirements are met:
- The total number of units does not increase above the number approved on the final or parcel map
- A perpetual estate or an estate for years in the remainder of the property is held by the condominium owners or by an association, and the estate in the remainder of the property is the same as the duration of the estate in the condominiums
- The three-dimensional portions are described on a condominium plan

Gov't Code § 66427

AGRICULTURAL LEASES AND AGRICULTURAL LABOR HOUSING

A lease of agricultural land for agricultural purposes is exempt from Map Act requirements. "Agricultural purposes" means the cultivation of food or fiber, or the grazing or pasturing of livestock. Gov't Code § 66412(k). What constitutes "agricultural land" is not defined by the Map Act. However, it is likely that agricultural land would include land designated as agricultural by a local zoning ordinance, general plan, or specific plan. Moreover, a Williamson Act contract is likely sufficient to establish the land as agricultural.

A lease of agriculturally zoned land to a nonprofit organization for the purpose of operating an agricultural labor housing project is exempt from Map Act requirements provided: (1) the property is not more than five acres; (2) the lease is for at least 30 years; and (3) the lease is signed before January 1, 2017. Gov't Code § 66412.9.

OTHER EXEMPTIONS

- The construction of removable commercial buildings having a floor area of less than 100 square feet, if so provided by local ordinance. Gov't Code § 66412.5
- The leasing of, or the granting of an easement for, wind-powered electrical generation devices if the project is subject to discretionary action by the city. Gov't Code § 66412(i)
- Dedication of land for cemetery purposes under the Health and Safety Code. Gov't Code § 66412(c)
- Mineral, oil, or gas leases. Gov't Code § 66412(b)
- The leasing, licensing, granting of an easement, use permit, or similar right on a portion of a parcel to a telephone corporation, exclusively for the placement and operation of cellular radio transmission facilities, if the project is subject to discretionary action by the city. Gov't Code § 66412(j)
- The leasing or granting of an easement of a parcel of land or any portion or portions of land in conjunction with financing, erection, and sale or lease of a solar electrical generation device on the land, provided the project is subject to review under other design and improvement local ordinances and is subject to other discretionary action by the advisory agency or legislative body. Gov't Code § 66412(l)

MAP WAIVERS

Condominium projects. A city may waive the requirement for a tentative and final map or a parcel map for construction of a condominium project on a single parcel. To do so, a city must enact an ordinance that provides a procedure for the waiver. The ordinance shall require a finding by the city council that the division of land complies with the Map Act and other local ordinances including, but not limited to, area, improvement and design, floodwater drainage control, appropriate improved public roads, sanitary disposal facilities, water supply availability, and environmental protection. Gov't Code § 66428(b).

Mobile home park conversions. The requirement for a tentative and final map or a parcel map may be waived in a mobile home conversion if at least two-thirds of the owners who are tenants in the mobile home park sign a petition showing their intent to purchase the park for a conversion to resident ownership. Additionally, a field survey must be performed. However, the requirement for a map cannot be waived if:

- There are design or improvement requirements necessitated by significant health and safety concerns

- A city determines that there is an exterior boundary discrepancy that would require a map
- The existing parcels were not created by a recorded final or parcel map
- The conversion would result in more units or interests than existed prior to the conversion

Gov't Code § 66428.1

Other parcel map waivers. The requirement of a parcel map can be waived pursuant to local ordinance. Every city is required to enact such a waiver ordinance. Gov't Code § 66428(b). A city must act upon a waiver application within 60 days of the application being deemed complete. Gov't Code § 66451.7. Before waiving a parcel map, a city must make certain specified findings, including, but not limited to, a finding that the proposed division of land complies with the Map Act and any local subdivision ordinance, and that the subdivision meets requirements relating to area, improvement and design, floodwater drainage control, public road improvements, sanitary disposal facilities, water supply availability, and environmental protection. Note that a city may still require a tentative map even if a parcel map is waived. Gov't Code § 66428(b).

TENTATIVE MAP PROCESSING

TENTATIVE MAPS

Necessity for tentative maps. When a final map is required, a tentative map is always required. Gov't Code § 66426. Contrast this with situations involving only parcel maps, which do not require a tentative map under the Map Act. However, local ordinances may, and often do, still require a tentative map where a parcel map is required.

If a subdivider desires to obtain vesting rights, the subdivider may file a vesting tentative map for a parcel map subdivision even if the local ordinance does not require a tentative map. Gov't Code § 66428(c).

Local ordinances. When processing a tentative and a final subdivision map, or a parcel map, it is imperative to consult the city's general plan, specific plans (if any), any applicable coastal plans, local ordinances, and procedures. The local subdivision ordinance specifies which type of governmental review is required and identifies the "advisory agency." In some cities, the advisory agency that approves the map is the planning commission, whose decision can be appealed to the city council; in other cities, the planning commission is purely advisory to the city council. In yet other cities, the approving body can be a city official or a committee of city officials.

It is important to determine when filing of the tentative map may be accomplished. Some cities require that all land use approvals be obtained before a tentative map is accepted for filing. *Benny v. City of Alameda*, 105 Cal. App. 3d 1006, 1011–12 (1980) (city's ordinance requiring zoning approval prior to filing of tentative map was valid).

Other regulations. Before a city accepts as complete an application for any development project, the applicant must submit a signed statement indicating whether the project and any alternatives are located on a site that is included on any of the local lists prepared by the California Integrated Waste Management Board of all solid waste disposal facilities from which there is a known migration of hazardous waste. Gov't Code §§ 65962.5(d), (f) ("Cortese List"). The Secretary for Environmental Protection maintains a statewide list and is responsible for distributing this information to any persons upon request. Gov't Code § 65962.5(e). The form of the Hazardous Waste and Substance Statement is contained in Government Code section 65962.5(f). *See Beck Dev. Co. v. Southern Pac. Transp. Co.*, 44 Cal. App. 4th 1160, 1202 (1996) (discussing this list).

In addition, a city must include in the information list for development projects, or on the application form for a building permit, specified requirements concerning compliance with statutes regulating hazardous materials and air pollution, the handling of acutely hazardous materials, and the emission of hazardous air emissions. Gov't Code § 65850.2. A city is prohibited from finding an application complete, approving a development project, or issuing a building permit for a project that requires only a building permit if the project meets specified requirements concerning hazardous materials and emissions, unless the owner or authorized agent complies with certain provisions, including submitting a risk management and prevention program (RMPP) if the administering agency makes a specified determination. This section, however, does not apply to applications solely for residential construction. Gov't Code § 65850.2(i).

Applicable time periods to act upon the tentative map. Under the Map Act, a city has 30 days to determine whether an application is complete if the application contains a statement that it is an application for a development permit. If the city does not respond within that time period, the application is "deemed complete" under the Permit Streamlining Act. Gov't Code § 65943(a).

Once the application is complete, the Map Act sets forth certain statutory time periods for reporting and acting upon maps, depending on which advisory agency is charged with approving the map. §§ 66452.1, 66452.2. If no action is taken within the specified time limits, the tentative map "shall be deemed approved" insofar as it complies with the requirements of the Map Act and local ordinances. Gov't Code § 66452.4. However, even if a city fails to act within these time limits, the map might not automatically be approved under Government Code section 66452.4 of the Permit Streamlining Act (discussed in the next section). Constitutional due process of notice and opportunity for hearing negates automatic approval under the provisions of the Map Act. *Horn v. County of Ventura*, 24 Cal. 3d 605, 615 (1979).

In addition, there must be an express finding of consistency with the applicable general plan as a prerequisite for approval of the tentative map, thereby precluding automatic approval. *Woodland Hills Residents Ass'n, Inc. v. City Council*, 44 Cal. App. 3d 825 (1975). Other courts, however, have held that automatic approval is proper under certain circumstances. In *Orsi v. City Council of Salinas*, the court found an application had been automatically deemed complete and a project, including its tentative map, had been deemed approved under both the Permit Streamlining Act and Government Code section 66452.4. 219 Cal. App. 3d 1576, 1584, 1588 (1990). In *Orsi*, public hearings had been held on the project and the court found it consistent with the general plan even though no specific findings were made. *See also Selinger v. City Council*, 216 Cal. App. 3d 259 (1989). If the map is automatically approved, it is entitled to the same treatment as if it were approved in a timely manner. 81 Ops. Cal. Atty. Gen. 166 (1998).

A city also must comply with the time periods for environmental review provided for in Public Resources Code section 21151.5 and other CEQA provisions. In *Sunset Drive Corporation v. City of Redlands*, the court held that a city can be subject to a writ of mandate and monetary damages for failing to complete and certify an EIR within one year after a complete application is accepted. 73 Cal. App. 4th 215, 222, 225 (1999); Pub. Res. Code § 21151.5. The time periods contained in the Map Act, including the basic time periods, commence after certification of the environmental impact report, adoption of a negative declaration, or an exemption determination. Gov't Code §§ 66452.1(c), 66452.2(c).

A city cannot disapprove a map based only on a failure to comply with the time limits specified in chapter 3 of the Map Act. Gov't Code § 66451 et seq.

TIME LIMITS IMPOSED BY THE PERMIT STREAMLINING ACT

In addition to the time limits contained within the Map Act, the time limits contained in the Permit Streamlining Act (Gov't Code § 65920 et seq.) must be followed. The Permit Streamlining Act requires that a city approve or disapprove a tentative map or a parcel map within the time limits set forth in the Act. Generally, the time limit is a 180-day period if an environmental impact report is required and 60 days if a negative declaration is issued, with certain exceptions. Gov't Code § 65950. If the city does not approve or disapprove a map within the time limits, the Permit Streamlining Act states that failure to do so shall be deemed approval of the project, provided that the prescribed public notice requirements have been met. There is no common law right to waive the time limits of the Permit Streamlining Act. In 1998, the Legislature made this clear when it expressly cited *Bickel v. City of Piedmont*, which found that an applicant had a common law right to waive the time limitations of the Act. 16 Cal. 4th 1040 (1997). The Legislature expressly stated its intent to clarify that the Permit Streamlining Act does not provide for a common law right of waiver. 1998 Cal. Stat., ch. 283, § 5.

However, the provisions of the Permit Streamlining Act do not apply to administrative appeals. Gov't Code § 65922(b). The Permit Streamlining Act also does not apply if map approval is contingent on a general plan amendment, rezoning, or other land use legislation. *Land Waste Mgmt. v. County of Contra Costa Bd. of Supervisors*, 222 Cal. App. 3d 950, 959 (1990); *Landi v. County of Monterey*, 139 Cal. App. 3d 934, 936 (1983). For a more detailed discussion of the Permit Streamlining Act, see chapter 17 (Rights of the Regulated).

Notice and hearing; processing. It is advisable in all subdivision approval processes—whether they involve tentative or parcel map approval or any other discretionary approval under the Map Act, such as an extension of a tentative map or the issuance of a conditional certificate of compliance—for notice to be given and an opportunity for hearing to be provided. In fact, the California Supreme Court has held that the due process requirements of the United States and California Constitutions require notice and opportunity for hearing if map approval will constitute a substantial or significant deprivation of the property rights of other landowners. *Horn v. County of Ventura*, 24 Cal. 3d 605, 612 (1979); see also *Kennedy v. City of Hayward*, 105 Cal. App. 3d 953, 962 (1980). In general, notice must be given pursuant to Government Code sections 65090 through 65091, and 66451.3(a).

In *Cohan v. City of Thousand Oaks*, the court held that the cumulative procedural errors committed by a city impaired the adequacy of the appeal hearing on the owners' subdivision, thus violating their due process rights. 30 Cal. App. 4th 547, 559–60 (1994). The errors in *Cohan* included (1) the council itself appealing the planning commission's decision without following either the Ralph M. Brown Act or the city's own ordinance provisions; (2) the failure to inform the owners of the grounds for the appeal; and (3) the unfair placement of the burden on the owners to convince the council of the correctness of the planning commission's decision. The court held that ignoring laws and regulations meant to ensure a fair process "stands due process on

> There is no common law right to waive the time limits of the Permit Streamlining Act.

its head." Id. at 560. In *Breakzone Billiards v. City of Torrance*, the court distinguished *Cohan* and upheld a councilperson's appeal of a planning commission's approval of a conditional use permit because the city's ordinance provisions were followed. 81 Cal. App. 4th 1205, 1222–1224 (2000).

Specific requirements apply when school districts and other agencies are affected. For example, a city must refer all maps to school districts that could be affected by the subdivision. Gov't Code § 66455.7. A city must also refer all maps to any water supplier that is, or may become, a public water system that may supply water for the subdivision, and also to Caltrans if Caltrans files a map with a city indicating territory in which it desires to make a recommendation. Gov't Code §§ 66455.3, 66455. There is a similar provision allowing the State Department of Water Resources to file a map of any territory within one mile of any facility of the State Water Resources Development System. If this occurs, the city must refer maps to the department for recommendations. Gov't Code § 66455.1. Furthermore, local agencies may make recommendations concerning proposed subdivisions in adjoining cities or unincorporated areas if the subdivision is located within the local agency's planning area and the local agency files a map with the neighboring jurisdiction that shows the territory for which it desires to make recommendations. Gov't Code § 66453. All such referrals to the recommending agency or district must be transmitted within five days after the map application is deemed complete. Such agencies and districts have 15 days after receiving a copy of the proposed map to provide their comments; the applicable city or county must consider the recommendations before acting. Gov't Code §§ 66453, 66455.1, 66455.7.

Any report or recommendation on a tentative map by the city staff shall be in writing and a copy served on the subdivider three days prior to any hearing, or prior to action on the map. Also, if there is a residential condominium conversion at issue, all tenants must receive the staff report. Gov't Code § 66452.3.

LIFE OF TENTATIVE MAPS

Initial life. The Map Act mandates an initial two-year life. By local ordinance, a city can extend that initial life for up to an additional 12 months. Gov't Code § 66452.6(a).

Multiple final maps. When the subdivider files multiple final maps pursuant to Government Code section 66456.1, the life of tentative maps can be extended by 36 months if the subdivider is required to construct, improve, or finance the construction of public improvements with a value of $236,790[8] or more outside of the boundaries of the tentative map. Gov't Code § 66452.6. This provision does not apply, however, if the improvements are public rights-of-way that abut the boundaries of the property to be subdivided, and that are reasonably related to the development of that property. Each 36-month extension affects the remaining portions of the tentative map upon the filing of each final map authorized by Government Code section 66456.1. Such an extension shall not extend the tentative map more than 10 years from its initial approval, taking into account the initial life of a map, but not any other mandatory or discretionary extensions.

---

[8] The amount of $236,790 is automatically increased each year according to the adjustment for inflation set forth in the statewide cost index for class B construction, as determined by the State Allocation Board at its January meeting. The effective date of the annual adjustment is March 1. The adjustment amount applies to tentative and vesting tentative maps whose applications were received after the effective date of the adjustment. Gov't Code § 66452.6(a)(2).

CALCULATING THE LIFE OF A TENTATIVE MAP

1. DETERMINE THE INITIAL LIFE OF THE MAP

- Identify the date the tentative map was *approved or conditionally approved* by the local agency.
- The tentative map will expire 24 months after this date, *unless* the local agency's ordinance extends the life up to an additional 12 months. Gov't Code § 66452.6(a)(1).

2. DETERMINE IF THE AUTOMATIC EXTENSION FOR PHASED, FINAL MAPS APPLIES

- To qualify for this automatic extension, the following two conditions must be met:

  —The subdivider must be authorized to file multiple final maps (§ 66456.1); and

  —The subdivider must be required to expend a minimum amount on public improvements[1] outside the tentative map boundary, *excluding* public right-of-way improvements that abut the property and are reasonably related to the property's development (§ 66452.6(a)(1)).

- If the conditions are met, *each time* a phased final map is filed before the tentative map expires, the life of the tentative map is extended for *36 months from the later of:* (1) the date of the tentative map's expiration; or (2) the date of the previously filed final map. § 66452.6(a)(1).

- These extensions cannot extend the tentative map more than 10 years from the date of its approval or conditional approval.[2] § 66452.6(a)(1).

3. DETERMINE IF THE LOCAL AGENCY HAS GRANTED ANY DISCRETIONARY EXTENSIONS

- If the subdivider applies for a discretionary extension before the tentative map expires, the local agency may approve an extension(s) up to a total of six years. § 66452.6(e).
- While the extension application is pending, the tentative map is automatically extended for 60 days *or* until the agency approves or denies the application, whichever comes first. § 66452.6 (e).

4. CHECK FOR SPECIAL EXTENSIONS GRANTED BY THE STATE LEGISLATURE

- Determine whether any statutory extensions apply to the map pursuant to provisions in §§ 66452.11, 66452.13, 66452.21, 66452.22, 66452.23 and 66452.24.

5. APPLY THE TOLLING PERIOD FOR DEVELOPMENT MORATORIA, IF APPLICABLE

- If a development moratorium is imposed after the tentative map is approved, do not include the moratorium period when calculating the life of the map. The tolling period resulting from the moratorium cannot exceed five years. § 66452.6(b)(1).
- If the remaining time on the map is less than 120 days when the moratorium is lifted, the map is valid for 120 days after the moratorium ends. § 66452.6(3).
- Development moratoriums include sewer and water moratoriums, and other public agency actions that delay or prohibit the approval of the final map. § 66452.6(f). They also include periods when map conditions cannot be satisfied because they require local agency action or acquisition of real property from a public agency. See § 66452.6(f)(1) for specific limitations.
- The tentative map may be tolled when a lawsuit is, or was, pending if the local agency approves. See § 66452.6(b)(2) for specific requirements.

6. APPLY THE TOLLING PERIOD FOR PENDING LITIGATION, IF APPLICABLE

- If a lawsuit is filed involving the map's approval or conditional approval, the subdivider may apply to the local agency for a "stay" while the lawsuit is pending. If the local agency approves the stay, the map's life will be tolled for up to five years. § 66452.6(c).

7. CHECK TO SEE IF THE MAP IS COVERED BY A DEVELOPMENT AGREEMENT

- Tentative maps on property subject to a development agreement authorized by §§ 65864 and 65869.5 may be extended for the period of time provided in the agreement, but not beyond the term of the agreement. § 66452.6(a)(1).

---

1 Public improvements include traffic controls, roads, bridges, over crossings, flood control or storm drain facilities, sewer facilities, water facilities, and lighting facilities. § 66452.6(a)(3).

2 However, an appellate court held the Map Act does not dictate the order in which discretionary and automatic extensions are used. The court rejected the argument that extensions beyond the tenth anniversary of the map may only be granted under the city's discretionary authority. *California Country Club Homes Ass'n, Inc. v. City of Los Angeles*, 18 Cal. App. 4th 1425 (1993).

The filing of a phased final map that does not conform to the tentative map's requirements would not entitle the map to a 36-month extension under section 66452.6(a)(1). *See Ailanto Properties, Inc. v. City of Half Moon Bay*, 142 Cal. App. 4th 572, 600 (2006). In *Ailanto*, an applicant filed, and the city rejected, a phased final map that did not include a coastal development permit required by the tentative map. The court found that the 36-month extension would not apply. The court stated that implicit in the extension provision is the requirement that the final map substantively complies with the Map Act. *Id.* Thus, timely delivery of a final map that did not conform with the tentative map would not be an effective filing; to conclude otherwise would permit an applicant to file nonconforming maps simply to secure an extension.

Development agreements. A tentative map for property subject to a development agreement authorized by Government Code sections 65864 and 65869.5 may be extended for the period of time provided for in the agreement, but not beyond the duration of the agreement. Gov't Code § 66452.6(a).

Discretionary extensions. Upon application by the subdivider, a city may extend the time at which the map expires for a period or periods not to exceed a total of six years. Gov't Code § 66452.6(e). These are called the discretionary extensions. *See Griffis v. County of Mono*, 163 Cal. App. 3d 414 (1985) (an ordinance restricting extensions to a one-year period was invalid). The application for extension must be filed prior to the expiration date. Once an application for an extension is timely filed, the map is automatically extended for 60 days or until the city acts on the extension, whichever occurs first.

An application to extend the life of a tentative map may be approved even after the automatic 60-day extension period has expired, so long as the application itself is filed prior to the expiration date. The issue of whether a timely filed application for an extension may be approved after the map's expiration date was addressed in *Bodega Bay Concerned Citizens v. County of Sonoma*, where the Board of Supervisors failed to consider a subdivider's timely filed application for extension of a tentative map until nearly one month after the map's expiration date. 125 Cal. App. 4th 1061, 1066 (2005). A citizen's group challenged the decision on the ground that the Board lacked the authority to grant the extension because the map had already expired. *Id.* at 1073. The appellate court disagreed and held that the Board may approve a timely application for an extension of a tentative map after the map has otherwise expired. The court based its holding in part upon Government Code section 66452.6(d), which allows local agencies to take action on "timely filings," even after expiration of the tentative map. *Id.* at 1069. According to the court, the statutory authority of an agency to act is expressed broadly and without limitation. Consequently, an agency may extend a tentative map after it has otherwise expired where an application for extension is timely filed, so long as the aggregate six-year period is not exceeded. *Id.* at 1073.

Statutory extensions. Recognizing the severe impact of a recession on developers, the Legislature in 1993, 1996, 2008, 2009, 2011, and again in 2013, extended the lives of tentative, vesting tentative, and parcel maps. The 1993 amendment added Government Code section 66452.11, which provided for a 24-month extension for all approved tentative maps that had not expired on the effective date, September 13, 1993. The extension was automatic, required no action by the city that approved the tentative maps, and provided no opportunity for the imposition of additional conditions of approval. This extension is in *addition* to all other extensions allowed or required by Government Code sections 66452.6 and 66463.5. Although not expressly stated, by extending the life of tentative maps, the 1993 amendment extended the

> An application to extend the life of a tentative map may be approved even after the automatic 60-day extension period has expired, so long as the application itself is filed prior to the expiration date.

rights conferred by a vesting tentative map, which last for at least one year beyond the recording of a final map.

The 1996 amendment is virtually identical to the 1993 amendment. The 1996 amendment provides for a 12-month extension in *addition* to all other extensions, for all tentative, vesting tentative, and parcel maps that had not expired as of May 14, 1996. Gov't Code §§ 66452.6, 66463.5.

The 2008 amendment provides for a 12-month extension of those tentative maps that: (a) had not expired prior to July 15, 2008; and (b) otherwise would expire before January 1, 2011. Gov't Code § 66452.21(a). The 2009 amendment provides for a 24-month extension of those maps that: (a) had not expired prior to July 15, 2009; and (b) otherwise would expire before January 1, 2012. Gov't Code § 66452.22(a). The 2011 amendment provides for a 24-month extension of those maps that (a) had not expired prior to July 15, 2011; and (b) otherwise would expire before January 1, 2014. Gov't Code § 66452.23(a). The determination of whether a tentative subdivision map or parcel map expires before a given date for purposes of applying the 2008, 2009, and 2011 statutory extensions shall count those discretionary extensions pursuant to Government Code sections 66452.6(e) and 66463.5(c) and any additional time in connection with the filing of a final map pursuant to section 66452.6(a) but shall not include any development moratorium tolling or litigation stay allowed or permitted by Government Code sections 66452.6 or 66453.5. Gov't Code §§ 66452.21(d), 66452.22(d), 66452.23(d).

Unlike the statutory extensions in 2008, 2009, and 2011, the 2013 extension is not limited to maps that are otherwise set to expire within a specified time. Rather, the 2013 legislation automatically extends by 24 months the life of all maps that were approved on or after January 1, 2000 and that had not expired on or before July 11, 2013. Gov't Code § 66452.24(a).

Maps approved prior to 2000 that are still in effect shall also be extended for 24 months under the 2013 extension, but only if: (1) the subdivider submits an application for the extension at least 90 days prior to expiration of the map, and (2) the city determines that the map is consistent with the applicable zoning and general plan requirements in effect when the application for extension is filed. Gov't Code § 66452.24(b). If the map is determined not to be consistent with applicable zoning and general plan requirements in effect when the extension application is filed, the city may deny or conditionally approve an extension for a period of 24 months. Where the extension application is made prior to expiration of the map, such application automatically extends the life of the map for 60 days or until the application is approved, conditionally approved, or denied, whichever occurs last. Denial of an extension by an advisory agency shall be appealable to the legislative body within 15 days. *Id.*

Each of the Legislature's statutory extensions in 1993, 1996, 2008, 2009, and 2011—Government Code sections 66452.11, 66452.13, 66452.21, 66452.22 and 66452.23—are automatic and require no action by the city that approved the tentative map. The 2013 statutory extension—Government Code section 66452.24—is automatic and requires no action except as applied to pre-2000 maps, which require the application and approval process described above. Statutory extensions provide no opportunity for the imposition of additional conditions of approval and are in addition to all other extensions of the expiration date allowed or permitted by Government Code sections 66452.6 and 66463.5. Gov't Code §§ 66452.11(b), 66452.13(b), 66452.21(b), 66452.22(b), 66452.23(b), 66452.24(c); *California Country Club Homes Ass'n, Inc. v. City of Los Angeles*; 18 Cal. App. 4th 1425 (1993) (order in which extensions are granted is immaterial).

The 1993, 1996, 2008, 2009, 2011, and 2013 extensions also apply to any legislative, administrative, or other approval by any agency of the State of California that pertains to a development project included in a map that is extended pursuant to the statutory extension provision. Gov't Code §§ 66452.11(c), 66452.13(c), 66452.21(c), 66452.22(c). The effect of this language is to extend related approvals issued by acknowledged state agencies such as the Coastal Commission, Department of Fish and Game, and the Regional Water Quality Control Boards. Note, however, that cities and counties are not agencies of the state, and their related approvals are not extended by these provisions.

For discussion of how certain of these statutory extensions affect the conditioning of approvals under the Map Act's "one bite of the apple" rule, see Timing of Conditions and Subsequent Conditions below.

Moratoria. The life of a tentative map does not include periods of time during which a development moratorium is in effect after the approval of the tentative map—provided, however, the length of the moratorium-based extension does not exceed five years. Gov't Code § 66452.6(b)(1). In 2006, a court of appeal clarified that the length of any moratorium-related tolling of the expiration of a vesting tentative map under section 66452(b)(1) was limited to five years, regardless of the duration of the development moratorium. *Ailanto Properties*, 142 Cal. App. 4th at 576. The court noted that interpreting section 66452.6(b)(1) to mean that development moratoria affecting maps shall automatically expire after five years regardless of whether the reasons for the moratoria were still in effect, as Ailanto had suggested, would lead to absurd practical results. The court also rejected Ailanto's arguments that multiple moratoria could lead to multiple tolling periods.

Development moratoria include a water and/or sewer moratorium, as well as other actions of public agencies that regulate land use, development, or the provision of services to the land. Thus, where a public agency with the authority to approve the tentative map, thereafter prevents, prohibits, or delays the approval of a final or parcel map, the life of the map is tolled. Gov't Code § 66452.6(f). Once the moratorium is lifted, the map will be valid for the shorter of five years or the period of time that remained on the map when the moratorium was imposed, but in any event, no less than 120 days. Gov't Code § 66452.6(b).

For a discussion of a development moratorium's effect on a tentative map, *see Ailanto Properties*, 142 Cal. App. 4th at 576, and *Native Sun/Lyon Communities v. City of Escondido*, 15 Cal. App. 4th 892, 914 (1993) (a city's development moratorium met the terms of Government Code section 66452.6(b)(1), and map was extended).

Litigation stays. The life of the tentative map also may be tolled during the time in which a lawsuit against the local agency challenging the approval or disapproval of the tentative map is, or was, pending. A litigation stay is not automatic; it requires approval from the local agency prior to the expiration of the tentative map. The subdivider may apply for the litigation stay after the local agency is served with the lawsuit. Within 40 days following the application for the stay, the agency must either stay the time period for up to five years or deny the request. The agency may adopt local procedures for reviewing such requests. Gov't Code §§ 66452.6(c), 66463.5(e).

In *Friends of Westhaven and Trinidad v. County of Humboldt*, the court held that a subdivider's application for a litigation stay must be submitted prior to expiration of the tentative map, even if litigation is still pending. 107 Cal. App. 4th 878, 887 (2003). The subdivider in this case received initial tentative map approval for two years. Litigation over the map ensued, and the case was resolved more than four months after the tentative map had expired. The subdivider waited until after the litigation had ended to

> The life of a tentative map does not include periods of time during which a development moratorium is in effect after the approval of the tentative map—provided, however, the length of the moratorium-based extension does not exceed five years.

apply for the stay. Although the county approved the request, the court overturned the extension, agreeing with project opponents that the stay request was not timely because the tentative map already had expired. Id.

Summary. The maximum life of a tentative map may not exceed an aggregate of mandatory extensions of up to 10 years and discretionary extensions not exceeding six years in addition, potentially, to statutory extensions depending on the applicability of Government Code sections 66452.11, 66452.13, 66452.21, 66452.22, and 66452.23. Gov't Code § 66452.6(e); *see, e.g., California Country Club Homes Ass'n, Inc. v. City of Los Angeles,* 18 Cal. App. 4th 1425, 1436–37 (1993) (the Map Act does not dictate the order in which discretionary and mandatory extensions must be used). However, the life of a tentative map might be extended even further by the tolling provisions triggered by development moratoria or litigation. Gov't Code §§ 66452.6(b), (c).

Following are the rules that determine the life of a tentative map:

- A map has an initial life of two years plus any additional time, to a maximum initial life of three years, allowed by local ordinance
- A map is automatically extended by three years upon the filing of each phased final map (to a maximum of 10 years) by a subdivider required to make substantial off-site public improvements as a condition of approval of the map
- A map may be extended for up to six years, at the discretion of the city, in addition to the initial life and the automatic extension
- A map may be extended by various tolling provisions triggered by development moratoria or litigation by up to five years
- If a map had not expired on September 13, 1993, it was automatically extended by two years in addition to any other extension
- In addition to any other extension, if a map had not expired on May 14, 1996, it was automatically extended one year
- In addition to any other extension, if a map had not expired prior to July 15, 2008, and would otherwise expire before January 1, 2011, it was automatically extended by one year
- In addition to any other extension, if a map had not expired prior to July 15, 2009, and would otherwise expire before January 1, 2012, it was automatically extended by two years
- In addition to any other extension, if a map had not expired prior to July 15, 2011, and would otherwise expire before January 1, 2014, it was automatically extended by two years. (To calculate whether a map would expire before the specified dates for purposes of these last three statutory extensions, *see* Government Code section 66452.21(d), 66452.22(d), and 66452.23(d)).
- In addition to any other extension, if a map was approved on January 1, 2000 or later and is still effective on July 11, 2013, it shall be automatically extended by 24 months. Maps approved prior to 2000 and not yet expired may be extended upon application by the subdivider and certain findings by the city.

Conditions imposed on extensions. Even though granting an extension under Government Code section 66452.6(e) is a discretionary act under Government Code section 66452.6(e), cities may not impose additional conditions other than those related to the length of time a map is valid. *See El Patio v. Permanent Rent Control Bd.,* 110 Cal. App. 3d 915, 928 (1980); *see also Bodega Bay Concerned Citizens v. County of Sonoma,* 125 Cal. App. 4th 1061 (2005). Application of the 2013 statutory extension to maps approved prior to 2000 is an exception to this rule, as the Legislature expressly

> A map has an initial life of two years plus any additional time, to a maximum initial life of three years, allowed by local ordinance.

provided that the approval of such extensions may be conditioned where the map is no longer consistent with applicable zoning and general plan requirements at the time of the extension application. Gov't Code § 66452.24(b).

A subdivider may agree to a new condition that a city imposes as a condition to an extension of the tentative map. However, if the subdivider chooses to do so, it may not later challenge the validity of that condition. *Rossco Holdings, Inc. v. State of California*, 212 Cal. App. 3d 642 (1989) (citing *County of Imperial v. McDougal*, 19 Cal. 3d 505 (1977)) (landowner cannot challenge condition on a permit after acquiescing to the condition by specific agreement, or by failure to challenge validity and accepting the benefits); *Pfeiffer v. City of La Mesa*, 69 Cal. App. 3d 74 (1977) (landowner waives right to assert invalidity of conditions and sue public entity for costs of compliance after acceptance of building permits and compliance with conditions).

If a subdivider does not agree to a new condition related to the extension, a city can deny the extension within its discretion under the reasonable exercise of the police power. If the city does so, the tentative map will expire and the subdivider will have to obtain a new tentative map that may have new conditions. Alternatively, unless the tentative map is a vesting tentative map, a city could permit the extension, but attach a new condition to a later approval, such as the issuance of a building permit, if permitted by its local regulations or ordinances. *See McMullan v. Santa Monica Rent Control Bd.*, 168 Cal. App. 3d 960, 962-963 (1985).

Expiration of other permits issued in conjunction with a tentative map. Unless an earlier expiration appears on the face of the permit, any permit issued in conjunction with a tentative subdivision map for a planned-unit development (PUD) shall expire no earlier than the approved tentative map, or any extension thereof, whichever occurs later. Gov't Code §§ 65863.9, 66452.12(a).

> PUD = planned-unit development

A local coastal development permit issued by a city in conjunction with a tentative subdivision map for a planned-unit development shall expire no earlier than the approved tentative map, and any extension of the map shall be in accordance with the applicable local coastal program, if any, that is in effect. Gov't Code § 65863.9.

For easy reference, a step-by-step approach to calculating the life of a tentative map is presented on the following page.

EFFECT OF APPROVAL OF MAP ON THE RIGHT TO DEVELOP—VESTED RIGHTS

Approval of a final map or a parcel map does not in itself confer a vested right to develop. *Avco Community Developers, Inc. v. South Coast Reg'l Comm'n*, 17 Cal. 3d 785, 739-94 (1976); *Consaul v. City of San Diego*, 6 Cal. App. 4th 1781, 1793 (1992); *Oceanic California, Inc. v. North Cent. Coast Reg'l Comm'n*, 63 Cal. App. 3d 57, 72-73 (1976). Zoning can still be changed, or other police power ordinances can be adopted, after even final maps, conditional use permits, PUDs, zoning, rezoning, grading, or other permits have been granted. *See Hafen v. County of Orange*, 128 Cal. App. 4th 133 (2005) (upholding zoning changes after tentative map approval because developer had not obtained a vested right to develop). There is no vested right to develop until actual building or other permits for identifiable buildings have been issued, and substantial work has been done thereafter in reliance on those permits. *Avco*, 17 Cal. 3d at 791; *see also Hafen*, 128 Cal. App. 4th at 142-43; *Golden State Homebuilding Ass'n v. City of Modesto*, 26 Cal. App. 4th 601, 611-12 (1994).

> There is no vested right to develop until actual building or other permits for identifiable buildings have been issued, and substantial work has been done thereafter in reliance on those permits.

Also, no contract regarding dedications will deprive the city of its rezoning power. *Call v. Feher*, 93 Cal. App. 3d 434, 441 (1979). For example, a condominium converter has no vested right through approval of a tentative or final map to bypass a later-enacted police power regulation including rent control provisions. *Santa Monica Pines, Ltd. v. Rent Control Bd.*, 35 Cal. 3d 858, 868-69 (1984); *People v. H & H Props.*, 154 Cal. App. 3d 894, 899-900 (1984); *see also Palmer v. Board of Supervisors*, 145 Cal. App. 3d 779, 783 (1983) (filing of a map is insufficient to exempt property from a subsequent zone change even though the original tentative map was improperly denied); *McMullan v. Santa Monica Rent Control Bd.*, 168 Cal. App. 3d 960, 962-63 (1985) (denial of a condominium conversion permit by the Rent Control Board was a proper exercise of the police power even though map approval was granted).

> The courts have carved out several narrow exceptions to the vested rights rule.

The courts have carved out several narrow exceptions to the vested rights rule. For example, the California Supreme Court held that a final map and the Bureau of Real Estate's issuance of a public report are all that is needed to allow a condominium converter to proceed, without complying with a later-enacted land use regulation. *City of W. Hollywood v. Beverly Towers, Inc.*, 52 Cal. 3d 1184 (1991). In another case, the court held that property owners could claim estoppel since the city had issued administrative regulations that were relied upon by the owners in proceeding with a condominium conversion—even though the city later enacted an ordinance that would have prevented the conversion. *Hock Inv. Co. v. City and County of San Francisco*, 215 Cal. App. 3d 438, 448-49 (1989).

The policy underlying the rule restricting vested rights was set forth by the California Supreme Court:

> If we were to accept the premise that the construction of subdivision improvements or the zoning of the land for a planned community are sufficient to afford a developer a vested right to construct buildings on the land in accordance with the laws in effect at the time the improvements are made or the zoning enacted, there could be serious impairment of the government's right to control land use policy.... Thus tracts or lots in tracts which had been subdivided decades ago, but upon which no buildings have been constructed could be free of all zoning laws enacted subsequent to the time of the subdivision improvement, unless facts constituting waiver, abandonment, or opportunity for amortization of the original vested right could be shown.

Avco Community Developers, 17 Cal. 3d at 797-798

In response to the *Avco* decision and other similar decisions, the Legislature adopted the Development Agreement Statute. Gov't Code § 65864 *et seq*. This statute provides that a city and a developer may enter into an agreement whereby the developer is insulated from future land use actions by the city that might otherwise prevent the developer from completing the approved development. Also as a result of *Avco*, the Legislature adopted the Vesting Tentative Map Statute. Gov't Code § 66498.1 *et seq*. For further discussion of vested rights, see chapter 10 (Vested Rights). *See also* David L. Callies, Cecily Talbert Barclay, and Julie Tappendorf, *Development by Agreement* (ABA Sect. of State and Local Gov't Law, 2012).

VESTING TENTATIVE MAP

Background. In 1984, the Legislature added Chapter 4.5 (Development Rights) to the Map Act, establishing a new form of tentative map for subdivisions in California—the "vesting tentative map." Gov't Code § 66498.1 *et seq*.

The approval of a vesting tentative map expressly confers a vested right to proceed with a development in substantial compliance with the ordinances, policies, and standards in effect at the time the application for approval of the vesting tentative map is deemed complete. Gov't Code § 66498.1(b). However, if a city has initiated proceedings changing its general or specific plan, zoning, or subdivision ordinances, by ordinance, resolution, or motion, and has published notice of this change, or if the subdivider has requested changes in connection with the same development project, the city may apply these new standards to any map for which an application has not been deemed complete. Gov't Code §§ 66474.2(b), (c). As stated by the court in *Bright Development Company v. City of Tracy*:

> The Subdivision Map Act (Act) permits a subdivider to file a "vesting tentative map" whenever the Act requires a tentative map. This procedure is intended to provide greater statutory protection to subdividers than was afforded under the common law vested rights doctrine. (Gov't Code §§ 66498.1–66498.9; California Subdivision Map Act Practice (Cont. Ed. Bar 1987) § 6.31; Curtin, Subdivision Map Act Manual (1992), p. 13.).

20 Cal. App. 4th 783, 792 (1993)

> In adopting these vesting tentative map statutes, the Legislature stated:
>
> By the enactment of this article, the Legislature intends to accomplish all of the following objectives:
>
> (a) To establish a procedure for the approval of tentative maps that will provide certain statutorily vested rights to a subdivider.
>
> (b) To ensure that local requirements governing the development of a proposed subdivision are established in accordance with Section 66498.1 when a local agency approves or conditionally approves a vesting tentative map. The private sector should be able to rely upon an approved vesting tentative map prior to expending resources and incurring liabilities without the risk of having the project frustrated by subsequent action by the approving local agency....

Gov't Code § 66498.9; *see also Bright Development Company*, 20 Cal. App. 4th at 792–93

The vesting tentative map statutes are applicable to residential, commercial, and industrial subdivisions. Cities are required to have their own implementing procedures in effect. Gov't Code §§ 66498.8, 66498.7. This statute is also applicable to parcel map filings. Gov't Code §§ 66428, 66463.5(g).

The primary exception to these vesting provisions provides that a city may condition or deny a permit, approval, extension, or entitlement if it determines any of the following: (1) a failure to do so would place the residents of the subdivision or the immediate community, or both, in a condition dangerous to their health or safety or both; or (2) the condition or denial is required in order to comply with state or federal law. Gov't Code § 66498.1(c); *see also N.T. Hill, Inc. v. City of Fresno*, 72 Cal. App. 4th 977, 981 (1999).

In *Pratt v. California Coastal Commission*, the court held that a Local Coastal Plan and the development permits issued by local agencies pursuant to the Coastal Act are not solely a matter of local law, but embody state policy. 162 Cal. App. 4th 1068, 1074–76 (2008). Noting that state laws and policies are not subject to the vesting provisions of Government Code section 66498.1(b), the court therefore held that a vesting tentative map did not protect the subdivider from application by the Coastal Commission of post-vesting state policies in an appeal to the Commission related to a land use approval within the coastal zone. *Id.*

The Vesting Tentative Map Statute represents one of the Legislature's responses to the long debate regarding the precise nature of vested rights for developers in California.

> The vesting tentative map statutes are applicable to residential, commercial, and industrial subdivisions. Cities are required to have their own implementing procedures in effect.

See, e.g., Avco, 17 Cal. 3d at 791 ("[I]f a property owner has performed substantial work and incurred substantial liabilities in good faith reliance upon a permit issued by the government, he acquires a vested right to complete construction in accordance with the terms of the permit.") Until the enactment of this statute, a developer's only means of obtaining assurance from a city that its project, for which a tentative map had been approved, would not be thwarted by subsequent changes in the city's land use laws (e.g., by a subsequent rezoning by the city council or by initiative) was through the approval of an agreement pursuant to the authority of the Development Agreement Statute. Gov't Code § 65864 *et seq.* Without such an agreement, the developer risked expending great sums of money for preliminary work, while being subject to the vagaries of the common law test for vested rights. The Vesting Tentative Map Statute offers developers a degree of assurance not previously available.

> The Vesting Tentative Map Statute offers developers a degree of assurance not previously available.

Until *Bright Development,* no appellate court cases discussed what was meant by the provisions to freeze in place those ordinances, policies, and standards in effect at the time the vesting tentative map application was accepted as or deemed complete. In *Bright Development,* Bright filed a vesting tentative map application with the city, which was deemed complete and approved by the city. 20 Cal. App. 4th at 789. A dispute later arose concerning whether Bright was required at its own expense to underground existing off-site utilities in the subdivision.

At the time Bright's vesting tentative map application was deemed complete, the city did not have in effect an ordinance, policy, or standard that required Bright, at its own expense, to underground existing off-site utilities fronting the development. *Id.* at 797. Accordingly, the city's action in imposing the off-site undergrounding requirement on Bright was illegal since it violated the provisions of the Vesting Tentative Map Statute. The court noted:

> The Legislature enacted these provisions to freeze in place those "ordinances, policies and standards in effect" at the time the vesting tentative map application is deemed complete. (Cal. Subdivision Map Act Practice, *supra,* § 6.31.) These provisions enable the private sector to rely on vesting maps to plan and budget development projects. (Gov't Code § 66498.9, subd. (b).) "The vesting tentative map statute now offers developers a degree of assurance, not previously available, against changes in regulations." (Longtin's California Land Use (2d ed. 1987) § 6.50[2]; Subdivision Map Act Manual, *supra,* pp. 13, 15.)

20 Cal. App. 4th at 793

Relying on *Bright Development,* another court held that a city's open-ended fee policy conflicted with the intent of the vesting tentative map. *Kaufman & Broad Cent. Valley, Inc. v. City of Modesto,* 25 Cal. App. 4th 1577, 1586-87 (1994). In *Kaufman & Broad,* the application for a vesting tentative subdivision map for a 31-acre residential development was deemed complete on June 22, 1988. At that time, the fee per unit was $1,434. The planning commission, on October 3, 1988, approved the developer's vesting tentative map for 134 lots, subject to a new fee escalator condition that was added to all new vesting tentative maps resulting from a new council policy adopted on August 16, 1988. That condition read as follows: "'The Capital Facilities Fee payable at the time of the issuance of a building permit for any construction in this subdivision map (parcel map) shall be based on the rates in effect at time of issuance of the building permit.'" *Id.* at 1581.

When the developer applied for building permits to construct individual units, the city charged capital facilities development fees of $4,890 per unit, which was the fee in effect at that time. The developer paid the fees under protest and filed a complaint and petition for writ of mandate, seeking reimbursement of all fees paid in excess of $1,434 per unit, the rate in effect when the vesting tentative subdivision map was deemed complete.

The issues were whether the city was entitled to attach the fee escalator condition to its approval of Kaufman's vesting tentative map application and, if so, whether the condition permitted imposition of fees in excess of those in effect when the map application was deemed complete. The court ordered the city to refund the fees for individual units in excess of those in effect when the vesting tentative map was deemed complete. "[D]ue process notice requirements implicit in the vesting tentative map statutes limit increases in developer's fees to those for which adequate standards for determining the scope and extent of the fee increases are in place at the time the vesting tentative map is deemed complete." *Id.* at 1579-80. In so doing, the court held that the city's open-ended fee policy conflicted with the intent of the vesting tentative map statutes, which were intended to create a vested right arising earlier in the development process and affording greater protection than the common law. *Id.* at 1588 (citing Curtin and Merritt, *California Subdivision Map Act and the Development Process*, sections 6.28, 6.31, pages 146-52 (Cal. CEB 1987); and Daniel J. Curtin, Jr., *California Land Use and Planning Law*, pages 187-188 (Solano Press, 14th ed. 1994)).

> The court held that the city's open-ended fee policy conflicted with the intent of the vesting tentative map statutes, which were intended to create a vested right arising earlier in the development process and affording greater protection than the common law.

In addition, the court found that the "vesting tentative map statutes also incorporate a notice requirement consistent with due process." *Id.*

> The private sector should be able to rely upon an approved vesting tentative map prior to expending resources and incurring liabilities without the risk of having the project frustrated by subsequent action by the approving local agency...." (§ 66498.9, subd. (b).). It follows that a developer is entitled to actual or constructive notice of the ordinances, policies, and standards with which it will be expected to comply.... Quite obviously one cannot rely on what one does not know or cannot reasonably discover.

Id. (quoting *Bright Development Company*, 20 Cal. App. 4th at 799)

With respect to timing of the notice, the court stated:

> The City argues at some length that Kaufman & Broad had actual or constructive notice of the fee increases later in the development process, both when the increases were approved and again when it acquired River Terrace. Be that as it may, the critical point in the process for the purposes of the vesting tentative map statutes is the date on which the map application is complete. Consequently, any notice Kaufman & Broad might have received afterward is of no particular significance to the present discussion.

Id. at 1589-90

Although the city's fee policy contemplated future increases in the amount of the fees, it did not foretell the comprehensive re-evaluation of the fee structure that the city later conducted. Government Code section 66498.1 conferred on the developer the vested right to develop its subdivision subject only to the capital facilities fees in effect when its vesting tentative map application was deemed complete.

This raises the question of what happens if a city changes the land use by a general plan amendment or adoption, amendment to a specific plan, or by a rezoning, after an application has been accepted as or deemed complete. From the holdings in *Bright Development* and *Kaufman & Broad*, and from the unambiguous language of the statute, it seems clear that there is no effect on the rights granted.

At least one superior court has held the "vesting effect" of the 1984 statute prohibits application of a later change in land use law to property subject to the vesting tentative map. In 1987, the Superior Court of Contra Costa County held that an initiative imposing a retroactive freeze on rezonings that increase density may not be applied to nullify a vested right to develop in accordance with a vesting tentative map. *Davidon Homes v. City of Pleasant Hill*, No. 297988 (Superior Court, Contra Costa County, April 3, 1987). The city did not appeal this trial court decision, and thus the decision cannot be cited as precedent in any other litigation.

As discussed above, the Vesting Tentative Map Statute gives subdividers who obtain approval of a vesting tentative map a statutory right to proceed with development in substantial compliance with the local ordinances, policies, and standards in effect at the time the map application is found complete. In *Davidon Homes*, the city had rezoned the project site and later approved a vesting tentative map for a sixty-nine-unit residential subdivision. Three weeks after the map was approved, an initiative that contained a retroactive limitation on rezonings was enacted. The city then refused to process Davidon's final map, claiming that the subdivision conflicted with the initiative's density limitations, and that the initiative operated to revoke the vested rights granted through the map. Based upon the Vesting Tentative Map Statute, the court rejected that argument, and Davidon was allowed to proceed.

Procedures. The vesting tentative map process begins when a subdivider files a tentative or parcel map with the words "vesting tentative map" printed conspicuously on the face of the map. Gov't Code § 66452(c).

When these prerequisites are met, a city must process the vesting tentative map and cannot deny it solely because it is an application for a vesting tentative map. The statute requires that vesting tentative maps be treated the same as tentative maps, except as otherwise provided by the Map Act or local ordinance adopted pursuant thereto. Gov't Code § 66452; *see McPherson v. City of Manhattan Beach*, 78 Cal. App. 4th 1252, 1259 (2000) (holding that developer's vested rights to build in accordance with city's previous height restrictions expired when developer failed to timely record a map relating to its approved tentative map).

The rights conferred by a vesting tentative map last for not less than one year, and no more than two years after the final map has been recorded, although they may be extended. Gov't Code §§ 66498.5(b), (c).

In adopting its implementing procedures, a city may require the subdivider to supply additional information before the map is processed. However, a city may not require more information than that related to ordinances, resolutions, policies, or standards for the design, development, or improvement relating to the conferred rights, except where necessary (1) to permit the city to make the determination whether an environmental impact report or negative declaration is required pursuant to Public Resources Code section 21080.1 (CEQA), or (2) to comply with federal or state requirements. Gov't Code § 66498.8(d).

If a subdivider files a vesting tentative map for a subdivision where the intended development is inconsistent with the zoning ordinance in existence at that time, that inconsistency must be noted on the map. A city may deny a vesting tentative map or approve it conditioned on the subdivider, or its designee, obtaining the necessary change in the zoning ordinance to eliminate the inconsistency. If the change in the zoning ordinance is obtained, then the approved or conditionally approved vesting tentative map, notwithstanding Government Code section 66498.1(b), confers the vested right to proceed with the development in substantial compliance with the change in the zoning ordinance and the map as approved. Gov't Code § 66498.3(a).

If the ordinances, policies, or standards described in Government Code section 66498.1(b) are changed subsequent to the approval or conditional approval of a vesting tentative map, the subdivider, or his or her assignee, at any time prior to the expiration of the vesting tentative map pursuant to Government Code sections 66498.5(b), (c), and (d) may apply for an amendment to the vesting tentative map to secure a vested right to proceed with the changed ordinances, policies, or standards. An application shall clearly specify the changed ordinances, policies, or standards for which the amendment is sought. Gov't Code § 66498.2.

EFFECT OF ANNEXATION TO CITY UPON MAPS

Under Government Code section 66413.5, if a subdivision is annexed to a city after a final map has been approved and filed for record, the final map as approved by the county and any related agreements shall continue to govern. Gov't Code § 66413(a). However, if a tentative or vesting tentative map has been approved by the county and no final map has been approved, or if a parcel map has not been finalized, and the subdivision is annexed to a city, all procedures and regulations of the annexing city shall govern. This means that the map shall comply with the city's regulations on the effective date of the annexation. Gov't Code § 66413(b).

Any subdivider may file with a city a tentative map of a proposed subdivision of unincorporated territory adjacent to such a city. The city may approve it conditioned upon annexation of the property to the city. Gov't Code § 66454.

> If a subdivision is annexed to a city after a final map has been approved and filed for record, the final map as approved by the county and any related agreements shall continue to govern.

EFFECT OF INCORPORATION INTO A NEWLY INCORPORATED CITY

Under Government Code section 66413.5, if an area in a subdivision or proposed subdivision is incorporated into a newly incorporated city, the newly incorporated city is required to approve the final map if:

- The final map meets the conditions of the tentative or vesting tentative map and all of the requirements for approval of final maps under the Map Act
- The county board of supervisors approved the tentative or vesting tentative map prior to the date of the incorporation election, and
- The application for the tentative or vesting tentative map was submitted prior to the date the first signature was affixed on the petition for incorporation pursuant to Government Code section 56704 (regardless of the first signature's validity) or the date a resolution was adopted pursuant to Government Code section 56800, whichever occurs first

Gov't Code § 66413.5(a) and (f); *City of Goleta v. Superior Court*, 40 Cal. 4th 270, 276-77 (2006). Where these conditions are not satisfied, a city retains discretion over a final map that relates to a county-approved tentative map, notwithstanding Government Code section 66474.1. *Id.*

An approved tentative or vesting tentative map will not limit a newly incorporated city from imposing reasonable conditions on subsequent required approvals or permits necessary for the development consistent with Government Code section 66474.2. Gov't Code § 66413.5(e). Furthermore, the newly incorporated city may condition or deny a permit, approval, or extension or entitlement if: (1) failure to do so would place the residents of the subdivision or the immediate community in a condition dangerous to their health and/or safety; and (2) the condition or denial is necessary to comply with state or federal law. Gov't Code § 66413.5(c).

CONDITIONS TO MAP APPROVAL

IN GENERAL

There is probably no issue in subdivision law that has generated more controversy than that of dedications and the imposition of impact fees. The concept is simple—a subdivider, in return for obtaining a map to sell, lease, or finance property and thus develop it, agrees to donate to the city an amount of land or money needed to provide certain services necessitated by the influx of new residents into the community that this development will attract.[9] *Trent Meredith, Inc. v. City of Oxnard*, 114 Cal. App. 3d 317, 361 (1981).

However, determining how far a city can go in imposing conditions in a particular case can be considerably more difficult. The authority for a city to impose conditions is the police power, and the test of its proper exercise is reasonableness. In general, cities must show through individualized findings that: (1) there is a "nexus" between the condition imposed and the state interest advanced; and (2) the condition imposed is "roughly proportional" to the subdivision's impacts. For more discussion on the "nexus" and "rough proportionality" tests set forth in the United States Supreme Court's *Nollan/Dolan* decisions, see chapter 11 (Takings) and chapter 12 (Exactions).

CONDITIONS IMPOSED THROUGH THE SUBDIVISION PROCESS

In the important dedication case of *Ayres v. City Council of Los Angeles*, 34 Cal. 2d 31, 40 (1949), the California Supreme Court held that dedication conditions can be imposed on a subdivision even though they are not expressly set forth in the Map Act or local ordinance. In determining which conditions to impose on a subdivision, cities generally look to three sources:

- The Map Act, which allows specific conditions to be imposed on subdivision maps either through the statutory authority of the Map Act itself, or by a local enabling ordinance adopted by the city
- CEQA and Government Code section 66474(e), which allow conditions to be imposed that will mitigate a subdivision's environmental impacts
- The city's general plan, or an applicable specific plan, to ensure that the subdivision, including its design and improvements, are consistent with such plans

All of these sources fall within the purview of the city's general police power.

SPECIFIC CONDITIONS ALLOWED BY THE MAP ACT AND LOCAL ORDINANCE

The Map Act identifies numerous conditions that can be imposed on the approval of subdivision maps. Some of these conditions are permissive, and the city must first adopt a local enabling ordinance following the criteria set forth in the Map Act, before imposing the condition on subdividers. Other conditions are mandatory, and must be imposed pursuant to the authority of the Map Act alone. *See, e.g.*, the requirements for public access to waterways (sections 66478.1–14), energy conservation (section

---

[9] *See* David L. Callies, Cecily Talbert Barclay, and Julie Tappendorf, *Development by Agreement* (ABA Sect. of State and Local Gov't Law, 2012).

66473.1), and proof of an adequate water supply for subdivisions that meet a certain size threshold (section 66473.7).

Parkland dedication (Gov't Code § 66477 (Quimby Act)). A city may, by ordinance, require the dedication of land or payment of fees for park or recreational purposes. Gov't Code § 66477; *Associated Home Builders, Inc. v. City of Walnut Creek*, 4 Cal. 3d 633, 641 (1971). However, according to Government Code section 66477, before such a condition can be validly attached to the approval of a map, certain criteria must be met:

- The ordinance must be in effect for a period of 30 days before the tentative or parcel map is filed. Gov't Code § 66477(a)(1)
- The ordinance must include definite standards for determining the proportion of the subdivision to be dedicated and the amount of the fee to be paid. The dedication or payment shall not exceed a proportionate amount necessary to provide three acres of park area per 1,000 subdivision residents unless the amount of existing neighborhood and park area exceeds that limit, in which case a higher standard may be allowed not to exceed five acres per 1,000 subdivision residents. Gov't Code § 66477(a)(2); *see Homebuilders Ass'n of Tulare/Kings Counties Inc. v. City of Lemoore*, 185 Cal. App. 4th 554, 565 (2010)
- Land required to be dedicated is to be used only for the purpose of developing new, or rehabilitating existing, park or recreational facilities to serve the subdivision. Previously, this same limitation applied also to fees collected in lieu of parkland dedication. However, as of January 1, 2014, parkland fees paid in connection with a subdivision may be used to develop new or rehabilitate existing park or recreational facilities in a neighborhood other than the one where the subdivision is located, provided: (1) the neighborhood where the fees are to be spent has fewer than three acres of park area per 1,000 members of the neighborhood population; (2) the neighborhood in which the subdivision for which fees are paid is located has a park area per 1,000 members of neighborhood population ratio that meets or exceeds the city's established park ratio (but in no event is less than three acres per 1,000 persons); (3) the legislative body holds a public hearing before using the fees; (4) the legislative body makes a finding supported by substantial evidence that it is reasonably foreseeable that future inhabitants of the subdivision for which the fee is imposed will use the proposed park and recreational facilities in the neighborhood where fees are used; and (5) the fees are used within a specified radius (planning area, zone of influence, geographic region, etc. established by the city) that complies with the city's parkland dedication ordinance and are consistent with the adopted general plan and any specific plan. Gov't Code § 66477(a)(3)(B).
- The amount and location of land to be dedicated or amount of fees paid shall bear a reasonable relationship to the use of the park and recreational facilities by the future inhabitants of the subdivision. Gov't Code § 66477(a)(3). There is no strict limitation on this criteria. Fees are justified if used for park and recreational facilities generally, but not exclusively, available to subdivision residents. *Associated Home Builders*, 4 Cal. 3d at 640 n.5
- A city must have a general plan or specific plan containing policies and standards for park and recreational facilities in accordance with definite principles and standards. Gov't Code § 66477(a)(4)
- The amount and location of land to be dedicated or the fees to be paid shall bear a reasonable relationship to the use of the park and recreational facilities by the future inhabitants of the subdivision. Gov't Code § 66477(a)(5)

> A city may, by ordinance, require the dedication of land or payment of fees for park or recreational purposes.

- A city shall develop a schedule specifying how, when, and where it will use the land or fees or both to develop park or recreational facilities. Any fees collected under the ordinance shall be committed within five years after payment of the fees or the issuance of building permits on one-half of the lots created by the subdivision, whichever occurs later. If the fees are not committed, they shall be distributed and paid to each record owner of the subdivision in the same proportion that the size of each lot bears to the total area of all lots in the subdivision. Gov't Code § 66477(a)(6)
- Only the payment of fees may be required for subdivisions containing 50 or fewer parcels. Gov't Code § 66477(a)(7)
- Subdivisions of fewer than five parcels that are not used for residential purposes shall be exempt unless a building permit for a residential structure is requested for one of the parcels within four years. The Quimby Act is not applicable to commercial and industrial subdivisions or condominium projects or stock cooperatives that consist of subdivision of airspace in an existing apartment building more than five years old when no new dwelling units are added. Gov't Code § 66477(a)(8)
- A city may provide developers of planned developments, real estate developments (Bus. & Prof. Code § 11003), community apartment projects, condominium projects, and stock cooperatives that contain private recreational open space credit for the value of that private open space. Gov't Code § 66477(e). However, unless a city has adopted legislation providing a credit for private open space, it has no clear, present, and ministerial duty to provide a specific amount of credit. *See Branciforte Heights, LLC v. City of Santa Cruz*, 138 Cal. App. 4th 914, 938-939 (2006) (noting that the court did not reach the question of whether a city could be compelled to enact an ordinance providing some credit for private open space consistent with Gov't Code § 66477(e))
- If the subdivider provides park and recreational improvements to the dedicated land, the value of the improvements, together with any equipment located thereon, shall be a credit against the payment of fees or dedication of land required by the ordinance. Gov't Code § 66477(a)(9). A city, as a condition of regulating and approving a subdivision, may not lawfully require the dedication of land improved for park and recreational purposes without credit being given to the subdivider for the value of the recreational improvements that are provided by the subdivider. 73 Ops. Cal. Atty. Gen. 152 (1990). However, this does not limit a city's use of other means by which it may obtain recreational fees and land, improvements, and fees for parks.
- Funds obtained as in-lieu fees under Government Code section 66477 may be used to purchase, construct, or acquire land for a theater for cultural activities. 81 Ops. Cal. Atty. Gen. 293 (1998)

Adequate water supply (Gov't Code § 66473.7). A condition requiring verification of water supply must be imposed on certain tentative maps. Gov't Code § 66473.7(b)(1). This requirement applies to proposed residential developments of more than 500 dwelling units. This requirement also applies when the public water system that will serve the subdivision has fewer than 5,000 service connections and the proposed residential development would account for an increase of ten percent or more in the number of the public water system's existing service connections. For a further discussion regarding water supply laws, see chapter 16 (Sustainable Development).

School site dedication (Gov't Code § 66478). The provision in the Map Act for school site dedication is not a true dedication provision. Instead, it is basically a reservation requirement for an elementary school site with a right to purchase at a later date. Its use appears to be minimal, since cities and school districts rely on other laws to require dedications. For further discussion regarding these laws, see chapter 12 (Exactions). Conditions related to school fees are discussed below, as well as in chapter 12 (Exactions).

Reservations (Gov't Code § 66479 et seq.). The Map Act provides that a city may impose by ordinance a requirement that real property within the subdivision be reserved for parks, recreational facilities, fire stations, libraries, or other public uses. As with parkland dedication, the ordinance must follow certain criteria contained in the statute.

The reserved area must be of a size and shape to permit the balance of the property to develop in an orderly, efficient manner. Gov't Code § 66479(c). Upon approval of the final map, a city must enter into a binding agreement with the subdivider to acquire the reserved area within two years after the completion and acceptance of all improvements, unless this time period is mutually extended. Gov't Code § 66480. The purchase price paid by the city for the reserved area shall be the market value at the time of filing of the tentative map, plus the taxes against the reserved area from the date of reservation, and maintenance costs (including interest costs) on any loans covering the reserved area. Gov't Code § 66480. If the city does not enter into an agreement, the reservation automatically terminates. Gov't Code § 66481.

Street and bicycle path dedications (Gov't Code §§ 66475, 66475.1). Dedications for streets, alleys, including access rights and abutters' rights, drainage, public utilities, and other public easements can be imposed by ordinance. Gov't Code § 66475. When a subdivider is required to dedicate roadways, the subdivider also may be required to dedicate land for bicycle paths. Gov't Code § 66475.1.

Dedication for local transit facilities (Gov't Code § 66475.2). A city may, by local ordinance, require dedication of land for local transit facilities, such as bus turnouts, benches, shelters, landing pads, and similar items that directly benefit the residents of a subdivision. However, only payment of fees in lieu of a dedication can be required for divisions in airspace of existing buildings into condominium projects, stock cooperatives, or community apartment projects.

Fees for drainage and sewer facilities (Gov't Code § 66483). This section details the requirements for payment of fees to defray actual or estimated costs of constructing planned drainage facilities and sanitary sewer facilities for local or neighborhood areas. The local ordinance requirement must meet certain criteria. A city must have a general drainage or sanitary sewer plan, and the fees shall be paid into a "planned local drainage facilities fund" and "a planned local sanitary sewer fund." Gov't Code § 66483(d). The fees that are required must be fairly apportioned within the areas, either on the basis of benefits conferred or on the need for the facilities created by the proposed subdivider. Disposition of surplus money is covered by Government Code sections 66483.1 and 66483.2.

In interpreting this section, the Attorney General has stated that a city, in regulating a subdivision, must comply with its requirements when enacting a drainage fee ordinance. 66 Ops. Cal. Atty. Gen. 120 (1983). But if it desires to use some other police power authority or taxation power, it need not follow the requirement of Government Code section 66483. Also, in calculating the maximum possible drainage fee under this section, the total acreage in the drainage area is to be the basis of the calculation.

> The Map Act provides that a city may impose by ordinance a requirement that real property within the subdivision be reserved for parks, recreational facilities, fire stations, libraries, or other public uses.

Fees for bridges and major thoroughfares (Gov't Code § 66484). A local ordinance may require the payment of a fee as a condition of approval or as a condition of issuing a building permit for purposes of defraying the actual or estimated costs of constructing bridges over waterways, railways, freeways, and canyons, or constructing major thoroughfares. As with other codes discussed in this section, the ordinance must meet certain criteria and must refer to the circulation element. This section reads as an assessment district procedure and provides for a majority protest. For San Diego and Los Angeles counties only, Gov't Code § 66404(i) establishes a special definition of "administrative costs" that may be included as construction costs.

Groundwater recharge (Gov't Code § 66484.5). A city may adopt an ordinance requiring, among other things, the payment of a fee or other consideration as a condition to approval of a final map or parcel map, or the issuance of a building permit to defray the cost of constructing planned recharge facilities for the replacement of surface waters into underground aquifers if the specified conditions are satisfied.

Fees for transportation facilities (Gov't Code § 66484.7). A city may require by ordinance the payment of a fee as a condition of approval of a final map or issuance of a building permit for purposes of defraying the actual or estimated cost of constructing pedestrian, bicycle, transit, and traffic-calming facilities. The ordinance must refer to the general plan's circulation element (including the provision identifying the transportation facilities), provide for determining in a public hearing a fair method of allocating and apportioning fees within the area to be benefitted, provide for the filing of protests by owners of a majority of property in the area to be benefitted, and meet other criteria in Government Code section 66484.7.

Supplemental improvements—reimbursement agreements (Gov't Code § 66485 et seq.). These sections allow a local ordinance to require that improvements be installed by the subdivider, for the subdivision's benefit, that contain supplemental size, capacity, number, or length for the benefit of property not within the subdivision. Supplemental length may include minimum-sized offsite sewer lines necessary to reach a sewer outlet in existence at that time. If a supplemental improvement requirement is imposed, a city shall enter into an agreement with the subdivider for reimbursement of the difference in cost. To pay costs of reimbursement, a city may collect a reasonable charge from persons or public agencies outside the subdivision for their use of supplemental improvements installed by the subdivider. For example, a city can collect reimbursement from a school district that is benefited by supplemental improvements to a storm drainage system. Gov't Code § 66487; 71 Ops. Cal. Atty. Gen. 163 (1988). Or a water district organized under the California Water District Law (Water Code § 3400 et seq.) can enter into an agreement with land developers for construction of oversized water facilities in support of anticipated growth in the area and enter into agreements with subsequent developers to reimburse the first developer for construction costs of the oversized facilities. 88 Ops. Cal. Atty. Gen. 172 (2005).

Soils investigations and reports (Gov't Code §§ 66490, 66491). These sections require that the preliminary soils report be prepared by a registered civil engineer and be based on adequate test borings. By local ordinance, a city may allow the report to be waived if it determines that it knows the qualities of the soils in the subdivision. In addition, by ordinance, a soils investigation may be required for each lot. If the preliminary report indicates the presence of critically expansive soils or other soils problems that, if not corrected, may lead to structural defects, then corrective action must be recommended. A city may approve the subdivision if recommended action is proposed to prevent structural damage to each structure and such action is imposed as a condition to issuance of a building permit. *See* Alquist-Priolo Special Studies Zones Act, Pub. Res. Code § 2621 *et seq.*

The state geologist is required to map earthquake fault zones. Pub. Res. Code § 2622. The State Mining and Geology Board establishes policy and criteria for approval of real estate development and structures for human occupancy in these special zones. Each development and structure must be approved for a city according to these criteria. Pub. Res. Code § 2623. Applications for all real estate developments and structures for human occupancy within earthquake fault zones must be accompanied by a geologist's report.

> Applications for all real estate developments and structures for human occupancy within earthquake fault zones must be accompanied by a geologist's report.

Setting of monuments (Gov't Code § 66495 *et seq.*). A city must require that at least one exterior boundary line of the land being subdivided be adequately monumented or referenced before the map is recorded. However, a city may, by ordinance, require additional monuments to be set.

Grading and erosion control requirements (Gov't Code § 66411). The local ordinance must provide for proper grading and erosion control, including the prevention of sedimentation or damage to off-site property.

Public access to public resources and dedication of public easements along banks of rivers and streams (Gov't Code § 66478.1 *et seq.*). Before approving a map, a city must require that there will be public access through the subdivision to public waterways, rivers, streams, coastlines, shorelines, lakes, and reservoirs, and must require dedication of public easements along banks of rivers and streams. This is based on definitive legislative policy:

> The Legislature finds and declares that the public natural resources of this state are limited in quantity and that the population of this state has grown at a rapid rate and will continue to do so, thus increasing the need for utilization of public natural resources. The increase in population has also increased demand for private property adjacent to public natural resources through real estate subdivision developments which resulted in diminishing public access to public natural resources.

Gov't Code § 66478.2

For a list of some of the navigable waters and public waterways, *see* Harbors and Navigation Code sections 100–107.

In interpreting Government Code sections 66478.1–66478.14, a court held that this law requires owners of a subdivision along a river not only to provide reasonable access to the riverbanks, but also to allocate a piece of the private land for public use. The court struck down an alternative access plan accepted by the city because it only provided access to an easement along the wrong part of the riverbank. *Kern River Pub. Access Com. v. City of Bakersfield*, 170 Cal. App. 3d 1205, 1214–15 (1985) (dedication of public easements must be "from a public access either across such tract or within a reasonable distance from such tract to that portion of the…[r]iver which borders or lies within that tract").

Energy conservation (Gov't Code § 66473.1). The design of a subdivision shall provide, to the extent feasible, for future passive or natural heating or cooling opportunities. The law shall not, however, be construed to require a reduction in allowable densities. This requirement does not apply to condominium projects that consist of the subdivision of air space in an existing building when no new structures are added. 64 Ops. Cal. Atty. Gen. 328 (1981).

Dedication for solar access easements (Gov't Code § 66475.3). This section gives a city the authority to require dedication of solar access easements as a condition of approval of a tentative map. However, an ordinance must be adopted to this effect that follows the criteria set forth in the section.

Indemnification (Gov't Code § 66474.9). A city may require, as a condition to a map application or approval, that the subdivider defend, indemnify, and hold harmless the city against any claim or action brought within the 90-day time period provided for in Government Code section 66499.37 to attack an approval by the city concerning a subdivision. Gov't Code § 66474.9(b)(1). Such condition may require indemnification of any agent, officer, and employee of the city, as well as indemnification of the city, the legislative body, and the planning commission or other advisory body. Id. However, a city may not condition map approval on a requirement that the subdivider indemnify it against a claim based on the city's action or inaction in reviewing, approving, or denying the map. Gov't Code § 66474.9(a). Any condition adopted under Government Code section 66474.9(b)(1) must include a requirement that the city promptly notify the subdivider of a claim against the city and that the city cooperate fully in the defense. Gov't Code § 66474.9(b)(2). In *Topanga Ass'n for a Scenic Community v. County of Los Angeles*, the court said that this section properly authorized the board of supervisors to require the developer to defend a legal action challenging the board's approval of a map. 214 Cal. App. 3d 1348, 1364 (1989); *see also* 85 Ops. Cal. Atty. Gen. 21 (2002) (county may require applicant to pay for defense of lawsuit challenging issuance of coastal development permit); P. Dallarda and K. Cold, Developers to the Rescue: Indemnifying Public Entities for *Litigation Arising Out of the Decision to Issue Development Permits*, 11 Cal. Land Use Law & Policy Rptr. 293 (2001).

Off-site improvements (Gov't Code § 66462.5). A city cannot postpone or refuse approval of a final map if a subdivider fails to construct or install off-site improvements on land owned by a third party. A court held that Government Code section 66462.5 only applies when approval of a final map is delayed or refused because the off-site improvements have not been completed. *Hill v. City of Clovis*, 80 Cal. App. 4th 438, 446-47 (2000). The city must act to acquire the land within 120 days of the filing of the final map or the condition is waived, unless the city, prior to final map approval, requires the subdivider to enter into an agreement to complete the off-site improvements at such time as the city acquires an interest in land that will permit the improvements to be made. In response to the *Hill* case, the Legislature amended the statute to provide that the waiver shall occur whether or not the city has postponed or refused approval of the final map. *See* Gov't Code § 66462.5(b). Note that this section is not applicable to parcel maps.

The legality of a city's consent to private condemnation of sewer and storm drainage easements, which was imposed as a condition of tentative map approval, was upheld in *L&M Professional Consultants, Inc. v. Ferreira*, 146 Cal. App. 3d 1038, 1059-60 (1983).

Standards and criteria for public improvements: residential subdivisions (Gov't Code § 65913.2). A city is prohibited from imposing on the developer of a residential subdivision more stringent standards and criteria for public improvements pursuant to the Map Act than those currently being applied by the city to its own publicly financed improvements located in similarly zoned districts within that city. In other words, a city cannot impose standards for improvements on a developer that exceed the city's own standards for constructing the same improvements with public funds.

If a city imposes engineering or surveying conditions on a tentative or a parcel map, those conditions must be reviewed by the city's engineer or surveyor to determine compliance with generally accepted engineering or surveying practices. Gov't Code § 66474.10.

CONDITIONS IMPOSED UNDER CITY'S AUTHORITY TO REGULATE "DESIGN" AND "IMPROVEMENT" AND ENSURE GENERAL AND SPECIFIC PLAN CONSISTENCY

The Map Act vests in cities the power to regulate and control the "design" and "improvement" of subdivisions. Gov't Code § 66411. These terms are broadly defined by Government Code sections 66418–66419.

The "McCarthy Legislation," passed in 1971, requires that a city, in approving a map, must make a finding that the subdivision, together with the provisions of its "design" and "improvement," are consistent with the general plan or any applicable specific plan. Gov't Code § 66473.5. This legislation, in addition to stressing the role of the general plan, expanded the power of cities to condition development. 58 Ops. Cal. Atty. Gen. 41 (1975).

The Attorney General has discussed the implications of this legislation, and concluded that a city is not limited to the traditional dedication requirements such as streets and parks, but, with proper general plan and regulatory ordinances, such dedication principles could be applied to other matters. 59 Ops. Cal. Atty. Gen. 129 (1976). The key portion of both definitions is the connection to the general plan. For example, the term "design" includes such other specific physical requirements in the plan and configuration of the entire subdivision as may be necessary to ensure consistency with or implementation of the general plan. The definition of "improvement" contains similar language. The Attorney General stated that the 1971 legislation, read together with the California Supreme Court's *Associated Home Builders* decision upholding parkland dedication, clearly indicated that the Legislature intended for cities to have greater power than they had previously. *Id.* at 132–36 (citing *Associated Home Builders, Inc. v. City of Walnut Creek*, 4 Cal. 3d 633 (1971)); *see also Ayres v. City Council*, 34 Cal. 2d 31, 35, 37 (1949) (upholding dedication and improvement conditions over a subdivider's objection that such conditions were not expressly provided for in the Map Act or local ordinance).

Courts have used these broader definitions to uphold the validity of conditions attached through the subdivision process. For example, one court found valid the conditions of approval imposed upon a condominium conversion that required building repairs and installation of smoke detectors in each unit. *Soderling v. City of Santa Monica*, 142 Cal. App. 3d 501, 509 (1983). The court pointed out that under these definitions of design and improvement, and in order to achieve one of the objectives of the city's general plan, "to promote safe housing for all," these conditions were valid, and the power to impose them need not be exercised by the specific enactment of an ordinance or the promulgation of a regulation. *See also Ayres v. City Council*, 34 Cal. 2d at 37 (finding that subdivision map conditions, even though not authorized in the Map Act or local ordinance, are lawful if they are not inconsistent with the Map Act and local ordinances and are reasonably required by the subdivision type and use).

Following the Attorney General's expansive interpretation of the McCarthy Legislation in the 1970s and the *Soderling* opinion in 1983, the California Legislature amended the Map Act in 1984 to limit the definition of "design" to "specific *physical* requirements" rather than "specific requirements" in general. 1984 Cal. Stat., ch. 1187, § 1. However, this amendment appears to have had little practical effect since: (1) it left untouched the Map Act's broad definition of "subdivision"; and (2) Government Code

> The Map Act vests in cities the power to regulate and control the "design" and "improvement" of subdivisions.

MAP ACT DEFINITIONS OF "DESIGN" AND "IMPROVEMENT"

DESIGN

(1) street alignments, grades, and widths; (2) drainage and sanitary facilities and utilities, including alignments and grades thereof; (3) location and size of all required easements and rights-of-way; (4) fire roads and firebreaks; (5) lot size and configuration; (6) traffic access; (7) grading; (8) land to be dedicated for park or recreational purposes; and (9) *other specific physical requirements in the plan and configuration of the entire subdivision as may be necessary to ensure consistency with, or implementation of, the general plan or any applicable specific plan as required pursuant to section 66473.5.*

IMPROVEMENT

(1) any street work and utilities to be installed, or agreed to be installed, by the subdivider on the land to be used for public or private streets, highways, ways and easements, as are necessary for the general use of the lot owners in the subdivision and local neighborhood traffic and drainage needs as a condition precedent to the approval and acceptance of the final map thereof; and (2) such other specific improvements or types of improvements, *the installation of which,* either by the subdivider, by public agencies, by private utilities, by any other entity approved by the local agency, or by a combination thereof, *is necessary to ensure consistency with, or implementation of, the general plan or any applicable specific plan.*

section 66473.5 requires that *subdivisions*, together with their *design and improvements*, be consistent with a city's general plan and any applicable specific plan. *See also DeVita v. County of Napa,* 9 Cal. 4th 763, 772-73 (1995) (referring to the McCarthy Legislation, the California Supreme Court observed that, "For the first time, proposed *subdivisions* and their *improvements* were required to be consistent with the general plan.... Thus after 1971 the general plan truly became, and today remains, a 'constitution' for future development.") (emphasis added).

Accordingly, utilizing the definitions of "design" and "improvement," and the independent treatment of "subdivision" under the law, a city has the authority, in proper circumstances, to require as a condition of subdivision approval the dedication of land or the payment of fees for various improvements not otherwise mentioned in the Map Act, such as child day care centers, public art, police stations, fire stations, and libraries. In addition, a city can require that certain "inclusionary" dwelling units be set aside for low- and moderate-income housing, and can impose deed restrictions to ensure that they remain so for a number of years. This authority is based on the principle that if a city's general plan requires these types of improvements, the subdivision must provide for them. Otherwise, the city must deny the map since it will not be consistent with the general plan. Gov't Code § 66474.

It is clear that if a city has the power to deny a map because it is not consistent with the general plan, then a city may impose conditions on map approval that would ensure the map's consistency with the general plan. This is predicated on the theory that the power to reject for a given factor implies the power to accept with conditions to obviate that factor. *See City of Buena Park v. Boyar,* 186 Cal. App. 2d 61, 68 (1960) (city may condition approval of a subdivision map on the installation of streets, curbs, gutters, sidewalks, etc. and payment of $50,000 to be spent by the city to construct an open drainage ditch or a concrete pipe to benefit the subdivided property).

MAP ACT REQUIREMENTS VS. GENERAL PLAN STANDARDS

If a dedication or fee condition is attached to a subdivision map approval based solely on the statutory authority of the Map Act, then the Map Act's criteria for that condition governs. For example, if a city wants to impose a condition requiring parkland dedication or payment of in-lieu park fees as part of the subdivision process, a city, by ordinance, may do so. Gov't Code § 66477; *see also Associated Home Builders, Inc. v. City of Walnut Creek,* 4 Cal. 3d 633, 640-41 (1971). Therefore, if the city attaches this condition to the approval of a map, it must adhere to the limitation of three to five acres per 1,000 residents as set forth in the Map Act.

However, a different rule applies if a dedication or fee is attached to a non-subdivision approval, such as an application for rezoning or a conditional use permit. In such situations, the imposition of dedications or fees is governed by a city's general police power, and subject to the United States Supreme Court's "nexus" and "rough proportionality" tests.[10] Consequently, if a city's general plan calls for six or seven acres per 1,000 residents, then a city may impose this higher standard under its general police power if this condition is attached to a non-subdivision approval, rather than a subdivision map approval, and the city has adopted a regulation to that effect. 73 Ops. Cal. Atty. Gen. 152, 156 (1990).

---

10 The "nexus" and "rough proportionality" test set forth in the *Nollan* and *Dolan* decisions is also discussed in chapter 11 (Takings) and chapter 12 (Exactions).

CONDITIONS THAT MAY BE IMPOSED THROUGH THE CEQA PROCESS

The California Environmental Quality Act of 1970 (Pub. Res. Code § 21000 et seq.) has a peculiar impact upon the application of Government Code section 66474(e), which states, in part, that a city shall deny a subdivision if it finds that the design of the subdivision or the proposed improvements are likely to cause substantial environmental damage or substantially injure fish or wildlife or their habitats. An environmental impact report that comments upon the amount of substantial environmental damage or injury to fish or wildlife caused by the subdivision could constitute the basis for a finding on those matters that would necessitate the denial of the subdivision map. CEQA requires that an EIR be prepared by a city before it approves a private project having a significant effect on the environment if the city has discretion to either approve or disapprove the project.

CEQA = California Environmental Quality Act

EIR = environmental impact report

It is clear that if the EIR points out negative impacts, the city may impose conditions to mitigate those impacts based on Government Code section 66474(e). The imposition of mitigating conditions is based on the theory that the power to reject because of a specific impact implies the power to accept with conditions that would obviate that impact. *See City of Buena Park v. Boyar*, 186 Cal. App. 2d 61, 66-7 (1960). A city cannot use its CEQA powers to attach conditions to approval (Pub. Res. Code § 21004), but that does not limit the city in the subdivision approval process since it is relying on its powers under Government Code section 66474(e).

There are special rules relating to school impact fees, since a city cannot levy these fees as a CEQA mitigation. Gov't Code § 65996(b). A line of cases had held that this prohibition did not apply to *legislative*, as opposed to adjudicatory, actions. For example, it did not apply to general plan amendments or rezonings. *Mira Dev. Corp. v. City of San Diego*, 205 Cal. App. 3d 1201, 1217 (1988); *see also Murrieta Valley Unified Sch. Dist. v. County of Riverside*, 228 Cal. App. 3d 1212, 1230-31 (1991); *William S. Hart Union High Sch. Dist. v. Reg'l Planning Comm'n*, 226 Cal. App. 3d 1612, 1625 (1991). Relying on these decisions, many cities required payment of school fees in excess of the statutory limits as a condition to granting rezoning, general plan amendments, and other legislative approvals.

In 1998, however, the Legislature enacted the Leroy F. Greene School Facilities Act (SB 50), 1998 Cal. Stat. ch. 407 (the "1998 Act"), which significantly amended the statutory scheme for school fees. Most important, it eliminated the rule of the *Mira-Hart-Murrieta* trilogy—i.e., that the statutory limitations on school impact fees and mitigation apply only to adjudicative, not legislative, actions. Gov't Code § 65995.

The 1998 Act amended Government Code section 65995(a) to prohibit state or local agencies from imposing school impact mitigation fees, dedications, or other requirements in excess of those provided in the statute in connection with "any legislative or adjudicative act...by any state or local agency involving...the planning, use, or development of real property...."

The legislation also amended Government Code section 65996(b) to prohibit local agencies from using the inadequacy of school facilities as a basis for denying or conditioning approvals of any "legislative or adjudicative act...involving...the planning, use or development of real property...." The express inclusion of "legislative" approvals in the statute evidences a legislative intent to overturn the *Mira-Hart-Murrieta* line of cases. For further discussion of this legislation, see chapter 12 (Exactions).

Further, a court has held that Government Code section 66474(e) provides for environmental review separate from and independent of the requirements of CEQA. *Topanga Ass'n for a Scenic Community v. County of Los Angeles*, 214 Cal. App. 3d 1348, 1355-56 (1989).

In *Topanga*, the court held that the finding required by that section is in addition to the requirements for the preparation of an EIR or a negative declaration. It further stated that this section requires disapproval of a project upon a finding that it is likely to cause substantial environmental damage; it does not require a finding of no substantial environmental damage as a condition of approval of a project. Finally, the court held that the term "substantial environmental damage" as used in Government Code section 66474(e) is the equivalent of "significant effect on the environment," which is defined in Public Resources Code section 21068 as "a substantial, or potentially substantial, adverse change in the environment." 68 Ops. Cal. Atty. Gen. 108, 111 n.2 (1985). However, the court held that the county made a proper finding of no substantial damage when it found:

> The design of the subdivision and the proposed improvements will not cause substantial environmental damage or substantial and avoidable injury to fish or wildlife or their habitat, since the project is not located in a Significant Ecological Area and the initial study for the project shows that the proposed development will not have a significant effect on the environment.

Topanga, 214 Cal. App. 3d at 1356

CONDOMINIUM, STOCK COOPERATIVE, AND COMMUNITY APARTMENT PROJECT CONVERSIONS

> Since condominium and stock cooperative conversions are governed by the Map Act, a city may be able to require dedications when a conversion is proposed.

Since condominium and stock cooperative conversions are governed by the Map Act, a city may be able to require dedications when a conversion is proposed. One of the leading condominium conversion cases is *Norsco Enters. v. City of Fremont*, which held that a city could require parkland dedication fees for condominium conversion even though no new residences had been added. 54 Cal. App. 3d 488, 498 (1976).

> Moreover, we find no unconstitutional legislative discrimination, as claimed by Norsco, in classifying differently, existing apartment buildings with rental units and similar apartment buildings for which the owner seeks municipal authorization for subdivision into condominium units....
>
> It seems not unreasonable that an apartment house owner seeking, for his presumable economic advantage, the City's permission to convert his already occupied rental units into condominiums, be assessed a reasonable amount for additional park and recreational facilities in the neighborhood.

Id. at 497-98

After this decision, the Legislature amended the law to provide that dedication cannot be required in condominium conversions where no new residences are added. Gov't Code § 66477(a)(9)(d). However, the principle that reasonable conditions can be imposed on condominium conversions enunciated in *Norsco* remains and might be applicable in other contexts.

For instance, in *Soderling v. City of Santa Monica*, the court held that since condominium conversion projects are subdivisions, a denial of map approval is required when there is a failure to fulfill design conditions authorized by local ordinance. 142 Cal. App. 3d 501, 506-07 (1983). That same year, the court held that a city acted properly in denying a conversion since it did not comply with present zoning. *Rasmussen v. City Council*, 140 Cal. App. 3d 842 (1983). Further, the court stated that a council finding that there may be a "domino effect" on other apartments (resulting in the conversion of other nearby apartments) was reasonable grounds for denial.

In addition, there are two important Attorney General opinions on condominium conversions. The first stated that cities possess powers necessary under the Map Act to set up condominium conversion restrictions. 58 Ops. Cal. Atty. Gen. 41 (1975). The second stated that the Map Act requires the processing of tentative and final subdivision maps to convert an existing apartment or house to a condominium, even though the condominium will be located on a single lot created by an earlier approved final subdivision map. 62 Ops. Cal. Atty. Gen. 410 (1979).

Also, before a final map is approved for a residential condominium conversion, special findings must be made relating to tenant notices. Those findings are contained in Government Code section 66427.1.

TIMING OF CONDITIONS AND SUBSEQUENT CONDITIONS

In determining whether to approve or disapprove an application for a tentative map, a city may impose only those ordinances, policies, and standards that are already in effect at the time the application for the tentative or parcel map has been deemed complete pursuant to Government Code section 65943 (the Permit Streamlining Act). Gov't Code § 66474.2(a). However, in certain circumstances, if the city has formally taken steps to change its requirements, it can attach the new requirements that are in effect at the time of approval. Gov't Code § 66474.2.

Further, under the so-called "one bite of the apple" rule, conditions that could have been placed on a tentative map, but were not, may not be placed on a subsequent building permit or other type of permit for residential construction with the following exceptions:

- More than five years have passed since the final map was recorded
- The condition is necessary to protect public health and safety
- The condition is necessary to comply with state or federal law
- The condition is necessary to ensure compliance with applicable zoning ordinances

Gov't Code § 65961; see also Beck Dev. Co. v. Southern Pac. Transp. Co., 44 Cal. App. 4th 1160, 1199–1200 (1996)

When it extended the life of valid tentative maps in 2009, 2011, and 2013, the Legislature also modified application of the "one bite of the apple" rule to maps relying on those extensions. For maps extended pursuant to Government Code sections 66452.22, 66452.23, or 66452.24, the five-year protection against imposition of certain new conditions under Government Code section 65961 is shortened to three years and the city is not prohibited from levying a fee or imposing a condition that requires the payment of a fee upon the issuance of a building permit, including, but not limited to, a fee defined in Government Code section 66000. See Gov't Code section 65961(e), (f).

In *Laguna Village, Inc. v. County of Orange*, the court held that Government Code section 65961 did not preclude the imposition of school impact fees at the time of issuance of the building permit, even though a map had been approved. 166 Cal. App. 3d 125, 131 (1985); see also *Golden State Homebuilding Ass'n v. City of Modesto*, 26 Cal. App. 4th 601, 608 (1994) (a city could lawfully condition issuance of building permits on development fees not yet established at the time of map approval). The court explicitly held that Government Code section 65961 did not protect the subdivider. *Laguna Village*, 166 Cal. App. 3d at 131. The "one bite of the apple" rule of section 65961 likewise provides no protection against zoning changes that occur after approval of a tentative map. *Hafen v. County of Orange*, 128 Cal. App. 4th 133, 142-43 (2005) (approval of a tentative map does not insulate developer from future zoning changes unless vested rights have been obtained). For further discussion of how to obtain and protect vested rights, see chapter 10 (Vested Rights).

REFUNDS

After a map has been recorded, the Map Act provides the exclusive procedures for obtaining refunds of unused and unnecessary subdivision fees after reversion to acreage (Gov't Code §§ 66499.17, 66499.19), park fees (Gov't Code § 66477(a)(6)), and storm drainage and sanitary sewer fees (Gov't Code § 66483.2). A request for a refund of development fees can be denied if the developer fails to comply with statutory refund procedures. *See B&P Dev. Corp. v. City of Saratoga*, 185 Cal. App. 3d 949 (1986). However, fees may be refunded if the subdivision map was not recorded. *See Wright Dev. Co. v. City of Mountain View*, 53 Cal. App. 3d 274, 276 (1975).

RECONVEYANCES

If a property is dedicated in fee to a local agency for a public purpose, and the agency determines that the purpose no longer exists, it must reconvey the property back to the subdivider or its successor in interest. Gov't Code § 66477(a). This rule does not apply to: (1) land dedicated for open space, parks, or schools; (2) land that was required to be dedicated before January 1, 1990; or (3) any portion of the land that is required for the public purpose or for public utilities. Gov't Code § 66477(a)-(e). The subdivider may pay a fee and request that the local agency determine whether the public purpose for which the land was dedicated still exists. Gov't Code § 66477(b). The determination may be based on a capital improvement plan, a general or specific plan, the subdivision map, or other public documents that identify the need for the dedication.

The law also provides that the city must give the subdivider 60 days' notice prior to vacating, leasing, selling, or otherwise disposing of the property, unless it will be used for the same public purpose for which it was dedicated. Gov't Code § 66477(d).

GROUNDS FOR MAP APPROVAL OR DENIAL

GROUNDS FOR APPROVAL

Before a tentative map or a parcel map is approved, a city must find that the proposed subdivision, together with the provisions for its design and improvement, is consistent with the general plan and any applicable specific plan. Gov't Code § 66473.5; *see also Woodland Hills Residents Ass'n, Inc. v. City Council*, 44 Cal. App. 3d 825, 832-33 (1975) (*Woodland Hills I*). However, the law does not require an exact match. The map need only be "in agreement with or in harmony with the general plan." *Sequoyah Hills Homeowners Ass'n v. City of Oakland*, 23 Cal. App. 4th 704, 707 (1993). In addition, a city should make a "housing balance finding," and a finding relating to future passive or natural heating or cooling opportunities. Gov't Code §§ 66412.3, 66473.1.

The importance of the consistency finding is reflected in the language of *Woodland Hills Residents Association, Inc. v. City Council* (*Woodland Hills II*):

> As plaintiffs suggest, the legislative history of the Subdivision Map Act illuminates the Legislature's acute awareness that approval of subdivisions which are inconsistent with a locality's general plan "subverts the integrity...

of the local planning process." (Subcommittee on Premature Subdivisions, Staff Recommendations for Legislative Action (January 15, 1971), p. 4.) To preserve the integrity of the "general plan" concept, the Legislature enacted Government Code sections 66473.5 and 66474.60, subd. (c)..., mandating that a subdivision map may not be approved unless the appropriate agencies first find that the subdivision is consistent with the applicable general plan. Plaintiffs argue, with much force, that once a general plan has been formulated, the public has an overriding interest in the faithful enforcement of the guidelines established by the plan as applied to proposed subdivisions.

23 Cal. 3d 917, 936 (1979)

However, any policies in the general plan related to school facilities are preempted by Government Code section 65996(a), which provides that the school facilities legislation is the exclusive method of mitigating school impacts. This section prevails over Government Code section 66473.5, since the former is more specific and was adopted later; therefore, a city cannot use the general plan consistency rule to deny a map where it does not comply with a school facilities policy. *See Corona-Norco Unified Sch. Dist. v. City of Corona*, 13 Cal. App. 4th 1577 (1993)

If a map is inconsistent with a city's general plan or if general plan elements relevant to the map are legally inadequate, the map is vulnerable to a legal challenge. *See, e.g., Camp v. Board of Supervisors*, 123 Cal. App. 3d 334, (1981). However, as with zoning consistency, a city's consistency finding will not be disturbed unless it is based on evidence from which no reasonable person could have reached the same conclusion. *Corona-Norco Unified Sch. Dist. v. City of Corona (Corona-Norco II)*, 17 Cal. App. 4th 985, 992 (1993); *see also Sequoyah Hills Homeowners*, 23 Cal. App. 4th 704 (1993).

When a proposed adoption or amendment to a general plan is at issue, the Governor's Office of Planning and Research conditions with respect to an extension of time to adopt or amend a general plan pursuant to Government Code section 65361 can require that tentative maps be consistent with the proposed general plan if the proposed general plan has been approved by the planning commission. *Harroman Co. v. Town of Tiburon*, 235 Cal. App. 3d 388, 393-94 (1991).

Before approving a tentative map, or a parcel map for which a tentative map was not required, for an area located in a state responsibility area or a very high fire hazard severity zone (as both are defined in Government Code section 51177), the City shall make: a) a finding supported by substantial evidence in the record that the design and location of each lot in the subdivision, and the subdivision as a whole, are consistent with any applicable regulations adopted by the State Board of Forestry and Fire Protection pursuant to Sections 4290 and 4290 of the Public Resources Code; b) a finding supported by substantial evidence in the record that structural fire protection and suppression services will be available for the subdivision through a county, city, special district, political subdivision of the state, other entity organized to provide fire protection services monitored and funded by a county or other public entity, or the Department of Forestry and Fire Protection through a contract entered into pursuant to Section 4133, 4142, or 4144 of the Public Resources Code; and c) a finding that, to the extent practicable, ingress and egress for the subdivision meets the regulations regarding road standards for fire equipment access adopted pursuant to Section 4290 of the Public Resources Code and any applicable local ordinance. Gov't Code § 66474.02. The requirement for these fire protection findings does not supersede any local ordinance that provides equivalent or more stringent minimum requirements on the same subject. *Id.*

> If a map is inconsistent with a city's general plan or if general plan elements relevant to the map are legally inadequate, the map is vulnerable to a legal challenge.

GROUNDS FOR DENIAL

In approving or disapproving a map, a city shall apply only those ordinances, policies, or standards in effect at the time the application was deemed complete, with certain exceptions. Gov't Code § 66474.2.

No city shall disapprove a tentative, final, or parcel map in order to comply with the time limits specified in chapter 3 of the Map Act (Gov't Code § 66451 et seq.), unless there are reasons for disapproval other than the failure to timely act in accordance with the time limits. Gov't Code § 66451.4.

If a city makes any of the following findings with respect to a tentative map or a parcel map, it must deny approval of the map. Gov't Code § 66474.

- The proposed map or the design or improvements of the proposed subdivision are inconsistent with the applicable general and specific plans (*Woodland Hills I*, 44 Cal. App. 3d at 825), or with a draft general plan being prepared under an OPR extension (*Harroman*, 235 Cal. App. 3d at 388; see also Gov't Code § 65361(e))

- The site is not physically suited for the proposed type or density of development (*Carmel Valley View, Ltd. v. Board of Supervisors*, 58 Cal. App. 3d 817, 822-23 (1976) (upholding the disapproval of a map because a site was not physically suited for the proposed development)). However, where such a finding has been made, the city may approve the map on conditions that will reduce the density. 56 Ops. Cal. Atty. Gen. 274 (1973)

- The design or proposed improvements are likely to cause substantial environmental damage, or substantially and unavoidably injure fish, wildlife, or their habitats, or cause serious public health problems. Regarding assessment of environmental impacts (Gov't Code § 66474(e)), see the California Environmental Quality Act of 1970 (Pub. Res. Code §§ 21000-21178.1) and 59 Ops. Cal. Atty. Gen. 129 (1976). Notwithstanding Government Code section 66474(e), a city may approve a map if an EIR was prepared and appropriate findings are made that specific economic, social, or other considerations make infeasible the mitigation measures or project alternatives identified in the EIR. Gov't Code § 66474.01

- The design or the types of subdivision improvements will conflict with public easements for access through or use of property within the proposed subdivision. A city may approve the map if alternative public easements will be provided

In addition to these specific grounds for denial contained in Government Code section 66474, a city must disapprove a map if the design of the subdivision does not provide for, to the extent feasible, future passive or natural heating or cooling opportunities. Gov't Code § 66473.1; 64 Ops. Cal. Atty. Gen. 328 (1981). Also, a city must disapprove a map for the applicant's failure to perform any of the requirements or conditions imposed by the Map Act or local ordinance pursuant thereto. Gov't Code § 66473.

A city may disapprove a tentative map if discharge of waste from the proposed subdivision would violate existing requirements prescribed by a regional water quality control board. Gov't Code § 66474.6.

A city must disapprove a map if the property is subject to a Williamson Act contract, open space easement, agricultural conservation easement, or conservation easement if the resulting parcels would be too small to sustain their agricultural use or will result in residential development not incidental to the agricultural uses. Gov't Code

§ 66474.4(a). Absent specific findings to the contrary, a parcel is too small to sustain agricultural use if it is less than 10 acres of prime agricultural land, or less than 40 acres of nonprime agricultural land. Gov't Code § 66474.4(b).

For further discussion of the Williamson Act, see chapter 9 (Design Review and Other Development Regulations).

In response to concerns over flood control, the legislature in 2007 added certain flood hazard conditions to those that require map disapproval. The 2007 legislation required each city and county within the Sacramento-San Joaquin Valley to amend its general plan to make provisions for the protection of lives and property from flood hazards. Gov't Code § 65302.9. Once those amendments become effective, the legislative bodies of these cities and counties are required to reject any tentative map, or parcel map for which a tentative map is required, for any subdivision lying within a "flood hazard zone" unless the body can make certain findings (Gov't Code § 66474.5(a)):

- The facilities of the State Plan of Flood Control or other management facilities protect the subdivision to the urban level of flood protection in urban or urbanizing areas, or to the national FEMA standard of flood protection in non-urban areas. Gov't Code § 66474.5(a)(1)
- The conditions imposed on the subdivision by the city or county will protect the subdivision to the relevant standard above. Gov't Code § 66474.5(a)(2), or
- The local flood management agency has made adequate progress on the construction of flood protection sufficient to provide protection to the relevant standard above. For urban or urbanizing areas, the protection level must be achieved by 2025. Gov't Code § 66474.5(a)(3)
- The property in an undetermined risk area has met the urban level of flood protection based on substantial evidence in the record. Gov't Code § 66474.5(a)(4)

The Sacramento-San Joaquin Valley is defined in Government Code section 65007 to include lands within the bed of the Sacramento or San Joaquin rivers and their tributaries, along or near the banks of these rivers or streams, and within their overflow basins, except lands in the Tulare Lake basin, including the Kings River.

FEMA = Federal Emergency Management Agency

FINDINGS FOR APPROVAL OR DENIAL

In approving or denying a map, a city must make findings that meet the test set forth in *Topanga Association for a Scenic Community v. County of Los Angeles*, 11 Cal. 3d 506 (1974). These findings are the legal footprints that a city must leave behind to explain how it progressed from the facts presented through established policies to the decision to grant or deny a map. Not only must findings be made, but more importantly, there must be evidence in the record to justify these findings. Evidence can be in the form of staff reports, written and oral testimony, exhibits, and the like. For a more detailed discussion of findings, see chapter 17 (Rights of the Regulated).

APPEALS AND JUDICIAL REVIEW

APPEALS

Under the Map Act, the subdivider may appeal the action of the advisory agency, e.g., a planning commission. Gov't Code § 66452.5(a). In addition, tenants in condominium conversions have the right to appeal. The Map Act provides a limited right of appeal of interested persons to appeal findings made by an advisory agency or appeals board concerning general and specific plan consistency, suitable siting, environmental concerns, and other items listed under Government Code sections 66474, 66474.1, and 66474.6. Gov't Code § 66474.7. In addition, the Map Act provides that any interested person adversely affected by a decision of the advisory agency may file an appeal with the city council. Gov't Code § 66452.5(d). Then, upon filing of the appeal, the city council shall set the matter for hearing and act on the appeal. For a general discussion on appeals, *see* 73 Ops. Cal. Atty. Gen. 338 (1990). Note that a city planning director can be an "interested person adversely affected" under Government Code section 66452.5(d), and may appeal a planning commission decision to the city council even without an enabling ordinance to that effect. 71 Ops. Cal. Atty. Gen. 326 (1988); *but see Cohan v. City of Thousand Oaks*, 30 Cal. App. 4th 547, 559-60 (1994) (a city council is not an interested person permitted to appeal a planning commission's approval of a tentative map). The *Cohan* court limited its holding so as not to invalidate all appeals taken by a city council or other governing body to itself from a decision of a subordinate body. The court emphasized that such a procedure should, however, be authorized by the ordinances or rules that govern appeals to such entity. These rules are necessary to ensure fairness and due process. "A fair trial in a fair tribunal is a basic requirement of due process." *Bullock v. City and County of San Francisco*, 221 Cal. App. 3d 1072, 1091 (1990). In *Cohan*, the city council disregarded the procedural and substantive due process rights of the developer. It was the cumulative effects of the council's actions that caused the court to nullify the council's appeal to itself. 30 Cal. App. 4th at 561.

However, one court held that when a city code specifically permitted filing of an appeal from a planning commission's decision by a city council member, such an appeal did not violate due process. *Breakzone Billiards v. City of Torrance*, 81 Cal. App. 4th 1205, 1239-41 (2000) (citing *Withrow v. Larkin*, 421 U.S. 35, 53, 56-57 (1975)). On appeal, the city council is not bound by the findings of the advisory agency and may hear the matter *de novo* and make its own determinations based on any relevant testimony or documents produced before it. Gov't Code § 66452.5(d); *see Langrutta v. City Council*, 9 Cal. App. 3d 890, 895 (1970).

JUDICIAL REVIEW

Exhaustion of administrative remedies. Before judicial relief is sought, all administrative remedies must be exhausted. If there is a failure to exhaust, there can be no judicial review. Gov't Code § 65009; *Sea & Sage Audubon Soc'y, Inc. v. Planning Comm'n*, 34 Cal. 3d 412, 417-18 (1983); *Tahoe Vista Concerned Citizens v. County of Placer*, 81 Cal. App. 4th 577, 589-90 (2000); *Coalition for Student Action v. City of Fullerton*, 153 Cal. App. 3d 1194, 1197-98 (1984). If a city seeks to invoke the doctrine of exhaustion, it must include a notice to this effect in its public hearing notice. Gov't Code § 65009(b)(2). If a city fails to do so, it may lose this defense in a court challenge. *Kings County Farm Bureau v. City of Hanford*, 221 Cal. App. 3d 692, 740 (1990). For further discussion of judicial review of tentative map approvals, see chapter 19 (Land Use Litigation).

Statute of limitations. Any action to attack a decision concerning a subdivision must be commenced and summons must be served within 90 days after the date of such decision. Gov't Code § 66499.37; *see also Maginn v. City of Glendale*, 72 Cal. App. 4th 1102, 1104 (1999) (statute of limitations to be strictly enforced); *Sprague v. County of San Diego*, 106 Cal. App. 4th 119 (2003) (dismissing case because summons was served late, although suit was filed on time). The time period runs from the date of the decision. For example, the time to attack conditions imposed by a tentative map runs from approval of the tentative map, not from final map approval. *Soderling v. City of Santa Monica*, 142 Cal. App. 3d 501, 505 (1983). The 90-day period applies to a failure to issue a certificate of compliance, as well as to map approvals, denials, conditions, and subdivision improvement agreements. *Hunt v. County of Shasta*, 225 Cal. App. 3d 432, 446 (1990); *see also Anthony v. Snyder*, 116 Cal. App. 4th 643 (2004) (holding that a lawsuit over a subdivision improvement agreement amounted to an action "concerning a subdivision" and therefore the 90-day limitations period applied); *Stell v. Jay Hales Dev. Co.*, 11 Cal. App. 4th 1214, 1228–29 (1992). The denial of an application to grant an extension for the life of a tentative map also triggers the 90-day statute of limitations. *Jamul v. Board of Supervisors*, 231 Cal. App. 3d 665, 670 (1991). As the court in *Jamul* stated, the broad language of Government Code section 66499.37 applies whenever "'the conduct of a local agency under the Subdivision Map Act is called into question,' even where it allegedly exercised no discretion under the act." *Id.* at 672 (citation omitted); *see also, Aiuto v. City and County of San Francisco*, 201 Cal. App. 4th 1347, 1360–61 (2011) (applying 90-day statute of limitations to facial challenge to ordinance amending provisions of city-wide below market rate housing program as "concerning a subdivision"). Failure to comply with the service of summons requirements can be a bar to litigation under the California Environmental Quality Act (Pub. Res. Code § 21000 et seq.). *See Friends of Riverside's Hills v. City of Riverside*, 168 Cal. App. 4th 793 (2008) (Gov't Code section 66499.37 applies to CEQA actions challenging subdivision approvals, despite CEQA's separate requirements); *see also Torrey Hills Community Coalition v. City of San Diego*, 186 Cal. App. 4th 429, 435–36 (2010).

In *Hensler v. City of Glendale*, the California Supreme Court addressed a claim that the application of a ridgeline ordinance in a condition of approval of the owner's subdivision map constituted a "taking" requiring just compensation. 8 Cal. 4th 1, 6 (1994). The court held that this claim was barred by the 90-day statute of limitations of the Map Act because the ridgeline ordinance was part of the city's subdivision regulations. In contrast, a court of appeal has ruled that a developer could sue for inverse condemnation within the five-year period applicable for such claims where the challenged condition was imprecisely drafted in that a condition the city sought to enforce was not contained in the language of the tentative map. *Uniwill L.P. v. City of Los Angeles*, 124 Cal. App. 4th 537, 542 (2004). The court reasoned that such a vague map condition is not subject to the Map Act's 90-day statute of limitations.

A claim alleging a breach of a subdivision-related development agreement is generally subject to the statute of limitations period for contract claims. However, those portions of the claim that could be challenged directly under the Map Act are subject to the shorter 90-day limitations period of section 66499.37. *Legacy Group v. City of Wasco*, 106 Cal. App. 4th 1305 (2003). In *Legacy*, a developer sued the city for breaching a development agreement by refusing to approve final subdivision maps, and for halting payments on improvements made to the property. The city argued the suit was time barred by the Map Act. The court held that the claim challenging denial of maps was subject to the Map Act's 90-day limitations period, but found the remaining claims were subject to the statute of limitations for contract claims. The court observed that this rule "precludes the parties from avoiding the application of section 66499.37 to decisions arising under the [Map Act] simply by restating as contractual covenants the responsibilities imposed on local government by the [Map Act]." *Id.* at 1313.

The statute of limitations period applicable to a claim challenging excessive fees imposed as a condition to the approval of a tentative map or parcel map depends on the manner in which the fee is challenged. When a party avails itself of the fee protest

> The statute of limitations period applicable to a claim challenging excessive fees imposed as a condition to the approval of a tentative map or parcel map depends on the manner in which the fee is challenged.

procedures of Government Code section 66020 to challenge allegedly excessive fees imposed upon a development project, the limitations period is the one established by section 66020 (180 days). However, where a party does not comply with the fee protest procedures of section 66020, a traditional mandate action must be brought within the 90-day limitations period specified by Government Code § 66499.37; *see Branciforte Heights, LLC*, 138 Cal. App. 4th at 928–29 (developer's compliance with the protest procedures set forth in section 66020 made 180-day statute of limitations applicable, rather than the 90-day period in a traditional mandate action); *see also Trinity Park L.P. v. City of Sunnyvale*, 193 Cal. App. 4th 1014, 1035–36 (2011) (affordable housing condition of approval was not intended to "defray all or a portion of the cost of public facilities related to the development project" and therefore did not constitute an "exaction" subject to Government Code section 66020 and its 180-day statute of limitations). For a more detailed discussion of Government Code section 66020, see chapter 19 (Land Use Litigation).

FINAL MAPS AND PARCEL MAPS

FINAL MAPS

Form and filing of final maps. The Map Act contains detailed provisions governing the content and form of the final map. Gov't Code § 66433 *et seq*. These sections establish the persons who are qualified to prepare the final map, the standard for preparation, and the various certificates and acknowledgments required for the final map.

The final map must be prepared under the direction of a registered civil engineer or a licensed land surveyor and be based on a survey. Gov't Code § 66434. Detailed requirements for its format are also contained in Government Code section 66434. Only final and parcel maps (not tentative maps) may be filed for recording in the county recorder's office. Gov't Code § 66429. The written consent of all parties having any record title interest in the real property proposed to be subdivided must be obtained as a prerequisite to the recordation of a final or parcel map. Gov't Code § 66430.

Various certificates, statements, and acknowledgments must accompany the final map under Government Code sections 66435–66443, including:

- A statement signed and acknowledged by all parties having any record title interest in the property consenting to preparation and recordation of the final map must appear on the map. Excluded from this requirement are various lienholders, parties owning easements, rights-of-way, owners of beneficial interests or trustees under deeds of trust (but not both), and holders of other interests that cannot ripen into a fee. Gov't Code § 66436
- Certain statements of dedication, including dedications of interests in real property for specified public purposes, such as streets and public utility easements. Gov't Code § 66439
- A certificate or statement for execution by the clerk of each approving legislative body, stating that the body approved the map and accepted any real property offered for dedication for public use. Gov't Code § 66440
- The certificate or statement of a city engineer or county surveyor. Gov't Code § 66442(a). The certificate/statement must state that the official has examined the map, that the subdivision is substantially the same as it appeared on the tentative map, that there has been compliance with all applicable provisions of the Map Act and local ordinances, and that the official is satisfied that the

map is "technically correct." This certificate or statement must be completed and filed with the appropriate legislative body within 20 days from the date the final map is submitted to the official by the subdivider for approval. Gov't Code § 66442(b). Government Code section 66442.5 identifies specific text to be included in the engineer's or surveyor's statement and a recorder's certificate or statement on the final map.

Multiple final maps may be filed before expiration of the tentative map if (1) at the time the tentative map is filed, the subdivider informs the city of its intent to file multiple final maps; or (2) the city and the subdivider later concur in the filing of multiple final maps. Gov't Code § 66456.1. The right of a subdivider to file multiple final maps under this section does not limit a city's authority to impose reasonable conditions relating to the filing of multiple final maps. Gov't Code § 66456.1.

Procedures for approval. It is important to file a final map with a city before the tentative map expires. The expiration of the tentative map terminates all proceedings, and no final map or parcel map can be filed without first processing a new tentative map. Once a timely filing is made, subsequent actions of the city, including but not limited to processing, approval, and recording, may lawfully occur after the date of expiration of the tentative map. Gov't Code § 66452.6(d). Delivery to the county surveyor or city engineer shall be deemed a timely filing for purposes of this section. The Map Act does not indicate what constitutes a "timely filing." It usually goes beyond presenting the map to the city, and includes such things as improvement agreements, bonds, evidence of other agency approvals, and a completed plan check. One must look at the local ordinances or procedures for specific requirements by a city in order for the map to be "timely filed."

> The Map Act does not indicate what constitutes a "timely filing." It usually goes beyond presenting the map to the city, and includes such things as improvement agreements, bonds, evidence of other agency approvals, and a completed plan check.

In *McPherson v. City of Manhattan Beach*, the court clarified that Government Code section 66452.6(d) was intended to protect the subdivider if the city failed to record the map through no fault of the subdivider. 78 Cal. App. 4th 1252, 1263 (2000). The developer filed a final parcel map with the city engineer, but did not pay the requisite property taxes or submit data for monument inspection approval. After the tentative map expired, the developer paid the taxes and submitted the monument data. The court held that under the unique circumstances of this case, delivery of the final parcel map to the city engineer did not constitute a timely filing. *McPherson*, 78 Cal. App. 4th at 1263; *see also Ailanto Props., Inc. v. City of Half Moon Bay*, 142 Cal. App. 4th 572 (2006) (following *McPherson* and holding that filing a phased final map that does not conform to the tentative map's requirements would not entitle the map to a 36-month extension under Government Code section 66452.6(a)(1); implicit in the extension provision is the requirement that the final map substantively complies with the Map Act).

The approval of a final map is ministerial if the final map is in substantive compliance with a properly approved tentative map, and the subdivider has satisfied the conditions of approval attached to the tentative map. *Youngblood v. Board of Supervisors*, 22 Cal. 3d 644, 656 (1978); *see also* Gov't Code § 66474.1. The developer is entitled to acceptance and approval of the final map, without the imposition of new or altered conditions, particularly those that are of a technical nature. *Anthony v. Snyder*, 116 Cal. App. 4th 643, 660, 664 (2004) (holding that the developer has a right to rely on the conditions established during tentative map approval). Accordingly, it is essential to make sure the final map is timely filed. *Santa Monica Pines, Ltd. v. Rent Control Bd.*, 35 Cal. 3d 858, 863 (1984); Gov't Code §§ 66458, 66474.1.

However, final maps cannot be ministerially approved if the map conditions are not fulfilled. The Map Act requires disapproval of a map if it fails to meet or perform any of the conditions imposed by the Map Act or local ordinance. Gov't Code § 66473; *see also Soderling,* 142 Cal. App. 3d at 507; *Kriebel v. City Council,* 112 Cal. App. 3d 693, 703 (1980) (observing that "[a]pproval of the final map in effect is a confirmation that the tentative map requirements have been fulfilled"). The disapproval of a final map must be accompanied by a finding that identifies the conditions that have not been met. Gov't Code § 66473. A local ordinance that implements the Map Act is required to set forth a procedure for waiving the requirements of Government Code section 66473 when failure of a map is due to a technical or inadvertent error that does not materially affect the map's validity.

The city council may delegate, by ordinance, the authority to approve or disapprove a final map to the city or county engineer, surveyor, or other designated official. Gov't Code § 66458(d). The ordinance that permits an official to approve or disapprove final maps must require the official to notify the city council when he or she is reviewing a map, contain specified time limits, provide notice of pending approval or disapproval by the official, state that the official's decisions may be appealed to the city council, and require periodic legislative review of the delegation of authority. Gov't Code § 66458(d).

If the city council or a designated official does not approve or disapprove the map within the prescribed time, or within any authorized extension, and the map conforms to all requirements and rulings, it shall be deemed approved, and the city clerk shall certify or state its approval thereon. Gov't Code § 66458(b).

A newly incorporated city may have discretion to disapprove a final map despite its substantial conformance with a county-approved tentative map depending on the timing and sequence of incorporation proceedings relative to the processing of the map. Gov't Code § 66413.5; *City of Goleta v. Superior Court,* 40 Cal. 4th 270, 276-77 (2006). For further discussion of the effect of incorporation upon a subdivision map, *see* Tentative Map Processing—Effect of Incorporation, this chapter.

FINAL MAP IS DEEMED VALID WHEN RECORDED

Unless otherwise provided by the county, if the final map or parcel map is not subject to Government Code section 66493 (relating to security for taxes), after the city's approval of a final map or parcel map, the city clerk shall transmit the map to the county recorder. Gov't Code § 66464(a). Once a final map or parcel map is recorded by the county recorder, it is deemed valid and imparts constructive notice to parties of interest. Gov't Code § 66468. Certain steps (set forth below) must occur, however, before the county records the final or parcel map.

Filing of certificates and security for tax liens. If at the time the final map is to be recorded, the subdivided property is subject to a lien for taxes (or special assessments collected as taxes) and those taxes are not yet payable, the subdivider must file the following two items with the clerk of the board of supervisors of the county where any part of the subdivision is located:

- A certificate of statement prepared by the appropriate state or local official, which estimates the amount of taxes or assessments subject to the lien. Gov't Code § 66493(a)(1), and
- Security conditioned upon the payment of all state, county, municipal, and local taxes and the current installment of principal and interest of all special assessments collected as taxes that are not yet payable. Gov't Code § 66493(a)(2). The security requirement may be waived by the county after consultation with the tax collector for a final parcel map of four or fewer parcels. Gov't Code § 66493(d)

Upon receipt of the certificate and security, the clerk of the board of supervisors then transmits the final map or parcel map to the county recorder for recording. Gov't Code § 66464(b). Other county officials also may transmit the final or parcel map to the county recorder, if authorized to do so by the board of supervisors. Gov't Code § 66494.1.

If the subdivided property has no tax liens, the subdivider must simply file a certificate or statement with the county where any part of the subdivision is located. The certificate or statement must show that county records indicate there are no liens against the property for unpaid taxes or special assessments, except for those taxes not yet payable. The certificate should be filed prior to submitting the final or parcel map to the legislative body. Gov't Code § 66492.

Subdivider to provide evidence of consent of record title holders. If a final or parcel map is not subject to the liens described in Gov't Code § 66493, then the appropriate city or county official can transmit the map directly to the county recorder. Gov't Code § 66464(a),(c). The subdivider must demonstrate that all parties with a record title interest in the subdivided property have consented in writing to the filing before the map is recorded. Gov't Code § 66465.

> The subdivider must demonstrate that all parties with a record title interest in the subdivided property have consented in writing to the filing before the map is recorded.

Recorder has 10 days to accept or reject map for filing. The county recorder has 10 days to examine the parcel or final map and make a determination about whether it should accept or reject it for filing (in this context, filing is the same as "recording"). Gov't Code § 66466. If the county recorder rejects the map, it must within 10 days mail a written notice of the reasons for the rejection to the city engineer or county surveyor and subdivider. It must also return the map to the city or county clerk so that the map can be placed on the agenda of the legislative body's next regular meeting.

The legislative body has 15 days after the meeting to rescind its approval and return the map to the subdivider, unless the subdivider demonstrates that the reason for the rejection by the recorder has been removed. The legislative body may continue the matter with the subdivider's consent, but the prior approval of the map shall be treated as rescinded during the continuation period. If the city or county determines that the map should be returned to the county recorder, the county recorder has a new 10-day period to decide whether to accept or reject the map for filing. After the map is filed, the surveyor or engineer who prepared the map must transmit a copy of the map with the recording information to the county surveyor, unless the county already requires automatic transmittal of the map to the surveyor. Gov't Code § 66466(f).

Condominium, stock cooperatives, and community apartment project conversions. Before the local agency may approve a final map for a subdivision to convert residential real property to a condominium project, community apartment project, or stock cooperative, it must make specific findings that each tenant of the project has received, or will receive:

- All applicable notices and rights required under chapters 2 or 3 of the Map Act (Gov't Code §§ 66425–66472.1) dealing with requirements and procedures. Gov't Code § 66427.1(a)(1). This requirement includes a finding that the applicable notices were also sent to each person applying for the rental of a unit in the property. Gov't Code § 66427.1(a)(1)
- Written notice of the intent to convert at least 60 days before the filing of a tentative map. Gov't Code § 66427.1(a)(2)(A)
- Ten days' written notice that an application was or will be submitted to the Bureau of Real Estate (BRE) for a public report, that the tenant's right to

> BRE = Bureau of Real Estate

purchase begins when the public report is issued, and that the report will be available on request. Gov't Code § 66427.1(a)(2)(B)

- Written notification that the subdivider has received the public report from the BRE. This notice is to be provided within five days after the date the subdivider receives the public report from the BRE

- Written notice within 10 days after approval of the final map. Gov't Code § 66427.1(a)(1)(D)

- One hundred and eighty days' written notice of the intent to convert, provided prior to termination of tenancy due to the conversion or proposed conversion pursuant to Government Code section 66452.14, but not before the local authority has approved a tentative map for the conversion. The text of this notification is given in Government Code section 66452.14(b). Gov't Code § 66427.1(a)(2)(E); see also California Subdivision Map Act and the Development Process, § 9.51A (Cal. CEB, 2d ed. 2001) (2013 Update). This provision does not alter any rights or obligations under the rental agreement or under Civil Code sections 1941–1941.2. Gov't Code § 66472.1(a)(1)(F)

- Notice of an exclusive right to contract for the purchase of his or her respective unit upon the same terms and conditions that the unit will be initially offered to the general public or terms more favorable to the tenant. Such notice shall be provided within five days of receipt of the subdivision public records. The exclusive right to purchase shall commence on the date the subdivision public report is issued and shall run for a period of not less than ninety (90) days, unless the tenant gives prior written notice of his or her intention not to exercise the right. Gov't Code § 66427.1(a)(2)(F); Gov't Code § 66452.15(a). The required form of the notice is given in Government Code section 66452.15(b). *See also California Subdivision Map Act and the Development Process*, § 9.51A. (For a waiver form, *see* Forming California Common Interest Developments § 4.38 (Cal. CEB 2013 Update).) Similar notice must be given to persons renting in a project subject to an approved final map, although failure to give notice renders the owner liable for actual moving expenses (up to $1,100) and first month's rent (up to $1,100) in the event the renter does not buy the unit, but does not give grounds to deny the conversion. Gov't Code § 66459(f)

- The written notices must be given in the language the rental agreement was negotiated in, if the agreement was negotiated in Spanish, Chinese, Tagalog, Vietnamese, or Korean. Gov't Code § 66427.1(d)

Dedications of streets, utilities, and other property. Dedications and offers to dedicate property for specified public uses must be made by acknowledged statement on the final map. Gov't Code § 66439(a). If a street is not offered for dedication, and there is a statement on the map to that effect, use of that street by the public will be with permission only. The offer of dedication includes public utility facilities located on or under the property only if there is a statement that the dedication includes these facilities. Gov't Code § 66439(c).

Once an offer of dedication is made, the city or a city official designated by ordinance must accept, accept subject to improvement, or reject all offers of dedication. Gov't Code § 66477.1. If the offer of dedication for streets, paths, alleys, public utility easements, rights-of-way for local transit facilities that directly benefit the residents of a subdivision, or storm drainage easements, is rejected, the offer will still remain open and a city may accept the offer in the future without any further action by the subdivider. Many cities will reject the offer when the final map is filed, and rescind that rejection and accept the offer once the improvements have been made. In this situation, the offer remains outstanding and cannot be revoked. However, no public interest is created until the offer of dedication is unconditionally accepted. *Mikels v. Rager*, 232 Cal. App. 3d 334, 354 (1991). Other cities will accept the dedication at the time of the final map approval subject to an agreement that the developer will pay for all the improvements. However, the offer will terminate without action by a city if all of the following conditions are satisfied:

- The offer was made by filing a map
- No acceptance of the dedication was made and recorded within 25 years after the map was filed
- The property was not used for the purpose for which the dedication was proposed within 25 years after the map was filed
- The property was sold to a third person after the map was filed and used free of the dedication

Code Civ. Proc. § 771.010

A legal action is still required to clear title under these circumstances. Code Civ. Proc. § 771.020. Otherwise the offer will remain open. In *Biagini v. Beckham*, the court held that "a statutory offer of dedication of land to use as a road may be revoked by the offeror to preclude later implicit acceptance by public use, even though the offer must remain open as to the public entity to which it was made under the provisions of the Subdivision Map Act." 163 Cal. App. 4th 1000, 1004 (2008).

Improvement agreements. If public improvements required by the city will not be completed and accepted until after filing of the final map (which is often the case), the legislative body, as a condition precedent to the approval of the final map, shall require the subdivider to enter into either: (1) an improvement agreement with the city upon mutually agreeable terms to thereafter complete the improvements at the subdivider's expense; or (2) an improvement agreement with the city to either initiate and consummate proceedings under an appropriate special assessment act or the Mello-Roos Community Facilities Act for the financing and completion of the improvements or, if the improvements are not completed under such proceedings, to complete the improvements at the subdivider's expense. Gov't Code § 66462(a). There is no right to a final map until the parties have entered into such an agreement. *South Cent. Coast Reg'l Comm'n v. Charles A. Pratt Constr. Co.*, 128 Cal. App. 3d 830, 834 (1982). If a city enters into an improvement agreement, it must require that performance be guaranteed by security. Gov't Code § 66462(c).

IMPROVEMENT SECURITY

Types of security. A city can require by ordinance that a subdivider post bonds, cash deposits, instruments of credit, a lien upon the property, or any other form of security acceptable to the city to secure completion of subdivision improvements. Gov't Code § 66499. The security ensures the faithful performance of the terms of the agreement and the securing of payment for labor, materials, and improvements, along with a guaranty and warranty for one year, plus costs, including reasonable attorneys' costs. Gov't Code §§ 66499.3, 66499.4. Courts will not interfere with a city's exercise of discretion in accepting or rejecting the security unless there is a showing of fraud, arbitrary action, or a clear abuse of discretion. Also, a city may adopt financial size criteria for insurers with respect to performance bonds. 74 Ops. Cal. Atty. Gen. 89 (1991). In addition, a city may have the obligation to ensure that the surety is sufficient. *Walt Rankin & Assocs., Inc. v. City of Murrieta*, 84 Cal. App. 4th 605, 627–28 (2000).

How much security is required? A city will determine the amount of security required for performance of an agreement to complete improvements. Gov't Code § 66499.3. However, Government Code section 66499.3 imposed the following requirements:

- The amount for faithful performance (performance bond) must be no less than fifty percent or more than 100 percent of the total estimated cost of the improvement or the act to be performed
- The amount for payment to the contractor, subcontractors, laborers, and anyone providing equipment must be no less than fifty percent or more than 100 percent of the total estimated cost of the improvement or the performance of the required act
- The amount must equal the amount determined by the city to fulfill the obligations for one year after completion of the improvement arising under a guaranty and warranty against defective work, labor, and materials

In addition to the face amount, the security must be sufficient to cover any costs, reasonable expenses, and fees, including attorneys' fees, that the city would have if it successfully enforced the security. Gov't Code § 66499.4. Some nonprofit organizations are exempt from the first two requirements listed above if certain conditions are met relating to how letters of credit are secured and how the contractor is paid. Gov't Code § 66499.3(c).

Rights and requirements. Once the improvement work begins, the subdivider and the entity that furnished the security (surety) are liable until all subdivision improvements are completed and accepted by the city. Therefore, subdividers and sureties must maintain and repair improvements after completion until all improvements guaranteed by the security are accepted by the city. *See County of Kern v. Edgemont Dev. Corp.*, 222 Cal. App. 2d 874, 879–80 (1963). A city's right to damages against a subdivider and the surety is not necessarily affected by modifications to an improvement agreement. *City of Sacramento v. Trans Pac. Indus., Inc.*, 98 Cal. App. 3d 389, 400–01 (1979).

A local agency is entitled to damages under a performance bond when a subdivider who is contractually responsible for constructing public improvements fails to perform, even if the agency incurs no out-of-pocket expense. In *City of Merced v. American Motorists Insurance Co.*, a developer entered into a subdivision agreement with the city under which it agreed to obtain a performance bond for deferred work identified in the agreement. 126 Cal. App. 4th 1316, 1318–1319 (2005). After completing construction of numerous residential units, the developer became insolvent. The insolvent developer then conveyed the remaining undeveloped property to another developer, who agreed to perform the first developer's deferred work. The city promised to obtain the bond proceeds and pay them to the second developer to defray the costs of completing the first developer's obligations. The city then sued to enforce the first developer's deferred work obligations.

The bonding company argued that the city should not be able to enforce the performance bond against it since the city was not damaged by the first developer's refusal to perform because the second developer agreed to timely perform the deferred work at no cost to the city. *Id.* at 1323. The appellate court disagreed and held that the city's damages were not limited to its actual costs. The city maintained a contractual right to expect the first developer to perform the deferred work, despite the city's agreement with the second developer. According to the court, the city was damaged once the first developer refused to perform. Thus, its damages are measured by the first developer's share of the uncompleted portion of the deferred work, and the surety is liable under the performance bond up to the bond amount. *Id.* at 1323.

There is conflicting authority as to whether the surety is liable under an improvement agreement when the subdivider has not actually commenced construction. In *County of Yuba v. Central Valley National Bank, Inc.*, the court held that if the project is abandoned after a final map has been recorded, even though an improvement agreement has been entered into by the subdivider and the city, the surety is exonerated as long as no construction has begun. 20 Cal. App. 3d 109, 113 (1971). If this occurs, the city cannot collect the amount of the bond or force the surety to install the improvements. The city may be able to proceed under Government Code section 66499.11 *et seq.* and "revert the subdivision to acreage," which has the practical effect of rescinding the subdivision map.

Conversely, in *City of Los Angeles v. Amwest Surety Insurance Co.*, the court held that the surety remained liable on the bond after the subdivider abandoned the project even though very minimal construction actually began. 63 Cal. App. 4th 378 (1998). The court distinguished *Yuba* based on the language of the security instrument, the fact that in *Amwest* the improvements were needed because the parcel was going to be developed by another developer, the money derived from the bond would be used to benefit the new development, and the parcel would not automatically revert to acreage because a reversion to acreage is a discretionary action, not a ministerial one.

It appears that the courts are limiting *Yuba* to its facts; thus, a surety will likely remain liable under an improvement agreement even if the subdivider has not begun construction. *See, e.g., City of Los Angeles v. Amwest Sur. Insurance Co.*, 63 Cal. App. 4th 378 (1998) (review denied (June 17, 1998)); *City of Merced v. American Motorists Ins. Co.*, 126 Cal. App. 4th 1316 (2005).

Releasing security. The Map Act allows a partial or complete release of the security for public improvements. Gov't Code § 66499.7. The security given for the faithful performance of an act (performance guarantee) must be released once the improvement is finally completed and accepted. Additionally, a city may establish rules that permit a partial release of the security as the work progresses. Gov't Code § 66499.7(a). The Map Act sets forth a detailed process for such partial release of performance security. For example, the subdivider may provide written notice to the city when it believes the required work has been completed. Gov't Code § 66499.7(b). The city then has 45 days to review and comment or approve the completion of the work. Gov't Code § 66499.7(b). If the city concludes that all required work has not been completed, it must provide a list of outstanding obligations to the subdivider. Gov't Code § 66499.7(b). The subdivider has 45 days from the date of receipt of the list to provide cost estimates to the city for all remaining work. Gov't Code § 66499.7(c). The city then has 45 days to review, comment, and approve, modify, or disapprove the subdivider's cost estimates. Gov't Code § 66499.7(d). If the city approves the cost estimate, it shall release all performance security except for security in an amount up to 200 percent of the cost estimate of the remaining work. Unless the city allows for earlier release, the process of partially releasing performance security must take place when the cost estimate of the remaining work does not exceed twenty percent of the original performance security. Gov't Code § 66499.7(d).

If the obligation must be approved by another agency other than the city, the city cannot release the security until the obligation is performed to the satisfaction of the other agency. The other agency has two months after completion to determine its satisfaction or dissatisfaction. If it reaches no decision after two months, the obligation shall be deemed to be satisfied. Gov't Code § 66499.8. The security given for labor and materials must be released (1) if no liens have been filed and the time has expired for a lien to be recorded pursuant to Civil Code section 8410 *et seq.*, and (2) the city has accepted the work. Gov't Code § 66499.7(h). If liens have been filed, upon expiration of the period for recording of liens, the city will hold an amount equal to the amount of the liens and release the remainder, provided the lien holders have given notice in writing to the city. Gov't Code § 66499.7(h). However, the release provisions do not apply to the release of the portion of security that covers any warranty or guaranty by the subdivider or reasonable costs and attorneys' fees pursuant to Government Code section 66499.9. Gov't Code § 66499.7(i).

Remedies. If a developer does not satisfy its obligations under the improvement agreement, the method of recovery depends on the type of security that is furnished. If the security is cash or negotiable bonds and is conditioned on payments to the contractor, subcontractor, and other persons furnishing labor, materials, or equipment, a city may recover from the holder of the deposit. If the security is a surety bond, a city may recover from the surety and sue if necessary to enforce the bond. If an irrevocable standby letter of credit is used, a city may draw on the letter of credit. Gov't Code § 66499.10. Although the Map Act authorizes a cause of action by a city against the financial institution obligated by the letter of credit, this should not be necessary in order for the city to collect on an irrevocable standby letter of credit.

The liability of a surety that issues a labor and materials bond for public improvements may extend to the benefit of contractors in addition to the city. *Sukut-Coulson, Inc. v. Allied Canon Co.*, 85 Cal. App. 3d 648, 651 (1978). This is because provisions of the Civil Code that would provide an appropriate remedy are not applicable to privately funded public improvements. *Id.* at 654; *see* Civ. Code § 8160 *et seq.*, § 9000 *et seq.*

PARCEL MAPS

Local ordinance requirements. Parcel map procedures and approvals are left up to the local ordinance, except as specifically provided in the Map Act. Gov't Code § 66463(a). However, even though notice and hearing requirements for parcel maps are not specifically set forth in the Map Act, constitutional prerequisites must be followed. *Horn v. County of Ventura*, 24 Cal. 3d 605, 616 (1979). For notice procedures, *see* Government Code sections 66451.3(a), 65090, 65091.

Parcel map requirements. When a parcel map is submitted, a city is more limited than with a tentative and final map in imposing fees and exactions. A city may only impose requirements for the dedication of rights-of-way, easements, and the construction of reasonable offsite and onsite improvements for the parcels that are being created. Gov't Code § 66411.1(a).

An important difference between final and parcel map conditions is that a city generally may not require that improvements be completed for subdivisions of four or fewer parcels until a permit for development is issued. However, satisfaction of conditions can be required at an earlier time upon a finding by the city that an earlier fulfillment of the construction improvements is necessary for the public health and safety or orderly development of the surrounding area. The completion of improvements can also be required earlier by agreement. Gov't Code § 66411.1; *see also* 78 Ops. Cal. Atty. Gen. 158 (1995).

While in subdivisions of five or more parcels security must be provided by the subdivider to ensure construction of the required improvements, cities *may*, by local ordinance, require similar security for subdivisions of four or fewer parcels. Such security may be in the form of bonds, money, or an instrument of credit. Gov't Code § 66411.1(a); *see also* 62 Ops. Cal. Atty. Gen. 175, 178 (1979).

Provisions regarding offers of dedication, approval of parcel maps, and the time limitations for a city to act on parcel maps are the same as for final maps. Gov't Code § 66463. Dedications or offers of dedication can be made either by a statement on the parcel map or by a separate written instrument recorded before or concurrently with the parcel map. Gov't Code § 66447. A subdivider may file multiple parcel maps if notice is given at the time of the filing of a tentative map or at a later date if the city concurs. Gov't Code § 66463.1. For details on the required content and form of parcel maps—including required statements by the preparing engineer or surveyor—see Government Code sections 66444 through 66450.

> A subdivider may file multiple parcel maps if notice is given at the time of the filing of a tentative map or at a later date if the city concurs.

Special case: four or fewer parcels and no dedications or improvements. Ordinarily, the map must be signed by all parties who have a record title interest in property to be subdivided. There must also be a statement that all of those parties consented to the preparation and recordation of the parcel map, unless the local ordinance provides for a different statement. A special case exists if there is a division of four or fewer parcels and no dedications or improvements are required. In that case, only the subdivider must sign the map. If the subdivider does not own the property, the city may require that the subdivider provide the city with evidence that owners have consented to the division. Gov't Code § 66445(e).

CORRECTION AND AMENDMENT OF MAPS

GROUNDS

Errors and omissions. After a final map or parcel map has been filed for recording, it may be amended in a limited number of situations by means of a certificate of correction or an amending map prepared by a civil engineer or licensed land surveyor. Gov't Code §§ 66469, 66470. An existing map may be amended to correct an error or omission in a course or distance on the map, or in the description of the real property shown on the map (Gov't Code §§ 66469(a)-(c)), but an existing course or distance may be corrected only if the error is ascertainable from data shown on the map (Gov't Code § 66469). A map also may be amended to indicate monuments that are set after the death, disability, or retirement of the engineer or surveyor responsible for setting the monuments (Gov't Code § 66469(d)), or to show the proper location or character of a monument that has been changed (Gov't Code § 66469(e)). Map amendments also are permitted under a catch-all provision to correct any other type of map error or omission if approved by either the county surveyor or the city engineer, provided the correction does not affect a property right. Gov't Code § 66469(g). Examples provided in Government Code section 66469(g) include correction of lot numbers, acreage, street names, and identification of adjacent record maps.

Changed circumstances. A recorded final map or parcel map may be amended if a city enacts an authorizing ordinance and makes certain specified findings. Gov't Code § 66472.1. To support the amendment, a city must find that:
- Changed circumstances make any or all map conditions no longer appropriate or necessary

- The modifications do not impose an additional burden on the existing fee owner
- The modifications do not alter any right, title, or interest in the property shown on the recorded map
- The modified map does not contain any of the grounds for denying a map under Government Code section 66474

The modifications must be set for public hearing as provided in Government Code section 66451.3, and the hearing must be confined to consideration of and action on the proposed modifications. Gov't Code § 66472.1.

AMENDMENT PROCEDURE

The amending map or certificate of correction must be prepared and signed by a registered civil engineer or licensed land surveyor in accordance with the standards applicable to a final map or a parcel map. Gov't Code § 66470. Each of the fee owners of property affected by the correction or omission at the time the original map was recorded must be listed on the amending map or "certificate of correction," but need not sign this document. Gov't Code § 66470. Within 60 days after recordation of a certificate of correction, the recorder must transmit a certified copy to the county engineer or surveyor, who must maintain an index of recorded certificates of correction. Gov't Code § 66470. After the corrected map or certificate of correction has been prepared, it must be submitted to the city engineer or county surveyor for certification that the changes made from the previously recorded map are only those specifically permitted by Government Code section 66469. Gov't Code § 66471. The amending map or certificate must then be filed with the recorder. The recorder must index the names of the fee owners and appropriate tract designation in the general index and map index. Gov't Code § 66472. On recordation, the original map is deemed to have been conclusively corrected, and the amending map or certificate imparts constructive notice of all corrections as though set forth in the original map. Gov't Code § 66472.

CHANGES AFFECTING PROPERTY RIGHTS

An amendment to a recorded final map or parcel map is not permitted by Government Code sections 66469(f) or 66472.1 if it would affect existing property rights. The Map Act contains no provision for amending a map when a property right is affected. In this situation, a subdivider might be able to effect an amendment by means of a lot line adjustment, which is excluded from Map Act regulation. Gov't Code § 66412(d).

Otherwise, even when the consent of all affected parties can be obtained, a subdivider may be required to process a new map in order to make amendments or corrections. When multiple legal parcels are involved, a subdivider might be able to correct an error or omission affecting a property right by filing a new final map or parcel map on only the affected property. Gov't Code § 66499.20½ (permitting merger and resubdivision of the property); Gov't Code §§ 66424, 66424.6 (permitting subdivision of a portion of a larger parcel).

In *Christian v. Flora*, where there was ambiguity in the manner by which a roadway easement had been moved, the court held that recordation of a later map that merged and resubdivided two lots operated as a matter of law to amend an earlier map of the same property and to substitute an easement alignment shown on the new map for one that had been eliminated through a series of quitclaim deeds. 164 Cal. App. 4th 539, 554 (2008). Adjacent landowners whose deeds made reference only to the earlier map were thus held to have rights to the easement shown on the later map that merged and resubdivided the property.

ENFORCEMENT

PROHIBITION

The Map Act prohibits the sale, lease, or financing of any parcels, or commencement of construction, except for model homes, on any parcel or parcels of real property for which a map is required before the map is filed. The Map Act also prohibits occupancy before the map is filed in compliance with the Map Act and local ordinance. Gov't Code § 66499.30.

However, this prohibition does not prohibit an offer or contract to sell, lease, or finance property or to construct improvements thereon so long as the offer or contract is expressly conditioned upon the approval and filing of the final map or parcel map. Gov't Code § 66499.30(e). In *Black Hills Investments, Inc. v. Albertsons, Inc.*, the court held that contracts for the sale of unsubdivided real property, which did not expressly condition the sale upon the recordation of a parcel map, were illegal and therefore void, not voidable. 146 Cal. App. 4th 883, 893-94 (2007). The *Black Hills* contract allowed the seller to waive the condition, which the court reasoned could have resulted in a violation of the Map Act. Therefore, the contract was void, not voidable. *Id.* The court in *Sixells v. Cannery Business Park* followed the *Black Hills* holding and specified that even if it was not the intent of the parties to circumvent the requirements of the Map Act, a real estate contract which allowed the buyer to waive the recording of a final map violated the Map Act and was void. 170 Cal. App. 4th 648, 653 (2008). An amendment adding the express condition required under section 66499.30 cured the illegality of an earlier option agreement without any such condition where the earlier option was never exercised, non-enforcement of the contract would result in unjust enrichment, and the amendment constituted a new and independent option contract. *Corrie v. Soloway*, 216 Cal. App. 4th 436, 449-51 (2013).

> The Map Act prohibits the sale, lease, or financing of any parcels, or commencement of construction, except for model homes, on any parcel or parcels of real property for which a map is required before the map is filed.

REMEDIES OF PRIVATE PERSONS

Any deed of conveyance, sale, or contract to sell that results in a violation of the Map Act is voidable at the sole option of the grantee, buyer, or person contracting to purchase within one year after the date of discovery of the violation. However, the deed of conveyance, sale, or contract of sale is binding upon any successor in interest of the grantee, buyer, or person contracting to purchase. Gov't Code § 66499.32(a). Nevertheless, any such grantee, or the successor in interest of real property that has been divided in violation of the Map Act, may, within one year of the date of discovery of such violation, bring an action to recover any damages suffered by reason of such division. Gov't Code § 66499.32(b). However, the grantee or successor in interest cannot bring such an action if a certificate of compliance has been issued, which serves to defeat a contention that the Map Act has been violated. *LeGault v. Erickson*, 70 Cal. App. 4th 369, 374 (1999).

In addition, any private individual has a right to bring a lawsuit to restrain or enjoin a violation of the Map Act. Gov't Code § 66499.33.

REMEDIES OF A CITY

There are several remedies available to a city for Map Act violations. First, it can bring a suit for declaratory relief or an action to restrain or enjoin a violation of the Map Act in superior court. Gov't Code § 66499.33; *City of Tiburon v. Northwestern Pac. R.R. Co.*, 4 Cal. App. 3d 160, 175–76 (1970). A city also may request that a criminal complaint be filed in court. Gov't Code § 66499.31. However, the most practical enforcement tool for a city is to withhold permits and approvals necessary to develop any property that has been divided in violation of the Map Act after making the necessary finding that the development is contrary to the public health or public safety. Gov't Code § 66499.34. As soon as a city has knowledge that there is a violation, it must process a notice of violation pursuant to Government Code section 66499.36.

CERTIFICATES OF COMPLIANCE

Any owner or vendee (that is, a person contracting to acquire property) may request that a city determine whether the property complies with the provisions of the Map Act and the local subdivision ordinance. Gov't Code § 66499.35; *see County of San Luis Obispo v. Superior Court*, 90 Cal. App. 4th 288 (2001). When such request is made, the city must issue a certificate of compliance or a conditional certificate of compliance. 74 Ops. Cal. Atty. Gen. 149 (1991); *see also Lakeview Meadows Ranch v. County of Santa Clara*, 27 Cal. App. 4th 593, 598–600 (1994); *Hunt v. County of Shasta*, 225 Cal. App. 3d 432, 438–39 (1990). If the city determines that the property complies with the provisions of the Map Act and local subdivision ordinances, it must issue a certificate of compliance. Gov't Code § 66499.35(a). If the city determines that the property does not comply, it must issue a conditional certificate of compliance. Gov't Code § 66499.35(b). Where property does not comply because parcels have been illegally created, the city may only issue a conditional certificate of compliance. *Fishback v. County of Ventura*, 133 Cal. App. 4th 896 (2005). A court described the legislative intent behind the certificate of compliance procedure:

> The Legislature in enacting a comprehensive scheme to regulate the creation and control of subdivisions and other divisions of land, past and present, and in an obvious effort to provide a fair and equitable scheme to settle the validity of divisions of land occurring in decades past under earlier provisions of law, also provided a means whereby land owners could request that a local government make a determination about the validity of any prior division of land. That means is presently embodied in Gov't Code § 66499.35.

Stell v. Jay Hales Dev. Co., 11 Cal. App. 4th 1214 (1992)

Government Code section 66499.35 allows two different standards of conditions to be imposed in issuing a conditional certificate of compliance. If the one who seeks the certificate is the one who initially violated the law and that person is the current owner, a city may impose such conditions as would be applicable to a current division of property. However, if the one who is requesting the certificate is not the violator, a city may impose only those conditions established by the Map Act or local ordinance that would have been applicable to the division at the time the applicant acquired its interest. Gov't Code § 66499.35(b). The two different standards were established on the assumption that conditions in effect at the current time would be more strict as compared to those in effect earlier. The Attorney General has opined that the conditions imposed could include the requirement that the subdivider apply for a subdivision map to legally create the parcel. 81 Ops. Cal. Atty. Gen. 144, 146 n.4 (1998).

> If the city determines that the property complies with the provisions of the Map Act and local subdivision ordinances, it must issue a certificate of compliance.

FIGURE A: CERTIFICATE OF COMPLIANCE FLOW CHART

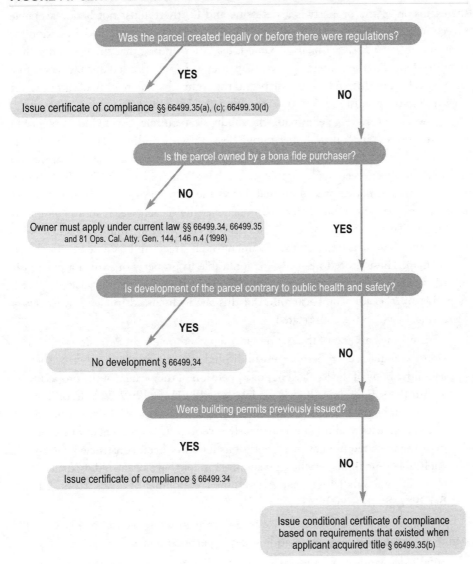

Certificates of compliance and conditional certificates of compliance must include the following notice:

> This certificate relates only to issues of compliance or noncompliance with the Subdivision Map Act and local ordinances enacted pursuant thereto. The parcel described herein may be sold, leased, or financed without further compliance with the Subdivision Map Act or any local ordinance enacted pursuant thereto. Development of the parcel may require issuance of a permit or permits, or other grant or grants of approval.

Gov't Code § 66499.35(f)(1)(e)

EXCLUSIONS AND REVERSIONS

Exclusions are governed by Government Code section 66499.21 *et seq.* and are rarely used. This procedure removes land from an existing subdivision and requires judicial action. It requires notice and a court hearing. A two-prong test must be met to exclude a parcel from a recorded subdivision map: (1) petitioners must prove to the court that the exclusion of the property is a necessity; and (2) there must not be a reasonable objection to the exclusion. Gov't Code § 66499.25. The court granted a petition for exclusion in *Van't Rood v. County of Santa Clara*, after finding that the petitioners had never consented to the contested parcel map, they were not afforded due process before their parcels were "merged" by the map, and the county had no reasonable grounds for objecting to the exclusion. 113 Cal. App. 4th 549, 577–578 (2003).

A reversion to acreage eliminates the subdivision entirely. Gov't Code § 66499.11 *et seq.* It requires city approval after public hearing, with findings (1) that the dedications to be vacated are unnecessary; and (2) that the owners have consented, or that no improvements have been made, or that no lots have been sold. Gov't Code § 66499.16. However, an alternative procedure that allows the filing of a new map over the old map that merges and re-subdivides without reverting to acreage, is more commonly used today. This procedure accomplishes, in one clean step by filing of a single map, the merger, re-subdivision, and abandonment of all streets and easements not shown on the map. These procedures only are applicable to property on which a previously recorded subdivision existed. Gov't Code § 66499.20½; *Negron v. Dundee*, 221 Cal. App. 3d 1502 (1990). The background of this law is discussed in *Gomes v. County of Mendocino*, in which the court stated:

> Article 1 of chapter 6 of the Act provides a procedure for the reversion of previously subdivided property to unsubdivided acreage, initiated either by the legislative body of the local agency or by petition of the owners of the property within the subdivision. ([Gov't Code] §§ 66499.11–66499.20¼.) According to one commentator, these formal reversion proceedings typically are initiated by local agencies to eliminate a previously approved subdivision map when the improvements required as map conditions have not been constructed within applicable time limits or when no subdivision lots have been sold. (Curtin *et al.*, California Subdivision Map Act and the Development Process (Cont. Ed. Bar 1987) § 9.1, p. 209.)

> Also appearing in the same article is Government Code section 66499.20½, the statute at issue in this case. The statute states in pertinent part:

>> Subdivided lands may be merged and resubdivided without reverting to acreage by complying with all the applicable requirements for the subdivision of land as provided by this division and any local ordinance adopted pursuant thereto. The filing of the final map or parcel map shall constitute legal merging of the separate parcels into one parcel and the resubdivision of such parcel, and the real property shall thereafter be shown with the new lot or parcel boundaries on the assessment roll.... Curtin suggests that this merger and resubdivision procedure is more commonly used than the formal reversion to acreage process because it enables an owner to resubdivide property for development in one relatively simple step. (Curtin *et al.*, Cal. Subdivision Map Act Practice, *supra*, § 9.4, p. 212.) 9.4, page 212.

37 Cal. App. 4th 977, 981–982 (1995)

Note that the reversion procedure is the exclusive method to obtain refunds of unused and unnecessary fees after recordation of a map, except for parkland dedication funds (Gov't Code § 66477(b)), and storm drainage and sanitary sewer fees (Gov't Code § 66483.2). *See B&P Dev. Corp. v. City of Saratoga*, 185 Cal. App. 3d 949, 961–62 (1986).

ANTIQUATED SUBDIVISIONS

ANTIQUATED SUBDIVISIONS—LEGALLY CREATED PARCELS?

California's first statewide Map Act was enacted in 1893. In *Gardner v. County of Sonoma*, the California Supreme Court examined whether a subdivision map recorded prior to 1893 could create legal lots. 29 Cal. 4th 990 (2003). The map in question was recorded in 1865 and showed a 1,000-acre property divided into 90 lots. *Id.* at 994. A 158-acre portion was conveyed intact through successive owners until it reached the plaintiffs. *Id.* at 995. The plaintiffs applied to the county for certificates of compliance to certify that the 12 lots shown on their property were valid under the Map Act, but the county only would recognize the land as a single parcel. *Id.*

> California's first statewide Map Act was enacted in 1893.

The California Supreme Court found that the map, despite its purported accuracy and the fact that it was adopted as the county's official map,[11] did not give rise to legally cognizable parcels. *Id.* at 999. The map did not satisfy either of the two main conditions required to establish a subdivision prior to 1893:

(1) Approval or exemption under a preexisting statute

(2) Separate conveyance of the parcels

Id.

If the map had been approved pursuant to, or exempted from, a statute governing local Sonoma County subdivisions in effect at the time the subdivision was established, it would have been grandfathered in under Sections 66499.30(d) and 66412.7. Because few local subdivision statutes existed prior to 1893, this occurrence would be extremely rare.[12] In the case of the Gardner map, the court found no legislation that authorized the creation of subdivided parcels in Sonoma County by map recordation before 1893. If the individual parcels had been separately conveyed from the surrounding land through a deed or patent after the map was recorded, they might have become eligible for legal status under the common law. The Gardners did not qualify for this consideration because their 158-acre portion of the map was conveyed intact through the years. *Gardner*, 29 Cal. 4th at 1001.

In holding that the 1865 map did not create legal parcels, the court cited strong public policy reasons for its decision:

> [I]f we were to adopt plaintiffs' position and hold that local agencies must issue a certificate of compliance for any parcel depicted on an accurate, antiquated subdivision map, we would, in effect, be permitting the sale, lease, and financing of parcels: (1) without regard to regulations that would otherwise require consistency with applicable general and specific plans... and require consideration of potential environmental and public health consequences...; (2) without consideration of dedications and impact mitigation fees that would otherwise be authorized by the Act; and (3) without affording notice and an opportunity to be heard to interested persons and landowners likely to suffer a substantial or significant deprivation of their property rights.

Id. at 1005 (internal citations omitted)

---

11 The court noted that the county's adopted map was not technically an "official map" for purposes of the Map Act because it did not meet the requirements of Gov't Code § 66499.50 *et seq. Gardner*, 29 Cal. 4th at 998.

12 See Daniel J. Curtin, Jr. and Robert E. Merritt, *California Subdivision Map Act and the Development Process*, section 2.37 (Cal. CEB, 2d ed. 2001) (2013 Update).

MAPS BEFORE 1929

In a footnote in the *Gardner* decision, the California Supreme Court left open the question of whether maps filed before 1929 can, by themselves, create legal lots. *Id.* at 1001 n.7. This date is significant because it was not until the 1929 amendments to the Map Act that cities and counties were given authority to regulate subdivisions. The court said it had no reason to resolve this question in *Gardner* because the map at issue predated the earliest statewide Map Act statute (1893).

MAPS AFTER 1893 GENERALLY

If a subdivision map was filed after the first Map Act was enacted in 1893, its validity is determined by whether it met the requirements of the version of the Map Act that was in effect at the time the subdivision was established. Gov't Code §§ 66451.10, 66499.30; 74 Ops. Cal. Atty. Gen. 149 (1991). For example, if a map was filed in 1935, the Map Act in effect in that year is the governing law and the map must have conformed to that law.

Two recent cases have analyzed this grandfathering provision and have specifically examined whether the statewide subdivision map law in effect at the time the subdivision was established was a law "regulating the design and improvement of subdivisions" pursuant to Government Code section 66499.30. *Abernathy Valley, Inc. v. City of Solano*, 173 Cal. App. 4th 42, 47–53 (2009); *Witt Home Ranch, Inc. v. County of Sonoma*, 165 Cal. App. 4th 543, 548 (2008). In both cases, the courts invalidated the map in question and upheld the denial of issuance of a certificate of compliance. In *Abernathy*, the 1909 map was not valid pursuant to the grandfather provision of the Map Act because the 1907 predecessor to the Map Act did not address design or improvement. 173 Cal. App. 4th at 51. In *Witt*, the court found the map to be invalid with reference to the 1915 predecessor of the Map Act on the same grounds. 165 Cal. App. 4th at 548.

U.S. SURVEY MAPS AND FEDERAL PATENTS

In *John Taft Corp. v. Advisory Agency*, the court held that a United States Government Survey Map is insufficient to create legal parcels. 161 Cal. App. 3d 749, 757 (1984). A patent (a grant of land) for more than 140 acres of land, including the three parcels at issue in this case, was granted to the landowner in 1895. While the survey described the land as separate parcels on a U.S. Survey Map, the patent was for the entire 140 acres. A subsequent landowner attempted to sell the separately described parcels and the court held that the U.S. Survey Map did not "create" parcels, and any transfer of these parcels was an illegal land division in violation of the Map Act. *Id.* at 757.

Conversely, a federal patent that itself divides the land can create legal parcels. In *Lakeview Meadows Ranch v. County of Santa Clara*, the parcel at issue was separately conveyed by the patent, and the court held that the patent created a parcel of land. 27 Cal. App. 4th 593, 597 (1994).

The Attorney General has followed the reasoning of *Taft* and *Lakeview Meadows*, and stated that a patent that granted land depicted on a United States Government Survey Map as contiguous "lots" does not create separate lots that must be recognized by a county. 81 Ops. Cal. Atty. Gen. 144 (1998).

MERGER AND UNMERGER

Merging parcels under one ownership. Under certain circumstances, contiguous legal parcels owned by the same person can be combined into one parcel. This is described as "merger."

For purposes of the Map Act's merger provisions, common ownership of contiguous parcels is determined not only by looking to proper title, but also by considering other indicators, including possession of or control over the affected property, whether a transfer occurred shortly before the planned merger, whether it occurred between family members, and the purpose of any recent transfer in title. *Kalway v. City of Berkeley*, 151 Cal. App. 4th 827, 834 (2007) (holding that parcels were in substance under common ownership at time city recorded notice of intent to determine status despite recent grant deed of parcel from landowner to his wife in effort to avoid merger).

Merger can occur by filing a final map or parcel map, which has the effect of creating a new subdivision. Gov't Code § 66499.20½. In addition, a city can adopt an ordinance permitting owner-initiated mergers. The ordinance must require recordation of an instrument evidencing the merger. Gov't Code § 66499.20¾. Finally, some jurisdictions permit a *de facto* merger using the lot line adjustment procedure by permitting lot lines dividing two or more parcels to be moved to correspond to the boundary lines of the parcels. Gov't Code § 66412(d).

The merger provisions of the Map Act provide the sole and exclusive authority for the merger of contiguous parcels initiated by a local agency. However, prior to 1983, merger was left largely to local law. *Moores v. Mendocino County*, 122 Cal. App. 4th 883, 886 (2004). In the *Moores* case, the court upheld the county's determination that four contiguous parcels were automatically merged by the county's merger ordinance adopted in 1981. The plaintiffs unsuccessfully argued that a merger had not occurred because the county did not follow its own local notice procedures enacted a year later in 1982. However, the court held that the "[c]ounty's subsequent enactment of an ordinance providing for recording of notice and a hearing did not result in unmerging parcels already automatically merged the previous year by operation of law." *Id.* at 890. Furthermore, the court observed that because the automatic merger of the parcels occurred as a result of a legislative enactment, due process did not require notice and an opportunity for a hearing. *Id.* at 889. The court said the intent of Government Code sections 66451.301 and 66451.302 was to preserve such mergers "accomplished through local law by exempting them from the requirement of recorded notice, and allowing the more informal notice outlined in Section 66451.302." *Id.* The County of Mendocino properly followed Government Code section 66451.302's required notice when it sent a form letter to the plaintiffs informing them that their parcels may have merged unless they qualified for one of the exemptions in section 66451.301.[13] *Id.* at 891.

The fact that the Map Act has provided exclusive authority for the merger of parcels since 1983 does not abrogate or limit the authority of a city to approve lot line adjustments, reversions to acreage, or parcel or final maps that combine lots and create fewer parcels. Gov't Code § 66451.10. Merger is not effective until notice of merger is filed for record with the county recorder. Before recording this notice, a city shall send by certified mail a notice of intention to determine status (Gov't Code § 66451.13), and the owner may request a hearing on determination of status (Gov't Code § 66451.14).

---

[13] For a discussion of the legislative history of the merger law, see *Gomes v. County of Mendocino*, 37 Cal. App. 4th 977 (1995).

Generally stated, the parcels must be contiguous, held by the same owner, and one of the parcels must not conform to the local standards for minimum parcel size.

The detailed requirements for parcel merger are contained in Government Code section 66451.11. Generally stated, the parcels must be contiguous, held by the same owner, and one of the parcels must not conform to the local standards for minimum parcel size. In addition:

- At least one of the parcels must not contain a structure for which a building permit was required, or must contain only an accessory structure, and
- With respect to any affected parcel, one or more of the following conditions exists:
    - It comprises less than 5,000 square feet at the time of merger, or
    - It was not created in compliance with applicable laws and ordinances in effect at the time of creation, or
    - It does not meet current standards for sewage disposal and water supply, or
    - It does not meet slope stability standards, or
    - It has no legal access, or
    - Its development would create health or safety hazards, or
    - It is inconsistent with the general plan or specific plan in areas other than minimum parcel size.

Gov't Code § 66451.11

The issue of merger was addressed in *Stell v. Jay Hales Development Co.*, 11 Cal. App. 4th 1214 (1992) (disapproved on other grounds by *Citizens for Covenant Compliance v. Anderson*, 12 Cal. 4th 345, 359 (1992)). In *Stell*, a landowner subdivided a single lot within a subdivision in 1960 that had conditions and restrictions stating that the lots could not contain more than one single-family dwelling and houses must be limited to one story in height. *Id.* at 1223. Both halves of that lot were sold to the defendant's predecessor in interest, and then the back half was conveyed to the defendant in 1989, who began building a two-story house after obtaining the proper permits from the city as well as a certificate of compliance on the back half of the lot. Plaintiffs contended that the divided lot was not lawfully subdivided in 1960 and, by operation of law, the two parcels comprising that lot were merged. *Id.* at 1224.

The court, after reviewing the history of merger law, held there was no merger by operation of law when the defendant's predecessor in interest became the owner of the contiguous parcels because there was no notice and hearing held by the city. *Id.* at 1227–28. The court stated that because the city issued and recorded the certificate of compliance for the lot, the city did not see fit to attempt any merger of the two parcels. The court stated that if the plaintiffs did not agree with the city's decision to issue the certificate of compliance, they should have filed a lawsuit within the 90-day statute of limitation period under Government Code section 66499.37. *Id.* at 1228–1229.

In 1994, the California Supreme Court struck down a local zoning ordinance requiring a merger of certain contiguous parcels in common ownership as a prerequisite to a development application involving one of the parcels. *Morehart v. County of Santa Barbara*, 7 Cal. 4th 725, 759 (1994). The court found that the local zoning regulations conflicted with the requirements of the merger provisions of the Map Act, and that the Map Act preempted such conflicting local laws. *Id.* at 765; Gov't Code § 66451.10 *et seq.*

In *Morehart*, the court reviewed the legislative history and intent of the Map Act merger provisions. Section 66451.11 enumerates specific and limited grounds for a local agency to require merger of parcels (e.g., failure to meet standards for sewage disposal, water supply, or vehicular access). The court held that these standards were intended to limit the conditions under which merger may be required, and that the county ordinance was invalid because it went beyond these standards and required merger to meet local density standards. The court found a "paramount state concern that statewide uniform standards govern the use of compulsory merger as a means of controlling development." *Morehart*, 7 Cal. 4th at 760. This paramount concern was sufficient to find *implied* preemption of the local ordinances. In describing the relationship between the county's zoning and subdivision authority, the court stated that the Map Act does not "affect the applicability of zoning ordinances requiring minimum parcel size for development so long as the requirements are not conditioned upon parcel merger." *Id*.

Unmerger or deemed not to have merged. Government Code section 66451.30 *et seq.* provides a procedure for the unmerger of certain contiguous parcels. Parcels for which no notices of merger were recorded as of January 1, 1984, shall be deemed not to have been merged if, as of that date, certain findings can be made. Gov't Code § 66451.30. This section was enacted to reverse automatic mergers occurring before the law was changed to require a hearing and recording of merger, and so has limited application.

PRESUMPTION OF LEGAL PARCELS

The fact that the Map Act has provided exclusive authority for the merger of parcels since 1983 does not abrogate or limit the authority of a city to approve lot line adjustments, reversions to acreage, or parcel or final maps that combine lots and create fewer parcels. Any parcel that was created prior to March 4, 1972, is conclusively presumed to be a legally created parcel if the parcel resulted from a division of land where fewer than five parcels were created, and no legal ordinances were in effect that regulated the division of land creating fewer than five parcels. Gov't Code § 66412.6(a). The presumption also exists for a parcel created before March 4, 1972 if a subsequent purchaser acquired the parcel for consideration without any actual or constructive knowledge of a violation of the Map Act or any applicable local ordinance. In that case, the owner must obtain a certificate of compliance or a conditional certificate of compliance before obtaining any grant of approval for development of the parcel. Gov't Code § 66412.6(b).

The Attorney General applied Government Code section 66412.6 to find that an agency had created two legal parcels under the Map Act when it acquired, through eminent domain, a significant portion of a 640-acre parcel to create a reservoir. 86 Ops. Cal. Atty. Gen. 70 (2003). The reservoir left two remaining areas of the parcel separated by 700 feet of water. Because the division occurred prior to March 4, 1972, and there was no local subdivision ordinance in effect at the time for four or fewer parcels, the Attorney General concluded the parcels were legally created for purposes of the Map Act. The Attorney General also found that the legal status of the two parcels was unaffected by the owner later obtaining a timberland production zone classification over the parcels, which required them to be managed contiguously as a single unit. *Id.*

CHAPTER 6

California Environmental Quality Act (CEQA)

Barbara Schussman

INTRODUCTION

The California Environmental Quality Act (CEQA) requires government agencies to consider the environmental consequences of their actions before approving plans and policies or committing to a course of action on a project. In enacting CEQA, the Legislature explained that this process is intended to: (1) inform government decisionmakers and the public about the potential environmental effects of proposed activities; (2) identify the ways that environmental damage can be avoided or significantly reduced; (3) prevent significant, avoidable environmental damage by requiring changes in projects, either by the adoption of alternatives or imposition of mitigation measures; and (4) disclose to the public why a project was approved if that project would have significant environmental effects.[1] Pub. Res. Code §§ 21000, 21001.

Consistent with these purposes, CEQA applies to most state, regional, and local agency decisions to carry out, authorize, or approve projects that could have adverse effects on the environment. CEQA requires that public agencies inform themselves about the environmental effects of proposed actions, consider all relevant information before they act, give the public an opportunity to comment on the environmental issues, and avoid or reduce potential harm to the environment when feasible.

> CEQA applies to most state, regional, and local agency decisions to carry out, authorize, or approve projects that could have adverse effects on the environment.

To ensure their validity, an agency's actions should comply with CEQA's statutory provisions as well as the state environmental guidelines that have been adopted by the Secretary of Resources and incorporated into the California Code of Regulations, title 14, section 15000 *et seq.* ("Guidelines").[2]

The CEQA process begins with a preliminary review of the proposal to determine whether CEQA applies to the agency action, or whether the action is instead exempt. Guidelines §§ 15060–15061. If the agency determines that the activity is not subject to CEQA, it may file a notice of exemption, and no further action to comply with CEQA is required. Guidelines §§ 15061, 15062. If the agency determines that the activity is a project subject to CEQA, the agency then must prepare either an environmental impact report (EIR) or a negative declaration. Pub. Res. Code §§ 21080, 21002.1.

> EIR = environmental impact report

---

1 For a more detailed summary of CEQA and its application, see Stephen L. Kostka and Michael H. Zischke, *Practice Under the California Environmental Quality Act* (Cal. Cont. Ed. Bar, 3rd ed. 2013).

2 At a minimum, the courts should afford great weight to the Guidelines. See *Laurel Heights Improvement Ass'n v. Regents of the Univ. of Cal.*, 47 Cal. 3d 376, 391 n. 2 (1988). However, if a guideline is inconsistent with CEQA's statutory provisions or case law, it may be invalidated. See *Communities for a Better Environment v. California Resources Agency*, 103 Cal. App. 4th 98 (2002).

DEFINITION OF A PROJECT UNDER CEQA

CEQA applies to discretionary actions proposed to be carried out or approved by a public agency.[3] Pub. Res. Code § 21080(a). An action is discretionary if the public agency is required to exercise judgment in deciding whether to approve or disapprove the particular activity, as distinguished from situations where the public agency merely has to determine whether there has been conformity with objective standards in applicable ordinances or other laws. Pub. Res. Code § 21080; Guidelines § 15357. "The statutory distinction between discretionary and purely ministerial projects implicitly recognizes that unless a public agency can shape the project in a way that would respond to concerns raised in an [environmental impact report], or its functional equivalent, environmental review would be a meaningless exercise." *Mountain Lion Found. v. Fish & Game Comm'n*, 16 Cal. 4th 105, 117 (1997). Thus, CEQA does not apply to proposed agency actions that are ministerial, rather than discretionary. *See Sierra Club v. Napa County Bd. of Supervisors*, 205 Cal. App. 4th 162 (2012) (deferring to County's determination that its process for considering sequential lot line adjustments was ministerial); *Health First v. March Joint Powers Authority*, 174 Cal. App. 4th 1135 (2009) (approval of design application was ministerial where plan review involved consistency determination with fixed standards included in an existing specific plan, an EIR prepared for the specific plan, and previously adopted design guidelines).

A city's decision to place a voter-sponsored initiative measure onto the ballot is a ministerial action, exempt from CEQA. *San Bernardino Assoc. of Governments v. Superior Ct.*, 135 Cal. App. 4th 1106 (2006) (county's decision to place transportation agency's measure on ballot was ministerial). By contrast, placement of the city's own initiative measure on the ballot is discretionary, and not exempt. *Friends of Sierra Madre v. City of Sierra Madre*, 25 Cal. 4th 165 (2001) (city's decision to place a city-sponsored initiative on the ballot is a discretionary action subject to CEQA). There is a split in authority as to whether a city's decision to adopt, rather than place on the ballot, a voter-sponsored measure is ministerial or discretionary. The California Supreme Court has accepted review of *Tuolumne Jobs & Small Business Alliance v. Superior Ct.*, a decision holding a city has discretion whether to adopt, rather than place on the ballot, a voter-sponsored initiative; therefore such action is subject to CEQA. 152 Cal. Rptr. 3d 808 (2013). That case conflicts with *Native American Sacred Site & Envtl. Protection Ass'n v. City of San Juan Capistrano*, 120 Cal. App. 4th 961 (2004), holding that because cities have a mandatory duty to place a voter-sponsored initiative on the ballot or adopt the initiative by ordinance, a city's decision to adopt the initiative by ordinance is ministerial and is not subject to CEQA.

CEQA also does not apply to activities that are not proposed for approval, or that will not directly or indirectly result in a change to the environment. CEQA defines a "project" as an activity that may cause either a direct physical change in the environment, or a reasonably foreseeable indirect physical change in the environment, and that is any of the following:

- An activity directly undertaken by any public agency
- An activity undertaken by a person that is supported, in whole or in part, through contracts, grants, subsidies, loans, or other forms of assistance from one or more public agencies

> There is a split in authority as to whether a city's decision to adopt, rather than place on the ballot, a voter-sponsored measure is ministerial or discretionary.

---

[3] The agency that is responsible for carrying out the mandates of CEQA is called the "lead agency." If a project will be carried out by a public agency, that agency will be the lead agency. Guidelines § 15051; *see also Planning & Conserv. League v. Dep't of Water Resources*, 83 Cal. App. 4th 892, 905 (2000) (if several agencies are involved in a project, the agency with principal responsibility for carrying out the project is the lead agency). For a private project, the lead agency is the public agency with the greatest responsibility for supervising or approving the project as a whole. Guidelines § 15051(b).

- An activity that involves the issuance to a person of a lease, permit, license, certificate, or other entitlement for use by one or more public agencies

Pub. Res. Code § 21065; Guidelines § 15378(a)

APPROVAL

CEQA compliance must occur before a public agency approves a project. The term "approval" refers to a public agency decision that "commits [it] to a definite course of action in regard to a project." Guidelines § 15352(a). Public agency approval of private projects is deemed to occur "upon the earliest commitment to issue or the issuance by the public agency of a discretionary contract, grant, subsidy, loan or other form of financial assistance, lease, permit, license, certificate, or other entitlement for use of the project." Guidelines § 15352(b). Approval of an agreement between a public agency and a private entity that is conditioned upon future CEQA compliance may not constitute "approval of a project" under CEQA where the agreement recognizes changes to the project may be made due to CEQA review, the agency does not commit itself to move forward with the project prior to CEQA compliance, and the agency does not limit its discretion in conducting its part of the CEQA analysis. *Concerned Citizens v. McCloud Community Services Dist.*, 147 Cal. App. 4th 181 (2007); *Cedar Fair v. City of Santa Clara*, 194 Cal. App. 4th 1150 (2011) (approval of a term sheet that provided for city discretion to modify the transaction to comply with CEQA and that bound the parties only to continue to negotiate in good faith, did not constitute a project approval; while the city may have been "politically dedicated" to a stadium project, it was not legally committed such that environmental review was foreclosed).

> CEQA compliance must occur before a public agency approves a project.

However, a contract's conditioning of final approval on CEQA compliance is not determinative. In *Save Tara v. City of West Hollywood*, 45 Cal. 4th 116, 130–32 (2008), the California Supreme Court struck down a conditional agreement between a city and two nonprofit developers for an affordable senior housing project on city-owned land. The court ruled that the city violated CEQA because it had impermissibly committed itself to proceed with the project before completing an environmental review under CEQA. The court expressly declined to adopt a bright line rule for when a public agency may approve an agreement that is contingent on future CEQA compliance. *Id.* at 138. Instead, the decision instructs courts to determine on a case-by-case basis, in light of all of the "surrounding circumstances," whether an agency has taken "any action that significantly furthers a project in a manner that forecloses alternatives or mitigation measures that would ordinarily be part of CEQA review." *Id.* at 138. *See also Riverwatch v. Olivenhain Municipal Water Dist.*, 170 Cal. App. 4th 1186 (2009) (where agency did not make clear that it reserved complete discretion under CEQA to adopt mitigation measures or alternatives to reduce significant impacts, approval of a sixty-year water supply agreement functioned as a project approval); *County of Amador v. City of Plymouth*, 149 Cal. App. 4th 1089 (2007) (approval of an agreement that is not conditioned on CEQA compliance and requires an agency to construct public works improvements that may have an effect on the environment is a project under CEQA).

For projects to be carried out by a public agency, approval does not occur until the agency is legally committed to proceed with the project. *See City of Vernon v. Board of Harbor Comm'rs*, 63 Cal. App. 4th 677, 688 (1998) (statement of intent signed by the agency's director did not constitute project approval, because statement did not legally bind agency to approve the project, nor did the agency commit to a definite course of action by merely advocating for a project or acting as a proponent for a project).

See also Chung v. City of Monterey Park, 210 Cal. App. 4th 394 (2012) (ballot measure requiring competitive bidding for future waste hauling contracts was not a "project" because it was a fiscal activity, and did not commit the city to a course of action); *City of Santee v. County of San Diego*, 186 Cal. App. 4th 55 (2010) (siting agreement was not a commitment to construct a jail facility); *Parchester Village Neighborhood Council v. City of Richmond*, 182 Cal. App. 4th 305 (2010) (agreement with tribe to support a casino application was not a project because the city had no control over a casino and did not commit to use funds from the tribe for any specific physical improvements); *Sustainable Transportation Advocates of Santa Barbara v. Santa Barbara Assoc. of Gov'ts*, 179 Cal. App. 4th 113 (2009) (ballot measure to approve a sales and use tax to fund transportation projects was not a "project" because it did not constitute a binding commitment to construct improvements listed in the investment plan attached to the measure); *Pala Band of Mission Indians v. County of San Diego*, 68 Cal. App. 4th 556, 576 (1998) (designation of potential waste disposal sites as "tentatively reserved" in county waste management plan did not trigger duty to prepare EIR because commitment to develop one or more of the sites could arise only after county found them consistent with general plan and designated them reserved); *Kaufman & Broad-South Bay, Inc. v. Morgan Hill Unified Sch. Dist.*, 9 Cal. App. 4th 464, 474 (1992) (formation of a community facilities district to provide funding for district activities was not a project, because the agency was not committed to a definite course of action relating to expenditure of funds); *Residents Ad Hoc Stadium Comm. v. Bd. of Trustees*, 89 Cal. App. 3d 274, 291 (1979) (in preparing an EIR for proposed athletic stadium, the agency did not have to consider other potential capital improvements in the university's master plan because other components were not proposed for approval). *But see County of Amador v. El Dorado County Water Agency*, 76 Cal. App. 4th 931, 950 (1999) (approval of a water supply program before adopting a revised general plan precludes proper review of significant growth issues).

ENVIRONMENTAL CHANGE

> To constitute a project under CEQA, the activity also must be one that might result in a physical change in the environment.

To constitute a project under CEQA, the activity also must be one that might result in a physical change in the environment. Pub. Res. Code § 21065; Guidelines § 15378(a). The term "environment" is defined as:

The physical conditions which exist within the area which will be affected by a proposed project, including land, air, water, minerals, flora, fauna, noise, and objects of historic or aesthetic significance.

Pub. Res. Code § 21060.5; Guidelines § 15360.

CEQA covers "tangible physical manifestations that are perceptible by the senses," and emphasizes "matters that can be seen, felt, heard, or smelled." *Martin v. City and County of San Francisco*, 135 Cal. App. 4th 392, 403 (2006) (project that affects only the interior of a house, even where the house is located in an historic district defined in part by the residential interiors, is not subject to CEQA). Impacts to a limited number of individual users of project facilities do not constitute impacts on the environment. *Eureka Citizens for Responsible Gov't v. City of Eureka*, 147 Cal. App. 4th 357 (2007). *See also Taxpayers for Accountable School Bond Spending v. San Diego Unified School Dist.*, 215 Cal. App. 4th 1013, 1042 (2013); *Mira Mar Mobile Community v. City of Oceanside*, 119 Cal. App. 4th 477, 492 (2004). Further, CEQA does not require an analysis of the impacts of the surrounding environment on the project. *Ballona Wetlands Land Trust v. City of Los Angeles*, 201 Cal. App. 4th 455, 473-74 (2011) (EIR was not required to address the impact of sea level rise on the project); *South Orange County Wastewater Auth. v. City of Dana Point*, 196 Cal. App. 4th 1604 (2011) (rejecting arguments that a negative declaration should have evaluated odor and noise impacts from an existing sewage treatment plant on new residents of a proposed project); *City of Long Beach v. Los Angeles Unified School Dist.*, 176 Cal. App. 4th 889, 905 (2009) (EIR for a new school was not required to address the impacts of emissions from nearby freeways on staff and students); *see also Baird v. Contra Costa County*, 32 Cal. App. 4th 1464 (1995).

The action reviewed under CEQA is the development or other physical activities that will result from the approval, not the approval itself. *Cal. Unions for Reliable Energy v. Mojave Desert Air Quality Mgmt. Dist.*, 178 Cal. App. 4th 1225, 1238 (2009). A public agency action that will not have an immediate effect on the environment but might culminate in a physical impact to the environment is a project under CEQA. *See Fullerton Joint Union High Sch. Dist. v. State Bd. of Educ.*, 32 Cal. 3d 779, 795 (1982). Thus, general plan amendments and other legislative policy enactments may be "projects" subject to CEQA even if further discretionary approvals will be necessary before development causing physical changes to the environment can occur. In *Christward Ministry v. Superior Court*, for example, the City of San Marcos argued that an EIR was not required for a general plan amendment relating to the siting of a landfill, because an EIR would be required for the development of the landfill itself. 184 Cal. App. 3d 180 (1986). The court rejected the city's argument, stating that general plans, though not directly effecting a physical change in the environment, do have an ultimate effect upon physical changes, and therefore require environmental review, where appropriate. Further, preparation of an EIR at the general plan stage comports with the policy that environmental consequences be considered at the earliest possible time. *Id.* at 193-194. *See also Muzzy Ranch Co. v. Solano County Airport Land Use Comm'n*, 41 Cal. 4th 372, 383 (2007) (adoption of an airport land use plan is a "project" under CEQA even if the plan merely freezes existing laws and even if future actions must be taken by other agencies); *but see Friends of Sierra Railroad v. Tuolumne Park & Recreation Dist.*, 147 Cal. App. 4th 643 (2007) (where development proposals have not yet been submitted, an action to transfer land may not be a "project" requiring CEQA review because not enough information is known to conduct a meaningful review).

> The action reviewed under CEQA is the development or other physical activities that will result from the approval, not the approval itself.

The action reviewed under CEQA must encompass all components of the activity that is being approved. The term "project" refers to the whole of an action. Guidelines § 15378. A public agency may not divide a single project into smaller individual subcomponents in order to avoid responsibility for considering the environmental impact of the project as a whole. *See Orinda Ass'n v. Board of Supervisors*, 182 Cal. App. 3d 1145, 1171 (1986). The "project" includes reasonably foreseeable consequences of the proposed approval, *Bozung v. Local Agency Formation Comm'n*, 13 Cal. 3d 263, 279-81, 289 (1975); *Laurel Heights Improvement Ass'n v. Regents of the Univ. of Cal.*, 47 Cal. 3d 376, 395-398 (1988) (*Laurel Heights I*); improvements necessary for the provision of public services to the project, *Santiago County Water Dist. v. County of Orange*, 118 Cal. App. 3d 818, 829-30 (1981); and components that are an integral part of the project, *No Oil, Inc. v. City of Los Angeles*, 196 Cal. App. 3d 223, 237 (1987).

PROCESS

If an agency determines that a proposed activity is a project under CEQA, it will usually take the following three-step approach: (1) determine whether the project is statutorily or categorically exempt from CEQA; (2) if the project is not exempt, prepare an initial study to determine whether the project may result in significant environmental effects; and (3) prepare a negative declaration, mitigated negative declaration, or EIR, depending upon the results of the initial study. For a more detailed discussion of these three steps, see *Gentry v. City of Murrieta*, 36 Cal. App. 4th 1359, 1371–72 (1995).

DETERMINING IF THE ACTIVITY IS EXEMPT FROM CEQA

If it can be seen with certainty that a project will not have a significant effect on the environment, it is exempt from further CEQA review. Guidelines § 15061(b)(3). Such a determination is known as the "common sense" exemption. This exemption can be relied upon only if substantial evidence in the record supports the determination that it applies. *Davidon Homes v. City of San Jose*, 54 Cal. App. 4th 106, 114 (1997). Such a decision need not necessarily be supported by detailed or extensive fact finding, at least where a project is consistent with existing general plan and zoning designations, and future effects will themselves require analysis under CEQA. *Muzzy Ranch*, 41 Cal. 4th at 388–89. Alternatively, a project may fit within a category of projects that expressly are excluded as exempt from CEQA compliance either by CEQA or the Guidelines. *See, e.g.*, Pub. Res. Code §§ 21080(b), 21080.01–21080.03, 21080.05–21080.08, 21080.7–21080.33, 21159.21–21159.24; Guidelines §§ 15062, 15260–15285, 15300–15332.

Statutory exemptions cover a wide range of activities, some limited to one particular project and some having more widespread application.[4] Statutory exemptions generally apply to classes of projects determined by the Legislature to promote an interest important enough to justify foregoing the benefits of environmental review. Unlike categorical exemptions, a project that falls within a statutory exemption generally is not subject to CEQA even if it has the potential to significantly affect the environment. *Del Cerro Mobile Estates v. City of Placentia*, 197 Cal. App. 4th 173 (2011) (approval of multiple grade separations was exempt from CEQA, and the city did not waive exemption by preparing an EIR that considered non-exempt alternatives). Several of the statutory exemptions provide limited environmental review for projects that are consistent with a previously adopted general plan, community plan, specific plan, or zoning ordinance. Gov't Code § 65457 (residential development or any zoning change undertaken to implement a specific plan); Pub. Res. Code § 21083.3 (limited environmental review of development proposals consistent with a previously adopted planning or zoning action). *See also* Pub. Res. Code § 21158.5(a) (limited environmental review of multiple family residential developments of not more than 100 units, and mixed use residential developments of not more than 100,000 square feet); Pub. Res. Code § 21080.14 (development of up to 100 units of low- and moderate-income housing); Pub. Res. Code § 21155.4 (residential, employment center, or mixed-use development projects within a transit priority area, consistent with a specific plan, and consistent with policies in a sustainable communities strategy or alternative planning strategy). Prior to conducting CEQA review of any project that is consistent with a prior planning action, each of these code sections should be reviewed carefully to determine whether all of the necessary conditions can be met. In *Concerned Dublin Citizens v. City of Dublin*, 214 Cal. App. 4th 1301 (2013), the court clarified that the substantial evidence test

---

[4] Most of CEQA's statutory exemptions are listed in Article 18 of the CEQA Guidelines, sections 15260–15285. However, because statutory exemptions may be found in various codes, all statutes regulating approval or development of a proposed project should be reviewed carefully to determine whether the project is exempt from CEQA. For examples of additional statutory exemptions that are not found in Article 18 of the CEQA Guidelines, see Stephen L. Kostka and Michael H. Zischke, *Practice Under the Environmental Quality Act*, section 5.5 (Cal. Cont. Ed. Bar, 3rd ed. 2013).

governs review of an agency's determination that a project is covered by the statutory exemption for residential projects that are consistent with a previously adopted specific plan, including the determinations whether the project is a residential development, whether it is consistent with a specific plan for which an EIR has been prepared, and whether any of the events triggering supplemental review under Public Resources Code section 21166 have occurred. Neither the fact that the specific plan also permitted nonresidential development nor the fact that the specific plan EIR was a program level EIR rather than project level EIR disqualified the project from the exemption. 214 Cal. App. 4th at 1312.

A different type of statutory exemption applies to certified regulatory programs. CEQA provides a mechanism for agencies implementing state regulatory programs to obtain certification from the Secretary of the Resources Agency confirming that compliance with the program will meet criteria ensuring environmental factors will be examined and considered during agency decisionmaking. Pub. Res. Code § 21080.5. When a regulatory program has been certified, action under the program is exempt from certain portions of CEQA. The practical effect of this exemption is that a state agency acting under a certified regulatory program need not comply with the requirements for preparing initial studies, negative declarations or EIRs. The agency's actions, however, remain subject to other provisions of CEQA. Guidelines § 15250. The same standard of review applies to judicial review of agency decisions made pursuant to a certified regulatory program as applies to decisions made pursuant to CEQA. *POET LLC v. Cal. Air Resources Bd.* 218, Cal. App. 4th 681 (2013). In addition, certified regulatory programs are not exempt from the timing requirements in Guidelines section 15004 for completion of environmental review prior to project approval. *Id.* (Air Resources Board improperly adopted low carbon fuel requirements prior to completing environmental review under its certified regulatory program).

Categorical exemptions are classes of projects that the Secretary of Resources has found do not have a significant effect on the environment. Pub. Res. Code § 21084(a); Guidelines § 15300. The categorical exemptions are set out in Article 19 of the CEQA Guidelines, sections 15301–15332. The categorical exemptions are not absolute. A categorical exemption generally will not apply if (1) there is a reasonable possibility of a significant effect on the environment due to unusual circumstances; (2) significant cumulative impacts from projects of the same type will result; or (3) the project will have impacts on a uniquely sensitive environment. Guidelines § 15300.2. The Guidelines also list several other specific exceptions to the categorical exemptions. Guidelines § 15300.2.

The two exceptions most often at issue are the "unusual circumstances" and "cumulative impacts" exceptions. Effects common to projects generally within a categorical exemption are not considered "unusual circumstances" triggering an exception. *See Fairbank v. City of Mill Valley*, 75 Cal App. 4th 1243, 1260 (1999) (traffic and parking effects from a small commercial structure in a downtown area not considered unusual circumstances); *see also Turlock Irrigation Dist. v. Zanker*, 140 Cal. App. 4th 1047 (2006) (no significant effect due to unusual circumstances shown from the water district's conservation measures); *San Lorenzo Valley Community Advocates for Responsible Education v. San Lorenzo Valley Unified School Dist.*, 139 Cal. App. 4th 1356 (2006) (traffic and parking effects associated with school closure and transfer of students not unusual circumstances). For the cumulative impact exception to apply, the combined effects of successive projects of the same type must be experienced in the same place. Guidelines § 15330(d); *see Robinson v. City and County of San Francisco*, 208 Cal. App.

> The two exceptions most often at issue are the "unusual circumstances" and "cumulative impacts" exceptions.

4th 950, 956-960 (2012) (upholding use of the small project exemption where the noise and visual effects of multiple installations of wireless transmission equipment would not be experienced at the same time in any particular location).

The project must qualify for statutory or categorical exemptions without modification; an agency cannot adopt mitigation measures in order to ensure that a project fits within a categorical exemption. *Salmon Protection and Watershed Network v. County of Marin*, 125 Cal. App. 4th 1098 (2004).

CEQA does not contain any required procedures for making an exemption determination. *See City of Pasadena v. State of California*, 14 Cal. App. 4th 810, 819-20 (1993); *San Lorenzo Valley Community Advocates for Responsible Education v. San Lorenzo Valley Unified School Dist.*, 139 Cal. App. 4th 1356 (2006); *Apartment Ass'n of Greater Los Angeles v. City of Los Angeles*, 90 Cal. App. 4th 1162, 1772-73 (2001) (initial study not required for determination that the city's housing code enforcement program is exempt). And, generally, neither CEQA nor the CEQA Guidelines require findings documenting the basis for an exemption. *See CalBeach Advocates v. City of Solana Beach*, 103 Cal. App. 4th 529, 540 (2002). The exemption for rate-setting under Public Resources Code section 21080(b)(8), however, requires that the "public agency shall incorporate written findings in the record of any proceeding...setting forth with specificity the basis for the claim of exemption." *See also* Guidelines § 15273(c). An agency can satisfy this requirement by tracking the language of section 21080(b)(8), and need not set forth with specificity its evidentiary sub-conclusions. *Great Oaks Water Co. v. Santa Clara Valley Water Dist.*, 170 Cal. App. 4th 956, 972 (2009) (court upheld the water district's findings that identified the ultimate factual bases for the claim of exemption, coupled with references in related findings to portions of the annual report and other information and evidence provided during the hearing process); *see also Bus Riders Union v. Los Angeles County Metropolitan Transportation Agency*, 179 Cal. App. 4th 101 (2009) (substantial evidence supported the conclusion that a bus fare increase fits within the rate-setting exemption).

In all exemption determinations, the agency should ensure the record demonstrates that the project falls within the claimed exemption. *See Magan v. County of Kings*, 105 Cal. App. 4th 468, 475 (2002). *See also Save Our Carmel River v. Monterey Peninsula Water Mgmt. Dist.*, 141 Cal. App. 4th 677 (2006) (replacement project exemption determination must be based on evidence from which the agency can compare the replacement structure and the existing structure to verify that the replacement structure will be on the same site with substantially the same purpose and capacity as the structure it replaces). On judicial review, the agency's determination that the project falls within the exempt category of projects will be affirmed if it is supported by substantial evidence. *Save the Plastic Bag Coalition v. County of Marin*, 218 Cal. App. 4th 209 (2013) (substantial evidence supported county's determination that plastic bag ban fit within exemptions in Guidelines §§ 15307 and 15308 for actions taken by regulatory agencies to assume maintenance, restoration or enhancement of a natural resource or to assure the maintenance, restoration, enhancement or protection of the environment).

An agency's determination that the project fits within a categorical exemption includes an implied finding that none of the exceptions identified in the Guidelines is applicable. The burden then shifts to the challenging party to produce evidence showing that one of the exceptions applies to take the project out of the exempt category. *See Committee to Save the Hollywoodland Specific Plan v. City of Los Angeles*, 161 Cal. App. 4th 1168, 1186 (2008); *Banker's Hill v. City of San Diego*, 139 Cal. App. 4th 249 (2006). Appellate districts are split as to whether the decision to apply an exception is subject to the substantial evidence standard or the "fair argument" test, in which an exemption cannot stand if the challenger presents evidence supporting a fair argument that an exception applies. *Compare Save Our Carmel River,* 141 Cal. App. 4th 677 (applying the substantial evidence test) *with Banker's Hill,* 139 Cal. App. 4th 249 (applying fair argument test to determine whether an infill housing project would have a significant effect on the environment due to unusual circumstances) and *Voices for Rural Living v. El Dorado Irrigation District,* 209 Cal. App. 4th 1096 (2012) (applying the fair argument test to determine whether constructing a small project necessary to supply increased water to a casino on tribal lands would have a significant effect due to unusual circumstances). In 2012, California Supreme Court accepted review of a case, *Berkeley Hillside Preservation v. City of Berkeley,* that is likely to lead to a decision on this issue in 2014. 142 Cal. Rptr. 3d 1 (2012).

Different procedural requirements apply to the exception for projects affecting a historic resource. Unless a resource has been listed, or officially determined eligible for listing, in the California Register of Historical Resources, the lead agency has discretion in determining whether the resource is historic. Such a determination will be upheld if there is substantial evidence in the record to support it, regardless of whether it is made in the context of a decision to exempt the project from CEQA, adopt a negative declaration, or certify an EIR. *Valley Advocates v. City of Fresno,* 160 Cal. App. 4th 1039 (2008).

> Different procedural requirements apply to the exception for projects affecting a historic resource.

An agency may elect to file a notice of exemption. A notice of exemption contains a brief project description; the location of a project; a finding that the project is exempt from CEQA, including a citation to the appropriate exemption; and a brief statement of the reasons to support the finding that the project is exempt. Guidelines § 15062(a). If a notice of exemption is filed after project approval, it will trigger a 35-day statute of limitations for challenging the agency's decision that the project is exempt from CEQA. Pub. Res. Code § 21167(d); Guidelines § 15062(d); *see Stockton Citizens for Sensible Planning v. City of Stockton,* 48 Cal. 4th 481 (2010) (suits alleging the agency "improperly determined" a project to be exempt from CEQA must be brought within 35 days of filing the notice of exemption); *but see Coalition for Clean Air v. City of Visalia,* 209 Cal. App. 4th 408 (2012) (notice of exemption filed before project approval is invalid). Further, the statute of limitation bars challenges to subsequent approvals for project components that are within the scope of the project determined to be exempt. *Madrigal v. City of Huntington Beach,* 147 Cal. App. 4th 1375 (2007) (challenge to a grading permit barred where subject fill activity was within the scope of original project approval). If the notice of exemption is not filed, the time period for challenging the action under CEQA is normally 180 days following the agency's approval. Pub. Res. Code § 21167(d); Guidelines § 15062(d).

PREPARATION OF AN INITIAL STUDY

If the project is not exempt, the public agency usually undertakes an "initial study." An initial study is:

> A preliminary analysis prepared by the lead agency (usually the city or the county having primary jurisdiction over the project) to determine whether an EIR or negative declaration must be prepared.

Guidelines §§ 15063, 15365; Pub. Res. Code §§ 21080.1, 21080.3.

The purpose of the initial study is to determine whether there may be a significant environmental impact. Pub. Res. Code § 21080(c); Guidelines §§ 15063–15065.

FIGURE B. CEQA FLOW CHART FOR LOCAL AGENCIES

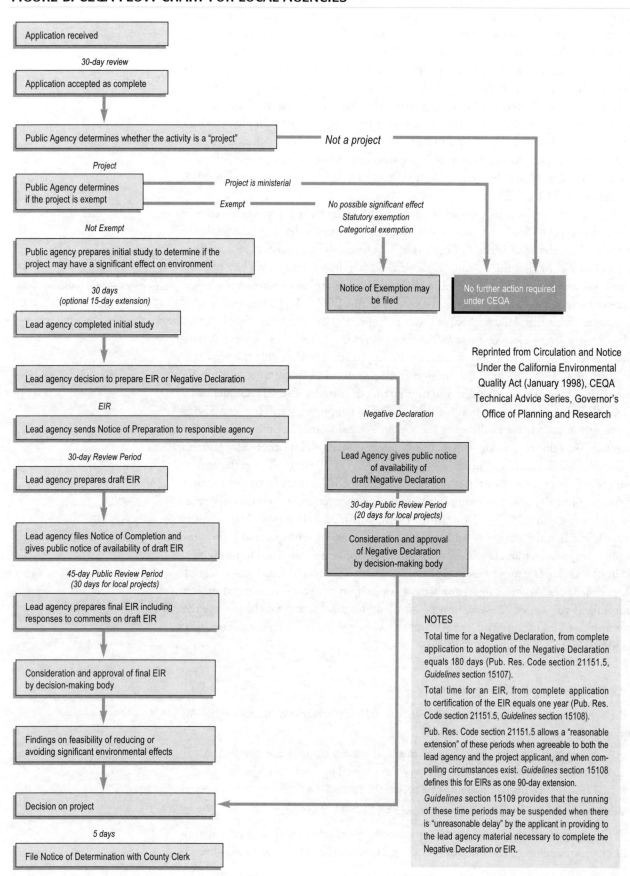

FIGURE C. LEAD AGENCY DECISION TO PREPARE AN EIR

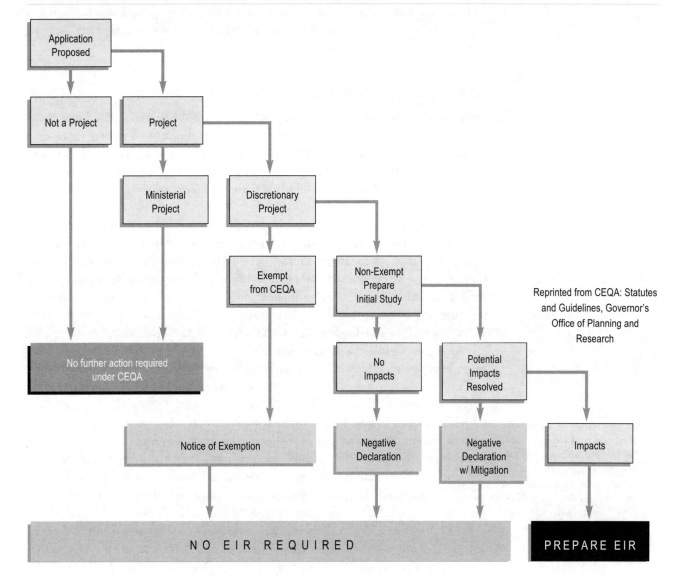

Reprinted from CEQA: Statutes and Guidelines, Governor's Office of Planning and Research

Appendix G to the CEQA Guidelines provides a suggested checklist for initial studies. In conducting the initial study, many agencies rely on a checklist, but, in doing so, they should disclose the data or evidence upon which the persons conducting the study relied. Mere conclusions as to the absence of the possibility of a significant effect are inadequate to support an agency's decision to proceed with a negative declaration. *See Citizens Ass'n for Sensible Dev. of Bishop Area v. County of Inyo*, 172 Cal. App. 3d 151, 171 (1985); *Sundstrom v. County of Mendocino*, 202 Cal. App. 3d 296, 305–06 (1988).

Where the proposed project would result in the adoption of revised policies that may result in adverse effects, those effects must be considered in the initial study. *See Lighthouse Field Beach Rescue v. City of Santa Cruz*, 131 Cal. App. 4th 1170 (2005). Indirect effects of a project also must be determined. *Inyo Citizens for Better Planning v. Bd. of Supervisors*, 180 Cal. App. 4th 1 (2009) (a change in the definition of net acreage in the county's general plan could increase development potential, resulting in adverse impacts to wildlife); *City of Arcadia v. State Water Resources Control Bd.*, 135 Cal. App. 4th 1392 (2006) (State Board's functional equivalent document should have evaluated potential construction and air quality effects from pollution control equipment likely to be installed in order to comply with "zero trash" water run-off standard). For a detailed discussion of the law on the initial studies, see *Gentry v. City of Murrieta*, 36 Cal. App. 4th 1359, 1376 (1995).

ADOPTION OF A NEGATIVE DECLARATION

If the initial study concludes that there will not be a significant effect on the environment, the agency can prepare a negative declaration and forego further CEQA compliance. Pub. Res. Code § 21080(c); Guidelines § 15070 et seq. (negative declaration process). A negative declaration is a written statement that an EIR is not required because a project will not have a significant adverse impact on the environment. Pub. Res. Code §§ 21064, 21080(c).

An agency may attach conditions to a negative declaration for the purpose of mitigating potential environmental effects. Such a negative declaration is referred to as a "mitigated negative declaration." Guidelines § 15070(b); Pub. Res. Code § 21064.5. A mitigated negative declaration states that revisions in the project made or agreed to by the applicant would avoid the potentially significant adverse impacts, and that there is no substantial evidence that the project, as revised, will have a significant effect on the environment. Pub. Res. Code § 21064.5; Guidelines § 15070(b)(2).

As a general rule, an agency may not adopt a negative declaration, and must instead prepare an EIR, if it can be fairly argued on the basis of substantial evidence that the project may have a significant environmental impact. *See No Oil, Inc. v. City of Los Angeles*, 13 Cal. 3d 68, 74–75 (1974); Guidelines § 15064(f)(1). Even where a project may result in a net benefit to the environment, if substantial evidence supports a fair argument that any adverse environmental impacts also may result, then an EIR must be prepared in order to explore potential mitigation measures and alternatives that would reduce or avoid such impact. *County Sanitation Dist. No. 2 v. County of Kern*, 127 Cal. App. 4th 1544 (2005). A significance determination requires the agency to exercise discretion. *See Citizen Action to Serve All Students v. Thornley*, 222 Cal. App. 3d 748, 755 (1990). In addition, the agency is entitled to make a fair assessment of the consequences of project approval; an agency need not place a finite limit on project activities. *Taxpayers for Accountable School Bond Spending v. San Diego Unified School Dist.*, 215 Cal. App. 4th 1013, 1038 (2013) (rejecting argument that district was required to limit evening events in order to assess impacts from installation of stadium improvements).

Substantial evidence means enough relevant information and reasonable inferences from this information that a fair argument can be made to support a conclusion, even though other conclusions may be reached. Guidelines § 15384(a). Reports prepared by experts, if based on fact, normally constitute substantial evidence. *See Sierra Club v. California Dept. of Forestry*, 150 Cal. App. 4th 370 (2007). Argument, speculation, inaccurate information, unsubstantiated opinion, or social or economic impacts unrelated to physical changes to the environment do not constitute substantial evidence. Pub. Res. Code §§ 21080(e), 21082.2(c). Similarly, the existence of public controversy over the environmental effects of a project does not, in and of itself, require preparation of an EIR if there is no substantial evidence before the agency that the project may have a significant effect on the environment. Pub. Res. Code § 21082.2(b); Guidelines § 15064(f)(4); *compare Taxpayers for Accountable School Bond Spending v. San Diego Unified School Dist.*, 215 Cal. App. 4th 1013, 1041 (2013) (given limited number of affected residences, limited operating hours and limited number of nighttime events, substantial evidence did not support a fair argument that new stadium lighting would result in sleep deprivation for a substantial number of people), *Bowman v. City of Berkeley*, 122 Cal. App. 4th 572 (2004) (differences of opinion regarding aesthetic effects in an urban area do not trigger preparation of an EIR when a project must undergo design review) *and Porterville Citizens for Responsible Hillside Development v. City of Porterville*, 157 Cal. App. 4th 885 (2007) (rejecting challenge based solely on aesthetic objections from neighbors, on grounds that such assertions were claims of effects on particular persons, not on persons in general) *with Citizens For Responsible & Open Gov't v. City of Grand Terrace*, 160 Cal. App. 4th 1323 (2008) (an EIR may be required when neighbors express concerns that project density and height may substantially change aesthetic conditions and neighborhood character for the public in general).

Courts conduct an independent review of the evidence that was before the agency under the fair argument standard, while giving the lead agency the benefit of the doubt on any legitimate, disputed issues of credibility. *Stanislaus Audubon Society, Inc. v. County of Stanislaus*, 33 Cal. App. 4th 144, 151 (1995). If a lead agency determines testimony and documents do not constitute substantial evidence due to lack of a credibility, it should identify the specific evidence and explain the conclusion in the record. *See Consolidated Irrigation District v. City of Selma*, 204 Cal. App. 4th 187 (2012) (refusing to defer to the city's decision to adopt a negative declaration when the city provided no citations to the record showing the council, planning commission or staff had addressed the credibility of any evidence presented).

The California Supreme Court has noted that common sense "is an important consideration at all levels of CEQA review." *Save the Plastic Bag Coalition v. City of Manhattan Beach*, 52 Cal. 4th 155, 175 (2011). In *Save the Plastic Bag Coalition*, the Court rejected arguments that increased effects from the life cycle of paper bag production and distribution as compared to the life cycle for plastic bags necessitated preparation of an EIR for a proposed plastic bag ban. The city and its retail sector were simply too small for the city's ban to cause significant impacts or a substantial contribution to cumulative impacts of similar bans in other jurisdictions.

A negative declaration must include a project description, the project location, the name of the project proponent, a finding of no significant effect on the environment, an attached copy of the initial study, and any mitigation measures that have been included in the project. Guidelines § 15071. The agency prepares the negative declaration and notifies the public that it is available for review, receives and considers comments on the negative declaration, considers and adopts the negative declaration, makes any necessary findings regarding mitigation measures, adopts a mitigation and monitoring program for any mitigation measures, and usually posts a notice of determination. Pub. Res. Code §§ 21092(b), 21092.2; Guidelines §§ 15072(a), 15075(a). It is important that the negative declaration also be provided to the State Clearinghouse for review by relevant state agencies prior to its approval. *See Fall River Wild Trout Found. v. County of Shasta*, 70 Cal. App. 4th 482, 490 (1999). If a fair argument based on substantial evidence can be made that significant impacts to biological resources may occur, the agency must consult with the California Department of Fish and Wildlife before conducting its initial study, and subsequently must notify CDFW of its intent to adopt a negative declaration. *Mejia v. City of Los Angeles*, 130 Cal. App. 4th 322 (2005).

CDFW = California Department of Fish and Wildlife

Any mitigation measures that will be incorporated into the project must be identified before the proposed negative declaration and initial study are released for public review. Pub. Res. Code § 21064.5; Guidelines § 15070(b). When a negative declaration has been substantially revised after public notice of its availability, but prior to its adoption, it must be recirculated before the agency may adopt it. Guidelines section 15073.5 states that recirculation is required upon (1) the identification of a new, avoidable significant effect that can be reduced to a less-than-significant level only through the adoption of mitigation; and (2) a determination that originally proposed mitigation is not sufficient to reduce a project's impact to a less-than-significant level, and that additional mitigation or project revisions are necessary. The section also provides detailed guidance as to how a negative declaration should be recirculated prior to its approval.

PREPARATION OF AN ENVIRONMENTAL IMPACT REPORT

If the project is one that the agency determines may have a significant effect on the environment, an EIR must be prepared. Pub. Res. Code §§ 21002.1, 21061, 21080, 21080.1 et seq.; Guidelines §§ 15080–15081.5. However, CEQA provides several optional tools for streamlining such environmental review when there is a series of projects or activities the agency is considering.

Master EIRs are designed to provide for analysis of broad policy issues, such as cumulative and growth-inducing impacts, to limit the environmental review of subsequent projects. Pub. Res. Code § 21156. The Public Resources Code, starting with section 21157.1, outlines the procedure for reviewing subsequent projects after a master EIR has been prepared. During the first five years after certification of a master EIR, an agency need not review the adequacy of the master EIR for projects included therein; after five years, the agency must determine whether a subsequent or supplemental EIR is needed. Pub. Res. Code § 21157.6.

Program EIRs generally can be used for the same types of actions as master EIRs, though this streamlining device is reserved for related actions that can be characterized as one large project. Guidelines § 15168. If the program EIR is sufficiently comprehensive, the agency may dispense with further environmental review for later activities within the program that are covered in the program EIR. Guidelines § 15168(c); *Concerned Dublin Citizens v. City of Dublin*, 214 Cal. App. 4th 1301, 1316 (2013) (rejecting the argument that a tiered CEQA document must be completed for a project specific approval relying on a previously certified program EIR). A program EIR also may be used to focus or simplify later environmental review or as the basis of a tiered EIR.

In determining whether a program EIR can be used for a later activity, the agency first should consider whether the activity at issue is within the geographic scope of the plan, program, or group of actions evaluated in the program EIR. Guidelines § 15168. The agency then must determine whether the later activity would have environmental effects that were not examined in the program EIR. Guidelines § 15168(c)(1). A written checklist should be used to document the evaluation of any site specific operations. Guidelines § 15168(c)(3). However, unlike an initial study for a new project that has not undergone any review at all, the question the agency asks in reviewing whether an action is within the scope of a program EIR is will there be any new or substantially more severe impacts compared to the impacts discussed in the program EIR. *See* Guidelines §§ 15168(c)(2); 15162. If substantial evidence supports the agency's determination that no new or substantially more severe impacts will occur, the agency can approve the later activity based upon the program EIR, and no further environmental review is required. *Citizens for Responsible Equitable Environmental Development v. City of San Diego Redevelopment Agency*, 134 Cal. App. 4th 598 (2005). If, however, the effects of the activity considered for approval were not addressed in the program EIR, a subsequent EIR must be prepared to consider such effects. *Center for Sierra Nevada Conservation v. County of El Dorado*, 202 Cal. App. 4th 1156, 1162 (2012) (program EIR for the county's general plan did not address environmental effects of a fee program to mitigate impacts on oak woodlands; accordingly adoption of an oak-woodland management plan necessitated preparation of a tiered EIR).

If a project is consistent with existing land use regulations, lead agencies should consider relying upon an EIR prepared for the general plan, community plan, or zoning ordinance. *See* Pub. Res. Code § 21083.3; Guidelines § 15183. Under Guidelines section 15183(a), projects that are consistent with the development density established by existing general plan policies for which an EIR has been certified "shall not require additional environmental review, except as might be necessary to examine whether there are project-specific significant effects which are peculiar to the project or its site." *See Wal-Mart Stores, Inc. v. City of Turlock*, 138 Cal. App. 4th 273, 286 (2006) (project opponent did not present evidence of a reasonably foreseeable project-specific significant change in the environment that was peculiar to a zoning ordinance to ban big box supercenters).

Tiering, under CEQA, refers to use of a broad EIR or negative declaration to analyze general matters (e.g., a plan, policy, or ordinance), coupled with use of later EIRs or negative declarations that focus on narrower projects that are consistent with or implement the more general project. To avoid repetition and wasted time, these later environmental documents may incorporate and build upon the earlier ones. Pub. Res. Code §§ 21068.5, 21093; Guidelines §§ 15152, 15385. Later EIRs or negative declarations need not examine environmental effects that the lead agency finds were mitigated or avoided as a result of the prior approval, or that were reviewed in the previous EIR or negative declaration in sufficient detail to allow those effects to be mitigated when the later project is approved. *See Sierra Club v. City of Orange*, 163 Cal. App. 4th 523 (2008) (supplemental EIR can limit its discussions of traffic baseline and impacts to that which went beyond what was evaluated in the earlier EIR); *Gilroy Citizens for Responsible Planning v. City of Gilroy*, 140 Cal. App. 4th 911 (2006) (EIR appropriately tiered from prior EIR for general plan and prior negative declaration for a retail center).

Tiering does not, however, allow deferral of review when a specific project is involved. In *Stanislaus Natural Heritage Project v. County of Stanislaus*, the court rejected an EIR for a 5,000 unit resort and residential project because the EIR did not analyze the impact of supplying water to most of the project. 48 Cal. App. 4th 182 (1996). The EIR indicated that the source of water was uncertain and concluded that this was a significant impact until a firm water supply could be established. The EIR also included a mitigation measure stating that development would not proceed until adequate water supply had been identified and evaluated under CEQA. The court held that the EIR did not need to identify a specific water source, but that the EIR must adequately disclose the impacts of supplying water to the site. *Id.* at 194–206.

EIR PROCEDURE

Scoping. The first step in preparing an EIR is to determine the scope of the EIR in consultation with agencies, the public, and the applicant. Guidelines §§ 15082, 15083. To do this, the agency prepares a notice of preparation of an EIR describing the project and soliciting comments on the scope of the EIR. The notice should be sent to specified public agencies, including responsible agencies, trustee agencies, and the Governor's Office of Planning and Research. Pub. Res. Code §§ 21080.4, 21092.4,

21104.2; Guidelines § 15082(a). Many agencies also publish the notice and solicit comments from members of the public. Written responses are due 30 days after receipt of the notice of preparation. Guidelines § 15082(b). Agencies also can hold scoping meetings with other agencies or members of the public. Guidelines § 15082(c). An agency is required to hold at least one scoping meeting in several instances, such as when a project is of statewide, regional, or areawide significance. Pub. Res. Code § 21083.9(a).

DEIR = draft environmental impact report

Draft EIR. Following the scoping process, either the agency must prepare a draft EIR or the applicant's consultant may prepare the CEQA documents, so long as the agency independently reviews, evaluates, and exercises judgment over the document and the issues it raises and addresses. *See Friends of La Vina v. County of Los Angeles,* 232 Cal. App. 3d 1446, 1452 (1991); Pub. Res. Code § 21082.1; Guidelines § 15084. The final responsibility to provide an adequate EIR lies with the lead agency. *See Mission Oaks Ranch, Ltd. v. County of Santa Barbara,* 65 Cal. App. 4th 713, 723–24 (1998).

The draft EIR is circulated to the public and to public agencies for review and comment. *See* Figure D, end of this chapter (Time Periods for Review of Environmental Documents), and Guidelines section 15105 for timing of review. Notice of availability of the draft EIR must be provided by newspaper publication, posting on- or off-site in the area where the project will be located, or direct mailing to the owners or occupants of contiguous properties. Pub. Res. Code § 21092(b)(3); *see also Gilroy Citizens for Responsible Planning v. City of Gilroy,* 140 Cal. App. 4th 911 (2006) (a newspaper notice published 42 days before the expiration of the 45-day comment period is insufficient; however, evidence of intent to mail combined with testimony of staff that notice was timely mailed and absence of contrary evidence constituted substantial evidence that the notice had been mailed on time). After receiving the comments, the agency must prepare responses to significant issues raised by the reviewers and, in some instances, revise the EIR. Pub. Res. Code §§ 21091–21092; Guidelines §§ 15085–15089.

Final EIR. The final EIR shall consist of:

- The draft EIR
- Comments and recommendations received on the draft EIR
- The responses of the lead agency to the significant environmental points raised in the review and consultation process
- A list of persons and agencies commenting on the draft EIR, and
- Any other information added by the lead agency

Guidelines § 15132

CEQA provides a "once-around" review system. There is no duty to make the final EIR available for public review and comment, but agencies may elect to do so. At least ten days before certifying a final EIR, the lead agency must provide any public agency that commented on the EIR with a written response to that agency's comments. Guidelines § 15088(b). This requirement may be met by providing the commenting agency with a copy of the final EIR or by making a separate response. Pub. Res. Code § 21092.5.

CONTENTS OF AN ENVIRONMENTAL IMPACT REPORT

To be complete, an EIR must contain the following:

- **Table of contents or index.** Guidelines § 15122
- **Summary of the proposed actions and their consequences.** Guidelines § 15123

- **Project description.** Guidelines § 15124
- **Environmental setting.** Guidelines § 15125
- **Evaluation of environmental impacts.** All phases of a project must be considered when evaluating its impact on the environment: planning, acquisition, development, and operation. Several of the subjects that must be discussed are listed below. Pub. Res. Code § 21100; Guidelines § 15126
- **Water supply assessment.** Water Code section 10911(b) requires that for certain large development projects, a water supply assessment must be included in any environmental document prepared for such projects, and findings must be made based on that assessment. Pub. Res. Code § 21151.9 (requiring compliance with Water Code section 10910 et seq.)
- **Significant environmental effects of the proposed project.** Guidelines § 15126.2
- **Effects not found to be significant.** Pub. Res. Code § 21100(c); Guidelines § 15128
- **Mitigation measures: proposed to avoid or minimize significant effects.** Guidelines § 15126.4
- **Cumulative impacts.** Pub. Res. Code § 21083(b); Guidelines § 15130
- **Alternatives to the proposed project.** Guidelines § 15126.6
- **Inconsistencies with applicable plans.** Guidelines § 15125(d)
- **A discussion of the growth-inducing impacts of the proposed project.** Pub. Res. Code § 21100(b)(5); Guidelines § 15126.2(d)
- **Organizations and persons consulted.** Pub. Res. Code §§ 21104, 21153; Guidelines § 15129

Several of these EIR requirements have been discussed extensively in the case law and are described in the CEQA Guidelines.

Project description. The project description should extend to the entire activity that will ultimately result from approval of the proposed project. All components of the project must be included. *See Santiago County Water Dist. v. County of Orange*, 118 Cal. App. 3d 818, 829 (1981) (EIR for a mining operation should have included an examination of the extension of waterlines to serve the mine); *Whitman v. Board of Supervisors*, 88 Cal. App. 3d 397, 414-15 (1979) (EIR for oil facilities should have considered pipelines needed to serve the facility); *Ass'n for a Cleaner Environment v. Yosemite Community College Dist.*, 116 Cal. App. 4th 629 (2004) (college was required to prepare an initial study for closure, clean up, and transfer of a shooting range where only some of the project components fit within categorical exemptions). Activities undertaken at the same time and location as the project that are required as conditions of project approval must be evaluated in the same EIR as the project, even if they theoretically could have occurred independent from the project. *Tuolumne County Citizens for Responsible Growth, Inc. v. City of Sonora*, 155 Cal. App. 4th 1214, 1231 (2007). The project description does not need to include ongoing activities that are unaffected by the proposed approvals. *Citizens for East Shore Parks v. Cal. State Lands Commission*, 202 Cal. App. 4th 549, 565 (2011) (proposed renewal of the lease for a marine terminal did not include refinery operations on private lands, unaffected by the lease).

The project description also must include reasonably foreseeable future activities that are consequences of the project. *See Laurel Heights Improvement Ass'n v. Regents of the Univ. of Cal.*, 47 Cal. 3d 376, 394-95 (1988) (future planned expansion of the project

> The project description should extend to the entire activity that will ultimately result from approval of the proposed project.

into the entire building should have been considered); *City of Santee v. County of San Diego*, 214 Cal. App. 3d 1438, 1452 (1989) (foreseeable extended duration of temporary facilities should have been examined). The project description need not include, however, potential future projects that exist only in concept and are not linked to the project the agency is considering. *See Save Round Valley Alliance v. County of Inyo*, 157 Cal. App. 4th 1437 (2007); *Berkeley Keep Jets Over the Bay Committee v. Board of Port Commissioners*, 91 Cal. App. 4th 1344, 1361 (2001). Further, where two proposed activities are independent of one another, they may be reviewed separately under CEQA, even though they may be similar. *Sierra Club v. West Side Irrigation Dist.*, 128 Cal. App. 4th 690 (2005) (transfers of water rights by two different agencies that could be implemented independently of one another and were not contingent on one another properly could be treated as separate projects). Adjacent projects also may be addressed in separate CEQA documents, even though infrastructure for one project will also serve the other as long as neither project is a consequence of the other. *Banning Ranch Conservancy v. City of Newport Beach*, 211 Cal. App. 4th 1209 (2012).

> Adjacent projects also may be addressed in separate CEQA documents, even though infrastructure for one project will also serve the other as long as neither project is a consequence of the other.

Environmental setting/baseline. An EIR must include a description of the environment in the vicinity of the project as it exists before the commencement of the project, at the time the notice of preparation is published, or if no notice of preparation is published, at the time environmental review is commenced, from both a local and regional perspective. Guidelines § 15125.

This existing environmental setting will normally constitute the point of comparison, or baseline, for determining whether a project will result in a significant effect. Guidelines § 15125(a). In *Communities for a Better Environment v. South Coast Air Quality Management District*, 48 Cal. 4th 310, 315 (2010), the Supreme Court explained: "[t]o decide whether a given project's environmental effects are likely to be significant, the agency must use some measure of the environment's state absent the project, a measure sometimes referred to as the 'baseline' for environmental analysis." The Court held that an agency should not compare project conditions to hypothetical conditions that might have occurred at the same facility had equipment been operated at maximum permit limits that had never been achieved in practice. Nevertheless, the court recognized that agencies enjoy discretion to determine how existing physical conditions can most realistically be measured. For example, where conditions are changing quickly, the baseline might appropriately be predicted conditions at the time of approval. *See also, Save Our Peninsula Comm. v. County of Monterey*, 87 Cal. App. 4th 99, 125 (2001); *Woodward Park Homeowners Ass'n v. City of Fresno*, 150 Cal. App. 4th 683, 708 (2007) (EIR cannot exclusively compare impacts of a project to impacts that might occur if the project site were developed according to existing land use plans and zoning). Subsequently, in *Neighbors for Smart Rail v. Exposition Metro Line Construction Authority*, 57 Cal. 4th 439 (2013), the Supreme Court confirmed that an EIR can use a baseline that departs from conditions existing at the time of commencement of environmental review, holding that future conditions that will exist when the project begins operations also can constitute an "existing conditions" baseline. *See also, Pfeiffer v. Sunnyvale*, 200 Cal. App. 4th 1552 (2011) (upholding use of background conditions consisting of existing peak-hour traffic volumes increased by a growth factor derived from the city's travel forecasting model, plus traffic from approved but not yet built projects, as the baseline for determining the project would not result in significant near-term traffic impacts). The Supreme Court also clarified that an agency may use both an existing conditions baseline and a future conditions baseline to analyze the project's significant adverse effects; use of future conditions need not be relegated to a cumulative impacts or "no project" alternative analysis. *Neighbors for Smart Rail*, 57 Cal. 4th at 454.

Moreover, an agency even has discretion to measure a project's impacts against a baseline of environmental conditions that are anticipated to exist far in the future and long after project operations have begun; however, to do so, the agency must "justify its decision by showing an existing conditions analysis would be misleading or without informational value." *Id.* The agency also has discretion whether to update baseline data over the course of environmental review; its decision will be upheld as long as it is supported by substantial evidence. *Citizens for Open Government v. City of Lodi*, 205 Cal. App. 4th 296, 318-19 (2012) (upholding the city's decision not to update baseline due to changes in economic conditions because such analysis could constitute a "moving target").

Even when actual conditions are in violation of current regulatory requirements, these conditions may form the baseline for environmental review. *Riverwatch v. County of San Diego*, 76 Cal. App. 4th 1428 (1999) (county's chosen baseline included illegal development that had occurred at a mining operation seeking a use permit; the court ruled the respondents could not turn back the clock and insist upon a baseline that excluded existing conditions). How current conditions came to exist is irrelevant to CEQA review. *Fat v. County of Sacramento*, 97 Cal. App. 4th 1270, 1277 (2002) (county acted within its discretion to use current airport operations as its CEQA baseline even though the airport developed without county authorization, environmental damage had occurred, and the airport had been the subject of zoning enforcement actions). Similarly, actual conditions constitute the proper baseline even where the approving agency can eliminate them by withholding its approval. *Citizens for East Shore Parks v. Cal. State Lands Commission*, 202 Cal. App. 4th 549, 560-61 (2011) (existing marine terminal operations constituted the proper baseline for evaluation of effects of lease renewal, even though the lease had expired and the applicant was a holdover tenant).

Evaluation of environmental impacts. An EIR should be prepared with a sufficient degree of analysis to provide decisionmakers with information that enables them to evaluate and review possible environmental consequences intelligently. An evaluation need not be exhaustive, and disagreement among experts does not make an EIR inadequate. See *Citizens of Goleta Valley v. Bd. of Supervisors*, 52 Cal. 3d 553, 564 (1990). The courts have looked not for perfection but for adequacy, completeness, and a good faith effort at full disclosure of impacts. Thus, it is not required that the body acting on an EIR "correctly" resolve a dispute among experts. All that is required is that, in substance, the material in the EIR be responsive to the opposition and that it responds to the most significant questions presented. See *Ass'n of Irritated Residents v. County of Madera*, 107 Cal. App. 4th 1383 (2003); *Browning-Ferris Indus. v. City Council*, 181 Cal. App. 3d 852, 862 (1986); *Greenebaum v. City of Los Angeles*, 153 Cal. App. 3d 391, 413 (1984). By contrast, an EIR that does not explain the basis for its conclusion may be deemed to not comply with CEQA's requirements. See *Californians for Alternatives to Toxics v. Dept. of Food and Agriculture*, 136 Cal. App. 4th 1 (2006); *Protect the Historic Amador Waterways v. Amador Water Agency*, 116 Cal. App. 4th 1099 (2004).

Defects and inaccuracies in an EIR that do not prejudice the environmental review process are not grounds for overturning an agency's decision to certify the EIR and approve the project. *Neighbors for Smart Rail v. Exposition Metro Line Construction Authority*, 57 Cal. 4th 439, 463-65 (2013) (use of future baseline conditions anticipated to occur 15 years after commencement of project operations was not adequately justified; however, the EIR did not deprive the agency or the public of substantial relevant information regarding the traffic and air quality impacts at issue); *Save Cuyama Valley v. County of Santa Barbara*, 213 Cal. App. 4th 1059, 1073 (2013) (error in significance determination was not prejudicial where the EIR set forth the pertinent data

> An EIR should be prepared with a sufficient degree of analysis to provide decisionmakers with information that enables them to evaluate and review possible environmental consequences intelligently.

and an adopted condition of approval ensured the impact would be negated); *Mount Shasta Bioregional Ecology Center v. County of Siskiyou*, 210 Cal. App. 4th 199 (2012) (alleged small discrepancy in baseline data and possible understatement of water supply impacts could not have precluded informed decisionmaking). *See also Citizens for Open Government*, 205 Cal App. 4th at 307-311 (appellant failed to show exclusion of 22 email messages resulted in prejudicial error).

If evidence is submitted to the decisionmaking body supporting a fair argument that a significant impact could occur, and the agency fails to consider the impact, then certification of an EIR may be overturned. *Bakersfield Citizens for Local Control v. City of Bakersfield*, 124 Cal. App. 4th 1184 (2004). In *Bakersfield*, opponents of two Wal-Mart supercenters submitted studies and reports indicating the centers could oversaturate the market, resulting in store closures and long-term vacancies in nearby retail areas. The city responded that such evidence showed an economic impact, not within CEQA's purview. The court ruled that when faced with such evidence, the city was required to determine whether indirect physical effects, such as urban decay or deterioration, may occur. By contrast, where an EIR does consider the potential for such effects, the agency's determination will be upheld so long as it is supported by evidence in the record, even if the evidence also would support the opposite determination. *See Gilroy Citizens for Responsible Planning*, 140 Cal. App. 4th 911 (2006); *Anderson First Coalition v. City of Anderson*, 130 Cal. App. 4th 1173 (2005). *See also Citizens for Open Government*, 205 Cal. App. 4th at 316-17 (contrasting blight with urban decay and finding no error with an EIR that did not discuss existing blight but addressed the potential for urban decay); *Melom v. City of Madera*, 183 Cal. App. 4th 41 (2010) (where there is no evidence that a "supercenter" will result in urban decay, there is no need to prepare a supplemental EIR for changes to a retail center to enable such use).

Thresholds of significance. After comparing project effects to baseline conditions, an EIR defines a "threshold of significance" to assess the environmental effect. A threshold of significance is "an identifiable quantitative, qualitative or performance level of a particular environmental effect, non-compliance with which means the effect will normally be determined to be significant by the lead agency and compliance with means the effect normally will be determined less than significant." Guidelines § 15064.7. A lead agency has discretion to determine whether to classify an impact as significant depending upon the nature of the area affected. *National Parks & Conservation Assn. v. County of Riverside*, 71 Cal. App. 4th 1341, 1357 (1999); *see also North Coast Rivers Alliance v. Marin Municipal Water Dist.*, 216 Cal. App. 4th 614, 625-27 (2013) (agency may decide, as a matter of policy, whether to classify an impact to visual resources as significant in light of the project setting). Many lead agencies use the checklist appended to the CEQA Guidelines as Appendix G for their significance thresholds. However, the CEQA Guidelines also encourage each public agency to develop and publish its own thresholds of significance. Guidelines § 15064.7(a). The Guidelines state that thresholds to be "adopted for general use must be adopted by ordinance, resolution or regulation and developed through a public review process and be supported by substantial evidence." Guidelines § 15064.7(b). Further, the requirement that thresholds for general use must be formally adopted does not preclude an agency from applying a threshold that is specific to an individual EIR, even if the threshold has not been formally adopted by the agency and it deviates from the Appendix G checklist. *Save Cuyama Valley v. County of Santa Barbara*, 213 Cal. App. 4th 1059, 1068 (2013) (agency need not explain why it did not use the Appendix G thresholds of significance; those thresholds are "only a suggestion").

In some cases CEQA and the CEQA Guidelines dictate thresholds of significance. For a residential, mixed-use residential, or employment center project on an infill site within a transit priority area, aesthetic and parking impacts shall not be considered significant effects on the environment. Pub. Res. Code § 21099(d)(1). There is a disagreement among the appellate districts as to whether a parking shortage created by a project may constitute a significant physical impact on the environment. *Compare San Franciscans Upholding the Downtown Plan v. City and County of San Francisco*, 102 Cal. App. 4th 656, 697-98 (2002) (the social inconvenience of having to hunt for scarce parking is not an environmental impact; the secondary impact of scarce parking on traffic and air quality is) *with Taxpayers for Accountable School Bond Spending v. San Diego Unified School Dist.*, 215 Cal. App. 4th 1013, 1051 (2013) (acknowledging parking impact was removed from Appendix G of the CEQA Guidelines, but reasoning because cars and other vehicles are physical objects that occupy space when parked, CEQA considers a project's impact on parking of vehicles to be a physical impact that could constitute a significant effect on the environment) and *Neighbors for Smart Rail*, 57 Cal. 4th at 465-66 (addressing the sufficiency of mitigation for "spillover" parking without questioning whether such an effect falls within CEQA's ambit).

The Legislature also has enabled cities and counties to designate "infill opportunity zones" in which traffic level of service standards do not apply. An infill opportunity zone must be located within one-half mile of a major transit stop or high-quality transit corridor (as defined by statute) and in an area identified in a regional transportation plan's sustainable communities strategy or alternative planning strategy as a "transit priority area." Gov't Code § 65088.4. In addition, the Legislature has directed the Office of Planning and Research to prepare revisions to the CEQA Guidelines for determining the significance of transportation impacts of projects within transit priority areas, meaning an area within one-half mile of a major transit stop that is existing or planned. The criteria must promote the reduction of greenhouse gas emissions, development of multimodal transportation networks, and a diversity of land uses. Pub. Res. Code § 21099(b)(1). Upon certification of the new guideline, automobile delay, as described by level of service or similar measures of vehicular capacity or traffic congestion, will not be considered a significant impact on the environment, expect in locations specified by the new guideline. Pub. Res. Code § 21099(b)(2).

CEQA specifically defines significance standards for effects on historic resources. A historic resource is a resource listed in, or determined by the State Historical Resources Commission to be eligible for listing in, the California Register of Historic Resources. Pub. Res. Code § 21084.1; Guidelines § 15064.5(a)(1). Historic resources listed in a local register or survey are presumed to be significant unless the preponderance of the evidence demonstrates the resource is not historically or culturally significant. Pub. Res. Code § 21084.1; Guidelines § 15064.5(a)(2). The fact that a resource has not been determined eligible for inclusion on the California Register and has not been included in a local register does not preclude an agency from determining whether it is a historic resource for purposes of CEQA. Pub. Res. Code § 21084.1. Generally, the lead agency applies the criteria for listing on the California Register of Historic Resources to determine whether the resource is significant, and such determination must be supported by substantial evidence. Guidelines § 15064.5(a)(3). Once the agency determines whether the resource is significant, it also must determine whether the project will result in a "substantial adverse change in the significance" of the resource. Guidelines § 15064.5(b). A substantial adverse change means physical demolition, destruction, relocation, or alteration of the resource or its immediate surroundings such that the

> Cumulative impacts are two or more individual effects that, when considered together, are considerable or that compound or increase other environmental impacts.

significance of the resource would be "materially impaired." Guidelines § 15064.5(b)(1). The significance of a resource is materially impaired when a project demolishes or materially alters in an adverse manner those physical characteristics of the resource that convey its historical significance and that justify its inclusion in the California Register, inclusion in the local register or identification in the local survey, or eligibility for inclusion in the California Register of Historic Resources as determined by the lead agency. Guidelines § 15064.5(b)(2); *see Taxpayers for Accountable School Bond Spending v. San Diego Unified School Dist.*, 215 Cal. App. 4th 1013, 1045 (2013) (the fact that stadium light standards would be visible from a historic resource does not create a reasonable inference that the resource's historical significance would be materially impaired).

Water supply. An EIR must consider whether there is sufficient available water to serve project demand in both the near term and the long term. The following general principles govern an EIR's analysis of water supply issues:

- CEQA's informational purposes are not satisfied by an EIR that ignores or assumes a solution to the problem of supplying water to proposed development; decisionmakers must be supplied with sufficient facts to evaluate the pros and cons of supplying the water the project will need

- An adequate environmental impact analysis for a long-range development proposal cannot be limited to water supply for the first stage of development

- Future water supplies identified and analyzed in an EIR must bear a likelihood of actually proving available; speculative sources and unrealistic allocations do not provide an adequate basis for decisionmaking under CEQA

- Where a full analysis leaves some uncertainty regarding the availability of anticipated future water sources, CEQA requires some discussion of possible replacement or alternative supply sources, and of the environmental consequences of resorting to these sources

Vineyard Area Citizens for Responsible Growth v. City of Rancho Cordova, 40 Cal. 4th 412 (2007) (citing *Santiago County Water Dist. v. County of Orange*, 118 Cal. App. 3d 818 (1981); *Stanislaus Natural Heritage Project v. County of Stanislaus*, 48 Cal. App. 4th 182 (1996); *Santa Clarita Organization for Planning the Environment v. County of Los Angeles* (SCOPE 1), 106 Cal. App. 4th 715 (2003); *Planning and Conservation League v. Dept. of Water Resources*, 83 Cal. App. 4th 892 (2000); *Cal. Oak Foundation v. City of Santa Clarita*, 133 Cal. App. 4th 1219 (2005); *Napa Citizens for Honest Gov't v. Napa County Bd. of Supervisors*, 91 Cal. App. 4th 342 (2001))

> CEQA does not require a definite water supply. Rather, CEQA's reporting requirements are satisfied when an EIR fully discloses the uncertainties, likely water sources, their impacts, and appropriate mitigation measures.

Under these principles, CEQA does not require a definite water supply. Rather, CEQA's reporting requirements are satisfied when an EIR fully discloses the uncertainties, likely water sources, their impacts, and appropriate mitigation measures. See *Vineyard Area Citizens*, 40 Cal. 4th at 434 (EIR's analysis of near-term supplies was sufficient, but the discussion of long-term supplies suffered from lack of evidentiary support); *Santa Clarita Organization for Planning the Environment v. County of Los Angeles* (SCOPE 2), 157 Cal. App. 4th 149 (2007) (EIR revealing legal uncertainty but explaining why, as a practical matter, water supply was likely to remain in place, supported the conclusion that water supply would be sufficient); *Clover Valley Foundation v. City of Rocklin*, 197 Cal. App. 4th 200 (2011) (a certified water supply assessment constituted substantial evidence supporting the conclusion that future water supplies were likely to be available and impacts would be less than significant); *Habitat and Watershed Caretakers v. City of Santa Cruz*, 213 Cal. App. 4th 1277, 1289-92 (2013) (upholding EIR that concluded water supplies would not be sufficient, revealed uncertainties in plans to secure more water and disclosed that forced conservation could occur during shortages). *But see Madera Oversight Coalition, Inc. v. County of Madera*, 199 Cal. App. 4th 48, 102-05 (2011) (analysis that failed to reveal uncertainty regarding the legal effect of a federal contract did not constitute a reasoned analysis or full discussion of the likelihood that alternative water supplies would be needed).

Courts have recognized that agencies are entitled to deference in determining the scope of analysis of water supply effects. A first-tier EIR evaluating water supply issues at a general level of detail may be sufficient if additional detail would be provided when specific projects are considered. *In re Bay-Delta Programmatic environmental impact report Coordinated Proceedings*, 43 Cal. 4th 1143 (2008).

Further, the water supplier and its experts have "substantial discretion" in selecting the appropriate methodology for conducting a water supply assessment. *O.W.L. Foundation v. City of Rohnert Park*, 168 Cal. App. 4th 568 (2008) (the court deferred to the city's decision to limit its evaluation of groundwater pumping to a defined study area). However, a court will not defer to an agency's interpretation as to whether a water supply assessment is required by statute. *See Center for Biological Diversity v. County of San Bernardino*, 185 Cal. App. 4th 866 (2010) (requiring a water supply assessment for a processing plant even though the project would use only 1.1 acre-feet of water per year). By contrast, an EIR is not adequate if substantial evidence fails to support the agency's determination that water supplies will be sufficient, and impacts of supplying water to the project will be less than significant. *Preserve Wild Santee v. City of Santee*, 210 Cal. App. 4th 260 (2012) (substantial unexplained discrepancy between the EIR's estimated water demand and the water supply assessment's lower estimated water demand demonstrated a lack of evidence supporting the EIR's conclusions).

> The water supplier and its experts have "substantial discretion" in selecting the appropriate methodology for conducting a water supply assessment.

Climate change. As is explained in more detail in chapter 16 (Sustainable Development), the CEQA Guidelines recognize that lead agencies have considerable discretion in assessing the significance of a project's greenhouse gas emissions. *See* Guidelines § 15064.4; *North Coast Rivers Alliance v. Marin Municipal Water Dist.*, 216 Cal. App. 4th 614, 650-53 (2013) (threshold of significance based on AB 32 standards was legally adequate; EIR analyzed whether project's power use would interfere with county's goal of reducing countywide greenhouse gas emissions by 15 percent compared with 1990 levels, by 2020); *Citizens for Responsible Equitable Environmental Development v. City of Chula Vista*, 197 Cal. App. 4th 327 (2011) (city properly exercised its discretion to utilize compliance with AB 32 as its threshold; a target of 20 percent below business as usual, which represents the midpoint between AB 32's goals for 2010 and 2020, was not arbitrary and unsubstantiated, particularly where the project reduced emissions by 29 percent below business as usual levels by 2020); *Rialto Citizens for Responsible Growth v. City of Rialto*, 208 Cal. App. 4th 899 (2012) (upholding climate change analysis where the EIR determined project-specific impacts on climate change were speculative, but determined the project's contribution to cumulate effects was cumulatively considerable and unavoidable). Adopted general plan provisions or climate protection plans, as well as significance thresholds published by regional air quality management districts, may be helpful to the lead agency in determining the appropriate standard.

In addition to articulating a significance standard, agencies performing CEQA review should make a good-faith effort, based to the extent possible on scientific and factual data, to describe, calculate or estimate the amount of greenhouse gases resulting from a project. Guidelines § 15064.4(a). The lead agency has discretion whether to use a model to quantify greenhouse gas emissions, or rely on a qualitative analysis or performance based standards. Guidelines § 15064.4(a)(1) and (2). However, the methodology that the agency uses to assess emissions should correlate with the significance standard the agency selects. If, for example, an agency elects to use compliance with AB 32 as its threshold, it cannot simply compare project-related greenhouse gas emissions to statewide emissions in order to find project emissions are so miniscule as to not impair compliance. Rather, the relevant question is whether emissions should be considered significant in light of the legislative policy to cut about 30 percent of business-as-usual emissions projected for 2020. *Friends of Oroville v. City of Oroville,* 219 Cal. App. 4th 832 (2013) (rejecting comparison to the AB 32 Scoping Plan measures to achieve compliance with AB 32 where such measures did not address the highest source of project-related emissions).

> Lead agencies shall consider feasible means of mitigating the significant effects of greenhouse gas emissions.

The Guidelines also state that lead agencies shall consider feasible means of mitigating the significant effects of greenhouse gas emissions. Guidelines § 15126.4(c). A court has rejected use of a "zero-increase" standard to reduce impacts to a less-than-significant level where the finding that the measure would be effective was not supported by facts demonstrating the standard could be achieved, and few specific measures were identified. *Communities for a Better Environment v. City of Richmond,* 184 Cal. App. 4th 70 (2010). On the other hand, where a project incorporated multiple greenhouse gas-reducing measures, and the lead agency found indirect transportation-related emissions to be significant and unavoidable, a court ruled the lead agency did not have to set forth an analysis of each of fifty general measures suggested in a paper drafted by the Attorney General's office. *Santa Clarita Organization for Planning the Environment v. City of Santa Clarita,* 197 Cal. App. 4th 1042 (2011) ("Considering the large number of possible mitigation measures set forth in the letter, as well as the letter's indication that not all measures would be appropriate for every project, it is unreasonable to impose on the city an obligation to explore each and every one.")

In some cases, an EIR or negative declaration will have been prepared for a project prior to the time period when lead agencies began including climate change analyses in their CEQA documents. In the first published opinion addressing this circumstance, an appellate court held that the petitioner had not satisfied exhaustion requirements, but that in any event, generalized statements that a project would result in greenhouse gas emissions were not sufficient to trigger preparation of a supplemental EIR. The court ruled that information about climate change and greenhouse gas emissions dated back to the 1970s and was not new information as defined by Public Resources Code section 21166 and Guidelines section 15162. "The effect of greenhouse gas emissions on climate change could have been raised in 1994 when the City considered the [EIR]." *Citizens for Responsible Equitable Environmental Development v. City of San Diego,* 196 Cal. App. 4th 515 (2011). *See also Concerned Dublin Citizens v. City of Dublin,* 214 Cal. App. 4th 1301, 1318-20 (2013) (adoption of thresholds of significance to address greenhouse gases did not constitute new information requiring supplemental review where earlier EIR addressed impacts on air quality and substantial evidence supported the conclusion that information about greenhouse gas emissions and climate change was available and could have been known when the EIR was certified in 2002). Please see chapter 16 (Sustainable Development) for a discussion of climate change effects under CEQA.

Cumulative impacts. An EIR must discuss significant cumulative impacts. Cumulative impacts are two or more individual effects that, when considered together, are considerable or that compound or increase other environmental impacts. Guidelines § 15355. The individual effects may be changes resulting from a single project or a number of separate projects. Thus, an EIR's cumulative impacts discussion should encompass "past, present and probable future projects." Guidelines §§ 15130(b)(1)(A), 15355.

The purpose of this requirement is to avoid "piecemeal" approval of projects without consideration of the total environmental effects the projects would have when taken together. *See San Joaquin Raptor/Wildlife Rescue Ctr. v. County of Stanislaus*, 27 Cal. App. 4th 713, 740 (1994).

The adequacy of an EIR's discussion of cumulative impacts is determined by standards of practicality and reasonableness. *Environmental Protection Information Center v. Cal. Dept. of Forestry and Fire Protection*, 44 Cal. App. 4th 459, 525 (2008); Guidelines § 15130(b). The discussion must reflect the severity of the impacts and the likelihood of their occurrence, but need not contain the same degree of detail as the EIR's discussion of impacts attributable to the project alone. Guidelines § 150130(b). The discussion may also rely upon previously approved land use documents, including general plans, specific plans, and local coastal plans. Pub. Res. Code § 21100(e); *see also* Guidelines § 15130(d).

The evaluation of cumulative impacts may be based upon a list of past, present, and probable future projects. Guidelines § 15130(b)(1)(A). *See also Env't Protection Info. Ctr. v. Cal. Dept. of Forestry & Fire Protection*, 44 Cal. 4th 459 (2008) (reaffirming the importance of analyzing past projects and historical context). Projects that are under environmental review may be sufficiently probable to be included in the analysis; however this is true only to the extent that the environmental review provides evidence that the proposed project is both probable and sufficiently certain to allow for meaningful cumulative impacts analysis. *Compare City of Maywood v. Los Angeles Unified School District*, 208 Cal. App. 4th 362 (2012) (assertion that notice of preparation of EIR for I-710 expansion had been issued did not show the potential interchange was probable or that enough technical information was available to analyze its cumulative traffic effects) *with Friends of the Eel River v. Sonoma County Water Agency*, 108 Cal. App. 4th 859 (2003) (finding the cumulative impacts analysis inadequate where the water agency reviewed the project for increased withdrawals from the river, but did not also review pending diversion curtailment proposals for the same river system even though proposals were undergoing NEPA review and all alternatives under review included the curtailment proposals). When using a list approach, the EIR also should define the relevant area affected and provide a reasonable explanation for the geographic limitation used. *Compare Kings County Farm Bureau v. City of Hanford*, 221 Cal. App. 3d 692, 723-24 (1990) (no explanation of why analysis of cumulative air quality impacts were limited to the Central Valley), *with East Bay Mun. Utility Dist. v. Cal. Department of Forestry & Fire Protection*, 43 Cal. App. 4th 1113, 1128-29 (1996) (the EIR explained the agency practice to define an assessment area that "was small enough to detect impacts, but not so small as to reduce any impact to insignificance"). *See also Bakersfield Citizens for Local Control v. City of Bakersfield*, 124 Cal. App. 4th 1184 (2004) (EIR could not arbitrarily define a project area so narrowly as to avoid discussion of cumulative effects); *City of Long Beach v. Los Angeles Unified School Dist.*, 176 Cal. App. 4th 889 (2009) (EIR defined the geographic scope of cumulative impact analysis for each resource).

Alternatively, the evaluation of cumulative impacts may be based on a summary of projections from an adopted general plan, related planning document, or previously adopted or certified environmental document that evaluates regional or areawide conditions contributing to the cumulative impact. Guidelines § 15130(b)(1)(B); *Schaeffer Land Trust v. San Jose City Council*, 215 Cal. App. 3d 612, 630-32 (1989); *see also Preserve Wild Santee*, 210 Cal. App. 4th at 260 (EIR's explanation that the project and other potential development must comply with the conservation goals of the adopted multispecies conservation plan, and that the project would not interfere with

NEPA = National Environmental Policy Act

the plan's goals, would attain its share of the goals and would mitigate its impacts to a less than significant level was adequate under a "reasonable and practical" standard); *Las Virgenes Homeowners Federation, Inc. v. County of Los Angeles*, 177 Cal. App. 3d 300, 307 (1986) (cumulative impacts analysis for a project may incorporate the information in an EIR prepared for a general plan or an adopted program).

It is improper for an EIR to conclude that a project's cumulative impacts are insignificant merely because the project contributes to an existing unacceptable environmental condition. *See Los Angeles Unified School Dist. v. City of Los Angeles*, 58 Cal. App. 4th 1019, 1025-26 (1997); *Kings County Farm Bureau*, 221 Cal. App. 3d at 718. Rather, in assessing cumulative impacts, the determination of whether the project's contribution is cumulatively considerable should take into account both the project's incremental effect and the nature and severity of the pre-existing significant cumulative effect. *Communities for a Better Environment v. Cal. Resources Agency*, 103 Cal. App. 4th 98, 119-120 (2002).

Where a project will make no contribution to a cumulative effect, and the only contributions will be made by other projects, the proposed project's EIR is not required to analyze the cumulative effect. *Santa Monica Baykeeper v. City of Malibu*, 193 Cal. App. 4th 1538 (2011) (project that reduced discharges to groundwater did not contribute to cumulative adverse impacts from groundwater mounding).

Mitigation. An EIR must describe feasible mitigation measures to minimize the project's significant environmental impacts. Pub. Res. Code §§ 21002.1(a), 21100(b)(3); Guidelines § 15126.4(a). The EIR also must analyze any significant effects of the mitigation measures it describes. Guidelines § 15126.4(a)(1)(D); *see also Stevens v. City of Glendale*, 125 Cal. App. 3d 986, 995 (1981). An EIR need not discuss alternative mitigation measures where the project's impacts have been found to be less than significant. *North Coast Rivers Alliance v. Marin Municipal Water Dist.*, 216 Cal. App. 4th 614, 648-50 (2013). Nor is an EIR required to consider mitigation measures that would be inconsistent with the project objectives. *San Diego Citizenry Group v. County of San Diego*, 219 Cal. App. 4th 1 (2013).

Generally, mitigation measures should be described specifically in the EIR and not left for future formulation. Guidelines § 15126.4(a)(1)(B); *see Preserve Wild Santee*, 210 Cal. App. 4th at 260 (mitigation requiring preparation of a future management plan without specifying performance standards, guidelines or activities to be undertaken was inadequate where the success of the mitigation efforts depended upon the management plan); *Endangered Habitats League, Inc. v. County of Orange*, 131 Cal. App. 4th 777 (2005) (mitigation that does no more than require a report to be prepared and followed, or allows approval by a county department without setting any standards, is insufficient); *San Joaquin Raptor Rescue Center v. County of Merced*, 149 Cal. App. 4th 645 (2007) (mitigation calling for future formulation of a habitat management plan is improper). One court faulted an EIR for including, as a first step in its mitigation program, verification of archaeological resources to confirm that they meet CEQA's significance criteria. In *Madera Oversight Coalition, Inc.*, 199 Cal. App. 4th at 81-82, the court held that a condition that enabled the agency to change the significance conclusion and avoid the remaining mitigation measures violates CEQA where the impact determination would occur subsequent to project approval, "outside an arena where public officials are accountable." Deferred mitigation also may be improper where an agency both defers formulation of the measure and delays implementation of mitigation, allowing the project to move forward without setting a timeline for achieving mitigation. *POET LLC v. Cal. Air Resources Bd.*, 218 Cal. App. 4th 681 (2013) (Air Resources

Board stated it would adopt rules to ensure biodiesel use would not result in increased NOx emissions, but did not specify how compliance would be monitored and did not commit to implement the measure prior to project implementation).

However, when an agency has evaluated the potential project impacts, and has shown the impact can be mitigated, it can defer formulation of the specifics of the mitigation measures and instead commit to mitigate the impact and specify "performance standards" that would mitigate the environmental effects, and that could be met in more than one way. Guidelines § 15126.4(a)(1)(B). The details of exactly how mitigation will be achieved under the identified measures can be deferred pending completion of a future study. *Cal. Native Plant Soc'y v. City of Rancho Cordova*, 172 Cal. App. 4th 603, 622 (2009). In *Sacramento Old City Association v. City Council*, for example, the court upheld an EIR that set forth a menu of possible mitigation measures to offset parking and traffic impacts, even though the EIR did not specify which mitigation measures the agency would adopt. 229 Cal. App. 3d 1011, 1032 (1991); *see also North Coast Rivers Alliance v. Marin Municipal Water Dist.*, 216 Cal. App. 4th 614, 630-31, 647-48 (2013) (upholding measures calling for future development of a landscaping plan to soften visual intrusion of water storage tanks and consultation with NOAA Fisheries to protect fish from pile driving noise); *Save Cuyama Valley v. County of Santa Barbara*, 213 Cal. App. 4th 1059, 1070-71 (2013) (upholding condition requiring compliance with surface mining regulations when adverse hydraulic impacts, as measured by the EIR's significance standard, occur); *City of Maywood*, 208 Cal. App. 4th at 409-13 (upholding a measure requiring further soil testing and remediation of contamination to specifications designed to protect public health and safety); *Oakland Heritage Alliance v. City of Oakland*, 195 Cal. App. 4th 884 (2011) (upholding a measure requiring compliance with state and local seismic requirements and additional analysis and review before building permit issuance); *Cal. Native Plant Soc'y v. City of Rancho Cordova*, 172 Cal. App. 4th 603, 622 (2009) (upholding a measure to mitigate loss of habitat by requiring preservation or creation of replacement habitat, off-site, in a specified ratio to acreage lost as a result of the project without describing location of mitigation site); *Clover Valley Foundation v. City of Rocklin*, 197 Cal. App. 4th 200 (2001) (upholding a measure requiring compliance with regulatory permits to avoid construction effects to a protected bird species because the EIR included performance criteria).

> The details of exactly how mitigation will be achieved under the identified measures can be deferred pending completion of a future study.

In some cases, payment of fees into established fee programs designed to fund off-site infrastructure projects and regional improvements may be an effective approach to reducing a project's effects. Accordingly, an agency carrying out its own development activities should consider the feasibility of voluntary payments into such programs, as well as the effectiveness of such programs, before it approves a project that will contribute to regional traffic congestion or other significant off-site environmental effects. *See City of Marina v. Bd. of Trustees of the Cal. St. Univ.*, 39 Cal. 4th 341 (2006); *see also County of San Diego v. Grossmont-Cuyamaca Community College District*, 141 Cal. App. 4th 86 (2006). A properly qualified program may serve to mitigate against both the direct effects of a project and its cumulative effects. Time-specific schedules for implementation of mitigation measures to be implemented under the fee program are not required; rather "[a]ll that is required by CEQA is that there be a reasonable plan for mitigation." *Save Our Peninsula Comm. v. County of Monterey*, 87 Cal. App. 4th 99, 141 (2001) (discussing mitigation of traffic impacts).

If implementation of a mitigation plan cannot reasonably be assured, payment of fair share funding toward future mitigation will not support a finding that impacts would be mitigated to a less-than-significant level. *Gray v. County of Madera*, 167 Cal.

App. 4th 1099 (2008) (the county could not rely on a measure calling for the project applicant to contribute "an equitable share" of the cost of constructing future highway improvements if requested by Caltrans or the county where there was no showing the Caltrans had scheduled improvements, or that the county had a mitigation plan in place). Further, if an in lieu mitigation fee has not undergone CEQA review, it cannot be presumed to fully mitigate the impact. *Cal. Native Plant Soc'y v. County of El Dorado*, 170 Cal. App. 4th 1026 (2009) (the agency could not rely on payment into a habitat mitigation fund where no CEQA review of the mitigation plan had occurred and the agency had not performed a specific evaluation of the plan's effectiveness to fully mitigate the project's impacts). On the other hand, where evidence supports the conclusion that mitigation within another agency's control can and should be adopted by the other agency, the lead agency can find the mitigation effectively will reduce the impact to a less than significant level. *Neighbors for Smart Rail v. Exposition Metro Line Construction Authority*, 57 Cal. 4th 439 (2013).

Substantial evidence also may support a finding that it is not feasible to mitigate on-site impacts, such as permanent conversion of prime agricultural land, through purchase of off-site conservation easements or similar measures. In *Citizens for Open Government v. City of Lodi*, 205 Cal. App. 4th 296, 322 (2012), the draft EIR for a project that would convert 40 acres of prime agricultural land to urban uses explained there was no mitigation to reduce this impact to a less-than-significant level "because the land 'once converted, loses its character as agricultural land and is removed from the stock of agricultural land.'" Although the city elected to condition the project approvals upon acquisition of off-site easements as partial mitigation, the court found the city did not need to demonstrate a higher ratio to be infeasible. The city's finding explained there were no feasible measures to avoid the loss of prime agricultural farmland because "it was not possible to recreate prime farmland on other lands." Under these facts, the court upheld the city's findings and deferred to its policy determination. However, in *Masonite Corporation v. County of Mendocino*, 218 Cal. App. 4th 230 (2013), the court issued an opinion that contradicts *City of Lodi*. In *Masonite*, the court rejected the same rationale that the City of Lodi had used to find purchase of offsite conservation easements infeasible, and instead ruled that the question whether conservation easements constitute mitigation is a question of law. The court found such easements may appropriately mitigate for the direct loss of farmland where a project converts agricultural land to a nonagricultural use. The court equated offsite agricultural easement to offsite habitat preservation and found both provide compensatory mitigation.

Project alternatives. The EIR must contain a meaningful discussion of project alternatives that would reduce adverse environmental impacts. *See Laurel Heights I*, 47 Cal. 3d at 403; Guidelines § 15126.6(a). The number of alternatives required to be analyzed in an EIR is subject to a "rule of reason." Guidelines § 15126.6(f); *Citizens of Goleta Valley v. Bd. of Supervisors*, 52 Cal. 3d 553, 565-66 (1990) (*Goleta II*). Alternatives that are not reasonable or feasible need not be discussed at length. Guidelines § 15126.6(a); *Village Laguna, Inc. v. Bd. of Supervisors*, 134 Cal. App. 3d 1022, 1028-29 (1982); *Goleta II*, 52 Cal. 3d at 574. Alternatives that do not offer substantial environmental advantages over the project can be rejected from consideration. Guidelines § 15126.6. In addition, alternatives that do not accomplish most of the basic objectives of the project can be excluded from the analysis. *In re Bay-Delta Programmatic Environmental Impact Report Coordinated Proceeding*, 43 Cal. 4th 1143 (2008) (EIR need not study alternatives that cannot achieve the fundamental objectives of the project); *Jones v. Regents of Univ. of Cal.*, 183 Cal. App. 4th 818 (2010) (EIR need not evaluate an off-site alternative that would not achieve project objectives to enhance collaboration, productivity and efficiency); *San Diego Citizenry Group v. County of San Diego*, 219 Cal. App. 4th 1 (2013). (County could reject alternatives that did not accomplish its policy objective to enact zoning that enabled development of boutique wineries as of right); *California Oak Foundation v. Regents of Univ. of Cal.*, 188 Cal. App. 4th 227 (2010) (EIR for integrated projects could limit evaluation to alternatives that would meet the collective objectives of the projects). *See also Save Our Residential Env't v. City of West Hollywood*, 9 Cal. App. 4th 1745, 1752–53 (1992); *but see Watsonville Pilots Ass'n v. City of Watsonville*, 183 Cal. App. 4th 1059 (2010) (reduced development alternative should have been evaluated, even if it would partially impede accomplishment of the project objectives); *San Bernardino Valley Audubon Soc'y, Inc. v. County of San Bernardino*, 155 Cal. App. 3d 738, 750 (1984) (reasonable alternatives must be considered, "even if they substantially impede the project or are more costly"); Guidelines § 15126(d).

Range of alternatives. The courts and CEQA Guidelines require that a "range of reasonable alternatives" be considered. *See Goleta II*, 52 Cal. 3d at 566; *Residents Ad Hoc Stadium Com. v. Board of Trustees*, 89 Cal. App. 3d 274, 287–88 (1979); Guidelines § 15126.6(c). The range of alternatives should include alternatives which feasibly attain most of the basic objectives of the project but would avoid or substantially lessen any of the significant effects of the project. Guidelines § 15126.6(a). The range must be sufficient "to permit a reasonable choice of alternatives so far as environmental aspects are concerned." *San Bernardino Valley Audubon Soc'y*, 155 Cal. App. 3d at 750–51; Guidelines §§ 15126.6(c), (f). "There is no ironclad rule governing the nature or scope of alternatives to be discussed other than the rule of reason." Guidelines § 15126.6.

An EIR's project objectives influence the range of alternatives that will be considered to be reasonable. "Although a lead agency may not give a project's purpose an artificially narrow definition, a lead agency may structure its EIR alternative analysis around a reasonable definition of underlying purpose and need and not study alternatives that cannot achieve that basic goal. *In re Bay-Delta Programmatic Environmental Impact Report Coordinated Proceedings*, 43 Cal. 4th 1143, 1166 (2008). A statement of objectives that focuses on the nature of the approvals requested may be improper where the statement does not illuminate the underlying project purpose and prevents an analysis of alternatives capable of reducing the project's significant impacts. *Habitat and Watershed Caretakers v. City of Santa Cruz*, 213 Cal. App. 4th 1277, 1300 (2013) (final EIR corrected inadequate statement of objectives in draft EIR).

An alternative need not be environmentally superior to the project in all respects; the CEQA Guidelines authorize consideration of alternatives that would reduce or lessen "any" of the significant effects of a project. *Sierra Club v. City of Orange*, 163 Cal. App. 4th 523 (2008). Further, an agency need not study alternatives that address existing environmental problems where those problems are not an impact of the proposed project. *Citizens of East Shore Parks v. Cal. State Lands Commission*, 202 Cal. App. 4th 549 (2011); *In re Bay-Delta Programmatic Environmental Impact Report Coordinated Proceedings*, 43 Cal. 4th at 1166.

> An alternative need not be environmentally superior to the project in all respects; the CEQA Guidelines authorize consideration of alternatives that would reduce or lessen "any" of the significant effects of a project.

Several cases support the view that not every alternative need be considered (even if it is reasonable) so long as the EIR's range of alternatives is itself reasonable. *See City of Maywood*, 208 Cal. App. 4th at 420 ("CEQA does not require that an agency consider specific alternatives that are proposed by members of the public or other outside agencies."). Numerous variations on the same theme need not be discussed. *See Village Laguna, Inc.*, 134 Cal. App. 3d at 1028–29 (EIR that discussed density alternatives of 7,500, 10,000, 20,000 and 25,000 units was not deficient for failure to discuss intermediate 16,000 unit alternative). The EIR may evaluate "prototypical" alternatives that demonstrate the advantages and disadvantages of a wider range of suggested alternatives. *See Save San Francisco Bay Ass'n v. San Francisco Bay Conserv. & Dev. Comm'n*, 10 Cal. App. 4th 908, 922 (1992). In some cases, an agency may conclude, after considering the possible options, there are no potentially feasible alternatives that would accomplish most of the basic project objectives. There is no rule specifying a particular number of alternatives that must be included. *Mount Shasta Bioregional Ecology Center*, 210 Cal. App. 4th at 184 ("An appellant may not simply claim the agency failed to present an adequate range of alternatives and then sit back and force the agency to prove it wrong."). *Compare Habitat and Watershed Caretakers v. City of Santa Cruz*, 213 Cal. App. 4th 1277, 1305 (2013) (EIR found to be inadequate because it did not explain why no feasible alternatives were discussed).

One of the alternatives studied, however, must be the "no project" alternative. Guidelines § 15126.6(e). The no-project analysis should discuss existing conditions as well as what would reasonably be expected to occur in the foreseeable future if the project were not approved, based on current plans and consistent with available infrastructure and community services. Guidelines § 15126.6(e); *but see Planning & Conserv. League v. Dep't of Water Resources*, 83 Cal. App. 4th 892, 913 (2000) (existing water contracts that "plausibly" could be interpreted to require reduced entitlements must be studied as part of the no-project alternative).

Consideration of alternative sites also may be required for both public and private development projects. *See Goleta II*, 52 Cal. 3d at 574-75. Whether alternative sites should be considered depends upon a variety of factors, including site ownership, whether the site is within the lead agency's jurisdiction, and current land use designations in a general plan or local coastal program. *Id.* at 573-75. If a development project is consistent with an adopted plan, evaluation of off-site alternatives may be unnecessary. *Mira Mar Mobile Community v. City of Oceanside*, 119 Cal. App. 4th 477 (2004); *but see Save Round Valley Alliance v. County of Inyo*, 157 Cal. App. 4th 1437 (2007) (potential alternative of government land exchange could not be excluded merely because zoning of federal land reflected its federal ownership).

A lead agency's ultimate finding that none of the alternatives fully satisfies the project objectives does not equate to a concession that the EIR failed to analyze a reasonable range of alternatives. *See Citizens for Open Government v. City of Lodi*, 205 Cal. App. 4th 296, 312-314 (2012) (upholding certification of an EIR where the city examined a reduced size alternative and an alternative project location, but rejected both after completion of the EIR because they would not "entirely fulfill" the project objectives and would be "substantially less effective" in meeting the city's goals.) *California Native Plant Society v. City of Santa Cruz*, 177 Cal. App. 4th 957, 998 (2009); *Mira Mar Mobile Community v. City of Oceanside*, 119 Cal. App. 4th 477 (2004). When drafting the EIR, the lead agency evaluates a range of alternatives that are potentially feasible. A lead agency may exclude from an EIR alternatives it concludes are not potentially feasible. *Save San Francisco Bay Association v. San Francisco Bay Conservation & Development Commission*, 10 Cal. App. 4th 908, 922 (1992); *Citizens of Goleta Valley v. Bd. Of Supervisors*, 52 Cal. 3d 553, 565 (1990). Once a range of potentially feasible alternatives has been evaluated, the agency's decisionmakers are entitled to weigh and balance the relative advantages and disadvantages of the alternatives and the project. *See California Native Plant Society*, 177 Cal. App. 4th at 981.

Extent of discussion. The CEQA Guidelines require that an EIR include sufficient information about each alternative "to allow meaningful evaluation, analysis and comparison with the proposed project." Guidelines § 15126.6(d). A matrix may be used to summarize comparisons. *Id.* However, as with the range of alternatives, there are no clear rules regarding the level of detail that must be provided. The extent of the analysis is subject to a rule of reason. *See Goleta II*, 52 Cal. 3d at 565.

Growth inducement. An EIR should discuss the "ways in which the proposed project could foster economic or population growth, or the construction of additional housing, either directly or indirectly, in the surrounding environment." Guidelines § 15126.2(d). This discussion should include projects that could remove obstacles to growth and projects that might facilitate other activities that could significantly affect the environment. If a project will create jobs and bring people into the area, the EIR must discuss the resulting housing needs and, if more housing will be required, its probable location. However, the "detail required in any particular case necessarily depends on a multitude of factors, including but not limited to, the nature of the project, the directness or indirectness of the contemplated impact and the ability to forecast the actual effects the project will have on the physical environment." *Napa Citizens for Honest Gov't v. County of Napa Bd. of Supervisors*, 91 Cal. App. 4th 342, 369 (2001). A detailed analysis of growth may not be required where a project's purpose is not to facilitate growth, the project removes only one of numerous obstacles to growth, and any future effects of additional development will undergo CEQA analysis, or already has undergone such analysis. *Clover Valley Foundation v. City of Rocklin*, 197 Cal. App. 4th 200 (2011); *see also Habitat and Watershed Caretakers v. City of Santa Cruz*, 213 Cal. App. 4th 1277, 1296 (2013) (upholding city's determination that because indirect population increase and housing demand was within existing city projections and city's expected housing units would satisfy this demand, impact would not be significant). The CEQA Guidelines caution, "[i]t must not be assumed that growth in any area is necessarily beneficial, detrimental, or of little significance to the environment." Guidelines § 15126.2(d); *see also Defend the Bay v. City of Irvine*, 119 Cal. App. 4th 1261 (2004) (upholding city's analysis of jobs-housing balance).

RESPONSES TO COMMENTS

The CEQA Guidelines state that the Final EIR is to include the comments and recommendations received on the draft EIR, and the "responses of the Lead Agency to significant environmental points raised in the review and consultation process." Guidelines § 15132(d). Reviewers of the draft EIR are advised to "explain the basis for their comments, and submit data or references offering facts, reasonable assumptions based on facts, or expert opinion supported by facts in support of the comments." Guidelines § 15204(c). Responsible and trustee agencies may submit mitigation measures to address significant impacts. Guidelines § 15204(f).

Lead agencies must evaluate comments on environmental issues from persons who reviewed the EIR, and prepare a written response to those comments raising significant environmental issues. Guidelines § 15088(a). The written response is to describe the disposition of significant environmental issues raised. Guidelines § 15088(c). In particular, if the Lead Agency does not agree with the recommendations or objections raised in the comments, the major issues raised should be addressed in detail, giving reasons why specific comments and suggestions were not accepted. *Id. See also, Flanders Foundation v. City of Carmel-by-the-Sea*, 202 Cal. App. 4th 603, 616-17 (2012) (invalidating an EIR where the city provided no response to a comment suggesting a method to reduce an impact that the EIR identified as significant and unavoidable). No responses

> Lead agencies must evaluate comments on environmental issues from persons who reviewed the EIR, and prepare a written response to those comments raising significant environmental issues.

are required when comments raise issues that are not required to be addressed under CEQA. *See Citizens for East Shore Parks v. Cal. State Lands Commission*, 202 Cal. App. 4th 549, 568 (2011). Further, the level of detail required in a response depends on the level of detail in the comment. "Where a general comment is made, a general response is sufficient." *Browning-Ferris Industries v. City Council*, 181 Cal. App. 3d 852, 862 (1986); *see also City of Maywood*, 208 Cal. App. 4th at 401 (finding a response listing the facts the agency relied on in concluding a future project was too speculative to qualify as a probable further project to be sufficient where commenter did not provide evidence demonstrating the future project to be probable).

When a court is asked to decide whether an agency has fulfilled its obligation to respond to significant environmental points raised in comments, it determines whether the failure to consider or respond to comments constitutes prejudicial error. In *Environmental Protection Information Center v. Department of Forestry and Fire Protection*, the California Supreme Court found that failure to respond to scholarly materials attached to comment letters was not prejudicial error because the lead agency had responded to the public comment letters themselves. 44 Cal. 4th 459 (2008). The Court also determined that failure to respond to a set of omitted oral and written comments was not prejudicial because it was undisputed that the comments were duplicative:

> When the material not considered was, on its face, demonstrably repetitive of material already considered, or so patently irrelevant that no reasonable person could suppose the failure to consider the material was prejudicial, or when the omitted material supports the agency action that was taken, then such omissions do not subvert the purpose of the public comment provisions and are nothing more than technical error.

Id. at 487.

> An agency may, but is not required to, respond to comments submitted after the end of CEQA's 45-day comment period.

An agency may, but is not required to, respond to comments submitted after the end of CEQA's 45-day comment period. Pub. Res. Code § 21091(d)(1); Guidelines § 15088. Thus, the inadequacy of an agency's responses to late comments "is not sufficient to render approval of the CEQA project ineffective or contrary to law." *Gray v. County of Madera*, 167 Cal. App. 4th 1099, 1111 (2008).

RECIRCULATION OF AN EIR

Normally, lead agencies are not required to provide an opportunity to review and comment on the final EIR. Guidelines §§ 15088.5(b), (e), 15089(b). However, when significant new information is added to an EIR after notice and consultation have occurred, but prior to certification, the agency must recirculate the final EIR for public comment. Pub. Res. Code § 21092.1. In *Laurel Heights Improvement Association v. Regents of University of California*, (*Laurel Heights II*), the California Supreme Court concluded that recirculation of a final EIR is required in four situations:

- When the new information shows a new, substantial environmental impact
- When new information shows a substantial increase in the severity of an environmental impact (unless mitigation measures reduce that impact to insignificance)
- When new information shows a feasible alternative or mitigation measure that clearly would lessen environmental impacts, but it is not adopted
- When the draft EIR was so fundamentally inadequate and conclusory that meaningful public review and comment were precluded

6 Cal. 4th 1112, 1129–30 (1993)

Guidelines section 15088.5(a) reflects *Laurel Heights II* and similarly defines "significant new information" for purposes of determining whether recirculation is required. The analysis of whether new information or project changes trigger a need for recirculation need not appear in the final EIR itself. It is sufficient that the decision not to recirculate the EIR is supported by evidence in the record. *Western Placer Citizens for an Agric. & Rural Env't v. County of Placer*, 144 Cal. App. 4th 890 (2006) (rejecting an argument that the final EIR must be revised to include project changes proposed after the final EIR was prepared but prior to certification).

PROJECT APPROVAL AND FINDINGS

After the final EIR is complete, the agency determines whether to approve the project. CEQA contains explicit requirements pertaining to approval of projects that have significant environmental impacts. Most importantly, agencies should not approve projects as proposed if there are feasible alternatives or feasible mitigation measures available that would substantially lessen the significant environmental effects of such projects unless (1) the agency finds that changes or alterations have been required in, or incorporated into the project to mitigate significant impacts; (2) such changes are within the responsibility of another agency and have been or can and should be adopted by that agency; or (3) specific economic, social, or other considerations make the mitigation measures or project alternatives identified in the EIR infeasible. Pub. Res. Code §§ 21002, 21081; Guidelines §§ 15091–15094.

CEQA does not, however, provide independent authority to require mitigation measures as project conditions:

> In mitigating or avoiding a significant effect of a project on the environment, a public agency may exercise only those express or implied powers provided by law other than this division. However, a public agency may use discretionary powers provided by such other law for the purpose of mitigating or avoiding a significant effect on the environment subject to the express or implied constraints or limitations that may be provided by law.

Pub. Res. Code § 21004; *see also Sierra Club v. Cal. Coastal Comm'n*, 35 Cal. 4th 839 (2005) (CEQA does not expand the Coastal Commission's authority to consider or require mitigation for impacts that would result from elements of the project outside the coastal zone).

In order to approve a project that would have significant environmental effects after mitigation, the lead agency must adopt findings identifying the specific considerations that make infeasible the environmentally superior alternatives. Pub. Res. Code § 21002.1(b); Guidelines § 15092. Evidence supporting the agency's ultimate findings of the infeasibility of alternatives studied in the EIR can be set forth elsewhere in the record; it need not appear in the EIR itself. *See Flanders v. City of Carmel-by-the-Sea*, 202 Cal. App. 4th 603, 618 (2012); *Sierra Club v. County of Napa*, 121 Cal. App. 4th 1490 (2004); *San Franciscans Upholding the Downtown Plan v. City & County of San Francisco*, 102 Cal. App. 4th 656, 679–80 (2002). However, an applicant's bald claims that an alternative is infeasible is not sufficient to support rejection of the alternative; the lead agency must independently analyze the alternatives to determine their feasibility. *Preservation Action Council v. City of San Jose*, 141 Cal. App. 4th 1336 (2006). *See also Uphold Our Heritage v. Town of Woodside*, 147 Cal. App. 4th 587 (2007) (that an applicant refuses to implement an alternative is not relevant; the question in evaluating

> In order to approve a project that would have significant environmental effects after mitigation, the lead agency must adopt findings identifying the specific considerations that make infeasible the environmentally superior alternatives.

economic feasibility of alternatives is whether the cost of the alternative, when compared with the cost of the project, is so great that a reasonably prudent property owner would not proceed with the alternative).

CEQA allows agencies to approve projects that damage the environment. If economic, social, or other considerations make it infeasible to mitigate the significant effects of a project on the environment, the project nevertheless may be carried out. Pub. Res. Code § 21002; Guidelines § 15091. In that case, however, the decision making body must adopt a Statement of Overriding Considerations to the effect that, although adverse impacts may result, specific overriding economic, legal, social, technological, or other considerations outweigh the project's significant, unmitigated impacts. Pub. Res. Code § 21081; Guidelines § 15093. These findings, which are adopted under Public Resources Code sections 21002.1 and 21081, must be supported by substantial evidence in the record. *See Sierra Club v. County of Contra Costa*, 10 Cal. App. 4th 1212, 1223 (1992). Nevertheless, a lack of evidence to support a particular reason justifying project approval will not invalidate the agency's findings if the agency specifies that each of the reasons is individually sufficient to outweigh the project's significant effects. *Habitat and Watershed Caretakers v. City of Santa Cruz*, 213 Cal. App. 4th 1277, 1308 (2013) (upholding findings even though several reasons lacked evidentiary support).

The agency also must include the following provisions in the findings or resolution of approval, in addition to the findings on mitigation measures, alternatives, and overriding considerations as required by Public Resources Code section 21081 and Guidelines sections 15091–15093:

- The lead agency "shall certify" that the EIR has been completed in compliance with CEQA. Guidelines § 15090(a)(1)
- The lead agency "shall certify" that the final EIR "was presented to the decisionmaking body of the lead agency and that the decisionmaking body reviewed and considered the information contained in the final EIR prior to approving the project." Guidelines § 15090(a)(2)
- The lead agency must independently review and analyze the EIR. Pub. Res. Code § 21082.1(c)(1). As part of the certification of the EIR, it must "find that the report...reflects the independent judgment of the lead agency." Pub. Res. Code § 21082.1(c)(3); Guidelines § 15090(a)(3)

CEQA provides that if a nonelected decisionmaking body of a local public agency certifies an EIR, that certification may be appealed to the agency's elected decisionmaking body, if any. Pub. Res. Code § 21151(c). For example, certification of an EIR for a tentative subdivision map by a city's planning commission may be appealed to the city council. Each local lead agency shall provide for such appeals. Guidelines § 15090(b). "Under CEQA, the 'decisionmaking body' is 'any person or group of people within a public agency permitted by law to approve or disapprove the project at issue.'" *Cal. Oak Foundation v. Regents of Univ. of Cal.*, 188 Cal. App. 4th 227, 289 (2010) (quoting Guidelines § 15356). The decisionmaking body need not be composed of the agency as a whole. *Id.* at 228-292. When certification of an EIR is appealed to the agency's elected decisionmaking body, a majority of that body must act to approve certification. *Vedanta Society of So. Cal. v. Cal. Quarters, Ltd.*, 84 Cal. App. 4th 517, 525-30 (2000). If the agency with final authority over a CEQA-triggering decision has no elected body, then CEQA does not necessitate an appeal to an elected body. *No Wetlands Landfill Expansion v. County of Marin*, 204 Cal. App. 4th 573, 584 (2012) (trial court erred in ordering appeal to the board of supervisors of decision by Marin Environmental Health Services Agency to certify an EIR for modification of a solid waste facility permit where

Marin EHS acted as the delegated local enforcement authority for Cal Recycle, and the board of supervisors had no authority to grant, deny or condition the permit).

The agency must file a notice of determination within five working days after it approves the project. Guidelines § 15094(a). The notice must identify the project and include a brief description of the project, the date when the agency approved the project, the agency's determination whether the project will have a significant effect on the environment, a statement that an EIR was prepared and certified, whether mitigation measures were made a condition of approval of the project, whether findings were made, whether a statement of overriding considerations was adopted, and the address where a copy of the final EIR and the record of project approval may be examined. Guidelines § 15094(a). If a notice of determination is properly filed and posted, then the notice will start a 30-day statute of limitations on court challenges to the approval under CEQA. Guidelines § 15094(f).

> If a notice of determination is properly filed and posted, then the notice will start a 30-day statute of limitations on court challenges to the approval under CEQA.

MITIGATION MONITORING AND REPORTING PROGRAMS

When an agency makes CEQA findings for any project that is approved subject to mitigation measures in an EIR, or when an agency adopts a mitigated negative declaration, the agency must impose a mitigation monitoring or reporting program to ensure implementation of the mitigation measures and project revisions that are required by the agency. Pub. Res. Code § 21081.6. *See also Fed'n of Hillside & Canyon Ass'ns v. City of Los Angeles*, 83 Cal. App. 4th 1252, 1261 (2000) (an agency must take steps to ensure that mitigation measures will be implemented). This requirement does not apply if the EIR does not recommend any mitigation measures, or if no mitigation measures are imposed. The statute does not require that the monitoring or reporting program be discussed in the EIR or mitigated negative declaration.

Guidelines section 15097(c) provides that "reporting" consists of a written compliance review that is to be submitted to the decisionmaking body or authorized staff person. The same section provides that "monitoring" is an ongoing periodic process of project oversight. The section explains that reporting is best suited to readily measurable or quantitative mitigation measures and to complex mitigation measures, particularly those to be implemented over a period of time. Monitoring or reporting programs must be "designed to ensure compliance during project implementation." Pub. Res. Code § 21081.6(1).

In *Rio Vista Farm Bureau Center v. County of Solano*, the court upheld a mitigation monitoring program for a countywide hazardous waste management plan. 5 Cal. App. 4th 351 (1992). The court stated that adequacy of a mitigation monitoring program must be assessed in accordance with a "rule of reason" that requires adherence to mitigation that is reasonably feasible. *Id.* at 376. The court upheld the plan in which the county committed to follow all CEQA, state law, and other applicable requirements for managing and disposing of hazardous waste, and described the federal, state, and local agencies that would monitor and report on hazardous waste practices or participate in implementing future projects. *Id.* at 376–77. *See also Christward Ministry v. County of San Diego*, 13 Cal. App. 4th 31, 49 (1993) (upholding a mitigation monitoring program that simply included a time for each measure to be implemented).

CEQA section 21081.6 itself does not give agencies the authority to modify mitigation measures if they later prove inadequate. However, an agency is not forever bound by mitigation measures that it adopts, at least where it is considering a subsequent discretionary approval for the same project or planning area. *See Napa Citizens*, 91 Cal.

App. 4th at 375. In recognition that land use plans need to be modified as circumstances change and that "the vision of a region's citizens or its governing body may evolve over time," an agency deleting an earlier-adopted mitigation measure need only state a legitimate reason for deleting the measure and support that statement with substantial evidence. *Id.* at 358.

SUPPLEMENTAL AND SUBSEQUENT EIRS AND NEGATIVE DECLARATIONS

Ordinarily, only one EIR or negative declaration is prepared for a project. Once an EIR has been prepared and a project has been approved, a public agency may not require additional environmental analysis. A supplemental or subsequent EIR (SEIR) may be required only if another discretionary approval for the same project is being considered and (a) there are substantial changes to the project; (b) there are substantial changes in the project's circumstances; or (c) new information that could not have been known at the time the EIR was certified becomes available and such changes or new information require major revisions to the previous EIR or negative declaration due to new significant environmental effects or a substantial increase in the severity of previously identified significant effects. Pub. Res. Code § 21166; Guidelines § 15162(a). *See also Benton v. Bd. of Supervisors*, 226 Cal. App. 3d 1467 (1991) and *Cucamongans United for Reasonable Expansion v. City of Rancho Cucamonga*, 82 Cal. App. 4th 473, 478 (2000) (applying the same once around rule to negative declarations).

Project changes standing alone normally will not trigger requirements for further CEQA review. An SEIR or subsequent negative declaration may be required only if there is a need to evaluate new significant environmental impacts that were not evaluated in the EIR for the project. *See Fund for Envtl. Defense v. County of Orange*, 204 Cal. App. 3d 1538, 1544-45 (1988). However, the lead agency must provide a reasoned basis supporting its conclusion that project changes would not result in new or substantially more severe significant impacts. *American Canyon Cmty United for Responsible Growth v. City of American Canyon*, 145 Cal. App. 4th 1062 (2006) (where the agency did not provide a reasoned basis for excluding portions of requested square footage from its analysis, the determination that project changes would not substantially increase traffic effects was not supported by substantial evidence). In addition, a city may be precluded from relying upon a prior mitigated negative declaration where the project at issue is considered to be a new project rather than a modification to a prior project. *Save Our Neighborhood v. Lishman*, 140 Cal. App. 4th 1288 (2006) (rejecting the city's attempt to rely on an addendum to a prior mitigated negative declaration where the city initially treated the proposed project as a new project, the project was proposed by a new applicant, and there was no evidence that any of the prior plans and drawings had been re-used). *But see Mani Brothers Real Estate Group v. City of Los Angeles*, 153 Cal. App. 4th 1385, 1399-1400 (2007) (distinguishing *Save Our Neighborhood* on the ground the project originally had been analyzed in a negative declaration rather than in an EIR and criticizing the "new project" test as not providing an objective or useful framework); *Moss v. County of Humboldt*, 162 Cal. App. 4th 1041 (2008) (renewed application for an expired subdivision map was not a new project, and could be evaluated based on information in a prior negative declaration).

New information can trigger an SEIR or subsequent negative declaration only if the information was not known and could not have been known at the time the EIR was certified as complete, shows new or substantially more severe significant

> SEIR = supplemental or subsequent environmental impact report

impacts or demonstrates the feasibility of mitigation measures or alternatives previously found infeasible, and is of substantial importance to the project. Pub. Res. Code § 21166(c); Guidelines § 15162(a)(3). *See Concerned Dublin Citizens v. City of Dublin*, 214 Cal. App. 4th 1301 (2013) (adoption of thresholds of significance to address greenhouse gases did not constitute new information requiring supplemental review); *Citizens for Responsible Equitable Environmental Development v. City of San Diego*, 196 Cal. App. 4th 515 (2011) (general assertions about climate change did not constitute new information that could not have been presented when the EIR was certified in 1994); *Fort Mojave Indian Tribe v. Cal. Dept. of Health Services*, 38 Cal. App. 4th 1574 (1995) (new regulation designating critical habitat for the desert tortoise was not significant new information where the physical effects of the project on the tortoise had been analyzed in the EIR).

An SEIR or subsequent negative declaration also is not required if the scope of the agency's discretion is limited to matters unrelated to the environmental effects at issue. In *San Diego Navy Broadway Complex Coalition v. City of San Diego*, 185 Cal. App. 4th 924 (2010), petitioners sought an analysis of greenhouse gas and climate change effects of a previously approved project. The court found subsequent approval regarding aesthetic aspects of the project did not trigger supplemental analysis of the project's climate change effects because petitioners did not demonstrate the agency had discretionary authority to address climate change concerns through project modification in other mitigation.

An agency's decision that an SEIR or subsequent negative declaration is not required will be upheld as long as it is supported by substantial evidence in the record. *See Moss v. County of Humboldt*, 162 Cal. App. 4th 1041 (2008); *Bowman v. City of Petaluma*, 185 Cal. App. 3d 1065, 1071–72 (1986) ("[A]fter a project has been subjected to environmental review, the statutory presumption flips in favor of the developer and against further review"); *Mani Brothers Real Estate Group v. City of Los Angeles*, 153 Cal. App. 4th 1385, 1398 (2007). *See also Abatti v. imperial Irrigation District*, 205 Cal. App. 4th 650, 671-74 (2012) (agreeing with the decision in *Benton v. Bd of Supervisors*, 226 Cal. App. 3d 1467 (1991), that the decision that no further review is required is reviewed under a substantial evidence standard, regardless of whether the original CEQA document was an EIR or a negative declaration). An explanation somewhere in the record as to why an SEIR or subsequent negative declaration is not required will assist a court reviewing the agency's determination. However, such an explanation is not required. *See Abatti*, 205 Cal. App. 4th at 682.

If the agency determines that an SEIR is warranted, it must be prepared and circulated for public review and comment in much the same manner as an original EIR. Guidelines § 15162(d).

USE OF AN ADDENDUM

If none of the three triggers for an SEIR exist, then an agency may use an addendum to make changes or additions to the prior EIR or negative declaration. Guidelines §§ 15164(a), (b). The addendum does not need to be circulated for public review, but it can be included in the final EIR or adopted negative declaration, and the agency must consider it before making a decision on the project. Guidelines §§ 15164(c), (d). A brief explanation of the decision not to prepare an SEIR should be included in the addendum, the findings, or elsewhere in the record. Guidelines § 15164(e).

EIR DEADLINES AND REQUIRED NOTICES

Various deadlines have been established by the Legislature for the EIR process. *See* Figure D (Time Periods for Review of Environmental Documents).

Also, a minimum of three notices must be prepared and properly filed in connection with the EIR. They are as follows:

- Notice of preparation of EIR. Pub. Res. Code § 21080.4; Guidelines § 15082
- Notice of completion of EIR. Pub. Res. Code § 21161; Guidelines § 15085
- Notice of approval or determination, which is filed and posted after the project is approved. Pub. Res. Code § 21152; Guidelines § 15094

JUDICIAL CHALLENGES TO AGENCY ACTION

TIME LIMITS FOR JUDICIAL CHALLENGES

A 30-day statute of limitations on judicial challenges to a project approval begins to run on the date the notice of determination is filed and posted. Pub. Res. Code §§ 21152(a), (c), 21167(b); Guidelines § 15075(e); *Citizens of Lake Murray Area Ass'n v. City Council*, 129 Cal. App. 3d 436, 440–41 (1982). *See also Sierra Club v. City of Orange*, 163 Cal. App. 4th 523 (2008) (limitations period does not start to run if the notice is substantially defective). The notice must include the determination whether the project will result in a significant impact to the environment, an indication whether an EIR has been prepared, and a certification that the final EIR with comments and responses, if one was prepared, is available to the general public. Pub. Res. Code §§ 21108, 21152; *see also* Figure D (Time Periods for Review of Environmental Documents). Further, the notice must have been filed and posted for the entire 30-day period, which excludes the first day of posting and includes the entirety of the last. *Latinos Unidos de Napa v. City of Napa*, 196 Cal. App. 4th 1154 (2011).

Absent the posting of a notice of determination, the statute of limitations to commence a lawsuit generally is 180 days. That period runs from the date of the decision to carry out or approve the project, or, if a project is undertaken without a formal decision, from the date of commencement of the project. Pub. Res. Code § 21167(a); Guidelines § 15112(c)(5). However, if a project is changed without any notice to the public after it is approved, a longer limitations period may apply. For example, in *Concerned Citizens of Costa Mesa, Inc. v. 32nd District Agricultural Association*, the project was substantially changed during construction, long after the EIR had been completed; the lawsuit was filed nearly a year after construction had begun. 42 Cal. 3d 929, 937–38 (1986). The California Supreme Court stated that the public reasonably could expect that the project under construction would be the project described in the EIR; therefore the failure to file a later EIR concerning the changes expanded the time period, so that the lawsuit could be filed within 180 days of the time the plaintiff knew, or should have known, that the project differed substantially from the one for which the EIR was prepared.

The 30-day statute of limitations also applies where an agency issues an approval after determining no additional CEQA review is necessary to address subsequent activities studied in a previous EIR. In *Committee for Green Foothills v. Santa Clara County Bd. of Supervisors*, 48 Cal. 4th 32 (2010), the California Supreme Court held that the 30-day statute applies not only when a notice of determination is filed after an EIR is first certified, but also when an NOD is filed after an agency determines no additional CEQA documentation is needed for a later approval. The Court also concluded that CEQA's 30-day statute of limitations does not depend on the merits of the petitioner's claims, but rather upon the notice to the public.

FIGURE D: TIME PERIODS FOR REVIEW OF ENVIRONMENTAL DOCUMENTS

ACTION GUIDELINES	EFFECT	TIME PERIOD	RELEVANT STATUTES
Review of application for completeness	If no determination is made within this period, it will be deemed complete.	30 days	Guidelines § 15101
Lead agency acceptance of a project as complete	Begins maximum one-year period to complete environmental review for certain projects.	1 year	Guidelines § 15108
Initial study	Provides 30 days to determine whether an EIR or negative declaration will be required.	30 days	Guidelines § 15102
Notice of preparation	Provides 30 days from receipt of NOP for agencies to review and comment.	30 days	Guidelines § 15103
Convening of scope and content meetings	Requires a meeting requested by an agency or by the applicant to be convened within 30 days of the request.	30 days	Guidelines § 15104
Public review	When an environmental document is submitted to the Clearinghouse, the public review period shall be at least as long as the review set by the Clearinghouse.	EIR: 30–60 days ND: 20–30 days	Guidelines § 15105
Review by state agencies	Provides standard 45 days for EIRs and standard 30 days for negative declarations.	EIR: 45 days ND: 30 days	Guidelines § 15105
Completion and certification of negative declaration	For a private project, the negative declaration must be completed in 180 days.	180 days	Pub. Res. Code § 21100.2(a)(1)(B)
Approval or disapproval of a project based on a negative declaration	A private project must be approved or disapproved within 60 days of the certification of the negative declaration.	60 days	Gov't Code § 65950(a)(2)
Completion and certification of EIR	For a private project, an EIR must be completed within one year. May be extended once for up to 90 days.	1 year	Guidelines § 15108
Approval or disapproval of a project based on an EIR	A private project must be approved or disapproved within 180 days of the certification of the EIR.	180 days	Gov't Code § 65950(a)(1)
Notice of determination—filing	Provides that the notice shall be filed within 5 days after project approval.	5 days	Guidelines § 15094(a)
Notice of determination	Filing and posting starts a 30-day statute approval of the project.	30 days	Guidelines § 15094(f)
Suspension of time limits	Unreasonable delay of document preparation caused by the applicant allows suspension of time period in Guidelines §§ 15107 and 15108.	varies	Guidelines § 15109
Projects with federal involvement	Time limits may be waived or superceded by federal time requirements.	varies	Guidelines § 15110

Filing additional notices of determination for subsequent discretionary determinations implementing a previously approved project does not reopen the statute of limitations to challenge the original CEQA document. *Citizens for a Megaplex-Free Alameda v. City of Alameda*, 149 Cal. App. 4th 91 (2007). Further, even where no notice of determination is filed, the limitations period is not re-opened each subsequent time that the public agency takes an action implementing the project. *Van de Kamps Coalition v. Bd. Of Trustees of Los Angeles Community College Dist.*, 206 Cal. App. 4th 1036 (2012).

JUDICIAL REVIEW

For a detailed discussion regarding judicial review of CEQA decisions, see chapter 19 (Land Use Litigation).

CHAPTER 7

Federal and State Wetland Regulation

Marc Bruner
Julie Jones

INTRODUCTION

Traditionally, land use regulation has been primarily a local responsibility. However, two major federal programs have taken on increasing importance over the past several decades. These are the federal wetlands regulatory program under Section 404 of the Clean Water Act (CWA), discussed in this chapter, and federal species protections under the Endangered Species Act (ESA), discussed in chapter 8. In California, as these chapters explain, the state also plays an active role in addressing wetlands and species issues.

CWA = Clean Water Act
ESA = Endangered Species Act

Wetlands perform important functions such as flood control, erosion protection, and pollutant removal. They also provide valuable fish and wildlife habitat, serving as spawning areas for many commercially important fisheries species, as well as playing a vital role in major waterfowl migration routes. It is estimated that in some areas of California, up to 90 percent of historic wetland areas have been lost to agricultural and urban development, leading to heightened public concern about further incremental losses.

The United States Army Corps of Engineers (Corps) is the federal agency with primary responsibility for issuing permits under Section 404 of the CWA for activities that involve filling a wetland. The Environmental Protection Agency (EPA) also plays an important role by defining, jointly with the Corps, when a wetland is covered by Section 404 and by establishing the criteria governing when development in a covered wetland may occur. Equally important, the EPA has the power to "veto" individual permit applications under Section 404. In California, in addition to the Corps and the EPA, the State Water Resources Control Board and the nine Regional Water Quality Control Boards are the agencies with the greatest involvement in wetlands regulation. The California Coastal Commission also regulates the development of wetlands in the coastal zone, and other agencies, such as the San Francisco Bay Conservation and Development Commission and local governments, may restrict development of wetlands within the geographic areas of their respective jurisdictions.

Corps = U.S. Army Corps of Engineers

EPA = Environmental Protection Agency

As often occurs where several agencies regulate a common resource, the various agencies responsible for wetlands regulation do not always agree on key issues, such as the definition of what constitutes a wetland, what role mitigation plays in the regulatory process, and whether particular projects should be allowed to proceed. Frequently, the responsibility for resolving these differences falls on the project proponent, and success in the permitting process often depends on guiding the agencies to a common conclusion. An understanding of the agencies' varying viewpoints, and how these viewpoints have evolved, can be essential to achieving the desired outcome.

This chapter presents an overview of the major aspects of the federal and state wetland regulatory programs. Following a brief history of the federal program, this chapter addresses the legal and scientific considerations governing the determination of whether a site contains wetlands or other "waters of the United States" subject to federal regulation. The chapter then presents an overview of the federal wetlands permitting program, including both nationwide and individual permits. Next is a more detailed discussion of the EPA's "Section 404(b)(1) Guidelines," which require that the Corps issue permits only for the "Least Environmentally Damaging Practicable Alternative" (LEDPA). For projects involving the fill of a wetland, this requirement has a direct and profound effect on the land use entitlement process. Other federal and state regulatory programs affecting development in wetlands also are summarized. The chapter concludes with a discussion of how the Corps, the EPA, and the courts enforce federal wetlands protections.

LEDPA = Least Environmentally Damaging Practicable Alternative

A BRIEF HISTORY OF THE FEDERAL PROGRAM

Modern wetlands regulation traces its roots to Sections 9 and 10 of the Rivers and Harbors Act of 1899, under which the Corps originally regulated streams and rivers to protect interstate commerce in navigable waterbodies. Section 9 of the Rivers and Harbors Act requires a permit from the Corps to construct a dike or dam in navigable waters of the United States. 33 U.S.C. § 401. Section 10 of the Rivers and Harbors Act requires a permit from the Corps to build structures in navigable waters such as piers, breakwaters, bulkheads, revetments, power lines, and aids to navigation, or to perform activities such as dredging, stream channelization, excavation, and filling that may interfere with navigation. 33 U.S.C. § 403. The Corps has largely integrated its permitting process under the Rivers and Harbors Act with the process for issuing permits under Section 404 of the CWA, which is discussed at length below.

Initially, the Corps administered the Rivers and Harbors Act to protect only actual navigation and navigable capacity. But in the late 1960s, the Corps began to expand the reach of its regulatory program by considering a broader range of "public interest" factors, including ecological and environmental concerns. In 1970, the Fifth Circuit upheld this approach in *Zabel v. Tabb*, 430 F. 2d 199 (5th Cir. 1970), *cert. denied*, 401 U.S. 910 (1971). The Corps' regulations codify the various "public interest" factors that it must consider as part of its permitting decisions, including effects on fish and wildlife; water quality; water supply; historic, cultural, scenic and recreational values; energy needs and conservation; flood protection; and property ownership and economics. *See generally* 33 C.F.R. § 320.4.

In 1972, the Corps further expanded its regulatory program by amending its administrative definition of "navigable waters" under the Rivers and Harbors Act. This definition, which codified the key court cases defining the extent of federal jurisdiction over navigable waters, included:

- All waters presently used for commerce. *See Ball v. United States*, 77 U.S. 557 (1870)
- All waters used in the past for interstate commerce. *See Economy Light & Power Co. v. United States*, 256 U.S. 113 (1921)

- All waters susceptible to use in their ordinary condition or with reasonable improvements as a means to transport interstate or foreign commerce. See *United States v. Appalachian Elec. Power Co.*, 311 U.S. 377 (1940)
- All waters subject to the ebb and flow of the tide. *Willink v. United States*, 240 U.S. 572 (1916)

Thus, despite retaining the term "navigable" in the definition, the Corps expanded its regulatory program in the late 1960s and early 1970s beyond a strict concept of actual navigability.

It was in this context that Congress passed the Federal Water Pollution Control Act of 1972, commonly known as the Clean Water Act. The goal of the CWA is to "restore and maintain the chemical, physical, and biological integrity of the Nation's waters." 33 U.S.C. § 1251(a). To meet this objective, Section 301 of the CWA prohibits the discharge of any pollutants into navigable waters, except as allowed by permits issued under Sections 402 and 404 of the CWA. See 33 U.S.C. §§ 1311, 1342, 1344. Section 402 of the CWA establishes the National Pollutant Discharge Elimination System (NPDES) program, which is administered by the EPA and the states. This program governs the discharge of wastewater and other pollutants into waters of the United States. Section 404 of the CWA authorizes the Corps to issue permits for the discharge of "dredged or fill material" into waters of the United States. 33 U.S.C. § 1344.

> NPDES = National Pollutant Discharge Elimination System

Pursuant to its authority under the Rivers and Harbors Act and Section 404 of the CWA, the Corps issues permits for seven general classes of activities, which are listed in 33 C.F.R. § 320.1(b):

- Dams or dikes in navigable waters of the United States (*see* 33 C.F.R. pt. 321)
- Other structures or work including excavation, dredging, and/or disposal activities in navigable waters of the United States (*see* 33 C.F.R. pt. 322)
- Activities that alter or modify the course, condition, location, or capacity of a navigable water of the United States (*see* 33 C.F.R. pt. 322)
- Construction of artificial islands, installations, or other devices on the outer continental shelf (*see* 33 C.F.R. pt. 322)
- Discharges of dredged or fill material into waters of the United States (*see* 33 C.F.R. pt. 323)
- Activities involving the transportation of dredged material for the purpose of disposal in ocean waters (*see* 33 C.F.R. pt. 324)
- Nationwide general permits for certain categories of activities (*see* 33 C.F.R. pt. 330)

HOW WETLANDS AND OTHER "WATERS OF THE UNITED STATES" ARE DEFINED UNDER THE CWA

Like the Rivers and Harbors Act, the CWA regulates "navigable waters." The CWA defines this term simply to mean "waters of the United States." 33 U.S.C. § 1362(7). This vague legal definition has generated substantial controversy concerning the extent of federal jurisdiction under Section 404.

One view is that Congress intended the term "waters of the United States" to include all waters that Congress has the power to regulate under the Commerce Clause of the United States Constitution. However, since Congress retained the term "navigable" and used it throughout the CWA, courts have struggled—and continue to struggle—with the implication that traditional notions of navigability still play a role in defining the boundaries of federal jurisdiction under Section 404.

There are also complex scientific and technical issues involved in answering the question "how wet is wet?" This line-drawing exercise, frequently requiring the assistance of experts, is of critical importance given the emphasis of the Section 404 permitting program on determining the amount of "waters of the United States" affected by a project.

LEGAL DEFINITIONS OF WETLANDS AND OTHER "WATERS OF THE UNITED STATES"

In adopting its initial regulations under the CWA in 1974, the Corps defined "waters of the United States" to match the definition of that term under the Rivers and Harbors Act. As explained above, this definition covered waters subject to the ebb and flow of the tide and waters currently being used, used in the past, or susceptible to use in the future for navigation. But in 1975, a federal district court found this definition to be too narrow, and agreed with the Natural Resources Defense Council (NRDC) that the Corps' Section 404 jurisdiction over "waters of the United States" extended to the maximum extent permissible under the Commerce Clause. See NRDC v. Callaway, 392 F. Supp. 685, 686 (D.D.C. 1975).

> NRDC = Natural Resources Defense Council

In response to *NRDC v. Callaway*, the Corps adopted regulations in 1977 that defined "waters of the United States" to the effective limits of the Commerce Clause. 42 Fed. Reg. 31722 (June 22, 1977). Those regulations, now found at 33 C.F.R. Part 328, define "waters of the United States" to include wetlands, as well as a broad range of other non-navigable aquatic features. The regulations extended the Corps' Section 404 jurisdiction to reach all of the following:

- All waters that are currently used, or were used in the past, or may be susceptible to use in interstate or foreign commerce, including all waters that are subject to the ebb and flow of the tide
- All interstate waters including interstate wetlands
- All other waters such as intrastate lakes, rivers, streams (including intermittent streams), mud flats, sand flats, wetlands, sloughs, prairie potholes, wet meadows, playa lakes, or natural ponds, where the use, degradation, or destruction of the waters could affect interstate or foreign commerce
- All impoundments of waters of the United States
- Tributaries of waters identified in the preceding four bullets
- Territorial seas
- Wetlands adjacent to the waters in the preceding six bullets

33 C.F.R. § 328.3(a)

Under the Corps' regulations, the origin of a wetland—whether it is natural or artificial—is largely irrelevant. For the most part, an area is treated as a wetland if it has physical wetlands characteristics. See *Leslie Salt Co. v. United States*, 896 F. 2d 354, 357–58 (9th Cir. 1990); but see *United States v. City of Fort Pierre*, 747 F. 2d 464, 465 (8th Cir. 1984) (Corps does not have jurisdiction over wetlands inadvertently created as a result of the Corps' own activity).

In 1985, the United States Supreme Court affirmed the Corps' power to regulate to the limits of the Commerce Clause in *United States v. Riverside Bayview Homes, Inc.*, 474 U.S. 121, 134 (1985). Bolstered by that ruling, during the late 1980s and 1990s the Corps adopted an ever expanding view of its jurisdiction, taking the position that Section 404 regulates waters and wetlands that are neither physically navigable nor connected in any way to navigable waters, so long as they provide habitat for migratory birds. The underlying legal theory was that hunting and bird watching are activities of interstate commerce and therefore are subject to Congressional jurisdiction under the Commerce Clause. 51 Fed. Reg. 41216 (Nov. 13, 1986). Several federal courts upheld this position, known as the "migratory bird rule." *See Leslie Salt Co. v. United States*, 896 F. 2d at 360; *Hoffman Homes, Inc. v. U.S. Environmental Protection Agency*, 999 F. 2d 256, 261-62 (7th Cir. 1993).

THE NARROWING OF FEDERAL JURISDICTION

In 2001, the United States Supreme Court reined in the Corps' expansive approach. *Solid Waste Agency of Northern Cook County (SWANCC) v. U.S. Army Corps of Eng'rs*, 531 U.S. 159 (2001). The *SWANCC* case involved a proposed solid waste disposal operation on the site of a former sand and gravel pit mine. The site contained numerous seasonal and permanent ponds, which were neither connected nor adjacent to any navigable waters—rather, they were "isolated" waters. The Corps determined that the ponds were "waters of the United States" because they were periodically used by migratory birds. The project proponent challenged the Corps' jurisdiction over the site. The challenge failed before the district court and the Seventh Circuit, but found a more receptive audience at the Supreme Court.

The *SWANCC* opinion began back where the CWA started—with the definition of "navigable waters." The Court concluded, by a slim 5-4 majority, that the migratory bird rule did not fit within this definition because it stretched the concept of navigability too far. The Court therefore invalidated the migratory bird rule and determined that the Corps lacked jurisdiction over the isolated ponds at the pit mine. In distinguishing its earlier decision in *Riverside Bayview Homes,* the Court explained that the wetlands at issue in that case were adjacent to, and therefore had a "significant nexus" to, navigable waters, whereas in *SWANCC* the ponds were isolated from any such waters. 531 U.S. at 167-68, 171-72. In holding that the migratory bird rule was inconsistent with the CWA's definition of navigable waters, the Court avoided the broader constitutional question of whether the rule violated the Commerce Clause. *Id.* at 174.

In January 2003, the Corps and the EPA published joint guidance concerning the scope of federal wetlands jurisdiction in light of *SWANCC*. 68 Fed. Reg. 1995 (Jan. 15, 2003). The guidance makes clear that the Corps now lacks the authority to regulate isolated, intrastate, non-navigable waters where the sole basis of jurisdiction is the use of those waters by migratory birds. The guidance further instructs Corps field staff to seek formal, project-specific approval from the Corps' headquarters in Washington, D.C. (the "phone home" rule), before asserting jurisdiction over such isolated waters on any *other* grounds (e.g., recreational use by interstate or foreign travelers or industrial uses in interstate commerce, *see* 33 C.F.R. § 328.3(a)(3)).

As the courts were grappling with how to interpret and apply the *SWANCC* decision, the Supreme Court in 2006 issued its fractured 4-1-4 opinion in *Rapanos v. United States*. 547 U.S. 715 (2006). The Court in *Rapanos* reviewed two decisions by the Sixth Circuit that had upheld the Corps' assertion of jurisdiction over wetlands that were remote and physically separated from navigable bodies of water. The first case, *United States v. Rapanos*, 376 F. 3d 629 (6th Cir. 2004), involved an enforcement action brought against a landowner who had filled wetlands to build a mall without a Corps permit.

> In January 2003, the Corps and the EPA published joint guidance concerning the scope of federal wetlands jurisdiction in light of *SWANCC*.

The wetland property was adjacent to a ditch that drained into a river and eventually to a lake. The second case, *Carabell v. U.S. Army Corps of Engineers*, 391 F. 3d 704 (6th Cir. 2004), centered on whether a Corps permit is required to fill wetlands separated by a manmade berm from a drainage ditch that led to a river. The landowners wanted to fill the wetlands to build condominiums, and sued after regulators denied their application for a Section 404 permit. In both cases, the Corps asserted jurisdiction over the wetlands because of their proximity to "tributary" ditches that eventually drained into navigable waters.

In voting to overturn the Sixth Circuit, the four most conservative members of the Court, in an opinion authored by Justice Scalia, said that the Corps' previously broad assertion of jurisdiction under Section 404 should be severely curtailed. Justice Scalia's opinion reasoned that only bodies of water with a "continuous surface connection" to navigable waters should fall under the CWA's aegis.

In a separate opinion, Justice Kennedy joined the decision to reverse the lower court, but found that Justice Scalia's view of the Corps' jurisdiction was too narrow and conflicted with the CWA. According to Justice Kennedy, the key question under Section 404 is whether the regulated waterbody has a "significant nexus" to currently or conceivably navigable waters. This fact-based inquiry requires a determination, based on a consideration of hydrologic and ecological factors, of whether the waterbody may "significantly affect the chemical, physical and biological integrity of other covered waters more readily understood as 'navigable.'"

In the dissenting opinion, the more liberal justices would have simply upheld the lower court's decision and the Corps' historically broad jurisdiction under the CWA.

With the opinions by Justices Scalia and Kennedy, a majority of the Court voted to overturn the Corps' assertion of jurisdiction. But there was no majority agreement on the standard to apply for determining when jurisdiction exists, and the cases interpreting *Rapanos* have failed to define with any degree of clarity the CWA's jurisdictional boundaries. Instead, the cases have borne out the prediction in Justice Roberts' concurring opinion that "[l]ower courts and regulated entities will now have to feel their way on a case-by-case basis." 547 U.S. at 758.

In the first case to interpret *Rapanos*, a district court in Texas followed Justice Scalia's narrow jurisdictional test, which was consistent with prior Fifth Circuit law, and dismissed Justice Kennedy's test as too "vague" and "subjective." The court ruled there was no CWA jurisdiction over an oil spill into the dry bed of an intermittent stream. *United States v. Chevron Pipe Line Co.*, 437 F. Supp. 2d 605 (D. Tex. 2006).

In contrast, the Ninth Circuit applied Justice Kennedy's significant nexus test as the "controlling rule of law" in a 2007 case involving the discharge of sewage to a pond containing wetlands that was adjacent to the Russian River. *Northern California River Watch v. City of Healdsburg*, 496 F. 3d 993, 999–1000 (9th Cir. 2007) *cert. denied*, 128 S. Ct. 1225 (2008). According to the court, there were two grounds for finding jurisdiction under the CWA. First, the fact that the wetlands in the pond were adjacent to the river was alone sufficient under Justice Kennedy's test to infer a significant nexus to the river. Second, the court emphasized that the pond water seeps into the river through both a surface and an underground connection, thus establishing a significant nexus to the river, irrespective of the adjacency issue. In deciding to apply Justice Kennedy's test, the court in *City of Healdsburg* relied on a prior opinion by the Seventh Circuit, which adopted that test in remanding a CWA penalty case for further fact-finding to determine whether a "significant nexus" existed. *United States v. Gerke Excavating*, 464 F. 3d 723 (7th Cir. 2006), *cert. denied*, 128 S. Ct. 45 (2007).

The Eleventh Circuit followed *City of Healdsburg* and *Gerke Excavation* in adopting Justice Kennedy's test as "the governing definition of 'navigable waters.'" *United States v. Robison*, 505 F. 3d 1208, 1219-22 (11th Cir. 2007), *cert. denied*, 129 S. Ct. 627 (2008). The defendants were convicted of violating the CWA for discharging contaminated water into Avondale Creek, based on evidence that the creek had a "continuous uninterrupted flow" into another creek that flowed into the Black Warrior River, a navigable water. Even though the evidence was sufficient to establish jurisdiction under Justice Scalia's opinion, the court ordered a new trial, on the ground that the jury instructions did not mention the need for—and the evidence did not establish—a "significant nexus" to the river. As the court explained: "The government presented no evidence...of the chemical, physical, or biological effect that Avondale Creek's waters had or might have had on the Black Warrior River." 505 F.3d at 1212. In reaching its ruling, the court rejected the position that the government could establish jurisdiction under *either* Justice Scalia's *or* Justice Kennedy's test.

The First Circuit, however, adopted precisely that position in remanding a CWA penalty case for further fact-finding. *United States v. Johnson*, 467 F. 3d 56 (1st Cir. 2006), *cert. denied*, 128 S. Ct. 375 (2007). The *Johnson* decision contained a lengthy discussion on the rules for interpreting Supreme Court decisions without a clear majority, and it criticized the reasoning in *City of Healdsburg* and *Gerke*. The Third and Eighth Circuits have followed the approach in *Johnson*, creating a significant divide among the federal courts. See *United States v. Bailey*, 571 F. 3d 791, 799 (8th Cir. 2009); *United States v. Donovan*, 661 F.3d 174 (3d Cir. 2011).

Meanwhile, the Fifth and Sixth Circuits, when faced with the issue, have declined to decide which of the different tests set out in *Rapanos* is controlling. See *United States v. Lucas*, 516 F. 3d 316, 327 (5th Cir.), *cert. denied*, 129 S. Ct. 116 (2008) (upholding the criminal conviction of a residential subdivider who installed septic systems in a wetland, based on the finding that the evidence presented at trial was sufficient to support jurisdiction under all three *Rapanos* standards); *United States v. Cundiff*, 555 F. 3d 200, 210-13 (6th Cir.), *cert. denied*, 130 S. Ct. 74 (2009) (in upholding a civil penalty imposed against a landowner who discharged fill material into a wetland, the court determined that it was not necessary to resolve which test in *Rapanos* had the force of law, since the Corps had jurisdiction regardless of which test was used).

Even where the parties agree that Justice Kennedy's significant nexus test governs, it is by no means clear how this test should be applied. In a case involving a proposed residential development in wetlands near a seasonal drainage ditch located seven miles from the nearest navigable water, the Corps found a "significant nexus" after extensively analyzing the role of the wetlands and the drainage ditch in mitigating downstream flood flows and in providing nutrients to fish species. But the court reversed and remanded to the Corps for further fact-finding. *Precon Dev. Corp. v. U.S. Army Corps of Eng'rs*, 633 F.3d 278, 294-95 (4th Cir. 2011). While the court acknowledged the significant nexus test does not require "laboratory tests" or "quantitative measurements," it found the evidence was not sufficient to establish the "comparative relationship between the wetlands at issue, their adjacent tributary, and traditional navigable waters." *Id.* at 294-95.

> Even where the parties agree that Justice Kennedy's significant nexus test governs, it is by no means clear how this test should be applied.

The confusion among the courts—coupled with Congress' inaction and the lack of regulations defining the extent of Section 404 jurisdiction—have led Justice Alito to make a dramatic plea:

> The reach of the Clean Water Act is notoriously unclear.... Real relief requires Congress to do what it should have done in the first place: provide a reasonably

clear rule regarding the reach of the Clean Water Act. When Congress passed the Clean Water Act in 1972, it provided that the Act covers "the waters of the United States." 33 U.S.C. § 1362(7). But Congress did not define what is meant by "the waters of the United States"; the phrase was not a term of art with a known meaning; and the words themselves are hopelessly indeterminate... For 40 years, Congress has done nothing to resolve this critical ambiguity; and the EPA has not seen fit to promulgate a rule providing a clear and sufficiently limited definition of the phrase.

Sackett v. Environmental Protection Agency, 132 S. Ct. 1367, 1376 (2012) (Justice Alito's concurring opinion)

The EPA also has highlighted the lack of clarity over the reach of the CWA. According to an EPA report published in 2009, the Rapanos decision has created "a lot of uncertainty" and has led to a significant increase in litigation over jurisdictional determinations under the CWA. See U.S. EPA, Office of Inspector General, Congressionally Requested Report on Comments Related to Effects of Jurisdictional Uncertainty on Clean Water Act Implementation (Apr. 30, 2009). As a result, the report explains, Rapanos has been "a major resource drain" on EPA's Office of Enforcement and Compliance Assurance, and has made it "difficult for EPA to craft jurisdictional determination guidance that is both legal and usable for field staff." Id.

CONTINUED UNCERTAINTY OVER THE BOUNDARIES OF FEDERAL JURISDICTION

As of late 2013, there still is no resolution of the significant uncertainties surrounding the key definition of "waters of the United States" that delineates the boundaries of Clean Water Act jurisdiction. In 2008, the Corps and EPA published joint guidance interpreting the extent of their permitting authority in light of the Rapanos decision. The guidance, however, was not legally binding and did little to clarify the limits of federal jurisdiction; for many smaller water bodies, the guidance required a highly fact-intensive scientific analysis by an environmental consultant to determine whether a "significant nexus" to a navigable waterway existed.

In April 2011, the agencies shifted course and issued new draft guidance that sought to expand their jurisdiction in comparison to the 2008 guidance. The 2011 draft guidance, however, unleashed a political firestorm and was never finalized.

The agencies recently embarked on a different path and have presented draft regulations to the Office of Management and Budget for intergovernmental review. As of late 2013, the draft regulations have yet to be formally proposed for public comment.

The draft regulations, if adopted in their current form, would establish an expansive definition of "waters of the United States" under the Clean Water Act. This expansive definition is based on a draft scientific report published by EPA in September 2013 entitled Connectivity of Streams and Wetlands to Downstream Waters: A Review and Synthesis of the Scientific Evidence. The draft report finds that all streams, regardless of their size or how frequently they flow, are connected to and have important effects on downstream waters. The draft report further finds that wetlands and open waters located in floodplains and riparian areas are integrated with and strongly influence downstream waters. These findings could be used to support a very broad reading of what constitutes a "significant nexus" under Justice Kennedy's opinion in Rapanos.

While it remains to be seen how the rulemaking process will play out, it is clear that the issue of how to define the boundaries of Clean Water Act jurisdiction will continue to generate controversy and uncertainty in 2014.

CALIFORNIA RESPONSE TO REDUCED FEDERAL WETLANDS JURISDICTION

As federal wetlands jurisdiction has receded in the wake of the SWANCC and Rapanos decisions, the State Water Resources Control Board (SWRCB or State Board) has moved in to fill the gap. Just a few weeks after the Supreme Court published its decision in SWANCC in January 2001, the State Board published a memorandum asserting that isolated wetlands that are no longer subject to federal jurisdiction remain subject to state regulation under the Porter-Cologne Water Quality Control Act (Water Code § 13000 et seq.).[1] In order to moderate the resulting permitting burden, the State Board in May 2004 issued a statewide general permit for discharges to waters deemed by the Corps to be outside of federal jurisdiction.[2] This general permit authorizes fills to isolated wetlands and other waters if the fill is not more than two-tenths of an acre in size, affects no more than 400 linear feet of waters of the state, and involves dredging of no more than fifty cubic yards within waters of the state. Coverage under the general permit is obtained through the filing of a notice of intent. For larger fills, individual waste discharge requirements must be obtained from the appropriate Regional Water Quality Control Board.

SWRCB/State Board = State Water Resources Control Board

The State Board also has launched a program to develop a statewide "wetland and riparian area protection policy." The first phase of this policy is to formulate a wetland definition that reliably captures the diverse array of California wetlands, develop statewide wetland delineation procedures based on the methods used by the Corps, and develop statewide procedures for the review and approval of discharges of dredged or fill material into waters of the state, including wetlands. In January 2013, the State Board published a "preliminary draft" policy, which proposes a state definition of "wetlands" (described below) and a set of procedures for the review and approval of state law permits for filling a wetland.[3]

The State Board has indicated that future phases of this statewide policy, which are not under consideration at this time, will seek to expand the regulatory program to cover not only discharges of dredged or fill material, but also other activities that may affect wetlands and upland riparian areas.

Thus, the restrictions on federal jurisdiction established by the United States Supreme Court in SWANCC and Rapanos have not decreased the level of wetland protection in California. Instead, these restrictions have spurred the emergence of a robust state law program to assume permitting responsibility for the filling of isolated wetlands and streams.

Restrictions on federal jurisdiction established by the United States Supreme Court in SWANCC and Rapanos have spurred the emergence of a robust state law program to assume permitting responsibility for the filling of isolated wetlands and streams.

---

1 See January 25, 2001 Memorandum from SWRCB Chief Counsel Craig Wilson, Effect of SWANCC v. United States on the 401 Certification Program (available at http://www.swrcb.ca.gov/water_issues/programs/cwa401/wrapp.shtml).

2 SWRCB Order No. 2004-0004-DWQ, Statewide General Waste Discharge Requirements for Dredged and Fill Discharges to Waters Deemed by the U.S. Army Corps of Engineers to be Outside of Federal Jurisdiction (May 4, 2004) (available at http://www.swrcb.ca.gov/board_decisions/adopted_orders/water_quality/wqo04.shtml).

3 SWRCB, Preliminary Draft Water Quality Control Policy for Wetland Area Protection and Dredged or Fill Permitting (Jan. 28, 2013) (available at http://www.swrcb.ca.gov/water_issues/programs/cwa401/wrapp.shtml).

THE SCIENTIFIC/TECHNICAL DEFINITION OF WETLANDS

The legal considerations outlined above merely set the stage for asking the frequently difficult question: what is the "point at which water ends and land begins?" *Riverside Bayview Homes*, 474 U.S. at 132. The Supreme Court has recognized that:

> Our common experience tells us that this is often no easy task: the transition from water to solid ground is not necessarily or even typically an abrupt one. Rather, between open waters and dry land may lie shallows, marshes, mudflats, swamps, bogs—in short, a huge array of areas that are not wholly aquatic but nevertheless fall far short of being dry land. Where on this continuum to find the limit of "waters" is far from obvious.

Id.

The Corps' regulations governing this determination define wetlands as:

> Those areas that are inundated or saturated by surface or ground water at a frequency and duration sufficient to support, and under normal circumstances do support, a prevalence of vegetation typically adapted for life in saturated soil conditions. Wetlands generally include swamps, marshes, bogs, and similar areas.

33 C.F.R. § 328.3(b)

Although this regulatory definition is simple, the field identification of wetlands can be quite complicated. For this reason, the Corps has developed a series of technical manuals to provide guidance on determining what constitutes a wetland. Generally, the Corps uses a three-part approach to define wetlands by the presence of:

- Permanent or periodic soil saturation or inundation (wetlands hydrology)
- Soils that exhibit anaerobic conditions in their upper part (hydric soils)
- Plants that grow in soils that are deficient in oxygen (hydrophytic vegetation)

Three major versions of the Corps' wetlands delineation manual were published in 1987, 1989, and 1991, respectively. All three versions follow the general three-part approach evaluating hydrology, soils, and vegetation, but differ in the details of their implementation (such as the number of days of inundation required to meet the hydrology criterion). However, controversy surrounding the 1989 Manual led Congress to suspend its use until a 1991 version could be adopted. In the meantime, Congress directed that the 1987 manual be used on an "interim" basis. *See* Energy and Water Development Appropriations Act of 1992 (H.R. 2427). But the 1991 Manual only was proposed for public comment, and never was finalized. As a result, the "interim" period has continued to the present, and the 1987 Manual is still in use.

The Corps has developed supplements to the 1987 Manual to address conditions that are specific to different regions of the country. These "Regional Supplements" are designed to address varying wetland characteristics in different geographic areas in order to improve the accuracy and efficiency of the procedures used for delineating wetlands. The supplements also describe how to deal with various situations that pose problems for delineating wetlands, such as soils with faint wetlands indicators or wetlands that periodically lack the requisite hydrology. The appropriate Regional Supplement is to be used in conjunction with the 1987 Manual and, where there are differences between the two documents, the Regional Supplement governs. The two Regional Supplements applicable to California, *Arid West Region* and *Western Mountains, Valleys, and Coast Region* were issued in September 2008 and May 2010, respectively.[4]

---

[4] The Regional Supplements are available at http://www.usace.army.mil/missions/civilworks/regulatoryprogramandpermits/reg_supp.aspx.

The Corps' manuals do not have the status of formal regulations, but regulators in the field use and rely on the manuals extensively to determine whether regulated wetlands are present.

WETLAND HYDROLOGY

The 1987 Manual defines an area as having wetlands hydrology where it is inundated either permanently or periodically at mean water depths of less than or equal to 6.6 feet, or where the soil is saturated to the surface at some point in time during the growing season of the prevalent vegetation. Generally speaking, areas that are seasonally inundated and/or saturated to the surface for more than 12.5 percent of the growing season are wetlands; areas saturated to the surface 5 to 12.5 percent of the growing season are sometimes wetlands; and areas saturated to the surface less than 5 percent of the growing season are non-wetlands. Wetland hydrology can be determined from recorded data, aerial photographs, or field indicators. Field indicators include visual evidence of flooding, water marks, scoured areas, and plant adaptations.

HYDRIC SOILS

The 1987 Manual defines hydric soil as soil that is saturated, flooded, or ponded long enough during the growing season to develop anaerobic conditions in the upper crust. The Natural Resources Conservation Service (NRCS) maintains national lists of hydric soils on soil maps; however, field investigation by soil scientists is needed to verify the mapping. The 1987 Manual provides examples of various field indicators of hydric soils.

NRCS = Natural Resources Conservation Service

WETLAND VEGETATION

The 1987 Manual defines wetland vegetation as vegetation that has the ability to grow, effectively compete, reproduce, and/or persist in anaerobic soil conditions due to morphological, physiological, and/or reproductive adaptations. The National List of Plant Species That Occur in Wetlands classifies approximately 7,000 plants into four categories of wetland indicator status:

- Obligate wetland plants that almost always occur in wetlands (greater than 99 percent of the time)
- Facultative wetland plants that usually occur in wetlands (67 percent to 99 percent of the time)
- Facultative plants that are equally likely to occur in wetlands or non-wetlands (34 percent to 66 percent of the time)
- Facultative upland plants that usually occur in non-wetlands but occasionally are found in wetlands (1 percent to 33 percent of the time)

To apply the vegetation criteria to a particular area, plant surveys must be performed and statistical formulas applied to determine whether the plant community as a whole is hydrophytic (i.e., thrives in wet conditions that are deficient in oxygen).

CALIFORNIA'S STATE LAW DEFINITION OF WETLANDS

California's emerging state law definition of wetlands is similar to, but slightly broader than, the federal definition. California's proposed definition, as set forth in the State Water Resources Control Board's January 2013 preliminary draft wetlands policy, is as follows:

An area is a wetland if, under normal circumstances, (1) the area has continuous or recurrent saturation of the upper substrate caused by groundwater or shallow surface water, or both; (2) the duration of such saturation is sufficient to cause anaerobic conditions in the upper substrate; and (3) the area either lacks vegetation or the vegetation is dominated by hydrophytes.

The key difference from the federal definition is that, under the State Board's proposed definition, vegetation is not needed to qualify as a wetland. In explaining this difference, the State Board has emphasized that areas such as mud flats and playas, while typically not vegetated, provide the same hydrological and ecological benefits as wetlands.

PROCEDURAL ISSUES IN DELINEATING WETLANDS

Due to the scientific and technical expertise required by the 1987 Manual, most wetlands delineations are performed by biologists or other specialists hired by a developer or landowner, and are presented to the Corps for review and approval. The Corps may approve the delineation in an Approved Jurisdictional Determination (or "Approved JD"), which is an official, written determination by the Corps that identifies the precise limits of the wetlands on the project site that are subject to CWA jurisdiction. *See* Regulatory Guidance Letter No 05-02 (June 14, 2005). An Approved JD remains valid for five years. A landowner or developer may contest an Approved JD by seeking a formal review by the Corps in accordance with the agency's administrative appeal procedures. *See* 33 C.F.R. Part 331.

> **Approved JD = Approved Jurisdictional Determination**

The Ninth Circuit has ruled, however, that an Approved JD that finds that a property contains jurisdictional wetlands cannot be challenged in court. *Fairbanks North Star Borough v. U.S. Army Corps of Engineers*, 543 F. 3d 586, (9th Cir. 2008), *cert denied*, 129 S. Ct. 2825 (2009). The court ruled that such an Approved JD is not a final agency action that is subject to judicial review, since it creates no legal rights and imposes no legal obligations. In the court's view, such an Approved JD does nothing more than put the developer on notice that the Corps believes a Section 404 permit would be necessary if the developer ultimately decides to develop his or her property. The court made clear, however, that a developer retains the ability to dispute the scope of CWA jurisdiction by challenging the final issuance or denial of a Section 404 permit, or as a defense in an administrative enforcement or criminal proceeding. The court also made clear that an Approved JD that finds there are no jurisdictional wetlands is a final, reviewable action, since it effectively terminates the Corps' decisionmaking process and establishes the developer's right to proceed without a Section 404 permit.

The Supreme Court reached a different result in ruling that two landowners were allowed to pursue a lawsuit to challenge an EPA compliance order asserting CWA jurisdiction over their property. *Sackett v. Environmental Protection Agency*, 132 S. Ct. 1367 (2012). The landowners had placed dirt on their land to build a home and the EPA issued a compliance order proclaiming the landowners in violation of the CWA and directing them to restore the site to its previous condition.

The Court held that the compliance order was subject to judicial review as a "final agency action" under the Administrative Procedure Act. Accordingly, the landowners did not have to wait to file a lawsuit until a final decision on a permit application or until the EPA filed an enforcement proceeding. The Court reasoned that the compliance order met the two requirements for final agency action under the APA in that it

(1) marked the consummation of the EPA's decisionmaking process on whether the site was a wetland, and (2) imposed legal obligations on the landowners to restore their property. The Court emphasized that the landowners were potentially liable for administrative penalties of up to $75,000 for each day they refused to comply ($37,500 per day for violating the CWA's requirement for a Section 404 permit and another $37,500 per day for violating the compliance order). In a sharp rebuke to the EPA, the Court declared "there is no reason to think that the Clean Water Act was uniquely designed to enable the strong-arming of regulated parties into 'voluntary compliance' without the opportunity for judicial review." 132 S. Ct. at 1374.

The question remains whether the Supreme Court's decision in *Sackett* will affect the Ninth Circuit's ruling in Fairbanks North Star Borough that an Approved JD is not a final agency action subject to challenge in court. As of late 2013, no federal circuit court of appeals had addressed this important question, although a few lower courts outside of California have adhered to the Ninth Circuit's position. The reasoning of these lower court cases is that, unlike the compliance order at issue in *Sackett*, an Approved JD does not by itself order a landowner to take any particular action and thus does not impose any legal obligations. *See, e.g., National Ass'n of Home Builders v. U.S. Environmental Protection Agency*, _F.Supp.2d_, 2013 WL 3863895 (D.D.C. July 26, 2013) (appeal filed on Sept. 24, 2013).

For landowners and developers who seek to expedite the wetland permitting process without contesting federal jurisdiction, the Corps has developed a procedure for landowners to obtain a "Preliminary JD." *See* Regulatory Guidance Letter No. 08-02 (June 26, 2008). Unlike an Approved JD, a Preliminary JD is not an official jurisdictional determination, but merely delineates all potential wetlands and other waters that may be subject to the Corps' jurisdiction. In other words, a Preliminary JD effectively *presumes* federal jurisdiction over all wetlands and other aquatic features on the site. By accepting a Preliminary JD, the permit applicant gives up the right to contest the scope of the Corps' jurisdiction, but in return avoids the time-consuming process required for an Approved JD, especially when a "significant nexus" determination must be made. As a practical matter, however, a Preliminary JD may pave the way for regulation by the Corps that exceeds the jurisdictional limitations established by the Supreme Court.

ACTIVITIES REGULATED BY THE CORPS

Under Section 404 of the CWA, the Corps is authorized to issue permits for the discharge of "dredged or fill material" into waters of the United States. The "discharge of fill material" means adding any material into waters of the United States that has the effect of replacing any portion of the water with dry land or changing the bottom elevation of the water. 33 C.F.R. §§ 323.2 (e), (f). The "discharge of dredged material" means adding into waters of the United States any materials, other than "incidental fallback," that have been excavated or dredged from a waterbody. 33 C.F.R. §§ 323.3(c), (d).

Dredging a wetland—as opposed to *discharging* dredged material into a wetland—is not directly regulated under Section 404 of the CWA. However, an early court decision established that the term "discharge" reasonably could be construed to include the redeposition of soils dredged from a wetland by mechanized land-clearing activities. *See Avoyelles Sportsmen's League, Inc. v. Marsh*, 715 F. 2d 897, 923-24 (5th Cir. 1983);

> In a sharp rebuke to the EPA, the Court declared "there is no reason to think that the Clean Water Act was uniquely designed to enable the strong-arming of regulated parties into 'voluntary compliance' without the opportunity for judicial review."

Regulatory Guidance Letter 90-5 (July 18, 1990). In 1993, in a significant departure from prior practice, the Corps adopted the so-called "Tulloch" rule, which required a permit for *any* such redeposit of soils. 58 Fed. Reg. 45008, 45035 (Aug. 25, 1993). The D.C. Circuit, however, invalidated the rule, concluding that the definition of discharge "cannot reasonably be said to encompass the situation in which material is removed from the waters of the United States and a small portion of it happens to fall back." *National Mining Ass'n v. U.S. Army Corps of Eng'rs*, 145 F. 3d 1399, 1404 (D.C. Cir. 1998). The court reasoned that because "incidental fallback" represents a net withdrawal, not an addition, of material into waters of the United States, it is not a discharge that can be regulated under the CWA.

The Corps subsequently adopted a revised rule in 2001 (the "Tulloch II" rule), which provided an exemption for "incidental fallback," defined as "the redeposit of small volumes of dredged material that is incidental to excavation activity in waters of the United States when such material falls back to substantially the same place as the initial removal." 66 Fed. Reg. 4550 (Jan. 17, 2001). This revised rule, however, suffered the same fate as the 1993 rule. In an unpublished decision in 2007, the federal district court in Washington, D.C., struck down the Corps' definition of "incidental fallback," concluding that the volume of material being redeposited was irrelevant.[5] According to the court, the difference between incidental fallback and a redeposit that requires a permit is best understood in terms of the time the material is held before being dropped to the earth and the distance between the place where the material is collected and the place where it is dropped. Because the Corps' definition did not address the timing issue and imposed an improper volume requirement, it was held to be invalid.

In response to the district court's decision, the Corps revised the rule in December 2008, again excluding "incidental fallback" from regulation under the CWA, but this time avoiding any definition of what this term means. *See* 73 Fed. Reg. 79641 (Dec. 30, 2008). Thus, the Corps' regulations still do not provide clear guidance on when the redeposit of dredged material requires a Corps permit, instead leaving this determination to be resolved on a case-by-case basis.

STATUTORY EXEMPTIONS

The Corps does not have regulatory authority over all discharges of dredged or fill materials into waters of the United States. Six classes of discharges, which would otherwise be subject to the Corps' jurisdiction, are exempted from regulation under Section 404(f) of the CWA. 33 U.S.C. § 1344(f). These exemptions are intended to avoid regulation of ordinary or minor actions, or to implement political compromises in the passage of the CWA. The exemptions include:

- Normal farming, silviculture, and ranching activities, such as plowing, seeding, cultivating, minor drainage, harvesting for the production of food, fiber, and forest products, and upland soil and water conservation practices
- Maintenance, including emergency reconstruction of recently damaged parts of currently serviceable structures, such as dikes, dams, levees, groins, riprap, breakwaters, causeways, and bridge abutments or approaches and transportation structures

---

5 *Nat'l Ass'n of Home Builders v. U.S. Army Corps of Eng'rs*, 64 ERC 2050, 2007 U.S. Dist. LEXIS 6366 (D.D.C. Jan. 30, 2007).

- Construction or maintenance of farm or stock ponds or irrigation ditches, or the maintenance of drainage ditches[6]
- Construction of temporary sedimentation basins on a construction site that does not include placement of fill materials into navigable waters
- Construction or maintenance of farm roads or forest roads, or temporary roads for moving mining equipment, where such roads are constructed and maintained in accordance with best management practices to assure that flow and circulation patterns and chemical and biological characteristics of the navigable waters are not impaired, that the reach of the navigable waters is not reduced, and that any adverse effect on the aquatic environment will be otherwise minimized
- Any activities for which a state administers an approved program for dredged or fill materials

33 U.S.C. § 1344(f); 33 C.F.R. § 323.4

These exemptions do not apply where the purpose of the discharge is to bring an area of navigable waters into a use for which it was not previously used, or where the discharge may impair the flow or circulation of navigable waters or reduce the reach of such waters. 33 U.S.C. § 1344(f)(2). As a result of this "recapture" provision, the "normal farming" exemption does not apply to deep ripping of soil for the purpose of converting ranch land to orchards and vineyards (i.e., a different use). *See Borden Ranch P'ship v. U.S. Army Corps of Eng'rs*, 261 F. 3d 810, 815–16 (9th Cir. 2001), *judgment aff'd*, 537 U.S. 99 (2002). Similarly, the silviculture exemption does not apply to timber clearing that converts wetlands to non-wetland uses. *See United States v. Larkins*, 852 F. 2d 189, 192–93 (6th Cir. 1988).

THE CORPS' PERMITTING PROCESS

Section 404 gives the Corps primary authority over the discharge of dredged or fill material into wetlands and other waters of the United States, and allows the Corps to issue permits for these activities. The EPA also plays an important role in the permitting process, as it shares authority with the Corps for determining the scope of Section 404 jurisdiction over waters of the United States. In addition, the Corps must follow guidelines established by the EPA when reviewing Section 404 permit applications to determine whether the discharge of dredged or fill materials may be permitted. 40 C.F.R. Part 230. Under Section 404(c) of the CWA, the EPA also has the authority to "veto" a decision by the Corps to issue a permit, and to prohibit a discharge of dredged or fill material even before a permit application is filed, where the EPA finds the discharge would cause an "unacceptable adverse effect" on municipal water supplies, fisheries, shellfishing, wildlife habitat, or recreational areas. 33 U.S.C. § 1344(c); 40 C.F.R. Part 231. The EPA's role in the permitting process is discussed later in this chapter.

The Corps issues both "general" and "individual" permits. Individual permits are for specific projects following review of an individual application, while general permits are available for a listed category of activities in specific geographic regions or nationwide. General permits typically cover activities that involve only minimal impacts to aquatic resources.

---

6 In 2007, the Corps issued detailed guidance on how to apply this statutory exemption with respect to the construction and maintenance of ditches. Regulatory Guidance Letter No. 07-02 (July 4, 2007) available at http://www.usace.army.mil/Missions/CivilWorks/RegulatoryProgramandPermits/GuidanceLetters.aspx.

NATIONWIDE PERMITS

NWP = nationwide permit

Nationwide permits (NWPs) are the most important type of general permit involving wetlands. 33 C.F.R. § 320.1(c). They cover discrete classes of activities and are applicable throughout the nation (hence their name). NWPs have been issued for a wide array of different activities involving discharges into waters of the United States. They are intended to allow dredging or filling to occur with little or no delay or paperwork. 33 C.F.R. § 330.1. The regulations governing NWPs are codified at 33 C.F.R. Part 330.

The Corps revises its NWPs every five years. In February 2012, the Corps reissued 48 out of 49 of its existing NWPs and added two new ones (NWPs 51 & 52) for specified renewable energy projects. *See* 77 Fed. Reg. 10184 (Feb. 21, 2012). Many of the NWPs have become fairly routine, although some are quite controversial for environmental or industry groups, such as NWP 21 (which authorizes surface coal mining activities) and NWP 46 (which asserts regulatory jurisdiction over certain kinds of ditches). The 2012 NWPs are briefly summarized in the table below. Details are available on the Corps' website (http://www.usace.army.mil/Missions/CivilWorks/RegulatoryProgramandPermits/NationwidePermits.aspx).

All activities under an NWP must comply with a series of general conditions. The Corps has established 31 general conditions, which serve as safeguards intended to ensure that an otherwise minor action does not cause unacceptable environmental impacts. The general conditions require, for example, that the permittee avoid breeding areas for migratory waterfowl, maintain appropriate soil erosion and sediment controls, implement appropriate mitigation, obtain a "water quality certification" from the applicable state or tribe, and, under specified circumstances, submit a preconstruction notification (PCN) to the Corps. Corps district offices may impose additional regional conditions.

PCN = preconstruction notification

For activities under an NWP that require the submission of a PCN, the Corps, upon receipt of the PCN, immediately will furnish a copy of the notification to the EPA, the United States Fish and Wildlife Service (Service), and other appropriate resource agencies. Generally, these agencies then have 10 calendar days to contact the Corps and inform the District Engineer that they will be submitting comments. The District Engineer then must wait an additional 15 calendar days before making a decision on the PCN.

If it determines use of an NWP is inappropriate, the Corps may require an individual permit on its own initiative, or at the request of the EPA or the Service, but the Corps has the sole authority to make this decision. The Corps has considerable discretion to require an individual permit if the combined direct and indirect adverse impacts of any NWP activity are more than minimal. NWP applicants can submit a proposed mitigation plan with a PCN to expedite the process, and the Corps will consider such optional mitigation in determining whether the project's net effects are minimal. Consequently, the nature and extent of mitigation proposed in a PCN can be of critical importance in determining what action the Corps will take.

THE CORPS' INDIVIDUAL PERMITTING PROCESS

Individual permits are required for any discharges of dredged or fill material into waters of the United States that are not authorized by an NWP or exempted. Unlike activities that are covered by an NWP, individual permit applications are subject to public notice and comment and environmental review under the National Environmental Policy Act (NEPA).

NATIONWIDE PERMITS

NO.	ACTIVITY	NO.	ACTIVITY
1	Aids to navigation*	27	Wetland and riparian restoration and creation activities
2	Structures in artificial canals	28	Modifications of existing marinas*
3	Maintenance activities	29	Single-family housing
4	Fish and wildlife harvesting, enhancement, and attraction devices and activities*	30	Moist soil management for wildlife
5	Scientific measurement devices*	31	Maintenance of existing flood control facilities
6	Survey activities, including core sampling and seismic exploratory activities*	32	Completed enforcement actions*
7	Outfall structures	33	Temporary construction, access, and dewatering
8	Oil and gas structures	34	Cranberry production activities
9	Structures in fleeting and anchorage areas*	35	Maintenance dredging at existing basins
10	Mooring buoys*	36	Boat ramps*
11	Temporary recreational structures*	37	Emergency watershed protection and rehabilitation
12	Utility line discharges*	38	Cleanup of hazardous and toxic waste*
13	Bank stabilization	39	Residential, commercial, and institutional developments
14	Linear transportation projects	40	Agricultural activities
15	U.S. Coast Guard-approved bridges	41	Reshaping existing drainage ditches
16	Return water from upland, contained disposal areas	42	Recreational facilities
17	Hydro-power projects	43	Stormwater management facilities
18	Minor discharges	44	Mining activities
19	Minor dredging	45	Repair of uplands damaged by discrete events
20	Oil spill cleanup*	46	Discharges in ditches
21	Surface coal mining activities	47	Reserved
22	Removal of vessels*	48	Existing commercial shellfish aquaculture activities
23	Approved categorical exclusions	49	Coal remining activities
24	State-administered Section 404 programs	50	Underground coal mining activities
25	Structural discharges	51	Land-Based Renewable Energy Generation Facilities
26	Reserved	52	Water-Based Renewable Energy Generation Pilot Projects

* Those NWPs with an asterisk have received water quality certification from the SWRCB (see http://www.swrcb.ca.gov/water_issues/programs/cwa401/generalorders.shtml). For the other NWPs, an individual certification must be obtained before permit coverage is effective.

In addition, the Corps must apply EPA regulations when making decisions on individual permit applications. 40 C.F.R. Part 230. These regulations are known as the Section 404(b)(1) Guidelines because that section of the CWA requires the EPA to develop criteria for the discharge of dredged or fill materials in environmentally sensitive areas such as wetlands.

The Section 404(b)(1) Guidelines prohibit the discharge of dredged or fill material into waters of the United States where:

- There is a practicable, less environmentally damaging alternative. 40 C.F.R. § 230.10(a)
- The discharge violates water quality or toxic effluent standards or jeopardizes the continued existence of species listed as threatened or endangered under the ESA. 40 C.F.R. § 230.10(b)
- The discharge will cause or contribute to significant degradation of the waters of the United States. 40 C.F.R. § 230.10(c)
- Appropriate and practicable steps have not been taken to minimize the potential adverse impact on the aquatic system. 40 C.F.R. § 230.10(d)

The alternatives analysis required under the first prong of the Section 404(b)(1) Guidelines is typically the most significant obstacle for project applicants, and is discussed in greater detail below.

Before issuing an individual permit, the Corps also conducts a "public interest" review. The Corps considers a variety of factors (including effects on fish and wildlife, water quality, water supply, aesthetics, recreation, navigation, property ownership, and so on) and balances the favorable aspects of the proposed activity against its reasonably foreseeable detriments. 33 C.F.R. § 320.4(a)(1). A recent court decision ruled that the Corps, in making a public interest determination, need not analyze each of the listed factors in depth or use a precise balancing formula. *Hoosier Environmental Council v. U.S. Army Corps of Engineers*, 722 F.3d 1053 (7th Cir. 2013). The Corps evaluates these factors in light of the following general criteria:

- The relative extent of the public and private need for the proposed structure or work
- Where there are unresolved conflicts as to resource use, the practicability of using reasonable altenative locations and methods to accomplish the objective of the proposed structure or work
- The extent and permanence of the beneficial and detrimental effects that the proposed structure or work is likely to have on public and private uses of the affected area

33 C.F.R. § 320.4(a)(2)

Upon completion of the public interest review, the Corps' regulations state that—if other permitting requirements are satisfied—a permit "will be granted unless the district engineer determines that it would be contrary to the public interest." 33 C.F.R. § 320.4(a)(1).

The Corps individual permitting process is schematically outlined in Figure E. The minimum time for processing an individual application is 60 days (33 C.F.R. § 325.2); however, the process usually takes considerably longer to complete. A complicated individual permit can take two or more years to process. To avoid delays, prior to submitting an individual permitting application, the applicant should meet with the Corps, the Service, and the EPA—and depending on the issues involved, with the responsible state agencies as well (such as the applicable Regional Water Quality Control Board

Chapter 7 Federal and State Wetland Regulation

FIGURE E: U.S. ARMY CORPS OF ENGINEERS PERMITTING PROCESS

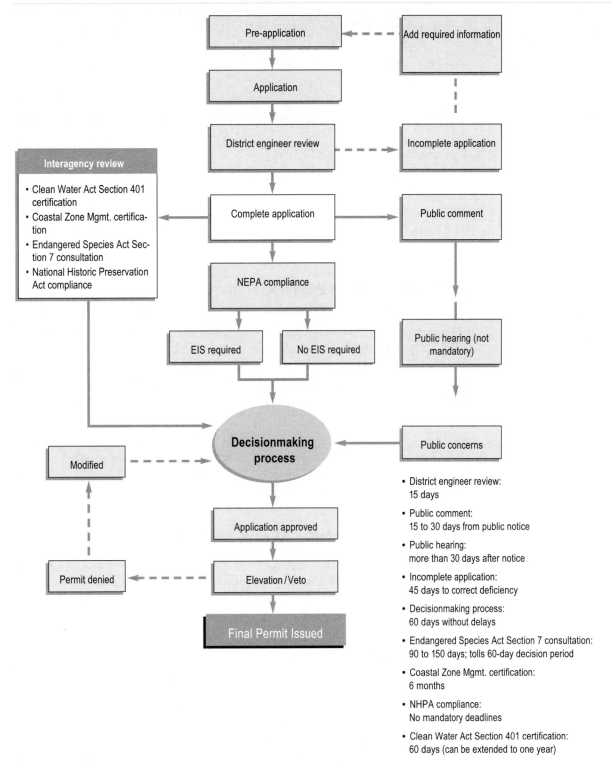

and the California Department of Fish and Wildlife)—to discuss the proposed activity, the type of permit required, and the information required to complete the application. See 33 C.F.R. § 325.1(b).

Applicants must use the Corps' standard application form and include a complete description of the proposed activity. 33 C.F.R. § 325.1(c). All activities the applicant plans to undertake that are reasonably related to the proposed project, and for which a Corps permit is required, must be included in the same application. 33 C.F.R. § 325.1(d)(2). For example, if a construction project involves structural fills in wetlands and bridges across navigable waterways, the permit application should include both of these activities. 33 C.F.R. § 325.l(d)(2).

Once a permitting decision has been made, the applicant may seek a formal review by the Corps, in accordance with the agency's administrative appeal procedures, of a permit denial or of the terms and conditions included in an approved permit. See 33 C.F.R. Part 331. The Corps' final decision on the permit may then be challenged in court.

REGULATORY GUIDANCE LETTERS

RGL = Regulatory Guidance Letter

The Corps periodically issues Regulatory Guidance Letters (RGLs), which often play an important role in the permitting process. RGLs are intended to provide guidance to the Corps' district and division offices on specific issues that may arise in the permitting context. They do not have the force of regulations published in the Federal Register and codified in the Code of Federal Regulations, and are not subject to formal rulemaking procedures. However, topics covered in RGLs often are incorporated into later Corps regulations and many Corps offices continue to follow some RGLs even after they have expired. Many of the RGLs (available at http://www.usace.army.mil/Missions/CivilWorks/RegulatoryProgramandPermits/GuidanceLetters.aspx) seek to clarify the types of activities that are subject to regulation and the extent of the Corps' permitting jurisdiction.

SCOPE OF ENVIRONMENTAL ANALYSIS UNDER NEPA

NEPA = National Environmental Policy Act

When the Corps issues an individual permit under Section 404, unless an exemption applies, the Corps must prepare an environmental analysis under NEPA. The Corps' regulations address a key question that often arises when the Corps issues a permit for a private development project: May the Corps limit its environmental analysis under NEPA to those aspects of the project that fall under its jurisdiction, or must the Corps evaluate the impacts of the entire project, including development on upland areas that are beyond its regulatory authority? The regulations state that the NEPA analysis should evaluate "the impacts of the specific activity requiring a [Corps] permit and those portions of the entire project over which the [Corps] has sufficient control and responsibility to warrant federal review." 33 C.F.R. § 325, App. B, ¶ 7(b).

In *Sylvester v. U.S. Army Corps of Engineers*, the Corps applied its regulations to a project in Squaw Valley consisting of skiing facilities, a resort village, and a golf course. 884 F. 2d 394 (9th Cir. 1988). In its NEPA review, the Corps evaluated only the impacts of the golf course, since this was the only part of the project that would require the filling of wetlands. The court upheld this approach and rejected claims that the Corps should have studied the environmental effects of the entire development project. The court reasoned that although the golf course and the remainder of the resort would each benefit from the other's presence, "each could exist without the other." *Id.* at 400. The court therefore concluded that the golf course and the rest of the resort were not "two links of a single chain" requiring a comprehensive environmental review.

The Ninth Circuit applied similar reasoning in *Wetlands Action Network v. U.S. Army Corps of Engineers*, 222 F. 3d 1105 (9th Cir. 2000). In that case, the court upheld the Corps' decision, in issuing a permit to fill 16 acres of wetlands to build a 600-acre mixed-use project, to focus its NEPA analysis on the wetland areas and to exclude any substantial consideration of the impacts of developing the surrounding uplands. The court explained that development of the upland areas could proceed without a Corps permit, even though the project would not be able to be built as planned. *Id.* at 1116-17. The court therefore concluded the Corps lacked sufficient control and responsibility over the upland areas to warrant their inclusion in the NEPA analysis.

In *Save Our Sonoran v. Flowers*, the Ninth Circuit reached a different result, ruling the Corps should have evaluated under NEPA the environmental effects of the entirety of the developer's proposal, and not just the effects of filling the jurisdictional washes on the property. 408 F. 3d 1113 (9th Cir. 2005). The court reasoned that—unlike in *Wetlands Action Network*, where the wetland and upland areas were separate and independent from each other—here, the washes ran through the property "like capillaries through tissue" and were inseparable from the uplands. *Id.* at 1122, 1124. The court concluded that because no development could occur on the site without impacting jurisdictional waters, the Corps had a duty under NEPA to evaluate the environmental effects of the entire development project.

> The court concluded that because no development could occur on the site without impacting jurisdictional waters, the Corps had a duty under NEPA to evaluate the environmental effects of the entire development project.

In *White Tanks Concerned Citizens v. Strock*, the Ninth Circuit found that the situation was similar to *Save Our Sonoran* and therefore ruled that the Corps should have evaluated the environmental impacts of the entire development proposal, and not just the effects of filling scattered washes on the project site. 563 F. 3d 1033 (9th Cir. 2009). The court explained that in *Wetlands Action Network*, the jurisdictional waters were concentrated in certain areas, "making it easy to build around them, so that substantial development can go forward without a Section 404 permit." *Id.* at 1040. *Save Our Sonoran* represents "the other end of the spectrum," where jurisdictional waters were dispersed throughout the site, "so that any construction on the site would be impossible without affecting the waters." *Id.* In *White Tanks*, although *some* development may have been possible without affecting jurisdictional waters, this development would have been so isolated and restricted that it was not economically feasible. The court therefore ruled that the case fell on the *Save Our Sonoran* side of the spectrum, requiring a full environmental review of the proposed project under NEPA.

In *Ohio Valley Environmental Coalition v. Aracoma Coal*, the Fourth Circuit took a different approach, suggesting that the ruling in *Save Our Sonoran* does not apply when a state agency has jurisdiction over the upland components of a project. 556 F. 3d 177, 197 n.11 (4th Cir. 2009). In *Ohio Valley*, the Corps, in approving a series of Section 404 permits for "mountaintop removal" coal mining operations, evaluated under NEPA only the effects of filling jurisdictional waters with rock and soil, and not the effects of filling the upland areas that surrounded these waters. The court upheld the Corps' approach, reasoning the Corps did not have sufficient control or responsibility over the filling of the upland areas, which instead were under the jurisdiction of the West Virginia Department of Environmental Protection.

In light of these judicial decisions, for projects involving both wetland and upland components, a careful evaluation of the different project elements, and of their relationship to one another, is required to determine the proper scope of the required environmental review.

ALTERNATIVES ANALYSIS UNDER EPA'S SECTION 404(B)(1) GUIDELINES

Under the EPA's Section 404(b)(1) Guidelines, the Corps may not issue a permit if there is a "practicable alternative" to the proposed discharge. 40 C.F.R. § 230.10(a). The practicable alternatives test prohibits the discharge of dredged or fill material into waters of the United States, including wetlands, if there is a practicable alternative to the proposed discharge that would have less adverse impact on the aquatic ecosystem, provided that the alternative does not have other, more adverse environmental impacts. 40 C.F.R. § 230.10(a). An alternative is "practicable" if it is "available and capable of being done after taking into consideration cost, existing technology, and logistics in light of overall project purposes." 40 C.F.R. §§ 230.3(q), 230.10(a)(2).

The practicable alternatives test is frequently the steepest hurdle a project proponent must overcome to obtain an individual permit from the Corps to fill wetlands or other jurisdictional waters. The test injects the Corps into local land use decisions and creates what is effectively a federal land use entitlement process.

In evaluating practicable alternatives, the Section 404(b)(1) Guidelines distinguish between water-dependent and non water-dependent projects. A water-dependent project requires access to waters to achieve its basic purpose. 40 C.F.R. § 230.10(a)(3). A marina is an example of a water-dependent project. A non water-dependent project does not need to be located in or adjacent to water to fulfill its basic purpose. Housing, shopping centers, restaurants, or office buildings are examples of non water-dependent activities.

For non-water-dependent projects that would fill wetlands, a permit application must overcome two presumptions under the Section 404(b)(1) Guidelines. First, the Guidelines presume, unless clearly demonstrated otherwise, that alternative sites are available that do not require a discharge of dredged or fill material into a "special aquatic site." 40 C.F.R. § 230.10(a)(3). Special aquatic sites include sanctuaries and refuges, wetlands, mudflats, vegetated shallows, coral reefs, and riffle and pool complexes in streams. 40 C.F.R. §§ 230.40–230.45. Second, the Guidelines presume, unless clearly demonstrated otherwise, that a practicable alternative that does not involve a discharge into a special aquatic site has less impact on the aquatic ecosystem than the proposed project. 40 C.F.R. § 230.10(a)(3).

An alternatives analysis is also required for water-dependent projects; however, there is no regulatory presumption that an alternative site with less adverse impacts exists.

The Guidelines make clear that the degree of rigor required for an alternatives analysis depends on the situation. Specifically, "compliance evaluation procedures will vary to reflect the seriousness of the potential for adverse impacts on the aquatic ecosystems posed by specific dredged or fill material discharge activities." 40 C.F.R. § 230.10. In 1993, the Corps and the EPA published joint guidance to clarify the appropriate level of analysis needed to satisfy the Guidelines (see http://water.epa.gov/lawsregs/guidance/wetlands/flexible.cfm). In some cases where an Environmental Impact Statement has been prepared, the alternatives analysis for a project under NEPA will provide the requisite information for evaluating alternatives under the Guidelines. See 40 C.F.R. § 230.10(a)(4); *Town of Norfolk v. U.S. Army Corps of Eng'rs*, 968 F. 2d 1438 (1st Cir. 1992). The Guidelines caution, however, that this approach is not always adequate and that where an alternatives analysis under NEPA does not provide sufficient detail, the Corps will need to supplement that analysis with additional information in order to satisfy the Guidelines.

> The practicable alternatives test is frequently the steepest hurdle a project proponent must overcome to obtain an individual permit from the Corps to fill wetlands or other jurisdictional waters.

PROJECT PURPOSE AND WETLANDS AVOIDANCE (SEQUENCING)

A critical first step in the Section 404(b)(1) analysis is determining the project's purpose, since the statement of the project's purpose forms the basis for evaluating the alternatives. From the early days of the wetlands regulatory program, the Corps demonstrated that it would not always accept uncritically an applicant's statement of purpose. For example, in 1976, the Corps rejected a proposal to build a waterfront resort project on Marco Island, Florida. The developer claimed that its purpose was to build an integrated waterfront project, that the project was water-dependent, and that there were no practicable alternatives to the project. The Corps rejected these claims in its decision to deny the permit. It said that the "basic purpose" of the project was housing and that the project was not water-dependent because housing does not have to be located near water or in wetlands. *See Report on Application for Department of Army Permit, Marco Island* (Apr. 15, 1976). Consequently, there were other "practicable" locations for accomplishing the basic project purpose. The courts upheld the Corps' decision. *See Deltona Corp. v. Alexander*, 504 F. Supp. 1280, 1283 (M.D. Fla. 1981); *Deltona Corp. v. United States*, 657 F. 2d 1184, 1185 (Ct. Cl. 1981) (permit denial was not a taking requiring compensation).

When the EPA adopted its practicable alternatives test in 1980, the tenor and language of the rulemaking was consistent with the Corps' decision on the Marco Island project. *See* 45 Fed. Reg. 85338–39 (Dec. 24, 1980). In adopting its test, the EPA emphasized the importance of the basic project purpose in evaluating alternatives and the importance of avoiding wetlands in the development process. During the 1980s, there was considerable controversy over the application of the practicable alternatives test, with several changes of position by the Corps regarding the degree of deference to be given to the project applicant's statement of purpose, and the priority to be given to avoiding wetlands.

In 1990, the role of the Section 404(b)(1) alternatives analysis was significantly magnified when the Corps and the EPA signed a Memorandum of Agreement (1990 MOA) on the application of the practicable alternatives test. 55 Fed. Reg. 9210 (Mar. 12, 1990). The 1990 MOA's stated objective was to unify the positions of the Corps and the EPA on how the test would be applied. Most importantly, it established a sequence for evaluating individual permit applications:

- Applicants must show first that there is no practicable alternative to avoid filling wetlands based on a comparison to available alternative sites
- Then, if there is no practicable alternative with less impact to aquatic resources, the applicant must minimize impacts to the project through on-site avoidance and other means
- Finally, applicants must provide compensatory mitigation for any lost aquatic values

The 1990 MOA effectively ended the former practice of mitigation buy-downs, where credit for mitigation was applied before the proposed project was tested against the other alternatives. Although the MOA is only a statement of goals and does not have the force and effect of law, as a general matter, the Corps and the EPA consistently use the 1990 MOA's sequencing approach in evaluating wetland permitting decisions.

The project's purpose plays a critical role in the practicable alternatives test, but there may be different purposes to consider. The "basic" project purpose is the fundamental goal to provide housing, transportation, or the like. The "overall" project purpose, by contrast, is more specific to the applicant's proposed project and takes

MOA = Memorandum of Agreement

into account additional considerations, such as the benefits of locating the project near other associated developments, or the need for the project to be profitable in order to be viable.

In at least one case, the EPA asserted that the "basic" and "overall" project purposes are one and the same. This position effectively eliminates the consideration of a broader range of factors (such as the cost or viability of the project) that could be used to reject potential alternatives. The EPA took this position in vetoing a Corps permit for the Two Forks Dam, a controversial water supply project for Denver. In its veto, the EPA stated:

> The 404(b)(1) Guidelines use the terms "basic purpose" and "overall project purposes" interchangeably. [I]t is clear that the two terms are not intended to have distinct meanings.... As such, we have read both phrases to have the same meaning, which is a generic basic purpose test.

Final Determination of the U.S. Environmental Protection Agency's Assistant Administration for Water Pursuant to Section 404(c) of the Clean Water Act Concerning the Two Forks Water Supply Impoundments, Jefferson and Douglas Counties, Colorado (November 23, 1990) at 2, n.2.

The EPA described the project purpose as providing a dependable water supply for Denver. It rejected the applicant's request to broaden the project purpose to include the provision of water at least cost.

The decision of the Ninth Circuit in *Sylvester v. U.S. Army Corps of Engineers* took a somewhat broader view, accepting a developer's assertion that it was necessary for a resort development to be located in association with an on-site, eighteen-hole golf course. 882 F. 2d 407 (9th Cir. 1989). Based on research conducted by the applicant demonstrating that such a golf course would be an essential element for the project's success, the court declined to set aside the proponent's project purpose statement, stating that "it would be bizarre if the Corps were to ignore the purpose for which the applicant seeks a permit and to substitute a purpose it deems more suitable." *Id.* at 409. The court therefore ruled the Corps did not need to consider an alternative, off-site location for the golf course.

PRACTICABILITY

The Section 404(b)(1) Guidelines require that the alternative selected be the "Least Environmentally Damaging Practicable Alternative" (LEDPA). The factors that come into play in a particular alternatives analysis will depend upon the characteristics of the alternatives being evaluated. For example, an alternative may be impracticable if its cost is unreasonably greater than the cost of other alternatives, considering the costs of acquisition, construction, infrastructure, and operation. Technological considerations affecting practicability could include such factors as access to a transportation system, water supplies, and other necessary infrastructure. Logistical considerations could include such factors as the need to rezone the alternative sites for the proposed use, existing barriers to the development such as the presence of improvements that would be difficult to move, and so on. Sometimes these criteria overlap, such as where a logistical or technological barrier could be overcome with an adequate investment of money.

A project applicant frequently will submit a written alternatives analysis evaluating a range of alternatives to demonstrate that no practicable alternatives to the proposed project exist. The level of analysis should be proportionate to the scale of the project and its environmental impacts.

Given the relatively open-ended and subjective nature of the practicability determination, it is common for disagreements to arise, both between the applicant and the Corps, and between the Corps and the EPA. As with the other determinations in the permitting process, the Corps retains the ultimate discretion to make the practicability determination, subject to judicial review and/or an EPA veto.

In a 2008 case involving the issuance of a Section 404 permit to fill nearly 350 acres of wetlands to develop a large gold mining project in Alaska, the Ninth Circuit upheld the Corps' determination that there were no practicable alternatives. *Bering Strait Citizens for Responsible Resource Development v. U.S. Army Corps of Engineers*, 524 F. 3d 938 (9th Cir. 2008). The Corps had evaluated 24 alternatives but determined they all were impracticable, because the nearby uplands were too steep to stabilize the project and the alternative designs would require the destruction of higher value wetlands, would expand the project's footprint, or were prohibitively costly. The court found that the Corps' rationale for rejecting the alternatives was "acceptable" under Section 404 and that the Corps "reasonably concluded that the proposed design was the best design alternative." *Id.* at 947–48.

Similarly, the Ninth Circuit upheld the Corps' consideration of a city's stated project purpose for "a medium to large parcel business park" that would create "synergy" among the park's occupants, and the resulting rejection of alternatives that would not provide parcels of a sufficient size to fulfill that purpose. *Butte Environmental Council v. U.S. Army Corps of Engineers*, 620 F.3d 936, 946 (9th Cir. 2010).

In another case involving the issuance of a Section 404 permit to fill approximately 54 acres of wetlands to build a town center, the D.C. Circuit upheld the Corps' determination that reducing the project size was impracticable for economic reasons. *Sierra Club v. Van Antwerp*, 661 F.3d 1147 (D.C. Cir. 2012). In assessing practicability, the Corps measured the expected rate of return against the project costs, which included the site's market value of nearly $73 million at the time of the permit application. The plaintiffs argued the Corps should have used instead the actual price the permit applicant paid for the site (about $52 million).

In rejecting the plaintiffs' claims, the court explained that use of the site's fair market value rather than the acquisition price appropriately reflected the opportunity costs the permit applicant forwent by developing the land instead of selling it. In another important ruling, the court upheld the Corps' decision that reducing the number of parking spaces was not a practicable alternative, noting that the purpose of the project was to build a "town center," which the evidence showed requires more parking than a traditional shopping mall.

> The court explained that use of the site's fair market value rather than the acquisition price appropriately reflected the opportunity costs the permit applicant forwent by developing the land instead of selling it.

Recently, the Seventh Circuit addressed the Corps' obligation to conduct a practicability analysis when it issues a Section 404 permit covering one part of a multi-phase project. In *Hoosier Environmental Center v. U.S. Army Corps of Engineers*, 722 F.3d 1053 (7th Cir. 2013), the Federal Highway Administration (FWHA) selected a corridor for a highway project in Indiana and the Corps subsequently considered whether to issue a permit needed for one segment of that corridor. The project opponents unsuccessfully claimed that the Corps was required, as part of its practicability analysis, to reconsider alternative alignments that the FHWA previously rejected for the segment. The court reasoned that the selection of a highway corridor was a task in the first instance for the transportation agencies, not the Corps. The court further explained that while the Corps has an independent responsibility to assess practicability, "it isn't required to reinvent the wheel." As a result, the Corps could rely on the FHWA's determination that the rejected alignments would not be practicable. The court concluded by emphasizing that the "wetlands tail" should not be allowed to wag the "highway dog."

AVAILABILITY

In addition to being practicable in view of costs, logistics, and technology, an alternative must be "available."

As a practical matter, a site not owned by an applicant cannot be available if the owner is unwilling to sell. The Corps, however, will not accept a statement that the applicant doesn't have access to the land and will require a high level of proof that any such site is truly not available to the applicant. Where the applicant is a public entity, this may be an even more difficult showing to make as the Corps may presume that the entity could exercise its eminent domain powers to acquire the land (if a "public purpose" can be shown). Sites may also be deemed unavailable for development for other reasons, for example, if they are subject to development restrictions such as a conservation easement, are located in areas where development is precluded because of adjacent uses such as military facilities, there is another project proposed on the site, or the site is owned by multiple owners such that acquiring interest in all the necessary areas is practically infeasible.

A key question is "available as of what time?" In describing alternative sites, the Guidelines refer to an area not "presently" owned by the applicant as being an acceptable site if it reasonably could be obtained or used. 40 C.F.R. § 230.10(a)(2). This seems to imply that the availability test is judged when the Corps considers the application. However, this is not the EPA's view, and the Corps' view on the issue is not settled.

In *Bersani v. U.S. Army Corps of Engineers*, a developer sought a Section 404 permit to build a shopping mall on an 80-acre site that contained a 49.5-acre wetland known as Sweedens Swamp. 850 F. 2d 36 (2d Cir. 1988), *cert denied*, 489 U.S. 1089 (1989). The Corps granted the permit but the EPA exercised its veto power under Section 404(c). 33 U.S.C. § 1344(c). The EPA concluded that because a practicable alternative was "available" when the developer "entered" the market to buy shopping center property, it could deny the permit for noncompliance with the practicable alternatives test even though the alternative site was no longer on the market when the EPA issued its veto. The court upheld the EPA's use of the "market entry approach" to determine availability under the practicable alternatives test, even though this approach is mandated neither by the CWA nor the Section 404(b)(1) Guidelines.

The Corps has not adopted the court-approved market entry approach for "availability." Given the problems with the market entry approach to the practicable alternatives test, it is unlikely that the Corps will use it unquestioningly. The *Bersani* opinion itself was a 2 to 1 decision, with the dissent arguing that Congress designed Section 404 "to preserve the environment consistent with reasonable accommodation to the economic and social needs of the public; it was not concerned with the identities or past activities of particular developers." *Bersani*, 850 F. 2d at 48.

Does the market entry approach to the practical alternatives test make sense? The market entry approach encourages buyers to look for properties that do not have wetlands, which arguably encourages avoidance. In a number of cases, the application of this approach has led to better decisions, resulting in the use of sites with reduced aquatic impact. The market entry approach makes very little sense, though, when applied to a developer who has owned property for a long time.

> The Corps has not adopted the court-approved market entry approach for "availability."

MITIGATION

In many circumstances, despite the avoidance of impacts to the extent practicable through the Section 404(b)(1) Guideline analysis, some residual impacts to wetlands will remain. The Corps' regulations require compensatory mitigation for these unavoidable impacts. Mitigation generally consists of off-site (or sometimes on-site) creation, enhancement, restoration, or preservation of wetlands.

The CWA does not require that all of the specific mitigation measures for a project be fully developed at the time the Corps issues a Section 404 permit. In *Bering Strait Citizens for Responsible Resource Development*, the Ninth Circuit rejected the claim that a permit condition requiring that the applicant meet with the Corps and the U.S. Fish and Wildlife Service within three months after the issuance of the permit to identify additional mitigation opportunities constituted an improper deferral of mitigation under the CWA. 524 F. 3d at 950–51. The court explained:

> Where the Corps has undertaken a genuine effort to develop a detailed mitigation plan, the mere fact that one aspect of the plan is not yet finalized will not necessarily lead to the conclusion that the Corps' decision was arbitrary and capricious.

There have long been concerns, however, with the effectiveness of compensatory mitigation. A 2001 study prepared by the National Research Council (NRC) and published by the National Academy of Sciences, entitled "Compensating for Wetland Losses under the Clean Water Act," criticized a number of common compensatory mitigation practices, concluding that in many circumstances approved mitigation plans either were not carried out, or failed to produce anticipated benefits.

NRC = National Research Council

In 2008, the Corps and the EPA adopted new regulations designed to establish more effective, consistent, and innovative mitigation practices. *See* 70 Fed. Reg. 19594 (Apr. 10, 2008) (codified at 33 C.F.R. Part 332 and 40 C.F.R. Part 230, Subpart J). The rules emphasize a watershed-based approach, with an eye towards consolidating mitigation projects and integrating mitigation with the overall needs of the watershed in order reduce the risk of failure and improve long-term sustainability.

The rules establish a primary preference for mitigation banks over other types of compensatory mitigation. A wetland mitigation bank is a wetland area that has been restored and protected and then set aside to compensate for future impacts to wetlands in other areas. The rationale behind the regulatory preference for mitigation banks is that they involve a significant degree of advance planning and financial investment because they typically are up and running before mitigation credits are sold to individual permittees. Banks also provide for mitigation that can be combined with mitigation for other projects.

In-lieu fee programs—which similarly provide opportunities for larger-scale mitigation—are second in preference. In-lieu fee programs provide funds for mitigation projects and typically are administered by public agencies or non-profit organizations. The regulations contain several requirements that are designed to address concerns over how these types of programs have been administered. These requirements include a cap on the number of advance mitigation credits that can be released for sale and rules for advance planning and improved financial accounting.

The third preference is for "permittee-responsible" mitigation. In contrast to mitigation banks and in-lieu fees, which both involve off-site mitigation conducted by a third party, permittee-responsible mitigation may be located at or adjacent to the impact site, and the permittee is responsible for the completion and success of the mitigation.

These preferences are not set in stone, and the local Corps District Engineer may override them based on the particular circumstances of each project. The local Corps office also has discretion to set the amount of required mitigation. This amount must be sufficient to replace the lost aquatic functions and values, but there is no required formula or ratio.

For all compensatory mitigation, the regulations require a detailed mitigation plan that must be approved by the Corps. Among other things, the plan must include adequate legal instruments (e.g., conservation easements) to protect the mitigation site; a methodology for calculating mitigation credits; objective, verifiable ecological performance standards; adequate financial assurances; and a long-term management plan. Monitoring must be sufficient to demonstrate that the compensatory mitigation project has met the applicable performance standards. *See* Regulatory Guidance Letter No. 08-03 (Oct. 10, 2008).[7]

THE EPA'S ROLE IN THE PERMIT PROCESS

Although the Corps issues permits under Section 404 of the CWA, the EPA often acts as an agency "watchdog," submitting extensive comments on individual permit applications to ensure compliance with the Section 404(b)(1) Guidelines (which EPA developed) and with other legal requirements such as NEPA. The EPA's comments become part of the administrative record for purposes of judicial review, and therefore are available for use by project opponents in litigation.

NEPA = National Environmental Policy Act

In recent years, the EPA has taken a more aggressive role under Section 404, including exercising its permit veto power under Section 404(c). *See* 33 U.S.C. § 404(c); 40 C.F.R. Part 231. In August 2008, the EPA, using its veto power for the first time since 1990, vetoed the Corps' proposal to build the Yazoo Backwater Area Pumps Project, a federal civil works project designed to reduce flooding in Mississippi. The EPA concluded that the large-scale hydrological alterations resulting from the project would result in unacceptable adverse effects on fisheries and wildlife.

In January 2011, the EPA took the unprecedented step of vetoing a permit that the Corps had already issued three years earlier for disposal of material from a surface mine project. 76 Fed. Reg. 3126 (Jan. 19, 2011). The federal district court struck down the veto, finding that the EPA lacked authority to veto a permit once it had been issued. But the D.C. Circuit reversed, holding that the text of Section 404(c) imposes no temporal limit on the EPA's veto authority. *Mingo Logan Coal Co. v. U.S. Environmental Protection Agency*, 714 F.3d 608 (D.C. Cir. 2013). As of late 2013, the permittee has filed a petition for certiorari and the Supreme Court has not yet decided whether to hear the case.[8]

Like the Corps' issuance or denial of a permit, the EPA's exercise of its veto authority is subject to judicial review. *See James City County, Virginia v. U.S. EPA*, 955 F. 2d 254 (4th Cir. 1992) (setting aside an EPA veto), 12 F. 3d 1330, 1331 (4th Cir. 1993) *cert. denied*, 513 U.S. 823 (1994) (affirming new EPA veto following remand).

In addition to its veto authority, pursuant to a 1992 Memorandum of Agreement (1992 MOA) between the EPA and the Corps, the EPA also may seek to "elevate" proposed Corps permitting decisions with which the EPA disagrees. Once elevated,

---

[7] More information about the federal wetland mitigation requirements is available on the EPA's website (http://water.epa.gov/lawsregs/guidance/wetlands/wetlandsmitigation_index.cfm).

[8] More information about the EPA veto process and recent actions taken by the EPA using that process is available at http://water.epa.gov/lawsregs/guidance/cwa/dredgdis/404c_index.cfm.

permitting decisions are then to be resolved between the agencies at higher levels within the respective agency hierarchies.[9]

The EPA, however, may only seek to elevate permitting decisions on individual projects when they involve impacts to "aquatic resources of national importance" or "ARNIs." The 1992 MOA does not define this important term. In practice, there has been no limitation on what wetlands or other waters the EPA asserts are ARNIs. Rather, if the EPA objects to a permitting decision, it appears to automatically assert that the wetlands or other waters in question are ARNIs, irrespective of their biological or other values, simply because classifying them as such is necessary under the 1992 MOA to begin the elevation process. However, the Corps has rejected this seemingly automatic characterization on at least one occasion, refusing to elevate a permit decision for a project in Stanislaus County involving seasonal wetlands and a creek with sparse riparian vegetation, because the Corps determined the site did not qualify as an ARNI.

ARNI = aquatic resource of national importance

In *Coeur Alaska, Inc. v. Southeast Alaska Conservation Council*, the United States Supreme Court addressed a different type of disagreement between the Corps and the EPA: the relationship between the Corps' authority to issue permits under Section 404 for the discharge of "fill," and the EPA's authority under the Section 402 NPDES program over discharges of wastewater and other "pollutants." 129 S. Ct. 2458 (2009). The case involved a Corps permit for the discharge of mining slurry (a mixture of mine tailings and water) into a lake in southeastern Alaska. The Court rejected the claim by several environmental groups that the EPA had NPDES permitting authority over the discharge. The Court found that the mining slurry constituted "fill" and ruled that under the CWA's language the Corps has exclusive permitting authority over all discharges of fill. The Court also ruled that the Corps' issuance of a fill permit was proper even though the EPA had previously published a "New Source Performance Standard" that prohibits discharges of "process wastewater" from the type of mining operation at issue. The Court concluded that these types of EPA standards do not apply to discharges of fill material.

OTHER FEDERAL STATUTES

Numerous other federal statutes also are involved in the permitting process. An outline of each statute and its relationship to the Corps' permitting process follows.

Section 401 of the Clean Water Act
33 U.S.C. § 1341
- Section 401 of the CWA requires all permittees to obtain certification from the state that the permitted activity will comply with applicable state effluent limitations and water quality standards. The Ninth Circuit has held that the Corps may accept a Section 401 certification from the relevant state authority, without having to conduct "its own independent analysis." *Bering Strait Citizens for Responsible Resource Development*, 524 F. 3d at 949-50.
- In California, the water quality certification must be obtained from the appropriate Regional Water Quality Control Board, both for individual permits and for any NWPs that have not already been "pre-certified." The Regional Water Boards have increasingly used their certification authority in recent years to regulate activities occurring in wetlands and streams.

---

[9] The 1992 MOA is available at http://water.epa.gov/lawsregs/guidance/wetlands/dispmoa.cfm.

National Environmental Policy Act
42 U.S.C. §§ 4321-4347

- For Corps individual permits, an environmental review is required under NEPA unless a "categorical exclusion" applies. If the permitted action will not result in any significant environmental impacts, the Corps complies with NEPA by preparing an environmental assessment (EA). If the permitted action will result in a significant environmental impact, an environmental impact statement (EIS) is required.

- The Corps' NEPA guidelines are codified at 33 C.F.R. Part 230 and 33 C.F.R. Part 325, Appendix B. As described above, there is a growing line of judicial decisions concerning the required scope of the environmental review under NEPA for the issuance of Corps permits for private development projects that contain both jurisdictional and upland components.

EA = environmental assessment
EIS = environmental impact statement

Endangered Species Act
16 U.S.C. § 1531 *et seq.*

- The Endangered Species Act (ESA) requires that the Corps consult with the United States Fish and Wildlife Service (or the National Marine Fisheries Service of the National Oceanic and Atmospheric Administration, depending on the particular species at issue) if it proposes to permit an activity that may affect a listed threatened or endangered species or designated critical habitat. Where protected species are present, the consultation process typically results in the adoption of mitigation measures to reduce the nature and extent of any adverse impacts. For a detailed discussion of the ESA, see chapter 8 (Endangered Species Protections).

- A Corps permit will not be granted if the Service determines that the permitted activities will jeopardize the continued existence of threatened or endangered species, or adversely modify critical habitat for such species.

ESA = Endangered Species Act

Fish and Wildlife Coordination Act
16 U.S.C. §§ 661-666(c)

- Prior to issuing a permit, the Corps must consult with the Service to prevent the direct and indirect loss of, or damage to, wildlife resources from the permitted activity.

- The Service has published guidelines that explain its consultation role under the Fish and Wildlife Coordination Act. 46 Fed. Reg. 7644 (Jan. 23, 1981).

Section 302 of the Marine Protection, Research and Sanctuaries Act of 1972
16 U.S.C. § 1432

- The Corps may not issue a Section 404 permit in areas designated as "marine sanctuaries" unless the dredge or fill activity is certified by the Secretary of Commerce.

National Historic Preservation Act of 1966
16 U.S.C. § 470

- The Advisory Council on Historic Preservation reviews and comments upon Corps permit applications that could have an effect upon historic properties listed, or eligible for listing, on the National Register of Historic Places.

- If the proposed activity will alter terrain so that significant historical or archeological data are threatened, the Secretary of the Interior may take action necessary to recover and preserve the data prior to the commencement of the activity.

- Obtaining the required cultural resource approvals can be a very complex and time-consuming process and may require extensive cultural resource surveys.
- The Corps' guidelines on its duties under the National Historic Preservation Act are codified at 33 C.F.R. Part 325, Appendix C.

Land Sales Full Disclosure Act
15 U.S.C. § 1701 *et seq.*
- If a subdivision lot is part of a project that requires a Corps permit prior to sale of the property, the developer must state whether or not a permit for the development has been applied for, issued, or denied by the Corps.

Coastal Zone Management Act of 1972
16 U.S.C. § 1456(c)
- In the event the proposed project is located in California's coastal zone, the California Coastal Commission (or the San Francisco Bay Conservation and Development Commission for projects located in or along the shores of the San Francisco Bay) must certify that the project is consistent with the state's coastal program before the Corps may issue a permit.

Food Security Act of 1985
16 U.S.C. §§ 3821-22
- The United States Department of Agriculture (USDA) has authority over certain activities in wetlands under the so-called "Swampbuster Provisions" of the Food Security Act, which address the agricultural conversion of wetlands. Under USDA regulations, any person producing agricultural commodities on certain converted wetlands is ineligible for crop insurance and other USDA benefits. 7 C.F.R. § 400.47(c).

USDA = United States Department of Agriculture

STATE STATUTORY AUTHORITY

In California, several state agencies are charged with regulating activities that may impact wetlands or other waters under the Corps' jurisdiction. In addition, local agencies also may promulgate wetland protection programs under their planning and zoning powers. An outline of the relevant state regulations follows.

Porter-Cologne Water Quality Control Act
Water Code § 13000 *et seq.*
- The Porter-Cologne Water Quality Control Act is California's comprehensive water pollution statute. It regulates the discharge of waste "that could affect the quality of the waters of the state." Water Code § 13260(1). The Porter-Cologne Act defines waste as "sewage and any and all other waste substances, liquid, solid, gaseous, or radioactive, associated with human habitation, or of human or animal origin, or from any producing, manufacturing, or processing operation, including waste placed within containers of whatever nature prior to, and for purposes of, disposal." Water Code § 13050(d). The Act broadly defines "waters of the state" as "any surface water or groundwater, including saline waters, within the boundaries of the state." Water Code § 13050(e). However, it does not mention, much less define, wetlands.
- Under the Porter-Cologne Act, the discharge of a waste into a water of the state requires the discharger to file with the appropriate Regional Water Quality Control Board (RWQCB or Regional Board) a "Report of Waste Discharge."

RWQCB/Regional Board = Regional Water Quality Control Board

Water Code § 13260(1). The Regional Board then determines whether a permit (called "Waste Discharge Requirements") is required.

- Historically, the State Water Resources Control Board and the nine individual Regional Boards have taken the position that wetlands constitute "waters of the state" subject to the Porter-Cologne Act. Likewise, they have taken the position that any fill of wetlands requires the filing of a Report of Waste Discharge and the issuance of Waste Discharge Requirements. Before *SWANCC* and *Rapanos*, in practice nearly every wetland fill was subject to Corps' jurisdiction under Section 404; the Regional Boards therefore obtained jurisdiction through the Section 401 water quality certification process, such that jurisdiction under the Porter-Cologne Act was not needed.

- But the Supreme Court's 2001 decision in *SWANCC*, which eliminated federal jurisdiction over many isolated waters and wetlands, suddenly brought to the fore the legal issue of state jurisdiction under the Porter-Cologne Act. In response to *SWANCC*, the State and Regional Boards have reiterated their position that the Porter-Cologne Act provides an independent basis for state regulation of wetlands, and have demanded that landowners file Reports of Waste Discharge prior to filling any isolated waters or wetlands that now escape Corps regulation. As noted above, the State Board has issued a statewide general permit to cover minor fills that meet specified criteria. The State Board also is developing a new wetland policy that seeks to establish uniform rules for review and approval of individual state law permits. Whether or not the Porter-Cologne Act actually confers to the state regulatory jurisdiction over wetlands is a question the courts have not yet addressed.

Streambed Alteration Agreement
Fish and Game Code § 1602

- The California Department of Fish and Wildlife (DFW) must be notified and given an opportunity to approve any work that substantially diverts, alters, or obstructs the natural flow or substantially changes the bed, channel, or banks of any river, stream, or lake. If the DFW does not grant or deny its approval within 60 days of the notification, the applicant may proceed with the work. Fish & Game Code §§ 1602(a)(4)(D), 1603(a).

- The DFW has specified that all waterways of the state, including intermittent streams, are subject to its jurisdiction. 14 Cal. Code Regs. § 720. Many waterways subject to DFW jurisdiction also will be subject to the Corps' jurisdiction.

- However, not all areas subject to the Corps' jurisdiction require a streambed alteration agreement. For example, wetlands under the Corps' jurisdiction are not regulated by section 1602, because they are not rivers, streams, or lakes.

Navigation Dredging Permit
Fish and Game Code § 5653

- A permit from the DFW is required before using a vacuum or suction dredge in any river, stream, or lake of the state. The DFW may prohibit suction dredging in certain areas.

- Dredging activity also may be regulated by the Corps under Section 10 of the Rivers and Harbors Act if the water body is navigable, or under Section 404 of the CWA if dredged material (other than "incidental fallback") is discharged into waters of the United States.

Coastal Zone Management
Public Resources Code § 30600 *et seq.*
- Developments proposed within the state's coastal zone (not including San Francisco Bay, which is regulated by the San Francisco Bay Conservation and Development Commission under the McAteer-Petris Act, Gov't Code § 66600 *et seq.*) must obtain a coastal development permit in addition to any other approvals or permits required. Pub. Res. Code § 30600. This permitting program is administered by the California Coastal Commission, or by cities or counties (with Commission oversight) that have an approved Local Coastal Program.
- The California Coastal Act prohibits the issuance of a coastal development permit for the diking, filling, or dredging of open coastal waters, wetlands, estuaries, and lakes—except for limited uses such as ports, boating facilities, and coastal-dependent industries, and only if (a) there is no feasible, less environmentally damaging alternative, and (b) feasible mitigation measures are provided to minimize adverse environmental effects. Pub. Res. Code § 30233(a). Obtaining a coastal development permit does not eliminate the need to obtain the applicable permits from the Corps, but that permit does serve to fulfill the federal consistency requirement under the Coastal Zone Management Act.
- In 1994, the Coastal Commission published a guidance document entitled "Procedural Guidance for the Review of Wetland Projects in California's Coastal Zone." This guidance document addresses the full range of issues raised by the permitting process, including the procedures for reviewing permit applications, the approach for delineating wetlands, and the requirements for mitigation. It should be noted that the Coastal Commission takes a more expansive approach to wetland delineations than the Corps takes in its 1987 Manual.
- In 1995, the Coastal Commission published a more detailed guidance document on the evaluation of mitigation proposals, entitled "Procedural Guidance for Evaluating Wetland Mitigation Projects in California's Coastal Zone." The purposes of this guidance are (1) to give those required to provide compensatory wetlands mitigation a clear idea of what will be acceptable to the Commission; and (2) to give the Commission staff a methodology to evaluate the post-approval performance of wetland mitigation projects. Online versions of these and other Coastal Commission publications are available at http://www.coastal.ca.gov/pubs.html.

ENFORCEMENT

CITIZEN SUITS

The CWA authorizes "citizen suits" to enforce the act's provisions. Under Section 505 of the CWA (33 U.S.C. § 1365), any citizen with standing to sue may file a civil action to stop an unpermitted discharge of dredged and fill material into waters of the United States and to require the discharger to obtain a Section 404 permit from the Corps. A citizen also may bring an action to compel a discharger with a Corps permit to comply with the permit's terms. The United States Supreme Court, however, has ruled that the CWA does not authorize citizen suits based on wholly past violations; rather, there must be a good-faith allegation of continuous or intermittent violations. *See Gwaltney of Smithfield v. Chesapeake Bay Foundation*, 484 U.S. 49 (1987). Finally, a citizen may bring

> The CWA does not authorize citizen suits based on wholly past violations; rather, there must be a good-faith allegation of continuous or intermittent violations.

suit to compel the EPA to perform a nondiscretionary duty under the CWA.[10] A prevailing citizen plaintiff may obtain injunctive relief and/or an award of attorneys' fees.

As a prerequisite to bringing a citizen suit, the plaintiff must give notice of the alleged violation at least 60 days before filing the lawsuit. Id. § 1365(b)(1). The purpose of the notice is two-fold. First, the notice gives the alleged violator an opportunity to come into compliance, thereby obviating the need for the citizen suit. Second, the notice allows governmental agencies to take responsibility for enforcing the CWA, similarly obviating the need for a citizen suit.

Under the CWA, a citizen suit may not be brought if the federal government (or the relevant state) has commenced and is diligently prosecuting either (1) a civil or criminal action in court seeking to remedy the alleged violation, or (2) an administrative proceeding to impose penalties for the violation. The Ninth Circuit, however, has held these two prohibitions against bringing a citizen suit are very limited. See *California Sportfishing Protection Alliance v. Chico Scrap Metal, Inc.*, 728 F.3d 868 (9th Cir. 2013).

The Ninth Circuit has strictly interpreted the notice requirements that must be met before a plaintiff may bring a citizen suit. In *Center for Biological Diversity v. Marina Point Development Co.*, 566 F. 3d 794 (9th Cir. 2009), the court dismissed a citizen suit alleging (among other things) that the discharger was filling wetlands and other waters of the United States in violation of the CWA. The plaintiffs sent four different 60-day notices, but the court found they were all insufficient because none of the notices provided enough detail about the alleged violations.

In cases where the CWA does not authorize a citizen suit, a plaintiff may nevertheless bring a lawsuit based on the Administrative Procedure Act to challenge final agency action under Section 404—such as the adoption by the Corps or the EPA of a final wetlands regulation, the granting of a Section 404 permit, a decision by the EPA to veto a Section 404 permit, or a final determination by the Corps that there are no jurisdictional waters on a particular site. These types of actions are not subject to the 60-day notice requirement.

A third avenue for judicial enforcement is a civil or criminal case brought by the federal government against a party alleged to be in violation of the CWA. Civil and criminal penalties are discussed further below.

STANDING TO SUE

One of the jurisdictional prerequisites to bringing a lawsuit to enforce Section 404 is that the plaintiff must have standing to sue. To establish standing, a plaintiff must prove three elements: (1) "injury in fact" as a result of the challenged action; (2) a causal connection between the injury and the challenged action; and (3) redressability of the injury by a favorable decision of the court. See *Lujan v. Defenders of Wildlife*, 504 U.S. 555, 560 (1992). With respect to the first element, a plaintiff must allege a concrete and particularized injury; generalized grievances, such as a challenge to an agency's failure to follow prescribed procedures, do not confer standing. Id. at 560, 571–79.

In 2009, the United States Supreme Court tightened the standing rules that apply when an environmental organization brings a lawsuit. *Summers v. Earth Island*

---

10 Section 505(a)(2) of the CWA, however, expressly authorizes such a suit only against the Administrator of the EPA, and the cases conflict on whether such a suit may be brought against the Corps. Compare *National Wildlife Federation v. Hanson*, 859 F. 2d 313 (4th Cir. 1988) (allowing citizen suit against the Corps), with *Cascade Conservation League v. M.A. Seagle, Inc.*, 921 F. Supp. 692 (W.D. Wash. 1996) (disagreeing with *Hanson* and ruling that Section 505(a)(2) did not permit citizen suit against the Corps).

Institute, 129 S. Ct. 1142 (2009). In a 5 to 4 decision, the Court rejected the claim that an environmental group has standing if it can show a "statistical probability" that some of its members face a threat of injury. The Court also rejected the notion that a "procedural injury"—such as the denial of a right to submit comments on a proposed project—is alone sufficient to confer standing. Rather, the group must submit evidence such as affidavits showing that specific individuals will suffer actual or imminent injury as a result of the project. For example, if a group alleges that a project will diminish the recreational enjoyment of its members, the group must submit evidence showing that specific members of the group have concrete plans to visit a specific tract of land that will be impacted by the project. While the case involved a discrete set of Forest Service regulations governing certain types of timber operations, the decision has broad implications for future environmental cases, including cases brought under Section 404.

INVESTIGATIONS AND COMPLIANCE ORDERS

While neither the Corps nor the EPA has an active wetlands inspection program, other state and federal resource agencies cooperate in identifying possible violators upon learning of a violation. The enforcement process begins with the discovery of an unauthorized activity—for example, the filling of a wetland without a permit or the failure to comply with a condition of a Corps-issued permit. Normally, the Corps will take the lead in investigating the potential violation. The Corps also acts as the lead agency for enforcement actions for violations of permit conditions and for many types of unpermitted fill activities. The EPA typically acts as the lead enforcement agency for unpermitted fills that involve significant environmental harm or repeat or flagrant violators.

Upon finding a violation, the Corps (or EPA) issues a formal notification to the landowner or responsible party and, if the activity is not complete, a cease-and-desist order. *See* 33 U.S.C. § 1319(a); 33 C.F.R. § 326.3(c). A cease-and-desist order also may require initial corrective actions to restore or stabilize the site. *See* 33 C.F.R. § 326.3(d). A cease-and-desist order is not subject to judicial review unless the Corps (or EPA) assesses an administrative penalty or the federal government brings a civil or criminal enforcement action. *See Rueth v. U.S. EPA*, 13 F. 3d 227 (7th Cir. 1993); *Southern Pines Ass'n v. United States*, 912 F. 2d 713 (4th Cir. 1990); *Hoffman Group, Inc. v. U.S. EPA*, 902 F. 2d 567 (7th Cir. 1990).

Following the completion of any required initial corrective measures, the Corps may, under certain circumstances, accept an "after-the-fact" permit application, which allows the agency to authorize an unpermitted fill after it has occurred. 33 C.F.R. § 326.3(e). For more serious violations, the Corps or the EPA may assess administrative penalties or refer the matter to the United States Department of Justice for criminal or civil court proceedings.

CRIMINAL, CIVIL, AND ADMINISTRATIVE PENALTIES

Section 309 of the CWA sets out the factors for determining the appropriate type and amount of penalty for violations of the CWA. 33 U.S.C. § 1319. Criminal, civil, or administrative penalties may be imposed.

The consequences for serious violations of the CWA can be substantial, since each day that a violator allows illegal fill material to remain in a wetland constitutes a separate violation. In one notable case, the Ninth Circuit upheld the district court's

> While neither the Corps nor the EPA has an active wetlands inspection program, other state and federal resource agencies cooperate in identifying possible violators upon learning of a violation.

finding that each pass of a deep ripping machine through a wetland constituted a separate violation of the CWA, yielding a total potential civil penalty of $8.95 million (although a much lower penalty was actually imposed). See Borden Ranch Partnership v. U.S. Army Corps of Engineers, 261 F. 3d 810 (9th Cir. 2001), judgment aff'd, 537 U.S. 99 (2002).

Criminal penalties are typically reserved for the most serious violations where the deterrence of future similar conduct is especially warranted. Criminal penalties may be sought for negligent or knowing violations, or violations that involve knowing endangerment to a person. 33 U.S.C. § 1319(c).

Simple negligence can result in criminal penalties of up to $25,000 per day of violation and one year in prison for first-time offenders, and up to $50,000 per day and two years in prison for repeat offenders. 33 U.S.C. § 1319(c)(1). In *United States v. Hanousek*, the Ninth Circuit ruled that because the CWA is a law designed to protect the public welfare, it may subject a person to criminal liability for ordinary negligence without violating constitutional due process principles. 176 F. 3d 1116 (9th Cir. 1999), cert. denied, 528 U.S. 1102 (2000).

As illustrated by the case of *United States v. Hong*, the penalties for even negligent violations of the CWA can be severe. 242 F. 3d 528 (4th Cir.), cert. denied, 548 U.S 823 (2001). In *Hong*, the owner of a wastewater treatment plant was sentenced to three years in prison for a series of negligent violations committed by the plant's employees. The court upheld the owner's conviction under the "responsible corporate officer" doctrine because he did not exercise reasonable care to prevent the violations, which consisted of discharges of untreated wastewater after the failure of a deficient filtration system.

For knowing violations, criminal penalties can reach $50,000 per day and three years in prison for first-time offenders, and $100,000 per day and six years in prison for repeat offenders. 33 U.S.C. § 1319(c)(2).

In *United States v. Wilson*, the Fourth Circuit held that, to prove a knowing violation, the government must show both that the defendant knew he was discharging dredge and fill material into a wetland and that the defendant was aware of the facts establishing the required jurisdictional link between the wetland and waters of the United States. 133 F. 3d 251 (4th Cir. 1997). But in *United States v. Cooper*, the same court ruled, in a case involving the discharge of sewage to a creek, that it was not necessary to show that the defendant knew that the creek was a water of the United States. 482 F. 3d 658 (4th Cir. 2007).

The federal government may decide to pursue civil actions against violators in cases where a criminal prosecution is not warranted but there is a need for a court order directing immediate or long-term compliance. The maximum civil penalty that may be imposed is $37,500 per violation. 40 C.F.R. § 19.4. The factors used to assess civil penalties for any particular violation are based on the seriousness of the violation, the economic benefit realized by the violator, any past history of violations, any good faith efforts to comply with the applicable requirements, the economic impact of the penalty on the violator, and other matters as justice may require. 33 U.S.C. § 1319(d).

Additionally, the EPA and the Corps both have the authority to assess administrative penalties. Two classes of administrative penalties may be imposed. 33 U.S.C. § 1319(g)(2)(A), (B); 40 C.F.R. § 19.4. Administrative penalties are assessed using a set of factors similar to those used for civil penalties. These factors include: the nature, circumstances, extent, and gravity of the violation; the violator's ability to pay the penalty; any prior history of violations; the degree of culpability; the economic benefit or savings resulting from the violation; and other matters as justice may require. 33 U.S.C. § 1319(g)(3).

PRACTICAL CONSIDERATIONS

Wetlands issues should be considered at each stage in the land development process: land acquisition, site planning, land use entitlement, and construction. Efforts should be made to coordinate federal wetlands permits with other needed state and local permits.

The five key steps in the federal permitting process are:
- First, in any complex situation, determine the extent of wetlands and other waters of the United States on the lands in question. Information on wetlands can be compiled or sent to the Corps for its approval. The applicant may seek an Approved Jurisdictional Determination from the Corps to delineate the precise boundaries on the site between jurisdictional and non-jurisdictional areas. Alternatively, the applicant may decide to agree to a Preliminary JD, which typically entails an expansive view of the Corps' jurisdiction but which can greatly expedite the permit process when complicated jurisdictional issues are involved. Whichever approach is used, reaching agreement with the Corps on the extent of its jurisdiction eliminates a major uncertainty in the permitting process.
- Second, the proposed project should be analyzed to determine whether it is possible to avoid filling wetlands and other waters of the United States. If such areas can be avoided practically, this will eliminate a major permitting obstacle.
- Third, if total avoidance is not possible, attempts should be made to minimize the amount of fill. Activities should be carefully examined to determine if an NWP is applicable. The NWP process is typically much less difficult than the individual permit process.
- Fourth, if compensatory mitigation is required (either under an NWP or an individual permit), the project proponent should be prepared to present a plan for how the mitigation will be achieved. Obtaining consensus on mitigation from the Corps, the EPA, and other federal and state agencies with a jurisdiction over the project is often a critical component of the permitting process.
- Finally, if the activity requires an individual permit, the applicant should recognize the complexity of the process and should be fully prepared to satisfy all of the regulatory hurdles that may arise.

CHAPTER 8

Endangered Species Protections

Marc Bruner
Julie Jones

INTRODUCTION

Protection of wildlife, fish, and plants has become increasingly important in California and much of the United States. Today it is difficult to avoid endangered species issues when developing land virtually anywhere in the state.

Congress passed the first legislation to protect endangered species in 1966. The 1966 Endangered Species Act (ESA) directed the Secretary of the Interior (Secretary) to carry out a federal program to protect endangered species and to prepare an official list of endangered species. It further directed the Departments of Interior, Agriculture, and Defense to preserve endangered species' habitats on their lands, consistent with the basic missions of these agencies. Unlike the current ESA, the 1966 ESA applied only to wildlife and fish, and not to plants. While the ESA has been amended several times since 1966, the compilation of a list of species in need of protection has remained the linchpin for applying the statute.

ESA = Endangered Species Act

In California alone, there are approximately 300 federally listed species—more than any other state except Hawaii. In addition to the protections provided by the federal ESA, California also has its own Endangered Species Act, which is discussed at the end of this chapter.

The ESA is jointly administered by the United States Fish and Wildlife Service (Service), which is part of the Department of the Interior, and the National Marine Fisheries Service of the National Oceanic and Atmospheric Administration Fisheries (NOAA Fisheries, also known as NMFS), which is part of the Department of Commerce. The Service has authority over most species, and for this reason the discussion below refers mainly to the Secretary of the Interior and the Service. However, the Secretary of Commerce and NOAA Fisheries have authority over marine species and anadromous fish such as salmon and steelhead.[1]

NOAA Fisheries/NMFS = National Oceanic and Atmospheric Administration Fisheries

The ESA has four major components:
- Provisions for listing species as threatened or endangered, and for designating "critical habitat" for listed species. 16 U.S.C. § 1533[2]

---

[1] Anadromous fish are born in fresh water, migrate to the ocean to grow into adults, and then return to fresh water to spawn.

[2] Detailed information about listed species is available on the Service's website at http://www.fws.gov/endangered.

- A requirement for consultation with the Service (or with NOAA Fisheries, depending on the affected species) by federal agencies on federal projects, including federal approvals of private projects (such as the issuance of a federal permit or license). 16 U.S.C. § 1536
- Prohibitions against the "taking" of listed species. 16 U.S.C. § 1538
- Provisions for authorizing the incidental taking of listed species. 16 U.S.C. §§ 1536, 1539

The ESA's reach not limited to the territorial boundaries of the United States. In considering whether to list a species as threatened or endangered, the Secretary is required to take into account the impacts of activities that occur outside the United States, and the ESA requires the Secretary to list species that are not found in the United States. The ESA also regulates the importation and exportation of species that are listed as threatened or endangered.

In its early years, the ESA focused largely on the consultation obligations of federal agencies. In recent years, the ESA has increasingly affected private landowners and developers, who can face serious penalties for violating the ESA's prohibition against the "taking" of an endangered or threatened species. This prohibition was initially targeted at shooting, trapping, and similar direct actions. But over the years the scope of the takings prohibition has expanded to include indirect impacts caused by habitat destruction or modification. Under this broad interpretation, the otherwise lawful action of a landowner in clearing or developing land can result in civil and criminal penalties.

> Over the years the scope of the takings prohibition has expanded to include indirect impacts caused by habitat destruction or modification.

LISTING PROCESS

LISTING OF A SPECIES AS THREATENED OR ENDANGERED

The listing of a species as threatened or endangered is a key starting point that triggers the ESA's protections. The term "species" is defined to include "any subspecies of fish or wildlife or plants, and any distinct population segment of any species of vertebrate fish or wildlife which interbreeds when mature." 16 U.S.C. § 1532 (16). The Secretary may list a species as threatened or endangered if the continued existence of the species is jeopardized by:

- The present or threatened destruction, modification, or curtailment of its habitat or range
- Overuse of the species or its habitat for commercial, recreational, scientific, or educational purposes
- Disease or predation
- The inadequacy of existing regulatory mechanisms to protect the species, or
- Other natural or man-made factors affecting the species' continued existence

16 U.S.C. § 1533(a)(1)

An endangered species is "any species which is in danger of extinction throughout all or a significant portion of its range...." 16 U.S.C. § 1532(6). A threatened species is "any species which is likely to become an endangered species within the foreseeable future throughout all or a significant portion of its range." 16 U.S.C. § 1532(20).

The primary considerations the Service likely will take into account when determining whether to list a species are:

- Is the species under consideration a species or subspecies of fish, wildlife, or plant, or a distinct population segment of any species of vertebrate fish or wildlife, that interbreeds when mature?

- What is the range of the species, subspecies, or population segment?
- Is the species, subspecies, or population segment in danger of extinction in all or any part of its range?
- If it is in danger of extinction in only part of its range, is that a significant part of its range?
- If the species, subspecies, or population segment is not in danger of extinction in all or part of its range, is it likely to become an endangered species within the foreseeable future in all or part of its range?

The Service determines whether a species is endangered or threatened based on "the best scientific and commercial data available...after conducting a review of the status of the species and after taking into account those efforts, if any, being made by any State or foreign nation or any political subdivision of a State or foreign nation, to protect such species...." 16 U.S.C. § 1533(b)(1)(A).

Two recent cases illustrate the difficulty of making listing decisions in the face of scientific uncertainty.

In *Tucson Herpetological Society v. Salazar*, 566 F. 3d 870 (9th Cir. 2009), the Service, after many years of litigation, withdrew a proposal to list the flat-tailed horned lizard. The Service, relying on population studies showing that the data on the lizard's decline was inconclusive, determined that the lizard remained viable throughout most of its range. The court struck down the withdrawal and remanded the matter to the Service to re-evaluate the species. The court explained that the Service "cannot reasonably infer that the absence of evidence of population decline equates to evidence of persistence." *Id.* at 879. The dissent, emphasizing the lack of reliable scientific information, called the case a "guessing contest" and questioned the majority's refusal to defer to the Service's expertise. *Id.* at 882-83.

In *Greater Yellowstone Coalition, Inc. v. Servheen*, 665 F.3d 1015 (2011), the Ninth Circuit struck down the Service's decision to delist the Yellowstone grizzly bear after the population had rebounded following a long decline. The Service acknowledged the worsening effects from climate change on the whitebark pine, a key food source for the bear. It also acknowledged the well-documented connection between reduced whitebark pine and increased bear mortality. But in making its delisting decision, the Service explained that the rate and distribution of the decline in whitebark pine, and the response of grizzlies to that decline, were highly uncertain. The Service also relied on evidence that other grizzly bear populations were thriving in the face of similar declines. The court, while acknowledging the significant scientific uncertainty, ruled that the Service did not adequately explain and support its findings. According to the court, "[i]t is not enough for the Service to simply invoke 'scientific uncertainty' to justify its actions.... The Service must rationally explain why the uncertainty regarding the impact of whitebark pine loss on the grizzly counsels in favor of delisting now, rather than, for example, more study. Otherwise, we might as well be deferring to a coin flip." 665 F.3d at 1028.

Although the economic impacts of listing a species as threatened or endangered can be enormous, by law these impacts may not be considered in the listing process. Only information concerning the species may be considered. This contrasts with the designation of critical habitat, where economic effects are taken into consideration.

As for the potential environmental impacts that may result from the decision to list a species under the ESA, the courts have held that the requirements of the National Environmental Policy Act (NEPA) do not apply to the listing process. *See Pacific Legal Found. v. Andrus*, 657 F. 2d 829, 835 (6th Cir. 1981); *see also Douglas County v. Babbitt*,

NEPA = National Environmental Policy Act

48 F. 3d 1495 (9th Cir. 1995) (relying on the Sixth Circuit's decision to conclude that NEPA does not apply to critical habitat designations).

LISTING OF A "DISTINCT POPULATION SEGMENT"

In 1996, the Service and NOAA Fisheries jointly adopted a policy statement on what constitutes a "distinct population segment" for purposes of the ESA's definition of "species." 61 Fed. Reg. 4722 (Feb. 7, 1996). The "DPS Policy" considers both the discreteness and the significance of the population segment in relation to the remainder of the species to which it belongs. Discreteness is satisfied if a population segment is separated from other populations of the same species as a result of physical, physiological, ecological, or behavioral factors. Significance is analyzed under four factors: (1) whether the population segment persists in a unique or unusual ecological setting; (2) whether the loss of the population segment would cause a significant gap in the species' range; (3) whether the population segment is the only surviving natural occurrence of a species; and (4) whether the population segment's genetic characteristics are markedly different from the rest of the species. If a population qualifies as a "distinct population segment," the inquiry then proceeds to whether the population should be listed as endangered or threatened.

In 2007, the Ninth Circuit ruled that the DPS Policy is entitled to judicial deference, is a reasonable interpretation of the ESA, and is legally binding. *Northwest Ecosystem Alliance v. U.S. Fish & Wildlife Serv.*, 475 F. 3d 1136 (9th Cir. 2007). The court concluded that Congress left it to the discretion of the Service and NOAA Fisheries to decide how best to define "distinct population segment," which is not defined in the ESA and has no generally accepted scientific meaning.

The court in *Northwest Ecosystem Alliance* upheld the Service's determination not to list the Washington population of the western gray squirrel as a threatened or endangered DPS. The court found that there was a reasonable basis for the Service to conclude that the population's ecological setting was not unique; that the loss of the population would not cause a significant gap in the squirrel's overall range; and that the population's genetic characteristics did not differ markedly from those of the squirrel's populations in Oregon and California. The court therefore upheld the Service's determination that the Washington population did not meet the criteria for "significance" in the DPS Policy. Compare *Nat'l Ass'n of Home Builders v. Norton*, 340 F. 3d 835 (9th Cir. 2003) (overturning the Service's decision to list Arizona pygmy owl population as an endangered population segment, where the evidence did not support the Service's conclusion that the population was significant under the DPS Policy).

Relying on *Northwest Ecosystem Alliance*, the Ninth Circuit in 2009 upheld NOAA Fisheries' policy of treating hatchery and natural steelhead as part of the same population segment in the Upper Columbia River and the agency's decision based on that policy to "downlist" the population from endangered to threatened. *Trout Unlimited v. Lohn*, 559 F. 3d 946 (9th Cir. 2009). The court rejected claims by environmentalists that NOAA Fisheries' listing decision should have been based solely on the status of the natural steelhead population, without any consideration of the hatchery population. The court also rejected claims by industry and farm groups that in making the listing decision NOAA Fisheries improperly gave greater weight to the status of the natural population, and limited its consideration of the hatchery population to its contributions to conserving the natural population. In response to both challenges, the court deferred to the agency's technical expertise, refusing to second-guess its resolution of the scientific issues involved.

The Ninth Circuit also upheld NOAA Fisheries' decision to list Central Valley steelhead as a distinct population segment separate from rainbow trout, even though the two fish interbreed. *Modesto Irrigation Dist. v. Gutierrez*, 619 F.3d 1024, 1033, 1036-37 (9th Cir. 2010). The two fish initially were treated as one "Evolutionarily Significant Unit" (ESU), which is the term used for Pacific salmon species to define the functional equivalent of a district population segment. Under NOAA's 1991 "ESU Policy" for these species, reproductive isolation is a prerequisite for a separate listing. *See* 56 Fed. Reg. 58612 (Nov. 20, 1991). But as concerns mounted over declining steelhead populations, NOAA Fisheries sought to list the steelhead as its own ESU in light of new scientific evidence illuminating the differences between the steelhead and the unthreatened rainbow trout. To justify the listing, NOAA Fisheries turned to the more broadly applicable 1996 DPS Policy, which does not place as much emphasis on interbreeding as the 1991 ESU Policy. The court again refused to second-guess NOAA Fisheries' decision, finding ample scientific support in the administrative record for the agency's change in approach and rejecting claims by Central Valley irrigation districts that the departure from prior policy was unlawful.

> ESU = evolutionarily significant unit

"SIGNIFICANT PORTION OF ITS RANGE"

A species will be listed under the ESA if it is found to be endangered or threatened "throughout all or a significant portion of its range...." 16 U.S.C. §§ 1532(6), (20). In 2001, the Ninth Circuit ruled that the Service, in deciding to withdraw its prior proposal to list the flat-tailed horned lizard, used an inappropriate standard in deciding whether the lizard faced the danger of extinction in "a significant portion of its range." *Defenders of Wildlife v. Norton*, 258 F. 3d 1136 (9th Cir. 2001). The Service took the position that a species is eligible for protection under the ESA "if it faces threats in enough key portions of its range that the *entire species* is in danger of extinction." *Id.* at 1141 (court's emphasis). In rejecting this position, the court adopted a more protective view, stating that a species qualifies for the ESA's protections "if there are major geographical areas in which it is no longer viable but once was." *Id.* at 1145. Thus, the entire species need not face the danger of extinction to trigger listing under the ESA.

> A species will be listed under the ESA if it is found to be endangered or threatened "throughout all or a significant portion of its range...."

In response to the Ninth Circuit's decision, the Service formulated a new interpretation to address the situation where a species faces the danger of extinction within a significant portion, but not all, of its range. In this situation, the Service would list the species only within the significant portion, and not within the remainder of the range. But several courts stuck down this interpretation, holding that the text of the ESA prohibits a decision to list only some members of a defined species, subspecies or DPS, but not other members of that same taxonomic group. *See, e.g., Defenders of Wildlife v. Salazar*, 729 F. Supp. 2d 1207 (D. Mont. 2010).

In late 2011, the Service and NOAA Fisheries jointly published a draft policy that seeks to harmonize the court decisions interpreting "significant portion of its range." *See* 76 Fed. Reg. 76987 (Dec. 9, 2011). The draft policy contains the following key elements:
- If a species is found to be endangered or threatened within a "significant portion of its range," then the species would be listed and the ESA's protections generally would apply to the species *throughout all of its range*; however, if the population of the species within that portion qualifies as a DPS, then only the DPS, and the not the entire species, would be listed

- A portion of a species' range would be considered significant if its contribution to the species' viability is so important that without the portion, the species would face the danger of extinction
- A species' range is the general geographical area where the species is found at the time the listing decision is made; lost historical range, while relevant to the overall status of the species, is not part of the "significant portion of its range"

The draft policy seeks to resolve years of debate and litigation, but controversy still abounds, as environmental groups have voiced their strong opposition to the draft policy, claiming it sets too high a threshold for protecting imperiled species. Until the draft policy is finalized, the Service and NOAA Fisheries have stated that they will follow the policy as "nonbinding guidance." As of late 2013, the agencies have not yet adopted a final policy.

LISTING PROCEDURES AND REQUIREMENTS

There are two ways in which a species can be considered for listing. The Service can initiate consideration on its own, or an individual can petition the Service to consider a species for listing. In California, a substantial portion of the listings have resulted from petitions to list.

Where the Service initiates the listing, the process begins with the publication of notice of a proposed rule in the Federal Register. 50 C.F.R. § 424.16. This notice must contain the complete text of the proposed rule, summarize the data on which the proposed rule is based, and show the relationship of the data to the proposed rule. 50 C.F.R. § 424.16(b).

The Service then allows at least 60 days for the public to comment on the proposal. The Service must hold at least one public hearing if any person requests a hearing within 45 days of publication of the proposed rule, and must provide at least 15 days' notice in the Federal Register of the time and place of the hearing. 50 C.F.R. § 424.16(b)(3).

The Service may extend or reopen the public comment period upon a finding that there is good cause to do so. 50 C.F.R. § 424.16(c)(2). When new information becomes available after the close of the public comment period that is critical to the listing decision, the Service must provide an additional opportunity for public review and comment. See *Idaho Farm Bureau Fed'n v. Babbitt*, 58 F. 3d 1392 (9th Cir. 1995) (Service should have reopened the comment period where new information of questionable accuracy was used to support key aspects of the agency's decision); *but see Kern County Farm Bureau v. Allen*, 450 F. 3d 1072 (9th Cir. 2006) (no duty to reopen the comment period where Service used new information merely to refine and expand pre-existing data, and not to introduce a new premise for the final decision, to independently justify that decision, or to reach a new conclusion).

Within one year after publishing a proposed rule to add a species to, or remove a species from, the endangered or threatened list, the Service is required either to adopt a final rule to implement the proposal; withdraw the proposed rule "upon a finding that available evidence does not justify the action proposed by the rule"; or extend the one-year period by an additional period of not more than six months because there is a "substantial disagreement among scientists knowledgeable about the species concerned regarding the sufficiency or accuracy of the available data relevant to the determination." 50 C.F.R. § 424.17(a).

Since the ESA was passed, the Service has listed hundreds of species yet has consistently faced a backlog of species to consider. In 1988, Congress noted that 950 species were prime candidates for listing for which the Service had taken no action. To address this issue, Congress amended the ESA to allow any person to petition the Service to add a species to, or remove a species from, the threatened or endangered list. Within 90 days of receiving such a petition, the Service must make a finding on whether the petition presents substantial scientific or commercial information indicating that the petitioned action may be warranted. If the Secretary makes an affirmative finding, he or she must promptly begin a review of the species' status. 16 U.S.C. § 1533(b)(3).

Within 12 months after receiving a petition where the Secretary determines further action may be warranted, the Secretary must publish in the Federal Register one of the following findings:
- That the petitioned action is not warranted
- That the petitioned action is warranted, in which case the Secretary shall promptly publish a proposed rule to that effect in the Federal Register
- That the action is warranted, but further action is precluded by other pending proposals considering whether various species are eligible or ineligible for listing

16 U.S.C. § 1533(b)(3). In *Center for Biological Diversity v. Norton*, the Ninth Circuit ruled the designation of a species as a "candidate" for future listing failed to satisfy the requirement to make and publish one of the specific findings listed in the statute. 254 F. 3d 833 (9th Cir. 2001).

The Secretary also is required to adopt a system to prioritize efforts for those species where further action is warranted but precluded by other pending proposals. The goal is for the Secretary to list those species that face the greatest danger of extinction. In furtherance of this goal, the Secretary periodically publishes a "Candidate Notice of Review" listing the species being considered for possible future listing actions. Candidate species, however, are not subject to the ESA's protections unless and until they are listed as threatened or endangered. Further information about candidate species is available at http://www.fws.gov/endangered (under "Find Endangered Species," choose "What species are candidates for listing?").

> The goal is for the Secretary to list those species that face the greatest danger of extinction.

Since 2007, petitions to the Service to list species have accelerated and the Service has fallen far behind in addressing them. In September 2011, the Service settled litigation with two frequent ESA litigants, WildEarth Guardians and the Center for Biological Diversity. The settlement agreements create work plans for the Service to process listing determinations for 251 species by September 30, 2016 and create disincentives for the plaintiffs to file new listing deadline-related litigation during that time. *See* http://www.fws.gov/endangered/improving_ESA/listing_workplan.html.

Once a species is listed, the Secretary is required to develop and implement a "recovery plan" that provides for the conservation and survival of the species. 16 U.S.C. § 1533(f). This requirement does not apply if the Secretary finds that such a plan will not promote the conservation of the species. The Service has published scores of recovery plans in recent years, but has not always been able to keep pace with the rate at which species are listed.

FIVE-YEAR REVIEW AND DELISTING

For each listed species, the Secretary is required to conduct a review at least once every five years to determine whether the species should be "delisted" (i.e., removed from the threatened or endangered list) or changed in status (i.e., from threatened to endangered or vice versa). 16 U.S.C. § 1533(c)(2). But in *Coos County Board of Supervisors v. Kempthorne*, the Ninth Circuit ruled that the appropriate procedure for a party seeking delisting of a species is to file a petition with the Secretary, rather than to challenge the outcome of the Service's five-year review. 531 F. 3d 792 (9th Cir. 2008). In *Coos County*, the Service had previously listed the "tri-state murrelet," a subpopulation of the marbled murrelet that lives in California, Oregon, and Washington. Based on a five-year review, the Service determined that this subpopulation did not qualify as a "distinct population segment." The Service nevertheless decided to keep the subpopulation on the threatened list pending a broader review of the species' entire geographic range, due to continued threats posed by the loss of old-growth forests from timber operations. In refusing to entertain a challenge to the merits of the Service's decision, the court emphasized that the five-year review process is separate and distinct from the citizen petition process, and that if the plaintiff wished to compel the Service to make a delisting decision on the tri-state murrelet, it should file a delisting petition.

EMERGENCY LISTINGS

In addition to its normal listing authority, the Service also has the authority at any time to take a listing action in response to "any emergency posing a significant risk to the well-being of a species of fish, wildlife or plant." 50 C.F.R. § 424.20. These emergency rules take effect immediately on publication in the Federal Register, but cease to have force and effect after 240 days. 50 C.F.R. § 424.20.

One example of an emergency listing is the Mojave Desert population of the desert tortoise. The Service explained that a variety of factors, including disease and predation by ravens, were causing a significant and dramatic decline of the species, and that an emergency listing was required to protect the species while further actions were considered.

The emergency listing of the desert tortoise caused serious problems for developers in Southern California and Las Vegas, and the action was challenged in *City of Las Vegas v. Lujan*, 891 F. 2d 927 (D.C. Cir. 1989). The court held that the ESA gave the Secretary considerable discretion and latitude in the emergency listing of endangered species, and refused to grant a preliminary injunction to halt the emergency listing of the desert tortoise. The court said that its "scrutiny of such emergency regulation is... less exacting on the Secretary than it would be if he enacted precisely the same regulation...after a normal rulemaking." *Id.* at 932.

DESIGNATION OF "CRITICAL HABITAT"

When a species is listed as endangered or threatened, the Service is required to publish concurrently, absent "extraordinary circumstances," a designation of "critical habitat" for the species. 16 U.S.C. § 1533(a)(3); *but see Center for Biological Diversity v. U.S. Fish and Wildlife Serv.*, 450 F. 3d 930 (9th Cir. 2006) (Service was not required to designate critical habitat for endangered fish species listed in 1970, since the ESA requirement to designate critical habitat concurrently with listing was not enacted until 1982 and did not apply to listings made before that date).

The term "critical habitat" means:
- The specific areas within the geographical area occupied by a species at the time it is listed where physical or biological features are found that are essential to the conservation of the species and may require special management considerations or protection

- Specific areas outside the geographical area occupied by a species at the time it is listed upon a determination by the Secretary that such areas are essential for the conservation of the species

50 C.F.R. § 424.02(d)

Unlike the listing determination, the Service must consider the economic impacts resulting from a designation of critical habitat. 50 C.F.R. § 424.19. In August 2013, the Service and NOAA Fisheries jointly published a final regulation that governs how the agencies evaluate economic effects when designating critical habitat. 78 Fed. Reg. 53058 (Aug. 28, 2013). With respect to timing, the regulation requires the economic impact analysis to be published at the same time as the proposed critical habitat designation. This approach should help to improve the consideration of economic impacts. Under prior practice, the economic analysis was published for comment later on in the process, which limited the agencies' ability to integrate changes in that analysis into the final habitat designation.

With respect to substance, the regulation adopts the "incremental" over the "baseline" approach, thereby addressing a longstanding dispute over the appropriate methodological starting point for the economic analysis. Under the incremental approach, the analysis considers only the economic impacts caused by the critical habitat designation itself, and does not consider the impacts caused by the initial decision to list the species. By contrast, the baseline approach posits that the costs associated with the listing and the critical habitat designation cannot be separated and should both be considered as part of the economic analysis. The conflict stems in part from dueling court decisions, with the Tenth Circuit favoring the baseline approach and the Ninth Circuit favoring the incremental approach. *Compare New Mexico Cattlegrowers Ass'n v. U.S. Fish & Wildlife Service*, 248 F.3d 1277 (10th Cir. 2001), *with Arizona Cattlegrowers Ass'n v. Salazar*, 606 F.3d 1160 (9th Cir. 2010) *and Gifford Pinchot Task Force v. U.S. Fish & Wildlife Service*, 378 F.3d 1059 (9th Cir. 2004). Industry groups generally oppose the incremental approach, on the ground that it tends to minimize the negative economic impacts resulting from critical habitat designations, since most of those impacts can be attributed to the initial listing decision.

Economic analyses for critical habitat designations have generated considerable controversy and litigation, and this trend likely will continue under the new regulation. The designation of critical habitat for 15 vernal pool species in California and southern Oregon illustrates the difficulties the Service faces in addressing economic issues. The Service's designation in 2003 excluded certain lands on economic grounds. In response to a lawsuit by environmentalists challenging the exclusions, the Service agreed to conduct a new economic analysis. The Service then issued a new designation in 2005, which was challenged again in court, by both environmentalists and the Home Builders Association of Northern California. In response to the court's determination that the Service did not adequately consider the economic benefits that could result from a critical habitat designation, the Service again reevaluated its economic exclusions, and while it retained its 2005 designation, it published a detailed analysis in the Federal Register to address the issues raised by the court. *See* 72 Fed. Reg. 30279 (May 31, 2007). The Ninth Circuit upheld the Service's 2007 designation and noted that the economic analysis from an outside consultant fulfilled the ESA's requirements. *Home Builders Ass'n of Northern California v. U.S. Fish and Wildlife Serv.*, 616 F.3d 983, 992 (9th Cir. 2010), *cert. denied*, 131 S.Ct 983 (2011).

With respect to NEPA compliance, there is some judicial disagreement as to whether NEPA's requirement for an environmental review applies to the designation of critical habitat. *Compare Douglas County v. Babbitt*, 48 F. 3d 1495, 1502–03 (9th Cir. 1995) (critical habitat designations do not require NEPA compliance) *with Catron County v. U.S. Fish and Wildlife Serv.*, 75 F. 3d 1429, 1433–34 (10th Cir. 1996) (environmental impact statement may be needed to support critical habitat designation). The Ninth Circuit's decision (holding that NEPA does not apply) is the governing law in California.

The requirement to designate critical habitat concurrently with the final listing of a species can be deferred for one year if the Secretary determines that it is essential that the species be listed promptly, even without a critical habitat designation, or if the Service determines that the critical habitat of the species is "not then determinable." 16 U.S.C. § 1533(b)(6)(C); 50 C.F.R. 424.17(b). Critical habitat is not determinable when either (1) information sufficient to perform the required analysis of the impacts of the designation is lacking, or (2) the biological needs of the species are not sufficiently known to permit a critical habitat designation. 50 C.F.R. § 424.12(a)(2); *see also Enos v. Marsh*, 769 F. 2d 1363, 1370–71 (9th Cir. 1985) (decision not to define critical habitat is proper where essential biological features are unknown). In addition, the Service may decide that it is "not prudent" to designate critical habitat if identifying the habitat can be expected to increase the threat posed by human activity, or if the designation would not be beneficial to the species. 40 C.F.R. § 424.12(a)(1); *see* 63 Fed. Reg. 54938 (Oct. 13, 1998) (Service declined to designate critical habitat immediately for several listed plants in Southern California due to fear that designation would result in purposeful vandalism and eradication efforts by landowners). However, the "imprudence" exception is narrow and is reserved for extraordinary circumstances. *See Natural Resources Defense Council v. U.S. Dept. of Interior*, 113 F. 3d 1121, 1126 (9th Cir. 1997).

The Service must state the reasons for not designating critical habitat, and its decision must be based on the best scientific data available. 50 C.F.R. § 424.12(a); *see Northern Spotted Owl v. Lujan*, 758 F. Supp. 621 (W.D. Wash. 1991) (Service abused its discretion when it decided not to designate critical habitat concurrently with the listing of the northern spotted owl, and failed to explain why critical habitat was not determinable); *Center for Biological Diversity v. Kempthorne*, 607 F. Supp. 2d 1078 (D. Ariz. 2009) (overturning Service's decision not to list critical habitat for the jaguar because the agency did not adequately consider the best scientific information available).

The controversy over critical habitat designations has intensified in recent years as environmental groups succeed in case after case forcing the Service to designate critical habitat against its will. The resulting accumulation of court orders, most containing deadlines for Service compliance, has resulted in a profusion of critical habitat proposals and designations.

Not surprisingly, legal challenges to critical habitat designations by both industry and environmental groups have followed. *See, e.g., New Mexico Cattle Growers Ass'n v. U.S. Fish and Wildlife Serv.*, 248 F. 3d 1277, 1283 (10th Cir. 2001) (critical habitat designation failed to account for all of the resulting economic impacts); *Home Builders Ass'n of N. Calif. v. Norton*, 293 F. Supp. 2d 1 (D.D.C. 2002) (court approved a settlement whereby the Service voluntarily rescinded its critical habitat designation for the California red-legged frog and agreed to new rulemaking proceedings); *Home Builders Ass'n of N. Calif. v. U.S. Fish and Wildlife Serv.*, 268 F. Supp. 2d 1197 (E.D. Cal. 2003) (Service's designation of critical habitat for the Alameda whipsnake was inadequately justified); *Center for Biological Diversity v. Norton*, 240 F. Supp. 2d 1090 (D. Ariz. 2003) (Service acted arbitrarily in failing to designate the full extent of Mexican spotted owl critical habitat).

As a result of court orders and settlement agreements, the Service recently has designated or proposed to designate critical habitat for a number of listed species in California affecting millions of acres. Recent critical habitat designations include:

- A designation of over 1.6 million acres in 27 California counties, ranging from Butte to Riverside, for the California red-legged frog. 75 Fed. Reg. 12815 (March 17, 2010) (the convoluted history of this designation included a 2004 Service proposal to designate more than four million acres, a lawsuit, a reduced Service proposal to cover less than 750,000 acres, a final designation in 2006 covering 450,000 acres, and the Service's agreement in 2007 to revise the designation in response to allegations of improper political meddling into critical habitat determinations)
- A designation covering thousands of square miles of freshwater, estuarine, and marine habitat for the Southern Distinct Population Segment of the North American Green Sturgeon. 74 Fed. Reg. 52300 (Oct. 9, 2009) (this designation includes California coastal waters north of Monterey Bay; San Francisco, San Pablo, and Suisun bays and the Sacramento-San Joaquin Delta; and the Sacramento, lower Feather, and lower Yuba rivers)
- A broad-reaching designation for west coast salmon and steelhead that includes riverine and estuarine habitats. 70 Fed. Reg. 52488 (Sept. 8, 2005)
- Designation of 200,000 acres in 19 counties for the Central California population of the tiger salamander (70 Fed. Reg. 49739 (Aug. 23, 2005)) and, following litigation, designation of approximately 47,000 acres for the Sonoma County population (76 Fed. Reg. 54346 (Aug. 31, 2011))
- Designation of over 850,000 acres in 34 California counties and one Oregon county for four vernal pool crustaceans and 11 vernal pool plant species. 70 Fed. Reg. 49739 (Aug. 23, 2005); 72 Fed. Reg. 30279 (May 31, 2007)
- Designation of over 150,000 acres in Northern California for the Alameda whipsnake. 71 Fed. Reg. 58176 (Oct. 2, 2006)
- Designation of 18,000 acres in San Mateo and Santa Clara Counties for the bay checkerspot butterfly. 73 Fed. Reg. 50406 (Aug. 26, 2008)
- A reduced designation covering approximately 60,000 acres in San Diego and Riverside Counties for the Quino checkerspot butterfly; the previous designation included more than 170,000 acres. 74 Fed. Reg. 28776 (June 17, 2009)
- Designation of 200,000 acres in Southern California for the coastal California gnatcatcher. 72 Fed. Reg. 72010 (Dec. 19, 2007)
- Designation of over 400,000 acres for the Sierra Nevada bighorn sheep. 73 Fed. Reg. 45534 (Aug. 8, 2008)
- A reduced designation covering 375,000 acres for the Peninsular bighorn sheep in southern California; the previous designation included approximately 850,000 acres. 74 Fed. Reg. 17288 (Apr. 14, 2009)
- A revised designation in November 2012 increasing the amount of critical habitat in California for the northern spotted owl from about 1.2 million acres to more than 2.1 million acres. 77 Fed. Reg. 71876 (Dec. 4, 2012)
- A revised designation for the marbled murrelet that removes about 190,000 acres in northern California and southern Oregon from the previous designation. 76 Fed. Reg. 61599 (Oct. 5, 2011)
- A revised designation that increases critical habitat for the Pacific Coast population of the western snowy plover. 77 Fed. Reg. 36728 (June 19, 2012)

> Given the combined effect of lawsuits by environmental groups to compel designations, and challenges to those designations once they have been made, the status of many of the Service's designations is in a constant state of flux.

Given the combined effect of lawsuits by environmental groups to compel designations, and challenges to those designations once they have been made, the status of many of the Service's designations is in a constant state of flux.[3]

CONSULTATION PROCESS

Section 7 of the ESA (16 U.S.C. § 1536) is a key provision that implements the protections afforded to listed species. Under Section 7, each federal agency must consult with the Service to ensure that any actions authorized, funded, or carried out by the agency are not likely to "jeopardize the continued existence of any endangered species or threatened species or result in the destruction or adverse modification of [critical] habitat." 16 U.S.C. §§ 1532(5), 1536(a)(2). The consultation process applies to all listed species, including plants. However, the process applies only to actions taken by federal agencies, and to actions taken by private parties that require federal agency permits, approval, or funding. It does not apply to private actions that do not require or involve a federal action, or to agency actions taken abroad. 51 Fed. Reg. 19926 (June 3, 1986); 50 C.F.R. § 402.01.

In 1998, the Service and NMFS published a detailed handbook on the Section 7 process. (*The Consultation Handbook* is available at http://www.fws.gov/endangered/esa-library/pdf/esa_section 7_handbook.pdf.)

Where a private project requires a federal approval (such as issuance of a wetlands permit by the Army Corps of Engineers), the burden of satisfying the consultation requirements, as a practical matter, typically falls on the project proponent. This includes identifying the presence or absence of listed species and their critical habitat, and preparing the required studies and reports. It is generally advisable for the project proponent to work with the federal permitting agency early in the review process to identify potential problems and to meet and consult informally with the Service. If possible, the project proponent should consider redesigning the project to avoid impacts to threatened or endangered species. If impacts cannot be avoided, the project proponent should work proactively to identify suitable mitigation.

COMPONENTS OF THE CONSULTATION PROCESS

Agency action. Section 7 applies to federal agency "action," which is defined as "all activities or programs of any kind authorized, funded or carried out, in whole or in part, by federal agencies in the United States or upon the high seas." 50 C.F.R. § 402.02.

Corps = U.S. Army Corps of Engineers

BLM = Bureau of Land Management

Examples of direct federal actions include the construction of a flood control dam by the Army Corps of Engineers (Corps), adoption of a new grazing policy by the Bureau of Land Management, and the EPA's registration of pesticides. The Ninth Circuit has held that Section 7 applies not only to the initial adoption by the Forest Service of a National Forest Land and Resource Management Plan, but also to the ongoing implementation of that plan. *See Pacific Rivers Council v. Thomas*, 30 F. 3d 1050, 1055–56 (9th Cir. 1994).

Examples of non-federal actions that require Section 7 consultation include the construction of a dam by a private entity where a Clean Water Act (CWA) Section 404 permit is required from the Corps (*Riverside Irr. Dist. v. Andrews*, 758 F. 2d 508

---

3 For a list of the Service's critical habitat designations, see http://criticalhabitat.fws.gov/crithab/.

(10th Cir. 1985)); development of a ski resort pursuant to a special use permit issued by the Forest Service (*Wilson v. Block*, 708 F. 2d 735 (D.C. Cir. 1983)); a federally financed state highway project (*National Wildlife Fed'n v. Coleman*, 529 F. 2d 359 (5th Cir.), *cert. denied*, 429 U.S. 979 (1976)); and operation of an oil refinery pursuant to an NPDES wastewater discharge permit issued by the EPA under Section 402 of the CWA (*Roosevelt Campobello Int'l Park Comm'n v. U.S. EPA*, 684 F. 2d 1041 (1st Cir. 1982)).

Section 7 consultation, however, is required only for "discretionary" actions by federal agencies. The United States Supreme Court, in reversing the Ninth Circuit, determined that the EPA's transfer of water pollution control authority to Arizona under Section 402(b) of the CWA did not trigger consultation, since the EPA was legally compelled by that provision to effectuate the transfer if certain conditions were met. *Nat'l Ass'n of Home Builders v. Defenders of Wildlife*, 127 S. Ct. 2518 (2007). The Court expressed concern that the EPA could not simultaneously obey the conflicting mandates set forth in Section 7 of the ESA and Section 402(b) of the CWA, and determined that where such a conflict exists, the consultation requirements of Section 7 must yield.

The Ninth Circuit found no such conflict in *Nat'l Wildlife Fed'n v. Nat'l Marine Fisheries Serv.*, 524 F. 3d 917 (9th Cir. 2008). In that case, the court rejected the claim that certain operations of the Federal Columbia River Power System (System) by the Corps and the United States Bureau of Reclamation were "non-discretionary," and therefore not subject to Section 7's consultation requirements, merely because those operations were being undertaken to implement a Congressional mandate. That mandate established non-discretionary goals that the System was required to achieve in relation to flood control, irrigation, and power production, but did not prescribe precisely *how* the System was to achieve those goals. As the court explained, "while the goals themselves may be mandatory, the agencies retain considerable discretion in choosing what specific actions to take in order to implement them. The agencies are therefore obligated to satisfy the ESA's requirements." *Id.* at 928-29.

> The court explained "while the goals themselves may be mandatory, the agencies retain considerable discretion in choosing what specific actions to take in order to implement them."

The Ninth Circuit found there was no duty to consult in *Grand Canyon Trust v. U.S. Bureau of Reclamation*, 691 F.3d 1008 (9th Cir. 2012), which involved the Bureau's annual operating plans for the Glen Canyon Dam. The plaintiff argued that the preparation of the plans constituted agency action triggering consultation, but the court disagreed. The court explained that the Bureau long ago completed ESA consultations on the flow regime adopted for the dam, and that the Bureau's preparation of annual plans describing the dam's operations was a non-discretionary task that was mandated by federal statute.

Consultation also is not required where a federal agency *fails* to act. *See, e.g., Western Watersheds Project v. Matejko*, 468 F.3d 1099 (9th Cir. 2006) (consultation not triggered by Bureau of Land Management's refusal to exercise its discretion to regulate private water diversions); *California Sportfishing Protection Alliance v. Federal Energy Regulatory Comm'n*, 472 F.3d 593 (9th Cir. 2006) (listing of a new species did not trigger consultation where private hydroelectric project was operating under a federal license issued in 1980 and did not require further federal approval to continue operating).

But in 2012, the Ninth Circuit held that the U.S. Forest Service took an affirmative, discretionary action triggering Section 7 consultation by not requiring a more in-depth agency review of a Notice of Intent to conduct recreational mining activities in a national forest. The dissent, which viewed the case as one of agency *inaction*, emphasized that the miners had a statutory right under the General Mining Law of 1872 to conduct mining on federal lands and that they were required only to follow a simple notification procedure, rather than having to file a formal permit application for federal review and approval. *Karuk Tribe of California v. U.S. Forest Service*, 681 F.3d 1006 (9th Cir. 2012).

The "Action Agency," "Action Area," and "Effects of the Action." Section 7's consultation requirement is triggered by a determination by the "action agency"—i.e., the federal agency that is carrying out, funding, or approving a project (such as the Corps when issuing a wetlands permit under Section 404 of the CWA)—that the project "may affect" a listed species or critical habitat. 50 C.F.R. § 402.14(a). The Ninth Circuit recently emphasized that the threshold for triggering consultation "is relatively low." *People of the State of California ex rel. Lockyer v. U.S. Dept. of Agriculture*, 575 F. 3d 999, 1018-19 (9th Cir. 2009); *see also Western Watersheds Project v. Kraayenbrink*, 632 F. 3d 472, 496 (9th Cir. 2011). The court explained that "any possible effect" triggers consultation and found the USDA acted arbitrarily in failing to consult with the Service with respect to a new rule governing roadless areas in national forests. The court rejected the USDA's claim that the new rule simply created different administrative procedures and would have "no effect" on listed species or habitat.

The "action area" and the "effects of the action" constitute the "scope of the action" subject to consultation. *See National Wildlife Fed'n*, 529 F. 2d at 371. Under the regulations implementing the ESA, "action area" means "all areas to be affected directly or indirectly by the Federal action and not merely the immediate area involved in the action." The regulations define "effects of the action" as "the direct and indirect effects of an action on the species or critical habitat, together with the effects of other activities that are interrelated or interdependent with that action...." Indirect actions "are those that are caused by the proposed action and are later in time, but still are reasonably certain to occur." 50 C.F.R. § 402.02. In *Jayne v. Sherman*, 706 F.3d 994 (9th Cir. 2013), the Ninth Circuit, in upholding a broad management plan governing roadless areas in national forests in Idaho, found that the Service appropriately relied on commitments made by Forest Service officials in finding that the impacts to species from potential future road construction were not reasonably certain to occur and therefore did not constitute indirect impacts of the proposed action.

The Service uses a "but for" test in deciding whether activities are "interrelated" (are part of a larger action and depend on the larger action for their justification) or "interdependent" (have no independent utility apart from the action under consideration), and therefore should be included within the scope of the action. *See Sierra Club v. Marsh*, 816 F. 2d 1376, 1387 (9th Cir. 1987); *see also* 51 Fed. Reg. 19932 (June 3, 1986).

In *Riverside Irrigation District v. Andrews*, the court held that in reviewing a Section 404 permit application for a dam, the Corps properly examined the indirect impacts resulting from increased upstream water use enabled by the dam, which would adversely affect whooping crane critical habitat located 150 miles downstream from the project. 758 F. 2d 508 (10th Cir. 1985). In *National Wildlife Federation v. Coleman*, the court similarly held that the impacts of a federal highway project included the indirect effects of private development resulting from the construction of highway interchanges. 529 F. 2d 359 (5th Cir. 1976).

The action agency and the Service sometimes disagree on whether consultation is required under Section 7. In such an instance, the Service lacks authority to require consultation, and it is up to the courts to decide the matter. *See Defenders of Wildlife v. Flowers*, 414 F. 3d 1066 (9th Cir. 2005) (no requirement to consult, even though the Service requested consultation, where the record showed no pygmy-owls had been found within the project area).

"Informal" vs. "formal" consultation. The consultation process typically begins with the action agency's request to the Service for information on whether there are any species listed or proposed to be listed, or any critical habitat, in the area of the proposed action. 16 U.S.C. § 1536(c)(1); 50 C.F.R. § 402.12(c). If no such species or critical habitat are present, no further consultation is required. 50 C.F.R. § 402.12(d)(1). If listed species or designated critical habitat may be present, then the action agency typically prepares a biological assessment to determine whether the proposed action is likely to have an adverse effect on the species or critical habitat. 16 U.S.C. § 1536(c)(1); *see generally* 50 C.F.R. § 402.12.[4] If the action agency determines, based on the biological assessment, that the proposed action is *not* likely to have any adverse effect on listed species or designated critical habitat, and if the Service concurs in writing with this determination, no further consultation is required. 50 C.F.R. § 402.13. This is referred to as "informal consultation."

In the absence of a "not likely to adversely affect" determination, the action agency must engage in "formal consultation" with the Service, which leads to the issuance of a biological opinion (as discussed below). 50 C.F.R. § 402.14.

Under the regulations implementing the ESA, formal consultation requires an assessment of whether the proposed action, alone or "taken together with cumulative effects, is likely to jeopardize the continued existence of listed species or result in the destruction or adverse modification of critical habitat." 50 C.F.R. § 402.14(g)(4). "Cumulative effects" are defined as "those effects of future State or private activities, not involving Federal activities, that are reasonably to occur within the action area of the Federal action subject to consultation." *Id.* § 402.02. However, the Ninth Circuit recently clarified that a consideration of cumulative effects is not required for informal consultations. *Conservation Congress v. U.S. Forest Service*, 720 F.3d 1048 (9th Cir. 2013).

During the consultation process, Section 7(d) of the ESA prohibits both the action agency and the project proponent from making any irreversible or irretrievable commitments of resources that would foreclose the formulation or implementation of measures to mitigate impacts to listed species and designated critical habitat. 16 U.S.C. § 1536(d).

Duty to use best available science. In conducting consultations, both the action agency and the Service must use the best available scientific and commercial information. 50 C.F.R. §§ 402.14(c), (d). This includes information that can be obtained during the consultation. *See, e.g., Resources Ltd. v. Robertson*, 35 F. 3d 1300, 1304–05 (9th Cir. 1993) (consultation was invalid where action agency selectively withheld information raising serious questions about potential effects on listed species); *Conner v. Burford*, 848 F.2d 1441, 1453-54 (9th Cir. 1988) (incomplete information does not excuse agency's failure to use the best information available, noting that the Service could have conducted additional analysis with the information it had); *Roosevelt Campobello Int'l Park Comm'n v. U.S. EPA*, 684 F. 2d 1041, 1052–55 (1st Cir. 1982) (EPA violated the ESA in issuing permit for refinery by failing to use "real time simulation studies" to assure low risk of an oil spill with a potential impact to endangered whales); *Consolidated Salmonid Cases*, 791 F. Supp. 2d 802, 821-27 (E.D. Cal. 2011) (NOAA Fisheries did not use the best available science in relying on "raw" fish salvage numbers, which were not scaled to reflect the size of the population from which the fish were salvaged); *NRDC v. Kempthorne*, 506 F. Supp. 2d 322, 362–67, 387 (E.D. Cal. 2007) (failure to analyze the

> In the absence of a "not likely to adversely affect" determination, the action agency must engage in "formal consultation" with the Service, which leads to the issuance of a biological opinion.

---

4 If only proposed species or proposed critical habitat are present, the action agency must confer with the Service, but preparation of a biological assessment is not required unless the proposal becomes final. 50 C.F.R. § 402.12(d)(1).

most recent fish abundance data made the information in the biological opinion unreliable); *Conservation Law Found. v. Watt,* 560 F. Supp. 561, 572 (D. Mass. 1983), *aff'd on other grounds sub nom., Massachusetts v. Watt,* 716 F. 2d 946 (1st Cir. 1983) (Section 7 imposes ongoing duty to assess new information as it arises during the consultation process).

On the other hand, the ESA allows the use of imperfect data, as long it is the best data available. *See Greenpeace Action v. Franklin,* 14 F. 3d 1324, 1337 (9th Cir. 1992) (upholding consultation based on uncertain data, since NOAA Fisheries made a reasonable evaluation of the best evidence available); *Stop H-3 Ass'n v. Dole,* 740 F. 2d 1442, 1460 (9th Cir. 1984), *cert. denied sub nom., Yamasaki v. Stop H-3 Ass'n,* 471 U.S. 1108 (1985) (upholding consultation where data "admittedly was weak" and there was contrary expert testimony, since there was no new or additional information the Service failed to evaluate); *Village of False Pass v. Clark,* 733 F. 2d 605, 610 (9th Cir. 1984) (minor differences between draft and final biological opinions did not fatally undermine the quality of the data).

Climate change impacts. Climate change is playing an increasingly important role in the land use planning and development process in California and is at the heart of the national debate over energy and environmental policy. Recent regulatory actions and court decisions under the ESA have begun to define the extent to which federal agencies must consider climate change impacts as part of the consultation process.

In December 2008, at the conclusion of the Bush Administration, the Service and NOAA Fisheries jointly adopted a controversial new regulation that would have substantially changed the consultation rules by limiting the obligation of federal agencies to consult under the ESA, especially with respect to climate change impacts resulting from emissions of greenhouse gases. *See* 73 Fed. Reg. 78272 (Dec. 16, 2008). A number of states, including California, sued to challenge the regulation. In March 2009, President Obama signed legislation authorizing the Secretaries of Commerce and the Interior to withdraw the regulation. In April 2009, the Secretaries jointly revoked the regulation and reinstated the prior rules on consultation.

GHG = greenhouse gas

On the other hand, the Obama Administration has kept in place a more narrow regulation that limits consideration of impacts caused by GHG emissions on the polar bear, which the Service listed as a threatened species in May 2008. Under this regulation, which was adopted on the same day as the Bush Administration's ill-fated consultation rule, the ESA's protections for the polar bear apply only to activities occurring within the bear's range. *See* 73 Fed. Reg. 76249 (Dec. 16, 2008). The regulation reflects the Service's position that consultation under the ESA is not required simply because a federal agency authorizes a project that emits GHGs. In other words, federal approval of a project in California does not require consultation on the polar bear, even though the project may emit GHGs that contribute to climate change, which in turn may adversely affect the polar bear and its habitat. The Service's rationale for this position is that "the best scientific data currently available do not show a causal connection between GHG emissions resulting from a specific Federal action and effects on listed species or critical habitat by climate change." 73 Fed. Reg. at 76266. In deciding to retain the rule, the Secretary stated in May 2009 that the ESA "is not the proper mechanism for controlling our nation's carbon emissions" and that a comprehensive climate change strategy is needed instead.[5]

---

5 The Service issued a strategy document in September 2010: *Rising to the Urgent Challenge: Strategic Plan for Responding to Accelerating Climate Change,* available at http://www.fws.gov/home/climatechange/strategy.html.

However, at least one federal court in California has ruled that the ESA requires consideration of climate change impacts when the scientific evidence shows that GHG emissions may affect specific future conditions in the area where the proposed action will occur. *See Natural Resources Defense Council v Kempthorne*, 506 F. Supp. 2d 322, 367-70 (E.D. Cal. 2007) (in evaluating the effects of water pumping operations on the Delta smelt, the Service violated the ESA by failing to include in its biological opinion any discussion of the potential effects from climate change on Delta hydrology and temperature); *Pac. Coast Fed'n of Fishermen's Ass'ns v. Gutierrez*, 606 F. Supp. 2d 1122, 1183-84 (E.D. Cal. 2008) (same conclusion with respect to NOAA Fisheries' biological opinion for salmon and steelhead).

Biological opinion. The formal consultation process under Section 7 culminates in a "biological opinion" prepared by the Service. The biological opinion evaluates whether the effects of the proposed action (including its direct and indirect effects, as well as the effects of any interrelated or interdependent actions)—taken together with any cumulative effects—are likely to jeopardize the continued existence of a listed species or destroy or adversely modify its designated critical habitat. 50 C.F.R. § 402.14(g).

If the Service makes a "jeopardy" finding (i.e., if it finds that the proposed action would jeopardize the continued existence of a listed species or adversely modify designated critical habitat), the Service must recommend reasonable and prudent alternatives to avoid the adverse impacts. 16 U.S.C. § 1536(b)(3). The action agency may depart from the Service's recommendations without violating the ESA, as long as the agency takes adequate steps to ensure the continued existence of the species. *See Tribal Village of Akutan v. Hodel*, 869 F. 2d 1185, 1193-94 (9th Cir. 1988). If there is no way to avoid jeopardizing the species, the action agency may not proceed with the project, or issue a permit for a private project, unless the Endangered Species Committee grants an exception. 16 U.S.C. § 1536(h).

"Jeopardize the continued existence" means:

[T]o engage in an action that reasonably would be expected, directly or indirectly, to reduce appreciably the likelihood of *both the survival and recovery* of a listed species in the wild by reducing the reproduction, numbers, or distribution of the species.

50 C.F.R. § 402.02 (emphasis added)

"Destruction or adverse modification of critical habitat" means:

[A] direct or indirect alteration that appreciably diminishes the value of critical habitat for *both the survival and recovery* of a listed species. Such alterations include, but are not limited to, alterations adversely modifying any of those physical or biological features that were the basis for determining the habitat to be critical.

50 C.F.R. § 402.02 (emphasis added)

As indicated by the italicized language above, under both regulatory definitions, the proposed action must appreciably diminish the survival, and not simply the recovery, of the species. In recent years, the "survival and recovery" standard has generated much controversy, with many on the conservation side of the debate arguing that the standard was not consistent with the ESA's overall purpose of conservation of engendered species and their habitat. The other side of this debate argued that Congress has implicitly approved the long-established jeopardy standard when it added the critical habitat provision to the statute.

In 2004, the Ninth Circuit invalidated the "survival and recovery" standard as applied to the adverse modification of critical habitat. The court reasoned that such a standard effectively required only consideration of the survival of the affected species, not its recovery. This was inconsistent, in the court's view, with the ESA's definition of critical habitat—which references the "conservation" of the species, a term the statute elsewhere equates to recovery. The court concluded that "the regulatory definition of 'adverse modification' gives too little protection to designated critical habitat." *Gifford Pinchot Task Force v. U.S. Fish and Wildlife Serv.*, 378 F. 3d 1059, 1069-70 (9th Cir. 2004).

In 2008, the Ninth Circuit made clear that the requirement to consider the recovery of a species, as set out in the *Gifford Pinchot* case, also applies to consideration of whether an action will jeopardize the continued existence of a species. *Nat'l Wildlife Fed'n*, 524 F. 3d at 931-33. The court flatly rejected NOAA Fisheries' claim that jeopardy is not triggered unless the action appreciably reduces *both* survival odds *and* the likelihood of recovery.

The Ninth Circuit's rulings in *Gifford Pinchot* and *National Wildlife Federation* throw into serious question the validity of many prior consultations that failed to consider recovery adequately, or even at all. *See, e.g., Oregon Natural Resources Council v. Allen*, 476 F. 3d 1031, 1032 (9th Cir. 2007) (noting that the Service voluntarily withdrew its biological opinion for part of a proposed timber harvest to consider recovery in accordance with *Gifford Pinchot*); *NRDC v. Kempthorne*, 506 F. Supp. 2d at 376-81 (biological opinion for water pumping operations did not adequately consider recovery of the Delta smelt); *Center for Biological Diversity v. Bureau of Land Management*, 422 F. Supp. 2d 1115, 1136 (N.D. Cal. 2006) (overturning biological opinion for a federal recreation area management plan where species recovery goals were ignored); *Natural Resources Defense Council v. Rogers*, 381 F. Supp. 2d 1212, 1224-34 (E.D. Cal. 2005) (Section 7 consultations on Bureau of Reclamation water contract renewals were invalidated for failure to consider recovery).

However, the Ninth Circuit recently referenced the ruling in *Gifford Pinchot* to conclude that "an area of a species' critical habitat can be destroyed without appreciably diminishing the value of critical habitat for the species' survial or recovery." *Butte Environmental Council v. United States Army Corps of Engineers*, 620 F.3d 936, 948 (9th Cir 2010). The court affirmed the Service's determination that destruction of critical habitat would not be inconsistent with a finding of no adverse modification, especially considering that a very small percentage of the species' critical habitat would be destroyed. The court quoted from the Service's handbook to explain that "adverse effects on individuals of a species or constituent elements or segments of critical habitat generally do not result in jeopardy or adverse modification determinations unless that loss, when added to the environmental baseline, is likely to result in significant adverse effects throughout the species' range, or appreciably diminish the capability of the critical habitat to satisfy essential requirements of the species."

In addition to recovery of the species, the evaluation of jeopardy in a biological opinion also must take into account the degree to which the environment has been degraded by past activities. The Ninth Circuit has rejected the view that jeopardy exists only if a project's effects are appreciably worse than the existing "baseline" conditions. *Nat'l Wildlife Fed'n*, 524 F. 3d at 929-30. The court stated that under this view, "a listed species could be gradually destroyed, so long as each step on the path to destruction is sufficiently modest. This type of slow slide into oblivion is one of the very ills the ESA seeks to prevent." *Id.* at 930. This decision makes it more difficult to make a no jeopardy finding where the baseline conditions are poor.

Where a biological opinion relies on mitigation measures for a "no jeopardy" finding, those measures must ensure that there will be no jeopardy to the continued existence of the species. *See Pac. Coast Fed'n of Fishermen's Assn's v. Bureau of Reclamation*, 426 F. 3d 1082 (9th Cir. 2005) (delayed in-stream flow requirements were insufficient to ensure near-term survival of Coho salmon in the Klamath River); *Sierra Club v. Marsh*, 816 F. 2d at 1386 (Corps violated ESA by allowing a construction project to proceed without first ensuring the acquisition and preservation of mitigation lands for the California least tern and the light-footed clapper rail); *NRDC v. Kempthorne*, 506 F. Supp. 2d at 350–59 (biological opinion was inadequate where there was no reasonable degree of certainty that mitigation actions for the Delta smelt would take place); *see also Nat'l Wildlife Fed'n*, 524 F.3d at 935-36 (finding in biological opinion that dam operations would not result in an adverse modification of critical habitat impermissibly relied on planned future structural improvements to aid fish passage, where the record showed "no clear, definite commitment of resources" to install the improvements). The degree of required mitigation can vary but the general objective is to ensure the short-term and long-term viability of the species in the area affected by the project. For animals and birds, habitat enhancement and habitat protection are likely mitigation measures. For plants, cultivation and protection of existing populations may be required.

Mitigation measures relied upon to make a no jeopardy finding must also be incorporated as requirements of the biological opinion. In *Center for Biological Diversity v. U.S. Bureau of Land Management*, 698 F.3d 1101 (9th Cir. 2012), the court overturned a biological opinion for a proposed natural gas pipeline that relied on conservation measures the project sponsor had voluntarily agreed to undertake. The biological opinion treated the measures as "cumulative" effects that lessened the project's impacts on fish species, but it did not incorporate the measures as requirements under the ESA. In rejecting this approach, the court ruled that when a biological opinion relies on mitigation measures to make a no jeopardy finding, the measures must be made enforceable under the provisions of the ESA, so that there is appropriate recourse under the ESA in the event the measures are not implemented.

As noted above, it is generally advisable for the project proponent to meet with the regulatory agencies early in the project review process. The regulations under the ESA specifically provide for "early consultation," which allows a project applicant to obtain advance approval of his or her project plans before submitting an actual permit application. 50 C.F.R. § 402.11. The early consultation results in a "preliminary biological opinion." 50 C.F.R. § 402.11(e). The preliminary biological opinion will be confirmed as final if there have been no significant changes in the proposed action or in the information used in the early consultation. 50 C.F.R. § 402.11(f).

Incidental take statement. If the proposed action will result in an "incidental take" of a listed species (i.e., a take that is incidental to the carrying out of an otherwise lawful activity), but will not result in jeopardy, the Service includes an "incidental take statement" in the biological opinion. The statement details the amount of take, the "reasonable and prudent" measures necessary to minimize the take, and mandatory terms and conditions to implement those measures. 50 C.F.R. § 402.14(i)(1). Reasonable and prudent measures and implementing terms and conditions are restricted to minor changes that do not alter the basic design, location, scope, duration, or timing of the action. 50 C.F.R. § 402.14(i)(2).

ITS = incidental take statement

The Service also imposes reporting requirements on the action to monitor the impacts of the incidental take. 50 C.F.R. § 402.14(i)(3). Any take that complies with the terms and conditions of the incidental take statement is not a prohibited act and is insulated from ESA liability. 50 C.F.R. § 402.14(i)(5).

In 2007, the Ninth Circuit published an opinion that contains several important rulings on incidental take statements. *Oregon Natural Resources Council v. Allen*, 476 F. 3d 1031 (9th Cir. 2007). First, when the Service withdraws its biological opinion for a proposed action, any incidental take statements based on the opinion are no longer valid. Second, the Service must adequately explain why a numerical standard is impractical if it decides not to include such a standard in an incidental take statement. *See also Center for Biological Diversity v. Salazar*, 695 F.3d 893 (9th Cir. 2012) (upholding ITS without a numeric take limit). Third, an incidental take statement must contain an adequate threshold (numerical or otherwise) that, if exceeded, will trigger the reinitiation of consultation (which is discussed below). A statement that simply allows the take of "all spotted owls" associated with the project is invalid, since it essentially shields the project from any requirement to reinitiate the Section 7 consultation process.

Reinitiation of consultation. Finally, there is the possible need to reinitiate consultation where discretionary federal involvement or control over the action has been retained or is authorized by law, and one or more of the following circumstances arises:
- The amount or extent of take specified in the incidental take statement is exceeded
- New information reveals that the action may affect listed species or critical habitat in a manner or to an extent not previously identified
- The action is modified in a manner that causes an effect to the listed species or critical habitat that was not considered in the biological opinion
- A new species is listed or critical habitat designated that may be affected by the action

50 C.F.R. § 402.16

In *Sierra Club v. Marsh*, the Ninth Circuit ruled that the Corps was required to reinitiate consultation where it failed to acquire 188 acres of wetlands that were needed to mitigate the impacts on two endangered birds from a combined highway and flood control project. The court explained: "We do not hold that every modification of or uncertainty in a complex and lengthy project requires the action agency to stop and reinitiate consultation." 816 F. 2d at 1388. However, the acquisition and preservation of the wetlands as a refuge for endangered birds was an essential mitigation measure, which the Service "considered absolutely necessary to insure that the project was not likely to jeopardize [the birds'] continued existence." *Id.; see also Forest Guardians v. Johanns*, 450 F. 3d 455 (9th Cir. 2006) (U.S. Forest Service was required to reinitiate consultation for the issuance of grazing permits, where it failed to comply with agreed-upon monitoring requirements and grazing limits were exceeded); *but see Envtl. Prot. Info. Ctr. v. Simpson Timber Co.*, 255 F. 3d 1073, 1081 (9th Cir. 2001) (new listing of a species did not trigger the requirement to reinitiate consultation for a permit authorizing private lumber operations where there was no ongoing federal authority or discretion over the operations).

EXEMPTIONS FROM THE ENDANGERED SPECIES ACT REQUIREMENTS

The Supreme Court's decision in *Tennessee Valley Authority v. Hill*, 437 U.S. 153 (1978), brought into sharp focus the tension between economic development and protection of endangered species. In that case, the Tennessee Valley Authority (TVA) had proposed to build a controversial dam on the Little Tennessee River. After nearly $100 million had been spent on the dam, a University of Tennessee ichthyologist discovered the tiny snail darter in the river. The Secretary designated the snail darter as an endangered species and designated the stretch of the Little Tennessee River in which the dam was located as "critical habitat."

Shortly thereafter, a group of scientists and local river users sued to halt completion and operation of the dam. The Court held that years of Congressional funding of the dam did not repeal by implication the ESA's mandate to protect endangered species. The Court upheld a lower court injunction prohibiting construction of the dam, finding that protection of endangered species had priority over the TVA's mission and the completion of the dam. *Id.* at 154. Ultimately, the dam was completed, as subsequent research found the snail darter could live in other streams, enabling the Service to determine that the dam would not jeopardize the snail.

In the wake of the *Hill* decision, Congress established the Endangered Species Committee—popularly known as the "God Squad"—to allow exemptions from the ESA's requirements. 16 U.S.C. § 1536(e). The Committee consists of seven members including the Secretaries of Agriculture, the Army, and the Interior, the Administrators of EPA and NOAA, and the Chairman of the Council of Economic Advisors. The seventh member is an individual from the affected state, appointed by the President. The Committee is authorized to allow an action that jeopardizes an endangered species to proceed if it finds that there are no reasonable and prudent alternatives and the benefits of the action "clearly outweigh the benefits of each considered alternative course of action." 50 C.F.R. § 451.02(5)(ii).

EPA = Environmental Protection Agency

In 1992, the Endangered Species Committee was convened in connection with the controversial listing of the northern spotted owl. The Director of the Bureau of Land Management sought an exemption from the ESA after the Service concluded that planned timber sales on 44 tracts of land in Oregon were likely to jeopardize the owl's continued existence. 56 Fed. Reg. 54562 (Oct. 22, 1991). The Committee granted an exemption to 13 of the proposed 44 sales, subject to mitigation and enhancement measures to be taken by BLM. 57 Fed. Reg. 23405 (June 3, 1992).

In *Portland Audubon Society v. Endangered Species Committee*, however, the Ninth Circuit upheld a challenge from environmental groups to the Committee's proceedings charging that the White House had improperly interfered with the Committee's decisionmaking process. 984 F. 2d 1534 (9th Cir. 1993). The court held the ban on *ex parte* communications found in the Administrative Procedure Act applies to the Committee's deliberations and to its communications with the White House. *Id.* at 1546; 5 U.S.C. § 577(d)(1). The court remanded the case to the Committee for an evidentiary hearing to determine the nature, content, and extent of any off-the-record communications.

Despite the Endangered Species Committee, and a few instances of special legislation overriding the ESA's requirements, compliance with the ESA remains a fundamental obligation of federal agencies, even where compliance may interfere with the agency's mission. As the Ninth Circuit has explained, the fact that federal agencies have competing interests as between their statutory mission and the mandates of the ESA does not relieve them of their "affirmative duty to satisfy the ESA's requirements, as a first priority." *Nat'l Wildlife Fed'n*, 524 F. 3d at 929.

PROHIBITIONS AGAINST TAKINGS

The consultation process under Section 7 of the ESA applies only to actions by federal agencies (including the issuance of federal permits or licenses to private parties).

In contrast, Section 9, which lists the acts prohibited by the ESA, applies to any person, including natural persons, corporations, and federal, state, and local agencies. 16 U.S.C. § 1538(a)(1).

FISH AND WILDLIFE

For fish and wildlife species listed as "endangered," Section 9(a)(1) makes it unlawful to:
- Import any such species into, or export any such species from, the United States
- Take any such species within the United States, its territorial sea, or the high seas
- Possess, sell, deliver, carry, transport, or ship, by any means whatsoever, any such species illegally taken
- Deliver, receive, carry, transport, or ship in interstate or foreign commerce, by any means whatsoever and in the course of a commercial activity, any such species
- Sell or offer for sale in interstate or foreign commerce any such species or
- Violate any regulation published by the Secretary under the ESA pertaining to any such species

16 U.S.C. 1538(a)(1)

The ESA defines the term "take" to mean "harass, harm, pursue, hunt, shoot, wound, kill, trap, capture, or attempt to engage in any such conduct." 16 U.S.C. § 1532(19).

The ESA does not directly apply these same prohibitions to "threatened" fish and wildlife species. Instead, Section 4(d) of the ESA leaves it to the Secretary to "issue such regulations as he deems necessary and advisable for the conservation of such species." 16 U.S.C. § 1533(d). The Service, however, has issued a blanket rule extending the prohibitions under Section 9 to all threatened species, unless the species is subject to its own special "4(d) rule." See 50 C.F.R. § 17.31. An example of such a 4(d) rule is the recent regulation concerning the threatened polar bear, which specifies that the ESA's protections for the bear apply only to activities occurring within the bear's range. See 73 Fed. Reg. 76249 (Dec. 16, 2008).

In contrast with the Service's blanket approach, NOAA Fisheries applies protections to threatened species under its jurisdiction on a case-by-case basis. See 50 C.F.R. pt. 223.

> In contrast with the Service's blanket approach, NOAA Fisheries applies protections to threatened species under its jurisdiction on a case-by-case basis.

PLANTS

For plant species listed as "endangered," Section 9(a)(2) makes it unlawful to:
- Import any such species into, or export any such species from, the United States
- Remove and reduce to possession any such species from areas under federal jurisdiction; maliciously damage or destroy any such species on any such area; or remove, cut, dig up, or damage or destroy any such species on any other area in knowing violation of any law or regulation of any state or in the course of any violation of a state criminal trespass law
- Deliver, receive, carry, transport, or ship in interstate or foreign commerce, by any means whatsoever and in the course of a commercial activity, any such species
- Sell or offer for sale in interstate or foreign commerce any such species, or
- Violate any regulation published by the Secretary under ESA pertaining to any such species

16 U.S.C. § 1538(a)(2). The Secretary has adopted regulations extending some, but not all, of these prohibitions to "threatened" plants. 50 C.F.R. § 17.71.

In several respects, the prohibitions applicable to plants are narrower than those applicable to fish and wildlife. First, with respect to listed wildlife species, Section 9 and its implementing regulations broadly prohibit any unauthorized "take," which includes actions that "harass" or "harm" a species through habitat destruction or modification. These broad take prohibitions do not apply to listed plants. Second, unlike for listed wildlife, the ESA provides more limited protections for listed plants on non-federal lands than for listed plants on federal land. *See* 16 U.S.C. § 1538(a)(2)(B); *Northern Callifornia River Watch v. Wilcox*, 620 F.3d 1075, 1089-90 (9th Cir. 2010) (interpreting "areas under federal jurisdiction" in Section 1538(a)(2)(B) as not including all of the "waters of the United States" as defined by the Clean Water Act and its regulations).

DEFINITION OF TAKE

A key issue under Section 9 is the scope of the "take" prohibition as applied to the modification or destruction of habitat. As noted above, the ESA's definition of "take" includes actions that "harm" or "harass" members of the species.

The ESA does not, however, define the term "harm." By regulation, the Service defines "harm" to mean "an act which actually kills or injures wildlife." 50 C.F.R. § 17.3. The regulation further states that such an act "may include significant habitat modification or degradation where it actually kills or injures wildlife by significantly impairing essential behavioral patterns, including breeding, feeding, or sheltering." *Id.*[6] This definition has led to considerable controversy regarding the type and amount of habitat modification that constitutes a prohibited "take," especially as the Service has increasingly directed its efforts at protecting habitat on both public and private lands.

In *Babbitt v. Sweet Home Chapter of Communities for a Great Oregon*, the United States Supreme Court upheld the regulatory definition of "harm," rejecting claims that the definition was facially inconsistent with the ESA. 515 U.S. 687 (1995). The Court concluded that the ordinary understanding of the word "harm," the broad species protection goals of the ESA, and the legislative history all supported the definition.

The Court acknowledged that in any particular case the Service might apply the "harm" regulation in a manner that was inconsistent with the ESA. For example, the Court stated that the plaintiffs had advanced "strong arguments" that activities that cause minimal or unforeseeable harm would not constitute a violation of the ESA, even though the Service might conclude otherwise by deciding that such activities fall within its definition of "harm." However, the Court declined to overturn the regulation, since the plaintiffs challenged only its facial validity and not its specific application, and since—in the words of Justice O'Connor's concurring opinion—the regulation "does not on its terms exceed the agency's mandate, and...has innumerable valid habitat-related applications." *Id.* at 714. Justice O'Connor's opinion nevertheless cautioned that harm occurs only where significant habitat modification "foreseeably" causes actual, "as opposed to hypothetical or speculative," death or injury to listed species. *Id.* at 708-09.

> A key issue under Section 9 is the scope of the "take" prohibition as applied to the modification or destruction of habitat.

---

6 The regulations define "harass" as "an intentional or negligent act or omission which creates a likelihood of injury to wildlife by annoying it to such an extent as to significantly disrupt normal behavioral patterns which include, but are not limited to, breeding, feeding, or sheltering." 50 C.F.R. 21 17.3

In the wake of the Supreme Court's decision in *Sweet Home*, the Ninth Circuit has in several cases applied a standard that evaluates whether death or injury to a member of a listed species is "reasonably certain to occur." In one such case, the plaintiff sued to stop the construction of a high school in Tucson, Arizona, on a site the Service designated as critical habitat for the cactus ferruginous pygmy owl, which at the time was listed as endangered. *See Defenders of Wildlife v. Bernal*, 204 F. 3d 920 (9th Cir. 2000). A biological survey showed that the only use by owls at the site involved an area the school district was not going to develop. The Ninth Circuit upheld the district court's finding that the plaintiff had not met its burden of showing that construction of the school would actually "harm" or "harass" the owl, because no owls actually used the area where construction would occur and there was evidence demonstrating the owls' ability to tolerate, and even benefit from, human activity. The court therefore allowed the project to proceed.

The court distinguished its prior decision in *Forest Conservation Council v. Rosboro Lumber Co.*, 50 F. 3d 781 (9th Cir. 1995). In that case, an expert biologist determined it was "reasonably certain" that a timber project would injure a pair of northern spotted owls by significantly impairing their breeding, feeding, and sheltering, due to the project's proximity to their nest. *See also Marbled Murrelet v. Babbitt*, 83 F. 3d 1060, 1066 (9th Cir. 1996) (upholding injunction where the evidence showed "a reasonably certain threat of imminent harm" to a protected species).

In another "harm" case, the Ninth Circuit held that the Service could not impose restrictions on grazing activities that were the subject of a Section 7 consultation, in the absence of evidence that a take was "reasonably certain to occur." *Arizona Cattle Growers Ass'n v. U. S. Fish and Wildlife Serv.*, 273 F. 3d 1229 (9th Cir. 2001). The court emphasized that the "mere potential" to harm a species does not suffice to impose conditions in an incidental take statement, and that the Service must instead demonstrate how the modification of habitat would "actually kill or injure" members of a protected species.

These decisions provide important guidance on the extent to which habitat modifications may result in a prohibited take under the ESA.

NO EXCEPTIONS FOR RELIGIOUS PRACTICES OR THE PROTECTION OF PRIVATE PROPERTY

In some cases, the taking of a threatened or endangered species is an historic part of Native American religion and tribal practices. Some wildlife protection acts, such as the Bald and Golden Eagle Protection Act, 16 U.S.C. § 668 *et seq.*, provide exceptions for these types of religious practices, but the ESA contains no exceptions. In *United States v. Billie*, the court found that the ESA's take prohibitions, as applied to the Florida black panther, did not constitute a burden on the freedom of expression or religion. 667 F. Supp. 1485 (S.D. Fla. 1987). The court found that the interest in hunting this particular species of panther was not central to the claimed tribal religious beliefs, and did not outweigh the government's interest in protecting the species.

The courts also have decided that the right to protect domestic livestock must give way to the mandates of the ESA. In *Christy v. Hodel*, the court upheld a fine of $2,500 against a rancher who shot an endangered grizzly bear that was killing his sheep. 857 F. 2d 1324, 1330 (9th Cir. 1988). Justice White, dissenting from the Supreme Court's denial of certiorari, commented that the right to protect one's property is a deeply rooted liberty interest and would have accepted the case to consider a possible Fifth Amendment claim. *See Christy v. Lujan*, 490 U.S. 1114, 1116 (1989).

The ESA, however, does not prohibit the take of a listed species in defense of one's own life or the lives of others. 50 C.F.R. § 17.21(c)(2).

HABITAT CONSERVATION PLANS AND INCIDENTAL TAKE PERMITS

The consultation process under Section 7 provides a means for a private landowner or developer to obtain permission from the Service, through the issuance of an incidental take statement in a biological opinion, for the incidental take of a listed species resulting from a development project such as the construction of homes, roads, or other facilities. But Section 7 applies only if there is an action by a federal agency, such as the provision of federal funding or the issuance of a federal permit or license.

In the absence of such a federal action, a private landowner or developer seeking authorization for an incidental take of a listed species must obtain an "incidental take permit" under Section 10 of the ESA (16 U.S.C. § 1539). To qualify for an incidental take permit, the taking of the species must be "incidental to, and not the purpose of, the carrying out of an otherwise lawful activity." 16 U.S.C. § 1539(a)(1)(B).

In addition, the landowner or developer must submit a habitat conservation plan (HCP) to the Service that specifies:

- The impacts that are likely to result from the taking
- The steps the applicant will take to mitigate and minimize the impacts
- The funding that will be available to implement such steps
- What alternative actions to the taking the applicant has considered
- The reason why the alternatives are not being adopted, and
- Such other measures as the Service may require

16 U.S.C. § 1539(a)(2)(A)

HCP = habitat conservation plan

The Service is authorized to issue an incidental take permit only if it finds that the permittee has, to the maximum extent practicable, minimized and mitigated the impacts of the taking; that adequate funding for the HCP will be provided; and that the taking will not appreciably reduce the likelihood of the survival and recovery of the species in the wild. 16 U.S.C. § 1539(a)(2)(B).

The Section 10 incidental take permit process can be quite time-consuming and complex. *See* 50 C.F.R. § 17, pts. C, D. An HCP typically takes several years to prepare and requires rigorous technical studies and extensive measures to protect the species.

Nevertheless, the Service advocates the use of HCPs as a creative and mutually beneficial way of resolving species concerns while allowing desired development to proceed. To encourage the use of HCPs, the Service in 1998 adopted the "No Surprises" rule—which is intended to assure landowners participating in an HCP that no additional land, land use restrictions, or financial compensation will be required from them in connection with their lawful land development activities in the event unforeseen circumstances arise, so long as the HCP is properly functioning. 50 C.F.R. § 17.22(b)(5). In 2007, the federal district court in Washington, D.C., upheld the rule. *Spirit of the Sage Council v. Norton*, 511 F. Supp. 2d 31 (D.D.C. 2007).

In 1996, the Service also published a handbook[7] on the Section 10 process, which contains guidance on developing and processing HCPs and applications for incidental take permits. The Service published an addendum to the handbook in 2000 to address a number of HCP issues pertaining to biological goals and objectives, adaptive

---

7 The HCP Handbook is available at http://www.fws.gov/endangered/esa-library/index.html.

management, monitoring, permit duration, and public participation. 65 Fed. Reg. 35242 (June 1, 2000).

In the absence of a Section 10 permit, purely private activity that is near or adjacent to the habitat of a listed species places the developer at risk of committing a prohibited "take," which can result in serious civil and criminal penalties and injunctive relief. The incidental take permit offers insurance against those penalties.

Despite its complexity, the HCP process is of increasing importance in California, where development often encroaches on territory inhabited by various listed species.

Multi-species planning is recognized as an effective way to protect species while minimizing economic disruptions, but such planning is difficult to implement from a practical standpoint. In 1991, at the urging of Governor Wilson, the California Legislature passed the Natural Community Conservation Planning Act (known as the NCCP Act and codified at Cal. Fish & Game Code § 2800 *et seq.*), which establishes a framework for multi-species habitat conservation planning. The NCCP Act was substantially revised in 2002 to include much greater detail regarding the procedures for the adoption of multi-species plans. The goal of the NCCP Act was to enable California to go beyond the single species focus of the ESA and to focus on preservation of entire ecosystems. The NCCP program provides for the use of scientific review panels, and calls for cooperation with the Service and development of interim measures to protect natural communities during the planning process by working closely with affected local communities.

The major NCCP efforts to date have typically been multi-agency efforts joined with HCPs, thereby providing coverage for both state and federally listed species.

SAFE HARBOR AND CANDIDATE CONSERVATION AGREEMENTS

Under the "safe harbor" policy, a private landowner may enter into an agreement with the Service whereby the landowner voluntarily agrees to manage his or her land to restore, enhance, or maintain habitats for listed species. In return, the Service assures the landowner that it will not require additional or different management activities to be undertaken without the landowner's consent in the event the species covered by the agreement become more numerous as a result of the landowner's conservation actions. The landowner also receives incidental take coverage for the actions contemplated in the agreement. At the end of the agreement period, the landowner may return the property to the baseline conditions that existed before the agreement was executed. The agreement must reasonably be expected to provide a net benefit to the affected species by contributing to its recovery. The regulations governing Safe Harbor Agreements are codified at 50 C.F.R. §§ 17.22(c), 17.32(c).

A landowner also may execute a "Candidate Conservation Agreement," through which similar incentives may be offered to a landowner who implements voluntary conservation measures for species that are candidates for listing under the ESA, as well as species likely to become candidate species. *See* 50 C.F.R. §§ 17.22(d), 17.32(d).

JUDICIAL REVIEW AND ENFORCEMENT

CITIZEN SUITS

Like the Clean Water Act, the ESA authorizes "citizen suits" to enforce the law's provisions. 16 U.S.C. § 1540(g). As a prerequisite for bringing suit, a citizen plaintiff must satisfy the requirements for "standing," which are discussed in chapter 7 (Federal and State Wetland Regulation).

The ESA's citizen suit provision authorizes three types of lawsuits: (1) suits to enjoin any person, entity, or governmental agency alleged to be in violation of the ESA or regulations issued under the authority of the ESA; (2) suits to compel the Secretary to enforce the ESA's prohibitions; and (3) suits to compel the Secretary to perform certain nondiscretionary duties, such as the obligation to designate critical habitat for listed species. The ESA does not authorize citizen suits against the Secretary concerning matters within his or her discretion. *See, e.g., Morrill v. Lujan*, 802 F. Supp. 424, 432 (S.D. Ala. 1992) (plaintiff could not utilize citizen suit provision to force the Secretary to add property to a critical habitat designation, as that was a matter left to the Secretary's discretion).

As with citizen suits under the Clean Water Act, the plaintiff must provide notice at least 60 days before filing suit. 16 U.S.C. §§ 1540(g)(2)(A)-(C). The Ninth Circuit has ruled that the failure to give the required notice requires dismissal of the suit. *See Save the Yaak Com. v. Block*, 840 F. 2d 714, 721 (9th Cir. 1988) (compliance with the 60-day notification provision is jurisdictional, and thus no citizen suit can be brought under the ESA unless and until the notification requirement is met); *but see Sierra Club v. Yeutter*, 926 F. 2d 429, 435 (5th Cir. 1991) (Fifth Circuit holding that while compliance with the 60-day notification provision is "mandatory," it is not jurisdictional "in the strictest sense of the term," and therefore may not be raised as a defense to a citizen suit for the first time on appeal). For citizen suits alleging that a party is in violation of the ESA—for example, by engaging in an activity that results in an unauthorized take of listed species—no suit may be brought if the Secretary has commenced an action to assess civil penalties or if the government has commenced and is diligently prosecuting a criminal action against the alleged violator. 16 U.S.C. §§ 1540(g)(2)(B), (C).

A six-year statute of limitations generally applies to ESA citizen suits. *See Center for Biological Diversity v. Hamilton*, 453 F. 3d 1331, 1334 (11th Cir. 2006) (dismissing as untimely lawsuit to compel Service to designate critical habitat, since more than six years had passed since the deadline for making the designation).

Successful citizen plaintiffs are entitled to attorneys' fees at the court's discretion. 16 U.S.C. § 1540(g)(4). At least in the Ninth Circuit, however, the converse is not true for prevailing defendants; they can recover fees from the plaintiff only if the court finds the plaintiff's claims were frivolous. *See Marbled Murrelet v. Babbitt*, 83 F. 3d 1060, 1094 (9th Cir. 1996).

SUITS UNDER THE ADMINISTRATIVE PROCEDURE ACT

In many instances, the ESA does not authorize citizen suits. For example, a plaintiff may not bring a citizen suit to challenge the issuance of a biological opinion, the decision to list or delist a species, the designation of critical habitat, the approval of an HCP and issuance of an incidental take permit, or the determination as a result of consultation that a proposed action is not likely to adversely affect a listed species. For these types of actions, the plaintiff instead must bring an action under the Administrative Procedure Act (APA), which provides for judicial review of final agency action. 5 U.S.C. § 704.

APA = Administrative Procedure Act

The basic standard of judicial review under the APA is the arbitrary and capricious test. 5 U.S.C. § 706. Under this test, the court may not substitute its judgment for that of that agency, but it "must engage in a careful, searching review to ensure that the agency has made a rational analysis and decision on the record before it." *Nat'l Wildlife Fed'n v. NMFS*, 524 F. 3d at 927; *see also Tucson Herpetological Society*, 566 F. 3d at 875 (agency must establish a rational connection between the facts and its final decision); *Oregon Natural Resources Council v. Allen*, 476 F. 3d 1031, 1036 (9th Cir. 2007) (agency acts arbitrarily if it fails to consider an important aspect of the problem). In addition, while a court may enjoin actions that violate the ESA, it may not fashion an injunction that eviscerates the agency's discretion. *See Sierra Club v. Yeutter*, 926 F. 2d 429, 439-40 (5th Cir. 1991) (district court acted properly in enjoining logging and in ordering preparation of a timber management plan to ensure the protection of the red-cockaded woodpecker, but the district court exceeded its authority in dictating the plan's specific contents).

JUDICIAL REMEDIES AND PENALTIES

A third avenue for judicial enforcement of the ESA (in addition to citizen suits and suits under the APA) is a civil or criminal action brought by the federal government. Any person who knowingly violates the ESA is subject to a civil penalty of not more than $25,000 for each violation. 16 U.S.C. § 1540(a)(1). Any person who knowingly violates the ESA also is subject to a criminal fine of not more than $50,000 or imprisonment for not more than one year in jail or both. *Id.* § 1540(b)(1).

With respect to criminal enforcement, at least one court has held that a "knowing" violation is a general intent crime, which means it is not necessary for the government to show that the defendant knew of the possession of an endangered species or that such possession was illegal. *See United States v. Nguyen*, 916 F. 2d 1016, 1018-19 (5th Cir. 1990). In *Nguyen*, the defendant captained a small fishing boat that the Coast Guard boarded for a safety check. During the inspection, the Coast Guard found four flippers from a threatened sea turtle. After being convicted of a misdemeanor, Nguyen appealed, claiming the instructions to the jury should have required a finding that he knew the turtle was a threatened species. In upholding his conviction, the Fifth Circuit held specific intent was not required, because Congress "clearly intended to proscribe certain acts regardless of the actor's mental state." *Id.* at 1019.

Violators also are subject to injunctive relief. In *United States v. Glenn-Colusa Irrigation District*, the court enjoined an irrigation district from operating a water pumping facility on the Sacramento River from July 15 through November 15 to protect endangered winter-run Chinook salmon. 788 F. Supp. 1126 (E.D. Cal. 1992). The court rejected arguments that enforcement required compliance with NEPA and that designation of critical habitat and designation of a recovery plan had to precede enforcement. *Id.* at 1135. In *Marbled Murrelet v. Babbitt*, the Ninth Circuit upheld an injunction prohibiting the defendant from cutting timber in an old-growth forest pursuant to a state-approved timber harvest plan. 83 F. 3d 1060, 1063 (9th Cir. 1996). The district court had found, after an eight-day trial, that the land contained habitat for the marbled murrelet, a threatened seabird, and that the proposed timber harvesting would "harm" and "harass" the bird so as to constitute a prohibited take.

CALIFORNIA ENDANGERED SPECIES ACT

CESA = California Endangered Species Act

The California Endangered Species Act (CESA) (Fish & Game Code §§ 2050-2098) provides the legal authority for the protection of threatened and endangered species by the state. The legislative policy expressed in the CESA is "to conserve, protect, restore and enhance" threatened and endangered species and their habitat and to acquire lands for habitat for threatened and endangered species. Fish & Game Code § 2052.

The CESA differs from the federal ESA in several important respects:
- Whereas the prohibitions in Section 9 of the ESA make a significant distinction between plants and animals, the take prohibitions in the CESA apply equally to *all* listed species
- Whereas the ESA authorizes the Secretary to impose lesser protections for "threatened" species than for "endangered" species, the CESA's take prohibitions apply equally to both listing categories
- Whereas the ESA does not prohibit the take of federally designated "candidate" species, the CESA prohibits the take of state-designated candidate species, unless the California Department of Fish and Wildlife (DFW) has authorized the take
- There are no provisions in the CESA for the designation of critical habitat
- There is no state consultation process, although, like the federal ESA, a take of state-listed species is prohibited without a CESA permit
- The CESA's definition of "take" is narrower than the federal definition and does not include actions that "harm" or "harass" a listed species

DFW = California Department of Fish and Wildlife

THE CESA LISTING PROCESS

The California Fish and Game Commission (Commission) is required to establish a list of threatened species and a list of endangered species. The Commission adds species to or removes them from the lists "upon the receipt of sufficient scientific information...that the action is warranted." Fish & Game Code § 2070. Interested persons may petition the Commission to add or remove a species. The petition process is described in detail in Title 14, California Code of Regulations, section 670.1. Once received by the Commission, a petition is referred to the DFW within 10 days. Fish & Game Code § 2073. The DFW must make a recommendation to the Commission within 90 days either that the petition should be accepted and considered or that the petition should be rejected. The DFW's recommendation is based on its determination of the sufficiency of the information in the petition to indicate whether or not the petitioned action may be warranted. Fish & Game Code § 2073.5.

Following the DFW's recommendation, the Commission must consider the petition and make a finding based on the DFW's recommendation at its next available meeting. If the Commission finds that a petition seeking to add a species to either list is sufficient to indicate that the petitioned action may be warranted, then the Commission publishes a notice to that effect and the species becomes a "candidate" species. Fish & Game Code § 2074.2. The CESA's take prohibitions apply to candidate species, although the DFW may authorize the take of candidate species subject to terms and conditions that it prescribes. Fish & Game Code §§ 2083, 2084.

A candidate species is evaluated by the DFW to determine whether listing is warranted, to identify preliminarily habitat that may be essential to the continued existence of the species, and to recommend management activities and other recommendations for recovery of the species. Fish & Game Code § 2074.6. The DFW has 12 months from the acceptance of the petition in which to review the status of the species and report to the Commission. Thereafter, the Commission considers the DFW's report, and makes a finding to list the species as threatened or endangered or to remove the species from candidacy. Fish & Game Code § 2075. Any finding by the Commission may be reviewed by the superior court by writ of mandate under section 1094.5 of the California Code of Civil Procedure.

In 2007, the California Court of Appeal upheld the Commission's decision to list separately under the CESA two "evolutionarily significant units" of the coho salmon. *California Forestry Ass'n. v. California Fish & Game Comm'n*, 156 Cal. App. 4th 1535 (2007). The court, deferring to the position of the Commission and the DFW, found that the definition of species under the CESA is broad enough to authorize the listing of ESUs. The court reached this conclusion even though the CESA—unlike the federal ESA—does not define species to include any taxon below a subspecies, and does not provide protections to "distinct population segments." *See* Fish & Game Code §§ 2062, 2067, 2068. The court also found that the term "range" under the CESA refers to a species' California range *only*, "thereby entitling a species to protection if it is threatened with extinction throughout all, or a significant portion, of its California range (as opposed to its worldwide range)." The court therefore rejected the view that the CESA requires the Commission and the DFW to consider the coho's *entire* geographic range, including areas outside of the state. Finally, the court determined that the state listings under the CESA were not duplicative, even though the ESUs were already protected under the federal ESA.

The case highlights the fact that the federal and state endangered species lists are distinct, with frequent dual listings under both programs. As a result, the regulatory status of a species needs to be evaluated under both programs in every instance.

In 2008, the same court that decided *California Forestry Ass'n* overturned the Commission's decision to reject a petition to list the California tiger salamander as an endangered species under the CESA. *Center for Biological Diversity v. Fish & Game Comm'n*, 166 Cal. App. 4th 597 (2008). The Commission had found there was insufficient data on population trends and loss of habitat to support the petition. But the court refused to defer to the Commission's findings, emphasizing that a petition must be accepted for consideration if it is supported by sufficient information to lead a reasonable person to conclude that there is a substantial possibility that the requested listing could occur. The court found the evidence before the Commission met this standard and, as a result, the Commission was required to accept the petition and to list the California tiger salamander as a candidate species. According to the court, the fact that the salamander is federally listed did not relieve the Commission of its duty under state law to accept and consider the petition.

Species protections have had a profound impact in recent years on water suppliers. In 2009, the Commission officially listed the longfin smelt as a threatened species under the CESA. This listing could lead to increased demands to restrict water diversions from the San Francisco Bay and Sacramento-San Joaquin Delta. Impacts to the Delta smelt and to salmon and steelhead populations already have resulted in significant restrictions on state and federal water pumping operations, and have placed immense pressures on water agencies that rely on the Delta for their water to find alternative supplies. These pressures are likely to intensify, given the growing scarcity of water in California and the importance of the Delta in supplying water to millions of Californians.

"TAKE" UNDER THE CESA

Section 2080 of the California Fish and Game Code prohibits, among other things, the "take" of species listed by the Commission as threatened or endangered. Unlike its federal counterpart, the CESA's take prohibitions do not distinguish between plants and wildlife. The actions that constitute a "take" under the CESA also differ from the federal ESA. Under Section 86 of the Fish and Game Code, "take" means to "hunt, pursue, catch, capture, or kill," or to attempt any of these acts. The definition does not by its terms cover actions that merely "harm" or "harass" a species. The California Attorney General accordingly concluded in 1995 that, in contrast to the federal ESA, the CESA does not prohibit indirect harm to listed species by way of habitat modification. 78 Ops. Cal. Atty. Gen. 137 (1995).

However, in *Department of Fish and Game v. Anderson-Cottonwood Irrigation District*, the court held that the CESA's definition of "take" is not limited to direct actions such as hunting or fishing. 8 Cal. App. 4th 1554 (1992). The court therefore concluded the CESA's take prohibitions applied to the incidental and inadvertent killing of winter-run chinook salmon at an irrigation district's pumping facilities. *Id.* at 1568.

In 2010, the court clarified that a state agency, such as the California Department of Water Resources, is a "person" within the meaning of Section 2080, which prohibits any "person" from taking an endangered or threatened species without appropriate permit authority from the DFW. *Kern County Water Agency v. Watershed Enforcers*, 185 Cal. App. 4th 969, 973 (2010).

INCIDENTAL TAKE PERMITS UNDER THE CESA

Before 1998, the CESA provided that the DFW, among other things, may authorize the "take" of threatened or endangered species for "management purposes" through permits or memoranda of understanding. Unlike the federal ESA, the CESA did not expressly provide DFW with the authority to issue permits for the "incidental take" of state-listed species. As a result, the DFW historically interpreted the term "management purposes" broadly to include land use or development projects that could result in the incidental take of a threatened or endangered species. It then issued a "Management Authorization" to the project proponent to authorize the take and to require mitigation.

But this practice was invalidated in *Planning and Conservation League v. Dep't of Fish and Game*, 55 Cal. App. 4th 479, 482 (1997). This left the DFW without any ability to authorize the take of state-listed species in connection with land use or development projects.

The Legislature quickly solved this problem by amending the CESA to provide the DFW with explicit incidental take authority. Senate Bill 879 amended section 2081 of the Fish and Game Code to authorize the DFW to issue permits allowing the "incidental take" of state-listed species, subject to several conditions:

- The impacts of the authorized take must be "fully mitigated"
- The mitigation must be "roughly proportional" to the impact
- The applicant must ensure adequate funding to implement the mitigation measures and to monitor the effectiveness of the measures
- Take permits cannot be issued if they would jeopardize the continued existence of the species

Fish & Game Code §§ 2081(b), (c)

For species listed under both the state and federal acts, the DFW may rely on a federal incidental take statement or permit to authorize a take under the CESA. Fish & Game Code § 2080.1. However, a recent decision by the California Supreme Court illustrates that there are important differences between federal and state law regarding incidental take permits. *See Envtl. Prot. and Info. Ctr. v. Cal. Dep't of Forestry*, 44 Cal. 4th 459 (2008) ("*EPIC*").

> In 2010, the court clarified that a state agency, such as the California Department of Water Resources, is a "person" within the meaning of Section 2080, which prohibits any "person" from taking an endangered or threatened species without appropriate permit authority from the DFW.

As explained above, there is a "No Surprises" policy under federal law, such that those who obtain an ESA Section 10 permit through preparation of an HCP are assured that they will not be required, if unforeseen events occur, to undertake mitigation that is above and beyond the measures set forth in the permit and HCP. But in *EPIC*, the California Supreme Court struck down the use of a No Surprises clause in a CESA incidental take permit issued to Pacific Lumber Company authorizing the take of the marbled murrelet incidental to logging activities.

The Court emphasized that, unlike the language of the federal ESA, the CESA's text requires that the impact of an incidental take be "fully mitigated." Fish & Game Code § 2081(b). This means that Pacific Lumber's mitigation obligations cannot be limited in advance to exclude mitigation for future impacts resulting from changed circumstances and unforeseen events such as natural disasters. The Court reasoned that when natural disasters change the baseline environmental conditions, logging activities may have adverse impacts, which they previously did not have, on protected species. The Court further posited that logging activities may even make disasters such as floods and fires more frequent or more severe, thus contributing to the impacts from the disaster on protected species. In the Court's view, the CESA requires permit holders to assume responsibility for mitigating these types of impacts. As a result, a permit clause that precludes the DFW's ability to impose additional mitigation to address future conditions as they arise is inconsistent with the CESA's mandates.

The decision in *EPIC* likely will complicate efforts in California to integrate federal and state permitting for endangered species. As a result of the decision, applicants for incidental take permits could face greater mitigation obligations under the CESA than under the federal ESA for the same actions affecting the same species. It also may become increasingly difficult for the DFW to rely on federal take authorizations to allow an incidental take of state-listed species, even though the CESA specifically authorizes this practice.

CHAPTER 9

Design Review, Historic Preservation, Williamson Act, Coastal Development, Stormwater, Prevailing Wage and Public Bidding

INTRODUCTION

This chapter discusses the following sources of regulation by which local, regional, state, and federal governments protect important resources and interests typically affected by development:
- Design review
- Historic preservation
- Williamson Act contracts
- Coastal development
- Storm water requirements
- Prevailing wage and public bidding

DESIGN REVIEW

When a city considers adopting or implementing a design or architectural review process, one issue that often arises is the legality of aesthetic control. Aesthetic regulation is permissible if it is reasonably related to public health, safety, or welfare. Broad latitude is given to cities in exercising this control. *See Metromedia, Inc. v. City of San Diego*, 26 Cal. 3d 848, 863 (1980); *see also Ehrlich v. City of Culver City*, 12 Cal. 4th 854, 881–882 (1996).

> Aesthetic regulation is permissible if it is reasonably related to public health, safety, or welfare.

Although design review might limit the use of, diminish the value of, or impose additional costs upon property, it does not impose requirements for either conveyances of land or monetary exactions. As a result, design review is a general regulation of land use that is not subject to the higher scrutiny test employed in *Nollan* and *Dolan*. *See Breneric Assocs. v. City of Del Mar*, 69 Cal. App. 4th 166, 176–77 (1998) (rejecting application of the *Nollan-Dolan* heightened scrutiny standard to design review). For a thorough discussion of *Nollan* and *Dolan*, see chapter 11 (Takings) and chapter 12 (Exactions). Therefore, denial of a design review application will be upheld so long as the denial substantially advances a legitimate governmental interest related to public health, safety or welfare and is supported by substantial evidence.

The leading case is *Novi v. City of Pacifica*, where the court upheld a city's ordinance that precluded "monotonous" developments and uses detrimental to the "general welfare." 169 Cal. App. 3d 678, 682 (1985). Responding to a claim the ordinance was unconstitutionally vague, the court stated, "[i]n fact, a substantial amount of vagueness is permitted in California zoning ordinances...." *Id.* For a more detailed discussion of the sufficiency of development standards in zoning ordinances, see chapter 4 (Zoning).

Similarly, the court in *Ross v. City of Rolling Hills Estates,* relying on *Novi,* held that a view protection ordinance was not unconstitutionally vague, and that such an ordinance supported denial of a building permit. 192 Cal. App. 3d 370, 376 (1987); *see also Echevarrieta v. City of Rancho Palos Verdes,* 86 Cal. App. 4th 472, 484–485 (2001) (ordinance prohibiting residents from significantly impairing a view by permitting foliage growth in excess of certain limitations was not unconstitutionally vague); *Briggs v. City of Rolling Hills Estates,* 40 Cal. App. 4th 637, 643 (1995) ("neighborhood compatibility" ordinance requiring that designs "respect the existing privacy of surrounding properties" was not void for vagueness).

In *Guinnane v. San Francisco City Planning Commission,* the court supported a city's concerns regarding neighborhood aesthetics. 209 Cal. App. 3d 732 (1989). Guinnane sought a building permit to construct a four-story, 6,000-square-foot house with five bedrooms, five baths, and parking for two cars. The planning commission rejected Guinnane's application during design review because the proposed building was too massive and "not in character" with the neighborhood. The board of permit appeals also denied the permit.

Upholding the city's action, the court stated the planning commission and the appeals board had the authority to exercise discretion in deciding whether to issue the permit. *Id.* at 742. The court noted such review is not limited to a determination of whether the applicant has complied with zoning ordinances and building codes. The San Francisco Planning Code specifically directed the commission to protect the "character and stability" of residential areas, and the court noted such concern for neighborhood aesthetics has long been justified as a legitimate governmental objective. Sufficient evidence existed to uphold the commission's finding the proposed house would increase traffic, cause parking problems, and have a negative effect on the neighborhood. *Id.*

Similarly, the court in *Saad v. City of Berkeley* upheld the City of Berkeley's denial of a use permit for a three-story home in a single-family zone because it would impair the view of neighboring property owners, and would have a towering effect. 24 Cal. App. 4th 1206, 1216 (1994); *see also Harris v. City of Costa Mesa,* 25 Cal. App. 4th 963, 973 (1994) (upholding denial of a use permit for second residential unit on one lot based on incompatibility with the neighborhood).

Another court clarified that a city can regulate tree growth for aesthetic reasons alone. *See Kucera v. Lizza,* 59 Cal. App. 4th 1141, 1149 (1997). There, the court upheld a land use ordinance preserving access to views and sunlight by regulating obstructing trees and tree growth as a valid exercise of police power. *Id.*

In *Crown Motors v. City of Redding,* the city adopted an urgency ordinance prohibiting electronic reader boards, finding the ordinance necessary for the immediate preservation of the public peace, health, and safety under Government Code section 36937(b), which allows cities to designate urgency ordinances that take effect immediately upon final passage. 232 Cal. App. 3d 173, 176 (1991). The court held the city council had the right to interpret "public health" to include the quality of life as it is affected by the aesthetics of the city, stating, "[m]ental health is certainly included in the public health." *Id.* at 178.

Tahoe Regional Planning Agency v. King further supports a city's power to regulate design of structures. 233 Cal. App. 3d 1365 (1991). There, the court held that *First English Evangelical Lutheran Church v. County of Los Angeles,* 482 U.S. 304 (1987), did not preclude the historic use of legitimate land use regulations for the removal of billboards

> The San Francisco Planning Code specifically directed the commission to protect the "character and stability" of residential areas, and the court noted such concern for neighborhood aesthetics has long been justified as a legitimate governmental objective.

after a reasonable amortization period. *Id.* at 1397, 1400. For a thorough discussion of *First English, see* chapter 11 (Takings). The court also held that *Nollan* did not eliminate aesthetics or scenic zoning as a legitimate focus of such regulations. *Id.* at 1401.

The court in *Friends of Davis v. City of Davis* upheld a city's interpretation of its own design review ordinance. 83 Cal. App. 4th 1004, 1014 (2000). There, citizens asked the city to use its design review ordinance to prevent a Borders bookstore from locating in the city. The city refused, taking the position its ordinance did not extend to tenant approval, but was limited to a detailed review of the exterior design and appearance of a proposed project. Upholding the city's interpretation, the court noted that a city is not required to have a design review ordinance, but when it chooses to do so, the scope of such review is determined by the city. *Id.* at 1014.

The court in *Friends of Davis* also clarified some limits with respect to a city's power to regulate aesthetics. A city may not exercise its discretion "carte blanche" to exclude a retailer that some citizens do not like. An ordinance proposing to do so "would confer on the City's planning department virtually unrestrained power to decide who may and who may not do business in the City." *Id.*

There are other significant limitations on a city's ability to exercise its police power to control aesthetics. For instance, a city cannot unduly infringe on a person's freedom of speech. The courts scrutinize more closely a city's action in furthering aesthetics when the action could jeopardize a citizen's right to free speech. The United States Supreme Court invalidated a city ordinance enacted to minimize visual clutter caused by signs, which was utilized to prohibit a sign reading "For Peace in the Gulf" on private property. *See City of Ladue v. Gilleo*, 512 U.S. 43, 54–55 (1994). In another case, the court held an ordinance prohibiting adult cabaret operations near a freeway violated First Amendment free speech rights, because the city did not have a legitimate interest in protecting its "image." *Gammoh v. City of Anaheim*, 73 Cal. App. 4th 186, 191 (1999).

Moreover, a city cannot infringe upon certain registered trademarks. *See Blockbuster Videos, Inc. v. City of Tempe*, 141 F. 3d 1295 (9th Cir. 1998). In *Blockbuster*, the Ninth Circuit held that section 1121(b) of the Lanham Act (15 U.S.C. § 1121 (b)) preempted the City's attempt to require alterations in the depictions of registered trademarks on outdoor signs. *Id.* at 1296. The city required all exterior signs in a shopping center to conform to a shopping center's sign package, which typically specified such things as the color, and allowed businesses to apply for variances. Blockbuster was denied permission to use the blue awning with yellow letters that is one of its own marks. In ruling partially against the city, the court stated that part of the legislative intent behind the Lanham Act was to protect registered marks from interference by state or local government. *Id.* at 1300. While the city could not require alterations of a registered mark, it retained the power of all municipalities to regulate whether and where signs may be placed and their size.

Aesthetic considerations in a city's design review process are distinct from considerations governing CEQA review of a project's visual impacts. This concept is underpinned by common practice and case law. In *Bowman v. City of Berkeley*, the court held that some aesthetic issues remain "the province of local design review, not CEQA," and that a "contrary holding that mandated redundant analysis would only produce needless delay and expense." 122 Cal. App. 4th 572, 594 (2004). Likewise, the court in *Guinnane v. San Francisco City Planning Commission* held "the environmental review process is not the same as the permit approval process" such that where a negative declaration found no significant impact for a proposed residence that was "not in character" and "significantly more massive and of a larger scale than adjoining dwellings," the city still

CEQA = California Environmental Quality Act

was justified in disapproving a permit because it "went beyond environmental concerns and focused instead on the suitability of the project within the affected neighborhood." 209 Cal. App. 3d 732, 735, fn.2, 742–43 (1989). Design review therefore can function as a complementary process, remaining distinct in its purview. *Bowman*, 122 Cal. App. 4th at 594. For example, the design review process itself can be found to mitigate purely aesthetic impacts to insignificance. *Id.*

Ultimately, what process should apply appears to hinge on the scope of the project impact at issue. CEQA review is concerned with bigger picture items, such as the effect of a project on the community at large, whereas a design review board concerns itself with a relatively narrow scope of persons—the neighbors and other circumscribed classes. Under CEQA, the question is "whether a project will affect the environment of persons in general, not whether a project will affect particular persons." *Porterville Citizens for Responsible Hillside Development v. City of Porterville*, 157 Cal. App. 4th 885, 900–901 (2007) (no CEQA aesthetic impacts where two neighbors complained that 219-home subdivision on hillside would harm views); *see also Banker's Hill, Hillcrest, Park West Community Preservation Group v. City of San Diego*, 139 Cal. App. 4th 249, 279 (2006) (no CEQA impact where inhabitants of a 14-story condominium building suffered view obstruction caused by construction of a same-height multifamily residential building); *Mira Mar Mobile Community v. City of Oceanside*, 119 Cal. App. 4th 477, 493 (2006) (no CEQA aesthetic impact where project obstructed ocean views enjoyed by members of 173-unit mobile home community); *Bowman*, 122 Cal. App. 4th at 586 "([O]bstruction of a few private views is not generally regarded as a significant environmental impact."); *Association for Protection of Environmental Values in Ukiah v. City of Ukiah*, 2 Cal. App. 4th 720, 734 (1991) (height, view, privacy, soil stability, and water runoff objections did not merit CEQA review where approximately 16 neighbors were impacted); *Topanga Beach Renters Assn. v. Dep't of Gen. Servs.*, 58 Cal. App. 3d 188, 195 (1976) (no CEQA study necessary for impacts on inhabitants of 79 structures where beach restoration required demolition of the buildings). For more discussion of CEQA, see chapter 6 (CEQA).

HISTORIC PRESERVATION

FEDERAL LEVEL

NHPA = National Historic Preservation Act

The National Historic Preservation Act is the primary federal historic preservation statute. 16 U.S.C. § 470 *et seq.* The NHPA sets forth a comprehensive program to carry out the national policy of protecting America's historic and cultural resources. It authorizes activities that implement the federal historic preservation program, including (1) the National Register of Historic Places (identifying and listing historic and cultural resources); (2) an expanded national register to include sites of state and local significance; (3) the matching grants-in-aid program, encouraging preservation activities at the state and local levels; (4) the Advisory Council on Historic Preservation, providing information on historic properties; and (5) the "section 106" review process.[1] For a thorough discussion of historic preservation at the federal, state, and local levels,

---

1 Section 106 (16 U.S.C. § 470(f)) provides the basic federal legal protection for historic sites. It requires agencies to identify and assess the effects of federal actions on cultural resources included in or eligible for listing in the National Register of Historic Places. It also requires federal agencies responsible for actions that affect National Register-listed or eligible properties to consult with the State Historic Preservation Office (SHPO), local officials, affected Indian tribes, applicants for federal assistance, and the public. The agency also must allow the Advisory Council to comment on the undertaking. The primary goal of section 106 consultation is to avoid adverse effects on National Register-eligible or listed properties. If avoidance is impossible, consulting parties must attempt to minimize or mitigate adverse effects.

see Juergensmeyer and Roberts, *Land Use Planning and Development Regulation Law* (3d ed. 2012).

STATE LEVEL

Public Resources Code section 5020 *et seq.* is California's state historic preservation statute. California law does not prohibit local control of historic properties; rather it assists local entities in encouraging historic preservation. Public Resources Code section 5020.1 established the California Register of Historic Resources, which is the authoritative listing and guide to be used by cities to identify existing historic resources deserving of protection. Once an historic site is included in the register, any project that may have an adverse impact on the site is deemed a project for CEQA purposes. *See* James Longtin, *Longtin's California Land Use*, § 3.11[7] (2012 update). CEQA defines historic resources more broadly than federal law, and includes both procedural and substantive project review requirements. Agencies must implement feasible mitigation measures or alternatives for projects that would cause significant adverse impacts. For further discussion of CEQA and historic resources, see chapter 6 (CEQA).

Although California imposes stricter environmental review requirements than required under the NHPA, the state also has created significant financial incentives to help preserve historic resources. The State Historical Building Code (SHBC) is an alternative building code that guides historic building rehabilitations and can offer substantial cost savings over the Uniform Building Code. The SHBC addresses accessibility, seismic, structural, infrastructure, and energy issues. The "triggers" for full upgrading to current standards that exist in other codes are not recognized by the SHBC, which concentrates instead on resolution of safety considerations. Note the SHBC is "designed to encourage private owners to preserve historically significant properties," and does not authorize the city to *prevent* changes to an historic structure. *See Prentiss v. City of South Pasadena*, 15 Cal. App. 4th 85, 96-98 (1993) (emphasis in original). If the property owner has complied with the Uniform Building Code, the city has no discretion to deny the building permit on historical preservation grounds.

SHBC = State Historical Building Code

LOCAL LEVEL

Some of the most important historic preservation work occurs at the local level. Cities have the authority under their general police power to protect property of historical and aesthetic significance. *See* David L. Callies, *Historic Preservation Law in the United States*, 32 Envtl. L. Rep. 10348 (March 2002). In the leading case of *Penn Central Transportation Company v. City of New York*, the United States Supreme Court affirmed the broad scope of authority the general police power provides cities to regulate property of historical interest. 438 U.S. 104, 131 (1978). There, the property owners claimed that New York City's landmark preservation law, which prohibited construction of a 54-story office building on top of Grand Central Station, constituted an unlawful taking. The Court rejected their claims, finding the local regulation valid, since it provided the owners with a reasonable beneficial use of their property, while fostering an important government interest.

Although the Court never mentioned the police power specifically, it made clear that local regulation of landmarks and historic districts falls within the scope of permissible government objectives. The Court observed that because it already had recognized "in a number of settings, that States and cities may enact land-use restrictions or controls to enhance the quality of life by preserving the character and desirable aesthetic features of a city," the property owners challenging the law did not even contest the legitimacy of the city's interest in preserving "structures and areas with special historic, architectural, or cultural significance." *Id.* at 129; *see also Bohannon v. City of San Diego*, 30 Cal. App. 3d 416, 423 (1973) (rejecting a takings challenge of a local measure that regulated the use of architectural styles in remodeling and repairs as a means of historic preservation; "[r]egulations and restrictions upon the use of property in an exercise of the police power for an authorized purpose do not constitute the taking of property without compensation or give rise to constitutional cause for complaint").

Under Government Code section 25373 (counties) and Government Code section 37361 (cities), local governments have the authority to acquire property for the preservation or development of an historical landmark, as well as the development of recreational purposes and facilities therein. These provisions also provide broad local authority to impose conditions to protect and enhance "places, building, structures, works of art, and other objects, having a special character or special historical or aesthetic interest or value." This local control "may include appropriate and reasonable control of the use or appearance of neighboring private property within public view, or both." Gov't Code § 31361(b).

As another incentive for the preservation of historical property listed in either federal, state or local registers, state law provides that an owner of any qualified historic property may enter into a contract with the city to restrict the use of the property in exchange for lowered assessment values. The city must inspect the interior and exterior of the property premises prior to a new agreement and every five years thereafter to ensure the property continues to meet the standards for a qualified historical property and the owner has not breached any conditions of the contract. *See* Gov't Code 50280 § *et seq.*

An exemption from local preservation laws does exist for non-commercial property owned by religious institutions. Gov't Code §§ 25373, 37361. The exemption applies even where the institution no longer uses or is capable of using a property for a religious purpose, or where it intends to sell the property for profit. *California-Nevada Annual Conference of the United Methodist Church v. City and County of San Francisco*, 173 Cal. App. 4th 1559, 1564–66 (2009) (church could sell property to condominium developer where it did not exist for profit, objected to imposition of landmarking regulations, and could show substantial hardship would result from regulations).

Generally, a city will initiate a preservation program through appropriate enabling legislation that establishes a preservation overlay zone, sets forth criteria for inclusion in the district, and creates an administrative body to review proposals. Under this regulatory scheme, property owners of designated historic sites must seek board approval prior to making any changes to the property. Cities also may impose duties on these property owners through local anti-neglect or minimum maintenance ordinances to prevent demolition by dereliction.

Careful drafting of local historic preservation ordinances can thwart constitutional challenges. For example, incorporating NHPA review standards, which have received extensive treatment in the case law, can protect an ordinance from a vagueness challenge. Similarly, the inclusion of flexible provisions or of "safety valves," which allow for exceptions where economic hardship would otherwise result, may reduce the risk of a potential takings challenge. Cities should consider inclusion of three elements when designing and implementing an historic preservation program: (1) a survey to establish the requisite nexus for designation and regulation of historic sites; (2) a way to provide technical and economic assistance to affected property owners; and (3) some means of synchronizing the preservation program with a city's general plan, zoning ordinances, or other regulatory programs.

PRESERVATION OF AGRICULTURAL LANDS BY WILLIAMSON ACT CONTRACT

As development expands into areas historically devoted to agricultural uses, it is important for cities and property owners to be familiar with restrictions on the development of farmland. California's primary farmland preservation law is the California Land Conservation Act of 1965, Government Code § 51200 *et seq.*, commonly known as the Williamson Act. The Williamson Act sets forth a framework based on traditional contract law whereby landowners within locally designated agricultural preserves may voluntarily place restrictions on agricultural lands in exchange for tax reductions and other incentives. *See County of Marin v. Assessment Appeals Bd.*, 64 Cal. App. 3d 319, 325-326 (1976) (to achieve the objectives of the Act, and give each party the benefit of its bargain, a Williamson Act contract is to be interpreted like any other form of contract).

The Williamson Act was adopted by the Legislature to maintain the agricultural economy of the state, to assure sufficient food supplies, to discourage the premature and unnecessary conversion of agricultural lands, to discourage discontiguous urban development patterns, and to preserve the open space and aesthetic values of agricultural lands. Gov't Code § 51220; *see also Kelsey v. Colwell*, 30 Cal. App. 3d 590, 594-595 (1973).

As of January 1, 2009, roughly 15 million of California's 30 million acres of farm and ranch land were restricted by Williamson Act contracts. *See The California Land Conservation (Williamson) Act Status Report*, California Department of Conservation (2010).[2] The Williamson Act is estimated to save agricultural landowners from 20 to 75 percent in property tax liabilities each year. *See* California Legislative Analyst's Office, *Analysis of the 2004-05 Budget Bill* (February 2004). For an overview of the Williamson Act and an analysis of its role in shaping national farmland preservation efforts, *see* Joshua Safran, *Contracting for Preservation: An Overview of State Agricultural District Programs*, 27 Zoning and Planning Law Report 7 (July/August 2004).

Any city may, by resolution and after a public hearing, establish an agricultural preserve under the Williamson Act. Preserves must be established to define the boundaries of those areas within which the city will be willing to enter into Williamson Act contracts. Proposals to establish an agricultural preserve must be submitted to the planning department of the city having jurisdiction over the land. Gov't Code § 51234. Agricultural preserves generally must consist of no less than 100 acres, but may be smaller if the city finds that smaller preserves are necessary due to the unique characteristics of the agricultural enterprises in the area and are consistent with the general plan. Gov't Code § 51230. While agricultural preserves are nominally limited to "agricultural land," the Williamson Act broadly defines this term to include lands within a scenic highway corridor, wildlife habitat areas, saltponds, managed wetland areas, submerged areas, or federal conservation reserve areas. Similarly, the required dedication of such lands to "agricultural uses" includes recreational and open space uses and greenhouses. Gov't Code §§ 51201, 51205. Agricultural preserves generally continue

> The Williamson Act was adopted by the Legislature to maintain the agricultural economy of the state, to assure sufficient food supplies, to discourage the premature and unnecessary conversion of agricultural lands, to discourage discontiguous urban development patterns, and to preserve the open space and aesthetic values of agricultural lands.

---

2 *Available at* http://www.consrv.ca.gov/dlrp/lca/stats_reports/Documents/2010%20Williamson%20Act%20Status%20Report.pdf.

in full effect following annexation, detachment, incorporation, or disincorporation of land within the preserve. Gov't Code § 51235.

Parcels proposed for inclusion under Williamson Act contract must be large enough to sustain agricultural uses; parcels are presumed to be large enough if the land is at least 10 acres in size in the case of prime agricultural land or at least 40 acres in size in the case of nonprime agricultural land. Gov't Code § 51222. Every Williamson Act contract must provide for the exclusion of all uses incompatible with agricultural uses. Gov't Code § 51243. While the determination of what uses are "compatible" with agricultural uses is generally left to the discretion of each city, such compatibility determinations must be accompanied by certain findings and conducted in a manner that recognizes that a permanent or temporary population increase often hinders or impairs agricultural operations. Gov't Code §§ 51220.5, 51238, 51238.1. Williamson Act contracts also must be binding upon and inure to the benefit of all successors in interest of the contracting landowner. Gov't Code § 51243. However, where a city files a protest to a Williamson Act contract with the county board of supervisors prior to the county's execution of the contract, the city may, where certain requirements are met, have the option not to succeed to the county's rights, duties, and powers under the contract upon annexation of the contracted land into the city. Government Code section 51243.5 identifies detailed requirements that must be met for such an option to exist.

> Cities are authorized to enter into contracts providing for restrictions, terms, and conditions, including payments and fees, more restrictive than called for in the Williamson Act.

Cities are authorized to enter into contracts providing for restrictions, terms, and conditions, including payments and fees, more restrictive than called for in the Williamson Act. Gov't Code § 51240. While not all contracts affecting land within a preserve need to be identical, discrepancies in terms must relate to differences in location and characteristics of the land, and all contracts must be made pursuant to uniform rules adopted by the city. Gov't Code §§ 51231, 51241.

Williamson Act contracts must provide for an initial term of no less than 10 years and must provide that on the anniversary date of the contract, or such other annual date as specified by the contract, a year will be added automatically to the initial term unless a notice of nonrenewal is given by the landowner or the city. Gov't Code § 51244. Where the initial term of the contract is more than 10 years, the contract may provide that on a specified annual date, beginning with the anniversary date on which the contract will have an unexpired term of nine years, a year will be added automatically to the initial term unless a notice of nonrenewal is given. Gov't Code § 51244.5. This requirement means that no matter when the notice of nonrenewal is given, the contract has at least nine additional years to run.

If either the landowner or the city desires not to renew the contract, that party must serve written notice of nonrenewal upon the other before the annual renewal date of the contract. Unless such written notice is served by the landowner at least 90 days before the renewal date or by the city at least 60 days before the renewal date, the contract is considered to be automatically renewed. Gov't Code § 51245. Once the notice of nonrenewal is timely served, the existing contract remains in effect for the balance of the period remaining under the contract. Gov't Code § 51246(a).

Because a notice of nonrenewal typically takes about a decade to become effective, landowners of restricted agricultural lands wishing to develop their lands for nonagricultural uses sooner often seek a contract cancellation. Any owner of lands restricted under the Williamson Act may petition the city council for cancellation of any Williamson Act contract as to all or any part of the subject lands. Gov't Code §§ 51281, 51282. The landowner's petition must be accompanied by a proposal for a specified alternative use of the land. Gov't Code § 51282(e). Prior to taking action on the petition for cancellation, the county assessor of the county in which the land is located must determine the current fair market value of the land as though it were free of the contractual restriction. Gov't Code § 51283(a). Because this valuation is the basis for calculating the cancellation fee that will be due if the petition for cancellation is approved, the landowner may contest the assessor's valuation. Gov't Code §§ 51203(b); 51283(a).

Prior to giving tentative approval to the cancellation of the contract, the city must determine and certify to the county auditor the amount of the cancellation fee that the landowner must pay the county treasurer upon cancellation. The fee is calculated as an amount equal to 12.5 percent of the current fair market value of the land as though it were free of the contractual restriction. Gov't Code § 51283(b). Under limited circumstances, the city council may waive some or all of the cancellation fee. Gov't Code § 51283(c). Cancellation fees also may be avoided in certain cases if the canceling landowner places an agricultural conservation easement on other land within the county that is of equal size or larger than the land subject to the contract, and is equally or more suitable for agricultural use. Gov't Code § 51256(c). Such an "easement exchange" requires approval by the State Department of Conservation. Gov't Code § 51256.1.

The city council may approve cancellation of a Williamson Act contract only if it finds, at a noticed public hearing, the cancellation is consistent with the purposes of the Williamson Act or is in the public interest. Gov't Code §§ 51282(a), 51284; *Sierra Club v. City of Hayward*, 28 Cal. 3d 840, 852 (1981) (holding that cancellation provisions of Williamson Act were included to deal with strictly "emergency situations" where the public interest no longer dictates that the contract be continued). Such findings must be supported by substantial evidence. *Friends of East Willits Valley v. County of Mendocino*, 101 Cal. App. 4th 191, 204 (2002).

A determination that cancellation is consistent with the Williamson Act's purposes must be supported by all of the following findings:
- Cancellation is for land on which a notice of nonrenewal has been served
- Cancellation is not likely to result in the removal of adjacent lands from agricultural use
- Cancellation is for an alternative use that is consistent with the city's general plan
- Cancellation will not result in discontiguous patterns of urban development
- There is no proximate noncontracted land which is available and suitable for the use proposed on the contracted land unless the use of such land would provide less contiguous patterns of urban development

Gov't Code § 51282(b)

A determination that cancellation is in the public interest must be supported by findings that other public concerns substantially outweigh the objectives of the Williamson Act, and that there is no proximate noncontracted land that is available and suitable for the use proposed on the contracted land unless the use of such land would provide less contiguous patterns of urban development. Gov't Code § 51282(c); *Save Panoche Valley v. San Benito County*, 217 Cal. App. 4th 503, 516–519 (2013) (upholding county's determination that cancellation for a proposed solar facility was in the public interest on basis of these findings, including finding that the public interest in renewable energy outweighed the purpose of the Williamson Act).

Upon approval of cancellation, a certificate of tentative cancellation is recorded. Once the landowner has satisfied all conditions and contingencies in the certificate of tentative cancellation, including payment of the cancellation fee, a certificate of cancellation of contract is recorded. Gov't Code § 51283.4. Judicial review of final city council determinations regarding contract cancellations must be brought within 180 days under Code of Civil Procedure section 1094.5. Gov't Code § 51286.

To facilitate a lot line adjustment pursuant to Government Code section 66412(d) the parties may mutually agree to rescind a Williamson Act contract or contracts and simultaneously enter into a new contract or contracts, provided that the board or council makes certain findings. Gov't Code § 51257. In the event the state fails to make payments or reduces a subvention required under Government Code sections 16142.1 or 16142.1 to replace revenues lost as a result of a Williamson Act contract, the affected property may be kept under such contract for a period of up to 10 years if the city approves a contract (entered into prior to January 1, 2016) between the landowner and a nonprofit land-trust organization, nonprofit entity or public agency in which the nonprofit entity or public agency agrees to make a contribution to the city equal to the foregone tax revenue. Gov't Code § 51257.5.

In 1998, the Legislature established an optional program within the Williamson Act allowing owners of certain important farmlands to create "farmland security zones." Gov't Code §§ 51296, 51296.1, 51296.8. Landowners may elect to rescind their traditional 10-year Williamson Act contracts by entering into 20-year farmland security zone contracts, which afford the benefits of significantly lower property tax bills and exemptions from parcel taxes, annexation, and designation for school use. Gov't Code §§ 51296.1, 51296.2(a); Rev. & Tax. Code § 423.4.

In addition, with approval by the Department of Conservation in consultation with the Department of Food and Agriculture, landowners and local officials may simultaneously rescind Williamson Act contracts and enter into easements allowing photovoltaic solar facilities on the same land for a term of no less than 20 years, except as specified. *See* Gov't Code § 51190 *et seq*.

Finally, in 2013, the Legislature enacted the Urban Agriculture Incentive Zones Act to authorize landowners and local agencies to enter into contracts that restrict the use of vacant, unimproved, or blighted lands between 0.10 and 3 acres for small-scale agricultural use, in exchange for a reduced tax assessment. *See* Gov't Code § 51040 *et seq*. Contracts must run for at least five years and may not be entered into or renewed after January 1, 2019. Gov't Code § 51042(b)(1), (e).

CALIFORNIA COASTAL COMMISSION

The California Coastal Commission was established by voter initiative in 1972 in order to control and regulate the use of land and water in the coastal areas of California. It was later made permanent by the Legislature through the adoption of the California Coastal Act of 1976 (Act). Pub. Res. Code § 30000 *et seq*. Under the Act, the mission of the Coastal Commission is to "protect, maintain and, where feasible, enhance and restore the overall quality" of the environmental and human-based resources of the California coast and ocean for environmentally sustainable and prudent use by current and future generations. Pub. Res. Code § 30001.5.

Composition. The Coastal Commission is an independent, quasi-judicial state agency. It consists of fifteen members (twelve voting members and three non-voting (ex-officio) agency representatives).[3] The twelve voting members are appointed equally (four each) by the Governor, the Senate Rules Committee, and the Speaker of the Assembly. Six out of the twelve voting members are locally elected officials; the other six are appointed from the public at large. Pub. Res. Code § 30301.

Constitutionality. Until 2003, all Commission members served "at the pleasure of their appointing authority." Pub. Res. Code § 30312. In 2002, a lawsuit was filed in which the petitioner claimed the structure of the Commission unconstitutionally failed to separate the legislative and executive branches of government. *Marine Forests Soc'y v. California Coastal Comm'n*, 36 Cal. 4th 1, 13 (2005). Marine Forests Society argued that because the majority of the Commission's voting members were appointed by and served at the will of the Legislature, the Commission was a legislative body without the authority to grant or deny permits. *Id.* The appellate court agreed in *Marine Forests Soc'y v. California Coastal Comm'n*, 104 Cal. App. 4th 1232 (2002) (review granted). The Legislature then passed urgency legislation which both lengthened the terms of the Commission members appointed by the Legislature, and provided they were not removable by their appointing authority. *Marine Forests Soc'y*, 36 Cal. 4th at 15. On appeal, the California Supreme Court determined that as revised, the Act was constitutional, concluding the Act's revised appointment structure and numerous safeguards ensured that members would adhere to statutory guidelines and be protected from improper interference by the Legislature. *Id.* at 10.

Development within the coastal zone may not commence until a coastal development permit has been issued either by the Coastal Commission or by a local government with a Commission-certified local coastal program. Pub. Res. Code § 30600.

CALIFORNIA COASTAL ACT OF 1976

The California Coastal Act was enacted by the State Legislature in 1976 to provide long-term protection of California's 1,100-mile coastline. The Act created a unique partnership between the state (acting through the Coastal Commission) and local governments (15 coastal counties and 58 coastal cities) to manage the conservation and development of coastal resources through a long-term and comprehensive planning program. The Act outlines standards for development in the coastal zone, including specific policies addressing shoreline public access, recreation, protection of marine and terrestrial habitats, visual resources, landform alteration, agricultural lands, commercial fisheries, industrial uses, water quality, offshore oil and gas development, transportation, development design, power plants, ports and public works. *See generally* Pub. Res. Code § 30200 *et seq.*

> The California Coastal Act was enacted by the State Legislature in 1976 to provide long-term protection of California's 1,100-mile coastline.

COASTAL ZONE

Excluding the coastal area of the San Francisco Bay (which is under the jurisdiction of the San Francisco Bay Conservation and Development Commission and is discussed further below), the coastal zone stretches for the entire 1,100-mile length of the California coastline, from Oregon to the Mexican border, encompassing approximately 1.5 million acres. The Act defines the coastal zone as the land and water area of the State of California, as specified by the maps identified and set forth in the Section 17 of the chapter enacting the Coastal Act. *Id.* In general, the boundaries of the coastal zone extend seaward to the

---

[3] The non-voting members represent the Resources Agency, the Business, Transportation and Housing Agency, and the State Lands Commission. Pub. Res. Code § 30301.

state's outermost line of jurisdiction, including all offshore islands, and inland to the point designated on the maps adopted by the Legislature. Pub. Res. Code § 30103(a). In significant estuary, habitat, and recreational areas, the inland boundary extends to the first major ridgeline paralleling the ocean, or five miles from the mean high tide line of the ocean, whichever is less. In developed urban areas, the boundary generally extends inland less than 1,000 yards. *Id.* The Commission may adjust the inland boundary upon the request of a city or county, to avoid the circumstance of the boundary bisecting an individual parcel of property. Pub. Res. Code § 30603.1.

DEVELOPMENT AND PERMITTING

With certain exceptions, development in the coastal zone requires a coastal development permit. The Act defines development very broadly:

> "Development" means, on land, in or under water, the placement or erection of any solid material or structure; discharge or disposal or any dredged material or...waste; grading, removing...or extraction of any materials; change in the density or intensity of use of land, including, but not limited to, subdivision... and any other division of land, including lot splits...; change in the intensity of use of water, or of access thereto; construction, reconstruction, demolition, or alteration of the size of any structure, including any facility...[or] utility; and the removal or harvesting of major vegetation....

Pub. Res. Code § 30106

Lot line adjustments also constitute development under the Act. *La Fe, Inc. v. County of Los Angeles*, 73 Cal. App. 4th 231, 240-42 (1999) (coastal development permit required for a lot line adjustment because, like a subdivision or a lot split, it can result in changes in the density or intensity of use). A subdivision approval constitutes a "development" as defined by section 30106 of the Coastal Act because a subdivision "may provide for a higher density than encompassed by a permitted use." *DeCicco v. California Coastal Comm'n*, 199 Cal. App. 4th 947, 951 (2011) (Coastal Commission lacks jurisdiction to review approval of a "principal permitted use" development, but when the development project also requires approval of a subdivision, Coastal Commission has appellate jurisdiction).

Despite the Act's broad definition of development, many types of development are statutorily exempt from coastal permitting requirements. Coastal development permits are not required for most repairs and improvements to existing single-family residences. They also are not required for development in areas subject to categorical exclusions, replacement of structures destroyed by disaster, and certain types of temporary development. Pub. Res. Code § 30610; *see also Gualala Festivals Comm. v. California Coastal Comm'n*, 183 Cal. App. 4th 60, 68-70 (2010) (proposed temporary fireworks display not exempt from coastal permitting requirements due to the proposed display's significant adverse impacts on coastal resources). Permit requirements also may be waived in cases of emergency. Pub. Res. Code § 30611.

Responsibility for issuing coastal development permits is shared between the Coastal Commission and local governments. The Commission will approve a coastal development permit if it finds "the proposed development is in conformity with Chapter 3 [the Coastal Resources Planning and Management Policies of the Coastal Act] and that the permitted development will not prejudice the ability of the local government to prepare a local coastal program that is in conformity with Chapter 3." Pub. Res.

Code § 30604(a). Most coastal development permits are issued by local governments through Commission-approved local coastal programs (discussed below), and subject to appeal to the Commission. Pub. Res. Code § 30603. However, the Commission retains original permit jurisdiction over the immediate shoreline, tidelands, submerged lands, public trust lands, and land within a certain distance of wetlands, estuaries, streams, and coastal bluffs. The Commission also has original permitting authority over developments constituting major public works projects or energy facilities. Pub. Res. Code § 30601.

Where the development of environmentally sensitive habitat is at stake, the Act imposes two restrictions: that development must cause no significant disruption of habitat values, and that the nature of the development must be dependent on the resources to be protected. Pub. Res. Code § 30240. However, local governments may relax this policy to avoid an unconstitutional taking so long as they make a specific finding a taking would occur. *McAllister v. California Coastal Comm'n*, 169 Cal. App. 4th 912, 939 (2008). Such a finding would, generally, have to show the restriction would deny the land owner substantially all economically viable use of the property, and would require analysis of such factors as the economic impact of the regulation, interference with the landowner's reasonable, investment-backed expectations, and the character of the government action. *Id.* at 40. In *McAllister*, the Commission did not make such a finding with regard to a proposal to build a single-family dwelling, and relied solely on the fact the project fell within residential zoning, causing the court to remand the matter for a new hearing on the permit application.

LOCAL COASTAL PROGRAMS

Local coastal programs (LCPs) contain the ground rules for future development and protection of coastal resources, and are the basic planning tools used by local governments to guide development in the coastal zone, in partnership with the Coastal Commission. LCPs identify the location, type, densities, and intensities of land uses, the applicable resource protection and development policies, and other ground rules for future development in the coastal zone portion of a local government, including mitigation fees. *See* Pub. Res. Code § 30108.6. Each LCP includes a land use plan and its implementing measures (e.g., zoning ordinances and maps). Pub. Res. Code §§ 30108.5, 30108.6. Prepared by local governments, these programs govern decisions that determine the short- and long-term conservation and use of coastal resources. *See, generally,* www.coastal.ca.gov for a description of LCPs and their function and *Douda v. California Coastal Comm'n*, 159 Cal. App. 4th 1181 (2008). The Act requires local governments to submit proposed LCPs to the Coastal Commission for the portion of the coastal zone within their jurisdiction. Pub. Res. Code § 30500. In lieu of preparing an LCP, local governments may request that the Commission prepare one on their behalf.

LCP = local coastal program

Although an LCP may be prepared by a local government and typically consists of parts of the local government's general plan and zoning ordinances, the Commission applies state law and policies in certifying an LCP. The Commission also applies state law and policy in determining whether a particular development permit complies with an LCP. *See Charles A. Pratt Construction Co., Inc. v. California Coastal Comm'n*, 162 Cal. App. 4th 1068, 1076 (2008).

Local governments may elect to divide their coastal zone jurisdictions into separate geographic segments, and prepare LCPs for each. Pub. Res. Code § 30500. Many of the 76 coastal counties and cities have done this, resulting in 128 LCP segments as of June

30, 2012. As of this date, the Commission has certified about 72 percent of the LCP segments, which represent about 85 percent of the coastal zone. *See* California Coastal Commission, Summary of LCP Program Activity in FY 11-12 (available at http://www.coastal.ca.gov/la/docs/lcp/FY11_12_LCPStatusSummaryChart_FINAL.pdf).

The Commission must certify or refuse certification of a proposed LCP within 90 days, based on whether it conforms with the requirements of Chapter 3 of the Act (Pub. Res. Code § 30200 *et seq.*) (Coastal Resources Planning and Management Policies). Pub. Res. Code § 30512. In addition to its role in approving LCPs, the Commission must also review and approve any amendments to previously certified LCPs. Pub. Res. Code § 30514. Although the Coastal Commission may override a local government's refusal to amend its LCP under specific narrow conditions, the Coastal Commission exceeds its jurisdiction when it approves amendments to an LCP at the request of state agencies over the objections of the city, where the amendments were not requested to undertake a public works project or energy facility, but instead changed the city's land use policies and development standards as they would apply to future plans for development within the city. *City of Malibu v. Cal. Coastal Comm'n*, 206 Cal. App. 4th 549 (2012) ("The Coastal Commission 'is not authorized by any provision of [the Coastal Act] to diminish or abridge the authority of a local government to adopt and establish, by ordinance, the precise content of its land use plan.'") (quoting Pub. Res. Code § 30512.2(a)).

After final certification of an LCP, with the exception of the limited areas over which the Commission retains jurisdiction, permitting authority under the Coastal Act is delegated to the local government which is implementing the LCP. Pub. Res. Code § 30519(a).

APPEALS

Any action taken by a local government on a coastal development permit application may be appealed to the Commission. Pub. Res. Code § 30600.5(d). After a local government's LCP is certified, its coastal development permitting decisions may be appealed to the Commission pursuant to Public Resources Code section 30603. Public Resources Code Section 30005 limits the Commission's appellate jurisdiction under certain circumstances, such as where a city or county acts to abate nuisances. *See* Pub. Res. Code § 30005(b). In *Citizens For a Better Eureka v. California Coastal Commission*, the court stated the application of the Coastal Act under section 30005(b) turns on "whether a development is limited to nuisance abatement." 196 Cal. App. 4th 1577, 1589 (2011). If so, a coastal development permit is not required. *Id.* Such a permit is required, however, where the development activity "exceeds the amount necessary... simply to abate the nuisance." *Id.* at 1585 (citations omitted). A subsequent decision has added that where a local government declares a nuisance and prescribes abatement measures, it must do so in good faith, and not as a pretext for avoiding obligations under its LCP, for the statutory limitation on the Commission's jurisdiction to apply. *City of Dana Point v. Cal. Coastal Comm'n*, 217 Cal. App. 4th 170, 199 (2013).

The following types of developments approved by local governments are appealable to the Commission:

- Developments between the sea and the first public road paralleling the sea or within 300 feet of the inland extent of any beach or of the mean high tideline of the sea where there is no beach
- Developments located on tidelands, submerged lands, public trust lands, within 100 feet of any wetland, estuary, or stream, or within 300 feet of the top of the seaward face of any coastal bluff

- Developments located in a sensitive coastal resource area
- Any development approved by a coastal county that is not designated as the principal permitted use under the zoning ordinance
- Any development which constitutes a major public works project or a major energy facility

Pub. Res. Code § 30603(a)

The grounds for an appeal of a local government's decision are limited to a claim the development does not conform to the standards set forth in the certified LCP, or with the access policies set forth in the Act. Pub. Res. Code §§ 30603(b), 30210-30214. *See Sec. Nat'l Guaranty, Inc. v. Cal. Coastal Comm'n*, 159 Cal. 4th 402, 421 (2008). Appeals must be filed within 10 days from the date the Commission receives notice of the local government's decision on a permit. If an appeal is not submitted within this time, the local government's action becomes final. Pub. Res. Code § 30603(c).

JUDICIAL REVIEW OF COMMISSION DECISIONS

Once it issues a decision on a permit, the Coastal Commission may be sued by an aggrieved person under Code of Civil Procedure section 1094.5 within 60 days of the Commission's decision. Pub. Res. Code § 30801. For a detailed discussion of litigation procedures, see chapter 19 (Land Use Litigation).

OTHER COASTAL COMMISSION RESPONSIBILITIES

The Coastal Commission has a variety of additional statutory functions that must be carried out on an ongoing basis:

- **Public works plans and university long-range development plans.** The Commission must review and approve these plans even when an LCP has been certified. Pub. Res. Code §§ 30605-30606
- **LCP, port master plan, university long-range development plan, and public works plan amendments.** The Commission must review and approve all amendments to these plans. Pub. Res. Code §§ 30514, 30515, 30716, 30605
- **Federal activities.** The Commission must review activities authorized, funded, or carried out by the federal government that affect coastal zone resources for consistency with the federally approved California Coastal Management Program, including the Coastal Act. Pub. Res. Code §§ 30330, 30400
- **Offshore energy projects.** The Commission must review all offshore oil and gas exploration, including any development on the federal outer continental shelf and projects in federal waters for consistency with the Coastal Act, and must regulate marine terminals, refineries, oil and gas pipelines, and other energy development in the coastal zone. Pub. Res. Code §§ 30260-30263
- **Oil spill program.** The Commission must assist in the implementation of a statewide oil spill prevention and response program for providing the best achievable protection for the state's coastal and marine resources under the California Oil Spill Prevention and Response Act (in coordination with other federal and state agencies)
- **Public access.** The Commission must implement a public coastal access program for the length of California's coastline, including maintaining and updating an access inventory, keeping records of easements and dedications, and expediting the opening of new accessways for public use. Pub. Res. Code §§ 30530-30534

- **Access guide.** The Commission has published and must periodically revise the popular Coastal Access Guide. 1979 Cal Stat. ch. 868
- **Energy projects and public works.** The Commission may amend a certified LCP (upon request or on its own motion) to accommodate energy and public works projects if the local government refuses to do so. Pub. Res. Code § 30515
- **LCP reviews.** The Commission must review each LCP at least every five years to determine whether the program is being effectively implemented in conformity with the Coastal Act. Pub. Res. Code § 30519.5
- **Power plant siting.** The Commission must update previously adopted maps of areas not suitable for new coastal electric power plants every two years, and must participate in Energy Commission decisions relative to other coastal power plant sites. Pub. Res. Code §§ 30413(c), (d)
- **Coastal resources information center.** The Commission is required to establish and maintain a centralized information center and clearinghouse of data about coastal resources for public and private use. Pub. Res. Code § 30343
- **Guide to coastal resources.** The Commission has published and must periodically revise the Coastal Resource Guide for public use. Pub. Res. Code § 30344
- **Public participation.** The Commission must make recommendations to state and local agencies to ensure effective public participation in their coastal resources management decisions. Pub. Res. Code § 30339
- **Wastewater treatment works.** The Commission must review coastal wastewater treatment works. Pub. Res. Code § 30412(c)
- **Restoration of wetlands.** The Commission must work on and promote wetland restoration. Pub. Res. Code §§ 30231, 30233, 30411(b), 30607.1
- **Local government costs.** The Commission must review all local government mandated cost claims resulting from Coastal Act duties and must make grants to local governments. Pub. Res. Code §§ 30350–30555, 30340.5
- **Federal pass-through grants.** The Commission is designated, under the federally approved California Coastal Management Program, as the state agency to receive and pass through federal grants to the San Francisco Bay Conservation and Development Commission and State Coastal Conservancy

SAN FRANCISCO BAY CONSERVATION AND DEVELOPMENT COMMISSION

Under the federal Coastal Zone Management Act of 1972, California's federally approved coastal management plan for the state consists of two segments: one for the coastline, administered by the California Coastal Commission, discussed above; and one for the San Francisco Bay, administered by the San Francisco Bay Conservation and Development Commission (BCDC). BCDC was created in 1965 by the McAteer-Petris Act, and has land use planning and regulatory authority over both private and public projects in and near the San Francisco Bay and its environs. *See* Gov't Code § 66600 *et seq.*

> BCDC = San Francisco Bay Conservation and Development Commission

Composition. BCDC is made up of 27 appointees from the following local governments and state and federal agencies: five, including the chairman and vice-chairman, appointed by the Governor; one appointed by the Speaker of the State Assembly; one appointed by the State Senate Rules Committee; one appointed by the Director of Finance; one each appointed by the Board of Supervisors of each of the nine Bay Area Counties; one each from a north, east, south, and west bay city appointed by the Association of Bay Area Governments; one from the California Business and

Transportation Agency; one from the California Resources Agency; one from the California State Lands Commission; one from the California Regional Water Quality Control Board, San Francisco Bay Region; one from the U.S. Army Corps of Engineers; and one from the U.S. Environmental Protection Agency. Gov't Code § 66620.

Jurisdiction. BCDC has jurisdiction over the open water, marshes, and mudflats of the greater San Francisco Bay along with the first 100 feet inland from the shoreline. This jurisdiction includes the bays of Suisun, San Pablo, Honker, Richardson, San Rafael, San Leandro, Grizzly, and the Carquinez Strait. BCDC also regulates the Suisun Marsh, portions of most creeks, rivers, sloughs, and other tributaries that flow into San Francisco Bay, as well as salt ponds, duck hunting preserves, game refuges, and other managed wetlands that have been diked off from San Francisco Bay. Gov't Code § 66610.

Permitting authority. Any person or governmental agency wishing to place fill in, extract materials from, or make any substantial change in the use of any water, land, or structure within the San Francisco Bay must obtain a permit from BCDC. Gov't Code § 66604. BCDC has the following responsibilities:

- Regulating all filling and dredging in San Francisco Bay (see "Jurisdiction" above)
- Administering the Suisun Marsh Preservation Act in cooperation with local governments
- Regulating new development within the first 100 feet inland from the bay to ensure that maximum feasible public access to the bay is provided
- Minimizing pressures to fill the bay by ensuring that the limited amount of shoreline area suitable for high priority water-oriented uses is reserved for ports, water-related industries, water-oriented recreation, airports, and wildlife areas
- Pursuing an active planning program to study bay issues so that BCDC plans and policies are based upon the best available current information
- Administering the federal Coastal Zone Management Act within the San Francisco Bay segment of the California coastal zone to ensure that federal activities reflect BCDC policies
- Participating in the region wide state and federal program to prepare a long-term management strategy (LTMS) for dredging and dredge material disposal in San Francisco Bay
- Participating in California's oil spill prevention and response planning program

BCDC is also authorized, with local governments, regional councils of governments, and interested parties, to develop regional strategies for addressing impacts of sea level rise and other impacts of global climate change on the Bay. Gov't Code § 66646.2. In 2011, BCDC adopted a series of amendments to its Bay Plans providing for the development of just such a regional strategy and establishing certain interim land use policies within BCDC's permitting jurisdiction until the regional strategy is developed.

LTMS = long-term management strategy

STORM WATER QUALITY REQUIREMENTS

Storm water quality is becoming increasingly important in the land use arena. The Environmental Protection Agency (EPA) and the California State Water Resources Control Board (State Board or SWRCB) have identified storm water pollution as the largest threat to water quality in the state and the nation. As a consequence, new regulatory restrictions have been imposed in recent years, and continue to be established,

EPA = Environmental Protection Agency

SWRCB or State Board = California State Water Resources Control Board to control storm water pollution resulting from development. The discussion below addresses the three main storm water requirements that pertain to development projects in California: (1) the statewide Construction General Permit issued by the State Water Resources Control Board, which regulates storm water runoff from construction sites disturbing one or more acres of land; (2) the statewide Industrial General Permit issued by the State Board, which regulates storm water associated with 10 specified classes of industrial activities; and (3) the requirements administered by the Regional Water Quality Control Boards (Regional Boards or RWQCBs) and by cities and counties to control post-construction storm water discharges from new development and redevelopment projects.

REGULATORY BACKGROUND

CWA = Clean Water Act

The federal Clean Water Act (CWA) prohibits the discharge of pollutants from a "point source" (which is broadly defined as "any discernible, confined and discrete conveyance") into "navigable waters" without a permit. CWA § 301(a), 33 U.S.C. § 1311(a). Under Section 404 of the CWA, the Army Corps of Engineers issues permits for the discharge of dredged and fill material into wetlands and other waters that are subject to federal jurisdiction. For further discussion of Section 404 and the extent of federal jurisdiction over "navigable waters," see chapter 7 (Federal and State Wetland Regulation). Discharges of wastewater to navigable waters are governed by a different provision of the CWA, Section 402, which requires the discharger to obtain a National Pollution Discharge Elimination System permit (NPDES permit). In California, NPDES permits are called "Waste Discharge Requirements" (or WDRs) and are issued by the Regional Boards, with State Board oversight.

NPDES = National Pollution Discharge Elimination System

WDR = Waste Discharge Requirement

Initially, the EPA exempted most storm water discharges from the NPDES permit requirement. But the courts rejected this approach and in 1987, Congress added Section 402(p) to the CWA to establish a framework and a timeline for regulating industrial and municipal storm water runoff. 33 U.S.C. § 1342(p). This provision serves as the basis for the three types of California permitting requirements discussed below.

BMP = Best Management Practice

In the early stages of the storm water regulatory program, compliance with the permitting requirements was achieved mainly by following a set of standardized Best Management Practices (BMPs) to reduce pollutants in storm water runoff. The selection of the appropriate BMPs was left to the permittee's discretion, and the standards to be achieved were presented in narrative or qualitative terms. But in recent years, the regulatory requirements have become increasingly more stringent, and the State and Regional Boards are now seeking to impose fixed numeric standards, as well as strengthened monitoring, reporting and enforcement provisions.

THE STATEWIDE CONSTRUCTION GENERAL PERMIT

In September 2009, the State Board adopted a new General Permit for Storm Water Discharges Associated with Construction Activity (Order 2009-0009-DWQ, as amended). This permit, which took effect in July 2010, applies throughout California and covers construction projects that disturb one or more acres of land, or that are part of a larger common plan of development that disturbs one or more acres in total. Construction is broadly defined and includes demolition, clearing, grading, and excavation activities. The "Construction General Permit" permit is available on the State Board's website at http://www.swrcb.ca.gov/water_issues/programs/stormwater/construction.shtml.

The permit represents a major shift in the way construction runoff is regulated in California. The new permit retains the core requirement in the previous version of the permit to prepare a Storm Water Pollution Prevention Plan (SWPPP), but there are now specific rules for the qualification and training needed to prepare a SWPPP. Most importantly, the new permit follows a risk-based approach that measures each construction project for its potential to discharge sediments and to degrade the quality of the receiving waters. For low-risk projects (Risk Level 1), the permit requires compliance with a list of minimum BMPs, including "good housekeeping" practices for use of construction materials, waste management, vehicle storage and maintenance, landscaping materials, and erosion and sediment control. For medium-risk projects (Risk Level 2), there are additional BMPs that must be followed, as well as increased monitoring and testing requirements. The permit also establishes "Numeric Action Levels" for pH and turbidity; if these levels are exceeded, the permittee must evaluate the problem and implement corrective action.

SWPPP = Storm Water Pollution Prevention Plan

For high-risk projects (Risk Level 3), the original version of the permit established the most stringent set of requirements, including expanded monitoring and "Numeric Effluent Limits" for pH and turbidity that, if exceeded, would constitute permit violations and expose the permittee to administrative or judicial enforcement, including the potential for citizen suits seeking fines and attorneys' fees. But the California Building Industry Association filed a lawsuit challenging the new permit and in December 2011 the Sacramento County Superior Court invalidated the Numeric Effluent Limits, finding that they were not based on actual performance data as required by the CWA. In July 2012, the State Board amended the permit to remove the Numeric Effluent Limits.

THE STATEWIDE INDUSTRIAL GENERAL PERMIT

The State Board has issued a separate statewide General Permit for Discharges of Storm Water Associated with Industrial Activities Excluding Construction Activities. This permit, adopted in 1997, applies throughout California to ongoing industrial activities falling into 10 broad categories, ranging from timber processing to chemical manufacturing to landfills to specified transportation facilities. *See* State Water Resources Control Board, Water Quality Order 97-03-DWQ, available at http://www.waterboards.ca.gov/water_issues/programs/stormwater/industrial.shtml. Like the prior version of the Construction General Permit, the 1997 Industrial General Permit uses a narrative and qualitative approach.

For the last decade, the State Board has been in the process of amending the 1997 permit with the goal of increasing water quality protections. In several important respects, the development of the new Industrial General Permit has paralleled that of the Construction General Permit. For both permits, the major area of controversy has been the Board's consideration of numeric requirements. Like the current version of the Construction General Permit, the latest draft of the Industrial General Permit, published in July 2013, proposes Numeric Action Levels that, if exceeded, would trigger the need to take corrective action, but excludes Numeric Effluent Limitations that, if exceeded, would give rise to a permit violation subject to enforcement and citizen suits. State Board staff expects to submit the final draft of the Industrial General Permit to the Board for its consideration in January 2014.

MUNICIPAL SEPARATE STORM SEWER SYSTEM (MS4) PERMITS

The post-construction runoff from new development and redevelopment projects that is discharged through municipal separate storm sewer systems is regulated for the most part through regional permits issued by the Regional Water Quality Control Boards, rather than by statewide permits. These regional permits, which are referred to as Phase 1 MS4 permits, cover discharges from municipal storm sewer systems serving 100,000 or more people.[4] Under these regional permits, local municipalities are designated as the permittees; in turn, the covered municipalities implement the permit requirements by imposing storm water controls on development projects within their respective jurisdictions through the land use approval process. The regional requirements may vary, so it is important to review the specific regional permit that may apply, as well as any additional requirements imposed by the applicable city or county.

The regional municipal storm water permit issued by the San Francisco Regional Water Quality Control Board in 2009 illustrates the types of storm water requirements that are being imposed on new development and redevelopment projects in California. See Municipal Regional Storm Water Permit, Order No. R2-2009-0074 (adopted Oct. 14, 2009, as amended) (available at http://www.waterboards.ca.gov/sanfranciscobay/water_issues/programs/stormwater/Municipal/index.shtml). The most important requirement is contained in Provision C.3 of the regional permit, which mandates that municipalities use their planning authorities to include appropriate storm water measures in approving new development or redevelopment projects that create or replace 10,000 square feet or more of impervious surface.[5] This provision establishes a number of "Low Impact Development" (LID) requirements, which are designed to reduce runoff and mimic a site's predevelopment hydrology by minimizing disturbed areas and impervious cover and then infiltrating, storing, detaining, evapotranspiring, or treating storm water runoff close to its source.

LID = Low Impact Development

Specifically, Provision C.3 requires minimum source controls to reduce the pollutants of concern in storm water runoff and site design features to limit the disturbance of natural drainage systems and the amount of runoff. More importantly, the provision requires covered projects to retain onsite a specified amount of the storm water runoff, either by infiltrating the storm water into the ground or by harvesting and reusing the storm water for irrigation or toilet flushing. If infiltration and harvest and reuse are not feasible due to site conditions, then regulated projects may use bioswales and other treatment methods that filter storm water through soils and vegetation to remove pollutants prior to discharge to the site's storm drain system.

Finally, for development and redevelopment projects that result in an increase in impervious surface area over the pre-project condition, Provision C.3 imposes a "hydromodification" requirement, which is designed to prevent any increase in the rate and duration of storm water runoff at the project site. A number of local jurisdictions in the Bay Area have prepared extensive technical guidance documents to address the detailed requirements of Provision C.3 of the regional municipal storm water permit. See, e.g., http://www.cleanwaterprogram.org/c3-guidance-table.html?view=item

---

4 *Discharges from municipal storm sewer systems serving fewer than 100,000 people, as well as storm sewer discharges from specified governmental facilities such as university campuses, military bases, prisons and hospitals, are regulated by the statewide "Phase II" MS4 permit issued by the State Board. See http://www.swrcb.ca.gov/water_issues/programs/stormwater/phase_ii_municipal.shtml.*

5 *The requirements of Provision C.3 also apply to designated projects (auto service facilities, retail gasoline outlets, restaurants, and uncovered parking lots) that create or replace 5,000 square feet or more of impervious surface.*

(Alameda County); http://www.flowstobay.org/newdevelopment (San Mateo County); http://www.scvurppp-w2k.com/nd_wp.shtml (Santa Clara County).

Over time, localized requirements imposed on development projects may increase as public agencies seek to protect themselves from liability for violations of their regional storm water permits. The Ninth Circuit recently found a county and its flood control district liable for storm water discharges that caused the receiving water bodies to exceed applicable water quality standards, even though the polluted storm water that flowed through the county's vast public conveyance systems came from a multitude of sources scattered across a sprawling urbanized area. *Natural Resources Defense Council, Inc. v. County of Los Angeles*, 725 F.3d 1194 (9th Cir. 2013).

In sum, storm water permitting requirements—which apply both during and after construction—are becoming increasingly important for development and redevelopment projects in California.

PREVAILING WAGE CONCERNS ON PRIVATE DEVELOPMENT PROJECTS

The California Labor Code generally requires that wage rates on all "public works" projects performed under contract be equal to or greater than the general prevailing rate per diem for work of a similar character in the locality in which the public work is performed. Labor Code § 1771.

The term "public works" is defined under the Labor Code to include all "work done under contract and paid for in whole or in part out of public funds." Labor Code § 1720(a)(1) (emphasis added). Under this broad language, payment of prevailing wages may be required for all work on an otherwise private development project even where only a small, discrete part of the project is paid for out of public funds.

The overall purpose of this prevailing wage law is to protect and benefit employees on public works projects. *Lusardi Construction Co. v. Aubry*, 1 Cal. 4th 976, 985 (1992). More specifically, prevailing wage law is designed to protect such employees from substandard earnings and to protect "local craftsmen who were losing work to contractors who recruited labor from distant cheap-labor areas." *O.G. Sansone Co. v. Dept. of Transportation*, 55 Cal. App. 3d 434, 458 (1976) (quoting federal authorities on the purpose of the federal Davis-Bacon Act). Courts will liberally construe prevailing wage statutes, but will not interfere where the Legislature "has demonstrated the ability to make its intent clear and chosen not to act." *McIntosh v. Aubry (Pricor)*, 14 Cal. App. 4th 1576, 1589 (1993).

Where the publicly funded portion of a project is arguably discrete and separate from the portion of a project funded solely with private funds, questions arise as to whether the project should be characterized as: (1) a single project with privately and publicly funded components, both subject to prevailing wage requirements; or (2) two separate projects, one that is publicly funded and subject to prevailing wage law, and a second privately funded project that is not. The Department of Industrial Relations (DIR) is authorized to make prevailing wage "coverage" determinations regarding prevailing wage requirements pursuant to Title 8, California Code of Regulations, section 16001(a). *Compare* Decision on Administrative Appeal Re Public Works Case No. 2003 028, *Baldwin Park Marketplace Project* (June 28, 2005) (construction of a Wal Mart "super center" found to be a project separate and distinct from a shopping center project in which Wal Mart was an "anchor tenant," despite the fact that Wal Mart was required to conform to "unifying design elements," and despite the fact that the site

DIR = Department of Industrial Relations

clearance, demolition, rough grading, and off-site infrastructure improvements were paid for out of public funds); with Public Works Case No. 2001 044, *Soledad Canyon Center Shopping Center, City of Santa Clarita* (Sept. 26, 2002) (development of a private shopping center was a public work subject to prevailing wage requirements because the private developer agreed to build a public library within the center and the library and certain off-site improvements were paid for, in part, out of public funds). Questions also arise regarding the scope of statutory exemptions to prevailing wage requirements. *See* Labor Code § 1720(c). For example, a private development project does not become a "public work" if the public contribution is *de minimis* in the context of the project as a whole. Labor Code § 1720(c)(3).

The DIR must issue its coverage determinations within 60 days of receiving the last notice of support or opposition relating to a project awarded or undertaken by an agency, or within 120 days of receipt for complex requests and for projects that are otherwise private development projects receiving public funds. Labor Code § 1773.5(b). An administrative appeal of the DIR's determination may be made within 30 days, with issuance of a decision ordinarily required within 120 days after receipt of the last notice of support or opposition related to the appeal. Labor Code § 1773.5(c).

The ultimate weight that can be given to the DIR's coverage determinations in the event of litigation is uncertain. In 2007, the DIR stripped past and present coverage determinations of their precedential status and announced that its determinations thereafter were to be considered "advisory" letters directed to specific individuals about whether a specific project is subject to prevailing wage requirements. In *State Building and Construction Trades Council v. Duncan*, 162 Cal. App. 4th 289 (2008), the court took note of the discontinuation of precedential coverage determinations and found that the DIR's decisions may not be entitled to "much, if any, deference." *Id.* at 302-03.[6] Nevertheless, in most circumstances the DIR's coverage determinations provide the only guidance on the scope of prevailing wage requirements.

Statutory exemptions to the prevailing wage law set forth in Labor Code section 1720 have been interpreted increasingly narrowly by the courts in recent years. Where a project required three kinds of funding sources, each of which individually and separately satisfied the criteria for exemption, a court held that based on the "express language of the statute" the exemptions could not be "combined" together to qualify the project for exemption from the prevailing wage law. *Housing Partners I, Inc. v. Duncan*, 206 Cal. App. 4th 1335, 1346 (2012). In considering the adverse impact of extending the prevailing wage law, thereby reducing developers' willingness to expand the stock of low-income housing, the court stated, "we decline to usurp the Legislature's treatment of these competing interests." *Id.* at 1347. In another recent case, a rent subsidy provided by a public agency to a private developer was held to constitute the use of public funds for construction of public works, thus triggering prevailing wage requirements. *See Hensel Phelps Const. Co. v. San Diego Unified Port Dist.*, 197 Cal. App. 4th 1020 (2011) (because rent credit provided by the port district to a tenant who would construct a hotel on port property subsidized construction of the hotel, the construction project was a "public work" paid for in part by public funds).

---

[6] The court relied on the principle that "a vacillating position...is entitled to no deference." *State Bldg.*, 162 Cal. App. 4th at 302, 307 n.11 (quoting *Yamaha Corp. of America v. State Bd. of Equalization*, 19 Cal. 4th 1, 13 (1998) and also noting previous application of non-deferential independent judgment standard of review in *McIntosh v. Aubry (Pricor)*, 14 Cal. App. 4th 1576 (1993)); *see also Greystone Homes, Inc. v. Cake*, 135 Cal. App. 4th 1, 8 (2005) (also adopting the non-deferential independent judgment standard).

Laws of charter cities trump state law, including the prevailing wage law, when it comes to "municipal affairs." The California Supreme Court has held that "construction of a city-operated facility for the benefit of a city's inhabitants is quintessentially a municipal affair, as is the control over the expenditure of a city's own funds" and the construction of the public buildings at issue was exempt from prevailing wage laws. *State Bldg. & Constr. Trades Council of Cal., AFL-CIO v. City of Vista*, 54 Cal. 4th 547, 559 (2012). Nevertheless, charter cities are prohibited from receiving or using state funding or financial assistance for most construction projects if the city has a charter provision or ordinance authorizing a contractor to not comply with prevailing wage law. Labor Code § 1782(a). The same prohibition also generally applies if, within the previous two years, a charter city has awarded a public works contract without requiring the contractor to comply with prevailing wage law. Labor Code § 1782(b).

Because of the broad scope of the "public works" language in the Labor Code, and the relative ease with which otherwise privately funded projects can be subjected to prevailing wage requirements, private developers and public agencies alike that may wish to avoid prevailing wage requirements should carefully evaluate DIR guidance on both the nature of "public works" and the scope of statutory exemptions.

PUBLIC BIDDING CONCERNS ON PRIVATE DEVELOPMENT PROJECTS

It is common practice for private developers of large parcels of land to construct and dedicate significant public facilities, such as schools, fire stations, and libraries within their developments. Public agencies may require the financing or construction of such facilities before approving the plans for development. *See, e.g.,* 69 Ops. Cal. Atty. Gen. 300, 301 (1986). Of increasing concern to public agencies and private developers alike is the issue of whether such facilities constitute "public works" or "public projects"—for which a public competitive bidding process must be conducted by a public agency—when they are being constructed by a developer on land to be transferred to such agency as a condition of development of a larger project.

Under existing law, there is no express requirement that public bidding be conducted for the construction of public facilities on private lands which will later be transferred to a public entity. However, due to a paucity of reported cases on the subject, private developers should expect that concerns about public bidding will arise and should be prepared to work with public agencies to satisfy such concerns.

The duty to solicit competitive bids for construction of public works is not a rule of general application, but rather the result of specific statutory mandates. "Competitive bidding is necessary only when required by statute." *County of Riverside v. Whitlock*, 22 Cal. App. 3d 863, 878 (1972). There is "no all-pervasive public policy that requires all public entities" to engage in competitive bidding. *San Diego Service Authority v. Superior Court*, 198 Cal. App. 3d 1466, 1469 (1988). Rather, "the Legislature imposes competitive bidding requirements on public entities within its purview when the Legislature determines it is in the public interest to do so." *Id.* "[A]bsent a statutory directive, a public entity is not bound to engage in competitive bidding." *Construction Indust. Force Account Council v. Amador Water Agency*, 71 Cal. App. 4th 810, 815 (1999).

The Public Contract Code specifically enumerates the entities that qualify as "public agencies" subject to public bidding requirements, and does not include private entities constructing public facilities as a condition of project approval within the meaning of "public agency." The statute does recognize that certain entities may act as agents of or proxies for "public agencies," but limits the application of the

> It is common practice for private developers of large parcels of land to construct and dedicate significant public facilities, such as schools, fire stations, and libraries within their developments.

competitive bidding requirements to certain nonprofit transit corporations. Pub. Cont. Code § 22002.

In *San Diego Service Authority*, the court held that absent an express statutory requirement, even a public entity which is an agent of or proxy for another public agency is not bound to engage in competitive bidding. 198 Cal. App. 3d at 1472. In *Service Authority*, San Diego County and a number of area cities established a service authority (which is a public entity) to implement an emergency call box system. Suit was brought against the service authority when it contracted to have the system installed by a party who did not offer the lowest bid. Although the cities and county that established the service authority would have been required to engage in competitive bidding under the Public Contract Code if they had individually let the contract, the court stated the service authority was a separate legal entity without any express statutory limitations upon its ability to contract. *Id.* The court held that if the Legislature wanted to require competitive bidding in all instances it would have done so specifically. It ruled a court should not presume the Legislature intended to legislate by implication. *Id.*

In *Service Authority*, the court also concluded it would be inconsistent with public policy to require the service authority to engage in competitive bidding. *Id.* at 1471. The purpose of competitive bidding is to guard against "favoritism, extravagance, fraud, and corruption; it serves the public by preventing waste and securing the best economic result." *Id.* at 1469. Where public bidding is not cost-effective or in the public interest it is unnecessary from a public policy perspective. *Id.* at 1470. Public policy considerations militate against application of public bidding requirements to developer-built facilities because private developers gain nothing by increasing expenditures on their projects. Because construction of public facilities are conditions of project approval and because any reimbursement provided by the public agency is usually capped at certain statutory limits (and less than the actual costs incurred), it is in the developer's best interest to diligently complete construction of the facilities as quickly and as cheaply as possible.

Even where projects are subject to the Public Contract Code's public bidding requirements, certain projects may be excused from bidding due to policy considerations. It is "well established that where requests for competitive proposals would be futile, unavailing, or would not produce an advantage, statutes requiring competitive bidding do not apply." *Meakin v. Steveland, Inc.*, 68 Cal. App. 3d 490, 498 (1977) (holding city's disposition of public land was excused from public bidding because the buyers were the only potential purchasers, and were willing to pay the full appraised price). This principle has been held applicable by California courts in a variety of situations involving the construction of public improvements and buildings where it has appeared that competitive bidding would be incongruous or would not result in any advantage to the public entity in efforts to contract for the greatest public benefit. *See, e.g., Graydon v. Pasadena Redevelopment Agency*, 104 Cal. App. 3d 631, 636 (1980).

CHAPTER 10

Vested Rights and Ability to Bind City by Contract

VESTED RIGHTS[1]

On occasion, at planning commission or city council meetings, a property owner will oppose a proposed general plan and/or zoning change and claim the city has no right to change the law governing its property because the owner already has completed significant planning, and perhaps some construction work, for development of the project. Unless the property owner previously has obtained statutory vested rights under a development agreement or a vesting tentative map, the property owner will need to establish that sufficient development activities have been undertaken to establish common law vested rights, thereby preventing a change in the law governing the use of the property.

> Unless the property owner previously has obtained statutory vested rights under a development agreement or a vesting tentative map, the property owner will need to establish that sufficient development activities have been undertaken to establish common law vested rights, thereby preventing a change in the law governing the use of the property.

THE *AVCO* RULE

The common law rule in California (the "*Avco* rule") is that if a city changes its land use regulations, a property owner cannot claim a vested right to build out a project under the prior land use regulations unless the owner has obtained a building permit, performed substantial work, and incurred substantial liabilities in good faith reliance upon the permit. This common law vested rights rule was affirmed in 1976 when the California Supreme Court stated:

> It has long been the rule in this state and in other jurisdictions that if a property owner has performed substantial work and incurred substantial liabilities in good faith reliance upon a permit issued by the government, he acquires a vested right to complete construction in accordance with the terms of the permit. Once a landowner has secured a vested right the government may not, by virtue of a change in the zoning laws, prohibit construction authorized by the permit upon which he relied.

Avco Community Developers, Inc. v. South Coast Regional Com., 17 Cal. 3d 785, 791 (1976) (citations omitted)

---

1 *See* David L. Callies, Cecily Talbert Barclay, and Julie Tappendorf, *Development by Agreement* (ABA Sect. of State and Local Gov't Law, 2012); Daniel J. Curtin, Jr., *Developer Claims of Vested Rights, Current Trends and Practical Strategies*, Land Use Law and Zoning 31 (Patricia E. Salkin ed., ABA, Sect. of State and Local Gov't Law, 2004).

The *Avco* court stated further, however, that:

> [N]either the existence of a particular zoning nor work undertaken pursuant to governmental approvals preparatory to construction of buildings can form the basis of a vested right to build a structure which does not comply with the laws applicable at the time a building permit is issued.

Id. at 793

Avco owned approximately 8,000 acres of land in Orange County, a small portion of which was located within the coastal zone. Prior to February 1, 1973, the date on which the coastal development permit requirement became effective under the California Coastal Act (Pub. Res. Code section 30000 *et seq.*), Avco had obtained zoning and tentative and final subdivision map approvals, and had completed or was in the process of constructing storm drains, improvements of utilities, and similar facilities for the subdivision tract. However, no building permits had been issued for vertical unit construction. The company had spent $2,000,000 and incurred additional liabilities of $750,000 for development of the subdivision. Based on this, Avco argued that it should be exempt from the new coastal development permit requirement. Although it had not yet obtained building permits, Avco believed that it had a vested right to proceed with its development because it had obtained all of its discretionary entitlements and had installed extensive utility improvements. The Coastal Commission disagreed, and denied Avco's requests for an exemption from the Coastal Act. The California Supreme Court held that Avco had no vested right to proceed:

> By zoning the property or issuing approvals for work preliminary to construction the government makes no representation to a landowner that he will be exempt from the zoning laws in effect at the subsequent time he applies for a building permit or that he may construct particular structures on the property, and thus the government cannot be estopped to enforce the laws in effect when the permit is issued.

Id. at 793

In summarizing the policy behind the vested right rule, the Court stated:

> Our conclusion that Avco has not acquired a vested right under the common law to proceed with its development absent a permit from the commission is not founded upon an obdurate adherence to archaic concepts inappropriate in the context of modern development practices or upon a blind insistence on an instrument entitled "building permit."

> If we were to accept the premise that the construction of subdivision improvements or the zoning of the land for a planned community are sufficient to afford a developer a vested right to construct buildings on the land in accordance with the laws in effect at the time the improvements are made or the zoning enacted, there could be serious impairment of the government's right to control land use policy. In some cases the inevitable consequence would be to freeze the zoning laws applicable to a subdivision or a planned unit development as of the time these events occurred.

> Thus tracts or lots in tracts which had been subdivided decades ago, but upon which no buildings have been constructed could be free of all zoning laws enacted subsequent to the time of the subdivision improvement, unless

facts constituting waiver, abandonment, or opportunity for amortization of the original vested right could be shown. In such situations, the result would be that these lots, as well as others in similar subdivisions created more recently or lots established in future subdivisions, would be impressed with an exemption of indeterminate duration from the requirements of any future zoning laws.

Id. at 797-98

Other cases have applied the same principle. See *Hill v. Manhattan Beach*, 6 Cal. 3d 279, 286-87 (1971) (application of a subsequent zoning ordinance to a previously divided parcel that prohibited development or sale of one of the lots was proper); *Oceanic California, Inc. v. North Cent. Coastal Reg'l Comm'n*, 63 Cal. App. 3d 57, 70 (1976) (although county repeatedly had approved developer's concept of a planned community development, such general approval was not sufficient basis for a claim of vested rights without securing the necessary coastal permit); *Hermosa Beach Stop Oil Coalition v. City of Hermosa Beach*, 86 Cal. App. 4th 534, 552 (2001) (no right to develop vests until all final discretionary permits have been authorized and significant "hard costs" have been expended in reliance on those permits, i.e., until substantial construction has occurred in reliance on a building permit); *Hafen v. County of Orange*, 128 Cal. App. 4th 133, 143 (2005) (county was authorized to enforce zoning changes that occurred after approval of a tentative parcel map since developer had not obtained a vested right).

REFINEMENTS OF THE *AVCO* RULE

Courts subsequently have refined and limited the *Avco* rule. First, the rights that may vest upon reliance on a governmental permit are no greater than those specifically granted by the permit itself. See *Santa Monica Pines, Ltd. v. Rent Control Bd.*, 35 Cal. 3d 858, 866 (1984); *People v. Thomas Shelton Powers*, 2 Cal. App. 4th 330, 337-38 (1992) (holding a city was not estopped from imposing a later-enacted ordinance restricting the resale price of units on a previously approved condominium conversion).

> Rights that may vest upon reliance on a governmental permit are no greater than those specifically granted by the permit itself.

Second, an owner of undeveloped land has no vested right in existing zoning, more valuable zoning that may have been anticipated, or zoning for the highest and best use of the property. See *Gilliland v. County of Los Angeles*, 126 Cal. App. 3d 610, 617 (1981).

Third, an invalid permit vests no rights. The California Supreme Court held that a developer cannot claim a vested right in reliance upon a permit he had reason to know might be defective. *Strong v. County of Santa Cruz*, 15 Cal. 3d 720, 725 (1975). Another court held that a property owner who had constructed improvements in reliance upon an invalid building permit could be required to remove the structure, even though the permit was regular on its face and the property owner acted without actual knowledge of any defect in it. *Pettitt v. City of Fresno*, 34 Cal. App. 3d 813, 823 (1973). The following year, in *People v. County of Kern*, the court held that a property owner could not obtain vested rights in reliance upon an approval obtained in accordance with the requirements of the county where the rules and practices adopted by the county did not conform strictly to the requirements of state law. 39 Cal. App. 3d 830, 837-38 (1974).

A property owner also cannot rely on written statements made by a public official unless the official is authorized to make those statements. See *Burchett v. City of Newport*

Beach, 33 Cal. App. 4th 1472, 1479-80 (1995). In *Burchett*, the property owners alleged a breach of a contract with the City of Newport Beach, claiming that the city agreed to allow the property owners to improve real property with a two-story condominium structure based on a letter from the owners to the planning department asking for a permit to use an existing, nonconforming driveway, on which an assistant planner had noted the facts were "correct." *Id.* at 1475.

In denying the petitioner's claim of a contractual right to develop, the court first noted the city's charter provided that it could not be bound by any contract unless that contract was in writing, approved by the city council, and signed on behalf of the city by the mayor and the city clerk or by another designated officer. *Id.* at 1479. Second, the assistant planner was neither the person to contact for an "encroachment permit" nor a member of the correct department. The court cited *Horsemen's Benevolent & Protective Association v. Valley Racing Association* for the proposition that "[n]o government, whether state or local, is bound to any extent by an officer's acts in excess of his authority." 4 Cal. App. 4th 1538, 1564 (1992). The court held that any purported right to develop was invalid. *Burchett*, 33 Cal. App. 4th at 1480. "One who deals with the public officer stands presumptively charged with a full knowledge of that officer's powers, and is bound at his peril to ascertain the extent of his powers to bind the government for which he is an officer, and any act of an officer to be valid must find express authority in the law or be necessarily incidental to a power expressly granted." *Id.*; *see also G.L. Mezzetta, Inc. v. City of American Canyon*, 78 Cal. App. 4th 1087, 1093 (2000) (general law city was not bound by an oral contract because it did not comply with Government Code section 40602 and relevant city code provisions).

Fourth, a vested right may be restricted or revoked if the use would be a menace to the public health and safety or a public nuisance. *See Davidson v. County of San Diego*, 49 Cal. App. 4th 639, 648 (1996) (although a zoning ordinance conferred a vested right to have a building permit application for a crematorium reviewed and considered in light of the regulations existing on the date of application, the county could require an application for a major use permit because vested rights may be impaired through subsequent police power enactments necessary to protect public health or safety).

Fifth, a city-promulgated administrative regulation relied on by an owner in proceeding with a condominium conversion may be a valid basis for estoppel against the city, even though the city later enacts an ordinance that would have prevented the conversion. *See Hock Investment Co. v. City and County of San Francisco*, 215 Cal. App. 3d 438, 449 (1989); *see also City of West Hollywood v. Beverly Towers, Inc.*, 52 Cal. 3d 1184, 1190-91 (1991). In *Beverly Towers*, several apartment building owners had obtained final map approval from Los Angeles County to convert their rental units into condominiums, and also had obtained permission to sell individual units as condominiums from the California Department of Real Estate. The owners did not need any further permits to complete the conversion. The California Supreme Court held that a newly incorporated city could not enforce new condominium regulations after final map and Department of Real Estate approval. *Id.* at 1191. The Court further held that it made no difference that the owners had not sold any units. *Id.* at 1190.

While these decisions narrowed the applicability of the *Avco* rule, California courts continue to rely on *Avco* to define when a property owner has acquired a vested right. For example, subdivision approval for condominium conversions does not give a developer a vested right against later-enacted police power ordinances. *See Santa Monica Pines, Ltd. v. Rent Control Board*, 35 Cal. 3d 858, 866 (1984) (converter had to obtain a permit from the rent control board since reliance upon tentative map approval was inadequate to establish vested rights); *Consaul v. City of San Diego*, 6 Cal. App. 4th 1781, 1794 (1992) (reaffirming *Avco*); *Hafen v. County of Orange*, 128 Cal. App. 4th 133 (2005) (developer required to comply with zoning changes as a tentative parcel map did not confer a vested right). In *People v. H & H Properties*, the developer was required to comply with the county's later enacted rent control ordinance even though he already had obtained tentative and final map approval. 154 Cal. App. 3d 894, 900 (1984). "Vested rights is not the question here. H & H is free to proceed. It simply must pay somewhat more than it expected for the privilege of engaging in a condominium conversion...." *Id*. at 902.

Open-ended conditions of approval may affect application of the *Avco* rule. In *Russ Building Partnership v. City and County of San Francisco*, developers were ordered to comply with a transit impact development fee even though they had acted on building permits and had begun construction before the fee ordinance went into effect. 44 Cal. 3d 839, 847 (1988). The fee was imposed pursuant to a generally worded condition of approval requiring the developer's participation in some type of transportation funding. The Court held that the developers did not have a vested right to develop free of imposition of the transit impact fee under the *Avco* rule because of the "open ended" condition attached to the earlier approval. *Id*.; *see also Blue Jeans Equities West v. City and County of San Francisco*, 3 Cal. App. 4th 164, 172 (1992).

> Open-ended conditions of approval may affect application of the *Avco* rule.

DEVELOPMENT AGREEMENTS[2]

In 1979, in an attempt to soften the impact of *Avco*, the Legislature established a property development agreement procedure. Gov't Code § 65864 *et seq*.; *see also The Legacy Group v. City of Wasco*, 106 Cal. App. 4th 1305, 1312 n.18 (2003).

The principal provisions of the legislation governing development agreements are as follows:

- Cities are given express authorization to enter into a development agreement and may adopt procedures to do so by resolution or ordinance. Gov't Code § 65865
- The development agreement is enforceable by any party to the agreement, notwithstanding a change in any applicable general or specific plan, zoning, subdivision, or building regulation adopted by the city. Gov't Code § 65865.4; *see also Beverly Towers*, 52 Cal. 3d at 1193 n.6; *Native Sun/Lyon Communities v. City of Escondido*, 15 Cal. App. 4th 892, 910 (1993); *Midway Orchards v. County of Butte*, 220 Cal. App. 3d 769, 773 (1990); 76 Ops. Cal. Atty. Gen. 227 (1994); 77 Ops. Cal. Atty. Gen. 94 (1994)
- Unless otherwise provided by the development agreement, the applicable rules, regulations, and policies are those that are in force at the time of the execution of the agreement. Gov't Code § 65866
- A city's exercise of its power to enter into a development agreement is a legislative act. *Mammoth Lakes Land Acquisition LLC v. Town of Mammoth Lakes*, 191 Cal. App. 4th 435, 442 (2010); *Santa Margarita Area Residents Together ("SMART") v. County of San Luis Obispo*, 84 Cal. App. 4th 221, 227–28 (2000).

---

2 *See* David L. Callies, Cecily Talbert Barclay, and Julie Tappendorf, *Development by Agreement* (ABA Sect. of State and Local Gov't Law, 2012); Daniel J. Curtin, Jr., *Exactions, Dedications and Development Agreements Nationwide and in California: When and How Do Nollan/Dolan Apply*, ch. 2, 33rd Annual Institute of Planning, Zoning and Eminent Domain (Matthew Bender, 2003); *Development Agreement Manual: Collaboration in Pursuit of Community Interest* (Institute for Local Self Government, 2002). *See also* Brad Schwartz, Development Agreements: Contracting for Vested Rights, 28 Boston College Envtl. Affairs L. Rev., no. 4,719 (Summer 2001).

It must be approved by ordinance, be consistent with the general plan and any specific plan, and is subject to repeal by referendum. Gov't Code § 65867.5

- Moreover, because entering into a development agreement is a legislative act, a city's decision not to enter into a development agreement need not be supported by findings. Gov't Code § 65867.5; *see also Native Sun/Lyon Communities v. City of Escondido,* 15 Cal. App. 4th 892, 910 (1993)

- There is a 90-day statute of limitations to challenge the adoption or amendment of a development agreement approved on or after January 1, 1996. Gov't Code § 65009(c)(1). An action by either a city or an applicant for breach of a development agreement is subject to the normal breach of contract statute of limitations, which generally is four years from accrual. *The Legacy Group v. City of Wasco,* 106 Cal. App. 4th at 1312–13 (holding that the Subdivision Map Act's 90-day statute of limitations to attack or review a "decision" of the city council "concerning a subdivision" does not apply to decisions concerning the adoption or amendment of a development agreement or interpretation of a clause therein); Code of Civ. Pro. § 337

- A city may terminate or modify a development agreement if it finds, on the basis of substantial evidence, that the applicant or successor in interest thereto has not complied in good faith with the terms or conditions of the agreement. Gov't Code § 65865.1

- A city is authorized to enter into a development agreement for property outside the city limits that is within its sphere of influence; the development agreement, however, does not become operative until annexation proceedings are completed within the period of time specified by the agreement. Gov't Code § 65865(b)

- A city shall not approve a development agreement that includes a residential subdivision of more than 500 dwelling units, unless the agreement provides that any tentative map prepared for the subdivision will comply with Government Code section 66473.7 relating to the availability of water supply. Gov't Code § 65867.5(c)

- If, prior to incorporation of a new city (or annexation to a city), a county has entered into a development agreement with the developer, that development agreement shall remain valid for the duration of the agreement, or for eight years from the effective date of the incorporation or annexation, whichever is earlier, or for up to 15 years upon agreement between the developer and the city. Gov't Code § 65865.3. This statute applies to incorporations where the development agreement was applied for prior to circulation of the incorporation petition and entered into between the county and the developer prior to the date of the incorporation election. The statute also allows the newly incorporated or annexed city to modify or suspend the provisions of the development agreement if it finds an adverse impact on public health or safety in the jurisdiction. However, as to annexations, if the proposal for annexation is initiated by a petitioner other than a city, the development agreement is valid unless the city adopts written findings that implementation of the development would create a condition injurious to the public health, safety, or welfare of the city's residents

- Pursuant to 2007 legislation, a city within the Sacramento-San Joaquin Valley shall make certain general plan amendments to provide for increased flood protection, and thereafter shall not enter into a development agreement for any property that is located within a flood hazard zone, unless the city makes one of three findings related to the adequacy of the flood protection. Gov't Code §§ 65302.9, 65860.1, 65865.5

A city's general plan, local ordinances, or policies may impose additional exactions or development conditions as a condition to obtaining the benefits of a development agreement, and all applicable local laws related to contract formations must be followed. Such local laws should be reviewed carefully before proceeding.

The California Supreme Court described the rights that may be vested pursuant to a development agreement as follows:

> [D]evelopment agreements...between a developer and a local government limit the power of that government to apply newly enacted ordinances to ongoing developments. Unless otherwise provided in the agreement, the rules, regulations, and official policies governing permitted uses, density, design, improvement, and construction are those in effect when the agreement is executed.

City of W. Hollywood v. Beverly Towers, Inc., 52 Cal. 3d 1184, 1193 n.6 (1991)

The Court in *Beverly Towers* noted that the purpose of granting vested rights in a development agreement is "to allow a developer who needs additional discretionary approvals to complete a long-term development project as approved, regardless of any intervening changes in local regulations." *Id.* at 1194.

Because a development agreement may offer a property owner or developer substantial assurance that its project can be completed "in accordance with existing policies, rules and regulations, and subject to conditions of approval" (Gov't Code § 65864(b)), it is advisable for the property owner and/or developer to retain a complete set of the local ordinances, policies, and standards into which the development vests. Otherwise, should a dispute arise years after the agreement has been executed, it may be difficult to piece together the operative law.

> A property owner and/or developer should retain copies of local laws in effect when the vesting tentative map application is complete. Otherwise, should a dispute arise years after the vesting tentative map was deemed complete, it may be extremely difficult to determine the operative law.

A city's decision to enter into a development agreement is a legislative act, and therefore is subject to referendum. However, the opportunity for such referendum expires 30 days after the city's adoption of the ordinance approving the agreement; thereafter, the project is immune to subsequent changes in zoning ordinances and land use regulations not consistent with those provided for in the agreement. Elec. Code § 9141. In *Midway Orchards v. County of Butte*, the court set aside the county's adoption of a development agreement because the general plan amendment needed for the agreement to be consistent with the general plan was timely referended. 220 Cal. App. 3d 765, 783 (1990). In setting aside adoption of the agreement, the court stated:

> The development agreement was therefore unlawfully approved and executed. A contract entered into by a local government without legal authority is "wholly void," ultra vires, and unenforceable. Such a "contract" can create no vested rights. Therefore, Midway can claim no right to develop its property based on a development agreement void from the beginning.

Id. at 783 (internal citations omitted)

Prior to expiration of the 30-day referendum period, the development agreement is not effective. *See* 216 *Sutter Bay Associates v. County of Sutter*, 58 Cal. App. 4th 860, 872–74 (1997) (an interim urgency zoning ordinance and a parallel "ordinary" urgency ordinance, adopted by a newly elected board of supervisors within the 30-day referendum period, successfully stopped a development agreement adopted by the preceding, lame-duck board).

CEQA = California Environmental Quality Act

A "fully negotiated" development agreement is a "project" under CEQA (Pub. Res. Code § 21000 et seq.), and is subject to environmental review. This is true even when the negotiated development agreement is submitted by a council-initiated ballot measure to the electorate for approval. See Citizens for Responsible Gov't v. City of Albany, 56 Cal. App. 4th 1199, 1215 (1997); see also Friends of Sierra Madre v. City of Sierra Madre, 25 Cal. 4th 165, 190–91 (2001) (holding that by voting to place a council-generated measure on the ballot, the city council had approved a "project" subject to CEQA, and thus did not fall within CEQA's exemption for proposals submitted to the voters).

Not infrequently, those who challenge projects governed by development agreements will argue that the agreements are invalid because the city is "contracting away" its police power. The courts have not been persuaded by this argument.

For example, in SMART v. County of San Luis Obispo, an area residents' association contended that because San Luis Obispo County had entered into a development agreement freezing zoning for a five-year period for a project before the project was ready for construction, the county improperly contracted away its zoning authority. 84 Cal. App. 4th 221, 232–33 (2000). In rejecting this contention, the court stated the development agreement statute should be liberally construed to permit "local government to make commitments to developers at the time the developer makes a substantial investment in a project." Id. at 230. The court noted that land use regulation is an established function of local government, providing the authority for a locality to enter into contracts to carry out the function. The county's development agreement required that the project be developed in accordance with the county's general plan, did not permit construction until the county had approved detailed building plans, retained certain of the county's discretionary authority in the future, and allowed a zoning freeze of limited duration only. The court found the zoning freeze in the county's development agreement was not a surrender of the police power but instead "advance[d] the public interest by preserving future options." Id. at 233.

Most recently, in Mammoth Lakes Land Acquisition LLC v. Town of Mammoth Lakes, the court upheld a $30 million damage award against the Town in favor of the developer for the Town's anticipatory breach of a 1997 development agreement in which the Town had agreed, among other things, to act reasonably in moving along the developer's proposed hotel/condominium project. 191 Cal. App. 4th 435 (2010). The court first reviewed the legislative history of development agreements in California and held that "a legislatively-approved development agreement gives both parties vested contractual rights." Id. at 444. The court then found the evidence of the Town's repudiation of the agreement and failure to cooperate with the developer in advancing the project supported the developer's breach of contract claim as well as the jury's damage award. In so ruling, the court rejected the Town's argument that the developer was required to first exhaust its administrative remedies, and instead focused on the contractual nature of a development agreement, which allowed the developer to pursue a breach of contract claim following the Town's failure to cure its default. Id. at 455.

Likewise, settlement agreements between city and developer do not surrender the city's police power. 108 Holdings LTD v. City of Rohnert Park, 136 Cal. App. 4th 186, 194 (2006). In 108 Holdings, the court held the city's execution of a settlement agreement with a preservation committee and subsequent acceptance of the stipulated judgment that bound the city to interpret and apply the general plan in a manner specified by the judgment did not constitute a surrender or bargaining away of the city's police power nor did it constitute an improper general plan amendment. Id. The court noted the stipulated judgment did not grant any party veto power over future general plan amendments. The court also agreed with the city's argument that the stipulated judgment did no more than set forth the manner in which the city would interpret certain provisions of its general plan, and that the provisions of the stipulated judgment were facially consistent with the general plan. *Id.* at 197. The fact that the city had agreed to include the provisions as an appendix to its general plan did not demonstrate they were amendments or that they constituted legislation. *Id.* at 202–03.

However, *Trancas Property Owners Association v. City of Malibu* presented a different situation. 138 Cal. App. 4th 172 (2006). After filing a lawsuit challenging the disapproval of its final subdivision maps, Trancas entered into a settlement agreement with the city in which it agreed to dismiss the suit and downsize its development in exchange for the city's approval of the final maps. In addition, the agreement exempted the downsized development from various current and future zoning provisions which would affect the project. The city council entered into the agreement after several closed sessions held under the Brown Act litigation exemption.[3] *See* Gov't Code § 54956.9.

The court set aside the agreement on two grounds. First, the court recognized that a city may lawfully agree to freeze the zoning governing a project, but that numerous procedural and substantive limitations attend the making and performance of such a "development agreement." *Trancas*, 138 Cal. App. 4th at 182. Without following the development agreement statutory process, the court held that the settlement agreement's commitment to refrain from zoning actions was invalid on the basis that it contracted away the city's right to exercise its police power. Second, the court held the settlement agreement was invalid as a municipal act because it violated the Brown Act. Although the court recognized that the litigation exemption to the Brown Act had previously been construed to permit a local legislative body to approve settlement agreements in closed sessions, the exemption is limited. The court held that the litigation exemption could not be construed to empower a city to enter into a settlement agreement in a closed session that in essence granted a zoning variance—an act that by statutory law requires a public hearing. *Id.* at 186–87.

> The court held that the litigation exemption could not be construed to empower a city to enter into a settlement agreement in a closed session that in essence granted a zoning variance—an act that by statutory law requires a public hearing.

Similarly, in *League of Residential Neighborhood Advocates v. City of Los Angeles*, the court held a "settlement agreement cannot override state law absent a specific determination that federal law has been or will be violated." 498 F. 3d 1052, 1053 (9th Cir. 2007). In this case, the city had entered into a settlement agreement with Congregation Etz Chaim to resolve the Congregation's lawsuit that denial of a conditional use permit violated the Congregation's federal and state constitutional rights. However, the court determined the settlement agreement was the functional equivalent of a conditional use permit for which public hearings are required. Since a city cannot bargain away its police powers by entering a settlement agreement that prevents it from enforcing applicable zoning restrictions. Thus, the settlement agreement was held invalid and unenforceable.

In *Hermosa Beach Stop Oil Coalition v. City of Hermosa Beach*, the court held a developer who entered into a lease agreement and who had failed to establish entitlement to vested rights to develop an oil business on property leased from the City of Hermosa Beach could have protected itself from subsequent regulatory changes by insisting the city enter into a development agreement. 86 Cal. App. 4th 534, 558 (2001). The court noted it was likely that the city would have demanded additional consideration for

---

3 For a further discussion on the Brown Act, see chapter 17 (Rights of the Regulated).

either a risk-adjustment provision in the existing lease or a separate development agreement, and that having at least implicitly decided to forego such protection against future regulatory changes, the developer must accept the consequences of this decision. *Id.*

Development agreements are adopted as a result of negotiations between a city and a developer; therefore, they are not subject to the *Nollan/Dolan* heightened scrutiny standard.[4] *See Leroy Land Dev. v. Tahoe Reg'l Planning Agency*, 939 F. 2d 696, 697-98 (9th Cir. 1991); *see also Nollan v. California Coastal Comm'n*, 483 U.S. 825 (1987); *Dolan v. City of Tigard*, 512 U.S. 374 (1994).

In *Leroy*, the developer entered into a settlement agreement, pursuant to which it agreed to certain restrictions on development. *Leroy*, 939 F. 2d at 697-98. After the United States Supreme Court subsequently decided *Nollan*, the developer sought to challenge the restriction as an inverse taking of private property. The Ninth Circuit rejected the challenge, holding that regardless of whether the restriction would have violated the Fifth Amendment Takings Clause if imposed as a condition of development, it could not be found invalid because the developer had voluntarily agreed to its imposition. *Id.* at 697.

> The threshold issue is whether, assuming arguendo that the mitigation provisions would constitute a taking under *Nollan* if imposed unilaterally by TRPA [the Tahoe Regional Planning Agency], they can be viewed as a "taking" when consented to as a part of a settlement agreement. We hold that they cannot. The mitigation provisions at issue here were a negotiated condition of Leroy's settlement agreement with TRPA in which benefits and obligations were incurred by both parties. Such a contractual promise which operates to restrict a property owner's use of land cannot result in a "taking" because the promise is entered into voluntarily, in good faith and is supported by consideration. Indeed we have found only one case in which an agreement negotiated before *Nollan* was challenged as a "taking" after *Nollan*, and it reached the same conclusion we reach. *See Xenia Rural Water Ass'n v. Dallas County*. To allow Leroy to challenge the settlement agreement five years after its execution, based on a subsequent change in the law, would inject needless uncertainty and an utter lack of finality to settlement agreements of this kind. We therefore hold that a takings analysis as articulated in *Nollan* is inapplicable where, as here, parties choose to terminate or avoid litigation by executing a settlement agreement supported by consideration.

Id. at 698 (internal citations omitted)

In *Meredith v. Talbot County*, a Maryland appellate court reached the same conclusion. 560 A. 2d 599, 604-05 (Md. App. 1989). For further discussion regarding when a taking occurs, see chapter 11 (Regulatory Takings).

Attempts to challenge a development fee contained in a development agreement as a taking also are unlikely to succeed. Under a line of cases starting with *Pfeiffer v. City of La Mesa*, acceptance and use of a land use approval waives any right to challenge the condition. 69 Cal. App. 3d 74, 78 (1977). In response, the Legislature enacted the pay-under-protest statute (Gov't Code § 66020), which allows a developer to protest and challenge a fee or condition without waiving the benefit of the

---

[4] For further discussion on this issue, see David L. Callies and Julie A. Tappendorf, *Unconstitutional Land Development Conditions and the Development Agreement Solution: Bargaining for Public Facilities After Nollan and Dolan*, 51 Case Western Reserve L. Rev., no. 4 (Summer 2001), and chapter 12 (Exactions).

permit. However, this provision is part of the Mitigation Fee Act and only applies to development fees as defined in the Act. Because the Act expressly excludes fees imposed under a development agreement, they are not subject to the protections of the Act. See Gov't Code §§ 66000 and 66020. Thus, it is difficult to argue that fees or exactions agreed to in a development agreement must meet common law and statutory nexus requirements. Many commentators reject the proposition that such fees can later be challenged as excessive, and one of the main attractions of a development agreement for a city is that it can negotiate for mitigation it could not otherwise exact.

However, where the terms of a development agreement provide that agreed-upon fees may be revised in the future where "reasonably justified," the city may be required to show a reasonable relationship between the amount of the revised fee and the deleterious impact of new development. *See Building Industry Ass'n of Central California v. City of Patterson*, 171 Cal. App. 4th 886 (2009). The development agreement in *BIA* recited that the City was working on a revised fee schedule and provided that the developer would be bound to the revised fees provided they were "reasonably justified." The court interpreted "reasonably justified" to mean in conformity with existing law, reasoning that "part of the way one would show a fee is reasonably justified is to show that it does not violate established legal principles." *Id.* at 896. The court concluded that the City's imposition of an increased affordable housing in lieu fee violated the "reasonably justified" requirement of the development agreement because the City had failed to meet the legal standards of the Mitigation Fee Act. *Id.* at 898-99. For further discussion of the Mitigation Fee Act, see chapter 12 (Exactions).

> Where the terms of a development agreement provide that agreed-upon fees may be revised where "reasonably justified," the city may be required to show a reasonable relationship between the amount of the fee and the deleterious impact of new development.

VESTING TENTATIVE MAPS

In 1984, in another legislative response to *Avco*, the Legislature adopted Chapter 4.5 (Development Rights) of the Subdivision Map Act, which established a new form of tentative map for subdivisions in California—the "Vesting Tentative Map." Gov't Code § 66498.1 *et seq*. The purpose of the Vesting Tentative Map Statute is to give a statutory vested right that will be effective earlier in the planning and development process than a common law vested right established pursuant to *Avco*. The vesting tentative map process starts when the subdivider files a tentative or parcel map with the words "Vesting Tentative Map" presented conspicuously on the face of the map. Gov't Code § 66452(c). For a general discussion of the legislative history of the statute and its application, see *Bright Development Company v. City of Tracy*, 20 Cal. App. 4th 783, 788-89 (1993) and *Kaufman & Broad Central Valley, Inc. v. City of Modesto*, 25 Cal. App. 4th 1577, 1587-88 (1994). The rights accruing to a subdivider upon approval of a vesting tentative map are expressly deemed "vested rights" to proceed with the development in substantial compliance with the local ordinances, policies, and standards in effect at the time the application for approval of the vesting tentative map is found or deemed complete. Gov't Code § 66498.1. That is, vesting tentative map provisions of the Map Act were designed to "freeze in place" ordinances, policies, and standards in effect at the time the vesting tentative map application is deemed complete. *Bright Development*, 20 Cal. App. 4th at 793. These vested rights extend for a substantial period of time, and therefore add a critical dimension to the approval process connected with such maps. For a detailed discussion of the life of vesting tentative maps, see chapter 5 (Subdivisions).

TABLE 1: A COMPARISON OF CALIFORNIA'S VESTED RIGHTS STATUTES

	VESTING TENTATIVE MAP GOV'T CODE §§ 66498.1–66498.9		DEVELOPMENT AGREEMENT GOV'T CODE §§ 65864–65869
1.	Processing mandatory: city cannot refuse application	1.	Processing elective: city's discretion whether to enter into an agreement
2.	Exactions subject to statutory and case law restrictions (e.g., "nexus")	2.	Ad hoc negotiation—exempt from development project fees requirements (Mitigation Fee Act, Gov't Code §§ 66000–66025); procedures for improvement deposits and accounting of such fees still apply (Gov't Code § 66006); waiver potential
3.	Permits are discretionary, subject to vested current law	3.	May alter future permit process; may have city commit to future issuance of entitlements
4.	Locks in rules when application "complete"	4.	Locks in rules at execution of agreement unless agreement provides otherwise
5.	Subdivision Map Act limits vesting life of tentative and final maps; incorporation exception	5.	Longer life for agreement; tentative (and vesting tentative) map and certain permits may be extended for life of agreement
6.	Does not limit other agencies (e.g., school districts)	6.	Does not limit agencies that are not parties (incorporation/annexation exception)
7.	Voters cannot referend (adjudicatory act)	7.	Subject to referendum (legislative act)
8.	No contrary future rules unless needed to prevent situation "dangerous" to health/safety or changes in state/federal law	8.	No contrary rules unless consistent with agreement
9.	City must have implementing regulations (if not, Subdivision Map Act governs)	9.	Local procedural regulations needed if requested by applicant, otherwise use statute
10.	Generally, 90-day statute of limitations after approval to file suit challenging	10.	Generally, 90-day statute of limitation to challenge adoption, amendment, or modifications occurring on or after January 1, 1996
11.	Incorporating city is subject to county-approved vesting tentative map; annexing city is not subject	11.	With certain exceptions, both incorporating city and annexing city are subject to county-approved agreement

VESTING TENTATIVE MAPS VS. DEVELOPMENT AGREEMENTS

A vesting tentative map differs from a development agreement in several respects. In particular, a vesting tentative map approval is unilateral, and a development agreement approval is bilateral. This means that cities must process a properly submitted vesting tentative map application and approve or deny it based on statutory criteria, whereas a development agreement is the result of negotiation. A vesting tentative map likely will vest rights earlier than a development agreement by vesting rights as of the date the map application is found or deemed complete. In comparison, development agreement rights, which generally vest on the date the agreement is executed, often vest significantly later in the process. Finally, as a legislative act, a development agreement is subject to referendum, while approval of a vesting tentative map is not.

A vesting tentative map does not provide a mechanism for controlling a city's future exercise of discretionary approvals. For example, if a subdivider needs a discretionary approval, such as a use permit, after the subdivider's tentative map vests, there is no guarantee of such approval. In approving or denying the use permit, however, a city will be governed by the ordinances, policies, and standards in effect at the time the tentative map application was complete, which may limit a city's exercise of discretion. Gov't Code § 66498.1(b).

A development agreement, by contrast, may provide negotiable conditions and requirements that will govern and limit the processing of future discretionary approvals. Gov't Code § 65865.2. Thus, its use is likely to provide a broader range of benefits than those obtained solely through a vesting tentative map.

A city's general plan, local ordinances, or policies may impose additional exactions or development conditions (e.g., increased inclusionary affordable housing) as a condition to entering into a development agreement. Local ordinances also may provide additional requirements necessary to obtain approval of a vesting tentative map. As is the case with all land use laws, such local laws should be reviewed carefully before proceeding with either a development agreement or a vesting tentative map.

> As is the case with all land use laws, local laws should be reviewed carefully before proceeding with either a development agreement or a vesting tentative map.

As with a development agreement, when a vesting tentative map is approved, the subdivider should retain a complete set of the local ordinances, policies, and standards in effect when the vesting tentative map application was deemed complete since the rights vested continue for some time. Otherwise, if a dispute should arise years after the vesting tentative map application was deemed complete, the operative law may be difficult to determine.

Neither a development agreement nor a vesting tentative map can insulate a project from changes in state or federal law. The California Court of Appeal in *Pratt v. California Coastal Comm'n* held that a local coastal plan and the development permits issued by local agencies pursuant to the California Coastal Act are not solely a matter of local law, but embody state policy. 162 Cal. App. 4th 1068, 1075 (2008). Noting that state laws and policies are not subject to the vesting provisions of Government Code section 66498.1(b), the court held that a vesting tentative map did not protect a subdivider in a coastal zone from the Coastal Commission's application of post-vesting policies in an appeal to the Commission. *Id.* at 1075-76. *Avco* likewise involved the Coastal Act. Therefore, neither a development agreement nor a vesting tentative map would have served to protect the developers in that case.

CHAPTER 11

Regulatory Takings

INTRODUCTION

The ability to regulate the use of land derives from the government's police power to regulate for the public health, safety, and welfare of its citizens. This power is, however, limited by the Fifth Amendment to the U.S. Constitution, which states in part, "nor shall private property be taken for public use, without just compensation." *See also* Cal. Const. Art. I, § 19. Thus, if a land use regulation becomes so unduly restrictive that it causes a "taking" of a landowner's property for public use, just compensation must be paid.

THE FOUR TYPES OF REGULATORY TAKINGS

The federal courts recognize that land use regulations can result in four types of regulatory takings: (1) permanent physical invasions; (2) denials of all economically beneficial use; (3) general regulatory takings in which the regulation goes too far; and (4) land use exactions. *Lingle v. Chevron U.S.A. Inc.*, 544 U.S. 528, 548 (2005): All four types of regulatory takings "share a common touchstone." *Lingle*, 544 U.S. at 539. According to the Court:

> Each aims to identify regulatory actions that are functionally equivalent to the classic taking in which government directly appropriates private property or ousts the owner from his domain. Accordingly, each of these tests focuses directly upon the severity of the burden that government imposes upon private property rights.

Id. Each type of regulatory takings is discussed below.

Regulation that effects a physical taking (*Loretto*). "Where government requires an owner to suffer a permanent physical invasion of her property—however minor—it must provide just compensation." *Lingle*, 544 U.S. 528, 538. The case most often cited to exemplify a regulation that effects a physical taking is *Loretto v. Teleprompter Manhattan CATV Corporation*, 458 U. S. 419 (1982). In *Loretto*, the Court addressed a state law that required landlords to permit cable companies to install cable facilities on privately owned apartment buildings, and held that the regulation effected a physical taking. It ruled that a government regulation that causes a physical intrusion on private property will be treated as a physical taking for which just compensation must be paid. *Id.* at 421. Because a physical regulatory taking is determined solely by the fact that the regulation

> The federal courts recognize that land use regulations can result in four types of regulatory takings: (1) permanent physical invasions; (2) denials of all economically beneficial use; (3) general regulatory takings in which the regulation goes too far; and (4) land use exactions.

allows a physical occupation of property, without an ad hoc or detailed factual analysis, it is deemed a "per se" or "categorical" regulatory taking.

Regulation that denies all economic use (*Lucas*). Another type of categorical taking occurs when government regulations deprive a landowner of "all economically beneficial use" of property. *Lucas v. South Carolina Coastal Council*, 505 U.S. 1003, 1015-16 (1992). In the event of such a total regulatory taking, the government must pay just compensation, except to the extent that "background principles of nuisance and property law" independently restrict the landowner's desired use of the land. *Id.* at 1052. In other words, when an owner of real property is called upon to sacrifice all economically beneficial uses in the name of the common good (i.e., to leave his property economically idle) this may constitute a taking. *Id.* at 1015.

In *Lucas*, the U.S. Supreme Court considered a landowner's challenge to a South Carolina regulation barring development of two beachfront lots in a developed subdivision. Findings in the state regulation stated new construction in the coastal zone threatened a valuable public resource. The Court suggested the property owner was entitled to compensation and remanded the case back to the state court for a final determination. On remand, the state court held that a taking had occurred and ordered payment to Lucas.

The Court limited its holding to situations in which owners are deprived of "all economically beneficial uses" of their property. *Id.* at 1027. The Court itself recognized such cases are relatively rare. *Id.* at 1018.

Other cases have emphasized *Lucas'* limited applicability. *See Tahoe-Sierra Preservation Council, Inc. v. Tahoe Reg'l Planning Agency*, 535 U.S. 302, 341-42 (2002) (a 32-month moratorium did not permanently deprive landowners of all economically viable use, and thus was not a categorical taking); *Palazzolo v. Rhode Island*, 533 U.S. 606, 609 (2001) (a regulation permitting a landowner to build a substantial residence on an 18-acre parcel did not leave the property "economically idle," and therefore did not result in a per se taking); *see also Blue Jeans Equities West v. City and County of San Francisco*, 3 Cal. App. 4th 164, 171 (1992) (*Lucas's* principles not applicable since all the property was not taken).

> The narrowness of the *Lucas* doctrine is reflected in the standards used to determine when a property owner has been deprived of all viable economic use.

The narrowness of the *Lucas* doctrine is reflected in the standards used to determine when a property owner has been deprived of all viable economic use. In *Keystone Bituminous Coal Association v. DeBenedictis*, the U.S. Supreme Court focused on how to evaluate whether property owners had been deprived of "economically viable use." 480 U.S. 470, 495-97 (1987). To determine this issue, the Court looked to the value that was left in the owners' property, rather than the value that was taken. *Id.* The plaintiffs were an association of coal mine owners who alleged that the Pennsylvania Bituminous Mine Subsidence and Land Conservation Act constituted a taking of their property by requiring them to forego mining almost 27 million tons of coal in their mines. But the Court focused on the fact that the total coal in the thirteen mines operated by the companies amounted to more than 1.46 billion tons. Noting the Act affected less than two percent of the owners' coal, the Court said the owners "have not shown any deprivation significant enough to satisfy the heavy burden placed upon one alleging a regulatory taking." *Id.* at 493.

In *Barancik v. County of Marin*, the Ninth Circuit held a rezoning that permitted only one residence per 60 acres, with a right to buy development rights, did not violate substantive due process because it did not deny the owner all beneficial use of his land. 872 F. 2d 834, 837 (9th Cir. 1988). The court said the ordinance was not irrational or arbitrary. The court in *Outdoor Systems Inc. v. City of Mesa* reiterated this position:

As for the question whether the sign codes deprive an owner of the economically viable use of the land, we recognize at the outset the term "economically viable use" has yet to be defined with such precision. We have held, however, that "the existence of permissible use [generally] determines whether a development restriction denies a property holder the economically viable use of its property."

997 F. 2d 604, 616 (9th Cir. 1993) (citation omitted); *see also William C. Haas & Co. v. City and County of San Francisco*, 605 F. 2d 1117, 1119 (9th Cir. 1979) (a zoning ordinance that reduced the value of private property by more than 90 percent, from two million dollars to $100,000, was constitutional); *Moore v. City of Costa Mesa*, 886 F. 2d 260, 263 (9th Cir. 1989) (invalid conditional use permit (variance) that caused a landowner a three-year delay in developing his property did not amount to a taking).

California courts likewise follow the "valuation rule," whereby the use of the property that *remains* determines whether a landowner has been deprived of economically viable use of his property. For example, in one case, the court held that the owners were not deprived of all use of their property when they could not demolish an existing building and erect a new multistory office structure, because they were not barred from remodeling the existing building. See *Terminals Equip. Co. v. City and County of San Francisco*, 221 Cal. App. 3d 234 (1990). The court stated:

> In every case in which a landowner seeks compensation for burdensome regulation of his or her property, the standard remains whether the regulations in issue have deprived the landowner of all use of the property. "When, as here, the claim is made that the regulation has significantly diminished the property value, the focus of the inquiry is on the uses of the property which remain. (*Penn Cent. Transp. Co. v. New York City*) Plaintiff cannot contend he was denied all use of his property. He was neither deprived of his right to exclude others from his land nor denied the right to sell the property." (*Guinnane v. City and County of San Francisco*)

Id. at 243 (citations omitted)

> California courts follow the "valuation rule," whereby the use of the property that *remains* determines whether a landowner has been deprived of economically viable use of his property.

The court in *Buena Park Motel Association v. City of Buena Park* held a city's restriction on extended stays at motels did not constitute a denial of all economically beneficial use. 109 Cal. App. 4th 302, 311 (2003). The City of Buena Park adopted ordinances limiting guest stays in motels to 60 days in a 180-day period. A motel association sued the city, alleging the ordinances were an unlawful taking of private property without just compensation. In ruling for the city, the court stated that whether an ordinance constitutes an unlawful taking depends on its economic effects. *Id.* at 309. Although the restrictions on stay length did diminish motel owners' use of their property, they were not considered unduly restrictive. The court held that while the motel owners undoubtedly would be economically impacted by the enforcement of the ordinances, they would not be deprived of all "economically viable use of their property." *Id.* at 311. The court noted that between 35 and 70 percent of the motel association's business would be unaffected by the ordinances, and that motel owners could modify their properties to meet criteria for allowing extended stays. *Id.*

Sometimes, however, the inquiry is focussed not on the magnitude of the economic impact, but on the nature of the right affected. For example, the California Supreme Court unanimously rejected a takings claim in *Regency Outdoor Advertising, Inc. v. City of Los Angeles*, 39 Cal. 4th 507, 513 (2006), where billboard owners claimed they were entitled to compensation when the city planted trees on city-owned property in the vicinity of their roadside billboards, obstructing views. The Court, after surveying more than 100 years of jurisprudence, found the owners' billboards had no "right to be seen" that would justify compensation for the allegedly lessened value of the billboards.

The courts have repeatedly held that denial of the highest and best use does not constitute a taking of the property. *See Long Beach Equities, Inc. v. County of Ventura,* 231 Cal. App. 3d at 1036; *see also MacLeod v. County of Santa Clara,* 749 F. 2d 541, 548 (9th Cir. 1984).

Regulation that goes too far (*Penn Central*). The third category of takings, general regulatory takings, is governed by *Penn Central Transportation Company v. City of New York,* 438 U.S. 104 (1978). Even if a governmental regulation does not cause a physical invasion or deprive a landowner of all economically beneficial use, it may nonetheless go too far in placing what should be a public burden on private shoulders. *Penn Central* established an ad hoc, fact-based inquiry that addresses three factors to be used in determining whether this type of regulatory taking has occurred: (1) "the economic impact of the regulation on the claimant," (2) "the extent to which the regulation has interfered with distinct investment-backed expectations," and (3) "the nature of the governmental action." *Id.* at 124. The Court applied these factors to an historic preservation ordinance that effectively barred construction of a high-rise office building over the Grand Central Terminal. The Court held that the regulation did not effect a taking because it did not have any economic impact upon the station. *Id.* at 138. Nor did the ordinance interfere with the landowner's investment-backed expectations, because there was no physical taking and the railroad could continue to earn a reasonable return under the existing use. *Id.* at 137.

In developing this test, the Court admitted that it never has been able to develop a "'set formula' for determining when 'justice and fairness' require that economic injuries caused by public action be compensated by the government, rather than remain disproportionately concentrated on a few persons." *Penn Central,* 438 U.S. at 124. Instead, the Court has observed that "whether a particular restriction will be rendered invalid by the government's failure to pay for any losses proximately caused by it depends largely 'upon the particular circumstances [in that] case.'" *Id.* Thus, the Court in *Penn Central* did not establish a categorical test for determining when a taking has occurred, but rather stated that a takings analysis proceeds on an essentially "ad hoc" basis.

Lingle v. Chevron U.S.A. 544 U.S. 528 (2005) clarified the role of the *Penn Central* test in takings jurisprudence. The *Lingle* Court considered an act passed by the Hawaii legislature to address the effects of market concentration on the retail price of gasoline. The act prohibited oil companies from charging lessee-dealers rent that exceeded 15 percent of the dealer's gross profits from gasoline sales plus 15 percent of gross sales of products other than gasoline.

Chevron challenged the rent cap on its face. It based its arguments on an older decision, *Agins v. City of Tiburon,* 447 U.S. 255 (1980), which had held that a regulation that failed to advance a legitimate governmental interest effected a taking. The Supreme Court rejected the arguments, announcing that the "substantially advances" inquiry is one of due process, that it has no place in takings jurisprudence, and that the language of *Agins* was "regrettably imprecise." *Id.* at 539-42. Moreover, none of the cases citing the "substantially advances" language actually concluded that there was a compensable taking. *Id.* at 545-47. The Court reasoned that a valid takings analysis should not demand heightened review of legislative determinations, "a task for which courts are not well suited," but rather should "help identify those regulations whose effects are functionally comparable to government appropriation or invasion of private property." *Id.* at 542-44. *See also Manufactured Home Communities, Inc. v. City of San Jose*, 420 F. 3d 1022, 1034 n.14 (9th Cir. 2005) (a takings claim based on the "substantially advances" test is foreclosed by *Lingle's* holding that such an inquiry is not a valid takings test); *Los Altos El Granada Investors v. City of Capitola*, 139 Cal. App. 4th 629, 651 (2006) (it is an error for a court to evaluate whether a rent control ordinance substantially advanced a legitimate government interest since such test is no longer available); *Allegretti & Co. v. County of Imperial*, 138 Cal. App. 4th 1261, 1280 (2006) (whether a county's action substantially advanced a state interest is no longer a valid standard to assess a taking under the Fifth Amendment since *Lingle*).

The *Lingle* Court explained the *Penn Central* factors serve "as the principal guidelines for resolving regulatory takings claims that do not fall within the physical takings or *Lucas* rules." 544 U.S. at 539 (citing *Palazzolo v. Rhode Island*, 533 U.S. 606, 617-18 (2001)); *see Tahoe-Sierra Preservation Council, Inc. v. Tahoe Reg'l Planning Agency*, 535 U.S. 302, 331 (2002) (noting that aside from categorical takings, its regulatory takings cases are characterized by "essentially ad hoc, factual inquiries"). The inquiry in a *Penn Central* case depends largely, but not exclusively, on "the magnitude of a regulation's economic impact and the degree to which it interferes with legitimate property interests." *Id.* at 539-40.

> The Court in *Lingle* explained the *Penn Central* factors serve "as the principal guidelines for resolving regulatory takings claims that do not fall within the physical takings or *Lucas* rules."

The California Supreme Court adopted the *Penn Central* test for general regulatory takings, but expanded it to include 10 additional, non-exclusive factors. In *Kavanau v. Santa Monica Rent Control Board*, the California Supreme Court addressed the role and application of the *Penn Central* test in a takings analysis. 16 Cal. 4th 761 (1997). The case involved a property owner's claim that Santa Monica's rent control regulations violated his right to due process and effected a taking. The Court ultimately ruled the property owner had no viable inverse condemnation claim. The Court departed from language previously used by California courts, stating that "a regulation...may effect a taking though it does not involve a physical invasion *and leaves the property owner some economically beneficial use of his property.*" *Id.* at 764. The Court observed that the U.S. Supreme Court in *Lucas* had "expressly rejected the 'assumption that the landowner whose deprivation is one step short of complete is not entitled to compensation.'" *Id.* at 774. Thus, the *Kavanau* Court reasoned that such an owner merely loses the benefit of the categorical determination that a taking occurs when a regulation deprives property of all use. The Court also concluded that when a regulation does not result in a physical invasion and does not deprive the property owner of all economically beneficial use of the property, a reviewing court must evaluate the regulation in light of the ad hoc three-part test established by the U.S. Supreme Court in *Penn Central* and discussed in numerous subsequent cases. The Court then listed 10 additional and nonexclusive factors that might be relevant in determining whether a regulatory taking has occurred. *Id.* at 776. Those factors include:

(1) Whether the regulation interferes with interests that are sufficiently bound up with the reasonable expectations of the claimant to constitute property for Fifth Amendment purposes

(2) Whether the regulation affects the existing or traditional use of the property and thus interferes with the property owner's primary expectation

(3) The nature of the State's interest in the regulation and, particularly, whether the regulation is reasonably necessary to the effectuation of a substantial public purpose

(4) Whether the property owner's holding is limited to the specific interest the regulation abrogates or is broader

(5) Whether the government is acquiring resources to permit or facilitate uniquely public functions such as government's entrepreneurial operations

(6) Whether the regulation permits the property owner to profit and to obtain a reasonable return on investment

(7) Whether the regulation provides the property owner benefits or rights that mitigate whatever financial burdens the law has imposed

(8) Whether the regulation prevents the best use of the land

(9) Whether the regulation extinguishes a fundamental attribute of ownership, and

(10) Whether the government is demanding the property as a condition for the granting of a permit

Id. at 775 (internal citations omitted)

The courts have not articulated a standard test for determining when circumstances comprise an acceptable diminution in value as compared to a regulation that "goes too far." *Pennsylvania Coal Co. v. Mahon*, 260 U.S. 393, 415 (1922) ("while property may be regulated to a certain extent, if regulation goes too far it will be recognized as a taking").

Measuring the diminution-in-value caused by the regulation is a difficult task. The courts tend to address the extent of diminution as one factor to consider in determining whether a taking has occurred, rather than in considering an amount of compensation. *See, e.g., Keystone Bituminous Coal Ass'n*, 480 U.S. 470, 496 (1987) (state statute requiring plaintiffs to forgo mining of two percent of the coal that might theoretically be mined was not a taking); *Euclid v. Ambler Realty Co.*, 272 U.S. 365, 384-85 (1926) (zoning ordinance that restricted property to residential use, allegedly resulting in a 75 percent diminution in value, did not operate to take plaintiff's property); *William C. Haas & Co. v. City and County of San Francisco*, 605 F. 2d 1117, 1120 (9th Cir. 1979) (downzoning of property, which benefitted public welfare but which allegedly reduced property value from about $2,000,000 to about $100,000 was not a taking); *HFH, Ltd. v. Superior Court*, 15 Cal. 3d 508, 512 (1975) (refusal to rezone property to commercial use, and subsequently zoning it for residential use, which allegedly reduced value of property from $400,000 to $75,000 held not to be a taking).

In *Brown v. Legal Foundation of Washington*, the U.S. Supreme Court held that where a taking occurs, "just compensation" required by the Fifth Amendment is measured by "the property owner's loss rather than the government's gain." 538 U.S. 216, 235-36 (2003). At issue in *Brown* was a rule requiring that all client funds paid to any Washington lawyer or law firm (or non-lawyer who is licensed to act as escrowee in real estate closings), which are individually insufficient to earn net interest for the client, be pooled into a trust account and the interest paid over to the Legal Foundation of Washington. *Id.* at 224-25. By the terms of the rule itself, the client funds subject to the rule would not have earned interest in any event, thus the requirement that interest be turned over to the Legal Foundation was constitutionally irrelevant. The fact the plaintiffs suffered no loss meant just compensation was not owed. *Id.* at 240.

The *Lucas* Court failed to provide direction as to how damages for a taking should be determined. Based upon a state court finding that the owner's property was rendered valueless by the state coastal zone regulations, the Court suggested the property owner was entitled to compensation. However, the Court did not decide how that compensation should be measured. Rather, it remanded the case to state court for a final decision on this issue. 505 U.S. at 1032.

The U.S. Claims Court addressed this issue when it awarded a developer $933,921 plus interest from the date of the Army Corps of Engineers' denial of a Section 404 permit to place fill in a wetland. *See Formanek v. United States*, 26 Cl. Ct. 332 (1992). The property in *Formanek* consisted of 12 acres of upland and 99 acres of wetland. Within the wetland acreage, there were 45 acres of calcareous fen, a rare wetland plant community. The developer wished to construct a multi-lot industrial project for which the Corps directed him to apply for an individual Section 404 permit, which ultimately was denied.

Ruling on the developer's subsequent lawsuit, the court held that the denial of the permit was proper. However, the court noted that "[t]he value before the taking was $933,921; the value after the permit denial was perhaps $112,000. This change clearly exceeds the 'mere diminution-in-value' which our society must tolerate in order for government to effectively operate." *Id.* at 340. After acknowledging that a substantial reduction in value alone will not effect a taking, the Court found that the permit denial interfered with the developer's investment-backed expectations and this, in combination with the "dramatic reduction," constituted a taking. *Id.* at 340-41.

Applying the *Penn Central* and *Kavanau* tests is often difficult. Government regulations, by their very nature, have an impact on property values. However, mere fluctuations in value are "incidents of ownership," and "cannot be considered a 'taking' in a constitutional sense." *Danforth v. U.S.*, 308 U.S. 271, 285 (1939). The U.S. Supreme Court consistently has "recognized, in a wide variety of contexts, that the government may execute laws or programs that adversely affect recognized economic values." *Penn Cent. Transp. Co. v. City of New York*, 438 U.S. at 124; *see also Long Beach Equities, Inc. v. County of Ventura*, 231 Cal. App. 3d 1016, 1030 (1991) (land use regulation is facially constitutional if it is substantially related to the public welfare, even where a substantial diminution in value is alleged).

> The U.S. Supreme Court consistently has "recognized, in a wide variety of contexts, that the government may execute laws or programs that adversely affect recognized economic values."

In *Herzberg v. County of Plumas*, 133 Cal. App. 4th 1 (2005), a California Court of Appeal noted that "[e]ven the wisest lawyers would have to acknowledge great uncertainty about the scope of the [the United States Supreme Court's] takings jurisprudence [citation omitted]" but acknowledged that "some general rules have taken shape in recent years" and were clarified by the U.S. Supreme Court in *Lingle*. *Id.* at 13. Relying on that clarification, the court in *Herzberg* ruled that an ordinance which does not cause a physical taking, impose conditions on development, or deprive a landowner of all economically beneficial use of land must be analyzed under the ad hoc balancing test of *Penn Central*. The court also applied and analyzed several of the additional factors described in *Kavanau v. Santa Monica Rent Control Board*. 16 Cal. 4th at 776.

In *Herzberg*, a group of landowners sued the county alleging that its "fencing out" ordinance, which declared certain areas of land to be devoted primarily to the grazing of livestock, caused a taking of their property under both the state and federal constitutions. The landowners argued the ordinance, which prohibited landowners from removing grazing animals from the landowners' properties unless the animals were found within a fenced area, unconstitutionally shifted the burden of controlling grazing animals to private landowners, since the ordinance required landowners to construct fences if they desired to prevent livestock from grazing upon their property.

Under the *Penn Central* ad hoc factual inquiry, the court concluded the "fencing out" ordinance was not a taking. It did not interfere with the landowners' investment-backed expectations, since the affected land was in a traditional open grazing area and the "occasional use of and damage to property caused by wandering cattle as they move on" could be avoided by fencing. 133 Cal. App. 4th at 19. Under *Kavanau*, the ordinance also did not restrict the landowners' use of their property or extinguish any fundamental attribute of ownership. *Id.* at 20. The court noted the ordinance supported important historic, traditional, and economic uses of rural property, and held that it "simply does not unconstitutionally 'forc[e] some people alone to bear public burdens which, in all fairness and justice, should be borne by the public as a whole.'" *Id.* (citations omitted) As a result, the ordinance did not effect a taking under either the state or federal constitutions.

Similarly, in *Allegretti & Company v. County of Imperial*, the court rejected a takings claim premised on the imposition of a conditional use permit that limited the total amount of groundwater that could be used on a 2,400-acre parcel of land. 138 Cal. App. 4th 1261, 1278–79 (2006). Analyzing the claim under the *Penn Central* ad hoc test, the court found the regulation was not a physical taking because it did not divert any water or physically invade the property, nor did it deny the landowner all economic use of the property. In applying the *Penn Central* factors, the court noted "the owner's entire property holdings at the time of the alleged taking, not just the adversely affected portion." *Id.* at 1277. The court held the regulation was not a taking because the only economic impact shown was a diminution in value resulting from the inability to farm the entire 2,400 acres, and mere interference with expectations of potential profits gained from farming the entire property was not a compensable interference with "distinct investment-backed expectations." *Id.* at 1278–79.

In *Guggenheim v. City of Goleta*, the Ninth Circuit, sitting *en banc*, held that the City of Goleta's mobile home rent control ordinance did not effect a taking under *Penn Central*. 638 F.3d 1111 (9th Cir. 2010) (en banc). The city's ordinance required the Guggenheims to rent spaces in their mobile home park at rates significantly lower than the market rate. Because mobile homes are almost never actually moved off the parcels on which they sit, the ordinance had the effect of transferring the market value that would otherwise accrue to the park owners through increased future rents to the tenants occupying the park. Because of the ordinance, current tenants selling their mobile homes would be able to charge a substantial premium that represents the present value of the future stream of rental discounts guaranteed by the ordinance.

The court noted that the mobile home rent control ordinance had been applied to the property since 1979 and the Guggenheims purchased the mobile home park in 1997. Thus, the Guggenheims' property was subject to the ordinance at the time they purchased it. Applying *Penn Central*, the Ninth Circuit held that the fact the ordinance applied to the Guggenheims' property at the time they purchased it was fatal to their takings claims. They could have no "distinct investment-backed expectations" that they would be able to charge rents in excess of those allowed under the rent control scheme. *Id.* at 1120. The court noted that "whatever unfairness to the mobile home park owner might have been imposed by rent control, it was imposed long ago, on someone earlier in the Guggenheims' chain of title." *Id.* at 1121–22; *see also MHC Financing Ltd. Partnership v. City of San Rafael*, 714 F.3d 1118, 1127-28 (9th Cir. 2013) (mobile home rent control ordinance did not constitute *Penn Central* taking where ordinance was in effect when plaintiff acquired the property as owner could not have reasonable investment-backed expectation that rent control regime would disappear); *Laurel Park Community, LLC v. City of Tumwater*, 698 F. 3d 1180, 1189-90 (9th Cir. 2012) (ordinance that foreclosed possibility of future conversion of manufactured-home park to multifamily use but allowed continuation of existing manufactured home use and resulted in 15 percent or less diminution in value did not result in a taking).

A contrary result was reached in *Palazzolo*, 533 U.S. at 627. Palazzolo did not own the property at the time the regulations went into effect, and therefore acquired the property with knowledge of the challenged regulations. The Court explained that certain enactments are unreasonable and do not become less so due to the passage of time. Therefore, the Court held, the post-regulation acquisition was not fatal either to the claim that Palazzolo had been deprived of all economically viable uses of the property (*Lucas*), or to the claim that Palazzolo had been deprived of his reasonable investment-backed expectations (*Penn Central*).

Exactions (*Nollan/Dolan*). The fourth type of regulatory taking claim recognized by the Supreme Court is that of exactions, where the government requires an exaction as a condition to issuance of a discretionary permit. These claims are analyzed under the principles set forth in the Court's decisions in *Nollan v. California Coastal Commission*, 483 U.S. 825 (1987), and *Dolan v. City of Tigard*, 512 U.S. 374 (1994). The issue in both *Nollan* and *Dolan* was whether the government could exact an easement as a condition for granting a development permit that it was entitled to deny, without the payment of compensation to the landowners that would otherwise be required for effecting such a taking. See chapter 12 (Exactions) for a more detailed discussion of exactions; *Nollan*, *Dolan*, and their application in California under *Ehrlich v. City of Culver City*, 12 Cal. 4th 854 (1996); and the United States Supreme Court's recent expansion of *Nollan* and *Dolan* in *Koontz v. St. Johns River Water Management District*, 133 S. Ct. 2586 (2013).

TEMPORARY TAKINGS

A temporary taking claim may be based on temporary physical invasion by the government, regulations such as an interim ordinance or a moratorium on development, an error in the processing of land use applications, inordinate delays, or other growth management measures. See *Arkansas Game and Fish Comm'n v. United States*, 133 S. Ct. 511, 519 (2012) (temporary but recurring physical invasion may constitute a taking); *First English Evangelical Lutheran Church v. County of Los Angeles*, 482 U.S. 304, 320 (1987) (temporary application of invalid law required just compensation); *but see City of Monterey v. Del Monte Dunes at Monterey, Ltd.*, 526 U.S. 687, 704 (1999) (U.S. Supreme Court has never provided a definitive statement of the elements of a temporary regulatory taking).

A temporary physical invasion of private property may require the payment of just compensation. *Arkansas Game*, S. Ct. 519. In *Arkansas Game*, the United States Army Corps of Engineers altered the flow of water from a dam between 1993 and 2000 at the request of local farmers. The alterations resulted in extended periods of flooding and allegedly interfered with the timber growing season on lands owned by the State of Arkansas. The Court held that government-induced flooding need not be permanent to be compensable as a taking. The Court noted that cases alleging temporary physical invasions require case-specific factual inquiries to determine whether a taking has occurred. *Id.* at 521 (citing *Penn Central* and *Loretto*).

Where a landowner is deprived of all use of property while an invalid law is in effect, mere withdrawal of the regulation is an insufficient remedy, and compensation for use of the property during the period in which the law was in effect must be paid. *First English*, 482 U.S. at 321. The landowner in *First English* operated a campground on which a number of buildings had been destroyed by a flood. An interim Los Angeles County ordinance prohibited construction or reconstruction of any building or structure in an interim flood protection area that included the owner's

> A temporary taking claim may be based on temporary physical invasion by the government, regulations such as an interim ordinance or a moratorium on development, an error in the processing of land use applications, inordinate delays or other growth management measures.

land. The Court assumed for purposes of the appeal that the ordinance deprived the owner of all economically beneficial use of its property. It then held that such deprivation constituted a temporary taking of the property for which compensation must be paid. "'[T]emporary' takings which…deny a landowner all use of his property, are not different in kind from permanent takings, for which the Constitution clearly requires compensation." *Id.* at 318. Thus, the Court held that "where the government's activities have already worked a taking of all use of property, no subsequent action by the government can relieve it of the duty to provide compensation for the period during which the taking was effective." *Id.* at 321.[1] Subsequent federal and state decisions have affirmed this principle.

Federal decisions. The U.S. Supreme Court's 2002 decision in *Tahoe-Sierra Preservation Council, Inc. v. Tahoe Regional Planning Agency* reaffirmed the ability of cities to use temporary development moratoria, such as interim ordinances that can be adopted under Government Code section 65858, as a planning tool without necessarily having to compensate property owners for the time period during which development is banned. 535 U.S. at 353.

In *Tahoe-Sierra*, the Tahoe Regional Planning Agency imposed two moratoria totaling 32 months on development in the Lake Tahoe basin while formulating a comprehensive land use plan for the area. Property owners filed suit, claiming the moratoria constituted a temporary categorical taking under *Lucas*. In rejecting this argument, the Court stated that because property subject to a temporary moratorium would recover its value when the moratorium was lifted, the moratorium did not permanently deprive the owner of all economically viable use. In effect, the Court held a moratorium is not a per se facial taking.

The landowners also had asked the Court to set a bright-line rule that any moratorium of longer than one year was a categorical taking. The Court refused, stating that formulation of a general rule of this kind was more suitable for the state legislatures. The Court noted many states (including California) have enacted legislation authorizing interim ordinances, including moratoria, with specific time limits. *See, e.g.,* Gov't Code § 65858 (authorizing interim moratoria of up to two years).

> The Court stated that unlike the "extraordinary circumstances" in which the government deprives a property owner of all economic use, moratoria are used widely among land use planners to preserve the status quo while formulating a more permanent development strategy.

The Court stated that unlike the "extraordinary circumstances" in which the government deprives a property owner of all economic use, moratoria are used widely among land use planners to preserve the status quo while formulating a more permanent development strategy. The Court refused to adopt the landowners' proposed categorical rule which would treat these interim measures as takings regardless of the good faith of the planners, the reasonable expectations of the landowners, or the actual impact of the moratorium on property values. 535 U.S. at 303–304.

The Court instead held that where a government enacts a temporary regulation that, while in effect, denies a property owner all viable economic use of the property, a reviewing court should apply the *Penn Central* factors to determine its constitutionality. *Id.* at 334–35; *see also Arkansas Game*, 133 S. Ct. at 519 (claims for temporary but recurring physical takings should be subject to "situation specific factual inquiries," citing *Penn Central*); *Loewenstein v. City of Lafayette*, 103 Cal. App. 4th 718, 736–37 (2002)

---

1 On remand, however, the California court of appeal held, for two independent reasons, that no taking had occurred:
- The interim ordinance in question substantially advanced the pre-eminent state interest in public safety and did not deny the church all use of its property.
- The interim ordinance only imposed a reasonable moratorium for a reasonable period of time while the county conducted a study and determined what uses, if any, were compatible with public safety.

First English, 210 Cal. App. 3d at 1372.

(where delay exists not for delay's sake but legitimate oversight, *Penn Central* factors are negated; a landowner cannot reasonably expect there will be no delays).

The Court stated the interest in facilitating informed decisionmaking by regulatory agencies would counsel against adopting a per se rule that would impose such severe costs on their deliberations. Otherwise, the financial constraints of compensating property owners during a moratorium might force cities to rush through the planning process or abandon the practice altogether. To the extent that communities would be forced to abandon using moratoria, landowners would have incentives to develop their property quickly before a comprehensive plan could be enacted, thereby fostering inefficient and ill-conceived growth.

Moreover, with a temporary ban on development there is less risk that individual landowners will be "singled out" to bear a special burden that should be shared by the public as a whole. At least with a moratorium, there is a "reciprocity of advantage," because it protects the interests of all affected landowners against immediate construction that might be inconsistent with the provisions of the plan that ultimately is adopted. "While each of us is burdened somewhat by such restrictions, we, in turn, benefit greatly from the restrictions that are placed on others." *Tahoe-Sierra*, 535 U.S. at 341.

Moratoria and other growth management measures based on documented health, safety, and general welfare concerns are more likely than other types of measures to withstand constitutional challenges. *See id.* at 329. In cases where the perceived problems of development can be mitigated, those measures that relax restrictions upon attainment of realistic service level goals also will be more likely to withstand attack.

California decisions. In *Landgate, Inc. v. California Coastal Commission*, 17 Cal. 4th 1006 (1998), the California Supreme Court addressed the issue of "temporary takings" in light of *First English*, 482 U.S. 304 (1987).

Plaintiff Landgate owned two long, thin parcels of land in the Malibu Hills. In the mid-1980s, the County of Los Angeles planned for a road that would run through the two lots. Landgate's predecessor and the county agreed the county would build the road in exchange for a lot line adjustment reconfiguring the lots into north of the road and south of the road. In October 1990, Landgate bought the northern lot and received the county's permission to grade the lot and build a single-family home. However, after an investigation raised objections regarding the grading plan and the height of the proposed home, along with contentions that the lot line adjustment had been illegal, the California Coastal Commission rejected Landgate's application. Landgate sued the Commission seeking compensation for a taking, contending the Commission had no jurisdiction over the lot line adjustment. While the Court ultimately agreed that the Commission had no jurisdiction over a lot line adjustment, it also found that the error did not result in a taking.

In ruling for the Commission, the California Supreme Court stated that "[v]irtually every court that has examined the issue has concluded...that a regulatory mistake resulting in delay does not, by itself, amount to a taking of property." *Id.* A government agency's error "in the development approval process does not necessarily amount to a taking even if the error in some way diminishes the value of the subject property, any more than the commission of state law error during a criminal trial is an automatic violation of the due process clause." *Id.* at 1016; *accord, Del Oro Hills v. City of Oceanside*, 31 Cal. App. 4th 1060, 1080 (1995) (an invalid regulation is not necessarily an unconstitutional one). Although the enforcement of a law or regulation that deprives property of all value is a compensable taking, land use regulations that are part of a reasonable regulatory process designed to advance legitimate government interests are not takings. *Landgate*, 17 Cal.4th at 1021.

> Moratoria and other growth management measures based on documented health, safety, and general welfare concerns are more likely than other types of measures to withstand constitutional challenges.

The *Landgate* Court also noted that *First English* emphasized the narrowness of its holding. "We...point out that the allegation of the complaint which we treat as true for purposes of our decision was that the ordinance in question denied appellant all use of its property. We limit our holding to the facts presented, and of course do not deal with the quite different questions that would arise in the case of normal delays in obtaining building permits, changes in zoning ordinances, variances, and the like which are not before us." *Landgate*, 17 Cal. 4th at 1017 (quoting *First English*, 482 U.S. at 321).

The significance of *Landgate* is its holding that an erroneous assertion of jurisdiction by the Coastal Commission, which prevented a landowner's development of his property for two years, was merely a "normal delay" in the development process and therefore did not amount to a taking. *See also Buckley v. California Coastal Comm'n*, 68 Cal. App. 4th 178, 183 (1998) (relying on *Landgate*, finding no taking even though the Coastal Commission acted erroneously in assuming jurisdiction over the development).

Landgate was distinguished in *Ali v. City of Los Angeles*, where the court held an unreasonable delay in issuing a demolition permit and the eventual denial of the permit was a temporary taking. 77 Cal. App. 4th 246, 254-55 (1999). The City of Los Angeles took approximately 19 months to issue a demolition permit for the plaintiff's building, which the city temporarily considered a single-room occupancy hotel, after a fire substantially destroyed the building. In a prior appeal, the court ruled this delay violated the Ellis Act (Gov't Code §§ 7060-7060.7), which precludes public agencies from forcing property owners to continue offering accommodations for rent or lease.

On remand, the trial court found a temporary taking. The parties stipulated as to the amount of compensation owed, and the judgment awarded Ali $1,199,237 plus interest. The appellate court affirmed. In so doing, it looked to the California Supreme Court decision in *Landgate* for guidance. In *Ali*, the court concluded the city's position, unlike the Coastal Commission's position in *Landgate*, was "so unreasonable from a legal standpoint as to lead to the conclusion that it was taken for no purpose other than to delay the development project before it." 77 Cal. App. 4th at 254-55. The city had contravened an earlier, unrelated published decision, in which the court held the Ellis Act preempted local laws, and that property owners were entitled to a demolition permit without having to comply with local conditions. The city's contrary position was arbitrary and unreasonable in light of this precedent. The delay in issuing the permit, therefore, was not a "normal delay" in the development process, and the property owner was entitled to damages for the temporary taking. *Id.* at 255.

In *Loewenstein v. City of Lafayette*, the court held a two-year delay precipitated by a city's erroneous action was not an unlawful temporary taking. 103 Cal. App. 4th 718, 729 (2002). In *Loewenstein*, property owners applied for a lot line adjustment, which would have allowed the owners to reconfigure one large and one small lot into two standard lots, and build an additional home. The city denied the project because it believed the adjustment would create an extra lot in a restricted subdivision. The city also was concerned the proposed lot line adjustment would violate municipal ordinances regarding hillside property. Eventually, a trial court ruled that the city had erred and taken plaintiff's property. Thereafter, the city approved the adjustment, thus rendering the taking temporary.

On appeal, the court reversed the trial court decision. It held that *Landgate* precluded a takings finding because the time spent resolving the legality of the lot line adjustment constituted a normal delay in the process of obtaining a land use permit. The delay in this case was not objectively unreasonable; it was not taken solely to delay the proposed project. Rather, the city merely was attempting to carry out reasonable land use policies. *Id.* at 733, citing *Littoral Dev. Co. v. San Francisco Bay Conser. & Dev. Comm'n*, 33 Cal. App. 4th 211, 221 (1995) (no taking where delay caused by the erroneous decision of a regulatory agency; there was no egregious bureaucratic overreaching and the agency's actions "were facially valid and supported by a plausible though erroneous legal argument").

Further, the court in *Lowenstein* held, the *Penn Central* factors are negated when *Landgate* applies because a property owner can have no reasonable expectation there will be no delays in the processing of his application. *Id.* at 736-37. In *Allegretti & Company v. County of Imperial*, the court agreed:

> Once a court determines that a governmental entity engaged in decisionmaking whose purpose is not delay for delay's sake but legitimate oversight, the question of whether a landowner has a reasonable investment-backed expectation that is impacted in a manner requiring compensation is, of necessity, answered in the negative. A landowner can have no reasonable expectation that there will be no delays or bona fide differences of opinion in the application process for development permits. Sometimes the application process must detour to the court process to resolve genuine disagreement. Because such delay comes within the *Landgate* category of normal delays in the development approval process, there is no taking even if the value of the subject property is diminished in some way.

138 Cal. App. 4th 1261, 1284-85 (2006) (quoting *Loewenstein*, 103 Cal. App. 4th at 736-37)

No temporary taking was found where an interim delay in acting on a building permit left some beneficial use of the property. *Guinnane v. City and County of San Francisco*, 197 Cal. App. 3d 862 (1987). In *Guinnane*, the landowner sued for damages, claiming that designation of his land as a possible site for a public park was an unreasonable precondemnation action, and that delays in processing his building permit application entitled him to damages for a temporary taking under *First English*.

First, the court rejected the claim that the city's designation of an area including the owner's property as open space and for study for possible acquisition as a public park amounted to unreasonable precondemnation activities. Mere planning activities of the city did not entitle the owner to require the city to condemn the property in question and pay the landowner the market value of the property that existed before the threat of condemnation arose. *Id.* at 867. The court distinguished the facts in this case from the situation where a city had actually announced or initiated eminent domain proceedings, thereby entitling the landowner to damages for inverse condemnation. *Id.* (citing *Klopping v. City of Whittier*, 8 Cal. 3d 39, 52 (1972)).

Mere planning activities of the city did not entitle the owner to require the city to condemn the property in question and pay the landowner the market value of the property that existed before the threat of condemnation arose.

Second, the court found the temporary suspension of land use that occurs during a normal governmental decisionmaking process, such as environmental review, does not constitute a taking. 197 Cal. App. 3d at 866-67. The court rejected the owner's claim that the city's delay in acting on his application was unusual, excessive, and unreasonable. To the contrary, the court found that many of the delays were directly attributable to the owner.

Finally, the court also indicated the landowner had not been deprived of all economically viable use of his land during the period of environmental review, noting that "the focus of the inquiry is on the uses of the property which remain." *Id.* at 868 (citing *Penn Central Transp. Co. v. City of New York*, 438 U.S. 104 (1978)). The court held, "Plaintiff cannot contend he was denied all use of his property. He was neither deprived of his right to exclude others from his land nor denied the right to sell the property." *Id.* (emphasis in original).[2]

Measure of compensation for a temporary taking. The Court in *First English* indicated there must be "payment of fair value for the use of the property during [the period of the taking]." *Id.* at 322. However, it did not indicate how fair value of the use is to be determined.

> There are many approaches to determining the value of use, including: rental value, reasonable investment-backed expectations, equity interest rate, the probability method, "before-and-after," and option value.

There are many approaches to determining the value of use, including: rental value, reasonable investment-backed expectations, equity interest rate, the probability method, "before-and-after," and option value. Each of these methods is briefly discussed below.

The rental value approach simply assigns damages at the fair market rental value multiplied by the period of the taking. *See Kimball Laundry Co. v. U.S.*, 338 U.S. 1, 7 (1949). Though simple, this approach is not readily applicable to claim that a property's *future* use is being restricted, e.g., where future development is unreasonably delayed. Other decisions, which were cited by the *First English* court in the context of discussing temporary takings, address compensation based on the value of a leasehold interest in the property taken. *First English*, 482 U.S. at 318 (citing *Kimball Laundry Co. v. United States*, 338 U.S. 1 (1949); *U.S. v. Petty Motor Co.*, 327 U.S. 372 (1946); and *United States v. General Motors Corp.*, 323 U.S. 373 (1945)).

Another approach is to relate damages to the owner's reasonable "investment-backed expectations." This measure generally favors owners who have overpaid (or at least paid top dollar) for their property. This was not likely the Court's intention, and the factor is generally used by courts as only one factor to consider in determining whether a taking has occurred, rather than the measure of compensation. The reasonable, investment-backed expectations argument was discussed in *Long Beach Equities, Inc. v. County of Ventura*, 231 Cal. App. 3d 1016 (1991). There, in upholding a local growth control regulation, the court referred to the developer's argument that its reasonable investment-backed expectations to profitably build a residential subdivision had been rendered economically infeasible because of past and future delays caused by the laws and the conduct of the defendants. *Id.* at 1039–40. The court said:

> There is considerable controversy whether the courts should consider a landowner's profit expectations in an inverse condemnation action. Although in some cases it may be a legitimate consideration, here LBE has not stated facts which enable it to proceed on this theory....
>
> Prediction of profitability is essentially a matter of reasoned speculation that courts are not especially competent to perform. The Fifth Amendment is not a panacea for less-than-perfect investment or business opportunities.

Id.

Other courts have invoked the equity interest approach. For example, the Eleventh Circuit ruled that an award for a temporary taking be based on the "market rate return computed over the period of the temporary taking on the difference between the property's fair market value without the regulatory restriction and its fair market value with the restriction." *Wheeler v. City of Pleasant Grove*, 896 F. 2d 1347, 1350 (11th Cir. 1990) (*Wheeler IV*). The court in *Wheeler IV* held it was erroneous for the district court to

---

[2] In *Dolan v. City of Tigard*, the U.S. Supreme Court emphasized the importance of this "right to exclude others" from the land, stating it is "'one of the most essential sticks in the bundle of rights that are commonly characterized as property.'" 512 U.S. 374, 384 (1994) (quoting *Kaiser Aetna v. U.S.*, 444 U.S. 164, 176 (1979)).

look to the fair market value of the land on which apartments were to be built. Instead, it should have focused on the "difference in the fair market value of appellants' right to develop their project when they received their building permit, and the fair market value of what remained after the city's actions against appellants." *Id.* at 1351. *Wheeler IV* provides the most significant attempt to define a formula for compensation, holding that the accurate measure of damages is based on the difference between the property's fair market value with the regulatory restriction and its fair market value without the restriction. *Id.* at 1350.

Although the equity interest approach is a more accurate statement of the owner's actual losses, this approach has been criticized because it requires the court to assume that projected development potential would have been realized. It also fails to consider other uses to which the land could be put under the restrictive regulations, and ignores other investment opportunities for capital that would have gone into the completed development.

The probability approach to is an attempt to strike a balance between avoiding the speculation inherent in the above approaches while still protecting a property owner from unreasonable delay in its attempts to develop land. This method assesses the probability that a development permit would have been approved in the absence of the restrictive regulation, taking into consideration the highest and lowest valuations of the property proposed by the parties. The full difference between these values may only be awarded if the landowner can show with certainty that its land would have been developed but for the restrictive ordinance. Then, the court determines compensation by applying a reasonable rate of return to the difference in the high and low valuations.

> The probability approach to is an attempt to strike a balance between avoiding the speculation inherent in the above approaches while still protecting a property owner from unreasonable delay in its attempts to develop land.

The probability method was articulated in *Herrington v. County of Sonoma*, 790 F. Supp. 909, 915-16 (N.D. Cal. 1991). The Herringtons owned a parcel of land for which they submitted a 32 lot subdivision proposal. After the county determined their proposal was inconsistent with the county's general plan, they sued the county for violations of due process and equal protection. Following a jury trial, the Herringtons were awarded $2,500,600 in damages. On appeal, the Ninth Circuit affirmed the finding of liability, but vacated the damages award and remanded for a retrial on this issue. *Herrington v. County of Sonoma*, 834 F. 2d 1488, 1503 (9th Cir. 1987), amended by 857 F. 2d 567 (9th Cir. 1988). The district court then considered the remanded issue of damages and used the probability method to determine that property owners were entitled to a reduced amount of damages for property value that was lost due to the county's rejection of their subdivision proposal. *Herrington*, 790 F. Supp. at 915-16.

The district court awarded a much smaller amount of damages to the Herringtons, construing their loss as temporary rather than permanent. The lost value of the property, as calculated by the Herringtons, was too high because approval of a 32-lot subdivision by the county was speculative. Furthermore, the Herringtons continued to own the property, which had appreciated substantially. The harm suffered due to the county's conduct was a temporary taking of the ability to use or develop the property. Such harm was valued at $52,123.52 plus interest. The total damages award came to $121,472.06, a far cry from the initial award of $2,500,600. *Id.* at 924-25. The district court's analysis was upheld on appeal. *Herrington v. County of Sonoma*, 12 F. 3d 901, 903 (9th Cir. 1993).

The "before and after" approach is a basic diminution of value approach that works in one of two ways. Under one approach, the court determines the difference between the value of a piece of property on the date the regulatory taking begins and then again on the date the taking ceases. 790 F. Supp. at 914. Under the second, the court finds the difference between the value immediately before the invalid regulation was imposed and the value immediately after its imposition. However, this approach is rarely used by the courts, likely because it does not value the use during the taking, but rather only the fee interest.

The option value approach calculates damages based on the value of a fictional option to buy the property in question for the period of the regulatory taking. Though this may be an accurate way of determining the value of the interest taken, it may not bear any relationship to the property owner's actual losses.

California courts have thus far bypassed the opportunity to clarify this confusing area of law. In *Ali v. City of Los Angeles*, the court affirmed a judgment in favor of the plaintiff landowner and an award for $1,199,237, based upon a stipulation as to the amount of compensation. 77 Cal. App. 4th at 249. The court did not discuss the calculation of compensation, making the case of little value in clarifying the issue.

SEGMENTATION—THE RELEVANT PARCEL ISSUE

The determination whether all economically viable use of a given property has been denied will depend on how "property" is defined. If, for example, a regulation precludes development on 90 percent of a parcel, should the regulation be considered to have deprived the owner of all use of that segment, or should the analysis focus instead on the use and value of the parcel viewed as a whole? If a court were to look only at the segment on which all use was prohibited, it would find a categorical taking under *Lucas*. If the parcel is viewed as a whole, however, then the burden remains on the property owner to prove the city's action unreasonably interferes with the owner's investment-backed expectations under *Penn Central*. The U.S. Supreme Court acknowledged in *Palazzolo v. Rhode Island* and again in *Lucas v. South Carolina Coastal Council* that the question remained open. *Palazzolo v. Rhode Island*, 533 U. S. 606, 631 (2001) (noting that the Court has "at times expressed discomfort with the logic of [the parcel as a whole] rule"); *Lucas v. South Carolina Coastal Council*, 505 U. S. 1003, 1017, n. 7 (1992) (recognizing that "uncertainty regarding the composition of the denominator in [the Court's] 'deprivation' fraction has produced inconsistent pronouncements by the Court," and that the relevant calculus is a "difficult question").

The Court addressed the issue to some extent in *Tahoe-Sierra Preservation Council, Inc. v. Tahoe Reg'l Planning Agency*, 535 U.S. 302 (2002). *Tahoe-Sierra* involved a pair of 32-month moratoria on development. The landowners argued that property ownership should be divided into discrete temporal segments, and that because the moratoria had denied them all use of their land during one such 32-month segment, the moratoria should be declared a categorical taking automatically entitling the landowners to compensation under *Lucas*. The Court rejected this argument, holding that the property interest in question must be evaluated as a whole, and that the length of time a regulation denies an owner the use of its property is only one factor to consider in determining whether or not a taking has occurred. The Court explained that the categorical rule of *Lucas* would not apply if the diminution in value were 95 percent instead of 100 percent of the property. Anything less than a "complete elimination of value" or a "total loss," the Court held, would require the kind of analysis applied in *Penn Central*. 535 U.S. at 330.

The Ninth Circuit chimed in with *Vacation Village, Inc. v. Clark County*, where owners of property near an airport claimed the county inversely condemned their property by restricting allowed uses. 497 F.3d 902 (2007). The Ninth Circuit determined the ordinance was not a regulatory taking under the *Penn Central* test in part because only five percent of the landowners' property was affected. However, it also based its decision on the fact that the affected portion could be put to other uses such as a water feature, some form of landscaping, or a parking lot. 497 F. 3d at 918-19.

California courts have not squarely decided the segmentation, or relevant parcel, issue. They have stated, however, that the question of whether differently zoned contiguous parcels are considered separately or as a whole depends on the facts, including the potential for development of each of the properties "from the standpoint of both economics and governmental cooperation." *Twain Harte Assocs., Ltd. v. County of Tuolumne*, 217 Cal. App. 3d 71, 87 (1990) (remanding to the trial court the issue of whether an undeveloped 1.7-acre parcel that had been downzoned from commercial to open space should be viewed as part of an 8.5-acre parcel on which the owner had built a shopping center). California courts also have identified as an important factor the availability of density transfers or other techniques for shifting burdens and benefits between the parcels. *See Aptos Seascape Corp. v. County of Santa Cruz*, 138 Cal. App. 3d 484, 497 (1982).

GROUNDS FOR DENIAL OF A TAKINGS CLAIM

The ripeness requirement. Courts have been strict with property owners in determining when they can bring an action challenging a regulation as a taking. A property owner must (1) not only receive a final determination from the city regarding use of the property, but also (2) seek compensation through the procedures the state has provided before a takings claim is ripe.[3] Some courts have held that this ripeness rule applies only to as applied challenges, and not when a plaintiff contends that a statute or ordinance is unconstitutional on its face. *See Rezai v. City of Tustin*, 26 Cal. App. 4th 443, 448 (1994).

> Courts have been strict with property owners in determining when they can bring an action challenging a regulation as a taking.

Courts are inconsistent in distinguishing between ripeness requirements and the requirement that a plaintiff exhaust administrative remedies. For example, one California court explained that the ripeness doctrine involves "a test of whether a developer has exhausted all administrative appeals regarding a particular application for development. The developer must show that it has submitted the appropriate applications necessary to proceed with the particular project and that it has received a final rejection of those applications." *Long Beach Equities, Inc. v. County of Ventura*, 231 Cal. App. 3d at 1034. Accordingly, some courts may treat the ripeness requirements addressed here as exhaustion of administrative remedies requirements.

Ripeness and the requirement for a final determination of the agency. As to the first ripeness requirement, the general rule is that a constitutional challenge to a land use regulation is ripe when the landowner has received the agency's "final, definitive position regarding how it will apply the regulations at issue to the particular land in question." *MacDonald, Sommer & Frates v. County of Yolo*, 477 U.S. 340, 351 (1986); *Williamson County Reg'l Planning Comm'n v. Hamilton Bank*, 473 U.S. 172 (1985). In both *MacDonald* and *Williamson County*, the U.S. Supreme Court required the submission and resubmission of development plans or the application for variances before the takings claim would be ripe for adjudication, unless such requests would be futile.

In *MacDonald*, the Court held mere rejection of one development application (a subdivision map) could not constitute a taking because denial of a single application

---

3 For a lengthy discussion of these two requirements, see *Levald Inc. v. City of Palm Desert*, 998 F. 2d 680 (9th Cir. 1993), and *Suitum v. Tahoe Regional Planning Agency*, 520 U.S. 725 (1997).

did not establish the county's final decision as to how land use regulation would be applied to the property in question. 477 U.S. at 342. The U.S. Supreme Court attempted to provide further clarification of the "final decision" aspect of a ripeness inquiry in *Palazzolo v. Rhode Island*, 533 U.S. 606 (2001). Palazzolo owned a waterfront parcel consisting mainly of salt marsh, subject to tidal flooding, over which the Rhode Island Coastal Resources Management Council had regulatory authority. Palazzolo's two separate applications for a private beach club were denied by the council. Palazzolo filed an inverse condemnation action claiming the council's action had deprived him of "all economically beneficial use" of his property, thus effecting a taking without just compensation. The Court stated the central question in resolving the ripeness issue under *Williamson County* is whether the petitioner obtained a final decision from the public agency determining the permitted use of the land. While a landowner must give a land use authority an opportunity to exercise its discretion, once it becomes clear that the agency lacks the discretion to permit any development, or the permissible uses of the property are known to a reasonable degree of certainty, a takings claim is likely to have ripened. *Palazzolo*, 533 U.S. at 620.

> While a landowner must give a land use authority an opportunity to exercise its discretion, once it becomes clear that the agency lacks the discretion to permit any development, or the permissible uses of the property are known to a reasonable degree of certainty, a takings claim is likely to have ripened.

The Court noted, however, that Palazzolo's claim was quite unlike those cases where an owner challenged a land use authority's denial of a substantial project, leaving doubt whether a more modest submission or an application for a variance would be accepted. *See MacDonald*, 477 U.S. at 350-51 (1986) (denial of 159-home subdivision); *Williamson County*, 473 U.S. at 182 (denial of 476-unit subdivision); *cf. Agins v. City of Tiburon*, 447 U.S. at 260 (1980) (the case was not ripe because no plan to develop was submitted). Those cases stand for the important principle that a landowner may not establish a taking before a land use authority has the opportunity, using its own reasonable procedures, to decide and explain the reach of a challenged regulation.

The *Palazzolo* Court took a somewhat innovative position by placing the burden on the government to indicate possible development options once the landowner had made a reasonable application for development. Nevertheless, this case still fails to provide predictability as to when a court will find a final decision has been made. The inquiry thus remains an essentially ad hoc endeavor, but one that *Palazzolo* indicates may now be resolved in favor of landowners when the record is unclear.

In *Dunn v. County of Santa Barbara*, the court relied on the analysis in *Palazzolo* to determine that a landowner's regulatory takings claims were ripe for adjudication. 135 Cal. App. 4th 1281, 1300-01 (2006). In *Dunn*, the County of Santa Barbara had denied the landowner's application to split a parcel into two parcels, each with a residence, concluding that only one residence could be built on the property. The court held that the permissible use of the property was known to a reasonably certain degree because the county had made it clear that its wetland and environmental regulations effectively limited development to one residence. *Id.* Dunn's regulatory takings claims and the derivative causes of action therefore were ripe even though he had not yet sought permission to build a single-family residence on his property. *Id.* at 1301.

Other California cases likewise have sought to clarify the final decision rule articulated in *Williamson County* and *MacDonald*. In *Kinzli v. City of Santa Cruz*, the property owner's takings claim was dismissed because there had been no attempt to secure a development permit prior to bringing suit. 818 F. 2d 1449, 1452-53 (9th Cir. 1987). Relying on *Williamson County*, the Ninth Circuit ruled that an inverse condemnation cause of action is not ripe until the landowner has secured a "final decision" on a permit application and a request for a variance. This prerequisite could be waived only upon a showing that such requests would be futile, i.e. "clear beyond peradventure that excessive delay in such a final determination [would cause] the present destruction of the property's beneficial use." Id. at 1454. The *Kinzli* court also suggested another test for futility: "[T]he submission of a plan for development is futile if a sufficient number of prior applications have been rejected by the planning authority." Id.

The *Kinzli* court ultimately held that a final decision by a city requires at least: "(1) a rejected development plan and (2) a denial of a variance or other similar land use relief such as a conditional use permit." 818 F. 2d at 1454; *see also Long Beach Equities, Inc.*, 231 Cal. App. 3d at 1016; *accord, Zilber v. Town of Moraga*, 692 F. Supp. 1195, 1199 (N.D. Cal. 1988) ("a property owner must make use of the development and variance application procedures even when the statute deprives the property owner of all beneficial uses and the application will therefore be denied....[N]o claim will be heard on the merits until rejection of development and variance applications."); *County of Alameda v. Superior Court of Alameda County*, 133 Cal. App. 4th 558, 570 (2005).

In *Milagra Ridge Partners Ltd. v. City of Pacifica*, the court further clarified an applicant's obligation to obtain a final determination of its development rights. 62 Cal. App. 4th 108, 119 (1998). In *Milagra*, the city denied a developer's original application as being inconsistent with the city's general plan. It later approved a different residential development plan and a corresponding general plan amendment, but the amendment was rejected by the electorate. The developer then sued for inverse condemnation. The court held the developer's claim was not ripe because the developer had not submitted a development application for the property as it was then zoned. The developer's request for a general plan amendment was not the equivalent of a request for a variance under the regulations then in effect. "[F]inality for purposes of a takings claim is determined by a denial of a requested deviation from the *present* land use scheme, not the rejection of an attempt to alter a comprehensive, long-range development scheme for the entire community." Id. The court noted that, under the present regulations, a substantially greater portion of the property was zoned commercial, which often carries a higher value than residential use. Thus, it was possible that some combination of commercial and residential use would be approved and would produce an economically viable use of the land. Id. Until a final determination was made under the present regulations, however, the claim was not ripe. *See also, Sinclair Oil Corp. v. County of Santa Barbara*, 96 F. 3d 401, 405-09 (9th Cir. 1996).

When, however, the agency has signalled that it has no intention of allowing the development reflected in its then-current plans, further applications may be futile. That was the case in *Hoehne v. County of San Benito*, 870 F.2d 529, 532-33 (1989), where the county downzoned the property to restrict further development. The court noted that when the county did so, "the supervisors themselves sent a clear, and we believe, final signal announcing their views as to the acceptable use of the property." Id. at 532-33. Accordingly, the court held, further applications would have been futile. Id.

A property owner's failure to attempt to sell or transfer development rights from the land that is claimed to have been taken may not bar a taking claim. *See Suitum v. Tahoe Regional Planning Agency*, 520 U.S. 725, 726 (1997). In *Suitum*, the U.S. Supreme Court held that the plaintiff's suit, which claimed that the Tahoe Regional Planning Agency had taken her property when it denied permission to build a house, could proceed even though the plaintiff had not attempted to sell or transfer the development rights associated with her property. *Suitum*, 520 U.S. at 744. The Court noted there was a "final decision" in this instance because the agency had determined irrevocably that

> When the agency has signalled that it has no intention of allowing the development reflected in its then-current plans, further applications may be futile.

Suitum could not build on her property. Furthermore, the agency lacked discretion to grant an exception to the development ban and the trial court could estimate the value of Suitum's transferrable development rights from evidence already presented to it. For these reasons, the Court held there was no need for Suitum to market her transferrable development rights before the trial court could decide her takings claim. *Id.* at 726.

Ripeness and the requirement to seek compensation through state procedures. The second ripeness requirement, applicable to suits brought in federal court, is that the owner first must seek compensation through the procedures the state has provided. *See Williamson County Regional Planning Commission v. Hamilton Bank*, 473 U.S. 172, 194 (1985); *Schnuck v. City of Santa Monica*, 935 F .2d 171, 173-74 (9th Cir. 1991) (there is a procedure available to a plaintiff in California for seeking compensation from the state). Unless the attempt would be futile, failure to seek compensation in state court requires dismissal of a federal takings case.

The Ninth Circuit applied this rule in *Ventura Mobilehome Communities Owners Association v. City of San Buenaventura*, 371 F. 3d 1046, 1053-54 (9th Cir. 2004). The plaintiffs there challenged as a taking a mobile home rent control ordinance passed by the city claiming that it allowed owners to realize a premium on the sale of their mobile homes amounting to the present value of future rent limitations. While the plaintiffs had engaged in substantial negotiations with the city to make changes to the ordinance and had even mediated their dispute, they had not filed a state court proceeding seeking compensation. *Id.* at 1053. Nor had they applied for relief from the rent restrictions under provisions available in the ordinance itself. *Id.* Plaintiffs' failure to seek such compensation or relief in state court made their claims unripe for review in federal court. *Id.* at 1054; *see also City of Monterey v. Dela Monte Dunes*, 526 U.S. 687, 688-89 (1999).

The practical result of the requirement that a property owner first seek just compensation through state procedures is that it will almost always preclude litigation of any taking claim in federal court. The landowner first must lose his or her takings challenge in state court in order to ripen a federal constitutional challenge; however, under the Full Faith and Credit Clause of the U.S. Constitution, the state court judgment usually will be given res judicata effect, precluding litigation of the issue in federal court. *See, e.g., Palomar Mobilehome Park Ass'n v. City of San Marcos*, 989 F. 2d 362, 364-65 (9th Cir. 1993); *but see Fields v. Sarasota Manatee Airport Auth.*, 953 F .2d 1299, 1303 (11th Cir. 1992) (describing a procedure for "reserving" federal claims for litigation in federal court); Thomas E. Roberts, *Procedural Implications of* Williamson County/First English *in Regulating Takings Litigation, Reservations, Removals, Diversity Supplemental Jurisdiction, Rooker-Feldman, and Res Judicata*, 31 Envtl. L. Rep. News & Analysis, no. 4 at 10353-70, Environmental Law Institute (April 2001).

The U.S. Supreme Court illustrated in *San Remo Hotel v. City and County of San Francisco* how "issue preclusion" typically occurs in the context of federal court takings challenges. 545 U.S. 323, 342-47 (2005). At issue in *San Remo* was a hotel conversion ordinance that prevented residential hotel owners from converting their units to tourist use unless they constructed new units, rehabilitated old ones, or paid an in lieu fee. Owners of the San Remo Hotel filed a series of administrative appeals and lawsuits in both state and federal court challenging the validity of the ordinance.

In a proceeding brought by the owners in federal court, the court held that because they had not sought and been denied just compensation in state court for the alleged taking effected by the ordinance, their claim was unripe under *Williamson County*. The owners then proceeded in state court seeking compensation for the alleged taking. They purported to reserve in the state court proceedings the right to later pursue a federal takings claim under the Fifth Amendment in federal court. The owners litigated the state court proceeding by raising a variety of regulatory takings issues, including whether the ordinance substantially advanced a legitimate state interest. The state court denied compensation and in doing so chose to address and apply federal standards.

The San Remo owners then returned to federal court. The U.S. Supreme Court held that issue preclusion prevented the owners from relitigating in federal court those claims that had been presented to and decided by a state court of competent jurisdiction. The owners argued the doctrine of issue preclusion ought not to apply where a litigant has been forced by *Williamson County* to proceed in state court to ripen a federal claim. The *San Remo* Court rejected this argument, noting a property owner does not necessarily have a right to try its federal claims in federal court. Rather, federal courts are required give preclusive effect to issues that were conclusively decided in state courts. *San Remo*, 545 U.S. at 343-347; *see also Adam Bros. Farming, Inc. v. County of Santa Barbara*, 604 F.3d 1142, 1149 (9th Cir. 2010) (applying res judicata to bar a landowner's federal takings claim after the landowner received state court relief under different causes of action arising from the same underlying facts as the takings claim); *Manufactured Home Communities, Inc. v. City of San Jose*, 420 F. 3d 1022, 1031 (9th Cir. 2005) (holding that federal takings claims challenging city's mobile home rent ordinance barred by doctrine of res judicata because those claims "depended on issues identical to those that had previously been resolved in the state-court action") (quoting *San Remo*).

> Federal courts are required give preclusive effect to issues that were conclusively decided in state courts.

The Court explained, however, that the requirement that a property owner first seek compensation in state court will not always preclude litigation in the federal courts. First, to the extent that a property owner asserts a facial takings claim, the relief sought would be "distinct from the provision of 'just compensation'" under the Fifth Amendment and therefore could be raised directly in federal court. Alternatively, the San Remo owners could have refrained from litigating in state court those facial takings challenges that they had indicated they intended to "reserve" for judgment in the federal court. *Id.* at 345.

A concurring opinion in *San Remo*, joined by four justices, questions the appropriateness of continuing to require litigants to seek compensation through state procedures before pursuing takings claims in federal court. While noting that the validity of this requirement was not among the issues before the Court, the concurring opinion reasoned that "it is not obvious that either constitutional or prudential principles require claimants to utilize all state compensation procedures before they can bring a federal takings claim." *Id.* at 349.

The requirement to challenge an unconstitutional condition in court before seeking compensation. A city may be able to avoid judgment if a plaintiff fails to pursue administrative and judicial remedies prior to filing a claim for a takings compensation. The decision in *Hensler v. City of Glendale* espouses this rule, and highlights a judicial tendency to invalidate a regulation or give the city the option to rescind the regulation, rather than award compensation to be paid by a local government that does not have the resources to pay. 8 Cal. 4th 1 (1994).

Hensler involved a claim that property was taken by a city's ridgeline ordinance, which had been applied to the plaintiff's property in a decision made under the Subdivision Map Act. The property owner sought compensation for the undevelopable portion of his property, without first seeking a writ invalidating the subdivision decision or giving the city an opportunity to grant an exception or revoke an unconstitutional decision. The

California Supreme Court unanimously rejected plaintiff's attempt to bypass administrative and judicial proceedings necessary to test the application of the ordinance to his property, and held his claim time-barred by the 90-day limitation period of the Subdivision Map Act (Gov't Code § 66499.37). The court explained:

> A complaint in inverse condemnation, even one which does not expressly attack the validity of the ordinance or its application, and seeks only compensation for an alleged taking, must be deemed a challenge to the local action. This follows because the constitutional validity of the governmental action if uncompensated must be determined in the course of ruling on the claim that compensation is owed. Moreover, the validity of the action must be determined to afford the local entity the opportunity to rescind its action rather than pay compensation for a taking. A landowner may not, by seeking only compensation, force a governmental agency to condemn the property.
>
> Therefore, unless the complaint alleges that the existence of a taking has already been judicially established, the complaint necessarily states a cause of action which requires judicial review of a decision of the local legislative body concerning a subdivision or of the reasonableness, legality, or validity of any condition attached to a permit decision within the meaning of section 66499.37. An action which requires that review is governed by section 66499.37 regardless of the plaintiff's characterization of the cause of action.

8 Cal. 4th at 7

The Court held that when restrictions on use of real property are the basis for a takings claim, the owner must pursue any available administrative permit process before seeking compensation or challenging the statute or regulation. California's permit process includes both administrative and judicial review. On this remedy issue, the Court noted:

> The disparity in resources between the federal government and local governmental entities both explains and justifies the state procedure. The likelihood that the impact of a federal regulatory statute may effect a taking of property of such value as to threaten the federal treasury with insolvency is remote. Congress has determined that providing a damage remedy for those cases in which a taking occurs will not cause undue hardship. Few local governments could afford the financial impact of a decision that a widely applicable zoning or regulatory ordinance brought about a taking of all affected property.[4]
>
> The California procedural requirements to which plaintiff objects do no more than ensure to the state its right to a prepayment judicial determination that the ordinance or regulation is excessive and will constitute a taking, thus affording the state the option of abandoning the ordinance, regulation, or challenged action, or exempting parcels from its scope if the regulation on use is excessive. As we noted above, the United States Supreme Court has recognized repeatedly the right of the state to reserve the option of rescinding a statute that imposes excessive regulation, and has reaffirmed the principle that a landowner may not compel the state to initiate an eminent domain action. These requirements extend that principle, to the inverse condemnation context.

Id. at 19

---

[4] The plaintiff sought damages of $10 million for the alleged taking of his property.

Numerous other decisions, issued both before and after *Hensler*, confirm that a property owner seeking to recover compensation on an inverse condemnation claim must first establish the invalidity of the regulation the public entity is seeking to impose through an administrative mandate proceeding. This rule serves the salutary purpose of promptly alerting the agency that its decision is being questioned and that it may be liable for inverse condemnation damages. *California Coastal Comm'n v. Superior Court (Ham)*, 210 Cal. App. 3d 1488, 1496 (1989), is one example. In *Ham*, the California Coastal Commission approved the demolition and rebuilding of a beachfront house on the condition that the property owner dedicate an easement for public access across a strip of beach in front of his home. The owner did not challenge the condition in a mandate action, but after some time had passed, sought compensation based on the U.S. Supreme Court ruling in *Nollan*. The court held that Ham's failure to file a mandate action precluded him from making a takings claim. *See also Serra Canyon Company Ltd. v. California Coastal Comm'n*, 120 Cal. App. 4th 663 (2004); *Patrick Media Group Inc. v. California Coastal Comm'n*, 9 Cal. App. 4th 592, 617 (1992); *Rossco Holdings, Inc. v. State of California*, 212 Cal. App. 3d 642, 657 (1989); *Rezai v. City of Tustin*, 26 Cal. App. 4th 443, 448 (1994) (a property owner must pursue mandate proceedings before seeking compensation for a taking alleged in connection with a use permit decision).

The requirement of a unique injury. A takings claim also may fail if a plaintiff cannot show any unique injury. In *Border Business Park, Inc. v. City of San Diego*, 142 Cal. App. 4th 1538 (2006), the court of appeal rejected an inverse condemnation claim because the landowner failed to produce evidence indicating the city's action had affected it in a unique manner. In *Border*, the owner purchased land to develop a business park. The city later annexed the area containing the property and announced plans to relocate its international airport there, only to drop such plans later. Border claimed, and trial court agreed, that the city's conduct in announcing its airport proposal was reckless and amounted to inverse condemnation (pursuant to *Klopping v. City of Whittier*, 8 Cal. 3d 39 (1972)) by causing a drop in sales at the business park. The court of appeal disagreed, finding that Border failed to show the city's announcements subjected it to "direct and special injury" or affected it in any unique manner different from other owners in the area. *Border*, 142 Cal. App. 4th at 1548-49. The court also rejected Border's claim that the city actions limiting truck routes to the property amounted to a compensable interference with the right of access because access, while reduced, still remained. *Id.* at 1557-58.

> A takings claim also may fail if a plaintiff cannot show any unique injury.

The role of California constitutional expenditure limitations. Once a city's obligation to pay just compensation arises, a city might not be able to avoid the obligation by claiming that the spending limits of California Constitution Articles XIIIA, XIIIB, XIIIC, and XVI make the expenditure impossible. *See F&L Farm Co. v. City of Lindsay*, 65 Cal. App. 4th 1345 (1998). In *F&L Farm Company*, the city was compelled to pay a $5 million inverse condemnation judgment when its handling of saline industrial waste caused damage to nearby farmlands. The court concluded that paying an inverse condemnation judgment "does not implement a municipal purpose" within the meaning of Article XIIIC, and thus is not covered by the spending limitations. *Id.* at 1355.

However, in *Ventura Group Ventures, Inc. v. Ventura Port District*, the California Supreme Court distinguished *F&L Farm Company*. 24 Cal. 4th 1089 (2001). In *Ventura Group*, the plaintiff developer obtained a judgment for damages resulting from the port district's breach of the covenant of good faith and fair dealing in relation to a contract between the developer and the district. The developer asserted that the *F&L Farm Company* decision supported its argument that the district, which was bankrupt, could levy property taxes higher than the one percent ceiling imposed by Article XIII of the California Constitution for the purpose of paying judgments against it. The Court found *F&L Farm Company* distinguishable on two grounds. First, unlike the inverse condemnation claim in *F&L Farm Company*, the claim at issue in *Ventura Group* was based upon a breach of contract, and thus was not covered by the statutory exemption to Article XIII. Second, unlike the city in *F&L Farm Company*, the district was not permitted to avoid satisfaction of the judgment on the grounds that it had no money. To the contrary, as a result of the district's bankruptcy proceeding, the developer already had received payment on nearly one-half of its judgment.

Moreover, *Ventura Group* criticized the reasoning in *F&L Farm Company*:

> The analysis of article XIII A in *F&L Farm Co.* got off on the wrong track because the case focused on whether, rather than how, the City was required to satisfy the judgment. [The court] got the whether right, but the how wrong. That is, article XIII A is most assuredly not a license to "stiff" judgment creditors with impunity....However, the fact that article XIII A does not absolutely shield a local public entity from a judgment creditor does not mean that a court can compel a county to levy property taxes in excess of article XIII A's one percent limit in order to satisfy the judgment.

24 Cal. 4th at 1101

Nuisance defense. In *Lucas v. South Carolina Coastal Council*, dicussed above, the United States Supreme Court indicated that a total regulatory taking requires the government to pay just compensation, except to the extent that "background principles of nuisance and property law" independently restrict the landowner's desired use of the land. Some public agencies have raised a defense to takings claims in which they claim the plaintiff's use of the land would be a nuisance that could lawfully be enjoined. 505 U.S. 1003, 1052. *Formanek v. United States*, 26 Cl. Ct. 332 (1992), is one example. The property owner wanted to develop 90 acres of wetlands, which included 45 acres of a rare wetland plant community. The U.S. Army Corps of Engineers denied a permit, and the owner sued, alleging a taking. The court agreed that a taking had occurred. It also held that the government's nuisance exception defense was not persuasive. The proposed development simply did not present the extreme threat to the public health, safety, and welfare that precluded the payment of compensation, such as had occurred in *Miller v. Schoene*, 276 U.S. 272 (1928) (destruction of trees to prevent spread of disease), and *Allied-General Nuclear Services v. United States*, 839 F. 2d 1572 (Fed. Cir. 1988) (prohibition of plutonium processing to prevent worldwide nuclear proliferation).

Similarly, a California court held in *Monks v. City of Rancho Palos Verdes* that an ordinance requiring landowners in a landslide-prone area to present data demonstrating a certain geological safety factor over the entire 130-acre neighborhood in order to build on their lots was a permanent taking requiring just compensation. 167 Cal. App. 4th 263 (2008). As in *Formanek*, the *Monks* court rejected the city's nuisance defense. It noted that the burden in asserting such a defense is upon the city to show that it could obtain an injunction against the affected construction by showing there is a reasonable probability that it would prevail on the merits of a nuisance claim.

TAKINGS IN THE FLOOD CONTROL CONTEXT

Where a local government interferes with private use of land for the sake of flood control, special rules apply. While a city or county is generally strictly liable when it damages or takes private land (i.e., the reasonableness of its behavior is not relevant), an agency undertaking a flood control project is not obliged to pay just compensation so long as its conduct is reasonable. *Hauselt v. County of Butte*, 172 Cal. App. 4th 550, 557 (2009). More precisely stated, "the public agency is liable if its conduct poses an unreasonable risk of harm to the plaintiff, the unreasonable conduct is a substantial cause of the damage to plaintiff's property, and the plaintiff has taken reasonable measures to protect his property." *Id.* This rule applies when a public agency tries to protect private property owners from a risk created by nature and, in doing so, may alter the risks created by nature, the rule does not apply where the agency diverts water to "private property in order to protect other property." *Id.* at 558, 561 (citing *Akin*, 61 Cal. App. 4th 1, 33 (1998)). The inquiry appears to be highly fact dependent, and likely will require comparison to previous cases that have applied the reasonableness standard. *Id.* at 557-58 (citing *Bunch v. Coachella Valley Water Dist.*, 15 Cal. 4th 432, 447 (1997); *Locklin v. City of Lafayette*, 7 Cal. 4th 327, 337-38 (1994)); *Belair v. Riverside County Flood Control Dist*, 47 Cal. 3d 550, 555-57 (1988); *see also Arkansas Game*, 133 S. Ct. at 519 (holding that temporary, recurring flooding caused by Army Corps of Engineers may result in a taking under the federal Takings Clause).

CIVIL RIGHTS ACTIONS UNDER SECTION 1983

Federal law provides a remedy when someone acting under color of state law deprives a person of federal rights, privileges, or immunities. 42 U.S.C. § 1983. Section 1983 does not apply to actions taken by federal officers. *See District of Columbia v. Carter*, 409 U.S. 418, 424 (1973). State action of some kind is required; a private person, acting alone, cannot be liable under section 1983. *See Taylor v. Nichols*, 558 F. 2d 561, 564 (10th Cir. 1977). A number of cases have held that damages may be recovered for overregulation of land under section 1983. *See, e.g., San Diego Gas & Elec. Co. v. City of San Diego*, 450 U.S. 621, 654-55 (1981); *Lake Country Estates, Inc. v. Tahoe Reg'l Planning Agency*, 440 U.S. 391, 402-03 (1979).

Procedural issues arising in Section 1983 cases. A landowner cannot recover under section 1983 when it is shown that provisions of the substantive statute under which relief is sought provide more limited remedies than those contained in section 1983. *City of Rancho Palos Verdes v. Abrams*, 544 U.S. 113, 127 (2005) (landowner sought injunctive relief and damages under the federal Telecommunications Act of 1986, 47 U.S.C. § 332(c)(7), based on city's denial of permission to construct a radio tower on his property).

Some courts have held that the ripeness doctrine applies equally to a civil rights claim and takings claim. *See Long Beach Equities, Inc. v. County of Ventura*, 231 Cal. App. 3d at 1041; *Herrington v. County of Sonoma*, 857 F. 2d 567, 570 (9th Cir. 1988). However, the U.S. Supreme Court indicated that the component of ripeness requiring that a plaintiff seek compensation via state remedies does not apply because plaintiffs in such cases are not seeking "just compensation." *See San Remo*, 545 U.S. at 345-46. The Ninth Circuit has found the ripeness doctrine inapplicable to a section 1983 claim. In *Carpinteria Valley Farms, Ltd. v. County of Santa Barbara*, a landowner sought to develop a home and personal polo field in Santa Barbara County. The county imposed numerous conditions on the development, including a requirement that he apply for a conditional use permit for the polo field, even though the county allowed others to build polo fields without such a permit. 334 F. 3d 796, 801 (2003), *as modified in* 344 F. 3d 822 (9th Cir. 2003). After a lengthy period of trying to resolve his differences with the county, the landowner sued under section 1983, claiming the county violated his constitutional rights by discriminating against him, primarily because he had been vocal in criticizing a group which supported a county supervisor. The Ninth Circuit stated that if the county's requirements were imposed in retaliation for the landowner's exercise of free speech rights to criticize the county, then he had suffered harm and did not need to wait for further action by the county. The same reasoning applied to the landowner's claims the county violated his equal protection and due process rights, and the Ninth Circuit found that his claims were ripe for adjudication. 344 F. 3d at 802.

The U.S. Supreme Court has held local governments are "persons" for purposes of section 1983, and that local governing bodies and local officials can, therefore, be sued directly in their official capacities for monetary, declaratory, and injunctive relief where an allegedly unconstitutional action implements or executes a policy, ordinance, regulation, or decision officially adopted or promulgated by those whose edicts or acts may fairly be said to represent official policy. See *Monell v. Dept. of Social Servs.*, 436 U.S. 658, 688 (1978); see also *Owen v. City of Independence*, 445 U.S. 622, 645-46 (1980) (section 1983 creates a species of tort liability that on its face admits of no immunities; thus, a municipality has no immunity flowing from its constitutional violations and may not assert the good faith of its officers as a defense to such liability).

In *Lake Country Estates, Inc. v. Tahoe Regional Planning Agency*, the U.S. Supreme Court entertained an action for inverse condemnation that had been dismissed at the district court level because the planning agency had no power of eminent domain and thus was not properly subject to an action in inverse condemnation. 440 U.S. at 401-03. The Court held a cause of action could be stated against the agency under section 1983 and opened the doors to litigation of allegations that police power and zoning regulations were excessive. *Id.* at 399-400.

Actions under section 1983 will lie in state courts as well as in federal courts. See *Williams v. Horvath*, 16 Cal. 3d 834, 837 (1976). Therefore, this section authorizes state courts to award monetary damages for improper land use decisions. See *Grupe Dev. Co. v. California Coastal Comm'n*, 166 Cal. App. 3d 148, 180 (1985); *MacLeod v. County of Santa Clara*, 749 F. 2d 541, 544 (9th Cir. 1984). In *Stubblefield Constr. Co. v. City of San Bernardino*, the court overturned an $11.5 million jury award and held there was no violation of section 1983 or substantive due process when a city acted in its legislative capacity in adopting new ordinances and regulations that prevented a development project from being approved, where the developer had no vested right to build an apartment complex. 32 Cal. App. 4th 687, 706-07 (1995).

Section 1983 provides a right to a jury trial for certain takings cases in federal court. See *Del Monte Dunes*, 526 U.S. at 707-08.

Substantive claims under Section 1983—equal protection and due process. Under section 1983, a plaintiff may allege a violation of the plaintiff's equal protection or due process rights.

An equal protection claim is established if: (1) the plaintiff is treated differently from other similarly situated persons; (2) the difference in treatment is intentional; and (3) there is no rational basis for the difference in treatment. *Genesis Environmental Services v. San Joaquin Unified Air Pollution Control Dist.*, 113 Cal. App. 4th 597, 605 (2003) (citing *Village of Willowbrook v. Olech*, 528 U.S. 562 (2000)). The plaintiff need not be a member of a larger group or class to bring an equal protection claim; as the U.S. Supreme Court made clear in *Olech*, courts have long recognized successful equal protection claims brought by a "class of one" and, in fact, the number of persons in the "class" is immaterial to the analysis. See *Olech*, 528 U.S. at 564 & fn.* (per curiam).

In *Olech*, the owners had asked the Village of Willowbrook to connect their property to the municipal water supply. The village at first conditioned the connection on the owners' granting the village a 33-foot easement. The Olechs objected, claiming other property owners seeking access to the village's water supply were only required to grant a 15-foot easement. After a three-month delay, the village agreed to connect the owners to the municipal water supply with a 15-foot easement.

The owners sued the village under the Fourteenth Amendment, claiming that the village's demand for a 33-foot easement was "irrational and wholly arbitrary." *Id.* at 564. In affirming the Seventh Circuit decision, the U.S. Supreme Court noted its prior opinions recognized successful "class of one" equal protection claims where "the plaintiff alleges that she has been intentionally treated differently from others similarly situated and that there is no rational basis for the difference in treatment." *Id.* The Court held the owners' complaint, alleging in part that the village's demand was "irrational and wholly arbitrary," was sufficient to state a claim for relief under traditional equal protection analysis. *Id.* at 565.

Nor does a plaintiff need to allege ill will to bring an equal protection claim. In *Olech*, the Supreme Court ruled the plaintiffs stated a viable equal protection claim, regardless of the town's subjective motivation. *Id.*; *see also Genesis Envtl. Servs.*, 113 Cal. App. 3d at 605 (animus or subjective ill will is an alternative legal theory that is separate from the traditional equal protection analysis, which evaluates whether there is a rational basis for the challenged difference in treatment).

A due process claim under the Fourteenth Amendment to the U.S. Constitution can allege the contested action was arbitrary and capricious and, thus, not a proper exercise of the police power. *See Lingle*, 544 U.S. at 548 (Kennedy, J., concurring) (noting that land use regulations that are arbitrary or irrational may violate a landowner's due process rights). However, the California Supreme Court has held that "an ordinance restrictive of property use will be upheld against due process attack, unless its provisions are 'clearly arbitrary and unreasonable, having no substantial relation to the public health, safety, morals or general welfare.'" *Nash v. City of Santa Monica*, 37 Cal. 3d 97, 103 (1984); *see also Kawaoka v. City of Arroyo Grande*, 17 F. 3d 1227, 1234 (9th Cir. 1994).

In *Barancik v. County of Marin*, the Ninth Circuit responded to the owner's argument that the zoning of one residence per 60 acres was a violation of his substantive due process rights by stating:

> The district court found that the County had a reasonable purpose in zoning as it did and applying the zoning as it did to Loma Alta Ranch. We agree. To prove his case Barancik had to show that the County's zoning was arbitrary and irrational. *Usery v. Turner Elkhorn Mining Co.*, 428 U.S. 1, 15 (1976). He attempted to do so by concentrating on the zoning in relation to his own property and arguing that just as many cows would graze there if there were 28 residences as would if there were nine. The argument, of course, is myopic. Zoning is of an area. The planner wants to preserve an area for a given use. Yielding to Barancik's arguments would set a precedent which, followed, would lead to the emulative destruction of agriculture in Nicasio Valley. The cowboy and the farmer may be friends as the song has it, but not the rancher and the urban commuter, at least not if commuters, with the roads they need and the cars they drive and the tastes they have, begin to predominate in the countryside. Marin's zoning no doubt preserves a bucolic atmosphere for the benefit of a portion of the population at the expense of those who would flow into the county if there was no zoning. The Constitution lets that decision be

> A due process claim under the Fourteenth Amendment to the U.S. Constitution can allege the contested action was arbitrary and capricious and, thus, not a proper exercise of the police power.

made by the legislature. The Countywide Plan is a legislative declaration that there will be a corridor in Marin agricultural in its use. The choice was not irrational, the application to Barancik is not arbitrary.

872 F. 2d 834, 836 (9th Cir. 1988)

The Ninth Circuit later held that a rent control ordinance restricting rent increases in mobile home parks was not a denial of substantive due process. *See Levald Inc. v. City of Palm Desert*, 998 F. 2d 680 (9th Cir. 1993). In so ruling, the court laid out the rule of judicial deference to the legislative body in such cases:

> In reviewing economic legislation on substantive due process grounds, we give great deference to the judgment of the legislature. "[O]rdinances survive a substantive due process challenge if they were designed to accomplish an objective within the government's police power, and if a rational relationship existed between the provisions and purpose of the ordinances." [T]here is no requirement that the statute actually advance its stated purpose; rather, the inquiry focuses on whether "the governmental body could have had no legitimate reason for its decision." "[T]he law need not be in every respect logically consistent with its aims to be constitutional. It is enough that there is an evil at hand for correction, and that it might be thought that the particular legislative measure was a rational way to correct it."

Id. at 690 (citations omitted); *see also MHC Financing Ltd. Partnership v. City of San Rafael*, 714 F. 3d 1118, 1130-31 (9th Cir. 2013) (mobile home park rent control ordinance did not violate substantive due process rights where members of city council could have rationally believed the ordinance would promote its objective).

SUBSTANTIVE DUE PROCESS AND RENT CONTROL

The California Supreme Court has recognized the viability of a substantive due process claim in the context of rent control ordinances. In *Kavanau v. Santa Monica Rent Control Board*, the Court interpreted and applied substantive due process principles to a local rent control law and held "a rent control law that merely allows a landlord to recoup the bare cost of a necessary capital improvement runs the risk of being confiscatory and thereby violating the landlord's right to [substantive] due process of law." 16 Cal. 4th at 773. The *Kavanau* court provided a conceptual distinction between takings and substantive due process in the rent control context. "[T]akings protection focuses on the impact of the government's action: whether the government has in effect appropriated private property for its use of the property," whereas "the due process protection focuses on the government's means and purpose: whether the government's method rationally furthers legitimate ends." *Id.* at 770-71.

In *Galland v. City of Clovis*, the plaintiff landlord brought a due process claim seeking damages for allegedly confiscatory rent control restrictions, as well as costs in the form of administrative and attorneys' fees, imposed on the landlord in the process of seeking a rent increases. 24 Cal. 4th 1003, 1008 (2001). The Court held a future rent adjustment (a "*Kavanau* adjustment") would preclude damages for violation of the right to constitutional due process under 42 U.S.C. section 1983. *Id.* at 1030-31. With regard to the due process claim based on costs incurred by the landlord in seeking rent increases, the Court concluded such a claim may lie when one of two conditions is present: (1) the costs imposed are part of a government effort to deliberately flout established law, e.g., obstruct legitimate rent increases; or (2) the landlord suffers confiscation as a result of the imposition of such costs. *Id.* at 1005.

In a case raising issues of both inverse condemnation and substantive due process in the rent control context, the court in *H.N. & Frances C. Berger Foundation v. City of Escondido*, 127 Cal. App. 4th 1 (2005) (*Berger Foundation*) relied upon *Galland* and *Kavanau*. In *Berger Foundation*, the owner of a mobile home park challenged a city resolution authorizing a smaller rent increase than the one for which it applied, on the grounds the authorized rent increase was confiscatory because it would not allow a reasonable return on investment. The court rejected this claim. According to the court, to avoid unconstitutional confiscation, a constitutionally valid rent control ordinance must allow landowners to earn a fair return on their investment. While such a fair rate of return has "a broad zone of reasonableness," it must allow profits to be adjusted for inflation so that the real value of profit does not unconstitutionally diminish over time. *Id.* at 8. However, there is no set formula for determining a reasonable return on investment, and annual rent increases do not have to be indexed so that they are equal to increases in inflation. *Id.* at 14-15. Cities therefore have wide latitude to balance the interests of property investors with those of tenants. Thus, there can be no taking or other civil rights violation if a city allows for future rent adjustments that allow a fair rate of return on investment. *Id.* at 16.

As the foregoing cases indicate, the substantive due process doctrine will rarely protect property rights in the land use context. That said, some California cases seem to recognize that substantive due process sometimes may provide protections in the rent control arena.

INTERPLAY BETWEEN TAKINGS CLAIMS AND SUBSTANTIVE DUE PROCESS CLAIMS

In contrast to a takings claim, a claim that a city has damaged property in violation of the owner's rights to due process and equal protection does not require proof that all use of the property has been denied. *See Herrington*, 834 F. 2d at 1498; *Harris v. County of Riverside*, 904 F .2d 497, 503-04 (9th Cir. 1990) (a county violated a landowner's due process rights when it deprived him of the commercial zoning on his property without prior notice of its proposed action).

Relying on *Harris*, the court in *Carpinteria Valley Farms* held a landowner's equal protection and due process claims were not takings claims within the meaning of *Williamson*, but rather independent section 1983 claims which were ripe for review. 334 F. 3d at 798-99, as modified in 344 F. 3d 822. The fact that the landowner's constitutional claims arose in the context of a county's permitting process did not render those claims "unripe," so long as the landowner otherwise met the ripeness requirements set forth in *Harris. Id.* at 802.

It is permissible to allege both a takings and civil rights claim in many circumstances. *Crown Point Development, Inc. v. City of Sun Valley*, 506 F. 3d 851, 852-53 (9th Cir. 2007) (discussing *Lingle*, 544 U.S. at 532). In *Crown Point Development*, a developer alleged that a city's arbitrary and irrational denial of its development applications violated its right to substantive due process. The district court dismissed the claim based on the rule of *Armendariz v. Penman*, 75 F. 3d 1311, 1391 (1996), which did not allow substantive due process claims pursuant to the Fourteenth Amendment when the interest at stake was real property.[5]

The Ninth Circuit reversed. It noted *Armendariz* was based upon a pre-*Lingle* view that a regulation that does not "substantially advance legitimate state interests" is a taking. It further explained:

> However, this understanding of the *Agins'* "substantially advances" language—i.e., that it is a "stand-alone regulatory takings test"—was rejected by the Supreme Court in *Lingle*. 544 U.S. at 540. The Court concluded "that this formula prescribes an inquiry in the nature of due process, not a takings, test, and that it has no proper place in our takings jurisprudence." *Id.* As the Court explained, the "substantially advances" test "does not help to identify those regulations whose effects are functionally comparable to government appropriation or invasion of private property; it is tethered neither to the text of the Takings Clause nor to the basic justification for allowing regulatory actions to be challenged under the Clause." *Id.* at 542.
>
> In this, *Lingle* pulls the rug out from under our rationale for totally precluding substantive due process claims based on arbitrary or unreasonable conduct. As the Court made clear, there is no specific textual source in the Fifth Amendment for protecting a property owner from conduct that furthers no legitimate government purpose.

Id. at 854–855

Accordingly, the Fifth Amendment would preclude a due process challenge only if the alleged conduct is actually covered by the Takings Clause. *Lingle* indicates a claim of arbitrary action is not such a challenge. It is therefore no longer possible to read *Armendariz* as imposing a blanket obstacle to all substantive due process challenges to land use regulation. Moreover, the Ninth Circuit explicitly held that the Fifth Amendment does not invariably preempt a claim that land use action lacks any substantial relation to the public health, safety, or general welfare. *Id.* at 856.

LEGISLATIVE ACTS GIVEN MORE DEFERENCE THAN ADJUDICATORY ACTS

In cases involving many types of alleged injury to property interests, the courts tend to grant more deference to an agency when it is acting in its legislative capacity as compared to its nonlegislative, "quasi-adjudicatory" administrative capacity. In *Cohan v. City of Thousand Oaks*, a court held that the cumulative procedural errors committed by the city impaired the adequacy of the appeal hearing on the Cohans' subdivision and that, therefore, their due process rights were violated. 30 Cal. App. 4th 547, 556-57 (1994). Some of the errors involved the council itself appealing the planning commission's decision, failure to inform the Cohans of the grounds for the appeal, and unfairly placing the burden on the Cohans "to convince the Council of the correctness of the Planning Commission's decision." *Id.* at 548. The court held that "this stands due process on its head." *Id.* at 560.

---

5 The Ninth Circuit previously ruled that substantive due process claims could not apply where the government has allegedly effected a taking violative of the Fifth Amendment, since the Takings Clause provided "an explicit textual source of constitutional protection" against the challenged governmental conduct. *Armendariz*, 75 F. 3d at 1319 (quoting *Graham v. Connor*, 496 U.S. 386, 395 (1989)); *see Squaw Valley Development Co. v. Goldberg*, 375 F. 3d 936, 949 (9th Cir. 2004). The court held where a regulation has denied economically viable use of property, the claim is one under the Takings Clause and a substantive due process argument based on the same set of facts is preempted by the takings claim.

In contrast, another court held there was no denial of civil rights or substantive due process when a city was acting in its legislative capacity and the plaintiff had no vested right to build an apartment complex. See *Stubblefield Constr. Co. v. City of San Bernardino*, 32 Cal. App. 4th at 707-08. In this case, one councilperson used everything in his power to stop the project. While arbitrary zoning actions directed at a specific property may be invalidated (see *Arnel Dev. Co. v. City of Costa Mesa*, 126 Cal. App. 3d 330, 334, 337 (1981)), the *Stubblefield* court said the actions it reviewed were general in application. Therefore, in the court's view, there was nothing arbitrary or unreasonable in the zoning actions taken. The city's revised multifamily zoning ordinance applied to all multifamily housing in the city; an urgency ordinance applied to all development applications pending at the time it was adopted; a moratorium ordinance applied to all foothill property north of a specified line; and a general plan revision affected all property in the city, while hillside provisions were based on slope percentages. These, the court said, were all rational classifications. It also noted that it was reluctant to minutely scrutinize the legislative processes of the city in the manner suggested by the Stubblefields. "[T]his is an ordinary dispute between a developer and a municipality and we conclude that the claims asserted simply do not qualify as a deprivation of substantive due process." *Id.* at 712.

In *City of Cuyahoga Falls v. Buckeye Community Hope Foundation*, the U.S. Supreme Court held the subjection of a local land use decision to a city's referendum process did not constitute per se arbitrary government conduct in violation of due process "regardless of whether that ordinance reflected an administrative or legislative decision." 538 U.S. 188, 199 (2003). The City of Cuyahoga Falls, Ohio, passed an ordinance authorizing developers to construct a low-income housing complex. Citizens submitted a referendum petition to the city asking that the ordinance be repealed or submitted to a vote. Pursuant to the city's charter, the referendum petition stayed the project until the voters voted. The city engineer, on advice from the city's law director, denied the developers' request for building permits. The developers sued the city, alleging violation of its rights to equal protection and due process.

In ruling for the city, the Supreme Court held the developers failed to present sufficient evidence of an equal protection or due process violation. They had not presented proof of racially discriminatory intent. Moreover, the petition was submitted to the voters pursuant to the city's charter, which set out a facially neutral petitioning procedure. The engineer performed a nondiscretionary ministerial act consistent with the city charter in refusing to issue permits while the referendum was pending. *Id.* His refusal to issue permits "in no sense constituted egregious or arbitrary government conduct." In light of the charter's provision that no challenged ordinance can go into effect until approved by the voters, the law director's instruction to the engineer represented an "eminently rational directive." *Id.* at 1396. Nor did the city's submission of an administrative land use determination to the charter's referendum procedures constitute per se arbitrary conduct. The Court noted the "people retain the power to govern through referendum with respect to any matter, legislative or administrative, within the realm of local affairs." *Id.* Because the developers did not challenge the referendum itself, they derived no benefit from the principle that a referendum's substantive result may be invalid if it is arbitrary or capricious. *Id.*

> The Court noted the "people retain the power to govern through referendum with respect to any matter, legislative or administrative, within the realm of local affairs."

CHAPTER 12

Exactions: Dedications and Development Fees

INTRODUCTION[1]

In nearly all aspects of land use approval, significant controversies arise over the amount and type of exactions a city may impose when approving a development, and whether they require dedications of property or the imposition of development fees. The concept is simple in theory: the developer, in return for receiving the city's approval to develop the land and realize a profit, agrees to provide to the city an amount of land or money needed for certain services and amenities necessitated by the anticipated influx of new residents or employees into the community as a result of such development. *See Associated Home Builders, Inc. v. City of Walnut Creek*, 4 Cal. 3d 633, 644 (1971); *Trent Meredith, Inc. v. City of Oxnard*, 114 Cal. App. 3d 317, 328 (1981).

Cities contend that this arrangement is only fair. Developers create new, sometimes overwhelming, burdens on city services; therefore, they should offset the additional responsibilities required of cities through dedication of land or the payment of fees. Developers, on the other hand, argue these extra expenses drive up the cost of development and result in higher costs for the home buyer or commercial users, thus eliminating affordable housing and/or driving away needed commerce. In an effort to avoid such costs, developers have challenged such fees by claiming they are special taxes illegally imposed without a vote of the people, or that dedications are takings of property without just compensation. Through the exercise of its police power, however, a city has the authority to impose these exactions, so long as they are reasonable and have the required nexus to the proposed development.

---

[1] For a good overview of exactions, see David L. Callies, Cecily Talbert Barclay and Julie A. Tappendorf, *Development by Agreement* (ABA Sect. of State and Local Gov't Law, 2012); Daniel J. Curtin, Jr., *Exactions, Dedications and Development Agreements Nationally and in California: When and How Do Dolan/Nollan Apply*, 33rd Annual Institute of Planning, Zoning and Eminent Domain, ch. 2 (Matthew Bender, 2003); Daniel J. Curtin, Jr., *Dolan and Nollan Takings and Exactions, California Style*, 32nd Annual Institute on Planning, Zoning and Eminent Domain (Matthew Bender, October 2002); William Abbott et al., *Exactions and Impact Fees in California* (Solano Press, 2012); Daniel J. Curtin, Jr., *How the West Was Won: Takings and Exactions—California Style*, Trends in Land Use Law from A to Z, ch. 9 (ABA 2001); see also Ronald H. Rosenberg, *The Changing Culture of American Land Use Regulation: Paying for Growth with Impact Fees*, 59 SMU L. Rev. 177 (2006).

PROPER EXERCISE OF POLICE POWER

A city relies on its police power authority to impose conditions on a development project through the dedication of land or the payment of fees. Cal. Const. Art. XI, § 7; *California Bldg. Indus. Ass'n v. Governing Bd. of the Newhall Sch. Dist.*, 206 Cal. App. 3d 212, 234 (1988). The U.S. Supreme Court and the California Supreme Court have long held the regulation of land use does not effect a taking of property if the regulation does not deny the property owner economically viable use of the land. *See Lingle v. Chevron U.S.A. Inc.*, 544 U.S. 528, 538 (2005); *Dolan v. City of Tigard*, 512 U.S. 374, 385 (1994); *Lucas v. South Carolina Coastal Council*, 505 U.S. 1003, 1016 (1992); *Nollan v. California Coastal Comm'n*, 483 U.S. 825, 834 (1987); *Landgate, Inc. v. California Coastal Comm'n*, 17 Cal. 4th 1006, 1017 (1998).

DEVELOPMENT: PRIVILEGE OR RIGHT?

> In California, courts repeatedly have held that there is no right to develop and that development is instead a privilege.

Over the years, there has been a great deal of controversy over whether development is a privilege or a right. In California, courts repeatedly have held that there is no right to develop and that development is instead a privilege. Examples of such decisions are:

- No right to subdivide. *Associated Home Builders, Inc. v. City of Walnut Creek*, 4 Cal. 3d 633, 638 (1971)
- Development is a privilege. *Trent Meredith, Inc. v. City of Oxnard*, 114 Cal. App. 3d 317, 325 (1981)
- No right to go out of business. *Nash v. City of Santa Monica*, 37 Cal. 3d 97, 103 (1984) (no taking where city requires a demolition permit under rent control laws; so long as tenants remain in landlord's apartment units and landlord continues to receive fair rate of compensation, landlord cannot evict tenants and demolish building)
- No right to convert an apartment to a condominium. *Griffin Dev. Co. v. City of Oxnard*, 39 Cal. 3d 256, 263 (1985); *Norsco Enters. v. City of Fremont*, 54 Cal. App. 3d 488, 497 (1976).
- No right to convert residential hotel units to other uses; conversion is a "privilege." *Terminal Plaza Corp. v. City and County of San Francisco*, 177 Cal. App. 3d 892, 907 (1986)
- Transit fees may be exacted if a developer voluntarily chooses to create new office space and the fees are "for the privilege of developing a particular parcel." *Russ Bldg. Partnership v. City and County of San Francisco*, 199 Cal. App. 3d 1496, 1506 (1987)

The U.S. Supreme Court has weighed in on this issue: "[T]he right to build on one's own property—even though its exercise can be subjected to legitimate permitting requirements—cannot remotely be described as a 'governmental benefit.'" *Nollan*, 483 U.S. at 833.

While the Court's decision in *Nollan* can be interpreted as stating a right to build *something* on one's own property, it cannot be read as recognizing any right to build a particular project. The court in *Lakeview Development Corporation v. City of South Lake Tahoe* explained:

> [Plaintiff] relies in particular on footnote 2 of *Nollan*, where the Court, in responding to Justice Brennan's dissent, said that "the right to build on one's own property—even though its exercise can be subject to legitimate permitting requirements—cannot remotely be described as a 'government benefit.'"

[Plaintiff] argues that the reference to building on one's property is a "right" and not a "benefit" is somehow inconsistent with the doctrine that a "right" to build a *particular project* vests only after substantial work is performed in reliance on a government permit. (emphasis in original)

There are two difficulties with this argument. First, the *Nollan* case dealt only with a property owner's right to build a single-family house, traditionally among the most minimally regulated uses [footnote omitted]. Second, and more important, the *Nollan* court's reference to a landowner's abstract "right" to build in no way suggests that a landowner has an unconditional right under the taking or deprivation clauses of the federal Constitution to build any particular project he chooses. The sentence quoted from the *Nollan* footnote is qualified by its reference to "legitimate permitting requirements." The footnote does not imply that a permitting requirement is "illegitimate" simply because it disallows a previously permitted use. It is well established that there is no federal Constitutional right to be free from changes in land use laws.

915 F. 2d 1290, 1294-95 (9th Cir. 1990)

To date, notwithstanding *Nollan*, California courts have not changed their position that development is merely a privilege. For example, in *Saad v. City of Berkeley*, the court rejected the property owner's "right to build" argument based on *Nollan*, where the owner had challenged the city's denial of a use permit for a home on the grounds that it would impair views and have a towering effect on the neighborhood. 24 Cal. App. 4th 1206, 1212-13 (1994). In another decision also rendered after *Nollan*, the court struck down a school district fee as being an invalid special tax. In so doing, it stated that "[t]ypically, a development fee is an exaction imposed as a precondition for the *privilege* of developing the land." *California Bldg. Indus. Ass'n v. Governing Bd. of the Newhall Sch. Dist.*, 206 Cal. App. 3d 212, 235 (1988) (citing *Candid Enters., Inc. v. Grossmont Union High Sch. Dist.*, 39 Cal. 3d 878 (1985) (emphasis added); *Associated Home Builders, Inc. v. City of Walnut Creek*, 4 Cal. 3d 633 (1971)); *see also Sinclair Paint Co. v. State Bd. of Equalization*, 15 Cal. 4th 866, 874 (1997) (it is a "voluntary decision to develop or to seek other government benefits or privileges"); *Clark v. City of Hermosa Beach*, 48 Cal. App. 4th 1152, 1178-84 (1996) (a denial of a fair hearing on a development application did not violate the owners' procedural or substantive due process rights, since the owners had no protected property right or interest in an application for a specific residence); *California Bldg. Indus. Ass'n*, 206 Cal. App. 3d at 236 (the fee is "triggered by the voluntary decision of the developer [to proceed with his development]"); *Russ Bldg. Partnership*, 199 Cal. App. 3d at 1505.

Whether development is a privilege or a circumscribed limited right, it is clear from California cases, as well as from *Nollan* and *Dolan* (discussed below) that a dedication or impact fee condition will be upheld so long as it does not deny an owner economically viable use of the land and the required nexus exists.[2] For a more detailed discussion on takings in general, *see* chapter 11 (Takings).

---

2 As is further discussed in chapter 11 (Takings), a city's ability to enact land use regulations, to require dedications, and to impose fees under its police power is limited by the Takings Clause of the Fifth Amendment of the U.S. Constitution, as made applicable to the states by the Fourteenth Amendment. The Takings Clause protects private property rights against governmental action by providing that a city shall not appropriate (take) private property for public use without compensating the owner of the property. Private property need not be physically seized to constitute a taking; regulation of property, such as land use regulation, may constitute a taking if it is determined to be excessive. *See Penn Cent. Transp. Co. v. City of New York*, 438 U.S. 104 (1978).

TEST OF REASONABLENESS/NEXUS REQUIREMENT

IN GENERAL

Given the rule that development is a privilege in California, courts have held that cities may impose conditions on development so long as the conditions are reasonable, and there exists a sufficient nexus between the conditions imposed and the projected burden of the proposed development. *See Associated Home Builders, Inc.*, 4 Cal. 3d at 644; *Ayres v. City Council*, 34 Cal. 2d 31, 42 (1949).

There is no single, precise rule that is applied by the courts to determine whether a dedication or a fee condition is reasonable and thus valid. In general, the degree of judicial review depends on whether an exaction is possessory or non-possessory (i.e., a physical exaction or a fee), and whether the local government applies it in an ad hoc manner, specific to a certain project, or as part of a generally applicable legislative enactment. The following general rules apply, subject to the explanations below:

1. For a condition requiring a dedication ("a possessory taking") that a city imposes in an ad hoc manner, the two-part *Nollan/Dolan* test will apply. First, there must be an "essential nexus," meaning the exaction must substantially advance a legitimate state interest. *Nollan*, 483 U.S. at 834, 837–39. Second, there must be a "rough proportionality" between the magnitude of the exaction and the nature and extent of the project impact that the exaction is intended to address. *Dolan*, 512 U.S. at 387 (1994).

2. For a possessory taking that a city imposes as part of generally applicable legislation (such as an ordinance requiring dedication of land for parks), courts will apply a more relaxed level of scrutiny known as the "reasonable relationship" test. *Home Builders Ass'n of Northern California v. City of Napa*, 90 Cal. App. 4th 188, 196–97 (2001); *see also Ehrlich v. City of Culver City*, 12 Cal. 4th 854, 865 (1996) (explaining difference between possessory and nonpossessory takings); *Shapell Indus., Inc. v. Governing Bd.*, 1 Cal. App. 4th 218, 234 (1991); *Balch Enters. v. New Haven Unified Sch. Dist.*, 219 Cal. App. 3d 783, 793 (1990); *Rohn v. City of Visalia*, 214 Cal. App. 3d 1463, 1471 (1989). Whereas *Nollan* and *Dolan* require an individualized and "factually sustainable proportionality between the effects of a proposed land use and a given exaction," the reasonable relationship test requires the exaction be theoretically or plausibly related to the governmental ends. *See Ehrlich*, 12 Cal. 4th at 876, 880; *see also Ocean Harbor House*, 163 Cal. App. 4th 215, 234 (2008) (to determine whether a fee is roughly proportionate under *Nollan* and *Dolan*, a court must "look behind the arithmetic" and evaluate the agency's measurements and analysis).

3. For a monetary ("nonpossessory") exaction that a city imposes in an ad hoc manner, the two-part *Nollan/Dolan* test will apply. *See Ehrlich*, 12 Cal. 4th at 880; *Koontz v. St. Johns River Water Mgmt. Dist.*, 133 S. Ct. 2586, 2599 (2013); *see also San Remo Hotel v. City and County of San Francisco*, 27 Cal. 4th 643, 666 (2002); *BIA of Central California v. City of Patterson*, 171 Cal. App. 4th 886, 898–99 (2009). A monetary exaction would include conditions requiring the payment of mitigation fees; in-lieu fees; funding for public facilities, infrastructure, and elements of capital improvement plans; and other development fees. It would not include building permit fees. In imposing such conditions, a city also need comply with the terms of the Mitigation Fee Act (Government Code § 66000 *et seq.*). While the main requirements of the Mitigation Fee Act codify the reasonable relationship test (*Ehrlich*, 12 Cal. 4th at 866), and therefore are redundant

of the *Nollan/Dolan* test (and somewhat watered down), the Act imposes other requirements not provided in *Nollan/Dolan* or their progeny (e.g., provisions governing how a city must deposit, invest, and account for collected fees, as in Government Code section 66006).

4. For a monetary exaction that a city imposes as part of generally applicable legislation, the reasonable relationship test applies, but as codified and modified by the Mitigation Fee Act. *See Ehrlich*, 12 Cal. 4th at 865-66, 876. The Mitigation Fee Act requires that the city identify (1) the fee's purpose and use; (2) the reasonableness of the relationship between the fee and a given project; and (3) the reasonableness of the relationship between the amount of the fee and the cost of the public facility attributable to the project. *Id.*; Gov't Code § 66001. As explained above, other requirements apply. *See, e.g.*, Gov't Code § 66006. For a full discussion of the Mitigation Fee Act, see California's "Nexus Legislation" in this chapter.

In applying these tests, courts use an ad hoc analysis, examining the facts of each case. For example, in applying the *Nollan/Dolan* test, the determination depends on the size of the development, the demand for services, the burden that will be created by the development, and the development's overall effect on the city and the surrounding community. *See, e.g., Ocean Harbor House Homeowners Ass'n v. California Coastal Comm'n*, 163 Cal. App. 4th at 222, 234 (calculating the value of an acre of beach by assessing the average amount a visitor spends to travel to the beach). Application of these tests is further discussed below.

> In applying these tests, courts use an ad hoc analysis, examining the facts of each case.

THE *NOLLAN* AND *DOLAN* DECISIONS

Nollan v. California Coastal Commission. In *Nollan*, the U.S. Supreme Court considered the constitutionality of a California Coastal Commission development permit condition requiring dedication of a lateral access easement along the owners' private beach. 483 U.S. 825 (1987). The easement purportedly was required to assist the public in viewing the beach and in overcoming a perceived "psychological barrier" to using the beach. *Id.* at 435. The owners, who had proposed building a house, challenged the easement, claiming the condition constituted a taking. The Court agreed and held that since there was no "nexus" between the burdens imposed by the owners' development and the permit condition, the dedication requirement failed to "substantially advance" a "legitimate state interest." *Id.* at 837. The Court reasoned that while protection of the public's ability to see the beach was a legitimate governmental interest, no nexus existed between the identified impact of the project (obstruction of the ocean view) and the easement condition (physical access across the beach). *Id.* at 839. "It is quite impossible to understand how a requirement that people already on the public beaches be able to walk across the *Nollan's* property reduces any obstacles to viewing the beach created by the new house," the Court said. *Id.* at 838.

If there is no such connection, the decision to impose the condition would not be proper and could amount to a taking. *Id.* at 837.

Nollan left unanswered the question of how close the nexus must be for a regulation to "substantially advance" the government's stated interest.[3] However, in the majority opinion authored by Justice Scalia, the Court acknowledged that, while it had not specified the showing necessary to pass the nexus test, a wide variety of land use regulations had met this burden:

---

[3] This issue was addressed seven years later by the U.S. Supreme Court's decision in *Dolan v. City of Tigard*, as discussed further below.

> Our cases have not elaborated on the standards for determining what constitutes a "legitimate state interest" or what type of connection between the regulation and the state interest satisfies the requirement that the former "substantially advance" the latter. They have made clear, however, that a broad range of governmental purposes and regulations satisfies these requirements. *See Agins v. City of Tiburon*, 447 U.S. 255, 260-62 (1980) (scenic zoning); *Penn Cent. Transp. Co. v. New York City*, *supra* (landmark preservation); *Euclid v. Ambler Realty Co.*, 272 U.S. 365 (1926) (residential zoning).

Id. at 834-35

Subsequent cases broadly construe the range of legitimate governmental interests to be advanced. Moreover, several California cases have interpreted the *Nollan* nexus requirement—that a regulation "substantially" advance a legitimate governmental interest—narrowly, as applying only where the regulation involves a physical encroachment. *See Saad*, 24 Cal. App. 4th at 1212-13; *City and County of San Francisco v. Golden Gate Heights Invs.*, 14 Cal. App. 4th 1203, 1209 (1993) (and cases cited therein); *Blue Jeans Equities W. v. City and County of San Francisco*, 3 Cal. App. 4th 164, 168-71 (1992); *see also San Remo Hotel v. City and County of San Francisco*, 27 Cal. 4th 663, 664-65 (2002).

In *Long Beach Equities, Inc. v. County of Ventura*, a California appellate court ruled the *Nollan* test was satisfied because there was a substantial relationship between the regulations and the "public welfare." The court found that the growth control ordinance was valid because it was designed "'to protect the unique, hill-surrounded environment; enhance the quality of life; promote public health, safety or welfare and the general well-being of the community....' By limiting the rate, distribution, quality, and type of residential development on an annual basis, with periodic reviews of the ongoing situation, City seeks 'to improve local air quality, reduce traffic demands... and ensure that future demands for such essential services as water, sewers and the like are met....'" *Id.*

In *Hotel & Motel Association of Oakland v. City of Oakland*, the Ninth Circuit Court of Appeals held that city ordinances enacted to improve the physical conditions in and around hotels were not an unconstitutional taking. 344 F. 3d 959, 967 (9th Cir. 2003). Studies showed a continued pattern of illegal activity, including prostitution and drug use, associated with poorly maintained hotels in the city of Oakland. In ruling for the city, the appellate court held that the ordinances advanced a legitimate governmental interest since they were adopted to protect the public from illegal activity and were directed toward protecting the health and welfare of citizens and visitors in Oakland.

In *Commercial Builders of Northern California v. City of Sacramento*, the court upheld a city's ordinance imposing a low-income housing fee on nonresidential development to assist in building low-income housing. 941 F. 2d 872 (1991). The court found evidence in the record that the commercial development proposed by the developers indirectly would affect the need for more affordable housing units, and so upheld the ordinance. In so doing, the court applied the "reasonable relationship" test of *Associated Home Builders*, and stated that *Nollan* stands only for the proposition that if there is no nexus, there is a taking. *Id.* at 874. "A purely financial exaction, then, will not constitute a taking if it is made for the purpose of paying a social cost that is reasonably related to the activity against which the fee is assessed." *Id.* at 876; *see also Garrick Dev. Co. v. Hayward Unified Sch. Dist.*, 3 Cal. App. 4th 320, 337 (1992). The court in *Commercial Builders* rejected the builder's argument that, under *Nollan*, an ordinance that imposes an exaction can be upheld only if it can be shown the development in question is directly responsible for the social ill that the exaction is designed to alleviate. Rather, the court held that *Nollan* did not create a stricter standard than prior federal law for judging how close the nexus must be. *Id.* at 874; *see also Tahoe Reg'l Planning Agency v. King*, 233 Cal. App. 3d 1365, 1400 (1991) (*Nollan* does not alter established law that aesthetic values are an appropriate subject of land use regulations; *Nollan* only requires that there be a nexus).

Other cases have applied *Nollan's* nexus holding to invalidate dedication requirements. For example, in *Rohn v. City of Visalia*, a city's requirement for a street widening was struck down since there was no evidence in the record the dedication was required to compensate for increased traffic produced by the project. 214 Cal. App. 3d at 1475. Citing *Associated Home Builders*, the *Rohn* court held that, although the facilities to be dedicated need not solely benefit the project, they at least must serve it in some capacity. This was not the case in *Rohn*, where substantial evidence existed that traffic problems would occur because of "poor planning during the original development" of the street, and not due to any increased vehicular traffic associated with the project. *Id.*

In another case, the court struck down an easement dedication allegedly required to prevent erosion, because there was no specific report or study to justify the dedication. *See Surfside Colony, Ltd. v. California Coastal Comm'n*, 226 Cal. App. 3d 1260, 1269 (1991). The Coastal Commission had relied on general studies of other areas to justify the exaction, but the court found they were inadequate to provide a legal nexus. *Id.*

> In another case, the court struck down an easement dedication allegedly required to prevent erosion, because there was no specific report or study to justify the dedication.

Dolan v. City of Tigard. In 1994, the *Dolan* Court addressed the question left unanswered by *Nollan*, adding the second prong of the Court's nexus test. In *Dolan*, a sharply divided court held that cities must prove that development conditions placed on a discretionary permit have a "rough proportionality" to the development's impact. If not, this action may constitute a taking. 512 U.S. 374, 391 (1994). In this 5-4 decision, the Court held for the first time that in making an adjudicative decision, a city must demonstrate a "required reasonable relationship" between the conditions to be imposed on a development permit and the development's impact. Even though the Court coined a new term ("rough proportionality") for the standard, it was basically the same reasonable relationship test that California and a majority of other states had followed for years, though more exacting than the rational basis test under the Equal Protection Clause of the Fourteenth Amendment (and distinguishable from the "reasonable relationship" standard that came to apply to generally applicable legislation). *See* discussion below.

Florence Dolan owned a plumbing and electrical supply store located in the business district of Tigard, Oregon, along Fanno Creek, which flows through the southwestern corner of the lot and along its western boundary. Dolan applied to the city for a building permit to develop the site. Her proposed plans called for nearly doubling the size of the store and paving a 39-space parking lot.

The planning commission granted Dolan's permit application subject to certain conditions, including the requirement that Dolan dedicate the portion of her property lying within the 100-year flood plain for improvement of a storm drainage system along Fanno Creek. In addition, she was required to dedicate an additional fifteen-foot strip of land adjacent to the flood plain as a pedestrian/bicycle pathway. In so doing, the city made a series of findings concerning the relationship between the dedicated conditions and the projected impacts on the Dolan property.

The U.S. Supreme Court granted certiorari "to resolve a question left open" in *Nollan*—what is the required degree of connection between the exactions imposed by a city and the projected impacts of the proposed development? *Id.* at 377. Significantly, the Court in *Dolan* noted that it was not dealing with a legislative determination regarding land use regulations, but instead with a city having made "an adjudicative decision to condition petitioner's application for a building permit on an individual parcel." *Id.* The Court also observed that "the conditions imposed were not simply a limitation on the use [the] petitioner might make of her own parcel, but a requirement that she deed portions of the property to the city." *Id.*

In evaluating the takings claim, the Court stated that it first must determine whether an "essential nexus" exists between the "legitimate state interest" and the exaction imposed. If a nexus exists, the next step is to determine whether the degree of connection is sufficient. The Court noted that in *Nollan*, there had been no nexus; thus, the Court did not move beyond the first step in the analysis. In *Nollan*, the absence of a nexus between the easement and the ocean view left the California Coastal Commission in the position of simply trying to obtain an easement "through gimmickry," which converted a valid regulation of land use into an "out-and-out plan of extortion." *Id.* at 387. In *Dolan*, however, the Court stated that no such "gimmickry" was evident. Rather, the Court concluded that the required nexus did, in fact, exist. Therefore, it was necessary for the Court to address the question left unanswered in *Nollan*—whether the *degree of exaction* demanded by the city's permit conditions bore the *required relationship* to the projected impact of the development.

Since state courts had a long history of dealing with this question, the Court then reviewed several representative state court decisions. The Court noted the decisions fell into three categories: first, a generalized nexus requirement, which the Court determined to be too lax; second, an exacting nexus described as the "specific and uniquely attributable test" (the so-called *Pioneer Trust* Rule from Illinois, 22 Ill. 2d 375 (1961)), which the Court rejected; and third, an intermediate position of a "reasonable relationship" nexus (highlighted in *Jordan v. Menomonee Falls*, 28 Wisc. 2d 608, 137 N.W. 2d 442 (1965)).

The *Dolan* Court noted the intermediate "reasonable relationship test," adopted by the majority of states (including California, *see Associated Home Builders*, 4 Cal. 3d at 640), was closer to the federal constitutional norm than the other two tests. However, it stated, "we do not adopt [the reasonable relationship test] as such, partly because the term 'reasonable relationship' seems confusingly similar to the term 'rational basis' which describes the minimal level of scrutiny under the Equal Protection Clause of the Fourteenth Amendment." 512 U.S. at 391. Instead, the Court coined the term "rough proportionality" to summarize what by the Fifth Amendment requires.[4] It then attempted to provide some meaning to the phrase. "No precise mathematical calculation is required, but the city must make some sort of individualized determination that the required dedication is related both in nature and extent to the impact of the proposed development." *Id.*

With the rough proportionality requirement in mind, the Court then reviewed the two required dedications and held the city had not met its burden of demonstrating the required relationship. After analyzing the city's findings, the Court stated the city had not shown the "required reasonable relationship" between the floodplain easement and the petitioner's proposed new building. *Id.* at 395.

Noting that Dolan's proposed development would have increased the amount of impervious surface—which in turn would increase the quantity and rate of storm water

---

4 After coining the term "rough proportionality," the Court, in its majority opinion, never used that term again in applying its analysis to the facts; instead it continued to use the words "required reasonable relationship" or "reasonably related."

flowing from the property—the Court determined the city could have required that Dolan simply keep the area open. But by requiring complete dedication of the land rather than simply restricting Dolan's ability to build on it, the city limited Dolan's ability to exclude others, which, the Court stated, is "'one of the most essential sticks in the bundle of rights that are commonly characterized as property.'" *Id.* at 393 (quoting *Kaiser Aetna v. United States*, 444 U.S. 164, 176 (1979)).

In addition, regarding the dedication of the pedestrian/bicycle pathway easement, the Court did not accept the city's conclusory statement that the creation of the pathway "could offset some of the traffic demand...and lessen the increase in traffic congestion." *Id.* at 381-82. "No precise mathematical calculation is required," the Court repeated, "but a city must make some effort to quantify its findings in support of the dedication for the pedestrian/bicycle pathway beyond the conclusory statement that it could offset some of the traffic demand generated." *Id.* at 395-96.

The Court concluded by stating:

> Cities have long engaged in the commendable task of land use planning, made necessary by increasing urbanization particularly in metropolitan areas such as Portland. The city's goals of reducing flooding hazards and traffic congestion, and providing for public greenways, are laudable, but there are outer limits to how this may be done. "A strong public desire to improve the public condition [will not] warrant achieving the desire by a shorter cut than the constitutional way of paying for the change."

Id. at 396 (quoting *Pennsylvania Coal Co. v. Mahon*, 260 U.S. 393, 416 (1922))

Subsequent case law has clarified that the *Dolan* rough proportionality rule applies when a court is determining whether dedications demanded as a condition of development are proportional to the development's anticipated impacts and was not intended to address, and is not applicable to, an analysis of whether or not a complete denial of development is a taking. *See City of Monterey v. Del Monte Dunes at Monterey, Ltd.*, 526 U.S. 687, 703 (1999). The United States Supreme Court in *Del Monte Dunes* unanimously held that it had not expanded the rough proportionality test of *Dolan* beyond the "special context of exactions—land use decisions conditioning approval of development on the dedication of property to public use." *Id.* at 702. The rough proportionality test was not designed to address, and is not readily applicable to, the much different questions arising where the landowner's challenge was based on denial of a development permit. California cases are consistent with the decision in *Del Monte Dunes. See, e.g., Breneric Assocs. v. City of Del Mar*, 69 Cal. App. 4th 166, 175-76 (1998) (rejecting Pacific Legal Foundation's argument in its amicus brief that the *Nollan/Dolan* "test should be applicable to denial of a design review permit").

In *Lingle v. Chevron U.S.A. Inc.*, the United States Supreme Court reaffirmed the role of *Nollan* and *Dolan* in cases involving challenges to adjudicative land use exactions. 544 U.S. 528 (2005).[5] In so doing, however, the Court clarified the limited holdings of those cases to adjudicative land use exactions only. The issue in both *Nollan* and *Dolan* was whether the government could demand an easement as a condition for granting a development permit. *Id.* at 546-47. The Court in *Nollan* held the exaction must substantially advance the same government interest that would furnish a valid

> Subsequent case law has clarified that the *Dolan* rough proportionality rule applies when a court is determining whether dedications demanded as a condition of development are proportional to the development's anticipated impacts and was not intended to address, and is not applicable to, an analysis of whether or not a complete denial of development is a taking.

---

[5] *See* Daniel J. Curtin, Jr., W. Andrew Gowder, Jr. and Bryan W. Wenter, *Exactions Update: The State of Development Exactions After Lingle v. Chevron U.S.A., Inc.*, 38 Urb. Law. 641 (2006); David L. Callies and Christopher T. Goodin, *The Status of Nollan v. California Coastal Commission and Dolan v. City of Tigard After Lingle v. Chevron U.S.A., Inc.*, John Marshall L. Rev. 539 (2007).

ground for denial of the permit, while in *Dolan* it held the required degree of connection must be "roughly proportional" both in nature and extent to the impact of the proposed development. Justice O'Connor's unanimous majority opinion emphasized that *Nollan* and *Dolan* do not address whether the challenged exactions "would substantially advance some legitimate state interests" but rather "whether the exactions substantially advanced the same interests" the government claimed would allow it to deny the permit itself. *Id.* at 547.

In *McClung v. City of Sumner*, the Ninth Circuit Court of Appeals held that legislative, generally applicable development conditions that do not require the owner to relinquish rights in real property (as opposed to adjudicative land use exactions) are not subject to *Nollan/Dolan* heightened scrutiny. 548 F. 3d 1219 (9th Cir. 2008). The ordinance at issue in *McClung* required that all new development include twelve-inch storm pipe, and the court noted this mandate was far from an adjudicative determination applicable solely to the McClungs. *Id.* at 1227, 1229. Rather, it was a "classic example" of the zoning laws that do not affect existing use of property and seek to promote health, safety, and welfare by prohibiting particular contemplated uses of land. *Id.* at 810. Such generally applicable legislative regulations are best kept in check, the court suggested, by ordinary restraints of the democratic political process. *Id.* at 1227 (citing *San Remo Hotel L.P. v. City and County of San Francisco*, 27 Cal. 4th at 671 (2002)).

What does *Dolan* mean in California? The United States Supreme Court has placed some limitations on a city's exercise of its police power to require dedication of land as a condition for issuing a development permit. *Dolan* requires a city to document the connection between the dedication and the projected impact of the proposed development. Not only must the required nexus exist, but findings must establish the required reasonable relationship between the required dedication and the impact. Thus, a two-part inquiry must be made to determine whether the essential nexus exists between the project and (1) the type of condition; and (2) the burden created by the condition. The "type of impact" nexus test requires that the type of condition imposed address the same type of impact caused by the development (*Nollan*) and the "burden created" nexus test requires an assessment of whether this condition is in reasonable proportion to the burden created by the new development (*Dolan's* rough proportionality). In California, the courts always have required a nexus based on a reasonable relationship. *Dolan* reiterates the need for a reasonable relationship, but emphasizes there must be something more than generalized or conclusory findings to support that connection.

As a result of *Dolan*, if a city seeks to require a dedication of land as a condition of approval (e.g., building permits, map approvals) as compared to legislative requirements (e.g., a determination applicable to all large development projects, where no individual bargaining is involved), the following rules should be followed:

- A city has the burden of proving a sufficient nexus exists between the required dedication and the impact of the proposed development
- No precise mathematical calculation is necessary to show the required reasonable relationship, but a city must make an individualized determination that the required dedication is related, both in nature and extent, to the impact of the proposed development (i.e., it is roughly proportional
- A city has the burden of proving why a dedication is necessary and why a land use regulation restricting the use of the property cannot suffice
- A city must tailor the conditions it demands to counter only the types of impacts expected from the development

- To meet the heightened *Nollan/Dolan* standard, a city should quantify its findings as much as possible, rather than relying on conclusory statements

For further discussion of the takings issue outside of the context of exactions, see chapter 11 (Regulatory Takings).

APPLICABILITY OF THE *NOLLAN/DOLAN* TEST TO IMPACT FEES AND EXACTIONS: *KOONTZ V. ST. JOHNS RIVER WATER MANAGEMENT DISTRICT* AND *EHRLICH V. CULVER CITY* [6]

In *Dolan*, where the City of Tigard conditioned a development permit on the property owner's dedication of land, the Supreme Court did not address whether the heightened standard enunciated applies to the situation when a city requires payment of an impact fee rather than a dedication of land. The Court addressed the issue in 2013 in *Koontz v. St. Johns River Water Management District*, at least as to the ad hoc imposition of monetary exactions. 133 S. Ct. 2586, 2602-03 (2013).

Koontz v. St. Johns River Water Management District: expansion of *Nollan* and *Dolan*. In *Koontz v. St. Johns River Water Management District*, the United States Supreme Court held that *Nollan*'s and *Dolan*'s nexus and rough proportionality requirements to apply to denials of permit applications where an applicant refuses to make requested concessions and where the local agency imposes *ad hoc* monetary exactions. 133 S. Ct. 2586 (2013).

Mr. Koontz had sought a permit from a Florida water management district to develop a portion of property that contained wetlands. Koontz proposed to develop the 3.7-acre northern portion of his property and to grant a conservation easement to the district over the approximately 11-acre southern portion of his property to mitigate the environmental effects of his proposed development. The district considered the 11-acre conservation easement to be inadequate and informed Mr. Koontz that it would approve the development only if he agreed to either (a) reduce the size of his development to one acre and deed to the district a conservation easement over the remaining 13.9 acres, or (b) proceed with development as proposed and also fund improvements for off-site wetland mitigation. Koontz declined to make either concession and filed suit in state court. The Florida Supreme Court rejected Koontz's claims, holding that *Nollan* and *Dolan* did not apply because the district had denied his application (rather than approving it with conditions that might constitute a taking) and the district's demand had been for money instead of an interest in real property.

The United States Supreme Court reversed, holding that *Nollan* and *Dolan* applied to the case. The Court unanimously agreed that *Nollan/Dolan* apply both to approval of a permit on the condition that the applicant turn over property and to denial of a permit because the applicant declines to turn over property. *Id.* at 2595.

The Justices disagreed on the significance of the water district's request for money rather than an interest in property. The Court's majority held that *Nollan*'s and *Dolan*'s nexus and rough proportionality requirements apply equally to the imposition of a property

> To meet the heightened *Nollan/Dolan* standard, a city should quantify its findings as much as possible, rather than relying on conclusory statements.

---

[6] For further discussion of impact fees and *Ehrlich*, see Daniel J. Curtin, Jr. and W. Andrew Gowder, Jr., *Recent Developments in Land Use, Planning and Zoning Law Relating to Exactions*, 36 Urb. Law. 519 (Summer 2004). *See also* Daniel J. Curtin, Jr., *Update on Exactions: The Legislative Versus Administrative Distinction (Ehrlich v. Culver City and Progeny)*, 34th Annual Institute on Planning, Zoning and Eminent Domain, ch. 8 (LexisNexis 2004).

or monetary exaction. *Id.* at 2599. The Court noted that otherwise local agencies would be able to evade the constitutional safeguards of *Nollan* and *Dolan* by allowing applicants to choose between dedicating an easement and making an in-lieu payment. This portion of *Koontz* dealing with the money/property distinction may prove to be of little significance here in California, where *Ehrlich* has long held that *Nollan* and *Dolan* requirements apply to the imposition of ad hoc fees imposed on an individual basis like those in *Koontz*.

Ehrlich v. City of Culver City: legislatively formulated vs. ad hoc development fees. The California Supreme Court previously had affirmatively answered the question of whether higher scrutiny should be used to examine the constitutionality of impact fees rather than dedications of land in *Ehrlich v. City of Culver City*, 12 Cal. 4th 854 (1996), and reaffirmed this position in *San Remo Hotel v. City and County of San Francisco*, 27 Cal. 4th 643 (2002). Prior to *Ehrlich*, courts had concluded that a higher level of scrutiny only applied in cases of possessory takings. See *Blue Jeans Equities W* at 169.[7]

In *Ehrlich*, the plaintiff closed his privately operated tennis club and recreational facility and applied for an amendment to the general plan and the specific plan, as well as a zoning change, to allow construction of a 30-unit condominium complex.

The city council voted to approve the project conditioned upon the payment of certain monetary exactions, including a $280,000 recreation mitigation fee for partial replacement of the lost private tennis and recreation facility and payment of $33,200 for art in public places. The amount of the $280,000 fee was based upon a city study that showed that the replacement costs for the recreational facilities "lost" as a result of amending the specific plan. Pursuant to Government Code sections 66020 and 66021,[8] Ehrlich challenged the recreation fee and the in-lieu art fee.

Citing *Nollan*, the Court in *Ehrlich* expressed concern that adjudicative, ad hoc conditions on development presented "an inherent and heightened risk that local government will manipulate the police power to impose conditions unrelated to legitimate land use regulatory ends, thereby avoiding what would otherwise be an obligation to pay just compensation." 12 Cal. 4th at 869. The Court emphasized the "extortion[ary]" danger of this "form of regulatory 'leveraging.'" *Id.* at 867. In response to this concern, the Court drew a distinction between legislatively-formulated development fees imposed on a class of property owners and individually-imposed conditions.

The Court held that in the "relatively narrow class of land use cases" that involve individual "land use 'bargains' between property owners and regulatory bodies...where the individual property owner-developer seeks to negotiate approval of a planned development...the combined *Nollan* and *Dolan* test quintessentially applies." *Id.* at 868. The discretionary aspect of conditioning an individual approval heightens the risk that a city may manipulate the police power to impose conditions unrelated to legitimate land use regulatory ends. On this point, the Court stated:

> It is the imposition of land-use conditions in individual cases, authorized by a permit scheme which by its nature allows for both the discretionary deployment of the police power and an enhanced potential for its abuse, that constitutes the sine qua non for application of the...standard of scrutiny formulated by the court in *Nollan* and *Dolan*.

Id. at 869

---

7 See also William Fulton and Paul Shigley, *Guide to California Planning*, chapter 10 (Solano Press, 4th ed. 2012).

8 Government Code sections 66020 and 66021 provide the exclusive method of challenging any fee, dedication, reservation, or other exaction imposed on a housing development. Any challenging party may file a protest by (1) tendering the dedication, fee, or exaction in full; and (2) providing the city written notice the payment is made under protest. For additional discussion of the procedure for challenging fees and dedications, see chapter 19 (Land Use Litigation).

By contrast, the Court reasoned, these dangers were not present in the context of legislatively adopted fees of general application. Accordingly, the court held, the *Nollan/Dolan* heightened scrutiny test did not apply to legislatively adopted fees. *See also Action Apartment Ass'n v. City of Santa Monica,* 166 Cal. App. 4th 456, 470-71 (2008) (holding that *Nollan/Dolan* heightened scrutiny did not apply to generally applicable, legislative inclusionary housing ordinance); *San Remo Hotel,* 27 Cal. 4th at 669-30 (relying on *Ehrlich,* holding an in-lieu fee for conversion of a residential hotel to tourist units was not subject to the *Nollan/Dolan* test); *Loyola Marymount Univ. v. Los Angeles Unified Sch. Dist.,* 45 Cal. App. 4th 1256, 1270-71 (1996) (applying *Ehrlich* to hold that the *Nollan/Dolan* test did not apply to a fee imposed pursuant to the Sterling Act (Educ. Code § 17620; Gov't Code § 65995)).

Applying the legislative vs. ad hoc distinction, the Court struck down the $280,000 recreational mitigation fee. Under the heightened scrutiny test of *Nollan/Dolan,* the Court found that although there was a nexus, it was not roughly proportional to the impact. *Ehrlich,* 12 Cal. 4th at 864. The record, the Court concluded, was "devoid of any individualized findings to support the required 'fit' between the monetary exactions and the loss of parcel zoned for commercial recreational use." *Id.* at 883. The Court remanded the matter to the city council to reconsider the amount of the fee in light of the court's decision. *Id.* at 885. In so doing, it observed this type of recreational fee could be proper as long as it was based on (1) the additional administrative expenses incurred in redesignating other property within a city for recreational use or (2) by the monetary incentives needed to induce private recreational development on other land.

On the other hand, the Court held that the public art fee was not a development exaction of the kind subject to the heightened *Nollan/Dolan* standard since it was more akin to traditional land use regulations, such as imposing minimal building setbacks, parking and lighting conditions, landscaping requirements, and other design conditions. The Court reasoned that such aesthetic control has long been held to be a valid exercise of a city's traditional police power, and does not amount to a taking merely because it might incidentally restrict a use, diminish the value, or impose a cost in connection with the property. *Id.* at 886.

Finally, the Court made it clear that "developers who wish to challenge a development fee on either statutory or constitutional grounds must do so via the statutory framework" of the Mitigation Fee Act (Gov't Code §§ 66000-66025, discussed below), which requires that for a fee to be challenged, it must first have been paid under protest, and then a suit must be brought within 180 days. *Id.* at 867.

The *Ehrlich* Court's key rulings may be summarized as follows:
- The *Nollan/Dolan* heightened scrutiny test applies only to development fees imposed on an individual, ad hoc basis in a discretionary permit granting process, and not to general legislatively formulated fees
- *Nollan/Dolan* does not apply to legislative acts applicable to a general class, e.g., transit fees imposed on downtown office developers (*Blue Jeans*), housing fees imposed on nonresidential developers (*Commercial Builders*), art fees (*Ehrlich*), nor in-lieu inclusionary housing fees (*City of Napa*). Applying this standard, it is clear from *Ehrlich* that cities have the authority to impose fees for a wide range of services, including transit fees, housing, and art, and so long as cities base development conditions on general legislative determinations, the conditions will almost always be within the police power
- If a developer wants to challenge an individually applied fee either statutorily or constitutionally, it must follow the statutory framework of the Mitigation

If a developer wants to challenge an individually applied fee either statutorily or constitutionally, it must follow the statutory framework of the Mitigation Fee Act.

Fee Act. This means that the challenger must file a written protest, pay the fee under protest, and bring suit within a 180-day time frame

- A city can legally charge a mitigation fee as a condition of a land use change if the discontinuation of the previous private use has public consequences, as long as the *Nollan/Dolan* test has been met
- An ordinance enacted for aesthetic purposes alone is well within the scope of a city's police power

The California Supreme Court reaffirmed the holding and rationale of *Ehrlich* in *San Remo Hotel v. City and County of San Francisco*, where the Court said that in-lieu fees required to pay for replacement housing in a hotel conversion from residential to tourist use were not subject to the heightened scrutiny test of *Nollan/Dolan*. 27 Cal. 4th 643, 670 (2002). In that case, the San Remo Hotel in San Francisco sought to convert the residential rooms to rooms for tourists rather than to longer-term residents. Pursuant to the city's Residential Hotel Unit Conversion and Demolition Ordinance (HCO), the Hotel paid an in-lieu fee into a governmental fund for the construction of low- and moderate-income housing.

The Court held that the in-lieu fee did not violate the Takings Clause, and was not subject to the heightened scrutiny test set forth in *Nollan, Dolan,* and *Ehrlich*. The Court declined to extend heightened takings scrutiny to all development fees, adhering instead to the distinction it drew in *Ehrlich, supra*, between ad hoc exactions and legislatively mandated, formulaic mitigation fees. The Court noted that while legislatively mandated fees do present some danger of improper leveraging, such generally applicable legislation is subject to the ordinary restraints of the democratic political process. A city council that charged extortionate fees for all property development, unjustifiable by mitigation needs, would likely face widespread and well-financed opposition at the next election. Echoing *Ehrlich*, the Court noted that ad hoc individual monetary exactions deserve special judicial scrutiny mainly because they affect fewer citizens and evade systematic assessment and, therefore, are more likely to escape such political redress.

The court in *Building Industry Association (BIA) of Central California v. City of Patterson* relied on *San Remo* in concluding that a legislatively-enacted, broadly-applicable in-lieu fee was unlawful where no reasonable relationship had been shown between the amount of the fee and "the deleterious public impact" of new development. 171 Cal. App. 4th 886, 898–99 (2009). The City of Patterson approved a development agreement for two residential subdivisions in the city. At the time the development agreement was approved, the city allowed developers to pay a fee of $734 per residential unit in lieu of constructing affordable housing. However, the development agreement recited that the developer agreed to be bound by revised fees, provided they were "reasonably justified." The city subsequently increased its in-lieu affordable housing fee to $20,946 per unit. The developer challenged the city's imposition of the revised fee to its project.

First, the court interpreted the agreement's use of the term "reasonably justified" to mean that any increase in the fee was required to conform to existing law. "In other words, part of the way one would show a fee is reasonably justified is to show that it does not violate established legal principles." *Id.* at 897. Like the fee in *San Remo Hotel*, the City of Patterson's in-lieu fee was formulaic and legislatively-mandated. It was not a discretionary ad hoc exaction. Relying on *San Remo Hotel*, the court in *Building Industry Association* therefore concluded the fee increase would pass muster only if "there is a reasonable relationship between the amount of the fee, as increased, and 'the deleterious public impact of the development.'" *Id.* at 898–99.

The city's Fee Justification Study failed to establish the required reasonable relationship between the fee of $20,946 and impacts created by the new residential units upon which this fee would be imposed. The study had arrived at the $20,946 fee by calculating the full estimated cost of subsidizing future development of the 642 affordable housing units allocated to the city through the Regional Housing Needs Assessment for Stanislaus County. It had then spread this entire cost among the unentitled future residential units anticipated by the city's General Plan. The study had not, however, shown a connection between the 642-unit figure and the need for affordable housing associated with new market-rate development, including the subdivisions subject to the development agreement. Thus, the court concluded the city had not established the necessary reasonable relationship.

The court in *Building Industry Association* reached no conclusion about whether—or how—Patterson and other cities could make the required showing in the context of an affordable housing in-lieu fee. The court made clear, however, that cities establishing and imposing affordable housing in-lieu fees must demonstrate a reasonable relationship between the amount of the fee and some deleterious impact associated with the development of new market-rate housing.

CALIFORNIA'S "NEXUS LEGISLATION"—THE MITIGATION FEE ACT

In 1987, the Legislature adopted Assembly Bill 1600 (AB 1600), often referred to as the 1987 "nexus legislation." AB 1600 added Government Code sections 66000 to 66011, which set forth certain requirements a city must follow in establishing or imposing fees. In 1996, the Legislature relabeled AB 1600 and other related sections (Gov't Code §§ 66000–66025) the "Mitigation Fee Act."

Section 66001(a) requires any city that establishes, increases, or imposes a fee as a condition of approval of a development project to do all of the following for both ad hoc fees and those established by legislation of general applicability:

- Identify the purpose of the fee
- Identify how the fee will be used
- Demonstrate there is a reasonable relationship between the purpose of the fee and the type of development project on which the fee is imposed
- Demonstrate that there is a reasonable relationship between the need for the public facility and the type of development project on which the fee is imposed

Next, Government Code section 66001(b) requires a city to show that there is a "reasonable relationship" between the specific amount of the fee imposed as a condition of approval on a particular development project and the cost of the public facility attributable to that project. Note, however, that impact and development fees imposed pursuant to a development agreement are exempt from the Act. Gov't Code § 60000(b).

While the Mitigation Fee Act requires a local government to establish a "reasonable relationship" between the exaction and the project's impact, which would appear to evoke a fairly deferential standard of review, the California Supreme Court has maintained that fees established in an ad hoc manner require the more searching inquiry articulated in the United States Supreme Court's decisions in *Nollan* and *Dolan*. See *Ehrlich*, 12 Cal. 4th at 880; see also *San Remo Hotel*, 27 Cal. 4th at 666; *BIA of Central California*, 171 Cal. App. 4th at 898–99. While the Legislature amended the Mitigation Fee Act to expressly apply to ad hoc monetary exactions in 1996, which occurred after some of the aforementioned decisions, the best reading of this statute is that the Act

> The California Supreme Court has maintained that fees established in an ad hoc manner require the more searching inquiry articulated in the United States Supreme Court's decisions in *Nollan* and *Dolan*.

imposes additional requirements on a local government in assessing an ad hoc fee, and is not intended to supplant *Nollan* and *Dolan* review for ad hoc fees.

The Mitigation Fee Act also contains provisions requiring a city to deposit, invest, account for, and expend such fees (Gov't Code § 66006);[9] to make findings once every fifth year regarding any portion of the fee remaining unexpended or uncommitted (Gov't Code § 66001(d)); to identify, within 180 days of determining that sufficient funds have been collected, an approximate date of commencing construction of improvements, or else to refund unexpended fees (Gov't Code § 66001(e)); and to adopt capital improvement plans (Gov't Code § 66002). Within 180 days of the close of each fiscal year, a city must make available to the public the beginning and ending balance for the fiscal year; the description and amount of fees, interest, and other income; the identification of public improvements on which fees were expended; the amount of expenditure by a city; and the amount of refunds made pursuant to section 66001 during the fiscal year. The city council is to review this information at the next regularly-scheduled meeting not less than fifteen days after it becomes available. Gov't Code § 66006(b).

Under the Mitigation Fee Act, a developer may challenge the imposition of a fee, dedication, or other exaction if the developer follows a specified procedure that includes protesting the fee in writing, "at the time of approval or conditional approval of the development or within 90 days after the date of the imposition of the...exactions." Gov't Code § 66020(d)(1). A city is required to provide written notice of the 90-day protest period to the developer at the time of project approval or imposition of the fees, though the statute is silent regarding any consequences of a city's failure to provide such notice. *Id*. Any party who files a protest may then file an action attacking the imposition of the fees within 180 days after delivery of the city's notice. Gov't Code § 66020(d)(2).

The California Supreme Court distinguished between the Act's remedies pertaining to fees imposed on a development project and fees for building inspections and permits in *Barratt American Inc. v. City of Rancho Cucamonga*, 37 Cal. 4th 685 (2005). In *Barratt*, a developer challenged a building permit fee and sought relief under Government Code section 66016(a), which provides a prospective fee reduction remedy if a development fee or service charge exceeds actual costs and create excess revenues, and sections 66020 and 66021, which authorize a refund of any unlawful part of fees imposed on a development project. The *Barratt* court clarified that building permit fees are not fees imposed on a development project. *Id*. at 696–700.

> The *Barratt* court clarified that building permit fees are not fees imposed on a development project.

In 2007, Barratt American challenged yet another fee resolution. *See County of Orange v. Barratt American Inc.*, 150 Cal. App. 4th 420 (2007). The county had resolved to expend its surplus fee revenue by reducing future developer fees and spending a portion of the surplus on related services and expenses. Barratt American argued that instead of spending any of the surplus, the county should further reduce future developer fees. The court held that section 66016(a) allowed the county to use any "surplus fee revenue to cover the reasonable and necessary costs of the services rather than merely lowering the fees until the surplus is dissipated." *Id*. at 433. However, the court further held the county had not shown its spending of $4.5 million of the surplus was reasonable and necessary and, therefore, ordered the county to lower its fees until that amount was dissipated.

---

[9] Government Code section 66006 is applicable to any public improvement fee received pursuant to a development agreement entered into on or after January 1, 2004. See Gov't Code § 65865(e).

In *Homebuilders Association of Tulare/Kings Counties, Inc. v. City of Lemoore,* the court upheld against a challenge under the Mitigation Fee Act a wide range of sometimes novel development fees, including fees for police equipment, garbage trucks, and a naval air museum, emphasizing the deference to be accorded an agency's choice of methodology in calculating the fees. 185 Cal. App. 4th 554 (2010). The court sustained the use of a so-called "standard-based" methodology for calculating fees, under which the cost of existing facilities is divided by the current population and the resulting figure multiplied by the number of projected future residents. *Id.* at 562-64. The court found this approach reasonable because the facilities at issue were intended for citywide use. The Mitigation Fee Act, the court held, does not require identification of specific facilities; references to types or categories of public facilities is sufficient. *Id.* at 564. Only one fee did not survive judicial review, for failing to show a nexus between new facilities and new development: a fire protection impact fee for an area of the city that already had facilities adequate to accommodate further development. *Id.* at 571-72.

Recently, the California Supreme Court held that the Mitigation Fee Act's pay under protest procedure applied to a challenge to a condition of approval requiring the developer to set aside units as below market rate units and make a cash payment to a city fund. *Sterling Park, L.P. v. City of Palo Alto,* 57 Cal. 4th 1193, 1209 (2013). The Supreme Court held that the term "other exactions"—as used to describe applicability of the pay under protest procedure in Government Code section 66020—includes "conditions on development a local agency imposes that divest the developer of money or a possessory interest in property." *Id.* at 1207. The Court distinguished such interests from restrictions on the manner in which a developer may use property, which are not subject to section 66020. The Court held that either component of the city's affordable housing program—the imposition of the in-lieu fee or the requirement that the developer sell units below market rate (including the city's reservation of an option to purchase)—would constitute an exaction. *Id.*

For a discussion of litigation under the Mitigation Fee Act, see chapter 19 (Land Use Litigation).

> The California Supreme Court held that the term "other exactions"—as used to describe applicability of the pay under protest procedure in Government Code section 66020—includes "conditions on development a local agency imposes that divest the developer of money or a possessory interest in property."

DOCUMENTING THE NEXUS

In order to meet the constitutional and statutory nexus requirement, a city must have strong factual support. A sufficient traffic fee study, for example, will anticipate development that is designated in the city's general plan, and estimate future traffic based upon that level of development. A strong study also will use established trip generation rates, or explain the rationale for deviating from those rates. A typical study then will project needed facilities based upon acceptable traffic levels and public transportation criteria set forth in the general plan, estimate the cost and schedule for building those facilities, and then allocate the cost of constructing those facilities to new and existing development on a proportional basis.

The decision in *Russ Building Partnership v. City and County of San Francisco* contains an example of a well-documented fee. 199 Cal. App. 3d 1496, 1496 (1987) (opinion certified for partial publication). In *Russ,* the court upheld a five-dollar-per-square-foot fee imposed on new office development for the San Francisco Municipal Railway System, based on the city's detailed study that documented the need and cost of the facilities. This case was decided before *Nollan* and before the effective date of the Mitigation Fee Act, but follows the principles later enunciated by those authorities.

In contrast, the decision in *Bixel Associates v. City of Los Angeles* provides an example of a poorly-documented fee. 216 Cal. App. 3d 1208, 1218–21 (1989). The court invalidated the City of Los Angeles' fire hydrant fees because there was no evidence of a proper nexus. The court then cited the proper methodology to analyze such exactions, citing *Russ Bldg. Partnership*, 199 Cal. App. 3d 1496, and *J.W. Jones Cos. v. City of San Diego*, 157 Cal. App. 3d 745 (1984). *Id.* at 1218.

DOUBLE TAXATION

Developers often have argued that the dedication of land or the payment of fees in return for approval of a project is a tax for a public purpose, thereby constituting double taxation. However, the California Supreme Court rejected this argument in *Associated Home Builders, Inc. v. City of Walnut Creek*:

> Double taxation occurs only when "two taxes of the same character are imposed on the same property, for the same purpose, by the same taxing authority within the same jurisdiction during the same taxing period." Obviously the dedication or fee required of the subdivider and the property taxes paid by the later residents of the subdivision do not meet this definition. If Associated's claim were valid the prior residents of a community could also claim double taxation since their tax dollars were utilized to purchase and maintain public facilities which will be used by the newcomers who did not contribute to their acquisition.

4 Cal. 3d 633, 642 (1971) (citations omitted)

EQUAL PROTECTION

Another course developers have pursued to avoid dedications of land or the payment of fees is to argue that such exactions violate the equal protection provisions of the Fourteenth Amendment to the U.S. Constitution. However, these arguments generally fail. The Fourteenth Amendment does not require that every law treat every person in exactly the same manner. Reasonable classifications can be established, and it only is necessary that the laws apply equally to persons within such classifications. With respect to economic regulation, the legislative determination of the propriety of the classification controls, so long as it meets the "rational relation" test. Thus, unless the classification is arbitrary or fails to rest upon any substantial distinction or apparent natural reason, such a determination will be upheld. *See Nordlinger v. Hahn*, 505 U.S. 1, 11 (1992) (upholding the acquisition value real property scheme of California's Proposition 13 (1978 ballot measure approving Article XIIIA of the California Constitution)); *Old Dearborn Distrib. Co. v. Seagram Distillers Corp.*, 299 U.S. 183, 197 (1936). Strict scrutiny of differential treatment will be applied only where there is a "suspect classification" or where a fundamental right is affected. As the California Supreme Court stated when it upheld a city's comprehensive condominium conversion ordinance:

> The vast majority of cities and counties in California has adopted comprehensive schemes of land use regulation. Except where such regulations have infringed upon fundamental constitutional rights or relied on suspect classifications such as race, they have generally been upheld in the face of due process and equal protection challenges.

Griffin Dev. Co. v. City of Oxnard, 39 Cal. 3d 256, 263 (1985); *see also Candid Enters., Inc. v. Grossmont Union High Sch. Dist.*, 39 Cal. 3d 878, 890 (1985) ("Developers do not constitute a 'suspect class,' and development is not a 'fundamental interest.'").

This equal protection argument was pursued by the developers in *Russ Building Partnership*, 199 Cal. App. 3d 1496, but to no avail. In *Russ Building Partnership*, office developers claimed the five-dollar-per-square-foot municipal railway fee ordinance discriminated against owners of office buildings constructed after 1979, denying them access to government benefits on the same footing as owners of pre-1979 buildings, and that it arbitrarily singled out commercial buildings while giving retail stores in the downtown area a free ride. The court rejected this contention, holding that there was no denial of equal protection:

> Under an equal protection analysis, the transit fee as an economic regulation is presumed to be constitutional....Likewise, the argument that retail stores, which are also responsible for increased ridership, somehow got a windfall also fails. The Ordinance imposes the fee on the projected ridership directly and reasonably arising from the new office space. The city may rationally conclude that office workers increase the need for transit services during peak hours. The conclusion that it is office space, and not retail stores, that is primarily responsible for the need for improved transit services is properly left to the sound discretion of the local governing body.

199 Cal. App. 3d at 1508

In other cases, developers have claimed equal protection violations based on the contention that a state law or city ordinance that applies only to subdividers, and exempts single lot or apartment house developers, denies subdividers equal protection. As part of this contention, the subdivider often argues that the occupants of an apartment house can impose as great a burden on the community as occupants of a single-family residential subdivision. However, the California Supreme Court has not been persuaded:

> This point has some arguable merit in the sense that the apartment builder, by increasing the population of an area, may add to the need for public recreational facilities to the same extent as the subdivider. However, the apartment is generally vertical, while the subdivision is horizontal. The Legislature could reasonably have assumed that an apartment house is thus ordinarily constructed upon land considerably smaller in dimension than most subdivisions and the erection of the apartment is, therefore, not decreasing the limited supply of open space to the same extent as the formation of a subdivision. This significant distinction justifies legislatively treating the builder of an apartment house who does not subdivide differently than the creator of a subdivision.

Associated Home Builders, Inc. v. City of Walnut Creek, 4 Cal. 3d at 643

OPPORTUNITIES FOR DEDICATIONS OR FEES

IN GENERAL

The land use approval process provides many opportunities for a city by using its police power to require dedication of land and payment of fees as conditions of approval of a development project. In *Ayres v. City Council*, the California Supreme Court upheld dedication conditions for a subdivision map approval based on the city's general police power, and rejected the subdivider's argument that the city needed an enabling ordinance. 34 Cal. 2d 31 (1949). Such opportunities include, but are not limited to, general and specific plan adoption or amendment, zoning, use permit, variance, subdivision or building permit approval, and approval of property development agreements.

> The land use approval process provides many opportunities for a city by using its police power to require dedication of land and payment of fees as conditions of approval of a development project.

Exactions and dedications can be required for a wide range of purposes, such as streets, sewers, drainage, parks, habitat conservation, and off-site improvements, and might include fees for building child day care centers in commercial developments, public art, financing a municipal transit system, or providing library sites, police or fire stations, or affordable housing.

THE GENERAL PLAN

Under the umbrella of its police power, a city can look to its zoning ordinance, subdivision ordinance, and use permit provisions as support for many of the standard types of dedications. However, more cities now are relying upon the general plan or applicable specific plan to support dedication or fee requirements. Given that the general plan is considered the constitution for development, it makes sense that dedication requirements can flow from goals and policies contained in such plans. See J.W. Jones Cos., 157 Cal. App. 3d at 749. Since all land use approvals must be consistent with the goals, policies, and objectives of the general plan, conditions can be attached to achieve these goals. For a thorough discussion of general plans and consistency requirements, see chapter 2 (General Plan).

For example, in *Soderling v. City of Santa Monica*, the court upheld a city's requirement that smoke detectors be installed in all units in a condominium conversion. In so doing, it reasoned that this requirement flowed from the city's general plan to "promote safe housing for all." 142 Cal. App. 3d 501, 506 (1983). This condition was seen as a valid means to achieve the goals of the city's general plan. Therefore, the power to impose the condition need not be expressed by the specific enactment of an ordinance or promulgation of a regulation, because the Subdivision Map Act requires consistency with the general plan.

Similarly, in *J.W. Jones Companies*, the court ruled that the City of San Diego properly exercised its police power to impose a facilities benefits assessment (FBA) on developers in order to carry out its general development scheme as "sketched in the general plan" of the city. 157 Cal. App. 3d at 758. An FBA would require the installation of a broad spectrum of public improvements by the developer, such as public libraries and fire stations, which in the past had been financed by general city revenues. The court stated, "[T]he ordinance is the key to implementing San Diego's controlled growth concept as formalized by the general plan and community plan.... The vision of San Diego's future as sketched in the general plan is attainable only through the comprehensive financing scheme contemplated by the FBA." Id. at 757–58.[10]

Thus, given the propriety of tying exactions to general plan goals, some cities have amended their general plans to adopt goals and policies relating to the need for child day care centers, public libraries, and fire stations and have, in turn, adopted ordinances requiring developers to pay a fee for those purposes.

SUBDIVISION PROCESS

Dedications and development fees are generated from three basic sources in the subdivision approval process:

FBA = facilities benefits assessment

---

[10] For a discussion of infrastructure finance mechanisms and the ability of the general plan to promote fairness and predictability, see Edward J. Sullivan and Ian Lester, *The Role of the Comprehensive Plan in Infrastructure Financing*, 37 Urb. Law. 53 (2005).

- Specific conditions that may be imposed by local ordinance through the specific statutory authorization contained in the Subdivision Map Act (Gov't Code §§ 66410–66499.58) and related statutes

- Environmental mitigation measures that may be imposed through the CEQA process (Pub. Res. Code §§ 21000–21177), and through Government Code section 66474(e), which requires denial of maps likely to cause substantial environmental damage

- Conditions that may be imposed through the definitions of "design" and "improvement" in the Subdivision Map Act and reliance on the general plan. *See* chapter 5 (Subdivisions)

CEQA = California Environmental Quality Act

If a dedication or fee requirement is attached to the approval of a map based on the specific statutory authorization of the Subdivision Map Act, then that criterion governs. However, a different rule applies if a dedication or fee is attached to a non-subdivision approval, e.g., a PUD or CUP. In these situations, the imposition of the requirement is governed by the city's general police power as interpreted under the nexus rules. For example, if a city wants to impose a condition requiring parkland dedication or payment of fees for park or recreational facilities as part of the subdivision process, a city, by ordinance, may do so. Gov't Code § 66477; *see also Associated Home Builders, Inc.*, 4 Cal. 3d at 640–41. Therefore, if the city attaches this condition to the approval of a map, it must adhere to the limitation of three to five acres per 1,000 residents set forth in the Map Act. But, if a city's general plan calls for six or seven acres per 1,000 residents, then a city may impose this higher standard under its general police power if this condition is attached to a non-subdivision approval, like a PUD or CUP, rather than the map approval, and the city has adopted a regulation to that effect. *See* 73 Ops. Cal. Atty. Gen. 152, 156 (1990).

PUD = planned-unit development
CUP = conditional use permit

BUILDING PERMITS

The dedication of land or the payment of fees can be required as a condition of issuance of building permits. The issuance of building permits once was viewed by developers as a right, so long as the project was in compliance with building codes and zoning regulations. *See Sunset View Cemetery Ass'n v. Kraintz*, 196 Cal. App. 2d 115, 118–19 (1961). However, courts no longer treat the issuance of building permits as ministerial only. Rather, courts consistently uphold local regulations that treat the issuance of building permits as discretionary, which allows cities to impose conditions on their issuance:

> The contention that Avco was entitled to a building permit because the county would have been compelled to issue it upon mere application has no merit. The Orange County Building Code (§ 302(a)) provides that a building permit may not issue unless the plans conform not only to the structural requirements of the Code but to "other pertinent laws and ordinances." This provision codifies the general rule that a builder must comply with the laws which are in effect at the time a building permit is issued, including the laws which were enacted after application for the permit.

Avco Community Developers, Inc. v. South Coast Reg'l Comm'n, 17 Cal. 3d 785, 795 (1976); *see also Friends of Westwood, Inc. v. City of Los Angeles*, 191 Cal. App. 3d 259, 276–77 (1987); *Fontana Unified Sch. Dist. v. City of Rialto*, 173 Cal. App. 3d 725, 732–33 (1985); *Slagle Constr. Co. v. County of Contra Costa*, 67 Cal. App. 3d 559, 563 (1977)

PROCESSING FEES—LAND USE AND BUILDING PERMIT FEES

Fees for building permits, zoning changes, use permits, and similar filing and processing fees may not exceed the estimated reasonable cost of providing the service for which they are charged. Gov't Code § 66014. Although Government Code section 66016 provides a prospective fee reduction remedy where fees have exceeded the cost of services, cities are not constitutionally required to conduct annual financial audits of their "proceeds of taxes," including regulatory fees that exceed the costs borne in providing regulatory services. *Barratt American*, 37 Cal. 4th at 702.

Before adopting such fees, a city must make available to the public "data indicating the amount of cost, or estimated cost, required to provide the service for which the fee or service charge is levied...." Gov't Code § 66016(a). Also, a city must hold at least one public meeting at which oral or written presentations can be made. *Id.*

Government Code section 66014 allows cities to include, as part of the fees they may charge, the costs reasonably necessary to prepare and revise the plans and policies they are required to adopt before making any necessary findings and determinations.

In *Barratt*, the California Supreme Court held that because building fees are not development fees, the applicable remedy and limitations period for excessive building fee claims are stated in sections 66016 and 66022. 37 Cal. 4th at 692. Under section 66016, the applicable remedy is a prospective fee reduction and, pursuant to section 66022(a), the applicable limitation period is 120 days from the effective date of the ordinance, resolution, or motion. *Id.* at 694. The court also found that if a city reenacts a building permit fee, even though the fee amount is unchanged, it does constitute a modification or amendment of an existing fee or service charge under section 66022, thus triggering a new limitations period. *Id.* at 703. The court reasoned that the city's reenactment of a permit fee changed the duration of the fee, extending its applicability, and by implication, its validity. Otherwise, without this interpretation, all subsequent reenactments of a fee not initially challenged would be immune from judicial challenges. *Id.*

SCHOOL DISTRICT FACILITIES FEE[11]

In 1985, the California Supreme Court held that a city could impose fees on new construction to mitigate impacts on school districts. *Candid Enterprises, Inc. v. Grossmont Union High Sch. Dist.*, 39 Cal. 3d 878, 886 (1985).

The current statutory scheme governing school fees, the Leroy F. Greene School Facilities Act, was adopted in 1998. The Act sets the base amount of allowable developer fees for residential, commercial, and industrial construction. Gov't Code § 65995(b). These base amounts are commonly referred to as Level 1 fees and are subject to adjustment for inflation. Gov't Code § 65995(b)(3). For updated information regarding statutory developer fees, see the State Allocation Board's website (www.opsc.dgs.ca.gov).

In certain circumstances, for residential construction, school districts can impose fees in excess of Level 1 fees. School districts can impose fees equal to 50 percent of land and construction costs (commonly referred to as Level 2 fees) if they prepare and

---

11 For an excellent historical review of the legislative and judicial history of school development fees, see *Grupe Development Co. v. Superior Court*, 4 Cal. 4th 911 (1993). In *Grupe*, the court held that the 1986 legislation preempted the field of school construction financing and declared invalid a special tax ($1,500 per unit) adopted after Proposition 13 and under its provisions by two-thirds vote. See also *Western/Cal. Ltd. v. Dry Creek Joint Elementary Sch. Dist.*, 50 Cal. App. 4th 1461 (1996).

adopt a school facilities needs analysis and meet at least two of the following four conditions (Gov't Code § 65995.5):

- At least 30 percent of the district's students are on a multitrack year-round schedule
- The district has placed on the ballot within the previous four years a local school bond that received at least 50 percent of the votes cast
- The district has passed bonds equal to (1) fifteen percent of its bonding capacity prior to November 4, 1998; or (2) 30 percent of its bonding capacity after November 4, 1998, or
- At least 20 percent of the district's teaching stations are relocatable classrooms

Also, if the state's bond funds are exhausted, a school district that is eligible to impose Level 2 fees will be authorized to impose even higher fees, which are commonly referred to as Level 3 fees, equal to 100 percent of land and construction costs of new schools required as a result of new developments.

The legislation also amended Government Code section 65996(b) to prohibit local agencies from using the inadequacy of school facilities as a basis for denying or conditioning approvals of any "legislative or adjudicative act...involving...the planning, use, or development of real property...." The former version of this statute extended only to approvals under the Subdivision Map Act or CEQA.

Nonprofit, private university is not exempt from school fees. In *Loyola Marymount University v. Los Angeles Unified School District,* the court held that a nonprofit, private university was not entitled to an exemption from school impact fees in connection with construction of its new business school. 45 Cal. App. 4th 1256, 1267-71 (1996).

Loyola Marymount University, a nonprofit Catholic institution, acquired vacant land adjacent to its Los Angeles campus. The university intended to construct a new building to house a postgraduate business school and a new parking structure. Loyola Marymount applied for a building permit, which would not be issued unless the university paid the school development fees authorized by the Sterling Act. Loyola Marymount paid $37,483 in school development fees under protest and then petitioned for a writ of mandamus. The trial court ordered the Los Angeles Unified School District to refund the fees with interest.

In ruling for the school district, the appellate court reversed, stating that to offset the burden imposed on school districts by new development, Education Code section 17620 (former Gov't Code § 53080(a)(1)) authorizes school districts to levy a fee to fund the construction of school facilities against all residential, commercial, and industrial development projects that are not subject to exemption. *Id.* at 1261. Loyola Marymount's proposed project qualified as commercial use since the school offered services in exchange for money. Moreover, Loyola Marymount did not qualify for an exemption from school facilities fees for state entities or facilities used exclusively for religious purposes.

Redevelopment construction is not exempt from school fees. In *Warmington Old Town Associates v. Tustin Unified School District,* a case of first impression, the court held that redevelopment construction is not exempt from the imposition of school-impact fees. 101 Cal. App. 4th at 845.

In *Warmington,* as part of a redevelopment project, the developer demolished 56 apartment units in the City of Tustin and replaced them with 38 single family homes. The school district then imposed $122,080 in school-impact fees, based on the total square footage of the 38 single family homes, considering them "new residential construction" within the meaning of Education Code section 17620(a)

(1)(B). The developer paid the fees under protest, then filed a petition for a writ of mandate, claiming that (1) he was owed a "credit" with respect to the 56 units that were replaced; and (2) the district failed to establish a sufficient nexus between the fee and the purported impact.

With respect to the developer's first contention, the court held that Education Code section 17620 permits school districts to impose school-impact fees to "new residential construction." These fees also apply to the resulting increase in space of "other residential construction." The court acknowledged that including an exemption for redevelopment projects would be consistent with the purpose of the statutory scheme, i.e., to address the impact on the affected school district related to the increase in students generated by the development; however, it rejected this argument because it would render section 17626 (exemption for remodeling projects) superfluous. Therefore, to harmonize the exemptions provided in sections 17620 and 17626, the court concluded the demolition of apartments and replacement with houses does not fall within the scope of "other residential construction" entitled to a credit. 101 Cal. App. 4th at 850–51.

The court also addressed the question of whether the fee study presented by the district in support of the imposition of school fees established the reasonable relationship required under Government Code section 66001. The fee study evaluated the impact of building new homes, which would generate new students, thereby impacting the district. However, the court held that the fee study was not sufficient to establish the required nexus between the amount of the fee imposed and the burden created. *Id.* at 851. In so holding, the court pointed out the flaws in this study as applied to redevelopment projects:

> [T]he Fee Study gives no thought to the extent of the impact of a tract of homes that are newly constructed in the place of older residential housing previously existing on the same site. It gives no consideration to whether those newly constructed replacement homes in fact generate additional numbers of students over and above those who occupied the previous homes at the site....
> It suggests no method for estimating the impact of new construction in the redevelopment context, in which new homes may generate no more students than replaced homes did previously or may even generate fewer students."

Id. at 859

Loyola Marymount University reaffirmed prior cases holding that the action of imposing a school fee was a legislative act reviewable under ordinary mandate (Code Civ. Proc. § 1085), and therefore the fee need only meet the "reasonable relationship" test. 45 Cal. App. 4th at 1270–71; *see also Western/Cal. Ltd. v. Dry Creek Joint Elementary Sch. Dist.*, 50 Cal. App. 4th 1461, 1492 (1996); *Garrick Dev. Co. v. Hayward Unified Sch. Dist.*, 3 Cal. App. 4th 320, 327–28 (1992).

HABITAT CONSERVATION PLANS AND NATURAL COMMUNITIES CONSERVATION PLANS

HCP = habitat conservation plan

NCCP = natural communities conservation plan

One area of increasing interest among cities and counties is the use of habitat conservation plans (HCPs) and natural communities conservation plans (NCCPs) to ensure the protection of certain species and certain types of habitat. Habitat conservation plans are the federal mechanism under the Endangered Species Act (ESA) for striking a balance between development and the protection of important habitat. Development and approval of an HCP acceptable to federal agencies would entitle a developer to a permit documenting compliance with the ESA. Natural communities conservation plans are a similar mechanism under state law for complying with the California ESA.[12] Impact fees on development and land exchanges among private, local, state, and even federal entities are among the ways HCPs and NCCPs are proposed to be funded.

ESA = Endangered Species Act

Certain local agencies have made moves to combine these federal and state conservation plans with their own local planning mechanisms. For example, Riverside County has coordinated its general plan update, transportation plan, and HCP. Riverside County's Multi-Species Habitat Conservation Plan was adopted by fourteen cities and was approved by state and federal regulators in June 2004.

Interestingly, as some local governments use their police power and planning authority to help implement the regional conservation goals of HCPs and NCCPs, others are frustrated that these plans circumvent the local planning process. They claim that the plans—with their promise of compliance with the Endangered Species Act—cede too much planning authority to federal and state statutes and authorities. They also argue that the result is a patchwork of ineffective conservation that does not reflect local preferences or local circumstances.

For more detailed information on HCPs, see chapter 8 (Endangered Species Protections).

CEQA

Although CEQA does not independently authorize a city to impose dedications or exactions, the statute is intended to be used in conjunction with the police powers or other discretionary powers granted to public agencies by other laws. Cal. Code Regs. tit. 14, § 15040. Therefore, so long as a dedication or exaction is carried out under some other authority, CEQA provides a basis for analyzing and considering the effects of a particular exaction. The CEQA Guidelines provide that "a lead agency for a project has the authority to require feasible changes in any or all activities involved in the project in order to substantially lessen or avoid significant effects on the environment, consistent with applicable constitutional requirements such as the 'nexus' and 'rough proportionality' standards established by case law." Cal. Code Regs. tit. 14, § 15041 (citing *Nollan v. California Coastal Comm'n*, 483 U.S. 825 (1987); *Dolan v. City of Tigard*, 512 U.S. 374 (1994)).

CEQA = California Environmental Quality Act

For further discussion of CEQA, see chapter 6 (CEQA).

SPECIAL REQUIREMENTS RELATING TO IMPOSITION OF FEES

WAITING PERIOD BEFORE FEES BECOME EFFECTIVE; PUBLIC HEARING REQUIRED

State law requires a 60-day waiting period before new fees or increased fees on development can go into effect. Gov't Code § 66017(a). This waiting period applies not only to processing fees but to development fees, such as circulation and drainage fees. Also, a properly noticed public hearing must be conducted pursuant to Government Code section 66016.

In addition, state law imposes a general ten-day newspaper notice and public hearing requirement for the adoption or increase of any fee, if that fee would not otherwise

---

[12] For a detailed discussion of habitat conservation plans and natural community conservation plans, see Paul Cylinder, et al., *Understanding the Habitat Conservation Planning Process in California* (Institute for Local Self Government, California League of Cities, 2004), *available at* http://www.ca-ilg.org/sites/ilgbackup.org/files/resources/HCP_book_2004_final.pdf.

be subject to other statutory notice requirements (i.e., Government Code sections 66017 and 66016). Gov't Code § 66018.

WHEN FEES ARE REQUIRED TO BE PAID

In general, a city that "imposes fees or charges for the construction of public improvements or facilities on a residential development" cannot require payment of the fee until the date of the final inspection or the date the certificate of occupancy is issued, whichever is first. Gov't Code § 66007.[13] Government Code section 66007 has two purposes: (1) to require cities to defer payment of general development fees so that developers will no longer be required to pay the fees as early in the process; and (2) to encourage cities to specify how money collected from fees will be spent prior to being able to collect such fees.

However, an exception exists. A city may collect fees at an earlier time if the city determines prior to the final inspection or the issuance of a certificate of occupancy that:

- The fees will be collected for public improvements or facilities for which an account has been established and funds appropriated, and the city has adopted a proposed construction schedule or plan for the project, or
- The fees are to reimburse the local agency for expenditures previously made

Gov't Code § 66007(b)(1)

This exception does not apply to units reserved for occupancy by lower income households where: (1) the units are included in a residential development proposed by a nonprofit housing developer; and (2) at least 49 percent of the total units are reserved for occupancy by lower income households at an affordable rent. Gov't Code § 66007(b)(2).

Another exception involves the collection of utility service fees. Utility service fees may be collected at the time an application for utility service is received. Gov't Code § 66007.

Cities also may require applicants for building permits to enter into a contract to pay the required fees. Gov't Code § 66007. The contracts must be recorded, and are enforceable against successors in interest to the applicant. The contracts may require notification to the city when any escrow for sale of a dwelling unit is opened, and may also require the fees to be paid from escrow before any sale proceeds are disbursed to the seller. *Id.*

In a 1990 case, a court held that Government Code section 66007 was not applicable to school impact fees. The court stated the specific provision relating to payment of school development fees (former Government Code § 53080) prevailed over the general provisions of Government Code section 66007. Therefore, the fees had to be paid before obtaining a building permit. *See RRLH, Inc. v. Saddleback Valley Unified Sch. Dist.*, 222 Cal. App. 3d 1602, 1611 (1990). The ruling in *RRLH* is probably also applicable to timing of fees specified in the Subdivision Map Act, such as fees for bridges and major thoroughfares. Gov't Code § 66484.

In response to high buyer cancellation rates and accompanying builder cash flow issues resulting from an economic downturn, the Legislature in 2008 amended Government Code section 66007 to allow—but not require—local agencies to collect impact fees (with the exception of school impact fees) at close of escrow. Gov't Code § 66007(g).

---

13 For a detailed discussion of fees in the context of open space programs, see *Funding Open Space Acquisition Programs: A Guide for Local Agencies in California* (Institute for Local Government, League of California Cities, 2005), *available at* http://www.cailg.org/sites/ilgbackup.org/files/2005-Open_Space-w.pdf.

REASONABLENESS OF DEVELOPMENT FEE AMOUNT

As discussed previously regarding the Mitigation Fee Act, when a city imposes any fees or exactions as a condition of approval of a proposed development, those fees or exactions shall not exceed the estimated reasonable cost of providing the service or facility for which the fees or exactions are imposed. Gov't Code § 66005. Furthermore, cities must comply with certain fee-identification and "reasonable relationship" requirements before establishing, increasing, or imposing a fee. Gov't Code § 66001. Cities may not include the cost attributable to existing deficiencies in public facilities, but may include the cost attributable to the increased demand for public facilities reasonably related to the development project. Gov't Code § 66001(g).

In 2008, the Legislature added Government Code section 66005.1, which provides that where a local agency imposes a fee on a housing development pursuant to Government Code section 66001 for the purpose of mitigating vehicular impacts and the housing development incorporates certain characteristics designed to reduce trip generation, the fee or the portion thereof relating to vehicular traffic impacts shall be set at a rate that reflects a lower rate of vehicular traffic impacts in comparison to projects without these characteristics. The characteristics necessary for section 66005.1 to apply include one-half mile proximity to transit coupled with barrier-free access; convenience retail uses within one-half mile; and maximum parking limits. Gov't Code § 66005.1(a).

> When a city imposes any fees or exactions as a condition of approval of a proposed development, those fees or exactions shall not exceed the estimated reasonable cost of providing the service or facility for which the fees or exactions are imposed.

FEES CANNOT BE LEVIED FOR MAINTENANCE AND OPERATION

Fees cannot be levied on development projects for the maintenance or operation of public capital facility improvements. Gov't Code § 65913.8. However, a maintenance and/or operation fee may be required if the improvement is designed and installed to serve only the specific development project on which the fee is imposed, and the improvement serves nineteen or fewer lots or units, so long as the city makes a finding, based upon substantial evidence, that it is infeasible or impractical to form an assessment district or to annex into one. In addition, this type of fee can be required if the improvement is within a water, sewer maintenance, street lighting, or drainage district if an assessment district will be created. This section does not affect developer fees for the construction of capital improvements.

DEDICATION OF LAND—RECONVEYANCE TO SUBDIVIDER

Government Code section 66477.5 provides that if a subdivider is required to make a dedication of land in fee title (not an easement) for public purposes (other than for open space, schools, or parks), the city to which the land is dedicated must record a certificate with the county recorder identifying the subdivider and the land being dedicated, and stating that the land shall be reconveyed to the subdivider if the same public purpose for which it was dedicated no longer exists, or the land or a portion thereof is not needed for public utilities. The subdivider may request that the city make such a determination and reconvey the land to the subdivider as provided above, but the city may assess a fee for making the determination. The fee may not, however, exceed the cost of making the determination.

If land is to be reconveyed, it shall be reconveyed to the subdivider or its successor in interest. The law also provides that the city must give the subdivider whose name appears on the certificate 60 days notice prior to vacating, leasing, selling, or otherwise disposing of the dedicated property, unless the dedicated property will be used for the same public purpose for which it was dedicated.

JUDICIAL REVIEW

Since the adoption of fees is a legislative act, it is reviewed under the narrow standards of ordinary mandate. Code of Civil Proc. § 1085. The court need only determine whether the action taken was arbitrary, capricious, or entirely lacking in evidentiary support, or whether it failed to conform to procedures required by law. Such a limited review is based on the doctrine of separation of powers, which (1) sanctions the legislative delegation of authority; and (2) acknowledges the presumed expertise of the agency. *See Canyon North Co. v. Conejo Valley Unified Sch. Dist.*, 19 Cal. App. 4th 243, 251 (1993) (upholding school fees); *Garrick Dev. Co. v. Hayward Unified Sch. Dist.*, 3 Cal. App. 4th 320, 328 (1992) (upholding school fees); *see also Western/Cal. Ltd. v. Dry Creek Joint Elementary Sch. Dist.*, 50 Cal. App. 4th 1461, 1492 (1996).

A party wanting to challenge the imposition of any fees, dedications, or other exactions must follow the procedures in the Mitigation Fee Act (Gov't Code §§ 66000-66025). Exactions are often challenged under the Mitigation Fee Act, or as aspects of an agency decision challenged in a mandate proceeding. For a detailed discussion of fee challenges, *see* chapter 19 (Land Use Litigation).

DEVELOPMENT FEE OR A TAX?

A fee is a "monetary exaction, other than a tax or special assessment, which is charged by a local agency to the applicant in connection with approval of a development project for the purpose of defraying all or a portion of the cost of public facilities related to the development project...." Gov't Code § 66000(b). Taxes are subject to their own constitutional requirements, discussed below, and the Mitigation Fee Act does not apply.

But distinguishing between a tax and a fee is not always easy, especially where a city assesses a tax on development. According to decisional law, an exaction is a tax where the city imposes it to raise revenue for the city's general fund, and not for the limited purpose of funding public facilities or services related to a new development. By contrast, "...[development] fees are commonly imposed on developers by local governments in order to lessen the adverse impact of increased population generated by the development.'" *Centex Real Estate Corp. v. City of Vallejo*, 19 Cal. App. 4th 1358, 1364-65 (1993) (citing *California Bldg. Industry Assn. v. Governing Bd. of the Newhall Sch. Dist.*, 206 Cal. App. 2d at 235 (1988)). Also, taxes generally are imposed for revenue purposes, rather than in return for a specific benefit conferred or privilege granted. *Sinclair Paint Co. v. State Bd. of Equalization*, 15 Cal. 4th 866, 874 (1997). For a good discussion of the distinctions between a "tax" and a "regulatory fee," see *Sinclair Paint Co.*, 15 Cal. 4th at 874-81.

HISTORICAL BACKGROUND

For many years, in particular before the passage of Proposition 218 in 1996, the courts had upheld a taxing approach by which cities and counties could distribute the burden of supporting community services. This approach could, for example, require the payment of a tax computed according to the number of bedrooms in the proposed structure, payable at the time of issuance of the building permit. The monies could then be used for various types of capital facilities. This bedroom tax approach was initially approved by the courts of appeal, which said a general law city's ordinance imposing such a tax was solely a revenue measure imposing a valid tax, rather than having any regulatory purpose. *See Associated Home Builders, Inc. v. City of Newark*, 18 Cal. App. 3d 107, 111 (1971).

For example, the California Supreme Court upheld a license tax on a company engaged in the business of acquiring, subdividing, improving, selling, and otherwise disposing of real property. *See City of Los Angeles v. Rancho Homes, Inc.*, 40 Cal. 2d 764, 771 (1953). In another case, a court upheld an environmental excise tax ordinance that levied $500 per bedroom with a maximum of $1,000 per dwelling unit. *See Westfield-Palos Verdes Co. v. City of Rancho Palos Verdes*, 73 Cal. App. 3d 486, 490 (1977).

EFFECT OF JARVIS INITIATIVES—PROPOSITION 13 (1978), PROPOSITION 62 (1986), AND PROPOSITION 218 (1996)

In 1978, the passage of Proposition 13, adding Article XIIIA to the California Constitution, dramatically changed local government finance by limiting most property taxes to one percent of the property value. In addition, Proposition 13 made the imposition of new state and local taxes more difficult by requiring a two-thirds vote of the Legislature for state taxes, or a two-thirds vote of the electorate for local taxes. *See Sinclair Paint Co.*, 15 Cal. 4th at 877–78 (considering whether the "fee" established by the Childhood Lead Poisoning Act, which the Legislature passed by a simple majority vote, was actually a "tax" requiring a two-thirds vote);[14] *see also Howard Jarvis Taxpayers Ass'n v. City of Riverside*, 73 Cal. App. 4th 679, 681–84 (1999) (overview of Proposition 13). Many cities were hit hard by the resulting loss in revenues and had to cut services sharply. To make up for the losses, cities increasingly turned to benefit assessments, special taxes, development fees, and other new revenue sources.

Proposition 62 (Gov't Code §§ 53720-53730) passed by the voters in November 1986, was designed to fill apparent gaps in Proposition 13. Proposition 62 specifically targeted loopholes through which local governments had continued to levy taxes—i.e., utility user taxes, transient occupancy taxes, and business license taxes—simply by a majority vote of the city council or board of supervisors without voter ratification. *See City and County of San Francisco v. Farrell*, 32 Cal. 3d 47, 56–57 (1982); *McBrearty v. Brawley*, 59 Cal. App. 4th 1441, 1448 (1997) (discussing the constitutionality of Proposition 62 and its retroactive application). Proposition 62 classifies all taxes as either "general taxes" or "special taxes." A "general tax" is a tax imposed for general governmental purposes, and under Proposition 62, no general tax may be imposed without a two-thirds vote of all members of the legislative body proposing to impose the tax, as well as a majority vote of the local electorate voting on the issue.

All taxes other than general taxes, including taxes for specific purposes, are "special taxes." No special tax may be imposed without a two-thirds vote of the local electorate voting on the question of whether to impose the tax. Gov't Code § 53722; *see also Santa Clara County Local Transp. Auth. v. Guardino*, 11 Cal. 4th 220, 231–32 (1995). The voter-approval requirement of Proposition 62 was upheld by the California Supreme Court, which determined that it did not violate the state constitutional prohibition

> All taxes other than general taxes, including taxes for specific purposes, are "special taxes."

---

14 In *Sinclair*, the California Supreme Court held a state-imposed charge on paint companies and other businesses that made products using lead was a "fee" and not a "tax" subject to the two-thirds vote requirement of Proposition 13. In November 2000, California voters endorsed the Court's opinion by defeating an initiative that would have required a two-thirds Legislative or voter approval for certain regulatory charges like the one in *Sinclair*.

against subjecting tax statutes to a referendum. *Id.* at 241; Cal. Const. Art. II, § 9. Thus, all new "taxes" sought to be imposed by local governments and districts are subject to voter approval.

However, Proposition 62 did not limit the authority of local governments to impose "special assessments," "fees," or "charges" under their police power in connection with the development of real property. This authority already was well established in California. *See, e.g., Russ Bldg. Partnership,* 199 Cal. App. 3d at 1503; *J.W. Jones Cos.,* 157 Cal. App. 3d 745, 758; *Trent Meredith, Inc. v. City of Oxnard,* 114 Cal. App. 3d 317, 325 (1981). Proposition 62 and the cases that followed it also left open the question of whether or not its restrictions and requirements applied to charter cities. *See Guardino,* 11 Cal. 4th at 260.

Proposition 218. California voters approved Proposition 218 in November 1996, adding articles XIIIC and XIIID to the California Constitution.[15] Proposition 218 was drafted by the Howard Jarvis Taxpayers Association, a group comprising many of the same people who championed Propositions 13 and 62. It was intended to close perceived loopholes in those earlier laws by placing in the state constitution the voter-approval requirements of Proposition 62, as well as by requiring voters to approve all locally-imposed special assessments and certain other fees and charges. Significantly, Proposition 218 expressly makes these restrictions and requirements applicable to both general law and charter law cities. *See Burbank-Glendale-Pasadena Airport Auth. v. City of Burbank,* 64 Cal. App. 4th 1217, 1226 (1998) (a charter city's enactment of a transient parking tax under Proposition 62 did not require voter approval, but, upon passage of Proposition 218, voter approval was required).

An official report by the Legislative Analyst in 1996 predicted that Proposition 218 would result in short-term local government revenue losses of more than $100 million; the long-term losses would total hundreds of millions of dollars annually. However, it appears that Proposition 218's actual impacts have been varied. Some cities have had significant revenue losses because their electorates have voted against taxes, assessments, fees, and charges needed to provide important municipal services. In other cities, including many in the San Francisco Bay Area, despite causing delays and increased administrative costs, Proposition 218 has had limited impacts on revenue because voters have supported existing and proposed assessments.

Impacts on local general taxes. Proposition 218 answered an important question not addressed in Propositions 13 and 62 by requiring all new or increased local, general taxes, including those in charter cities, to be approved by a majority vote of the local electorate. It also required existing general taxes that were imposed, extended, or increased after January 1, 1995 to be approved by a majority of voters within two years, unless the tax had been approved previously by a majority vote.

Proposition 218 requires that elections to approve general taxes be held at the same time as the regularly scheduled general election for the members of the local governing body. However, special elections to approve general taxes can be held upon a unanimous vote of the governing body declaring a case of emergency. It also prohibits special purpose districts or agencies, including school districts, from levying general taxes.

---

15 For a summary of the historical background that led to the adoption of Proposition 218, see *Howard Jarvis Taxpayers Ass'n v. City of Riverside,* 73 Cal. App. 4th at 681–683. Also, for an informative discussion of Proposition 218, see Robert E. Merritt and Rajiv Parikh, *The Proposition 218 Odyssey: New Challenges for Real Property Development,* 20 CEB Real Prop. L. Rep. 70 (May 1997). *See also* Proposition 218—Implementation Guide (League of California Cities 2007), *available at* http://www.cacities.org/resource_files/newCybrary/2007/legalresource/ 26003.PROP%20218%20final.pdf.

Under subsequent legislation clarifying Proposition 218 (Stats. 1997, chap. 38), resolutions presented to voters for taxes may state a range of rates or amounts. In addition, such resolutions may provide for an automatic inflation adjustment pursuant to a clearly-identified formula, unless the tax rate itself is determined by a percentage calculation. Gov't Code §§ 53739(a), (b).

Impacts on local special taxes. Proposition 218 reaffirms that special taxes may be imposed, extended, or increased only upon a two-thirds vote of the electorate. As with general taxes, resolutions proposing special taxes may state a range of rates or amounts, and may provide for an automatic inflation adjustment unless the special tax is determined by a percentage calculation.

Impacts on special assessments. Special assessments, also known as benefit assessments, are charges levied on real property to pay for benefits the property receives from a local improvement. See Silicon Valley Taxpayers Ass'n, Inc. v. Santa Clara County Open Space, 44 Cal. 4th 431, 441–42 (2008) (benefit must affect the assessed property in a way that is particular and distinct from its effect on other nearby non-assessed parcels). Cities can levy special assessments to finance improvements such as sidewalks, street lighting, parks, open space, and recreational programs. Following passage of Proposition 13, special assessments became popular among local governments because the assessments were exempt from the tax limits of Proposition 13 and usually were not subject to a public vote.

Prior to the enactment of Proposition 218, statutory law contained a number of requirements for establishing a valid special assessment. An assessment could not be levied against property that did not benefit from the improvement being financed, or against property outside the area receiving the special improvement. Each property within the area subject to the assessment could be assessed only a share of the costs of the improvements that was proportional to the benefits it received from those improvements. Assessment statutes also contained procedural requirements such as notice, hearings, and a right to protest. Proposition 218 supersedes and significantly expands those requirements for existing, new, or increased special assessments.[16]

Proposition 218 defines "assessment" as "any levy or charge upon real property by an agency for a special benefit conferred upon the real property." Cal. Const. Art. XIIID, § 2(b). Thus, to constitute an "assessment," the levied amount must be based on property ownership. See Howard Jarvis Taxpayers Ass'n v. City of San Diego, 72 Cal. App. 4th at 236-37 (Proposition 218 does not apply to an assessment levied by a Business Improvement District because that assessment was levied on all businesses, not on real property).

> Proposition 218 defines "assessment" as "any levy or charge upon real property by an agency for a special benefit conferred upon the real property."

The California Supreme Court in *Richmond v. Shasta Community Services District* held that a capacity charge levied on new water connections did not constitute an "assessment" under Proposition 218. 32 Cal. 4th 409, 419-20 (2004). Plaintiffs in *Richmond* were property owners who challenged the local water district's adoption of an ordinance establishing capacity charge for all new water connections. Plaintiffs claimed the capacity charge was an assessment and that its adoption by ordinance had failed to comply with Proposition 218's requirements for such assessments. The Court disagreed, noting the district's capacity charge is not imposed upon particular identifiable parcels. Rather, it is imposed upon a self-selected group of individuals requesting new water service. The charge therefore could not be described as a "charge upon real property" and was not an assessment for purposes of Proposition 218. *Id.* at 419.

---

16 For a discussion of what constitutes an "increase," see 82 Ops. Cal. Atty. Gen. 35 (1999).

The California Constitution provides that "no assessment shall be imposed on any parcel which exceeds the reasonable cost of the proportional special benefit conferred on that parcel." Cal. Const. Art. XIII D, § 4(a). The court in *Dahms v. Downtown Pomona Property* held that an assessment could be discounted for non-profit property owners without violating this requirement. 174 Cal. App. 4th 708, 716-19 (2009). The court reasoned that Article XIII D permits an assessment that is less than the benefit (i.e., includes a discount) because the Constitution requires only that an assessment not exceed the reasonable cost of providing proportional special benefit. For this same reason, an assessment formula would be permitted to calculate the amount of an assessment based on "front footage" (the length of street relating only to one's address) rather than total street frontage along all streets, even though this formula results in corner lots receiving proportionally greater benefits than others. *Id.* at 720-21. While subsection (f) of Article XIII D requires an agency to prove "the amount of any contested assessment is proportional to, and no greater than, the benefits conferred on the property or properties in question," the *Dahms* court concluded that this language means only that the agency bears the burden of proof that the assessment imposed on a parcel does not "exceed[ ] the reasonable cost of the proportional special benefit conferred on that parcel." *Id.* at 1210.

Importantly, Proposition 218 raises to the constitutional level the procedures by which a local government can impose a special assessment. It also addresses the distinction between general benefits and special benefits by defining a special benefit as a "particular and distinct benefit over and above general benefits conferred on real property located in the district at large," and expressly excludes a "[g]eneral enhancement of property value." Cal. Const. Art. XIIID, § 2(i). This provision appears to distinguish the common law definition of special benefit set forth in *Knox v. City of Orland*, in which the Court stated that a special benefit is a benefit that "particularly and directly" benefits the assessed property, and is "over and above" any benefit received by the general public. 4 Cal. 4th 132, 143 (1992).

Perhaps most importantly, Proposition 218 requires an assessment ballot proceeding, similar to an election, for every type of assessment previously addressed by existing statutes (e.g., Streets and Highways Code sections 2800-3012 (Majority Protest Act)). *See* Elec. Code § 4000(c)(9) (Proposition 218 Omnibus Implementation Act of 1997). Specifically, Government Code section 53753 sets out notice, protest, and hearing requirements, including procedures in preparation, processing, and counting ballots. In addition, ballots in such proceedings must be weighted based on the proportional financial obligation of each assessed parcel. This is a change from previous law, which required a majority protest of property owners owning more than 50 percent of the area of assessable land in order to block an assessment, but did not require an election or a ballot proceeding. Proposition 218 requires the agency to mail a ballot to each property owner of record. When ballots are counted, a majority of ballots actually received must favor the assessment. Thus, a small group of very interested voters submitting protests can defeat the assessment if the majority of eligible voters favor the assessment, but do not vote. Significantly, in contrast to prior law, the legislative body cannot override a protest. Under Government Code section 53753(c), added in 1997, voters may change or withdraw an assessment ballot at any time prior to the conclusion of the public testimony offered at the required public hearing. *See Not About Water Com. v. Board of Supervisors*, 95 Cal. App. 4th 982, 999-1000 (2002) (use of voting tied proportionally to property ownership in the context of a voting scheme employed by district officials in the formation of a water assessment district does not violate due process).

The notice requirements described above, as clarified by the 1997 legislation, supersede virtually all other existing statutory notice, protest, and hearing requirements. Gov't Code §§ 53753, 53753.5, 53755.

Proposition 218 exempts the following benefit assessments if they existed on or before November 6, 1996:

- Assessments to finance the capital costs or operation and maintenance of sidewalks, streets, sewers, water, flood control, drainage systems, or vector control
- Assessments imposed pursuant to a petition signed by all the owners of the parcels subject to the assessment
- Assessments previously approved by a majority vote in an election on the assessment

See *Howard Jarvis Taxpayers Ass'n v. City of Riverside*, 73 Cal. App. 4th at 683

All other existing assessments that Proposition 218 does not exempt must have been approved by a ballot proceeding held no later than July 1, 1997. *See Consolidated Fire Protection Dist. v. Howard Jarvis Taxpayers Ass'n*, 63 Cal. App. 4th 211, 220 (1998) (district's assessment for fire suppression equipment that was authorized in 1991, but which the district had to levy on an annual basis, required voter approval under Proposition 218).

Impacts on fees and charges. Proposition 218 also creates significant procedural requirements for new and increased fees or charges. "Fee" or "charge" is defined as "any levy other than an ad valorem tax, a special tax, or an assessment, imposed by an agency upon a parcel or upon a person as an *incident of property ownership, including user fee or charge for a property related service*." Cal. Const. Art. XIIID, § 2(e) (emphasis added).

While "property related service" is defined as "a public service having a direct relationship to property ownership," the phrase "an incident of property ownership" is not defined. Proposition 218 does clarify that fees for the provision of electrical and gas service are not fees or charges imposed as an incident of property ownership. These ambiguous definitions and the distinctions made among gas, electric, and other basic services (e.g., water and sewer) have been the subject of several California Attorney General Opinions. *See, e.g.*, 82 Ops. Cal. Atty. Gen. 43 (1999) (where a water *usage-based* surcharge is imposed only on property-owners already paying a *property-based* charge for the same service, the usage-based charge is subject to Proposition 218's notice and hearing, but not voter approval, requirements); 81 Ops. Cal. Atty. Gen. 104 (1998) (fees for storm drain maintenance do not fall within Proposition 218's exception to voter approval requirement for sewer or water services because storm drain maintenance is distinct from sewer or water services); 80 Ops. Cal. Atty. Gen. 183 (1997) (certain water charges were not subject to Proposition 218 because they were based on water usage, not imposed as an "incident of property ownership").

> Proposition 218 clarifies that fees for the provision of electrical and gas service are not fees or charges imposed as an incident of property ownership.

The Court in *Richmond v. Shasta Community Services District* held that a fire suppression fee imposed on new water connections did not constitute a "fee" subject to Proposition 218. 32 Cal. 4th at 426. The Court reasoned that a water connection charge is not imposed simply by virtue of property ownership, but instead it is imposed as an incident of the voluntary act of the property owner in applying for a water service connection. The fees for connection to the system therefore were not imposed as "an incident of property ownership" and were not subject to Proposition 218. *Id.*

In *Bighorn-Desert View Water Agency v. Verjil*, the California Supreme Court upheld the provisions of a voter-initiative that reduced current water delivery charges, but overturned those provisions that required future voter pre-approval for new increases or charges. 39 Cal. 4th 205, 218–20 (2006). The Court found that Proposition 218 protects the initiative power in matters reducing any local fee, but that Proposition 218 did not permit an initiative to require further voter approval for future increases in fees or new charges. *Id.* The Court also acknowledged there was a question whether the provision of Proposition 218 at issue applied only to "property-related fees" as do other parts of Proposition 218, but held that it applied to such fees at a minimum, and concluded that ongoing water delivery fees, as opposed to new water connections, are imposed as an incident of property ownership. *Id.* at 216–17.

In 2007, a court of appeal relied upon *Bighorn-Desert* and ruled that a groundwater augmentation charge could not be validly imposed without complying with the provision of Proposition 218 because the fee was imposed "as an incident of property ownership." *Pajaro Valley Water Mgmt. Agency v. Amrhein*, 150 Cal. App. 4th 1364, 1370 (2007).

Like the requirements for assessments, fees and charges on a parcel may "not exceed the proportional cost of the service attributable to the parcel." Cal. Const. Art. XIIID, § 1(b)(3); *see* 81 Ops. Cal. Atty. Gen. 106 (1998) (storm drain fees imposed only on property owners connected to a district's sewer system violate Proposition 218; the fees are not proportional to the benefit received by those owners because they are subsidizing other property owners who contribute to storm water flows but who are not charged the fee). However, it is unclear whether the proportionality requirement will prevent cities from subsidizing rates for low-income users with revenues from other ratepayers.

Fees or charges cannot be imposed for general governmental services that are available to the public at large, such as police, fire, and library services. In *Silicon Valley Taxpayers Ass'n, Inc. v. Santa Clara County Open Space Authority*, 44 Cal. 4th 431 (2008), taxpayers sued a county open space authority that had proposed a special assessment on all taxpayers to fund the purchase of open space. The accompanying engineer's report included statements that the additional open space would "'provide a degree of general benefit to the public at large.'" *Id.* at 454. In invalidating the fee, the California Supreme Court found that the authority failed to demonstrate the properties in the assessment district received a particular and distinct special benefit not shared by the district's property in general or by the public at large. *Id.* at 456. *See also Concerned Citizens for Responsible Government v. West Point Fire Protection Dist.*, 196 Cal.App.4th 1427, 1438 (2011) (citing and affirming *Silicon Valley Taxpayers*, and invalidating a "special assessment" for fire suppression services because it conferred general benefits of fire protection to all parcels in the district); *Golden Hill Neighborhood Association, Inc., v. City of San Diego*, 199 Cal. App. 4th 416 (2011) (invalidating a "special assessment" purportedly for specific properties in a district, because the required engineer's report failed to "adequately separate" and quantify the amount of general and special benefits conferred upon owners of assessed properties).

Fees and charges also may be levied only for services that are "actually used or immediately available;" therefore, charges based on future use of a service are not permitted.

Proposition 218 further states that fees and charges "shall not exceed the funds required to provide the property related service." Cal. Const. Art. XIIID, § 6(b)(1). Although cities may recover all of their costs for particular services through user fees, the constitutional limits on the amount of the fee or charge imposed restrict the manner in which they may do so. Cal. Const. Art. XIIID, § 1(b)(3). As the court explained in *Howard Jarvis Taxpayers Ass'n v. City of Fresno*, a city that seeks "to recover all of its utilities costs from user fees [must] reasonably determine [citation omitted] the unbudgeted costs of utilities enterprises and that those costs be recovered through rates proportional to the cost of providing service to each parcel." 127 Cal. App. 4th 914, 923 (2005).

Proposition 218 imposes procedural requirements for fees and charges that are different from those for assessments in two important ways. First, voters effectively get "two bites at the apple" because they have an opportunity to block the fee or charge first at a public hearing held on the issue, and second at a ballot election held no earlier than 45 days following the hearing. If a majority of the affected property owners files written protests against the proposed fee or charge at the hearing, the agency shall not impose it. If there is not a majority protest against the fee or charge at the hearing, then the agency proceeds to hold a ballot election on the issue (except in the case of fees or charges for sewer, water, and refuse collection services, which do not require an election). In conducting the election, a local agency may use procedures similar to those set forth by Proposition 218 for an assessment election. The fee or charge cannot be imposed unless it is approved either by a majority vote of the affected property owners, or by a two-thirds vote of the electorate.

The second important way the procedures for fees and charges differ from those for assessments is that the votes on proposed fees and charges are not weighted according to the proportional financial obligation of the affected property as they are for assessments. This means that the majority protest procedure for fees and charges may underrepresent owners of large parcels. For example, it would allow the owners of two parcels that total only five acres and are worth a total of only $500,000 to block a charge supported by the owner of an adjacent 50-acre parcel worth $5,000,000.

Possible impacts on new development fees. Proposition 218 states that it shall not be construed to "affect *existing* laws relating to the imposition of fees or charges as a condition of property development." Cal. Const. Art. XIIID, § 1(b) (emphasis added). However, it is unclear whether this exemption for development fees will apply to new laws imposing development fees adopted after July 1, 1997. The Attorney General has suggested that school impact fees are not subject to the voter approval requirements of Proposition 218. *See* 81 Ops. Cal. Atty. Gen. 181 (1998); *but see Apartment Ass'n v. City of Los Angeles*, 24 Cal. 4th 830, 844 (2001) (Proposition 218 inapplicable to a housing inspection fee; and stating the exemption for development fees applies only to fees already in existence).

Impacts on standby charges. Despite its name, a standby charge is an "assessment" for the purposes of Proposition 218. Cal. Const. Art. XIIID, § 6(b)(4); *see also Keller v. Chowchilla Water Dist.*, 80 Cal. App. 4th 1006, 1011 (2000). Thus, the procedural rules concerning assessments apply to standby charges. Accordingly, the Attorney General has opined that Proposition 218's exception for increases in fees, charges, or taxes (but not assessments), in accordance with a schedule of adjustments adopted prior to November 6, 1996, does not apply to such increases in standby charges. *See* 82 Ops. Cal. Atty. Gen. 35 (1999); *see also Howard Jarvis Taxpayers Ass'n v. City of Los Angeles*, 85 Cal. App. 4th 79, 83 (2000) (fees for water usage rates are commodity charges rather than fees under Prop. 218, since they were not "levies or assessments" incident to property ownership).

However, as assessments, standby charges are exempt from the procedural rules concerning assessments if they are imposed exclusively to finance certain capital costs

> Despite its name, a standby charge is an "assessment" for the purposes of Proposition 218.

or maintenance and operation expenses, e.g., sidewalks and water. See Keller, 80 Cal. App. 4th at 1012; Cal. Const. Art. XIIID, § 5(a). The court in Keller addressed this issue. There, the question was whether a standby charge imposed by the water district for its purchase of water was exempt. The court found that the district's standby charge was an "assessment imposed exclusively to finance the...maintenance and operation expenses for water" and was exempt from Proposition 218's procedures and approval process for assessments. Keller, 80 Cal. App. 4th at 1014.

Use of initiatives. Proposition 218 specifically authorizes the use of initiatives to repeal or reduce local taxes, assessments, fees, or charges. Cal. Const. Art. XIIIC, § 3. Thus, it appears that virtually all sources of local revenue may be repealed or reduced through the initiative process. As a result, the rating, valuation, and marketing of local agency bonds may be affected significantly if the revenue sources that support these bonds can be repealed or reduced.

> Proposition 218 specifically authorizes the use of initiatives to repeal or reduce local taxes, assessments, fees, or charges.

It is unclear whether an initiative that affects such a revenue source can withstand a challenge based on an impairment-of-contract theory. The 1997 legislation clarifying Proposition 218 bolsters the impairment-of-contract argument by adding a provision that Proposition 218 "shall not be construed to mean that owners of municipal bonds assume the risk of, or consent to, any action by initiative that constitutes an impairment of contractual rights protected under the Contract Clause of the U.S. Constitution." Gov't Code § 5854. For a discussion of impairment-of-contract doctrine in the context of Proposition 218's balloting requirements as applied to pre-existing assessments, see Consolidated Fire Protection Dist. v. Howard Jarvis Taxpayers Ass'n, 63 Cal. App. 4th 211, 219 (1998).

For a more thorough discussion of initiatives, see chapter 13 (Initiative and Referendum).

CONDITIONS ATTACHED TO LAND USE APPROVALS FOR FINANCING AND MAINTAINING PUBLIC FACILITIES

In order to relieve themselves of the burden of constructing and, particularly, of maintaining new infrastructure, cities attempt to establish various funding vehicles through state law to shift the cost to project owners and new inhabitants. For example, a city could form a Mello-Roos district pursuant to the 1982 Mello-Roos Community Facilities Act (Gov't Code § 53311 et seq.) and impose special taxes on the developing property to fund the installation of public facilities, including streets, sidewalks, storm drains, fire stations, and other improvements. The city could also form a landscaping and lighting district, or require an annexation into one, pursuant to the Landscaping and Lighting Act of 1972 (Sts. & High. Code § 22500 et seq.), or form a Geologic Hazard Abatement District (GHAD) pursuant to Public Resources Code section 26500 et seq.[17] Further, certain cities, such as the City of San Diego, have set up conditions relating to facilities benefits.

The assessments levied by these districts must comply with Proposition 218. But compliance usually is easily accomplished, because the developer initially owns all the property in the proposed district, and is therefore the only voter required to cast a ballot in approving the assessments. Today, conditions regarding such financing are just as important as the conditions for exactions relating to fees and dedications.

---

[17] GHADs are empowered to finance the prevention, mitigation, abatement, or control of actual or potential geologic hazards by levying and collecting special assessments.

GHADs in particular.[18] Geologic Hazard Abatement Districts are local governmental districts formed specifically to address geologic hazards and related concerns. The law authorizing their formation (Pub. Res. Code § 26500 et seq.) was enacted in 1979 to address the aftermath of the Portuguese Bend landslides in the Palos Verdes area of Southern California. A GHAD may be formed for the purpose of prevention, mitigation, abatement, or control of a geologic hazard, and also for mitigation or abatement of structural hazards that are partly or wholly caused by geologic hazards. Pub. Res. Code § 26525. A "geologic hazard" is broadly defined as an actual or threatened landslide, land subsidence, soil erosion, earthquake, fault movement, or any other natural or unnatural movement of land or earth. Pub. Res. Code § 26507.

A GHAD is a political subdivision of the state and is not an agency or instrumentality of a local agency. Pub. Res. Code § 26570. The legislative body of a city or county conducts the formation proceedings. Once the GHAD has been formed, the legislative body must select the district's initial board of directors—either five landowners from the GHAD area, or the legislative body itself. If the legislative body selects five landowners, the initial term shall be four years; thereafter, the landowner board shall be elected from the district. Pub. Res. Code §§ 26567, 26583. Otherwise, the legislative body remains as the board of directors.

A GHAD is empowered to acquire, construct, operate, manage, or maintain improvements on public or private lands. "Improvement" is defined as any activity that is necessary or incidental to the prevention, mitigation, abatement, or control of a geologic hazard, including, but not limited to, the acquisition of property or any interest therein, construction, and maintenance, repair, or operation of any improvement.

A GHAD may include property in more than one city or county, and the property may be publicly or privately owned. Pub. Res. Code §§ 26531, 26532. The property comprising the district need not be contiguous so long as all included property is specially benefited by the proposed construction to be undertaken by the GHAD in a plan of control. Pub. Res. Code §§ 26530, 26534. However, no parcel of real property shall be divided by the boundaries of the proposed district. Pub. Res. Code § 26533. Land may be annexed into an existing GHAD following formation; however, the district's board of directors assumes the responsibilities of the legislative body of the city or county. Nonetheless, annexation is subject to the approval of the legislative body that ordered formation of the district. Pub. Res. Code § 26581.

A GHAD is authorized to finance improvements through the Improvement Act of 1911, the Municipal Improvement Act of 1913, and the Improvement Bond Act of 1915. Pub. Res. Code § 26587. It also may accept financial or other assistance from any public or private source (Pub. Res. Code § 26591), and may borrow funds from a local agency, the state, and the federal government. Pub. Res. Code § 26593.

A GHAD may assess landowners for operation and maintenance of improvements acquired or constructed under the GHAD law. Pub. Res. Code § 26650. These assessments, which attach as liens on property, may be collected at the same time and in the same manner as general taxes on real property. Pub. Res. Code § 26654. All assessment proceedings must also comply with the requirements of Proposition 218.

GHADs are public agencies that operate locally for the sole and specific purpose of addressing geologic hazards and related concerns. As such, they offer several

> Geologic Hazard Abatement Districts (GHADs) are local governmental districts formed specifically to address geologic hazards and related concerns.

---

18 *See* Daniel J. Curtin, Jr. and Shawn Zovod, *GHADs: California's Experience with Hazard Mitigation through Special Districts*, Landslide Hazards and Planning, ch. 4, page 62, APA (2005); *see also* S. Jeer, *Weighing the Benefits of GHADs*, *id.*, page 69.

distinct advantages. Through the development and implementation of a Plan of Control, a GHAD acts to prevent damage resulting from earth movement by identifying and monitoring potential geologic hazards and undertaking improvements as appropriate. When unforeseen hazards arise, GHADs, as existing agencies, are in place with the technical and organizational resources and funding capability necessary to respond quickly and effectively. Since GHADs are authorized to collect assessments along with the general property tax, there is no need for separate collection by a private entity, such as a homeowners' association. Finally, under state law (Gov't Code § 865 *et seq.*), GHADs are given a degree of immunity from liability for actions they undertake. The Legislature intended that these provisions encourage local public entities to take remedial action to abate earth movement. In addition, the Tort Claims Act (Gov't Code § 810 *et seq.*) in general provides immunities to GHADs as it does to other local public agencies.

> When unforeseen hazards arise, GHADs are in place with the technical and organizational resources and funding capability necessary to respond quickly and effectively.

CHAPTER 13

Initiative and Referendum

Ballot box planning, the practice of placing land use measures before the voters, is common in California. Frequently it is citizens, unhappy with the current state of affairs in their communities, who propose initiatives or referenda to adopt general and specific plans or zoning measures, or prevent council- or board-enacted measures from taking effect. Sometimes a developer will use the ballot box to advance its own proposal. Finally, city councils and boards of supervisors frequently submit land use measures directly to the citizens for their approval or rejection.

Ballot box planning, the practice of placing land use measures before the voters, is common in California.

INTRODUCTION[1]

The United States Constitution has no provision for initiative or referendum. Consequently, many states have chosen to adopt one or both of these powers in their state constitutions. California reserved the power of the initiative, referendum, and recall mechanisms in its 1911 Constitution.[2] With respect to local ordinances, local initiatives and referenda are based upon Article II, section 11, which provides:

> Initiative and referendum powers may be exercised by the electors of each city or county under procedures that the legislature shall provide. Except as provided in subdivisions (b) and (c), this section does not affect a city having a charter.[3]

Initiative and referendum proceedings provide a way to obtain a direct popular vote on proposed or recently enacted legislation. The California Supreme Court held that an initiative can be used only to enact a statute—a legislative act—and cannot be used merely to declare policy or guide lawmakers in future decisions. *See American Fed'n of Labor v. Eu, 36 Cal. 3d 687, 708 (1984); see also Marblehead v. City of San Clemente, 226 Cal. App. 3d 1504, 1509 (1991).* In short, the local initiative process is used to adopt ordinances or resolutions, and the referendum process is used to reject them.

Since the people reserved to themselves the powers of initiative and referendum through the Constitution, the courts have carefully guarded these rights. For example,

---

1 For a good discussion on the use of the initiative process as a means to manage growth, see *California 2025: Taking on the Future* (Ellen Harak and Mark Baldassare eds., Public Policy Institute of California, 2005).
2 See – 9 Cal. 4th 688 (1995), for an interesting discussion of the historical background of these constitutional provisions.
3 Many charter cities have initiative and referendum procedures similar to those in the general law, but at times the procedures vary from the general law in certain particulars (e.g., number of signatures required, filing deadlines).

when the California Supreme Court upheld Proposition 140 (term limitations on state legislators) in *Legislature v. Eu*, it noted:

> Accordingly, the initiative power must be *liberally construed* to promote the democratic process. Indeed, it is our solemn duty to jealously guard the precious initiative power, and to resolve any reasonable doubts in favor of its exercise. As with statutes adopted by the Legislature, all presumptions favor the validity of initiative measures and mere doubts as to validity are insufficient; such measures must be upheld unless their unconstitutionality clearly, positively, and unmistakably appears.

54 Cal. 3d 492, 501 (1991) (emphasis in original) (citations omitted); *see also DeVita v. County of Napa*, 9 Cal. 4th 763, 784 (1995) (upholding a county land use element initiative amending the county's general plan); *Rossi v. Brown*, 9 Cal. 4th 688, 702 (1995) (upholding an initiative prospectively repealing a local tax ordinance and barring future adoption of a tax); *Associated Home Builders, Inc. v. City of Livermore*, 18 Cal. 3d 582, 591 (1976) ("If doubts can reasonably be resolved in favor of the use of this reserve power, courts will preserve it.").

In 1978, the California Supreme Court upheld the general validity of Proposition 13 (the Jarvis-Gann Tax Initiative). In so doing, it stated:

> [T]he initiative is in essence a *legislative battering ram* which may be used to tear through the exasperating tangle of the traditional legislative procedure and strike directly toward the desired end. Virtually every type of interest group has on occasion used this instrument. It is deficient as a means of legislation in that it permits very little balancing of interests or compromise, but it was designed primarily for use in situations where the ordinary machinery of legislation had utterly failed in this respect.

Amador Valley Joint Union High Sch. Dist. v. State Bd. of Equalization, 22 Cal. 3d 208, 228 (1978) (quoting Key & Crouch, *The Initiative and the Referendum in Cal.*, p. 485 (1939))

Wielding this "legislative battering ram," voters in cities and counties across the state have taken matters into their own hands and adopted planning and zoning laws. Most often, they have done so when the council or board failed to heed their demands for specific legislation.

THE INITIATIVE

The California Constitution defines the initiative as "the power of the electors to propose statutes and amendments to the Constitution and to adopt or reject them." Cal. Const. Art. II, § 8(a); *see also Marblehead*, 226 Cal. App. 3d at 1509; *American Fed'n of Labor*, 36 Cal. 3d at 708-09. At the local level, this process empowers the voters to enact ordinances or resolutions through a local election. The local initiative power reserved in a city charter may be even broader than the initiative power reserved in the Constitution. *See Rossi*, 9 Cal. 4th at 696.

THE REFERENDUM

The California Constitution defines the referendum as "the power of the electors to approve or reject statutes or parts of statutes...." Cal. Const. Art. II, § 9(a). As contrasted with the initiative power, the referendum applies only to newly enacted legislation and is subject to express constitutional limitations, among them the exemption of tax measures from referendum. *See Rossi*, 9 Cal. 4th at 697. For purposes of local government, referendum is the power to reject an ordinance or resolution that a council or board recently passed to accomplish a legislative act, such as the adoption of a general plan or specific plan, a rezoning ordinance, or adoption of a development agreement.

PROCEDURAL REQUIREMENTS FOR PLACING A LOCAL INITIATIVE OR REFERENDUM MEASURE ON THE BALLOT

Initiatives proposed by council or board. In both cities and counties, the council or board may choose, on its own, to submit proposals to the voters. Elec. Code §§ 9140 (counties); 9222 (cities). Before doing so, however, the council or board must comply with CEQA. *Friends of Sierra Madre v. City of Sierra Madre*, 25 Cal. 4th 165, 194-95 (2001); *see also Citizens for Responsible Government v. City of Albany*. 56 Cal. App. 4th 1199, 1219 (1997) (city council-sponsored measure to approve and implement a "fully negotiated" development agreement could not be submitted to the electorate without CEQA review).

3653333333. With respect to voter-sponsored initiatives, and for referenda, the California Elections Code sets out detailed provisions for the format and circulation of petitions for initiatives and referenda. Elec. Code §§ 9100 *et seq.* (counties) and 9200 *et seq.* (cities). The Elections Code also contains procedures for qualifying initiative and referendum petitions for the ballot in special districts. Elec. Code § 9300 *et seq.* A ballot measure in a general law city or county is subject to the procedures in the Elections Code. A ballot measure in a charter city whose charter "makes any provision for the direct initiation of ordinances by the voters" is governed by the charter, unless the measure would amend the charter. Elec. Code § 9247. If the charter has no provisions setting forth initiative and referendum procedures, then the Elections Code provisions govern.

> A ballot measure in a general law city or county is subject to the procedures in the Elections Code.

The procedures in the Elections Code for submitting a voter-sponsored initiative measure are similar for general law cities and counties, although they differ in particular details. In general, the procedural steps to qualify such an initiative in either a city or county are:

(1) Submittal of a notice of intent to circulate a petition and the text of the initiative measure to the elections official of the county or city (usually the county or city clerk), along with a request that a ballot title and summary be prepared. Elec. Code §§ 9103, 9105(a) (counties); 9202, 9203(a) (cities)

(2) Preparation of ballot title and summary by county counsel or city attorney. Elec. Code §§ 9105 (counties); 9203 (cities)

(3) Publication and/or posting of notice of intent to circulate an initiative petition, and ballot title and summary. Elec. Code §§ 9105(b) (counties); 9205 (cities)

(4) Circulation of an initiative petition for signatures. Elec. Code §§ 9108-9110 (counties); 9207-9209 (cities)

(5) Filing of an initiative petition and examination of signatures. Elec. Code §§ 9113-9115 (counties); 9210-9211 (cities)

(6) Optional reports on the effect of the initiative measure. Elec. Code §§ 9111 (counties); 9212 (cities)

(7) Adoption of the initiative measure by board of supervisors or city council, or alternatively, placement of the measure on the ballot. Elec. Code §§ 9116, 9117 (counties); 9214, 9215 (cities)

(8) Preparation of impartial analysis and arguments to appear on ballot. Elec. Code §§ 9120, 9160 *et seq.* (counties); 9219, 9220, 9280 *et seq.* (cities)

(9) Election campaign and vote. Elec. Code §§ 9121, 9122 (counties); § 9217 (cities)

The procedural steps for qualifying a referendum also are similar in cities and in counties. The steps are:

(1) Circulation of referendum petition (no notice required) and submittal of petition to county or city elections official prior to date when subject legislation would otherwise take effect (usually 30 days after enactment). Elec. Code §§ 9141–9144, 9146 (counties); 9235–9238 (cities)

(2) Examination of petition form and signatures. Elec. Code §§ 9146 (counties); 9239–9240 (cities)

(3) Repeal by board of supervisors or city council of subject legislation, or alternatively, placement of referendum on ballot. Elec. Code §§ 9145 (counties); 9241 (cities)

(4) Preparation of impartial analysis and ballot arguments. Elec. Code §§ 9146 (counties); 9243 (cities)

(5) Election campaign and vote. Elec. Code §§ 9146 (counties); 9243 (cities)

FORM OF PETITION

Initiative petitions in counties and cities must be designed so that each signer may personally affix onto the petition the following:

(a) The signer's signature;

(b) The signer's printed name;

(c) The signer's residential address, giving street number or, if no street number exists, adequate designation of residence so that the location may be readily ascertained; and

(d) The name of the incorporated city or unincorporated community in which the signer resides.

Elec. Code § 9020

Each "section" of the petition, meaning each separate printed copy of the petition, must include the text of the measure proposed for enactment. Elec. Code §§ 9101 (counties); 9201 (cities). The ballot title and summary must appear across the top of each page of the petition where signatures are to appear. Elec. Code §§ 9105(c) (counties); 9203(b) (cities). Each section of an initiative petition also shall bear a copy of the notice of intention to circulate. Elec. Code §§ 9108 (counties); 9207 (cities).

In a county, the form of a referendum petition is subject to the Elections Code provisions regarding form of initiative petitions. Elec. Code § 9146. Across the top of each page of a county referendum petition there shall be printed the following: "Referendum Against an Ordinance Passed by the Board of Supervisors." Elec. Code § 9147(a). In a city, the form of a referendum petition must be substantially the same as that required for statewide initiative or referendum petitions. Elec. Code § 9238(a). The heading "Referendum Against an Ordinance Passed by the City Council" must appear across the top of each page of a city referendum petition. *Id.* Each section of a referendum petition must contain the ordinance's identifying number or title, and must include the text of the ordinance or the portion of the ordinance that is the subject of the referendum. Elec. Code §§ 9147(b) (counties); 9238(b) (cities).

The form of a petition need only be in "substantial compliance" with statutory and constitutional requirements. This, however, means "actual compliance" with essential statutory requirements. *See Assembly v. Deukmejian*, 30 Cal. 3d 638, 649-52 (1982). A petition can be deemed in substantial compliance with the Elections Code, despite a technical defect, when the purpose of the technical requirement established by the Elections Code is not frustrated by the defective form of the petition. *See Costa v. Superior Court*, 37 Cal. 4th 986, 1013 (2006) (minor defects that do not affect the integrity of the electoral process do not warrant invalidation of a petition and preclusion of a vote as long as the fundamental purposes underlying applicable statutory and constitutional requirements have been fulfilled).

Courts have reached inconsistent results when evaluating whether a defect is substantial, and courts have sometimes held that requirements may be ignored by city or county clerks. (See "Filing; Examination of Signatures," below.) Nonetheless, courts generally focus on the common sense issue of whether the petition signers were fully informed. For example, if a resolution adopting a general plan incorporates by reference as an exhibit the contents of the general plan, the entire general plan must be attached to each petition circulated to referend the resolution, even if it consists of several hundred pages and is 2.5 inches thick. *See Nelson v. Carlson*, 17 Cal. App. 4th 732, 738-39 (1993). However, the petition to referend an ordinance that adopts a development plan need not include the plan if the ordinance does not incorporate the plan by reference, at least when the ordinance describes the development project and includes a number of details about the property and the development project. *Lin v. City of Pleasanton*, 176 Cal. App. 4th 408 (2009).

> Courts generally focus on the common sense issue of whether petition signers were fully informed.

In *Hebard v. Bybee*, three words were dropped from the lengthy ordinance title on some, but not all, of the referendum petitions that were circulated for signatures. 65 Cal. App. 4th 1331 (1998). The court concluded that the omission created an ambiguity regarding the effect of the ordinance, and that any voter who did not read the text of the ordinance (which was attached to the petition) was not clearly informed about its full effect. Thus, the court affirmed an order directing the city clerk not to count the signatures on the defective petitions. *Id.* at 1338; *see also Myers v. Patterson*, 196 Cal. App. 3d 130, 136 (1987) (registrar had a duty to reject petitions that did not include the notice of intent to circulate, which was required by statute).

In *Mervyn's v. Reyes*, the court set aside an initiative petition that did not contain the "full text" of the general plan provisions to be enacted by the initiative, as required by Elections Code section 9201, and held that the petition's reference to those sections was not substantial compliance. 69 Cal. App. 4th 93 (1998).[4] However, section 9201 requires only the text of the measure proposed to be enacted, not all the information an informed voter would want. *We Care-Santa Paula v. Herrera*, 139 Cal. App. 4th 387, 391 (2006). Section 9201 does not require that a petition include the text of every plan, law, or ordinance the measure might affect. *Id.* at 390.

In *Hayward Area Planning Association v. Superior Court*, the court held that the lack of the required title, "Referendum Against an Ordinance Passed by the City Council," did not invalidate the petition because the language of the petition furnished the information that would have been provided by the statutorily required title. 218 Cal. App. 3d 53, 59 (1990).

---

[4] The *Mervyn's* opinion contains a good summary of cases concerning whether an initiative or referendum measure substantially complied with statutory requirements.

NOTICE OF INTENTION TO CIRCULATE; BALLOT TITLE AND SUMMARY

A notice of intention to circulate an initiative petition must be filed with the county or city clerk prior to circulating copies of the petition for signatures. Elec. Code §§ 9104 (counties); 9202 (cities). The notice of intention must be accompanied by the written text of the initiative, and may be accompanied by a written statement of up to 500 words giving reasons for the proposed initiative. No notice of intention to circulate is required for referendum petitions.

Sections 9104 and 9202(a) of the Elections Code provide that a notice of intention to circulate shall be in "substantially" the form provided in those sections. The notice of intention in a county must include the names and addresses of at least one, but not more than five proponents. Elec. Code § 9104. In a city, the notice of intention must be signed by at least one, but not more than three, proponents. Elec. Code § 9202(a). A county or city elections official has a ministerial duty to reject an initiative petition that does not include a notice of intention. *See Myers*, 196 Cal. App. 3d at 136.

In counties, when the elections official receives the notice of intention to circulate, the official must immediately transmit a copy of the proposed initiative to the county counsel for preparation of a ballot title and summary. Elec. Code § 9105. In cities, initiative proponents or any other "interested" person shall request preparation of a ballot title and summary upon submission to the city elections official of the notice of intention. The elections official must then immediately transmit the proposed measure to the city attorney. Elec. Code § 9203. The county counsel or city attorney must return the official ballot title and summary within 15 days after the proposed measure is filed. The ballot title and summary must be a "true and impartial" statement of the purpose of the proposed measure, not to exceed 500 words in length. Elec. Code §§ 9105(a) (counties); 9203(a) (cities). The ballot title and summary must appear across the top of each page of the initiative petition where signatures are to appear. Elec. Code §§ 9105(c) (counties); 9203(b) (cities).

Any elector of the county or city may seek a writ of mandate requiring the ballot title or summary to be amended. A peremptory writ will not issue unless there is clear and convincing evidence that the ballot title or summary is false, misleading, or otherwise fails to conform to the statutory requirements. Elec. Code §§ 9106 (counties); 9204 (cities).

PUBLICATION AND POSTING

The notice of intention to circulate, ballot title, and summary must be published and posted prior to circulation of an initiative petition for signatures. *See Ibarra v. City of Carson*, 214 Cal. App. 3d 90, 96 (1989). The requirements for publication and posting in a county and in a city are different. In counties, the notice of intention, the ballot title, and the summary of the proposed measure must be published in a newspaper of general circulation published in the county. The initiative proponents must file a proof of publication with the county elections official. Elec. Code § 9105(b). In cities, the notice of intention and the title and summary of the proposed measure must be published or posted or both. The notice, title, and summary must be published at least once in a newspaper that has been adjudicated as being of general circulation in the city in which the petition is to be circulated. If there is no such newspaper in the city, the notice, title, and summary must be published at least once in a newspaper circulated in the city and adjudicated as being of general circulation in the county in which the city is located, and also must be posted in three public places within the city that are used for posting ordinances. If there is no adjudicated newspaper of general circulation that is circulated in the city, the notice, title, and summary need not be published, but must be posted in three public places within the city that are used for posting ordinances. Elec. Code § 9205.

These provisions are designed to serve the important purpose of educating the public about the petition campaign before it begins. Therefore, strict compliance with the publication and posting requirements is necessary. *Ibarra*, 214 Cal. App. 3d at 95-96.

CIRCULATION; SIGNATURE

Circulation of an initiative petition may commence after the notice, ballot title, and summary are published and/or posted, as required. Elections Code section 101 requires that petitions for local initiatives contain a notice that the petition may be circulated by either a paid signature gatherer or a volunteer, and that members of the public have the right to ask about the circulator's status. Only a voter who is eligible and registered to vote in the jurisdiction for which an initiative or referendum measure is proposed may sign a petition. Elec. Code § 100. The voter's signature must be written on the petition; electronic signatures are not suffient. *See Ni v. Slocum*, 196 Cal. App. 4th 1636, 1649 (2011). Initiative proponents have 180 days from receipt of a ballot title and summary, or from termination of any action for writ of mandate regarding the title and summary, whichever occurs later, in which to collect sufficient signatures. Elec. Code §§ 9110 (counties); 9208 (cities).

In a county, an initiative petition must be signed by at least 10 percent of the entire vote cast in the county at the last gubernatorial election in order to qualify the initiative for a regular election, and by at least 20 percent of such a vote to qualify for a special election. Elec. Code §§ 9101, 9116, 9117. In a city with more than 1,000 registered voters, initiative petitions must be signed by not less than 10 percent of the city's registered voters to qualify the measure for the regular election, and by not less than 15 percent of registered voters to qualify for a special election. Elec. Code §§ 9201, 9214, 9215. In a city with 1,000 or fewer registered voters, an initiative petition must be signed by 25 percent of the registered voters, or 100 registered voters, whichever is the lesser number, compelling the legislative body to adopt the ordinance without alteration, or submit the ordinance without alteration to the voters at a special election. Elec. Code §§ 9214, 9215.

Charter cities, and charter cities and counties, are subject to special requirements. If an initiative in a charter city proposes an ordinance that does not amend the charter, the city charter will determine the number of signatures required. If the charter does not address the required number of signatures, then the Elections Code provisions governing general law cities apply. Elec. Code § 9247. When an amendment to a city or county charter is at issue, the Elections Code determines the required number of petition signatures. It contains a separate article governing charter amendments. Elec. Code §§ 9255 *et seq.* For amendments to a city charter initiated by petition, 15 percent of the registered voters must sign the petition. Elec. Code § 9255 (a)(3). For amendments to the charter in a city and county (i.e. San Francisco) that are initiated by petition, only 10 percent of the registered voters' signatures are required. Elec. Code § 9255 (a)(4).

A county or city ordinance may be referended by filing a petition protesting the adoption of the ordinance with the elections official of the local legislative body before the effective date of the ordinance (usually within 30 days of adoption of the ordinance). In a county, a referendum petition must be signed by not less than 10 percent of the entire vote cast within the county at the last gubernatorial election. Elec. Code § 9144. In a city with more than 1,000 registered voters, referendum petitions must be signed by not less than 10 percent of the city's registered voters. Elec. Code § 9237. In a city with 1,000 or fewer registered voters, a referendum petition must be signed by 25 percent of the registered voters, or 100 registered voters, whichever is the lesser number. Id. When a valid referendum petition is filed, the ordinance does not go into effect, and the legislative body must reconsider the ordinance. Elec. Code §§ 9144 (counties); 9237 (cities).

FILING; EXAMINATION OF SIGNATURES

The provisions of the Elections Code governing filing and examination of petitions in cities and counties are applicable to petitions for both initiatives and referenda. Elec. Code §§ 9146 (counties); 9239 (cities). After sufficient signatures are collected, a petition may be filed by proponents or any person so authorized in writing by the proponents. All sections of a signed petition must be filed with the elections official of the jurisdiction in which the measure is proposed at the same time. Elec. Code §§ 9113 (counties); 9208 (cities). In counties an affidavit, and in cities a declaration, signed by the circulator must be attached to each section. Elec. Code §§ 9109 (counties); 9209 (cities). The forms of the county affidavit and city declaration are provided in the Elections Code. Elec. Code §§ 104 (counties); 9022 (cities).

The local elections official has 30 days, excluding Saturdays, Sundays, and holidays, from the date of filing in which to examine the petition and determine if it contains the required number of signatures. Elec. Code §§ 9114, 9115 (counties); 9211 (cities). Random sampling techniques may be employed to examine petitions bearing more than 500 signatures; however, verification of each signature is required where statistical sampling shows that the number of signatures is between 95 and 110 percent of the number required. Elec. Code §§ 9115 (counties); 9211 (cities). The elections official is to attach a certificate to the petitions showing the results of the examination, and to notify the proponents of the petition as to its sufficiency. Id.

The duties of an election official in examining an initiative or referendum petition are ministerial and not judicial. It is not the function of the official to determine whether a proposed measure is within the power of the electorate to adopt or will be valid if enacted. If the petition satisfies formal requirements and contains a sufficient number of valid signatures, the official must certify the petition as sufficient. See Truman v. Royer, 189 Cal. App. 2d 240, 243 (1961); Farley v. Healey, 67 Cal. 2d 325, 327 (1967). In Alliance for a Better Downtown Millbrae v. Wade, 108 Cal. App. 4th 123 (2003), the court ruled that elections officials are not authorized under state law to consider extrinsic evidence or engage in "discretionary factfinding" to determine whether an initiative petition complies with the Elections Code. Id. In Wade, the city clerk of Millbrae found that an initiative petition was circulated in violation of the Elections Code and refused to certify the petition. The clerk's finding was based on a number of factors: the signature page showing greater wear than the full text and notice of intention pages; unidentified persons told her they saw circulation of the petition without the full text and notice of intention; a folder with signature pages by themselves were found; and she believed the circulators had violated the Elections Code in the past. Id. at 134. In ruling for the petitioner, the court held that the city clerk impermissibly went beyond the face of the petition, made unauthorized adjudicative decisions based on extrinsic evidence, and violated her ministerial duty to accept the petition. *Id.* at 131-134. If initiative petitions are adequate on their face, the courts, not elections officials, are the proper forum for enforcing the provisions of the Elections Code. *Id.* at 136.

However, the election official's duties, though ministerial, are not mechanical. The official must exercise some judgment, e.g., when comparing signatures on the petition with those on voter registration affidavits. *See Wheelwright v. County of Marin,* 2 Cal. 3d 448, 455-56 (1970); *see also Truman,* 189 Cal. App. 2d at 243 (city clerk may refuse to certify petitions because of noncompliance with election procedures). Nonetheless, if the clerk chooses to examine the signatures and finds them sufficient the clerk "must certify the petition as sufficient." *Truman,* 189 Cal. App. 2d at 243-44. The court in *Truman* upheld the clerk's certification of petitions notwithstanding the circulators' failure to comply with the circulators' affidavit requirement. "The defective affidavits accompanying the referendum petition are not part of the petitions themselves, and failure of such should not invalidate a petition which was in fact signed by the requisite number of qualified voters...." *Id.* at 244.

The decision in *Truman* was distinguished in *Myers v. Patterson,* where the court noted that a failure of a referendum petition to include a notice required by the city charter "directly affected the content of the petition sections circulated to voters...[and] the information was not just for the benefit of the City official." 196 Cal. App. 3d 130, 137 (1987). Accordingly, the court in *Myers* held that *Truman* was not applicable since, in contrast to *Truman,* the defect directly affected the content of the petition sections circulated to the voters. *Id.* at 136. If the elections official determines that the petition bears an insufficient number of valid signatures, no further action is taken. Elec. Code §§ 9114, 9115 (counties); 9211 (cities). Failure to secure sufficient signatures does not preclude the filing of an entirely new initiative petition on the same subject at a later date. *Id.* Failure to secure sufficient signatures on a referendum petition usually does terminate the referendum effort, since there will generally be insufficient time to prepare and circulate another referendum petition. If the number of signatures on a petition is found to be sufficient, the elections official certifies the results to the local legislative body at its next regular meeting. *Id.* § 9146, 9237.5.

> If the elections official determines that the petition bears an insufficient number of valid signatures, no further action is taken.

ACTION BY LOCAL LEGISLATIVE BODIES ON INITIATIVE AND REFERENDA PETITIONS

INITIATIVES

Once the valid signatures on an initiative petition are certified to the city council as sufficient, the Elections Code allows the city council to refer the qualified initiative measure to staff or any city or county agencies for a report on its fiscal impact, consistency with the general plan, and any other matters. The report must be completed within 30 days after the initiative petition is certified as having a sufficient number of signatures. Elec. Code §§ 9111 (counties); 9212 (cities). The city council may request such a report prior to certification of signatures by the elections official to allow for a longer period for completion of the report. A council or board may request a limited environmental analysis of an initiative measure as part of the 30-day report permitted for initiative measures. Elec. Code §§ 9111(a)(3) (counties); 9212(a)(3) (cities). Although the information gained from that process could presumably assist the voters in passing judgment on the initiative, this review cannot be used to modify the initiative. The board of supervisors or city council is allowed to refer the proposed initiative measure to any county or city agency, respectively, for a report or reports on a number of issues related to the measure. Topics for which reports may be commissioned include the fiscal impact of the measure, its effect on the internal consistency of the county's or city's general and specific plans, including the housing element, consistency between planning and zoning, limitations on city or county actions under various sections of the Government Code, and any other matters the board or council request to be in the report.

Legislative amendments in 2000 further expanded the list of specifically allowable topics to include many quality of life and environmental issues. The expanded list includes the effect of the measure on the use of land, the impact on the availability and location of housing, the ability of the city or county to meet its regional housing needs, the impact of the measure on funding for infrastructure of all types, including whether or not the proposed measure would result in increased infrastructure costs or savings to current residents and businesses, the impact of the measure on the community's ability to attract and retain business and employment, the impact on the uses of vacant parcels of land, and the impacts on agricultural lands, open space, traffic congestion, existing business districts, and developed areas designated for revitalization. Although these sections are useful to governments in ensuring that the public is well-informed as to all the potential impacts of a proposed initiative measure, the measure must be submitted to the voters as drafted by its sponsors, and cannot be modified based on conclusions reached in the course of generating any reports.

After receiving a valid initiative petition (and perhaps the requested report(s)), the board of supervisors or city council must either pass the proposed ordinance without change or submit the ordinance, without alteration, to the city electorate. Elec. Code §§ 9118, 9214, 9215. There is an open question whether CEQA compliance is required when a city council adopts a voter-sponsored initiative rather than placing the measure on the ballot In *Native American Sacred Site & Envtl. Protection Ass'n v. City of San Juan Capistrano*, 120 Cal. App. 4th 961 (2004), the court held that because cities have a mandatory duty either to place a voter-sponsored initiative on the ballot or adopt the initiative, a city's decision to adopt the initiative by ordinance is ministerial and is not subject to CEQA. Another court reached the opposite result in *Tuolumne Jobs & Small Business Alliance v. Superior Ct.*, formerly published at 210 Cal. App. 4th 1006 (2012) (city has discretion whether to adopt, rather than place on the ballot, a voter-sponsored initiative; therefore such action is subject to CEQA). The California Supreme Court granted review in *Tuolumne*, with a decision expected in 2014.

A city council has the authority to delay the election on an initiative. In *Jeffrey v. Superior Court*, more than 22,000 Huntington Beach residents sought to amend the city charter in 2002 by placing the Fair Apportionment and Individual Representation (FAIR) initiative on the ballot. The initiative proposed to modify the city council's term limits and change the city council from seven members elected at large to five members elected by districts, with changes becoming effective two years in the future, during the November 2004 general municipal election. 102 Cal. App. 4th 1 (2002). Though Huntington Beach had an upcoming general election in 2002, the city council placed the FAIR initiative on the March 2004 ballot instead, for the express purpose of giving the city council more time to defeat the initiative. FAIR supporters petitioned the court to have the initiative placed on the November 2002 ballot. The trial court denied the petition after concluding council members have the authority to delay the initiative. The appellate court affirmed, relying on Elections Code sections 9255(a)

CEQA = California Environmental Quality Act

FAIR = Fair Apportionment and Individual Representation

and 1415, which detail the minimum time limits but not the maximum time limits in which a proposal must be submitted to voters. The Court noted that nothing in these provisions requires a city council to "order" an election at the next available opportunity. *Id.* at 4.

If the majority of the voters on a proposed ordinance vote in its favor, the ordinance becomes a valid and binding ordinance. Elec. Code §§ 9122 (counties); 9217 (cities). No ordinance proposed by initiative petition and adopted either by the voters or the city council can be repealed or amended except by a vote of the people, unless the ordinance provides to the contrary. Elec. Code §§ 9125 (counties); 9217 (cities).

REFERENDA

If a referendum petition is submitted with sufficient signatures, the subject ordinance or resolution is suspended and the city council must reconsider it. Elec. Code §§ 9144, 9237. If the city council does not, upon reconsideration, entirely repeal the ordinance or resolution, it must submit the ordinance or resolution to the voters. Such ordinance or resolution then shall not become effective unless a majority of the electorate vote in favor of it. Elec. Code §§ 9145, 9241.

Cities may not avoid this stay provision by reenacting materially identical laws as an interim measure until the referendum election. *Lindelli v. Town of San Anselmo (Marin Sanitary Service)*, 111 Cal. App. 4th 1099 (2003). In *Lindelli*, the Town of San Anselmo maintained a waste management services contract with North Bay Corporation from 1994 to 2002. In August 2002, the town passed a resolution awarding a new franchise grant to a competitor, Marin Sanitary Service (MSS). A referendum petition challenging the award was certified. The town then awarded an interim contract to MSS until the referendum election and set an election for the referendum for November 4, 2003. The terms were identical to the original agreement, except for the duration. Lindelli and North Bay petitioned for writ of mandate, arguing that the interim contract violated the stay provision of Elections Code section 9241.

In ruling against the town, the court held that the function of the stay provision is to enforce the electorate's power to approve or reject legislation provisionally adopted before it takes effect. Granting of a franchise is a legislative act subject to the referendum stay, and the legislative body may not violate the stay by enacting an essentially identical measure on the same subject matter. The interim contract to MSS differed from the original award only in the length of time—one year versus five years. It was the change in provider, not the length of the award, that inspired the referendum advocates. Because the interim contract was essentially the same as the challenged franchise ordinance, the court held that it violated the stay provision. The court further held that the contract did not fall within any exception to the referendum stay, including the urgency exception, because there was no imminent risk that garbage would pile up in the streets without immediate legislative action since alternative waste management providers were available.

> Granting of a franchise is a legislative act subject to the referendum stay, and the legislative body may not violate the stay by enacting an essentially identical measure on the same subject matter.

A municipal ordinance or resolution rejected by referendum cannot again be enacted by the council for a period of one year after the date of its repeal by council or disapproval by the voters. Elec. Code § 9241. *See generally, Assembly v. Deukmajian*, 30 Cal. 3d 638, 678 (1982). A city council may enact an ordinance that is essentially different from the ordinance that was suspended by referendum even if it addresses the same subject matter. In *Rubalcava v. Martinez*, 158 Cal. App. 4th 563 (2007), the court held the city council did not violate voters' rights by enacting an "Airport Hospitality

Enhancement Zone" ordinance within less than a year after a "Hotel Workers Living Wage" ordinance had been repealed by voter referendum. The court concluded that the new provisions of the subsequent zone ordinance, requiring street improvements, investments for attracting new businesses, and training programs for hotel workers, were substantiated and were aimed at responding to the specific objections made to the first ordinance, even though the later ordinance had similar, though phased, minimum wage levels. Id. at 568; see also Reagan v. City of Sausalito, 210 Cal. App. 2d 618, 630 (1962).

LIMITATIONS ON THE USE OF INITIATIVE AND REFERENDUM

Cannot be unconstitutional. If the content of an initiative ordinance violates the California or United States Constitutions, it is invalid. Constitutional challenges typically involve claims that the initiative, especially a growth management measure, is an improper exercise of the city's police power because it violates the due process or equal protection rights of affected property owners. See, e.g., Building Indus. Ass'n v. City of Camarillo, 41 Cal. 3d 810, 824 (1986). For example, in Hawn v. County of Ventura, an initiative giving approval power over airport site selection to the voters of a city, but not nearby residents of unincorporated territory, was ruled an unconstitutional denial of equal protection. 73 Cal. App. 3d 1009, 1018 (1977).

In adjudicating constitutional challenges, courts hold initiative measures to the same standards as council-enacted measures. In Arnel Development Co. v. City of Costa Mesa, the court held that "[t]he city's authority under the police power is no greater than otherwise it would be simply because the subsequent rezoning was accomplished by initiative." 126 Cal. App. 3d 330, 337 (1981). Arnel involved an initiative that rezoned some property in order to defeat development approvals the council had just granted. The court invalidated the initiative on the ground that the people may not use an initiative to discriminate against a particular parcel of land, and that the courts may properly inquire as to whether the classification scheme had been applied fairly and impartially. Id. As the Costa Mesa ordinance clearly would have been held invalid as arbitrary and discriminatory if adopted by the city council, it was also invalid when adopted by initiative. The initiative failed also because it lacked a substantial and reasonable relationship to the public welfare. Id. The court held that no attempt had been made to accommodate the competing public interests that were present, namely, the acute shortage of moderate-income housing in the region versus a desire for lower-density development. The court concluded that "the initiative ordinance, which completely precludes development of multiple family residences in the area, does not effect a reasonable accommodation of the competing interests on a regional basis and is therefore not a valid exercise of the police power." Id. For a general discussion of the police power, see chapter 1 (Local Land Use Authority).

Two ballot initiatives were held to be invalid in Howard Jarvis Taxpayers Association v. City of San Diego because they were inconsistent with the California Constitution and therefore exceeded the city's police power. 120 Cal. App. 4th 374 (2004). The plaintiff taxpayer group in Howard Jarvis had qualified Proposition E, which sought to amend San Diego's charter so as to require a super-majority two-thirds vote to approve any new general tax or increase in an existing tax. In response, the city placed onto the same ballot Proposition F, which sought retroactively to require a two-thirds super-majority vote in order to amend the city charter, thus imposing a higher threshold for passage of Proposition E. Both measures received greater than 50 percent affirmative votes.

The court held that both initiatives violated the Constitution and were invalid. The charter measure ran afoul of Article XI, section 3(a) of the California Constitution, which expressly provides that a city may adopt or amend its charter by majority vote of its electors. *Id.* at 385–86. The tax measure conflicted with Proposition 218, a constitutional amendment providing that general taxes may be enacted or increased by a simple majority vote of the electorate. *Id.* at 392–93. For further discussion of Proposition 218, *see* chapter 12 (Exactions).

In *Bighorn-Desert View Water Agency v. Verjil*, the California Supreme Court held that, pursuant to section 3 of Article XIII C of the California Constitution (enacted by Proposition 218), an initiative could be used to reduce the rate charged by a public water district for domestic water. 39 Cal. 4th 205 (2006). However, the court ruled that the California Constitution did not support the premise that the initiative power could be used to grant local voters a right to impose a voter-approval requirement on all future adjustments of, or creation of new, water delivery charges. *Id.* at 218–19. *See also, Birkenfeld v. City of Berkeley*, 17 Cal. 3d 129 (1976) (rent control charter amendment enacted by initiative invalidated because it unconstitutionally imposed heavy burdens on landlords not related to the measure's legitimate governmental objectives, and because it conflicted with state law eviction procedures).

The United States Supreme Court addressed federal constitutional issues in *City of Cuyahoga Falls v. Buckeye Community Hope Foundation*, 538 U.S. 188 (2003). In *Cuyahoga Falls*, the city passed an ordinance authorizing developers to construct a low-income housing complex. Project opponents submitted a referendum petition to the city asking that the ordinance be repealed or submitted to a vote. Pursuant to the city's charter, the referendum petition stayed the project approvals until the election. The city engineer, on advice from the city's law director, denied the developers' request for building permits. The developers sued the city, alleging that submission of the ordinance to voters violated the Equal Protection and Due Process Clauses. They argued that the city's actions gave effect to racial bias reflected in the public's opposition to the project. The Supreme Court held that the developers failed to present sufficient evidence of an equal protection violation, and could not ascribe the motivations of a handful of citizens backing the referendum to the city. Submitting the petition to voters was action taken pursuant to the city's charter, which set out a facially neutral procedure. *Id.* at 194.

The Court also found no arbitrary government conduct in violation of due process. The Court noted that the "people retain the power to govern through referendum 'with respect to any matter, legislative or administrative, within the realm of local affairs.'" *Id.* Because the developers did not challenge the referendum itself, they derived no benefit from the principle that a referendum's substantive result may be invalid if it is arbitrary or capricious. *Id.*

Cannot conflict with state law. The California Constitution prohibits general law cities from enacting ordinances that conflict with general state law. Cal. Const. Art. XI, § 7. Charter cities may enact local laws that conflict with general state law provided the local law addresses a strictly municipal affair. *See* Cal. Const. Art. XI, § 5(a). With regard to matters of statewide concern, even charter cities are precluded from enacting measures that conflict with state law. *See Bishop v. City of San Jose*, 1 Cal. 3d 56, 61 (1969). The limitation against enacting conflicting local laws applies to measures adopted either by the legislative body or by the voters directly. *See Legislature v. Deukmejian*, 34 Cal. 3d 658, 675 (1983); *Galvin v. Bd. of Supervisors of Contra Costa County*, 195 Cal. 686, 692 (1925). Thus, for example, a local initiative that granted a

> The California Constitution prohibits general law cities from enacting ordinances that conflict with general state law.

franchise for a toll bridge was invalidated because it failed to comply with requirements set by state law, such as obtaining the approval of the state engineer. *See Galvin,* 195 Cal. at 696–98.

In *Shea Homes L.P. v. County of Alameda,* the court addressed procedural issues related to a claim that an initiative violates state law. 110 Cal. App. 4th 1246 (2003). The court held that claims alleging that a local ordinance conflicts with a state statutory scheme implicate questions of law, not fact. The first step in the reviewing court's inquiry is to determine whether a genuine conflict exists between the local ordinance and the state law. In that case, the court examined Measure D, which redesignated land for open space and agricultural uses, and determined that although it reduced the amount of vacant land available for development, Measure D did not conflict with state housing laws. It noted that Measure D allowed for an expansion of the urban growth boundary and stated that none of its provisions would be applied so as to preclude the county's compliance with state law housing obligations. Section 7 also authorized the county board of supervisors to approve housing beyond that boundary to meet state housing requirements if certain factors were demonstrated and certain guidelines as to location of that housing were adhered to. In concluding on this point, the court said that clauses such as section 7, together with the rule that initiatives are to be upheld when possible, may defeat a challenged cause of action as a matter of law. *Id.* at 1266.

The prohibition against initiatives that conflict with state law has been applied even in the face of constitutional language prohibiting restrictions on the initiative power. In *Mission Springs Water District v. Verjil,* 218 Cal. Appl. 4th 892 (2013), the court addressed language in the California Constitution that was added by Proposition 218. See chapter 12 (Exactions) for a discussion of Proposition 218. The relevant language of Proposition 218 states "notwithstanding any other provision of the Constitution, . . . the initiative power shall not be prohibited or otherwise limited in matters of reducing or repealing any local tax, assessment, fee or charge." Proponents of initiatives setting water and sewer rates argued that the question whether their initiatives conflicted with state law requirements regarding minimum rates was not relevant in light of this constitutional language. The court disagreed, ruling that the constitutional language "does not alter this traditional limitation on the initiative power." 218 Cal. App. 4th at 545. The constitutional language, the court explained, presupposes an otherwise valid use of the initiative power. Because the voters have no more power than the board to set rates, and because Water Code section 31007 precludes the board from setting rates below costs, the voters were also prohibited from setting rates that low. "If the rule were otherwise, the voters of a city, county or special district could essentially exempt themselves from statewide statutes." 218 Cal. App. 4th at 545.

One application of the rule prohibiting initiatives that violate state law that is common in the land use context involves state laws requiring General Plan consistency.[5]

Vertical consistency. As explained more fully in chapters 2 (General Plan), 3 (Specific Plan), 4 (Zoning) and 5 (Subdivisions) above, California law requires that most land use approvals be consistent with the jurisdiction's general plan. Gov't Code §§ 65454 (specific plan), 65860 (zoning for general law cities and charter cities that adopt the requirement), 65460.8 (transit village plan), 65867.5 (development agreement), 66473.5 (subdivision map); *Lesher Commc'ns, Inc. v. City of Walnut Creek,* 52 Cal. 3d 531, 540 (1990). If a subordinate land use regulation, whether enacted by the legislative

---

5 For a detailed discussion of general plans and consistency requirements, see chapter 2 (General Plan).

body or directly by the voters, is inconsistent with the applicable general plan, it is void *ab initio. Lesher*, 52 Cal. 3d at 545-46.

Horizontal or internal consistency. State law also requires that a general plan have "horizontal" or internal consistency within itself. Gov't Code § 65300.5. Any measure, whether enacted by initiative or the local legislative body, that will result in inconsistency within the general plan is vulnerable to legal challenge. See *DeVita*, 9 Cal. 4th at 796 n. 12. For a thorough discussion of general plan internal consistency, *see* chapter 2 (General Plan).

> Any measure, whether enacted by initiative or the local legislative body, that will result in inconsistency within the general plan is vulnerable to legal challenge.

Cannot invade a duty delegated exclusively to the council or board or imposed on an agent of the state. In *Committee of Seven Thousand (COST) v. Superior Court*, the California Supreme Court explained the doctrine of exclusive delegation, under which legislative power granted exclusively to boards or councils cannot be exercised by voters. 45 Cal. 3d 491 (1988). COST involved an initiative that precluded the council from adopting or imposing fees to fund projects within a proposed major thoroughfare and bridge fee program unless those projects were approved by the voters. The court explained that references in the state law applicable to such programs to "city council" or "board of supervisors," while not conclusive, supported an inference that the Legislature's intent was to preclude action by initiative or referendum. 45 Cal. 3d at 501. The degree to which the initiative or referendum addresses municipal affairs as opposed to matters of statewide concern is also important to the analysis. 45 Cal. 3d at 505. Applying these rules, the court held the initiative invalid, concluding that the power to adopt and impose such fees addressed a matter of statewide concern, and had been delegated exclusively to the city council.

In another case, the Court found that Government Code section 66484.3 granted exclusive authority to impose the developer fees at issue to boards of supervisors and to city councils, rather than to the voters. The Court held that the voters' imposition of the fees conflicted with state law because of the exclusive delegation by the Legislature to the local legislative body. See *DeVita v. County of Napa*, 9 Cal. 4th 763, 786 (1995)

The opposite result was obtained in *Pettye v. City and County of San Francisco*. The court there held that the enactment of standards for providing general assistance to the indigent was a legislative act that was properly subject to a voter initiative. 118 Cal. App. 4th 233, 244-45 (2004). In November 2003, voters in San Francisco passed the "Care Not Cash" initiative, which called for the city to change the nature of the "general assistance" it is required to provide under state law by replacing most outright cash grants to homeless recipients with in-kind benefits for housing, utilities, and meals. The court noted that by declaring a new goal and public policy with respect to aid and care for the indigent homeless, the San Francisco initiative had a "quintessential legislative character." *Id.* at 244. The court rejected the petitioners' claim that the state general assistance amounted to an exclusive delegation of power to the local legislative body that preempted the involvement of the local electorate. *Id.* at 245-46. Recognizing also that it must "construe constitutional and charter provisions in favor of the people's right to exercise their reserved power of initiative," the court held that the initiative had been a proper exercise of that power. *Id.* at 240. See also *Citizens for Planning Responsibly v. County of San Luis Obispo*, 176 Cal. App. 4th 357, 373-375 (2009) (rejecting claim that the airport land use laws delegated exclusive authority to airport land use commissions).

Voter action can be precluded also when the Legislature has occupied the entire field, and provided that only certain boards or commissions may exercise powers within that field, to the exclusion of the voters. *L.I.F.E. Committee v. City of Lodi*, 213 Cal. App. 3d 1139, 1148–49 (1989) (initiative that required voter approval of a general plan amendment prior to annexation was preempted by state laws pertaining to annexation, which allowed elections only in very limited circumstances).

A prime example of "invading a duty imposed on a city as an agent of the state" was found in the context of redevelopment prior to the dissolution of redevelopment agencies in 2012. Local redevelopment agencies that functioned pursuant to the Community Redevelopment Law (Health & Safety Code § 33000 *et seq.*) were administrative agents of the state. By statute, the deactivation of the redevelopment agency and the adoption or the amendment of a redevelopment plan were made subject to the referendum process. Health & Safety Code §§ 33141, 33365, 33450. However, outside that exception, the general rule precluding initiatives that seek to invade a duty imposed upon agents of the state prevailed.

In one case, a citizens' group opposed part of a 1967 redevelopment plan that called for building the West Berkeley Industrial Park. *Redevelopment Agency v. City of Berkeley*, 80 Cal. App. 3d 158 (1978). The group objected to the elimination of numerous old residences in the project area. The initiative would have amended the plan and rezoned a six-square-block area to retain the residences. The court held that the development of the project pursuant to the redevelopment plan was an administrative act carrying out state policy even though adopted by ordinance, and therefore was not subject to amendment by initiative. The court further stated that the statutory provisions authorizing the use of the referendum on certain redevelopment decisions did not authorize the use of the initiative in the redevelopment field. *Id.* at 169.

The same citizens' group had lost an earlier court battle launched to stop the razing of the old residences for development of the West Berkeley Industrial Park. *Kehoe v. City of Berkeley*, 67 Cal. App. 3d 666 (1977). In 1973, the group had secured the adoption of an initiative to restrict the razing of old homes by controlling the issuance of demolition permits. The court held that the provisions of the "Neighborhood Preservation Ordinance" could not be applied to the redevelopment project area because they conflicted with general state law (the Community Redevelopment Law). *Id.* at 674.

Cannot adopt non-legislative measures. The powers of initiative and referendum extend only to legislative acts, and do not encompass administrative or other non-legislative matters. *See Yost v. Thomas*, 36 Cal. 3d 561, 570 (1984); *Arnel Dev. Co.*, 28 Cal. 3d at 514–16 (1980). Accordingly, actions that are administrative in nature can neither be enacted nor overturned by initiative or referendum.

In the land use area, the courts have drawn generic classifications, viewing zoning ordinances as legislative and other decisions, such as variances, use permits, and subdivision map approvals, as nonlegislative or administrative. *Id.* Similarly, the adoption or amendment of general plans, specific plans, or Local Coastal Programs are legislative acts subject to initiative and referendum even though enacted by a resolution rather than by an ordinance. *See Midway Orchards v. County of Butte*, 220 Cal. App. 3d 765, 773–74 (1990); *Yost*, 36 Cal. 3d at 569–70; *DeVita*, 9 Cal. 4th at 775–76; *San Mateo County Coastal Landowners' Ass'n*, 38 Cal. App. 4th at 534. However, a city's agreement with a Native American tribe to mitigate casino impacts, even though approved by resolution, was held to be an administrative act not subject to referendum. *Worthington v. City Council of the City of Rohnert Park*, 130 Cal. App. 4th 1132, 1143 (2005). The court found that based on the extensive federal regulation of Indian gaming, federal and state governments have sole authority to exercise legislative power in this area, and that

> The powers of initiative and referendum extend only to legislative acts, and do not encompass administrative or other non-legislative matters.

the city was acting merely as an administrative agent of the state in its negotiation and approval of the agreement. Further, the court rejected the argument that the city's decision to negotiate with the tribe and then publicly oppose the casino plan was a policy decision subject to referendum, stating that "policy" is a broad term not synonymous with legislation. *Id.* at 1142.

In a variation on the "legislative acts only" theme, a court struck down an initiative because it directed the city council to adopt legislation, rather than enacting the legislation itself. In *Marblehead v. City of San Clemente*, the court invalidated an initiative that tied future development to the ability to meet specified service levels for traffic and a range of public services. 226 Cal. App. 3d 1504, 1507 (1991). The court held that the initiative, which contemplated amendments to the city's general plan but did not enact those amendments, violated the California Constitution's provisions authorizing initiatives. *Id.* at 1510. The court noted that the measure did not actually enact legislation, which is the constitutional authorization. Rather, the initiative directed the city council to enact legislation, in the form of a general plan amendment, in order to implement the policies in the initiative.

Cannot impair an essential governmental function. An initiative may not interfere with the efficacy of an essential governmental power, such as a city's power to grant a franchise (*Newsom v. Bd. of Supervisors*, 205 Cal. 262, 271-72 (1928)) or site a courthouse (*Simpson v. Hite*, 36 Cal. 2d 125, 134 (1950)). For instance, the decision in *Citizens for Jobs and the Economy v. County of Orange* involved an initiative measure passed by the voters in Orange County, which placed a number of spending and procedural restrictions upon the Board of Supervisors regarding the planning and implementation process for the conversion of the El Toro Marine Base to a civilian airport. 94 Cal. App. 4th 1311 (2002). Although "mindful that initiative measures are not to be stricken down lightly," the court found this measure defective. *Id.* at 1324.

> The court reasoned:
>
> Measure F impermissibly intrudes into Board prerogatives, particularly with respect to the functions of the Board in managing its financial affairs and in carrying out the public policy declared by [a prior measure]. The terms of Measure F seek to broadly limit through procedural restrictions the power of future legislative bodies to carry out their duties, as prescribed to them by their own inherent police power. As such, the measure should not be considered to have proper legislative subject matter.

Id. at 1331

This limitation on the impairment of an essential governmental function has been relied upon as the basis for voiding an initiative that would impair a city's fiscal management abilities. *See, e.g., City of Atascadero v. Daly*, 135 Cal. App. 3d 466, 470 (1982) (initiative is invalid if it will impede city's taxing power). However, in *Rossi v. Brown*, the Court upheld a tax-repeal initiative as not impairing a city's fiscal management, distinguishing the facts from those in *Atascadero*. 9 Cal. 4th 688, 698-99 (1995). The *Rossi* decision stated that it cannot be assumed that every initiative that repeals a tax will impermissibly interfere with a local legislative body's responsibility for fiscal management. It may do so, however, if the repeal initiative eliminates a major revenue source, and no other revenue source is available that may be tapped to offset a resulting budget deficit or to avoid future deficits. *Id.* at 710; *see also Santa Clara County Local Transp. Auth. v. Guardino*, 11 Cal. 4th 220, 235-36 (1995) (the requirement of Proposition 62 for a vote by the people on all general and special taxes did not impair a local

> An initiative may not interfere with the efficacy of an essential governmental power, such as a city's power to grant a franchise or site a courthouse.

government's fiscal powers). The Constitution also limits statewide referenda regarding tax matters. Cal. Const. Art. II, § 9(a).

Must address a single subject. The California Constitution states that an initiative can embrace only one subject. Cal. Const. Art. II, § 8(d). The single subject rule is equally applicable to both state and local measures. *See San Mateo County Coastal Landowners' Ass'n v. County of San Mateo*, 38 Cal. App. 4th 523, 553 (1995).

> The California Constitution states that an initiative can embrace only one subject. The single subject rule is equally applicable to both state and local measures.

The California courts have taken a broad view as to what constitutes a single subject. *See, e.g., Brosnahan v. Brown*, 32 Cal. 3d 236, 248-49 (1982). For instance, in *Raven v. Deukmejian*, the Court held that "an initiative measure does not violate the single subject requirement if, despite its varied collateral effects, all of its parts are 'reasonably germane' to each other and to the general purpose or object of the initiative." 52 Cal. 3d 336, 346 (1990); *but see Senate v. Jones*, 21 Cal. 4th 1142, 1153-54 (1999) (rejecting in a preelection challenge Proposition 24, the "Let the Voters Decide Act of 2000," which would significantly have revised the role of the California Citizens Compensation Commission in setting salaries of legislators, and which would also have transferred the power to reapportion congressional, legislative, and Board of Equalization districts from the Legislature to the Supreme Court); *Chemical Specialties Mfg. Ass'n, Inc. v. Deukmejian*, 227 Cal. App. 3d 663, 667-68 (1991) (striking down Proposition 105, the "Public Right to Know Act," enacted by the voters in November 1988, as violating the single subject rule of the California Constitution).

In *Shea Homes L.P. v. County of Alameda*, the court held that an initiative altering a county's solid waste management practices, and designating more land for agriculture and open space and less land for urban growth, did not violate the single subject rule. 110 Cal. App. 4th 1246 (2003). Measure D, a "Citizens for Open Space Initiative Plan to Protect Agriculture and Open Space," was adopted in November 2000 by the electorate of Alameda County, and relocated the urban growth boundary to coincide with existing or proposed city urban growth boundaries, generally redesignating previous urban development use designations with agricultural uses. In addition, Measure D altered the county's solid waste management and planning practice.

Property owners affected by Measure D brought suit and argued that because the initiative constricted the county's urban growth boundary and altered its solid waste policies, it violated the single subject rule of the California Constitution and violated various state housing laws. In ruling for the county, the court held that the purpose of the single subject rule is to avoid voter confusion and subversion of the electorate's will. An initiative that is entitled "Save Agriculture and Open Space Lands" reasonably and naturally encompasses provisions that will (1) limit a use of the land at issue, such as a landfill, that is incompatible with this title; and (2) promote an activity, such as coordination of solid waste recycling and management, that fosters this title by reducing a cause for encroachment on open space. *Id.* at 1258-59. Consequently, such provisions, even if they may effectively realign agency responsibility for solid waste management, would not mislead a voter as to Measure D's purpose because, like all the provisions in the measure, they are germane to achieving its clearly stated objective of preserving and enhancing specifically defined open space and agricultural lands within the county. *Id.*

Cannot be used to reject urgency measures. Other constitutional limitations provide that a referendum may not be used to reject "urgency statutes, statutes calling elections, and statutes providing for tax levies or appropriations for usual current expenses." Cal. Const. Art. II, § 9(a); *Rossi v. Brown*, 9 Cal. 4th 688, 697-98 (1995) (relating to tax measures).

INITIATIVES AND REFERENDA ARE NOT SUBJECT TO THE SAME PROCEDURAL REQUIREMENTS AS CITY COUNCIL MEASURES

Procedural requirements (i.e., notice, hearing, and findings) necessary for adoption of a general plan or amendment, a specific plan adoption or amendment, or a zoning ordinance enacted by a city council do not apply to the voters. The California Supreme Court stated: "It is well established in our case law that the existence of procedural requirements for the adoption of local ordinances generally does not imply a restriction of the power of initiative or referendum." *DeVita*, 9 Cal. 4th at 785 (1995). This position is consistent with an earlier case where the Court held that an initiative zoning measure was valid without complying with the general law requirements of public hearings before the planning commission and the city council and notice to affected property owners. *See Associated Home Builders, Inc. v. City of Livermore*, 18 Cal. 3d 582, 596-97 (1976). The same principle applies to general plan and specific plan procedures (*DeVita*, 9 Cal. 4th at 785), or locally enacted plan procedures (*San Mateo County Coastal Landowners' Ass'n*, 38 Cal. App. 4th at 539).

The basis for excluding voter-sponsored initiatives from certain procedural requirements applicable to council actions was explained by the California Supreme Court in *Building Industry Association v. City of Camarillo*, 41 Cal. 3d 810 (1986). The voters of the City of Camarillo adopted a restricted growth ordinance limiting the number of dwelling units constructed in the city to 400 per year. The Building Industry Association (BIA) challenged the initiative as failing to meet the requirements of Government Code section 65863.6, which requires a city to balance housing needs against public service needs before passing growth control ordinances, and to list findings in those ordinances as to the public health, safety, and welfare promoted by the ordinance that justify reducing housing opportunities in the region. BIA further argued that the city failed to meet the requirements of Evidence Code section 669.5, which shifts to a city the burden of proving that a growth control ordinance is necessary to promote public health, safety, and welfare. The Court held that Evidence Code section 669.5 applied to initiative measures, but that Government Code section 65863.6 did not. It pointed out that the "[p]rocedural requirements which govern council action...generally do not apply to initiatives, any more than the provisions of the initiative law govern the enactment of ordinances in council." *Id.* at 823 (citing *Livermore*, 18 Cal. 3d at 596). The Court further cautioned that "a statute which made compliance with *procedural* requirements a prerequisite to enactment of local ordinances would be constitutionally suspect if applied to preclude enactment by initiative of an ordinance on a subject on which the city council could legislate." *Id.* at 821. The Court concluded that requiring the electorate to make the findings required by Government Code section 65863.6 would "place an insurmountable obstacle in the path of the initiative process." *Id.* at 824. However, Evidence Code section 669.5 "places no procedural barriers on the ability of the electorate to legislate through the power of initiative." *Id.* at 822. The Court emphasized that limiting the applicability of certain procedural requirements did not affect the general rule that "the people may [not] enact a statute which the Legislature has no power to enact." *Id.* at 821.

This position is consistent with an earlier case where the Court held that an initiative zoning measure was valid without complying with the general law requirements of public hearings before the planning commission and the city council and notice to affected property owners. *See Associated Home Builders, Inc. v. City of Livermore*, 18 Cal. 3d 582, 596-97 (1976). The same principle applies to general plan and specific plan procedures (*DeVita*, 9 Cal. 4th at 785), or locally enacted procedures (*San Mateo*

> Procedural requirements (i.e., notice, hearing, and findings) necessary for adoption of a general plan or amendment, a specific plan adoption or amendment, or a zoning ordinance enacted by a city council do not apply to the voters.

County Coastal Landowners' Ass'n, 38 Cal. App. 4th at 539). Similarly, the voters need not comply with the procedural requirements that apply to councils and boards when they enact land use laws within an area covered by an Airport Land Use Plan. *Citizens for Planning Responsibly v. County of San Luis Obispo*, 176 Cal. App. 4th 357 (2009).

Another major prerequisite to adoption of most land use ordinances or resolutions is California Environmental Quality Act (CEQA) review. Pub. Res. Code § 21000 et seq. Courts have held that this requirement does not apply to voter-sponsored initiatives. *See Stein v. City of Santa Monica*, 110 Cal. App. 3d 458, 460-61 (1980) (initiative ordinance to adopt rent control); *DeVita*, 9 Cal. 4th at 769 (general plan amendment initiative); Cal. Code Regs. tit. 14, § 15378(b)(4).

PRE-ELECTION CHALLENGES TO INITIATIVES AND REFERENDA

Pre-election challenges to initiatives and referenda have been successful when the claim is that there has been a failure to comply with procedural requirements in the following circumstances:

- Referendum petition misstated the title of the challenged ordinance. *Hebard v. Bybee*, 65 Cal. App. 4th 1331, 1338 (1998)
- Referendum petition contained only the number and title of the challenged ordinance, rather than its complete text. *Creighton v. Reviczky*, 171 Cal. App. 3d 1225, 1229 (1985); see also *Billig v. Voges*, 223 Cal. App. 3d 962, 968 (1990); Elec. Code § 9238
- Referendum petition failed to include an exhibit setting forth the technical legal description and location of the affected real property. *Chase v. Brooks*, 187 Cal. App. 3d 657, 664 (1986); see also *Nelson v. Carlson*, 17 Cal. App. 4th 732, 739-740 (1993); Elec. Code § 9238
- Initiative petition was signed after notice of intent to circulate the petition was published, but prior to that notice being posted. *Ibarra*, 214 Cal. App. 3d at 95-96; Elec. Code § 9202(a)
- Initiative petition contained indisputably false statements about the reasons for signing the petition. *San Francisco Forty-Niners v. Nishioka (Comstock)*, 75 Cal. App. 4th 637, 649-50 (1999); Elec. Code § 18600

Procedural challenges may be considered moot after the election. *Costa v. Superior Court*, 37 Cal. 4th at 1005-1088; *Assembly v. Deukmejian*, 30 Cal. 3d 638, 652-53 (1982).

Pre-election challenges that raise claims of substantive invalidity fare a little differently. At least one court has indicated that the board of supervisors should not usurp a judicial function by refusing to place a duly certified initiative on the ballot; the board had a duty to do so unless it obtains a court order barring the matter from the ballot. *Save Stanislaus Area Farm Econ. (SAFE) v. Bd. of Supervisors*, 13 Cal. App. 4th 141, 148 (1993); but see *Worthington v. City Council of the City of Rohnert Park*, 130 Cal. App. 4th 1132 (2005) (court did not address the city's refusal to place a referendum on the ballot based on determination that subject agreement was an administrative act not subject to referendum). Although they generally prefer post-election review, the California courts have indicated an increased willingness to review an initiative or referendum measure for legal validity *prior* to its submission to the electorate if the measure would conflict with state law or if the drive to qualify the measure is procedurally defective. The effect of a pre-election challenge can be substantial. After a successful trial court challenge, the initiative can remain off the ballot and ineffective unless and until an appeal succeeds and the initiative is subsequently enacted. Compare this to the case

> The effect of a pre-election challenge can be substantial. After a successful trial court challenge, the initiative can remain off the ballot and ineffective unless and until an appeal succeeds and the initiative is subsequently enacted.

of a post-election challenge to a measure that already has been enacted by the voters. The challenged measure often remains in effect until the judicial process, including all appeals, has been exhausted. For example, the growth management measure enacted in Walnut Creek in November 1985 and challenged in *Lesher* was found invalid by the trial court in February 1987. 52 Cal. 3d at 535. The measure's limitations remained in effect, however, until the California Supreme Court's decision affirming the trial court in December 1990.

The decision whether to review a measure's validity prior to its submission to the electorate lies wholly within the discretionary power of the court. *See deBottari v. City Council*, 171 Cal. App. 3d at 1209. In one case, the court stated that the opponents of a duly qualified initiative must make a compelling showing that the measure should be removed from the ballot and that only a court, and not a board of supervisors, could refuse to place a duly qualified initiative on the ballot. *See Save Stanislaus Area Farm Econ. (SAFE) v. Bd. of Supervisors*, 13 Cal. App. 4th at 148-49 (1993); *but see Worthington v. City Council of the City of Rohnert Park*, 130 Cal. App. 4th 1132 (2005) (court did not address a city's refusal to place referendum on the ballot despite the lack of a court order).

Generally, the courts weigh two competing considerations when deciding whether to undertake pre-election review. On the one hand, courts are concerned with preventing the waste of public funds in pointless elections. *See, e.g., Gayle v. Hamm*, 25 Cal. App. 3d 250, 257 (1972). On the other hand, courts are reluctant to delay the exercise of the public's right to vote on a measure while its legality is determined. If a court does find a measure facially invalid, it will order either that the measure be removed from the ballot or that any vote taken be disregarded. Balancing these concerns is relatively straightforward when a measure is invalid on its face. Where the issues are not so apparent, it is difficult to predict when a court will agree to review an initiative or referendum measure prior to an election.

Two decisions by the California Supreme Court demonstrate the reluctance of courts to delay exercise of the public's right to vote while the legality of a ballot measure is being determined: *Independent Energy Producers Ass'n v. McPherson*, 31 Cal. Rptr. 3d 852, and *Costa v. Superior Court*, 37 Cal. 4th 986 (2006). In *Independent Energy Producers*, the court vacated a stay issued by the court of appeal restraining Proposition 80 on the November 8, 2005 ballot. The court quoted *Brosnahan v. Eu*, 31 Cal. 3d 1 (1982), which held "it is usually more appropriate to review constitutional and other challenges to ballot propositions or initiative measures after an election rather than to disrupt the electoral process by preventing the exercise of the people's franchise, in the absence of some clear showing of invalidity." 31 Cal. 3d at 4. Disagreeing with the court of appeal that the initiative, which would have given the Public Utilities Commission additional authority and jurisdiction over the California electricity market, was clearly precluded by the Constitution, the Court concluded that its validity should not be determined prior to the election. *Id*. Using similar reasoning, the Court in *Costa v. Superior Court* issued a stay of a superior court judgment directing the Secretary of State not to place any version of Proposition 77 on the November 8, 2005 ballot. 37 Cal. 4th 986 (2006). The initiative, which would have amended the California Constitution's redistricting process, was circulated for signatures and received a sufficient number for placement on the ballot. However, the proponents failed to disclose that the measure circulated was a different version than that originally submitted to the California Attorney General as required by law. Despite this discrepancy, the Court concluded that it would be inappropriate to deny the electorate the opportunity to vote on Proposition 77, and directed the Secretary of State to place the circulated version on the November ballot. Id. at 1004. While Proposition 77 was defeated by the voters, the Court issued a full opinion to provide guidance in future cases. The Court stated that, even when a pre-election challenge was appropriate—such as a challenge to procedural defects in Proposition 77—considerable caution must be exercised before a court intervenes to remove or withhold a measure with qualified signatures from an imminent election, and should only occur when a court is confident that a pre-election challenge is meritorious and justifies withholding the measure from the ballot. Id. at 1007–08.[6]

Reaching a different result, in *deBottari*, the court of appeal considered the appropriateness of pre-election judicial review in the context of a referendum measure that sought to reject rezoning ordinances enacted by the city council. 171 Cal. App. 3d at 1209–10. After a referendum petition was successfully circulated, the city council refused to either repeal the ordinances or submit the referendum to the voters as required by Elections Code section 9241. The council relied on its determination that rejection of the ordinances would result in zoning inconsistent with the city's general plan. First, the court held that the city council had a mandatory duty under the referendum laws either to repeal the challenged ordinances or to submit them to referendum unless "'directed to do otherwise by a court on a compelling showing that a proper case has been established for interfering with the [referendum] power.'" Id. at 1209 (quoting *Farley v. Healey*, 67 Cal. 2d 325, 327 (1967)).

The *deBottari* court assessed whether such a showing had been made by the city council. As an initial matter, the court noted two exceptions to the general rule from *Brosnahan* that "'it is usually more appropriate to review constitutional and other challenges to...initiative measures after an election rather than to disrupt the electoral process by preventing the exercise of the people's franchise.'" 31 Cal. 3d at 4. First, a court may review challenges to initiative measures prior to an election where the electorate "lacks the 'power to adopt the proposal'," as when the initiative proposed would affect an administrative, rather than a legislative, matter. Id. Second, a court may review a measure prior to a vote when "the substantive provisions of the proposed measure are legally invalid." Id. at 1210.

The court analyzed the referendum at issue in *deBottari* under the second of these exceptions. It held that because rejection of the zoning ordinance would result in the property being zoned in a manner inconsistent with the City's general plan, the "invalidity of the proposed referendum [had] been compellingly demonstrated," and the "referendum, if successful, would enact a clearly invalid zoning ordinance.... Judicial deference to the electoral process does not compel judicial apathy towards patently invalid legislative acts." Id. at 1212–13; see also *City of Irvine v. Irvine Citizens Against Overdevelopment*, 25 Cal. App. 4th 868, 875–76 (1994) (permitting a city to bring a pre-election challenge to keep a referendum of a pre-zoning ordinance off the ballot to protect consistency with general plan).

Under the *deBottari* rule, a challenging party might be successful if it could show, for example, that an initiative is inconsistent with a city's general plan or would cause the general plan to become internally inconsistent. See *Lesher*, 52 Cal. 3d at 531, 541; *Concerned Citizens of Calaveras County v. Bd. of Supervisors*, 166 Cal. App. 3d 90, 95

> Under the *deBottari* rule, a challenging party might be successful if it could show, for example, that an initiative is inconsistent with a city's general plan or would cause the general plan to become internally inconsistent.

---

[6] The Court found that the proponents of the initiative had substantially complied with the constitutional and statutory requirements that the version of the initiative submitted to the Attorney General be identical to the version printed on petitions and circulated for signatures. The Court found the differences between the two to be relatively minor and did not mislead the public or otherwise defeat purposes of the constitutional and statutory provisions. *Costa*, 37 Cal. 4th at 1022.

(1985); *Sierra Club*, 126 Cal. App. 3d at 704. Such inconsistencies could be shown by a report ordered by the city council pursuant to Elections Code sections 9111 or 9212. For example, if the report requested by a city council shows that an initiative would be inconsistent with the city's general plan, the challenger could use that official report as the basis for seeking a court order to keep the initiative off the ballot. See *SAFE v. Bd. of Supervisors*, 13 Cal. App. 4th 141, 145–46 (1993).

In *Committee of Seven Thousand (COST) v. Superior Court*, the California Supreme Court upheld the pre-election invalidation of a proposed initiative measure, finding that the measure was correctly kept off of the ballot by the trial court because it conflicted with state law. 45 Cal. 3d 491, 495 (1988). A city also may bring a declaratory relief action to keep a referendum of a pre-zoning ordinance off the ballot on the basis that if the referendum passed it would create an inconsistency between the pre-zoning and the general plan. See *Irvine Citizens Against Overdevelopment*, 25 Cal. App. 4th at 879.

Standing to challenge initiative and referendum measures can be problematic. See *City of Santa Monica v. Stewart*, 126 Cal. App. 4th 43 (2005) (city lacked standing for a post-election challenge to the constitutionality of an initiative amending the city charter as there was no actual or threatened action which would injure the city or violate its rights). Initiative proponents, however, can have standing. See *Perry v. Brown*, 52 Cal. 4th 1116, 1117 (2009), ("In a postelection challenge to a voter-approved initiative measure, the official proponents of the initiative are authorized under California law to appear and assert the state's interest in the initiative's validity and to appeal a judgment invalidating the measure when the public officials who ordinarily defend the measure or appeal such a judgment decline to do so.")

INITIATIVES LIMITING HOUSING: BURDEN OF PROOF

As a general rule, zoning and other land use regulations adopted by council-enacted ordinance or initiative are presumed to be valid, and the burden of proving the contrary rests with the person attacking the regulation. Pursuant to Evidence Code section 669.5, however, in any action challenging the validity of an ordinance that limits housing development by number, the burden is on a city to prove that the ordinance is reasonably related to the public health, safety, or welfare. Thus, with respect to measures seeking to limit housing development, the ordinary presumption in favor of the validity of ordinances has been reversed; accordingly, such measures are more susceptible to successful challenge. However, at least one court, in ruling on the validity of a city's housing element, stated that Evidence Code section 669.5 does not come into play unless there is a violation of the "least cost zoning law" contained in Government Code section 65913.1. *Hernandez v. City of Encinitas*, 28 Cal. App. 4th 1048, 1075 (1994).

The California Supreme Court has made clear that Evidence Code section 669.5 applies to ordinances enacted by the initiative process. *Building Indus. Ass'n v. City of Camarillo*, 41 Cal. 3d 810, 817–18 (1986). The Court stated that pursuant to section 669.5, "if the electorate exercises its initiative power, the local government must bear the burden of showing that the ordinance is reasonably related to the protection of the public health, safety, or welfare of the affected population." *Id.* at 822.

CONFLICTING INITIATIVES ON THE SAME BALLOT

A phenomenon that appears to be increasing at the local level, as well as in California's statewide elections, is for competing initiatives to appear on the same ballot. See, e.g.,

> A phenomenon that appears to be increasing at the local level, as well as in California's statewide elections, is for competing initiatives to appear on the same ballot.

Taxpayers to Limit Campaign Spending v. Fair Political Practices Comm'n, 51 Cal. 3d 744 (1990) (considering two measures regulating political campaign contributions and spending). The Elections Code addresses this issue and provides that, if the provisions of two or more ordinances adopted at the same election conflict, the ordinance receiving the highest number of affirmative votes shall control. Elec. Code §§ 9123 (counties); 9221 (cities).

Some initiatives have attempted to ensure applicability of these provisions of state law by including a "killer" clause as part of the initiative. A killer clause will state that the measure's provisions are intended to, and do, conflict with the provisions of a rival initiative. Thus, the initiative receiving the most votes should "kill" the rival initiative, even if both pass. See *Taxpayers*, 51 Cal. 3d at 767.

An example of the efficacy of Elections Code sections 9123 and 9221, and of a killer clause, was provided in *Concerned Citizens v. City of Carlsbad*, 204 Cal. App. 3d 937 (1988). In *Carlsbad*, the court ruled that a city can refuse to enforce a citizens' initiative that had been passed by the voters where a city's own ballot measure on the same subject, which was inconsistent with the citizens' initiative, received more affirmative votes. *Id.* at 941.

Concerned Citizens presented the City of Carlsbad with an initiative (Proposition G) to regulate housing development for a 10-year period. The measure would have created annual limits on new residential construction. In response to Proposition G, the city council placed an alternative measure on the ballot, Proposition E, which tied the rate of development to the development of new public facilities. In its killer clause, Proposition E stated that it was inconsistent with Proposition G. The voters passed both measures, but the council's measure received more votes. Accordingly, the council enacted Proposition E and refused to enact Proposition G.

Concerned Citizens sought to have Proposition G enforced, claiming that it was not inconsistent with Proposition E. The court held that Proposition E was clearly inconsistent with Proposition G, stating that Proposition E expressed "an unambiguous intent to supplant any [annual] numerical limit [on the rate of residential construction.]" *Id.*

In *Taxpayers to Limit Campaign Spending v. Fair Political Practices Commission*, the California Supreme Court addressed the degree to which the provisions of two measures dealing with political campaign reform should be made operative. 51 Cal. 3d 744 (1990). *Taxpayers* involved rival statewide initiatives passed on the same ballot, but its holding is probably applicable to local initiatives as well. The court relied on the California Constitution, which states that if provisions of two or more measures approved at the same election conflict, those of the measure receiving the highest affirmative vote shall prevail. Cal. Const. Art. II, § 10(b). The court noted that both measures established a comprehensive regulatory scheme. *Taxpayers*, 51 Cal. 3d at 768–69.

The Taxpayers group argued that only those provisions from the "losing" measure that conflict with the provisions of the "winning" measure, and those provisions that cannot be severed from the conflicting provisions, need be invalidated. The court rejected that argument, and held that Article II, section 10(b) does not permit the court to graft onto one regulatory scheme provisions which are intended to be part of a different one.

> [U]nless a contrary intent is apparent in competing, conflicting initiative measures which address and seek to comprehensively regulate the same subject, only the provisions of the measure receiving the highest affirmative vote become operative upon adoption. If the measures propose alternative

regulatory schemes, a fundamental conflict exists. In those circumstances, [the Constitution] does not require or permit either the court or the agency charged with the responsibility of implementing the measure or measures to enforce any of the provisions of the measure which received the lesser affirmative vote.

Id. at 770–71

In a footnote, the court addressed when provisions of a "losing" measure may be given effect:

> Our construction of Section 10(b) [of the Constitution] does not foreclose operation of an initiative measure that receives an affirmative vote simply because one or more minor provisions happen to conflict with those of another initiative principally addressed to other aspects of the same general subject. In the latter circumstance, if the principal purpose of the initiative can be accomplished notwithstanding the excision of the minor, incidental conflicting provisions, the remainder of the initiative can be given effect.

Id. at 771 n. 12

In *Yoshisato v. Superior Court,* the California Supreme Court expanded upon its ruling in *Taxpayers.* 2 Cal. 4th 978 (1992). As in *Taxpayers,* the *Yoshisato* court relied on Article II, section 10(b) of the California Constitution to address the problem of two conflicting statewide initiatives. In *Yoshisato,* the question before the court was the degree to which the provisions of two measures that amended portions of the Penal Code should be made operative. The court held that the *Taxpayers* approach to conflicting initiatives should be employed only when the two measures are "competing," as opposed to merely "complementary." *Id.* Under *Yoshisato,* the threshold question is whether the measures are "competing" or whether the measures are "complementary" (i.e., noncompeting). *Id.* at 988. If the measures are "competing," the *Taxpayers* bright-line interpretation of section 10(b) governs, and only the provisions of the measure with the highest affirmative vote are operative. *Id.* at 987–88. However, if the measures are "complementary or supplementary," the court held that:

> The measures should be compared "provision by provision," and the provisions of the measure receiving the lower number of affirmative votes are operative so long as they do not conflict with the provisions of the measure receiving the higher number of affirmative votes, and so long as those nonconflicting provisions are severable from any that do conflict.

Id. at 988

In *Yoshisato,* the court considered two factors to determine whether the measures were "competing" or "complementary." It first considered whether the materials presented to the voters expressly or impliedly indicated that the measures were "competing" or "complementary." *Id.* at 989. The court then considered whether it was the voters' intention when they enacted each measure to create a comprehensive scheme related to the same subject matter. Ultimately, the court found the measures did not seek to create a comprehensive scheme, and the material presented to the voters indicated both measures sought to amend the code in a complementary fashion. *Id.* at 990–91. Based on this assessment, the court employed the more accommodating interpretation of section 10(b), and compared the measures provision by provision to determine which provisions of the measure receiving the lower number of votes were operative. *Id.* at 991.

> Under *Yoshisato*, the threshold question is whether the measures are "competing" or whether the measures are "complementary" (i.e., noncompeting).

RESTRICTIONS ON A CITY'S ROLE IN CAMPAIGNS

As a general rule, California law does not allow local governments to campaign either for or against an initiative or referendum. It is a "fundamental precept" of the American democratic electoral process that the government may not "take sides" in election contests or bestow an unfair advantage on one of several competing factions. *Stanson v. Mott*, 17 Cal. 3d 206, 217 (1976) (holding that such partisanship is an "improper distortion" of the democratic process); *League of Women Voters v. Countywide Crim. Justice Coordination Comm.*, 203 Cal. App. 3d 529, 546 (1988) (holding that while such partisanship may be allowed in "totalitarian, dictatorial or autocratic governments" it cannot be tolerated in a democracy).

A city is prohibited from expending funds on activities that reasonably are characterized as campaign materials or activities—including, for example, bumper stickers, mass media advertisement spots, billboards, door-to-door canvassing, or the like—even if those activities do not comprise express advocacy for one position or another. *Vargas v. City of Salinas*, 46 Cal. 4th 1, 8 (2009).

At the same time, however, local governments are authorized to engage in legislative "lobbying" for or against proposed state, federal, and other legislation. *See, e.g.*, Government Code § 50023 (authorizing city councils to lobby the Legislature, Congress, and state, federal, and local agencies on behalf of or to oppose legislative actions). Rather than attempting to determine whether an activity constitutes impermissible "campaigning" or permissible "lobbying," the courts have adopted an "audience test" whereby it is not the subject of the promotional activities that matters, but the audience to which it is directed. *Miller v. Miller*, 87 Cal. App. 3d 762, 768 (1978). Under the "audience test," local governments may undertake promotional activities directed at other government bodies but not targeting the electorate itself. *Id.*

Although prohibited from targeting the electorate with "promotional" communications, local governments are authorized, and often required, to provide the electorate with educational "informational" materials on pending initiatives and referenda. To determine whether a city's action is proper in this regard depends upon a careful consideration of such factors as the style, tenor, and timing of the communication. *See Stanson v. Mott*, 17 Cal. 3d at 222; *Keller v. State Bar*, 47 Cal. 3d 1152, 1170-71 (1989); 73 Ops. Cal. Atty. Gen. 255 (1990). In general, courts focus on whether the city discussed the concerns of both sides and presented all the facts in a fair manner. *See, e.g., California Common Cause v. Duffy*, 200 Cal. App. 3d 730, 748 (1987) (holding that distribution of postcards to voters was a political and not an informational activity where the postcards presented not merely the facts, both good and bad, regarding the issue, but rather only one side); *Schroeder v. Irvine City Council*, 97 Cal. App. 4th 174, 187 (2002) (holding that a voter registration program was a proper use of public funds where it did not expressly advocate a partisan position and was conducted without regard to political affiliation); *see also Stanson v. Mott*, 17 Cal. 3d at 211.

The California Supreme Court confirmed these principles in *Vargas*, 46 Cal. 4th 1. Salinas residents proposed an initiative measure that would reduce and eventually repeal the city's utility users tax. The city council adopted a budget listing the facilities that would be closed and programs and services that would be eliminated if the measure passed. The city posted the council's resolution, minutes, and related matters on its website. It produced a document that briefly described the measure and listed each facility, program, and service that would be affected by the measure, which it made available on its website and at public locations. The city also included similar contents in its quarterly newsletter, which it routinely mailed to residents.

The Court upheld Salinas' use of public funds for these activities. It noted that the information conveyed generally involved past and present facts, such as how the original tax was enacted, what proportion of the budget was produced by the tax, and how the city council had voted to modify the budget in the event the measure passed; that the communications avoided argumentative or inflammatory rhetoric and did not urge voters to vote in a particular manner or take other actions in support of or in opposition to the measure; and that the information provided and the manner in which it was disseminated were consistent with established practice regarding use of the website and regular circulation of the city's official newsletter. *Id.* at 40.

Citizens alleging misuse of government funds for impermissible promotional activities may bring a taxpayer action against the city or city officials under Code of Civil Procedure section 526a and common law theories. Section 526a is liberally construed to allow "citizens to challenge asserted illegal expenditures of public funds." *See Blair v. Pitchess,* 5 Cal. 3d 258, 268-267 (1971); *California Ass'n for Safety Educ. v. Brown,* 30 Cal. App. 4th 1264, 1281 (1994); *Bledsoe v. Watson,* 30 Cal. App. 3d 105, 108 (1973). Taxpayers may bring an action against a city at common law as well, but only in cases involving fraud, collusion, ultra vires, or failure by the governmental body to perform a duty specifically enjoined. *See Gogerty v. Coachella Valley Junior Coll. Dist.,* 57 Cal. 2d 727, 730 (1962); *Los Altos Property Owners Ass'n v. Hutcheon,* 69 Cal. App. 3d 22, 26 (1977).

The general restrictions on promotional or campaign activities directed at the electorate by cities do not prohibit the city council itself or individual members of the city government from taking sides in an initiative or referendum campaign. *See City of Fairfield v. Superior Court,* 14 Cal. 3d 768, 780 (1975) (holding that a council member "has not only a right but an obligation to discuss issues of vital concern with his constituents and to state his views on matters of public importance"). For further discussion on this subject, *see* the *California Municipal Law Handbook,* § 3.211-3.222 (2010), concerning rules for city participation in ballot measures, lobbying measures, and drafting ballot measures. *See also Ballot Measure Advocacy and the Law: Legal Issues Associated with City Participation in Ballot Measure Campaigns,* League of California Cities (September 2003); Steven Lucas and Betsy Strauss, *Ballot Measure Fund Raising: Some Legal Do's and Don'ts,* Western City, at 19, League of California Cities (March 2004).

CONCLUSION

A relatively small, but still significant, backlash to the use of initiatives to enact land use measures—particularly those with the far-reaching impacts of growth management measures—has surfaced in California due to the fact that such measures can make good land use planning difficult, if not impossible. The hallmarks of good land use planning are decisions that are well informed, a planning process that is flexible and responsive to changing circumstances and values, and decisions reflecting a comprehensive planning process and accommodation of competing public interests.[7]

> The hallmarks of good land use planning are decisions that are well informed, a planning process that is flexible and responsive to changing circumstances and values, and decisions reflecting a comprehensive planning process and accommodation of competing public interests.

Critics of land use initiatives claim that voters never have as much information available to them in making land use decisions as compared to the knowledge,

---

7 *See* Lora A. Lucero, *Ballot Box Zoning,* 28 Zoning and Planning Law Report, no. 6 (June 2005); Lora A. Lucero, *Ballot Box Zoning: Good Planning or Vigilantism,* Zoning News, APA (May 2003); S. Meyers and R. Mandleman, *Planning by Plebiscite; The Ballot Box Is the Wrong Forum for California's Growth Wars,* 24 State and Local Law News, no. 4, ABA (Summer 2001).

The fact that initiatives are generally exempt from the requirement of environmental review under CEQA means that decisions with a potentially enormous environmental impact may be made without the extensive review that CEQA requires.

information, and resources available to a professional planning staff, planning commission, or city council. More specifically, the fact that initiatives are generally exempt from the requirement of environmental review under CEQA means that decisions with a potentially enormous environmental impact may be made without the extensive review that CEQA requires. *See Stein v. City of Santa Monica*, 110 Cal. App. 3d 458, 461 (1980); *DeVita v. County of Napa*, 9 Cal. 4th 763, 793-94 (1995). Another criticism is that that voters will rely on titles and perhaps summaries of proposed legislation, rather than carefully review the proposed initiative in order to understand and appreciate its impacts. These concerns were highlighted by the California Supreme Court in *Taxpayers*:

> We observed many years ago that even the most conscientious voters may lack the time to study ballot measures with that degree of thoroughness. Noting the tendency of voters to rely on the title to describe the content of an initiative, we agreed implicitly with the Supreme Court of Oregon whose observation we quoted.
>
> > "The majority of qualified electors are so much interested in managing their own affairs that they have no time carefully to consider measures affecting the general public. A great number of voters undoubtedly have a superficial knowledge of proposed laws to be voted upon.... We think the assertion may safely be ventured that it is only the few persons who earnestly favor or zealously oppose the passage of a proposed law initiated by petition who have attentively studied its contents and know how it will probably affect their private interests. The greater number of voters do not possess this information and usually derive their knowledge of the contents of a proposed law from an inspection of the title thereof, which is sometimes secured only from the very meager details afforded by a ballot which is examined in an election booth preparatory to exercising the right of suffrage."
>
> Those observations are no less pertinent today. "Voters have neither the time nor the resources to mount an in depth investigation of a proposed initiative. Often voters rely solely on the title and summary of the proposed initiative and never examine the actual wording of the proposal."

51 Cal. 3d at 770 (citations omitted)

This issue was addressed to some degree in the 1987 amendments to the Elections Code. *See* Elec. Code §§ 9111, 9212. Under these amendments, which were adopted to establish procedures designed to better equip the local legislative body and the electorate to evaluate initiatives when a petition is circulated (*see DeVita v. County of Napa*, 9 Cal. 4th 763), a city council may request and receive reports from any city agency on such issues as the measure's fiscal impact, its effect on the internal consistency of the city's general and specific plans, the consistency between planning and zoning, environmental impact, and any other matters the council identifies. Elec. Code §§ 9111 (counties); 9212 (cities). The insights that might result from such reports, however, can only influence the council's decision to enact the initiative measure or place it on the ballot, or the voters' decision on whether to enact the measure should it be placed before them. The measure itself may not be changed from its form when circulated for signature. Thus, these council-ordered reports are very different from environmental impact reports prepared under CEQA, which often have the effect of modifying the land use decisions under review.

The charge that land use initiatives frustrate the flexibility and responsiveness to change that are required of good land use planning is supported by the fact that generally, ordinances adopted by local initiative may not be repealed or amended except by a subsequent vote of the electorate. Elec. Code §§ 9125 (counties); 9217 (cities). This statutory provision stands to reason. The purpose for granting the initiative power—empowering an electorate confronted by an unresponsive legislative body—would be vitiated if the legislative body were allowed to "undo" what the people had accomplished through the initiative. The California Supreme Court has emphasized that these sections have their roots in the constitutional right of the electorate to initiative, ensuring that successful initiatives will not be undone by subsequent hostile legislative bodies. See *DeVita*, 9 Cal. 4th at 797.

As a result, however, a land use regulation adopted by initiative may be very difficult to amend. Even though the concerns that prompted the measure's passage may have subsided, generating sufficient voter interest in updating or repealing the measure to conform to changed circumstances may present a real problem. Further, regulations appropriate for a particular period in a city's development may linger well past their usefulness and may, in fact, impede orderly development. On this point, in answering the claim that the rigidity of a general plan initiative amendment frustrates the basic purpose of the planning law, the Court in *DeVita* recognized that some degree of flexibility is desirable in the planning process. *Id.* at 789 (citing Daniel J. Curtin, Jr. and Thomas Jacobson, *Growth Control by the Ballot Box: California's Experience*, 24 Loyola L.A. Law R. 1073, 1102 (1991)). However, the *DeVita* court noted, citing Government Code section 65300, that "[o]n the other hand, it is also desirable that plans possess some degree of stability so that they can be 'comprehensive [and] long-term' guides to local development." *Id.*

Another disturbing aspect of land use initiatives is that the balancing of competing public interests may be lost from the land use planning and regulation process. In upholding Proposition 13, California's tax reform initiative enacted in 1978 (Cal. Const. Art. XIIIA, § 16), the California Supreme Court characterized the initiative as deficient as a means of lawmaking, in that it permits very little balancing of interests or compromise. See *Amador Valley Joint Union High Sch. Dist. v. State Bd. of Equalization*, 22 Cal. 3d 208, 228-29 (1978) (quoting V. Key and W. Crouch, The Initiative and the Referendum in California, page 485 (1939)). For example, an initiative measure that places numerical restrictions on housing development is exempt from the requirement of findings that address health, safety, and welfare concerns. Likewise, the fact that CEQA's environmental review provisions do not generally apply to initiative measures means that the balancing procedures that are a part of that process are not brought to bear on the formulation of the proposed policies and standards.

Occasionally, a controversial court decision regarding a land use issue will trigger initiatives seeking to reverse the ruling. Such has been the response to the United States Supreme Court's *Kelo v. City of New London*, 545 U.S. 469 (2005) decision, which upheld the use of eminent domain to take property from one private owner in order to further private economic development that the city determined would provide a public benefit. Although *Kelo* did not represent an extension of existing law in terms of takings jurisprudence, it sparked public outcry over the abuse of government power. In response, a statewide initiative, Proposition 90, qualified for the November 2006 ballot in California, but was defeated at the polls. The debate over Proposition 90 went to the heart of concerns over an initiative eliminating local governments' ability to balance competing public interests and respond to changing circumstances and values.

Proposition 90 would have prohibited the use of eminent domain to take property and give it to another private party even if such a transfer provided a public benefit, and would have required compensation to owners whose property suffered an economic loss as a result of a city's land use decision.[8]

A blanket statement that initiative measures are completely free of requirements to balance competing interests would, however, be inaccurate. The three-part balancing test set forth in *Livermore* to determine whether the initiative measure bears a reasonable relationship to a legitimate governmental interest, and is thus a valid exercise of the police power, requires post-election inquiry into how competing interests were balanced. *Associated Home Builders, Inc.*, 18 Cal. 3d at 601; *see also DeVita*, 9 Cal. 4th at 796 n. 12.

> A blanket statement that initiative measures are completely free of requirements to balance competing interests would be inaccurate.

---

8 For a further discussion of Proposition 90, see Paul Shigley, Property Rights Measure Reaches Ballot, California Planning & Development Report (August 2006); Boalt Hall California Center for Environmental Law & Policy, Proposition 90: An Analysis, U.C. Regents (Oct. 2006).

CHAPTER 14

Local Agency Formation Commissions: Local Agency Boundary Changes

INTRODUCTION

Local Agency Formation Commissions (LAFCOs or Commissions) determine public agency boundaries, urban service areas and spheres of influence. Gov't Code §§ 56001, 56375, 56425. In California, each of the 58 counties have a LAFCO, which collectively make determinations regarding the boundary changes of more than 3,500 government agencies composed of the 58 counties, almost 500 incorporated cities and towns, and 3,000-plus special districts.[1]

LAFCO = Local Agency Formation Commission

The primary purpose of LAFCOs is to: (1) facilitate orderly growth and development by determining logical local agency boundaries; (2) preserve prime agricultural lands by guiding development away from presently undeveloped prime agricultural preserves; and (3) discourage urban sprawl and encourage the preservation of open space by promoting development of vacant land within cities before annexation of vacant land adjacent to cities. Gov't Code §§ 56001, 56301; *see also Sierra Club v. San Joaquin LAFCO*, 21 Cal. 4th 489, 495 (1999); *Placer County LAFCO v. Nevada County LAFCO*, 135 Cal. App. 4th 793, 798 (2006); *McBail & Co. v. Solano LAFCO*, 62 Cal. App. 4th 1223, 1228 (1998); *City of Santa Cruz v. LAFCO*, 76 Cal. App. 3d 381, 385 (1977).

LAFCOs also ensure that agency boundaries logically relate to one another, thereby minimizing inefficiencies in service provision and overlapping responsibilities. LAFCOs have been described as watchdogs, guarding "against the wasteful duplication of services that results from indiscriminate formation of new local agencies or haphazard annexation of territory to existing local agencies." *City of Ceres v. City of Modesto*, 274 Cal. App. 2d 545, 553 (1969).

HISTORY OF LAFCO LAW

The Cortese-Knox Local Government Reorganization Act of 1985 consolidated three major laws previously used by the state's cities and special districts to secure boundary changes: (1) the Knox-Nesbit Act of 1963 (former Gov't Code § 54722 *et seq.*); (2) the District Reorganization Act of 1965 (former Gov't Code § 56000 *et seq.*); and (3) the Municipal Reorganization Act of 1977 (former Gov't Code § 35000 *et seq.*).

---

1 For further information concerning LAFCOs, see California Association of Local Agency Formation Commissions materials, available at http://www.calafco.org.

Growth Within Bounds recognized that California did not have a plan for growth, and recommended numerous substantive changes to laws relating to LAFCOs' powers, orderly growth and resource protection, the sphere of influence provisions, and various boundary change procedures.

The next major revision to LAFCO law began in the late 1990s. In 1997, the Legislature created the Commission on Local Governance for the 21st Century for the purposes of assessing governance issues and making appropriate recommendations regarding LAFCO law. This 15-member commission, which included city, county, special district, and private members, rendered its lengthy report in Spring 2000. Entitled *Growth Within Bounds*,[2] the report recognized that California did not have a plan for growth, and recommended numerous substantive changes to laws relating to LAFCOs' powers, orderly growth and resource protection, the sphere of influence provisions, and various boundary change procedures. The report listed eight major recommendations:

- The policies and procedures of LAFCOs should be streamlined and clarified
- LAFCOs should be neutral and independent, and provide balanced representation for counties, cities, and special districts
- The powers of LAFCOs should be strengthened to prevent urban sprawl and to ensure the orderly formation and extension of government services
- LAFCO policies that are designed to protect prime agricultural lands and open space should be strengthened
- The state-local fiscal relationship should be comprehensively revised
- The state should develop incentives to encourage compatibility and coordination of plans and actions of all local agencies within each region, including school districts, as a way to encourage an integrated approach to public service delivery and to improve overall governance
- Enhancements should be made to communication and coordination, and to the procedures of LAFCOs and local governments
- Opportunities for public involvement, active participation, and information regarding government decisionmaking should be increased

In response to the Commission's report, the Legislature again substantially revised LAFCO law by enacting the Cortese-Knox-Hertzberg Local Government Reorganization Act of 2000 (Gov't Code §§ 56000–57550), incorporating many of the Commission's recommendations. Specifically, LAFCO law was amended to include the following significant changes:[3]

- LAFCOs' powers were strengthened to ensure the logical and orderly extension of services and to prevent urban sprawl
- LAFCOs' neutrality, independence, and balance in membership were emphasized
- LAFCOs' policies and procedures were clarified and streamlined
- Additional opportunities for public involvement in LAFCO processes were provided
- Coordination and communication between LAFCOs and local agencies were enhanced

Government Code section 56001 sets forth the legislative findings and declarations of LAFCO law, reinforcing policies that encourage orderly growth and development, which are characterized as essential to the social, fiscal, and economic well-being of California. The Legislature recognized that the logical determination of local agency

---

[2] A copy of *Growth Within Bounds: Report of the Commission on Local Governance for the 21st Century* can be found on the Commission's website (http://opr.ca.gov/docs/79515.pdf).

[3] For a more detailed discussion of the Cortese-Knox-Hertzberg Act, see the California Assembly Committee on Local Government's *Guide to the Cortese-Knox-Hertzberg Local Government Reorganization Act of 2000* (2011), available at http://www.calafco.org/docs/CKH/2011_CKH_Guide.pdf.

boundaries is an important factor in balancing the state's interest in promoting orderly development with the sometimes competing state interests of discouraging urban sprawl, preserving open space and prime agricultural lands, and efficiently extending government services. The Legislature declared that the policy favoring orderly development should be realized through the logical formation and modification of the boundaries of local agencies. The Legislature also recognized that providing housing for persons and families of all incomes is an important factor in promoting orderly development. A preference was granted to accommodating additional growth within, or through the expansion of, boundaries of the local agencies that can provide necessary governmental services and housing for persons and families of all incomes in the most efficient manner feasible.

COMPOSITION AND FUNCTION OF LAFCOs

Each county in California has a LAFCO. Except as specifically provided by statute with respect to certain counties, each LAFCO is composed of seven members: two members appointed by the county board of supervisors from its own membership; two members selected by the majority vote of cities in the county, each of whom must be a mayor or councilmember; two special district members; and one member of the general public appointed by the other members of the commission. Gov't Code §§ 56325, 56326-56328, 56329, 56332.

The counties excepted from this general rule, which include Los Angeles, Sacramento, Santa Clara, San Diego, and Kern, as well as any county with no city, are governed by individual rules of creation and composition in the Government Code. *See* Gov't Code §§ 56326-56329.

The powers and duties of LAFCOs are set forth in Government Code section 56375. In particular, LAFCOs make determinations regarding boundary changes to local agencies, including the incorporation and disincorporation of cities, the formation and dissolution of most special districts, and the annexation, detachment, consolidation, merger, and reorganization of cities and districts. Gov't Code §§ 56001, 56375. They also establish, update, and amend spheres of influence for cities and districts. Gov't Code §§ 56425, 56428. In addition, LAFCOs have authority to permit a city or district to provide new or extended services outside its jurisdictional boundaries under certain limited circumstances. Gov't Code §§ 56133, 56375(p). *See also Community Water Coal. v. Santa Cruz County LAFCO*, 200 Cal. App. 4th 1317 (2011) (LAFCO's jurisdiction to approve extraterritorial extension of urban services does not depend upon the identity of the person who filled out the application; a prospective recipient of the services may apply for LAFCO's approval so long as the city or district that will provide the services is a party to the agreement for which approval is sought and is required to join the request by affirmatively indicating its willingness to provide the services).

Pursuant to Government Code section 56325.1, in making determinations, commission members must "exercise their independent judgment on behalf of the interests of residents, property owners, and the public as a whole in furthering the purposes of this division." Members appointed on behalf of local governments "shall represent the interests of the public as a whole and not solely the interests of the appointing authority." This section does not require the abstention of any member of the commission on any matter. *Id.*

The nature of LAFCOs' power is generally treated as both legislative and political. *Sierra Club v. San Joaquin LAFCO*, 21 Cal. 4th 489, 495 (1999); *City of Santa Cruz v. LAFCO*, 76 Cal. App. 3d 381, 387 (1978). Accordingly, LAFCOs have broad discretion in making decisions regarding boundary changes and spheres of influence. *Oxnard Harbor Dist. v. LAFCO*, 16 Cal. App. 4th 259, 262 (1993); *City of Agoura Hills v. LAFCO*, 198 Cal. App. 3d 480, 489 (1988). This discretion, however, must be exercised within legislative parameters. LAFCOs are a creation of the Legislature and have only the powers that are expressly granted by statute or that are necessarily implied in order to exercise the powers expressly granted. *City of Ceres v. City of Modesto*, 274 Cal. App. 2d 545, 550 (1969); *Tillie Lewis Foods, Inc. v. City of Pittsburg*, 52 Cal. App. 3d 983, 999 (1975). The subject matters LAFCOs address are not within the purview of the electorate, except as expressly provided in LAFCO law. *L.I.F.E. Comm. v. City of Lodi*, 213 Cal. App. 3d 1139 (1989) (no initiative or referendum power).

SPHERES OF INFLUENCE

Pursuant to Government Code section 56425, LAFCOs must develop and determine a "sphere of influence" for each city and each special district within its county.

> A sphere of influence is a plan for the probable physical boundaries and service area of a local government agency.

A sphere of influence is a plan for the probable physical boundaries and service area of a local government agency. Gov't Code § 56076. The boundary of the sphere of influence should be designed to provide for the needs of the county and its communities.

To this end, Government Code section 56425(a) provides:

> In order to carry out its purposes and responsibilities for planning and shaping the logical and orderly development and coordination of local governmental agencies subject to the jurisdiction of the commission to advantageously provide for the present and future needs of the county and its communities, the commission shall develop and determine the sphere of influence of each city and each special district, as defined by section 56036, within the county and enact policies designed to promote the logical and orderly development of areas within the sphere.

Once it has determined and adopted a sphere of influence, the commission must review and update it as necessary, but not less than once every five years.[4] Gov't Code § 56425(g). The law imposed an initial deadline for LAFCOs to review and update each sphere of influence on or before January 1, 2008, and then every five years thereafter. *Id.*

Every boundary change determination made by LAFCOs must be consistent with the sphere of influence established for the local agency affected by such determination. Gov't Code § 56375.5.

Prior to submitting an application to LAFCO to amend or update a sphere of influence, representatives from the city and county must meet to discuss the proposed sphere to "explore methods to reach agreement on development standards, and planning and zoning requirements within the sphere." If an agreement is reached, LAFCO must give great weight to this agreement in making its sphere determination. Gov't Code § 56425(b).

---

4 There is some ambiguity in the law about a sphere of influence "amendment," "revision," and "update." These ambiguities have implications for the requirement of LAFCOs to prepare municipal service reviews (as discussed further below). For an interesting discussion on this and related issues, see CALAFCO Subcommittee on Spheres of Influence and Municipal Service Reviews, Final Report on Review of MSR/SOI Statutes (September 2005), available at http://www.calafco.org/docs/COMBINED_SOI-MSR_REPORT.pdf.

In determining each local agency's sphere of influence, the commission must consider several factors and prepare a written statement of its determinations with respect to the following:

- The present and planned land uses in the area, including agricultural and open space lands
- The present and probable need for public facilities and services in the area
- The present capacity of public facilities and adequacy of public services that the agency provides or is authorized to provide
- The existence of any social or economic communities of interest in the area if the commission determines that they are relevant to the agency
- The present and probable need for certain public facilities and services of any disadvantaged unincorporated communities within the existing sphere of influence (for certain updates to a sphere of influence)

Gov't Code § 56425(e)

LAFCOs may adopt, amend, or revise a sphere of influence after notice and a public hearing called and held for that purpose. Gov't Code § 56427. An amendment may also be requested by any person or local agency, if a proposal for a boundary change is not consistent with the current sphere of influence. Often, this request is made in connection with a specific boundary change request, and the commission may act on both requests at the same hearing. Gov't Code § 56428(g).

> LAFCOs may adopt, amend, or revise a sphere of influence after notice and a public hearing called and held for that purpose.

MUNICIPAL SERVICE REVIEW REQUIREMENT

When establishing and updating spheres of influence, LAFCOs are required to conduct municipal service reviews.

These reviews are designed to be a tool for collecting information and evaluating the provision of services from a broader perspective. Specifically, service reviews are designed to ensure that the proposed extension of services or creation of new service providers is consistent with the LAFCO's purposes, policies, and procedures, including promoting orderly development, discouraging urban sprawl, preserving open space and prime agricultural lands, providing housing for persons and families of all incomes, and the efficient extension of government services. Gov't Code § 56434(g).

As part of this review process, the commission prepares a written statement of its determinations with respect to each of the following seven categories:

(1) Growth and population projections for the affected area

(2) The location and characteristics of any disadvantaged unincorporated communities within or contiguous to the sphere of influence

(3) Present and planned capacity of public facilities, adequacy of public services, and infrastructure needs or deficiencies

(4) Financial ability of agencies to provide services

(5) Status of and opportunities for shared facilities

(6) Accountability for community service needs including governmental structure and operational efficiencies

(7) Any other matter related to effective or efficient service delivery, as required by commission policy

Gov't Code § 56430(a)

In conducting a service review, the commission also comprehensively reviews all of the agencies that provide the identified service or services within the designated geographic area. Gov't Code § 56430(b). In addition, the commission may review whether the agencies under review are in compliance with the Safe Drinking Water Act. Gov't Code § 56430(c). The commission also may review and comment upon the following:

(1) The extension of services into previously unserved territory within unincorporated areas

(2) The creation of new service providers to extend urban type development into previously unserved territory within unincorporated areas

Gov't Code § 56434(a)

> OPR = Governor's Office of Planning and Research

The Governor's Office of Planning and Research (OPR) has issued municipal service review guidelines that provide direction to LAFCOs in implementing the service review requirements.[5] However, OPR makes clear that these are only advisory "guidelines," not "regulations." The guidelines recommend how LAFCOs should evaluate each of the categories for which written determinations must be rendered. They also suggest several methodologies for identifying an appropriate geographic scope for the municipal service review. For example, depending upon local conditions, circumstances, and geography, LAFCOs may choose to use geographic and growth boundaries, geo-political boundaries, existing planning areas, or multi-county study areas when conducting municipal service reviews. The guidelines also discuss environmental justice considerations that may be considered in the LAFCO decision-making process.

The guidelines encourage LAFCOs to collaborate and coordinate with all stakeholders, including other affected and interested LAFCOs and government agencies, as well as members of the public. Several opportunities for public participation during the municipal service review process are identified, including stakeholder meetings, public hearings or workshops to initiate municipal service reviews, a public review period of the draft municipal service review report, and a public hearing to consider that report.

LAFCOs' JURISDICTION OVER CHANGES OF ORGANIZATION AND REORGANIZATIONS

AUTHORITY TO MAKE DETERMINATIONS REGARDING CHANGES OF ORGANIZATION OR REORGANIZATIONS

LAFCOs are charged with reviewing and approving or disapproving proposals for local agency changes of organization or reorganizations brought by individuals or affected public agencies. Gov't Code § 56375. Although LAFCOs make determinations regarding changes of organization or reorganizations, they do not have the authority to directly regulate land use density or intensity, property development, or subdivision requirements. Gov't Code § 56375(a)(6).

A "change of organization" is any one of the following boundary changes (Gov't Code § 56021):

- **Annexation**—defined as the inclusion, attachment, or addition of territory to a city or district. Gov't Code § 56017

---

5 OPR's *Local Agency Formation Commission Municipal Service Review Guidelines* (2003) are available at http://opr.ca.gov/docs/MSRGuidelines.pdf. The guidelines emphasize the importance of LAFCOs retaining flexibility to modify OPR's recommendations to reflect local conditions and circumstances, and the types of services under review.

- **Detachment**—defined as the exclusion, deletion, or removal from a city or district of any portion of the territory of that city or district. Gov't Code § 56033
- **Incorporation**—defined as the creation or establishment of a city. Gov't Code § 56043
- **Formation**—defined as the creation of a district. Gov't Code § 56039
- **Disincorporation**—defined as the dissolution, extinguishment, or termination of the existence of a city and the cessation of its corporate powers, except for the purpose of winding up the affairs of the city. Gov't Code § 56034
- **Dissolution**—defined as the disincorporation, extinguishment, or termination of the existence of a district and the cessation of all its corporate powers, except as the commission may otherwise provide pursuant to Government Code section 56886 or for the purpose of winding up the affairs of the district. Gov't Code § 56035
- **Consolidation**—defined as the uniting or joining of two or more cities located in the same county into a single new successor city or two or more districts into a single new successor district. Gov't Code § 56030
- **Merger**—defined as the termination of the existence of a district when the responsibility for the functions, services, assets, and liabilities of that district are assumed by a city as a result of proceedings taken pursuant to this division. Gov't Code § 56056
- **Establishment of Subsidiary District**—defined as the establishment of a district in which a city council is designated as, and empowered to act as, the ex officio board of directors of the district. Gov't Code § 56078
- **Change of Functions or Services**—defined as the exercise of new or different functions or classes of services, or divestiture of the power to provide particular functions or classes of services, within all or part of the jurisdictional boundaries of a special district. Gov't Code § 56021(m)

A "reorganization" is defined as a proceeding involving two or more changes of organization initiated in a single proposal. Gov't Code § 56073.

While LAFCOs have authority to consider proposals for boundary changes, they do not have the power to initiate them, except for those involving: (1) the formation, consolidation, or dissolution of districts; (2) merger of districts; (3) establishment of subsidiary districts; or (4) a reorganization that involves any of these changes of organization. Gov't Code § 56375(a).

LAFCOs may only initiate these proceedings if the change of organization or reorganization is consistent with a recommendation or conclusion of a study prepared pursuant to section 56378, 56425, or 56430, and the commission can make certain required findings. Gov't Code § 56375(a)(3).

AGENCIES OVER WHICH LAFCOs HAVE JURISDICTION

Each LAFCO has jurisdiction over all cities and most districts that serve land within the county in which the LAFCO is located. When an agency provides services to land located in more than one county, the LAFCO in the county having the majority of the assessed value of the district's taxable property has jurisdiction. See Gov't Code §§ 56387, 56066 (definition of principal county); *Placer County LAFCO v. Nevada County LAFCO*, 135 Cal. App. 4th 793, 809 (2006). Under certain circumstances, however, jurisdiction may be transferred from the principal

> Each LAFCO has jurisdiction over all cities and most districts that serve land within the county in which the LAFCO is located.

county to another county in accordance with the provisions of Government Code section 56388.

Certain agencies are expressly excluded from LAFCOs' jurisdiction. Gov't Code §§ 56036(b), 56036.5(a). These include:

- School districts or community college districts
- Assessment districts or special assessment districts
- Improvement districts
- Community facilities districts formed pursuant to the Mello-Roos Community Facilities Act of 1982
- Permanent road divisions formed pursuant to section 1160 *et seq.* of the Streets and Highways Code
- Air pollution control districts or air quality maintenance districts
- Zones of any special districts
- Unified or union high school library districts
- Bridge and highway districts
- Joint highway districts
- Transit or rapid transit districts
- Metropolitan water districts
- Separation of grade districts

In addition, under Government Code section 56036.6, the following entities are not within a LAFCO's jurisdiction if the commission of the principal county determines that the entity is not a "district" or "special district":

- Flood control districts
- Flood control and flood water conservation districts
- Flood control and water conservation districts
- Conservation districts
- Water conservation districts
- Water replenishment districts
- The Orange County Water District
- California water storage districts
- Water agencies
- County water authorities
- Water authorities

Further, some entities are excluded from LAFCO's jurisdiction pursuant to the statutes relevant to their formation. *See, e.g.,* Gov't Code § 26550 *et seq.* (formation of geologic hazard abatement districts); *Las Tunas Beach Geologic Hazard Abatement Dist. v. Superior Court,* 38 Cal. App. 4th 1002 (1995) (general provisions of LAFCO law do not apply to the formation of geologic hazard abatement districts, as the law addressing GHADs contains its own more specific formation procedures). The Community Services District law excludes from LAFCO's control the internal zones of community services districts.[6] In addition, County Service Area (CSA) law limits LAFCO's jurisdiction in two respects: (1) a LAFCO is prohibited from issuing a certificate of filing (i.e., completing the annexation process) for the annexation of incorporated territory

GHAD = geologic hazard abatement district

CSA = County Service Area

---

[6] The Community Services District law (Gov't Code § 61000 et seq.) has several implications for LAFCO proceedings. *See Community Services District Law Update: CSDs and LAFCO: What's New?* (September 2005), *available at* http://www.calafco.org/docs/CSD_Update.doc.

to a CSA (or a reorganization that would result in the annexation of incorporated territory to a CSA, unless the City Council has adopted a resolution consenting to the annexation (Gov't Code § 25210.7(c); § 25211.4);[7] (2) a LAFCO is prohibited from approving any change of organization or reorganization that would result in the inclusion of land devoted primarily to the commercial production of agricultural products, timber, or livestock in a CSA unless the relevant Board of Supervisors finds that the land will benefit from the services and facilities that the CSA provides. Gov't Code § 25210.7(d).[8]

PROCEDURES FOR CHANGES OF ORGANIZATION AND REORGANIZATIONS

LAFCO law sets out detailed procedures for the initiation, processing, and approval or disapproval of proposals for changes of organization and reorganizations. *See generally* Gov't Code § 56650 *et seq*. In addition to following these procedures, proponents must comply with the local written policies and procedures of the particular LAFCO reviewing the proposal (Gov't Code § 56300), and any enabling statutes relevant to the formation of any special districts at issue (*see, e.g.,* Mello-Roos Community Facilities Act, Gov't Code §§ 53311–53368.3).

A proposal for a change of organization or reorganization may be initiated by landowner or registered voter petition (Gov't Code § 56700) or by resolution of application (Gov't Code § 56650) from the legislative body of an affected agency. Gov't Code § 56654, 56658(a). *But see* Gov't Code §§ 56654(a), (b) (a proposal for a change of organization that involves the exercise of new or different functions or classes of services, within all or part of the jurisdictional boundaries of a special district, shall be initiated only by the legislative body of that special district). The petitioner or legislative body (as the case may be) must submit an application to the executive officer of the affected LAFCO that contains, at minimum, the following information:

- Petition or resolution of application initiating the proposal
- Description of the nature of the proposal
- Map and description of the boundaries of the subject territory
- Names of officers or persons, not to exceed three, to receive copies of the LAFCO report and to be given mailed notice of the hearing
- Any additional data and information pertaining to the proposal required by the executive officer or by any regulation of the commission

Gov't Code § 56652

In general, proponents should be prepared to take the following steps as part of the application process:

(1) Arrange for a presubmittal meeting with the executive officer to discuss the process

(2) Compile information regarding the property site (e.g., map of the affected territory, assessors' parcel numbers, general plan/zoning designations, development plans)

(3) Complete a resolution or petition pursuant to Government Code section 56654 or 56700, as applicable

(4) Provide any environmental review documents prepared pursuant to CEQA

CEQA = California Environmental Quality Act

---

[7] *But see* Gov't Code § 25211.4(c)(2) (if the incorporated territory is removed from the boundaries of the CSA, then LAFCO may proceed without the city council's consent).

[8] *See also* Government Code section 25211.4 for additional limitations on LAFCOs' approved authority on CSAs.

(5) Present evidence that a satisfactory property tax exchange agreement is in place or provide needed information to assist LAFCO in making the determination of the amount of property tax revenue to be exchanged in the event of a city incorporation or district formation[9]

(6) Present evidence that the subject territory has been prezoned as required by Government Code section 56375(a)(7)

(7) Remit the required processing fees and service charges as well as any required deposit pursuant to Government Code section 56383[10]

If the proposal is initiated by a local agency's submission of a resolution of application, then a plan for services must be submitted as well, which must include all of the following information and any additional information required by the commission or the executive officer:

- An enumeration and description of the services to be extended to the affected territory
- The level and range of those services
- An indication of when those services can feasibly be extended to the affected territory
- An indication of any improvement or upgrading of any structures, roads, or service or water facilities, or other conditions the local agency would impose or require within the affected territory if the change of organization/reorganization is completed
- Information with respect to how those services will be financed

Gov't Code § 56653; *see also* Government Code section 56824.12 for the required contents of a plan for services for proposals to provide new or different services or the divestiture of the power to provide particular functions or classes of services.

The executive officer must render a decision on the completeness of the application for a change of organization or reorganization within 30 days of receipt, and must determine the status of CEQA review.

The executive officer, who is responsible for conducting the day-to-day business of the commission (Gov't Code § 56384), must render a decision on the completeness of the application for a change of organization or reorganization within 30 days of receipt, and must determine the status of CEQA review. Gov't Code § 56658(c).

Immediately after receiving an application for a boundary change (and prior to issuing a certificate of filing), the executive officer must provide mailed notice to each affected agency, the county committee on school district organization, each school superintendent whose school district overlies the affected territory, and all landowners within 300 feet of the subject territory. Gov't Code § 56157, 56658(b). The executive officer then must wait for at least 20 days after giving this required notice before issuing the certificate of filing. Gov't Code § 56658(d). After this 20-day period has passed and the application is determined to be complete, the executive officer must issue a certificate of filing to the applicant. Gov't Code § 56658(f). If the application is determined to be incomplete, the executive officer must immediately inform the applicant in writing of the additional information or supplemental documents that are required before the proposal can be heard by the commission. Gov't Code § 56658(g). If the executive officer fails to make a completeness determination within 30 days of

---

9 *See* Revenue and Taxation Code sections 99 and 99.1 regarding the requirement of a satisfactory property tax exchange. Note that master property tax agreements may be applicable or separate property tax exchange resolutions may be required. The mandatory process for negotiating property tax sharing agreements between a county and city in the event of an annexation of unincorporated land is scheduled to sunset in 2015. *See also* Gov't Code §§ 56810 (determination), 56811 (formation of district), 56812 (incorporation of city), and 56815 (revenue neutrality).

10 Any mandatory time limits may be deferred until the applicant pays the required fee, service charge, or deposit. Gov't Code § 56383(e).

receiving the application, and the required fees, service charges, and deposits have been paid, an application is automatically deemed accepted for filing. Gov't Code § 56658(e). The executive officer then must set the LAFCO hearing within 90 days of the issuance of the certificate of filing, or the date on which the application was deemed accepted, whichever is earlier. Gov't Code § 56658(h). Except as provided in Government Code section 56662, notice of the hearing must be given at least 21 days prior to the hearing by mailing, publication, and posting. However, in certain limited circumstances, LAFCOs may make determinations without notice and a hearing. Gov't Code § 56662.

After reviewing the complete application, public or other agency comments, and other relevant information, the executive officer must prepare a staff report, including recommendations, on the application. The staff report must be completed not less than five days before the hearing, and copies must be furnished to each individual designated in the application, each affected local agency[11] requesting a report, each local agency whose boundaries or sphere of influence would be changed, the executive officer of another affected county when a district is or will be located in that other county, and each affected city. Gov't Code § 56665.

Under certain circumstances, proceedings may be terminated prior to the hearing. Pursuant to Government Code section 56857, any special district to which annexation of territory is proposed may adopt and transmit to the commission a resolution requesting termination of the proceedings. This resolution must be based on written findings supported by substantial evidence in the record that the request is justified by a financial or service related concern. The resolution is subject to judicial review prior to the commission's termination of proceedings. Gov't Code § 56857(b). If the commission timely receives a resolution requesting termination, but has not received notice that judicial review of the resolution is being sought, the commission must terminate the proceedings no sooner than 30 days from receipt of the resolution. Gov't Code § 56857(c). Similarly, a city from which detachment of territory is proposed may adopt and transmit to the commission a resolution requesting termination of the city detachment proceedings. Gov't Code § 56751. However, unlike the provision addressing district authority to terminate annexation proceedings, the provision addressing a city's ability to terminate detachment proceedings does not reference any requirement to justify the request based on financial or service related concerns.

FACTORS LAFCOs MUST CONSIDER WHEN REVIEWING A BOUNDARY CHANGE PROPOSAL

GENERAL FACTORS

Under Government Code section 56668, LAFCOs must consider the following factors when reviewing a boundary change proposal:
- Population and population density; land area and land use; per capita assessed valuation; topography, natural boundaries, and drainage basins; proximity to other populated areas; and the likelihood of significant growth in the area and in adjacent incorporated and unincorporated areas during the next 10 years

---

11 LAFCO law defines an "affected local agency" as any local agency that contains, or would contain, or whose sphere of influence contains or would contain, any territory for which a change of organization is proposed or ordered, either singularly or as part of a reorganization or for which a study is to be reviewed by the commission. Gov't Code § 56014.

FIGURE F: LAFCO PROCEEDINGS

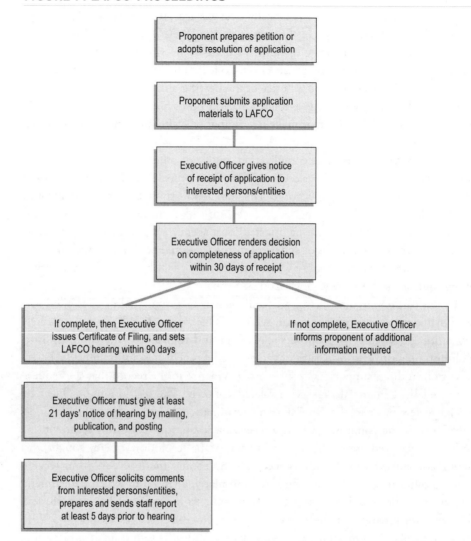

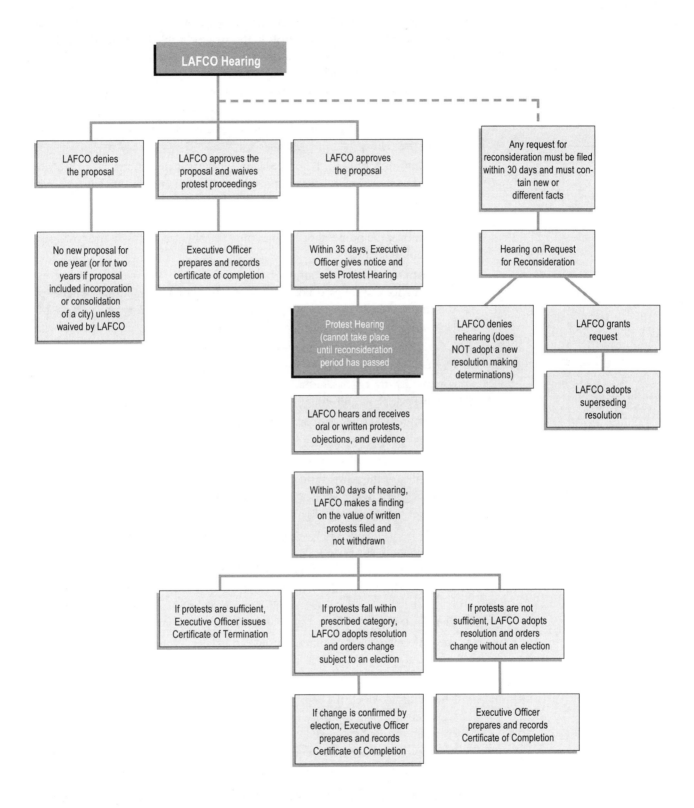

- The need for organized community services; the present cost and adequacy of governmental services and controls in the area; probable future needs for those services and controls; probable effect of the proposed incorporation, formation, annexation, or exclusion and of alternative courses of action on the cost and adequacy of services and controls in the area and adjacent areas
- The effect of the proposed action and of alternative actions on adjacent areas, on mutual social and economic interests, and on the local government structure of the county
- The conformity of both the proposal and its anticipated effects with both the adopted commission policies on providing planned, orderly, efficient patterns of urban development, and the open space land use policies and priorities specified under LAFCO law
- The effect of the proposal on maintaining the physical and economic integrity of agricultural lands
- The definiteness and certainty of the boundaries of the territory, the nonconformance of proposed boundaries with lines of assessment or ownership, the creation of islands or corridors of unincorporated territory, and other similar matters affecting the proposed boundaries
- Consistency with city or county general and specific plans
- Consistency with the regional transportation plan, including the sustainable community strategy or alternative planning strategy it contains (for more discussion of such plans and strategies, see chapter 16 (Sustainable Development)
- The sphere of influence of any local agency that may be applicable to the proposal being reviewed
- The comments of any affected local agency or other public agency
- The ability of the newly formed or receiving entity to provide the services that are the subject of the application to the area, including the sufficiency of revenues for those services following the proposed boundary change
- Timely availability of water supplies adequate for projected needs as specified in Government Code section 65352.5
- The extent to which the proposal will affect a city or cities and the county in achieving their respective fair shares of the regional housing needs, as determined by the appropriate council of governments consistent with Housing Element law
- Any information or comments from landowners, voters or residents of the affected territory
- Any information relating to existing land use designations
- The extent to which the proposal will promote environmental justice; as used here, "environmental justice" means the fair treatment of people of all races, cultures, and incomes with respect to the location of public facilities and the provision of public services

ADDITIONAL FACTORS THAT LAFCO MUST CONSIDER IN CERTAIN PROCEEDINGS

If the proposal involves the annexation of territory to a city, prezoning is required.

If the proposal involves the annexation of territory to a city, prezoning is required. Gov't Code § 56375(a)(7). To meet this as a condition of annexation, a city must have prezoned the territory to be annexed or present evidence satisfactory to LAFCO either that the existing development entitlements on the territory to be annexed are vested or that the territory is already at buildout and is consistent with the city's general plan. *Id.* The decision of the commission with regard to a proposal to annex territory to a city shall be based upon the general plan and the prezoning. Gov't Code § 56375(a)(7). The commission does not have the authority to specify how, or in what manner, the territory shall be prezoned. *Id.* Once the territory is annexed, the city may not make any subsequent change to the general plan or the zoning for the annexed territory for a period of two years after the completion of the annexation, unless it makes a finding at a public hearing that a substantial change has occurred in circumstances that necessitate a departure from the prezoning relied upon in the annexation application to the commission. Gov't Code § 56375(e).

LAFCO law requires special consideration of proposals to annex "islands," which are unincorporated areas that are surrounded or substantially surrounded by a city. In particular, LAFCO law encourages annexation of islands since urban service delivery to these islands is often very inefficient, if not impossible, and residents generally receive fewer and lower levels of services for which they may pay the same taxes and fees as those in a nearby city. Urban islands of less than 150 acres may be annexed without holding protest proceedings or elections provided certain requirements are met. Gov't Code §§ 56375.3, 56375.4.

Additional factors LAFCO must consider when the proposal involves a city detachment or district annexation include:

- In the case of district annexation, whether the proposed annexation will be for the interest of landowners or present or future inhabitants within the district and within the territory proposed to be annexed to the district
- In the case of a city detachment, whether the proposed detachment will be for the interest of the landowners or present or future inhabitants within the city and within the territory proposed to be detached from the city
- Any of the factors set forth in Government Code section 56668 (*see* Factors LAFCO Must Consider When Reviewing a Boundary Change Proposal, this chapter)
- Any resolution raising objections to the action that may be filed by an affected agency
- Any other matters that LAFCO deems material

LAFCO must give great weight to any resolution raising objections to the action that is filed by a city or district. However, LAFCO's consideration shall be based only on financial or service related concerns expressed in the protest. Gov't Code § 56668.3(b). *But see* Gov't Code § 56751 (does not address requirement to justify termination request regarding detachment based on financial or service-related concerns).

In connection with special districts, recent amendments require that for proposals to establish new or different functions or a different class of services, LAFCO may not approve the proposal unless it determines that the special district will have sufficient revenues to carry out the proposal; or, in the alternative, LAFCO may condition approval on the district's concurrent approval of sufficient revenues to carry out the proposal. Gov't Code § 56824.14.

ADDITIONAL FACTORS THAT LAFCO MAY CONSIDER

In addition, LAFCO may, but is not required to, consider the regional growth goals and policies established by a collaboration of elected officials, only formally representing their local jurisdictions in an official capacity on a regional or subregional basis. Gov't Code § 56668.5.

LAFCOs' CONSIDERATION OF BOUNDARY CHANGE PROPOSALS

When considering the above factors, LAFCOs must evaluate proposals with the purposes of the Cortese-Knox-Hertzberg Act in mind. *McBail & Co. v. Solano LAFCO*, 62 Cal. App. 4th 1223, 1227–29 (1998); *Simi Valley Recreation & Park Dist. v. LAFCO*, 51 Cal. App. 3d 648, 668 (1975); *see also Opinion of Brown* (07-206) (June 27, 2008) (authorizing a LAFCO to enlarge the boundaries of a proposed incorporation beyond those set forth in the petition based on LAFCO's authority to promote the efficient extension of services).

Within 35 days of the conclusion of the hearing, LAFCO must adopt a resolution making determinations approving or disapproving the proposal. Gov't Code § 56375(a), 56880. With respect to boundary change decisions, formal written findings of fact are not required. *City of Santa Cruz v. LAFCO*, 76 Cal. App. 3d at 387. *See also* Gov't Code § 56668.3(b). To enable a court to scrutinize the substantiality of the evidence supporting the agency's decision, however, the record of the proceedings must adequately reflect the reason for the decision. *McBail & Co.*, 62 Cal. App. 4th at 1230. LAFCOs have express authority to impose certain conditions specified by statute when approving a change of organization or reorganization. *See, e.g.*, Gov't Code § 56886; AG Opinion, 89 Ops. Cal. Atty. Gen. 173 (2006) (LAFCOs may condition approval of the incorporation of a city upon voters within the proposed city approving a general tax, and may do so by a majority vote). *See also Voices for Rural Living v. El Dorado Irrigation District*, 209 Cal. App. 4th 1096, 1116 (2012) (irrigation district may not disregard annexation conditions by treating them as void *ab initio* on the theory they were unconstitutional). However, these conditions may not directly regulate land use. Gov't Code §§ 56375(a)(6), 56886. If denied, no new proposal can be made for one year unless this restriction is waived by LAFCO. Gov't Code § 56884. If the proposal included incorporation or consolidation of a city, no new proposal can be made for two years unless this restriction is waived by the commission. Gov't Code § 57090.

LAFCO decisions may be challenged in court. Gov't Code § 56107 (recognizing judiciary's authority to independently review LAFCO decision). In any action or proceeding to attack a LAFCO decision, judicial review extends only to whether there was fraud or a prejudicial abuse of discretion. *Id.*; *see also Resource Def. Fund v. LAFCO*, 191 Cal. App. 3d 886 at 890; *City of Santa Cruz*, 76 Cal. App. 3d at 391. Prejudicial abuse of discretion is established if the court finds that LAFCO's decision was not supported by substantial evidence in light of the whole record. Gov't Code § 56107. *See also City of Agoura Hills*, 198 Cal. App. 3d at 489; *Simi Valley Recreation & Park Dist.*, 51 Cal. App. 3d at 686; *City of Livermore v. LAFCO*, 184 Cal. App. 3d 531, 540 (1986).

The court's role is to ensure that LAFCO adequately considered all relevant factors and demonstrated a rational connection between these factors, the choice made, and the purposes of the enabling statute. *McBail & Co.*, 62 Cal. App. 4th at 1228; *see also Ridgecrest Charter Sch. v. Sierra Sands Unified Sch. Dist.*, 130 Cal. App. 4th 986, 1006–07 (2005). The petitioner has the affirmative burden to establish this is not the case. *Cequel III Commc'ns I, LLC. v. LAFCO*, 149 Cal. App. 4th 310, 329 (2007).

For the purpose of any action to determine or contest the validity of any change of organization or reorganization, it shall be deemed to be completed and in existence upon execution by the executive officer of the certificate of completion. Gov't Code § 56102. If, at the time the challenge is brought, the boundary change is not "complete," some case law suggests the LAFCO decision is reviewable by ordinary mandamus. *McBail & Co.*, 62 Cal. App. 4th at 1227; *see also Bozung v. LAFCO*, 13 Cal. 3d 263, 271 (1975); *Hills for Everyone v. LAFCO*, 105 Cal. App. 3d 461, 466 (1980); *Norlund v.*

Thorpe, 34 Cal. App. 3d 672, 676 (1973); *Los Angeles County v. City Council of Lawndale*, 202 Cal. App. 2d 20, 26 (1962); *Cothran v. Town Council of Los Gatos*, 209 Cal. App. 2d 647, 650 (1962); *Campbell v. Mosk*, 197 Cal. App. 2d 640, 645 (1961); *Hazelton v. City of San Diego*, 183 Cal. App. 2d 131, 135 (1960); *Jefferson Union Sch. Dist. of Santa Clara City v. City Council of City of Sunnyvale*, 129 Cal. App. 2d 264, 267-68 (1954); *American Distilling Co. v. City Council of City of Sausalito*, 34 Cal. 2d 660, 667 (1950); *but see Cequel III Commc'ns I, LLC*, 149 Cal. App. 4th at 316 (because LAFCO's approval was not complete until after certification of completion was issued, a legal challenge filed immediately after adoption of the resolution and before LAFCO's issuance of a certificate of compliance would have been premature).

Once a boundary change or sphere of influence decision is complete, it may be challenged only by a validation action pursuant to Code of Civil Procedure section 860 *et seq.* A validation action provides a uniform procedure for prompt resolution of the validity of a completed annexation by an *in rem* action. This procedure is necessary to settle any questions respecting the city's jurisdiction over the annexed territory, including any uncertainties regarding the applicable land use regulations, or the city's responsibilities to provide police, fire, and other municipal services to the area. The procedure prescribed by the validating statute assures due process notice to all interested persons and settles the validity of the annexation once and for all by a single lawsuit. *Hills For Everyone*, 105 Cal. App. 3d at 467-68; *see also Katz v. Campbell Union High Sch. Dist.*, 144 Cal. App. 4th 1024, 1028 (2006); *Embarcadero Mun. Improvement Dist. v. City of Santa Barbara*, 88 Cal. App. 4th 781, 789 (2001); *Friedland v. City of Long Beach*, 62 Cal. App. 4th 835, 844 (1998).

Validation actions must be brought within 60 days. Gov't Code § 56103; *see also Hills for Everyone*, 105 Cal. App. 3d at 467; *Environmental Coal. of Orange County, Inc. v. LAFCO of Orange County*, 110 Cal. App. 3d 164, 170 (1980); *Campbell*, 197 Cal. App. 2d at 645; *Crowl v. Bd. of Trustees of City of Southgate*, 292 P. 985, 215-16 (1930); *Coe v. City of Los Angeles*, 183 P. 822, 480-81 (1919). Some case law indicates this is generally true even if there are allegations that the boundary change is only complete because of a failure to adhere to legal requirements. *Coe*, 183 P. 822 at 481; *but see City of Anaheim v. City of Fullerton*, 102 Cal. App. 2d 395, 401 (1951) (since the annexation was only "complete" because of "subterfuge and evasion," validation action not required based on court's conclusion that city had neither actual nor de facto exercise of dominion over annexed land).

RECONSIDERATION HEARING

After LAFCO adopts a resolution approving, modifying, or denying a proposal determining a boundary change, the executive officer is required to send the resolution to the proponents and to each affected local agency whose boundaries will be changed by the proposal. Gov't Code § 56882. Any person or affected agency may file a written request with the executive officer requesting amendments to or reconsideration of the resolution. The request must state the specific modification to the resolution being requested, and what new or different facts exist that could not have been presented previously, or what applicable new law is claimed to warrant the requested reconsideration. Gov't Code § 56895(a). The request must be filed within 30 days after adoption of the resolution by the commission. Gov't Code § 56895(b).

Upon receipt by the executive officer of a timely and proper request for reconsideration, the executive officer shall place the request for reconsideration on the agenda

> Any person or affected agency may file a written request with the executive officer requesting amendments to or reconsideration of the resolution.

of the commission's next meeting for which proper notice can be given. The time to file an action, including an action pursuant to CEQA, shall be tolled during the time the commission takes to act on the reconsideration request. Gov't Code § 56895(d). The executive officer must give notice of the commission's hearing on the reconsideration request in the same manner as for the original proposal and also may give notice in any other manner that he or she deems necessary or desirable. Gov't Code § 56895(e).

At the reconsideration hearing, the commission must consider the request and receive any oral or written testimony. The commission's consideration of the request may be continued from time to time, but such continuances cannot exceed 35 days from the hearing date first specified in the notice. The person or agency that filed the request for reconsideration may withdraw the request at any time prior to the conclusion of the commissioners' consideration. Gov't Code § 56895(f).

At the conclusion of its consideration, the commission may approve or disapprove the requested modifications to its resolution. If it disapproves the request to modify its resolution, the commission shall not adopt a new resolution making determinations. If it approves the request, with or without amendment, the commission shall adopt a new resolution that supersedes the previous resolution. Gov't Code § 56895(g). The determinations of the commission are final and conclusive, and no person or agency shall make any further request for the same change or a substantially similar change, as determined by the commission. Gov't Code § 56895(h). Since seeking reconsideration is permissive, pursuing reconsideration of a LAFCO decision is not required to exhaust administrative remedies. *Sierra Club v. LAFCO*, 21 Cal. 4th 489 (1999).

PROTEST PROCEEDINGS

After a LAFCO adopts a resolution approving or modifying a proposed boundary change, it generally must take on the ministerial role of "conducting authority" and conduct protest proceedings (except for certain changes of reorganization pursuant to Government Code sections 57077-57077.4), unless the proceedings have been waived pursuant to Government Code sections 56662, 56663 and 57002. Gov't Code §§ 57000, 56029. If, however, a LAFCO wholly disapproves any proposal, "no futher proceedings shall be taken on that proposal" and no "similar proposal involving the same or substantially the same territory" may be initiated for one year, unless LAFCO waives these requirements. Gov't Code § 56884.

The purpose of the protest proceedings is to provide a forum in which registered voters and property owners (if the territory is inhabited) or property owners (if the territory is uninhabited) can formally voice their approval or opposition for the particular change of organization or reorganization.[12] However, the protest process does not implicate a fundamental right to vote. *Citizens for Responsible Open Space v. San Mateo County LAFCO*, 159 Cal. App. 4th 717, 725 (2008).

The executive officer must set the protest hearing and give proper notice within 35 days of the commission's adoption of its resolution making determinations regarding the boundary change. Gov't Code §§ 57025, 57026 (noticing requirements); *but see Citizens for Responsible Open Space*, 159 Cal. App. 4th at 717 (upholding annexation without election despite minor technical deficiencies in notice). This hearing shall not be held, however, prior to the expiration of the reconsideration period. Gov't Code § 57002(a). The date of the protest hearing must be within 60 days, but not less than 21

---

[12] "Inhabited territory" means territory within which there reside 12 or more registered voters. Gov't Code § 56046.

days, from the date of published notice.[13] Gov't Code § 57050(a). The hearing may be continued from time to time, not to exceed 60 days from the date specified for the hearing in the notice. Gov't Code § 57062(a).

At the protest hearing, the commission must hear and receive any oral or written protests, objections, or evidence that are presented. Gov't Code §§ 57050(b), 57051. At any time prior to the conclusion of the protest hearing, any owner of land or any registered voter within the affected territory may file a written protest. Gov't Code § 57051. *See Citizens for Responsible Open Space*, 159 Cal. App. 4th at 733 (upheld LAFCO's exclusion of protests that did not include protester's residence address). However, in contrast to the original LAFCO proceedings on the proposal, the commissioners at a protest hearing have no decisionmaking power. Rather, the action taken at this hearing is based solely on the *number* of written protests received. Written protests may be withdrawn during the protest hearing.

Upon conclusion of the protest hearing, if no written protests have been filed, the commission must adopt a form of resolution ordering the change of organization or reorganization without an election. However, if written protests have been filed, within 30 days after the conclusion of the hearing the commission must, except under certain limited circumstances (*see* Gov't Code §§ 57077-57077.4), make a determination on the value of written protests filed and not withdrawn.[14] Gov't Code § 57052. *See also Citizens for Responsible Open Space*, 159 Cal. App. 4th at 729-30 (rejected claim that LAFCO improperly delegated to County elections division the task of counting and verifying protests).

The commission then must take one of the following actions, depending on the nature of the change of organization or reorganization:

- Issue a Certificate of Termination terminating the LAFCO proceedings
- Adopt a resolution making determinations and ordering the change of organization or reorganization without an election, or
- Adopt a resolution making determinations and ordering the change of organization or reorganization subject to confirmation by the voters

If the proceedings are terminated, then no substantially similar proposal may be made for one year, except in the case of an incorporation or city consolidation, in which case no substantially similar proposal may be made for two years. These waiting periods, however, may be waived by LAFCO. Gov't Code § 57090.

FINAL ACTIONS, FILINGS, AND NOTIFICATIONS

Immediately after the protest hearing is completed and if the LAFCO proceedings are not terminated, upon satisfaction of any conditions contained in LAFCO's resolution-making determinations that are required to be completed prior to filing a certificate of completion, the executive officer must prepare, execute, and file a certificate of completion. Gov't Code §§ 57200, 57201. The certificate then must be recorded in the county recorder's office within 90 days. Gov't Code § 57203. The change of organization or reorganization is complete on the date the certificate of completion is executed and effective on the dates specified in the resolution. If no effective date is specified in the LAFCO resolution, then the date of recordation of the certificate of completion is the

> Immediately after the protest hearing is completed and if the LAFCO proceedings are not terminated, upon satisfaction of any conditions contained in LAFCO's resolution-making determinations that are required to be completed prior to filing a certificate of completion, the executive officer must prepare, execute, and file a certificate of completion.

---

13 With respect to subsidiary districts, the hearing shall be held not less than 90 days but no more than 135 days following notice. Gov't Code § 57002(b).

14 See Gov't Code §§ 57075, 57075.5 for additional information regarding the resolution of protest proceedings. For an evaluation of the effects of protests, see Table 2.

TABLE 2. LAFCO PROTEST PROCEEDINGS—EFFECT OF PROTESTS

Most changes of organization or reorganization proceed in a three-step fashion: (1) application, (2) LAFCO decision, and (3) protest proceedings. The purpose of protest proceedings (also known as conducting authority proceedings) is to allow landowners or voters to have a say in whether the changes or organization or reorganization will proceed. The conducting authority—LAFCO—holds a hearing to receive protests. The number of protests determine whether LAFCO must terminate proceedings, approve the change, or approve the change subject to an election. This chart details what number of protests trigger which actions.

REGISTERED-VOTER DISTRICTS* OR CITIES WHERE THE ONLY CHANGES OF ORGANIZATION OR REORGANIZATION CONSIST OF ANNEXATIONS, DETACHMENTS, OR FORMATION OF COUNTY SERVICE AREAS**		
	INHABITED	**UNINHABITED**
Who May Protest	Any owner of land within the territory, or any registered voter residing within the territory may protest. Gov't Code § 57026(g)	Any owner of land within the territory may protest. Gov't Code § 57026(h)
Actions That Require Termination of Proceedings	Majority protest by ≥ 50% of the voters residing in the territory. Gov't Code §§ 57075(a)(1), 57078(b)	Majority protest by landowners owning ≥ 50% of the assessed value of the land within the territory. Gov't Code §§ 57075(b)(1), 57078(a)
Actions That Require Approval of Change Subject to Election	Election of voters residing in the affected territory if written protests from either: (a) ≥ 25% but < 50% of registered voters residing within affected territory OR (b) ≥ 25% of the number of owners of land who also own at least 25% of the assessed value of land within the affected territory. Gov't Code § 57075(a)(2)	Not provided for
Actions That Require Approval of Change Without Election	Protests from: (a) < 25% of registered voters OR (b) < 25% of the number of owners of land owning < 25% of the assessed value of the land within the affected territory. Gov't Code § 57075(a)(3)	Protests from owners of land who own < 50% of the total assessed value of the land within the affected territory. Gov't Code § 57075(b)(2)
LANDOWNER-VOTER DISTRICTS* WHERE THE ONLY CHANGES OF ORGANIZATION OR REORGANIZATION CONSIST OF ANNEXATIONS AND DETACHMENTS**		
Who May Protest	The provisions of Government Code sections 57026(g) and (h) are written to apply to any protest hearing. These discuss the ability of registered voters and landowners to protest in inhabited territory, and only landowners to protest in uninhabited territory. However, the provisions specifically related to protests in landowner-voter districts, noted below, do not distinguish between inhabited and uninhabited territory, and indicate that only those who hold voting power are entitled to protest.	
Actions That Require Termination of Proceedings	Majority protest by ≥ 50% of the voting power of the voters entitled to vote as a result of owning land within the district. (Note that the reference is to the district, not just the affected territory.) Gov't Code §§ 57076(a), 57078(c)	
Actions That Require Approval of Change Subject to Election	Election within affected territory if protests from: (a) ≥ 25% of the number of owners of land who also own ≥ 25% of the assessed value of land within the territory OR (b) ≥ 25% of the voting power of landowner voters entitled to vote as a result of owning property within the territory. Gov't Code § 57076(b)	
Actions That Require Approval of Change Without Election	Protests from < 25% of the number of owners of land who own < 25% of the assessed value of land within the affected territory. Gov't Code § 57076(c)	

* Registered-voter district means a district whose principal act provides that registered voters residing within the district are entitled to vote for the election of district officers, incurring of bonded indebtedness, or any other district matter. Gov't Code § 56072.

** Does not include inhabited territory that is proposed to be annexed to a city with more than 100,000 residents and that is located in a county with a population of more than 4 million. Gov't Code § 57075.5.

*** Landowner-voter district means a district whose principal act provides that owners of land within the district are entitled to vote upon the election of district officers, the incurring of bonded indebtedness, or any other district matter. Gov't Code § 56050.

effective date. Gov't Code § 57202. A statement of boundary change or creation will then be issued by the executive officer and filed along with appropriate fees with the State Board of Equalization and the County Assessor. If it is a city change, notice will be provided to the Secretary of State. Gov't Code § 57204. Property tax resolutions, if any, will be forwarded to the County Auditor to enable property tax transfers. The executive officer must provide a notice of completion and effective date to affected agencies and county departments. Gov't Code § 57203. Any other agencies, utilities, and other affected parties also will be notified, as appropriate. Gov't Code § 57204. After receiving notice, affected agencies are required to recognize completion of the jurisdictional changes and implement any amended processes such as the redistribution of property tax.

PROCESSING MULTI-COUNTY CHANGES OF ORGANIZATION OR REORGANIZATION

More than one LAFCO may be involved in a particular proposal—for example, in the case of a district that is, or as a result of a proposed boundary change would be, located in more than one county. Under these circumstances, exclusive jurisdiction shall be vested in the commission of the principal county. Gov't Code §§ 56123, 56387; *Placer County LAFCO*, 135 Cal. App. 4th at 808. "Principal county" is defined as the county having the greater portion of the entire assessed value, as shown on the last equalized assessment roll of the county or counties, of all taxable property within a district or districts for which a change of organization or reorganization is proposed. Gov't Code § 56066.

However, exclusive jurisdiction can be vested in the commission of an affected county other than the commission of the principal county if all of the following occur: (1) the commission of the principal county approves the request to transfer jurisdiction; (2) the commission of the principal county designates the other affected county to assume jurisdiction; and (3) the commission of the other affected county agrees to assume jurisdiction. Gov't Code §§ 56124, 56388.

ENVIRONMENTAL REVIEW

As a public agency, LAFCO must comply with the provisions of the California Environmental Quality Act (Pub. Res. Code § 21000 *et seq.*). As the California Supreme Court noted, "LAFCO must recognize that [LAFCO law] dovetails with CEQA." *Bozung*, 13 Cal. 3d at 282. Under *Bozung*, if a LAFCO approval starts in motion a chain of events that ultimately can lead to a development project that will cause environmental impacts, the need for analysis under CEQA is triggered. *Id.* at 278. This is true even though numerous further steps in the approval process will be required prior to any actual development. *Id.* at 282; *see also Pistoresi v. City of Madera*, 138 Cal. App. 3d 284, 287 (1982); *City of Santa Clara v. LAFCO*, 139 Cal. App. 3d 923, 930-31 (1983); *People v. LAFCO*, 81 Cal. App. 3d 464, 478-79 (1978).

CEQA = California Environmental Quality Act

Usually, the city, county, or special district that is involved in the annexation or other boundary change takes some action that triggers CEQA, and becomes the lead agency under CEQA. For example, prior to annexing territory into a city, that city must prezone the territory (Gov't Code § 56375(a). LAFCO decisions become subsequent decisions on the project, which results in LAFCOs generally functioning as responsible agencies. California Code of Regulations, title 14, section 15096(d).

There are, however, situations where LAFCOs take on lead CEQA responsibility. LAFCOs should be mindful of the potential application of CEQA to their decisions to adopt or amend LAFCO policies. *City of Livermore*, 184 Cal. App. 3d at 538 (new guidelines regarding spheres of influence required preparation of an EIR since they would "influence LAFCO decisions about development plans and future growth of cities and service areas").

LAFCOs also can act as lead agencies when amending spheres of influence or conducting municipal service reviews. *Compare City of Agoura Hills*, 198 Cal. App. 3d at 495 (amendment to sphere did not trigger CEQA; "[t]he fact that spheres of influence are recognized as important factors in annexations does not compel the conclusion that they are per se 'projects' subject to CEQA") *with* Gov't Code § 56428 (requests for a sphere amendment must be placed on the LAFCO agenda after "compliance" with CEQA).

The question of whether the preparation of a municipal service review triggers CEQA remains unsettled as well. If a service review is treated as merely "information gathering" or as a "planning and feasibility study," then it is exempt under CEQA. CEQA Guidelines §§ 15262, 15306. *Cf. Calfornia Water Impact Network v. Newhall County Water Dist.*, 161 Cal. App. 4th 1464, 1471 (2008) (holding that preparation of a study that is merely "a technical, informational document" is "not a 'final' act or determination subject to direct mandamus review"). However, if it involves something that actually will influence growth patterns or otherwise affect land use in a way that results in environmental impacts, it may trigger application of CEQA. *City of Livermore*, 184 Cal. App. 3d at 538; Governor's Office of Planning and Research, Municipal Service Review Guidelines (Aug. 2003) *available at* http://opr.ca.gov/docs/MSR Guidelines.pdf.

In the event of a CEQA challenge of a completed boundary change or sphere decision, the validation rule discussed above still applies. For example, in *Hills for Everyone*, the petitioner argued the case should not be dismissed for missing the 60-day statute of limitations period under validation actions because the challenge was grounded in CEQA claims. The court rejected this argument, stating:

> Although grounded on alleged violations of CEQA, petitioner's action is one seeking to invalidate a completed municipal annexation; it is not just an action to review and set aside LAFCO approval of a proposed annexation. Petitioner should have proceeded under the validating statute and its action was subject to dismissal for failure to do so.

Hills for Everyone, 105 Cal. App. 3d at 468

For a more detailed discussion on the requirements regarding the environmental review process, *see* chapter 6 (CEQA).

CHAPTER 15

Affordable Housing

INTRODUCTION: THE AFFORDABLE HOUSING CRISIS IN CALIFORNIA[1]

Even with the prolonged downturn in the housing market, communities across California continue to confront the challenges posed by a scarcity of housing, particularly affordable housing. In the last several decades, housing production in the state has lagged behind population and job growth, resulting in a housing deficit.[2] Census Bureau figures show that housing costs continue to consume much more than the recommended 30 percent of the monthly paycheck for millions of Americans.[3] While all citizens feel the impact of this housing shortage at some level, those with incomes at the lowest end of the economic spectrum often bear the brunt of the shortage. In 2011, 8.5 million very low-income families without housing assistance paid more than 50 percent of their incomes for housing—an increase of 43 percent since 2007.[4]

While the long-term impacts of the recent housing downturn on the affordability of housing in California are yet to be fully understood, the impacts of a limited supply of housing over the past few decades remain far reaching.[5] As the Legislature continues to acknowledge, the "lack of housing is a critical problem that threatens the economic, environmental, and social quality of life in California." Gov't Code § 65589.5(a)(1). Housing remains a linchpin of sustainable development and smart growth, and is inextricably linked to economic and social opportunity. The level of access to quality employment, education, and support systems, as well as the availability of a wide range of services and amenities are, in significant part, determined by where one lives. As the Millennial Housing Commission emphasized:

> The Legislature continues to acknowledge that the "lack of housing is a critical problem that threatens the economic, environmental, and social quality of life in California."

---

1 For a thorough discussion of local, state, and federal regulatory responses to the issue of affordable housing, see *The Legal Guide to Affordable Housing Development* (T. Iglesias & R.E. Lento eds., 2nd ed. 2011).

2 *See e.g.*, California Budget Project, *Locked Out 2008: The Housing Boom and Beyond* (2008) at 29, 30, *available at* http://www.cbp.org/pdfs/2008/080212_LockedoutReport.pdf.

3 *See* John Leland, *Housing Costs Consumed More of Paychecks in 2006*, N.Y. Times, Sept. 12, 2007, *available at* http://www.nytimes.com/2007/09/12/us/12housing.html; U.S. Census Bureau, 2010 American Community Survey.

4 *See The Affordable Housing Crisis*, N.Y. Times, December 5, 2012, available at http://www.nytimes.com/2012/12/05/opinions/the-affordable-housing-crisis.

5 For a good overview of the impacts of the housing market collapse on California's housing policies, see William Fulton and Paul Shigley, *Guide to California Planning*, Chapter 16, pp. 323-338 (Solano Press 4th Ed. 2012).

Decent, affordable, and accessible housing fosters self-sufficiency, brings stability to families and new vitality to distressed communities, and supports overall economic growth.[6]

Following is a discussion of various aspects of state law that are designed to eliminate unnecessary constraints on residential development and provide housing opportunities to meet the needs of all Californians.

STATE HOUSING ELEMENT LAW

PURPOSE OF THE MANDATED HOUSING ELEMENT

The Legislature has declared: "the availability of housing is of statewide importance, and the early attainment of decent housing and a suitable living environmental for every Californian, including farmworkers, is a priority of the highest order;" "the provision of housing affordable to low- and moderate-income households requires the cooperation of all levels of government;" and "governments have a responsibility to use their powers to make adequate provision for the housing needs of all economic segments of the community." Gov't Code § 65580.

To facilitate the improvement and development of housing for all economic segments of the community (pursuant to Gov't Code § 65580(d)), every city in the state is required to adopt a housing element as part of its general plan. Gov't Code § 65302(c). This mandate helps to ensure that "counties and cities recognize their responsibilities in contributing to the attainment of the state housing goal" by planning for future housing needs of all income levels. Gov't Code § 65581(a). *See Committee for Responsible Planning v. City of Indian Wells*, 209 Cal. App. 3d 1005, 1013 (1989); *Buena Vista Gardens Apartments Ass'n v. City of San Diego*, 175 Cal. App. 3d 289, 295 (1985).

REQUIRED CONTENTS OF THE HOUSING ELEMENT

While cities have considerable flexibility in drafting other elements of the general plan, the housing element must comply with detailed statutory provisions. *See* Gov't Code § 65580 *et seq*.

Government Code section 65583(a)–(c) sets forth an extensive list of the analyses, information, and programs that are required to be included in a city's housing element. Among other things, it must contain an assessment of the jurisdiction's existing and projected housing needs, including special needs of the elderly, the disabled, female-headed households, large families, farmworkers, homeless persons and families, and emergency shelters, as well as an inventory of resources and constraints relevant to meeting those needs. Gov't Code § 65583(a). The existing and projected needs assessment must include its share of the regional housing need in accordance with Government Code section 65584. It also must contain a land inventory (Gov't Code § 65583(a)(3)), and identify adequate sites to provide for the housing needs of households at all income levels.

The element must contain a program that sets forth actions, each with a timeline for implementation, the city intends to undertake during the planning period to implement the policies and achieve the identified goals and objectives. Gov't Code § 65583(c). In addition, it must include an analysis of governmental and non-governmental

---

[6] Millenial Housing Commission, *Meeting Our Nation's Housing Challenge* (2002) at 10, *available at* http://govinfo.library.unt.edu/mhc/MHCReport.pdf.

constraints (Gov't Code § 65583(c)(5)), and a statement of the community's goals, quantified objectives, and policies relative to the maintenance, preservation, improvement, and development of housing. Gov't Code § 65583(b)(1). *See Hoffmaster v. City of San Diego*, 55 Cal. App. 4th 1098, 1107 (1997); *Buena Vista Gardens*, 175 Cal. App. 3d at 302. If available resources are inadequate to satisfy a city's identified fair share housing needs, the city may set as its "quantified objectives" the maximum number of housing units by income category that can be constructed, rehabilitated, and conserved over a five-year period. Gov't Code § 65583 (b) (2). The housing element must contain quantitative analyses supporting these projections and the conclusion that the city cannot meet its acknowledged need for housing. *Hoffmaster*, 55 Cal. App. 4th at 1108.

REGIONAL HOUSING NEEDS ALLOCATION PROCESS

In recognition of the need to evaluate housing and growth issues in a regional context, state law has established a regional housing needs allocation (RHNA) process, which determines existing and projected housing needs during the planning period for each jurisdiction. Gov't Code § 65584 *et seq.*

RHNA = regional housing needs allocation

HCD = Department of Housing and Community Development

COG = Council of Government

The Department of Housing and Community Development (HCD), in consultation with each Council of Government (COG), determines the existing and projected housing needs for each region. Gov't Code § 65584.01 (describing the manner in which the needs determination shall be made). Then, the applicable COG determines each city's fair share of that regional housing need. Where a COG does not exist, this determination is made by HCD. Gov't Code § 65584(b). COGs are authorized under the law to charge a fee to cities to cover the projected reasonable, actual costs in completing the allocation process. A city also may charge a fee to developers to support the work of the planning agency and to reimburse it for the cost of any fee charged by the COG, although there are some limitations on cities in this regard. Gov't Code § 65584.1; Health & Safety Code §§ 17021.6, 18021.7, 50451, 50452, and 50453.

Each city's share of the regional housing need is further distributed among four income categories to ensure planning for all income levels. These categories are based on the percentage of an area's median income (i.e., the County's median income per Gov't Code § 65589.5(h)(4)), as periodically established by HCD pursuant to Health and Safety Code section 50093:

Income level	Percentage of median income
Very low income	0–50
Low income	51–80
Moderate income	81–120
Above moderate income	121+

Gov't Code §§ 65584(a)(1) & (e); Health & Safety Code §§ 50105, 50079.5, 50093

If a city disagrees with the COG's (or HCD's) initial determination, it must follow the applicable procedures contained in Government Code section 65584.05 or 65584.06 to obtain revisions.

Over time, the Legislature has significantly revised the allocation process to include: the establishment of overall policy objectives for the regional allocation; the requirement of COGs to incorporate specific factors into their methodologies; the inclusion of an alternative process to allocate housing needs to subregions; and the provision for a detailed process to determine the allocation, to allow for public participation, and to hear appeals. Gov't Code §§ 65584.01–65584.04.

The allocation plan must be consistent with the following objectives: (1) increasing the housing supply and the mix of housing types, tenure, and affordability within the region in an equitable manner, which must result in each jurisdiction receiving an allocation for low- and very low-income units; (2) promoting infill development and socioeconomic equity, the protection of environmental and agricultural resources, and the encouragement of efficient development patterns; (3) promoting an improved intraregional relationship between jobs and housing; and (4) allocating a lower proportion of housing needs to an income category when a jurisdiction already has a disproportionately high share of households in that category. Gov't Code § 65584(d).

To the extent sufficient data is available, the allocation methodology factors must include: existing and projected jobs and housing relationships; opportunities and constraints to development of additional housing in each member jurisdiction; household growth distribution and opportunities to maximize the use of public transportation; market demand for housing; city-county agreements to direct growth toward incorporated areas; loss of existing affordable units; high housing cost burdens; housing needs of farmworkers; housing needs generated by the presence of a university or college; and any other factors adopted by the COG. Gov't Code § 66584.04(d). Further, the law provides that any direct or indirect local growth control ordinances shall not be justification for reducing a city's share of the regional housing need.

Recent changes to the law emphasize the Legislature's intent that planning for housing be coordinated and integrated with the regional transportation plan. For further discussion, see Chapter 16 (Sustainable Development). To achieve this goal, the allocation plan shall allocate housing units consistent with the development pattern included in the region's sustainable communities' strategy (pursuant to Government Code section 65080 *et seq.*). Gov't Code § 65584.04(i)(1) The final allocation plan must ensure the total regional housing need by income category is maintained, and that each jurisdiction in the region receive an allocation of units for low- and very low-income households. The resolution approving the final housing need allocation plan must demonstrate that the plan is consistent with the development pattern included in the sustainable communities' strategy in the regional transportation plan. Gov't Code § 65584.04(i)(2) and (3).

The city shall provide an annual report to HCD that describes the city's progress in meeting its share of regional housing needs, the actions taken by the city towards removing constraints to the maintenance, improvement and development of housing and completion of the housing element programs, and the status of the city's compliance with deadlines in the housing element. Gov't Code § 65400(2)(A), (B).

PREPARING THE LAND INVENTORY AND IDENTIFYING ADEQUATE SITES

The housing element must demonstrate site development capacity equivalent to, or exceeding, the projected housing need. This requires preparation of a land inventory. Gov't Code § 65583(a)(3). The inventory's purpose is to identify specific sites suitable for residential development in order to compare the city's projected new housing need with its residential development capacity. The land inventory also must contain information regarding any environmental constraints and the availability of utilities, as well as other detailed site-specific information. Gov't Code § 65583.2(b).

The statute defines "land suitable for residential development" in an inventory as (1) vacant sites zoned for residential use; (2) vacant sites zoned for nonresidential use that also allows residential development; (3) underutilized residentially zoned sites that are capable of being developed at a higher density or with greater intensity; and (4) sites zoned for nonresidential use that can be redeveloped for, and as necessary, rezoned for, residential use. Gov't Code § 65583.2(a).

To substantially comply with the adequate sites requirement under Government Code section 65583(c)(1), a city must identify actions that will be taken to make sufficient sites available during the planning period—with appropriate zoning and development standards and with services and facilities—in an amount adequate to meet its regional fair share of housing need.[7] *See also City of Irvine v. S. Cal. Ass'n of Gov'ts*, 175 Cal. App. 4th 506, 513 (2009) and *Hoffmaster*, 55 Cal. App. 4th at 1111. This requires the city to provide specific information to demonstrate the identified sites actually will be available for development during the planning period, and that these sites will accommodate the amount of development the city has attributed to them. *Id. See* Gov't Code §§ 65583.2(b); 65583(c)(1)(B) (specifying the kind of information that must be included when a city identifies sites). *See also* 70 Ops. Cal. Atty. Gen. 231 (1987). As the *Hoffmaster* court emphasized when it found the City of San Diego's housing element inadequate:

> Substantial compliance with the legislative mandate requires more than merely designating every unoccupied mote within City's boundaries, each of which is subject to City-imposed developmental and separate restrictions....

55 Cal. App. 4th at 1111.

In *Hoffmaster*, the plaintiffs challenged the City of San Diego's housing element on the ground that it failed to identify adequate sites that would be made available as part of a plan designed to facilitate development of homeless emergency shelters and transitional housing. San Diego's housing element merely identified in its land inventory the amount of "available" land zoned at various density levels, and then assumed the maximum possible buildout to support its claim that it could meet its projected housing need. The court acknowledged that as a matter of mathematics, the amount of acreage identified, if truly "available," could satisfy the city's housing need for all income groups. However, the court emphasized that the law requires more. To demonstrate the adequacy of the sites for residential development that it has identified, a site-specific analysis should consider the following analysis by the *Hoffmaster* court:

> An adequate site is one available for immediate development, which is located within reasonable access to public agencies and transportation services; will not require unusually high site development costs; has available public services and facilities; is consistent with the general plan designation and site zoning so as to permit the development of...housing without undue regulatory approval; and is consistent with applicable parking requirements, fire regulations and design standards.

Id.; cf. St. Vincent's Sch. for Boys, Catholic Charities CYO v. City of San Rafael, 161 Cal. App. 4th 989, 1012 (2008) (housing element law does not require city to demonstrate substantial compliance by showing how its housing strategy will "actually produce" a specific number of units).

In instances where the land inventory does not identify sites sufficient to meet the city's share of the regional housing need for groups of all household income levels,

> A city must identify actions that will be taken to make sufficient sites available during the planning period—with appropriate zoning and development standards and with services and facilities—in an amount adequate to meet its regional fair share of housing need.

---

[7] *See also* Cal. Dep't of Housing and Cmty. Dev., *Housing Element Questions and Answers: A Guide to the Preparation of Housing Elements* (2006) at 36-57, *available at* http://sustainca.org/content/housing_element_questions_and_answers_guide_preparation_housing_elements.

sites must be identified in the housing element and then rezoned for development, including adoption of minimum density and development standards. Gov't Code § 65583(c)(1)(A)

For cities with an eight-year planning period (pursuant to Government Code section 65588), such rezoning must be completed no later than three years after the element is adopted by the City Council, or three years and 120 days after the city's statutory deadline for adopting a housing element if the city fails to adopt a housing element by the deadline. *Id.* Those sites identified to meet the needs of very low- and low-income households as determined by the RHNA process discussed above must be rezoned to allow owner-occupied and rental multifamily residential "use by right," with minimum density and development standards that permit at least 16 to 20 units per acre. Gov't Code § 65583.2(h). Once a site is rezoned, the city cannot require a conditional use permit, planned unit development permit, or other discretionary approval that would constitute a "project" for purposes of CEQA. However, the Subdivision Map Act still applies, and cities may require design review subject to certain restrictions. Gov't Code § 65583.2(i).

If a city fails to complete the rezoning within the mandated timeframe, it will be prohibited from: (1) disapproving a housing development project; (2) requiring a discretionary approval (e.g., conditional use permit, planned unit development permit); or (3) imposing a condition that would render the project infeasible, if the project is proposed on a site required to be rezoned and complies with the applicable, objective general plan and zoning standards and criteria. The only exception to such prohibitions is if the city can make findings that: (1) the project would have a specific adverse impact upon the public health or safety; and (2) there is no feasible method to mitigate that impact. Gov't Code § 65583(g)(1), (2). For purposes of this section, "housing development project" means a project to construct residential units for which the developer provides sufficient legal commitments to the city to ensure the continued availability and use of at least 49 percent of the units for very low-, low-, and moderate-income households. Gov't Code § 65583(g)(4). The project applicant or any interested person may bring an action to enforce these provisions. Gov't Code § 65583(g)(3). If the court finds the city disapproved or conditioned a project in violation of section 65583(g)(2), it shall issue an order compelling compliance within 60 days and shall return jurisdiction to ensure its order is carried out and if not, may issue further orders to ensure compliance. Gov't Code § 65583(g)(3). The city bears the burden of proof in such action. *Id.*

If a city in a prior planning period failed to identify or make available adequate sites to accommodate its fair share of regional housing needs, then the city is required, in its next housing element, within the first year of the planning period, to zone or rezone adequate sites to accommodate the unaccommodated portion of regional housing need allocation from the prior planning period. Gov't Code § 65584.09.

ANALYSIS OF GOVERNMENTAL AND NON-GOVERNMENTAL CONSTRAINTS

In preparing a housing element, potential and actual governmental constraints upon the maintenance, improvement, or development of housing for persons of all income levels and for persons with disabilities must be analyzed. Gov't Code § 65583(a)(5). For each policy, requirement, or procedure identified as a governmental constraint, the element must include an appropriate action program to modify or eliminate the

CEQA = California Environmental Quality Act

constraint or demonstrate how its impacts will be effectively offset. HCD provides a number of strategies that communities may use to reduce or eliminate regulatory barriers, including modifications to land use controls, codes, and enforcement procedures, on- and off-site improvement requirements, fees and exactions, and processing and permit procedures. HCD's "Building Blocks for Effective Housing Elements" reference materials provide helpful implementation information.[8]

Housing elements also must identify and mitigate to the extent feasible nongovernmental constraints, such as land prices, construction costs, and financing availability. Gov't Code § 65583(a)(6). HCD recognizes that although nongovernmental constraints are primarily market-driven and generally outside direct government control, cities can significantly influence and offset the negative impact of such constraints through responsive programs and policies.

CONSISTENCY WITH GENERAL PLAN, PREPARATION OF ANNUAL REPORT, AND NOTIFICATION REQUIREMENTS

Other housing element requirements that must be satisfied include: (1) maintaining consistency with other elements of the city's general plan (Gov't Code § 65300.5); (2) preparing an annual report to the legislative body, the Office of Planning and Research (OPR), and HCD (Gov't Code § 65400(a)(2)); and (3) notifying retail water and sewer providers upon the completion of an amended or adopted housing element. Gov't Code § 65589.7.

OPR = Office of Planning and Research

With respect to the consistency requirement, a city is not required to ensure an adopted housing element be consistent with other elements of its general plan upon adoption of the updated element. In *Friends of Aviara v. City of Carlsbad*, the court held that so long as a city adopts a timeline to achieve future consistency, as required by Government Code section 65583(c)(7), such temporary inconsistency is lawful. 210 Cal. App. 4th 1103, 1112-1113 (2012). The *Aviara* court recognized the legislature manifested a clear preference that municipalities adopt a housing plan to meet the city's urgent housing obligations, even at the cost of creating temporary general plan inconsistencies. *Id.*

With respect to the annual report requirement, each planning agency, after a general plan has been adopted, must provide an annual report, on or before April 1st of each year, to the legislative body, OPR, and HCD on the status of the general plan and the city's progress in meeting its share of regional housing needs and local efforts to remove governmental constraints. The report must include the degree to which the approved general plan complies with OPR's general plan guidelines and the date of the last revision to the general plan. Gov't Code § 65400(b)(3). If litigation is brought, a court is required to issue an order or judgment compelling compliance with this reporting requirement within 60 days, if the housing element portion of the report is untimely. Gov't Code § 65400(c).

SPECIAL PROVISIONS REGARDING HOUSING NEEDS WITHIN THE COASTAL ZONE

Special attention is given to housing needs within the state's coastal zone. *See* Gov't Code §§ 65588(d), 65590, and 65590.1. When coastal zone jurisdictions review their housing elements, such reviews must provide the following additional information:

---

[8] This publication is available at http://www.hcd.ca.gov/hpd/housing_element/.

- The number of new housing units approved for construction within the coastal zone
- The number of housing units for persons and families of low and moderate income required to be provided in new housing developments either within the coastal zone or within three miles of it
- The number of existing residential units occupied by low- and moderate-income households that have been authorized to be demolished or converted in the coastal zone
- The number and location of residential units for low- and moderate-income households that have been required for replacement of those units being demolished or converted in the coastal zone

Gov't Code §§ 65588(d)(1-4)

The case of *Coalition of Concerned Cmtys, Inc. v. City of Los Angeles*, involved a question of the interpretation of a California statute (Gov't Code § 65590(d)) that imposes an inclusionary requirement on new housing developments constructed within the coastal zone. 34 Cal. 4th 733 (2004). Plaintiff citizen groups claimed this provision applied to a proposed project located partially within the coastal zone, even though no housing units would actually be constructed within that zone.

The court rejected this contention, holding that the inclusionary requirement does not apply if the development does not propose to construct any housing or private amenities within the coastal zone. In the case at hand, the project included only construction of infrastructure and a public view park within the coastal zone. The court determined that since the project did not affect existing affordable housing or have a new housing impact within the zone the statute did not apply. *Id.* at 739. The court, however, did leave open the possibility the inclusionary requirement might apply if the project proposed to build private amenities within the coastal zone, such as a golf course or other sporting facility.

REVIEW, CERTIFICATION, AND LEGAL ADEQUACY OF HOUSING ELEMENTS

The housing element shall be reviewed "as frequently as appropriate" in order to evaluate the appropriateness of the housing goals, objectives, and policies, the element's effectiveness, and the progress made in implementation of the housing element. Gov't Code § 65588(a). Recent changes in the law have modified the timeframe for revising a housing element. Previously, housing elements needed to be revised as necessary, but not less frequently than once every five years. This timing has been modified to provide that, except under certain limited circumstances, the housing element shall be revised as appropriate—but not less frequently than every eight years—in those cities that are located within (1) a metropolitan planning organization in a region classified as nonattainment for one or more pollutants regulated by the federal Clean Air Act; or (2) a metropolitan planning organization or regional transportation planning agency that has elected to adopt a regional transportation plan not less than every four years. A city that does not adopt a housing element within 120 days of the statutory deadline shall revise its housing element as appropriate, but not less frequently than every four years. All cities not subject to the four-year or eight-year revision schedules shall revise their housing elements at five-year intervals. Gov't Code § 65588 (a), (e).

The above-described revision schedule is unique to the housing element. The remainder of the general plan need be reviewed only periodically and updated only when warranted by changing circumstances. Gov't Code § 65103(a). *See also Citizens* of Goleta Valley v. Board of Supervisors, 52 Cal. 3d 553, 572 (1990); *Garat v. City of Riverside*, 2 Cal. App. 4th 259, 298 (1991), disapproved on other grounds by *Morehart v. County of Santa Barbara*, 7 Cal. 4th 725 (1994) with the timetable for cities to revise their housing elements as set forth in Government Code sections 65588 and 65588.1. Failure to comply does not automatically invalidate a general plan or its housing element. *San Mateo County Coastal Landowners' Ass'n v. County of San Mateo*, 38 Cal. App. 4th 523, 544 (1995). Rather, to invalidate a housing element on the basis that it has not been timely revised, a plaintiff must show how the failure to timely revise the housing element is connected to a substantive deficiency in the general plan or the housing element.

In preparing its housing element, a city must consider the guidelines adopted by HCD. However, these guidelines are advisory only. Gov't Code § 65585(a). Prior to adopting or amending the housing element, a city must submit a draft of the element to HCD for review. HCD must prepare written findings regarding whether the draft substantially complies with the statutory provisions.

A city must consider HCD's findings before adopting or amending its housing element, unless the findings are not available within specified time limits. If HCD finds that the draft does not comply with the law, the city may change the draft to substantially comply or adopt it without changes. If the city elects to adopt it without changes, then its resolution of adoption must include written findings explaining its conclusions that the draft substantially complies with the law despite HCD's findings to the contrary. Gov't Code § 65585(f).

> If HCD finds that a city's draft housing element does not comply with the law, the city may change the draft to substantially comply or adopt it without changes.

There are several effects of a determination by HCD that a housing element substantially complies with the state's housing laws. First, such a finding creates a rebuttable presumption of the housing element's validity in any court challenge. Gov't Code § 65589.3. Second, a city, with certain exceptions, is prohibited from reducing, requiring, or permitting the reduction of residential density for *any parcel* to a "lower residential density." Gov't Code § 65863(b). If a city's housing element has been determined in substantial compliance by HCD, "lower residential density" means the following: (a) for sites on which the zoning designation permits residential use and that are identified in the city's inventory, fewer units on the site than were projected by the city to be accommodated on the site pursuant to section 65583.2(c); and (b) for sites that have been or will be rezoned, fewer units for the site than were projected to be developed on the site in the housing element program. Gov't Code § 65863(g)(1). If the city has not adopted a housing element for the current planning period, or if the adopted housing element has not been found to be in substantial compliance with the housing element law, "lower residential density" means the following: for residential zoning sites, a density below 80 percent of the maximum allowable residential density for the parcel; and for sites on which residential and nonresidential uses are permitted, a use that would result in the development of fewer than 80 percent of the number of residential units that would be allowed under the maximum residential density for that site. Gov't Code § 65863(g)(2).

A city may allow for a reduction of residential density if it makes the following findings supported by substantial evidence:
- The reduction is consistent with the adopted general plan, including the housing element
- The remaining sites identified in the housing element are adequate to accommodate the city's share of regional housing needs

Gov't Code § 65863(b)(1), (2)

Alternatively, the reduction may be approved if a city can establish through written findings based on substantial evidence that there are "sufficient, additional, adequate, and available sites with an equal or greater residential density in the jurisdiction so that there is no net loss of residential unit capacity." Gov't Code § 65863(e). An amendment to the "no downzoning" law makes the city solely responsible for compliance, unless the applicant initially requests the reduction in zoning density. Gov't Code § 65863(c). The law also clarifies that development agreements and applications for subdivision maps made prior to January 1, 2003 are not subject to this statute. Gov't Code § 65863(f). If a plaintiff is successful in challenging a city's action under this statute, the court shall award reasonable attorneys' fees and costs except under limited circumstances. *Id.* HCD issues a Housing Element Compliance Report, as required by Health and Safety Code section 54059(c).[9]

In evaluating the adequacy of a housing element, a court will limit its review to determining whether a city has "substantially complied" with the statutory requirements. Gov't Code § 65587(b). "Substantial compliance means *actual* compliance in respect to the substance essential to every reasonable objective of the statute, as distinguished from mere technical imperfections of form." *Camp v. Board of Supervisors*, 123 Cal. App. 3d 334, 348 (1981). *See also Hoffmaster*, 55 Cal. App. 4th at 1111 (providing guidance regarding what constitutes "substantial compliance"). A court is prohibited, however, from probing the merits or wisdom of the housing element. *See Hernandez v. City of Encinitas*, 28 Cal. App. 4th 1048, 1067-68 (1994) (a city's housing element withstood attack by low-income and homeless petitioners since it substantially complied with statutory requirements). If a court finds that an action taken by a city does not comply with its housing element, the city must bring its action into compliance within 60 days, unless it can make a showing of undue hardship, in which case the court may extend this deadline by 60 days. Gov't Code § 65587(c). If a city fails to adopt the required rezonings, the court shall issue an order or judgment, after considering the equities presented by all the parties, compelling the city to do so within 60 days or the earliest time consistent with public noticing requirements. Gov't Code § 65587(d)(1). An action to compel compliance shall be brought pursuant to Civil Code of Procedure section 1085, and may be brought pursuant to the notice and accrual provisions of Government Code section 65009(d). In any such action, the city shall bear the burden of proof. Gov't Code § 65587(d)(2).

RESTRICTIONS ON THE DISAPPROVAL OF CERTAIN HOUSING PROJECTS

In 1982, in response to the housing crisis, which was viewed as threatening the "economic, environmental and social quality of life in California," the Legislature enacted Government Code section 65589.5. Commonly referred to as the "Anti-Nimby" legislation, but officially named the "Housing Accountability Act" by legislation passed in 2006, this statute restricts a city's ability to disapprove, or require density reductions in, certain types of residential projects.[10] The Housing Accountability Act's requirement to make findings applies by its terms to any "housing development project," which is defined to include any project consisting of "residential units only" and is not limited

---

9 *See* Div. of Housing Policy Dev., Dep't of Housing and Cmty. Dev., *Housing Element Compliance Report* (2012), available at http://www.hcd.ca.gov/hpd/hrc/plan/he/status.pdf.

10 *See also* Gov't Code § 65008 (action by a city is "null and void" if it denies an individual, or a group of individuals, the enjoyment of residence, landownership, tenancy, or any other land use for enumerated reasons including intended occupancy of a residential development by persons of very low, low, moderate, or middle income).

to projects that include affordable units. *Honchariw v. County of Stanislaus*, 200 Cal. App. 4th 1066, 1073 (2011) (Housing Accountability Act prohibited the county from denying a subdivision map for a housing project in absence of specific findings and evidentiary support, even though the project did not include any affordable units.)

The basis of this statute is the Legislature's finding that "the excessive cost of the state's housing supply is partially caused by activities and policies of many local governments that limit the approval of housing, increase the cost of land for housing, and require that high fees and exactions be paid by producers of housing." Gov't Code § 65589.5(a)(2). The purpose of the legislation is to help ensure that a city "not reject or make infeasible housing developments, including emergency shelters, that contribute to meeting the housing need determined pursuant to [Housing Element Law] without a thorough analysis of the economic, social, and environmental effects of the action and without complying with subdivision (d)." Gov't Code § 65589.5(b).

Although this statute affords various protections to certain affordable housing projects (Gov't Code § 65589.5(d)) and certain housing projects generally (Gov't Code § 65589.5(j)), it does not relieve a city from complying with provisions of the Congestion Management Program, the California Coastal Act, CEQA, or other state or local requirements. Gov't Code § 65589.5(e). It also does not limit a city's ability to impose fees or exactions otherwise authorized by law that are essential to provide necessary public services and facilities to the project. Gov't Code § 65589.5(f). Further, it does not prohibit a city from enforcing written development standards, conditions, and policies appropriate to, and consistent with, meeting the jurisdiction's share of the regional housing need. However, the standards relied upon must be "objective" and "quantifiable," and must be applied to facilitate and accommodate development at the density permitted on the site and proposed by the project. *Id.*

The Housing Accountability Act provides that the court shall award reasonable attorneys' fees and costs of suit to the plaintiff or petitioner who successfully challenges the disapproval or improper conditioning of a project under the Act. Gov't Code § 65589.5(k). However, this attorneys' fees provision has been interpreted to apply only to successful challenges involving housing development projects containing affordable housing, not those involving housing development projects generally. *Honchariw v. County of Stanislaus*, 218 Cal. App. 4th 1019, 1037 (2013) (ambiguity in the plain language of section 65589.5(k) prompts reliance on legislative history, which indicates attorneys' fees provision was intended to be limited to cases involving affordable housing projects).

> The Housing Accountability Act does not limit a city's ability to impose fees or exactions otherwise authorized by law that are essential to provide necessary public services and facilities to a project.

DISAPPROVAL RESTRICTIONS ON AFFORDABLE HOUSING PROJECTS

Under Government Code section 65589.5(d), a city may not disapprove a housing development project[11] affordable to very low-, low-, or moderate-income households, or emergency shelters, or condition approval of such a project in a manner that makes the project infeasible, unless it finds, based on substantial evidence, one of the following:

- The city has adopted a housing element that has been revised in accordance with Government Code section 65588, is in substantial compliance with the

---

11 For purposes of this statute, "housing development project" means a use consisting of: (1) residential units only, (2) mixed-use developments consisting of residential and nonresidential uses in which the nonresidential uses are limited to neighborhood commercial uses and to the first floor of buildings that are two or more stories, or (3) transitional housing or supportive housing. Gov't Code § 65589.5(h)(2). At least one court has held that a specific plan, rejected by the voters by the referendum process, does not constitute a "housing development project." *Chandis Sec. Co. v. City of Dana Point,* 52 Cal. App. 4th 475, 486–87 (1996).

Housing Element law, and the city has met or exceeded its share of the regional housing need for the income category proposed for the housing development project (if it includes a mix of income categories, and the jurisdiction has not met its fair share housing needs, then this paragraph cannot be used as a basis to deny or condition approval)

- The project as proposed would have a specific adverse impact upon the public health and safety that cannot be satisfactorily mitigated without rendering the housing development project unaffordable, or development of the emergency shelter financially infeasible; inconsistency with the zoning ordinance or general plan land use designation shall not constitute a specific, adverse impact upon public health and safety
- The denial of the project or imposition of conditions is required in order to comply with state or federal law (e.g., CEQA), and there is no feasible method to comply without rendering the housing development project unaffordable or development of the emergency shelter financially infeasible
- The project is proposed on land zoned for agriculture or resource preservation that is surrounded on at least two sides by land being used for agriculture or preservation purposes, or the site does not have an adequate water or wastewater facility to serve the project
- The project is inconsistent with both the city's zoning ordinance and general plan land use designation as specified in the general plan as it existed on the date the application was deemed complete, and the city has adopted a revised housing element in accordance with section 65588 that is in substantial compliance with the Housing Element law

In the absence of such findings, Government Code section 65589.5(d)(5)(A) limits a city's discretion to deny a housing development project if it is proposed on a site that is identified as suitable or available for very low, low-, or moderate-income households in the city's housing element and is consistent with the density specified in the city's housing element, even though it is inconsistent with *both* the city's zoning ordinance and general plan land use designation. Moreover, a city cannot disapprove an affordable housing development by declaring it is not needed unless the community has actually met its fair share housing needs. This provision is intended to preclude a city from relying on speculative projects not yet approved to justify denial.

To qualify for the protections provided by Government Code section 65589.5(d), an affordable housing project must propose development of housing for "very low-, low- or moderate-income households," which includes:

- Projects in which at least 20 percent of the total units shall be sold or rented to lower income households (as defined in Health and Safety Code section 50079.5)
- Project in which 100 percent of the units shall be sold or rented to moderate-income households (as defined in Health and Safety Code section 50093), or to middle-income households (as defined in Government Code section 65008)
- Supportive housing, transitional housing, and certain mixed use projects as defined in the Code

Gov't Code § 65589.5(h)(3)

Housing units targeted for lower income households must be made available at a monthly housing cost that does not exceed 30 percent of 60 percent of the median income for the area, adjusted for family size. Housing units targeted for moderate-income households shall be made available at a monthly housing cost that does not exceed 30 percent of 100 percent of median income for the area, adjusted for family size. Gov't Code § 65589.5(h)(3). In addition, the developer must provide sufficient legal commitments to ensure continued affordability of low- and very low-income units for 30 years. Gov't Code § 65589.5(h)(4).

The applicant for the housing development project or any person who would be eligible to apply for residency in the development may bring an action to enforce this law. Gov't Code § 65589.5(k). In any legal action challenging a city's denial or conditional approval of an affordable housing project under Government Code section 65589.5(d), the city shall have the burden of proof to show that its decision is consistent with the requisite findings and supported by substantial evidence. Gov't Code § 65589.5(i). If the city cannot meet this burden, then the court shall issue an order compelling compliance within 60 days, including, without limitation, an order to take action on the proposed project. The court shall retain jurisdiction to ensure its order or judgment is carried out and shall award reasonable attorneys' fees and costs of the suit to the petitioner, except under extraordinary circumstances in which the court finds that awarding fees would not further the purposes of the statute. If the court determines that its order or judgment has not been carried out within 60 days, the court may issue further orders to ensure the purposes and policies of this law are fulfilled, including vacating the city's decision, deeming the project approved, and imposing fines if the court finds that the city acted in bad faith. Gov't Code § 65589.5(k). As described in the preceding section, the attorneys' fees provision of section 65589.5(k) has been held to apply only to successful challenges involving housing development projects that include affordable housing. *Honchariw*, 218 Cal. App. 4th at 1037.

DISAPPROVAL OF HOUSING DEVELOPMENT PROJECTS GENERALLY

Under Government Code section 65589.5(j), a city's ability to deny approval or impose conditions on housing development projects that do not contain the required affordable housing also may be restricted under certain circumstances. When a proposed housing development project complies with applicable, objective general plan and zoning standards and criteria, the city shall not disapprove the project or condition approval on a density reduction unless it makes written findings based upon substantial evidence that both of the following conditions exist:

- The housing project would have a specific, adverse impact upon the public health and safety unless the project is disapproved or approved only on condition that the project be developed at a lower density. "Specific, adverse impact" is defined as "a significant, quantifiable, direct, and unavoidable impact, based on objective, identified written public health or safety standards, policies, or conditions...." Gov't Code § 65589.5(j)(1), and
- There is no feasible way to satisfactorily mitigate or avoid the adverse impact identified, other than the disapproval of the project or the approval conditioned on developing the project at a lower density. Gov't Code § 65589.5(j)(2)

There is no requirement under subsection (j) that the development project contain any affordable units. *Sequoyah Hills Homeowners Ass'n v. City of Oakland*, 23 Cal. App. 4th 704, 715-16 (1993) (when there are findings that a proposed residential project complies with all general plan and zoning policies, Government Code section 65589.5 prevents a city from requiring a reduction in the density of the project without first establishing the project poses a "specific adverse impact upon the public health or safety"). *See also North Pacifica, LLC v. City of Pacifica*, 234 F. Supp. 2d 1053, 1057 (N.D.

Cal. 2002) (Government Code section 65589.5(j) applies to all "housing development projects" regardless of the income level of the intended occupants).

PRIORITIZATION OF SERVICES TO CERTAIN AFFORDABLE HOUSING PROJECTS

Each public agency or private entity providing water or sewer services must grant a priority for the provision of available and future resources or services to proposed housing developments that help meet a city's affordable housing needs. These service providers must adopt a written policy with "specific objective standards" for allocation of water and sewer services to affordable housing developments. In addition, such service providers are prohibited from denying, conditioning approval, or reducing the amount of service for a proposed affordable housing development unless certain findings are made. Gov't Code § 65589.7.

CERTAIN MULTIFAMILY HOUSING PROJECTS MAY BE A PERMITTED USE

Pursuant to Government Code section 65589.4, under certain circumstances, attached housing developments shall be a permitted use not subject to a conditional use permit on any parcel zoned for attached housing. This law applies to a broad range of projects, including all attached housing developments (with the exception of second units and existing structures converted to condominiums) with two or more units. This law is applicable to charter cities.

To qualify under this statute, the project must meet one of the following affordability criteria:

- At least 10 percent of the project's units shall be affordable to very low-income households, as defined in Health and Safety Code section 50105
- At least 20 percent of the project's units shall be affordable to lower-income households, as defined in Health and Safety Code section 50079.5, or
- At least 50 percent of the project's units shall be affordable to moderate-income households, consistent with Health and Safety Code section 50052.5

Gov't Code § 65589.4(b)

The developer must provide sufficient legal commitments to ensure the units will remain affordable for a period of at least 30 years. In addition to satisfying the affordability criteria specified above, the project must either:

- Qualify for one of three CEQA exemptions relating to the development of housing for agricultural employees (Pub. Res. Code § 21159.22), certain small affordable projects (Pub. Res. Code § 21159.23), or certain infill projects (Pub. Res. Code § 21159.24), or
- Meet all of the following criteria:
  - The project is subject to a discretionary decision other than a conditional use permit, and a negative declaration or mitigated negative declaration has been adopted for the project under CEQA
  - The project is consistent with both the city's zoning ordinance and general plan as it existed on the date the project application was deemed complete, except that a project shall not be deemed to be inconsistent with the general plan only because the project site has not been rezoned to conform with the most recent adopted general plan
  - The project is located in an area that is covered by one of the following documents that has been adopted by the city within five years of the date the

project application was deemed complete: (1) a general plan; (2) a revision or update to the general plan that includes at least the land use and circulation elements; (3) an applicable community plan; or (4) an applicable specific plan

- The project consists of not more than 100 residential units with a minimum density of not less than 12 units per acre or a minimum density of not less than 8 units per acre if the project consists of 4 or fewer units
- The project is located in an urbanized area (as defined in Pub. Res. Code § 21071), or within a census-defined place with a population density of at least 5,000 persons per square mile, or, if the project consists of 50 or fewer units, within an incorporated city with a population density of at least 2,500 persons per square mile and a total population of at least 25,000 persons
- The project is located on an infill site (as defined in Pub. Res. Code § 21061.0.5)

However, a city is not prohibited from applying design and site review standards in existence on the date the application was determined complete. Gov't Code § 65589.4(c)

OTHER STATE LAWS DESIGNED TO FACILITATE HOUSING PRODUCTION

In addition to state housing element provisions, the Legislature has provided a number of reforms and incentives to encourage development of affordable housing. Gov't Code § 65582.1 (cataloging such laws).

LEAST COST ZONING LAW

State laws have been enacted in order to (1) expedite the entitlement process; (2) assure that cities zone sufficient land at densities high enough for affordable housing production; and (3) assure that cities make a diligent effort to significantly reduce development costs and facilitate the development of affordable housing.

Under Government Code section 65913.1, commonly known as the "Least Cost Zoning" law, cities must designate and zone sufficient vacant land with "appropriate standards" for residential use to meet the housing needs of all income levels. Gov't Code § 65913.1. This requirement is in addition to the mandate under Government Code section 65583(c)(1) imposed upon cities to identify adequate sites in their housing elements to meet fair share housing needs.

Under Government Code section 65913.1, "appropriate standards" means densities and requirements imposed on residential lots that contribute significantly to the economic feasibility of producing housing at the lowest possible cost including requirements with respect to minimum floor areas, building setbacks, rear and side yards, parking, the percentage of a lot that must be occupied by a structure, and amenities. These standards must take into consideration economic and environmental factors, public health and safety, and the need to facilitate the development of affordable housing.

> Under the "Least Cost Zoning" law, cities must designate and zone sufficient vacant land with "appropriate standards" for residential use to meet the housing needs of all income levels.

DENSITY BONUSES

Density bonuses for affordable housing are addressed in Government Code section 65915 *et seq.* A density bonus means an increase in density over the otherwise maximum allowable residential density. Gov't Code § 65917.5(2). The Legislature adopted this law to "encourage, to the maximum extent practicable, the location of housing developed pursuant to [Density Bonus Law] in urban areas with adequate infrastructure to serve the housing." This law requires a city to grant a density bonus and a certain number of concessions or incentives to a developer who agrees to construct certain housing developments that provide either affordable or senior housing and meet certain criteria.[12] Gov't Code § 65915(a), (b)(1). *See also Wollmer v. City of Berkeley*, 193 Cal. App. 4th 1329 (2011) (density bonus laws allow developers to receive a density bonus for renting to Section 8 tenants even though property owners would receive Section 8 subsidies in addition to receiving "affordable rents" capped under state law); *Friends of Lagoon Valley*, 154 Cal. App. 4th 807 (2007); *Shea Homes Ltd. P'ship v. County of Alameda*, 110 Cal. App. 4th 1246, 1263 (2003) (density bonus laws "reward a developer who agrees to build a certain percentage of low-income housing with the opportunity to build more residences than would otherwise be permitted by the applicable local regulations"). In addition, this law requires a city to adopt an ordinance that specifies how local compliance to the state density bonus law will be implemented, although failure to adopt such an ordinance shall not relieve the city from complying with the law.

The density bonus law provides for greater bonuses as a project's number of affordable units increases. Over time, the law has been modified to reduce the percentage of units required to earn the density bonus, while increasing both the level of density bonus and the incentives and concessions the city must provide. A city must grant a density bonus when a developer applies to reserve 10 percent of its development for low-income households, or 5 percent for very low-income households. Gov't Code § 65915(b)(1)(A)–(B). There is, however, no density bonus for reserving units for moderate-income households, except in the context of common interest developments where all of the units, including the moderate-income units, are available for sale to the public. Gov't Code § 65915(b)(1)(D). In addition, a city must grant a bonus if a developer applies to develop any senior citizen housing development with at least 35 units, including mobile home parks that limit residence by age. A city may not condition availability of a density bonus upon provision of more affordable units than the minimum number required by the Density Bonus Law. *Latinos Unidos del Valle de Napa y Solano v. County of Napa*, 217 Cal. App. 4th 1160, 1169 (2013) (implementing ordinance that failed to credit affordable units satisfying the county's inclusionary requirements towards satisfaction of state density bonus thresholds and thus requires developer to dedicate larger percentage of units than required by section 65915 violates the Density Bonus Law and is void).

For purposes of determining whether a project would qualify for a density bonus, "total units" does not include units added by a density bonus awarded pursuant to section 65915 or any local law granting a greater density bonus.

To qualify for a density bonus, the applicant must propose to construct a housing development meeting certain criteria. The definition of "housing development" means development projects for five or more residential units, which shall be on contiguous sites that are the subject of one development application, but do not have to be based upon individual subdivision maps or parcels. This on has been expanded over time as well to include a subdivision or a common interest development. Gov't Code § 65915(i). If an applicant qualifies, it must be granted, except under certain limited circumstances, at least one development concession or incentive. These may include the following:

---

[12] For the American Planning Association's model density bonus ordinance, see Marya Morris, *Smart Codes (PAS 556): Model Land-Development Regulations* (2009).

- A reduction in site development standards
- A modification of zoning code requirements or architectural design requirements that exceed the minimum building standards
- Approval of mixed-use zoning in conjunction with the housing project if commercial, office, industrial, or other land uses will reduce the cost of the housing development, and if such nonresidential uses are compatible with the project and the existing and planned development in the area
- Other regulatory incentives or concessions proposed by the developer or the city that result in identifiable, financially sufficient, and actual cost reductions

The amount of density bonus depends on how many affordable units are reserved. If a developer reserves 10 percent of its project for low-income units, state law mandates the developer must receive a 20 percent density bonus. For every 1 percent beyond the minimum amount, the developer will receive an addition 1.5 percent density bonus, up to a maximum of 35 percent. Gov't Code § 65915(g). While state law sets 35 percent as the maximum amount that local agencies can be required to provide, cities may decide to provide an additional density bonus above this amount. Gov't Code § 65915(n). *See also Friends of Lagoon Valley*, 154 Cal. App. 4th at 825. All fractional results will be rounded up to the next whole number. Gov't Code § 65915(q). If a developer reserves 5 percent of its project for very low-income housing, state law mandates the developer must receive a 20 percent density bonus. For every 1 percent beyond the minimum amount, state law mandates the developer must receive an additional 2.5 percent density bonus, up to a maximum of 35 percent. Gov't Code § 65915(q).

The provision of direct financial incentives for such housing by the city is not limited or required, and the waiver of fees or dedication requirements may be retained. Gov't Code § 65915(l).

To deny a particular concession or incentive requested by the applicant, the city must adopt findings that the particular concession or incentive is not needed to achieve affordability or would threaten public health and safety or a historic structure, or would be contrary to state or federal law. Gov't Code § 65915(d)(1). *See also Building Indus. Ass'n v. City of Oceanside*, 27 Cal. App. 4th 744, 755–66 (1994) (zoning initiative that imposed a numerical residential growth cap conflicted with Government Code section 65915). If a city is unable to make these findings and still refuses to grant the required incentives or concessions, the developer may initiate judicial proceedings. In such a proceeding, a court must award reasonable attorneys' fees and costs of suit if the plaintiff succeeds in showing that a city violated the statute. Gov't Code §§ 65915(d)(1) and (e).

Affordability rates and processing requirements are set forth in Government Code section 65915(c). The requirement that the developer and the city agree to the continued affordability of moderate-income units for 10 years has been removed, although the 30-year affordability requirement for the low- and very low-income units which qualified the applicant for the density bonus has been retained. However, the developer must agree, and the city must ensure, that the initial occupants of moderate-income units meet the moderate-income standard, as statutorily defined. Upon the subsequent sale of such units, the seller is allowed to keep the value of any improvements, the down payment, and an allocated share of appreciation. The city also may recapture an allocated share of appreciation, but must use that share within five years for the promotion of affordable home ownership. Upon the developer's request, the city is prohibited from requiring parking standards greater than one on-site parking space for units with zero to one bedroom, two on-site spaces for two- to three-bedroom units, and 2.5 parking spaces for units with four or more bedrooms. Cities may grant density bonuses greater than what is provided in the statute or lower in cases where the statutory requirements are not met.

The law also provides a 15 percent density bonus for the entire project to the developer of any market-rate housing project who donates land to a city that could accommodate housing for very low-income households equal to at least 10 percent of the number of units in the market-rate development. Gov't Code § 65915(g). To be eligible for this bonus, the applicant must donate and transfer the land no later than the approval of the final subdivision map, parcel map, or development application. The transferred land also must be at least one acre or of sufficient size to accommodate 40 units and be located within, or if the city agrees, within one-quarter mile of, the proposed development. The land must be subject to deed restrictions ensuring continued affordability and must be donated to the city or to a developer approved by the city. Further, it must have the appropriate general plan designation, be appropriately zoned with development standards for development at the requisite density, have the necessary permits and approvals, and the ability to be served by infrastructure.

In addition, when an applicant proposes to construct a project that conforms to the requirements of the statute and includes a child care facility that will be located on the premises of, as part of, or adjacent to the project, the city shall grant either an additional density bonus equal to or greater than the square footage of the child care facility, or an additional concession or incentive that contributes significantly to the economic feasibility of the construction of the child care facility. Gov't Code § 65915(h)(1). An applicant must meet certain conditions in order to receive the additional child care density bonus, including: (1) continued operation of the facility for a duration of time equal in length to the period of time the affordable units within the project must remain affordable; and (2) a requirement that, of the children who attend the facility, the children of very low-income households, lower-income households, and moderate-income households shall constitute a percentage that is equal to or greater than the percentage of affordable units required to qualify for the density bonus. Gov't Code § 65915(i)(2).

There also are incentives for low-income housing development provided for in connection with condominium conversions. Gov't Code § 65915.5.

To ensure its purposes are implemented, the Density Bonus Law prevents a city from applying any development standard that would have the effect of physically precluding development of a project that otherwise qualifies for the bonus. Gov't Code § 65915(e)(1). "Development Standard" includes a site or construction condition including a height limitation, a setback requirement, a floor area ratio, an on-site open space requirement, or a parking ratio. Gov't Code § 65915(o)(1).

SECOND UNITS

Facilitating the development of second units is recognized by the Legislature as a means to increase the supply of affordable housing. In enacting California's second unit statute, the Legislature found:

> [S]econd units are a valuable form of housing in California. Second units provide housing for family members, students, the elderly, in-home health care providers, the disabled, and other, at below market prices within existing neighborhoods. Homeowners who create second units benefit from added income, and an increased sense of security.

Gov't Code § 65852.150

Similarly, HCD encourages the use of secondary units as affordable housing:

> Second units (i.e., in-law apartments, granny flats, or accessory apartments) provide an important source of affordable housing. By promoting the development of second-units, a community may ease a rental housing deficit, maximize limited land resources and existing infrastructure and assist low and moderate-income homeowners with supplemental income. Second-units can increase the property tax base and contribute to the local affordable housing stock.[13]

In keeping with this philosophy, HCD allows local governments to meet a portion of their fair share of the region's housing need through the provision of secondary units.[14] *See* Gov't Code § 65583.1(a) (authorizing HCD to allow cities and counties to identify, in the housing elements of their general plans, sites for secondary units based on certain factors).

"Second unit" means an attached or detached residential unit that provides complete independent living facilities for one or more persons. Gov't Code § 65852.2(i)(4). Government Code section 65852.2 sets forth procedures by which second units in single-family and multifamily residential zones may be established. Government Code section 65852.150 permits a city to establish a procedure by ordinance to allow these types of units. In addition, it requires cities without second unit ordinances to consider applications for such units ministerially, without discretionary review and a hearing unless they adopt such an ordinance within 120 days after receiving the application. The law also requires that the city grant a variance or special use permit for the creation of a second unit if the applicant's proposal meets all of the criteria set forth in Government Code section 65852.2(b)(1). These criteria also establish the maximum standards that cities are allowed to use in evaluating second unit applications. Gov't Code § 65852.2(b)(3).

Cities are not permitted to restrict the use of second units to specific categories of people. *Coalition Advocating Legal Hous. Options v. City of Santa Monica*, 88 Cal. App. 4th 451 (2001) (invalidating ordinance that restricted the creation of second units in single-family residential zones only to those units where either the property owner or the owner's dependent or caregiver would reside). Prior legislation granted a city authority to approve what were commonly referred to as "granny" units. Changes to the law have repealed a city's authority in this regard in favor of the newer law addressing second units. However, such "granny" units constructed or with approved permits issued before this date are legal. Gov't Code § 65852.1(b).

> Cities are not permitted to restrict the use of second units to specific categories of people.

GROWTH MANAGEMENT AND AFFORDABLE HOUSING

Over the past several decades, various cities have enacted growth management measures, both council- and voter-initiated. To ensure they do not unduly hamper the production of housing, California law imposes special requirements on such measures.

If a city, including a charter city, adopts or amends a general plan element that operates to limit the number of housing units that may be constructed on an annual basis,

---

[13] Memorandum from Cathy E. Creswell, Deputy Director, HCD Division of Housing Policy Development, to Planning Directors and Interested Parties, at 2 (Aug. 6, 2003), available at http://www.hcd.ca.gov/hpd/hpd_memo_ab1866.pdf.

[14] California Dep't of Housing & Community Development, Second Units, htt;://www.hcd.ca.gov/hpd/housing_element2/SIA_secondunits.php.

such action must be based on findings that justify reducing the housing opportunities of the region. Gov't Code § 65302.8. The findings shall include all of the following:
- A description of the city's appropriate share of the regional need for housing
- A description of the specific housing programs and activities being undertaken by the city to fulfill the requirements of the state housing element law
- A description of how the public health, safety, and welfare would be promoted by such adoption or amendment, and
- The fiscal and environmental resources available to the city

Any zoning ordinance that, by its terms, limits the number of housing units that may be constructed on an annual basis shall contain findings as to the public health, safety, and welfare of the city to be promoted by the adoption of the ordinance that justify reducing the housing opportunities of the region. Gov't Code § 65863.6. These requirements are not applicable, however, if the numerical restrictions are imposed by initiative. *Building Indus. Ass'n v. City of Camarillo*, 41 Cal. 3d 810, 815 (1986).

When a growth limitation is adopted, the burden of proving the ordinance or regulation is reasonably related to the protection of public health, safety, and welfare of the affected population is on the city and not the attacking party. Evid. Code § 669.5(b). *See also Building Industry Ass'n v. Superior Court*, 211 Cal. App. 3d 277, 292-93 (1989); *Lee v. City of Monterey Park*, 173 Cal. App. 3d 798, 806-07 (1985). *But see Hernandez*, 28 Cal. App. 4th at 1076 (Evidence Code section 669.5 does not come into play unless there is a violation of the "least cost zoning law" contained in Government Code section 65913.1). This burden shifting applies even if the restriction is imposed by initiative. *City of Camarillo*, 41 Cal. 3d at 815. However, there are certain exceptions. For example, if the initiative exempts affordable housing projects, Evidence Code section 669.5 does not apply.

Any growth management measure also must comply with state law, including substantive requirements for the general plan. HCD has devised a compliance test to determine the validity of a growth management measure under the housing element requirements of state law, taking into consideration the following:
- Is the measure based upon actual and clearly defined environmental or public facility constraints (e.g., limited sewer, water, or school capacity)?
- Does the measure set the city's new construction maximums above its new construction need, including its share of the region's housing needs?
- Does the measure provide adequate incentives to encourage the development of housing affordable to low- and moderate-income households, consistent with the city's share of the region's housing needs for all income levels?
- Is the city taking all reasonable and available steps to relieve the constraints that made the growth limitation necessary?
- Does the measure also equitably limit industrial and commercial development that may increase the need for housing?
- Is the growth limitation measure conditioned to expire upon removal of the justifying constraint?

If a particular measure appears to preclude the locality from meeting its housing element obligations, HCD will report that, in its opinion, the housing element does not comply with state law. Such a finding could serve as evidence in a legal action seeking a judgment that the city's general plan is inadequate. *See, e.g., Buena Vista Gardens Apartments Ass'n*, 175 Cal. App. 3d at 304.

INCLUSIONARY HOUSING

INTRODUCTION

In general, inclusionary housing regulations[15] either mandate or encourage developers of new residential projects to set aside a certain percentage of a project's residential units for lower- and moderate-income households. These programs are typically effectuated by ordinance, zoning codes, policy statements, or a city's housing element or fair share plan.[16]

> In general, inclusionary housing regulations either mandate or encourage developers of new residential projects to set aside a certain percentage of a project's residential units for lower- and moderate-income households.

Components of inclusionary housing programs may include: the specification that a certain percentage of affordable units must or should be provided as part of a project; the establishment of affordability criteria for those units based upon a percentage of median income; and the provision for future price or rent restrictions in order to preserve the long-term affordability of such units. In addition, inclusionary housing programs often provide certain incentives and concessions to encourage the provision of affordable units, as well as various alternatives to on-site affordable housing production, such as in-lieu fees, land dedication, and off-site development.[17] Such benefits to developers may include density bonuses, expedited processing, local tax abatements, waiver of permit fees or land dedication requirements, reduction of required developer-provided amenities, and subsidization or provision of infrastructure by the jurisdiction for the developer's project.

Reliance on the tool of inclusionary housing continues to be apparent as communities seek ways to increase their affordable housing stock.[18] In the absence of a statewide approach to inclusionary housing, each jurisdiction has the option of whether to implement inclusionary practices and, if so, how to design an inclusionary program to match its local needs and political reality.

Based on currently available information, one-third of California localities (170 jurisdictions) have adopted some form of inclusionary housing.[19] At least 30 other jurisdictions in the state are considering adopting some kind of inclusionary housing policy. Nearly two-thirds of these programs have been adopted since 1990.[20] Inclusionary practices are also being employed in increasingly diverse kinds of neighbor-

---

15 Although the term "inclusionary housing" is sometimes used interchangeably with "inclusionary zoning," not all inclusionary regulations are zoning overlays. *See generally* Brian R. Lerman, *Mandatory Inclusionary Zoning: The Answer to the Affordable Housing Problem*, 33 B.C. Envtl. Aff. L. Rev. 383 (2006).

16 *See* David L. Callies, Leigh Anne King, James C. Nicholas, and Cecily Talbert Barclay, *Workforce and Affordable Housing: Local Government Inclusionary Housing Programs and the Courts*, 63 Plan. & Envtl. Law no. 10, page 8 (2011); Cecily T. Talbert & Alison L. Krumbein, *Inclusionary Zoning: How to Strengthen the Defensibility of This Popular Tool to Meet Your Community's Affordable Housing Needs*, 46 Mun. Law. 7 (May/June 2005). *See also* Barbara Ehrlich Kautz, *In Defense of Inclusionary Zoning: Successfully Creating Affordable Housing*, 36 U.S.F. L. Rev. 973, 983–85 (2002) for a thorough history of the use of inclusionary housing across the nation.

17 *See generally* Dr. Robert W. Burchell & Catherine C. Galley, *Inclusionary Zoning: Pros and Cons*, in The California Inclusionary Housing Reader (Bill Higgins ed., Institute for Local Self Government, 2003), *available at* http://www.cailg.org/sites/ilgbackup.org/files/resources/California_Inclusionary_Housing_Reader.pdf.

18 *See* Nico Calavita, *Origins and Evolution of Inclusionary Housing in California*, in Inclusionary Housing: The California Experience, 3(1) NHC Affordable housing Policy Rev. 1 (Feb. 2004), *available at* http://www.nhc.org/media/documents/IZ_CA_experiencet.pdf. *See also* D. Porter, *Inclusionary Zoning for Affordable Housing* (Urban Land Institute, 2004), for analysis of these issues as well as case studies of inclusionary housing programs throughout the nation.

19 *See* Cal. Coal. for Rural Hous. & Non-Profit Hous. Ass'n of N. Cal., *Affordable by Choice: Trends in California Inclusionary Housing Programs* (2007), *available at* http://nonprofithousing.org/pdf_attachments/IHIReport.pdf.

20 *Id. See also* Calavita, *supra* note 21.

hoods.[21] The reliance on inclusionary housing in large cities like San Francisco, San Diego,[22] and Sacramento is of particular note.[23] Other large-city jurisdictions, including Los Angeles and Oakland, are considering the adoption of some form of inclusionary housing.[24]

Determining the actual number of units produced as a result of inclusionary housing is a challenge, due in part to the difficulties faced by implementing jurisdictions in collecting and maintaining the necessary data.[25] However, available reports indicate that, in total, inclusionary housing may well have produced approximately 30,000 affordable units in California.[26]

In addition to increasing a community's affordable housing stock, advocates of inclusionary practices point to other related benefits, including: (1) facilitating racial and economic integration;[27] (2) encouraging implementation of smart growth principles; (3) providing housing for a diverse work force, which helps foster a strong

> Available reports indicate that, in total, inclusionary housing may well have produced approximately 30,000 affordable units in California.

---

[21] See *Expanding Housing Opportunity in Washington, D.C.: The Case for Inclusionary Zoning* (PolicyLink, Winter 2005) at 16 (discussing the potentially positive impact of using inclusionary housing in different kinds of neighborhoods, including those that are gentrifying, new and expanding, expensive, and those that have high concentrations of poverty); Jesse M. Keenan, *Affordable Housing Policy in Miami: Inclusionary Zoning and the Median-Income Demographic*, 14(2) J. Affordable Housing & Cmty. Dev. Law 110 (Winter 2005) (arguing that Miami should institute some form of an inclusionary housing policy).

[22] In 2006, a superior court invalidated the City of San Diego's inclusionary housing ordinance, holding that on its face the ordinance did not include a "complete waiver" provision and therefore did not allow the city to avoid the unconstitutional application of the ordinance. San Diego Sup. Ct. Case No. 6JC817064. The city settled the suit by adding a waiver provision to the ordinance and adjusted how in-lieu fees are calculated. Lori Weisberg, *City, Builders Settle Ordinance Fight*, San Diego Union-Trib. (July 26, 2006).

[23] For a historical perspective on development patterns that resulted in metropolitan decentralization, see Blackwell & Fox, *supra* note 5, at 3–4. *See also* Nicholas Brunick, *Inclusionary Housing: Proven Success in Large Cities*, Zoning Prac. no. 10 (Oct. 2004) (discussing the reasons for the growth of inclusionary housing in large cities, and describing several large-city programs), *available at* http://www.inclusionaryhousing.ca/wp-content/uploads/2010/01/ ResourceUS_APA_IZPracticesOct04.pdf.

[24] *See* Bill Higgins, *Inclusionary Zoning and Affordable Housing After Homebuilders Ass'n of Northern California v. City of Napa*, page 3 (Inst. on Planning, Zoning, and Eminent Domain, 2003). *See also* David Paul Rosen & Associates, *Los Angeles Inclusionary Housing Study: Final Report* (2002), *available at* http://lahd.lacity.org/lahdinternet/; *Oakland Moving Forward Community Task Force Report on Housing* (December 2006), *available at* http://www.oaklandnet.com/TaskForceInfo/Housing_v6.pdf.

[25] Inclusionary housing programs remain controversial. Debate about their level of effectiveness in terms of unit production continues. For differing perspectives regarding the effectiveness of mandatory programs, see Nicholas Brunick, Lauren Goldberg, & Susannah Levine, *Voluntary or Mandatory Inclusionary Housing Production, Predictability and Enforcement* (Business and Professional People for the Public Interest, August 2004) (concluding that mandatory programs produce more units for a wider range of income levels), *available at* http://www.bpichicago.org/documents/ mandatoryv.voluntary5.06.pdf; Benjamin Powell & Edward Stringham, *Housing Supply and Affordability: Do Affordable Housing Mandates Work?* (The Reason Public Policy Institute, April 2004) (finding that mandatory programs produce relatively few units at very high costs), *available at* http://reason.org/files/02062493 3d4c04a615569374fdbeef41.pdf; Victoria Basolo & Nico Calavita, *Policy Claims with Weak Evidence: A Critique of the Reason Foundation Study on Inclusionary Housing Policy in the San Francisco Bay Area* (June 2004) (disputing claims that inclusionary housing programs are too costly and ineffective). *See also* David Rosen, *Inclusionary Housing and Its Impact on Housing and Land Markets*, 3(1) NHC Affordable Housing Policy Rev. 38 (Feb. 2004) (evaluating the effect inclusionary housing policies have on housing production in California cities), *available at* http://www.nhc.org/media/documents/ IZ_CA_experiencet.pdf.

[26] *See Affordable by Choice*, *supra* note 22; Cal. Coal. for Rural Hous. & Non-Profit Hous. Ass'n of N. Cal., *Inclusionary Housing in California: 30 Years of Innovation* (2003) at 7, *available at* http://calruralhousing.org/drupal/sites/default/files/Inclusionary30Years.pdf.

[27] *See generally* Angela Glover Blackwell, *Urban Equity: Consideration of Race and the Road Towards Equitable Allocation of Municipal Services: It Takes a Region*, 31 Fordham Urb. L. J. 1303 (2004); Edward G. Goetz, Karen Chapple, & Barbara Lukermann, *The Minnesota Land Use Planning Act and the Promotion of Low- and Moderate-Income Housing in Suburbia*, 22 Law & Ineq. J. 31 (2004); Thomas A. Brown, *Democratizing the American Dream: The Role of a Regional Housing Legislature in the Production of Affordable Housing*, 31 U. Mich. J.L. Ref. 599 (2004); Christopher Courchesne, *What Regional Agenda?: Reconciling Massachusetts' Affordable Housing Law and Environmental Protection*, 28 Harv. Envtl. L. Rev. 215 (2004).

economic environment; and (4) protecting against displacement of lower-income households when new investment occurs.[28]

JUDICIAL TREATMENT OF INCLUSIONARY HOUSING

Despite the increasing use of inclusionary housing regulations to encourage the development of affordable housing, debate regarding the legality and effectiveness of inclusionary housing remains.[29] Decisions addressing inclusionary housing challenges have recognized the legitimate governmental interest in promoting affordable housing and in imposing regulations intended to achieve that objective. While the courts have not yet fully addressed the constitutionality of imposing inclusionary housing obligations on private developers, at least one appellate court recently found a city's in-lieu affordable housing fee unreasonable, while another placed strict limits on a city's ability to impose restrictions on rental units that have not received a public subsidy. *BIA of Central California v. City of Patterson*, 171 Cal. App. 4th 886 (2009); *Palmer/Sixth St. Properties, L.P. v. City of Los Angeles*, 175 Cal. App. 4th 1396 (2009). Recently, the California Supreme Court granted a petition seeking review of a court of appeal decision upholding San Jose's inclusionary housing ordinance as a valid exercise of the police power. *California Building Industry Ass'n v. City of San Jose*, 161 Cal. Rptr. 3d 699 (2013). San Jose's ordinance required all new development of 20 units or more to make 15 percent of their units affordable or to pay an in-lieu fee. The trial court had invalidated the ordinance, concluding the city had not established the required linkage between the impact of new residential and the need for affordable housing. The court of appeal reversed, holding the ordinance was a valid exercise of the city's police power. The Supreme Court is expected to hear the case in 2014. Its decision likely will have significant ramifications for the future of inclusionary housing programs throughout the state.

> Despite the increasing use of inclusionary housing regulations to encourage the development of affordable housing, debate regarding the legality and effectiveness of inclusionary housing remains.

HISTORY OF INCLUSIONARY HOUSING—THE PRE-*NOLLAN* AND *DOLAN* ERA

Nationwide, there are relatively few published decisions considering the legality of inclusionary housing. The first court to address this issue was in the Virginia case of *Board of Supervisors v. De Groff Enterprises*, 198 S.E. 2d 600 (Va. 1973). In that decision, despite acknowledging the "urgent need for housing units for low and moderate income families," the Virginia Supreme Court invalidated a mandatory inclusionary housing ordinance that required 15 percent of multifamily units in new residential projects be affordable. It did so based on the grounds that the ordinance exceeded the city's police power, as well as constituted a taking under the Virginia State Constitution.

Subsequent cases, however, have not followed suit. New Jersey, where the courts have tended to take on a more legislative role than is typically seen in most states, has

---

28 *See* Angela Glover Blackwell, *Urban Equity, supra* note 30; *Expanding Housing Opportunity in Washington, D.C., supra* note 24, at 9, 16; Nicholas Brunick, *The Impact of Inclusionary Zoning on Development* (2003) at 2–3, *available at* http://www.bpichicago.org/documents/impact_iz_development.pdf.

29 For a discussion regarding the legal issues, see, e.g., Kautz, *supra* note 18; Laura M. Padilla, *Reflections on Inclusionary Housing and a Renewed Look at Its Viability*, 23 Hofstra L. Rev. 539 (1995). For differing perspectives on the costs and benefits of inclusionary housing, see generally Burchell & Galley, *supra* note 20; Powell & Stringham, *supra* note 28 (finding that mandatory programs produce relatively few units at very high costs); Andrew G. Dietderich, *An Egalitarian's Market: The Economics of Inclusionary Zoning Reclaimed*, 24 Fordham Urb. L.J. 23 (1996); Lawrence Berger, *Inclusionary Zoning Devices as Takings: The Legacy of the Mount Laurel Cases*, 70 Neb. L. Rev. 186 (1991); Robert C. Ellickson, *The Irony of "Inclusionary" Zoning*, 54 S. Cal. L. Rev. 1167 (1981).

been in the forefront. In 1983, in the case of *Southern Burlington County N.A.A.C.P. v. Township of Mt. Laurel* ("*Mt. Laurel I*"), the New Jersey Supreme Court issued the first decision in the country to explicitly recognize the importance of combating exclusionary zoning practices. 336 A.2d 713 (N.J. 1983).[30] In that case, the plaintiffs, representing minority, low-income residents, attacked a local zoning ordinance that had both the intent and effect of excluding low- and moderate-income residents from the city. The ordinance accomplished this goal by: (1) permitting only single-family detached dwelling units in residentially zoned areas; and (2) requiring significant minimum lot sizes and floor areas for new units. The New Jersey Supreme Court found this ordinance to be unconstitutional, violating basic principles of fairness. While the court stopped short of endorsing mandatory price controls on new housing, it ruled that all developing cities have an affirmative obligation, through their local land use regulations, to "make realistically possible" an appropriate variety and choice of housing without excluding low- and moderate-income housing opportunities. *Id.* at 724.

In a subsequent decision that year, *Southern Burlington County N.A.A.C.P v. Township of Mt. Laurel* ("*Mt. Laurel II*"), the state high court made it clear that it would not back away from its holding in *Mt. Laurel I*. 456 A.2d 390 (N.J. 1983). Rather, it extended the duty to provide an appropriate variety of housing to *all* cities in New Jersey and advocated mandatory set-aside programs as one way for cities to fulfill their *Mt. Laurel* obligations. The court directed cities to accommodate their fair share of housing needs and went so far as to direct certain cities to accommodate certain specific needs.

On the constitutional question regarding the legality of singling out developers of new projects to bear the burden of remedying the affordable housing crisis, the court gave mixed signals. On the one hand, the court recognized the need to "assur[e] developers of an adequate return on their investment." *Id.* at 446. On the other hand, the court held that mandatory set-asides did not suffer from the infirmities identified in an earlier case, which had overturned a rent control ordinance that precluded rent increases for certain tenants. The *Mt. Laurel II* court reconciled these situations by emphasizing that in the case at hand, the inclusionary rental units would not be exempt from rent increases, which would likely track increases in the median incomes of lower income families. Thus, the result could not be considered confiscatory to the developer, since "the builder who undertakes a project that includes a mandatory set-aside voluntarily assumes the financial burden, if there is one, of that condition." *Id.* at 446, n.30.

INCLUSIONARY HOUSING IN CALIFORNIA IN THE POST-*NOLLAN* AND *DOLAN* ERA

Between 1987 and 1994, in the cases of *Nollan v. California Coastal Comm'n*, 483 U.S. 825 (1987), and *Dolan v. City of Tigard*, 512 U.S. 374 (1994), the United States Supreme Court applied an intermediate level of judicial review referred to as "heightened scrutiny" to examine certain conditions applied to development projects. In contrast to a more deferential standard, heightened scrutiny places the burden of proof on the city to establish an "essential nexus" and a "rough proportionality" between a project's impacts and the particular requirement imposed, a more difficult task. *Nollan*, 483

---

[30] For articles discussing the continuing implications of Mt. Laurel, exclusionary zoning, and potential housing, see Adam Gordon, *Making Exclusionary Zoning Remedies Work: How Courts Applying Title VII Standards to Fair Housing Cases Have Misunderstood the Housing Market*, 24 Yale L. & Pol'y Rev. 437 (2006); Catherine Durkin, *The Exclusionary Effect of "Mansionization": Area Variances Undermine Efforts to Achieve Housing Affordability*, 55 Cal. U. L. Rev. 439 (2006).

U.S. at 839-40; *Dolan*, 512 U.S. at 391. How the *Nollan/Dolan* heightened scrutiny standard would be applied to inclusionary housing regulations became a key issue in the debate surrounding the legality of such regulations.

In 1991, a federal appellate court in *Commercial Builders of Northern California v. City of Sacramento*, which involved the relationship between commercial development and affordable housing requirements, weighed in on the issue. 941 F. 2d 872 (9th Cir. 1991). In that case, the ordinance conditioned approval of certain types of non-residential building permits upon the developer's payment of a fee dedicated to an affordable housing trust fund. The plaintiff, citing *Nollan*, argued the ordinance constituted an impermissible means of advancing the city's legitimate interest in increasing the supply of affordable housing, since it placed a burden of paying for low-income housing on non-residential development without establishing a sufficient nexus between such development and the stated need. However, the court was not persuaded. Refusing to require a direct causal relationship,[31] it held that *Nollan* did not materially change the level of scrutiny. The court upheld the ordinance, relying on the fact that it was implemented only after a careful study revealed the amount of low-income housing that would likely become necessary as a direct result of the influx of workers as a result of the new non-residential development.

In 2001, in the *Home Builders Ass'n of Northern California v. City of Napa*, the plaintiff challenged the City of Napa's inclusionary housing ordinance, which imposed a mandatory 10 percent affordability requirement on new residential projects. 90 Cal. App. 4th 188 (2001). Plaintiffs contended the ordinance was facially invalid because it (1) was an impermissible taking under both state and federal law; and (2) violated the federal Due Process Clause. In ruling for the city, the court affirmed the trial court's decision and upheld the ordinance against the facial constitutional attacks.

The plaintiff's principal constitutional claim was that the city's ordinance was invalid under the heightened scrutiny standard required by *Nollan* and *Dolan*. It contended there was no "essential nexus" or "rough proportionality" between the exaction required by the ordinance and the impacts caused by development of the project.

However, the court rejected this argument, holding the *Nollan/Dolan* heightened scrutiny test was inapplicable to a facial challenge to an ordinance generally applicable throughout the city. The court reasoned that this higher level of review was reserved for situations involving land use "bargains" between property owners and regulatory bodies, whereby the city sought to impose ad hoc requirements on individual developers in exchange for project approval. The court found that since the ordinance was generally applicable to all development in Napa, and the risk of extortionate behavior on the part of the city was therefore minimized, the more deferential standard of scrutiny applied.

After acknowledging the legitimate governmental interest in encouraging the development of affordable housing, the court rejected the facial challenge to Napa's ordinance. In so doing, it found dispositive the fact that the ordinance contained an administrative relief clause, which allowed for a complete waiver of the inclusionary requirements should the developer establish that the requirements were unconstitutional or unlawful. The court did not address the issue of the appropriate standard of review to be applied in the event a developer brought a subsequent challenge based on the city's refusal to grant a waiver for lack of nexus or rough proportionality to that developer's specific project.

---

31 This case was decided prior to the *Dolan* decision, which imposes the requirement of "rough proportionality." Therefore, the court did not address the question of "how close a fit" is required between the project and its impacts on the affordable housing supply.

In 2002, the California Supreme Court, in *San Remo Hotel v. City and County of San Francisco*, addressed a unique situation involving the imposition of affordable housing fees as a condition of approval for a permit to convert a hotel from long-term residential use to tourist use. 27 Cal. 4th 643 (2002). Here, the plaintiff hotel owners were required to pay $567,000 to convert 62 residential hotel rooms to tourist rooms under San Francisco's Hotel Conversion Ordinance. Upon imposition of those requirements, the owners paid the fee under protest and sued the city for inverse condemnation.

The California Supreme Court upheld the fee, declining to extend the heightened scrutiny standard to the San Francisco ordinance. Instead, the court found that challenges to "generally applicable legislation," which impose fees that are calculated according to a nondiscretionary formula such as the ordinance at issue, are subject only to a deferential standard of review, under which a court assesses whether the exaction or fee is reasonably related to a project's impacts. The court clarified that "generally applicable legislation" under *Ehrlich v. City of Culver City*, 12 Cal. 4th 854 (1996), need not apply to every property in a city, so long as it applies to "all property in the class logically subject to its strictures." *Id.* at 669. The court then held that because the housing replacement fee bore a reasonable relationship to the loss of housing caused by converting residence hotels to tourist hotels, the fee was valid. In so doing, the decision reaffirmed the ruling in *Ehrlich* which held that the "heightened scrutiny" test for exactions required under the *Nollan* and *Dolan* decisions does not generally apply to fees; accordingly, fees imposed under an inclusionary housing program enacted by general legislation in California would not be subject to heightened scrutiny.

In 2009, a California court addressed the reasonableness of an in-lieu affordable housing fee imposed on a developer by means of a development agreement. *BIA of Central California v. City of Patterson*, 171 Cal. App. 4th 886 (2009). *BIA* involved a development agreement that required the developer to pay an in-lieu affordable housing fee that could be revised over time by the city if the revised amount was "reasonably justified." Subsequently, the city sought to substantially increase the fee based on an updated fee study. This study provided for a per-unit fee that was determined by dividing the cost of bridging the "affordability gap" between the cost of the number of affordable units the city needed and the cost to produce those new units divided by the number of homes projected to be built in the city. The court concluded the increased fee was not "reasonably justified," as required by the development agreement, finding the fee did not bear any reasonable relationship to any deleterious impact associated with the project. *Id.* at 891–92. Rather, the fee simply represented the city's decision to shift all costs of providing affordable housing to new housing developments. While *BIA* did not involve a challenge to imposition of a city's inclusionary housing requirements per se, it provides significant guidance to cities as they prepare or update fee studies to support inclusionary fees.

Also in 2009, another court addressed the question whether affordable housing requirements imposed by a city as a condition of project approval are preempted by the Costa-Hawkins Act and therefore void as a matter of law.

In *Palmer/Sixth St. Props., L.P. v. City of Los Angeles*, 175 Cal. App. 4th 1396 (2009) the court considered a specific plan adopted by the City of Los Angeles that required developers of certain projects within the plan area to either provide affordable units that would be subject to long-term rental restrictions, or pay in-lieu fees that the city would use to build affordable housing elsewhere. The city imposed these affordable housing requirements as a condition of approval on a particular mixed-use project, requiring either construction of 60 affordable rental units or payment of over $6.7 million in in-lieu fees. The developer challenged this condition on the basis that it was preempted by the Costa-Hawkins Act, which allows only the owner—and not the city—to set initial rent levels.

The court agreed with the developer, and held that the Costa-Hawkins Act preempted these locally-imposed affordable housing requirements. 175 Cal. App. 4th at 1410. The court reasoned that under the plain language of Civil Code section 1954.52(a), a condition of approval that forces a developer to provide affordable housing units at regulated rental rates in order to obtain project approval is "clearly hostile" to the rights afforded under the Costa-Hawkins Act. Accordingly, the court affirmed the trial court's decision to issue a writ of mandate prohibiting the city from enforcing the affordability requirements at issue. Id. at 1399. The court held the in-lieu fee also was invalid because it was "inextricably intertwined" with the invalid inclusionary rental requirements. Id. at 1412.

One question left unanswered by *Palmer* is the proper scope and interpretation of an exception to the pre-emption under the Costa-Hawkins Act. Under Civil Code §§ 1954.52(b) and 1954.53(a)(2), the Costa-Hawkins Act does not apply when "[t]he owner has otherwise agreed by contract with a public entity in consideration for a direct financial contribution or any other forms of assistance specified in Chapter 4.3 [the State Density Bonus Statute]." This statutory language could be construed as ambiguous as to whether the exception would be triggered only in circumstances where the owner has actually received a density bonus under state law, or more broadly where the owner has received other forms of financial assistance. Pending further clarification, cities will need to evaluate whether the exception applies on a project-by-project basis.

> Pending further clarification, cities will need to evaluate whether the exception applies on a project-by-project basis.

Recently, the California Supreme Court addressed the procedure for challenging conditions requiring the provision of affordable housing. In *Sterling Park, L.P. v. City of Palo Alto*. 57 Cal. 4th 1193 (2013), the Court held that the Mitigation Fee Act's pay under protest procedure in Government Code section 66020—which allows an applicant to proceed with development while pursuing a challenge to a contested fee or exaction—applied to a challenge to a condition of approval requiring the applicant to set aside units in its project as affordable units and to pay into a city's affordable housing fund. *Sterling Park, L.P. v. City of Palo Alto*, 57 Cal. 4th 1193, 1209 (2013).

Finally, as discussed above, the California Supreme Court recently granted a petition for review of a case involving a facial challenge to the City of San Jose's inclusionary housing ordinance. The Supreme Court's decision in that case likely will have significant ramifications for the furture of affordable housing programs throughout the state.

LEGAL ISSUES TO CONSIDER WHEN ADOPTING AND IMPLEMENTING AN INCLUSIONARY HOUSING PROGRAM

It is anticipated that inclusionary practices will continue as cities seek to address the lack of affordable housing in their communities, though many cities will need to revisit their particular regulations in light of the *Patterson* and *Palmer* decisions. Whether revising or enacting inclusionary regulations, there are a number of additional legal issues a city should consider.

METHOD OF ENACTMENT

Cities enact inclusionary housing programs pursuant to their local police power. *Euclid v. Ambler Realty Co.*, 272 U.S. 365 (1926) (discussing the scope of the local police power). These programs can be implemented in several ways, including through ordinances, zoning codes, general policy statements, a city's housing element, or various permit approval procedures. To date, the majority of jurisdictions in California—approximately 78 percent—have enacted inclusionary housing programs by local ordinances.[32]

Although cities may adopt inclusionary housing in various ways, there are benefits to enacting these programs through a generally applicable zoning ordinance. Adoption of a zoning regulation is a legislative act and is entitled to judicial deference. It is presumed the enactment of the regulation is justified under the police power and was adopted for the purpose of promoting the public health, safety, and general welfare. Hence, a zoning regulation may be invalidated only if it bears no reasonable relationship to a legitimate public purpose. *Candid Enters., Inc. v. Grossmont Union High Sch. Dist.*, 39 Cal. 3d 878 (1985).

In addition, the adoption of an inclusionary housing program through a generally applicable ordinance reduces its legal vulnerability by helping to avoid the kind of individualized ad hoc application that invites takings or other legal challenges. In *Home Builders Ass'n of Northern California v. City of Napa*, the court held that since the ordinance was enacted legislatively, the more deferential standard of scrutiny applied "because the heightened risk of the 'extortionate' use of the police power to exact unconstitutional conditions is not present." 90 Cal. App. 4th at 197.

While some flexibility can be retained to allow for discretionary decisions that may be necessary when applying the ordinance to specific projects, it is important to minimize such discretion where possible. The specific requirements—the type and percentage of affordable units to be produced, affordability levels and controls, availability of alternatives to on-site production and developer incentives, and selection of beneficiaries—should be generally applicable and sufficiently detailed rather than individually negotiated.[33] In addition, the ordinance should contain clear definitions and requirements, defining all terms precisely and providing clear statements regarding the applicable standards.

Taking these steps limits the risk of misinterpretation and arbitrary application. Such limits on discretion give the ordinance a better chance of withstanding constitutional challenge.

FACTUAL RECORD TO SUPPORT ENACTMENT AND APPLICATION

Inclusionary housing regulations are less vulnerable to legal attack when based on empirical data that justifies the city's policy decisions. In particular, adequate findings supported by substantial evidence should be made to demonstrate a legitimate governmental interest in providing affordable housing in the community and the ways in which inclusionary housing will substantially advance this interest.[34]

---

32 See *Inclusionary Housing in California: 30 Years of Innovation*, supra note 29, at 8.
33 See Kautz, supra note 18 at 1021-22.
34 For example, in the *City of Napa* case, the court relied in part on its finding that the inclusionary housing ordinance, which imposed a 10 percent affordability requirement, substantially advanced a legitimate state interest. The court reasoned that both the California Supreme Court and the State Legislature had recognized the creation of affordable housing for low- and moderate-income households as a legitimate state interest. The court then assumed that the city's inclusionary ordinance would necessarily result in the substantial advancement of this important interest by increasing the affordable housing stock in the community. 90 Cal. App. 4th at 195.

Even assuming the general proposition that the creation of affordable housing is a legitimate interest,[35] cities are well served to show the need for additional affordable housing in their particular communities. There are numerous existing sources of data upon which a city can rely. For example, this information can be gathered as the calculation of each community's "fair share" of the regional housing need is made every five years. In addition, cities can rely on public input or may decide to conduct a nexus study to establish such local need. For more information about the use of residential nexus analysis in California, see Adam F. Cray, *The Use of Residential Nexus Analysis in Support of California's Inclusionary Housing Ordinances: A Critical Evaluation* (November 2011), *available at* http://www.cbia.org/go/linkservid/06D3172D-35C3-4C71-9A9098D439C63874/showMeta/0/.

Developing and collecting evidence demonstrating that imposition of the inclusionary requirements will not deny property owners all economically viable use of their property and will not interfere with their reasonable investment-backed expectations may help further insulate an inclusionary housing program from a takings challenge.

Cities also should consider documenting how their inclusionary programs actually increase the affordable housing stock. This evidence can be used to counter the argument that inclusionary housing requirements actually diminish the amount of overall residential construction, thereby hampering rather than advancing the interest of providing more affordable housing.[36]

Finally, with respect to affordable housing fees in particular, cities should strongly consider demonstrating a proposed fee is "reasonably justified." *See BIA v. City of Patterson*, 171 Cal. App. 4th at 891–92.

INCLUSION OF "SAFETY VALVE" PROVISIONS

The inclusion of a provision that would allow a city to waive the inclusionary requirements or permit an alternative means of compliance can reduce the legal vulnerability of an inclusionary housing program. *See City of Napa*, 90 Cal. App. 4th at 199 (availability of a waiver provision was noted as a basis for upholding the regulations). This provision permitted city officials to reduce, modify, or waive the requirements contained in the ordinance if the developer could demonstrate that there was no reasonable relationship or nexus between the impact of the development and the inclusionary requirement. As the court stated, "Since City has the ability to waive the requirements imposed by the ordinance, the ordinance cannot and does not, on its face, result in a taking." *Id.* at 194.

An inclusionary housing program also may contain a provision that permits a developer to comply with the affordable housing requirements without producing units on site. Typical alternatives to on-site production include allowing developers (1) to pay an in-lieu fee that is deposited in an affordable housing trust fund to be used for construction of affordable units; (2) to dedicate land for construction of affordable units; or (3) to build affordable units on another site.

It remains an open question whether an alternative compliance provision is necessary to withstand constitutional scrutiny. In *City of Napa*, the court acknowledged the

> The inclusion of a provision that would allow a city to waive the inclusionary requirements or permit an alternative means of compliance can reduce the legal vulnerability of an inclusionary housing program.

---

35 The assumption that inclusionary housing requirements necessarily leads to the creation of more affordable housing has been questioned. *See* Ellickson, *supra* note 32, at 1167 (concluding that inclusionary housing aggravates housing shortages, which results in less housing "filtering down" to lower-income families and an increase in overall housing prices).

36 *See* Kautz, *supra.* note 18.

alternative compliance provision in the ordinance at issue, noting that although the ordinance placed "significant burdens" on developers, it also provided "significant benefits" to developers who complied with its terms. However, it did not rely on this provision to uphold the ordinance. Rather, its key concern was the city's ability to waive the inclusionary requirements if necessary to avoid unconstitutional applications.

From a policy perspective, there is support for the position that permitting such flexibility will result in the construction of more affordable units in the community than on-site production, alone, could attain.[37] Accordingly, numerous jurisdictions include such alternative compliance provisions.

However, providing the option of paying in-lieu fees or dedicating land could increase the likelihood a court would review the ordinance as an exaction as opposed to a land use regulation which, in turn, could result in the imposition of a higher level of scrutiny to evaluate the constitutionality of the program. For example, a city could enact an inclusionary ordinance that applies to all residential developments, regardless of size. However, because it would not be feasible to require on-site production where a developer proposes a one-unit project, this ordinance could require that such developer pay an in-lieu fee instead. If the fee is one of general applicability, then the city would need to establish an adequate factual basis to demonstrate a connection between the ordinance's requirements and the impacts of development. *San Remo Hotel*, 27 Cal. 4th at 669; *see also BIA v. City of Patterson*, 171 Cal. App. 4th at 891–92. However, if the fee is determined on a case-by-case basis, the heightened scrutiny standard may well apply.

> If the fee is one of general applicability, then the city would need to establish an adequate factual basis to demonstrate a connection between the ordinance's requirements and the impacts of development.

In addition, allowing an in-lieu fee option raises two additional issues involving the Mitigation Fee Act and Proposition 218. The Mitigation Fee Act (Gov't Code §§ 66000–66025) provides that a fee or exaction imposed as a mandatory condition for approval of development cannot exceed the estimated reasonable cost of providing the public facility for which the fee is imposed. Gov't Code § 66005. If an in-lieu fee provision in an inclusionary housing program is viewed as a "fee" under the Mitigation Fee Act, then such fee would be subject to said statutory restrictions.[38]

In cases concerning affordable housing in-lieu fee increases, the Mitigation Fee Act also may operate to determine what is a "reasonably justified" fee increase. In the *BIA* decision, the court adopted the "test" set forth in Government Code section 66001 of the Mitigation Fee Act, which states:

> In the action imposing a fee as a condition of approval of a development project by a local agency, the local agency shall determine how there is a reasonable relationship between the amount of the fee and the cost of the public facility or portion of the public facility attributable to the development on which the fee is imposed.

171 Cal. App. 4th at 891

---

[37] *See, e.g.*, Cal. Affordable Hous. Law Project & W. Ctr. on Law and Poverty, *Inclusionary Zoning: Policy Considerations and Best Practices* (2002) at 15–19 (discussing potential benefits of providing alternatives to on-site production), *available at* http://www.oaklandnet.com/BlueRibbonCommission/PDFs/BlueRibbon11-WCLP.pdf. This kind of provision may be particularly appropriate in jurisdictions that seek to impose inclusionary requirements on all projects, including those that propose to develop only one unit; otherwise, the inclusionary program could be subject to legal challenge for imposing an entirely economically infeasible requirement. Of course, there also are policy arguments against the broad use of such alternatives. *See, e.g., Expanding Housing Opportunity in Washington, D.C., supra* note 24, at 33–34.

[38] In *City of Napa*, the plaintiff raised this argument, claiming that the ordinance's in-lieu fee provision violated the Mitigation Fee Act. The court did not address the merits of this claim, as it was deemed waived in an unpublished portion of the court's decision. 90 Cal. App. 4th at 198. *See Inclusionary Zoning: Policy Considerations and Best Practices, supra* note 41, at 30–31 (2002) for a discussion regarding the applicability of the Mitigation Fee Act to an in-lieu fee option in an inclusionary ordinance.

Proposition 218 added Article XIIID to the California Constitution, which prohibits a city from imposing a fee on property owners for services that are available to the public in general. A fee may not be assessed "as an incident of property ownership" except as specified in the article. Therefore, the issue is whether an in-lieu fee option constitutes a "fee" and thus is subject to the constitutional restrictions of Proposition 218.[39] It could be argued that such a fee is subject to Proposition 218, since it imposes a cost on property owners in connection with the development of their property. However, it is important to note the *City of Napa* court rejected this position. In so doing, it reasoned that the fees come into play only when an owner acts to develop property and not "solely by virtue of property ownership." 90 Cal. App. 4th at 200. *See also Richmond v. Shasta Cmty. Servs. Dist.*, 32 Cal. 4th 409, 419–20, 426 (2004) (upholding a water connection fee challenged under Proposition 218, holding the fee was imposed not on real property as such, but upon individuals who apply for new service connections; it thus is not a fee imposed on incident of property ownership).

PROVISION OF INCENTIVES AND CONCESSIONS TO DEVELOPERS

Many inclusionary housing programs provide incentives or concessions to developers in order to elicit compliance and further support the position that the program does not constitute an impermissible taking.[40] There are a range of incentives and concessions that jurisdictions can consider, including:

- Waivers of zoning requirements, including density, area, height, open space, use, or other provisions
- Local tax abatements
- Waiver of permit fees or land dedication requirements
- Reduction of required developer-provided amenities
- Fast-track permitting
- Subsidization or provision of infrastructure by the jurisdiction for the developer's project

> Many inclusionary housing programs provide incentives or concessions to developers in order to elicit compliance and further support the position that the program does not constitute an impermissible taking.

RELATIONSHIP TO THE COSTA-HAWKINS (ANTI-RENT CONTROL) ACT

Cities also may wish to consider the implications of providing incentives or concessions such as those listed above in order to limit challenges to rental restriction in the inclusionary program on the basis that such restriction have been preempted by state law. *See Palmer*, 175 Cal. App. 4th at 1410. *See also Town of Telluride v. Lot Thirty-Four Venture, L.L.C.*, 3 P. 3d 30 (Col. 2000) (town's "affordable housing mitigation" ordinance, which required developers to create affordable housing for 40 percent of the employees generated by the new development, as well as setting a base rental rate, constituted "rent control," thereby violating the state's anti-rent control statute).

---

[39] See *Inclusionary Zoning: Policy Considerations and Best Practices*, supra note 41, at 33 for a discussion regarding the applicability of Proposition 218 to an in-lieu fee alternative.

[40] The majority of jurisdictions in California provide some kind of developer incentive or concession. About half of the cities authorize their councils to grant a density bonus, often on a one-to-one basis (i.e., for each affordable unit provided, the developer is entitled to one additional market-rate unit). A number of programs provide a list of possible incentives to be granted only at the city's discretion. Numerous others provide "priority processing" or fast track review, which may have little practical value if every new residential project qualifies. Only one city specifically lists financial assistance as an incentive. About 35 percent of inclusionary programs provide no incentives to a developer providing inclusionary housing. *See* Kautz, *supra* note 18, at 981.

The Costa-Hawkins Rental Housing Act invalidates local rent control ordinances that do not permit owners of residential real property to set initial rents at a certain level or to establish subsequent rents when the unit is later vacated. Cal. Civ. Code §§ 1954.50–1954.535. As discussed above, inclusionary programs that impose initial and long-term affordability covenants on rental units[41] are subject to legal challenge for violating the Act. *See Palmer*, 175 Cal. App. 1396 (Costa-Hawkins Act preempts city-imposed rental restrictions).[42]

POLICY ISSUES TO CONSIDER WHEN CRAFTING AN INCLUSIONARY HOUSING PROGRAM

Along with legal considerations, there are a number of policy issues cities should evaluate when designing and implementing inclusionary housing. In so doing, a city can better tailor inclusionary housing to meet specific community needs as well as potentially bolstering the program's legal viability.

NATURE OF THE PROGRAM—MANDATORY OR VOLUNTARY?

Cities should consider whether the inclusionary housing program they adopt will be mandatory or voluntary. Advocates of a mandatory approach contend that voluntary programs lack sufficient incentives over typical market-based conditions to encourage the development of affordable units.[43] They further argue that even if there were enough incentives to offset the costs, other issues may hamper voluntary participation. These can include: (1) a lack of understanding on the part of developers regarding the economics of the inclusionary program; (2) a concern that inclusion of an affordable housing component, particularly when accomplished through higher levels of density than otherwise would be permitted, may heighten public opposition; and (3) issues relating to the administration and enforcement of the inclusionary requirements.[44]

However, there is support for voluntary programs as well. These programs rely solely on incentives to encourage developers to provide the affordable units. To be effective, the incentives must be sufficiently attractive to balance the percentage of units that are affordable and the income ranges they target. Advocates of this approach cite to the fact that voluntary programs are harder to attack legally, and their administration can be more flexible, thereby improving efficiency and effectiveness.[45] The

---

41 The Costa-Hawkins Act only applies to rental units. Accordingly, the Act cannot be applied to inclusionary for-sale units even if such units are subject to lifetime affordability covenants.

42 For informative articles on this issue, see Nadia I. El Mallakh, *Does the Costa-Hawkins Act Prohibit Local Inclusionary Zoning Programs?*, 89 Cal. L. Rev. 1849 (2001); Kautz, *supra* note 18, at 1010–11 (Summer 2002) and Institute for Local Self Government, *Legal Issues Associated with Inclusionary Housing Ordinances*, in The California Inclusionary Housing Reader, (Bill Higgins ed., Institute for Local Self Government, 2003) at 112–117, *available at* http://www.cailg.org/sites/ilgbackup.org/files/resources/California_Inclusionary_Housing_Reader.pdf.

43 For arguments in support of mandatory inclusionary programs, see *Expanding Housing Opportunity in Washington, D.C.*, *supra* note 24, at 24 (citing a study to demonstrate the superior delivery power of mandatory inclusionary housing); District of Columbia Office of Planning, *Inclusionary Zoning: A Primer* (2002) (arguing that the most successful inclusionary housing programs in the country in terms of number of affordable units built are the mandatory programs that also offer incentives to provide some compensation to the requirements); Nicholas J. Brunick, *The Inclusionary Housing Debate: The Effectiveness of Mandatory Programs Over Voluntary Programs*, Zoning Prac. no. 9 (Sept. 2004) at 2, *available at* http://www.inclusionaryhousing.ca/wpcontent/uploads/2010/01/ResourceUS_APA_IZ-PracticesSep04.pdf; Lerman, *supra* note 17.

44 *See* Kautz, *supra* note 18, at 975.

45 *See* Enterprise Foundation, *Inclusionary Zoning: Program Design Considerations (with a Program Design Checklist)* (2004), *available at* http://www.practitionerresources.org/showdoc.html?id=26115&topic=Supportive%20Housing&doctype=Model%20Document (select "view the full document").

recent *Palmer* decision also may provide additional support for voluntary programs to avoid claims of preemption. 175 Cal. App. 4th 1396 (2009).

A hybrid voluntary-mandatory inclusionary housing approach has emerged in a number of fast-growing cities that have adopted growth management ordinances. In these communities, a growth restriction is imposed by ordinance that limits the number of dwelling units that can be constructed in any given year. To determine which development applications will be approved, the city holds a "beauty contest" whereby project sponsors compete to present the most desirable project. By awarding points for the inclusion of affordable units in the proposed development, the city is able to leverage its growth cap by encouraging developers to "volunteer" to include affordable units so as to enhance their opportunity to be awarded their approvals.[46]

DETERMINING THE CLASSES AND SIZE OF DEVELOPMENT THAT WILL BE SUBJECT TO THE INCLUSIONARY HOUSING PROGRAM

Cities need to consider what classes of development, i.e., residential, mixed-use, commercial, or industrial, will be subject to inclusionary housing. The majority of inclusionary programs apply only to new residential developments. If this approach is taken, a city must then determine whether they apply to single-family or multifamily development, or both, and whether residential components of mixed-use projects will be included.

> The majority of inclusionary programs apply only to new residential developments.

Some cities also apply inclusionary requirements to commercial or industrial developments. These are often referred to as "linkage programs" because they assume a link exists between the development of a new commercial or industrial project and an increase in affordable housing needs, presumably from the new workers that the project brings to an area.[47]

In addition to determining the classes of development that will trigger application of inclusionary requirements, cities also must define the size of the project at which those requirements apply. Typically, the threshold ranges from 10 to 50 units, with small projects being exempted. However, some cities have adopted programs that set a relatively low threshold, while others are applying inclusionary policies to all projects, regardless of size.[48]

The designation of a threshold for triggering application of inclusionary requirements is a policy decision to be based on numerous factors. However, one key consideration must be an understanding of the community development patterns; otherwise, an ineffective inclusionary program may well result. For example, consider a community that has a limited supply of available land, and thus, few development applications for projects over 50 units are submitted. An inclusionary program that applied only to projects with 50 or more units, therefore, would not result in the production of much affordable housing.[49] Since the success of inclusionary housing depends on the approval and production of market-rate projects, jurisdictions are well advised to assess construction patterns and establish an inclusionary program that captures the majority of that development.

---

46 Higgins, *supra* note 27, at 3.
47 *See* Institute for Local Self Government, *Inclusionary Zoning Issues Briefing Paper*, in *The California Inclusionary Housing Reader* (2003) at 43, *available at* http://www.cailg.org/sites/ilgbackup.org/files/resources/California_Inclusionary_Housing_Reader.pdf.
48 *See Expanding Housing Opportunity in Washington, D.C., supra* note 24, at 31.
49 Several jurisdictions have adjusted the project triggers in their inclusionary ordinances to reflect shifting development patterns. For example, San Francisco amended its inclusionary housing program to eliminate the exemption for live-work developments.

REQUIRED AMOUNT AND AFFORDABILITY LEVELS OF INCLUSIONARY UNITS

There is considerable variation among inclusionary housing programs with respect to the percentage of affordable units required. Affordability levels generally range from 4 to 30 percent, with most cities imposing requirements from 10 to 15 percent.[50] Numerous considerations come into play in making this policy determination. Some cities choose to require a percentage of affordable units at the higher end of the range, with the goal of further increasing the affordable housing supply.[51] However, there are risks associated with doing so. Among others, this approach will likely heighten the risk of legal challenge and could enhance the plaintiff's chance at success should litigation ensue. Further, it actually may hamper the goals of the inclusionary program by increasing the costs of residential construction so much that developers simply cannot afford to build in that community.[52]

In addition to determining the total amount of affordable housing that will be required, cities also must consider whether their inclusionary programs will target certain lower income households. If a program merely sets forth a percentage of affordable units required, but does not specify whether these units will be affordable to very low-, low- or moderate-income households, moderate units are more likely to be produced, given the associated costs of development. Accordingly, many programs designate specific targets for each major income category in order to achieve deeper levels of affordability.[53]

Given the increased costs associated with constructing units affordable to households with low and very low incomes, cities may consider decreasing this financial burden by providing income-targeting incentives in their inclusionary programs. For example, the program could provide a credit against part of the moderate-income obligation in return for the developers producing a greater number of very low- and low-income units. Thus, if a city requires 20 percent affordability (with a mix of 10 percent moderate-, 5 percent low- and 5 percent very low-income units) and a developer exceeds the 5 percent very low-income requirement, the ten percent obligation on the moderate end could be reduced in a commensurate amount.[54]

TIMING ISSUES AND DESIGN STANDARDS FOR INCLUSIONARY UNITS

Cities may want to consider specifying the timing of when the inclusionary units are planned for completion within the context of the overall development. For a variety of reasons, affordable units may not, actually, result unless certain timing requirements are imposed. Among others, financing issues can impair a developer's long-term ability to produce such units. In addition, there is a risk of public opposition to the construction of affordable units within the project from new residents, who might not have understood that affordable units were part of the project when they bought their homes. To counter these problems and help ensure that inclusionary units are built, some cities require that the inclusionary units be constructed up front or be phased in a way that is proportional to the rest of the development.

---

50 *See Cal. Affordable Hous. Law Project & W. Ctr. on Law and Poverty, supra* note 41, at 5.
51 *Id.*
52 *See* Ellickson, *supra* note 32, at 1215-16.
53 *See* Higgins, *supra* note 27, at 3, 6.
54 *Cal. Affordable Hous. Law Project & W. Ctr. on Law and Poverty, supra* note 41, at 6.

Along with timing issues, cities should consider what design standards will be applied to the affordable units. The inclusionary program should clarify the extent to which these units must be built to the same development standards and design guidelines as the market-rate units. Conformity assures that the affordable units will consist of quality construction and will not be stigmatized within the project or the community. However, imposing such requirements can increase the cost of these units tremendously, potentially making their development infeasible.

> Cities should consider what design standards will be applied to affordable units.

In order to balance these competing concerns, many cities require stricter controls for the exterior of the affordable units, but allow for the use of less expensive (but still quality) materials for interior features and the provision of fewer interior amenities. Another means of addressing this issue is to provide the developer with incentives to construct affordable and market-rate units in a uniform manner. For instance, in return for providing affordable homes that mirror the more expensive housing in the project, developers could be permitted to charge an additional amount (perhaps five or ten percent) for the affordable homes.[55]

PRESERVING AFFORDABILITY OF INCLUSIONARY UNITS

In order to ensure that inclusionary units remain affordable for a significant period of time, most programs contain some kind of affordability controls. Otherwise, inclusionary units would be "lost" in the system and sold or rented at market rates, thereby creating a windfall to the owner at the expense of lost public and private investment. Avoiding this pitfall may require the establishment of various controls, including: (1) sales price restrictions; (2) a program for determining eligibility of applicants; (3) the setting of a specific period of time during which the inclusionary units must remain affordable; and (4) enforcement and monitoring mechanisms to ensure these requirements are met.

To effectively implement such affordability controls and related monitoring and enforcement mechanisms, a considerable amount of staff supervision is required. Accordingly, cities need to consider these administrative issues when crafting their inclusionary programs. Cities take various approaches in this regard based on the amount of supervision required under their specific programs. While some administer inclusionary housing with existing staff, others contract with outside sources such as local housing authorities to administer this staff-intensive activity.[56]

SALES PRICE LIMITATIONS

Most cities include formulas to calculate the maximum sales price for housing units, adjusted by bedroom size (which relates to family size) and appropriate income level. Different standards often are used with respect to for-sale housing. In addition, some formulas will include the cost of utilities in the rental price. Ownership units typically will include utilities, homeowners' association dues, taxes, and mortgage insurance.[57] As discussed above, cities should consider the *Palmer* decision for limitations on their ability to impose rental restrictions.

---

55 *See* Karen Destorel Brown, *Expanding Affordable Housing Through Inclusionary Zoning: Lessons from the Washington Metropolitan Area* (The Brookings Institute, Discussion Paper Series, Oct. 2001) at 26, *available at* http://www.brookings.edu/~/media/Files/rc/reports/2001/10metropolitanpolicy_brown/inclusionary.pdf.
56 *Id.*
57 *See* Higgins, *supra note 27, at 9.*

QUALIFICATION OF APPLICANTS

Criteria should be established to screen the applicants for the affordable units to ensure their income qualifies them for such units. Inclusionary programs should establish clear guidelines to assist in the administration of the program, reduce confusion, and ensure fairness. Among the issues to consider is how the inclusionary program will define very low-, low-, and moderate-income households. To ensure consistency, most inclusionary ordinances use the definitions provided by the U.S. Department of Housing and Urban Development. Another item to consider is how the income limits will be adjusted for family size and the method by which income limits will be updated.

LENGTH OF TIME THAT INCLUSIONARY UNITS MUST REMAIN AFFORDABLE

Typically, units are required to remain affordable for a period of 20 to 30 years, although the length of time can range from five years to perpetuity depending upon the city. Various policy considerations come into play when cities are determining what this time period should be. On the one hand, if affordability is required for only a short period of time, this imposes a significant burden on the community to produce additional affordable units within a relatively short time frame in order to maintain the affordable housing stock. In addition, this approach can increase the legal vulnerability of the inclusionary program by providing support for the argument that it is not, in fact, substantially advancing a legitimate interest since the increase in affordable units is more of an illusion than a reality. On the other hand, a requirement that units remain affordable in perpetuity may unreasonably penalize developers and disserve individual owners of inclusionary units by reducing their ability to benefit from the financial opportunities afforded by home ownership or their ability to remodel or refurbish units.[58]

ENFORCEMENT AND MONITORING MECHANISMS

With respect to ownership units, affordability controls generally are implemented, enforced, and monitored through resale restrictions. Such restrictions can include the following: (1) "soft" second mortgages for the difference between the appraised value and the delivered price; (2) terms for repayment of such mortgages upon sale and/or forgiveness over 10 to 20 years; (3) ownership of the underlying land by a land trust; and (4) other related devices such as the city's right of first refusal. Regulatory agreements are another tool that can be utilized to lock in specific commitments of owners, tenants, and inclusionary homeowners over time.

In order to evaluate the effectiveness of their inclusionary programs, some cities have initiated reviews or refinements once they have been in place for a number of years. One way to accomplish this objective is to build in a defined program review milestone to ensure that the inclusionary program is effective and is maximizing inclusionary opportunities.

The case of *Dieckmeyer v. Redevelopment Agency* raised issues of enforcement and monitoring. 127 Cal. App. 4th 248 (2005). In that case, the petitioner purchased a condominium under an affordable housing program (adopted pursuant to redevelopment law), wherein the city helped her finance the purchase of the unit. The parties executed

---

[58] To balance the goals of preserving affordability and promoting wealth-building opportunities of home ownership, many inclusionary programs establish shared appreciation formulas to allow the program and the inclusionary homeowner to share resale profits. *See Expanding Housing Opportunity in Washington, D.C., supra* note 24, at 33.

a loan agreement, note, and deed of trust, and certain restrictions were imposed as a condition of purchasing the home through recorded covenants, conditions, and restrictions (CC&Rs). One such condition required the homeowner to pay an "equity share," i.e., a percentage of the profit earned on the sale of the home, under certain circumstances.

The petitioner filed suit when the city sought payment of the equity share at the time petitioner sought to prepay the loan. While the court agreed with the petitioner the terms of the loan agreement did not require payment of the equity share at the time of prepayment, it refused to eliminate the equity share requirement altogether. Rather, it would remain due upon sale of the unit to a buyer who did not qualify as a low- or moderate-income household, or upon any of the other specific trigger conditions set forth in the agreement.

In so doing, the court rejected the petitioner's argument that imposing the equity share violated a legislative intent to expand housing opportunities for people of all economic levels. It noted the equity share is designed to recapture some of the profit (which would then be used to support development of additional affordable units) if the unit is sold at a market price during the 30-year affordability period in effect. The court held that the purpose of the programs would be undermined if the equity share could be eliminated by the simple expedient of prepaying the city's small down payment and closing costs loan. Since the petitioner chose to take advantage of the benefits provided by the affordable housing program, the court noted that she could not now complain about terms she accepted.

CC&Rs = covenants, conditions, and restrictions

The court noted the equity share is designed to recapture some of the profit (which would then be used to support development of additional affordable units) if the unit is sold at a market price during the 30-year affordability period in effect.

CHAPTER 16

Sustainable Development

Julie Jones

INTRODUCTION

Sustainable development has been defined as "development that meets the needs of the present without compromising the ability of future generations to meet their own needs."[1] Two primary factors have led California to focus on sustainable development in recent years. The first is population growth. Between 1980 and 2010, California's population grew from 23.7 million to 37.3 million. Even taking into account recently reduced growth projections, the state's population is expected to reach 50 million by 2049.[2] For decades, state and local governments have attempted to manage the effects of population growth, often citing sustainable development or "smart growth" principles.

> Sustainable development has been defined as "development that meets the needs of the present without compromising the ability of future generations to meet their own needs."

The second key factor in California's sustainable development focus is climate change, which has attracted great attention with the enactment of California's landmark Global Warming Solutions Act of 2006 and its many legislative and regulatory progeny.

This chapter discusses the following sustainable development efforts as they relate to land use:

- Growth management and smart growth
- Traffic congestion management
- Water supply planning and water conservation legislation
- Assembly Bill 32—the Global Warming Solutions Act of 2006
- Senate Bill 375—the Sustainable Communities and Climate Protection Act of 2008
- Guidance for evaluating climate change impacts in CEQA documents
- CEQA streamlining provisions intended to encourage infill and renewable energy development

> CEQA = California Environmental Quality Act

- Green building standards
- Renewable energy development
- Adaptation to climate change

Regulation in the area of sustainable development is evolving at a rapid pace. It is crucial to confirm the status of any legislation or regulation discussed in this chapter before relying on it.

---

1 See *Our Common Future, The World Commission on Environment and Development—Brundtland Commission* (1987), *available at* http://www.un-documents.net/ocf-02.htm.

2 California Department of Finance, Population Projections, 2010-2060. Press Release (Jan. 2013) *available at* http://www.dof.ca.gov/research/demographic/reports/projections.

GROWTH MANAGEMENT MEASURES

Since the 1970s, California cities and counties have enacted a variety of growth management measures, citing many reasons for doing so. Some measures are related directly to a lack of adequate infrastructure—limited sewer capacity, water shortages, revenue shortages, school overcrowding, and traffic congestion. Others are adopted to maintain quality of life—the community's unique character, open space, low densities, and scenic views. A desire to retain agricultural lands has become yet another reason to restrict growth in certain communities.

Environmentalists cite growth management as a means of preventing air pollution, reducing fossil fuel dependence, curbing global warming, and stopping the destruction of quickly disappearing habitat for endangered species. Growth management can, however have the opposite of this desired effect, by displacing development from a centrally located community and leading to "leapfrog" development in outlying areas.

"Growth management" also can mask exclusionary zoning, motivated by a desire to prevent lower-income families from finding affordable housing in the community, or a desire to benefit financially from the increased housing prices that often result when the housing supply is restricted. California courts have expressed concern over this "drawbridge mentality." *Building Indus. Ass'n v. City of Camarillo*, 41 Cal. 3d 810, 825 (1986) (Mosk, J., concurring). For a discussion of measures used to combat exclusionary zoning, see chapter 15 (Affordable Housing).

The California Supreme Court has emphasized that when a city adopts growth management measures that will have effects beyond its borders, the city must consider those regional effects. *Associated Home Builders, Inc. v. City of Livermore*, 18 Cal. 3d 582 (1976). To judge whether a measure limiting development within a jurisdiction bears a substantial and reasonable relationship to the *regional* welfare, the Court asked:

- What is the probable effect and duration of the ordinance?
- What are the competing interests affected by the ordinance (e.g., environmental protection versus the opportunity of people to settle where they choose)?
- Does the ordinance, in light of its probable impact, represent a reasonable accommodation of the competing interests?

Id. at 608–09.

Using this test, the *Livermore* court upheld the city's growth management ordinance, finding that the challengers had failed to meet their burden of proving that the ordinance lacked a reasonable relationship to the regional welfare. *Id.*

In 1980, the Legislature reversed this burden of proof, amending the Evidence Code to impose the burden on the city or county enacting restrictions on residential construction (including limits on the number of residential building permits allowed) to prove "that such ordinance is necessary for the protection of the public health, safety, or welfare of the population of such city, county, or city and county." Evid. Code § 669.5. *See also Building Indus. Ass'n v. City of Oceanside*, 27 Cal. App. 4th 744, 762 (1994) (finding an initiative growth control ordinance inconsistent with the city's general plan housing goals, viewed as distinguishable from the ordinance upheld in *Livermore*).

Cities and counties have used seven broad categories of tools to manage growth: housing caps; commercial and industrial caps; infrastructure adequacy ordinances; downzoning or rezoning; urban growth boundaries; voter approval requirements; and other controls such as General Plan growth management elements.[3] Most cities attempt to achieve their growth management goals by using the most basic of land use tools: the general plan, specific plans,

---

3 *See* W. Fulton, et al., *Growth Management Ballot Measures in California* (June 2002) (section 3), *available at* http://www.lgc.org/freepub/docs/community_design/reports/ca_growth_mgmt_report.pdf.

and zoning ordinances. For a complete discussion on the many types of land use techniques available, see chapter 2 (General Plan), chapter 3 (Specific Plan), and chapter 4 (Zoning).

One popular technique in California is the urban growth boundary (UGB), by which a city delineates the area beyond which it will not extend municipal services such as sewers and street maintenance. The concept behind establishing a UGB is that the area within the UGB will be made available for urban development, while land outside the UGB will remain primarily rural for farming, forestry, or low-density residential development. UGBs are meant to provide something to both developers and environmentalists—the developers are given assurance that development will be allowed to occur *somewhere*, while environmentalists are given assurance that there are certain places where development *will not* occur.

UGB = urban growth boundary

Drawing a line on a map, however, is not enough. In order for UGBs to work properly, several supporting factors need to be in place. First, cities should revise their land use laws within the UGB to allow for more dense development. Otherwise the UGB will not provide any mechanism for a city to accommodate new growth. Second, effective UGBs require some inter-jurisdictional cooperation. In large, highly developed places like the metropolitan areas of California, if a city draws its UGB at the edge of its jurisdiction, there is nothing to stop the county from picking up where the city left off, just on the other side of the line. A truly effective UGB requires regional cooperation on matters such as planning, tax revenue, and transportation.

"SMART GROWTH"

The Smart Growth movement emerged as a reaction to urban sprawl and the ill effects often associated with it—including disinvestment in central cities, environmental degradation, traffic congestion, increasing separation by race and income, conversion of prime agricultural lands, and loss of community character. The Smart Growth Network provides the following list of 10 smart growth principles:

- Mix land uses
- Take advantage of compact building design
- Create a range of housing opportunities and choices
- Create walkable neighborhoods
- Foster distinctive, attractive development with a strong sense of place
- Make development decisions predictable, fair and cost-effective
- Preserve open space, farmland, natural beauty and critical environmental areas
- Provide a variety of transportation choices
- Strengthen and direct development towards existing communities
- Encourage community and stakeholder collaboration in development decisions[4]

In 2002, the Urban Land Institute's California Smart Growth Initiative[5] identified a number of barriers that prevented or impeded the spread of Smart Growth practices. More than ten years later, these barriers remain to some degree and some have increased.

- **Fiscal zoning.** Since the passage of Proposition 13 in 1978, many of California's cities have preferred tax-generating commercial uses over housing. Such fiscal zoning discourages infill residential development.

---

[4] *See* Smart Growth Network website (http://www.smartgrowth.org/principles/mix_land.php).

[5] Urban Land Institute, *Putting the Pieces Together: State Actions to Encourage Smart Growth Practices in California (2002)*, available at http://www.uli.org/wp-content/uploads/2012/07/PuttingthePiecesTogether.ashx_.pdf.

- **Neighborhood opposition to new development.** NIMBY (Not In My Back Yard) attitudes prevail in communities that fear new development will cause traffic congestion, loss of open space, or aesthetic impacts.
- **Fragmented decisionmaking.** Piecemeal planning decisions and failure by local officials to develop and adhere to a comprehensive planning framework prohibit the integration of, for instance, a transportation system linked to efficient development. The same problem is repeated on the regional level with a lack of coordination among jurisdictions.
- **Insufficient funding for infrastructure.** Infill development requires the updating of sewer, water, street, and public transportation infrastructure. Infrastructure deficits hinder efforts to make these necessary improvements.
- **Limited funding for planning.** Funding for Smart Growth planning strategies often falls victim to perennial budget shortfalls in many localities.
- **CEQA redundancies.** CEQA procedures that have evolved to evaluate the potential environmental impacts of proposed plans and projects contain redundancies that create uncertainties, delays and additional costs in the development process.
- **Brownfield development issues.** The federal, state, and local regulatory regimes governing the development of even slightly contaminated building sites cause uncertainty and delay that discourage developers, lenders, and insurers from investing in them.
- **Construction defect litigation.** By 2002, the rise in lawsuits brought by homeowners against developers and builders had made the construction of multifamily residential units expensive and risky. In 2002, the Legislature enacted a law intended to address this problem by setting out clear performance standards for many aspects of construction, and by providing pre-litigation dispute resolution procedures to facilitate lower cost solutions to residents' grievances. *See* Civ. Code § 895 *et seq.*

> "Smart growth" principles, whether or not so labeled, have continued to be incorporated into California law, culminating in Senate Bill 375, the land use element of the Legislature's response to global climate change.

"Smart growth" principles, whether or not so labeled, have continued to be incorporated into California law, culminating in Senate Bill 375, the land use and transportation element of the Legislature's response to global climate change, enacted in 2008 and discussed in detail later in this chapter.

In addition, in 2004, the Legislature amended the State Environmental Goals and Policy Report, which is used to direct state budget resources, to include goals of infill development, redevelopment of land already served by infrastructure and transit, efficient development in greenfields, and the preservation of natural resources and agricultural land. Gov't Code § 65041 *et seq.*

In 2002, 2004, 2005, and 2008, the Legislature amended the state's density bonus law, which requires a city to provide incentives or concessions to developers who agree to construct affordable housing. A city must grant a density bonus and certain incentives or concessions, unless it makes written findings to show that the development would have an adverse effect on health, safety, or the environment, that the incentive is not required to provide for affordable housing costs, or that the incentive would be contrary to state or federal law. Gov't Code § 65915(d)(1). "In no case may a city...apply any development standard that will have the effect of precluding the construction of a development meeting the criteria of [the density bonus law] at the densities or with the concessions or incentives permitted by this section." Gov't Code § 65915(e). If a city refuses to grant the density bonus and incentive or concession, the developer may initiate judicial proceedings, and may recover reasonable attorneys' fees and costs of suit for violation of the statute. Gov't Code §§ 65915(d)(3) and (e). For further discussion of the state density bonus law, see chapter 15 (Affordable Housing).

SUSTAINABLE DEVELOPMENT AND TRANSPORTATION POLICY

CONGESTION MANAGEMENT PLANNING

Even prior to the enactment of Senate Bill 375 in 2008, California has used transportation policy—and transportation funding—in an attempt to reduce vehicle emissions and encourage infill development and alternative transportation opportunities.

In 1990, the voters adopted Proposition 111, which substantially increased gas tax and truck fee revenues to fund road, bicycle, pedestrian, and public transit projects, in addition to traditional highway and road improvements. *See* Chapter 2.6 (Congestion Management) of Title 7 (Planning and Land Use) of the Government Code, Gov't Code § 65088 *et seq.*

The law requires each county that does not opt out (*see* Gov't Code § 65088.3) to designate a Congestion Management Agency (CMA). A CMA is either a county transportation commission or another public agency. Every two years, the CMA must issue a Congestion Management Program (CMP). In developing the CMP, the CMA must consult and cooperate with the transportation planning agency, regional transportation providers, local governments, the Transportation Department, and the air pollution control or air quality management district. Gov't Code § 65089(a).

> CMA = Congestion Management Agency
>
> CMP = Congestion Management Program

The CMP must include five elements:

- Traffic level of service standards established for, at a minimum, all state highways and principal arterials. Except in infill opportunity zones (described below), when the level of service on a roadway segment or at an intersection fails to attain the established level of service, the local jurisdiction also must adopt a deficiency plan to address the deficiency, unless it shows that certain external factors account for the deficiency
- A performance element to evaluate current and future multimodal system performance for the movement of people and goods, including performance measures that support mobility, air quality, land use, and economic objectives
- A travel demand element that promotes alternative transportation methods "including, but not limited to, carpools, vanpools, transit, bicycles, and park-and-ride lots; improvements in the balance between jobs and housing; and other strategies, including, but not limited to, flexible work hours, telecommuting, and parking management programs"
- A program to analyze the impacts of land use decisions made by local jurisdictions on regional transportation systems, including an estimate of the costs associated with mitigating those impacts
- A seven-year capital improvement program

Gov't Code §§ 65089(b), 65089.4

If the CMA, after conducting annual monitoring and a noticed public hearing, determines that a city is not conforming to the requirements of the CMP, the CMA must notify the city in writing of the specific areas of nonconformance. Gov't Code § 65089.5(a). If the city does not come into conformance with the CMP, the CMA must make a finding of nonconformance and submit the finding to the California Transportation Commission and the California Controller. Upon receiving notice of nonconformance from the CMA, the Controller must withhold apportionments of funds generated by Proposition 111 to the nonconforming city until the Controller is notified by the CMA that the city is in conformance. Id.

In 2002, the CMP law was amended allow cities, until December 31, 2009, to create "infill opportunity zones" within 1/3 of a mile of major public transit routes, for new compact residential and mixed-use development in population centers of more than 400,000 people. Some cities established such zones, which are exempt from traffic level of service requirements normally required by a CMP. The Legislature's intent was to encourage dense infill development near transit where traffic level of service requirements would otherwise preclude higher densities.

In 2013, concerned that traditional level of service standards and traffic impact assessment methodologies continued to inhibit infill development, the Legislature took further action. First, it reinstated the ability of cities and counties to designate infill opportunity zones, which now must be within 1/2 mile of a major transit stop or high-quality transit corridor and must be a "transit priority area" within an SB 375 sustainable communities strategy or alternative development strategy.[6] Gov't Code §§ 65088.1, 65088.4. CMP level of service standards "shall not apply to the streets and highways" within these new infill opportunity zones. Gov't Code § 65088.4(b). In addition to reviving infill opportunity zones, the Legislature called for modernization of transportation analysis for transit-oriented infill projects. The Secretary of Resources is to adopt new CEQA Guidelines under which "automobile delay, as described solely by level of service or similar measures of vehicular capacity or traffic congestion shall not be considered a significant impact on the environment" of transit-oriented infill projects under CEQA. Pub. Res. Code § 21099. Local governments remain free, however, to impose conditions under local law. Pub. Res. Code § 21099(b)(4).

RELATIONSHIP BETWEEN CMPs AND REGIONAL TRANSPORTATION PLANS

> MPO = metropolitan planning organization

A county CMP is different from a regional transportation plan and a regional transportation improvement program, the latter of which are developed by one of the 18 regional metropolitan planning organizations (MPOs). However, a CMP must be consistent with the pertinent regional transportation plan and the supporting improvement program. Gov't Code §§ 65080, 65089.2(a). Once the MPO finds the CMP is consistent, it will incorporate the CMP into the regional transportation improvement program. Gov't Code §§ 65089.2(b), 65082. Inclusion has implications that may improve the federal funding of local transportation projects. As discussed later in this chapter, the enactment of Senate Bill 375 in 2008 strengthened the link between transportation funding and land use planning.

"COMPLETE STREETS"

In 2007, citing Assembly Bill 32 (2006), the Legislature revised the requirements for city and county general plan circulation elements. Effective January 1, 2011, "upon any substantive revision of the circulation element," the circulation element shall be modified "to plan for a balanced, multimodal transportation network that meets the needs of all users of streets, roads, and highways," i.e., "bicyclists, children, persons with disabilities, motorists, movers of commercial goods, pedestrians, users of public transportation, and seniors." Gov't Code § 65302(b)(2). The legislation, co-sponsored by the California Bicycle Coalition and AARP California, is referred to as the "Complete

---

[6] These strategies are discussed further below under "Senate Bill 375: The Sustainable Communities and Climate Protection Act of 2008."

Streets Act." The Act reflects increasing demand for roadways that accommodate bicyclists, pedestrians and transit.

WATER SUPPLY PLANNING AND CONSERVATION

Water supply planning and conservation has assumed ever-increasing importance due to California's population growth, the effects of climate change on water supplies, and the GHG emissions associated with pumping water throughout the state.

GHG = greenhouse gas

SENATE BILLS 610 AND 221

In 2001, California enacted two bills that address the marriage of land use planning and water supply planning. Senate Bill 610, which typically comes into play for planning level approvals, requires water supply assessments, and Senate Bill 221, which applies to certain residential subdivision maps, requires water supply verifications. Both bills require cities and counties[7] to contact the water agency proposed to serve a large development project to analyze whether water supplies are sufficient to serve the project. For a summary of the requirements of SB 610 and SB 221, and a comparison between the two bills, see Table 3 on the following pages.

As the California Supreme Court has explained:

> Taken together, Water Code sections 10910 to 10912 and Government Code section 66473.7 thus demand...that water supplies must be identified with more specificity at each step as land use planning and water supply planning move forward from general phases to more specific phases. The plans and estimates that Water Code section 10910 mandates for future water supplies at the time of any approval subject to CEQA must, under Government Code section 66473.7, be replaced by firm assurances at the subdivision map approval stage.

Vineyard Area Citizens for Responsible Growth v. City of Rancho Cordova, 40 Cal. 4th 412, 433-434 (2007) (quotations omitted).

The water agency's water supply assessment or water supply verification should be based on its current Urban Water Management Plan (UWMP).[8] Most urban water suppliers are required to prepare UWMPs every five years. Water Code section 10635 requires that the supplier's UWMP include "an assessment of the reliability of its water service to its customers during normal, dry, and multiple dry water years. This water supply and demand assessment shall compare the total water supply sources available to the water supplier with the total projected water use over the next 20 years, in five-year increments, for a normal water year, a single dry water year, and multiple dry water years. The water service reliability assessment shall be based on the information compiled pursuant to section 10631, including available data from state, regional, or local agency population projections within the service area of the urban water supplier." Compliance with SB 610 and SB 221 is generally more difficult if a current, comprehensive UWMP is not in place.

UWMP = Urban Water Management Plan

Under SB 610, the water supply and demand projections that the assessment contains need not be certain. For example, a water supplier that relies on groundwater supplies does not necessarily need to take account of the entire groundwater basin before

---

7 SB 610 applies only to cities and counties, not to other agencies. SB 221, because it applies only to agencies that have the power to approve tentative subdivision maps, also applies only to cities and counties.

8 *See generally Guidebook for Implementation of Senate Bill 610 and Senate Bill 221 of 2001*, California Department of Water Resources (2003), *available at* http://www.water.ca.gov.

TABLE 3. COMPARISON OF SB 610 AND SB 221

	SB 610 ASSESSMENT	SB 221 VERIFICATION
Codified	Water Code (WC) §§ 10631, 10656, 10657, 10910–10912; Pub. Res. Code § 21151.9	Business & Prof. Code § 11010 (report to DRE to include verification); Government Code (GC) §§ 65867.5 (development agreement); 66455.3 (process); 66473.7 (tentative map condition)
Projects covered	Large projects approved by a city or county—various land uses: • Residential > 500 units • Shopping center or business establishment > 1,000 employees or > 500,000 sf of floor space • Office building > 1,000 employees or > 250,000 sf of floor space • Hotel or motel > 500 rooms • Industrial, manufacturing or processing plant, or industrial park housing > 1,000 persons, > 40 acres or > 650,000 sf of floor space • Mixed-use project that includes one or more of above • Project that would demand water ≥ the amount of water required by 500 dwelling units	Large subdivisions—residential only: • Residential subdivisions of > 500 units; or if public water system has < 5,000 connections, a residential development that would generate an increase of 10 percent or more in connections. GC § 66473.7(a) • Development agreements that include such a subdivision. GC § 65867.5(c)
	• If public water system has < 5,000 connections, an increase of 10 percent or more, or a project with equivalent water demand WC § 10912	
Exceptions	None stated	• Project proposed for a site within an urbanized area that has previously been developed for urban uses or where the immediate contiguous properties surrounding the site are, or previously have been, developed for urban uses • Housing projects that are exclusively for very low and low-income households GC § 66473.7(i)
Context	**Processing.** An evaluation of a 20-year water supply for the project must be included in an EIR, Negative Declaration, or Mitigated Negative Declaration prepared for the project.	**Map Act.** The tentative map approval must be conditioned on a requirement that water supply be verified before final map approval.
Water supply analysis required	An assessment of water supplies which addresses whether "the total projected water supplies available during normal, single-dry and multiple-dry water years during a 20-year projection will meet the projected water demand associated with the proposed project, in addition to...existing and planned future uses, including agricultural and manufacturing uses." WC § 10910(c).	A verification that a sufficient water supply shall be available, meaning "the total water supplies available during normal, single-dry, and multiple-dry years within a 20-year projection that will meet the projected demand associated with the proposed subdivision, in addition to existing and planned future uses, including, but not limited to, agricultural and industrial uses." GC § 66473.7(a).
Agency that analyzes water supply and form of determination	A public water system, which means a system for the provision of piped water to the public for human consumption that has 3,000 or more service connections. WC § 10912(c). The city or county must identify any public water system that may supply water for the project and request an assessment from each. WC §§ 10910(b), (c). The governing body of the water supplier must approve the assessment at a regular or special meeting. WC § 10910(g)(1) If there is no public water system, then the city or county prepares the assessment after consulting with any domestic water supplier whose service area includes the project site, LAFCO, and any public water system adjacent to the project site. WC § 10910(b)	A public water system, which means a system for the provision of piped water to the public for human consumption that has 3,000 or more service connections, that may supply water for a subdivision. GC § 66473.7(a)(3); WC § 10912. The public water system must "deliver the written verification" to the local agency. GC § 66473.7(b) If there is no public water system, the local agency approving the map shall make a finding of sufficient water supply based on the same evidence, and identify the mechanism for providing water to the subdivision. GC § 66473.7(e)

COMPARISON OF SB 610 AND SB 221 *continued*

	SB 610 ASSESSMENT	SB 221 VERIFICATION
Initial step in process	The "city or county, at the time that it determines whether an environmental impact report, a negative declaration, or a mitigated negative declaration is required for any project subject to the California Environmental Quality Act..." must identify the water provider. WC § 10910(b); Pub. Res. Code § 21151.9	"Not later than five days after a city or county has determined that a tentative map application for a proposed subdivision... is complete," the city or county must send a copy of the application to the water supplier. GC § 66455.3 For a development agreement, the city or county need only ensure that the agreement requires that the tentative map(s) comply. GC § 65867.5
Timing	The public water system is to provide the assessment not later than 90 days after receiving a request from the city or county. WC § 10910(g) (1). Before that time expires, the public water system may request an extension of up to 30 days from the city or county. WC § 10910(g)(2). If the public water system does not meet these deadlines, the city or county may seek a writ compelling compliance. WC § 10910(g)(3)	Proof of the availability of a sufficient water supply "shall be based on a written verification from the applicable public water system within 90 days of a request." If the water system fails to deliver the verification, the local agency or any interested party may seek a writ compelling compliance. If the water system fails to provide a verification notwithstanding a writ, then the local agency may make a finding—on the record and supported by substantial evidence—that sufficient water supplies are, or will be, available prior to completion of the subdivision. GC § 66473.7(b)
Proof of supplies	The assessment must identify relevant, existing water supply entitlements, water rights, or water service contracts, and describe the quantities of water received in prior years. The identification shall be demonstrated by providing information related to all of the following: • Written contracts or other proof of entitlement to an identified water supply • Copies of a capital outlay program for financing the delivery of a water supply that has been adopted by the public water system • Federal, state, and local permits for construction of necessary infrastructure associated with delivering the water supply • Any necessary regulatory approvals that are required in order to be able to convey or deliver the water supply If no water has been received in prior years under an existing entitlement, right, or contract, the assessment must identify the other public water systems or water service contractholders that receive a water supply or have existing entitlements, rights, or contracts, to the same source of water. WC §§ 10910(d)(2), (e)	In determining a "sufficient water supply," all of the following factors shall be considered: • The availability of water supplies over a historical record of at least 20 years • The applicability of an urban water shortage contingency analysis prepared pursuant to Section 10632 of the Water Code that includes actions to be undertaken by the public water system in response to water supply shortages. • The reduction in water supply allocated to a specific water use sector pursuant to a resolution or ordinance adopted, or a contract entered into, by the public water system, as long as that resolution, ordinance, or contract does not conflict with Section 354 of the Water Code. • The amount of water that the water supplier can reasonably rely on receiving from other water supply projects, such as conjunctive use, reclaimed water, water conservation, and water transfer, including programs identified under federal, state, and local water initiatives such as CALFED and Colorado River tentative agreements, to the extent that these water supplies meet the criteria of subdivision (d) [regarding projected supplies] GC § 66473.7(a)(2) In addition, the verification shall be supported by substantial evidence which may include, but is not limited to: • The public water system's most recently adopted urban water management plan • A water supply assessment that was completed pursuant to Part 2.10 (commencing with section 10910) of Division 6 of the Water Code • Other information relating to the sufficiency of the water supply that contains analytical information that is substantially similar to the assessment equired by section 10635 of the Water Code* GC § 66473.7(c)

* Section 10635 requires that an Urban Water Management Plan include "an assessment of the reliability of its water service to its customers during normal, dry, and multiple dry water years. This water supply and demand assessment shall compare the total water supply sources available to the water supplier with the total projected water use over the next 20 years, in five-year increments, for a normal water year, a single dry water year, and multiple dry water years. The water service reliability assessment shall be based upon the information compiled pursuant to section 10631, including available data from state, regional, or local agency population projections within the service area of the urban water supplier."

COMPARISON OF SB 610 AND SB 221 *continued*

	SB 610 ASSESSMENT	SB 221 VERIFICATION
Other water supplies	**Supplies to remedy insufficiency.** If the public water system's total projected water supplies available during a 20-year projection are insufficient, then the water agency must identify plans to acquire additional supplies that may include, but are not limited to: • The estimated total costs, and the proposed method of financing the costs, associated with acquiring the additional water supplies • All federal, state, and local permits, approvals, or entitlements that are anticipated to be required in order to acquire and develop the additional water supplies • Based on the considerations set forth in paragraphs (1) and (2), the estimated timeframes within which the public water system expects to be able to acquire additional water supplies WC §§ 10910(c)(3), 10911(a)	**Projected supplies.** For projected supplies not currently available to the public water system, the verification shall be based on all of the following, to the extent each is applicable: • Written contracts or other proof of valid rights to the identified water supply that identify the terms and conditions under which the water will be available to serve the proposed subdivision • Copies of a capital outlay program for financing the delivery of a sufficient water supply that has been adopted by the applicable governing body • Securing of applicable federal, state, and local permits for construction of necessary infrastructure associated with supplying a sufficient water supply to the subdivision GC § 66473.7(d) **Supplies not considered by the water supplier.** The local agency may make a finding, after consideration of the written verification by the applicable public water system, and based on substantial evidence, that additional supplies not accounted for by the public water system are, or will be, available prior to completion of the subdivision that will satisfy the requirements for a verification of a 20-year water supply. GC § 66473.7(b)(3)
Groundwater	If a water supply for a proposed project includes groundwater, the following additional information shall be included in the water supply assessment: • (f)(1) A review of any information contained in the urban water management plan relevant to the identified water supply for the proposed project • (f)(2) A description of any groundwater basin or basins from which the proposed project will be supplied. For those basins for which a court or the board has adjudicated the rights to pump groundwater, a copy of the order or decree adopted by the court or the board and a description of the amount of groundwater the public water system...has the legal right to pump under the order or decree. For basins that have not been adjudicated, information as to whether the department has identified the basin or basins as overdrafted or has projected that the basin will become overdrafted if present management conditions continue, in the most current bulletin of the department that characterizes the condition of the groundwater basin, and a detailed description by the public water system...of the efforts being undertaken in the basin or basins to eliminate the long-term overdraft condition. • (f)(3) A detailed description and analysis of the amount and location of groundwater pumped by the public water system...for the past five years from any groundwater basin from which the proposed project will be supplied. The description and analysis shall be based on information that is reasonably available, including, but not limited to, historic use records. • (f)(4) A detailed description and analysis of the amount and location of groundwater that is projected to be pumped by the public water system,...from any basin from which the proposed project will be supplied. The description and analysis shall be based on information that is reasonably available, including, but not limited to, historic use records.	Where a water supply for a proposed subdivision includes groundwater, the public water system serving the proposed subdivision shall evaluate, based on substantial evidence, the extent to which it or the landowner has the right to extract the additional groundwater needed to supply the proposed subdivision. Nothing in this subdivision is intended to modify state law with regard to groundwater rights. GC § 66473.7(h)

COMPARISON OF SB 610 AND SB 221 *continued*

	SB 610 ASSESSMENT	SB 221 VERIFICATION
Groundwater *(continued)*	• (f)(5) An analysis of the sufficiency of the groundwater from the basin or basins from which the proposed project will be supplied to meet the projected water demand associated with the proposed project A water supply assessment shall not be required to include the information required by this paragraph if the public water system determines, as part of the review required by paragraph (1), that the sufficiency of groundwater necessary to meet the initial and projected water demand associated with the project was addressed in the description and analysis required by paragraph (4) of subdivision (b) of Section 10631.** WC § 10910(f)	
Analyses regarding issues other than sufficiency	The assessment is to be included in an environmental document, which will address other impacts of the project. WC § 10911(b)	The verification must also include a description, to the extent information is reasonable available based on published records of federal and state agencies, and public records of local agencies, of the impacts of a proposed subdivision on the availability of water resources for agricultural and industrial uses within the public water system's service area that are not receiving water from the public water system, but are taking from the same source. If this issue was evaluated in a prior environmental document, that information may be used. GC § 66473.7(g)
City or county's ability to override public water agency's determination	The city or county may include an evaluation of the assessment in the EIR, Negative Declaration, or Mitigated Negative Declaration. WC § 10911(c). The city or county is ultimately responsible for determining whether supplies will be sufficient. WC § 10911(c) (see next cell).	Local agency may make a finding, after consideration of the written verification by the applicable public water system, and based on substantial evidence, that additional supplies not accounted for by the public water system are, or will be, available prior to completion of the subdivision that will satisfy the requirements for a verification of a 20-year water supply. GC § 66473.7(b)(3)
City or county findings	"The city or county shall determine, based on the entire record, whether projected water supplies will be sufficient to satisfy the demands of the project, in addition to existing and planned future uses. If the city or county determines that water supplies will not be sufficient, the city or couty shall include that determination in its findings for the project." WC § 10911(c)	The initial requirement is to include as a condition on the tentative map "a requirement that a sufficient water supply shall be available." GC § 66473.7(b)(1) If the water agency reports that supplies are not sufficient, the local agency may find that additional supplies support a verification. This finding "shall be made on the record and supported by substantial evidence." GC § 66473.7(b)(3) If no verification is provided by the water agency despite requests and a court order, the local agency "may make a finding that sufficient water supplies are, or will be, available prior to completion of the subdivision that will satisfy the requirements of this section. This finding shall be made on the record and supported by substantial evidence." GC § 66473.7(b)(4)
Prior and later analyses	If the project has been the subject of an assessment that complies with the requirements of SB 610, then no additional water supply assessment shall be required for subsequent projects that were part of a larger project for which water supplies were found sufficient. Exceptions are: • Changes in the project that will substantially increase water demand • Changes in circumstances that substantially affect the ability to provide a sufficient water supply • Significant new information becomes known WC § 10910(h)	A water supply assessment prepared under SB 610 may constitute evidence for the SB 221 verification. GC § 66473.7(c)(2)

** SB 610 proposed amendments to section 10631(b)(4) to require "A detailed description and analysis of the location, amount, and sufficiency of groundwater that is projected to be pumped by the urban water supplier. The description and analysis shall be based on information that is reasonably available, including, but not limited to, historic use records." Subdivision (b)(4) now provides: "A detailed description and analysis of the amount and location of groundwater that is projected to be pumped by the urban water supplier. The description and analysis shall be based on information that is reasonably available, including, but not limited to, historic use records."

projecting how much groundwater will be available to it in the future. *O.W.L. Foundation v. City of Rohnert Park,* 168 Cal. App. 4th 568 (2008). Projections about water supply entitlements the water agency expects to gain in the future may be even less certain:

> With regard to *existing* supply entitlements and rights, a water supply assessment must include assurances such as written contracts, capital outlay programs and regulatory approvals for facilities construction..., but as to additional *future* supplies needed to serve the project, the assessment need include only the public water system's plans for acquiring the additional supplies, including cost and time estimates and regulatory approvals the system anticipates needing.

Vineyard Area Citizens supra, 40 Cal. 4th at 433.

Nor does the statute dictate that any particular methodology be used to assess sufficiency; rather, the statute affords the water supplier substantial discretion in determining how to measure sufficiency. *O.W.L. Foundation,* 168 Cal. App. 4th 568.

SB 610 requires a city to include the assessment in "any environmental document prepared for the project pursuant to [CEQA]." Water Code § 10911. The city also may include its own evaluation of the water agency's assessment in that same document. SB 610 then leaves the ultimate determination whether water supplies will be sufficient to the city and requires the city to include that information in its findings for the project. *See* Water Code § 10911(c). Until these final steps are taken, a water supply assessment will generally not be ripe for judicial review. *O.W.L. Foundation,* 168 Cal. App. 4th at 580–585; *California Water Impact Network v. Newhall County Water Dist.,* 161 Cal. App. 4th 1464 (2008). If an SB 610 assessment concludes that supplies will be sufficient for a large project, no additional assessment shall be required for subsequent projects that are part of that larger project. Water Code § 10910(h).

SENATE BILL X7-7

In 2009, the Legislature enacted SB X7-7, requiring the state to achieve a 20 percent reduction in urban per capita water use by December 31, 2020, and to make progress toward this goal by reducing per capita water use by at least 10 percent on or before December 15, 2015. Water Code §§ 10608-10608.64. Urban retail water suppliers are required to identify their targets in Urban Water Management Plans that were due by August 1, 2011. SB X7-7 also imposed new water management requirements on agricultural water suppliers; the first agricultural water management plans incorporating SB X7-7 requirements were due from the agricultural water suppliers by December 31, 2012. Water Code §§ 10800-10853. The "20 percent by 2020" rule has placed increased pressure on urban water retailers to require water conservation, and this requirement trickles down to cities and counties through the SB 610 water supply assessment and SB 221 water supply verification requirements.

GRAYWATER SYSTEMS

Graywater systems use water from showers, bath tubs, washing machines and bathroom sinks for landscape irrigation. In 2012, the Legislature amended the Water Code to encourage the use of graywater by curtailing the ability of a city, county or other local agency to adopt building standards that are more restrictive than the graywater building standards adopted by the state (Chapter 16A of the California Plumbing Code). Local agencies may adopt more restrictive graywater rules only if they identify "the local climatic, geological, topographical, or public health conditions that necessitate building standards that are more restrictive than the graywater building standards adopted to pursuant to state requirements and shall be limited to the specific area of the city, county, or local agency where the conditions exist." Water Code § 14877.3.

ASSEMBLY BILL 32: THE CALIFORNIA GLOBAL WARMING SOLUTIONS ACT OF 2006

Assembly Bill 32 is the state's primary legislative response to rising GHG emissions.[9] The bill calls for both the establishment of GHG reduction targets and the implementation of measures to ensure the state will meet those objectives.

AB 32 commits California, by the year 2020, to reduce greenhouse gas emissions to their 1990 level, which the California Air Resources Board (CARB) has determined is 427 million metric tons of carbon dioxide equivalent.[10]

CARB = California Air Resources Board

AB 32 required CARB to adopt a "scoping plan" to identify ways to "achieve the maximum technologically feasible and cost-effective reduction in greenhouse gas emissions...by 2020." CARB completed its scoping plan in 2008 and has since updated its projections.[11] The current scoping plan includes the following key strategies for reducing California GHG emissions:

- Expand and strengthen existing energy efficiency programs and building and appliance standards
- Achieve a statewide renewables energy mix of 33 percent
- Develop a California cap-and-trade program
- Establish targets for transportation-related GHG emissions in the state and pursue policies and incentives to achieve those targets
- Adopt and implement emissions reduction measures under existing California laws and policies, such as California's Clean Car Standards and Low Carbon Fuel Standard[12]
- Create targeted fee programs, such as a public goods charge on water usage that can be used to fund water efficiency programs and improvements, and fees to fund the administrative costs of implementing AB 32

The reduction of transportation-related GHG emissions is the element of AB 32 that most directly affects the planning and approval of development projects in California.

The AB 32 Scoping Plan must be updated every five years. In October 2013, CARB released its discussion draft of the first five-year update. The draft Scoping Plan Update finds that California is on track to meet AB 32's GHG reduction goal for 2020, and it

---

9 GHGs include carbon dioxide, methane, nitrous oxide, hydrofluorocarbons, perfluorocarbons, and sulfur hexafluoride. Health & Safety Code § 38505(g); CEQA Guidelines § 15364.4.

10 Carbon dioxide equivalent is a metric used to compare the effects of emissions from various greenhouse gases; for example, a few pounds of some gases (e.g., nitrogen trifluoride) can have the same effect on climate change as several tons of carbon dioxide.

11 See *Climate Change Scoping Plan* (December 2008) *available at* http://www.arb.ca.gov/cc/scopingplan/document/adopted_scoping_plan.pdf *and Status of Scoping Plan Recommended Measures, available at* http://www.arb.ca.gov/cc/scopingplan/status_of_scoping_plan_measures.pdf (updating 2008 Scoping Plan). Like many regulatory actions associated with GHG reduction, the 2008 Scoping Plan was controversial and was challenged in litigation. *See Association of Irritated Residents v. California Air Resources Board,* 206 Cal. App. 4th 1487 (2012) (upholding Scoping Plan).

12 CARB's Low Carbon Fuel Standard regulations have been challenged in both state and federal courts. A state appellate court held that CARB unlawfully adopted the regulations before completing a CEQA review, but the court allowed the LCFS to remain in place while CARB takes action to comply with CEQA. *POET, LLC v. California Air Resources Board,* 218 Cal. App. 4th 681 (2013). The Ninth Circuit Court of Appeal has rejected claims that the LCFS constitutes a facially impermissible burden on interstate commerce and an unconstitutional extra-territorial regulation on out-of-state fuel producers, but has left other challenges to be resolved on remand. *Rocky Mountain Farmers Union v. Corey,* 730 F.3d 1070 (9th Cir. 2013).

recommends actions to ensure that the 2020 goal is met and to meet the state's climate goals beyond 2020.[13] CARB anticipates adopting the Scoping Plan Update in Spring 2014.[14]

SENATE BILL 375: SUSTAINABLE COMMUNITIES AND CLIMATE PROTECTION ACT OF 2008

Senate Bill 375 seeks to reduce California's GHG emissions by reducing vehicle miles traveled. The bill begins by noting that cars and light trucks account for almost 30 percent of GHG emissions and 50 percent of all air pollution in California. 2008 Cal. Stat. Ch. 728, Section 1(a) & (d) (uncodified). To reduce vehicle miles traveled, SB 375 addresses leapfrog and sprawling development patterns by tying land use planning to transportation planning. SB 375 relies on incentives (CEQA streamlining)[15] and disincentives (potential loss of transportation funding) to strongly encourage local agencies to establish complementary land uses such as housing, job centers and transit hubs in closer proximity to each other.

SUSTAINABLE COMMUNITIES STRATEGIES

The centerpiece of SB 375 is the new "sustainable communities strategy" that now must be included in the federally mandated regional transportation plan prepared every four or five years by each California metropolitan planning organization (MPO). California has 18 MPOs in total, covering 37 counties and 98 percent of the state's population. The four largest of these (the Southern California Association of Governments [SCAG], the Bay Area's Metropolitan Transportation Commission [MTC], the San Diego Association of Governments [SANDAG], and the Sacramento Area Council of Governments [SACOG]) include 82 percent of the state's population. Under SB 375, CARB was tasked with establishing targets that address emissions from automobiles and light trucks for each region of California that has an MPO. After a two-year process (see Gov't Code § 65080(b)(2)), CARB established these targets in early 2011.

The targets, described as the "most ambitious achievable," represent a per capita percentage of GHG emission reduction, relative to 2005 levels. The targets are designed to be achieved through regional land use and transportation strategies, and not to reflect changes in vehicle emissions standards or fuel economy that are expected to independently reduce GHG emissions. The reduction targets for the four largest MPOs and the group of eight MPOs that make up the San Joaquin Valley region currently are:

MPO	2020	2035
SCAG	8%	13%
MTC	7%	15%
SANDAG	7%	13%
SACOG	7%	16%
San Joaquin MPOs	5%	10%

---

13 In 2005, Governor Schwarzenegger targeted a statewide reduction of GHG emissions to 80 percent below 1990 levels by 2050 (Exec. Order 5-3-5). In 2012, Governor Brown specified that the transportation sector should achieve the same target of an 80 percent reduction from 1990 (Exec. Order B-16-2012).

14 See CARB's news release at http://www.arb.ca.gov/newsrel/newsrelease.php?id=509 and the Discussion Draft Climate Change Scoping Plan First Update at http://arb.ca.gov/cc/scoping plan/2013_update/discussion_draft.pdf.

15 Streamlining under SB 375 is discussed in Table 4 below, along with other CEQA streamlining measures.

With these targets in place, SB 375 next requires that each MPO develop its sustainable communities strategy. Gov't Code §§ 65080(b)(2)(A), (B)(2), and (G). The sustainable communities strategy must include a development pattern that, when integrated with the regional transportation network and policies, will reduce emissions from cars and trucks to achieve the CARB targets for the region "if there is a feasible way to do so." Gov't Code § 65080(b)(2)(B). The authoring MPO must quantify the expected reduction in GHG emissions and state whether it will meet the regional target. Gov't Code § 65080(b)(2)(H).

To develop the strategies, the MPOs must use information from general plans and other sources to forecast the requisite development pattern; that is, the plan must be based on estimates of current and future population and assumptions regarding employment, travel, and congestion. *See* 40 CFR § 93.110, incorporated by Gov't Code § 65080(b)(2)(B) (plan must be based on recent planning assumptions, including "estimates of current and future population, employment, travel, and congestion most recently developed by the MPO").

If the MPO finds that it cannot meet the targets (e.g., due to lack of funding for infrastructure), the MPO must prepare an "alternative planning strategy" that identifies the impediments to achieving the targets, and how the targets would be achieved through alternate development patterns, infrastructure, or additional measures or policies. Gov't Code § 65080(b)(2)(H). An alternative planning strategy is not to be included in the regional transportation plan.

MPOs must submit sustainable communities strategies and alternative planning strategies to CARB for review, and CARB must accept or reject an MPO's demonstration that a sustainable communities strategy would meet its GHG reduction target. As of November 2013, the status of the sustainable communities strategies for the four largest MPOs and the San Joaquin Valley MPOs is:

- SANDAG: SCS completed and accepted by CARB November 2011; San Diego Superior Court overturned December 2012
- SCAG: SCS completed and accepted by CARB June 2012
- SACOG: SCS completed and accepted by CARB June 2012
- MTC: SCS completed July 2013; three legal challenges pending; no CARB action
- San Joaquin MPOs: SCS adoption anticipated 2014

CARB tracks the progress of sustainable communities strategies on its website at www.arb.ca.gov/cc/sb375/sb375.htm.

A sustainable communities strategy does not supersede a city's or county's general plan, specific plan, or zoning ordinance. Gov't Code § 65080(b)(2)(J). Nor does SB 375 require any consistency between the sustainable communities strategy and these planning documents. Nevertheless, because transportation funding is now tied to SB 375 compliance by way of the regional transportation plan, local agencies are likely to take those strategies seriously in their land use decisionmaking. Moreover, as discussed below, the regional housing needs allocations that form the basis of each city's and county's general plan housing element must, under SB 375, be consistent with the sustainable communities strategy, so SB 375 is expected to affect local planning and zoning for housing.

> A sustainable communities strategy does not supersede a general plan, specific plan, or local zoning ordinance.

TRAFFIC MODEL GUIDANCE

Another component of SB 375 requires the California Transportation Commission to develop guidelines for traffic models so that they more accurately account for emissions. Gov't Code § 14522.1. The new guidelines are required to account for:

- The relationship between land use density and household vehicle ownership and vehicle miles traveled, in a way that is consistent with statistical research

- The impact of enhanced transit service levels on household vehicle ownership and vehicle miles traveled
- Changes in travel and land development likely to result from highway or passenger rail expansion
- Mode splitting that allocates trips between automobile, transit, carpool, and bicycle and pedestrian trips
- Speed and frequency, days, and hours of operation of transit service

The Department of Transportation issued its new guidelines in April 2010. *See* http://www.catc.ca.gov/programs/rtp.htm.

AFFORDABLE HOUSING

SB 375 alters the affordable housing landscape by adding a requirement that final housing need allocation plans demonstrate consistency with the GHG-sensitive development patterns in the sustainable communities strategies. Gov't Code §§ 65584.04(i); 65080(b)(2)(B). In addition, when engaging in the threshold step of calculating a region's existing and projected housing need, a council of governments must factor in the employment projections from the regional transportation plan that contains the sustainable communities strategy. Gov't Code § 65584.01(d)(1).

ACCOUNTING FOR CLIMATE CHANGE IMPACTS IN CEQA DOCUMENTS: GUIDANCE FROM CEQA GUIDELINES, REGIONAL AIR QUALITY MANAGEMENT DISTRICTS, AND THE COURTS

After passage of AB 32, questions quickly arose regarding how lead agencies should account for climate change impacts in documents prepared under the California Environmental Quality Act. The scientific literature on climate change does not provide guidance for understanding the impact of a particular development project, leaving agencies with the basic question of how much GHG emission is too much.

Compounding the problem is that CEQA was not originally designed to address this type of issue. CEQA defines impacts as physical conditions "within the area which will be affected by a project" and changes to the environmental setting "in the vicinity of the project." Pub. Res. Code § 21060.5; CEQA Guidelines § 15125(a). Unlike other air pollutants, GHG emissions do not produce impacts on a local or even a regional level, but rather on a global scale. Even as to cumulative impacts, CEQA did not originally address any global issue like climate change; its provision for a list of projects producing related or cumulative impacts is tailored to local or regional environmental concerns. *See* CEQA Guidelines § 15130(b)(1).

2010 CEQA GUIDELINES CHANGES

In 2007, the Legislature enacted Senate Bill 97, which required the Governor's Office of Planning and Research (OPR) to develop and propose "guidelines for the mitigation of greenhouse gas emissions or the effects of greenhouse emissions as required [by CEQA], including, but not limited to effects associated with transportation or energy consumption." Pub. Res. Code § 21083.05(a). The California Natural Resources Agency (CRNA) adopted amendments to the CEQA Guidelines that became effective on March 18, 2010.

The CEQA Guidelines on climate change do not dictate a specific metric lead agencies should use to determine whether project-related GHG emissions are cumulatively considerable. Rather, they set out a basic framework of analysis for assessing a project's contribution to GHG emission levels.

Among other things, the Guidelines provide:
- A lead agency should make a good-faith effort, based to the extent possible on scientific and factual data, to describe, calculate or estimate the amount of GHG emissions resulting from a project. § 15064.4(a)
- A lead agency shall have discretion to determine, in the context of a particular project, whether to:
    —Use a model or methodology to quantify GHG emissions resulting from a project, and which model or methodology to use; and/or
    —Rely on a qualitative analysis or performance based standards. § 15064.4(a)(1) & (2)
- A lead agency should consider the following factors, among others, when assessing the significance of impacts from GHG emissions on the environment:
    —The extent to which the project may increase or reduce GHG emissions as compared to the existing environmental setting
    —Whether the project emissions exceed a threshold of significance that the lead agency determines applies to the project
    —The extent to which the project complies with regulations or requirements adopted to implement a statewide, regional, or local plan for the reduction or mitigation of GHG emissions. If there is substantial evidence that the possible effects of a particular project are still cumulatively considerable notwithstanding compliance with the adopted regulations or requirements, an EIR must be prepared for the project. § 15064.4(b)
- Lead agencies shall consider feasible means of mitigating the significant effects of greenhouse gas emissions. Measures to mitigate the significant effects of GHG emissions may include, among others:
    —Measures in an existing plan or mitigation program for the reduction of emissions that are required as part of the lead agency's decision
    —Reductions in emissions resulting from a project through implementation of project features, project design, or other measures, such as those described in Appendix F to the CEQA Guidelines
    —Off-site measures, including offsets that are not otherwise required, to mitigate a project's emissions
    —Measures that sequester GHGs
    —In the case of the adoption of a plan, such as a general plan, long-range development plan, or plan for the reduction of GHG emissions, mitigation may include the identification of specific measures that may be implemented on a project-by-project basis. Mitigation may also include the incorporation of specific measures or policies found in an adopted ordinance or regulation that reduces the cumulative effect of emissions. Guidelines § 15126.4(c)
- Agencies may choose to analyze and mitigate significant GHG emissions in a plan for the reduction of GHG emissions or similar document—adopted in a public process following environmental review—and may determine that a project's incremental contribution to a cumulative effect is not cumulatively considerable if the project complies with the requirements in a previously adopted plan or mitigation program under specified circumstances.

Again, while the adopted Guidelines go to some length to instruct agencies how to proceed with a CEQA discussion on climate change impacts, they ultimately leave

EIR = environmental impact report

While the adopted Guidelines go to some length to instruct agencies how to proceed with a CEQA discussion on climate change impacts, they ultimately leave the establishment of significance thresholds to the discretion of a lead agency.

the establishment of significance thresholds to the discretion of a lead agency. While some agencies are developing local climate action plans, which the adopted Guidelines recognize, many others look to the significance thresholds formulated by their regional air quality management districts. The South Coast Air Quality Management District (SCAQMD), the San Joaquin Valley Air Pollution Control District (SJVAPCD), and the Bay Area Air Quality Management District (BAAQMD) have all been active in developing significance thresholds.

BAAQMD adopted a set of significance thresholds for GHG emissions under CEQA on June 2, 2010. However, BAAQMD withdrew its thresholds following a 2012 superior court ruling that they were adopted in violation of CEQA. As of November 2013, BAAQMD had not reinstated its thresholds despite an appellate court decision reversing the superior court's ruling. *California Building Industry Ass'n v. Bay Area Air Quality Management Dist.*, 218 Cal. App. 4th 1171 (2013). The California Supreme Court has granted a petition for review of that appellate court decision. 161 Cal. Rptr. 3d 128 (2013).

Other courts have provided some guidance on the handling of climate change impacts in CEQA documents:

- No climate change analysis is required where the public agency has no discretion to address a project's potential climate change impacts. *San Diego Navy Broadway Complex Coal. v. City of San Diego*, 185 Cal. App. 4th 924, 938 (2010)
- An EIR that identifies mitigation consisting only of a "generalized goal" of no net increase in GHG emissions over the project baseline impermissibly defers mitigation. *Communities for a Better Env't v. City of Richmond*, 184 Cal. App. 4th 70 (2010)
- A city properly selected and applied a GHG emissions threshold asking whether a project would "conflict with or obstruct the goals or strategies" of AB 32. *Citizens for Responsible Equitable Environmental Development v. City of Chula Vista*, 197 Cal. App. 4th 327, 335-337 (2011)
- An agency need not explore every GHG mitigation measure on a long list of potential measures attached to a commenter's letter. *Santa Clarita Organization for Planning the Environment v. City of Santa Clarita*, 197 Cal. App. 4th 1042 (2011)
- Where a water district's drought plan concludes that future climate change might intensify risks to the district's water supplies, the district must analyze that issue under CEQA before approving a large increase in its promised water deliveries. *Voices for Rural Living v. El Dorado Irrigation Dist.*, 209 Cal. App. 4th 1096 (2012)
- Where a project is otherwise entitled to rely on an existing environmental impact report, the adoption of new air district significance thresholds for GHG emissions does not constitute "significant new information" requiring preparation of a new CEQA document. *Concerned Dublin Citizens v. City of Dublin*, 214 Cal. App. 4th 1301 (2013)
- An EIR that analyzes a project's GHG emissions by comparing them to the GHG emissions of the entire state of California is inadequate. *Friends of Oroville v. City of Oroville*, 219 Cal. App. 4th 832 (2013)

CEQA STREAMLINING FOR SUSTAINABLE DEVELOPMENT

As noted earlier in this chapter, CEQA requirements, and particularly redundant CEQA processes, are widely seen as a factor discouraging "smart" infill development in California. One means of encouraging sustainable development is for the Legislature to

TABLE 4: SUMMARY OF CEQA STREAMLINING PROVISIONS FOR SUSTAINABLE DEVELOPMENT

CEQA STREAMLINING PROVISION	PROJECT TYPE	STREAMLINING TYPE	RESTRICTIONS
CEQA Guidelines (14 Cal. Code Regs.) § 15332 (1998)	Infill development on no more than 5 acres, in city, substantially surrounded by urban uses, consistent with general plan and zoning.	CEQA categorical exemption.	Site must have no value as habitat for endangered, rare, or threatened species; project must not cause significant traffic, noise, air quality or water quality effects; site must be adequately served by all required utilities and services. Exemption not available if "the cumulative impact of successive projects of the same type in the same place, over time is significant"; if project would have significant impact due to "unusual circumstances," if project is on a listed hazardous waste site; or if project would cause substantial impact on a scenic highway or historical resource. 14 Cal. Code Regs. § 15300.2.
Public Resources Code (PRC) §§ 21159.24, 21159.21 (2002)	Residential infill of no more than 100 units on no more than 4 acres, providing for affordable housing and within 1/2 mile of major transit stop (PRC § 21159.24)	CEQA statutory exemption (PRC § 21159.24)	Requires community-level environmental review that preceded project application by no more than 5 years; no single-level building exceeding 100,000 square feet. No exemption if "reasonable possibility" of significant impacts due to unusual circumstances, or if substantial changes or new information shown after community-level environmental review was completed. (PRC § 21159.24) See PRC § 21159.21 for two additional pages of restrictions.
PRC §§ 21155-21155.3 (SB 375) (2008)	Transit Priority Projects consistent with SB 375 sustainable communities strategy or alternative planning strategy. Transit Priority Project is at least 50% residential, high density, and within 1/2 mile of major transit stop or high-quality transit corridor (PRC § 21155)	CEQA statutory exemption, "sustainable communities environmental assessment," or reduced EIR scope (PRC §§ 21155.1, 21155.2)	CEQA exemption available only if project would be adequately served by existing utilities; all applicable in-lieu or development fees are paid; site does not include wetlands or riparian areas; project would not harm any protected species; site is not a listed hazardous waste site; preliminary hazardous substance endangerment prepared and addressed; project has no significant effect on historical resources; project not subject to unusually high fire risk or seismic, landslide, or flood risks not mitigated through general plan or zoning ordinance; site not located on developed open space. (PRC § 21155.1(a)) CEQA exemption also requires that project be no more than 8 acres and 200 residential units, not result in any net loss in the number of affordable housing units in the project area, not include any single level building that exceeds 75,000 square feet, incorporate applicable mitigation or performance standards in prior EIRs, not conflict with nearby operating industrial uses, and be within 1/2 mile of a rail transit station or ferry terminal included in a regional transportation plan or within 1/4 mile of a high-quality transit corridor. PRC § 21155.1(b). The CEQA exemption further requires that the project meet at least one of the following: provide specified affordable housing; provide equivalent affordable housing in-lieu fees; or provide public open space equal to or greater than 5 acres per 1,000 residents of the project. Projects satisfying some, but not all, of the exemption prerequisites are eligible for a sustainable communities environmental assessment or a reduced-scope EIR.

SUMMARY OF CEQA STREAMLINING PROVISIONS FOR SUSTAINABLE DEVELOPMENT *continued*

CEQA STREAMLINING PROVISION	PROJECT TYPE	STREAMLINING TYPE	RESTRICTIONS
PRC § 21159.28 (SB 375) (2008)	Residential or mixed-use residential (at least 75% residential or a Transit Priority Project) that is consistent with SB 375 sustainable communities strategy or alternative planning strategy	No requirement of CEQA findings re growth-inducing impacts, or project-specific or cumulative impacts from cars and light-duty truck trips generated by the project on global warming or the regional transportation network. An EIR is not required to discuss a reduced residential density alternative to address the effects of car and light-duty truck trips.	Project must incorporate mitigation measures required by an applicable prior environmental document.
PRC § 21094.5, 21095.5.5 (SB 226) (2011)	Infill projects that are consistent with the SB 375 sustainable communities strategy or alternative planning strategy, or are "small walkable community projects" or, if located in an MPO lacking a sustainable communities strategy or alternative planning strategy, have residential density of at least 20 units per acre or FAR of at least 0.75. Project must also meet eligibility requirements adopted by regulation in 2013.	CEQA statutory exemption or reduced scope of CEQA documentation	"Infill project" is residential, retail or commercial with no more than 1/2 of project area used for parking, a transit station, a school, or a public office building, and must be located on a site that has previously been developed or meets other requirements. PRC § 21094.5(e). A "small walkable community project" is in an incorporated city but not within an MPO, and must meet certain additional requirements. The CEQA Guidelines specify that the statutory exemption is available only if the project's effects were analyzed in a prior planning-level EIR or, if the effect was not analyzed in that EIR or is more significant than previously analyzed, uniformly applicable development policies or standards would substantially mitigate that effect. If the exemption is not available, a negative declaration or "infill EIR" must be prepared. 14 Cal. Code Regs. § 15183.3. Performance standards limit infill streamlining eligibility for various types of projects. 14 Cal. Code Regs. §§ 15000-15387, Appendix M.
PRC § 21080.35 (SB 226) (2011)	Solar energy systems on roofs of existing buildings or at existing parking lots, including "associated equipment"	CEQA statutory exemption	"Associated equipment" for solar energy systems does not include substations, must not use more than 500 square feet of ground surface, and must be located on or near the same parcel as the building. An "existing parking lot" must have been used as such for at least two years prior to the solar energy system application. Associated equipment must not be located on a site that contains plants protected by the Native Plant Protection Act, and must not require an individual permit or WDRs under the Clean Water Act or the Porter-Cologne Act, an individual take permit for listed species, or a streambed alteration agreement under the Fish and Game Code. The exemption does not apply if a solar energy system in an existing parking lot would require the removal of certain trees, including any native tree over 25 years old.

SUMMARY OF CEQA STREAMLINING PROVISIONS FOR SUSTAINABLE DEVELOPMENT continued

CEQA STREAMLINING PROVISION	PROJECT TYPE	STREAMLINING TYPE	RESTRICTIONS
PRC §§ 21178–21189.3 (AB 900) (2011)	"Environmental leadership development projects," i.e., 1) infill residential, retail, commercial, sports, cultural, entertainment, or recreational use projects certified as LEED Silver or better, achieving "a 10-percent greater standards for transportation efficiency than for comparable projects," and consistent with any SB 375 sustainable communities strategy or alternative planning strategy; 2) clean renewable energy projects that generate electricity exclusively through wind or solar; 3) clean energy manufacturing projects. (PRC § 21180)	CEQA litigation streamlining: Any CEQA lawsuit must be filed in Court of Appeal; other claims challenging the land use approvals must be filed concurrently; Court of Appeal must issue decision within 175 days of the filing of the petition. (PRC § 21185)	Notification to lead agency and certification by Governor. Certification criteria include: Project will result in a minimum investment of $100,000,000 in California; prevailing and living wages and reduction of unemployment; no net additional emission of GHGs; binding mitigation agreement; applicant agreement to pay costs of Court of Appeal in hearing and deciding case and in costs of preparing of administrative record concurrent with review and consideration of the project. (PRC § 21186)

offer CEQA "streamlining," often in the form of CEQA exemptions, to such development. Over the past 25 years, the Legislature has made many such efforts, particularly for infill and sustainable energy projects. But because any reduction in CEQA requirements—even for projects that are intended to improve California's environment—is hotly debated and often opposed, the bills as ultimately enacted have been so tightly circumscribed that only a few projects have been able to take advantage of them. See Table 4 on the following pages for a summary and comparison of the CEQA streamlining programs that are intended to encourage sustainable development projects.

GREEN BUILDING

"Green building," according to one definition, "is the practice of creating structures and using processes that are environmentally responsible and resource-efficient throughout a building's life-cycle from siting to design, construction, operation, maintenance, renovation, and deconstruction."[16] Both state agencies and local jurisdictions have set ambitious goals with respect to green building to foster sustainable development in general and to help address climate change in particular.

STATE GREEN BUILDING STANDARDS

At the state level, green building standards are found in two parts of the building code, Part 6 (Energy Code) and Part 11 (Green Building Code):

---

16 Document available at www.epa.gov/greenbuilding/pubs/about.htm.

CEC = California Energy Commission

Energy Code, Title 24, Part 6. Since 1977, one of the California Energy Commission's (CEC's) statutory responsibilities has been to "[p]rescribe, by regulation, energy and water conservation design standards for new residential and nonresidential buildings." Pub. Res. Code § 25402(b). Building Energy Efficiency standards are implemented through the Energy Code (Title 24, Part 6). The CEC regularly updates the Building Energy Efficiency Standards, and its efforts have been credited for keeping California's per capita electricity use steady since the mid-1970 s while other states' per capita use has risen. In 2007, the CEC set the goal that all new homes will be "zero net energy" by 2020 and that new commercial buildings will be zero net energy by 2030. A zero net energy building "consumes only as much energy on an annual basis as can be generated with an on-site renewable energy system."[17]

The subsequent 2008 Building Energy Efficiency Standards went into effect on January 1, 2010. On January 1, 2014, the 2013 Standards took effect and require 25 percent improved efficiency for residential construction and 30 percent improved efficiency for nonresidential construction compared to the previous 2008 standards.[18]

Green Building Code, Title 24, Part 11. The California Building Standards Commission adopted the nation's first Green Building Standards Code in 2007.[19]

CALGreen = Green Building Standards Code

The Green Building Standards Code, also known as "CALGreen," first took effect as voluntary standards in August 2009. The code was updated and became mandatory on January 1, 2011. 24 Cal. Code Regs., Part 11. The CALGreen standards include requirements for reducing water use, increasing waste diversion from landfills, and using low-pollutant-emitting interior finish materials such as paints, carpet, vinyl flooring and particle board. CALGreen also layers voluntary "reach" standards for energy efficiency onto the CEC's mandatory standards set forth in the Energy Code. CALGreen establishes tiered energy performance levels 15 percent and 30 percent more stringent than the mandatory 2008 CEC standards, and provides that local jurisdictions may adopt them.

Electric Vehicle Charging Stations. In 2013, the Legislature enacted new Health and Safety Code section 18941.10, which mandates that the next edition of the California Building Standards Code include requirements for electric vehicle charging infrastructure in parking facilities for multifamily dwellings and nonresidential developments.

LOCAL GREEN BUILDING STANDARDS

Even as statewide green building regulation increases, many local governments have adopted their own green building ordinances, and many are doing so by adopting third-party rating systems for green building. The most commonly used rating system is the Leadership in Energy and Environmental Design system, more commonly known as LEED, developed by the U.S. Green Building Council, a nonprofit organization. Another popular rating system in California for residential construction is the GreenPoint Rated system developed by Build it Green, another nonprofit organization.

LEED = Leadership in Energy and Environmental Design

These rating systems require raters to assign points to a building using various criteria to determine how "green" a building is. For example, points in the LEED system are allocated for such criteria as "alternative transportation," "site development,"

---

17 *See Background on the 2013 Building Energy Efficiency Standards, available at* www.energy.ca.gov/title24/2013standards/background.html.

18 *See* News Release *available at* www.energy.ca.gov/releases/2012-05-31_energy_commission_approves_more_efficient_buildings_nr.html.

19 Cal. Code. Regs., title 24, pt. 11.

"water efficiency," and "energy and atmosphere." The point totals translate into building ratings within tiers: "Certified," "Silver," "Gold," and "Platinum." Some local governments are requiring that all new residential and nonresidential construction attain enough points to fall within one of these tiers.

> Points in the LEED system are allocated for such criteria as "alternative transportation," "site development," "water efficiency," and "energy and atmosphere."

POTENTIAL ISSUES ARISING FROM A CITY'S USE OF RATING SYSTEMS

If a city adopts a third-party rating system such that changes in the rating system are automatically applied without further action by the city, the regulation may be vulnerable to challenge based upon the non-delegation doctrine. This issue was addressed in *International Association of Plumbing & Mechanical Officials v. California Building Standards Commission*, 55 Cal. App. 4th 245 (1997). In discussing the scope of the powers of the Building Standards Commission, the court ruled that private associations (such as the U.S. Green Building Council) must not be accorded the "power to initiate or enact rules that acquire the force of law." 55 Cal. App. 4th at 254-55. Specifically, the court said:

> In providing for state building standards the Legislature could have adopted a particular model code, either directly or by depriving the Commission of any discretion by specifically compelling it to adopt the model code. However, such an act could adopt only an existing version of the model code and could not take into account future revisions without improperly delegating lawmaking authority to the private entity that produced the code.

Id. at 255; *see also Plastic Pipe and Fittings Association v. California Buildings Standards Commission*, 124 Cal. App. 4th 1390 (2004) (model code may only be deemed approved by Building Standards Commission's inaction where code was already considered and adopted by another agency).[20]

Determining whether a regulation or ordinance should be construed as attempting to adopt changing versions of a third-party rating system, or instead construed as adopting the third-party rating system as it existed at the time of the enactment of the regulation or ordinance, will require a close examination of case law and the text of the regulation or ordinance. *See, e.g., Palermo v. Stockton Theatres*, 32 Cal. 2d 53 (1948).

STATE PREEMPTION AND REQUIRED FINDINGS

In adopting a statewide building code in 1970, the California Legislature found:

> ...that the uniformity of codes throughout the State of California is a matter of statewide interest and concern since it would reduce housing costs and increase the efficiency of private housing construction industry and its production. [¶] Uniformity can be achieved within a framework of local autonomy, by allowing local governments to adopt changes making modifications in such codes based on differences in local conditions, but requiring express findings as reasons for those changes which would serve as a deterrent to the excessive adoption of changes or modifications.

Stats. 1970, ch. 1436, § 7

---

[20] *See generally* Barbara Schussman, Verne Ball, and Jessica Tucker-Mohl, *The Rapid Rise of Local Green Building Ordinances—Will They Survive Legal Challenge?*, Climate Change L. Policy R., Vol. 2, No. 2, 35 (2009).

The California Building Standards Code, of which the Green Building Standards Code is a part, preempts local building codes. *See Leslie v. Superior Court*, 73 Cal. App. 4th 1042, 1048 (1999). For a city to adopt "more restrictive requirements" than the California Building Standards Code, it must find that the modifications "are reasonably necessary because of local climatic, geological, or topographical conditions." Health & Safety Code §§ 17958.5, 18941.5. The passage of AB 210 in 2009 makes clear that this finding requirement applies to "green building standards."[21] The finding must be filed with the California Building Standards Commission,[22] but the Commission does not review the merits of the finding. Health & Safety Code § 17958.7. If a city fails to make and file the finding, the building ordinance is void. *Id.*; *Briseno v. City of Santa Ana*, 6 Cal. App. 4th 1378, 1380 (1992). One court has held that a city need not show that local conditions deviate from statewide conditions to satisfy the requirements of section 17958.5. *ABS Institute v. City of Lancaster*, 24 Cal. App. 4th 285, 294 (1994). The *Briseno* court previously had reached the opposite conclusion, albeit in dicta. 6 Cal. App. 4th at 1383 n.3.

While Title 24 preempts local regulations where the required procedures for deviating from it have not been followed, its application is flexible. The Health and Safety Code allows local governments to make case-by-case exceptions to the requirements of Title 24 if the local building department "finds that the proposed design is satisfactory and that each such material, appliance, installation, device, arrangement, method, or work offered is" equivalent to the requirements in the California Building Standards Code. Health & Safety Code § 17951(e)(2).

Public Resources Code section 25402.1(h)(2) allows cities to apply to the CEC to adopt energy consumption requirements more stringent than the California Energy Code. Cities must provide the CEC with a study of how the local standards will save more energy than the current statewide standards, and they also must state the basis of their determination that the local standards are cost-effective.[23]

FEDERAL PREEMPTION OF STATE AND LOCAL GREEN BUILDING CODES

Some state and local green building codes may be federally preempted by the Energy Policy and Conservation Act (EPCA), 42 U.S.C. § 6201 *et seq.*, *as amended by* the National Appliance Energy Conservation Act (NAECA), Pub.L. No. 100-102 (1987), and the Energy Policy Act of 1992 (EPACT), 42 U.S.C. §§ 6311–6317. EPCA establishes nationwide standards for the energy efficiency and energy use of major appliances and HVAC equipment used in both residential and commercial settings. 42 U.S.C. § 6291 *et seq.*; *id.* § 6311 *et seq.*[24] As amended, EPCA's purposes are twofold: "to reduce the Nation's consumption of energy and to reduce the regulatory and economic burdens on the appliance manufacturing industry through the establishment of national energy conservation standards for major residential appliances." S. Rep. 100-6, at 1.

---

21 SB 1473 was not intended to affect the preemption of local building ordinances one way or another. It contains an uncodified finding that "It is the intent of the Legislature that [SB 1473] shall not affect the ability of a city, county, or city and county to adopt changes, modifications, amendments, additions, or deletions to the California Building Standards Code, including, but not limited to, green building standards." SB 1473, stats. 2008, ch. 719 § 1(a).

22 All "building standards" must be submitted to the State Buildings Standards Commission. Health & Safety Code § 18930. The term "building standard" is very broadly defined. *See id. at* § 18909. However, a city may have authority to adopt regulations on subjects not covered by the state code. *See Baum Electric Co. v. City of Huntington Beach*, 33 Cal. App. 3d 573, 584 (1973).

23 24 Cal. Code Regs § 10-106.

24 Title 42 also requires energy codes to meet federally adopted standards, or explain to the Department of Energy why they will not. 42 U.S.C. § 6833.

EPCA explicitly preempts state regulation "concerning" the "energy efficiency, energy use, or water use" of covered products. 42 U.S.C. § 6297(c); *see also* 42 U.S.C. § 6316(b)(2) (preempting state standards for certain "commercial" equipment). But under the statute, "a regulation or other requirement contained in a State or local building code for new construction concerning the energy efficiency or energy use" of a covered product is not superseded by the EPCA's general preemption provision if the code complies with seven specified requirements. 42 U.S.C. § 6297(f)(3).

> EPCA explicitly preempts state regulation "concerning" the "energy efficiency, energy use, or water use" of covered products.

Two recent federal district court cases have applied EPCA's preemption standards to green building codes. The first case addressed the City of Albuquerque, New Mexico's green building code, which created two menus of compliance options, one applying to commercial and multi-family buildings, and one applying to single- and two-family residential buildings. Each menu included a LEED silver option, other performance-based options, and a "prescriptive" option requiring HVAC equipment that was more energy-efficient than EPCA required. An industry association sued and, in a published opinion, the federal court ruled that the prescriptive option was preempted by EPCA. *Air Conditioning, Heating and Refrigeration Institute v. City of Albuquerque*, 835 F. Supp. 2d 1133 (D.N.M. 2010). The court reserved judgment on the LEED and other menu options, but the city then stipulated that the non-prescriptive options were not severable from the prescriptive options and that the menus would not have been enacted in the absence of the prescriptive options. In an unreported decision, the court then invalidated the entire program. *Air Conditioning, Heating and Refrigeration Institute v. City of Albuquerque*, Civ. No. 08-633, Doc. 185 (D.N.M. Jan. 25, 2012).

The second case concerned a challenge to the State of Washington's 2009 update to its building energy code. This update required a 15 percent improvement in building energy performance compared to the state's 2006 code, and used a menu of options to achieve that goal: a systems analysis performance pathway, a building envelope trade-off performance pathway, and a prescriptive pathway. But Washington's "prescriptive pathway," unlike Albuquerque's, itself included a long list of options for achieving "credits," some of which dictated particular equipment but many of which did not. A building association challenged the 2009 code update, alleging that as a practical matter the options would require equipment exceeding EPCA standards. After ruling that the case represented a facial challenge to the constitutionality of Washington's code, and therefore that the association had to show "that no set of circumstances exists under which the [code] would be valid," the district court found that the association did not meet that burden. *Building Industry Ass'n v. Washington State Building Code Council*, 2011 WL 485895 (W.D.Wash. Feb. 7, 2011) (not reported in F. Supp. 2d).

DEVELOPMENT OF RENEWABLE ENERGY

California has set ambitious goals for the development and use of renewable energy. The state continues to establish numerous laws, policies, and collaborative efforts to provide incentives for, or to prohibit barriers to, the development of renewable energy generation.

REQUIRED RENEWABLE PROCUREMENT

The most prominent policy is the state's Renewable Portfolio Standard (RPS), which requires retail sellers of electricity to procure 33 percent of their electricity from

> RPS = Renewable Portfolio Standard

renewable energy sources by 2020.[25] See Pub. Res. Code §§ 25740 et seq.; Pub. Util. Code §§ 399.11 et seq. And in 2003, California's first Energy Action Plan established a "loading order," under which the state and its utilities should meet electricity demand first with energy efficiency and demand-side resources, second with renewable resources, and third with "clean" conventional electricity supply.[26]

LOWERING BARRIERS TO DEVELOPMENT AND PERMITTING OF RENEWABLE ENERGY

Subdivision Map Act exemptions for solar projects. The Subdivision Map Act requires that a landowner may not subdivide its property without obtaining approval of tentative and final parcel maps from the local governing body. See Gov't Code §§ 66410 et seq. Assembly Bill 1510 exempts from this requirement leases and easements entered into in connection with the financing, erection, sale, or lease of solar electrical generation devices on the land. See Gov't Code §§ 66412. The exemption applies only if the project is subject to review under local ordinances regulating design and improvement, or if the project is subject to discretionary action by the advisory agency or legislative body. For further discussion of the Subdivision Map Act, see chapter 5 (Subdivisions).

Permitting process for wind systems outside urbanized areas. Legislation in 2009 authorized counties to adopt ordinances that would provide for the installation of small wind systems outside urbanized areas. Gov't Code § 65896(a). The law also established a conditional use permit process for the approval of such systems, though its applicability depends on the timing of an ordinance's adoption, as further explained below.

The law provides that an "ordinance may impose conditions on the installation of small wind energy systems that include, but are not limited to, notice, tower height, setback, view protection, aesthetics, aviation, and design-safety requirements." Gov't Code § 65896(b). A county also may impose, as a condition of approval, a requirement that the system be removed if it remains inoperable for 12 consecutive months. Gov't Code § 65896(c).

However, the county is not permitted to impose certain conditions that are more restrictive than some of the conditions and requirements established under Government Code section 65896(b). These benchmarks relate to notice, tower height, setback, noise level, visual effects, turbine approval, tower drawings, engineering analysis, line drawings, and other system aspects. See Gov't Code §§ 65896(b)(1)–(17). Compliance with federal aviation laws and certain state and local land use plans (e.g., a local coastal program or a Williamson Act contract) also is required. Id.

The timing of an ordinance's adoption is an issue, however. For those ordinances adopted prior to January 1, 2011, the requirements of section 65896 do not apply. Gov't Code § 65895(a) (ordinance is exempt from compliance). If a small wind energy system is proposed between January 1, 2011 and the subsequent adoption of an ordinance, the county must approve an application for a system that meets the requirements and conditions of section 65896(b) through a ministerial permit. Gov't Code § 65895(b)(3). Finally, where a system is proposed on or after January 1, 2011 and a conditional use permit ordinance already exists, the ordinance must comply with section

---

[25] For purposes of the RPS, eligible renewable facilities must have a capacity of at least 1.5 megawatts and include solar thermal, photovoltaic, wind, biomass, geothermal, fuel cells using renewable fuels, small hydroelectric, digester gas, municipal solid waste conversion, landfill gas, ocean wave, ocean thermal, and tidal current facilities.

[26] See 2012 Integrated Energy Policy Report Update, available at www.energy.ca.gov.

65896 and project approvals may be awarded within the discretion of the county. Gov't Code § 65895(a).

Williamson Act express inclusion of biofuels and probable inclusion of wind. Under the Williamson Act, local governments may enter into contracts with private landowners under which the landowners receive relatively low property tax assessments for parcels of land restricted to open space, agricultural, or agricultural compatible use. *See* Gov't Code § 51200 *et seq.* In 2008, Assembly Bill 1764 amended the definition of "agricultural commodity" in the Act to include plant products used in biofuels. Local governments thus no longer have the discretion to determine whether biofuel production qualifies as an agricultural use for Williamson Act purposes. *See* Gov't Code § 51201.

Local governments retain the discretion in implementing the Williamson Act, however, to determine whether the use of land for wind or solar facilities constitutes an "agricultural compatible" use of the reserved land. In making compatibility determinations, cities and counties must find that the intended use will not significantly compromise the long-term productive agricultural capability of the contracted land, significantly displace or impair current or reasonably foreseeable agricultural operations on the contracted land, or result in the significant removal of adjacent contracted land from agricultural or open space use. Gov't Code § 51238.1(a). Several local governments have determined that operation of wind energy projects constitutes an "agricultural compatible" use of land contracted under the Williamson Act.[27] Solar projects, on the other hand, are unlikely to be deemed compatible with agricultural use of contracted land. Because of the relatively large ground surface area covered by solar energy generating facilities, such projects are likely to displace or impair agricultural operations. *See* Gov't Code § 51238.1.

> In making compatibility determinations, cities and counties must find that the intended use will not significantly compromise the long-term productive agricultural capability of the contracted land, significantly displace or impair current or reasonably foreseeable agricultural operations on the contracted land, or result in the significant removal of adjacent contracted land from agricultural or open space use.

Additionally, although the erection and maintenance of gas and electric facilities are considered "de facto" compatible uses under the Act, such electric facilities are likely limited to utility lines and other transmission facilities and likely do not extend to renewable energy generating facilities. *See* Gov't Code § 51238.

Public interest cancellation of Williamson Act contract to allow solar facility. Williamson Act contracts may be cancelled in the public interest. A utility-scale solar facility meets the public interest test such that county may cancel a Williamson Act contract to permit the solar project to proceed. *Save Panoche Valley v. San Benito County*, 217 Cal. App. 4th 503 (2013).

Minimizing private entity restrictions on solar energy systems. The Solar Rights Act, enacted in 2000, provides that any provision in legal instruments affecting the transfer or sale of real property that unreasonably restricts or effectively prohibits the installation or use of solar energy systems is void and unenforceable. Civ. Code § 714. The law permits only reasonable restrictions—those that do not significantly increase the cost of the solar energy system or significantly decrease its efficiency or specified performance, or that allow for an alternative system of comparable cost efficiency and energy conservation benefits. *Id.* The court in *Palos Verdes Home Association v. Rodman* established that an installer of a solar energy system cannot ignore homeowners' association guidelines if following the guidelines would only minimally increase installation costs. 182 Cal. App. 3d 324, 324-29 (1986).

Assembly Bill 2180, enacted in 2008, amends the Solar Rights Act to extend the prohibition against unreasonable restrictions to legal instruments governing common

---

27 *See, e.g.,* Kern County Resolution 2007-017 (2007); Solano County Uniform Rules and Procedures Governing Agricultural Preserves *and* Land Conservation Contracts (effective Jan 3, 2008), page 42.

interest developments. In addition, the bill provides that homeowners' associations that are not public entities must process and approve or deny applications for approval of solar installations in the same manner as applications for approval of an architectural modification to the property. The approving entity must not wilfully avoid the application or delay in addressing it. An application for approval of a solar installation will be deemed approved in the absence of a written denial within 60 days, unless the delay is the result of a reasonable request for additional information. Civ. Code § 714.

Minimizing public entity restrictions on solar energy systems. Local governments must use non-discretionary permitting for solar energy systems and cannot pass ordinances that impose unreasonable restrictions on them. *See* Gov't Code § 65850.5; Civ. Code § 714(h). Review of solar energy systems must be limited to "those standards and regulations necessary to ensure that the solar energy system will not have a specific, adverse impact upon the public health or safety." Gov't Code § 65850.5. Local governments that do not comply with these provisions are ineligible to receive state-sponsored grant funding or loans for solar energy programs. Civ. Code § 714(h). In 2012, the Legislature added section 66015 to the Government Code, placing limits on the fees local agencies can charge for permits for rooftop solar energy systems.

The Solar Rights Act creates a right to receive sunlight for use by a solar energy system, thereby adding solar easements to the list of the state's recognized easements. *See* Civ. Code §§ 801, 801.5. Solar easements are limited to the sole purpose of accessing sunlight to create thermal or electric energy. *Id.* An instrument creating a solar easement must include a description of the easement's dimensions in measurable terms, a list of restrictions that would impair the passage of sunlight through the easement, and the terms or conditions, if any, under which the easement may be terminated or revised. Civ. Code § 801.5. Case law has established that the instrument creating the easement must be created in writing to be enforceable. *See Zipper v. County of Santa Clara*, 133 Cal. App. 4th 1013 (2005).

Solar panels as a standard option on new homes. The "Million Solar Roofs" law, enacted as Senate Bill 1 in 2006, requires that all new homes built in California include solar panels as a standard option for homebuyers. Pub. Res. Code § 25405.5.

Geothermal heat pump and geothermal ground loop technologies. Geothermal heat pump and ground loop technologies take advantage of the relatively constant temperature of the earth to heat and cool buildings, reducing the use of electricity and natural gas for heating and cooling. In 2012, the Legislature added section 25228 to the Public Resources Code, requiring the CEC to evaluate and recommend policies and implementation strategies to overcome barriers to the deployment and use of these technologies, and to include its evaluation and recommendations in the 2013 Integrated Energy Policy Report (IEPR). The draft 2013 IEPR calls on the geothermal heat pump industry to propose an "alternative calculation methodology" for energy efficiency, propose protocols for proper heat pump ground loop systems, standardize training for installers, propose a model local ordinance, and coordinate with federal, state and local agencies to resolve permitting issues.[28]

ADAPTATION TO EFFECTS OF CLIMATE CHANGE

In addition to attempting to reduce California's contribution to climate change by reducing GHG emissions, state regulators are planning for adaptation to the effects of

---

[28] *See* Draft Lead Commissioner Report, 2013 Integrated Energy Policy Report, *available at* www.energy.ca.gov.

climate change. In 2009, California adopted a Climate Adaptation Strategy (CAS).[29] An update was planned for 2013 but no draft had been released as of November 2013. Key recommendations from the 2009 strategy that are directly relevant to land use decisionmaking include:

CAS = Climate Adaptation Strategy

Key Recommendation 3. Consider project alternatives that avoid significant new development in areas that cannot be adequately protected...from flooding, wildfire and erosion due to climate change.... State agencies should generally not plan, develop, or build any new significant structure in a place where that structure will require significant protection from sea level rise, storm surges, or coastal erosion during the expected life of the structure. However, vulnerable shoreline areas containing existing development that have regionally significant economic, cultural, or social value may have to be protected, and in-fill development in these areas may be accommodated. State agencies should incorporate this policy into their decisions and other levels of government are also encouraged to do so.

Key Recommendation 5. To the extent required by CEQA Guidelines section 15126.2, all significant state projects, including infrastructure projects, must consider the potential impacts of locating such project in areas susceptible to hazards resulting from climate change. Section 15126.2 is currently being proposed for revision by the California Natural Resources Agency to direct lead agencies to evaluate the impacts of locating development in areas susceptible to hazardous conditions, including hazards potentially exacerbated by climate change.

Key Recommendation 7. Using existing research the state should identify key California land and aquatic habitats that could change significantly during this century due to climate change. Based on this identification, the state should develop a plan for expanding existing protected areas or altering land and water management practices to minimize adverse effects from climate change induced phenomena.

Key Recommendation 9. Communities with General Plans and Local Coastal Plans should begin, when possible, to amend their plans to assess climate change impacts, identify areas most vulnerable to these impacts, and develop reasonable and rational risk reduction strategies using the Climate Adaptation Strategy as guidance. Every effort will be made to provide tools, such as interactive climate impact maps, to assist in these efforts.

In 2010, the California Natural Resources Agency reported progress in implementing the Climate Adaptation Strategy. Among other items, the report noted the ongoing development of the CalAdapt mapping tool for identifying locations where future climate impacts are likely to occur. As of November 2013, however, CalAdapt, like previous mapping efforts, still does not include a sea level rise map that takes into account protective structures such as levees.[30]

The progress report also noted the amendment of CEQA Guidelines section 15126.2 to treat as an environmental impact the effects of locating development where it would be vulnerable to climate change effects such as sea level rise or catastrophic wildfire. This success may have been short-lived, however. In the case of *Ballona Wetlands*

---

29   *See* 2009 California Climate Adaptation Strategy, *available at* http://www.climatechange.ca.gov.
30   *See* http://cal-adapt.org/tools/#sealevel.

Trust v. City of Los Angeles, the Second District Court of Appeal held that an environmental impact report need not evaluate the impacts of possible future sea level rise on a project or the project's occupants. *See* 201 Cal. App. 4th 455, 473-74 (2011). Citing the rule that CEQA is concerned with the effects of a project on the environment, not the effects of the environment on a project, the court held that contrary provisions of Guidelines section 15126.2 were inconsistent with the CEQA statute.

Regardless of whether CEQA will ultimately be used as a tool to address the impacts of climate change, efforts in the planning arena are expected to continue. In October 2011, following more than two years of controversy, the Bay Conservation and Development Commission amended the San Francisco Bay Plan to address the expected impacts of climate change within BCDC's jurisdiction—San Francisco Bay, the Delta, and the "shoreline band" extending 100 feet inland. Among other requirements, sea level rise "risk assessments" are now required for planning shoreline areas or designing larger shoreline projects, and these projects must be designed to cope with anticipated flooding. New projects on Bay fill that are likely to be affected by future sea level rise and storm activity must be set back far enough from the shoreline to avoid flooding, be elevated above expected flood levels, be designed to tolerate flooding, or employ other means of addressing flood risks.[31] The California Coastal Commission, which has jurisdiction over the entire California coast that is not under BCDC's purview—a jurisdiction comprising 1.5 million acres and a wider shoreline band than BCDC's—released Draft Sea-Level Rise Policy Guidance for public review in October 2013.[32]

BCDC = San Francisco Bay Conservation and Development Commission

Also in 2013, the Legislature added Public Resources Code section 6311.5, which requires many local agencies that have been granted tidelands and submerged lands (i.e., public trust lands) to prepare assessments of how they propose to address the impacts of sea level rise. The assessments must include specified topics and are due by July 1, 2019.

---

[31] *See* New Sea Level Rise Policies Fact Sheet, *available at* http://www.bcdc.ca.gov/planning/climate_change/SLRfactSheet.shtml.

[32] *See* DRAFT Sea-Level Rise Policy Guidance, *available at* http://www.coastal.ca.gov/climate/SLRGuidance.html.

CHAPTER 17

Rights of the Regulated

IN GENERAL

Property owners are entitled to certain protections when a city regulates development. Affected citizens also are entitled to have their rights protected. A city must act rationally in exercising its police power. When acting in its adjudicatory capacity in granting use permits, variances, or subdivisions, a city must ensure that the property owner and affected citizens each receive adequate notice of all hearings, and that the required findings are made regarding the particular decision. For a discussion on damages resulting from a city's violation of an individual's rights to due process and equal protection, see chapter 11 (Takings).

Citizens also enjoy certain statutory rights relating to the regular business of their local governments. The Ralph M. Brown Act (Gov't Code §§ 54950-54963) requires that, with certain exceptions, meetings of city bodies be open and public. The Permit Streamlining Act (Gov't Code § 65920 et seq.) is designed to ensure timely consideration by the city of many types of applications relating to development. These statutes are discussed later in this chapter.

> When acting in its adjudicatory capacity in granting use permits, variances, or subdivisions, a city must ensure that the property owner and affected citizens each receive adequate notice of all hearings, and that the required findings are made regarding the particular decision.

NOTICE AND HEARING[1]

As a general rule, the constitutional, statutory, or common law requirements of notice and an opportunity to be heard apply only in adjudicatory hearings, and not in the adoption of general legislation. *See Horn v. County of Ventura*, 24 Cal. 3d 605, 612 (1979) (neighbors are entitled to notice of a hearing on a subdivision map application); *see also Kennedy v. City of Hayward*, 105 Cal. App. 3d 953, 961-62 (1980). However, the requirement of notice and an opportunity to be heard extends to certain legislative acts, such as rezonings, because of specific state statutory provisions. Thus, a city is required to notify all city and non-city residents if they fall within the distance requirements of the notice provisions or if, pursuant to *Horn*, the decision will affect their property rights. *See Scott v. Indian Wells*, 6 Cal. 3d 541, 549 (1972) (neighbors are entitled to due process notice of a hearing on a conditional use permit application).

---

1 For a good discussion on how public agencies can maximize the effectiveness of public hearings, see *Getting the Most Out of Public Hearings: Ideas to Improve Public Involvement*, Institute for Local Government (2005) *available at* http://www.ca-ilg.org/publichearings.

The notice given must adequately describe what action is being requested, because the courts view inadequate notice as equivalent to providing no notice at all. *See Drum v. Fresno County Dep't of Public Works,* 144 Cal. App. 3d 777, 782 (1983) (notice was inadequate because it did not show that a variance request for a garage included a second-story dwelling unit).

For example, a city must provide notice of the subjects that may be discussed. *See Clark v. City of Hermosa Beach,* 48 Cal. App. 4th 1152, 1173 (1996). The court in *Clark* found the city did not provide a fair hearing where it raised concerns relating to lot coverage and open space only after it closed the public portion of the hearing and then denied a permit, in part, because of these issues. *Id.*

Under the Planning and Zoning Law, notice regarding a legislative body's potential action on a matter that requires a recommendation from the planning commission cannot be given until after the planning commission issues its recommendation. *Envtl. Defense Project of Sierra County v. County of Sierra,* 158 Cal. App. 4th 877, 888 (2008) (interpreting Government Code section 65094, which requires that the notice include a "general explanation of the matter to be considered").

Notice need not be given by mail unless a statute or ordinance so requires; publication and posting can be constitutionally adequate. *See Hayssen v. Bd. of Zoning Adjustments,* 171 Cal. App. 3d 400, 405 (1985). If a citizen, developer, or property owner would like to ensure actual notice of a land use matter, he or she should submit a request in writing to the city asking to receive copies of all planning commission and city council notices and agendas. Actual notice of a hearing satisfies due process. *See Benson v. California Coastal Comm'n,* 139 Cal. App. 4th 348, 354 (2006). In *Benson,* a developer received actual notice of a Coastal Commission appeal hearing regarding his previously approved project, but failed to attend after being told by Commission staff that no substantive action was likely to be taken. In fact, the Commission found the appeal raised substantive issues. Benson challenged the Commission's finding on the ground that he was denied due process because of inadequate notice. The court held the written notice given was adequate and Benson could not reasonably rely on staff recommendations and comments. *Id.* at 355. The court noted that predictions and suggestions from staff could be misleading, and therefore a party should take such advice with caution. *Id.* at 581.

Failure to receive notice that is properly given may not invalidate an action. *See Newberry Springs Water Ass'n v. County of San Bernardino,* 150 Cal. App. 3d 740, 745–46 (1984). In *Newberry Springs,* the court referred to the uncodified section 4 of Chapter 131 of the 1980 Statutes, which reads in part:

> [T]he Legislature...affirm[s] the general principle that statutory requirements for public notice are fulfilled if the public agency [responsible for giving the notice] makes a good faith effort to follow the procedures prescribed by law for giving notice.

Id. at 746

Failure to receive notice, however, can be a factor in a court's decision that a permit application must be reheard because the applicant was denied a fair hearing. *See Clark,* 48 Cal. App. 4th at 1173. In *Clark,* the court found that the applicants had been denied a fair hearing in several respects. First, the city raised issues and concerns for the first time after the public portion of a hearing was closed; the applicants had not received notice of these issues and were not permitted to address them by having the hearing reopened. Second, the city exhibited unfair bias against the project by unsuccessfully attempting to impose a moratorium against construction. Third, a council member with a common law conflict of interest voted on the project. Together, these defects amounted to a denial of a fair hearing. The court's remedy was to have the city council rehear the matter and provide the applicants with a fair hearing. Id. at 1169.

In Cohan v. City of Thousand Oaks, the court held that the cumulative procedural errors committed by a city and its city council impaired the adequacy of the appeal hearing on the developers' subdivision, thereby violating their due process rights. See 30 Cal. App. 4th 547, 559-60 (1994). The court vacated the city council's decision without ordering that further hearings be held. Id. at 562. The procedural errors in Cohan included the council itself appealing the planning commission's decision without complying with the Brown Act and the local ordinance, failure to inform the developers of the grounds for the appeal, and unfairly placing the burden on the developers "to convince the council of the correctness of the planning commission's decision." Id. at 548. The court held that "[t]his stands due process on its head." Id. at 560. In ruling for the developer, the court concluded:

> As real estate developers, appellants [developers] took the risk that their proposed project may not be approved or, if approved, may be severely conditioned. They may even incur the risk of a seemingly unfair decision. However, they should not be subjected to the blatant disregard of their due process rights. The Council simply submitted to the roar of the crowd.

Id. at 561

Cohan was distinguished in BreakZone Billiards v. City of Torrance, 81 Cal. App. 4th 1205 (2000). The issue in BreakZone Billiards was whether a city council member's appeal of a conditional use permit satisfied the city's requirements. The court found that, unlike the ordinance in Cohan, the applicable ordinance prescribed only that there be a written statement of appeal articulating the grounds for the appeal, with which the city council member complied. Id. at 1223. Further, the notice of appeal appropriately informed the applicant that it had the burden of establishing to the satisfaction of a majority of the city council that the application should be approved. Id. at 1222. Finally, unlike the cumulative effect of procedural errors in Cohan, there were no individual procedural errors in BreakZone Billiards resulting in a violation of the applicant's procedural and substantive due process rights. Id. at 1243. For a discussion of what constitutes a "fair hearing," see chapter 19 (Land Use Litigation).

THE ONE WHO DECIDES MUST REVIEW EVIDENCE

In a landmark administrative law case, Chief Justice Hughes of the United States Supreme Court coined the phrase "The one who decides must hear." Morgan v. United States, 298 U.S. 468, 481 (1936) ("Morgan I"). The phrase is often still quoted, and the constitutional rule regarding consideration of evidence has been refined and explained. The portion of Morgan I that indicated a court could inquire into whether a decisionmaker actually considered every piece of evidence was overruled in United States v. Morgan, 313 U.S. 409, 421-22 (1941) ("Morgan IV"). See National Nutritional Foods Ass'n v. FDA, 491 F. 2d 1141, 144 (2d Cir. 1974) ("[Morgan IV] took back most or all of what the first decision had given [on this point]."). It is now clear that the federal constitution requires that decisionmakers consider the evidence in some rational form. See,

> In a landmark administrative law case, Chief Justice Hughes of the United States Supreme Court coined the phrase "The one who decides must hear."

e.g., *KFC National Management Corp. v. National Labor Relations Board*, 497 F. 2d 298, 305–07 (2d Cir. 1974). However, the federal constitution does not prohibit a decisionmaker from delegating the collection of evidence to others; it allows that evidence to be sifted and analyzed by subordinates before being presented to the decisionmaker, and it allows those who take the evidence to present preliminary, proposed decisions to the decisionmaker. *Id.* at 303–05.

California courts have reached similar results. The California Supreme Court, in *Cooper v. State Bd. of Medical Examiners*, 35 Cal. 2d 242, 246 (1950), expressly confirmed that a decisionmaker need not be present to hear evidence:

> We conclude here that participation in a decision by a board member who has read and considered the evidence, or a transcript thereof, even though he was not physically present when the evidence was produced, does not violate the requirements of due process.

Other courts reach similar results in interpreting laws or regulations that specifically require that decisionmakers hear the evidence. *See, e.g., Old Santa Barbara Pier Co. v. State of California*, 71 Cal. App. 3d 250, 255–56 (1977) (interpreting former 14 Cal. Code Regs § 13347, which required that Coastal Zone Conservation Commission members who had missed a prior hearing formally disclose for the record before voting that they had familiarized themselves with those proceedings or the materials relating to the appeal). The court held that such requirements mean only that the decisionmaker must be familiar with the presentation made at the earlier meeting and with the material relating to the appeal. *Id.*

> **The members of the decisionmaking body must be present or, if absent, must familiarize themselves with the record before voting.**

In sum, the members of the decisionmaking body must be present or, if absent, must familiarize themselves with the record before voting. *See* Charles S. Rhyne, The Law of Local Government Operations, pages 764–65 (1980).[2]

Therefore, it is good practice to follow these procedures: If a commissioner or council member is to vote on a matter to be heard at a public hearing, then that individual should not only be present during the public hearing, but should be sure to remain attentive throughout. If an individual is absent and the public hearing has been closed and continued for a decision to another date, or the hearing continued to another date, the absent member should review the tape of the earlier part of the public hearing, read all of the documents involved, examine all aspects of the issue presented, and state on the record that such review and examination was completed. *See* Charles S. Rhyne, The Law of Local Government Operations, page 765.

For further discussion on information that local officials may consider in the decision-making process, see chapter 4 (Zoning). For further information regarding the requirements of a "fair hearing" under Code of Civil Procedure section 1094.5, see chapter 19 (Land Use Litigation).

---

2 Slightly different procedures may apply under the California Administrative Procedures Act. (APA) Under the APA, an agency may adopt the decision of an administrative hearing officer even though the agency has not considered the evidence, if certain requirements are met. *See Ventimiglia v. Board of Behavioral Sciences*, 168 Cal. App. 4th 296, 308–11 (2008). Land use matters rarely, if ever, involve proceedings under the APA.

FINDINGS

WHEN ARE FINDINGS REQUIRED?

Findings are generally not required for legislative actions, but are required for quasi-judicial decisions.

LEGISLATIVE ACTS

Findings are not required for legislative acts unless a statute or local ordinance so requires. *See Mountain Defense League v. Board of Supervisors*, 65 Cal. App. 3d 723, 732, n.5 (1977). Thus, findings are generally not required for approval of zoning ordinances since they are legislative in nature. *See Ensign Bickford Realty Corp. v. City Council*, 68 Cal. App. 3d 467, 473 (1977); *Towards Responsibility In Planning v. City Council*, 200 Cal. App. 3d 671, 685 (1988) (summary of fiscal finding is not required in a general plan amendment or a rezoning).

Under certain circumstances, however, local ordinances or state law require findings for a legislative act. For example, state law requires findings when a general plan limits the number of newly constructed housing units, when a local ordinance has an effect on the housing needs of a region, or when a housing development project that complies with the applicable general plan and zoning is disapproved because it would have an adverse effect on public health or safety. Gov't Code §§ 65302.8, 65863.6, 65589.5(j); *see also Mira Dev. Corp. v. City of San Diego*, 205 Cal. App. 3d 1201, 1222 (1988) (Government Code section 65589.5 does not require findings to support denial of a rezoning application (citing *Arnel Dev. Co. v. City of Costa Mesa*, 28 Cal. 3d 511, 522 (1980))). The Mitigation Fee Act requires that certain determinations be made by the legislative body when it establishes or increases development impact fees. Gov't Code § 66001.

Other statutes require that certain determinations be made regardless of whether the decision at issue is adjudicatory or legislative. For example, CEQA requires that certain findings be made whenever a project is approved and an EIR has been prepared that identifies significant impacts. Pub. Res. Code § 21081. *See also* chapter 6 (CEQA). The Water Code requires, for certain large projects, that the city "shall determine, based on the entire record, whether projected water supplies will be sufficient to satisfy the demands of the project, in addition to existing and planned future uses." Water Code § 10911(c). *See also* chapter 16 (Sustainable Development). Findings requirements are generally applied only to councils and boards, and not to the electorate. *See Building Indus. Ass'n v. City of Camarillo*, 41 Cal. 3d 810, 823–24 (1986).

CEQA = California Environmental Quality Act

EIR = environmental impact report

ADJUDICATIVE ACTS UNDER 1094.5

Findings are required whenever a city acts in its adjudicatory role as opposed to its legislative capacity. A city usually acts in its legislative capacity when it establishes a basic principle or policy, such as a general plan adoption or amendment, or a rezoning. *Ensign Bickford Realty Corp. v. City Council*, 68 Cal. App. 3d at 474. The quasi-judicial capacity usually involves applying a fixed rule, standard, or law to a specific circumstance, such as a specific parcel of land. Examples of such nonlegislative actions include granting or denying variances, use permits, subdivision maps, design proposals, and the like. See chapter 19 (Land Use Litigation) for further discussion of the difference between adjudicatory and legislative approvals.

This findings requirement stems from Code of Civil Procedure section 1094.5 The California Supreme Court has set forth definitive requirements for adequate findings under section 1094.5. *Topanga Ass'n for a Scenic Community v. County of Los Angeles*, 11 Cal. 3d 506, 513–17 (1974). In *Topanga*, the Court overturned a zoning variance because it was not supported by adequate findings. The Court interpreted Code of Civil Procedure section 1094.5, which requires that certain adjudicatory decisions be supported by findings that bridge "the analytical gap between evidence and ultimate decision or order," and held that findings must be supported by substantial evidence. *Id.* at 514–15. The Court explained that the findings requirement serves five salutary purposes:

- Providing a framework for making principled decisions, thereby enhancing the integrity of the administrative process
- Facilitating orderly analysis and reducing the likelihood the city will leap randomly from evidence to conclusions
- Serving a public relations function by helping to persuade parties that administrative decisionmaking is careful, reasoned, and equitable
- Enabling the parties to determine whether and on what basis they should seek judicial review and remedies
- Apprising the reviewing court of the basis for the city's decisions

11 Cal. 3d at 516–517

Findings can take many forms. Although findings must be discernable, strict formality is not required. *Craik v. County of Santa Cruz*, 81 Cal. App. 4th 880, 884 (2001). For example, a city's "written findings" are not the sole means by which *Topanga* requirements can be satisfied. See *Harris v. City of Costa Mesa*, 25 Cal. App. 4th 963, 971 (1994). The *Harris* court said in addition to the findings stated in the city council resolution, it could look to the transcript of the hearing for findings contained in statements made by council members. The court further held it is proper to look for findings in oral remarks made at a public hearing where both parties were present, which were recorded, and of which a written transcript could be made. *Id.*

One court held that a summary of factual data, the language of the motion, and the reference in a motion to a staff report can constitute findings; however, that court made clear a transcript of a council debate that did not set forth the basis of the Council's decision was inadequate. See *Pacifica Corp. v. City of Camarillo*, 149 Cal. App. 3d 168, 179 (1983). "The Council debate, although reflective of the views of individual councilmen, is not the equivalent of *Topanga* findings." *Id.* Findings can also satisfy legal requirements by incorporating a staff report. See *McMillan v. American Gen. Fin. Corp.*, 60 Cal. App. 3d 175, 184 (1976).

Boilerplate or conclusory findings that do not recite the specific facts upon which the findings are based are not legally sufficient. See *Village Laguna, Inc. v. Board of Supervisors*, 134 Cal. App. 3d 1022, 1033–34 (1982). Similarly, a finding that was made "perfunctorily" and "without discussion or deliberation and thus does not show the Board's analytical route from evidence to finding" will be struck down. *Honey Springs Homeowners Ass'n v. Board of Supervisors*, 157 Cal. App. 3d 1122, 1151 (1984).

For example, in *City of Poway v. City of San Diego*, the City of Poway alleged that San Diego's findings on a land use project were insufficient under the *Village Laguna* standard. 155 Cal. App. 3d 1037, 1044-45 (1984). The court disagreed and held that San Diego's written findings provided sufficient information and factual discussion of the issues before the city. *Id.* at 1049. This comports with *Craik v. County of Santa Cruz,* in which the court stated that "findings need not be stated with judicial formality. Findings must simply expose the mode of analysis, not expose every minutia." 81 Cal. App. 4th at 884.

Similar findings were upheld in *Jacobson v. County of Los Angeles,* 69 Cal. App. 3d 374 (1977). In this case, the ordinance pertaining to conditional use permits required the zoning board to reach seven specific subconclusions and described these as the "findings" that must be made. *Id.* at 391 n.3 (citing *Topanga,* 11 Cal. 3d at 516). The court found these specific subconclusions sufficient.

The record must contain evidence supporting the findings. There must be substantial evidence in the record to support the findings. *Topanga,* 11 Cal. 3d at 515. Evidence may consist of staff reports, written and oral testimony, the EIR, exhibits, and the like. Opinions of neighbors may constitute evidence, and sufficient evidence can be found in presentations by neighbors opposing a project. *Harris,* 25 Cal. App. 4th. at 973.

Relevant personal observations also may be evidence. An adjacent property owner may testify to traffic conditions based upon personal knowledge. *See Citizens Ass'n for Sensible Dev. of Bishop Area v. County of Inyo,* 172 Cal. App. 3d 151, 173 (1985). Also, testimony at a public hearing describing various problems posed by the proposed development, including increased flooding and traffic, security problems, and health and safety risks, can support a city's findings in denying a development plan. *See Lindborg/Dahl Investors, Inc. v. City of Garden Grove,* 179 Cal. App. 3d 956, 962-63 (1986); *Placer Ranch Partners v. County of Placer,* 91 Cal. App. 4th 1336, 1342 (2001) (holding that the opinion of area residents was an appropriate factor to consider in making zoning decisions, citing *Stubblefield Construction Co. v. City of San Bernardino,* 32 Cal. App. 4th 687, 711 (1995)); *see also Browning-Ferris Indus. v. City Council,* 181 Cal. App. 3d 852, 866 (1986) (a city may rely upon staff's opinion as substantial evidence in reaching decisions).

> Relevant personal observations also may be evidence.

MAINTAINING SEPARATION BETWEEN PROSECUTORIAL AND ADJUDICATORY FUNCTION

Court decisions reflect concern that cities establish and maintain adequate separation between prosecutorial and adjudicatory functions in administrative hearings. *See Morongo Band of Mission Indians v. State Water Resources Control Board,* 45 Cal. 4th 751 (2009); *Quintero v. City of Santa Ana,* 114 Cal. App. 4th 810, 816 (2003); *Nightlife Partners, Ltd. v. City of Beverly Hills,* 108 Cal. App. 4th 81, 92 (2002).[3]

In *Nightlife Partners,* the plaintiff claimed the city had blurred the lines between prosecutorial and adjudicatory functions, thereby violating plaintiffs' due process rights. 108 Cal. App. 4th at 92. Nightlife Partners had submitted an application for renewal of a use permit. On the advice of an assistant city attorney that the application was incomplete, the city refused to renew the permit. At the administrative hearing on the plaintiff's appeal from that decision, the hearing officer announced the same assistant city attorney would be "advising [him] and assisting [him] as necessary in these proceedings." *Id.* at 85.

---

3 *See also* League of California Cities City Attorneys Department, *Report of the Department's Ad Hoc Due Process Committee on the Commingling of Functions in Quasi-Judicial Proceedings in the Wake of Nightlife Partners and Quintero* (2005), *available at* http://www.localgovlaw.com/Civica/filebank/blobload.asp?BlobID=2209.

In ordering that Nightlife Partners be granted a new hearing, the court held there had been an "objectionable overlapping of the role of advocate and decisionmaker" where the attorney had both advocated the City's position on the denial of the permit and then advised the decisionmaker at the administrative hearing relating to that permit denial. *Id.* at 94.

The court in *Quintero* went a step further than *Nightlife Partners*, holding that due process was violated where a lawyer who had advised the decisionmaker on *other* matters represented the city as an advocate before that decisionmaker. 114 Cal. App. 4th at 817. Quintero, a former detention officer, appealed his termination to the city's personnel board. He claimed the board's hearing violated due process because the deputy city attorney who represented the city at the hearing had at times served as a legal advisor to the board on various other matters, including other termination cases and the development of new procedural rules for appeals and standards for the adoption of findings. *Id.* at 813.

In granting Quintero's request for a new hearing, the court concluded that, while the deputy city attorney had not acted as both advocate and advisor in Quintero's particular case, the nature and extent of his relationship with the personnel board created the appearance of bias. *Id.* at 814. The court noted, "dual representation is not barred so long as there is adequate separation of the two roles and the attorneys performing them." *Id.* at 817 (citation omitted). But it held that the totality of the circumstances of the deputy city attorney's relationship with the board created a substantial risk that the board's judgment in Quintero's case was "skewed in favor of the prosecution." *Id.* at 817.

Quintero was narrowed in *Morongo Band of Mission Indians v. State Water Resources Control Bd.*, 45 Cal. 4th 731 (2009). In *Morongo*, the California Supreme Court held that an agency attorney prosecuting a matter before a board may simultaneously serve as an advisor to that board on an unrelated matter. It interpreted *Quintero* to be based upon two circumstances. First, there had been no internal separation of adjudicatory and prosecutorial functions in prior matters involving the parties. Second, the record suggested that one particular attorney had become the board's sole or primary legal adviser. The *Morongo* Court also disapproved of language in the *Quintero* that could be read to bar agency attorneys from simultaneously exercising advisory and prosecutorial functions, even in unrelated proceedings. *Morongo*, 45 Cal. 4th at 740 fn. 2 (disapproving language such as "[w]hat is inappropriate is one person simultaneously performing both functions" and "the attorney may occupy only one position at a time and must not switch roles from one meeting to the next").

The *Morongo* Court noted that the case before it did not involve the two factors determined in *Quintero*, and announced the rule that representation as a prosecutor on one matter, and as an advisor to the decisionmaking body on an unrelated matter, is lawful and constitutional.

RALPH M. BROWN ACT[4]

The Ralph M. Brown Act (Brown Act) details the various requirements to be followed by local bodies, including city councils and planning commissions, in conducting their

---

4 For further discussion of the Brown Act, see League of California Cities, *The California Municipal Law Handbook*, §§ 2.36-2.118 (2010); Ted Fourkas, *Open and Public III, A User's Guide to the Ralph M. Brown Act* (revised 2003, published by the Open and Public Participants including the League of California Cities); *The Brown Act: Open Meetings for Local Legislative Bodies* (California Attorney General's Office, 2003), *available at* http://ag.ca.gov/publications/brownAct2003.pdf.

meetings.[5] Gov't Code §§ 54950-54963. The Brown Act states that all meetings of city bodies shall be open and public, and all persons shall be permitted to attend any meeting with certain statutory exceptions, such as meetings for personnel matters and litigation. Gov't Code § 54953. The legislative intent of the Brown Act is contained in Government Code section 54950:

> In enacting this chapter, the Legislature finds and declares that the public commissions, boards and councils and the other public agencies in this State exist to aid in the conduct of the people's business. It is the intent of the law that their actions be taken openly and that their deliberations be conducted openly.
>
> The people of this State do not yield their sovereignty to the agencies which serve them. The people, in delegating authority, do not give their public servants the right to decide what is good for the people to know and what is not good for them to know. The people insist on remaining informed so that they may retain control over the instruments they have created.

Gov't Code § 54950

Meetings "that are subject to the Brown Act requirements" means:

Any congregation of a majority of the members of a legislative body at the same time and location, including teleconference location as permitted by section 54593 to hear, discuss, deliberate or take action on any item that is within the subject matter jurisdiction of the legislative body.

Gov't Code § 54952.2(a)

However, the Brown Act does not impose requirements upon any of the following:
- Individual contacts or conversations between a member of a legislative body and any other person that do not constitute "seriatim meetings" (as explained below)
- The attendance of a majority of the members of a legislative body at a conference or similar gathering open to the public that involves a discussion of issues of general interest to the public or to public agencies of the type represented by the legislative body, provided that a majority of the members do not discuss among themselves, other than as part of the scheduled program, business of a specified nature that is within the subject matter jurisdiction of the local agency
- The attendance of a majority of the members of a legislative body at an open and publicized meeting organized to address a topic of local community concern by a person or organization other than the local agency, provided that a majority of the members do not discuss among themselves, other than as part of the scheduled program, business of a specific nature that is within the subject matter jurisdiction of the legislative body of the local agency
- The attendance of a majority of the members of a legislative body at an open and noticed meeting of another body of the local agency, or at an open and noticed meeting of a legislative body of another local agency, provided that a majority of the members do not discuss among themselves, other than as part of the scheduled meeting, business of a specific nature that is within the subject matter jurisdiction of the legislative body of the local agency
- The attendance of a majority of the members at a purely social or ceremonial occasion, provided that a majority of the members do not discuss among

---

[5] A ballot measure approved by voters in November 2004 gives constitutional status to the notion that meetings of public bodies shall be open to public scrutiny. Proposition 59 amended the California Constitution to provide that statutes furthering the people's right of access shall be broadly construed while those limiting the right of access shall be narrowly construed. Cal. Const. art. I, § 3.

themselves business of a specific nature that is within the subject matter jurisdiction of the legislative body of the local agency
- The attendance of a majority of the members of a legislative body at an open and noticed meeting of a standing committee of that body, provided the members of the legislative body who are not members of the standing committee attend only as observers

Gov't Code § 54952.2(e)

As noted above, the Brown Act's definition of "meeting" does not include individual contacts between one member of a legislative body and any other person. However, separate meetings do violate the Brown Act if they are used in concert to build consensus between the council members by conveying the opinions of other council members behind closed doors. These meetings, called "seriatim meetings," are identified as a series of closed meetings held between members of a legislative body and others, with the goal of gathering information to be conveyed between respective members of the public body, while ensuring that a quorum of the legislative body is never present at any one meeting. The prohibition is against using intermediaries "to discuss, deliberate, or take action on any item of business that is within the subject matter jurisdiction of the legislative body." Gov't Code § 54952.2(b). There is no prohibition against individual conversations in which there is no attempt to use such conversations to achieve a collective deliberation between the members.

The Attorney General's office further explained the distinction. It concluded that the Brown Act clearly prohibits seriatim meetings, in which the members of the legislative body are "engaged in '*collective* discussion' and '*collective* acquisition and exchange of facts preliminary to the ultimate decision' albeit they do so in a series of meetings and not in a single meeting." 65 Ops. Cal. Atty. Gen. 63 at 65 (1982) (quoting 63 Ops. Cal. Atty. Gen. 820 (1980)) (emphasis added). The opinion clarified, however, that there was no intention to preclude individual councilpersons or commissioners from discussing matters of public concern with their constituents, nor to prevent private citizens from approaching and discussing their public business with individual members of the council or commission. Were it otherwise, public agencies effectively would be prohibited from conducting business in an efficient manner; if all communications outside the context of a public meeting were prohibited, then councilmembers would never be permitted even to read correspondence submitted to them on matters of public concern before attending a noticed meeting. *Id.; see also Wolfe v. City of Fremont,* 144 Cal. App. 4th 533, 549 (2006) (serial non-public discussions among city councilmembers resulting in collective concurrence on issue prior to public meeting would violate Brown Act).

> The Brown Act expressly allows a public agency to meet in closed session on a variety of topics, including those concerning personnel.

The Brown Act expressly allows a public agency to meet in closed session on a variety of topics, including those concerning personnel. Gov't Code § 54957(b)(1). The purpose of the personnel exception is to allow free and candid discussions of such matters, and to protect employees from public embarrassment.

The Brown Act also allows public agencies to meet in closed session to discuss pending or threatened litigation. Gov't Code § 54956.9. This exception from the general open meeting rule is designed to ensure the local agency's position in the litigation not be prejudiced. However, this exception is not unlimited. The court in *Trancas Property Owners Association v. City of Malibu* invalidated a settlement agreement adopted in a closed meeting because the agreement, which granted a zoning variance, violated the Brown Act. 138 Cal. App. 4th 172, 186 (2006). The court said a zoning variance requires a public hearing, and concluded:

The statutory exemption of discussions with counsel remains plenary: under section 54956.9, governing bodies may discuss with their counsel, in closed session, any settlement proposals or terms they deem worthy of consideration. And they generally may agree to such terms and settlements in closed session. What they may not do is decide upon or adopt in closed session a settlement that accomplishes or provides for action for which a public hearing is required by law, without such a hearing.

Id. at 187

The Brown Act provides that "[a]t least 72 hours before a regular meeting, the legislative body of the local agency, or its designee, shall post an agenda containing a brief general description of each item of business to be transacted or discussed at the meeting, including items to be discussed in closed session. A brief general description of an item generally need not exceed 20 words. The agenda shall specify the time and location of the regular meeting and shall be posted in a location that is freely accessible to members of the public and on the local agency's Internet Web site, if the local agency has one." Gov't Code § 54954.2(a)(1). The Act forbids action or discussion on any item not appearing on the posted agenda. Id. Where an agency will consider both approval of a project and adoption of a CEQA document for the project at a meeting, both items should be disclosed on the agenda. San Joaquin Raptor Rescue Center v. County of Merced, 216 Cal. App. 4th 1167, 1176-77 (2013) (failure to disclose planning commission's consideration of mitigated negative declaration on meeting agenda violated Brown Act).

The Brown Act's requirements apply to "legislative bodies," which is defined to include the governing body of a local agency as well as decisionmaking or advisory commissions, committees, boards, or other bodies of the agency. Gov't Code §§ 54952(a), (b). It also includes a board, commission, committee, or other multimember body that governs a private corporation, limited liability company, or other entity that either:

- Is created by the elected legislative body to exercise authority delegated by the governing body or
- "Receives funds from a local agency and the membership of whose governing body includes a member of the legislative body of the local agency appointed to that governing body as a full voting member by the legislative body of the local agency"[6]

Gov't Code § 54952(c)(1)

A member who attends a meeting during which action is taken in violation of the Brown Act, with wrongful intent to deprive the public of information to which it is entitled under the Brown Act, is guilty of a misdemeanor. Gov't Code § 54959. Further, a court can enjoin a city from violating the Brown Act, and can declare null and void an action taken in violation of the Brown Act. Gov't Code §§ 54960, 54960.1.

EX PARTE CONTACTS

Due process concerns may arise when a developer or a citizen contacts a planning commissioner or councilmember outside of a public hearing or outside the presence of other interested parties concerning projects that may come before the city. *Ex parte*

---

[6] For example, where a chamber of commerce is funded in part by a city and the mayor is appointed by the city council to sit on the chamber's board of directors, the chamber would be subject to the Brown Act. Ted Fourkas, *Open and Public III, A User's Guide to the Ralph M. Brown Act* (revised 2003).

contacts during the course of a quasi-judicial proceeding may lead to claims of bias on the part of the public official or violation of an interested party's right to know what evidence is used by the council or commission in reaching its decision.[7]

The problem of *ex parte* contacts in the land use arena has been largely ignored by the Legislature and California courts.[8] The leading California case on this issue is *City of Fairfield v. Superior Court of Solano County*, 14 Cal. 3d 768 (1975). In *Fairfield*, the California Supreme Court discussed whether three city councilmembers should be disqualified from voting on a land use permit in a quasi-judicial hearing because of previous spoken opposition during an election campaign. The Court stated: "that fact would not disqualify them from voting on the application." *Id.* at 779. Because even quasi-judicial decisions may significantly influence the nature and direction of future economic growth, a councilmember "has not only a right but an obligation to discuss issues of vital concern with his constituents and to state his views on matters of public importance." *Id.* at 780; *see also Todd v. City of Visalia*, 254 Cal. App. 2d 679 (1967); League of California Cities, *The California Municipal Law Handbook*, § 2.180 (2010).

Local officials are not and cannot be held to the same standards that apply to judges.[9] Councilmembers and planning commissioners have a statutory duty to apprise themselves of all of the facts in any given issue. In addition, local officials dealing with land use issues have much more exposure to the public, particularly in smaller cities.

PERMIT STREAMLINING ACT

Protecting California's economy, the health of its citizens, and its environment requires sophisticated consideration of development proposals. By adopting the Permit Streamlining Act (Gov't Code § 65920 *et seq.*), the California Legislature declared the protection of those interests also involves the "statewide need to ensure clear understanding of the specific requirements which must be met in connection with the approval of development projects and to *expedite* decisions on such projects." Gov't Code § 65921 (emphasis added). The Permit Streamlining Act was adopted to relieve permit applicants from protracted and unjustified governmental delays in processing their project applications.

The Permit Streamlining Act applies to certain local land use decisions and requires a city to follow a standardized process with respect to those decisions. It also requires completion of review and decisions on development applications within strict time limits. Gov't Code § 65943. Pursuant to the Act, failure by a city to approve or disapprove a development project within those time limits may result in the project being "deemed" approved, provided that the prescribed public notice requirements

---

[7] Only those governmental decisions that are adjudicative or "quasi-judicial" in nature are subject to procedural due process principles. Legislative action is not burdened by such requirements. See *Horn v. County of Ventura*, 24 Cal. 3d 605, 612 (1979).

[8] Other states such as Oregon and Washington have enacted legislation regulating *ex parte* contacts with local officials. *See, e.g.*, Oregon's planning procedure guidelines, Or. Rev. Stat. § 227.180, and Washington's *Appearance of Fairness* Statute, Wash. Rev. Code § 42.36.060. The Idaho Supreme Court addressed this issue in *Idaho Historic Preservation Council, Inc. v. City Council of Boise*, 134 Idaho 651 (2000). *See also* Edward J. Sullivan and Carrie Richter, *Out of the Chaos: Towards a National System of Land-Use Procedures*," 34 Urb. Law. 449 (2002).

[9] For a good overview of the competing approaches to this issue, see 32 *Fed. Prac. & Proc. Judicial Review*, section 8260 (2007); Edward H. Ziegle, 2 *Rathkopf's Law of Zoning and Planning*, sections 32:10–11 (4th ed. September 2007); John W. Witt, *The Problem of Ex Parte Contacts*, 3 Land Use & Env. Forum 24 (CEB, Winter 1994); Daniel J. Curtin, Jr., *Ex Parte Contacts: A Less Restrictive View*, 3 CEB Land Use & Env. Forum 31 (Winter 1994); *see also* William W. Eigner and Robert L. Wernli, Jr., *Lobbying Guidelines and Rules for Ex Parte Contact*, 21 California Real Prop. J., no. 2 (Spring 2003).

have been met. *Id.* The Permit Streamlining Act does not apply to ministerial permits or permits to operate. Gov't Code § 65928. Morever, as explained more fully below, the deemed approved or automatic approval provisions do not apply to legislative acts, such as rezonings and general plan amendments. *See Landi v. County of Monterey*, 139 Cal. App. 3d 934, 937 (1983).

Under the Act, a city is required to compile one or more lists specifying in detail the information needed from a project applicant, and to make such lists available to all applicants and anyone else who requests them. Gov't Code § 65940; *see also Bickel v. City of Piedmont*, 16 Cal. 4th 1040, 1046 (1997). These lists must be revised so that they are current and accurate at all times. Gov't Code § 65942. In general, revisions may be prospective only and cannot be applied to applications submitted before the revisions took effect. The lists must indicate the criteria that will be applied in determining whether an application is complete and the time limits for the review and approval of applications. Gov't Code §§ 65941, 65941.5; *see also Beck Dev. Co. v. Southern Pac. Transp. Co.*, 44 Cal. App. 4th 1160, 1198 (1996).

A city must include in the information list for development projects, or in the application form for a building permit, specified requirements concerning compliance with statutes regulating hazardous materials and air pollution, the handling of acutely hazardous materials, and the emission of hazardous air emissions. Gov't Code § 65850.2. This section prohibits a city from finding an application complete, or from approving a development project or a building permit for a project that requires only a building permit, if the project meets specified requirements concerning hazardous materials and emissions, unless the owner or authorized agent complies with certain provisions. It also requires the owner or authorized agent to substantially meet the requirements for submitting a risk management and prevention program if the administering agency makes a specified determination. This section does not apply to applications solely for residential construction. Gov't Code § 65850.2(i).

Also, state law requires that the applicant to indicate whether the property is located on any of several lists of sites compiled by state agencies. Gov't Code § 65962.5. For example, the list prepared by the California Integrated Waste Management Board contains the list all solid waste disposal facilities from which there is a known migration of hazardous waste. Gov't Code §§ 65962.5(d), (f) (Cortese List). The Secretary for Environmental Protection maintains a statewide list and is responsible for distributing this information to any persons upon request. Gov't Code § 65962.5(e). Governmnet Code Section 65962.5(e) contains the form of the Hazardous Waste and Substance Statement.

Submittal of a project application is the first step in the streamlined permitting process. Within 30 calendar days of receiving an application, a city must inform the applicant in writing whether the application is complete and accepted for filing. Gov't Code § 65943. If the application is complete, a city proceeds with the evaluation of the development project. If it finds the application incomplete, the city must indicate in detail where the application is deficient and specify the additional information needed. Gov't Code § 65943.

If the city fails to notify the applicant whether it is complete, the application is deemed "complete and accepted" 30 days after it the city received it. *See Bickel*, 16 Cal. 4th at 1046; *Orsi v. City Council*, 219 Cal. App. 3d 1576, 1584 (1990). Once an application is accepted as complete or is deemed complete, the city cannot ask for new information, although it may require the applicant to clarify or supplement the material provided in the accepted application. Gov't Code § 65944; *Bickel*, 16 Cal. 4th at 1046.

> Under the Permit Streamlining Act, a city is required to compile one or more lists specifying in detail the information needed from a project applicant, and to make such lists available to all applicants and anyone else who requests them.

The date on which an application is accepted as complete or deemed complete is important because it may dictate what laws apply to a project or what actions a city may take. For example:

- To address the problem of affordable housing, when a proposed housing development project complies with the applicable general plan, zoning, and development policies in effect at the time the application is determined to be complete, a city cannot disapprove it or approve it at a lower density without making written findings stating that certain specific conditions exist. Gov't Code § 65589.5
- With certain exceptions, a city, when approving or disapproving a tentative subdivision map, can apply only those ordinances, policies, and standards that were in effect at the time the application was determined to be complete. Gov't Code § 66474.2
- When a city approves a vesting tentative map, that approval confers a vested right to proceed with development in substantial compliance with the ordinances, policies, and standards that are in effect at the time the application is complete (much like Government Code section 66474.2). Gov't Code § 66498.1(b)
- Finally, all deadlines under the Permit Streamlining Act begin from the day an application is accepted as complete or deemed complete

The completion date also starts the clock running on processing the application. Subject to certain exceptions, under the Permit Streamlining Act, a city acting as the lead agency for a project for which an EIR is prepared shall approve or disapprove the project within 180 days from the date of the EIR's certification. Gov't Code § 65950(a)(1); *see Eller Media Co. v. City of Los Angeles*, 87 Cal. App. 4th 1217, 1220 (2001) (Permit Streamlining Act measures time limits for approval or disapproval of an application from specific CEQA actions, including: the determination that a project is exempt from CEQA, the adoption of a negative declaration, or the certification of an EIR).

A 60-day time limit is provided when a negative declaration is adopted or if the project is exempt from the CEQA. Gov't Code § 65950(a)(3). The Permit Streamlining Act provides a one-time-only 90-day extension to these deadlines upon consent of the city and the applicant. Gov't Code § 65957. Legislation enacted in 1998 amended Government Code section 65957 so that no other extension, continuance, or waiver of these time limits by either the applicant or the lead agency is permitted. The Legislature included a declaration that it was aware of *Bickel v. City of Piedmont*, which held that an applicant had a common law right to waive the time limits prescribed by the Permit Streamlining Act, and stated its intent to clarify that the Act "does not provide for the application of the common law doctrine of waiver by either the act's purpose or its statutory language." 1998 Cal. Stat. ch. 283, § 5. There is a statutory prohibition against a city's requiring extensions or waivers of the time limits for approval or disapproval. Gov't Code § 65940.5.

If approval or disapproval of a project does not occur within these deadlines, the project shall be deemed approved provided the prescribed public notice requirements have been met. Gov't Code § 65956; *see also Orsi v. City Council of Salinas*, 219 Cal. App. 3d at 1585. Due process may require that a hearing be held first for some applications. *See Horn v. County of Ventura*, 24 Cal. 3d 605, 616 (1979) (referring to "deemed approved" provision in Subdivision Map Act); *Selinger v. City Council*, 216 Cal. App. 3d 259, 272–74 (1989) (holding "deemed approved" provisions unconstitutional insofar as they contravened *Horn*.) Further, the time period for an appeal is not included within the prescribed time limits. Gov't Code § 65922.

The Act provides two methods for an applicant to ensure the public notice requirements for a project to be deemed approved are met: (1) the applicant may use the civil mandamus remedy to compel a city to provide the required public notice (Gov't Code § 65956(a)); or (2) the applicant may provide public notice of the project if the city fails to do so. Gov't Code § 65956(b). Section 65956(b) specifically states that if the applicant provides public notice, the notice must include the fact that failure of the city to act on the application within 60 days will result in the application being deemed approved.

Although not explicitly set out in the statute, a 2006 court of appeal decision held a local agency's notice also must state that a failure to act will result in the application being deemed approved. *Mahon v. County of San Mateo*, 139 Cal. App. 4th 812, 822 (2006). Mahon applied for design review and building permits for two small projects. The county determined that each project was exempt from CEQA review, starting the 60-day period for the county to approve or disapprove the projects. Neither the mailed nor the posted notices advised that the permits would be deemed approved if the county failed to act within a specified period. The county failed to approve or disapprove the permit applications within this 60-day deadline, and Mahon sued, arguing that the applications had been deemed approved by the Act.

CEQA = California Environmental Quality Act

The court held that, although it was undisputed the county failed to act within the 60-day deadline, the notice given by the county was not the "public notice required by law" necessary for deemed approval under Gov't Code § 65956(b), in that it did not contain language stating the permits would be deemed approved if the county failed to act within the 60-day period. *Id.* at 822. The court rejected Mahon's argument that this requirement was only applicable to notices that an applicant must give. The court concluded, "we see no reason why...'public notice required by law' would mean one thing if notice is provided by the agency and another if provided by the applicant." *Id.* Since section 65956(b) requires an applicant's notice to include a warning regarding the potential for deemed approval, the court found the requirement must be considered part of "public notice required by law"—a term not otherwise defined in the statute. *Id.* at 821–22.

As to the proper method of noticing under Government Code section 65956(b), the court in *Ciani v. San Diego Trust and Savings Bank* held an applicant must follow notice distribution requirements under the applicable law that governs the particular permit in question. 233 Cal. App. 3d 1604, 1616–17 (1991). In that case, the court found a "deemed approved" permit bears all the legal entitlements of a tangible permit issued by the agency, including availability of the statutory appeal provided for agency-issued permits. *Id.* at 1613. In *Ciani*, the 10-day appeal period provided in the statute and regulation for a coastal permit was applicable. Because the applicant failed to provide notice to the Coastal Commission prior to commencement of the 10-day appeal period, its permit was not deemed approved. *Id.* at 1616–17. For an introduction to some of the issues faced by an applicant when its project is deemed approved, see Robert E. Merritt, *The Permit Streamlining Act*, 1 CEB Land Use Forum 30 (Fall 1991).

Several cases uphold application of the Act's automatic approval provisions to particular projects. In 1986, a court held the Act was applicable to a development project for a subdivision, conditional use permit, and building permits when a city failed to act within a one-year time limit. In this situation, the general plan and zoning permitted the use. *See Palmer v. City of Ojai*, 178 Cal. App. 3d 280, 293 (1986).

The Act's time limits for acting on a development application are not tolled by a building moratorium. *See Selinger v. City Council*, 216 Cal. App. 3d 259 (1989). The court in *Selinger* also rejected the City's argument that the automatic approval provision was not applicable because a tentative map cannot be deemed approved without the city council making the express finding the map is consistent with the City's general plan as required by the Subdivision Map Act. The court held the City's duty to make findings cannot be reconciled with the Act's automatic approval provision and that the latter prevailed. *Id.* at 270 (discussing Gov't Code §§ 66473.5, 66474). *But see id.* at 274 (holding "deemed approval" provisions unconstitutional insofar as they fail to provide adequate notice and opportunity to be heard to affected, neighboring landowners).

In 1990, another court held there was an automatic approval for a planned unit development when a city failed to notify the developer the application was incomplete within the first 30 days. *See Orsi v. City Council of Salinas*, 219 Cal. App. 3d at 1586. Also, the court stated the developer's resubmittal at the request of the City after the time had expired did not change the effect of the automatic approval. In this case, a negative declaration was adopted, notice was given, and hearings were held.

However, the courts also have strictly limited application of the Permit Streamlining Act. One court held that the Act was not meant to impose a rigorous timetable on a city's exercise of its policy-making "legislative" powers, but only on the exercise of its "adjudicatory" powers. *See Landi v. County of Monterey*, 139 Cal. App. 3d 934, 937 (1983). Thus, the Act has been declared not to apply to an application for a legislative approval, such as a general plan amendment or a rezoning. In *Landi*, the court held that because the applicant had requested a rezoning, which is a legislative act, the Act and its time limits for approval did not apply. *Id.; see Meridian Ocean Sys., Inc. v. State Lands Comm'n*, 222 Cal. App. 3d 153, 166 (1990) (whether an EIR should be prepared is a policy decision, and thus a quasi-legislative action under *Landi*).

Further, the Act does not require automatic approval of a nonlegislative or adjudicatory project (e.g., a site plan or map approval permit application) when such permit application would require legislative changes in applicable general plans, zoning ordinances, or other controlling land use regulations. If the nonlegislative or adjudicatory permit is tied to legislative change, then the deemed approved provisions of the Act are not applicable. *See Land Waste Mgmt. v. County of Contra Costa Bd. of Supervisors*, 222 Cal. App. 3d 950, 959 (1990). Significantly, the Act also does not cause an automatic certification of an EIR or automatic approval of a negative declaration or other review required by CEQA. *Id.*

The Act was found not to apply to a request for a certificate of compliance under the Subdivision Map Act since "development project" as defined in the Permit Streamlining Act does not include ministerial acts. *See Findleton v. Bd. of Supervisors*, 12 Cal. App. 4th 709, 714 (1993); *see also Meridian Ocean Sys.*, 222 Cal. App. 3d at 166 (holding that the Act applies only to approval of development projects as defined and not to a permit to operate; thus, the Act was not applicable to an application for a permit to conduct geophysical research).

OTHER PROCEDURAL REQUIREMENTS

A subdivider as well as tenants in condominium conversions are entitled to the city staff's written report at least three days before the hearing on a subdivision. Gov't Code § 66452.3. Tenants also must be notified by a subdivider when a final map has been approved for a condominium project, community apartment project, or stock

EIR = environmental impact report

cooperative project. Gov't Code § 66459. A planning commission must follow the minimal procedural standards set forth in Government Code section 65804. Many cities have enacted ordinances or resolutions that require staff reports to be made available to the public prior to the hearing.

DEVELOPER MISREPRESENTATIONS

A developer's misrepresentations, unfulfilled promises, and negligent predictions of future actions made to induce political support may be actionable. *See Lacher v. Superior Court*, 230 Cal. App. 3d 1038, 1046-47 (1991). In *Lacher*, the court held that willful and negligent misrepresentations made to a homeowners' association that its members' views would not be affected by the developer's residential beachfront project were actionable since they induced the association to support the proposed development before the local planning commission. *Id*. at 1046.

Significantly, the *Lacher* court also found no merit in the developer's claim the Planning and Zoning Law and the Subdivision Map Act precluded the homeowners' cause of action for fraud and negligent misrepresentation. The court held those laws were meant to limit a party's ability to challenge a city's land use decisions, but that the Legislature did not intend to supplant the common law with respect to actions brought against third-party developers. 230 Cal. App. 3d at 1050.

> A developer's misrepresentations, unfulfilled promises, and negligent predictions of future actions made to induce political support may be actionable.

CHAPTER 18

Enforcement of Land Use Laws

INTRODUCTION

This chapter discusses some of the enforcement mechanisms a city may use when confronting violations of its land use regulations or noncompliance with the conditions imposed on a permit approval or development. This chapter also discusses the possible defenses to enforcement actions.

ADMINISTRATIVE AND CRIMINAL SANCTIONS

MISDEMEANOR

The scope of a city's authority to impose administrative or criminal sanctions for violations of ordinances or codes is set by Government Code section 36900, which provides that "[v]iolation of a city ordinance is a misdemeanor unless by ordinance it is made an infraction."

The maximum penalties are set forth in Government Code section 36901, which provides that "a fine shall not exceed one thousand dollars," and "[i]mprisonment shall not exceed six months." However, it allows both penalties to be imposed for the same violation, which is permitted by Penal Code section 19. The violation may be prosecuted by city authorities (or by the district attorney) in the name of the people of the State of California. Gov't Code § 36901.

The right of a city to impose multiple penalties for continuous conduct was upheld in *People v. Djekich*, 229 Cal. App. 3d 1213, 1224 (1991). There, the conduct at issue involved illegal conversion of a building into a duplex and the disregard of multiple notices of continuing violation. The court stated that a zoning ordinance may specifically authorize a separate punishment for each violation and define each day's continuance as a distinct offense. Thus, "a penal provision reflecting a clear legislative intent to permit pyramiding of punishment through cumulative convictions by providing for a separate offense for each day a defendant continues his/her criminal conduct is valid... providing the fine imposed is not unconstitutionally excessive or the sentence imposed does not constitute cruel and/or unusual punishment." *Id.*

> The right of a city to impose multiple penalties for continuous conduct was upheld in *People v. Djekich*.

INFRACTION

Under Government Code section 36900, a violation of an ordinance or code determined to be an infraction is punishable by (1) a fine not exceeding one hundred dollars for a first violation; (2) a fine not exceeding two hundred dollars for a second violation of the same ordinance within one year; and (3) a fine not exceeding five hundred dollars for each additional violation of the same ordinance within one year. For violations of local building and safety codes, the maximum fines are $100, $500, and $1,000, respectively. As with the misdemeanor violations, penalties for infractions can be cumulated based both on the number of violations and their duration. However, in contrast to misdemeanor prosecutions, infraction proceedings lack procedural protections such as a trial.

The infraction procedure is typically used when dealing with small land use infractions, such as sign violations.

ADMINISTRATIVE PENALTIES

Government Code section 53069.4 permits a city to adopt an ordinance that subjects any person who violates an ordinance to an administrative fine or penalty. Under this law, a city must adopt an ordinance setting forth the administrative procedures that govern the imposition, enforcement, collection, and administrative review of these fines or penalties. Where the violation otherwise would be an infraction, the administrative fine or penalty cannot exceed the maximum fine or penalty for infractions set forth in Government Code sections 25132 and 36900, except in the case of building or safety code violations where the maximum fines are greater. Gov't Code §§ 25132(c), 36900(c). When a code violation pertains to building, plumbing, electrical, or other similar structural or zoning issues that do not create an immediate danger to health or safety, the administrative procedures must give the person responsible for the continuing violation a reasonable amount of time to remedy the violation before imposing fines or penalties.

In addition, if fees, costs, and expenses incurred in the enforcement of state or local zoning, building, and housing laws and regulations, or in the abatement of a nuisance, are not paid within 45 days, a city can impose a lien against the property that is the subject of the enforcement activity. Gov't Code § 54988. However, the power to impose enforcement costs as a penalty in a criminal prosecution of code infractions is not valid under the general law. See *People v. Minor*, 96 Cal. App. 4th 29, 32 (2002).

WARRANT

When inspecting private property in the field, enforcement agents step into the domain of law enforcement. Although not police or peace officers, they are public employees seeking to enforce applicable municipal regulations or ordinances. Thus, enforcement agents, like the police, must adhere to legal and constitutional limits of search of private property. *Camara v. Municipal Court*, 387 U.S. 523, 539–540 (1967).

An administrative inspection warrant must (1) be in writing (Code of Civil Procedure (CCP) § 1822.50); (2) be in the name of the people (CCP § 1822.50); (3) signed by a judge of a court of record (CCP § 1822.50); (4) issued upon "cause" (CCP § 1822.51); and (5) be supported by an affidavit that particularly describes the place, dwelling, structure, etc. to be inspected (CCP § 1822.51). The affidavit must contain

CCP = Code of Civil Procedure

either a statement that consent was sought and refused or facts or circumstances reasonably justifying the failure to seek such consent. CCP § 1822.51.

Cause shall be deemed to exist if either reasonable legislative or administrative standards for conducting a routine or area inspection are satisfied with respect to the particular place, dwelling, structure, premises, or vehicle, or there is reason to believe that a condition of nonconformity exists with respect to the particular place, dwelling, structure, premises, or vehicle. CCP § 1822.52

A warrant remains valid for a maximum of 14 days. CCP § 1822.55.

ENFORCEMENT UNDER THE REVENUE AND TAXATION CODE

Where there is a violation of a local code dealing with health, safety, or building conditions associated with rental housing, cities also may use Revenue and Taxation Code sections 17274 and 24436.5 for enforcement. Under these provisions, after following specific procedures set forth in the law, a city may file a written notice of violation with the Franchise Tax Board. If the owner of the rental income property fails to remedy the violation within a certain time period, he or she is then precluded from taking a deduction for interest, taxes, depreciation, or amortization paid or incurred in a taxable year. Rev. and Tax. Code § 24436.5. All state revenue that normally would have accrued to the property owner by way of tax deductions is returned to the city that notified the Franchise Tax Board of the violation. To initiate this procedure, the Franchise Tax Board has adopted a "Notice of Non-Compliance" (SRH 1010 (10-78)) that can be obtained from the Board.

ENFORCEMENT UNDER THE SUBDIVISION MAP ACT

For violation of subdivision regulations, the Subdivision Map Act provides its own detailed enforcement procedures. *See* Gov't Code § 66499.30 *et seq.* In addition to these various remedies for noncompliance, once a city makes a finding that development is contrary to the public health or safety, it must refuse to issue any permit or grant any approval necessary to develop the property that is in violation of the law. Gov't Code § 66499.34.

A city may also encourage compliance with its subdivision regulations through the notice-and-hearing procedure set forth in state law. *See* Gov't Code § 66499.36. Whenever a city has knowledge that property has been illegally subdivided, it must inform the property owner of its intention to file a notice of violation. This notice will cloud title to the property, encouraging compliance.

ENFORCEMENT UNDER CEQA

The California Environmental Quality Act (CEQA) also provides cities with a mechanism to remedy a developer's failure to implement mitigation measures required by law. If changes have been incorporated into a development project, or conditions have been proposed on the project, to mitigate or avoid significant adverse environmental effects of the project upon the environment (as may be required by an environmental impact report or mitigated negative declaration), an agency must adopt a mitigation monitoring program at the time the project is approved. Doing so ensures the developer will comply with the mitigation measures during project implementation. Pub. Res. Code § 21081.6(a); Cal. Code Regs. tit. 14, § 15091(d). As part of the mitigation

CEQA = California Environmental Quality Act

monitoring program, a city must ensure that mitigation measures are fully enforceable as conditions of development of the project. Pub. Res. Code § 21081.6(b).

The conditions of approval generally are incorporated into the resolution or ordinance approving the project. The conditions must address each of the mitigation measures adopted by the city, and must expressly provide that approval of a final map or other approvals is conditioned upon completion of certain mitigation measures. If a developer fails to implement a mitigation measure, the conditions then provide a city with the mechanism for permit revocations, stop work orders, or denial of subsequent approvals that are needed to complete, operate, or occupy the project. For further discussion of the requirements of CEQA, see chapter 6 (CEQA).

ENFORCEMENT UNDER THE BUSINESS AND PROFESSIONS CODE

Another method to enforce land use regulations is found in Business and Professions Code section 17200 (the unfair competition statute). In 1997, a court found that Squaw Valley Ski Resort had engaged in unfair competition by committing unlawful business practices when it violated not only conditions of a conditional use permit, but also the Forest Practices Act (Pub. Res. Code § 4511 et seq.) by resorting to self-help and cutting down more than 1,800 trees without a permit. See *Hewlett v. Squaw Valley Ski Corp.*, 54 Cal. App. 4th 499, 520 (1997). The court rejected Squaw Valley's claim that the tree-cutting should not be prosecuted as an unlawful business practice, holding the intent at the time of cutting, rather than the final use of the timber, controlled. *Id.* at 523-24. However, later decisions have found reasons not to apply section 17200 to environmental disputes, for example, *Center for Biological Diversity v. FPL, Inc.*, 166 Cal. App. 4th 1349 (2008) (court declined to reach section 17200 claim challenging operation of windfarms on environmental grounds).

POSSIBLE DEFENSES TO A CITY'S ENFORCEMENT ACTION

DENIAL OF DUE PROCESS OR EQUAL PROTECTION

At times, a violator will claim as a defense that there is a denial of due process or equal protection because the relevant laws are not being enforced against similarly situated people. However, courts generally have rejected this argument. For example, in *City of Banning v. Desert Outdoor Advertising, Inc.*, the court stated that it was not a defense that zoning officials permitted similar violations by others to continue over a number of years. 209 Cal. App. 2d 152, 155-56 (1962); see also *Sutherland v. City of Fort Bragg*, 86 Cal. App. 4th 13, 24 (2000) (a fire chief's duty to enforce fire code was discretionary, and therefore enforcement of the code against one party but not another did not subject him to liability). *Riggs v. City of Oxnard*, 154 Cal. App. 3d 526, 531 (1984) (zoning enforcement is a discretionary function); *City and County of San Francisco v. Burton*, 201 Cal. App. 2d 749, 755 (1962) (unintentional discriminatory enforcement of a zoning ordinance is not a defense to prosecution).

Disparate treatment of individual violators of a law or ordinance is subject to rational basis scrutiny—and therefore will not give rise to an equal protection or due process claim—so long as it bears some rational relation to a legitimate state interest. See *Squaw Valley Development Co. v. Goldberg*, 375 F. 3d 936, 948 (9th Cir. 2004) (recognizing that more aggressive enforcement against a violator could be rationally related to a legitimate state interest).

However, to the extent the "rational basis" used to justify selective enforcement is shown to be merely a pretext for differential treatment, a plaintiff may establish an equal protection violation. *Squaw Valley Development Co.*, 375 F. 3d at 944-45. The plaintiff in *Squaw Valley* claimed an equal protection violation by the executive officer of the regional water quality control board with oversight of the plaintiff's property. Squaw Valley claimed that it was singled out and subjected to stricter enforcement by the board's management because of personal animus on the part of the board's executive officer. *Id.* at 944. The Ninth Circuit held that, while there may have been a rational basis for selective enforcement against Squaw Valley, there also was evidence to support a conclusion that the purported rational basis was merely a pretext. *Id.* at 948. Most notably, the defendant regulator was unable to recollect a single instance when the plaintiff Squaw Valley had failed to comply with water quality laws so as to arguably justify the stricter enforcement he claimed was necessary. The Ninth Circuit therefore reversed the trial court's grant of summary judgment as to the board's executive officer and allowed Squaw Valley's equal protection claim against him to proceed. *Id.* at 949.

In *Lim v. City of Long Beach*, owners and operators of adult businesses claimed the city violated their equal protection rights by forcing existing adult businesses to relocate under a new zoning ordinance. The ordinance restricted the locations in which adult businesses could operate, while allowing non-adult businesses to remain in place even when in violation of other city ordinances. In denying the adult business owners' claim, the court stated the city's actions only needed to be rationally related to a permissible government objective. 217 F. 3d 1050, 1056 (9th Cir. 2000). The court found sufficient the city's proffered reason for enforcing its adult business ordinance as its interest in curbing the secondary effects of adult businesses. The city did not have a similar interest in enforcing its other zoning ordinances. *Id.* at 1057.

However, not all enforcement of planning and zoning provisions is discretionary. In *Terminal Plaza Corporation v. City and County of San Francisco*, Terminal Plaza filed a petition for writ of mandate, contending the city had refused to enforce a project condition requiring the construction of a mid-block pedestrian way. 186 Cal. App. 3d 814, 831 (1986). The court held that in light of the clear language of the condition, the zoning administrator had a ministerial duty to enforce its requirements. *Id.* The zoning administrator had no discretion to determine whether an express condition had been violated or to interpret it, and did not have the discretionary enforcement authority of a prosecuting attorney. *Id.* at 834.

> Not all enforcement of planning and zoning provisions is discretionary.

In *Lockyer v. City and County of San Francisco*, the California Supreme Court held that local officials did not have any judicial or quasi-judicial discretionary authority in their enforcement of the state family law statute that limits the granting of a marriage license to a couple comprised of a man and a woman. 33 Cal. 4th 1055, 1093 (2004). At the Mayor's direction, the San Francisco County Clerk had removed mention of gender from marriage forms created by the State Registrar of Vital Statistics and had begun to solemnize marriages between same-sex couples. The Mayor had directed such action based on his belief that the state law violated the equal protection clause of the California Constitution.

The *Lockyer* court held that once a statute is duly enacted, it is presumed constitutional and the scope of a public official's statutorily derived authority to act is defined by the terms of the statute itself. *Id.* at 1086. In this instance, the state law governing the issuance of marriage licenses did not grant city officials discretion in issuing licenses, but rather created a ministerial duty to grant licenses in accordance with the statute.

The County Clerk therefore had no authority to disregard the statutory mandate based on her own determination that the statute was unconstitutional. *Id.* at 1092-93.

ESTOPPEL

> The estoppel theory is very difficult to use successfully against a city because courts have a strong policy against applying this doctrine where the interests of the public may be adversely affected.

Another defense that may surface in an enforcement action is a claim that the city is estopped from enforcing its own regulations because the city itself has acted contrary to them. The estoppel theory is very difficult to use successfully against a city because courts have a strong policy against applying this doctrine where the interests of the public may be adversely affected.

To establish a claim of estoppel against the government a litigant must (1) prove the same four elements as make up a cause of action for equitable estoppel against a private party; and (2) satisfy a fifth element which applies only to the government. *La Canada Flintridge Development Corporation v. Department of Transportation*, 166 Cal. App. 3d 206, 219 (1985). The first four elements are:

(1) the party to be estopped must be apprised of the facts

(2) it must intend that its conduct shall be acted upon, or must so act that the party asserting the estoppel had a right to believe it was so intended

(3) the other party must be ignorant of the true state of facts

(4) the other party must rely upon the conduct to its injury

Driscoll v. City of Los Angeles, 67 Cal. 2d 297, 305 (1967)

The fifth element requires the plaintiff to demonstrate the injury to its personal interests if the government is not estopped exceeds the injury to the public interest if the government is estopped. Thus an estoppel will not be applied against the government if to do so would effectively nullify "a strong rule of policy, adopted for the benefit of the public...." *La Canada*, 166 Cal. App. 3d at 219 (quoting *County of San Diego v. California Water and Telephone Co.*, 30 Cal. 2d 817, 829-30 (1947)). As a result of this principle, courts rarely enforce an estoppel defense against local governments. *See, e.g., Smith v. County of Santa Barbara*, 7 Cal. App. 4th 770, 775-76 (1992) (county not estopped from revoking erroneously issued land use permit to install microwave dishes); *County of Sonoma v. Rex*, 231 Cal. App. 3d 1289, 1295 (1991) (county not estopped from enforcing a zoning ordinance against an innkeeper).

However, there are several cases where property owners have successfully asserted an estoppel theory. In *Congregation Etz Chaim v. City of Los Angeles*, the Ninth Circuit Court of Appeals estopped the City of Los Angeles from revoking building permits upon which the plaintiff congregation had relied. 371 F. 3d 1122, 1125 (9th Cir. 2004). Congregation Etz Chaim and the city had reached a settlement agreement to resolve their disagreement over permit requirements in connection with renovation of the Congregation's facility. The Congregation thereafter submitted renovation plans for the facility. After requiring numerous changes to the plans, the city approved them and issued a building permit. Within a week after the Congregation began work and in response to complaints from neighbors, the city issued a stop-work order and notified the Congregation that it intended to revoke the building permit. The city claimed the permit was issued in violation of other provisions of its code.

The Ninth Circuit held the city could not revoke the permit, finding that the facts of the case "provide particularly strong support for the Congregation's estoppel argument." *Id.* The court found the city's own grant of the building permit, after having reviewed and approved the plans along with the settlement agreement, amounted to a representation by the city that the plans complied with the agreement. Moreover, the Congregation had performed substantial work and incurred substantial liabilities in reliance on the permit. *Id.*

In another case, a court held that reliance by a property owner on an administrative regulation of the City and County of San Francisco was a valid basis for an estoppel against the city in enforcing a later-enacted ordinance. *See Hock Inv. Co. v. City and County of San Francisco*, 215 Cal. App. 3d 438, 450-51 (1989). Also, the City of Laguna Beach was estopped from enforcing its second-dwelling unit ordinance because the city had intentionally evaded its obligations under the state law regarding second dwelling units before enacting the ordinance. *See Wilson v. City of Laguna Beach*, 6 Cal. App. 4th 543, 558 (1992).

While a city may be estopped by a property owner's reliance on a validly issued permit or administrative regulation, it is not usually bound by statements made by public officials. A property owner cannot rely on statements—whether oral or written—made by an official unless the official is authorized to make such statements. In *Burchett v. City of Newport Beach*, the court held: "[N]o government, whether state or local, is bound to any extent by an officer's acts in excess of his [or her] authority." 33 Cal. App. 4th 1472, 1479 (1995).

The *Burchett* court went on to state:

> One who deals with the public officer stands presumptively charged with a full knowledge of that officer's powers, and is bound at his [or her] peril to ascertain the extent of his [or her] powers to bind the government for which he [or she] is an officer, and any act of an officer to be valid must find express authority in the law or be necessarily incidental to a power expressly granted.

Id. (quoting *Horsemen's Benevolent & Protective Ass'n v. Valley Racing Ass'n*, 4 Cal. App. 4th 1538, 1563-64 (1992))

> While a city may be estopped by a property owner's reliance on a validly issued permit or administrative regulation, it is not usually bound by statements made by public officials.

CHAPTER 19

Land Use Litigation

Geoffrey Robinson
Marie Cooper

INTRODUCTION

This chapter discusses the procedures most frequently used to challenge local land use decisions in court: traditional mandate and administrative mandate. This chapter also discusses litigation challenging exactions, including dedications and development fees. Procedural rules and standards of review that apply specifically to the type of land use decision being challenged are discussed in the chapters pertaining to those decisions.

OVERVIEW AND TERMINOLOGY

A writ of mandate is the most common method by which courts compel or set aside actions by a local agency.[1] Mandate proceedings—also called "mandamus proceedings" or "writ proceedings"—are commenced with the filing of a petition. A petition functions much like a complaint in an ordinary civil action in that it states the petitioner's claimed bases for relief, and seeks an order directing the respondent agency to implement the remedy sought.

When land use decisions are challenged, there is often a party with a particular interest that may be affected by the action, who must be named as the "real party in interest." For example, a petitioner challenging a city's approval of a development project must name the city as respondent and the developer as real party in interest. Likewise, if a petitioner is challenging a city clerk's decision to place a citizen-sponsored initiative on the ballot, the petitioner must name the city clerk as respondent and the initiative sponsors as real parties in interest.

A mandate proceeding functions essentially as an appeal to a court of a local agency's decision or failure to act. After the petition is filed, one of the parties (usually the respondent agency) prepares a record consisting of the documents and minutes or transcripts of testimony upon which the local agency based its decision. The parties lodge the record with the court and establish a hearing and briefing schedule. Generally, the petitioner files an opening brief, the respondent and real party in interest file opposition briefs that respond to the petitioner's arguments, and the petitioner files a reply brief.

> A writ of mandate is the most common method by which courts compel or set aside actions by a local agency.

---

1 In this chapter, when the term "local agency" is used it includes a city, a county, special district, and other local government agencies. The local agency most often sued in a land use case is a city or county.

The court typically does not hold a traditional trial with testimony and exhibits; it instead hears oral argument, reviews the briefs and the record, and issues its decision. Because the trial court is reviewing a local agency's decision in light of the evidence that was presented to the agency, in most cases the court's review is similar to an appellate court's review of a traditional trial.

If it finds no merit in the challenge, the court denies the petition and enters judgment in favor of the respondent and real party in interest. If it rules in favor of the petitioner, the court enters a judgment directing that a writ issue. The court clerk then issues a writ of mandate directing the local agency either to vacate its decision or to take some other specified action. The agency then files a return to the writ indicating how it has complied with the writ, or that it has appealed the judgment.

TYPES OF MANDATE PROCEEDINGS

There are, broadly, two broad types of mandate proceedings: traditional mandate and administrative mandate. Code of Civil Procedure sections 1084 to 1097 specify the procedures for both traditional and administrative mandate. Traditional mandate proceedings involve judicial review of legislative and ministerial acts. Administrative mandate[2] proceedings involve judicial review of certain types of quasi-judicial decisions made after a hearing in which the agency received evidence. As explained below, the two types of mandate proceedings differ primarily in the standard the court employs when reviewing the legality of the agency action.

The difference between quasi-judicial and legislative decision making is not always easy to discern. The distinction turns on the function being performed by the agency (see *Pitts v. Perluss*, 58 Cal. 2d 824, 834 (1962)), rather than the particular procedure by which the decision was reached. See *Wilson v. Hidden Valley Mun. Water Dist.*, 256 Cal. App. 2d 271, 280 (1967); *Pacifica Corp. v. City of Camarillo*, 149 Cal. App. 3d 168, 176 (1983) (classification of a decision as adjudicatory does not depend on the procedural characteristics of the administrative process). In general, legislative decisions involve adoption of local laws, policies, or regulations of general applicability. See, e.g., *Karlson v. City of Camarillo*, 100 Cal. App. 3d 789, 799 (1980) (adoption or amendment of general plan is quasi-legislative). Quasi-judicial decisions, by contrast, involve application of pre-existing laws, policies, or regulations in a specific factual context. See, e.g., *San Diego Bldg. Contractors Ass'n v. City Council*, 13 Cal. 3d 205, 211 (1974). A ministerial decision is one a local agency is required to make by law, without the exercise of judgment as to the wisdom or manner of carrying out the activity. *Mountain Lion Found. v. Fish and Game Comm'n*, 16 Cal. 4th 105, 117 (1997).

In practice, rather than engaging in a case-by-case determination, courts have tended to classify types of land use decisions as quasi-judicial or legislative according to the subject matter of the decision rather than the function being performed in each particular case. See *Arnel Dev. Co. v. City of Costa Mesa*, 28 Cal. 3d 511, 519 n. 8 (1980)

> The difference between quasi-judicial and legislative decision making is not always easy to discern.

---

2 Administrative mandate is technically a subset of mandate—with specific procedural rules and standards—rather than a separate form of proceeding. As the California Supreme Court observed, "mandamus pursuant to...section 1094.5, commonly denominated 'administrative mandamus' is mandamus still. It is not possessed of 'a separate and distinctive legal personality.' It is not a remedy removed from the general law of mandamus or exempted from the latter's established principles, requirements and limitations.' The full panoply of rules applicable to 'ordinary' mandamus applies to 'administrative' mandamus proceedings except where modified by statute." *County of San Diego v. State of California*, 15 Cal. 4th 68, 109 (1997) (even where the petitioner pleads the wrong mandate statute—1085 instead of 1094.5—the error does not affect the court's ability to grant mandate relief and a demurrer on this ground should be overruled); see also *Woods v. Superior Court*, 28 Cal. 3d 668, 674 (1981) (ordinary mandate statutes and cases interpreting them govern administrative mandate proceedings unless they conflict with section 1094.5).

("The courts have not resolved the legislative or adjudicative character of administrative land use decisions on a case by case basis, but instead have established a generic rule that variances, use permits, subdivision maps, and similar proceedings are necessarily adjudicative").

TRADITIONAL MANDATE PROCEEDINGS UNDER SECTION 1085 CHALLENGE LEGISLATIVE AND MINISTERIAL ACTS

Code of Civil Procedure sections 1085 through 1094 and 1095 through 1097 create a set of procedures commonly called "traditional" or "ordinary" mandate proceedings. These rules supplement the rules generally applicable to ordinary civil actions. Code Civ. Proc. § 1109 (code provisions pertaining to ordinary civil actions apply to writ proceedings except as otherwise provided in the statutes pertaining to special proceedings such as a writ proceeding). Traditional mandate proceedings are used to review two types of agency decisions: legislative and ministerial actions.

Legislative acts.[3] In general, legislative actions establish rules or standards of general applicability and are political in nature, involving "the exercise of a discretion governed by considerations of the public welfare." *Wilson*, 256 Cal. App. 2d at 280. Legislative actions tend to declare a public purpose and make provision for the ways and means of its accomplishment. *See, e.g., Meridian Ocean Sys., Inc. v. State Lands Comm'n*, 222 Cal. App. 3d 153, 167 (1990); *Fishman v. City of Palo Alto*, 86 Cal. App. 3d 506, 509 (1978).

> In general, legislative actions establish rules or standards of general applicability and are political in nature, involving "the exercise of a discretion governed by considerations of the public welfare."

The following have been held to be legislative actions:

- The adoption or amendment of a general plan or specific plan. *See, e.g., Yost v. Thomas*, 36 Cal. 3d 561, 570 (1984); *Sierra Club v. Gilroy City Council*, 222 Cal. App. 3d 30, 39 (1990); *O'Loane v. O'Rourke*, 231 Cal. App. 2d 774, 784-85 (1965). For further discussion of general and specific plans, see chapter 2 (General Plan) and chapter 3 (Specific Plan).

- Zoning or rezoning. *See Arnel Dev. Co.*, 28 Cal. 3d at 514; *San Diego Bldg. Contractors Ass'n*, 13 Cal. 3d at 212-13; *William S. Hart Union High Sch. Dist. v. Reg'l Planning Comm'n*, 226 Cal. App. 3d 1612, 1625 (1991); *but see Southwest Diversified, Inc. v. City of Brisbane*, 229 Cal. App. 3d 1548, 1555-58 (1991) (adjustment of zoning boundaries in accordance with settlement agreement held not to be legislative); *W.W. Dean & Assoc. v. City of South San Francisco*, 190 Cal. App. 3d 1368, 1374-80 (1987) (amendment of development plan not legislative even though adoption of plan was legislative). For further discussion of zoning, see chapter 4 (Zoning).

- Adoption or amendment of a redevelopment plan under the California Redevelopment Act. *PR/JSM Rivara LLC v. Community Redevelopment Agency of the City of Los Angeles*, 180 Cal. App. 4th 1475, 1482 (2010).

- Incorporation or annexation decisions. *See Bookout v. Local Agency Formation Comm'n*, 49 Cal. App. 3d 383, 386 (1975); *Richards v. City of Tustin*, 225 Cal. App. 2d 97, 100 (1964) (deannexation). For further discussion of incorporation and annexation, see chapter 14 (LAFCO).

- Adoption of rules or regulations by a regulatory body. *See Western States Petroleum Ass'n v. Superior Court*, 9 Cal. 4th 559, 567 (1995); *Dunn-Edwards Corp. v. Bay Area Air Quality Management Dist.*, 9 Cal. App. 4th 644, 665 (1992).

---

[3] The phrase "legislative acts" as used in this chapter includes quasi-legislative acts.

Ministerial acts. Ministerial acts involve no exercise of subjective judgment:

> The public official merely applies the law to the facts as presented but uses no special discretion or judgment in reaching a decision. A ministerial decision involves only the use of fixed standards or objective measurements, and the public official cannot use personal subjective judgment in deciding whether or how the project should be carried out.

Mountain Lion Found. v. Fish and Game Comm'n, 16 Cal. 4th 105, 117 (1997) (quotations and citation omitted)

When a local agency is required by law to make a decision, that duty usually is held to be ministerial, even though the substance of the decision may be wholly within the agency's discretion. Thus, a writ of mandate may be used to compel an agency to exercise its discretion, but not to control the manner in which that discretion is exercised. *See Arnel Dev. Co.*, 28 Cal. 3d 511; *Sunset Drive Corp. v. City of Redlands*, 73 Cal. App. 4th 215 (1999) (writ may issue even if duty is directory, not mandatory); *Mitchell v. County of Orange*, 165 Cal. App. 3d 1185 (1985); *Benny v. City of Alameda*, 105 Cal. App. 3d 1006 (1980); *Ensign Bickford Realty Corp. v. City Council*, 68 Cal. App. 3d 467 (1977).

The following have been held to be ministerial acts:

- Approval of a final subdivision map that substantially conforms to the tentative map. *See Youngblood v. Board of Supervisors*, 22 Cal. 3d 644 (1978)

- Issuance of a building permit for a development that is consistent with the zoning and applicable building codes. *See Prentiss v. City of South Pasadena*, 15 Cal. App. 4th 85 (1993). However, the question of whether building permit issuance is ministerial may depend on the local agency's ordinances or on potential environmental impacts. *See, e.g., Friends of Westwood, Inc. v. City of Los Angeles*, 191 Cal. App. 3d 259 (1987); *Slagle Constr. Co. v. County of Contra Costa*, 67 Cal. App. 3d 559 (1977)

- Approval of a lot line adjustment. *See Loewenstein v. City of Lafayette*, 103 Cal. App. 4th 718, 721 (2002)

- Issuance of a conditional use permit for second units that meet the requirements of the state's "secondary unit" statutes, when the city has not adopted its own ordinance regulating second units. *See Wilson v. City of Laguna Beach*, 6 Cal. App. 4th 543 (1992)

- Adoption of forestry regulations required by statute, even though the contents of the regulations are a matter of agency discretion. *See Redwood Coast Watersheds Alliance v. State Bd. of Forestry & Fire Prot.*, 70 Cal. App. 4th 962, 970 (1999)

- Implementation by a local agency or administrator of non-discretionary duties imposed by ordinance or statute. *See, e.g., Terminal Plaza Corp. v. City and County of San Francisco*, 186 Cal. App. 3d 814, 830–32 (1986) (zoning administrator required to enforce permit condition)

- Placing an initiative measure proposed by voter-signed petition on the ballot, or adopting it without change. *See, e.g., Native American Sacred Site & Envtl. Prot. Ass'n v. City of San Juan Capistrano*, 120 Cal. App. 4th 961 (2004); *Stein v. City of Santa Monica*, 110 Cal. App. 3d 458 (1980)

ADMINISTRATIVE MANDATE PROCEEDINGS UNDER SECTION 1094.5 CHALLENGE ADMINISTRATIVE AND QUASI-JUDICIAL DECISIONS

Administrative mandate proceedings, which are governed by Code of Civil Procedure section 1094.5, challenge a third type of agency decision, called "administrative," "adjudicatory," or "quasi-judicial."[4]

Administrative decisions are those in which a local agency applies existing policies, laws, or regulations to a given set of facts. *See San Diego Bldg. Contractors Ass'n*, 13 Cal. 3d at 211; *Pacifica Corp.*, 149 Cal. App. 3d at 176.

Section 1094.5 applies only when there is a challenge to:

> ...any final administrative order or decision made as the result of a proceeding in which by law a hearing is required to be given, evidence is required to be taken, and discretion in the determination of facts is vested in the inferior tribunal, corporation, board, or officer....

Code Civ. Proc. § 1094.5. Section 1094.5 applies only when all of these specific requirements are met. *See Western States Petroleum Ass'n*, 9 Cal. 4th at 567–68. *See also Topanga Ass'n for a Scenic Cmty. v. County of Los Angeles*, 11 Cal. 3d 506, 514 n. 12 (1974). For section 1094.5 to apply, the hearing must be required by law and the agency must be legally required to take evidence, not merely *permitted* to take evidence. *See Lightweight Processing Co. v. County of Ventura*, 133 Cal. App. 3d 1042, 1049 (1982); *see, e.g., Mahdavi v Fair Employment Practices Comm'n*, 67 Cal. App. 3d 326 (1977) (applicable law must mandate a hearing; if it gives the agency discretion on whether to hold a hearing, that requirement is not satisfied).

Many of the decisions that have been categorically held to be subject to administrative mandate review are made after relatively informal proceedings (such as decisions on zoning variances, use permits, and subdivision maps made at city council or planning commission meetings) that have none of the usual indicia of a trial-type proceeding involving formal presentation of evidence, such as sworn testimony, cross-examination, rules of evidence, or neutral decisionmakers. *See Topanga Ass'n for a Scenic Cmty.*, 11 Cal. 3d at 518 (land use decisions are often made after procedures that may be characterized as casual).

On the other hand, a proceeding that meets all requirements of section 1094.5 may nonetheless not be subject to administrative mandate review because it is categorically defined as "quasi-legislative." *See, e.g., Western States*, 9 Cal. 4th at 567 (quasi-legislative actions must be challenged in traditional mandate proceedings even if administrative agency was required by law to conduct hearing and take evidence).

The following kinds of land use decisions have been held subject to section 1094.5:
- Variances from zoning ordinances. *See Topanga*, 11 Cal. 3d at 517
- Tentative subdivision maps and parcel maps. *See Horn v. County of Ventura*, 24 Cal. 3d 605, 612 (1979). For further discussion of subdivision and parcel maps, see chapter 5 (Subdivisions)

> Administrative decisions are those in which a local agency applies existing policies, laws, or regulations to a given et of facts.

---

[4] These are collectively referred to as "administrative" decisions. Land use decisions, which are typically made by cities, counties, or special districts, seldom involve an adversary proceeding that is subject to rules of evidence. However, courts commonly refer to them as "quasi-judicial."

- Most types of use permits. *See Horn,* 24 Cal. 3d at 614; *Johnston v. City of Claremont,* 49 Cal. 2d 826, 834 (1958); *Neighborhood Action Group v. County of Calaveras,* 156 Cal. App. 3d 1176, 1186 (1984)
- Many types of planned unit development permits. *See City of Fairfield v. Superior Court,* 14 Cal. 3d 768, 773 (1975)
- Adoption of design guidelines by a redevelopment agency covering matters such as floor area ratios, height of buildings, and design criteria for redevelopment project area. *PR/JSM Rivara LLC v. Community Redevelopment Agency of the City of Los Angeles,* 180 Cal. App. 4th 1475, 1483 (2010) (Agency's actions carrying out redevelopment plan are administrative in nature, not legislative)
- Coastal development permits. *See Patterson v. Central Coast Reg'l Comm'n,* 58 Cal. App. 3d 833, 840-41 (1976)
- Tentative cancellation of Williamson Act contracts. *See Sierra Club v. City of Hayward,* 28 Cal. 3d 840, 849 (1981)
- Timber harvesting plans. *See Laupheimer v. State of California,* 200 Cal. App. 3d 440 (1988)

ADMINISTRATIVE MANDATE IS THE EXCLUSIVE PROCEDURE FOR CHALLENGING ADMINISTRATIVE DECISIONS

Administrative mandate generally is held to be the exclusive method of challenging an administrative decision. *See State of California,* 12 Cal. 3d at 249; *Guilbert v. Regents of Univ. of Cal.,* 93 Cal. App. 3d 233, 244-45 (1979).[5] Failing to bring such a challenge within the applicable statute of limitations renders the agency decision final and immune from attack under the doctrine of administrative res judicata. *See Hensler v. City of Glendale,* 8 Cal. 4th 1 (1994); *State of California v. Superior Court,* 12 Cal. 3d 237 (1974); *City and County of San Francisco v. Padilla,* 23 Cal. App. 3d 388, 396-97 (1972) (discussing application of doctrine against local agency that made the administrative decision). Under the principle of administrative collateral estoppel,[6] it may also preclude the party involved in the administrative proceeding from relitigating, in any subsequent judicial action, any issue that was raised and expressly or necessarily decided in the administrative proceeding. This principle is sometimes known as the doctrine of exhaustion of judicial remedies.

Mandate is the exclusive procedure for challenging an administrative decision whether the challenge raises statutory, constitutional, or other grounds. *See Johnson v. City of Loma Linda,* 24 Cal. 4th 61, 70 (2000) (failure to bring mandate action challenging agency's findings and decision barred later action for violation of Fair Employment and Housing Act); *Knickerbocker v. City of Stockton,* 199 Cal. App. 3d 235, 240-44 (1988) ("Unless the administrative decision is [judicially] challenged, it binds the parties on

---

5 When section 1094.5 was first adopted, its primary purpose was to provide a procedure for prompt judicial review of administrative licensing decisions and discipline of private citizens. *Royal Convalescent Hosp. v State Bd. of Control,* 99 Cal. App. 3d 788, 793 (1979); *Brock v. Superior Court,* 109 Cal. App. 2d 594, 599 (1952). Use of administrative mandate has now been expanded beyond these parameters to include a wide range of land use decisions made by city councils, planning commissions, zoning appeals boards, and other bodies during relatively informal meetings. *Royal Convalescent Hosp.,* 99 Cal. App. 3d at 794; *see also Topanga Ass'n for a Scenic Cmty. v. County of Los Angeles,* 11 Cal. 3d 506, 518 (1974) (commenting on informality of proceedings involving land use decisions).

6 The doctrine of administrative collateral estoppel applies to decisions made by administrative agencies if (1) the issues were determined at a fair hearing by the agency acting in its quasi-judicial capacity; (2) the agency resolved disputed issues of fact properly before it; and (3) the parties had an adequate opportunity to present the issue or issues. *People v. Sims,* 32 Cal. 3d 468, 478-81 (1982).

the issues litigated and if those issues are fatal to a civil suit, the plaintiff cannot state a viable cause of action."). In an appropriate situation, even claims for violations of federal civil rights are subject to this doctrine. See Mola Dev. Corp. v. City of Seal Beach, 57 Cal. App. 4th 405, 412 (1997) (rejecting a developer's arguments that the doctrine cannot be applied in federal civil rights actions, and that the doctrine cannot be applied unless the administrative hearing contained procedural safeguards such as the right to cross-examine and subpoena witnesses); see also Briggs v. City of Rolling Hills Estates, 40 Cal. App. 4th 637, 645–46 (1995) (failure to challenge building permit condition by administrative mandate precluded 42 U.S.C. section 1983 federal civil rights action).

However, mandate is not the exclusive remedy if the issue sought to be raised in court was one that the administrative agency was not qualified to decide. See State of California, 12 Cal. 3d at 251 (issue of constitutionality of a statute under which an agency functioned could be raised for the first time in court action).

If a petitioner brings a timely mandate proceeding together with other claims that are dependent upon the validity or propriety of the agency's decision,[7] the mandate issues must be resolved first. See Hensler v. City of Glendale, 8 Cal. 4th 1, 13–15 (1994); Patrick Media Group Inc. v. California Coastal Comm'n, 9 Cal. App. 4th 592, 612 (1992) (challenges to administrative actions allegedly constituting takings must be brought initially by mandate).

STANDARDS COURTS APPLY IN REVIEWING LAND USE DECISIONS

The standard under which a court reviews a local agency's actions depends upon both the type of agency action involved (legislative or administrative) and the rights affected by the agency's decision. Land use decisions ordinarily do not implicate fundamental vested rights, as, for example, those involved in revocation or suspension of a business or professional license (see Bixby v. Pierno, 4 Cal. 3d 130, 146 (1971)), or termination of social welfare benefits (see Harlow v. Carleson, 16 Cal. 3d 731, 737 (1976)). See Interstate Brands v. Unemployment Ins. Appeals Bd., 26 Cal. 3d 770, 779 n. 5 (1980) (fundamental vested right is one that an individual presently possesses and is so significant that it cannot be extinguished or abridged by any entity lacking judicial power); see also chapter 10 (Vested Rights). Rather, they typically involve proceedings relating to issuance of a new permit or entitlement to which there is no right. See, e.g., Bank of America v. State Water Resources Control Bd., 42 Cal. App. 3d 198, 206 (1974). Accordingly, writ proceedings that challenge land use decisions ordinarily do not employ the independent judgment test, in which a court reweighs evidence and makes its own determination. Code Civ. Proc. § 1094.5(c). Instead, such proceedings are subject to standards of review that grant varying degrees of deference to the agency's decision.[8] For further discussion of vested rights, see chapter 10 (Vested Rights).

> The standard under which a court reviews a local agency's actions depends upon both the type of agency action involved (legislative or administrative) and the rights affected by the agency's decision.

Additionally, in a limited range of cases, a more stringent standard of review may be required by statute. See Voices of Wetlands v. SWRCB (Duke Energy), 52 Cal. 4th 499 (2011) (under Porter-Cologne Act, decisions of the State Water Board on appeals from Regional Water Boards—including decisions regarding NPDES penalties—are

---

7 See discussion under heading "Joining Other Causes of Action with a Writ Claim," below.

8 Mandate proceedings involving ministerial acts are an exception to the rule. In most such cases, the court is not reviewing a specific decision by an agency, but is instead determining whether, by law, the agency acted in accordance with its ministerial duty. Accordingly, the court does not grant any deference to the agency, but rather simply determines whether the agency acted as required by law. Stated differently, agencies have no discretion not to follow the law; thus the court accords no deference when the issue is whether the agency has failed to comply with a mandatory legal requirement.

reviewable by administrative mandamus proceedings in which the court is obligated to exercise its independent judgment).

STANDARD OF JUDICIAL REVIEW OF LEGISLATIVE DECISIONS

The "arbitrary-and-capricious" standard of review. When local agencies make legislative decisions, they generally are adopting local laws or policies. The local agency is granted the discretion to make these policy decisions by statute and sometimes by the California Constitution. Courts do not have this discretion. Accordingly, courts cannot interfere with legislative discretion, and may overturn an agency's legislative decision only if that decision is arbitrary, capricious, wholly lacking in evidentiary support, or fails to conform to the procedures required by law. See, e.g., *Fullerton Joint Union High Sch. Dist. v. State Bd. of Educ.*, 32 Cal. 3d 779, 786 (1982) ("In reviewing...legislative decisions, the trial court does not inquire whether, if it had the power to act in the first instance, it would have taken the action taken by the administrative agency. The authority of the court is limited to determining whether the decision of the agency was arbitrary, capricious, entirely lacking in evidentiary support, or unlawfully or procedurally unfair."). This standard often is called the "arbitrary-and-capricious" standard of review.

This limited review is grounded in the doctrine of separation of powers, which sanctions the legislative delegation of authority to the agency and acknowledges the agency's presumed expertise. See *Baldwin v. City of Los Angeles*, 70 Cal. App. 4th 819, 836 (1999). Courts have consistently refused to substitute judicial judgment for the legislative judgment of the governing body of a local agency. So long as the enactment bears a reasonable relationship to the public welfare, it is upheld. See *Associated Home Builders, Inc. v. City of Livermore*, 18 Cal. 3d 582, 604 (1976); see also *California Hotel & Motel Ass'n v. Indust. Welfare Comm'n*, 25 Cal. 3d 200, 211-12 (1979) (judicial review of legislative administrative decisions limited "out of deference to the separation of powers between the Legislature and the judiciary [and] to the legislative delegation of administrative authority to the agency").

> *So long as the enactment bears a reasonable relationship to the public welfare, it is upheld.*

A California court explained this general principle as follows:

> In considering the scope or nature of appellate review in a case of this type we must keep in mind the fact that the courts are examining the act of a coordinate branch of the government—the legislature—in a field in which it has paramount authority, and not reviewing the decision of a lower tribunal or of a fact finding body.
>
> Courts have nothing to do with the wisdom of laws or regulations, and the legislative power must be upheld unless manifestly abused so as to infringe on constitutional guaranties. The duty to uphold the legislative power is as much the duty of appellate courts as it is of trial courts, and under the doctrine of separation of powers neither the trial nor appellate courts are authorized to "review" legislative determinations.

Carty v. City of Ojai, 77 Cal. App. 3d 329, 333 n. 1 (1978) (citations and quotations omitted)

Individual legislator's motives are irrelevant. The motives of *individual members* of a legislative body in enacting local land use laws are immaterial absent an unconstitutional motivation, such as racially discriminatory animus, motivation arising from a conflict of interest, or a bias sufficient to deprive an applicant of a fair hearing where one is required. The court explained this principle in *County of Butte v. Bach*:

The Bachs suggest that, by advancing the interests of the neighbors who opposed commercial use of the corner lots, Supervisor Wheeler, and by attribution the County of Butte, acted improperly. The implication is that Wheeler's affiliation with the cause of those constituents who opposed the commercial use is an illicit motivation for her official acts in the course of the controversy. With few exceptions, e.g., racially discriminatory animus, none of which are made out in this case, the motive of officials enacting a zoning ordinance is immaterial. Absent such an unconstitutional motivation, we discern no legal impropriety in an elected official siding with one faction in what is, so long as the alternative chosen is not unreasonable, ultimately a political contest.

172 Cal. App. 3d 848, 862 n. 1 (1985) (internal citations omitted)

The intent and purpose of the legislative body is relevant. The prohibition against inquiries into the motives and intent of the individual members of the legislative body does not preclude judicial inquiry into the intent, purpose, and effect of local land use laws. Motives and purposes of the legislative body as a whole—or even the electorate—are factors to be considered in determining whether a land use law is invalid as discriminatory. *See Arnel Dev. Co. v. City of Costa Mesa*, 126 Cal. App. 3d 330 (1981) (court reviewed ballot arguments in determining that an initiative ordinance discriminated against a particular parcel of land).

The legislative body's motive and intent are to be determined from a review of the evidence before the legislative body. "Resolution of that question is an objective determination, drawn not from an inquiry into individual motives, but from an analysis of the evidence supporting the government agency's official findings. 'The proper inquiry is not into the subjective motive of the government agency, but whether there is, objectively, sufficient connection between the land use regulation in question and a legitimate governmental purpose....'" *Loewenstein v. City of Lafayette*, 103 Cal. App. 4th 718, 731 (2002) (quoting *Landgate, Inc. v. California Coastal Comm'n*, 17 Cal. 4th 1006, 1022 (1998)); *see also Kissinger v. City of Los Angeles*, 161 Cal. App. 2d 454, 462 (1958) (objective evidence showed that the city's purpose in zoning property was to depress its value so that it might be acquired for airport purposes at a lower cost).

Due process and fair hearing requirements. There is no statutory requirement for a "fair hearing" when a local agency is making a legislative decision. *Contrast*, Code Civ. Proc. § 1094.5 (fair hearing required for administrative decisions). Courts grant a high degree of deference to the local agency and allow decisionmakers to vote based on predispositions, campaign promises made before the matter has come before the agency, and *ex parte* communications and information.[9] This is because great leeway is required when a council is establishing local policy and addressing political issues. *See* John W. Witt and Daniel J. Curtin, Jr., *The Problem of Ex Parte Contacts*, 3 CEB Land Use & Env. Forum 24 (Winter 1994). For a discussion of *ex parte* contacts, see chapter 17 (Rights of the Regulated).

Nonetheless, even legislative actions may be subject to fair hearing or due process requirements under some circumstances. *See Harris v. County of Riverside*, 904 F. 2d 497

> The legislative body's motive and intent are to be determined from a review of the evidence before the legislative body.

---

[9] Decisionmakers who have a conflict of interest (such as ownership of neighboring property) in a matter may be prohibited from involvement in the decision under specific laws such as Government Code section 1090 *et seq.* and the Political Reform Act (Gov't Code § 87100 *et seq.*). *See* California Attorney General's Office, *Conflicts of Interest* (1998). *See also Providing Conflict of Interest Advice Handbook*, City Attorneys Department, Continuing Legal Education Seminar (League of Cal. Cities, Feb. 2004).

(9th Cir. 1990) (procedural due process required when change in land use designation from commercial to residential has particularized effect on plaintiff); *Scott v. City of Indian Wells*, 6 Cal. 3d 541, 548–49 (1972) (discussing due process notice requirements in the context of a zoning decision). Additionally, the public is entitled to certain notices and the right to be heard at most legislative body hearings pursuant to the Ralph M. Brown Act, Government Code section 54950 *et seq.*, and, as relevant, specific provisions of the Planning and Zoning Law. Gov't Code §§ 65854, 65856 (notice and hearing requirements for proposed adoption or amendment of zoning ordinance), for example. See chapter 17 (Rights of the Regulated) for a discussion of the Brown Act.

STANDARD OF JUDICIAL REVIEW OF ADMINISTRATIVE DECISIONS

Courts grant less deference to administrative decisions than to legislative decisions. Because an administrative proceeding adjudicates individual rights and interests, findings are required and a reviewing court looks to whether the evidence supports the findings. *Topanga Ass'n for a Scenic Cmty.*, 11 Cal. 3d at 514 (1974). The standard of review in an administrative mandate proceeding is set forth in Code of Civil Procedure section 1094.5(b), which states that the judicial inquiry extends to:

- Whether the respondent has proceeded without, or in excess of, jurisdiction
- Whether there was a fair hearing
- Whether there was any prejudicial abuse of discretion

Abuse of discretion is established when:

- The respondent has not proceeded in the manner required by law
- The order or decision is not supported by the findings
- The findings are not supported by the evidence

Code Civ. Proc. § 1094.5(b)

The degree of deference accorded the administrative decision differs according to the specific ground for challenge of the decision, as described more specifically in the following sections.

"Excess of jurisdiction." In determining whether a local agency has proceeded in excess of its jurisdiction, courts generally grant no deference to the agency's determination of whether jurisdiction existed, and decide the issue as a matter of law. See *State of California v. Superior Court*, 12 Cal. 3d 237, 248 (1974) (agency decision could not be upheld if the agency did not have jurisdiction to hear appeal).

"Fair hearing." Code of Civil Procedure section 1094.5 expressly mandates that there be a "fair trial" when an agency makes an administrative decision. In the land-use context, this is generally interpreted to require a fair hearing, since there is no "trial" in the usual sense. In determining whether an agency afforded a "fair hearing" pursuant to section 1094.5, courts generally use due process principles to evaluate the fairness of the agency action. See *Nasha v. City of Los Angeles*, 125 Cal. App. 4th 470, 482 (2004) ("procedural due process principles apply to quasi-judicial decisionmaking"); *Clark v. City of Hermosa Beach*, 48 Cal. App. 4th 1152, 1169 (1996) ("foundational factual findings must be sustained if supported by substantial evidence; however, the ultimate determination of whether the administrative proceedings were fundamentally fair is a question of law to be decided on appeal") (citation omitted).

Generally speaking, in light of the fundamentally political nature of land use decisions, there is no denial of a fair hearing when council members come to the hearing with pre-determined notions regarding the desirability of the type of project before them. Even when council members have publicly announced their opposition to the very project being considered, there is generally no denial of a fair hearing. *City of Fairfield v. Superior Court*, 14 Cal. 3d 768, 779–80 (1975) (city did not deny a developer a fair hearing under section 1094.5 when it denied a PUD permit, even if council members had previously announced their positions on the developer's proposed shopping center, which could significantly influence the nature and direction of future economic growth in the city). *See also Breneric Assocs. v. City of Del Mar*, 69 Cal. App. 4th 166, 184 (1998) (allegations that council members were hostile to the developers seeking design review approval failed to state a claim of arbitrary action because motives for voting on land use issues are irrelevant to assessing the validity of the action taken); *Stubblefield Constr. Co. v. City of San Bernardino*, 32 Cal. App. 4th 687 (1995) (no violation of civil rights or substantive due process when city's actions were not arbitrary or irrational, even though one council member sponsored numerous procedural and substantive ordinances designed to stop and delay the project); 78 Ops. Cal. Atty. Gen. 77 (1995) (council member who signs a petition opposing a land use project is not disqualified from participating in the council proceeding regarding that project).

PUD = planned-unit development

At some point, however, a council member's personal stake in or animus towards a project or a developer may be so extreme as to constitute a denial of a fair hearing. *See Clark v. City of Hermosa Beach*, 48 Cal. App. 4th 1152, 1173 (1996) (city denied a fair hearing on application for permits, in part because a council member had a common law conflict of interest and "personal animosity toward the [applicants] contributed to his conflict of interest; he was not a disinterested, unbiased decisionmaker").

Similarly, a planning commissioner's authorship of a newsletter article characterizing a project site as an "absolutely crucial habitat corridor" while the project was pending before the commission, can result in the denial of a fair hearing, by establishing an unacceptable probability of actual bias. *Nasha*, 125 Cal App. 4th 470. The project at issue in *Nasha* was approved by the city planning director and appealed to the planning commission by a group of neighborhood residents. *Id.* at 473–75. Before the planning commission hearing, the residents association, of which one of the planning commissioners was the president, published an unsigned news update on the project, contending that it was a threat to the wildlife corridor. The court overturned the commission's decision, holding that while the standard of impartiality at an administrative hearing is less exacting than that required in judicial proceedings, procedural due process requires that the hearing be conducted before a reasonably impartial uninvolved reviewer. *Id.* at 483. In this case, authorship of the article gave rise to an unacceptable probability of actual bias, and precluded the commissioner from serving as an impartial reviewer. *Id.* at 484.

"Proceeding in the manner required by law." In determining whether a local agency's actions conform to the procedures required by law, the courts simply apply the law at issue to the agency's actions. *See Azusa Land Reclamation Co., Inc. v. Main San Gabriel Basin Watermaster*, 52 Cal. App. 4th 1165, 1192 (1997); *Bright Dev. v. City of Tracy*, 20 Cal. App. 4th 783 (1993) (court determined whether the agency's denial of a subdivision map conformed to state law requirement that only certain ordinances be applied, without giving deference to agency's decision). The "law" to which the procedure must adhere may be either the applicable statute or ordinance (*e.g., Georgia-Pacific Corp. v. California Coastal Comm'n*, 132 Cal. App. 3d 678, 701 (1982)), or the requirement of due process (*e.g., Negrete v. State Pers. Bd.*, 213 Cal. App. 3d 1160, 1165 (1989)). As discussed more fully below, courts do not grant deference to a city's interpretation of state or constitutional law, but will defer to a city's interpretation of *local* laws and procedures.

In determining whether a local agency's actions conform to the procedures required by law, the courts simply apply the law at issue to the agency's actions.

"Supported by the findings and evidence." In determining whether a local agency's decisions are supported by findings and whether the findings are supported by the evidence, the court accords differing degrees of deference to the agency. The court gives substantial deference in determining whether the evidence is sufficient:

> In reviewing the evidence...all conflicts must be resolved in favor of the [prevailing party], and all legitimate and reasonable inferences indulged in to uphold the [finding] if possible. It is an elementary, but often overlooked principle of law, that when a [finding] is attacked as being unsupported, the power of the...court begins and ends with a determination as to whether there is any substantial evidence, contradicted or uncontradicted, which will support the [finding]. When two or more inferences can be reasonably deduced from the facts, the reviewing court is without power to substitute its deductions for those of the [agency].

Western States Petroleum Ass'n, 9 Cal. 4th at 571 (quotations and citations omitted). However, the court must review the entire record and consider all relevant evidence, including evidence that fairly detracts from the evidence supporting the agency decision. *California Youth Authority v. SP Board*, 104 Cal. App. 4th 575, 585 (2002); *Young v. Gannet*, 97 Cal. App. 4th 209, 225 (1997).

The court accords less deference in determining whether the decision is supported by proper findings, but still recognizes the expertise of the local agency. In *Topanga Association for a Scenic Community*, the court explained the fundamental rules that apply to judicial review of findings in an administrative mandate proceeding:

> Implicit in [Code Civ. Proc.] section 1094.5 is a requirement that the agency which renders the challenged decision must set forth findings to bridge the analytic gap between the raw evidence and ultimate decision or order.
>
> ...[The agency] must render findings sufficient both to enable the parties to determine whether and on what basis they should seek review and, in the event of review, to apprise a reviewing court of the basis for the board's action.

11 Cal. 3d at 514–15

The substantial evidence test compels courts only to sustain existing findings supported by such evidence, not to hypothesize new findings. As the court explained in *Sierra Club v. City of Hayward*, even the existence of substantial evidence to support a necessary determination will not compel a conclusion that the determination was in fact made. 28 Cal. 3d 840, 859 (1981). Findings do not however, require judicial precision. "[F]indings need not be stated with judicial formality. Findings must simply expose the mode of analysis, not expose every minutia." *Craik v. County of Santa Cruz*, 81 Cal. App. 4th 880, 891 (2000). For further information regarding the required content of findings, see chapter 17 (Rights of the Regulated).

> The substantial evidence test compels courts only to sustain existing findings supported by such evidence, not to hypothesize new findings.

STANDARD OF JUDICIAL REVIEW OF AGENCY DECISIONS WITH BOTH LEGISLATIVE AND ADMINISTRATIVE ASPECTS

The case law is unclear as to the applicable standard when agency decisions possess both legislative and administrative aspects. Some courts have held that the nature of the agency's "dominant concern" in making the decision determines the decision's character, which then determines whether review is in traditional or administrative mandate. See *Del Mar Terrace Conservancy, Inc. v. City Council*, 10 Cal. App. 4th 712,

725–28 (1992) (dominant concern of challenged action regarding location of a highway was legislative); *Meridian Ocean Sys., Inc.*, 222 Cal. App. 3d at 167–68 (court looked to an agency's dominant concern in making a decision relating to high energy permits connected with geophysical research and concluded it was legislative); *City of Rancho Palos Verdes v. City Council*, 59 Cal. App. 3d 869, 883–85 (1976) (where the city's dominant concern in vacating a public street was the effect on a few individuals, the action was adjudicatory).

Other courts have held that the stricter standard of substantial evidence is controlling where agency decisions involve both judicial and legislative functions. *See City of Carmel-By-The-Sea v. Bd. of Supervisors*, 183 Cal. App. 3d 229, 239 (1986) (board action determining a wetlands demarcation line was subject to substantial evidence test when the action involved a determination of specific rights in regard to a particular factual situation, even though the demarcation line was established as part of a zoning decision). *See also Mountain Def. League v. Bd. of Supervisors*, 65 Cal. App. 3d 723, 729 (1977) ("[where]...an agency in two capacities is simultaneously disposing of two legally required functions with but one decision, review of that determination must be by the more stringent standard").

In general, where an agency's "final act" is legislative, the steps preceding it also are deemed to be legislative. *See Prentis v. Atlantic Coast Line Co.*, 211 U.S. 210, 227 (1908). Holding hearings and taking evidence before reaching a legislative decision do not make the final action administrative. *See Patterson*, 58 Cal. App. 3d at 841; *Wilson*, 256 Cal. App. 2d at 279.

STANDARD OF JUDICIAL REVIEW OF AN ASPECT OF AN AGENCY DECISION THAT INTERPRETS OR APPLIES LAW

Many local land use decisions involve the interpretation and application of law. The degree of judicial deference afforded these aspects of a local agency's decision depends not on whether review is under traditional or administrative mandate but on whether the agency is interpreting law and what law it is interpreting. When the issue involves construction of general state law, unless the agency is charged with interpreting and applying that law, courts accord no deference to the agency decision. *See County of San Diego v. State of California*, 15 Cal. 4th at 68, 109 (1997); *Baldwin*, 70 Cal. App. 4th at 836. *See also Azusa Land Reclamation Co.*, 52 Cal. App. 4th at 1192 ("The issue is one of law because it turns on the interpretation of the [CEQA] Guidelines. An issue involving a rule of law is one which this court decides de novo.").

CEQA = California Environmental Quality Act

When, however, the contention raises a question of an agency's interpretation and application of its own local laws, courts grant deference to the agency's interpretation: "There is a strong policy reason for allowing the governmental body which passed legislation to be given a chance to interpret or clarify its intention concerning that legislation." *City of Walnut Creek v. County of Contra Costa*, 101 Cal. App. 3d 1012, 1021 (1980). Courts likewise give deference when an interpretation of state or local law is rendered by an agency that is charged with applying and interpreting the law or regulation at issue. *Id.*; *see also Rizzo v. Board of Trustees*, 27 Cal. App. 4th 853, 861 (1994) (long-standing, consistent construction by the administrative agency is entitled to great weight and should not be disturbed unless it is clearly erroneous).

This distinction is important in land use cases because local agencies frequently interpret and apply their own general plans, zoning ordinances, and other local laws in determining whether to issue a permit or grant a project approval. In these instances, courts will overturn the local agency's interpretation only if "a reasonable person could not have reached the same conclusion." *No Oil, Inc. v. City of Los Angeles*, 196 Cal. App. 3d 223, 243 (1987) (referring to determination that project was consistent with the city's general plan); *see also Sequoyah Hills Homeowners Ass'n v. City of Oakland*, 23 Cal. App. 4th 704, 719-20 (1993) ("[o]nce a general plan is in place, it is the province of elected city officials to examine the specifics of a proposed project to determine whether it would be 'in harmony' with the policies stated in the plan. It is, emphatically, *not* the role of the courts to micromanage these development decisions.") (internal citation omitted)

Judicial deference does not give agencies license to interpret their plans in whatever manner they desire. In *Families Unafraid to Uphold Rural El Dorado County v. Board of Supervisors of El Dorado County*, the court overturned the county's findings of consistency because the general plan provision at issue was "fundamental, mandatory and unambiguous" in prohibiting the action the County approved. 62 Cal. App. 4th 1332 (1998). Similarly, in *Napa Citizens For Honest Government v. Napa County Bd. of Supervisors*, the court found a specific plan to be inconsistent with the general plan when the county acknowledged that the specific plan's circulation element did not actually implement the goals and policies identified in the general plan, and recognized that the specific plan required no specific action that would further the general plan's housing goals, policies, or objectives. 91 Cal. App. 4th 342 (2001). For further discussion of the general plan consistency requirements, see chapter 2 (General Plan).

DEADLINES FOR BRINGING ACTIONS

Statutes of limitations in the land use area are unusually short, and the statutes sometimes overlap or conflict, or are simply confusing. The purpose of the relatively short limitations periods is "to provide certainty for property owners and local governments regarding decisions made pursuant to [the Planning and Zoning Law]." Gov't Code § 65009(a)(3); *see Wagner v. City of South Pasadena*, 78 Cal. App. 4th 943, 948-49 (2000). To achieve these ends, the statutes of limitations applicable to land use decisions—particularly those governing planning and zoning decisions (Gov't Code § 65009), and decisions regarding subdivisions (Gov't Code § 66437)—employ expansive language to describe the scope of decisions covered. *Hensler*, 8 Cal. 4th at 25 (referencing "broad language" in section 66499.37); *Ching v. San Francisco Bd. of Permit Appeals*, 60 Cal. App 4th 888, 893 (1998) (legislative intent underlying section 65009 was to give zoning decisions certainty, giving property owners the necessary confidence to proceed with approved projects).

Most limitations periods applicable to land use entitlements apply regardless of whether the challenged decision is to grant or to deny the entitlement. *See General Development Co. v. City of Santa Maria*, 202 Cal. App. 415 1391 (2012) (90-day limitations period under Gov't Code section 65009 applies to decisions to deny zoning change). The principal exception is Code of Civil Procedure section 1094.6, which imposes a 90-day deadline to file an administrative mandamus action challenging a decision to deny (but not to grant) a permit.

The general rule requiring narrow construction of statutes of limitation (*see, e.g., Steketee v. Lintz, Williams & Rothberg*, 38 Cal. 3d 46, 56 (1985)) does not apply where the governing statute reflects a legislative policy in favor of expeditious resolution of disputes. *Maginn v. City of Glendale*, 72 Cal. App. 4th 1102, 1109-10 (1999) (rule of narrow construction not appropriate in litigation involving the Subdivision Map Act

(Gov't Code §§ 66410–66499.37), which reflects legislative intent that disputes should be resolved as quickly as possible consistent with due process); *see also Util. Cost Mgmt. v. Indian Wells Valley Water Dist.*, 26 Cal. 4th 1185, 1191 (2001) (broad construction required for Gov't Code section 66022, addressing challenges to fees and exactions); *Stockton Citizens for Sensible Planning v. City of Stockton*, 210 Cal. App. 4th 1484 (2012) (decision of zoning administrator constitutes a decision of a "legislative body" for purposes of Government Code section 65009(c)'s 90-day limitations period). The importance CEQA places upon prompt resolution of disputes led the court in *Alliance for the Protection of the Auburn Community Environment v. County of Placer*, to hold that Code of Civil Procedure section 473, which allows relief from default, mistake or excusable neglect in other circumstances, did not apply to a party's failure to file a lawsuit within CEQA's statute of limitations. 215 Cal. App. 4th 25 (2013). As a result, not only are the limitations periods in land use cases very short, courts are more likely than in the ordinary civil context to select the *shorter* of two applicable limitations periods if there is any doubt on the subject.

The event triggering the statute of limitations—such as the filing of a Notice of Determination (NOD) or Notice of Exemption (NOE) under CEQA—commences the running of the statute regardless of the validity of the underlying decision or action. *Stockton Citizens for Sensible Planning v. City of Stockton*, 48 Cal. 4th 481 (2010); *Committee for Green Foothills v. Santa Clara County Board of Supervisors*, 48 Cal. 4th 32 (2010). In *Stockton Citizens for Sensible Planning*, the City filed a Notice of Exemption under CEQA, stating that its approval of a Wal-Mart Supercenter fell within CEQA's exemption for ministerial acts. Plaintiffs argued that because the approval was manifestly not ministerial, the project was not exempt, and the city therefore could not rely on a Notice of Exemption. The California Supreme Court disagreed, finding the plaintiffs confused the *timeliness* of the lawsuit with its *merits*. It held that the validity of the agency's underlying action had no bearing on the effectiveness of the Notice of Exemption to trigger the statute of limitations. It reached a similar conclusion in *Committee for Green Foothills v. Santa Clara County Board of Supervisors, supra*. There, the County filed a CEQA Notice of Determination that reflected a decision to require a supplemental or subsequent EIR for an agreement implementing prior approvals. The court rejected petitioners' claims that the County's decision should be treated as a failure to make a CEQA determination, triggering a 180-day statute of limitations. It ruled that the proper filing of an NOD triggers a 30-day period to bring all CEQA challenges to the decisions announced in an NOD, regardless of the validity of those decisions.

NOD = Notice of Determination

NOE = Notice of Exemption

EIR = environmental impact report

On the other hand, the statute of limitations that is triggered by a notice will not apply if the notice itself is defective. *See County of Amador v. El Dorado County Water Agency*, 76 Cal. App. 4th 931, 963 (1999) (30-day limitations period under CEQA not triggered if notice of exemption is procedurally defective). In *Latinos Unidos de Napa v. City of Napa*, 196 Cal. App. 4th 1154 (2011), the court held that because a CEQA notice of exemption was posted for only part of the thirtieth day of posting, the 30-day limitations period under Pub. Res. Code section 21152(a) was not triggered, and the action was subject to the 180-day limitations period under section 21152(c).

Many land use statutes of limitations require that an action not only be filed but also served within a specific period. When that is the case, the service must be *completed*—not merely commenced—by the indicated deadline. *See Royalty Carpet Mills, Inc. v. City of Irvine*, 125 Cal. App. 4th 1110 (2005) (petition was dismissed even though it was timely filed, because it was not timely served); *Wagner*, 78 Cal. App. 4th at 948 (because the statute applicable to notice and acknowledgment of receipt of the summons provides that service is not complete until the notice is signed; mailing the notice and acknowledgment on the last day to file and serve an action was insufficient). Moreover, the duty to serve a summons may be enforced even when a trial court makes it difficult to fulfill that duty. *Torrey Hills Community Coalition v. City of San Diego*, 186 Cal. App. 4th 429 (2010) (Map Act's 90-day statute of limitations requiring service of summons not tolled under Code Civ. Proc. § 583.240 for impossibility even though the trial court refused to issue summons on a CEQA petition, because the plaintiffs made no effort to obtain the summons after an appellate decision was published that made clear that a CEQA case could be dismissed for failure to serve summons in a timely manner). If, however, the respondent appears in the action before the deadline for serving the action has passed, the respondent likely will be held to have waived any arguments about service. Both *Kriebel v. City Council*, 112 Cal. App. 3d 693 (1980), and *Sprague v. County of San Diego*, 106 Cal. App. 4th 119 (2003), discussed application of the 90-day file and serve statute to claims arising under the Subdivision Map Act and noted that appearance within the 90-day statutory period waived any claims relating to failure to serve the summons.

ACTIONS SUBJECT TO MORE THAN ONE STATUTE

In land use cases, it is not uncommon for the same decision to be subject to more than one statute of limitations and/or service requirement. For example, an action challenging a general plan amendment or rezoning for failure to comply with CEQA is subject to the 90-day limitations period under Government Code section 65009 and either a 30-day or 180-day statute of limitations under Public Resources Code section 21152 depending on whether the city posts a notice of determination. The action is also subject to the requirement under section 65009(c)(1) that the petition be served within 90 days and the requirement under CEQA that the petition be served on the agency within 10 business days after the petition is filed. Pub. Res. Code § 21167.6(a).

In such instances, the general rule is that the more specific statute controls. *Royalty Carpet Mills v. City of Irvine*, 125 Cal. App. 4th 1110, 1118 (2005). *See, e.g., Okasaki v. City of Elk Grove*, 203 Cal. App. 4th 1043 (2012) (because Gov't Code section 65009 applied more specifically to variance decision than Code of Civil Procedure section 1094.6, challenge was subject to § 65009). However, courts must first attempt to reconcile and apply both statutes regardless of which is more specific. If the two statutes cannot be reconciled (as, for example, when two different limitations period apply), the court will apply the more specific statute. *Committee for a Progressive Gilroy v. State Water Resources Control Bd.*, 192 Cal. App. 3d 847, 857 (1987) (180-day limitations period under CEQA was more specific and hence prevailed over conflicting 30-day period under Water Code).

If, on the other hand, the provisions of the two statutes can be reconciled, courts must give "concurrent effect to both, even though one is specific and the other general." *Friends of Riverside's Hills v. City of Riverside*, 168 Cal. App. 4th 743, 753 (2008) (where procedures specified by CEQA and Subdivision Map Act could be harmonized, petitioner required to comply with both). *See, e.g., Royalty Carpet Mills*, 125 Cal. App. 4th at 1118 (where limitations and service periods set forth in Government Code and Public Resources Code could be reconciled, mandamus action dismissed for failure to comply with 90-day service requirement of Gov't. Code section 65009). *See also Torrey Hills Community Coalition v. City of San Diego*, 186 Cal. App. 4th 429 (2010) (non-compliance with 90-day service of summons requirement under Map Act, Gov't Code section 66499.37, mandated dismissal notwithstanding evidence that clerk had previously refused to issue summons in CEQA cases). If the action includes a CEQA claim, the petitioner must also comply with other procedural requirements of CEQA, including the requirement under Public Resources Code section 21167.4 that a hearing be requested within 90 days of the date of filing of the petition. *See Torrey Hills Community Coalition*, 186 Cal. App. 4th at 442 (oral request for hearing did not satisfy requirement of section 21167.4, where other provisions of same statute referred to "filing" of request).

The requirement of harmonization of statutes does not apply if the legislature has indicated that a statute specifies the exclusive procedures for challenging the agency's action. *See Ehrlich v. City of Culver City*, 12 Cal. 4th 854, 866 (1996) (Legislature intended that all challenges to development fees—regardless of the legal basis for challenge—be subject to the procedures specified in the Mitigation Fee Act); *Branciforte Heights v. City of Santa Cruz*, 138 Cal. App. 4th 914, 925 (2006) (challenges to development fees must be brought in compliance with Mitigation Fee Act and are not subject to 90-day statute of limitations under Gov't Code section 66499.37 for challenges to condition imposed on subdivision map).

> The requirement of harmonization of statutes does not apply if the legislature has indicated that a statute specifies the exclusive procedures for challenging the agency's action.

Different statutes of limitation can also apply where land use disputes involve issues of free speech, such as those raised when a project involves signs, billboards, or controversial uses such as adult businesses. Where a permit applicant or the issuing public agency brings an action in connection with a permitting decision that involves a prior restraint on expressive conduct, a 21-day statute of limitation applies under Code of Civil Procedure section 1094.8. In *Stearn v. County of San Bernardino (General Outdoor Advertising)*, 170 Cal. App. 4th 434, 440–42 (2009), the court noted the 21-day deadline does not apply to actions brought by third parties challenging a local agency's decision. The court held the expedited review process functions, in part, to preclude delay by public agencies and has no relevance where a private party is acting to protect business, personal, environmental, or other private interests. *Id.* at 443. The appellant in *Stearn* challenged a board of supervisor's decision to approve conditional use permits that would have allowed the siting of billboards in desert areas, and did so as a resident concerned about protecting private vistas and "visual pollution." In rejecting the trial court's dismissal of the action on procedural grounds, the court held the resident "neither derives the benefit of the expedited process nor is subject to its statutes of limitations." *Id.* at 438, 443. Under the principles discussed above, a mandamus action challenging denial of a conditional use permit allowing a billboard or adult business would also be subject to Government Code section 65009, which requires that the action be served within 90 days.

Calculation of the period under the statute of limitations is governed by Code of Civil Procedure section 12, under which the first day is excluded and the last day, which must consist of the entire day, included. *Latinos Unidos de Napa v. City of Napa*, 196 Cal. App. 4th 1154, 1161 (2011) (30-day limitations period for CEQA challenge calculated by excluding the first day of posting of the notice of determination and including the last day of posting).

HOW TO FIND THE APPLICABLE STATUTE OF LIMITATIONS

In the land use litigation context, the applicable statute is most commonly determined by the *type* of decision being challenged. For example, Government Code section 65009(c) creates a 90-day statute applicable to many planning and zoning decisions such as amendment of a general plan or zoning ordinance. Similarly, Government Code section 56103 and Code of Civil Procedure section 860 require challenges to

TABLE 5. STATUTES APPLICABLE TO COMMON LAND USE DECISIONS

TIME PERIOD	TYPE OF ACTION CHALLENGED	AUTHORITY
21 days from permitting decision	Grant or denial of permitting decision permit involving expressive conduct, such as signs, billboards, or adult businesses	Code Civ. Proc. § 1094.8
30 days of decision to carry out or approve project	Approval of a project pursuant to a specific plan without having previously certified a supplemental EIR for the specific plan	Pub. Res. Code § 65457(b)
30 days after CEQA notice of determination is filed	Adoption of Negative Declaration under CEQA	Pub. Res. Code § 21167(b)
30 days after CEQA notice of determination is filed	Certification of EIR under CEQA	Pub. Res. Code § 21167(c)
30 days after the last date on which reconsideration could have been ordered	Agency proceedings subject to the Administrative Procedure Act	Gov't Code § 11523
30 days after assessment is levied	The validity of an assessment or supplemental assessment against real property for public improvements, the proceedings for which are prescribed by the legislative body of any chartered city	Code Civ. Proc. § 329.5
35 days after CEQA notice of exemption is filed	Determination that project is exempt from CEQA	Pub. Res. Code § 21167(d)
35 days following 30-day period to cure or correct, following demand given within 30 days or 90 days of violation	Open meeting law (Brown Act) violation	Gov't Code § 54960.1
60 days	Completed change of organization or reorganization (LAFCO decisions)	Gov't Code § 56103; Code Civ. Proc. § 860
60 days	Any decision or action of the Coastal Commission	Pub. Res. Code § 30801
90 days to commence action and serve legislative body	Adoption or amendment of general plan*	Gov't Code § 65009(c)(1)(A)
90 days to commence action and serve legislative body	Adoption or amendment of zoning ordinance	Gov't Code § 65009(c)(1)(B); Pub. Res. Code § 21167(d)
90 days to commence action and serve legislative body	Adoption or amendment of a specific plan or any regulation attached to a specific plan	Gov't Code § 65009(c)(1)(A); (c)(1)(C)
90 days to commence action and serve legislative body	Adoption or amendment of a development agreement	Gov't Code § 65009(c)(1)(D)
90 days to commence action and serve legislative body	Decision on conditional use permit, decision of board of zoning adjustment or zoning administrator, authorization for board of zoning adjustment or zoning administrator to decide variances without a public hearing	Gov't Codes § 65009(c)(1)(E); 65901; 65903
90 days to commence action and serve legislative body zoning administrator	Decision of board of appeals on appeal of decision of board of zoning adjustment or zoning administrator	Gov't Code § 65009(c)
90 days to commence action and serve legislative body	Challenge to condition attached to variance, conditional use permit "or any other permit"	Gov't Code § 65009(c)
90 days to commence action and serve legislative body	Determination that zoning is consistent with the general plan	Gov't Code § 65860(b)
90 days to commence action and serve summons	Decision concerning a subdivision****	Gov't Code § 66499.37
90 days to commence action and serve summons		Gov't Code §§ 66473.7(o), 66499.37
90 days from date of decision (or from mailing of decision if a written decision or findings are required)**	Decision revoking or denying an application for a permit, license, or other entitlement	Code Civ. Proc. § 1094.6

STATUTES APPLICABLE TO COMMON LAND USE DECISIONS *continued*

120 days	Adoption of ordinance or resolution to establish, increase or modify specified sewer or water fees, capacity charges, or processing fees	Gov't Code § 66022(a)
180 days after imposition; protest must be delivered within 90 days of imposition	Imposition of fees, dedications, or exactions on a development project	Gov't Code §§ 66020(d), 66021
180 days after determination***	CEQA determination made but no notice of determination or notice of exemption filed	Pub. Res. Code § 21167(a); 14 Cal. Code Regs. § 15112(c)(5)
180 days after project approved or agency begins to carry it out	Approval or carrying out of project without CEQA determination	Pub. Res. Code § 21167(a)
180 days after decision on cancellation petition	Cancellation of Williamson Act contract	Gov't Code § 51286
180 days to one year from date challenger provides certain notice to commence action and serve legislative body	Certain challenges to planning and zoning decisions related to affordable housing and accommodation of fair share housing needs.	Gov't Code § 65009(d)
Two years	Action alleging violation of federal civil rights under 42 U.S.C. § 1983	*Wallace v. Kato,* 549 U.S. 384, 387 (2007); Code Civ. Proc. § 335.1
Three years of accrual of action	Challenge to ordinance based on claim it has been preempted by later-enacted statute	*Travis v. County of Santa Cruz,* 33 Cal. 4th 757 (2004)
Three years after assessor establishes cancellation value	State of California's challenge to a cancellation fee made pursuant to a decision to cancel a Williamson Act Contract	*People ex rel. Dept. of Conservation v. Triplett,* 48 Cal. App. 4th 233 (1996)

* Not all general plan provisions are protected by the 90-day statute. Even general plan provisions that were enacted years ago may be challenged in certain instances. A petitioner may claim that a general plan amendment or project approval is invalid because there is no legally adequate general plan to support a determination of general plan consistency. In that instance, the petitioner may challenge the legal adequacy of the portions of the general plan that are relevant to the consistency determination. See *Garat v. City of Riverside,* 2 Cal. App. 4th 259 (1991).
** This period may be extended if the agency has a provision for reconsideration or if petitioner requests the record within ten days of the decision becoming final. CCP § 1094.6(d).
*** *County of Amador v. El Dorado County Water Agency,* 76 Cal. App. 4th 931, 963 (1999) ("If notice of exemption is not filed, or is defective in any material manner, the limitations period is extended to 180 days after the project is approved.") The 180-day period also may apply when an agency determines that no supplemental or subsequent EIR is required, but files no notice of determination. See *Cumming v. City of San Bernardino Redevelopment Agency,* 101 Cal. App. 4th 1229 (Aug. 9, 2002) (petition time-barred because not filed within 180 days after city made finding that no further environmental review was required. See also *Kraus v. Trinity Management Servs., Inc.,* 23 Cal. 4th 116, 129 (2000). *Cortez v. Purolator Air Filtration Products Co.,* 23 Cal. 4th at 168 (2000)).
**** At least some lot line decisions are not covered by this 90-day statute. *People ex rel. Brown v. Tehama County Bd. of Supervisors,* 149 Cal. App. 4th 420, 430–31 (2007) (approval of lot line adjustment by planning director not subject to 90-day statute in section 66499.37).

annexations, formations, and detachments of property to be brought within 60 days. The type of decision is not, however, always obvious. "To determine the statute of limitations which applies to a cause of action it is necessary to identify the nature of the cause of action, i.e., the 'gravamen' of the cause of action. [T]he nature of the right sued upon and not the form of action nor the relief demanded determines the applicability of the statute of limitations...." *Hensler,* 8 Cal. 4th at 22-23 (internal citation omitted). In *Hensler,* the plaintiff claimed that the city took his property without just compensation when it applied a ridgeline ordinance to his project. He argued that his lawsuit was timely because the statute of limitations on such "takings" claims is five years, according to Code of Civil Procedure sections 318 and 319. However, the court concluded that the plaintiff actually was challenging the adoption and application of a land use ordinance to the proposed project. It held that (1) the plaintiff's as-applied claims were barred by Government Code section 66499.37, which contains a 90-day statute of limitations for proceedings involving the Subdivision Map Act; and (2) the plaintiff's facial challenges to the ordinance were subject to Government Code section 65009, which provided for a 120-day limitation period for actions challenging the facial validity of a land use ordinance. *Id.* at 22.

In *Honig v. San Francisco Planning Department*, the court applied the 90-day statute of limitations governing challenges to zoning actions to a challenge of a building permit issuance. 127 Cal. App. 4th 520 (2005). It reasoned that the complaint, although nominally seeking rescission of the building permit, was actually challenging the validity of the underlying variance that allowed the issuance of the building permit. The court stated that it "would exalt form over substance to refuse to apply [Section 65009] to a challenge to a different zoning and planning decision where that decision rested entirely on the variance." *Id.* at 528. *See also Gonzales*, 65 Cal. App. 4th 777 (where two statutes of limitation—Government Code sections 65009 and 65860—both governed challenge to zoning enactment for inconsistency with general plan, petitioner was required to comply with service requirements of section 65009, even though section 65860 was the shorter and more specific statute and had no service deadline).

The applicable statute of limitations may instead be found in the laws that pertain to all decisions made by the agency. For example, Public Resources Code section 30801 directs that actions challenging any decision of the California Coastal Commission be brought within 60 days.

A party attempting to determine the applicable deadline should also review Code of Civil Procedure section 1094.6, which applies to decisions "revoking, denying an application for a permit, license, or other entitlement," and provides for a 90-day statute of limitations.[10] For section 1094.6 to apply, however, the local agency must provide formal notice to the party that section 1094.6 governs the time within which judicial review of the decision must be sought. Code Civ. Proc. § 1094.6(f). The 90-day limitations period does not begin to run until this notice is given. *Donnellan v. City of Novato*, 86 Cal. App. 4th 1097, 1102 (2001); *El Dorado Palm Springs, Ltd. v. Rent Review Comm'n*, 230 Cal. App. 3d 335, 345 (1991). Code of Civil Procedure section 1094.6(b) requires that a verified or testimonial statement attesting to the date the decision was mailed to the party by first-class mail, postage prepaid, be mailed with the decision. *Donnellan*, 86 Cal. App. 4th at 1102. An after-the-fact declaration stating that the notice was mailed on a particular date does not satisfy the requirements of section 1094.6 because the statute expressly requires that "the facts of the mailing must be attested to in a written statement *included* with the written decision." *Id.* at 1107 (emphasis in original).

The party should also determine whether the agency proceedings were subject to the Administrative Procedure Act (APA) (Gov't Code § 11500 *et seq.*), which applies to most state agencies and any local agency that acts on behalf of a state agency subject to the APA. *See Garner v. City of Riverside*, 170 Cal. App. 3d 510 (1985). If so, the mandate action must be filed within 30 days of the last date on which reconsideration could have been ordered by the agency. Gov't Code § 11523. The statute applies regardless of whether reconsideration actually was sought. *Id.*

If no specific limitations period applies to the particular decision or agents, the statute of limitations applicable to the right being asserted will govern. *See* Code Civ. Proc. § 1109; *Peralta Fed. of Teachers v. Peralta Cmty. Coll. Dist.*, 24 Cal. 3d 369, 386 (1979). For example, Code of Civil Procedure section 338(a) creates a three-year statute

---

[10] The former requirement under Code of Civil Procedure section 1094.6(g) that the local agency formally have adopted an ordinance approving section 1094.6 was deleted by 1993 legislation.

for "an action upon a liability created by statute." This three-year limitation runs from accrual of the action, but does not apply "where, in special cases, a different limitation is prescribed by statute." *Travis v. County of Santa Cruz*, 33 Cal. 4th 757, 769 (2004); *see also Howard Jarvis Taxpayer Ass'n v. City of Los Angeles*, 79 Cal. App. 4th 242, 248 (2000) (Gov't Code § 65009 prevailed over Code Civ. Proc. § 338). Accordingly, the three-year statute would apply in the land use context only in the rare instance where land use laws do not prescribe a more specific statute of limitations applicable to the right being asserted. *E.g., id.* at 769, (challenge to zoning ordinance, to the extent it was based on preemption by later-enacted state law, held subject to the three-year limit of Code of Civil Procedure section 338 rather than the 90-day limit of Government Code section 65009).

One case suggests that local agencies may establish local statutes of limitations. In *Pan Pacific Properties, Inc. v. County of Santa Cruz*, the court held that a county ordinance that established a 30-day statute of limitations for judicial review of county zoning ordinances was not preempted by state law, since at the time the Planning and Zoning Law contained no statute specifically applicable to such challenges. 81 Cal. App. 3d 244 (1978). However, since *Pan Pacific* was decided, the Legislature has enacted and amended Government Code section 65009 to establish statutes of limitations applicable to most, if not all, planning and zoning decisions. In *Hittle v. Santa Barbara County Employees Retirement Ass'n*, the court overturned a local agency's attempt to establish a shorter period of limitations than allowed under Code of Civil Procedures section 1094.6. 39 Cal. 3d 374, 387 (1985).

If no other statute of limitations applies, the catch-all statute of Code of Civil Procedure section 343 provides a four-year statute for "an action for relief not hereinbefore provided for." Code Civ. Proc. § 343.

Administrative mandate is an equitable proceeding in which the defense of laches may be invoked. *Concerned Citizens of Palm Desert, Inc. v. Bd. of Supervisors*, 38 Cal. App. 3d 257, 265 (1974). Laches applies independently of any statute of limitations and may bar an action filed within the appropriate statute. *Holt v. County of Monterey*, 128 Cal. App. 3d 797, 801 (1982) (delay in challenging a specific plan, during which developers expended significant sums, warranted dismissal under laches doctrine); *Concerned Citizens*, 38 Cal. App. 3d at 265 (action challenging conditional use permit barred by laches where the recipient incurred significant financial liabilities in reliance on permit during the period of delay); *People v. Dep't of Hous. & Cmty Dev.*, 45 Cal. App. 3d 185, 195 (1975).

Under some circumstances (usually involving lack of notice) a statute of limitations may be tolled by operation of law. *Compare Concerned Citizens of Costa Mesa, Inc. v. 32nd District Agric. Ass'n*, 42 Cal. 3d 929, 937–39 (1986) (CEQA statute tolled when no public notice was given of changes to project) *with Cumming v. City of San Bernardino Redev. Agency*, 101 Cal. App. 4th 1229 (2002) (no tolling of a CEQA statute on redevelopment project). Statutes are automatically tolled if the parties agree to mediation pursuant to Government Code sections 66030 *et seq*. Also, a seemingly time-barred facial challenge to a legislative enactment may sometimes be pursued as a challenge to the application of that legislation to a particular project. *See, e.g., Travis*, 33 Cal. 4th 757 ("[A] challenge to a permit or permit condition, timely under section 65009, subdivision (c)(1)(E), is [not] rendered untimely merely because the theory of challenge is the facial invalidity of the ordinance upon which the permit or condition is based." Court permitted a challenge to the constitutionality of the second unit ordinance because the petitioner challenged the application of that ordinance

> Under some circumstances (usually involving lack of notice) a statute of limitations may be tolled by operation of law.

to its project); *Garat v. City of Riverside*, 2 Cal. App. 4th 259 (1991) (court indicated that an otherwise time-barred challenge to the adequacy of certain general plan provisions may be pursued when those general plan provisions have a nexus with a project that was recently approved and timely challenged). Such a challenge may be valid even where the basis for the challenge is some defect in the ordinance as originally enacted, not the validity of the application of the ordinance to the petitioner.

Statutes of limitations may generally be extended, or "tolled" by agreement. *County of Los Angeles v. Raytheon Co.*, 159 Cal. App.4th 27, 39–40 (2008). Code of Civil Procedure section 360.5 limits the duration of tolling agreements to four years. Such agreements are favored under the law because they allow parties to negotiate and resolve issues without resort to litigation. In the land use context, there are countervailing public policy reasons favoring prompt filing and disposition of such matters. However, the one decision to date addressing this issue came out squarely in favor of tolling agreements, holding that the public policy in favor of tolling agreements was not outweighed by the public policy of prompt resolution of CEQA and land use cases. *Salmon Protection and Watershed Network v. County of Marin*, 205 Cal. App. 4th 195, 201 (2012). The court pointed to the multiple benefits of tolling agreements, including increasing chances of successful settlement, conserving judicial and local agency resources, avoiding the costs and time of litigation, and minimizing the inevitable delay while project approval is litigated. *Id.* at 202-03. While the court's decision involved CEQA and Government Code section 65009, its broad reasoning appears applicable to other land use statutes of limitation, such as the 90-day period for actions concerning a subdivision map (Gov't Code § 66499.37) and the 180-day period for challenges to fees and exactions (Gov't Code § 66020).

In a typical land use case, involving a petitioner, a public agency and a project proponent, a tolling agreement must have the assent of all three parties to be valid. *Salmon Protection*, 159 Cal. App.4th at 204. Where there is no project opponent or other real party in interest, however, only the petitioner and public agency need consent to the tolling agreement. *Id.* The agreement of other affected parties—such as neighbors—is not required. *Id.* at 205 ("[T]he primary purpose of limitations periods is to protect project proponents from extended delay, uncertainty and potential disruption of a project caused by a belated challenge to the validity of the project's authorization. While others may be incidentally affected by an agreement to defer potential litigation, their indirect concerns are not sufficient to prevent those directly affected to waive or agree to extend the limitation period.")

PROCESS OF A MANDATE PROCEEDING

PREREQUISITE TO LITIGATION: EXHAUSTION OF ADMINISTRATIVE REMEDIES

The common law exhaustion doctrine. A court has no power to make a land use decision in the first instance; it can act only to review a decision made by a local agency. Accordingly, a court generally cannot consider a claim regarding a land use decision unless the petitioner presented that claim to the agency and pursued all available appeals before bringing suit. This requirement is called the exhaustion of administrative remedies doctrine and is frequently referred to as a "jurisdictional" prerequisite to bringing an action that challenges an agency decision. *See Abelleira v. District Court of Appeal*, 17 Cal. 2d 280 (1941). However, it is doubtful that the exhaustion doctrine is truly jurisdictional in the sense that a court lacks the power to review a decision or action unless administrative remedies are exhausted. As one court explained:

> The exhaustion requirement does not implicate subject matter jurisdiction in its fundamental sense. "Although earlier cases tended to view the exhaustion doctrine as invaliding a court's subject matter jurisdiction, thus allowing a defendant to raise it at any time [citations], later cases have generally [concluded] a defendant waives the defense by failing to timely assert it. [Citations.]" (*Mokler v. County of Orange* (2007) 157 Cal. App. 4th 121, 135 [68 Cal. Rptr. 3d 568].) Thus, "[t]he exhaustion of an administrative remedy is a procedural prerequisite to an action at law, and the failure to exhaust it does not divest a trial court of subject matter jurisdiction. [Citations.]" (*Holland v. Union Pacific Railroad Co.* (2007) 154 Cal. App. 4th 940, 946 [65 Cal. Rptr. 3d 145].) Indeed, the exhaustion doctrine is subject to numerous equitable exceptions, confirming that failure to exhaust administrative remedies does not deprive a court of fundamental jurisdiction to act. (*Cf. Green v. City of Oceanside* (1987) 194 Cal. App. 3d 212, 222 [239 Cal. Rptr. 470] [listing various equitable exceptions to exhaustion requirement].)

O.W.L. Foundation v. City of Rohnert Park, 168 Cal. App. 4th 568, 583-584 (2008). *Accord, Green v. City of Oceanside*, 194 Cal. App. 3d 212, 222 (1987) (doctrine is a "procedural prerequisite originally devised for convenience and efficiency"); *Mokler v. County of Orange*, 157 Cal. App. 4th 121, 135 (2007) (although earlier cases tended to view the exhaustion doctrine as jurisdictional, later cases have generally concluded that a defendant waives the defense by failing to timely assert it.); *Holland v. Union Pacific R. R. Co.*, 154 Cal. App. 4th 940, 946 (2007) (exhaustion doctrine is a procedural prerequisite to an action at law, and the failure to exhaust it does not divest a trial court of subject matter jurisdiction).

Under the exhaustion of administrative remedies doctrine, where an administrative remedy is provided (e.g., review of a staff determination by the planning commission or an appeal to the city council), "relief must be sought from the administrative body and this remedy exhausted before the courts will act." *Abelleira*, 17 Cal. 2d at 292. However, court decisions have differed as to which administrative remedies must be exhausted or what constitutes a "remedy." Some courts use the phrase "exhaustion of administrative remedies" only in its most technical, literal sense. These courts hold that the exhaustion doctrine applies only when there is an administrative process available for the complainant to seek a remedy for a past wrong and does not require presentation of claims in the proceeding in which the challenged decision is first made. *Tahoe Vista Concerned Citizens v. County of Placer* represents this variant of the exhaustion doctrine:

> Ordinarily we use the word remedy as meaning a device to redress a wrong. It is decidedly inappropriate to speak of remedying a wrong which has not occurred and may not occur. Prior to the adoption of a negative declaration under the scheme here in issue there is no wrong to be remediated. Hence, the mere public opportunity to participate in an administrative proceeding prior to the adoption of a negative declaration is not a remedy. The exhaustion of administrative remedies doctrine has never applied where there is no available administrative remedy.

81 Cal. App. 4th 577, 590 (2000) (quoting *California Aviation Council v. County of Amador*, 200 Cal. App. 3d 337, 348 (1988) (Blease, J., concurring)) (internal citation omitted); *see also Lindelli v. Town of San Anselmo*, 111 Cal. App. 4th 1099, 1105-06 (2003) (holding that a public hearing did not constitute a remedy because it was scheduled before

any action was taken). By this reasoning, the exhaustion of administrative remedies doctrine has no application to the wide gamut of public hearings preceding approval of development projects because there is no "wrong to be remedied" until the agency has made a decision to which a party objects.

A less restrictive (and the most widespread) approach to the exhaustion doctrine is founded principally on the twin purposes of avoiding judicial interference into administrative proceedings and promoting judicial economy. See *Abelleira*, 17 Cal. 2d at 306 ("[T]o permit the initial consideration of these matters by the courts would not only preclude the efficient operation of the [administrative proceedings], but would overwhelm the courts with cases of a technical, specialized character, and seriously impair their capacity to handle their normal work."). Courts have characterized the doctrine as furthering a variety of practical and policy considerations, including "bolstering administrative autonomy, mitigating damages, giving agencies opportunity to make factual findings, encouraging settlement, filtering out frivolous claims, fostering better prepared litigation, and promoting judicial economy." *Wright v. State*, 122 Cal. App. 4th 659, 666 (2004). The unifying theme of these cases, however, is that a court should not review claims that an agency has not had a full and fair opportunity to resolve. *Coal. for Student Action v. City of Fullerton*, 153 Cal. App. 3d 1194, 1197–98 (1984) ("[T]he agency should be given an opportunity to meet all the issues and defenses during administrative hearings and offer opposing evidence and argument, so that appropriate rulings and findings may be made.... The essence of the exhaustion doctrine is the public agency's opportunity to receive and respond to articulated factual issues and legal theories *before* its actions are subjected to judicial review.") (emphasis in original).

The exhaustion requirement has two components. First, "issue exhaustion" requires that all legal and factual issues be presented to the administrative agency before being asserted in court. Second, "appeal exhaustion" requires that all available administrative appeals be taken before resorting to the court.

Issue exhaustion. Petitioners must submit all factual and legal issues to the administrative agency before seeking judicial review. Generalized concerns or conclusory arguments, unsupported by specific factual or legal arguments against the challenged actions, are not sufficient. See *Corona-Norco Unified Sch. Dist.*, 13 Cal. App. 4th 1577; *Coal. for Student Action*, 153 Cal. App. 3d at 1197; *City of Walnut Creek*, 101 Cal. App. 3d at 1020. "Less specificity is required to preserve an issue for appeal in an administrative proceeding than in a judicial proceeding," since citizens are not expected to bring legal expertise to the administrative proceeding. *Citizens Ass'n for Sensible Dev. of Bishop Area v. County of Inyo*, 172 Cal. App. 3d 151, 163 (1985). However, recent cases suggest a stricter trend. *See, e.g., Jones v. Regents of Univ. of Cal.*, 183 Cal. App. 4th 818 (2010) (generalized comments about failure to adequately analyze water quality impacts not sufficient to preserve claims that analysis was deficient for failure to consider "numerical benchmarks or standards" or to factor in exceedance of stormwater discharge limits); *Evans v. City of San Jose*, 128 Cal. App. 4th 1123 (2005) (objections raised regarding the redevelopment plan during the administrative proceedings were too general to alert the agency to the host of alleged technical deficiencies subsequently asserted in court); *Park Area Neighbors v. Town of Fairfax*, 29 Cal. App. 4th 1442 (1994) (generalized objections to a traffic study are insufficient; specific objections to the methodology employed must be raised administratively);. Exhaustion is not required if the gravamen of the case is one for which no administrative remedy exists. See *Mammoth Lakes Land Acquisition LLC v. Town of Mammoth*, 191 Cal. App. 4th 435 (2010) (no administrative remedy existed for a developer's claim that the city had failed to cure a default under development agreement).

Appeal exhaustion. The petitioner also must obtain a final decision on the merits at the highest available administrative level before seeking judicial review. If an appeal can be taken to a higher administrative body—such as from the planning commission to the council—that appeal must be pursued and the issues must be presented to the final decisionmaker before they can be presented in court. For example, in *Tahoe Vista Concerned Citizens*, the petitioner in a CEQA case argued that it had exhausted its administrative remedies by presenting its comments on a negative declaration before the close of the last public hearing, as required under CEQA (Public Resources Code § 21177). 81 Cal. App. 4th 577. The court disagreed, noting that while petitioners had presented all their comments to the planning commission, they had appealed only a planning issue, and not the environmental review issues, to the board of supervisors. The court held that compliance with section 21177 did not excuse them from bringing their CEQA concerns to the board of supervisors.[11] See also *Edgren v. Regents of Univ. of Cal.*, 158 Cal. App. 3d 515, 520 (1984).

So long as the issues are presented to the final decisionmaking body, it does not matter that the petitioner did not appear before or present issues to the lower body. For example, in *Browning-Ferris Industries v. City Council of the City of San Jose*, the court found it irrelevant that the petitioner did not present comments to the planning commission when comments had been presented to the city council. 181 Cal. App. 3d 852 (1986).

> So long as the issues are presented to the final decisionmaking body, it does not matter that the petitioner did not appear before or present issues to the lower body

Additionally, the petitioner must comply with all procedural requirements applicable to such an appeal, such as payment of a fee, verification of the application, and provision of proper notice. See *Park Area Neighbors v. Town of Fairfax*, 29 Cal. App. 4th 1442, 1452 (1994). In *Park Area Neighbors*, petitioners challenged the planning commission's approval of a development project. The city's code provided that a planning commission action could be appealed to the town council by verified application. The petitioners did not file such an appeal. Instead, they presented the council with a list of signatures opposing the project. The court found that the petitioners had not pursued the correct appellate remedy and thus had failed to exhaust administrative remedies. It reached this result despite the petitioners' claims that (1) they were not represented by counsel; and (2) they had relied on erroneous advice by a member of the planning commission that the correct remedy was a petition to the council rather than an appeal. The court stated:

> We conclude that neither lack of legal representation, nor any consequent vulnerability to purported misadvice on matters of administrative procedure, relaxes the requirement that [the petitioners] must have exhausted [their] administrative remedies as a jurisdictional prerequisite to resort to the courts, or excuses [their] failure to do so. The exhaustion doctrine is well rooted in *stare decisis*, and courts should be loathe to carve out exceptions to such established procedural rules absent compelling reasons to do so.

Id. at 1450 (emphasis in original)

---

11 The court in *Tahoe Vista* held that the petitioners' presentations of issues to the planning commission conferred standing under section 21177, but did not suffice to exhaust administrative remedies absent appeal of the CEQA issues to the Board of Supervisors. *Tahoe Vista*, 81 Cal. App. 4th at 590-91. In *Waste Mgmt. of Alameda County, Inc. v. County of Alameda*, in contrast, the court ruled that section 21177 addressed only exhaustion, and did not confer standing:

Public Resources Code section 21177 is a statutorily imposed requirement of the exhaustion of administrative remedies before bringing a judicial action. Exhaustion of administrative remedies is an entirely separate issue from the requirement of standing to pursue a judicial action. The exhaustion of administrative remedies does not automatically confer standing to seek judicial review, and nothing in Public Resources Code section 21177 states or implies otherwise. 79 Cal. App. 4th 1223, 1239 (2000) (internal citations omitted)

A party challenging a legislative act is not required to exhaust administrative remedies unless exhaustion is otherwise required for the specific claim by statute. (*See* Codification of the Exhaustion Doctrine, *infra*). In *Howard v. County of San Diego*, 184 Cal. App. 4th 1422 (2010), plaintiffs claimed the County had inversely condemned their property by denying a building permit for a barn on the ground that the construction would interfere with a road shown on the County's general plan. The County contended that the claim was barred for failure to exhaust administrative remedies because plaintiffs had not sought a general plan amendment to eliminate the road. The court held that because a general plan amendment is a legislative act, plaintiffs were not required to seek such relief in order to adequately exhaust administrative remedies. *Id.* at 1432.

Rehearing/reconsideration. Where a request for reconsideration is mandatory under the applicable statute, such reconsideration must be sought in order to exhaust administrative remedies. However, when a reconsideration application is permitted but not required, applying for reconsideration is not necessary to exhaust remedies. *Sierra Club v. San Joaquin Local Agency Formation Commission*, 21 Cal. 4th 489 (1999). The Sierra Club Court cautioned, however, that even where permissive, reconsideration may be necessary to exhaust remedies on issues that have not previously been presented to the local agency:

> We emphasize this conclusion does not mean the failure to request reconsideration or rehearing may never serve as a bar to judicial review. Such a petition remains necessary, for example, to introduce evidence or legal arguments before the administrative body that were not brought to its attention as part of the original decisionmaking process. Our reasoning here is not addressed to new evidence, changed circumstances, fresh legal arguments, filings by newcomers to the proceedings and the like. Likewise, a rehearing petition is necessary to call to the agency's attention errors or omissions of fact or law in the administrative decision itself that were not previously addressed in the briefing, in order to give the agency the opportunity to correct its own mistakes before those errors or omissions are presented to a court.

Id. at 510 (internal citation omitted)

In the case of an administrative decision, if rehearing or reconsideration is not provided for by statute or local ordinance or rule, an agency has no power to rehear or reconsider a final decision. *Heap v. City of Los Angeles*, 6 Cal. 2d 405, 407 (1936) (city civil service commission, having made its final decision on the discharge of a city employee, "had no jurisdiction to retry the question and make a different finding at a later time"); *Olive Proration Program Comm. v. Agric. Prorate Comm'n*, 17 Cal. 2d 204, 209 (1941) (agency could not change its prior final decision without express authorization to do so).

Exceptions to the exhaustion requirement. The courts have developed several exceptions to the exhaustion requirement that may excuse a petitioner from having to present issues to the agency before presenting them to a court.[12]

---

12 The existence of several exceptions to the exhaustion requirement casts further doubt on whether the doctrine is jurisdictional in the fundamental sense. *Green v. City of Oceanside*, 194 Cal. App. 3d 212, 222 (1987) (exhaustion is subject to "numerous exceptions...including...unreasonable delay,...when the subject matter lies outside the administrative agency's jurisdiction,...irreparable harm,...when the agency is incapable of granting an adequate remedy,... and when resort to the administrative process would be futile because it is clear what the agency's decision would be."); *see also Acme Fill Corp. v. San Francisco Bay Conservation etc. Com.*, 187 Cal. App. 3d 1056 (1986) (although plaintiff failed to exhaust administrative remedies, court could proceed to decision because case posed questions of broad public interest that were likely to recur).

Exhaustion of administrative remedies is not required where an administrative remedy is not expressly provided for by statute or local law. See *Branciforte Heights, LLC v. City of Santa Cruz*, 138 Cal. App. 4th 914, 925 (2006) (developer seeking private open space credit against park fees was not required to exhaust where municipal code did not provide procedural mechanism for obtaining administrative review of city's denial of credit); *Endangered Habitats League, Inc. v. State Water Resources Control Bd.*, 63 Cal. App. 4th 227, 238-39 (1997) (State Board provided no opportunity to comment before implementing a plan without a second tier of environmental review); *City of Coachella*, 210 Cal. App. 3d at 1287 (administrative remedy provided only where the agency is required to accept, evaluate, and resolve disputes or complaints); *Envtl. Law Fund v. Town of Corte Madera*, 49 Cal. App. 3d 105, 115 (1975) (where petitioners had no statutory right to an administrative appeal of a tentative map approval, no further exhaustion was required). The fact that the city holds a hearing does not trigger the exhaustion requirement if the city is not legally required to hold a hearing and consider and act upon public input. *City of Coachella v. Riverside County Airport Land Use Comm'n*, 210 Cal. App. 3d 1277 (1989) ("An administrative remedy is provided only in those instances where the administrative body is required to actually accept, evaluate, and resolve disputes of complaints.")

Exhaustion of administrative remedies is likewise not required when the petitioner challenges the validity of the statute from which the administrative agency derives its authority. See *State of California v. Superior Court of Orange County*, 12 Cal. 3d at 251 ("It would be heroic indeed to compel a party to appear before an administrative body to challenge its very existence and to expect a dispassionate hearing before its preponderantly lay membership on the constitutionality of the statute establishing its status and functions."). A petitioner also may be excused when the agency is proposing to exceed its jurisdiction. *California-Nevada Annual Conference of the United Methodist Church v. City and County of San Francisco*, 173 Cal. App. 4th 1359 (2009), and where the administrative body or official has no power to grant the relief sought. See *Bernstein v. Smutz*, 83 Cal. App. 2d 108, 115 (1947) (zoning administrator lacked power to grant variance). However, the exhaustion doctrine applies to the agency's construction and application of its governing statute in the course of exercising its administrative functions.

A petitioner need not exhaust administrative remedies when it would be futile to do so. See *Howard v. County of San Diego*, 184 Cal. App. 4th 1422 (2010); *Twain Harte Assocs., Ltd. v. County of Tuolumne*, 217 Cal. App. 3d 71, 91-92 (1990); see also *Furey v. City of Sacramento*, 24 Cal. 3d 862, 871 (1979). However, futility can be shown only if it is certain what the agency's decision in the case would be. See *County of Contra Costa v. State of California*, 177 Cal. App. 3d 62, 77-78 (1986); *Doyle v. City of Chino*, 117 Cal. App. 3d 673, 683 (1981) (the futility exception applies only where a petitioner can positively state that the agency has already declared what its decision will be in a particular case). The question of whether it would have been futile to pursue administrative remedies further may be a question of fact. *Howard v. County of San Diego*, 184 Cal. App. 4th 1422, 1431 (2010) (where plaintiffs alleged that county staff repeatedly stated that building permit would never be issued because of planned road and that general plan amendment was necessary to eliminate the road, triable issue of fact existed as to whether plaintiffs exhausted administrative remedies).

A petitioner also is excused from presenting issues to a local agency when the agency did not give proper notice of the action it was considering. In *McQueen v. Board of Directors*, 202 Cal. App. 3d 1136 (1988), the petitioner was excused from exhausting remedies when the project description the agency gave did not disclose that the

> A petitioner need not exhaust administrative remedies when it would be futile to do so.

property to be acquired contained PCBs. However, incomplete notice does not excuse exhaustion unless it is the equivalent of *no* notice of the matter at issue. In *Temecula Band of Luiseno Mission Indians v. Rancho California Water District*, the court clarified the rule of *McQueen*, holding that "an incomplete or misleading notice may be treated as equivalent to no notice only to the extent that the notice's deficiencies prevented the petitioner from invoking administrative remedies." 43 Cal. App. 4th 425, 434 (1996). The petitioner still must raise the objections and exhaust the administrative remedies available at the time. In *Temecula*, the court concluded that the petitioner had failed to exhaust its administrative remedies because, although the public notice had failed to state that the project was a modification of the earlier project, the agency had announced this fact at a public hearing attended by petitioner, and petitioner had failed to object that the project description was inaccurate. *Id.*

Finally, petitioners are *not* excused from the exhaustion requirement merely because they comprise a public interest group, provided the agency gave proper notice of the hearing. *Res. Def. Fund v. LAFCO*, 191 Cal. App. 3d 886, 895 (1987).

Codification of the exhaustion requirement. The exhaustion of administrative remedies doctrine has been codified in the Planning and Zoning Law and in CEQA. The Planning and Zoning Law provides:

> In an action or proceeding to attack, review, set aside, void, or annul a finding, determination, or decision of a public agency made pursuant to this title[13] at a properly noticed public hearing, the issues raised shall be limited to those raised in the public hearing or in written correspondence delivered to the public agency prior to, or at, the public hearing, except where the court finds either of the following:
> (A) The issue could not have been raised at the public hearing by persons exercising reasonable diligence.
> (B) The body conducting the public hearing prevented the issue from being raised at the public hearing.

Gov't Code § 65009(b)(1)

In order to rely on this statute, the agency must give notice that the exhaustion doctrine will apply to any subsequent litigation. The notice must be substantially in the following form:

> If you challenge the (nature of the proposed action) in court, you may be limited to raising only those issues you or someone else raised at the public hearing described in this notice, or in written correspondence delivered to the (public entity conducting the hearing) at, or prior to, the public hearing.

Gov't Code § 65009(b)(2)

This statutory codification of the exhaustion of administrative remedies doctrine supersedes the common law doctrine. *See Kings County Farm Bureau v. City of Hanford*, 221 Cal. App. 3d 692, 740-41 (1990) ("A public agency cannot claim the protection of the exhaustion doctrine despite noncompliance with a statutory mandate to provide notice of the doctrine's application.... The provisions of Government Code section 65009 supersede the requirements of the common law doctrine of exhaustion of remedies"). Accordingly, an agency's failure to provide the notice required by Government Code section 65009(b)(2) excuses the petitioner from the exhaustion requirement. *Id.*

---

[13] The title referenced is Title 7 of the Government Code, the Planning and Zoning Law, which includes Division 1, Planning and Zoning; Division 2, the Subdivision Map Act; and Division 3, Official Maps.

In CEQA, the exhaustion requirement is embodied in Public Resources Code section 21177. See Litigation Under CEQA, below.

RIPENESS AND FINALITY

Disputes over the validity or effect of legislative or administrative decisions are not ripe for adjudication unless those decisions have generated a "justiciable controversy." The point in time at which a dispute becomes ripe for judicial action—as distinct from a non-justiciable controversy that calls for an "advisory opinion"—is often difficult to discern in land use cases. The cases frequently involve decisions by agencies on matters of broad public interest and generate controversy during as well as after the decision is made. In *Zetterberg v. State Dept. of Public Health*, 43 Cal. App. 3d 657, 662 (1974), the court distinguished between disagreements as to the performance or policies of local agencies, which do not give rise to justiciable actions, and challenges to the exercise of powers or application of policies in specific instances. The court observed that the "wisdom or effectiveness of the exercise of either legislative or administrative discretion is judged essentially by the political process.... A difference of opinion as to the interpretation of a statute as between a citizen and a governmental agency does not give rise to a justiciable controversy, and provides no compelling reason for a court to attempt to direct the manner by which the agency shall administer the law." *Id.* at 662-64 (citations omitted).

> Disputes over the validity or effect of legislative or administrative decisions are not ripe for adjudication unless those decisions have generated a "justiciable controversy."

By contrast, disputes over the effect of acts taken or decisions made by a public entity, or establishment of policies affecting a party's rights that violate applicable law, may present justiciable controversies. *Alameda County Land Use Ass'n v. City of Hayward*, 38 Cal. App. 4th 1716, 1723 (1995). Similarly, where a controversy exists between landowners and a local agency as to the status of property in relation to specific controlling regulations, such legal and factual issues are generally ripe for adjudication. *City of Tiburon v. Northwestern Pac. R.R. Co.*, 4 Cal. App. 3d 160, 170-73 (1970).

Ripeness is analyzed under a two-part test. At the first stage, the inquiry focuses on "fitness" of the issues for judicial decision. An issue is fit for judicial decision when it is "definite and concrete" and "admit[s] of specific relief through a decree of a conclusive character, as distinguished from an opinion advising what the law would be upon a hypothetical state of facts." *Alameda County Land Use Assn., supra*, 38 Cal. App. 4th at 1722. At the second stage, the court considers "the hardship to the parties of withholding court consideration." *Id.* at 1723.

Ripeness issues frequently arise when landowners claim that a city's decision to deny a development proposal has resulted in a taking of their property. "[T]he developer bears a heavy burden of showing that a regulation as applied to a particular parcel is ripe for a taking claim. Before such a claim is made, the plaintiff must establish that it has submitted at least one meaningful application for a development project which has been thoroughly rejected...." *Milagra Ridge Partners Ltd. v. City of Pacifica*, 62 Cal. App. 4th 108, 117 (1998). The City must also make "a final and authoritative determination of the type and intensity of development legally permitted on the subject property." (citations omitted) The application of the ripeness doctrine in the context of takings and substantive due process cases is discussed in greater detail in Chapter 11 (Takings).

Ripeness issues can also arise in the context of a multi-agency proceeding. In *California Water Impact Network v. Newhall County Water District*, 161 Cal. App. 4th 1464, 1471 (2008), the court refused to consider a challenge to a Water Supply Assessment adopted by a water supplier because the assessment would be included in an EIR by a city that had yet to be completed. *See also, O.W.L. Found. v. City of Rohnert Park*, 168 Cal. App. 4th 568 (2008) (distinguishing *California Water Impact Network* and entertaining a challenge to a water supply assessment that had been filed before EIR was completed). Courts also may entertain challenges before an agency has issued its final decision if it is clear the agency is about to exceed its jurisdiction and act unlawfully. *See California-Nevada Annual Conference of the United Methodist Church v. City and County of San Francisco*, 173 Cal. App. 4th 1559 (2009) (where a church wished to sell church property, petitioner was permitted to obtain relief without exhausting remedies and before city made final decision on whether to designate the church property as a landmark). Even a fully ripe decision, in circumstances where petitioners have exhausted all available remedies, may not be subject to judicial review. *City of Irvine v. Southern California Ass'n of Governments*, 175 Cal. App. 4th 506 (2009) (decision to allocate regional housing needs is not subject to judicial review).

IDENTIFYING THE PROPER PARTIES

Petitioner Standing. Although standing is a general requirement in all cases, it has particular importance in mandate cases. Standing is a jurisdictional issue that may be raised at any time during the proceedings, even on appeal. *See Common Cause v. Bd. of Supervisors*, 49 Cal. 3d 432, 438 (1989). Thus, it is important for the petitioner to plead and prove facts demonstrating standing, either by showing a beneficial interest in the litigation or by establishing some other basis for standing (such as a citizen or taxpayer action), discussed below.

Beneficial interest. Under Code of Civil Procedure section 1086, a writ of mandate may be issued only "upon the verified petition of the party *beneficially interested*" (emphasis added). "The requirement that a petitioner be 'beneficially interested' has generally been interpreted to mean that one may obtain the writ only if the person has some special interest to be served or some particular right to be preserved or protected over and above the interest held in common with the public at large. "One who is in fact adversely affected by governmental action should have standing to challenge that action if it is judicially reviewable." *Save The Plastic Bag Coalition v. City of Manhattan Beach*, 52 Cal. 4th 155,165 (2011). (quotations and citations omitted) *See Carsten v. Psychology Examining Comm.*, 27 Cal. 3d 793, 796 (1980); *Braude v. City of Los Angeles*, 226 Cal. App. 3d 83 (1990).

These requirements for beneficial interest standing are usually met easily in CEQA cases. General allegations that the petitioner is within a class of persons beneficially interested and is a citizen or resident of the affected area normally are sufficient. *See Kane v. Redevelopment Agency*, 179 Cal. App. 3d 899, 904 (1986). While a mere claim of geographic proximity may be insufficient to establish a beneficial interest, the courts recognize that "[e]ffects of environmental abuse are not contained by political lines; strict rules of standing that might be appropriate in other contexts have no application where broad and long-term effects are involved." *Bozung v. Local Agency Formation Comm'n*, 13 Cal. 3d 263, 272 (1975). Accordingly, "a property owner, taxpayer, or elector who establishes a geographical nexus with the site of the challenged project has standing." *Citizens Ass'n for Sensible Dev. of Bishop Area*, 172 Cal. App. 3d at 158.

The petitioner's interest need not be an environmental one, and can encompass economic issues. In response to a claim that a petitioner must be affected by a particular adverse *environmental* impact to qualify for beneficial interest standing under CEQA, the California Supreme Court explained, "We have never so limited the scope of the beneficial interest requirement. It is not unusual for business interests whose operations are directly affected by a government project to raise a CEQA challenge to the government's environmental analysis." *Save the Plastic Bag*, 52 Cal. 4th at 170. Public agencies have beneficial interest standing if programs or resources administered by them may be affected by the challenged decision. *Consolidated Irrigation District v. City of Selma*, 204 Cal. App. 4th 187, 201-02 (2012) (irrigation district's operation of a groundwater recharge program gave the district a special interest—one not held by the public at large—in potential environmental impacts of a development project that would use groundwater from the same basin).

Associational standing. An association (whether or not incorporated) has standing to bring suit on behalf of its members when: (a) its members otherwise would have standing to sue in their own right; (b) the interests it seeks to protect are germane to the organization's purpose; and (c) neither the claim asserted nor the relief requested requires the participation of individual members in the lawsuit. *Property Owners of Whispering Palms, Inc. v. Newport Pacific, Inc.*, 132 Cal. App. 4th 666, 673 (2005).

Public interest standing. Standing may also exist where the petitioner is enforcing an important public right. "[W]here the question is one of public right and the object of the mandamus is to procure the enforcement of a public duty, the [petitioner] need not show that he has any legal or special interest in the result, since it is sufficient that he is interested as a citizen in having the laws executed and the duty in question enforced. This 'public right/public duty' exception to the requirement of beneficial interest for a writ of mandate promotes the policy of guaranteeing citizens the opportunity to ensure that no governmental body impairs or defeats the purpose of legislation establishing a public right." *Save The Plastic Bag Coalition*, 52 Cal. 4th at 166. (citations and quotations omitted) Corporations may qualify for public interest standing under the same standards that apply to individual citizens. *Id.* at 167 (disapproving rule from *Waste Management of Alameda County, Inc. v. County of Alameda*, 79 Cal. App.4th 1223 (1980), holding corporations to a higher standard in qualifying for public interest standing). A public interest can also exist in the unique circumstance involving voter-approved laws that public officials fail to defend. In *Perry v. Brown*, 52 Cal. 4th 1116 (2009), the California Supreme Court ruled that "[i]n a postelection challenge to a voter-approved initiative measure, the official proponents of the initiative are authorized under California law to appear and assert the state's interest in the initiative's validity and to appeal a judgment invalidating the measure when the public officials who ordinarily defend the measure or appeal such a judgment decline to do so." 52 Cal. 4th at 1117. Presumably, the same rule applies in the context of the local initiatives that are now common in the land use context. *See Mission Springs Water District v. Verjil*, 218 Cal. App. 4th 892 (2013) (applying various rulings of *Perry* in a case involving local initiatives).

> Corporations may qualify for public interest standing under the same standards that apply to individual citizens.

To establish public interest standing, entities and individuals must be pursuing public interests; a business competitor, with no demonstrable concern for protecting the environment would not qualify. *Id.* at 169. *Accord Laidlaw Envtl. Servs., Inc. v. County of Kern*, 44 Cal. App. 4th 346, 354 (1996). Citizen's action standing has also been denied when the petitioner's action was motivated by other factors not relevant to a neutral interest in seeing the laws enforced. *See Carsten*, 27 Cal. 3d at 799 (in denying a member of an administrative board standing to pursue a citizen's action, the court noted that "[h]er interest in the subject matter was piqued by service on the board, not by virtue of the neutrality of citizenship").

Taxpayer suits. Taxpayers have standing under Code of Civil Procedure section 526a to challenge any action alleged to involve illegal expenditure or waste of public funds, or injury to funds or property. The purpose of the statute is to permit any individual or corporate taxpayer to challenge wasteful governmental action that might otherwise go unchallenged because of the standing requirement. *See Blair v. Pitchess*, 5 Cal. 3d 258, 267–68 (1971). Although it refers to actions for injunctive relief against cities and counties, the statute has been judicially extended to all state and local agencies and officials (*Farley v. Cory*, 78 Cal. App. 3d 583, 589 (1978)), and to mandamus actions (*Van Atta v. Scott*, 27 Cal. 3d 424, 449–50 (1980)). The statute has been broadly construed to give taxpayers standing to enjoin enforcement or application of allegedly unlawful or unconstitutional ordinances. *See, e.g., Tobe v. City of Santa Ana*, 9 Cal. 4th 1069 (1995). Standing is permitted under section 526(a) when the waste is alleged to be simply the time spent by government employees performing illegal acts, and even where the challenged procedures result in a net savings. *See Blair v. Pitchess*, 5 Cal. 3d at 267.

To establish taxpayer standing, a petitioner must cite specific facts and reasons for a belief that some illegal expenditure or injury to public funds is occurring or will occur. General allegations, innuendo, and legal conclusions are not sufficient. *Waste Mgmt.*, 79 Cal. App. 4th at 1240.

Taxpayer organizations also have been held to have standing. *See Common Cause v. Bd. of Supervisors*, 49 Cal. 3d 432, 439 (1989) (county taxpayer and organizations concerned with voting rights had standing to seek a mandate concerning a voter outreach program).

Respondent. The correct respondent in a mandate action is:
- If the writ petition seeks review of a decision, the person or entity with final responsibility for making that decision
- If the writ petition seeks to compel a particular act, the person or entity with authority to carry out that act

The identity of the appropriate respondent generally can be derived from the review of the statute or ordinance governing the decision or action in question. In general, the appropriate respondent is:
- The board, council, or commission—not its individual members
- The city council or board of supervisors—not the planning commission board of zoning appeals or zoning administrator (unless there is no provision for appeal to the council or board)
- The state agency with responsibility for the act—not the state

In an action seeking review of a decision made on behalf of a city, it is common practice to name both the city council (or other city board, department, or agency) and the city itself as respondents in writ petitions. *See Dierkes v. City of Los Angeles*, 25 Cal. 2d 938 (1945) (although the City Board of Pensions had exclusive control over the pensions at issue, a writ was appropriately directed at the city as well). Additionally, there may be instances in which the city itself is an indispensable party as, for example, where the petition relies, in part, upon a contractual obligation of the city. *See, e.g., Roccaforte v. City of San Diego*, 89 Cal. App. 3d 877, 888 (1979) (in mandamus action seeking reinstatement of police officer, the "real party in interest" was the city, which was "bound by contractual agreements with [the officers]," and "[w]hile the city [had] many departments and sub-departments, [] it [was] a single entity in its contractual obligation"). In order to avoid any such issues, the best course is to name the local entity as a respondent in all cases since its inclusion is, at worst, harmless error. *See Shannon v. City of Los Angeles*, 205 Cal. 366, 372 (1928) (in mandamus proceeding challenging petitioner's dismissal by Department of Building and Safety, the city was "a proper, though perhaps not a necessary, party" to proceedings).

It is generally not good practice to name *only* the city as respondent. Doing so may create uncertainty regarding appropriate service and enforcement of the writ, responsibility for the return to the writ, and sanctions for noncompliance with the writ. For example, section 1097 of the Code of Civil Procedure, which addresses sanctions for noncompliance with a writ of mandate, specifically refers to disobedience of the writ by "any *member* of [the] tribunal, corporation, or [b]oard or such *person* upon whom the writ has been personally served...." (emphasis added) Moreover, it has been held that failure to name the respondent with specific authority to carry out the requested writ may result in dismissal. See *Valley Motor Lines, Inc. v. Riley*, 22 Cal. App. 2d 233, 257 (1937).

When the challenged decision is made by a multi-member board, council or commission, the proper respondent is the board, council, or commission, not its individual members. See *State of California v. Superior Court*, 12 Cal. 3d 237, 255 (1974). However, it also is permissible to name the individual members in their official capacity as respondents. See, e.g., *Moran v. State Bd. of Med. Exam's.*, 32 Cal. 2d 301, 314 (1948) (in mandamus action regarding board decision, in the absence of a legislative provision to the contrary, naming of individual members of the board was proper although not necessary); *Harmer v. Superior Court*, 275 Cal. App. 2d 345, 350 (1969) (individual members of commission were proper but not necessary parties to mandamus proceeding; commission itself was the only indispensable party), *see also* 43 Cal. Jur. 3d, *Mandamus and Prohibition*, § 38 (3d ed., 2002).

Real party in interest. Any real party in interest also should be named as a party. See *Inland Counties Reg'l Ctr., Inc. v. Office of Admin. Hearings*, 193 Cal. App. 3d 700 (1987); *see also* Code Civ. Proc. § 389(c). The real party in interest usually is the person or entity in whose favor the agency decision operates, or anyone having a direct interest in the result. See *Sonoma County Nuclear Free Zone*, 189 Cal. App. 3d 167, 173 (1987). Similarly, anyone who received a permit or benefit that would be lost if the petitioner were successful is a real party in interest. A real party in interest has a right to be served with the petition, to file an answer or other pleadings, and to be heard before the trial or appellate court issues a peremptory writ. *Sonoma County Nuclear Free Zone '86 v. Superior Court*, 189 Cal. App. 3d 167, *see* *Harris v. Alcoholic Beverage Control Appeals Bd.*, 245 Cal. App. 2d 919, 923 (1966) (real party in interest who did not participate in superior court proceedings had the right to appeal the trial court's judgment). Any real party in interest must also be a party to an agreement to toll the statute of limitations for such an agreement to be valid.

> A real party in interest has a right to be served with the petition, to file an answer or other pleadings, and to be heard before the trial or appellate court issues a peremptory writ.

The failure to include a real party in interest in the action does not necessarily preclude maintenance of the action, unless that party is "indispensable," in which case the court may refuse to hear the petition unless that party is added before the statute of limitations expires. See, e.g., *Citizens Ass'n for Sensible Dev. of Bishop Area*, 172 Cal. App. 3d 151 (owner of property proposed for shopping center development deemed a real party in interest, but not an indispensable party); *Sierra Club, Inc. v. California Coastal Comm'n*, 95 Cal. App. 3d 495 (1979). However, the court may limit the relief in order to avoid harm to the real party in interest or restrict the action to avoid potentially inconsistent judgments or collateral attack on the judgment. Therefore, the better practice is to include any party whose interests are or may be directly affected by the outcome of the mandate proceeding in the absence of authority indicating that such a party is categorically not an indispensable party.

Failure to name an indispensable real party in interest prior to expiration of the statute of limitations may result in dismissal under the compulsory joinder rules of Code of Civil Procedure section 389(a). See, e.g., *Save Our Bay, Inc. v. San Diego Unified Port Dist.*, 42 Cal. App. 4th 686, 696 (1996); *Beresford Neighborhood Ass'n v. City of San Mateo*, 207 Cal. App. 3d 1180, 1189 (1989). In a broad application of the indispensable party rule, the court in *Save Our Bay* held that an owner whose property would have been acquired for a port marina project was an indispensable party in interest in an action challenging the project. 42 Cal. App. 4th at 695.

The developer of a project whose entitlements are challenged generally is considered an indispensable party to the litigation. However, it is usually not necessary to name the owner of the property on which the developer has an option since it is assumed that the developer will adequately represent the interests of the property owner in the litigation. See *Citizens Ass'n for Sensible Dev. of Bishop Area*, 172 Cal. App. 3d at 158 (developer could adequately represent the interests of the property owner); see also *Deltakeeper v. Oakdale Irrig. Dist.*, 94 Cal. App. 4th 1092, 1102 (2001) ("A party's ability to protect its interest is not impaired or impeded as a practical matter where a joined party has the same interest in the litigation"). By contrast, courts have held that the city or county issuing the land use approval cannot reasonably be expected to represent the interests of either the landowner or the developer under such circumstances. See, e.g., *Beresford Neighborhood Ass'n*, 207 Cal. App. 3d at 1189; *Buena Vista Gardens Apartments Ass'n v. City of San Diego Planning Dept.*, 175 Cal. App. 3d 289 (1985).

In determining whether a party in the land use context is indispensable, courts have drawn a distinction between challenges to quasi-legislative approvals (such as a general plan amendment or rezoning) and administrative approvals (such as a tentative map approval). In the former case, the owners of the affected property are generally not deemed real parties in interest, and the action may proceed solely against the respondent agency. See, e.g., *Buena Vista Gardens Apartments Ass'n*, 175 Cal. App. 3d 289; *Camp v. Board of Supervisors*, 123 Cal. App. 3d 334 (1981) (sphere of influence plan). The rationale is that unless a challenge is aimed at a specific developer or landowner, the developer or landowner is not exposed to "the prejudice necessary to make it an indispensable party." *Sierra Club, Inc. v. California Coastal Comm'n*, 95 Cal. App. 3d 495; see, e.g., *City of Livermore v. Local Agency Formation Comm'n*, 184 Cal. App. 3d 531, 544 (1986) (in action to prevent a LAFCO from implementing revised sphere-of-influence guidelines, developer who had proposed to build a project outside the city's sphere of influence was not an indispensable party because the developer had the same interest as any other potential developer).

In *Kaczorowski v. Mendocino County Board of Supervisors*, the court held that where an appeal is taken to the Coastal Commission and the Commission conducts a *de novo* proceeding, the Commission is an indispensable party in any subsequent challenge to the administrative decision. 88 Cal. App. 4th 564, 569 (2001). It reasoned that because the Commission is the entity that issues permits or sets conditions, failure to join it in the action would not bind the Commission and would render the decision open to collateral attack.[14]

---

14 Conversely, the Coastal Commission's participation in a writ proceeding may deprive it of authority to hear an appeal of a coastal development permit. In *City of Half Moon Bay v. Superior Court*, the Coastal Commission intervened in a writ proceeding that challenged a city's decision to deny a coastal development permit. 106 Cal. App. 4th 795 (2003). The court issued a writ ordering the City to issue the permit, and the City complied. The Coastal Commission then attempted to hear an appeal of the permit and impose additional conditions relating to the issues addressed in the writ proceeding. The court held that the effect of the Commission's action was to overturn a valid court order, which it could not do.

JOINING OTHER CAUSES OF ACTION WITH A WRIT CLAIM

The rules governing joinder of other causes of action with a writ petition can be confusing, as claims for declaratory relief, damages, injunctions, and other remedies sometimes are allowed and sometimes are prohibited in the case law. The key distinction is between non-mandate claims that attempt to seek review of a local agency's decision—which are not allowed—and claims that are based on independent grounds, which are permitted. For example, a claim for declaratory relief based on the alleged invalidity or impropriety of the agency's action is prohibited, since that is the central issue in the mandate action. By contrast, a request for a declaratory judgment regarding the constitutionality of a statute under which the agency acted may properly be joined with a mandate action. See State of California, 12 Cal. 3d at 251 (declaratory relief was the appropriate remedy to challenge constitutionality of Coastal Act but not Commission's application of Act to petitioner).

When an action that should be brought in mandate is improperly labeled as an action for declaratory relief or injunction, the complaint is subject to demurrer, *State of California*, 12 Cal. 3d at 249, although the court has discretion to treat it as a mandate petition. See *Scott v. City of Indian Wells*, 6 Cal. 3d at 541, 546 (1972).

A petition for writ of mandate includes an implied claim for injunctive relief. See *Camp*, 123 Cal. App. 3d at 356. Accordingly, the petitioner need not state a separate cause of action for an injunction, nor pray for an injunction as a remedy separate from the writ.

A claim for a writ may be joined with a claim of inverse condemnation. See *Hensler v. City of Glendate*, 8 Cal. 4th 1, 13 (1994), *Patrick Media Group Inc. v. California Coastal Comm'n*, 9 Cal. App. 4th 592, 603 (1992). However, when mandate claims questioning the validity or propriety of an agency's administrative decision are joined with an inverse condemnation claim, the mandate issues must be resolved first. See *Hensler*, 8 Cal. 4th at 10; *Patrick Media Group, Inc.*, 9 Cal. App. 4th at 606 (challenges to administrative actions constituting takings must be brought initially by mandate). All claims must be resolved before any decision on any particular claim may be appealed. See *Morehart v. County of Santa Barbara*, 7 Cal. 4th 725, 743 (1994).

All claims based on the same underlying factual circumstances as the mandamus claim (such as denial of a permit or approval), must be asserted in the same action or may be barred by the doctrine of *res judicata*. *Busick v. Workmen's Compensation Appeals Bd.*, 7 Cal. 3d 967, 975 (1972) (res judicata bars not only claims actually litigated in a prior proceeding, but also claims that *could have been* litigated). This includes claims involving federal constitutional rights, such as due process and inverse condemnation. See *Clark v. Yosemite Community College Dist.*, 785 F.2d 781, 786 (9th Cir. 1986) (a claim involving federal constitutional rights may be joined to a California mandamus action). In *Adam Brothers Farming, Inc. v. County of Santa Barbara*, 604 F.3d 1142 (9th Cir. 2010), plaintiffs sued the county challenging an erroneous wetlands designation of part of their property. After prevailing in that action, they filed a federal claim for inverse condemnation. The court held the claim barred by res judicata. It found that the substance of plaintiff's state and federal complaints was nearly identical in that both alleged that the county had improperly delineated part of its property as a restricted wetland and claimed that plaintiff was thereby injured because it could not farm as it had intended. For purposes of res judicata, the court held, "it is irrelevant that Adam Bros. attempts to recover under different legal theories.... By choosing to proceed in state court without the takings claim, Adam Bros. risked that the state court's later judgment would forever bar that takings claim." *Id*. at 1152.

EARLY MEDIATION

The Planning and Zoning Law provides for voluntary mediation at the outset of cases relating to most land use and CEQA cases. Early mediation is available in cases addressing approval or denial of a development project, CEQA, the Permit Streamlining Act, school impact fees, the Mitigation Fee Act, the adequacy of a general or specific plan, sphere of influence, annexation, urban service area and other decisions made under the Cortese-Knox-Herzberg Local Government Reorganization Act, zoning, and airport land use commission decisions. Gov't Code § 66031. In such cases, within five days after the deadline for the response to file its reply or answer, the court may invite the parties to consider mediation. Gov't Code § 66031(b). If the parties do not agree upon a mediator within 30 days, the action proceeds. Gov't Code § 66031(d). If the parties do agree, then mediation occurs and most deadlines in the action are tolled, but the action is reactivated 90 days later and every 90 days thereafter unless the parties either settle or present a written stipulation to extend the mediation for another 90-day period. Gov't Code § 66032(d).

The code section that addresses the tolling of litigation deadlines, Gov't Code § 66032, has two versions. One version applies before January 21, 2016 and one applies after. The pre-2016 version of section 66032 provides that all litigation deadlines are tolled excepted as specified in the provisions of CEQA that relate to a required settlement conference.[15] The post-2016 version of section 66032 states instead that all time limits are tolled "notwithstanding any provision of law to the contrary." CEQA provides for an additional mediation opportunity, which is addressed below under Special Procedures for a CEQA Action.

PREPARATION OF THE RECORD

With rare exceptions, mandate cases are heard and decided on the basis of the record of proceedings before the local agency. In broad terms, the record includes all of the documents presented to or considered by the agency and minutes or transcripts of hearings before the agency. If hearings are held before more than one person or body, such as a zoning administrator, planning commission, and city council, the record includes all materials relating to each of the proceedings. For land use decisions, the record normally will include application materials, memos and correspondence to and from staff, notices, agendas, staff reports, minutes, transcripts of proceedings, all documents presented to the decisionmaking body by staff, applicant, or others, and proposed and final versions of findings, resolutions, and ordinances.

Although the mandate statutes specify the contents of and procedures for the record in actions subject to Code of Civil Procedure section 1094.6 (applicable to proceedings for revocation or denial of a permit, license, or other entitlement and to employment and retirement benefits), they are silent as to procedures for the record in all other mandate cases. Also, with the exception of CEQA cases, there is no statutory provision for "certification" of the record by the local agency. Thus the timing, scope, and content of the record frequently are matters of negotiation between the parties and motions to the court to limit or augment the record.

The procedures for preparation of the record in a CEQA case are contained in Public Resources Code section 21167.6. These procedures, although not binding in

---

15 The CEQA provision, Public Resource Code section 21167.8, also has pre-2016 and post-2016 versions. Both versions require settlement conferences in CEQA actions and state that "the settlement meeting may be continued from time to time without postponing or otherwise delaying other applicable time limits in the litigation." Pub. Res. Code § 21167.8(c).

other mandate cases, often serve as a useful reference point for parties and courts dealing with issues regarding the scope and content of the record. *See* "Litigation Under CEQA" (this chapter).

DISCOVERY AND EVIDENCE OUTSIDE THE RECORD

Whether evidence outside the record may be discovered and admitted depends upon the issue to which the evidence relates.

Evidence outside the record generally is inadmissible and undiscoverable to determine whether a local agency's decision is valid. When the issue in controversy is whether an agency's decision is supported by the evidence or findings, or whether the decision was arbitrary and capricious, the court reviews the agency's decision in light of the matters considered by the agency, as reflected in the record before it. *See Toyota of Visalia, Inc. v. New Motor Vehicle Bd.*, 188 Cal. App. 3d 872, 881 (1987); "Standards Courts Apply in Reviewing Land Use Decisions" (this chapter). Accordingly, only the evidence in the record is relevant on this issue (Evid. Code § 350), and it is an error for the court to consider any other evidence. *See Gong v. City of Fremont*, 250 Cal. App. 2d 568, 573 (1967). Because discovery directed to evidence outside the record could not possibly lead to the discovery of evidence admissible on this issue (Code Civ. Proc. § 2107), such discovery is not permitted. *State of California*, 12 Cal. 3d 237 (discovery of evidence outside the record not permitted; joinder of claim for declaratory relief did not entitle the petitioner to discovery).

The rule limiting evidence to the record before the agency applies in traditional mandate proceedings that challenge legislative decisions. *See Western States Petroleum Ass'n v. Superior Court*, 9 Cal. 4th 559 (1995). It is codified for administrative mandate proceedings that challenge adjudicatory decisions in Code of Civil Procedure section 1094.5(e). *See Cadiz Land Co., Inc. v. Rail Cycle, L.P.*, 83 Cal. App. 4th 74, 120 (2000); *Fort Mojave Indian Tribe v. Department of Health Servs.*, 38 Cal. App. 4th 1574 (1995); *Sacramento Old City Ass'n v. City Council*, 229 Cal. App. 3d 1011, 1039 n. 13 (1991).

> The rule limiting evidence to the record before the agency applies in traditional mandate proceedings that challenge legislative decisions.

An exception to this rule exists when there is "relevant evidence that, in the exercise of reasonable diligence, could not have been produced or that was improperly excluded at the hearing." Code Civ. Proc. § 1094.5(e) (administrative mandate); *see also Western States Petroleum Ass'n*, 9 Cal. 4th at 578 (analogizing to section 1094.5(e) in traditional mandate proceeding challenging legislative action). However, in order to conduct discovery aimed at augmenting the administrative record, the moving party must demonstrate to the court:

- What evidence is sought to be discovered for the purpose of augmenting the record
- How that evidence is relevant
- Either that the evidence could not have been produced at the hearing with the exercise of reasonable diligence or that it was improperly excluded

See Pomona Valley Hosp. Med. Ctr. v. Superior Court, 55 Cal. App. 4th 93 (1997)

If the moving party fails to make this showing, it is an abuse of the court's discretion to allow discovery. *Id.*

This exception does not apply, and evidence is limited to the record, even when the petitioner is claiming that the evidence presented to the decisionmakers was tainted or incomplete. In *Cadiz Land Company, Inc.*, the petitioner propounded discovery intended to solicit information explaining why certain evidence was not presented to the board of supervisors, contending that an individual took actions that tainted the administrative process. 83 Cal. App. 4th 74 (2000). The court acknowledged that the individual had received a prison term for conspiring to wiretap, receive, and conceal stolen property, manipulate computer data, misuse trade secrets, and commit fraud in connection with sale of stock, all in matters related to the landfill project before the board. The court nonetheless held the discovery impermissible, because the petitioner could not establish under section 1094.5(e) that the evidence it sought "could not have been produced or...was improperly excluded at the hearing." Id. at 118 n29.

The court also upheld a decision not to permit the petitioner to depose the individual. While the petitioner presented evidence that this individual might testify to bribing members of the board of supervisors, there was inadequate evidence that the deposition would lead to evidence of fraud or corruption. Id. at 121-23.

Evidence outside the record regarding issues other than the validity of a local agency's decision generally is admissible and discoverable. Evidence outside the record concerning such issues as the court's jurisdiction, or procedural issues or defenses, generally is admissible in mandate cases. See Running Fence Corp. v. Superior Court, 51 Cal. App. 3d 400, 424, n.14 (1975). Unlike the issue of the validity of a local agency's decision, these issues are *not* determined based solely on a review of the record. Evidence outside the record therefore is relevant to the court's decision. Because evidence outside the record often is relevant and admissible on these issues, it also is discoverable.

These issues include such matters as:
- Petitioner's standing (or "beneficial interest")
- Whether petitioner properly exhausted all available administrative remedies, and whether any exception (e.g., futility) applied
- Whether the action is barred by laches
- Whether the action is moot (e.g., because of subsequent agency action)
- Whether an injunction or stay is appropriate because of impending irreparable harm
- Issues related to a request for attorneys' fees
- Whether a real party in interest should have been included in the action
- Accuracy and completeness of the record of proceedings
- Any affirmative defense that relies on extra-record evidence

Evidence outside the record may be admissible in traditional mandate proceedings that challenge ministerial acts. Evidence outside the record in traditional mandate actions challenging ministerial or informal administrative actions is admissible if the facts are in dispute. See Western States, 9 Cal. 4th at 576. As a practical matter, in many such cases, there is no record of proceedings because the agency has not taken any action with regard to the alleged ministerial act at issue.

Decisionmakers' thought processes. Evidence regarding the mental processes of individual decisionmakers is not discoverable or admissible. See City of Fairfield v. Superior Court, 14 Cal. 3d 768, 772-73 (1975); State of California, 12 Cal. 3d at 257-58; County of Los Angeles v. Superior Court, 13 Cal. 3d 721, 726 (1975). This "deliberative process privilege" means that evidence regarding individual decisionmaker's motives or mental processes cannot be presented to the court, and that discovery regarding these matters is not permitted. See Bd. of Supervisors v. Superior Court, 32 Cal. App. 4th 1616, 1623 (1995).

The doctrine prohibits any inquiries "to determine what evidence [the decisionmakers] relied upon, or what reasoning they employed, in voting...." City of Fairfield, 14

Cal. 3d at 772. The privilege applies to attempts to determine when a legislator decided to vote a particular way. *Id.* at 774. Discovery seeking to determine what materials were considered and relied upon by a decisionmaker in reaching a decision also is prohibited by the privilege. *See State of California*, 12 Cal. 3d at 257-58 (interrogatories were improper because they sought to determine whether the Commission was aware of certain facts at the time of the hearing).

The privilege also prohibits disclosure of discussions in which local officials participated prior to voting. *See County of Los Angeles*, 13 Cal. 3d at 729; *see also City of Santa Cruz v. Superior Court*, 40 Cal. App. 4th 1146, 1148 (1995) ("[D]iscovery into the subjective motives or mental processes of legislators is forbidden, and [ ] this proscription may not be circumvented by deposing others about the factors that may have led to the legislators' votes."). It also prohibits discovery into council members' recollections of a closed session even when there is no other means of ascertaining whether the session was conducted lawfully. *See Kleitman v. Superior Court*, 74 Cal. App. 4th 324 (1999) (court refused to allow the plaintiff to conduct discovery into the council members' recollections, even though there were no other means of proving a violation of the Brown Act).

Discovery regarding whether a council member relied on information acquired outside the hearing room likewise is impermissible. *See Bd. of Supervisors*, 32 Cal. App. 4th 1616 (plaintiff could not conduct discovery concerning whether members of the board of supervisors took a judges' vote into advisement before reaching their decision to consolidate court-related services in the county sheriff's office instead of in the marshal's office).

> Discovery regarding whether a council member relied on information acquired outside the hearing room is impermissible.

The privilege applies to documents as well as testimony. *See Times Mirror Co. v. Superior Court*, 53 Cal. 3d 1325, 1342 (1991) (materials reflecting deliberative or decisionmaking processes are exempt from disclosure under the Public Records Act). Even if the content of a document is purely factual, it still is exempt from public scrutiny if it is "actually...related to the process by which policies are formulated or inextricably intertwined with policy-making processes" (internal citations omitted). *Id.* at 1342-43 (the deliberative process privilege protects from disclosure the appointment calendars and schedules of the governor, and "[d]isclosing the identity of persons with whom the governor has met and consulted is the functional equivalent of revealing the substance or direction of the governor's judgment and mental processes").

The privilege applies to both administrative and legislative decisions. *See State of California*, 12 Cal. 3d at 257-58 (applying privilege to decision of state commission to deny land use permit).

Attorney-client privilege and work product doctrine. The attorney-client privilege and work product doctrine apply in the context of an administrative record. Documents that are otherwise protected are excluded from the record. *California Oak Found. v. County of Tehama*, 174 Cal. App. 4th 1217, 1221 (2009). This rule applies in CEQA cases as in other land use cases, even though CEQA directs that a record include all written documents and internal agency communications relevant to the agency's compliance with CEQA. *Id.* (citing Pub. Res. Code § 21167.6). Moreover, the attorney-client privilege and work product protection are not waived by the agency's disclosure to others when that disclosure is reasonably necessary for the accomplishment of the purpose for which the lawyer was consulted. *Id.* at 1222-23 (court addressed "common interest doctrine" and held that public agency's disclosure to developer's counsel did not waive privilege).

Judicial notice. It is common in land use cases for petitioners or respondents to attempt to supplement the record through a request for judicial notice. However, the doctrine is frequently misused, and care should be taken to ensure that the facts identified are properly subject to judicial notice. Judicial notice is not merely a substitute for introducing or authenticating evidence or a way to eliminate hearsay objections, but instead is a manner of establishing a fact as incontrovertible. "The underlying theory of judicial notice is that the matter being judicially noticed is a law or fact that is not reasonably subject to dispute." *Lockley v. Law Office of Cantrell, Green, Pekich, Cruz & McCort,* 91 Cal. App. 4th 875, 882 (2001). "The appropriate setting for resolving facts reasonably subject to dispute is the adversary hearing." *Id.* Accordingly, "the weight of the authority is that, where notice is mandatory, the effect is substantially that of a *conclusive* presumption; *i.e.,* the fact must be accepted and no evidence can be offered to dispute it." 1 Witkin, *Calif. Evidence, Judicial Notice,* section 3 (4th ed. 2000).

> Judicial notice is not merely a substitute for introducing or authenticating evidence or a way to eliminate hearsay objections, but instead is a manner of establishing a fact as incontrovertible.

Additionally, judicial notice cannot be used to evade other evidentiary problems. Rather, judicial notice may be taken only of evidence that otherwise meets evidentiary requirements. *Mozzetti v. City of Brisbane,* 67 Cal. App. 3d 565, 578 (1977) ("[T]he purpose of judicial notice is to expedite the production and introduction of *otherwise admissible* evidence.") (emphasis added); *Marocco v. Ford Motor Co.,* 7 Cal. App. 3d 84, 89 (1970); *Love v. Wolf,* 226 Cal. App. 2d 378, 403 (1964).

Moreover, judicial notice of documents is not judicial notice of the truth of statements contained in those documents. "Taking judicial notice of a document is not the same thing as accepting the truth of its contents or accepting a particular interpretation of its meaning." *Joslin v. H.A.S. Ins. Brokerage,* 184 Cal. App. 3d 369, 374 (1986); *see also StorMedia Inc. v. Superior Court,* 20 Cal. 4th 449, 456-57 n.9 (1999) (when judicial notice is taken of a document, the truthfulness and proper interpretation of the document may be subject to dispute). Thus, if documents are judicially noticeable as official acts of a governmental agency, the court may take judicial notice of only the fact that an agency generated the document, not of the substance or conclusions of the document. *Beckley v. Reclamation Bd. of the State,* 205 Cal. App. 2d 734, 741-42 (1962); *see also Mangini v. R. J. Reynolds Tobacco Co.,* 7 Cal. 4th 1057, 1063 (1994) (judicial notice of the authenticity of an official document does not establish the truth of the statements it makes); *People v. Long,* 7 Cal. App. 3d 586, 591 (1970).

At least one court has held that even judicial findings are subject to this rule. *Sosinsky v. Grant,* 6 Cal. App. 4th 1548, 1565 (1992) (disagreeing with Jefferson's California Evidence Benchbook and cases following it, and holding that court cannot take judicial notice of truth of court findings, even though made after a contested adversary hearing).

Finally, care should also be taken when seeking judicial notice of documents alleged to comprise legislative history. One Court of Appeal emphatically criticized the practice of many attorneys submitting requests contending that "every scrap of paper that is generated in the legislative process constitutes the proper subject of judicial notice." *Kaufman & Broad Cmtys, Inc. v. Performance Plastering, Inc.,* 133 Cal. App. 4th 26, 29 (2006). The court directed, "This must stop." *Id.* The court produced a list both of documents constituting cognizable legislative history, such as conference committee reports and different versions of the bill, and documents that may not be noticed, such as letters to the Governor urging signing of a bill. *Id.* at 31-39.

SETTING A BRIEFING AND HEARING SCHEDULE

There are two procedures for bringing a writ proceeding to hearing: noticed motion made by either party, or application for an alternative writ by the petitioner. Both procedures allow for short briefing schedules and a prompt hearing date. Both procedures presume that the record will be prepared and presented to the court quickly. In cases challenging a general plan or any element thereof on the grounds that it fails to comply with the Planning Law, the petitioner must request a hearing with 90 days of filing a petition. Gov't Code § 65753.[16]

In practice, many parties stipulate to a hearing and briefing schedule and present the stipulation to the court for approval.

Alternative writ. An alternative writ is an interim order issued by the court, usually at the outset of the case, that commands the respondent to carry out the act requested by the petitioner, or to show cause before the court at a specified date and time why it has not done so. Code Civ. Proc. § 1087. The practical effect of the alternative writ is to establish a hearing and briefing schedule, except in rare instances in which the agency decides, in response to the writ, to carry out the act sought by petitioners.

Additionally, the alternative writ (which must be served in the same manner as a civil summons) constitutes the process whereby the court acquires personal jurisdiction over the respondent and any real party in interest. If no alternative writ is obtained, there is no court process to compel the respondent and real party in interest to appear unless a summons is served. Service of the petition itself is not sufficient to bring parties before the court. See *Wagner v. City of South Pasadena*, 78 Cal. App. 4th 943, 947–51 (2000); see also *Bd. of Supervisors v. Superior Court*, 23 Cal. App. 4th 830, 840 (1994) (the apparently optional use of summons procedures authorized by Code of Civil Procedure section 1107 for mandate proceedings is actually mandatory).

To obtain an alternative writ, the petitioner submits an application for an alternative writ *ex parte*, i.e., without formal notice. Generally, the petitioner must give at least twenty-four hours' informal notice to the other parties of the *ex parte* application, to comply with local court rules.

The alternative writ process is detailed, requiring submittal of an application, memorandum, proposed order, and proposed alternative writ, and service upon the respondent agency and real party in interest twice. See Geoffrey L. Robinson, *Handling Administrative Mandamus*, Step 28 (Cal. CEB, Action Guide, Spring 2000). The petitioner must prepare a memorandum of points and authorities to accompany the application, showing the legal basis for the court's issuance of the alternative writ, and specifying the reasons the writ should issue.

Alternative writs are a useful vehicle for bringing all parties before the court quickly and establishing a short hearing and briefing schedule. Alternative writs are therefore most commonly issued when time is of the essence.

> Alternative writs are most commonly issued when time is of the essence.

Noticed motion. A mandate proceeding also may be brought to hearing by a noticed motion "by any party."[17] Code Civ. Proc. § 1094. See also Code Civ. Proc. § 1088. A noticed motion in a writ proceeding is governed by the rules applicable to noticed motions generally. Code Civ. Proc. § 1109. These provisions arguably include the notice provisions of Code of Civil Procedure section 1005, although Code of Civil Procedure section 1088 states only that notice of the application for writ must be given *at least* 10 days before the writ issues.

---

16 This is also true in CEQA cases. Pub. Res. Code § 21167.4(a). See "Special Procedures for CEQA Actions" (below).

17 As noted above, however, a summons should be served with the petition if the matter is to be brought to hearing other than by alternative writ. See *Wagner*, 78 Cal. App. 4th at 947–51.

Because the notice period required for a motion for judgment on the writ is short, and because the noticed motion procedure is not limited to petitioners, it is sometimes often used by the respondent or real party in interest to bring a case to hearing quickly.

Informal means of obtaining hearing date. Land use practitioners have developed informal means of setting a hearing and briefing schedule. Experienced practitioners generally will enter into a stipulation covering both preparation and lodging of the record and a briefing and hearing schedule, and present it to the court for approval and entry as an order. Even when a party brings an *ex parte* application for an alternative writ, the parties often stipulate to a hearing and briefing schedule, which the court then inserts into the alternative writ.

Some courts assign a specific judge or judges to hear writ proceedings.[18] In that situation, a practitioner often will call the clerks of those departments to determine the preferred method for setting a hearing date. Other courts hear writ matters on their law and motion calendars, even if the matter proceeds pursuant to an alternative writ. In those courts, the process for obtaining a hearing date in a writ proceeding is the same method specified in the local court rules for other noticed motions.

SUMMARY JUDGMENT

Although there is no express limitation on the use of summary judgment in mandate proceedings, its applicability is limited by pragmatic considerations. The court's review is limited to the record. Because a court must review the entire record to determine whether substantial evidence supports the decision, the summary judgment procedure (in which review is limited to the evidence tendered in the moving and opposing papers) is effectively unavailable. *Dunn v. County of Santa Barbara*, 135 Cal. App. 4th 1281, 1292 (2006). The court in *Dunn* held that where the requirements for a motion for judgment on the peremptory writ under Code of Civil Procedure section 1094 are met (i.e., where the petition presents no triable issue of fact or is based solely on an administrative record), a motion for judgment under section 1094 "is the proper, and exclusive, procedural means for seeking a streamlined review of an agency's decision." *Id.* at 1293.

On the other hand, summary judgment may be granted in mandate proceedings where evidence outside of the administrative record disposes of the petition as a matter of law. *See, e.g., Stanton v. Dumke*, 64 Cal. 2d 199 (1966) (summary judgment appropriate in administrative mandate proceeding upon showing that petition was moot); *California Rifle and Pistol Assn. v. City of West Hollywood*, 66 Cal. App. 4th 1302, 1309 (1998) (summary judgment granted in favor of defendant City in a mandate proceeding challenging gun control ordinance on grounds of preemption, equal protection, and due process). Where such evidence is judicially noticeable, the same result may be accomplished by demurrer or motion for judgment on the pleadings.

PREPARING THE BRIEFS

Courts apply varying rules to briefs in mandate cases. Some courts consider mandate briefs subject to the rules normally applicable to law and motion practice. In that case,

---

18 CEQA requires that the superior courts in all counties with a population of more than 200,000 designate one or more judges to develop expertise in CEQA and related land use and environmental laws. Pub. Res. Code § 21167.1(b). A list of CEQA judges can be found at the California Environmental Resources Evaluation System (CERES), a web-based information system developed by the California Resources Agency (http://ceres.ca.gov/ceqa), and in the *California Planners' Book of Lists* published annually by the Governor's Office of Planning and Research (OPR) available at http://opr.ca.gov.s_publications.php.

court permission to file a brief that exceeds the relatively short page limits allowed in law and motion practice usually is required. Other courts consider the briefs to be trial briefs, and impose no page limits. Still others have special rules applicable to mandate cases, "writs and receivers," or CEQA cases. Local rules should be checked. The issue often is addressed in a stipulated order regarding the hearing and briefing schedule. *See* "Informal Means of Obtaining a Hearing Date" (above).

A petitioner should be especially aware of the burden it faces in preparing a brief, and ensure that all recitations of fact are supported by citations to the record and that the brief addresses evidence that supports as well as contradicts the agency's findings. In *Jacobson v. County of Los Angeles*, the petitioners brought an administrative mandate proceeding challenging the decision of a zoning board. 69 Cal. App. 3d 374 (1977). The court chastised the petitioners for failing to address the evidence in the record that supported the zoning board's findings. With an analogy to appellate review of trial court proceedings, the court explained how the petitioners failed to establish their case:

> No fair statement of the evidence has been undertaken by petitioners. [¶] Here appellants have made no effort to comply with the rules of court and have failed to set forth the evidence of the matter under consideration. What is said in *Hickson v. Thielman*, is particularly appropriate: "The first contention of defendants is that the findings are unsupported by the evidence. In this connection, we repeat what every lawyer should know, namely, that when an appellant urges the insufficiency of the evidence to support the findings it is his duty to set forth a fair and adequate statement of the evidence which is claimed to be insufficient. He cannot shift this burden onto respondent, nor is a reviewing court required to undertake an independent examination of the record when appellant has shirked his responsibility in this respect."

Id. at 388. (citation omitted) Similarly, in *Stolman v. City of Los Angeles*, the court faulted the City for not providing citations to the record to support its contention, stating that "[i]ts cursory argument on this point, unsupported by citations to the record, is clearly deficient. '[S]tatements of fact contained in the briefs which are not supported by the evidence in the record must be disregarded.'" 114 Cal. App. 4th 916, 926-27 (2003) (quoting *Tisher v. California Horse Racing Bd.* 231 Cal. App. 3d 349, 361 (1991)); *see also Defend the Bay v. City of Irvine*, 119 Cal. App. 4th 1261, 1266 (2004) ("[A]n appellant challenging an EIR for insufficient evidence must lay out the evidence favorable to the other side and show why it is lacking. Failure to do so is fatal. A reviewing court will not independently review the record to make up for appellant's failure to carry his burden."); *Markley v. City Council*, 131 Cal. App. 3d 656, 673 (1982) (quoting *Jacobson*).

A STAY OR PRELIMINARY INJUNCTION MAY ISSUE PENDING A FINAL DECISION ON THE WRIT PETITION

A petitioner challenging a development project often will seek to halt construction of the project pending the court's final decision. Two interim orders are available in writ proceedings to maintain the status quo pending a final decision on the merits: a stay and a temporary restraining order followed by an injunction.

Stays. A stay of a local agency's decision in an administrative mandamus proceeding is available under Code of Civil Procedure section 1094.5(g). The stay operates to preclude the agency decision from taking effect. A stay may be issued unless the court determines that a stay would be against the public interest. Code Civ. Proc. § 1094.5(g).

The decision whether to issue a stay is discretionary with the trial court. *West Coast Home Improvement Co. v. Contractors' State License Bd.*, 68 Cal. App. 2d 1, 4 (1945).

The court also has discretion to require the petitioner to post a bond when a stay is issued. *See Venice Canals Resident Home Owners Ass'n v. Superior Court*, 72 Cal. App. 3d 675, 679–80 (1977) (bond properly required to protect developer from losses resulting from stay of project issued at request of neighbors). A bond is designed to protect the respondent or real party in interest from the damages that would be caused by the stay if the court later determines the agency action was valid, up to the limit of the bond. *Id.*

TROs and preliminary injunctions. Temporary restraining orders (TROs) last only a few days, until a hearing can be held on a request for preliminary injunction, which, if granted, generally maintains the status quo until the merits of the writ petition are decided. These orders are permitted in writ proceedings. *See* Code Civ. Proc. § 1109; *Camp v. Bd. Of Supervisors*, 123 Cal. App. 3d 334, 356 (1981); Code Civ. Proc. § 1109. A TRO or injunction typically prohibits the real party in interest—often a developer—from carrying out the activity approved by the local agency. A TRO or injunction requires a showing of a probability of prevailing on the merits and irreparable harm in the absence of an order. *See Cohen v. Bo. of Supervisors*, 40 Cal. 3d 277 (1985).

> TRO = temporary restraining order

A bond is required for an injunction to issue. Code Civ. Proc. §§ 529 (general provisions), 529.1 (bond in action to enjoin a construction project that has received all legally required licenses and permits), 529.2 (bond in action to enjoin low- or moderate-income housing development project). The bond is designed to protect the respondent or real party in interest against damages sustained by reason of the injunction if the court finally decides that the petitioner was not entitled to the injunction. Code Civ. Proc. § 529.

The damages that may be recovered against a bond are those that appear with reasonable certainty to be the necessary and proximate result of the injunction, up to the limit of the bond. 6 Witkin, *Calif. Procedure, Provisional Remedies*, section 416, (5th ed. 2008). Those damages may include attorneys' fees the respondent or real party in interest incurs in defending the main action, on the theory that defending the main action is necessary to establish that the injunction should not have issued. *Id.*, § 417. Thus, by seeking an injunction, a petitioner may open itself up to an award of attorneys' fees where none would otherwise be recoverable.

In CEQA cases, by statutory mandate, if no stay or injunction is issued, responsible agencies are required to assume that the EIR or negative declaration is adequate, and decide whether to approve the project accordingly. A responsible agency's approval of the project in that circumstance constitutes permission to proceed with the project at the applicant's risk pending final determination of the CEQA action. Pub. Res. Code § 21167.3(b). The same rules implicitly apply in non-CEQA cases by virtue of the presumption of validity that attaches to public agency decisions. Evid. Code § 664 ("It is presumed that official duty has been regularly performed.").

ISSUANCE OF THE WRIT

The writ issued at the end of a case is a peremptory writ of mandate. The writ cannot be granted by default. The case must be heard by the court whether the adverse party appears or not. Code Civ. Proc. § 1088.

If the petition challenges a local agency decision, and the court determines that the petition has merit, it enters a judgment directing issuance of a writ. The clerk of the court then issues the writ. *See* 31 *California Forms of Pleading and Practice*, ch. 358, forms

18 and 20 (Matthew Bender) 2004. The writ typically directs the respondent agency to vacate and set aside the decision, and not to take similar action until there has been compliance with the law. Code Civ. Proc. § 1087. If the petition seeks to compel specific action and the court determines that remedy is appropriate, the writ directs the respondent agency to take the action. At least one court held that the writ must specify a return date to ensure compliance. It explained:

> A writ of mandate is a piece of paper. If its purpose is to declare the rights of parties, its existence suffices. If its purpose is to compel someone to do something, its existence does not suffice. The proper way to ensure compliance is to require a return on the writ, which commands a party to do something and report to the court that the act has been done. (See Cal. Administrative Mandamus (Cont. Ed. Bar 1989) Procedures After Trial, §§ 13.10-13.11, pp. 411-14 [providing form for this purpose].)

Endangered Habitats League, Inc. v. State Water Res. Control Bd., 63 Cal. App. 4th 227, 244 (1997). Notwithstanding this statement, many peremptory writs do not expressly require a return.

If the court determines that the writ proceeding has no merit, it issues a judgment denying the petition for writ of mandate, and declaring that the petitioner take nothing by its action. A statement of decision ordinarily is not required, since a writ proceeding typically involves no factual findings. *See City of Coachella v. Riverside County Airport Land Use Comm'n.*, 210 Cal. App. 3d 1277, 1291-92 (1989).

APPEAL IN A WRIT OF MANDATE CASE

Appeals of judgments in mandate cases generally are subject to the rules applicable to appeals in civil cases. Code Civ. Proc. § 1109; California Rules of Court, Rules 1-55. However, caution is warranted in applying these general rules to the peculiarities of mandate proceedings.

> Appeals of judgments in mandate cases generally are subject to the rules applicable to appeals in civil cases.

Time to appeal. In *Laraway v. Pasadena Unified School District*, the court held that the time to appeal started to run upon the trial court's order granting a motion for writ of mandate, rather than the subsequent judgment. 98 Cal. App. 4th 579 (2002). The court held that the order was appealable, since it contemplated no further action and disposed of all issues between all parties. It explained that once a final, appealable order or judgment has been entered, the time to appeal begins to run, and the time cannot be restarted or extended by the filing of a subsequent judgment or appealable order making the same decision. *Id.*

Effect of appeal on judgment. The statutes governing the effect of appeals on judgments in mandate cases also are somewhat confusing, because some provisions address the effect of the appeal on the *trial court's* decision and others deal with the effect on the underlying *agency* action. The guiding principle, however, is simply stated: during appeal from a judgment granting a writ in an administrative mandate case, the agency's decision is automatically stayed. *See Agric. Labor Relations Bd. v. Tex-Cal Land Mgmt., Inc.*, 43 Cal. 3d 696, 706 n.9 (1987); Code Civ. Proc. § 1094.5(g). In all other cases (i.e., denial of a writ in an administrative mandate case or denial or grant of a writ in a traditional mandate case), the agency's decision or order remains in effect pending appeal absent a contrary order issued by the trial court or the court of appeal. Code Civ. Proc. §§ 916(a) (general rule is that appeal stays judgment), 917.1-917.9 (exceptions to general rule, which do not include a writ of mandate), 1109 (code provisions pertaining to ordinary civil actions apply to writ proceedings except as otherwise provided in writ statutes), 1110(b) (court may direct that an appeal of a judgment granting a writ of mandate does not stay the judgment), 1094.5(g) (agency decision not stayed upon appeal of judgment denying administrative writ unless court order otherwise). *See also Union Pacific R.R., Co. v. State Bd. of Equalization*, 49 Cal. 3d 138, 158 (1989) (traditional writ of mandate automatically stayed pending appeal; writ of prohibition, which maintains status quo, is not automatically stayed pending appeal).

Administrative mandate. Appeal in an administrative mandate case is governed by Code of Civil Procedure section 1094.5(g), under which (1) in an appeal from denial of the writ, the order or decision of the agency is not stayed except upon the order of the appellate court; and (2) an appeal from the granting of the writ automatically stays the order or decision of the agency pending the determination of the appeal unless the appellate court directs otherwise.

Traditional mandate. A petitioner's appeal from the grant or denial of a writ of traditional mandate is governed by general rules on appeals in civil actions. Code Civ. Proc. § 1109 (except as otherwise provided, general rules of civil procedure govern special proceedings). Under Code of Civil Procedure section 916, "an appeal stays proceedings in the trial court upon the judgment or order appealed from...." Thus, if a court either grants or denies a writ of traditional mandate, its order is automatically stayed by appeal. The practical effect in both cases is to leave the agency decision or order in effect pending appeal.

Injunction. The situation is further complicated, however, if the judgment includes a permanent injunction, such as an injunction prohibiting the developer from pursuing its project. Mandatory injunctions are automatically stayed pending appeal, while prohibitory injunctions are not. 1 *Calif. Civil Appellate Practice*, § 6.19 (Cal. CEB, 3d ed. 1997); 9 Witkin, *Calif. Procedure, Appeal*, § 276 (5th ed. 2008); 6 Witkin, *Calif. Procedure, Provisional Remedies*, § 403 (5th ed. 2008).

LITIGATION UNDER CEQA

CEQA actions are brought as mandate actions, but are subject to several unique procedural rules that dictate the pace of the litigation to a significant degree.

SPECIAL PROCEDURES FOR CEQA ACTIONS

> CEQA = California Environmental Quality Act

The petitioner in a CEQA proceeding must request a hearing within 90 days of filing the petition. Pub. Res. Code § 21167.4(a).[19] The hearing need not be held within the 90-day period, but the request for a hearing must be made within that time. *Id.; see also Ass'n for Sensible Dev. at Northstar, Inc. v. Placer County*, 122 Cal. App. 4th 1289, 1293-95 (2004) (disagreeing with *McCormick v. Board of Supervisors*, 198 Cal. App. 3d 352 (1988), which held that the mere filing of a request for a hearing was insufficient); *Mitchell v. County of Orange*, 165 Cal. App. 3d 1185 (1985). The hearing must be on the merits of the petition itself; setting a hearing on provisional remedies or collateral matters within 90 days of filing the action is insufficient. *See Miller v. City of Hermosa Beach*, 13 Cal. App. 4th 1118, 1135 (1993). The failure to request a hearing can result in dismissal of the case, and relief from that dismissal under Code of Civil Procedure

---

[19] A similar requirement to request a hearing within 90 days applies to certain challenges to general plans. Gov't Code § 65753.

section 473 has been held to be unavailable when the failure to request a hearing was due to an attorneys' inexcusable mistake. *Nacimiento Reg'l Water Mgmt. Advisory Comm. v. Monterey County Water Res. Agency*, 122 Cal. App. 4th 961 (2004). The request for hearing must be in writing; an oral request is insufficient. *Torrey Hills Com'ty. Coal. v. City of San Diego*, 186 Cal. App. 4th 429, 442 (2010).

> The request for hearing must be in writing; an oral request is insufficient.

CEQA provides for an additional mediation opportunity before a CEQA lawsuit is filed. Within five days of the filing of a Notice of Determination, a person "wishing to bring" a CEQA action may file a request for mediation with the respondent public agency. Pub. Res. Code § 21167.10(a). Unless the agency accepts, the request is deemed denied five business days later. Pub. Res. Code § 21167.10(c). If mediation occurs, the limitations periods provided for in Chapter 6 of CEQA, Pub. Res. Code §§ 21165-21177, are tolled pending completion of the mediation. The statute addressing this mediation potential remains in effect only until January 1, 2016, except that the tolling of the limitation periods continues to apply if a mediation is completed on or after January 1, 2016.

CONTENTS OF A CEQA RECORD

The contents of a record in a CEQA proceeding are specified by statute. Public Resources Code section 21167.6(e) provides that the record must include certain materials. In general terms, it requires the following:

- All project application materials
- All staff reports and related documents prepared by the agency and written testimony or documents submitted by any person relevant to the agency's action on the project, compliance with CEQA, and any related findings adopted by the agency
- Any transcripts or minutes[20] of proceedings at which the decisionmaking bodies at the agency heard testimony or considered any environmental document on the project, and any transcripts or minutes of proceedings before any advisory body that were presented to the decisionmaking body prior to taking action on the environmental documents or the project
- Any other written materials relevant to the agency's compliance with CEQA and its final decision on the merits of the project (such as the initial study, copies of studies or other documents relied upon in any environmental document prepared for the project and either made available to the public or included in the agency's files, and all internal agency communications, including staff notes and memoranda related to the project or compliance with CEQA)[21]
- Local court rules sometimes add a myriad of procedural and substantive requirements regarding preparation of a record

Web-based materials. The statute does not provide guidance regarding inclusion or exclusion of materials available on the web that are referenced or linked to in documents in the record. In *Consolidated Irrigation District v. Superior Court*, 205 Cal. App. 4th

---

20 In *Consolidated Irrigation District v. City of Selma*, 204 Cal. App. 4th 187 (2012), the court held that the reference to "transcripts or minutes" must be read conjunctively—both must be included. If no transcript exists of a recorded meeting, the tape recording of the meeting must be included in the record. The court indicated that a party requesting a transcript under such circumstances must prepare or pay for preparation of the transcript.

21 The record does not, however, include documents that are privileged or protected. *California Oak Foundation v. County of Tehama*, 174 Cal. App. 4th 1217 (2009). See "Attorney-Client Privilege and Work Product Doctrine" (this chapter).

697 (2012), the court ruled that documents referenced in correspondence submitted to the agency and accessible on the web constituted "written evidence submitted to the agency" for purposes of CEQA and had to be included in the record if they met certain criteria established by the court. The court's guiding principle was that documents made "readily available" to the agency would be deemed to have been "submitted to" the agency for purposes of Public Resources Code section 21167.6(e). The court applied this principle as follows:

Documents for which a general website address is provided. If correspondence submitted to the agency refers only to a general website, such as an organization's home page, and requires further searching to locate the specific document, the document is not part of the record even if the correspondence expressly requests that it be made part of the record.

Documents for which a specific web address is provided. If the correspondence provides a specific web address (url) that calls up the referenced document, the document is part of the record *even if the correspondence does not specifically request that it be made part of the record.*

Documents for which no website address is provided. If the correspondence references a web document but provides no website, the document is not part of the record, even if the document can easily be located on the web. *Id.* at 724-25.

Presumably, citation to a web page should also be sufficient to include the cited document in the record presented to the court, without producing a physical copy. Despite these rules, parties seeking to include specific web pages in the record before the agency or before a court would be better protected by providing paper or electronic copies of the web page, to ensure that the version of the web page as it exists on the day it is cited is preserved and available for later reference.

The court further found that where correspondence references documents previously submitted to the agency (whether or not available on the web) and expressly requests that such documents be made part of the record and offers to provide another copy upon request, these documents must be included in the record. *Id.* at 724.

Documents in consultant and subconsultant files. Disputes often arise regarding whether documents prepared by and retained in files of consultants involved in preparation of the EIR must be included in the record. The record must include "copies of studies other documents relied upon in any [EIR and] included in the...public agency's files on the project...." (Pub. Res. Code § 21167.6(e)(10)). The court in *Consolidated Irrigation District* interpreted the term "public agency files" to mean files owned by the agency or in its custody or control—not necessarily in its actual possession. 214 Cal. App. 4th at 710-11. This means that documents in the files of consultants must be included in the record if the contract between the agency and the consultant gives the agency an ownership interest in those documents. *Id.* On the other hand, documents in files of subconsultants—those contracting with the main EIR consultant but not the public agency—need not be included since the agency neither possesses nor has any ownership interest in such documents. *Id.* at 711.

Responsibility of preparation of the record. CEQA allows a petitioner to prepare the record, presumably to allow the petitioner to keep costs down. Pub. Res. Code § 21167.6(b)(2); *but see St. Vincent's School for Boys, Catholic Charities CYO v. City of San Rafael*, 161 Cal. App. 4th 989 (2008) (petitioner's election to prepare the record did not preclude the agency from recovering costs it incurred in locating emails).

The responsibility for an adequate, well-organized, and comprehensive record always remains, however, with the respondent agency, and "[t]he consequences of providing a record to the courts that does not evidence the agency's compliance with CEQA is severe—reversal of project approval." *Protect Our Water v. County of Merced*, 110 Cal. App. 4th 362, 373 (2003).

> The responsibility for an adequate, well-organized, and comprehensive record always remains with the respondent agency,.

Protect Our Water presented an extreme example of poor record preparation, with the court assigning blame to the petitioner, the agency, and the project applicant. The petitioner had exercised its election to prepare the record, and had failed to organize or index the documents coherently. The court noted that "it is nearly impossible to locate the pertinent documents...[the] majority... are neither properly indexed nor coherently organized," and it was not even clear whether the court had complete copies. *Id.* at 372. There was only a master index, which identified only broad categories of documents spanning hundreds of pages. The county, for its part, failed to prepare coherent documents. It failed to properly label documents, and some appeared incomplete. The court could not differentiate between documents and attachments. "We find it inconceivable that, given the scope and magnitude of this project, the documents comprising the administrative record are so defectively drafted. This responsibility fell squarely on the County." *Id.* at 372-73. The project applicant also received court censure on the ground that project applicants often assist in the preparation of the record, as they are the parties with an indisputable interest in upholding an agency action approving a project. *Id.* at 373.

CEQA EXHAUSTION AND STANDING RULES

CEQA has it own version of the exhaustion doctrine as well. It is codified in section 21177, which provides in relevant part:

> An action or proceeding shall not be brought pursuant to Section 21167 unless the alleged grounds for noncompliance with this division were presented to the public agency orally or in writing by any person during the public comment period provided by this division or prior to the close of the public hearing on the project before the issuance of the notice of determination.

Pub. Res. Code § 21177(a). Section 21177, by its terms, remains in effect only until 2016. Pub. Res. Code § 21177(f).

Section 21177 alters the common law exhaustion doctrine in that it requires a potential litigant to raise CEQA issues if the agency holds any hearing on the project, even if a hearing is not required by law. *Tomlinson v. County of Alameda*, 54 Cal. 4th 281 (2012). The conclusion follows from the language of Public Resources Code section 21177(a), which states that a project can only be challenged on grounds "that were presented to the public agency...prior to the close of the public hearing on the project before the issuance of a notice of determination." In *Tomlinson*, the California Supreme Court explained that the phrase "before issuance of a notice of determination" does not limit the statute's reach to only those projects for which such a notice is filed:

> *If* a notice of determination is filed, the public hearing provision requires a party wishing to challenge the project in court to raise the party's objections to the project at a public hearing held before the notice of determination is filed. But if no such notice is filed, the public hearing provision nonetheless applies. In that situation, the challenging party is still required to exhaust its administrative remedies by presenting its objections to the project to the

pertinent public agency, so long as it is given the opportunity to do so at a public hearing held *before the project is approved*. When, as in this case, a party is given such an opportunity, and it fails to raise a particular objection to the project, it may not raise that objection in court, because it has not satisfied the exhaustion requirement of section 21177's subdivision (a).

54 Cal. 4th at 290 (emphasis in original). Thus, if the agency holds a hearing on the project, whether or not required by law, CEQA issues must be raised at or before that hearing in order to exhaust administrative remedies under section 21177(a).

Public Resources Code section 21177(a) essentially codifies the "issue exhaustion" requirement, discussed above. Although the statute is silent on the "appeal exhaustion" requirement, courts have held that a petitioner also must satisfy the common law exhaustion requirement by appealing to the final decisionmaking body. *See Tahoe Vista Concerned Citizens v. County of Placer*, 81 Cal. App. 4th 577, 590–91 (2000).

Ordinarily, a petitioner in a mandate case need not have personally objected to the proposed action in order to have standing. In CEQA cases, however, section 21177(b) states:

(b) No person shall maintain an action or proceeding unless that person objected to the approval of the project orally or in writing during the public comment period provided by this division or prior to the close of the public hearing on the project before the issuance of the notice of determination.

Section 21177(b) essentially creates an additional "standing" requirement. *Id.* However, compliance with section 21177(b) is not sufficient, by itself, to confer standing. *Waste Mgmt. of Alameda County, Inc.*, 79 Cal. App. 4th at 1239 (compliance with section 21177(b) does not confer standing on a petitioner that has no beneficial interest in CEQA compliance).

> CEQA also expressly provides that an organization formed after the approval of a project may sue if a member of that organization exhausted remedies under the statute.

CEQA also expressly provides that an organization formed after the approval of a project may sue if a member of that organization exhausted remedies under the statute. Pub. Res. Code § 21177(c). Section 21177 allows for exhaustion through submittal of comments at the last public hearing on a project, even though the comment period provided for by CEQA has passed. *See Galante Vineyards v. Monterey Peninsula Water Mgmt. Dist.*, 60 Cal. App. 4th 1109 (1997).

STANDARD OF JUDICIAL REVIEW OF CEQA DECISIONS

Judicial review of CEQA determinations made in connection with a legislative decision is governed by Public Resources Code section 21168.5. That section states that "the inquiry shall extend only to whether there was a prejudicial abuse of discretion. Abuse of discretion is established if the agency has not proceeded in a manner required by law or if the determination or decision is not supported by substantial evidence." Pub. Res. Code § 21168.5.

Judicial review of CEQA decisions made in connection with administrative decisions is governed by Public Resources Code section 21168. That section provides that review "shall be in accordance with the provisions of section 1094.5 of the Code of Civil Procedure." Pub. Res. Code § 21168.

The courts have explained that while the standards under these two sections appear different, they are essentially the same. *See Laurel Heights Improvement Ass'n v. Regents of the Univ. of Cal.*, 47 Cal. 3d 376, 392 n.5 (1988). Accordingly, review of any CEQA decision will be made under a standard that essentially is the same as the substantial evidence standard of review of an administrative decision under Code of Civil Procedure section 1094.5. The California Supreme Court has described the standard as follows:

> In reviewing agency actions under CEQA, Public Resources Code section 21168.5 provides that a court's inquiry shall extend only to whether there was a prejudicial abuse of discretion. Abuse of discretion is established if the agency has not proceeded in a manner required by law or if the determination or decision is not supported by substantial evidence. Thus, the reviewing court does not pass upon the correctness of the EIR's environmental conclusions, but only upon its sufficiency as an informative document. We may not set aside an agency's approval of an EIR on the ground that an opposite conclusion would have been equally or more reasonable. Our limited function is consistent with the principle that [ ] the purpose of CEQA is not to generate paper, but to compel government at all levels to make decisions with environmental consequences in mind. CEQA does not, indeed cannot, guarantee that these decisions will always be those which favor environmental considerations. We may not, in sum, substitute our judgment for that of the people and their local representatives. We can and must, however, scrupulously enforce all legislatively mandated CEQA requirements.

Citizens of Goleta Valley v. Bd. of Supervisors, 52 Cal. 3d 553, 564 (1990) (citations and quotations omitted)

> Review of any CEQA decision will be made under a standard that essentially is the same as the substantial evidence standard of review of an administrative decision under Code of Civil Procedure section 1094.5.

The high court also has explained that "[i]n applying the substantial evidence standard, 'the reviewing court must resolve reasonable doubts in favor of the administrative finding and decision.'" *Laurel Heights Improvement Ass'n*, 47 Cal. 3d at 393. (citation omitted) *See also National Parks and Conservation Ass'n v. County of Riverside*, 71 Cal. App. 4th 1341 (1999) (limiting inquiry to whether the agency had substantial evidence to support its decision to approve the EIR).

Because this standard of review applies to CEQA issues regardless of whether the CEQA review is challenged in connection with an administrative decision or a legislative decision, an action that challenges a legislative decision on both CEQA and non-CEQA grounds will be reviewed under two different standards of review. For example, a claim that a general plan amendment fails to conform to state law will be reviewed under the arbitrary and capricious standard that generally applies in traditional mandate proceedings. *See, e.g., Karlson v. City of Camarillo*, 100 Cal. App. 3d 789, 803-04 (1980). But a claim that the EIR prepared for the general plan amendment fails to comply with CEQA will be reviewed under the stricter CEQA standard, which requires an evaluation of whether there is substantial evidence to support the agency's certification of the EIR, and whether the agency abused its discretion by failing to proceed in the manner required by law.[22]

REMEDIES IN A CEQA CASE

Courts are vested with broad discretion to craft an appropriate remedy to ensure compliance with CEQA and simultaneously to ensure that the local agency understands the appropriate corrective action that is necessary to comply with the law. Pub. Res. Code § 21168.9. Public Resources Code section 21168.9 allows the court wide latitude in determining whether to suspend all activity and void a decision or allow part of the project to move forward. This type of specifically tailored remedy was applied in *Laurel*

---

22 Stephen L. Kostka and Michael H. Zischke, *Practice Under the California Environmental Quality Act*, §§ 12.4, 12.5, 23.33 (Cal. CEB, 2d ed. 2008, 2013 Update).

Heights Improvement Association, in which the California Supreme Court allowed the University to continue its existing uses at the project site when the EIR was inadequate only as to future uses. 47 Cal. 3d at 422.

LITIGATION UNDER THE MITIGATION FEE ACT

Challenges to fees and exactions are governed by the Mitigation Fee Act, Government Code section 66000 *et seq.,* and are the subject of two potentially applicable limitations periods.

As Applied Challenges to Development Fees. The first limitations period, contained in Government Code section 66020, governs "as-applied" challenges to development fees or other exactions[23] that are imposed as a condition of approval of specific development projects. *Sterling Park, L.P. v. City of Palo Alto,* 57 Cal.4th 1193, 1207 (2013). Under Government Code section 66020, a party wishing to challenge the imposition of development fees on its project must file a written protest "at the time of approval or conditional approval of the development or within 90 days after the date of the imposition of the...exactions." Gov't Code § 66020(d)(1). Fees are deemed imposed "when they are imposed or levied on a specific development." Gov't Code § 66020(h). In addition to serving a written protest setting forth the factual and legal elements of the dispute, the party must either tender any required payment in full or provide satisfactory evidence of arrangements to pay the fee when due. Gov't Code § 66020(a)(1). A party that satisfies these protest requirements may file an action challenging imposition of the fees within 180 days after delivery of a notice from the local agency containing a statement of the amount of the fees and notification that the protest period has begun. Gov't Code § 66020(d)(1). The pay-under-protest procedures and limitations period under Government Code section 66020 apply only to fees imposed on a development project as a condition of approval of development. *Barratt American, Inc. v. City of Rancho Cucamonga,* 37 Cal. 4th 685, 699 (2005) ("[A] fee does not become a 'development fee' simply because it is made in connection with a development project."); *Capistrano Beach Water Dist. v. Taj Development Corp.,* 72 Cal. App. 4th 524, 529-530 (1999). They do not apply to water and sewer service connection fees and capacity charges or fees and charges for processing of permits, which may only be challenged under Government Code section 66022 (discussed below). *Barratt American,* 37 Cal. 4th at 699. Nor do they apply to regulatory fees charged to cover the reasonable cost of a service or program connected to a particular activity. *California Building Industry Assn. v. San Joaquin Valley Air Pollution Control Dist.,* 178 Cal. App. 4th 120, 124-125 (2009) (Indirect Source Review fee to mitigate indirect pollution created by development projects not a development fee).

Facial Challenges To Sewer and Water Fees, Capacity Charges and Processing Fees. The second limitations period, Government Code section 66022, governs challenges to the adoption of an ordinance or resolution levying or increasing specified fees or service charges. Such an action must be filed within 120 days of the effective date of the challenged ordinance or resolution. Gov't Code § 66022(a). The action must be brought as a validation proceeding pursuant to Code of Civil Procedure section 860 *et seq.* Gov't Code § 66022(b). However, Government Code section 66022, by

---

[23] Government Code § 66020 applies to "any fees, dedications, reservations, or other exactions" imposed on a development project. *See Sterling Park, L.P. v. City of Palo Alto,* 57 Cal.4th 1193, 1207 (2013) (statute governs conditions on development a local agency imposes that divest the developer of money or a possessory interest in property). For convenience, these are collectively referred to as "development fees" or "fees."

its terms, applies only to (1) sewer and water connection fees and "capacity charges" described in Government Code section 66013, and (2) to fees and service charges for processing of zoning changes, use permits, and other permits described in Government Code section 66014(a). Challenges to these fees and charges may not be brought under the pay-under-protest procedures of Government Code section 66020. A validation action under section 66022 is the exclusive procedure for challenging these fees. *Barratt American Inc.*, 37 Cal. 4th 685 (fees and charges defined in Government Code sections 66014 and 66016 do not qualify as "development project fees" under section 66020). In contrast to section 66020, which provides for a refund of excessive or invalid development fees, there is no right to a refund of fees or charges challenged under section 66022; the sole remedy is the reduction of future fees or charges. *Id.*

The two statutes of limitation—Government Code section 66020, governing as applied challenges to imposition of development fees, and Government Code section 66022, governing facial challenges to specified water, sewer, capacity, and processing charges—are discussed in further detail below.

CHALLENGE TO IMPOSITION OF FEES ON A DEVELOPMENT PROJECT (GOV'T CODE § 66020)

A party seeking to challenge the imposition of any fees, dedications, or other exactions on a development project must follow the procedures in Government Code section 66020. These procedures apply to any conditions of approval on a development project imposed by a local agency "that divest the developer of money or a possessory interest in property...." *Sterling Park*, 57 Cal. 4th at 1207.24. They do not apply to zoning restrictions such as setbacks, floor area ratios, density limitations or other "restrictions on the manner in which a developer may use its property." *Id.* Under the statute, the party must first protest the fee in writing "at the time of approval or conditional approval of the development or within 90 days after the date of the imposition of the...exactions...." Gov't Code § 66020(d)(1). The written protest must be served on the "governing body" of the local agency (such as the city council of a city) and must set forth "the factual elements of the dispute and the legal theory forming the basis for the protest." Gov't Code § 66020(a)(2). Fees are considered imposed "when they are imposed or levied on a specific development" (Gov't Code § 66020(h)) as distinct from when they are adopted. The date of imposition is not necessarily the date on which the fees are paid. *See Ponderosa Homes, Inc. v. City of San Ramon*, 23 Cal. App. 4th 1761 (1994) (tentative map condition requiring payment of traffic mitigation fee prior to issuance of building permits constituted "imposition" of such fees for purposes of Government Code section 66020). However, adoption of an ordinance or resolution applying the fee to broad classes of projects does not constitute "imposition" of the fee for purposes of Government Code section 66020. *See N.T. Hill, Inc. v. City of Fresno*, 72 Cal. App. 4th 977, 989–90 (1999) ("[S]ection 66020 applies to a developer's challenge to an agency's adjudicative decision to impose upon a particular development project a fee adopted by a generally applicable legislative decision."); *Trend Homes, Inc. v. Central Unified Sch. Dist.*, 220 Cal. App. 3d 102, 111 (1990). The applicant must follow

> At the time of project approval or imposition of the fees, the local agency is required to provide written notice to the project applicant describing the exactions and notifying the applicant that the 90-day protest period has begun.

---

24 Although the statute defines "fee" as a monetary exaction imposed "for the purpose of defraying all or a portion of the cost of public facilities related to the development project," the California Supreme Court has held that the pay-and-protest procedures are not limited to exactions imposed for the purpose of funding public facilities or services. *Sterling Park*, 57 Cal. 4th at 1205 (statute is not restricted to exactions imposed to defray project costs, but includes exactions arbitrarily imposed for purposes entirely unrelated to the project).

a specified procedure, including tendering any required payment in full or committing to performance of any necessary conditions. At the time of project approval or imposition of the fees, the local agency is required to provide written notice to the project applicant describing the exactions and notifying the applicant that the 90-day protest period has begun. Gov't Code § 66020(d)(1). The 180-day statute does not begin to run unless the agency provides the required notice. *Branciforte Heights, LLC v. City of Santa Cruz*, 138 Cal. App. 4th 914, 925 (2006).

Compliance with the protest procedures allows a party to challenge the exaction within 180 days of delivery of the notice. Gov't Code § 66020(d)(2). By providing for an action that challenges the imposition of a fee or other exaction upon a development project, Government Code section 66020 creates a vehicle for bringing an "as applied" challenge to a fee ordinance.

Other provisions of the Mitigation Fee Act indicate that a facial challenge to an ordinance or resolution establishing a fee may be combined with the as-applied claim. Government Code section 66024 states that a developer upon whom a fee has been imposed may seek to invalidate "any order or resolution providing for the imposition" of such fee if such a fee is an invalid "special tax," i.e., if the fee exceeds the cost of the service or facility for which it is imposed. Government Code section 66021 likewise allows a developer who protests the imposition of a fee also to protest "the *establishment* ...of the fee, tax, assessment, dedication, reservation, or other exaction...." (emphasis added) Further, an action filed within the limitations period for challenges to application of a fee to a specific project may include a claim that the ordinance enacting the fee is facially invalid; such a claim need not be brought within 120 days, or other specific period following enactment or amendment of the underlying ordinance. See *Travis v. County of Santa Cruz*, 33 Cal. 4th 757 (2004). By contrast, as discussed below, a facial challenge, brought as a validation proceeding, is the *exclusive* procedure for challenging adoption or amendment of water and sewer connection charges, fees and charges for permits, and other fees and charges described in Government Code sections 66013 and 66014—they cannot be challenged under Government Code section 66020. *Barratt American Inc.*, 37 Cal. 4th 685 (Gov't Code section 66020, by its own terms, applies only to "development fees" that mitigate the effects of development on the community and does not include fees for water or sewer connections or specified service charges).

Government Code section 66024 requires that at least 30 days prior to initiating an action asserting that the fee constitutes a special tax, the petitioner must have requested that the local agency provide a copy of the documents establishing that the development fee did not exceed the cost of the service for which it was imposed. The purpose of requiring a party to request documents before suing is not to cause the agency to discontinue collecting the disputed fees, but to provide the party with a factual basis for its claim before filing suit. Therefore, a suing party cannot claim it was futile to ask. See *Trend Homes, Inc. v. Central Unified Sch. Dist.*, 220 Cal. App. 3d 102 (1990).

> The statutory "pay and protest" procedure was enacted to negate the harsh common law rule under which a developer was forced to choose between accepting a permit in order to pursue development, and giving up the ability to develop under the permit by suing to invalidate unlawful conditions.

The statutory "pay and protest" procedure was enacted to negate the harsh common law rule under which a developer was forced to choose between accepting a permit in order to pursue development, and giving up the ability to develop under the permit by suing to invalidate unlawful conditions. See *Sterling Park*, 57 Cal. 4th at 1199; *Pfeiffer v. City of La Mesa*, 69 Cal. App. 3d 74 (1977) (acceptance and use of permit waives right to challenge conditions). If a developer follows the statutory protest procedure, a city cannot use the protest as a basis to withhold approval of the project while the protest is pending. Gov't Code § 66020(b). However, a local agency can make certain findings that the construction of public facilities, the need for which is directly attributable to the proposed development, is required for the public health, safety, and welfare, and then suspend the permit or other approval that was granted on condition that the developer construct such facilities, pending withdrawal or resolution of the protest against those conditions. Gov't Code § 66020(c).

The pay-and-protest procedure prescribes the exclusive method for an as-applied challenge to fees and exactions imposed on a development project as a condition of development approval. See *Ehrlich v. City of Culver City*, 12 Cal. 4th 854, 866 (1996) ("[T]he Legislature intended to require all protests to a development fee that challenge the sufficiency of its relationship to the effects attributable to a development project—regardless of the legal underpinnings of the protest—to be channeled through the administrative procedures mandated by the [Mitigation Fee Act]."); accord, *Sterling Park*, 57 Cal. 4th at 1205 (city requirement that the developer provide it with a below-market option for affordable housing amounted to an "other exaction" under Mitigation Fee Act and was therefore subject to its pay-and-protest provisions); *California Ranch Homes Dev. Co. v. San Jacinto Unified Sch. Dist.*, 17 Cal. App. 4th 573 (1993) (Government Code section 66020 describes the exclusive procedure for challenging the imposition of school fees on a project). Accordingly, the statutory protest procedure supplants the common law exhaustion requirement (discussed above), and allows developers to protest imposition of fees within 90 days after project approval without having raised the issue during the approval process. See *Kings County Farm Bureau v. City of Hanford*, 221 Cal. App. 3d 692, 740 (1990) (statutory codification of exhaustion requirement supersedes common law). It also supplants the more general 90-day limitations period for challenges to "the reasonableness, legality or validity of any condition" attached to a subdivision map. Gov't Code § 66499.37. See *Branciforte Heights, LLC*, 138 Cal. App. 4th at 925 (party challenging fees imposed under Quimby Act may use pay-and-protest provisions of Mitigation Fee Act in lieu of compliance with Map Act procedures and limitations).[25] On the other hand, the pay-and-protest procedure is not available to challenge conditions or restrictions that do not involve exactions or dedication requirements. See *Sterling Park*, 57 Cal. 4th at 1207 (procedure is not applicable to restrictions on the use of land such as a limit on the number of units that can be built); *Fogarty v. City of Chico*, 148 Cal. App. 4th 537 (2007) (land use restrictions imposed as a condition of approval are not "exactions" even if they allegedly render property valueless).

> The pay-and-protest procedure is not available to challenge conditions or restrictions that do not involve exactions or dedication requirements.

Because lawsuits contesting the imposition of a condition or exaction challenge agency decisions, such actions usually are brought as writ proceedings. See discussion above regarding mandate as the exclusive procedure for challenging administrative agency actions.

CHALLENGE TO ENACTMENT OR INCREASE OF WATER, SEWER, CAPACITY OR PROCESSING FEES (GOV'T CODE § 66022)

Facial challenges to ordinances or resolutions that enact or amend water or sewer fees or capacity charges and processing fees are governed by Government Code section 66022, which sets a 120-day limitations period for challenge.

---

25 There is some question about whether *Branciforte* will remain good law since Government Code section 66000 expressly excludes Quimby Act fees and dedication requirements from the scope of the Mitigation Fee Act (an issue apparently not raised by the parties or noted by the court).

TABLE 6. SUMMARY OF GOVERNMENT CODE SECTION 66022 AND RELATED PROVISIONS

Section 66022 applies to "fees, capacity charges, and service charges described in and subject to Sections 66013, 66014, and 66016" Gov't Code § 66022(c).

Section 66013 addresses fees related to:
- sewer connection (the connection of a structure or project to a public sewer system)
- water connection (the connection of a structure or project to a public water system)
- capacity charge (a charge for public facilities in existence at the time a charge is imposed or charges for new public facilities to be acquired or constructed in the future that are of proportional benefit to the person or property being charged, including supply or capacity contracts for rights or entitlements, real property interests, and entitlements and other rights of the local agency involving capital expense relating to its use of existing or new public facilities)

Section 66014 pertains for processing fees. It specifically addresses fees for:
- zoning variances
- zoning changes
- use permits
- building inspections
- building permits
- filing and processing applications and petitions filed with the local agency formation commission or conducting preliminary proceedings or proceedings under the Cortese-Knox-Hertzberg Act
- the processing of maps under the provisions of the Subdivision Map Act
- planning services under the authority of Chapter 3 (commencing with Section 65100) of Division 1 of Title 7 of the Government Code, or under any other authority

Section 66016 references fees "as described in Sections 51287, 56383, 65104, 65456, 65584.1, 65863.7, 65909.5, 66013, 66014, and 66451.2 of this code, Sections 17951, 19132.3, and 19852 of the Health and Safety Code, Section 41901 of the Public Resources Code, and Section 21671.5 of the Public Utilities Code." Sections 66013 and 660154 are listed above. The remainder of these code sections reference the following fees:

- Gov't Code § 51287 – the reasonable cost of services provided by the city or county under the contract cancellation provisions of the Williamson Act
- Gov't Code § 56383 – fees and service charges for proceedings under the Cortese-Knox-Hertzberg Act
- Gov't Code § 65104 – fees to support the work of the planning agency, which shall not exceed the reasonable cost of providing the service for which the fee is charged
- Gov't Code § 65456 – specific plan fee imposed upon persons seeking governmental approvals which are required to be consistent with the specific plan, which fees as estimated do not exceed, the cost of preparation, adoption, and administration of the specific plan, including costs incurred pursuant to CEQA
- Gov't Code § 65584.1 – councils of government may charge a fee to local governments to cover the projected reasonable, actual costs of the council in distributing regional housing needs, and the city or county may then charge a fee to reimburse the fee it paid to the council of governments
- Gov't Code § 65863.7 – fees for reviewing, and potentially mitigating, the impact of a mobile home conversion on the displaced residents of the mobilehome park, and advising the owner of requirements relevant to the conversion
- Gov't Code § 65909.5 – fees for the processing of use permits, zone variances, or zone changes
- Gov't Code § 66451.2 – fees for the processing of tentative, final and parcel maps and for other procedures required or authorized by the Subdivision Map Act or local ordinance
- Health & Safety Code § 17951 – fees for permits, certificates, or other forms or documents required or authorized by, and for enforcement of, laws pertaining to buildings for human habitation
- Health & Safety Code § 19132.3 – fees related to building permits and compliance with building requirements related to earthquake protection
- Health & Safety Code § 19852 – fees for maintaining copies of plans for which building permits have issued
- Pub. Res. Code § 41901 – fees to pay the costs of preparing, adopting, and implementing a countywide integrated waste management plan, and the costs of the setting and collection of local fees
- Pub. Util. Code § 21671.5 – fees charged by an Airport Land Use Commission for services to fulfill the duties imposed on it by law

A party challenging water, sewer, or processing fees pursuant to section 66022, must bring the action within 120 days of the effective date of the ordinance and cannot wait until the fee is imposed and then rely upon the pay-and-protest procedure described above. *Barratt American Inc.*, 37 Cal. 4th 685 (fees and charges described in Gov't Code sections 66013 and 66014 are not "fees imposed on a development project" and are not subject to the pay-under-protest procedures and limitations periods of Gov't Code § 66020); *N.T. Hill, Inc.*, 72 Cal. App. 4th 977 (a developer must comply with the procedures of Government Code section 66022, rather than Government Code section 66020, when seeking a court ruling that a legislative decision adopting a capacity charge cannot be enforced due to some substantive illegality in the decision-making process). As discussed above, the California Supreme Court has held that a challenge to the facial validity of an ordinance or resolution enacting or increasing development impact fees (as distinct from water and sewer fees or processing charges) is timely if brought within the limitations period for an as-applied challenge to imposition of the impact fees to a specific project. *Travis v. County of Santa Cruz*, 33 Cal. 4th 757 (2004).

The sole remedy upon invalidation of a fee or service charge under section 66022 is a prospective reduction in the amount of the future fee or charge, not a refund. *Barratt American Inc.*, 37 Cal. 4th 685 (remedy upon invalidation of processing fees is a *reduction* of such fees based on revenues in excess of actual cost, not a refund of the excess fees); *Capistrano Beach Water Dist. v. Taj Dev. Corp.*, 72 Cal. App. 4th 524 (1999) (water and sewer fees and capacity charges are not "development impact fees," and no refund remedy is available); *see also* Gov't Code section 66016(a) (if "fees or service charges create revenues in excess of actual cost, those revenues shall be used to reduce the fee or service charge creating the excess").

A facial challenge under Government Code section 66022 must be brought as a validation action pursuant to the procedures described in Code of Civil Procedure section 860 *et seq.* Gov't Code § 66022(b). *Barratt American Inc.*, 37 Cal. 4th 685. The Legislature created the validation procedure to provide finality and protection from attacks for important, usually financial, transactions of public agencies. A validation proceeding is an action *in rem*, in which the court takes jurisdiction over the ordinance or resolution being challenged. Code Civ. Proc. § 860; *see also Bernardi v. City Council*, 54 Cal. App. 4th 426, 439 (1997). The validation statutes provide for publication of the summons in order to serve "all persons interested" in the matter being validated. Code Civ. Proc. § 861.1. The statutes also impose a short, 30-day period within which any party may appeal from the judgment. Code Civ. Proc. § 870(b). Once the appeal period has passed without an appeal being filed, or once an appeal finally is resolved, the judgment is final as against all persons, not merely the parties involved in the action:

> The judgment...shall, notwithstanding any other provision of law,...thereupon become and thereafter be forever binding and conclusive, as to all matters therein adjudicated or which at that time could have been adjudicated, against the agency and against all other persons, and the judgment shall permanently enjoin the institution by any person of any action or proceeding raising any issue as to which the judgment is binding and conclusive.

Code Civ. Proc. § 870(a)

Because a validation proceeding determines the absolute validity or invalidity of the ordinance or resolution at issue, all claims relating to the validity of that ordinance or resolution must be consolidated with the validation proceeding, and a single judgment must be entered in the consolidated action. Code Civ. Proc. § 865; *see also Comm. for Responsible Planning v. City of Indian Wells*, 225 Cal. App. 3d 191, 196 (1990). The resulting judgment then binds all persons not only as to claims that were adjudicated, but as to all claims relating to the enactment that "at that time *could have been* adjudicated." Code Civ. Proc. § 870 (emphasis added)

The validation statutes also expressly allow a party who did not appear in the action, in certain circumstances, to appeal the judgment, and they provide that such a party may, on appeal, challenge the trial court's jurisdiction to enter a validation judgment. Code Civ. Proc. § 870(b). However, at least one court has held that parties who do not answer within the time period specified in the published summons have no right to appear in the action later. *See Green v. Cmty. Redev. Agency*, 96 Cal. App. 3d 491, 494 (1979).

REMEDY

If a public agency does not calculate its development fee correctly, only the unlawful portion of the fee—i.e., the amount that exceeds the estimated reasonable cost of providing the service for which the fee is imposed—need be refunded to the developer. *See Shapell Indus., Inc. v. Governing Bd.*, 1 Cal. App. 4th 218, 241 (1991).

ANTI-SLAPP STATUTE

> SLAPP = Strategic Lawsuit Against Public Participation

In 1992, the Legislature enacted Code of Civil Procedure section 425.16, commonly known as the anti-SLAPP statute. "SLAPP" is an acronym for Strategic Lawsuit Against Public Participation, and the statute frequently has been invoked in actions filed by a land developer against those who object publicly to the development project. *See Wilcox v. Superior Court*, 27 Cal. App. 4th 809 (1994); *see generally*, 4 Witkin, *Calif. Procedure, Pleading*, sections 1017 *et seq.* (5th ed. 2008). SLAPP suits have been described as:

> ..."civil lawsuits...that are aimed at preventing citizens from exercising their political rights or punishing those who have done so." (citations omitted) They are brought, not to vindicate a legal right, but rather to interfere with the defendant's ability to pursue his or her interests. Characteristically, the SLAPP suit lacks merit; it will achieve its objective if it depletes defendant's resources or energy. The aim is not to win the lawsuit but to detract the defendant from his or her objective, which is adverse to the plaintiff.

Church of Scientology v. Wollersheim, 42 Cal. App. 4th 628, 645 (1996); *see also, Wilcox*, 27 Cal. App. 4th at 815-16; *Hull v. Rossi*, 13 Cal. App. 4th 1763, 1769 (1993)

The anti-SLAPP statute is intended to protect those exercising free speech rights. It imposes a procedural burden on plaintiffs who file suits arising from the exercise of a person's right of free speech or right to petition the government. The anti-SLAPP statute allows a defendant who has been unjustly sued to bring a special motion to strike the offending cause of action early in the litigation. To rule on a special motion to strike, the court must first decide whether the defendant has made the threshold showing that the challenged cause of action is one "arising from" protected activity. If so, the court must then move to the second stage, in which it determines whether the plaintiff has demonstrated a probability of prevailing on its claim, and grant the motion to dismiss if the plaintiff has not established a probability of prevailing. E.g., *Oasis West Realty, LLC v. Goldman*, 51 Cal. 4th 811, 819-20 (2011). The statute also provides for an attorneys' fees award to either the plaintiff or defendant.

APPLICATION OF THE ANTI-SLAPP STATUTE TO THE LAND USE CONTEXT

Many SLAPP cases arise in the land use context, or involve issues relevant to land use practice. See *Tuchscher Dev. Enter., Inc. v. San Diego Unified Port Dist.*, 106 Cal. App. 4th 1219 (2003) (developer's action against the port district for inducing breach of contract, based on alleged interference with an agreement between the developer and the city granting the developer exclusive rights to negotiate to develop bayfront property, dismissed as SLAPP suit). Cases involving land use initiatives have been the subject of SLAPP decisions. *Rosenaur v. Scherer*, 88 Cal. App. 4th 260 (2001) (court granted the SLAPP motion of project opponents sued by a property owner whom they accused of being a thief during a campaign regarding the property owner's pro-development initiative); *City of San Diego v. Dunkl*, 86 Cal. App. 4th 384 (2001) (no SLAPP dismissal of the city's lawsuit against initiative proponents regarding the validity of their proposed ballpark redevelopment project initiative).

> Many SLAPP cases arise in the land use context, or involve issues relevant to land use practice.

The statute also has been invoked in a lawsuit between competing developers. In *Ludwig v. Superior Court*, a developer's attacks on a competing mall in nearby Barstow were held subject to the protection of the anti-SLAPP statute. 37 Cal. App. 4th 8 (1995). "The development of the Barstow mall, with potential environmental effects such as increased traffic and impaction on natural drainage, was clearly a matter of public interest." *Id.* at 15.

CEQA issues have also been addressed in SLAPP decisions. The court in *Mission Oaks Ranch, Ltd. v. County of Santa Barbara* applied the SLAPP statute to dismiss a developer's claims against an environmental consultant and a county regarding the county's denial of the developer's project and the accuracy of an EIR's evaluation of the developer's project. 65 Cal. App. 4th 713 (1998). In *Dixon v. Superior Court*, the firm that had performed the archeological testing of the site sued a university professor who opposed the development through a letter-writing campaign. 30 Cal. App. 4th 733 (1994). The court held that the professor's SLAPP motion should have been granted. It explained that because the professor's comments were made during CEQA's required public comment period, they were made in response to a matter of public concern. It further concluded that because CEQA invites public comment, the statements were entitled to absolute immunity, so the archeological testing firm could not establish a probability of prevailing at trial.

Actions to enforce, interpret or invalidate local laws generally are subject to differing court treatments under the anti-SLAPP statute. Although anti-SLAPP protection extends to statements and writings of governmental entities and public officials on matters of public interest and concern (*Vargas v. City of Salinas*, 46 Cal. 4th 1, 17 (2009)), this protection does not extend to decisions and actions by a public agency interpreting or enforcing local laws or policies, even when these are the result of public proceedings. In *USA Waste of California, Inc. v. City of Irwindale*, 184 Cal. App. 4th 53 (2010), the owner of a quarry operation challenged the city's issuance of a notice of violation (NOV) regarding its operations. The city brought a special motion to strike the quarry owner's claims, arguing that its suit arose out of the NOV issued as a result of an "official proceeding authorized by law" under section 425.16(e)(I)(2) of the anti-SLAPP statute. The court disagreed, observing that the thrust of the owner's claim was that the NOV was based on erroneous interpretation of compaction guidelines for the operation, not on the city's exercise of its free speech rights. Suits arising from interpretation or enforcement of laws, it held, were "generally not subject to being stricken under the anti-SLAPP statute." *Id.* at 64. Otherwise, the court reasoned, "efforts to challenge governmental action would be burdened." *Id.*

> NOV = notice of violation

On the other hand, an action addressing the legality of local initiatives was held subject to the anti-SLAPP statute in *Mission Springs Water District v. Verjil*, 218 Cal. App. 4th 892 (2013). In that case, the Mission Springs Water District brought a pre-election challenge against initiative proponents, seeking a declaration that two initiatives the proponents had sponsored were invalid and should be kept off the ballot. The district claimed that the initiatives violated requirements of state law that water and sewer rates be set high enough to cover costs. The plaintiffs brought a special motion to strike under the anti-SLAPP statute. The court first agreed that the district's claim "arose out of" the initiative proponents' protected right to petition. It acknowledged that this holding might hinder pre-election declaratory relief actions regarding the validity of initiatives. It reasoned, however, a plaintiff wishing to bring such a claim was still free to show a probability of prevailing, which it called "not a particularly high hurdle." *Id.* at 907. Because the district had introduced uncontradicted evidence that the rates proposed by the initiative fell below costs, the court found the district had established a probability of prevailing and affirmed an order denying the special motion to strike.

ATTORNEYS' FEES IN LAND USE CASES

Attorneys' fees may be awarded to a prevailing petition in a land-use case under Code of Civil Procedure section 1021.5, which allows for award of attorneys' fees in cases resulting in a public benefit under the private attorney general doctrine. *See Margolin v. Regional Planning Comm'n*, 134 Cal. App. 3d 999 (1982):

> The private attorney general theory recognizes citizens frequently have common interests of significant societal importance, but which do not involve any individual's financial interests to the extent necessary to encourage private litigation to enforce the right. To encourage such suits, attorneys' fees are awarded when a significant public benefit is conferred through litigation pursued by one whose personal stake is insufficient to otherwise encourage the action. Section 1021.5 was not designed as a method for rewarding litigants motivated by their own pecuniary interests who only coincidentally protect the public interest. This last requirement effectuates public policy by focusing "on the financial burdens and incentives involved in bringing the lawsuit."

Beach Colony II Ltd. v. California Coastal Comm'n, 166 Cal. App. 3d 106, 114 (1985) (citations omitted) (fees denied to private developer)

The private attorney general doctrine grants broad discretion to the trial court to award fees, but requires a showing that the litigation:
- Served to vindicate an important public right
- Conferred a significant benefit on the general public or large class of persons
- Imposed a financial burden on the petitioner that was out of proportion to its stake in the matter

Families Unafraid to Uphold Rural El Dorado County v. County Bd. of Supervisors, 79 Cal. App. 4th 505, 511 (2000) (*Families Unafraid II*)

The most controversial factor in this analysis in land use litigation is usually the financial burden criteria. "The issue, in short, is whether the cost of litigation is out of proportion to the litigant's stake in the litigation." *California Licensed Foresters Ass'n v. State Bd. of Forestry*, 30 Cal. App. 4th 562, 574 (1994) (overturning award of fees and holding that the interest of association is to be measured according to the financial interests of the members it was representing); *see Riverwatch v. County of San Diego Dept.*

of *Environmental Health*, 175 Cal. App. 4th 768 (2009) (casino owners claiming fees had no economic interest as approved landfill would not have impacted operations).

The litigant's stake is determined by looking at its financial interest; personal nonpecuniary motives (such as desire to maintain the character of a building or avoid loss of historic resources) may not be used to disqualify the litigant from obtaining fees under section 1021.5. *In re Conservatorship of Whitley*, 50 Cal. 4th 1206 (2010); *see also City of Maywood v. Los Angeles Unified School District*, 208 Cal. App. 4th 362 (2012) (Nonpecuniary motives do not preclude recovery of attorney's fees for either public or private litigants). The financial stake is weighed and balanced against the outcome and probability of success to determine whether an award is appropriate. In *Whitley*, the California Supreme Court laid out the steps courts should follow in determining how to factor a litigant's stake in the proceedings into the appropriate attorneys' fees award:

> The trial court must first fix—or at least estimate—the monetary value of the benefits obtained by the successful litigants themselves.... Once the court is able to put some kind of number on the gains actually attained it must discount these total benefits by some estimate of the probability of success at the time the vital litigation decisions were made which eventually produced the successful outcome.... Thus, if success would yield...the litigant group... an aggregate of $10,000 but there is only a one-third chance of ultimate victory they won't proceed—as a rational matter—unless their litigation costs are substantially less than $3,000.
>
> "After approximating the estimated value of the case at the time the vital litigation decisions were being made, the court must then turn to the costs of the litigation—the legal fees, deposition costs, expert witness fees, etc., which may have been required to bring the case to fruition.... [¶] The final step is to place the estimated value of the case beside the actual cost and make the value judgment whether it is desirable to offer the bounty of a court-awarded fee in order to encourage litigation of the sort involved in this case.... [A] bounty will be appropriate except where the expected value of the litigant's own monetary award exceeds by a substantial margin the actual litigation costs." (*Los Angeles Police Protective League v. City of Los Angeles*, 188 Cal. App. 3d 1, 9-10 (1986).)

In re Conservatorship of Whitley, 50 Cal. 4th at 1215-16

The amount of fees awarded depends upon the reasonableness of the attorneys' hourly rates, the time spent, the probability of a favorable outcome, the type of remedy achieved and the nature of the issues involved. The analysis typically begins with the "lodestar," which is the number of hours reasonably expended, multiplied by a reasonable hourly rate, which is dependent upon the rate prevailing in the community for comparable work. E.g., *Center for Biological Diversity v. County of San Bernardino*, 185 Cal. App. 4th 866, 895-896 (2010). The lodestar may include fees for time spent during the administrative proceedings, to the extent necessary to exhaust administrative remedies. *Edna Valley Watch v. County of San Luis Obispo*, 197 Cal. App. 4th 1312 (2011). The lodestar is then adjusted to account for "a number of factors, including the nature of the litigation, its difficulty, the amount involved, the skill required in its handling, the skill employed, the attention given, the success or failure, and other circumstances in the case." *Center for Biological Diversity*, 185 Cal. App. 4th at 896.

Fees will be limited to those incurred by the petitioner when it obtained its initial victory. Fees incurred in unsuccessful subsequent challenges to an agency's actions regarding the same development project cannot be recovered. *See National Parks & Conser. Ass'n v. County of Riverside*, 81 Cal. App. 4th 234 (2000) (association that recovered fees on a successful challenge to an EIR held not entitled to recover fees on an unsuccessful challenge to the county's return to the writ in the same case). Moreover, the reversal of a judgment under which a petitioner was awarded fees ensures reversal of the fee award. *See Metropolitan Water Dist. v. Imperial Irr. Dist.*, 80 Cal. App. 4th 1403, 1436 (2000) (citing cases and explaining "[t]he parties have also appealed from the trial court's post-judgment order variously awarding and denying costs and attorney's fees. Our reversal of the judgment in favor of defendants requires we vacate the attorney fee and cost award in their favor.").

The fee award may run against not only the respondent agency, but also a developer that was named a real party in interest. In *San Bernardino Valley Audubon Soc'y, Inc. v. County of San Bernardino*, the court required both the county and developer to pay the attorney's fees incurred by the Audubon Society. 155 Cal. App. 3d 738 (1984). The court reasoned that the developer should share in the blame for the county's failure to follow CEQA requirements since the developer was involved in filing the application and should have been monitoring the process. On the other hand, an *amicus curiae* is not liable for attorneys' fees under CCP section 1021.5 where its role is to advocate a position based on its own views of what is legally correct and beneficial to the public rather than out of direct interest in the litigation. *Connerly v. State Personnel Board*, 37 Cal. 4th 1169, 1183 (2006).

The fee award also may run against one public agency in favor of another. In 1993, the Legislature amended Code of Civil Procedure section 1021.5 to provide that "[w]ith respect to actions involving public entities, this section applies to allowances against, but not in favor of, public entities, and no claim shall be required to be filed therefore, unless one or more successful parties and one or more opposing parties are public entities...." *See also City of Hawaiian Gardens v. City of Long Beach*, 61 Cal. App. 4th 1100 (1998) (fees denied to petitioner city because it did not show that its burden of litigation outweighed its interest in the controversy, as the case was tried primarily on the pre-existing administrative record with a brief trial court hearing).

Attorneys' fees are also available to a defendant who prevails in a SLAPP motion, and to a plaintiff who successfully defends against a meritless anti-SLAPP motion. Code Civ. Proc. § 425.16(c).

LEGAL LIABILITY OF LOCAL AGENCIES AND PERSONNEL

Two other laws are sometimes involved in land use cases—the California Tort Claims Act and the Federal Civil Rights Act. The former limits the legal liability of government officials and agencies while the latter renders them liable for violations of federal civil rights.

CALIFORNIA TORT CLAIMS ACT

The California Tort Claims Act (Gov't Code §§ 810–996.6) declares that "[e]xcept as otherwise provided by statute, [a] public entity is not liable for an injury, whether such injury arises out of an act or omission of the public entity or a public employee or any other person." Gov't Code § 815; *see also Cochran v. Herzog Engraving Co.*, 155 Cal. App. 3d 405, 409 (1984).

In *Caldwell v. Montoya*, the California Supreme Court described the basic structure of the Act as comprising the following four general rules:
- Public entities are immune from liability except as provided by statute. Gov't Code § 815(a)
- Public employees are liable for their torts except as otherwise provided by statute. Gov't Code § 820(a)
- Public entities are vicariously liable for the torts of their employees. Gov't Code § 815.2(a)
- Public entities are immune where their employees are immune, except as otherwise provided by statute. Gov't Code § 815.2(b)

10 Cal. 4th 972, 980 (1995)

LIABILITY OF PUBLIC EMPLOYEES AND ENTITIES

Employees. Government Code section 820 provides that a public employee is liable for any injury caused by his or her act or omission "to the same extent as a private person," except as provided by statute. In general, therefore, employees are liable for their own common law torts just as any other individual would be unless shielded by the immunities, discussed below. *See* Gov't Code §§ 820.2–823.

Entities. The Tort Claims Act provides four principal avenues through which a public entity may be held liable for its actions. These are vicarious liability (Gov't Code § 815.2(a)), liability for independent contractors (Gov't Code § 815.4), liability for breach of a mandatory duty imposed pursuant to enactment (Gov't Code § 815.6), and dangerous condition liability (Gov't Code § 835). Although all four types of liability are equally actionable, breach of mandatory duty is the claim most likely to be asserted in the land use context. The Act describes the mandatory duty theory of liability as follows:

> Where a public entity is under a mandatory duty imposed by an enactment that is designed to protect against the risk of a particular kind of injury, the public entity is liable for an injury of that kind proximately caused by its failure to discharge the duty unless the public entity establishes that it exercised reasonable diligence to discharge the duty.

Gov't Code § 815.6

An "enactment" is defined as "a constitutional provision, statute, charter provision, ordinance or regulation." Gov't Code § 810.6. When alleging a cause of action for breach of a mandatory duty, a claimant must specifically identify the enactment alleged to create the mandatory duty. *Lehto v. City of Oxnard*, 171 Cal. App. 3d 285, 292 (1985).

Whether an enactment is "designed to protect against the risk of a particular kind of injury" is determined under a three-part test. To impose liability:
- The enactment must impose a mandatory, not discretionary, duty
- The Legislature must have intended that the statute protect against the risk of the kind of injury suffered by the claimant, and
- The breach of the mandatory duty must be a proximate cause of the injury

State of California v. Superior Court (Perry), 150 Cal. App. 3d 848, 854 (1984)

In order to be considered a mandatory duty, the enactment must be obligatory and must require that a particular action be taken. *Haggis v. City of Los Angeles*, 22 Cal.

> An "enactment" is defined as "a constitutional provision, statute, charter provision, ordinance or regulation."

4th 490, 498 (2000). For cases discussing whether a particular enactment imposes a mandatory duty, see *California Government Tort Liability Practice*, section 9.25 *et seq.* (Cal. CEB, 4th ed. 2012).

IMMUNITY OF PUBLIC EMPLOYEES AND ENTITIES

For purposes of land use practice, the most relevant immunity conferred under the Act is that involving discretionary acts and omissions. Under Government Code section 820.2, "[e]xcept as otherwise provided by statute, a public employee is not liable for an injury resulting from his act or omission where the act or omission was the result of the exercise of the discretion vested in him, whether or not such discretion be abused." See *Caldwell v. Montoya*, 10 Cal. 4th 972, 988 (1995) (school board members immune against claims of the terminated superintendent as the decision to replace the school district's highest official was a basic governmental policy decision and a "quintessential discretionary act of government"). Under Government Code section 815.2(b), public entities have the same immunity for discretionary acts and omissions as public employees.

There are a variety of factors to consider when determining whether a public employee or entity has exercised a "discretionary" function that would be eligible for immunity if challenged. The two most important factors are:

- **Statutory provisions.** When statutory provisions entrust authority and discretion to a branch of government, a court is likely to find that actions taken under those statutes are subject to discretionary immunity. See *Leyva v. Nielsen*, 83 Cal. App. 4th 1061, 1066–67 (2000) (parole board decision to deny parole immunized due to statutory powers); and

- **Distinction between planning and operational functions.** In *Johnson v. State*, which involved a suit by a foster mother injured by a violent youth placed into her care without a warning, the court recognized a distinction between the planning and operational functions of government. 69 Cal. 2d 782, 793 (1968). The planning function, as described by the court, involves a basic, conscious policy decision, in which an employee can show a deliberate balancing of risks and objectives within the policymaking arena of government. *Id.* at 795. Such decisions are subject to discretionary immunity. In the case at bar, the court determined the decision to place the youth into parole was a policy decision. However, the decision of whether or not to warn the foster mother of the youth's violent history, was not discretionary, but merely an implementing or "operational" decision, and thus not subject to immunity. *Id.* at 794. See also *Barner v. Leeds*, 24 Cal. 4th 676, 714 (2000) (original decision to represent a criminal defendant immunized as a basic policy decision but the services of a public defender in actual representation of a criminal defendant are operational as merely implementing the initial decision to represent, and thus are not immunized).

Attorney's fees may be awarded to the prevailing party in a civil action under the Tort Claims Act. *See* Gov't Code § 800. For an in-depth discussion of public employee and entity liability and immunity under the Tort Claims Act, see *California Government Tort Liability Practice* (Cal. CEB, 4th ed. 2012).

FEDERAL CIVIL RIGHTS ACT

The Federal Civil Rights Act of 1871 (42 U.S.C. § 1983) authorizes a court to grant relief when an individual's constitutional or other federally protected rights have been violated by a state or local official or other person acting under color of state law. The basic purpose of section 1983 is to allow redress for injuries inflicted by an official or other person acting on behalf of the government. Two basic questions arise under section 1983: (1) when does a deprivation of federal rights occur under color of state law; and (2) who is a person subject to suit?

> The basic purpose of section 1983 is to allow redress for injuries inflicted by an official or other person acting on behalf of the government.

COLOR OF LAW

A claim for relief under section 1983 only may be asserted against persons who acted under color of state law. As a general rule, the official conduct of state and local officials is almost always found to have occurred under color of state law. *See* Martin A. Schwartz, *Section 1983 Litigation* (4th ed. 2011) § 5.05[A]; *see also United States v. Classic*, 313 U.S. 299, 326 (1941) ("Misuse of power, possessed by virtue of state law and made possible only because the wrongdoer is clothed with the authority of state law, is action taken 'under color of' state law.").

Because local agencies, including cities and counties, are authorized or created by state law and endowed with police powers and/or other authority (see Cal. Const. art. XI), anyone acting under local laws enacted pursuant to those grants of authority is acting under color of state law for purposes of section 1983. *See generally Lugar v. Edmondson Oil Co.*, 457 U.S. 922, 929-34 (1982) (discusses approach to determining whether action is taken under color of state law).

TREATMENT OF PERSONS AND PUBLIC ENTITIES UNDER SECTION 1983: MUNICIPAL LIABILITY AND LEGISLATIVE IMMUNITY

Most relevant in the land use context, local governments, municipal corporations, school boards, special assessment districts, and their agents acting under color of "state" law (which may encompass implementation or enforcement of a municipal or local law, regulation, policy or custom) are "persons" subject to liability under section 1983. *Monell v. Dept. of Social Servs.*, 436 U.S. 658, 690-91 (1978). This liability does not arise under a theory of respondeat superior, but rather "when execution of a government's policy or custom, whether made by its lawmakers or by those whose edicts or acts may fairly be said to represent official policy, inflicts the injury." *Id.* at 694. In *Brandon v. Holt*, the Court held that a suit against a municipal official acting in his official capacity is the same as a suit against the municipal entity. 469 U.S. 464, 471-72 (1985). A city itself may also be held liable under section 1983 in some instances for failure to comply with land use laws. *See Sunset Drive Corp. v. City of Redlands*, 73 Cal. App. 4th 215, 225 (1999) (developer's allegations that a city had acted arbitrarily in failing to complete and certify an EIR within one year, as required by CEQA, stated a valid claim for damages under section 1983).

Liability of individual officials is limited substantially, however, by the doctrine of legislative immunity. Of particular relevance to land use decisions is the holding of *Tenney v. Brandhove*, in which the United States Supreme Court held that officials acting in a legislative capacity are absolutely immune from section 1983 liability for official conduct within "the sphere of legitimate legislative activity." 341 U.S. 367, 376 (1951). This absolute legislative immunity applies regardless of the official's motive. *Id.* at 377; *see also Bogan v. Scott-Harris*, 523 U.S. 44, 54 (1998) (city officials were immune from a claim that their legislative act of eliminating a city agency violated the Civil Rights Act, regardless of their subjective motivation); *Chappell v. Robbins*, 73 F. 3d 918,

921 (9th Cir. 1996) (legislator convicted of accepting bribes for sponsoring and voting for legislation was entitled to legislative immunity). Local legislators also are protected by absolute legislative immunity. *See Cinevision Corp. v. City of Burbank*, 745 F. 2d 560, 577 (9th Cir. 1984); *Kuzinich v. Santa Clara*, 689 F. 2d 1345, 1349-50 (9th Cir. 1982). Absolute legislative immunity protects individual legislators and may not be asserted by municipal entities sued under section 1983. *See Schwartz, supra* at § 7.02.

By contrast, no immunity exists where officials are acting in an administrative rather than a legislative capacity. In *Kaahumanu v. County of Maui*, commercial wedding arrangers filed a section 1983 suit against the Maui County Council for denying a conditional use permit for a commercial wedding business on beach-front residential property. 315 F. 3d 1215, 1223-24 (9th Cir. 2003). The councilmembers argued they were entitled to absolute legislative immunity under section 1983 because the use permit was formally legislative in character. *Id.* at 1223. In ruling against the county council, the court held that the decision to deny the use permit was administrative and not legislative because it was based on the individual circumstances of the case and did not effectuate policy or create a binding rule of conduct. *Id.* at 122. Accordingly, the councilmembers were not entitled to absolute legislative immunity for the use permit denial under section 1983.

> **Legislative immunity does not apply to actions merely related to a legislative act.**

Legislative immunity also does not apply to actions merely related to a legislative act. *See San Pedro Hotel Co. v. City of Los Angeles*, 159 F. 3d 470, 478 fn. 11 (9th Cir. 1998) (legislative immunity does not extend to a retaliation claim against a council member under the federal Fair Housing Act, even though the alleged retaliation grew out of a legislative act).

Attorneys' fees may be awarded to a plaintiff under section 1983, and in narrow circumstances, to the defendant. *See* 42 U.S.C. § 1988.

For an in-depth discussion of legislative immunity and municipal liability, along with other relevant provisions of the Federal Civil Rights Act, *see Schwartz, supra; see also California Government Tort Liability Practice, Federal Civil Rights Act*, ch. 13 (Cal. CEB, 4th ed. 2012).

For further discussion of civil rights actions, in the context of takings claims, see chapter 11 (Takings).

Glossary

Portions of this glossary were derived from the "Quick List," prepared by the staff of the Senate Local Government Committee, and the *Planners Pocket Guide* published by the League of California Cities.

abandonment
A cessation of the use of the property by the owner with the intention neither of transferring rights to another owner nor resuming use of the property.

abatement
The method of reducing the degree and intensity of a problem or pollution.

abutting
Having property or zone district boundaries in common; e.g., two lots abut if they have property lines in common.

access
A way of approaching or entering a property. In zoning and subdivision regulations, a lot of record usually is required to have direct access to a public street or highway or to a private street meeting public standards. In the context of land use controls, access includes ingress, the right to enter, and egress, the right to leave.

accessory building or use
An activity or structure on a property that is incidental and subordinate to the main use.

adaptive reuse
The development of a new use for an older building. Often used in reference to a proposal to convert buildings of historic significance to a use different from the original intended use.

Administrative Procedures Act
The procedures for state departments to adopt their administrative regulations. Gov't Code § 11340 *et seq.*

advisory election
Local officials can put nonbinding questions on local ballots. Elec. Code § 9603.

agricultural conservation easement
Landowners and local officials can voluntarily restrict land to an agricultural use. Pub. Res Code § 10260 *et seq.* Also see, "conservation easement" and "open space easement."

air rights
The rights to the space above a property, for development, usually for a dissimilar use.

Airport Land Use Commission
Every county with a public use airport has an ALUC that must adopt binding land use plans. Pub. Util. Code § 21670 *et seq.*

Alquist-Priolo Earthquake Fault Zoning Act
Local officials must adopt earthquake fault zoning, based on state maps. Pub. Res. Code § 2621 *et seq.*

ambient air
The unconfined outside atmosphere.

amendment, zoning (rezoning)
An amendment to or a change in the zoning ordinance.

amortization
The process by which nonconforming uses and structures must be discontinued or made to conform to requirements of the ordinance at the end of a specified period of time.

annexation
The inclusion of a land area into an existing city or special district with a resulting change in the boundaries of that local agency.

anti-NIMBY law
Cities and counties must approve certain housing developments, even if neighbors object. Gov't Code § 65589.5. In 2006, the title of the anti-NIMBY law was changed to the "Housing Accountability Act."

appeal
Request that another, usually higher, authority review or reconsider a decision.

assessed valuation
The value at which property is appraised for tax purposes.

Bagley-Keene Open Meeting Law
The open meeting law for state agencies, similar to the Brown Act. Gov't Code § 11120 *et seq.*

base map
A map having sufficient points of reference, such as state, county or municipal boundary lines, streets, easements, and other selected physical features to allow the plotting of other data.

BCDC (San Francisco Bay Conservation and Development Commission)
The state commission that plans and regulates land use under and around the San Francisco Bay. Gov't Code § 66600 *et seq.*

benefit (special) assessment
Involuntary charge on property owners to pay for public works that directly benefit property.

biota
All the species of plants and animals occurring within a certain area.

blighted area
In redevelopment law, predominately urbanized area prevalently characterized by the conditions contained in Health and Safety Code section 33031.

Board of Zoning Adjustment
A local body that considers requests for variances, i.e., deviations from normal zoning ordinances.

bond
Most local bonds require voter approval or a property owner's approval; e.g., general obligation bonds for cities, counties, and special districts need two-thirds voter approval. Cal. Const. Art. XVI, § 18(a); general obligation bonds for school districts require 55 percent voter approval. Cal. Const. Art. XVI, § 18(b); revenue bonds require majority-voter approval. Gov't Code § 54300 *et seq.*; assessment bonds require property owner's approval in a weighted ballot election. Cal. Const. Art. XIII D, § 4 and Gov't Code § 53753.

bond oversight
Local officials must issue annual reports on how they spend bond funds. Gov't Code § 53410 et seq.

Bradley-Burns Uniform Local Sales and Use Tax Law
Counties and cities levy sales taxes for general purposes. Rev. & Tax. Code § 7200 et seq.

Brown Act
Open meeting law for local governments. Gov't Code § 54950 et seq.

buffer zone
A strip of land zoned to protect one type of land use from another with which it is incompatible.

building coverage
The amount of land covered or permitted to be covered by a building, usually measured in terms of percentage of a lot, or floor area ratio.

building envelope
The space remaining on a site for structures after building setbacks, height limits, and bulk requirements are met.

California Environmental Quality Act
The statute requiring public agencies to identify and consider the environmental effects of a development project. Pub. Res. Code § 21000 et seq.

capital improvement program
A governmental budget that schedules the construction of public facilities to fit its fiscal capability into the future. A planning commission reviews the capital improvement program, thereby linking planning to the annual budgeting process.

census tract
A small portion of a populated area where data is collected for statistical analysis.

Central Business District
A major commercial and business area usually located near the center of the community that has historically served as the city's primary commercial district.

CEQA Guidelines
The state regulations that interpret the California Environmental Quality Act. 14 Cal. Code Reg. § 15000 et seq.

certificate of compliance
This term has three distinctly different meanings: (1) it is commonly used synonymously with a zoning permit in which an official certifies that the plans for a proposed use conform with the zoning ordinance; (2) certificate issued pursuant to Map Act which states that the division of property is in compliance with the State Subdivision Map Act and local subdivision ordinances; (3) the term may also mean an enforcement device that, in reference to a certain class of structure (usually multiple-family dwellings), incorporates in one document an indication of conformance, or lack thereof, with the several municipal codes—zoning, building, housing, occupancy—that may apply to a specific property.

certificate of occupancy
Official certification that the premises conforms to provisions of the zoning ordinance (and building code) and may be used or occupied. Such a certificate is granted for new construction or for alteration or additions to an existing structure. Unless such a certificate is issued, a structure cannot be occupied.

charter city
A city incorporated under its own charter rather than under the general laws of the state. Charter cities have broader powers than do general law cities in matters of municipal affairs. Cal. Const. Art. XI, § 3 and § 5; Gov't Code § 34400 et seq. and § 34450 et seq.

city council district
Voters can elect city council members "by divisions" or "from divisions." Gov't Code § 34870 et seq.

city council vacancy
A vacancy on a city council is filled by appointment or election. Gov't Code § 1770 and § 36513.

city ordinance
Procedures for adopting city ordinances and penalties for violations. Gov't Code § 36900 et seq.

Clean Air Act
A federal act establishing national air quality standards.

Coastal Act
State law requires special planning and permits for development in the coastal zone. Pub. Res. Code § 30000 et seq.

Coastal Commission
State agency that reviews development plans within the Coastal Zone according to the California Coastal Act of 1976.

common open space
Land within or related to a development, not individually owned or dedicated for public use, that is designed and intended for the common use or enjoyment of the development's residents.

common ownership
Ownership by one or more individuals of two or more contiguous parcels of property in any form of ownership.

Community Facilities District (Mello-Roos)
Local agencies can levy special taxes to pay for public works and some public services. Gov't Code § 53311 et seq.

Community Redevelopment Law (redevelopment)
Redevelopment agencies use tax increment revenue and eminent domain in blighted areas. Health & Safety Code § 33000 et seq.

comprehensive plan
See general plan.

condemnation
The exercise by a governmental agency of the right of eminent domain to acquire property.

conditional rezoning
The attachment of special conditions to a rezoning that are not spelled out in the text of the zoning ordinance.

conditional use permit (special use permit)
Permit allowing a use under specified conditions which assure that the use will not be detrimental to the public health, safety, and welfare and will not impair the integrity and character of the zoned district.

condominium
A dwelling unit in a residential development (or space in an office or commercial project) that is under a legal arrangement specifying that the unit is individually owned but the common areas are owned, controlled, and maintained through an organization consisting of all the individual owners.

condominium association
The community association that administers and maintains the common property and common elements of a condominium.

conflict of interest
Public officials may not participate in decisions in which they have a financial interest. Gov't Code § 1090 et seq. and § 87100 et seq.; 2 Cal. Code Reg. § 18700.

conservation easement
Landowners can grant an easement to preserve open space and prohibit future or additional development. Civ. Code § 815 et seq.

contract city ("Gonsalves Act")
A city can contract with the county for municipal services. Gov't Code § 51350.

contracts and bidding
State law spells out bidding and contract procedures for cities, counties, and special districts. See city (Pub. Cont. Code § 20160 et seq.); county (Pub. Cont. Code § 20120 et seq.

and § 20150 et seq.); and district (chart at Pub. Cont. Code § 20100 et seq.).

Cortese-Knox-Hertzberg Local Government Reorganization Act
State law that governs city and special district boundaries; and also creates a LAFCO in every county. Gov't Code § 56000 et seq.

Council of Government
A regional planning agency between counties and cities that prepares regional plans primarily concerned with transportation planning and housing. Gov't Code § 6500 et seq.

county charter
A county can adopt and revise its charter giving it limited local autonomy. Cal. Const. Art. XI § 4; Gov't Code § 23700 et seq.

county formation
Procedures for forming a new county. Gov't Code § 23300 et seq.

county officers, named and classified
State law spells out the names and duties of county officers. Gov't Code § 24000 et seq. and § 24300 et seq.

county ordinance
Procedures for adopting county ordinances and penalties for violations. Gov't Code § 25120 et seq.

covenants, conditions, and restrictions (CC&Rs)
The requirements and limitations placed on each lot of a subdivision or condominium project intended to protect the individual property as well as the general public regarding placement, construction, appearance, and maintenance of buildings and common areas.

culvert
Drain, ditch, or conduit not incorporated in a closed system that carries drainage water under a driveway, roadway, railroad, pedestrian walk, or public way.

cut
A portion of land surface or area from which earth is removed by excavation; also, the depth below the original ground surface.

Davis-Stirling Common Interest Development Act
State law that governs common interest developments (homeowners' associations). Civ. Code § 1350 et seq.

decibel (dB)
Unit of sound pressure level that is used to express noise level.

dedication
Action by a property owner that turns over private land for a public use, and its acceptance for such use by the government agency in charge of the public function for which it will be used. Dedications for streets, parks, school sites, or other public uses are often made conditions for approval of a development.

dedication, payment in lieu of
Cash payment required from a property developer as a substitute for a dedication of land.

deed restriction
A private legal restriction on the use of land that is contained in the deed to the property or otherwise formally recorded.

demolition permit
A permit a local authority issues to allow a building or structure to be razed.

density
The average number of families, persons, or housing units per unit of land; usually density is expressed "per acre." Gross density typically includes the area necessary for streets, schools, and parks. Net density does not typically include land for public facilities.

density bonus
Financial incentive to a developer that builds affordable housing. Gov't Code § 65915 et seq.

density transfer
Process that permits unused allowable densities in one area to be used in another area. Where density transfer is permitted, the average density over an area would remain constant, but allow for internal variations.

density zoning
Device for averaging residential density over an entire parcel and placing no restrictions on lot size or dwelling type. Under this approach, any type of dwelling is permitted, from a detached house to an apartment anywhere on the site, so long as total density does not exceed the maximum permitted. The only development standards imposed are: distance between buildings, distance between facing windows, amount of parking, and minimum open space. Conventional setback and lot-size requirements are dropped.

detention basin (pond)
An open storage pond for the temporary storage of stormwater runoff.

developer fee or development impact fee
Counties and cities can charge a developer an impact fee to pay for public facilities. Gov't Code § 66000 et seq.

development agreement
An agreement adopted by ordinance between a developer and a city or county establishing the conditions under which a particular development may occur. The local government "freezes" the regulations applicable to the site for an agreed-upon period prior to actual development to allow preparation and approval of plans. Gov't Code § 65864 et seq.

development rights
Broad range of less-than-fee-simple ownership interests, mainly referring to easements. The property owner would keep title but agree to continue using the land as it had been used in the past, with the right to develop resting with the holder of the development rights. Such rights usually are expressed in terms of the density allowed under existing zoning.

development timing or development phasing
Rate and geographic sequence of the development of a project.

district
Section of a city or county designated in the zoning ordinance text and usually delineated on the zoning map within which certain zoning or development regulations apply.

downzoning
Change in the zoning classification of land to one permitting development that is less intensive or dense, such as from multi- to single-family or from commercial to residential. A change in the opposite direction is called upzoning.

due process
Generally, a requirement that legal proceedings be carried out in accordance with established rules and principles. Procedural due process assures that all parties to a proceeding are treated fairly and equally; citizens have a right to have their views heard; necessary information is available for informed opinions to be developed; conflicts of interest are avoided; and, generally, the appearance, as well as the fact of fairness exists.

easement
The portion of a property for which access or use is allowed by a person or agency other than the owner.

effluent
Discharge of pollutants, with or without treatment, into the environment.

eminent domain
Legal right of public entities to acquire or take private property for public use or public purpose upon paying just compensation and due process to the owner. Cal. Const. Art. I, § 19; Code Civ. Proc. § 1230.010 et seq.

emission standard
Maximum amount of a pollutant legally permitted to be discharged from a single source, either mobile or stationary.

encroachment
Any obstruction or protrusion into a right of way or adjacent property, whether on the land or above it.

environmental impact report
An EIR is the public document used by government agencies pursuant to CEQA that analyzes the significant environmental effects of a proposed project, compares alternatives and discusses possible methods to reduce or avoid the environmental impacts. When no significant environmental impact will result, a "negative declaration" is issued.

environmental impact statement
Environmental impact document prepared in accordance with the National Environmental Policy Act.

ethics training
Elected and key appointed officials must take biennial ethics training courses. Gov't Code § 53234 et seq.

exclusionary zoning
Zoning regulations that result in the exclusion of low- and moderate-income or minority persons from a community.

Fair Political Practices Commission
The state commission that administers the Political Reform Act. Gov't Code § 81000 et seq. and § 83100 et seq.

fair share housing plan
Plan designed to promote equitable distribution of low- and moderate-income housing opportunities among all the communities in a region.

final subdivision map
Map of an approved subdivision that is recorded, usually showing surveyed lot lines, street rights-of-way, easements, monuments, and distances, angles, and bearings pertaining to the exact dimensions of all parcels, street lines, etc.

findings
Specific facts and required statements serving as the legal basis for certain actions by the local decision-making body.

fire protection district
Special district that provides fire protection and other emergency services. Health & Safety Code § 13800 et seq.

flood plain
The channel and the adjoining area of a natural stream or river that is susceptible to flooding.

floor area, gross
The sum of the gross horizontal areas of all the floors of a building measured from the exterior face of exterior walls, or from the center line of a wall separating two buildings, but not including interior parking spaces, loading space for motor vehicles, or any space where the floor-to-ceiling height is less than six feet.

floor area ratio
Gross floor area of all buildings on a lot divided by the lot area.

form-based zoning
Zoning regulations emphasizing design and physical form of buildings, streetscapes and public places with less emphasis on allowed uses inside buildings.

general law city
Most cities rely on state laws to spell out their governance structure and duties. Gov't Code § 36501 et seq.

general plan
Required legal document adopted by the local legislative body to establish the policies of a city or county regarding its jurisdiction and long-term development in the form of a map and accompanying textual elements. Sometimes called a comprehensive plan or master plan, it is the constitution for development. Gov't Code § 65300 et seq.

general plan guidelines
OPR's advisory guidelines on preparing a general plan. Gov't Code § 65040.2.

general tax
General tax revenues are used for general purposes and require approval by a majority of the voters. Cal. Const. Art. XIII C, § 2; Gov't Code § 53720 et seq.

geologic hazard abatement district
District that finances the prevention, mitigation, abatement, or control of geologic hazards. Pub. Res Code § 26500 et seq.

grade
The rate of rise or descent of a sloping surface, usually expressed in degrees or in a percentage calculated by the number of feet of rise or drop per 100-foot horizontal distance.

granny unit
A dwelling unit for the sole occupancy of one or two adults, 62 years or older, comprising less than 30 percent of the existing primary living area or 1,200 square feet. Gov't Code § 65852.1.

gross leasable area
Total floor area for which a tenant pays rent that is designed for that tenant's occupancy and exclusive use.

ground coverage
The amount of land covered or permitted to be covered by a building, usually measured in terms of percentage of a lot.

groundwater
Supply of freshwater under the earth's surface in an aquifer or soil that forms the natural reservoir for potable water.

group care facility
Facility or dwelling unit housing persons unrelated by blood or marriage that provides care beyond simply lodging. Such facilities may include halfway houses; recovery homes; and homes for orphans, foster children, the elderly, battered children, and women, etc.

highest and best use
The use of a property that will bring to its owners the greatest profit.

home occupation
Any activity a resident conducts for monetary gain that is an accessory use in the resident's dwelling unit.

homeowner association
Nonprofit organization representing the particular interests of homeowners. Homeowner associations normally operate under recorded legal agreements attached to ownership of land.

housing element
Part of a general plan that spells out housing data, goals, and implementation programs. Gov't Code § 65580 et seq.

hydrology
A branch of science that deals with the properties, distribution, and circulation of water and snow.

impervious surface
Any material that prevents absorption of water into previously undeveloped land.

incentive zoning
The granting by local authority of additional development capacity in exchange for the developer's provision of a public benefit or amenity.

inclusionary zoning
A zoning policy and program to require the provision of affordable housing as part of new residential development.

infill development
Development of new housing or other buildings on scattered vacant sites in a built-up area.

infrastructure
Physical facilities and services needed to sustain industry, residential and commercial activities, such as streets, sewers, utilities, etc.

infrastructure finance
State law provides several ways for local governments to pay for public works.

infrastructure financing district
District that uses property tax increment revenues to pay for public works in nonblighted areas. Gov't Code § 53395 et seq.

initial study
Under CEQA, a preliminary analysis of the potential environmental impacts of a proposed project. Where the lead agency finds that the project may individually or cumulatively have a significant effect on the environment, an EIR must be prepared. The potential environmental impacts identified in the initial study become the focus of the EIR.

initiative
A ballot measure used to enact new legislation. In California, city and county initiative measures may be placed on the ballot by petition of the voters or action of the legislative body.

interim zoning development control
Device to freeze or severely restrict development of an area for a short period, during which a comprehensive plan or new land use regulations are prepared.

inverse condemnation
The effective taking or reduction in value of a property as a result of public action, in contrast to a direct taking through eminent domain.

joint powers agreement, joint powers agency
Public agencies can enter into agreements to jointly exercise any common power. Gov't Code § 6500 et seq.

just compensation
The appropriate payment made to a private property owner by an agency with power of eminent domain when the private property is taken for public use.

Landscaping and Lighting Act of 1972
Local officials can charge a benefit assessment to pay for public works and public services. Sts. & High. Code § 22500 et seq.

lead agency
Public agency with the principal responsibility for carrying out or approving a project. Under CEQA, the lead agency is also responsible for preparing and certifying an adequate EIR.

local agency formation commission
Commission in each county that regulates annexations, detachments, and incorporations. Gov't Code § 56000 et seq.

lot, coverage
Portion of a lot covered by buildings and structures.

lot line, front
The frontage or front of a lot is usually defined as the side nearest the street. The definition used is important because it may affect yard requirements.

lot line, rear
Ordinarily that line of a lot that is opposite and farthest from the front lot line. In triangular or other odd-shaped lots, the planning commission or other public body with jurisdiction may need to define the rear lot line.

lot line, side
Any lot line other than ones for the front or rear of a property.

lot of record
Lot that is part of a subdivision or a parcel of land that has been recorded, usually at a county recorder's office where property tax records are kept.

lot split
See parcel map.

lot, through (or double frontage)
Lot abutting on two parallel or approximately parallel streets.

low-income housing
Housing that is economically feasible for persons whose income level is categorized as low within the standards set by the U.S. Department of Housing and Urban Development or the appropriate state housing agency.

Mello-Roos Community Facilities Act (Mello-Roos Act)
Local agencies can levy special taxes to pay for public works and some public services. See also "community facilities district." Gov't Code § 53311 et seq.

metes and bounds
System of describing or identifying land using measure (metes) and direction (bounds) from an identifiable point of reference such as a monument or other marker, the corner of intersecting streets, or, in rural areas, a tree or other permanent feature.

Mills Act (historic preservation)
An owner can contract to preserve an historic property and thereby obtain a lower property tax assessment. Gov't Code § 50280 et seq.; Rev. & Tax. Code § 439.

minor land division
A division of contiguous property into four or fewer lots.

mitigated negative declaration
Under CEQA, a negative declaration that includes measures needed to mitigate or avoid a project's significant effects on the environment.

mitigation
Actions, improvements, features, modifications, or requirements intended to eliminate or reduce the significant environmental effects of a project.

mitigation monitoring program
Program adopted as part of a mitigated negative declaration or environmental impact report that establishes a reporting system designed to ensure compliance with the conditions adopted as part of the MND or EIR during project implementation.

mixed use development
Development of a tract of land or building with two or more different uses.

mixed use zoning
Zoning that permits a combination of usually separated uses within a single development. Many planned unit development ordinances permit combinations of various residential densities and commercial uses.

mobile home
A structure transportable in one or more sections that is at least 8 feet in width and 32 feet in length, built on a permanent chassis, and designed for use as a dwelling unit, with or without a permanent foundation, when connected to the required utilities.

moderate-income housing
Housing that is economically feasible for families whose income level is categorized as moderate within the standards set by the U.S. Department of Housing and Urban Development or the appropriate state housing agency.

moratorium
In planning, a temporary freeze or restriction on all new development pending completion and adoption of certain planning or zoning ordinance requirements, e.g., general plan, zoning ordinance amendment, sewer line installations, or growth management programs.

multiple use
Harmonious use of the land for more than one purpose; not necessarily the combination of uses that will yield the highest economic return, e.g., a mix of residential and commercial development in the same area.

National Environmental Policy Act
Enacted in 1969, NEPA contains a declaration of policy expressing a commitment to environmental values and a requirement that federal agencies prepare an environmental impact statement for any project that may adversely affect the environment.

negative declaration
Under CEQA, a statement that describes why a project will not have a significant adverse effect on the environment, and that may propose measures to avoid all possible adverse effects.

net area of lot (net acreage)
The area of the lot excluding those features or areas that the development ordinance excludes from the calculations.

nonconforming lot
Lot that does not meet current zoning requirements.

nonconforming structure or building
Building that does not meet current zoning requirements.

nonconforming use
Land use that does not meet current zoning requirements.

notice of completion
A notice issued and properly filed by the lead agency upon completion of a draft EIR. The NOC contains a description of the project and its location, an address where copies of the draft EIR are available, and the period during which comments will be received on the draft EIR.

notice of determination
A notice issued and properly filed by an agency upon its approval of a project subject to CEQA regulation indicating whether the project will have a significant effect on the environment and whether an EIR has been prepared. (The NOD is filed with the State Secretary of Resources if the lead agency is a state agency and with the county clerk if the lead agency is a local agency.)

notice of preparation
A notice sent by a lead agency announcing its intention to prepare an EIR for a proposed project, inviting responsible and trustee agencies and other interested parties to state their concerns regarding potential impacts. The responses are then used to further define the EIR's scope.

occupancy permit
Permit needed for a new tenant to move into a commercial or industrial building.

Office of Planning and Research
Part of the Office of the Governor that works on land use planning and environmental quality. Gov't Code § 65025 *et seq.*

off-site improvement
Improvement or facility that may be required of a project—such as the installation of streets, curbs, gutters, sidewalks, street trees, etc., that are located adjacent to publicly-owned property.

open space easement
A landowner can grant an easement to protect open space and prohibit development. *See also* "conservation easement." Gov't Code § 51070 *et seq.*

ordinance
Law adopted by a city council or board of supervisors. *See* Gov't Code § 36900 *et seq.* (cities); Gov't Code § 25120 *et seq.* (counties).

overlay zone
Set of zoning requirements in addition to those of the underlying district. Developments within an overlay zone must conform to the requirements of both zones or the more restrictive one.

parcel
Lot, or contiguous group of lots in single ownership or under single control, and usually considered a unit for purposes of development.

parcel map
A subdivision map that divides a parcel into four or fewer lots.

parcel tax (special tax)
A special tax levied by local governments with two-thirds voter approval. Gov't Code § 50075 *et seq.*

partial taking
Condemnation of part of a property.

payment in lieu
Payment of cash that is authorized in subdivision regulations when requirements for mandatory dedication of land cannot be met because of the site's physical conditions or other reasons.

peak-hour traffic
The largest number of vehicles passing over a designated section of a street during the busiest one-hour period of a 24-hour period.

performance standard
Minimum requirement or maximum allowable limit on the effects or characteristics of a use, usually written in the form of regulatory language. Performance standards in zoning might describe allowable uses with respect to smoke, odor, noise, heat, vibration, glare, traffic generation, visual impact, etc., instead of the more traditional classifications of "light" or "heavy" uses.

Permit Streamlining Act
Public agencies must meet statutory deadlines for decisions on development projects. Gov't Code § 65920 *et seq.*

permitted use
Use specifically authorized in a particular zoning district, in contrast to a conditional use that is authorized only if certain requirements are met and after review and approval by the appropriate public agency.

phased development control (phased control)
Term that refers to programs or techniques to guide the timing and sequence of development. In one form of phased zoning, land designated for residential use but presently undeveloped could receive permission to subdivide only if the developer can show the availability of adequate public services such as sewers, drainage, park sites, and roads.

planned development (P-D)
Self-contained development, often with a mixture of land uses and densities, in which the subdivision and zoning controls are applied to the project as a whole rather than to individual lots. Commercial and even industrial uses are combined with different types of residential uses. A planned development with only residential uses is referred to as a planned residential development (PR-D).

planned-unit development
Land use zoning that allows for adoption of a set of development standards specific to a particular project. PUD zones usually do not contain the kind of detailed development standards that are established when proposals are being considered and subsequently adopted by ordinance upon project approval.

Planning Commission
The body, appointed by the city council or board of supervisors, charged with developing the general plan, formulating and administering the zoning map and ordinance, and reviewing development applications.

Planning Director
A planning department's chief administrator.

plat
(1) A map representing a tract of land, showing the boundaries and location of individual properties and streets; (2) a map of a subdivision or site plan.

plot
Often an indefinite term usually referring to a piece of usable property; often used

synonymously with parcel or site, and mistakenly, to mean plat.

point source
A stationary source of a large individual emission, generally industrial in nature; for example, a waste discharge pipe or a waste dump.

police power
The authority of government to exercise controls to protect the public's health, safety, and general welfare. Cal. Const. Art. XI, § 7.

Political Reform Act of 1974
Prohibits a public official from having an economic conflict of interest. Gov't Code § 81000 et seq.

PPM
Parts per million.

prezoning
The zoning of unincorporated territory by a city before annexation. Gov't Code § 65859.

property tax allocation
Allocation of property tax revenue to local governments and schools. Revenue and Taxation Code § 95 et seq.

Proposition 1A (1998)
Protects local governments' financing from the state government. Cal. Const. Art. XI § 15, Art. XIII § 25.5, and Art. XIII B § 6.

Proposition 13 (1978)
Limits property tax rate to one percent, limits reassessments, requires voter approval for special taxes. Cal. Const. Art. XIII A.

Proposition 62 (1986)
Requires voter approval for local special taxes and most local general taxes. Gov't Code § 53720 et seq.

Proposition 218 (1996)
Requires voter or property owner approval for local taxes, assessments, and fees. Cal. Const. Arts. XIII C and XIII D; Gov't Code § 53750 et seq.

public domain
All land owned by government.

public hearing
A meeting announced and advertised in advance and open to the public, at which the public has an opportunity to talk and participate.

public improvement
Any improvement, facility, or service together with its associated public site or right-of-way intended to provide transportation, drainage, public or private utilities, energy, or similar essential services.

Public Records Act
Requires public access to public records, with limited exceptions. Gov't Code § 6250 et seq.

publication requirements
Laws governing the publication of public notices. Gov't Code § 6000 et seq.

Quimby Act
Cities and counties can require a subdivider to dedicate land for parks. Gov't Code § 66477.

Redevelopment (Community Redevelopment Law)
A redevelopment agency can use tax-increment revenues and eminent domain to revitalize a blighted area. Cal. Const. Art. XVI, § 16; Health & Safety Code § 33000 et seq.

referendum
A citizen challenge to legislative action taken by a city or county. If enough citizen signatures are filed, the city council or board of supervisors must either rescind its decision or call an election on the issue.

responsible agency
Any public agency other than the lead agency with the power of discretionary project approval. A responsible agency sends comments to the lead agency regarding environmental impacts about which they have expertise.

restrictive covenant
A restriction on the use of land usually set forth in the deed.

reuse
A use for an existing building or parcel of land other than the one for which it was originally intended.

right-of-way
Strip of land acquired by reservation, dedication, forced dedication, prescription, or condemnation and that is occupied or intended to be occupied by a road, crosswalk, railroad, electric transmission line, oil or gas pipeline, water line, sanitary storm sewer, and other similar uses.

riparian land
Land traversed or bounded by a natural watercourse or adjoining tidal lands.

riparian rights
Rights of a landowner to the water on or bordering his property, including the right to make use of such waters and to prevent diversion or misuse of upstream water.

"run with the land"
Term for a covenant or restriction—either contained in a deed or imposed by local government through an ordinance—that is binding on the present and all future owners of the property.

scenic easement
Legal device for protecting scenic views and associated aesthetic qualities of a site by restricting change in existing features without government approval.

school developer fees
A school district can levy developer fees to pay for a new school. Education Code § 17620; Gov't Code § 65995.

second unit
Attached or detached residential dwelling providing complete independent living facilities for one or more persons. Gov't Code § 658522.

setback
Minimum distance that zoning requires be maintained between two structures or between a structure and a property line.

site plan
A plan, to scale, showing uses and structures proposed for a parcel of land. The site plan includes lot lines, streets, building sites, public open space, buildings, major landscape features—both natural and man-made—and, depending on requirements, the locations of proposed utility lines.

Soil Erosion and Sediment Control Plan
A plan that indicates necessary land treatment measures, including a schedule for installation, that will effectively minimize soil erosion and sedimentation.

solar access
A property owner's right to have sunlight shine on his land or buildings.

solid waste management
A program providing for the collection, storage, and disposal of solid waste including, where appropriate, recycling and recovery.

special assessment (benefit assessment)
Fee a local authority levies for the financing of a local improvement that is primarily of benefit to the landowners who must pay the assessment.

special district
A local government that provides limited services and facilities to a defined geographic area. Gov't Code § 50077(d); Rev. & Tax. Code § 95(m).

special district's principal acts
State laws that govern each type of special district. For example, Community Services District Law is Government Code section 61000 et seq.

special tax
Special tax revenues are restricted to special uses. Special taxes require two-thirds voter approval. Cal. Const. Arts. XIII A, § 4 and XIII C, § 2; Gov't Code § 50075 et seq., § 53722 et seq., and § 53970 et seq.

specific plan
Plan adopted by a city or county to implement its general plan for designated areas. A special plan contains the locations and standards for land use densities, streets, and other public facilities in greater detail than the general plan map and text. Gov't Code § 65450 et seq.

sphere of influence
The probable ultimate physical boundary and service limits of a local agency as approved by a LAFCO, identifying the area available to a city for future annexation.

spot zoning
Zoning of an isolated parcel in a manner inconsistent or incompatible with surrounding zoning or land uses, particularly if done to favor a particular landowner.

State Clearinghouse
Part of the Governor's Office of Planning and Research that is responsible for distributing environmental documents to state agencies, boards, and departments.

stormwater detention
Any storm drainage technique that retards or detains runoff, such as a detention or retention basin, parking lot storage, rooftop storage, porous pavement, dry wells, or any combination thereof.

street, arterial
A street with access control, channelized intersections, and restricted parking that collects and distributes traffic from one area of a community to another.

street, collector
A street that collects traffic from local streets and connects with arterials.

street, local
A street designed to provide vehicular access to abutting property and discourage through traffic.

strip zone
A zone normally consisting of a ribbon of uses fronting on one or both sides of a major street and extending inward for approximately one-half block. Strip commercial development is the most common form.

Subdivided Lands Act
Land can be divided into five or more parcels for sale, lease, or finance. Bus. & Prof. Code § 11000 et seq.

subdivision
Division of any unit or units of land for the purpose of sale, lease, or financing.

Subdivision Map Act
State law regulates the subdivision of land with tentative maps and parcel maps. Gov't Code § 66410 et seq.

taking
The appropriation by government of private land for which compensation must be paid.

tentative subdivision map
A map showing the design and improvement of a proposed subdivision of five or more lots that includes existing conditions in and around a subdivision. At this stage a city or county must place on the map all the restrictions deemed necessary. The term "tentative" is misleading, because additional conditions or substantive design changes cannot be required once a tentative subdivision map is approved.

transfer of development right
The separation of development rights from the land where a community wishes to limit development. Because it permits the selling of rights to an area where high-density development is desirable, TDR is promoted as a way to retain farmland, preserve endangered natural environments, protect historic areas, stage development, promote low- and moderate-income housing, and achieve other land use objectives.

transitional area
(1) An area in the process of changing from one use to another or changing from one racial or ethnic occupancy to another; (2) an area that acts as a buffer between two different land uses.

transitional use
Land use with an intermediate intensity between a more and less intensive use.

transportation systems management
A program coordinating many forms of transportation (car, bus, carpool, rapid transit, bicycle, etc.) in order to distribute the traffic impacts of new development. Instead of emphasizing road expansion or construction, TSM examines methods of increasing road efficiency.

tribal consultation
Cities and counties must consult with tribes before adopting or amending a general plan. Gov't Code § 65352.3.

trip generation
The total number of one-way vehicle trips produced by a specific land use or activity.

turbidity
A thick, hazy condition of air or water resulting from the presence of suspended particulates or other pollutants.

urban limit line (urban service area)
An area, identified through official public policy, within which urban development will be allowed during a specified time period. Beyond this line—using a variety of growth management tools such as acreage zoning and limits on capital improvements—development is prohibited or strongly discouraged.

urban service boundary
A defined region, not always coincidental with a municipality's corporate boundary, that defines the geographical limit of government-supplied public facilities and services.

use
Purpose or activity for which a piece of land or its buildings is designed, arranged, or intended, or for which it is occupied or maintained.

validation suit
Lawsuit that asks a court to validate bonds, boundaries, or other decisions. Code Civ. Proc. § 860 et seq.

variance
Permission to depart from the literal requirements of a zoning ordinance. For a variance to be granted, the local decision-making body must make findings that a hardship would exist if a variance were not granted and that granting it would not constitute a special privilege.

vested right
A right that has become absolute and fixed and cannot be defeated or denied by subsequent conditions or a change in regulations, unless it is taken and paid for.

water table
The upper surface of groundwater, or that level below which the soil is seasonally saturated with water.

Williamson Act
The California Land Conservation Act of 1965 (Gov't Code § 51200 et seq.). The Williamson Act authorizes local governments to designate "agricultural preserves" and allows for taxation of land within those preserves based on agricultural use, rather than the "highest and best use," which might be residential, industrial, or commercial. In return for this preferential tax treatment, the landowner must agree to maintain the land in agricultural uses for a minimum of ten years.

zero lot line
Development approach in which a building is sited on one or more lot lines to allow more flexibility in site design and to increase the amount of usable open space on the lot. Conceivably, three of the four sides of a building could be on the lot lines.

zoning
Ordinances enacted by a city or county that divide a community into districts or zones within which permitted and special uses are established, as well as regulations governing lot size, building bulk, placement, and other development standards. Gov't Code § 65800 *et seq.*

zoning administrator
An appointed official in charge of carrying out public policy regarding zones and empowered to make decisions concerning design permits, administrative use permits, and other permits as stated in the zoning ordinance.

zoning map
The map or maps that are part of the zoning ordinance, delineating the boundaries of zoning districts.

zoning ordinance
A local law that contains detailed standards and procedures to implement the general plan. The ordinance divides the city or county into various zoning districts with different land uses permitted in each.

Acronyms

ABAG	=	Association of Bay Area Governments
AEP	=	Association of Environmental Professionals
ALUC	=	Airport Land Use Commission
ALUP	=	Airport Land Use Plan
APA	=	Administrative Procedures Act
APA	=	American Planning Association
ARNI	=	Aquatic Resources of National Importance
BAAQMD	=	Bay Area Air Quality Management District
BCDC	=	San Francisco Bay Conservation and Development Commission
BIA	=	Building Industry Association
BLM	=	Bureau of Land Management
BMP	=	best management practice
BRE	=	Bureau of Real Estate
CALGreen	=	Green Building Standards Code
Caltrans	=	Department of Transportation
CAPCOA	=	California Air Pollution Control Officers Association
CARB	=	California Air Resources Board
CBD	=	central business district
CC&Rs	=	covenants, conditions, and restrictions
CCP	=	Code of Civil Procedure
CDFW	=	California Department of Fish and Wildlife
CEC	=	California Energy Commission
CEQA	=	California Environmental Quality Act
CERES	=	California Environmental Resources Evaluation System
CESA	=	California Endangered Species Act
CMA	=	Congestion Management Agency
CMP	=	Congestion Management Program
COG	=	Council of Government
Corps	=	U.S. Army Corps of Engineers
CSA	=	County Service Area
CUP	=	conditional use permit
CWA	=	Clean Water Act
DEIR	=	draft environmental impact report
DFW	=	Department of Fish and Wildlife
DIR	=	California Department of Industrial Relations
DPS	=	distinct population segment
DWR	=	Department of Water Resources
EA	=	environmental assessment
EAP	=	Energy Action Plan
EIR	=	environmental impact report
EIS	=	environmental impact statement
EPA	=	Environmental Protection Agency
EPACT	=	Energy Policy Act of 1992
EPCA	=	Energy Policy and Conservation Act
ESA	=	Endangered Species Act
ESU	=	evolutionary significant unit
FAIR	=	Fair Apportionment and Individual Representation
FAR	=	floor area ratio
FBA	=	facilities benefits assessment
FEMA	=	Federal Emergency Management Agency
FPPC	=	Fair Political Practices Commission
GHAD	=	geologic hazard abatement district
GHG	=	greenhouse gas
GIS	=	geographic information system
GLA	=	gross leasable area
HCD	=	Department of Housing and Community Development
HCO	=	Hotel Unit Conversion and Demolition Ordinance
HCP	=	habitat conservation plan
IEPR	=	Integrated Energy Policy Report
IFD	=	infrastructure financing district
IGRA	=	Indian Gaming Regulatory Act
IOLTA	=	interest on lawyers' trust account
ITS	=	incidental take statement
JPA	=	joint powers agency
JPA	=	joint powers agreement
LAFCO	=	Local Agency Formation Commission
LCP	=	local coastal program
LEDPA	=	least environmentally damaging practicable alternative
LEED	=	Leadership in Energy and Environmental Design
LID	=	Low Impact Development
LTMS	=	long-term management strategy
MERA	=	Marin Emergency Radio Authority
MND	=	mitigated negative declaration
MOA	=	memorandum of agreement
MOU	=	memorandum of understanding
MPO	=	metropolitan planning organization
MS4	=	municipal separate storm sewer system
MSS	=	Marin Sanitary Service
MTC	=	Metropolitan Transportation Commission
NAECA	=	National Appliance Energy Conservation Act
NCCP	=	natural communities conservation plan
NEPA	=	National Environmental Policy Act
NHPA	=	National Historic Preservation Act
NIMBY	=	Not in My Back Yard
NOAA	=	National Oceanic and Atmospheric Administration
NOAA Fisheries/NMFS	=	National Oceanic and Atmospheric Administration Fisheries
NOC	=	Notice of Completion
NOD	=	Notice of Determination
NOE	=	Notice of Exemption
NOI	=	Notice of Intent
NOP	=	Notice of Preparation
NPDES	=	National Pollutant Discharge Elimination System
NRC	=	National Research Council
NRCS	=	Natural Resources Conservation Service
NRDC	=	Natural Resources Defense Council
NWP	=	nationwide permit
OPR	=	Governor's Office of Planning and Research
PCN	=	pre-construction notification
PUD	=	planned-unit development
PD	=	planned-unit development
RES	=	renewable electricity standard
RFRA	=	Religious Freedom and Restoration Act of 1993
RGL	=	Regulatory Guidance Letter
RHNA	=	regional housing needs allocation
RLUIPA	=	Religious Land Use and Institutionalized Persons Act
RMPP	=	Risk Management and Prevention Program
RPS	=	Renewable Portfolio Standard
RWQCB	=	Regional Water Quality Control Board
SCAQMD	=	South Coast Air Quality Management District
SJVAPCD	=	San Joaquin Valley Air Pollution Control District
SEIR	=	supplemental environmental impact report
SHBC	=	State Historical Building Code
SLAPP	=	Strategic Lawsuit Against Public Participation
SRB	=	State Reclamation Board
SWANCC	=	Solid Waste Agency of Northern Cook County
SWPPP	=	Storm Water Pollution Prevention Plan
SWRCB	=	State Water Resources Control Board
TDR	=	transfer of development rights
TEIR	=	Tribal Environmental Impact Report
TRO	=	temporary restraining order
TRPA	=	Tahoe Regional Planning Agency
TSM	=	transportation systems management
UGB	=	urban growth boundary
USDA	=	U.S. Department of Agriculture
UWMP	=	Urban Water Management Plan
WDR	=	Waste Discharge Requirement

Suggested Reading

California Land Use Practice
August 2012 (with annual supplement)
Adam U. Lindgren and Steve T. Mattas, eds.

Provides comprehensive information on the complex world of California land use law, and covers all major topics encountered in land use practice, including general and specific plans, regulatory takings and exactions, constitutional protections, zoning and variances, conditional use permits, environmental review, code enforcement, design review, growth management, land use litigation, vested rights, and development conditions.

Continuing Education of the Bar • California
2100 Franklin St., Suite 500
Oakland, CA 94612-3098
1-800-232-3444

Outside California:
(510) 302-2000
www.ceb.com

California Municipal Law Handbook
2012 edition

This collaborative work of over 300 municipal attorneys from the City Attorneys' Department of the League of California Cities that provides municipal law practitioners an excellent source of first resort in researching a given area of California municipal law including land use.

Continuing Education of the Bar • California
2100 Franklin St., Suite 500
Oakland, CA 94612-3098
1-800-232-3444
Outside California:
(510) 302-2000
www.ceb.com

California Planners' 2012 Book of Lists

Practical information that is useful to local, regional, and state planners and resource managers.

State of California
Governor's Office of Planning and Research
1400 10th Street, Suite 100
Sacramento, CA 95814
(916) 322-2318
www.opr.ca.gov

California Planning Guide: An Introduction to Planning in California
2005 edition

A lay person's introduction to the world of planning.

State of California Governor's Office of Planning and Research
1400 10th Street, Suite 100
Sacramento, CA 95814
(916) 322-2318
www.opr.ca.gov

California Subdivision Map Act and the Development Process
November 2001 (second) edition, supplemented annually by Matthew S. Gray
Daniel J. Curtin, Jr. and Robert E. Merritt

A detailed analysis of the Subdivision Map Act intended for lawyers.

Continuing Education of the Bar • California
2100 Franklin St., Suite 500
Oakland, CA 94612-3098
1-800-232-3444
Outside California:
(510) 302-2000
www.ceb.com

CEQA Deskbook
A Step-by-Step Guide on How to Comply with the California Environmental Quality Act
2013 (third) edition
Ronald E. Bass, Terry Rivasplata, and Kenneth M. Bogdan

Practical user's guide that explains how to proceed from the beginning to the end of the environmental review process. It summarizes the California Environmental Quality Act and the Guidelines, focusing on CEQA's procedural and substantive requirements.

Solano Press Books
P.O. Box 773
Point Arena, CA 95468
(800) 931-9373

Development by Agreement
2012 edition
A Tool Kit for Land Developers and Local Governments
David L. Callies, Cecily T. Barclay, and Julie A. Tappendorf

Provides guidance for and explores principles behind development conditions, vested rights, development/annexation agreements, and numerous other public-private agreements that facilitate development; extensive appendices provide useful forms.

American Bar Association
321 North Clark Street
Chicago, IL 60654-7598
(312) 988-5000

Exactions and Impact Fees in California
A Comprehensive Guide to Policy, Practice, and the Law
2012 (third) edition
William W. Abbott et al.

A comprehensive source of information regarding the history, policy, and law of development fees and exactions, including practice tips.

Solano Press Books
P.O. Box 773
Point Arena, CA 95468
(800) 931-9373

General Plan Guidelines
October 2003

Complete guide to the planning process and to the preparation of general plans. (The Governor's Office of Planning and Research has begun its 2013 update of the General Plan Guidelines. The OPR website will include the latest information on the update, including documents and meeting notifications.)

State of California
Governor's Office of Planning and Research
State Clearinghouse
P.O. Box 3044
Sacramento, CA 95812
(916) 445-0613
www.opr.ca.gov

Growing Pains: Airport Expansion and Land Use Compatibility Planning in California
September 2006

Grant Boyken

The result of Senator Christine Kehoe's request that the California Research Bureau examine opportunities and challenges faced by airport operators throughout the state as they cope with pressures to expand operations to meet future demand, while dealing with local land use impacts including noise, traffic and compatibility issues.

California State Library, California Research Bureau, State Information and Reference Center
P.O. Box 942837
Sacramento, CA 94237
(916) 654-0261
www.library.ca.gov

Guide to California Planning
2012 (fourth) edition

William Fulton and Paul Shigley

An extensive account of land use planning in California, including processes and laws that must be observed and how they are used for better or for worse. Written by a well-respected journalist and urban planner, this book is a must for all those students who wish to understand the fundamentals of the practice of land use planning in California.

Solano Press Books
P.O. Box 773
Point Arena, CA 95468
(800) 931-9373

The Legal Guide to Affordable Housing Development
May 2011

Tim Iglesias and Rochelle E. Lento, eds.

A clearly written, practical resource for attorneys representing local governments (municipalities, counties, housing authorities, and redevelopment agencies), housing developers (both for-profit and nonprofit), investors, financial institutions, and populations eligible for housing.

American Bar Association
321 North Clark Street
Chicago, IL 60654-7598
(312) 988-5000

Longtin's California Land Use
2012 (second) edition (supplemented annually)

James Longtin

A detailed, strictly legal analysis of California land use law.

Local Government Publications
P.O. Box 2596
Walnut Creek, CA 94595
(925) 962-9617

An Ounce of Prevention: Best Practices for Making Informed Land Use Decisions
2006

Focuses on the underlying procedures common to all land use decisions.

Institute for Local Government
League of California Cities
1400 K Street, Suite 400
Sacramento, CA 95814
(916) 658-8200
www.cacities.gov

The Planning Commissioner and the California Dream
Plan It Again, Sam
July 2005

Marjorie W. Macris, FAICP

Reference and guidelines directed at the practical needs of city and county planning commissioners in California, with practice tips.

Solano Press Books
P.O. Box 773
Point Arena, CA 95468
(800) 931-9373

Planning Commissioner's Handbook
2004 edition

Primary Contributors: Bill Higgins, Anya Lawler, Gary Binger

Identification of the tools available for planning commissioners and others to assist in reaching the community's goal of quality planning.

League of California Cities
1400 K Street, Suite 400
Sacramento, CA 95814
(916) 658-8200
www.cacities.gov

Planning, Zoning and Development Laws
2012

An important tool provided by OPR to help land use professionals keep abreast of the ever-changing land use regulatory environment.

State of California
Governor's Office of Planning and Research
1400 10th Street, Suite 100
Sacramento, CA 95814
(916) 322-2318
www.opr.ca.gov

Practice Under the California Environmental Quality Act
2013 (third) edition

Stephen L. Kostka and Michael H. Zischke

An encyclopedic, step-by-step guide to the California Environmental Quality Act, covering preparation and judicial review of EIRs and other CEQA documents. Features detailed discussion of legal requirements and practical considerations. Indispensable to attorneys and environmental professionals.

Continuing Education of the Bar • California
2100 Franklin St., Suite 500
Oakland, CA 94612-3098
1-800-232-3444
Outside California
(510) 302-2000
www.ceb.com

State and Local Government Land Use Liability
2013, updated annually

Michael A. Zizka, Timothy S. Hollister, Marcella Larsen, Patricia E. Curtin

The goal of this book is to help government attorneys and officials understand, adopt, administer, and enforce land use regulations and ordinances in a way that will minimize their exposure to liability.

Available at: http://legalsolutions.thompsonreuters.com

Table of Authorities

CASES

108 Holdings LTD v. City of Rohnert Park, 136 Cal. App. 4th 186 (2006), 280, 281

1119 Delaware v. Continental Land Title Co., 16 Cal. App. 4th 992 (1993), 55

216 Sutter Bay Assocs. v. County of Sutter, 58 Cal. App. 4th 860 (1997), 62, 63, 279

A Local & Reg'l Monitor v. City of Los Angeles, 16 Cal. App. 4th 630 (1993), 43

Abatti v. imperial Irrigation District, 205 Cal. App. 4th 650, 671-74 (2012), 169

Abelleira v. District Court of Appeal, 17 Cal. 2d 280 (1941), 524, 525, 526

Abernathy Valley, Inc. v. City of Solano, 173 Cal. App. 4th 42 (2009), 134

ABS Institute v. City of Lancaster, 24 Cal. App. 4th 285 (1994), 470

Acme Fill Corp. v. San Francisco Bay Conservation etc. Com., 187 Cal. App. 3d 1056 (1986), 528

Action Apartment Ass'n v. City of Santa Monica, 166 Cal. App. 4th 456 (2008), 331

Adam Bros. Farming, Inc. v. County of Santa Barbara, 604 F.3d 1142 (9th Cir. 2010), 307, 537

Agins v. City of Tiburon, 447 U.S. 255 (1980), 290, 304, 324

Agric. Labor Relations Bd. v. Tex-Cal Land Mgmt. Inc., 43 Cal. 3d 696 (1987), 547

Ailanto Properties, Inc. v. City of Half Moon Bay, 142 Cal. App. 4th 572 (2006), 89, 91, 119

Air Conditioning, Heating and Refrigeration Institute v. City of Albuquerque, 835 F. Supp. 2d 1133 (D.N.M. 2010), 471

Air Conditioning, Heating and Refrigeration Institute v. City of Albuquerque, No. 08-633, Doc. 185 (D.N.M. Jan. 25, 2012), 471

Aiuto v. City and County of San Francisco, 201 Cal. App. 4th 1347 (2011), 117

Alameda County Land Use Ass'n v. City of Hayward, 38 Cal. App. 4th 1716 (1995), 531

Allegretti & Co. v. County of Imperial, 138 Cal. App. 4th 1261 (2006), 58, 291, 294, 299

Alliance for a Better Downtown Millbrae v. Wade, 108 Cal. App. 4th 123 (2003), 364, 365

Allied-General Nuclear Services v. United States, 839 F. 2d 1572 (Fed. Cir. 1988), 310

Amador Valley Joint Union High Sch. Dist. v. State Bd. of Equalization, 22 Cal. 3d 208 (1978), 358, 385

American Canyon Cmty United for Responsible Growth v. City of American Canyon, 145 Cal. App. 4th 1062 (2006), 174

American Distilling Co. v. City Council of City of Sausalito, 34 Cal. 2d 660 (1950), 403

American Fed'n of Labor v. Eu, 36 Cal. 3d 687 (1984), 357, 358

Anderson First Coalition v. City of Anderson, 130 Cal. App. 4th 1173 (2005), 24, 158

Anthony v. Snyder, 116 Cal. App. 4th 643 (2004), 117, 119

Anza Parking Corp. v. City of Burlingame, 195 Cal. App. 3d 855 (1987), 55

Apartment Ass'n of Greater Los Angeles v. City of Los Angeles, 90 Cal. App. 4th 1162 (2001), 146

Apartment Ass'n v. City of Los Angeles, 24 Cal. 4th 830 (2001), 353

Aptos Seascape Corp. v. County of Santa Cruz, 138 Cal. App. 3d 484 (1982), 303

Arizona Cattle Growers Ass'n v. U. S. Fish and Wildlife Serv., 273 F. 3d 1229 (9th Cir. 2001), 240

Arizona Cattle Growers' Ass'n v. Salazar, 606 F.3d 1160 (9th Cir. 2010), 255

Arkansas Game and Fish Comm'n v. United States, 133 S. Ct. 511 (2012), 295, 296, 311

Armendariz v. Penman, 75 F. 3d 1311 (1996), 315, 316

Arnel Dev. Co. v. City of Costa Mesa, 126 Cal. App. 3d 330 (1981), 41, 42, 48, 317, 368, 511

Arnel Dev. Co. v. City of Costa Mesa, 28 Cal. 3d 511 (1980), 39, 44, 46, 372, 481, 504, 505, 506

Ass'n for a Cleaner Environment v. Yosemite Community College Dist., 116 Cal. App. 4th 629 (2004), 155

Ass'n for Sensible Dev. at Northstar, Inc. v. Placer County, 122 Cal. App. 4th 1289 (2004), 584

Ass'n of Irritated Residents v. County of Madera, 107 Cal. App. 4th 1383 (2003), 157

Assembly v. Deukmejian, 30 Cal. 3d 638 (1982), 361, 367, 376

Associated Home Builders, Inc. v. City of Livermore, 18 Cal. 3d 582 (1976), 1, 4, 40, 41, 212, 358, 375, 386, 448, 510

Associated Home Builders, Inc. v. City of Newark, 18 Cal. App. 3d 107 (1971), 347

Associated Home Builders, Inc. v. City of Walnut Creek, 4 Cal. 3d 633 (1971), 101, 107, 108, 319, 320, 321, 336, 337

Association for Protection of Environmental Values in Ukiah v. City of Ukiah, 2 Cal. App. 4th 720 (1991), 252

Association of Irritated Residents v. California Air Resources Board, 206 Cal. App. 4th 1487 (2012), 459

Association of Plumbing & Mechanical Officials v. California Building Standards Commission, 55 Cal. App. 4th 245 (1997), 469

Audubon Soc'y, Inc. v. Planning Comm'n, 34 Cal. 3d 412 (1983), 116

Avco Community Developers, Inc. v. South Coast Reg'l Comm'n, 17 Cal. 3d 785 (1976), 93, 94, 96, 273, 274, 275, 276, 277, 283, 285, 339

Avoyelles Sportsmen's League, Inc. v. Marsh, 715 F. 2d 897 (5th Cir. 1983), 191

Ayres v. City Council of Los Angeles, 34 Cal. 2d 31 (1949), 71, 100, 107, 322, 337
Azusa Land Reclamation Co., Inc. v. Main San Gabriel Basin Watermaster, 52 Cal. App. 4th 1165 (1997), 513, 515
B&P Dev. Corp. v. City of Saratoga, 185 Cal. App. 3d 949 (1986), 132, 133, 134
Baird v. Contra Costa County, 32 Cal. App. 4th 1464 (1995), 57, 143
Bakersfield Citizens for Local Control v. City of Bakersfield, 124 Cal. App. 4th 1184 (2004), 158, 163
Balch Enters. v. New Haven Unified Sch. Dist., 219 Cal. App. 3d 783 (1990), 322
Baldwin v. City of Los Angeles, 70 Cal. App. 4th 819 (1999), 510, 515
Ball v. United States, 77 U.S. 557 (1870), 180
Ballona Wetlands Land Trust v. City of Los Angeles 201 Cal. App. 4th 455 (2011), 142, 475, 476
Bank of America v. State Water Resources Control Bd., 42 Cal. App. 3d 198 (1974), 509
Bank of the Orient v. Town of Tiburon, 220 Cal. App. 3d 992 (1990), 5, 63
Banker's Hill v. City of San Diego, 139 Cal. App. 4th 249 (2006), 146, 147, 252
Banning Ranch Conservancy v. City of Newport Beach, 211 Cal. App. 4th 1209 (2012), 156
Barner v. Leeds, 24 Cal. 4th 676 (2000), 566
Barratt American Inc. v. City of Rancho Cucamonga, 37 Cal. 4th 685 (2005), 334, 340, 554, 555, 556, 559
Bauer v. City of San Diego, 75 Cal. App. 4th 1281 (1999), 57
Baum Electric Co. v. City of Huntington Beach, 33 Cal. App. 3d 573 (1973), 470
Bd. of Supervisors v. Superior Court, 23 Cal. App. 4th 830 (1994), 543
Beach Colony II Ltd. v. California Coastal Comm'n, 166 Cal. App. 3d 106 (1985), 11, 562
Beck Dev. Co. v. Southern Pac. Transp. Co., 44 Cal. App. 4th 1160 (1996), 39, 62, 85, 111, 489,
Beckley v. Reclamation Bd. of the State, 205 Cal. App. 2d 734 (1962), 542
Belair v. Riverside County Flood Control Dist, 47 Cal. 3d 550 (1988), 311
Benny v. City of Alameda, 105 Cal. App. 3d 1006 (1980), 72, 84, 506
Benson v. California Coastal Comm'n, 139 Cal. App. 4th 348 (2006), 478
Benton v. Bd of Supervisors, 226 Cal. App. 3d 1467 (1991), 174, 175
Beresford Neighborhood Ass'n v. City of San Mateo, 207 Cal. App. 3d 1180 (1989), 536
Bering Strait Citizens for Responsible Resource Development v. U.S. Army Corps of Engineers, 524 F. 3d 938 (9th Cir. 2008), 203, 207
Berkeley Keep Jets Over the Bay Committee v. Board of Port Commissioners, 91 Cal. App. 4th 1344 (2001), 156
Berman v. Parker, 348 U.S. 26 (1954), 1, 2
Bernardi v. City Council, 54 Cal. App. 4th 426 (1997), 559
Bernstein v. Smutz, 83 Cal. App. 2d 108 (1947), 529
BIA of Central California v. City of Patterson, 171 Cal. App. 4th 886 (2009), 332, 333, 434, 437, 438
Big Creek Lumber Co. v. City of Santa Cruz, 38 Cal. 4th 1139 (2006), 2
Billig v. Voges, 223 Cal. App. 3d 962 (1990), 376
Birkenfeld v. City of Berkeley, 17 Cal. 3d 129 (1976), 2, 3, 369
Bixby v. Pierno, 4 Cal. 3d 130 (1971), 509
Blackmore v. Powell, 150 Cal. App. 4th 1593 (2007), 75, 76
Blair v. Pitchess, 5 Cal. 3d 258 (1971), 383, 534
Bldg. Indus. Ass'n v. City of Camarillo, 41 Cal. 3d 810 (1986), 40, 48, 368, 375, 379, 428, 448, 481

Bledsoe v. Watson, 30 Cal. App. 3d 105 (1973), 383
Blockbuster Videos, Inc. v. City of Tempe, 141 F. 3d 1295 (9th Cir. 1998), 251
Blue Jeans Equities W. v. City and County of San Francisco, 3 Cal. App. 4th 164 (1992), 277, 288, 324, 330, 331
Board of Supervisors v. De Groff Enterprises, 198 S.E. 2d 600 (Va. 1973), 431
Board of Supervisors v. Superior Court, 32 Cal. App. 4th 1616 (1995), 47, 540, 541
Bodega Bay Concerned Citizens v. County of Sonoma, 125 Cal. App. 4th 1061 (2005), 89, 92
Bogan v. Scott-Harris, 523 U.S. 44 (1998), 567
Bohannon v. City of San Diego, 30 Cal. App. 3d 416 (1973), 254
Bookout v. Local Agency Formation Comm'n, 49 Cal. App. 3d 383 (1975), 505
Borden Ranch P'ship v. U.S. Army Corps of Eng'rs, 261 F. 3d 810 (9th Cir. 2001), judgment aff'd, 537 U.S. 99 (2002), 193, 214
Border Business Park, Inc. v. City of San Diego, 142 Cal. App. 4th 1538 (2006), 309
Bowman v. City of Berkeley, 122 Cal. App. 4th 572 (2004), 151, 251, 252
Bowman v. City of Petaluma, 185 Cal. App. 3d 1065 (1986), 175
Bozung v. Local Agency Formation Comm'n, 13 Cal. 3d 263 (1975), 143, 402, 407, 532
Branciforte Heights v. City of Santa Cruz, 138 Cal. App. 4th 914 (2006), 102, 118, 519, 529, 556, 557
Brandon v. Holt, 469 U.S. 464 (1985), 532
Braude v. City of Los Angeles, 226 Cal. App. 3d 83 (1990), 532
Breakzone Billiards v. City of Torrance, 81 Cal. App. 4th 1205 (2000), 87, 116, 479
Breneric Assocs. v. City of Del Mar, 69 Cal. App. 4th 166 (1998), 47, 249, 327, 513
Briggs v. City of Rolling Hills Estates, 40 Cal. App. 4th 637 (1995), 46, 250, 509
Bright Development Company v. City of Tracy, 20 Cal. App. 4th 783 (1993), 95, 96, 97, 283, 513
Bright v. Board of Supervisors, 66 Cal. App. 3d 191 (1977), 77
Briseno v. City of Santa Ana, 6 Cal. App. 4th 1378 (1992), 470
Brock v. Superior Court, 109 Cal. App. 2d 594, 599 (1952), 508
Brosnahan v. Eu, 31 Cal. 3d 1 (1982), 377, 378
Browning-Ferris Indus. v. City Council, 181 Cal. App. 3d 852 (1986), 157, 170, 483, 527
Buckley v. California Coastal Comm'n, 68 Cal. App. 4th 178 (1998), 298
Buena Park Motel Association v. City of Buena Park, 109 Cal. App. 4th 302 (2003), 108, 109, 289
Buena Vista Gardens Apartments Ass'n v. City of San Diego Planning Dept., 175 Cal. App. 3d 289 (1985), 18, 19, 30, 410, 411, 428, 536
Building Indus. Ass'n v. City of Oceanside, 27 Cal. App. 4th 744 (1994), 24, 43, 425, 448
Building Indus. Ass'n v. Superior Court, 211 Cal. App. 3d 277 (1989), 24, 428
Building Indus. Legal Defense Found. v. Superior Court, 72 Cal. App. 4th 1410 (1999), 63
Building Indus. Ass'n of Central California v. City of Patterson, 171 Cal. App. 4th 886 (2009), 283, 322, 332, 333, 431, 434, 437, 438
Building Indus. Ass'n v. Washington State Building Code Council, 2011 WL 485895 (W.D.Wash. Feb. 7, 2011), 471
Bullock v. City and County of San Francisco, 221 Cal. App. 3d 1072 (1990), 116

Burbank-Glendale-Pasadena Airport Auth. v. City of Burbank, 64 Cal. App. 4th 1217 (1998), 378

Busick v. Workmen's Compensation Appeals Bd., 7 Cal. 3d 967 (1972), 537

Bus Riders Union v. Los Angeles County Metropolitan Transportation Agency, 179 Cal. App. 4th 101 (2009), 143

Butte Environmental Council v. U.S. Army Corps of Engineers, 620 F.3d 936 (9th Cir. 2010), 203, 234

Cadiz Land Co., Inc. v. Rail Cycle, L.P., 83 Cal. App. 4th 74 (2000), 539, 540

Cal. Native Plant Soc'y v. County of El Dorado, 170 Cal. App. 4th 1026 (2009), 166

Cal. Oak Foundation v. City of Santa Clarita, 133 Cal. App. 4th 1219 (2005), 160

Cal. Unions for Reliable Energy v. Mojave Desert Air Quality Mgmt. Dist., 178 Cal. App. 4th 1225 (2009), 143

CalBeach Advocates v. City of Solana Beach, 103 Cal. App. 4th 529 (2002), 146

Caldwell v. Montoya, 10 Cal. 4th 972 (1995), 565, 566

California Water Impact Network v. Newhall County Water Dist., 161 Cal. App. 4th 1464 (2008), 408, 458, 531

California Ass'n for Safety Educ. v. Brown, 30 Cal. App. 4th 1264 (1994), 383

California Aviation Council v. City of Ceres, 9 Cal. App. 4th 1384 (1992), 26

California Bldg. Indus. Ass'n v. Governing Bd. of the Newhall Sch. Dist., 206 Cal. App. 3d 212 (1988), 320, 321

California Building Industry Ass'n v. Bay Area Air Quality Management Dist., 218 Cal. App. 4th 1171 (2013), 464

California Building Industry Ass'n v. City of San Jose, 161 Cal. Rptr. 3d 699 (2013), 431

California Building Industry Ass'n v. San Joaquin Valley Air Pollution Control Dist., 178 Cal. App. 4th 120 (2009), 554

California Coastal Comm'n v. Granite Rock Co., 480 U.S. 572 (1987), 66

California Coastal Comm'n v. Superior Court (Ham), 210 Cal. App. 3d 1488 (1989), 309

California Coastal Comm'n v. Quanta Inv. Corp., 113 Cal. App. 3d 579 (1980), 72, 313

California Common Cause v. Duffy, 200 Cal. App. 3d 730 (1987), 382

California Country Club Homes Ass'n, Inc. v. City of Los Angeles 18 Cal. App. 4th 1425 (1993), 88, 90, 92

California Forestry Ass'n. v. California Fish & Game Comm'n, 156 Cal. App. 4th 1535 (2007), 246

California Hotel & Motel Ass'n v. Indust. Welfare Comm'n, 25 Cal. 3d 200 (1979), 510

California Licensed Foresters Ass'n v. State Bd. of Forestry, 30 Cal. App. 4th 562 (1994), 562

California Native Plant Society v. City of Rancho Cordova, 172 Cal. App. 4th 603 (2009), 21, 22, 24, 165

California Native Plant Society v. City of Santa Cruz, 177 Cal. App. 4th 957 (2009), 168

California Oak Found. v. County of Tehama, 174 Cal. App. 4th 1217 (2009), 541, 549

California Oak Foundation v. Regents of Univ. of Cal., 188 Cal. App. 4th 227 (2010), 167, 172

California Ranch Homes Dev. Co. v. San Jacinto Unified Sch. Dist., 17 Cal. App. 4th 573 (1993), 557

California Rifle and Pistol Assn. v. City of West Hollywood, 66 Cal. App. 4th 1302 (1998), 544

California Sportfishing Protection Alliance v. Federal Energy Regulatory Comm'n, 472 F. 3d 593 (9th Cir. 2006), 229

California v. Cabazon Band of Mission Indians, 480 U.S. 202 (1987), 68

California Youth Authority v. SP Board, 104 Cal. App. 4th 575 (2002), 514

California-Nevada Annual Conference of the United Methodist Church v. City and County of San Francisco, 173 Cal. App. 4th 1559 (2009), 54, 254, 532

Californians for Alternatives to Toxics v. Dept. of Food and Agriculture, 136 Cal. App. 4th 1 (2006), 157

Camara v. Municipal Court, 387 U.S. 523 (1967), 496

Camp v. Board of Supervisors, 123 Cal. App. 3d 334 (1981), 12, 13, 16, 18, 20, 21, 29, 30, 33, 113, 418, 536, 537, 546

Campbell v. Mosk, 197 Cal. App. 2d 640 (1961), 403

Candid Enters., Inc. v. Grossmont Union High Sch. Dist., 39 Cal. 3d 878 (1985), 214, 321, 336, 340, 436

Canyon North Co. v. Conejo Valley Unified Sch. Dist., 19 Cal. App. 4th 243 (1993), 346

Capistrano Beach Water Dist. v. Taj Dev. Corp., 72 Cal. App. 4th 524 (1999), 554, 559

Carabell v. U.S. Army Corps of Engineers, 391 F. 3d 704 (6th Cir. 2004), 184

Cardin v. De La Cruz, 671 F. 2d 363 (9th Cir. 1982), 68

Carmel Valley View, Ltd. v. Board of Supervisors, 58 Cal. App. 3d 817 (1976), 114

Carsten v. Psychology Examining Comm., 27 Cal. 3d 793 (1980), 532, 533

Carty v. City of Ojai, 77 Cal. App. 3d 329 (1978), 41, 510

Catron County v. U.S. Fish and Wildlife Serv., 75 F. 3d 1429 (10th Cir. 1996), 226

Cedar Fair v. City of Santa Clara, 194 Cal. App. 4th 1150 (2011), 141

Center for Biological Diversity v. Bureau of Land Management, 422 F. Supp. 2d 1115 (N.D. Cal. 2006), 234

Center for Biological Diversity v. County of San Bernardino, 185 Cal. App. 4th 866 (2010), 161, 563

Center for Biological Diversity v. Fish & Game Comm'n, 166 Cal. App. 4th 597 (2008), 246

Center for Biological Diversity v. FPL, Inc., 166 Cal. App. 4th 1349 (2008), 498

Center for Biological Diversity v. Kempthorne, 607 F. Supp. 2d 1078 (D. Ariz. 2009), 226

Center for Biological Diversity v. Norton, 240 F. Supp. 2d 1090 (D. Ariz. 2003), 223. 226

Center for Biological Diversity v. Salazar, 695 F.3d 893 (9th Cir. 2012), 236

Center for Biological Diversity v. U.S. Bureau of Land Management, 698 F.3d 1101 (9th Cir. 2012), 235

Center for Biological Diversity v. U.S. Fish and Wildlife Serv., 450 F. 3d 930 (9th Cir. 2006), 224

Center for Sierra Nevada Conservation v. County of El Dorado, 202 Cal. App. 4th 1156 (2012), 153

Centex Real Estate Corp. v. City of Vallejo (1993), 19 Cal. App. 4th 1358, 346

Cequel III Commc'ns I, LLC. v. LAFCO, 149 Cal. App. 4th 310 (2007), 402, 403

Chandis Sec. Co. v. City of Dana Point, 52 Cal. App. 4th 475 (1996), 419

Chappell v. Robbins, 73 F. 3d 918 (9th Cir. 1996), 567

Charles A. Pratt Construction Co., Inc. v. California Coastal Comm'n, 162 Cal. App. 4th 1068 (2008), 95, 261, 285

Chemical Specialties Mfg. Ass'n, Inc. v. Deukmejian, 227 Cal. App. 3d 663 (1991), 374

Ching v. San Francisco Bd. of Permit Appeals, 60 Cal. App 4th 888 (1998), 516

Chino MHC, LP v. City of Chino, 210 Cal. App. 4th 1049 (2012), 73

Christward Ministry v. County of San Diego, 13 Cal. App. 4th 31 (1993), 173

Chung v. City of Monterey Park, 210 Cal. App. 4th 394 (2012), 142

Church of Scientology v. Wollersheim, 42 Cal. App. 4th 628 (1996), 560

Cinevision Corp. v. City of Burbank, 745 F. 2d 560 (9th Cir. 1984), 568

Citizen Action to Serve All Students v. Thornley, 222 Cal. App. 3d 748 (1990), 150

Citizens Ass'n for Sensible Dev. of Bishop Area v. County of Inyo, 172 Cal. App. 3d 151 (1985), 23, 149, 483, 526, 532, 535, 536

Citizens for a Megaplex-Free Alameda v. City of Alameda, 149 Cal. App. 4th 91 (2007), 177

Citizens for Covenant Compliance v. Anderson, 12 Cal. 4th 345 (1992), 136

Citizens for East Shore Parks v. Cal. State Lands Commission, 202 Cal. App. 4th 549 (2011), 155, 157, 167, 170

Citizens for Open Government v. City of Lodi, 205 Cal. App. 4th 296 (2012), 157, 158, 166, 168

Citizens for Planning Responsibly v. County of San Luis Obispo, 176 Cal. App. 4th 357 (2009), 36, 371, 376

Citizens For Responsible & Open Gov't v. City of Grand Terrace, 160 Cal. App. 4th 1323 (2008), 151

Citizens for Responsible Equitable Environmental Development v. City of Chula Vista, 197 Cal. App. 4th 327 (2011), 161, 464

Citizens for Responsible Equitable Environmental Development v. City of San Diego, 196 Cal. App. 4th 515 (2011), 162, 175

Citizens for Responsible Equitable Environmental Development v. City of San Diego Redevelopment Agency, 134 Cal. App. 4th 598 (2005), 152

Citizens for Responsible Gov't v. City of Albany, 56 Cal. App. 4th 1199 (1997), 280, 359

Citizens for Responsible Open Space v. San Mateo County LAFCO, 159 Cal. App. 4th 717 (2008), 404, 405

Citizens of Goleta Valley v. Bd. of Supervisors, 52 Cal. 3d 553 (1990), 10, 15, 23, 30, 157, 166, 168, 553

Citizens of Lake Murray Area Ass'n v. City Council, 129 Cal. App. 3d 436 (1982), 176

Citizens to Enforce CEQA v. City of Rohnert Park, 131 Cal. App. 4th 1594 (2005), 70

City of Agoura Hills v. LAFCO, 198 Cal. App. 3d 480 (1988), 390, 402, 408

City of Anaheim v. City of Fullerton, 102 Cal. App. 2d 395 (1951), 403

City and County of San Francisco v. Burton, 201 Cal. App. 2d 749 (1962), 498

City and County of San Francisco v. Farrell, 32 Cal. 3d 47 (1982), 347

City and County of San Francisco v. Golden Gate Heights Invs., 14 Cal. App. 4th 1203 (1993), 324

City and County of San Francisco v. Padilla, 23 Cal. App. 3d 388 (1972), 508

City of Arcadia v. State Water Resources Control Bd., 135 Cal. App. 4th 1392 (2006), 149

City of Atascadero v. Daly, 135 Cal. App. 3d 466 (1982), 373

City of Bakersfield v. Miller, 64 Cal. 2d 93 (1966), 58

City of Boerne v. Flores, 521 U.S. 507 (1997), 52

City of Buena Park v. Boyar, 186 Cal. App. 2d 61 (1960), 108, 109

City of Carmel-By-The-Sea v. Bd. of Supervisors, 183 Cal. App. 3d 229 (1986), 515

City of Carmel-by-the-Sea v. Board of Supervisors, 137 Cal. App. 3d 964 (1982), 21, 55

City of Ceres v. City of Modesto, 274 Cal. App. 2d 545 (1969), 387, 390

City of Coachella v. Riverside County Airport Land Use Comm'n, 210 Cal. App. 3d 1277 (1989), 296, 529, 547

City of Cuyahoga Falls v. Buckeye Community Hope Foundation, 538 U.S. 188 (2003), 317, 369

City of Dana Point v. Cal. Coastal Comm'n, 217 Cal. App. 4th 170 (2013), 262

City of Del Mar v. City of San Diego, 133 Cal. App. 3d 401 (1982), 41, 42

City of Fairfield v. Superior Court of Solano County, 14 Cal. 3d 768 (1975), 47, 383, 488, 508, 513, 540

City of Fontana v. Atkinson, 212 Cal. App. 2d 499 (1963), 59

City of Goleta v. Superior Court, 40 Cal. 4th 270 (2006), 99, 120

City of Hawaiian Gardens v. City of Long Beach, 61 Cal. App. 4th 1100 (1998), 564

City of Irvine v. Irvine Citizens Against Overdevelopment, 25 Cal. App. 4th 868 (1994), 22, 42, 43, 48, 61, 378

City of Irvine v. S. Cal. Ass'n of Gov'ts, 175 Cal. App. 4th 506 (2009), 413, 532

City of Ladue v. Gilleo, 512 U.S. 43 (1994), 251

City of Lafayette v. East Bay Mun. Util. Dist., 16 Cal. App. 4th 1005 (1993), 67

City of Las Vegas v. Lujan, 891 F. 2d 927 (D.C. Cir. 1989), 224

City of Littleton, Colorado v. Z.J. Gifts D-4, LLC, 541 U.S. 774 (2004), 51, 52

City of Livermore v. LAFCO, 184 Cal. App. 3d 531 (1986), 402, 408, 536

City of Long Beach v. Los Angeles Unified School Dist., 176 Cal. App. 4th 889 (2009), 143, 163

City of Los Altos v. Barnes, 3 Cal. App. 4th 1193 (1992), 46

City of Los Angeles v. Amwest Sur. Insurance Co., 63 Cal. App. 4th 378 (1998) (review denied (June 17, 1998)), 125

City of Los Angeles v. Gage, 127 Cal. App. 2d 442 (1954), 60

City of Los Angeles v. Superior Court, 193 Cal. App. 4th 1159 (2011), 6

City of Los Angeles v. Wolfe, 6 Cal. 3d 326 (1971), 58

City of Malibu v. Cal. Coastal Comm., 206 Cal. App. 4th 549 (2012), 262

City of Marina v. Bd. of Trustees of the Cal. St. Univ., 39 Cal. 4th 341 (2006), 165

City of Maywood v. Los Angeles Unified School District, 208 Cal. App. 4th 362 (2012), 163, 165, 167, 170, 563

City of Merced v. American Motorists Ins. Co., 126 Cal. App. 4th 1316 (2005), 124, 125

City of Monterey v. Del Monte Dunes at Monterey, Ltd. (1999), 526 U.S. 687, 295, 306, 312, 327

City of National City v. Wiener, 3 Cal. 4th 832 (1992), 49

City of Pasadena v. State of California, 14 Cal. App. 4th 810 (1993), 146

City of Poway v. City of San Diego, 229 Cal. App. 3d 847 (1991), 28, 29, 482

City of Rancho Palos Verdes v. City Council, 59 Cal. App. 3d 869 (1976), 515

City of Renton v. Playtime Theatres, Inc., 475 U.S. 41 (1986), 49, 50

City of Sacramento v. Trans Pac. Indus., Inc., 98 Cal. App. 3d 389 (1979), 124

City of Salinas v. Ryan Outdoor Adver., Inc., 189 Cal. App. 3d 416 (1987), 60

City of San Diego v. Dunkl, 86 Cal. App. 4th 384 (2001), 561

City of Santa Ana v. City of Garden Grove, 100 Cal. App. 3d 521 (1979), 9

City of Santa Clara v. LAFCO, 139 Cal. App. 3d 923 (1983), 407

City of Santa Cruz v. LAFCO, 76 Cal. App. 3d 381 (1977), 387, 390, 402

City of Santa Cruz v. Superior Court, 40 Cal. App. 4th 1146 (1995), 47, 541

City of Santa Monica v. Stewart, 126 Cal. App. 4th 43 (2005), 379

City of Santee v. County of San Diego, 186 Cal. App. 4th 55 (2010), 142

City of Santee v. County of San Diego, 214 Cal. App. 3d 1438 (1989), 156

City of Sausalito v. County of Marin, 12 Cal. App. 3d 550 (1970), 48

City of Tiburon v. Northwestern Pac. R.R. Co., 4 Cal. App. 3d 160 (1970), 72, 130, 531

City of Vernon v. Board of Harbor Comm'rs, 63 Cal. App. 4th 677 (1998), 141

City of Walnut Creek v. County of Contra Costa 101 Cal. App. 3d 1012 (1980), 24, 515, 526

City of West Hollywood v. Beverly Towers, Inc., 52 Cal. 3d 1184 (1991), 55, 82, 94, 276, 2779

Clark v. City of Hermosa Beach, 48 Cal. App. 4th 1152 (1996), 321, 478, 512, 513

Clark v. Yosemite Community College Dist., 785 F.2d 781 (9th Cir. 1986), 537

Clover Valley Foundation v. City of Rocklin, 197 Cal. App. 4th 200 (2011), 160, 165, 169

Cmty. Dev. Comm'n v. City of Fort Bragg, 204 Cal. App. 3d 1124 (1988), 56

Coalition Advocating Legal Hous. Options v. City of Santa Monica, 88 Cal. App. 4th 451 (2001), 427

Coalition for Clean Air v. City of Visalia, 209 Cal. App. 4th 408 (2012), 147

Coalition for Student Action v. City of Fullerton, 153 Cal. App. 3d 1194 (1984), 116, 526

Cochran v. Herzog Engraving Co., 155 Cal. App. 3d 405 (1984), 564

Coe v. City of Los Angeles, 183 P. 822 (1919), 403

Cohan v. City of Thousand Oaks, 30 Cal. App. 4th 547 (1994), 86, 87, 116, 316, 479

Cohen v. Bd. of Supervisors, 40 Cal. 3d 277 (1985), 546

Colony Cove Properties LLC v. City of Carson, 187 Cal. App. 4th 1487 (2010), 73

Comm. for Responsible Planning v. City of Indian Wells, 225 Cal. App. 3d 191 (1990), 560

Commercial Builders of Northern California v. City of Sacramento, 941 F. 2d 872 (1991), 324, 331, 433

Committee for a Progressive Gilroy v. State Water Resources Control Bd., 192 Cal. App. 3d 847 (1987), 518

Committee for Green Foothills v. Santa Clara County Bd. of Supervisors, 48 Cal. 4th 32 (2010), 176, 517

Committee for Responsible Planning v. City of Indian Wells, 209 Cal. App. 3d 1005 (1989), 14, 34, 410

Common Cause v. Bd. of Supervisors, 49 Cal. 3d 432 (1989), 532, 534

Communities for a Better Environment v. City of Richmond, 184 Cal. App. 4th 70 (2010), 162, 464

Communities for a Better Environment v. California Resources Agency, 103 Cal. App. 4th 98 (2002), 139, 164

Communities for a Better Environment v. South Coast Air Quality Management District, 48 Cal. 4th 310 (2010), 156

Community Water Coal. v. Santa Cruz County LAFCO, 200 Cal. App. 4th 1317 (2011), 389

Concerned Citizens for Responsible Government v. West Point Fire Protection Dist., 196 Cal.App.4th 1427 (2011), 352

Concerned Citizens of Calaveras County v. Board of Supervisors, 166 Cal. App. 3d 90 (1985), 13, 18, 22, 29, 30, 378

Concerned Citizens of Costa Mesa, Inc. v. 32nd District Agric. Ass'n, 42 Cal. 3d 929 (1986), 176, 523

Concerned Citizens of Palm Desert, Inc. v. Bd. of Supervisors, 38 Cal. App. 3d 257 (1974), 57, 523

Concerned Citizens v. City of Carlsbad, 204 Cal. App. 3d 937 (1988), 380

Concerned Citizens v. McCloud Community Services Dist., 147 Cal. App. 4th 181 (2007), 141

Concerned Dublin Citizens v. City of Dublin, 214 Cal. App. 1301 (2013), 144, 152, 162, 175, 464

Conner v. Burford, 848 F.2d 1441 (9th Cir. 1988), 231

Connerly v. State Personnel Board, 37 Cal. 4th 1169 (2006), 564

Consaul v. City of San Diego, 6 Cal. App. 4th 1781 (1992), 93, 277

Conservation Law Found. v. Watt, 560 F. Supp. 561 (D. Mass. 1983), aff'd on other grounds sub nom., Massachusetts v. Watt, 716 F. 2d 946 (1st Cir. 1983), 232

Consolidated Fire Protection Dist. v. Howard Jarvis Taxpayers Ass'n, 63 Cal. App. 4th 211 (1998) , 351, 354

Consolidated Irrigation District v. City of Selma, 204 Cal. App. 4th 187 (2012), 151, 533, 555

Consolidated Irrigation District v. Superior Court, 205 Cal. App. 4th 697 (2012), 549

Consolidated Rock Prods. Co. v. City of Los Angeles, 57 Cal. 2d 515 (1962), 4

Construction Indust. Force Account Council v. Amador Water Agency, 71 Cal. App. 4th 810 (1999), 271

Cooper v. State Bd. of Medical Examiners, 35 Cal. 2d 242 (1950), 480

Cormier v. County of San Luis Obispo, 161 Cal. App. 3d 850 (1984), 47

Corona-Norco Unified Sch. Dist. v. City of Corona (Corona-Norco II), 17 Cal. App. 4th 985 (1993), 113

Corona-Norco Unified Sch. Dist. v. City of Corona, 13 Cal. App. 4th 1577 (1993), 23, 25, 113, 526

Costa v. State of California, 177 Cal. App. 3d 62 (1986), 529

Costa v. Superior Court, 37 Cal. 4th 986 (2006), 361, 376, 377, 378

County of Alameda v. Superior Court of Alameda County, 133 Cal. App. 4th 558 (2005), 305

County of Amador v. City of Plymouth, 149 Cal. App. 4th 1089 (2007), 141

County of Amador v. El Dorado County Water Agency, 76 Cal. App. 4th 931 (1999), 142, 517, 521

County of Butte v. Bach, 172 Cal. App. 3d 848 (1985), 47, 510, 511

County of Imperial v. McDougal, 19 Cal. 3d 505 (1977), 55

County of Kern v. Edgemont Dev. Corp., 222 Cal. App. 2d 874 (1963), 124

County of Los Angeles v. Raytheon Co., 159 Cal. App.4th 27 (2008), 524

County of Los Angeles v. Sahag-Mesrob Armenian Christian School, 188 Cal. App. 4th 851 (2010), 53

County of Los Angeles v. Superior Court, 13 Cal. 3d 721 (1975), 540, 541

County of Marin v. Assessment Appeals Bd., 64 Cal. App. 3d 319 (1976), 255

County of Orange v. Barratt American Inc., 150 Cal. App. 4th 420 (2007), 334

County of Riverside v. Whitlock, 22 Cal. App. 3d 863 (1972), 271

County of San Diego v. Grossmont-Cuyamaca Community College District, 141 Cal. App. 4th 86 (2006), 165

County of San Diego v. McClurken, 37 Cal. 2d 683 (1951), 58

585

County of San Diego v. State of California, 15 Cal. 4th (1997), 504, 515

County of San Luis Obispo v. Superior Court, 90 Cal. App. 4th 288 (2001), 130

County of Sonoma v. Rex, 231 Cal. App. 3d 1289 (1991), 498, 499, 500, 501

County Sanitation Dist. No. 2 v. County of Kern, 127 Cal. App. 4th 1544 (2005), 150

Craik v. County of Santa Cruz, 81 Cal. App. 4th 880 (2001), 56, 482, 483, 514

Crown Point Development, Inc. v. City of Sun Valley, 506 F. 3d 851 (9th Cir. 2007), 315

Cucamongans United for Reasonable Expansion v. City of Rancho Cucamonga, 82 Cal. App. 4th 473 (2000), 174

Cumming v. City of San Bernardino Redev. Agency, 101 Cal. App. 4th 1229 (2002), , 521, 523

Danforth v. U.S., 308 U.S. 271 (1939), 293

Daro v. Superior Court, 151 Cal. App. 4th 1079 (2007), 72

Davidon Homes v. City of Pleasant Hill, No. 297988 (Superior Court, Contra Costa County, April 3, 1987), 98

Davidon Homes v. City of San Jose, 54 Cal. App. 4th 106 (1997), 144

Davidson v. County of San Diego, 49 Cal. App. 4th 639 (1996), 276

deBottari v. City Council, 171 Cal. App. 3d 1204 (1985), 43, 48, 377, 378

DeCicco v. California Coastal Commission, 199 Cal. App. 4th 947 (2011), 260

Defend the Bay v. City of Irvine, 119 Cal. App. 4th 1261 (2004), 169, 545

Defenders of Wildlife v. Flowers, 414 F. 3d 1066 (9th Cir. 2005), 230

Defenders of Wildlife v. Norton, 258 F. 3d 1136 (9th Cir. 2001), 221

Defenders of Wildlife v. Salazar, 729 F. Supp. 2d 1207 (D. Mont. 2010), 221

Del Cerro Mobile Estates v. City of Placentia, 197 Cal. App. 4th 173 (2011), 144

Del Mar Terrace Conservancy, Inc. v. City Council, 10 Cal. App. 4th 712, 514

Del Oro Hills v. City of Oceanside, 31 Cal. App. 4th 1060 (1995), 297

Delta Wetlands Props. v. County of San Joaquin, 121 Cal. App. 4th 128 (2004), 67

Deltakeeper v. Oakdale Irrig. Dist., 94 Cal. App. 4th 1092 (2001), 536

Deltona Corp. v. Alexander, 504 F. Supp. 1280 (M.D. Fla. 1981), 201

Deltona Corp. v. United States, 657 F. 2d 1184 (Ct. Cl. 1981), 201

Denny's Inc. v. City of Agoura Hills, 56 Cal. App. 4th 1312 (1997), 60

DeVita v. County of Napa, 9 Cal. 4th 763 (1995), 2, 9, 11, 27, 29, 30, 108, 358, 371, 372, 375, 376, 384, 385, 386

Dienelt v. County of Monterey, 113 Cal. App. 2d 128 (1952), 58, 59

Dierkes v. City of Los Angeles, 25 Cal. 2d 938 (1945), 534

Disney v. City of Concord, 194 Cal. App. 4th 1410 (2011), 3

Dolan v. City of Tigard, 512 U.S. 374 (1994), 33, 100, 249, 277, 282, 295, 300, 319, 320, 321, 322, 323, 325, 326, 327, 328, 329, 330, 331, 332, 333, 334, 343, 431, 432, 433, 434

Donnellan v. City of Novato, 86 Cal. App. 4th 1097 (2001), 522

Douda v. California Coastal Commission, 159 Cal. App. 4th 1181 (2008), 261

Douglas County v. Babbitt, 48 F. 3d 1495 (9th Cir. 1995), 219, 220, 226

Doyle v. City of Chino, 117 Cal. App. 3d 673 (1981), 529

Driscoll v. City of Los Angeles, 67 Cal. 2d 297 (1967), 500

Drum v. Fresno County Dep't of Public Works, 144 Cal. App. 3d 777 (1983), 478

Dunex v. City of Oceanside, 218 Cal. App. 4th 1158 (2013), 73

Dunn v. County of Santa Barbara, 135 Cal. App. 4th 1281 (2006), 304, 305, 544

Dunn-Edwards Corp. v. Bay Area Air Quality Management Dist., 9 Cal. App. 4th 644 (1992), 505

East Bay Asian Local Dev. Corp. v. State of California, 24 Cal. 4th 693 (2000), 54, 540, 541

East Bay Mun. Utility Dist. v. Cal. Department of Forestry & Fire Protection, 43 Cal. App. 4th 1113 (1996), 163

Echevarrieta v. City of Rancho Palos Verdes, 86 Cal. App. 4th 472 (2001), 250

Economy Light & Power Co. v. United States, 256 U.S. 113 (1921), 180

Edgren v. Regents of Univ. of Cal., 158 Cal. App. 3d 515 (1984), 527

Edna Valley Watch v. County of San Luis Obispo, 197 Cal. App. 4th 1312 (2011), 563

Ehrlich v. City of Culver City, 12 Cal. 4th 854 (1996), 3, 249, 295, 322, 323, 329, 330, 331, 332, 333, 434, 519, 557

El Dorado Palm Springs, Ltd. v. Rent Review Comm'n, 230 Cal. App. 3d 335 (1991), 522

El Patio v. Permanent Rent Control Bd., 110 Cal. App. 3d 915 (1980), 92

Eller Media Co. v. City of Los Angeles, 87 Cal. App. 4th 1217 (2001), 490

Embarcadero Mun. Improvement Dist. v. City of Santa Barbara, 88 Cal. App. 4th 781 (2001), 403

Employment Division v. Smith, 494 U.S. 872 (1990), 52

Endangered Habitats League, Inc. v. County of Orange, 131 Cal. App. 4th 777 (2005), 24, 111, 164

Endangered Habitats League, Inc. v. State Water Resources Control Bd., 63 Cal. App. 4th 227 (1997), 529, 547

Enos v. Marsh, 769 F. 2d 1363 (9th Cir. 1985), 226

Ensign Bickford Realty Corp. v. City Council, 68 Cal. App. 3d 467 (1977), 481, 506

Env't Protection Info. Ctr. v. Cal. Dept. of Forestry & Fire Protection, 44 Cal. 4th 459 (2008), 163, 170, 247

Environmental Coal. of Orange County, Inc. v. LAFCO of Orange County, 110 Cal. App. 3d 164 (1980), 403

Environmental Council v. Board of Supervisors, 135 Cal. App. 3d 428 (1982), 33

Environmental Defense Project of Sierra County v. County of Sierra, 158 Cal. App. 4th 877 (2008), 45, 478

Envtl. Defense Project of Sierra County v. County of Sierra, 158 Cal. App. 4th 877 (2008), 45, 478

Envtl. Law Fund v. Town of Corte Madera, 49 Cal. App. 3d 105 (1975), 529

Envtl. Prot. Info. Ctr. v. Simpson Timber Co., 255 F. 3d 1073 (9th Cir. 2001), 236

Essick v. City of Los Angeles, 34 Cal. 2d 614 (1950), 57

Eureka Citizens for Responsible Gov't v. City of Eureka, 147 Cal. App. 4th 357 (2007), 142

Evans v. City of San Jose, 128 Cal. App. 4th 1123 (2005), 526

Ewing v. City of Carmel-by-the-Sea, 234 Cal. App. 3d 1579 (1991), 3, 4, 41, 46

Fairbank v. City of Mill Valley, 75 Cal App. 4th 1243 (1999), 145

Fairbanks North Star Borough v. U.S. Army Corps of Engineers, 543 F. 3d 586 (9th Cir. 2008), cert denied, 129 S. Ct. 2825 (2009), 190

Fall River Wild Trout Found. v. County of Shasta, 70 Cal. App. 4th 482 (1999), 151

Families Unafraid to Uphold Rural El Dorado County v. Board of Supervisors of El Dorado County, 62 Cal. App. 4th 1332 (1998), 24, 25, 32, 516

Families Unafraid to Uphold Rural El Dorado County v. County Bd. of Supervisors, 79 Cal. App. 4th 505 (2000) (Families Unafraid II), 562
Farley v. Cory, 78 Cal. App. 3d 583 (1978), 534
Farley v. Healey, 67 Cal. 2d 325 (1967), 364
Fat v. County of Sacramento, 97 Cal. App. 4th 1270 (2002), 157
Fed'n of Hillside & Canyon Ass'ns v. City of Los Angeles, 83 Cal. App. 4th 1252 (2000), 173
Federation of Hillside & Canyon Assns. v. City of Los Angeles, 126 Cal. App. 4th 1180 (2004), 23
Felice v. City of Inglewood, 84 Cal. App. 2d 263 (1948), 57
Fields v. Sarasota Manatee Airport Auth., 953 F.2d 1299, 306
Findleton v. Bd. of Supervisors, 12 Cal. App. 4th 709 (1993), 492
First English Evangelical Lutheran Church v. County of Los Angeles, 482 U.S. 304 (1987), 60, 63, 250, 251, 295, 296, 297, 298, 299, 300, 306
Fishback v. County of Ventura, 133 Cal. App. 4th 896 (2005), 130
Fishman v. City of Palo Alto, 86 Cal. App. 3d 506 (1978), 505
Flanders Foundation v. City of Carmel-by-the-Sea, 202 Cal. App. 4th 603 (2012), 169, 171
Flavell v. City of Albany, 19 Cal. App. 4th 1846 (1993), 20, 21
Fogarty v. City of Chico, 148 Cal. App. 4th 537 (2007), 557
Fontana Unified Sch. Dist. v. City of Rialto, 173 Cal. App. 3d 725 (1985), 339
Forest Conservation Council v. Rosboro Lumber Co., 50 F. 3d 781 (9th Cir. 1995), 240
Forest Guardians v. Johanns, 450 F. 3d 455 (9th Cir. 2006), 236
Formanek v. United States, 26 Cl. Ct. 332 (1992), 293, 310
Fort Mojave Indian Tribe v. Department of Health Servs., 38 Cal. App. 4th 1574 (1995), 175, 539
Friedland v. City of Long Beach, 62 Cal. App. 4th 835 (1998), 403
Friends of Aviara v. City of Carlsbad, 210 Cal. App. 4th 1103 (2012), 15, 23, 415
Friends of "B" St. v. City of Hayward, 106 Cal. App. 3d 988 (1980), 21, 22, 23
Friends of East Willits Valley v. County of Mendocino, 101 Cal. App. 4th 191 (2002), 357, 341
Friends of H Street v. City of Sacramento, 20 Cal. App. 4th 152 (1993), 26
Friends of La Vina v. County of Los Angeles, 232 Cal. App. 3d 1446 (1991), 154
Friends of Lagoon Valley v. City of Vacaville, 154 Cal. App. 4th 807 (2007), 10, 23, 24, 424, 425
Friends of Oroville v. City of Oroville, 219 Cal. App. 4th 832 (2013), 162, 464
Friends of Riverside's Hills v. City of Riverside, 168 Cal. App. 4th 743 (2008), 518
Friends of Riverside's Hills v. City of Riverside, 168 Cal. App. 4th 793 (2008), 117
Friends of Sierra Madre v. City of Sierra Madre, 25 Cal. 4th 165 (2001), 140, 280, 359
Friends of Sierra Railroad v. Tuolumne Park & Recreation Dist., 147 Cal. App. 4th 643 (2007), 143
Friends of the Eel River v. Sonoma County Water Agency, 108 Cal. App. 4th 859 (2003), 66, 163
Friends of Westwood, Inc. v. City of Los Angeles, 191 Cal. App. 3d 259 (1987), 339, 506
Fullerton Joint Union High Sch. Dist. v. State Bd. of Educ., 32 Cal. 3d 779 (1982), 143, 510
Fund for Envtl. Defense v. County of Orange, 204 Cal. App. 3d 1538 (1988), 174

Furey v. City of Sacramento, 24 Cal. 3d 862 (1979), 529
G & D Holland Constr. Co. v. City of Marysville, 12 Cal. App. 3d 989 (1970), 4, 48
G.L. Mezzetta, Inc. v. City of American Canyon, 78 Cal. App. 4th 1087 (2000), 276
Galante Vineyards v. Monterey Peninsula Water Mgmt. Dist., 60 Cal. App. 4th 1109 (1997), 552
Gammoh v. City of Anaheim, 73 Cal. App. 4th 186 (1999), 49, 251
Gardner v. County of Sonoma, 29 Cal. 4th 990 (2003), 131, 132, 133, 134
Garner v. City of Riverside, 170 Cal. App. 3d 510 (1985), 522
Garrick Dev. Co. v. Hayward Unified Sch. Dist., 3 Cal. App. 4th 320 (1992), 324, 342, 346
Gayle v. Hamm, 25 Cal. App. 3d 250 (1972), 377
General Development Co. v. City of Santa Maria, 202 Cal. App. 4th 1391 (2012), 516
Genesis Environmental Services v. San Joaquin Unified Air Pollution Control Dist., 113 Cal. App. 4th 597 (2003), 312
Gentry v. City of Murrieta, 36 Cal. App. 4th 1359 (1995), 144, 150
Georgia-Pacific Corp. v. California Coastal Comm'n, 132 Cal. App. 3d 678 (1982), 513
Gifford Pinchot Task Force v. U.S. Fish and Wildlife Service, 378 F. 3d 1059 (9th Cir. 2004), 225, 234
Gilliland v. County of Los Angeles, 126 Cal. App. 3d 610 (1981), 275
Gilroy Citizens for Responsible Planning v. City of Gilroy, 140 Cal. App. 4th 911 (2006), 153, 154, 158
Gobin v. Snohomish County, 304 F. 3d 909 (9th Cir. 2002), 68
Gogerty v. Coachella Valley Junior Coll. Dist., 57 Cal. 2d 727 (1962), 383
Golden Hill Neighborhood Association, Inc., v. City of San Diego, 199 Cal. App. 4th 416 (2011), 352
Golden State Homebuilding Ass'n v. City of Modesto, 26 Cal. App. 4th 601 (1994), 93, 111
Gomes v. County of Mendocino, 37 Cal. App. 4th 977 (1995), 132, 135
Gong v. City of Fremont, 250 Cal. App. 2d 568 (1967), 539
Gonzalez v. County of Tulare, 65 Cal. App. 4th 777 (1998), 43, 522
Grand Canyon Trust v. U.S. Bureau of Reclamation, 691 F.3d 1008 (9th Cir. 2012), 229
Gray v. County of Madera, 167 Cal. App. 4th 1099 (2008), 165, 170
Graydon v. Pasadena Redevelopment Agency, 104 Cal. App. 3d 631 (1980), 272
Great Oaks Water Co. v. Santa Clara Valley Water Dist., 170 Cal. App. 4th 956 (2009), 146
Greater Yellowstone Coalition, Inc. v. Servheen, 665 F.3d 1015 (2011), 219
Green v. City of Oceanside, 194 Cal. App. 3d 212 (1987), 252, 528
Green v. Cmty. Redev. Agency, 96 Cal. App. 3d 491 (1979), 560
Greenebaum v. City of Los Angeles, 153 Cal. App. 3d 391 (1984), 25, 157
Greenpeace Action v. Franklin, 14 F. 3d 1324 (9th Cir. 1992), 232
Griffin Dev. Co. v. City of Oxnard, 39 Cal. 3d 256 (1985), 3, 72, 320, 336
Griffis v. County of Mono, 163 Cal. App. 3d 414 (1985), 72, 89
Groch v. City of Berkeley, 118 Cal. App. 3d 518 (1981), 56
Grupe Dev. Co. v. California Coastal Comm'n, 166 Cal. App. 3d 148 (1985), 312
Grupe Development Co. v. Superior Court, 4 Cal. 4th 911 (1993), 340
Gualala Festivals Comm. v. California Coastal Comm'n, 183 Cal. App. 4th 60 (2010), 260

Guardians of Turlock's Integrity v. City Council, 149 Cal. App. 3d 584 (1983), 21

Guilbert v. Regents of Univ. of Cal., 93 Cal. App. 3d 233 (1979), 508

Guinnane v. City and County of San Francisco, 197 Cal. App. 3d 862 (1987), 289, 299, 300

Guru Nanak Sikh Society of Yuba City v. County of Sutter, 456 F. 3d 978 (9th Cir. 2006), 53

Gwaltney of Smithfield v. Chesapeake Bay Foundation, 484 U.S. 49 (1987), 211

H.N. & Frances C. Berger Foundation v. City of Escondido, 127 Cal. App. 4th 1 (2005), 315

Habitat and Watershed Caretakers v. City of Santa Cruz, 213 Cal. App. 4th 1277 (2013), 160, 167, 168, 169, 172

Hafen v. County of Orange, 128 Cal. App. 4th 133 (2005), 93, 112, 275, 277

Haggis v. City of Los Angeles, 22 Cal. 4th 490 (2000), 565

Hall v. City of Taft, 47 Cal. 2d 177 (1956), 66, 134

Harlow v. Carleson, 16 Cal. 3d 731 (1976), 509

Harmer v. Superior Court, 275 Cal. App. 2d 345 (1969), 535

Harris v. Alcoholic Beverage Control Appeals Bd., 245 Cal. App. 2d 919 (1966), 535

Harris v. City of Costa Mesa, 25 Cal. App. 4th 963 (1994), 250, 315, 482, 483

Harris v. County of Riverside, 904 F. 2d 497, (9th Cir. 1990), 315, 511

Harroman Co. v. Town of Tiburon, 235 Cal. App. 3d 388 (1991), 31, 32, 113, 114

Hauselt v. County of Butte, 172 Cal. App. 4th 550 (2009), 311

Hayssen v. Bd. of Zoning Adjustments, 171 Cal. App. 3d 400 (1985), 478

Hazelton v. City of San Diego, 183 Cal. App. 2d 131 (1960), 403

Health First v. March Joint Powers Authority, 174 Cal. App. 4th 1135 (2009), 140

Heap v. City of Los Angeles, 6 Cal. 2d 405 (1936), 528

Hebard v. Bybee, 65 Cal. App. 4th 1331 (1998), 357, 361, 376

Hellweg v. Cassidy, 61 Cal. App. 4th 806 (1998), 80

Hensel Phelps Const. Co. v. San Diego Unified Port Dist., 197 Cal. App. 4th 1020 (2011), 270

Hensler v. City of Glendale, 8 Cal. 4th 1 (1994), passim

Hermosa Beach Stop Oil Coalition v. City of Hermosa Beach, 86 Cal. App. 4th 534 (2001), 275, 281

Hernandez v. City of Encinitas, 28 Cal. App. 4th 1048 (1994), 12, 14, 18, 30, 33, 40, 379, 418, 428

Hernandez v. City of Hanford, 41 Cal. 4th 279 (2007), 42

Herrington v. County of Sonoma, 12 F. 3d 901 (9th Cir. 1993), 301

Herrington v. County of Sonoma, 790 F. Supp. 909 (N.D. Cal. 1991), 301

Herrington v. County of Sonoma, 834 F. 2d 1488 (9th Cir. 1987), amended by 857 F. 2d 567 (9th Cir. 1988), 301, 315

Herrington v. County of Sonoma, 857 F. 2d 567 (9th Cir. 1988), 311

Herzberg v. County of Plumas, 133 Cal. App. 4th 1 (2005), 293, 294

HFH, Ltd. v. Superior Court, 15 Cal. 3d 508 (1975), 292

Hill v. City of Clovis, 80 Cal. App. 4th 438 (2000), 106

Hill v. Manhattan Beach, 6 Cal. 3d 279 (1971), 275

Hills for Everyone v. LAFCO, 105 Cal. App. 3d 461 (1980), 402, 403, 408

Hock Inv. Co. v. City and County of San Francisco, 215 Cal. App. 3d 438 (1989), 94, 276, 501

Hoehne v. County of San Benito, 870 F.2d 529 (1989), 305

Hoffman Group, Inc. v. U.S. EPA, 902 F. 2d 567 (7th Cir. 1990), 213

Hoffman Homes, Inc. v. U.S. Environmental Protection Agency, 999 F. 2d 256 (7th Cir. 1993), 183

Hoffmaster v. City of San Diego, 55 Cal. App. 4th 1098 (1997), 14, 411, 413, 418

Holland v. Union Pacific R. R. Co., 154 Cal. App. 4th 940 (2007), 525

Holt v. County of Monterey, 128 Cal. App. 3d 797 (1982), 523

Home Builders Ass'n of N. Calif. v. Norton, 293 F. Supp. 2d 1 (D.D.C. 2002), 226

Home Builders Ass'n of N. Calif. v. U.S. Fish and Wildlife Serv., 268 F. Supp. 2d 1197 (E.D. Cal. 2003), 226

Home Builders Ass'n of Northern California v. City of Napa, 90 Cal. App. 4th 188 (2001), 322, 433, 436

Home Builders Ass'n of Northern California v. U.S. Fish and Wildlife Serv., 616 F.3d 983 (9th Cir. 2010), cert. denied, 131 S.Ct 983 (2011), 225

Homebuilders Ass'n of Tulare/Kings Counties Inc. v. City of Lemoore, 185 Cal. App. 4th 554 (2010), 101, 335

Honchariw v. County of Stanislaus, 200 Cal. App. 4th 1066 (2011), 14, 414, 419

Hoosier Environmental Center v. U.S. Army Corps of Engineers, 722 F.3d 1053 (7th Cir. 2013), 196, 203

Hopkins v. MacCulloch, 35 Cal. App. 2d 442 (1939), 59

Horn v. County of Ventura, 24 Cal. 3d 605 (1979), 44, 85, 86, 126, 477, 488, 490, 507, 508,

Horsemen's Benevolent & Protective Association v. Valley Racing Association 4 Cal. App. 4th 1538 (1992), 276

Hotel & Motel Ass'n of Oakland v. City of Oakland, 344 F. 3d 959 (9th Cir. 2003), 46, 324

Housing Partners I, Inc. v. Duncan, 206 Cal. App. 4th 1335 (2012), 270

Howard Jarvis Taxpayer Ass'n v. City of Los Angeles, 79 Cal. App. 4th 242 (2000), 523

Howard Jarvis Taxpayers Ass'n v. City of Los Angeles, 85 Cal. App. 4th 79 (2000), 353

Howard Jarvis Taxpayers Ass'n v. City of Riverside, 73 Cal. App. 4th 679 (1999), 347, 351

Howard Jarvis Taxpayers Ass'n v. City of San Diego, 72 Cal. App. 4th, 349

Howard v. County of San Diego, 184 Cal. App. 4th 1422 (2010), 529

Hull v. Rossi, 13 Cal. App. 4th 1763 (1993), 560

Hunt v. County of Shasta, 225 Cal. App. 3d 432 (1990), 117, 130

Idaho Farm Bureau Fed'n v. Babbitt, 58 F. 3d 1392 (9th Cir. 1995), 222

Idaho Historic Preservation Council, Inc. v. City Council of Boise, 134 Idaho 651 (2000), 488

Ideal Boat & Camper Storage v. County of Alameda, 208 Cal. App. 4th 301 (2012), 24

In re Bay-Delta Programmatic environmental impact report Coordinated Proceedings, 43 Cal. 4th 1143 (2008), 161, 167

In re Conservatorship of Whitley, 50 Cal. 4th 1206 (2010), 563

Independent Energy Producers Ass'n v. McPherson, 31 Cal. Rptr. 3d 852, 377

Inland Counties Reg'l Ctr., Inc. v. Office of Admin. Hearings, 193 Cal. App. 3d 700 (1987), 535

International Church of the Foursquare Gospel v. City of San Leandro, 634 F.3d 1037 (9th Cir. 2011), 53

Interstate Brands v. Unemployment Ins. Appeals Bd., 26 Cal. 3d 770 (1980), 509

Inyo Citizens for Better Planning v. Bd. of Supervisors, 180 Cal. App. 4th 1 (2009), 149

Isbell v. City of San Diego, 258 F. 3d 1108 (9th Cir. 2001), 50, 51

J.W. Jones Cos. v. City of San Diego, 157 Cal. App. 3d 745 (1984), 32, 33, 336, 338, 348

Jacobson v. County of Los Angeles, 69 Cal. App. 3d 374 (1977), 483, 545

James City County, Virginia v. U.S. EPA, 955 F. 2d 254 (4th Cir. 1992), 12 F. 3d 1330 (4th Cir. 1993) cert. denied, 513 U.S. 823 (1994), 206

Jamul v. Board of Supervisors, 231 Cal. App. 3d 665 (1991), 117, 290

Jayne v. Sherman, 706 F. 3d 994 (9th Cir. 2013), 230

Jefferson Union Sch. Dist. of Santa Clara City v. City Council of City of Sunnyvale, 129 Cal. App. 2d 264 (1954), 403

Johnson v. City of Loma Linda, 24 Cal. 4th 61 (2000), 508

Johnston v. City of Claremont, 49 Cal. 2d 826 (1958), 508

Jones v. City Council, 17 Cal. App. 3d 724 (1971), 57

Jones v. Regents of Univ. of Cal., 183 Cal. App. 4th 818 (2010), 166, 526

Joslin v. H.A.S. Ins. Brokerage, 184 Cal. App. 3d 369 (1986), 542

Kalway v. City of Berkeley, 151 Cal. App. 4th 827 (2007), 135

Kane v. Redevelopment Agency, 179 Cal. App. 3d 899 (1986), 532

Karlson v. City of Camarillo, 100 Cal. App. 3d 789 (1980), 23, 503, 553

Karuk Tribe of California v. U.S. Forest Service, 681 F.3d 1006 (9th Cir. 2012), 230

Katz v. Campbell Union High Sch. Dist., 144 Cal. App. 4th 1024 (2006), 403

Kaufman & Broad Cent. Valley, Inc. v. City of Modesto, 25 Cal. App. 4th 1577 (1994), 96, 97, 283

Kaufman & Broad Cmtys, Inc. v. Performance Plastering, Inc., 133 Cal. App. 4th 26 (2006), 542

Kaufman & Broad-South Bay, Inc. v. Morgan Hill Unified Sch. Dist., 9 Cal. App. 4th 464 (1992), 142

Kawaoka v. City of Arroyo Grande, 17 F. 3d 1227 (9th Cir. 1994), 37, 313

Kehoe v. City of Berkeley, 67 Cal. App. 3d 666 (1977), 372

Keller v. Chowchilla Water Dist., 80 Cal. App. 4th 1006 (2000), 353, 354

Keller v. State Bar, 47 Cal. 3d 1152 (1989), 382

Kelsey v. Colwell, 30 Cal. App. 3d 590 (1973), 255

Kennedy v. City of Hayward, 105 Cal. App. 3d 953 (1980), 86, 477

Kern County Farm Bureau v. Allen, 450 F. 3d 1072 (9th Cir. 2006), 222

Kern County Water Agency v. Watershed Enforcers, 185 Cal. App. 4th 969 (2010), 247

Kern River Pub. Access Com. v. City of Bakersfield, 170 Cal. App. 3d 1205 (1985), 105

KFC National Management Corp. v. National Labor Relations Board, 497 F. 2d 298 (2d Cir. 1974), 480

Kieffer v. Spencer, 153 Cal. App. 3d 954 (1984), 63

Kimball Laundry Co. v. U.S., 338 U.S. 1 (1949), 300

Kings County Farm Bureau v. City of Hanford, 221 Cal. App. 3d 692 (1990), 20, 29, 68, 116, 163, 164, 530, 557

Kissinger v. City of Los Angeles, 161 Cal. App. 2d 454 (1958), 48, 511

Kleitman v. Superior Court, 74 Cal. App. 4th 324 (1999), 47, 541

Klopping v. City of Whittier, 8 Cal. 3d 39 (1972), 309

Knickerbocker v. City of Stockton, 199 Cal. App. 3d 235 (1988), 508

Koontz v. St. Johns River Water Management District, 133 S. Ct. 2586 (2013), 295, 322, 329, 330

Kriebel v. City Council, 112 Cal. App. 3d 693 (1980), 120, 518

Kucera v. Lizza, 59 Cal. App. 4th 1141 (1997), 250

Kuzinich v. Santa Clara, 689 F. 2d 1345 (9th Cir. 1982), 568

L&M Professional Consultants, Inc. v. Ferreira, 146 Cal. App. 3d 1038 (1983), 106

L.I.F.E. Community v. City of Lodi, 213 Cal. App. 3d 1139 (1989), 372, 390

La Canada Flintridge Development Corporation v. Department of Transportation, 166 Cal. App. 3d 206 (1985), 500

La Fe, Inc. v. County of Los Angeles, 73 Cal. App. 4th 231 (1999), 79, 260

Lacher v. Superior Court, 230 Cal. App. 3d 1038 (1991), 493

Laidlaw Envtl. Servs., Inc. v. County of Kern, 44 Cal. App. 4th 346 (1996), 533

Lake Country Estates, Inc. v. Tahoe Reg'l Planning Agency, 440 U.S. 391 (1979), 311

Lakeview Development Corporation v. City of South Lake Tahoe, 915 F. 2d 1290 (9th Cir. 1990), 320

Lakeview Meadows Ranch v. County of Santa Clara, 27 Cal. App. 4th 593 (1994), 130, 134

Landgate, Inc. v. California Coastal Comm'n, 17 Cal. 4th 1006 (1998), 293, 297, 298, 320

Landi v. County of Monterey, 139 Cal. App. 3d 934 (1983), 86, 489, 492

Langrutta v. City Council, 9 Cal. App. 3d 890 (1970), 116

Las Tunas Beach Geologic Hazard Abatement Dist. v. Superior Court, 38 Cal. App. 4th 1002 (1995), 394

Las Virgenes Homeowners Federation, Inc. v. County of Los Angeles, 177 Cal. App. 3d 300 (1986), 164

Latinos Unidos de Napa v. City of Napa, 196 Cal. App. 4th 1154 (2011), 176, 517, 519

Latinos Unidos del Valle de Napa y Solano v. County of Napa, 217 Cal. App. 4th 1160 (2013), 424

Laupheimer v. State of California, 200 Cal. App. 3d 440 (1988), 508

Laurel Heights Improvement Ass'n v. Regents of the Univ. of Cal., 47 Cal. 3d 376 (1988), 139, 143, 155, 166, 170, 171, 552, 553

Laurel Park Community, LLC v. City of Tumwater, 698 F. 3d 1180 (9th Cir. 2012), 294

Lawler v. City of Redding, 7 Cal. App. 4th 778 (1992), 68

League of Residential Neighborhood Advocates v. City of Los Angeles, 498 F. 3d 1052 (9th Cir. 2007), passim

League of Women Voters v. Countywide Crim. Justice Coordination Comm., 203 Cal. App. 3d 529 (1988), 382

Lee v. City of Monterey Park, 173 Cal. App. 3d 798 (1985), 40, 428

Legacy Group v. City of Wasco, 106 Cal. App. 4th 1305 (2003), 117, 277, 278, 536

LeGault v. Erickson, 70 Cal. App. 4th 369 (1999), 129

Legislature v. Deukmejian, 34 Cal. 3d 658 (1983), 382

Lehto v. City of Oxnard, 171 Cal. App. 3d 285 (1985), 565

Leroy Land Dev. v. Tahoe Reg'l Planning Agency, 939 F. 2d 696 (9th Cir. 1991), 282

Lesher Commc'ns, Inc. v. City of Walnut Creek, 52 Cal. 3d 531 (1991), 10, 20, 43, 48, 370, 371, 377, 378

Leslie Salt Co. v. United States, 896 F. 2d 354 (9th Cir. 1990), 182, 183

Leslie v. Superior Court, 73 Cal. App. 4th 1042 (1999), 470

Levald Inc. v. City of Palm Desert, 998 F. 2d 680 (9th Cir. 1993), 303, 314

Leyva v. Nielsen, 83 Cal. App. 4th 1061 (2000), 566

Lighthouse Field Beach Rescue v. City of Santa Cruz, 131 Cal. App. 4th 1170 (2005), 149

Lightweight Processing Co. v. County of Ventura, 133 Cal. App. 3d 1042 (1982), 507

Lin v. City of Pleasanton, 176 Cal. App. 4th 408 (2009), 361

Lincoln Property Co. No. 41 v. Law, Inc. 45 Cal. App. 3d 230 (1975), 64

Lindborg/Dahl Investors, Inc. v. City of Garden Grove, 179 Cal. App. 3d 956 (1986), 483

Lindelli v. Town of San Anselmo (Marin Sanitary Service), 111 Cal. App. 4th 1099 (2003), 367, 525

Lingle v. Chevron U.S.A. Inc., 544 U.S. 528 (2005), 287, 290, 291, 293, 313, 315, 316, 320, 327

Littoral Dev. Co. v. San Francisco Bay Conser. & Dev. Comm'n, 33 Cal. App. 4th 211 (1995), 276

Livingston Rock & Gravel Co. v. County of Los Angeles, 43 Cal. 2d 121 (1954), 58, 60

Lockard v. City of Los Angeles, 33 Cal. 2d 453 (1949), 40

Lockley v. Law Office of Cantrell, Green, Pekich, Cruz & McCort, 91 Cal. App. 4th 875 (2001), 542

Loewenstein v. City of Lafayette, 103 Cal. App. 4th 718 (2002), 296, 298, 299, 506, 511

Long Beach Equities, Inc. v. County of Ventura, 231 Cal. App. 3d, 290, 293, 300, 303, 305, 311, 324

Loretto v. Teleprompter Manhattan CATV Corporation, 458 U. S. 419 (1982), 287

Los Altos El Granada Investors v. City of Capitola, 139 Cal. App. 4th 629 (2006), 291

Los Altos Property Owners Ass'n v. Hutcheon, 69 Cal. App. 3d 22 (1977), 383

Los Angeles County v. City Council of Lawndale, 202 Cal. App. 2d 20 (1962), 403

Los Angeles Police Protective League v. City of Los Angeles, 188 Cal. App. 3d 1 (1986), 563

Los Angeles Unified School Dist. v. City of Los Angeles, 58 Cal. App. 4th 1019 (1997), 164

Love v. Wolf, 226 Cal. App. 2d 378 (1964), 542

Loyola Marymount Univ. v. Los Angeles Unified Sch. Dist., 45 Cal. App. 4th 1256 (1996), 331, 341

Lucas v. South Carolina Coastal Council, 505 U.S. 1003 (1992), 288, 291, 292, 295, 296, 302, 310, 320

Lugar v. Edmondson Oil Co., 457 U.S. 922 (1982), 567

Lujan v. Defenders of Wildlife, 504 U.S. 555 (1992), 212

Lusardi Construction Co. v. Aubry, 1 Cal. 4th 976 (1992), 269

Mack v. Ironside, 35 Cal. App. 3d 127 (1973), 48

MacLeod v. County of Santa Clara, 749 F. 2d 541 (9th Cir. 1984), 290, 312

Madera Oversight Commission, Inc. v. County of Madera, 199 Cal. App. 4th 48 (2011), 161, 164

Madrigal v. City of Huntington Beach, 147 Cal. App. 4th 1375 (2007), 147

Magan v. County of Kings, 105 Cal. App. 4th 468 (2002), 146

Maginn v. City of Glendale, 72 Cal. App. 4th 1102 (1999), 116, 516

Mahdavi v Fair Employment Practices Comm'n, 67 Cal. App. 3d 326 (1977), 507

Mahon v. County of San Mateo, 139 Cal. App. 4th 812 (2006), 491

Malibu Mountains Recreation, Inc. v. County of Los Angeles, 67 Cal. App. 4th 359 (1998), 57

Mammoth Lakes Land Acquisition LLC v. Town of Mammoth Lakes, 191 Cal. App. 4th 435 (2010), 277, 280, 526

Mangini v. R. J. Reynolds Tobacco Co., 7 Cal. 4th 1057 (1994), 542

Manhattan Sepulveda v. City of Manhattan Beach, 22 Cal. App. 4th 865 (1994), 59

Mani Brothers Real Estate Group v. City of Los Angeles, 153 Cal. App. 4th 1385 (2007), 174, 175

Manufactured Home Communities, Inc. v. City of San Jose, 420 F. 3d 1022 (9th Cir. 2005), 291, 307

Masonite Corporation v. County of Mendocino, 218 Cal. App. 4th 230 (2013), 166, 370

Marbled Murrelet v. Babbitt, 83 F. 3d 1060 (9th Cir. 1996), 240, 243, 244

Marblehead v. City of San Clemente, 226 Cal. App. 3d 1504 (1991), 357, 358, 373

Margolin v. Regional Planning Comm'n, 134 Cal. App. 3d 999 (1982), 562

Marine Forests Soc'y v. California Coastal Comm'n, 104 Cal. App. 4th 1232 (2002), (review granted), 259

Marine Forests Soc'y v. California Coastal Comm'n, 36 Cal. 4th 1 (2005), 259

Markley v. City Council, 131 Cal. App. 3d 656 (1982), 545

Marocco v. Ford Motor Co., 7 Cal. App. 3d 84 (1970), 542

Martin v. City and County of San Francisco, 135 Cal. App. 4th 392 (2006), 142

Maryland-Nat'l Capital Park Planning Comm'n v. U.S. Postal Serv., 487 F. 2d 1029 (D.C. Cir. 1973), 65

Mayo v. United States, 319 U.S. 441 (1943), 65

McAllister v. California Coastal Commission, 169 Cal. App. 4th 912, (2008), 261

McBail & Co. v. Solano LAFCO, 62 Cal. App. 4th 1223 (1998), 387, 402

McCormick v. Board of Supervisors, 198 Cal. App. 3d, 548

McManus v. KPAL Broad. Corp., 182 Cal. App. 2d 558 (1960), 57

McMillan v. American Gen. Fin. Corp., 60 Cal. App. 3d 175 (1976), 482

McMullan v. Santa Monica Rent Control Bd., 168 Cal. App. 3d 960 (1985), 72, 93, 94

McPherson v. City of Manhattan Beach, 78 Cal. App. 4th 1252 (2000), 98, 119

McQueen v. Board of Directors, 202 Cal. App. 3d 1136 (1988), 529, 530

Mejia v. City of Los Angeles, 130 Cal. App. 4th 322 (2005), 151

Melom v. City of Madera, 183 Cal. App. 4th 41 (2010), 158

Melton v. City of San Pablo, 252 Cal. App. 2d 794 (1967), 57

Meridian Ocean Sys., Inc. v. State Lands Comm'n, 222 Cal. App. 3d 153 (1990), 492, 505, 515

Metromedia, Inc. v. City of San Diego, 26 Cal. 3d 848 (1980), void on other grounds, 453 U.S. 490 (1981), 1, 3, 60, 249

Metropolitan Water Dist. v. Imperial Irr. Dist., 80 Cal. App. 4th 1403 (2000), 564

MHC Financing Ltd. Partnership v. City of San Rafael, 714 F.3d 1118 (9th Cir. 2013), 294, 314

Midrash Sephardi, Inc. v. Town of Surfside, 366 F. 3d 1214 (11th Cir. 2004), 53

Midway Orchards v. County of Butte, 220 Cal. App. 3d 765 (1990), 27, 277, 279, 372

Mikels v. Rager, 232 Cal. App. 3d 334 (1991), 123

Milagra Ridge Partners Ltd. v. City of Pacifica, 62 Cal. App. 4th 108 (1998), 305, 531

Miller v. City of Hermosa Beach, 13 Cal. App. 4th 1118 (1993), 548

Miller v. Miller, 87 Cal. App. 3d 762 (1978), 382

Miller v. Schoene, 276 U.S. 272 (1928), 310

Mingo Logan Coal Co. v. Environmental Protection Agency, 850 F. Supp. 2d 133 (D.D.C. 2012), 202

Mira Dev. Corp. v. City of San Diego, 205 Cal. App. 3d 1201 (1988), 109, 481

Mira Mar Mobile Cmty. v. City of Oceanside, 119 Cal. App. 4th 477 (2004), 10, 142, 168, 252

Mission Oaks Ranch, Ltd. v. County of Santa Barbara, 65 Cal. App. 4th 713 (1998), 154, 311, 561

Mission Springs Water District v. Verjil, 218 Cal. App. 4th 892 (2013), 421, 533, 562

Mitchell v. County of Orange, 165 Cal. App. 3d 1185 (1985), 24, 37, 506, 548

Mitcheltree v. City of Los Angeles, 17 Cal. App. 3d 791 (1971), 57

Modesto Irrigation Dist. v. Gutierrez, 619 F.3d 1024 (9th Cir. 2010), 221

Mokler v. County of Orange, 157 Cal. App. 4th 121 (2007), 525

Mola Dev. Corp. v. City of Seal Beach, 57 Cal. App. 4th 405 (1997), 509

Monell v. Dept. of Social Servs., 436 U.S. 658 (1978), 312, 567

Moore v. City of Costa Mesa, 886 F. 2d 260 (9th Cir. 1989), 289

Moores v. Mendocino County, 122 Cal. App. 4th 883 (2004), 135

Moran v. State Bd. of Med. Exam's., 32 Cal. 2d 301 (1948), 535

Morehart v. County of Santa Barbara, 7 Cal. 4th 725 (1994), 5, 12, 42, 72, 136, 137, 417, 537

Morgan v. United States, 298 U.S. 468 (1936), 479

Morongo Band of Mission Indians v. State Water Resources Control Board, 45 Cal. 4th 751 (2009), 484

Morrill v. Lujan, 802 F. Supp. 424 (S.D. Ala. 1992), 243

Moss v. County of Humboldt, 162 Cal. App. 4th 1041 (2008), 174, 175

Mount Shasta Bioregional Ecology Center v. County of Siskiyou, 210 Cal. App. 4th 199 (2012), 158, 168

Mountain Def. League v. Bd. of Supervisors, 65 Cal. App. 3d 723 (1977), 481, 515

Mountain Lion Found. v. Fish and Game Comm'n, 16 Cal. 4th 105 (1997), 140, 504, 506

Mozzetti v. City of Brisbane, 67 Cal. App. 3d 565 (1977), 542

Murrieta Valley Unified Sch. Dist. v. County of Riverside, 228 Cal. App. 3d 1212 (1991), 109

Muzzy Ranch Co. v. Solano County Airport Land Use Comm'n, 41 Cal. 4th 372 (2007), 26, 143, 144

Myers v. Patterson, 196 Cal. App. 3d 130 (1987), 361, 362, 365

N.T. Hill, Inc. v. City of Fresno, 72 Cal. App. 4th 977 (1999), 95, 555, 559

Nacimiento Reg'l Water Mgmt. Advisory Comm. v. Monterey County Water Res. Agency, 122 Cal. App. 4th 961 (2004), 549

Napa Citizens for Honest Gov't v. Napa County Bd. of Supervisors, 91 Cal. App. 4th 342 (2001), 25, 35, 160, 169, 173, 516

Nash v. City of Santa Monica, 37 Cal. 3d 97 (1984), 42, 313, 320

Nasha v. City of Los Angeles, 125 Cal. App. 4th 470 (2004), 48, 512, 513

Nat'l Adver. Co. v. County of Monterey, 1 Cal. 3d 875 (1970), 58

Nat'l Ass'n of Home Builders v. Defenders of Wildlife, 127 S. Ct. 2518 (2007), 229

Nat'l Ass'n of Home Builders v. Norton, 340 F. 3d 835 (9th Cir. 2003), 220

Nat'l Wildlife Fed'n v. Nat'l Marine Fisheries Serv., 524 F. 3d 917 (9th Cir. 2008), 229, 234, 235, 237, 243

National Ass'n of Home Builders v. U.S. Environmental Protection Agency, F.Supp.2d, 2013 WL 3863895 (D.D.C. July 26, 2013) (appeal filed on Sept. 24, 2013), 191

National Mining Ass'n v. U.S. Army Corps of Eng'rs, 145 F. 3d 1399 (D.C. Cir. 1998), 188

National Nutritional Foods Ass'n v. FDA, 491 F. 2d 1141 (2d Cir. 1974), 479

National Parks & Conser. Ass'n v. County of Riverside, 81 Cal. App. 4th 234 (2000), 564

National Parks and Conservation Ass'n v. County of Riverside, 71 Cal. App. 4th 1341 (1999), 158, 553

National Wildlife Fed'n v. Coleman, 529 F. 2d 359 (5th Cir.), cert. denied, 429 U.S. 979 (1976), 229, 230

Native Am. Sacred Site & Envtl. Protection Ass'n v. City of San Juan Capistrano, 120 Cal. App. 4th 961 (2004), 140, 366, 506

Native Sun/Lyon Communities v. City of Escondido 15 Cal. App. 4th 892 (1993), 91, 277, 278

Natural Resources Defense Council v. Rogers, 381 F. Supp. 2d 1212 (E.D. Cal. 2005), 234

Natural Resources Defense Council v. U.S. Dept. of Interior, 113 F. 3d 1121 (9th Cir. 1997), 226

Negrete v. State Pers. Bd., 213 Cal. App. 3d 1160 (1989), 513

Negron v. Dundee, 221 Cal. App. 3d 1502 (1990), 132

Neighborhood Action Group v. County of Calaveras, 156 Cal. App. 3d 1176 (1984), 20, 32, 55, 508

Neighbors for Smart Rail v. Exposition Metro Line Construction Authority, 57 Cal. 4th 439 (2013), 156, 157, 159, 166

Neighbors in Support of Appropriate Land Use v. County of Tuolumne, 157 Cal. App. 4th 997 (2007), 55

Nelson v. Carlson, 17 Cal. App. 4th 732 (1993), 361, 376

New Mexico Cattle Growers Ass'n v. U.S. Fish and Wildlife Serv., 248 F. 3d 1277 (10th Cir. 2001), 225, 226

Newberry Springs Water Ass'n v. County of San Bernardino, 150 Cal. App. 3d 740 (1984), 478

Newsom v. Bd. of Supervisors, 205 Cal. 262 (1928), 373

Ni v. Slocum, 196 Cal. App. 4th 1636 (2011), 363

Nightlife Partners, Ltd. v. City of Beverly Hills, 108 Cal. App. 4th 81 (2002), 483, 484

No Oil, Inc. v. City of Los Angeles, 13 Cal. 3d 68 (1974), 150

No Oil, Inc. v. City of Los Angeles, 196 Cal. App. 3d 223 (1987), 24, 143, 416, 516

No Wetlands Landfill Expansion v. County of Marin, 204 Cal. App. 4th 573 (2012), 172

Nollan v. California Coastal Comm'n, 483 U.S. 825 (1987), 60, 100, 108, 249, 251, 282, 295, 309, 319, 320, 321, 322, 323, 324, 325, 326, 327, 328, 329, 330, 331, 332, 333, 334, 335, 343, 431, 432, 433, 434

Nordlinger v. Hahn, 505 U.S. 1 (1992), 336

Norsco Enters. v. City of Fremont, 54 Cal. App. 3d 488 (1976), 110, 320

North Coast Rivers Alliance v. Marin Municipal Water Dist., 216 Cal. App. 4th 614 (2013), 158, 161, 164, 165

North Pacifica, LLC v. City of Pacifica, 234 F. Supp. 2d 1053 (N.D. Cal. 2002), 421

Northern California River Watch v. City of Healdsburg, 496 F. 3d 993 (9th Cir. 2007) cert. denied, 128 S. Ct. 1225 (2008), 184, 185

Northern Spotted Owl v. Lujan, 758 F. Supp. 621 (W.D. Wash. 1991), 226

Northwest Ecosystem Alliance v. U.S. Fish & Wildlife Serv., 475 F. 3d 1136 (9th Cir. 2007), 220

Not About Water Com. v. Board of Supervisors, 95 Cal. App. 4th 982 (2002), 350

Novi v. City of Pacifica, 169 Cal. App. 3d 678 (1985), 45, 46, 249, 250

NRDC v. Callaway, 392 F. Supp. 685 (D.D.C. 1975), 182

NRDC v. Kempthorne, 506 F. Supp. 2d 322 (E.D. Cal. 2007), 231, 233, 234, 235

O.G. Sansone Co. v. Dept. of Transportation, 55 Cal. App. 3d 434 (1976), 269

O.W.L. Found. v. City of Rohnert Park, 168 Cal. App. 4th 568 (2008), 161, 458, 525, 532

O'Loane v. O'Rourke, 231 Cal. App. 2d 774 (1965), 39, 505

O'Mara v. Council of City of Newark, 238 Cal. App. 2d 836 (1965), 59

Oakland Heritage Alliance v. City of Oakland, 195 Cal. App. 4th 884 (2011), 165

Oasis West Realty, LLC v. Goldman, 51 Cal. 4th 811 (2011), 560

Ocean Harbor House Homeowners Ass'n v. California Coastal Comm'n, 163 Cal. App. 4th, 222, 234, 322, 323

Oceanic California, Inc. v. North Cent. Coastal Reg'l Comm'n, 63 Cal. App. 3d 57 (1976), 93, 275

Okasaki v. City of Elk Grove, 203 Cal. App. 4th 1043 (2012), 518

Old Dearborn Distrib. Co. v. Seagram Distillers Corp., 299 U.S. 183 (1936), 336

Old Santa Barbara Pier Co. v. State of California, 71 Cal. App. 3d 250 (1977), 480

Olive Proration Program Comm. v. Agric. Prorate Comm'n, 17 Cal. 2d 204 (1941), 528

Oregon Natural Resources Council v. Allen, 476 F. 3d 1031 (9th Cir. 2007), 234, 236, 244

Orinda Ass'n v. Board of Supervisors, 182 Cal. App. 3d 1145 (1986), 56, 143

Orinda Homeowners Comm. v. Board of Supervisors, 11 Cal. App. 3d 768 (1970), 64

Orsi v. City Council, 219 Cal. App. 3d 1576 (1990), 85, 489, 490, 492

Owen v. City of Independence, 445 U.S. 622 (1980), 312

Oxnard Harbor Dist. v. LAFCO, 16 Cal. App. 4th 259 (1993), 390

Pac. Coast Fed'n of Fishermen's Assn's v. Bureau of Reclamation, 426 F. 3d 1082 (9th Cir. 2005), 235

Pacific Legal Found. v. Andrus, 657 F. 2d 829 (6th Cir. 1981), 219

Pacific Palisades Bowl Mobile Estates, LLC v. City of Los Angeles, 55 Cal 4th 703 (2012), 73

Pacifica Corp. v. City of Camarillo, 149 Cal. App. 3d 168 (1983), 482, 504, 507

Pajaro Valley Water Mgmt. Agency v. Amrhein, 150 Cal. App. 4th 1364 (2007), 352

Pala Band of Mission Indians v. County of San Diego, 68 Cal. App. 4th 556 (1998), 142

Palazzolo v. Rhode Island, 533 U.S. 606 (2001), 288, 295, 302, 304

Palermo v. Stockton Theatres, 32 Cal. 2d 53 (1948), 469

Palmer v. Board of Supervisors, 145 Cal. App. 3d 779 (1983), 94

Palmer v. City of Ojai, 178 Cal. App. 3d 280 (1986), 491

Palmer/Sixth St. Props., L.P. v. City of Los Angeles, 175 Cal. App. 4th 1396 (2009), 431, 434, 435, 439, 440, 441, 443

Palomar Mobilehome Park Ass'n v. City of San Marcos, 989 F. 2d 362 (9th Cir. 1993), 306

Parchester Village Neighborhood Council v. City of Richmond, 182 Cal. App. 4th 305 (2010), 142

Park Area Neighbors v. Town of Fairfax, 29 Cal. App. 4th 1442 (1994), 526, 527

Patrick Media Group Inc. v. California Coastal Comm'n, 9 Cal. App. 4th 592 (1992), 309, 509, 537

Patterson v. Central Coast Reg'l Comm'n, 58 Cal. App. 3d 833 (1976), 508, 515

Penn Central Transportation Company v. City of New York, 438 U.S. 104 (1978), 3, 63, 253, 289, 290, 291, 293, 294, 295, 296, 297, 299, 302, 303, 321, 324

People ex rel. Deukmejian v. County of Mendocino, 36 Cal. 3d 476 (1984), 5

People of the State of California ex rel. Lockyer v. U.S. Dept. of Agriculture, 575 F. 3d 999 (9th Cir. 2009), 230, 499

People v. Dep't of Hous. & Cmty Dev., 45 Cal. App. 3d 185 (1975), 523

People v. Djekich, 229 Cal. App. 3d 1213 (1991), 495

People v. Gates, 41 Cal. App. 3d 590 (1974), 45

People v. H & H Properties, 154 Cal. App. 3d 894 (1984), 94, 277

People v. LAFCO, 81 Cal. App. 3d 464 (1978), 407

People v. Long, 7 Cal. App. 3d 586 (1970), 542

People v. Minor, 96 Cal. App. 4th 29 (2002), 496

People v. Sims, 32 Cal. 3d 468, 478-81 (1982), 508

People v. Thomas Shelton Powers, 2 Cal. App. 4th 330 (1992), 275

Peralta Fed. of Teachers v. Peralta Cmty. Coll. Dist., 24 Cal. 3d 369 (1979), 522

Perry v. Brown, 52 Cal. 4th 1116 (2009), 379, 533

Personal Watercraft Coalition v. Marin County Board of Supervisors, 100 Cal. App. 4th 129 (2002), 46

Pettitt v. City of Fresno, 34 Cal. App. 3d 813 (1973), 275

Pfeiffer v. City of La Mesa, 69 Cal. App. 3d 74 (1977), 93, 282, 556

Pfeiffer v. Sunnyvale, 200 Cal. App. 4th 1552 (2011), 156

Pines v. City of Santa Monica, 29 Cal. 3d 656 (1981), 72, 82

Pistoresi v. City of Madera, 138 Cal. App. 3d 284 (1982), 407

Pitts v. Perluss, 58 Cal. 2d 824 (1962), 504

Placer County LAFCO v. Nevada County LAFCO, 135 Cal. App. 4th 793 (2006), 387, 393, 407

Placer Ranch Partners v. County of Placer, 91 Cal. App. 4th 1336 (2001), 481

Planning and Conservation League v. Dep't of Fish and Game, 55 Cal. App. 4th 479 (1997), 247

Planning and Conservation League v. Dept. of Water Resources, 83 Cal. App. 4th 892 (2000), 140, 160, 168

Plastic Pipe and Fittings Association v. California Buildings Standards Commission, 124 Cal. App. 4th 1390 (2004), 469

POET LLC v. Cal. Air Resources Bd., 218 Cal. App. 4th 681 (2013), 164, 459

Pomona Valley Hosp. Med. Ctr. v. Superior Court, 55 Cal. App. 4th 93 (1997), 539

Ponderosa Homes, Inc. v. City of San Ramon, 23 Cal. App. 4th 1761 (1994), 555

Porterville Citizens for Responsible Hillside Development v. City of Porterville, 157 Cal. App. 4th 885 (2007), 151, 252

PR/JSM Rivara LLC v. Community Redevelopment Agency of the City of Los Angeles, 180 Cal. App. 4th 1475 (2010), 505, 508

Pratt v. Adams, 229 Cal. App. 2d 602 (1964), 75, 77

Precon Dev. Corp. v. U.S. Army Corps of Eng'rs, 633 F.3d 278 (4th Cir. 2011), 185

Prentis v. Atlantic Coast Line Co., 211 U.S. 210 (1908), 515

Prentiss v. City of South Pasadena, 15 Cal. App. 4th 85 (1993), 253, 506

Preservation Action Council v. City of San Jose, 141 Cal. App. 4th 1336 (2006), 171

Preserve Wild Santee v. City of Santee, 210 Cal. App. 4th 260 (2012), 161, 163, 164

Property Owners of Whispering Palms, Inc. v. Newport Pacific, Inc., 132 Cal. App. 4th 666 (2005), 533

Protect Our Water v. County of Merced, 110 Cal. App. 4th 362 (2003), 551

Protect the Historic Amador Waterways v. Amador Water Agency, 116 Cal. App. 4th 1099 (2004), 157

Qwest Communications, Inc. v. City of Berkeley, 433 F.3d 1253 (9th Cir. 2006), 6

Rancho La Costa v. County of San Diego, 111 Cal. App. 3d 54 (1980), 2, 143

Rapanos v. United States. 547 U.S. 715 (2006), 183, 184, 187, 369

Rapp v. County of Napa Planning Comm'n, 204 Cal. App. 2d 695 (1962), 57

Rasmussen v. City Council, 140 Cal. App. 3d 842 (1983), 110

Reagan v. City of Sausalito, 210 Cal. App. 2d 618 (1962), 363

Redevelopment Agency v. City of Berkeley, 80 Cal. App. 3d 158 (1978), 372

Redwood Coast Watersheds Alliance v. State Bd. of Forestry & Fire Prot., 70 Cal. App. 4th 962 (1999), 506

Regency Outdoor Advertising, Inc. v. City of Los Angeles, 39 Cal. 4th 507 (2006), 289

Regents of Univ. of Cal. v. City of Santa Monica, 77 Cal. App. 3d 130 (1978), 66

Remmenga v. California Coastal Comm'n, 163 Cal. App. 3d 623 (1985), 4

Res. Def. Fund v. County of Santa Cruz, 133 Cal. App. 3d 800 (1982), 20, 32, 43

Res. Def. Fund v. LAFCO, 191 Cal. App. 3d 886 (1987), 402, 530

Residents Ad Hoc Stadium Comm. v. Bd. of Trustees, 89 Cal. App. 3d 274 (1979), 142, 167

Resource Defense Fund v. County of Santa Cruz, 133 Cal. App. 3d 800 (1982), 20, 32, 43

Resources Ltd. v. Robertson, 35 F. 3d 1300 (9th Cir. 1993), 231

Rezai v. City of Tustin, 26 Cal. App. 4th 443 (1994), 303, 309

Rialto Citizens for Responsible Growth v. City of Rialto, 208 Cal. App. 4th 899 (2012), 161

Ricciardi v. County of Los Angeles, 115 Cal. App. 2d 569 (1953), 59

Richards v. City of Tustin, 225 Cal. App. 2d 97 (1964), 505

Richeson v. Helal, 158 Cal. App. 4th 268 (2007), 4, 5

Richmond v. Shasta Community Services District, 32 Cal. 4th 409 (2004), 349, 351, 352, 439

Ridgecrest Charter Sch. v. Sierra Sands Unified Sch. Dist., 130 Cal. App. 4th 986 (2005), 402

Riggs v. City of Oxnard, 154 Cal. App. 3d 526 (1984), 498

Riverwatch v. County of San Diego, 76 Cal. App. 4th 1428 (1999), 157

Riverwatch v. Olivenhain Municipal Water Dist., 170 Cal. App. 4th 1186 (2009), 141

Rizzo v. Board of Trustees, 27 Cal. App. 4th 853 (1994), 515

Robinson v. City and County of San Francisco, 208 Cal. App. 4th 950 (2012), 145

Robinson v. City of Alameda, 194 Cal. App. 3d 1286 (1987), 73, 75

Roccaforte v. City of San Diego, 89 Cal. App. 3d 877 (1979), 534

Rocky Mountain Farmers Union v. Corey, 730 F.3d 1070 (9th Cir. 2013), 459

Rohn v. City of Visalia, 214 Cal. App. 3d 1463 (1989), 322, 325

Roosevelt Campobello Int'l Park Comm'n v. U.S. EPA, 684 F. 2d 1041 (1st Cir. 1982), 229, 231

Rosenaur v. Scherer, 88 Cal. App. 4th 260 (2001), 561

Ross v. City of Rolling Hills Estates, 192 Cal. App. 3d 370 (1987), 46, 250

Rossco Holdings, Inc. v. State of California, 212 Cal. App. 3d 642 (1989), 93, 309

Rossi v. Brown, 9 Cal. 4th 688 (1995), 358, 359, 373, 374, 560

Royal Convalescent Hosp. v State Bd. of Control, 99 Cal. App. 3d 788, 793 (1979, 508

Royalty Carpet Mills, Inc. v. City of Irvine, 125 Cal. App. 4th 1110 (2005), 515, 518

RRLH, Inc. v. Saddleback Valley Unified Sch. Dist., 222 Cal. App. 3d 1602 (1990), 344

Rubalcava v. Martinez, 158 Cal. App. 4th 563 (2007), 367, 368

Rueth v. U.S. EPA, 13 F. 3d 227 (7th Cir. 1993), 213

Running Fence Corp. v. Superior Court, 51 Cal. App. 3d 400 (1975), 540

Russ Bldg. Partnership v. City and County of San Francisco, 199 Cal. App. 3d 1496 (1987), 277, 320, 321, 335, 336, 337, 348

Saad v. City of Berkeley, 24 Cal. App. 4th 1206 (1994), 57, 250, 321, 324

Sabek, Inc. v. County of Sonoma, 190 Cal. App. 3d 163 (1987), 60

Sackett v. Environmental Protection Agency, 132 S. Ct. 1367 (2012) (Justice Alito's concurring opinion), 186, 190, 191

Sacramento Old City Ass'n v. City Council, 229 Cal. App. 3d 1011 (1991), 165, 539

Salmon Protection and Watershed Network v. County of Marin, 125 Cal. App. 4th 1098 (2004), 146, 524

Salmon Protection and Watershed Network v. County of Marin, 205 Cal. App. 4th 195 (2012), 524

San Bernardino Assoc. of Governments v. Superior Ct., 135 Cal. App. 4th 1106 (2006), 140

San Bernardino Valley Audubon Soc'y, Inc. v. County of San Bernardino, 155 Cal. App. 3d 738 (1984), 167, 564

San Diego Bldg. Contractors Ass'n v. City Council, 13 Cal. 3d 205 (1974), 504, 505, 507

San Diego Gas & Elec. Co. v. City of San Diego, 450 U.S. 621 (1981), 311

San Diego Navy Broadway Complex Coal. v. City of San Diego, 185 Cal. App. 4th 924 (2010), 175, 464

San Diego Service Authority v. Superior Court, 198 Cal. App. 3d 1466 (1988), 271

San Franciscans Upholding the Downtown Plan v. City & County of San Francisco, 102 Cal. App. 4th 656 (2002), 24, 159, 171

San Francisco Forty-Niners v. Nishioka (Comstock), 75 Cal. App. 4th 637 (1999), 376

San Joaquin Raptor Rescue Center v. County of Merced, 149 Cal. App. 4th 645 (2007), 164

San Joaquin Raptor/Wildlife Rescue Ctr. v. County of Stanislaus, 27 Cal. App. 4th 713 (1994), 163

San Jose Christian College v. City of Morgan Hill, 360 F. 3d 1024 (9th Cir. 2004), 53, 106, 479

San Lorenzo Valley Community Advocates for Responsible Education v. San Lorenzo Valley Unified School Dist., 139 Cal. App. 4th 1356 (2006), 145, 146

San Mateo County Coastal Landowners' Ass'n v. County of San Mateo, 38 Cal. App. 4th 523 (1995), 15, 372, 374, 375, 417

San Pedro Hotel Co. v. City of Los Angeles, 159 F. 3d 470 (9th Cir. 1998), 568

San Remo Hotel v. City and County of San Francisco, 545 U.S. 323 (2005), 302, 303, 306, 307

San Remo Hotel v. City and County of San Francisco, 27 Cal. 4th 643 (2002), 322, 324, 328, 330, 331, 332, 434, 438

Santa Clara County Contractors and Homebuilders Ass'n v. City of Santa Clara, 232 Cal. App. 2d 564 (1965), 72

Santa Clara County Local Transp. Auth. v. Guardino, 11 Cal. 4th 220 (1995), 347, 348, 373

Santa Clarita Organization for Planning the Environment v. City of Santa Clarita, 197 Cal. App. 4th 1042 (2011), 162, 464

Santa Clarita Organization for Planning the Environment v. County of Los Angeles (SCOPE 1), 106 Cal. App. 4th 715 (2003), 160

Santa Clarita Organization for Planning the Environment v. County of Los Angeles (SCOPE 2), 157 Cal. App. 4th 149 (2007), 160

Santa Margarita Area Residents Together ("SMART") v. County of San Luis Obispo, 84 Cal. App. 4th 221 (2000), 277, 280

Santa Monica Baykeeper v. City of Malibu, 193 Cal. App. 4th 1538 (2011), 164

Santa Monica Beach, Ltd. v. Superior Court, 19 Cal. 4th 952 (1999), 4, 276, 371, 379

Santa Monica Pines, Ltd. v. Rent Control Bd., 35 Cal. 3d 858 (1984), 72, 82, 94, 119, 275, 276

Santa Rosa Band of Indians v. Kings County, 532 F. 2d 655 (9th Cir. 1975), 68

Santiago County Water Dist. v. County of Orange, 118 Cal. App. 3d 818 (1981), 143, 155, 160

Save Cuyama Valley v. County of Santa Barbara, 213 Cal. App. 4th 1059 (2013), 157, 158, 165

Save El Toro Ass'n v. Days, 74 Cal. App. 3d 64 (1977), 16, 21

Save Our Bay, Inc. v. San Diego Unified Port Dist., 42 Cal. App. 4th 686 (1996), 536

Save Our Carmel River v. Monterey Peninsula Water Mgmt. Dist., 141 Cal. App. 4th 677 (2006), 146, 147

Save Our Neighborhood v. Lishman, 140 Cal. App. 4th 1288 (2006), 174

Save Our Peninsula Comm. v. County of Monterey, 87 Cal. App. 4th 99 (2001), 23, 156, 165

Save Our Residential Env't v. City of West Hollywood, 9 Cal. App. 4th 1745 (1992), 167

Save Round Valley Alliance v. County of Inyo, 157 Cal. App. 4th 1437 (2007), 156, 168

Save San Francisco Bay Ass'n v. San Francisco Bay Conserv. & Dev. Comm'n, 10 Cal. App. 4th 908 (1992), 162

Save Stanislaus Area Farm Econ. (SAFE) v. Bd. of Supervisors, 13 Cal. App. 4th 141 (1993), 376, 379

Save Tara v. City of West Hollywood, 45 Cal. 4th 116 (2008), 141

Save the Yaak Com. v. Block, 840 F. 2d 714 (9th Cir. 1988), 243

Schaeffer Land Trust v. San Jose City Council, 215 Cal. App. 3d 612 (1989), 163

Schnuck v. City of Santa Monica, 935 F.2d 171, 173-74 (9th Cir. 1991), 306

Scott v. Indian Wells, 6 Cal. 3d 541 (1972), 477, 512, 537

Scrutton v. County of Sacramento, 275 Cal. App. 2d 412 (1969), 2, 63, 64

Sec. Nat'l Guaranty, Inc. v. Cal. Coastal Comm'n, 159 Cal. 4th 402 (2008), 263

Segundo v. City of Rancho Mirage, 813 F. 2d 1387 (9th Cir. 1987), 68

Selinger v. City Council, 216 Cal. App. 3d 259 (1989), 85, 490, 491, 492

Senate v. Jones, 21 Cal. 4th 1142 (1999), 374

Sequoia Park Associates v. County of Sonoma, 176 Cal. App. 4th 1270 (2009), 5, 72, 89

Sequoyah Hills Homeowners Ass'n v. City of Oakland, 23 Cal. App. 4th 704 (1993), 25, 112, 113, 421, 516

Serra Canyon Company Ltd. v. California Coastal Comm'n, 120 Cal. App. 4th 663 (2004), 309

Shapell Indus., Inc. v. Governing Bd., 1 Cal. App. 4th 218 (1991), 322, 560

Shea Homes L.P. v. County of Alameda, 110 Cal. App. 4th 1246 (2003), 370, 374, 424

Shelter Creek Dev. Corp. v. City of Oxnard, 34 Cal. 3d 733 (1983), 71, 72

Sierra Club, Inc. v. California Coastal Comm'n, 95 Cal. App. 3d 495 (1979), 535, 536

Sierra Club v. Bd. of Supervisors, 126 Cal. App. 3d 698 (1981), 13, 19, 20, 23, 29, 379

Sierra Club v. Cal. Coastal Comm'n, 35 Cal. 4th 839 (2005), 171

Sierra Club v. California Dept. of Forestry, 150 Cal. App. 4th 370 (2007), 150

Sierra Club v. City of Hayward, 28 Cal. 3d 840 (1981), 257, 508, 514

Sierra Club v. City of Orange, 163 Cal. App. 4th 523 (2008), 153, 167, 176

Sierra Club v. County of Napa, 121 Cal. App. 4th 1490 (2004), 37, 171, 172

Sierra Club v. Gilroy City Council, 222 Cal. App. 3d 30 (1990), 505

Sierra Club v. Marsh, 816 F. 2d 1376 (9th Cir. 1987), 230, 235, 236

Sierra Club v. Napa County Bd. of Supervisors, 205 Cal. App. 4th 162 (2012), 79, 140

Sierra Club v. San Joaquin LAFCO, 21 Cal. 4th 489 (1999), 387, 390, 404, 528

Sierra Club v. West Side Irrigation Dist., 128 Cal. App. 4th 690 (2005), 156

Sierra Club v. Yeutter, 926 F. 2d 429 (5th Cir. 1991), 243, 244

Silicon Valley Taxpayers Ass'n, Inc. v. Santa Clara County Open Space, 44 Cal. 4th 431 (2008), 349, 352

Silvera v. City of S. Lake Tahoe, 3 Cal. App. 3d 554 (1970), 62

Simi Valley Recreation & Park Dist. v. LAFCO, 51 Cal. App. 3d 648 (1975), 402

Simpson v. Hite, 36 Cal. 2d 125 (1950), 373

Sinclair Oil Corp. v. County of Santa Barbara, 96 F. 3d 401 (9th Cir. 1996), 305

Sinclair Paint Co. v. State Bd. of Equalization, 15 Cal. 4th 866 (1997), 321, 346, 347

Sladovich v. County of Fresno, 158 Cal. App. 2d 230 (1958), 48

Smith v. County of Santa Barbara, 203 Cal. App. 3d 1415 (1988), 65

Smith v. County of Santa Barbara, 7 Cal. App. 4th 770 (1992), 500

Snow v. City of Garden Grove, 188 Cal. App. 2d 496 (1961), 57

Socialist Party v. Uhl, 155 Cal. 776 (1909), 6

Soderling v. City of Santa Monica, 142 Cal. App. 3d 501 (1983), 32, 71, 107, 110, 117, 120, 338

Solid Waste Agency of Northern Cook County (SWANCC) v. U.S. Army Corps of Eng'rs, 531 U.S. 159 (2001), 183, 187, 210

Sonoma County Nuclear Free Zone '86 v. Superior Court, 189 Cal. App. 3d 167, 535

Sosinsky v. Grant, 6 Cal. App. 4th 1548 (1992), 542

Sounhein v. City of San Dimas, 11 Cal. App. 4th 1255 (1992), 45

South Cent. Coast Reg'l Comm'n v. Charles A. Pratt Constr. Co., 128 Cal. App. 3d 830 (1982), 123

South Orange County Wastewater Auth. v. City of Dana Point, 196 Cal. App. 4th 1604 (2011), 143

Southern Pines Ass'n v. United States, 912 F. 2d 713 (4th Cir. 1990), 213

Southwest Diversified, Inc. v. City of Brisbane, 229 Cal. App. 3d 1548 (1991), 505

Sprague v. County of San Diego, 106 Cal. App. 4th 119 (2003), 116, 518

Squaw Valley Development Co. v. Goldberg, 375 F. 3d 936 (9th Cir. 2004), 316, 498, 499

St. Vincent's Sch. for Boys, Catholic Charities CYO v. City of San Rafael, 161 Cal. App. 4th 989 (2008), 413, 550

Stanislaus Audubon Society, Inc. v. County of Stanislaus, 33 Cal. App. 4th 144 (1995), 151

Stanislaus Natural Heritage Project v. County of Stanislaus, 48 Cal. App. 4th 182 (1996), 150, 155

Stanson v. Mott, 17 Cal. 3d 206 (1976), 382

Stanton v. Dumke, 64 Cal. 2d 199 (1966), 544

State Bldg. & Constr. Trades Council of Cal., AFL-CIO v. City of Vista, 54 Cal. 4th 547 (2012), 271

State Building and Construction Trades Council v. Duncan, 162 Cal. App. 4th 289 (2008), 270

State of California v. Superior Court (Perry), 150 Cal. App. 3d 848 (1984), 565

State of California v. Superior Court, 12 Cal. 3d 237 (1974), 508, 509, 512, 529, 535, 537, 539, 540, 541

Stearn v. County of San Bernardino (General Outdoor Advertising), 170 Cal. App. 4th 434 (2009), 519

Stein v. City of Santa Monica, 110 Cal. App. 3d 458 (1980), 376, 384, 506

Steketee v. Lintz, Williams & Rothberg, 38 Cal. 3d 46 (1985), 516

Stell v. Jay Hales Dev. Co., 11 Cal. App. 4th 1214 (1992), 117, 130, 136

Sterling Park, L.P. v. City of Palo Alto, 57 Cal. 4th 1193 (2013), 335, 435, 554, 555, 556, 557

Stevens v. City of Glendale, 125 Cal. App. 3d 986 (1981), 164

Stockton Citizens for Sensible Planning v. City of Stockton, 210 Cal. App. 4th 1484 (2012), 517

Stockton Citizens for Sensible Planning v. City of Stockton, 48 Cal. 4th 481 (2010), 147, 517

Stoddard v. Edelman, 4 Cal. App. 3d 544 (1970), 57

Stop H-3 Ass'n v. Dole, 740 F. 2d 1442 (9th Cir. 1984), *cert. denied sub nom., Yamasaki v. Stop H-3 Ass'n,* 471 U.S. 1108 (1985), 232

StorMedia Inc. v. Superior Court, 20 Cal. 4th 449 (1999), 542

Strong v. County of Santa Cruz, 15 Cal. 3d 720 (1975), 275

Stubblefield Constr. Co. v. City of San Bernardino, 32 Cal. App. 4th 687 (1995), 47, 312, 317, 513

Suitum v. Tahoe Regional Planning Agency, 520 U.S. 725 (1997), 303, 305, 306

Sukut-Coulson, Inc. v. Allied Canon Co., 85 Cal. App. 3d 648 (1978), 126

Summers v. Earth Island Institute, 129 S. Ct. 1142 (2009), 212, 213

Sundstrom v. County of Mendocino, 202 Cal. App. 3d 296 (1988), 149

Sunny Slope Water Co. v. City of Pasadena, 1 Cal. 2d 87 (1934), 68

Sunset Drive Corp. v. City of Redlands, 73 Cal. App. 4th 215 (1999), 85, 506, 567

Sunset View Cemetery Ass'n v. Kraintz, 196 Cal. App. 2d 115 (1961), 339

Surfside Colony, Ltd. v. California Coastal Comm'n, 226 Cal. App. 3d 1260 (1991), 325

Sustainable Transportation Advocates of Santa Barbara v. Santa Barbara Assoc. of Gov'ts, 179 Cal. App. 4th 113 (2009), 142

Sutherland v. City of Fort Bragg, 86 Cal. App. 4th 13 (2000), 498

Tahoe Reg'l Planning Agency v. King, 233 Cal. App. 3d 1365 (1991), 60, 250, 251, 325

Tahoe Vista Concerned Citizens v. County of Placer, 81 Cal. App. 4th 577 (2000), 116, 525, 527, 552

Tahoe-Sierra Preservation Council, Inc. v. Tahoe Reg'l Planning Agency, 535 U.S. 302 (2002), 63, 288, 291, 296, 297, 302, 312

Taxpayers for Accountable School Bond Spending v. San Diego Unified School Dist. 215 Cal. App. 4th 1013 (2013), 142, 150, 159, 160

Taxpayers to Limit Campaign Spending v. Fair Political Practices Comm'n, 51 Cal. 3d 744 (1990), 380, 384

Taylor v. Nichols, 558 F. 2d 561 (10th Cir. 1977), 311

Tennessee Valley Authority v. Hill, 437 U.S. 153 (1978), 232

Tenney v. Brandhove, 341 U.S. 367 (1951), 563

Terminal Plaza Corp. v. City and County of San Francisco, 177 Cal. App. 3d 892 (1986), 320

Terminal Plaza Corp. v. City and County of San Francisco, 186 Cal. App. 3d 814 (1986), 499, 506

Terminals Equip. Co. v. City and County of San Francisco, 221 Cal. App. 3d 234 (1990), 289

Tillie Lewis Foods, Inc. v. City of Pittsburg, 52 Cal. App. 3d 983 (1975), 390

Times Mirror Co. v. Superior Court, 53 Cal. 3d 1325 (1991), 541

Tobe v. City of Santa Ana, 9 Cal. 4th 1069 (1995), 534

Todd v. City of Visalia, 254 Cal. App. 2d 679 (1967), 488

Tomlinson v County of Alameda, 54 Cal. 4th 281 (2012), 551, 552

Topanga Ass'n for a Scenic Cmty. v. County of Los Angeles, 11 Cal. 3d 506 (1974), 55, 56, 115, 482, 483, 507, 508, 512, 514

Topanga Ass'n for a Scenic Community v. County of Los Angeles, 214 Cal. App. 3d 1348 (1989), 106, 109, 110

Topanga Beach Renters Assn. v. Dep't of Gen. Servs., 58 Cal. App. 3d 188 (1976), 252

Torrey Hills Community Coalition v. City of San Diego, 186 Cal. App. 4th 429 (2010), 117, 518, 519, 549

Towards Responsibility In Planning v. City Council, 200 Cal. App. 3d 671 (1988), 46, 481

Town of Norfolk v. U.S. Army Corps of Eng'rs, 968 F. 2d 1438 (1st Cir. 1992), 200

Toyota of Visalia, Inc. v. New Motor Vehicle Bd., 188 Cal. App. 3d 872 (1987), 539

Travis v. County of Santa Cruz, 33 Cal. 4th 757 (2004), 521, 523, 556, 559

Trend Homes, Inc. v. Central Unified Sch. Dist., 220 Cal. App. 3d 102 (1990), 555, 556

Trent Meredith, Inc. v. City of Oxnard, 114 Cal. App. 3d 317 (1981), 100, 319, 320, 348

Tribal Village of Akutan v. Hodel, 869 F. 2d 1185 (9th Cir. 1988), 233

Trinity Park L.P. v. City of Sunnyvale, 193 Cal. App. 4th 2014 (2011), 118

Trout Unlimited v. Lohn, 559 F. 3d 946 (9th Cir. 2009), 220

Truman v. Royer, 189 Cal. App. 2d 240 (1961), 364, 365

Tuchscher Dev. Enter., Inc. v. San Diego Unified Port Dist., 106 Cal. App. 4th 1219 (2003), 561

Tucson Herpetological Society v. Salazar, 566 F. 3d 870 (9th Cir. 2009), 219, 243

Tuolumne County Citizens for Responsible Growth, Inc. v. City of Sonora, 155 Cal. App. 4th 1214 (2007), 155

Turlock Irrigation Dist. v. Zanker, 140 Cal. App. 4th 1047 (2006), 145

Twain Harte Assocs., Ltd. v. County of Tuolumne, 217 Cal. App. 3d 71 (1990), 303, 529

Twain Harte Homeowners Ass'n v. County of Tuolumne, 138 Cal. App. 3d 664 (1982), 11, 13, 18, 30

Union Oil Co. v. South Coast Regional Com., 92 Cal. App. 3d 327 (1979), 59

Union Pacific R.R., Co. v. State Bd. of Equalization, 49 Cal. 3d 138 (1989), 548

United Outdoor Adver. Co. v. Business, Transp. and Hous. Agency, 44 Cal. 3d 242 (1988), 20

United States v. Appalachian Elec. Power Co., 311 U.S. 377 (1940), 181

United States v. Bailey, 571 F. 3d 791 (8th Cir. 2009), 185

United States v. Chevron Pipe Line Co., 437 F. Supp. 2d 605 (D. Tex. 2006), 184

United States v. City of Fort Pierre, 747 F. 2d 464 (8th Cir. 1984), 182

United States v. Classic, 313 U.S. 299 (1941), 567

United States v. Cundiff, 555 F. 3d 200 (6th Cir.), *cert. denied,* 130 S. Ct. 74 (2009), 185

United States v. Donovan, 661 F.3d 174 (3d Cir. 2011), 185

United States v. Gerke Excavating, 464 F. 3d 723 (7th Cir. 2006), *cert. denied,* 128 S. Ct. 45 (2007), 184

United States v. Johnson, 467 F. 3d 56 (1st Cir. 2006), *cert. denied,* 128 S. Ct. 375 (2007), 185

United States v. Larkins, 852 F. 2d 189 (6th Cir. 1988), 193

United States v. Lucas, 516 F. 3d 316 (5th Cir.), *cert. denied,* 129 S. Ct. 116 (2008), 185

United States v. Rapanos, 376 F. 3d 629 (6th Cir. 2004), 183

United States v. Riverside Bayview Homes, Inc., 474 U.S. 121 (1985), 182, 188

United States v. Robison, 505 F. 3d 1208 (11th Cir. 2007), cert. denied, 129 S. Ct. 627 (2008), 185

Uniwill L.P. v. City of Los Angeles, 124 Cal. App. 4th 537 (2004), 117

Uphold Our Heritage v. Town of Woodside, 147 Cal. App. 4th 587 (2007), 171

Upton v. Gray, 269 Cal. App. 2d 352 (1969), 56, 57

USA Waste of California, Inc. v. City of Irwindale, 184 Cal. App. 4th 53 (2010), 561

Usery v. Turner Elkhorn Mining Co., 428 U.S. 1 (1976), 313

Util. Cost Mgmt. v. Indian Wells Valley Water Dist., 26 Cal. 4th 1185 (2001), 371, 517

Valley Advocates v. City of Fresno, 160 Cal. App. 4th 1039 (2008), 147

Valley Motor Lines, Inc. v. Riley, 22 Cal. App. 2d 233 (1937), 535

Van Atta v. Scott, 27 Cal. 3d 424 (1980), 534

Van de Kamps Coalition v. Bd. Of Trustees of Los Angeles Community College Dist., 206 Cal. App. 4th 1036 (2012), 177

Van Sicklen v. Browne, 15 Cal. App. 3d 122 (1971), 57

Vargas v. City of Salinas, 46 Cal. 4th 1 (2009), 382, 383, 561

Vedanta Society of So. Cal. v. Cal. Quarters, Ltd., 84 Cal. App. 4th 517 (2000), 172

Venice Canals Resident Home Owners Ass'n v. Superior Court, 72 Cal. App. 3d 675 (1977), 546

Ventimiglia v. Board of Behavioral Sciences, 168 Cal. App. 4th 296 (2008), 480

Ventura County v. Gulf Oil Corp., 601 F. 2d 1080 (9th Cir. 1979), 65

Ventura Group Ventures, Inc. v. Ventura Port District, 24 Cal. 4th 1089 (2001), 309, 310

Ventura Mobilehome Communities Owners Association v. City of San Buenaventura, 371 F. 3d 1046 (9th Cir. 2004), 306

Verdugo Woodlands Homeowners Ass'n v. City of Glendale, 179 Cal. App. 3d 696 (1986), 42

Viacom Outdoor, Inc. v. City of Arcata, 140 Cal. App. 4th 230 (2006), 5

Village Laguna, Inc. v. Board of Supervisors, 134 Cal. App. 3d 1022 (1982), 166, 167, 482, 483

Village of Belle Terre v. Boraas, 416 U.S. 1 (1974), 2

Village of Euclid v. Ambler Realty Co., 272 U.S. 365 (1926), 2, 292, 324, 436

Village of False Pass v. Clark, 733 F. 2d 605 (9th Cir. 1984), 232, 478

Vineyard Area Citizens for Responsible Growth v. City of Rancho Cordova, 40 Cal. 4th 412 (2007), 160, 453, 458

Vo v. City of Garden Grove, 115 Cal. App. 4th 425 (2004), 57, 58

Voices for Rural Living v. El Dorado Irrigation District, 209 Cal. App. 4th 1096 (2012), 147, 402, 464

Voices of Wetlands v. SWRCB, 52 Cal. 4th 499 (2011), 509

W.W. Dean & Assoc. v. City of South San Francisco, 190 Cal. App. 3d 1368 (1987), 64, 505

Wagner v. City of South Pasadena, 78 Cal. App. 4th 943 (2000), 516, 517, 543

Wal-Mart Stores, Inc. v. City of Turlock, 138 Cal. App. 4th 273 (2006), 3, 153

Walt Rankin & Assocs., Inc. v. City of Murrieta, 84 Cal. App. 4th 605 (2000), 124

Waste Management of Alameda County, Inc. v. County of Alameda, 79 Cal. App.4th 1223 (1980), 527, 533, 534, 552

Watsonville Pilots Ass'n v. City of Watsonville, 183 Cal. App. 4th 1059 (2010), 167

We Care-Santa Paula v. Herrera, 139 Cal. App. 4th 387 (2006), 361

West Coast Home Improvement Co. v. Contractors' State License Bd., 68 Cal. App. 2d 1 (1945), 546

Western Placer Citizens for an Agric. & Rural Env't v. County of Placer, 144 Cal. App. 4th 890 (2006), 171

Western States Petroleum Ass'n v. Superior Court, 9 Cal. 4th 559 (1995), 505, 507, 514, 539, 540

Western Watersheds Project v. Kraayenbrink, 632 F. 3d 472 (9th Cir. 2011), 226

Western Watersheds Project v. Matejko, 468 F. 3d 1099 (9th Cir. 2006), 229

Western/Cal. Ltd. v. Dry Creek Joint Elementary Sch. Dist., 50 Cal. App. 4th 1461 (1996), 340, 342, 346

Westfield-Palos Verdes Co. v. City of Rancho Palos Verdes, 73 Cal. App. 3d 486 (1977), 347

Wetlands Action Network v. U.S. Army Corps of Engineers, 222 F. 3d 1105 (9th Cir. 2000), 199

Wheeler v. City of Pleasant Grove, 896 F. 2d 1347 (11th Cir. 1990) (Wheeler IV), 300, 301

Wheelwright v. County of Marin, 2 Cal. 3d 448 (1970), 365

Whitman v. Board of Supervisors, 88 Cal. App. 3d 397 (1979), 155

Wilcox v. Superior Court, 27 Cal. App. 4th 809 (1994), 560

William C. Haas & Co. v. City and County of San Francisco, 605 F. 2d 1117 (9th Cir. 1979), 289, 292

William S. Hart Union High Sch. Dist. v. Reg'l Planning Comm'n, 226 Cal. App. 3d 1612 (1991), 109, 505

Williams v. Horvath, 16 Cal. 3d 834 (1976), 312

Williamson County Reg'l Planning Comm'n v. Hamilton Bank, 473 U.S. 172 (1985), 303, 304, 306, 307

Willink v. United States, 240 U.S. 572 (1916), 181

Wilson v. Block, 708 F. 2d 735 (D.C. Cir. 1983), 214, 229, 242

Wilson v. City of Laguna Beach, 6 Cal. App. 4th 543 (1992), 501, 506

Wilson v. Hidden Valley Mun. Water Dist., 256 Cal. App. 2d 271 (1967), 504, 505, 515

Witt Home Ranch, Inc. v. County of Sonoma, 165 Cal. App. 4th 543 (2008), 134

Wolfe v. City of Fremont, 144 Cal. App. 4th 533 (2006), 486

Wollmer v. City of Berkeley, 193 Cal. App. 4th 1329 (2011), 424

Woodland Hills Residents Ass'n, Inc. v. City Council, 44 Cal. App. 3d 825 (1975), 85, 112, 114

Woods v. Superior Court, 28 Cal. 3d 668 (1981), 504

Woodward Park Homeowners Ass'n v. City of Fresno, 150 Cal. App. 4th 683 (2007), 156

Worthington v. City Council of the City of Rohnert Park, 130 Cal. App. 4th 1132 (2005), 70, 372, 376, 377

Wright Dev. Co. v. City of Mountain View, 53 Cal. App. 3d 274 (1975), 112

Wright v. State, 122 Cal. App. 4th 659 (2004), 526

Yost v. Thomas, 36 Cal. 3d 561 (1984), 29, 36, 372, 505

Young v. Am. Mini Theatres, Inc., 427 U.S. 50 (1976), 40, 49

Young v. Gannet, 97 Cal. App. 4th 209 (1997), 514

Youngblood v. Board of Supervisors, 22 Cal. 3d 644 (1978), 25, 119, 506

Zabel v. Tabb, 430 F. 2d 199 (5th Cir. 1970), cert. denied, 401 U.S. 910 (1971), 180

Zack v. Marin Emergency Radio Auth., 118 Cal. App. 4th 617 (2004), 67

Zetterberg v. State Dept. of Public Health, 43 Cal. App. 3d 657 (1974), 531

Zilber v. Town of Moraga, 692 F. Supp. 1195 (N.D. Cal. 1988), 305

Zipper v. County of Santa Clara, 133 Cal. App. 4th 1013 (2005), 474

Table of Authorities

UNITED STATES CONSTITUTION

Article IV, § 3, 65
Article IV, § 19(f), 69
Article VI, § 2, 65
Commerce Clause, 175, 176, 177
Contract Clause, 349
Due Process Clause, 293, 374, 431
Equal Protection Clause, 51, 321, 322, 374, 497
Establishment Clause, 54
Fifth Amendment, 240, 282, 287, 291, 292, 300, 307, 316, 326, 321
First Amendment, 46, 49, 51, 52, 54, 57, 58, 251
Fourteenth Amendment, 313, 316, 321, 325, 326, 336, 343,
Free Exercise Clause, 54
Freedom of Speech Clause, 49
Full Faith and Credit Clause, 302
Property Clause, 65
Supremacy Clause, 5, 65
Takings Clause, 32, 282, 311, 316, 321, 332

FEDERAL STATUTES

5 U.S.C. § 577(d)(1), 237
5 U.S.C. § 704, 243
5 U.S.C. § 706, 243
15 U.S.C. § 1121 (b)), 251
15 U.S.C. § 1701 et seq., 209
16 U.S.C. § 470, 208
16 U.S.C. § 470 et seq., 252
16 U.S.C. § 470(f), 252
16 U.S.C. §§ 661–666(c), 208
16 U.S.C. § 668 et seq., 240
16 U.S.C. § 1432, 208
16 U.S.C. § 1456(c), 209
16 U.S.C. § 1531 et seq., 208
16 U.S.C. § 1532(5), 228
16 U.S.C. § 1532(6), 218
16 U.S.C. § 1532(16), 218
16 U.S.C. § 1532(19), 238
16 U.S.C. §§ 1532(20), 218, 221
16 U.S.C. § 1533, 217
16 U.S.C. § 1533(a)(1), 218
16 U.S.C. § 1533(a)(3), 224
16 U.S.C. § 1533(b)(1)(A), 219
16 U.S.C. § 1533(b)(3), 223
16 U.S.C. § 1533(b)(6)(C), 226
16 U.S.C. § 1533(c)(2), 224
16 U.S.C. § 1533(d), 238
16 U.S.C. § 1533(f), 223
16 U.S.C. § 1536, 218
16 U.S.C. § 1536(a)(2), 228
16 U.S.C. § 1536(b)(3), 233
16 U.S.C. § 1536(c)(1), 231
16 U.S.C. § 1536(d), 231
16 U.S.C. § 1536(e), 237
16 U.S.C. § 1536(h), 233
16 U.S.C. § 1538, 218

16 U.S.C. § 1538(a)(1), 238
16 U.S.C. § 1538(a)(2), 239
16 U.S.C. § 1538(a)(2)(B), 239
16 U.S.C. § 1539, 218, 241
16 U.S.C. § 1539(a)(1)(B), 241
16 U.S.C. § 1539(a)(2)(A), 241
16 U.S.C. § 1539(a)(2)(B), 241
16 U.S.C. § 1540(a)(1), 244
16 U.S.C. § 1540(g), 242
16 U.S.C. §§ 1540(g)(2)(A)–(C), 243
16 U.S.C. § 1540(g)(2)(B), 243
16 U.S.C. § 1540(g)(2)(C), 243
16 U.S.C. § 1540(g)(4), 243
16 U.S.C. §§ 3821–22, 209
25 U.S.C. § 2701 et seq., 68
25 U.S.C. § 2703(6), 69
25 U.S.C. §§ 2703(7), 69
25 U.S.C. § 2710, 69
25 U.S.C. § 2710(d)(1)(B), 69
25 U.S.C. § 2710(d)(3), 69
25 U.S.C. § 2710(d)(7), 69
25 U.S.C. § 2710(d)(7)(B)(iii), 69
31 U.S.C. § 6506, 65
33 U.S.C. §301(a), 266
33 U.S.C. § 401, 180, 207, 210
33 U.S.C. § 403, 180
33 U.S.C. § 404, 179, 180, 181, 182, 183, 184, 185, 190, 191, 193, 198, 199, 203, 204, 205, 206, 207, 208, 210, 211, 212, 213, 228, 230, 266, 293
33 U.S.C. § 404(b)(1), 180, 196, 200, 201, 202, 204, 205, 206
33 U.S.C. § 404(c), 193, 202, 204, 206
33 U.S.C. § 404(f), 192
33 U.S.C. § 1251(a), 181
33 U.S.C. § 1311, 181
33 U.S.C. § 1311(a), 266
33 U.S.C. § 1319, 213
33 U.S.C. § 1319(a), 213
33 U.S.C. § 1319(c), 214
33 U.S.C. § 1319(c)(1), 214
33 U.S.C. § 1319(c)(2), 214
33 U.S.C. § 1319(d), 214
33 U.S.C. § 1319(g)(2)(A), 214
33 U.S.C. § 1319(g)(2)(B), 214
33 U.S.C. § 1319(g)(3), 215
33 U.S.C. § 1342, 181
33 U.S.C. § 1342(p), 266
33 U.S.C. § 1344, 181
33 U.S.C. § 1344(c), 193, 204
33 U.S.C. § 1344(f), 192, 193
33 U.S.C. § 1344(f)(2), 193
33 U.S.C. § 1362(7), 181, 186
33 U.S.C. § 1365, 211
42 U.S.C. § 1983, 311, 312, 314, 315, 509, 521, 566, 567, 568
42 U.S.C. § 1988, 568
42 U.S.C. § 2000 et seq., 52
42 U.S.C. § 4321 et seq., 65
42 U.S.C. §§ 4321–4347, 208

42 U.S.C. § 6201 et seq., as amended by the National Appliance Energy Conservation Act (NAECA), Pub.L. No. 100-102 (1987), 470, 471
42 U.S.C. § 6291 et seq., 470
42 U.S.C. § 6297(c), 471
42 U.S.C. § 6297(f)(3), 471
42 U.S.C. §§ 6311–6317, 470
42 U.S.C. § 6316(b)(2), 471
42 U.S.C. § 6833, 470
42 U.S.C § 7506, 15
47 U.S.C. § 253, 5, 6
47 U.S.C. § 332(c)(7), 311

FEDERAL REGULATIONS

7 C.F.R. § 400.47(c), 209
33 C.F.R. § 320.1(b), 181
33 C.F.R. § 320.1(c), 194
33 C.F.R. § 320.4, 180
33 C.F.R. § 320.4(a)(1), 196
33 C.F.R. § 320.4(a)(2), 196
33 C.F.R. § 321, 181
33 C.F.R. § 322, 181
33 C.F.R. § 323, 181
33 C.F.R. §323.2(e), 191
33 C.F.R. § 323.2(f), 191
33 C.F.R. § 323.3(c), 191
33 C.F.R. § 323.3(d), 191
33 C.F.R. § 323.4, 193
33 C.F.R. § 324, 181
33 C.F.R. § 325, Appendix B, 208
33 C.F.R. § 325, Appendix B, ¶ 7(b), 198
33 C.F.R. § 325, Appendix C., 209
33 C.F.R. § 325.1(b), 198
33 C.F.R. § 325.1(c), 198
33 C.F.R. § 325.1(d)(2), 198
33 C.F.R. § 325.2, 196
33 C.F.R. § 326.3(c), 213
33 C.F.R. § 326.3(d), 213
33 C.F.R. § 326.3(e), 213
33 C.F.R. § 328, 182
33 C.F.R. § 328.3(a), 182
33 C.F.R. § 328.3(a)(3), 183
33 C.F.R. § 328.3(b), 188
33 C.F.R. § 328, 182
33 C.F.R. § 330, 181, 194
33 C.F.R. § 331, 190, 198
33 C.F.R. § 330.1, 194
40 C.F.R. § 19.4, 214
40 C.F.R § 93.110, 461
40 C.F.R. § 230, 193, 196, 208
40 C.F.R. § 230.3(q), 200
40 C.F.R. § 230.10, 200
40 C.F.R. § 230.10(a), 196, 200
40 C.F.R. § 230.10(a)(2), 204
40 C.F.R. § 230.10(a)(3), 200
40 C.F.R. § 230.10(a)(4), 200
40 C.F.R. § 230.10(b), 196
40 C.F.R. § 230.10(c), 196

40 C.F.R. § 230.10(d), 196
40 C.F.R. §§ 230.40-230.45, 200
40 C.F.R. § 231, 193, 206
40 C.F.R. § 424.12(a)(1), 221, 226
50 C.F.R. § 17, part C, 241
50 C.F.R. § 17, part D, 241
50 C.F.R. § 17.3, 235
50 C.F.R. § 17.21(c)(2), 241
50 C.F.R. § 17.22(b)(5), 241
50 C.F.R. § 17.22(c), 242
50 C.F.R. § 17.22(d), 242
50 C.F..R § 17.32(c), 242
50 C.F.R. § 17.32(d), 242
50 C.F.R. § 17.31, 238
50 C.F.R. § 17.71, 239
50 C.F.R. § 21.17.3, 239
50 C.F.R. § 223, 238
50 C.F.R. § 402.01, 228
50 C.F.R. § 402.02, 228, 230, 233
50 C.F.R. § 402.11, 235
50 C.F.R. § 402.11(e), 235
50 C.F.R. § 402.11(f), 235
50 C.F.R. § 402.12, 231
50 C.F.R. § 402.12(c), 231
50 C.F.R. § 402.12(d)(1), 231
50 C.F.R. § 402.13, 231
50 C.F.R. § 402.14, 231
50 C.F.R. § 402.14(i)(1), 235
50 C.F.R. § 402.14(i)(2), 235
50 C.F.R. § 402.14(i)(3), 235
50 C.F.R. § 402.14(i)(5), 236
50 C.F.R. § 402.14(a), 230
50 C.F.R. § 402.14(c), 231
50 C.F.R. § 402.14(d), 231
50 C.F.R. § 402.14(g), 233
50 C.F.R. § 402.14(g)(4), 231
50 C.F.R. § 402.16, 236
50 C.F.R. § 424.02(d), 225
50 C.F.R. § 424.12(a), 226
50 C.F.R. § 424.12(a)(2), 226
50 C.F.R. § 424.16, 222
50 C.F.R. § 424.16(b), 222
50 C.F.R. § 424.16(b)(3), 222
50 C.F.R. § 424.16(c)(2), 222
50 C.F.R. § 424.17(a), 222
50 C.F.R. § 424.17(b), 226
50 C.F.R. § 424.19, 225
50 C.F.R. § 424.20, 224
50 C.F.R. § 451.02(5)(ii), 237
42 Fed. Reg. 31722, 182
45 Fed. Reg. 85338-39, 201
46 Fed. Reg. 7644, 208
51 Fed. Reg. 19926, 228
51 Fed. Reg. 19932, 230
51 Fed. Reg. 41216, 183
55 Fed. Reg. 9210, 201
56 Fed. Reg. 54562, 237
56 Fed. Reg. 58612, 221
57 Fed. Reg. 23405, 237
58 Fed. Reg. 45008, 192
58 Fed. Reg. 45035, 192
61 Fed. Reg. 4722, 220
63 Fed. Reg. 54938, 226
65 Fed. Reg. 35242, 242
66 Fed. Reg. 4550, 192
68 Fed. Reg. 1995, 183
70 Fed. Reg. 19594, 205
70 Fed. Reg. 49739, 227
70 Fed. Reg. 52488, 227
71 Fed. Reg. 58176, 227
72 Fed. Reg. 30279, 225, 227
72 Fed. Reg. 72010, 227
73 Fed. Reg. 45534, 227
73 Fed. Reg. 50406, 227
73 Fed. Reg. 76249, 232, 238
73 Fed. Reg. 76266, 232
73 Fed. Reg. 78272, 232
73 Fed. Reg. 79641, 192
74 Fed. Reg. 17288, 227
74 Fed. Reg. 28776, 227
74 Fed. Reg. 52300, 227
75 Fed. Reg. 12815, 227
76 Fed. Reg. 3126, 206
76 Fed. Reg. 54346, 227
76 Fed. Reg. 61599, 227
76 Fed. Reg. 76987, 221
77 Fed. Reg. 10184, 194
77 Fed. Reg. 36728, 227
77 Fed. Reg. 71876, 227
78 Fed. Reg. 53058, 225

CALIFORNIA CONSTITUTION

Cal. Const. Art. I, § 3, 485
Cal. Const. Art. I, § 19, 287
Cal. Const. Art. II, § 11, 353
Cal. Const. Art. II, § 8(a), 358
Cal. Const. Art. II, § 8(d), 374
Cal. Const. Art. II, § 9, 348
Cal. Const. Art. II, § 9(a), 358, 374
Cal. Const. Art. II, § 10(b), 380, 381
Cal. Const., Art. IV, § 19(f), 69
Cal. Const. Art. XI, 567
Cal. Const. Art. XI § 1(b), 6
Cal. Const. Art. XI, § 7, 71, 320, 369
Cal. Const. Art. XI, § 3(a), 350
Cal. Const. Art. XI, § 5(a), 369
Cal. Const. Art. XIII, 305, 310
Cal. Const. Art. XIIIC, 369
Cal. Const. Art. XIIID, 348
Cal. Const. Art. XIIID, § 2(b), 349
Cal. Const. Art. XIIID, § 2(e), 351
Cal. Const. Art. XIIID, § 2(i), 350
Cal. Const. Art. XIIID, § 5(a), 354
Cal. Const. Art. XIIID, § 6(b)(1), 351
Cal. Const. Art. XIIID, § 6(b)(4), 352

CALIFORNIA STATUTES

Business & Professions Code

Bus. & Prof. Code § 5200 et seq., 5
Bus. & Prof. Code § 5490 et seq., 60
Bus. & Prof. Code § 5499, 60
Bus. & Prof. Code § 8762, 79
Bus. & Prof. Code § 11000 et seq., 72, 78
Bus. & Prof. Code § 11010, 454
Bus. & Prof. Code § 11003, 102
Bus. & Prof. Code § 17200, 498

Civil Code

Civ. Code § 714, 473, 474
Civ. Code § 714(h), 474
Civ. Code § 801, 474
Civ. Code § 801.5, 474
Civ. Code § 895 et seq., 450
Civ. Code § 1351(e), 81, 82
Civ. Code §§ 1941-1941.2, 122
Civ. Code §§ 1954.50-1954.535, 435, 440
Civ. Code § 1954.52(a), 435
Civ. Code § 1954.52(b), 435
Civ. Code § 1954.53(a)(2), 435
Civ. Code § 3109 et seq., 125
Civ. Code § 3114 et seq., 125
Civ. Code § 3179 et seq., 125
Civ. Code § 4290, 81, 82
Civ. Code § 4295, 81, 82
Civ. Code § 8160 et seq., 126
Civ. Code § 8410 et seq., 126
Civ. Code § 9000 et seq., 126

Code of Civil Procedure

Code Civ. Proc. § 12, 519
Code Civ. Proc. § 318, 521
Code Civ. Proc. § 319, 521
Code Civ. Proc. § 329.5, 520
Code Civ. Proc. § 335.1, 521
Code Civ. Proc. § 337, 278
Code Civ. Proc. § 338, 523
Code Civ. Proc. § 338(a), 522
Code Civ. Proc. § 343, 523
Code Civ. Proc. § 360.5, 524
Code Civ. Proc. § 389(a), 536
Code Civ. Proc. § 389(c), 535
Code Civ. Proc. § 425.16, 560
Code Civ. Proc. § 425.16(c), 564
Code Civ. Proc. § 473, 517, 549
Code Civ. Proc. § 526a, 383, 534
Code Civ. Proc. § 529, 546
Code Civ. Proc. § 583.240, 518
Code Civ. Proc. § 771.010, 123
Code Civ. Proc. § 771.020, 123
Code Civ. Proc. § 860 et seq., A, 403, 554, 559
Code Civ. Proc. § 860, 519, 520, 559
Code Civ. Proc. § 861.1, 559
Code Civ. Proc. § 865, 560

Code Civ. Proc. § 870, 560
Code Civ. Proc. § 870(a), 559
Code Civ. Proc. § 870(b), 559, 560
Code Civ. Proc. § 872.040, 75
Code Civ. Proc. § 916, 548
Code Civ. Proc. § 916(a), 547
Code Civ. Proc. §§ 917.1-917.9, 547
Code Civ. Proc. § 1005, 543
Code Civ. Proc. § 1021.5, 562, 563, 564
Code Civ. Proc. § 1084, 42, 504
Code Civ. Proc. § 1085, 34, 37, 342, 346, 418, 504, 505
Code Civ. Proc. §§ 1085-1094, 505
Code Civ. Proc. § 1086, 532
Code Civ. Proc. § 1087, 543, 547
Code Civ. Proc. § 1088, 543, 546
Code Civ. Proc. § 1094, 543, 544
Code Civ. Proc. § 1094.5, 245, 258, 263, 480, 481, 482, 504, 507, 508, 509, 512, 513, 514, 552, 553
Code Civ. Proc. § 1094.5(b), 512
Code Civ. Proc. § 1094.5(c), 25, 509
Code Civ. Proc. § 1094.5(e), 539, 540
Code Civ. Proc. § 1094.5(g), 545, 547, 548
Code Civ. Proc. § 1094.6, 516, 518, 520, 522, 523, 538
Code Civ. Proc. § 1094.6(b), 522
Code Civ. Proc. § 1094.6(d), 521
Code Civ. Proc. § 1094.6(f), 522
Code Civ. Proc. § 1094.6(g), 522
Code Civ. Proc. § 1094.8, 519, 520
Code Civ. Proc. §§ 1095-1097, 505
Code Civ. Proc. § 1097, 533, 535
Code Civ. Proc. § 1107, 543
Code Civ. Proc. § 1109, 505, 522, 543, 546, 547, 548
Code Civ. Proc. § 1822.50, 496
Code Civ. Proc. § 1822.51, 496, 497
Code Civ. Proc. § 1822.52, 497
Code Civ. Proc. § 1822.55, 497
Code Civ. Proc. § 2107, 539

Education Code

Educ. Code § 17620, 331, 341, 342
Educ. Code § 17620(a)(1)(B), 373
Educ. Code § 17626, 373

Elections Code

Elec. Code § 100, 363
Elec. Code § 101, 363
Elec. Code § 104, 364
Elec. Code § 1415, 362
Elec. Code § 4000(c)(9), 350
Elec. Code § 9020, 360
Elec. Code § 9022, 360
Elec. Code § 9100 et seq., 359
Elec. Code § 9101, 360, 363
Elec. Code § 9103, 359
Elec. Code § 9104, 362
Elec. Code § 9105, 359, 362
Elec. Code § 9105(a), 359
Elec. Code § 9105(b), 359, 362
Elec. Code § 9105(c), 360, 362
Elec. Code § 9106, 362
Elec. Code § 9108, 360
Elec. Code §§ 9108-9110, 359
Elec. Code § 9109, 364
Elec. Code § 9110, 363
Elec. Code § 9111, 359, 365, 379, 384
Elec. Code § 9111(a)(3), 365
Elec. Code § 9113, 364
Elec. Code §§ 9113-9115, 359
Elec. Code § 9114, 364, 365
Elec. Code § 9115, 364
Elec. Code § 9116, 359, 363
Elec. Code § 9117, 359, 363
Elec. Code § 9118, 366
Elec. Code § 9120, 360
Elec. Code § 9121, 360, 367
Elec. Code § 9122, 360, 362, 367
Elec. Code § 9123, 380
Elec. Code § 9125, 367, 385
Elec. Code § 9140, 359
Elec. Code § 9141, 279
Elec. Code §§ 9141-9144, 360
Elec. Code § 9144, 363, 364, 367
Elec. Code § 9145, 363, 360, 367
Elec. Code § 9146, 360, 364
Elec. Code § 9147(a), 360
Elec. Code § 9147(b), 360
Elec. Code § 9160, 360
Elec. Code § 9200 et seq., 355
Elec. Code § 9201, 361, 363
Elec. Code § 9202(a), 362, 376
Elec. Code § 9203, 362
Elec. Code § 9205, 363
Elec. Code § 9209, 360
Elec. Code § 9212, 382
Elec. Code § 9214, 363, 366
Elec. Code § 9215, 363, 366
Elec. Code § 9217, 355
Elec. Code § 9221, 380
Elec. Code § 9237, 364, 367
Elec. Code § 9237.5, 361
Elec. Code §§ 9238, 376
Elec. Code § 9238(a), 360
Elec. Code § 9241, 367, 378
Elec. Code § 9247, 359, 363
Elec. Code § 9255(a), 366
Elec. Code § 9255 (a)(3), 363
Elec. Code § 9255 (a)(4), 363
Elec. Code § 9255 et seq., 363
Elec. Code § 9300 et seq., 359
Elec. Code § 18600, 376

Evidence Code

Evid. Code § 350, 359
Evid. Code § 664, 546
Evid. Code § 669.5, 40, 375, 379, 428, 448
Evid. Code § 669.5(b), 428

Fish & Game Code

Fish & Game Code § 86, 246
Fish & Game Code § 1602, 210
Fish & Game Code § 1602(a)(4)(D), 210
Fish & Game Code § 1603(a), 210
Fish & Game Code § 5653, 206
Fish & Game Code §§ 2050-2098, 244
Fish & Game Code § 2052, 244
Fish & Game Code § 2062, 246
Fish & Game Code § 2067, 246
Fish & Game Code § 2068, 246
Fish & Game Code § 2070, 245
Fish & Game Code § 2073, 245
Fish & Game Code § 2073.5, 245
Fish & Game Code § 2074.2, 245
Fish & Game Code § 2074.6, 245
Fish & Game Code § 2075, 245
Fish & Game Code § 2080, 246, 247
Fish & Game Code § 2080.1, 247
Fish & Game Code § 2081, 243
Fish & Game Code § 2081(b), 247, 248
Fish & Game Code § 2081(c), 247
Fish & Game Code § 2083, 245
Fish & Game Code § 2084, 245
Fish & Game Code § 2800 et seq., 237, 242

Government Code

Gov't Code § 800, 566
Gov't Code § 810 et seq., 564
Gov't Code §§ 810-996.6, 564
Gov't Code § 810.6, 565
Gov't Code § 815, 564
Gov't Code § 815(a), 565
Gov't Code § 815.2(a), 565
Gov't Code § 815.2(b), 565, 566
Gov't Code § 815.4, 565
Gov't Code § 815.6, 565
Gov't Code § 820, 565
Gov't Code § 820(a), 565
Gov't Code §§ 820.2-823, 565
Gov't Code § 835, 565
Gov't Code § 865 et seq., 356
Gov't Code § 1090 et seq., 501
Gov't Code § 5854, 354
Gov't Code §§ 7060-7060.7, 298
Gov't Code § 8670.1 et seq., 263
Gov't Code § 8875, 17
Gov't Code § 8875.3, 17
Gov't Code § 8876, 17
Gov't Code § 11340 et seq., 480
Gov't Code § 11523, 522
Gov't Code § 12012.40, 69
Gov't Code § 12012.45, 69
Gov't Code § 14522.1, 461
Gov't Code § 16142.1, 254, 258
Gov't Code § 23005, 6
Gov't Code § 25131, 46
Gov't Code § 25132, 495, 496
Gov't Code § 25132(c), 496
Gov't Code § 25210.7(c), 395

Gov't Code § 25210.7(d), 395
Gov't Code § 25211.4, 395
Gov't Code § 25211.4(c)(2), 395
Gov't Code § 25373, 54, 254
Gov't Code § 26550 et seq., 394
Gov't Code § 27281.5, 55
Gov't Code § 31361(b), 254
Gov't Code § 34900, 6
Gov't Code § 35000 et seq., 387
Gov't Code § 36501, 6
Gov't Code § 36801, 6
Gov't Code § 36802, 6
Gov't Code § 36900, 493, 496
Gov't Code § 36900(c), 496
Gov't Code § 36901, 495
Gov't Code § 36934, 46
Gov't Code § 36937(b), 250
Gov't Code § 37361, 53, 54, 250, 254
Gov't Code § 40602, 276
Gov't Code § 40605, 7
Gov't Code § 43007, 59
Gov't Code § 50023, 382
Gov't Code § 50280 et seq., 254
Gov't Code § 51040 et seq., 258
Gov't Code § 51042(b)(1), 258
Gov't Code § 51042(e), 258
Gov't Code § 51177, 113
Gov't Code § 51190 et seq., 258
Gov't Code § 51200 et seq., 251, 255, 471, 473
Gov't Code § 51201, 255
Gov't Code § 51201, 473
Gov't Code § 51203(b), 257
Gov't Code § 51205, 255
Gov't Code § 51220, 255
Gov't Code § 51220.5, 256
Gov't Code § 51222, 256
Gov't Code § 51230, 255
Gov't Code § 51231, 256
Gov't Code § 51234, 255
Gov't Code § 51235, 256
Gov't Code § 51238, 256, 473
Gov't Code § 51238.1, 256, 473
Gov't Code § 51238.1(a), 473
Gov't Code § 51241, 252
Gov't Code § 51243, 256
Gov't Code § 51243.5, 256
Gov't Code § 51244, 256
Gov't Code § 51244.5, 256
Gov't Code § 51245, 256
Gov't Code § 51246(a), 256
Gov't Code § 51256(c), 257
Gov't Code § 51256.1, 257
Gov't Code § 51257, 258
Gov't Code § 51257.5, 258
Gov't Code § 51281, 256
Gov't Code § 51282, 256
Gov't Code § 51282(a), 257
Gov't Code § 51282(b), 257
Gov't Code § 51282(c), 257
Gov't Code § 51282(e), 257

Gov't Code § 51283(a), 257
Gov't Code § 51283(b), 257
Gov't Code § 51283(c), 257
Gov't Code § 51283.4, 258
Gov't Code § 51284, 257
Gov't Code § 51286, 258, 521
Gov't Code § 51287, 558
Gov't Code § 51296, 258
Gov't Code § 51296.1, 258
Gov't Code § 51296.2(a), 258
Gov't Code § 51296.8, 258
Gov't Code § 53069.4, 496
Gov't Code § 53080, 344
Gov't Code § 53080(a)(1), 341
Gov't Code § 53090-53091, 67
Gov't Code § 53090-53091, 68
Gov't Code § 53090 et seq., 66
Gov't Code § 53091, 66
Gov't Code § 53091, 67
Gov't Code § 53096, 67
Gov't Code § 53096(a), 67
Gov't Code § 53311 et seq., 354
Gov't Code §§ 53720-53730, 347
Gov't Code § 53722, 347
Gov't Code § 53739(a), (b), 349, 350
Gov't Code § 53753, 351, 382
Gov't Code § 53753(c), 350
Gov't Code § 53753.5, 351
Gov't Code § 53755, 351
Gov't Code § 54722 et seq., 387
Gov't Code § 54950, 485
Gov't Code § 54950 et seq., 6, 8, 512
Gov't Code §§ 54950-54963, 485
Gov't Code § 54952(a), (b), 487
Gov't Code § 54952(c)(1), 487
Gov't Code § 54952.2(a), 485
Gov't Code § 54952.2(b), 486
Gov't Code § 54952.2(e), 486
Gov't Code § 54953, 485
Gov't Code § 54954.2(a)(1), 487
Gov't Code § 54956.9, 281, 484, 486, 487
Gov't Code § 54956.9, 484
Gov't Code § 54957(b)(1), 486
Gov't Code § 54960, 487
Gov't Code § 54960.1, 520
Gov't Code § 54988, 496
Gov't Code § 56000 et seq., 387, 388
Gov't Code § 56001, 387, 389
Gov't Code § 56014, 397
Gov't Code § 56017, 392
Gov't Code § 56021, 392
Gov't Code § 56021(m), 393
Gov't Code § 56030, 393
Gov't Code § 56033, 393
Gov't Code § 56034, 393
Gov't Code § 56035, 393
Gov't Code § 56036(b), 394
Gov't Code § 56036.5(a), 394
Gov't Code § 56036.6, 394
Gov't Code § 56039, 393

Gov't Code § 56043, 393
Gov't Code § 56046, 404
Gov't Code § 56050, 406
Gov't Code § 56056, 393
Gov't Code § 56066, 393, 407
Gov't Code § 56072, 406
Gov't Code § 56073, 393
Gov't Code § 56076, 390
Gov't Code § 56078, 393
Gov't Code § 56102, 402
Gov't Code § 56103, 403, 520, 579
Gov't Code § 56107, 402
Gov't Code § 56123, 407
Gov't Code § 56124, 407
Gov't Code § 56133, 389
Gov't Code § 56157, 397
Gov't Code § 56300, 395
Gov't Code § 56301, 387
Gov't Code § 56325, 389
Gov't Code § 56325.1, 389
Gov't Code §§ 56326-56329, 389
Gov't Code § 56332, 389
Gov't Code § 56375, 61, 387, 389, 392
Gov't Code § 56375(a), 391, 402, 405
Gov't Code § 56375(a)(3), 393
Gov't Code § 56375(a)(6), 392, 402
Gov't Code § 56375(a)(7), 396, 400, 401
Gov't Code § 56375(e), 401
Gov't Code § 56375(p), 389
Gov't Code § 56375.3, 401
Gov't Code § 56375.4, 401
Gov't Code § 56375.5, 390
Gov't Code § 56383, 396, 558
Gov't Code § 56383(e), 396
Gov't Code § 56384, 396
Gov't Code § 56387, 393, 407
Gov't Code § 56388, 394, 405
Gov't Code § 56425, 387, 389, 390, 393
Gov't Code § 56425(a), 390
Gov't Code § 56425(b), 390
Gov't Code § 56425(e), 391
Gov't Code § 56425(g), 391
Gov't Code § 56427, 391
Gov't Code § 56428, 389, 408
Gov't Code § 56428(g), 391
Gov't Code § 56430(a), 391
Gov't Code § 56430(b), 392
Gov't Code § 56434(a), 392
Gov't Code § 56434(g), 391
Gov't Code § 56650, 395
Gov't Code § 56650 et seq., 395
Gov't Code § 56652, 395
Gov't Code § 56653, 395
Gov't Code § 56654, 395
Gov't Code § 56654(a), 395
Gov't Code § 56654(b), 395
Gov't Code § 56658(a), 395
Gov't Code § 56658(b), 397
Gov't Code § 56658(c), 397
Gov't Code § 56658(d), 397

Gov't Code § 56658(e), 397
Gov't Code § 56658(f), 397
Gov't Code § 56658(g), 397
Gov't Code § 56658(h), 397
Gov't Code § 56662, 396, 397, 402, 404
Gov't Code § 56663, 404
Gov't Code § 56665, 397
Gov't Code § 56668, 397, 401
Gov't Code § 56668.3(b), 401, 402
Gov't Code § 56668.5, 401
Gov't Code § 56700, 395
Gov't Code § 56704, 99
Gov't Code § 56751, 397, 399
Gov't Code § 56800, 99
Gov't Code § 56810, 396
Gov't Code § 56824.12, 396
Gov't Code § 56824.14, 401
Gov't Code § 56857, 397
Gov't Code § 56857(b), 397
Gov't Code § 56857(c), 397
Gov't Code § 56880, 402
Gov't Code § 56882, 403
Gov't Code § 56884, 402, 404
Gov't Code § 56886, 403
Gov't Code § 56886, 393, 402
Gov't Code § 56895(a), 403
Gov't Code § 56895(b), 403
Gov't Code § 56895(d), 404
Gov't Code § 56895(e), 404
Gov't Code § 56895(f), 404
Gov't Code § 56895(g), 404
Gov't Code § 56895(h), 404
Gov't Code § 57000, 404
Gov't Code § 57002, 404
Gov't Code § 57002(a), 404
Gov't Code § 57002(b), 405
Gov't Code § 57025, 404
Gov't Code § 57026, 404
Gov't Code § 57026(g), 406
Gov't Code § 57026(h), 406
Gov't Code § 57050(a), 405
Gov't Code § 57050(b), 405
Gov't Code § 57051, 403, 405
Gov't Code § 57052, 405
Gov't Code § 57062(a), 405
Gov't Code § 57075, 405
Gov't Code § 57075(a)(1), 406
Gov't Code § 57075(a)(2), 406
Gov't Code § 57075(a)(3), 406
Gov't Code § 57075(b)(1), (2) 406
Gov't Code § 57075.5, 405, 406
Gov't Code § 57076(b), (c), 406
Gov't Code § 57077, 404, 405
Gov't Code § 57078(a), (b), 406
Gov't Code § 57090, 402, 405
Gov't Code § 57200, 405
Gov't Code § 57201, 405
Gov't Code § 57202, 407
Gov't Code § 57203, 405, 407
Gov't Code § 60000(b), 333

Gov't Code § 61000 et seq., 394
Gov't Code § 65007, 115
Gov't Code § 65008, 418, 420
Gov't Code § 65009, 34, 37, 116, 516, 518, 519, 522, 523, 524, 530
Gov't Code § 65009(a)(3), 516
Gov't Code § 65009(b)(1), 530
Gov't Code § 65009(b)(2), 116, 530
Gov't Code § 65009(c), 34, 519, 520
Gov't Code § 65009(c)(1), 27
Gov't Code § 65009(c)(1)(A), (B), (D), 520
Gov't Code § 65009(d), 418, 521
Gov't Code § 65009(d), 42
Gov't Code § 65010, 48
Gov't Code § 65010(a), 48
Gov't Code § 65010(b), 49
Gov't Code § 65030.2, 46
Gov't Code § 65040.2, 7, 11, 13, 28
Gov't Code § 65040.2(g), 11
Gov't Code § 65040.5, 30
Gov't Code § 65041 et seq., 450
Gov't Code § 65080, 452
Gov't Code § 65080(b)(2)(B)(2), 461
Gov't Code § 65080(b)(2)(G), 461
Gov't Code § 65080(b)(2)(L), 15
Gov't Code § 65080(b)(2), 460
Gov't Code § 65080(b)(2)(a), 461
Gov't Code § 65080(b)(2)(b), 461
Gov't Code § 65080(b)(2)(h), 461
Gov't Code § 65080(b)(2)(j), 461
Gov't Code § 65080 et seq., 412
Gov't Code § 65082, 452
Gov't Code § 65088 et seq., 451
Gov't Code § 65088.1, 452
Gov't Code § 65088.3, 451
Gov't Code § 65088.4, 159, 452
Gov't Code § 65088.4(b), 452
Gov't Code § 65089(a), 451, 452
Gov't Code § 65089(b), 451
Gov't Code § 65089.2(a), 452
Gov't Code § 65089.2(b), 452
Gov't Code § 65089.4, 451
Gov't Code § 65089.5(a), 451, 452
Gov't Code § 65090, 126
Gov't Code §§ 65090–65091, 86
Gov't Code § 65091, 126
Gov't Code § 65094, 478
Gov't Code § 65100 et seq., 6
Gov't Code § 65100, 7
Gov't Code § 65101, 7
Gov't Code § 65103, 7
Gov't Code § 65103(a), 15, 21, 30, 31, 416
Gov't Code § 65104, 558
Gov't Code § 65300, 10, 12, 22, 29, 30, 385
Gov't Code § 65300 et seq., 6, 9, 71
Gov't Code § 65300.5, 12, 22, 29, 31, 371, 415
Gov't Code § 65300.7, 20
Gov't Code § 65300.9, 20
Gov't Code § 65301, 12

Gov't Code § 65301(a), 20
Gov't Code § 65301(c), 30
Gov't Code § 65302, 11, 12, 20, 29, 31
Gov't Code § 65302(a), 13, 19, 30
Gov't Code § 65302(a)(2), 13
Gov't Code § 65302(b), 12, 13, 19, 30
Gov't Code § 65302(b)(2), 452
Gov't Code § 65302(c), 410
Gov't Code § 65302(d), 15
Gov't Code § 65302(f), 16
Gov't Code § 65302(f)(4), 16
Gov't Code § 65302(g), 17, 18, 31
Gov't Code § 65302(g)(2), 18
Gov't Code § 65302.3, 29
Gov't Code § 65302.3(a), 26
Gov't Code § 65302.3(b), 26
Gov't Code § 65302.4, 13
Gov't Code § 65302.5(a)(2), 17
Gov't Code § 65302.5, 17
Gov't Code § 65302.5(a)(1), 17
Gov't Code § 65302.5(a)(3), 17
Gov't Code § 65302.5(b), 18
Gov't Code § 65302.5(c), 18
Gov't Code § 65302.7, 18
Gov't Code § 65302.8, 46, 428, 481
Gov't Code § 65302.9, 115, 275, 279
Gov't Code § 65302.9(a), 18, 43
Gov't Code § 65303, 19
Gov't Code § 65350 et seq., 27
Gov't Code § 65351, 7
Gov't Code § 65352, 7, 28
Gov't Code § 65352(c)(1), 28
Gov't Code § 65352.2, 67
Gov't Code § 65352.3, 31
Gov't Code § 65352.5, 400
Gov't Code § 65353, 7
Gov't Code § 65353(a), 27
Gov't Code § 65354, 27
Gov't Code § 65354.5, 27
Gov't Code § 65356, 27
Gov't Code § 65357, 29
Gov't Code § 65357(b)(2), 28
Gov't Code § 65358(b), 27
Gov't Code § 65358(c), 27
Gov't Code § 65360, 31
Gov't Code § 65361, 113
Gov't Code § 65361(a), 32
Gov't Code § 65361(a), 31
Gov't Code § 65361(b), 32
Gov't Code § 65361(c), 31
Gov't Code § 65361(d), 32
Gov't Code § 65361(e), 32, 114
Gov't Code § 65361(f), 32
Gov't Code § 65400, 7, 28
Gov't Code § 65400(2)(a), 412
Gov't Code § 65400(2)(b), 412
Gov't Code § 65400(a)(2), 415
Gov't Code § 65400(b)(3), 415
Gov't Code § 65400(c), 415
Gov't Code § 65401, 7

601

Gov't Code § 65402, 7
Gov't Code § 65402(b), 68
Gov't Code § 65403, 7
Gov't Code § 65450, 35
Gov't Code § 65451(a), 35
Gov't Code § 65451(b), 35
Gov't Code § 65452, 36
Gov't Code § 65454, 370
Gov't Code § 65456, 558
Gov't Code § 65456(a), 36
Gov't Code § 65457, 36, 144
Gov't Code § 65560, 16
Gov't Code § 65560(b), 16
Gov't Code § 65560(b)(6), 16
Gov't Code § 65561, 29
Gov't Code § 65561(a), 16
Gov't Code § 65561(b), 16
Gov't Code § 65562.5, 16, 31
Gov't Code § 65563, 16, 21
Gov't Code § 65564, 16, 31
Gov't Code § 65567, 16
Gov't Code § 65580, 29, 410
Gov't Code § 65580(a), 14
Gov't Code § 65580(b)–(d), 14
Gov't Code § 65580(d), 410
Gov't Code § 65580(e), 13
Gov't Code § 65580 et seq., 13, 410
Gov't Code § 65581(a), 410
Gov't Code § 65582.1, 423
Gov't Code § 65583, 13, 31
Gov't Code § 65583(a), 14, 408
Gov't Code § 65583(a)(3), 14, 408, 410
Gov't Code § 65583(a)(5), 414
Gov't Code § 65583(a)(6), 415
Gov't Code § 65583(a)(8), 31
Gov't Code § 65583(a)–(c), 410
Gov't Code § 65583(b)(1), 14, 411
Gov't Code § 65583(b)(2), 411
Gov't Code § 65583(c), 410
Gov't Code § 65583(c)(1), 413, 423
Gov't Code § 65583(c)(1)(a), 14, 414
Gov't Code § 65583(c)(3), 7, 14, 28
Gov't Code § 65583(c)(4), 19
Gov't Code § 65583(c)(5), 411
Gov't Code § 65583(c)(7), 415
Gov't Code § 65583(f), 14
Gov't Code § 65583(g), 14
Gov't Code § 65583(g)(1), 412
Gov't Code § 65583(g)(2), 412
Gov't Code § 65583(g)(3), 14, 414
Gov't Code § 65583(g)(4), 414
Gov't Code § 65583.1(a), 427
Gov't Code § 65583.2(a), 413
Gov't Code § 65583.2(b), 412, 413
Gov't Code § 65583.2(h), 414
Gov't Code § 65583.2(i), 414
Gov't Code § 65584, 7, 14, 408
Gov't Code § 65584(a)(1), 411
Gov't Code § 65584(b), 411
Gov't Code § 65584(d), 412

Gov't Code § 65584(e), 411
Gov't Code § 65584 et seq., 411
Gov't Code § 65584.01, 28, 411, 558
Gov't Code § 65584.01(d)(1), 462
Gov't Code § 65584.01–65584.04, 411
Gov't Code § 65584.04(i), 462
Gov't Code § 65584.04(i)(1), 412
Gov't Code § 65584.04(i)(2), 412
Gov't Code § 65584.04(i)(3), 412
Gov't Code § 65584.05, 411
Gov't Code § 65584.09, 414
Gov't Code § 65585(a), 417
Gov't Code § 65585(b), 28, 31, 170
Gov't Code § 65585(f), 417
Gov't Code § 65587(a), 32
Gov't Code § 65587(b), 34, 418
Gov't Code § 65587(c), 34, 418
Gov't Code § 65587(d)(1), 418
Gov't Code § 65587(d)(2), 418
Gov't Code § 65587(b), 34
Gov't Code § 65587(c), 34
Gov't Code § 65588, 15, 414, 417, 419, 420
Gov't Code § 65588(a), 15, 416
Gov't Code § 65588(b), 15
Gov't Code § 65588(d), 15, 415
Gov't Code § 65588(d)(1-4), 416
Gov't Code § 65588(e), 15, 416
Gov't Code § 65589.3, 417
Gov't Code § 65589.4, 420
Gov't Code § 65589.4(b), 422
Gov't Code § 65589.4(c), 423
Gov't Code § 65589.5, 5, 39, 418, 421, 481, 490
Gov't Code § 65589.5(a)(1), 409
Gov't Code § 65589.5(a)(2), 419
Gov't Code § 65589.5(b), 419
Gov't Code § 65589.5(d), 14, 26, 419, 420, 421
Gov't Code § 65589.5(d)(5), 20, 22
Gov't Code § 65589.5(d)(5)(a), 420
Gov't Code § 65589.5(e), 419
Gov't Code § 65589.5(f), 419
Gov't Code § 65589.5(h)(2), 419
Gov't Code § 65589.5(h)(3), 420, 421
Gov't Code § 65589.5(h)(4), 411, 421
Gov't Code § 65589.5(i), 421
Gov't Code § 65589.5(j), 481
Gov't Code § 65589.5(j), 419, 421, 422
Gov't Code § 65589.5(j)(1), 421
Gov't Code § 65589.5(j)(2), 421
Gov't Code § 65589.5(k), 419, 421
Gov't Code § 65589.7, 415, 422
Gov't Code § 65590, 15, 415
Gov't Code § 65590(d), 416
Gov't Code § 65590.1, 15, 415
Gov't Code § 65700, 22
Gov't Code §§ 65750–65763, 34
Gov't Code § 65753, 34, 543, 548
Gov't Code § 65754, 34
Gov't Code § 65755, 34

Gov't Code § 65800 et seq., 6, 39, 72
Gov't Code § 65803, 22, 23, 39, 42
Gov't Code § 65804, 39, 44, 493
Gov't Code § 65850, 44, 46
Gov't Code § 65850.2, 85, 489
Gov't Code § 65850.2(i), 85, 489
Gov't Code § 65850.4, 52
Gov't Code § 65850.5, 474
Gov't Code § 65852, 55
Gov't Code § 65852.1, 80
Gov't Code § 65852.1(b), 427
Gov't Code § 65852.2, 427
Gov't Code § 65852.2(b)(1), 427
Gov't Code § 65852.2(b)(3), 427
Gov't Code § 65852.2(i)(4), 80, 427
Gov't Code § 65852.25(a), 59
Gov't Code § 65852.150, 426, 427
Gov't Code § 65853, 44
Gov't Code § 65854, 7, 44
Gov't Code § 65855, 44, 512
Gov't Code § 65856, 44, 512
Gov't Code § 65857, 45
Gov't Code § 65858, 5, 44, 62, 63, 296
Gov't Code § 65858(b), 62
Gov't Code § 65858(d), 62
Gov't Code § 65858(e), 62
Gov't Code § 65858(f), 62
Gov't Code § 65858(g), 62
Gov't Code § 65858(h), 62
Gov't Code § 65859, 61
Gov't Code § 65860, 9, 522
Gov't Code § 65860(a), 42
Gov't Code § 65860(b), 43, 520
Gov't Code § 65860(c), 43
Gov't Code § 65860(d), 22, 42
Gov't Code § 65860.1, 43
Gov't Code § 65860.1, 22, 23
Gov't Code § 65860.1, 279
Gov't Code § 65863(b), 417
Gov't Code § 65863(b)(1),(2), 417
Gov't Code § 65863(c), 418
Gov't Code § 65863(e), 418
Gov't Code § 65863(f), 418
Gov't Code § 65863(g)(1), 417
Gov't Code § 65863(g)(2), 417
Gov't Code § 65863.4(a), 59, 60
Gov't Code § 65863.6, 46, 375, 428, 481
Gov't Code § 65863.7, 558
Gov't Code § 65863.9, 91, 93
Gov't Code § 65864, 88
Gov't Code § 65864(b), 275
Gov't Code § 65864 et seq., 6, 95, 96, 277
Gov't Code §§ 65864–65869, 284
Gov't Code § 65865, 277
Gov't Code § 65865(b), 278
Gov't Code § 65865(e), 334
Gov't Code § 65865.1, 278
Gov't Code § 65865.2, 285
Gov't Code § 65865.3, 278
Gov't Code § 65865.4, 277

Gov't Code § 65865.5, 279
Gov't Code § 65866, 277
Gov't Code § 65867.5, 35, 278, 454, 455
Gov't Code § 65867.5(c), 278, 454
Gov't Code § 65869.5, 88, 89
Gov't Code § 65895(a), 472, 473
Gov't Code § 65895(b)(3), 472
Gov't Code § 65896(a), 472
Gov't Code § 65896(b), 470, 472
Gov't Code §§ 65896(b)(1)–(17), 472
Gov't Code § 65896(c), 472
Gov't Code § 65901, 56
Gov't Code § 65906, 55, 56
Gov't Code § 65909.5, 558
Gov't Code § 65910, 16
Gov't Code § 65912, 16
Gov't Code § 65913.1, 379, 423, 428
Gov't Code § 65913.2, 105
Gov't Code § 65913.8, 345
Gov't Code § 65915, 424, 425
Gov't Code § 65915(a), 424
Gov't Code § 65915(b)(1), 424
Gov't Code §§ 65915(b)(1)(a)–(b), 424
Gov't Code § 65915(b)(1)(d), 424
Gov't Code § 65915(c), 425
Gov't Code § 65915(d)(1), 425, 450
Gov't Code § 65915(d)(3), 450
Gov't Code § 65915(e), 450, 425, 451
Gov't Code § 65915(e)(1), 426
Gov't Code § 65915(g), 425, 426
Gov't Code § 65915(h)(1), 426
Gov't Code § 65915(i), 424
Gov't Code § 65915(i)(2), 426
Gov't Code § 65915(l), 425
Gov't Code § 65915(n), 425
Gov't Code § 65915(o)(1), 426
Gov't Code § 65915(q), 425
Gov't Code § 65915 et seq., 423
Gov't Code § 65915.5, 426
Gov't Code § 65917.5(2), 423
Gov't Code § 65919 et seq., 28
Gov't Code § 65919.3, 28
Gov't Code § 65920 et seq., 6, 72, 86, 477, 488
Gov't Code § 65921, 488
Gov't Code § 65922, 490
Gov't Code § 65922(b), 86
Gov't Code § 65928, 489
Gov't Code § 65940, 489
Gov't Code § 65940.5, 490
Gov't Code § 65941, 489
Gov't Code § 65941.5, 489
Gov't Code § 65942, 489
Gov't Code § 65943, 111
Gov't Code § 65943, 486, 487
Gov't Code § 65944, 489
Gov't Code § 65950, 86
Gov't Code § 65950(a)(1), 170, 490
Gov't Code § 65950(a)(2), 177
Gov't Code § 65950(a)(3), 490

Gov't Code § 65956, 490
Gov't Code § 65956(a), 491
Gov't Code § 65956(b), 491
Gov't Code § 65957, 490
Gov't Code § 65961, 111
Gov't Code § 65961(e), 111
Gov't Code § 65961(f), 111
Gov't Code § 65962, 18
Gov't Code § 65962.5, 489
Gov't Code § 65962.5(d), 84, 489
Gov't Code § 65962.5(e), 84, 489
Gov't Code § 65962.5(f), 84, 85, 489
Gov't Code § 65995, 109, 331
Gov't Code § 65995(a), 109
Gov't Code § 65995(b), 372
Gov't Code § 65995(b)(3), 340
Gov't Code § 65995.5, 341
Gov't Code § 65996, 25
Gov't Code § 65996(a), 113
Gov't Code § 65996(b), 109, 341
Gov't Code § 66000, 111, 283, 333, 557
Gov't Code § 66000(b), 346
Gov't Code § 66000 et seq., 6, 322, 554
Gov't Code §§ 66000–66011, 333
Gov't Code §§ 66000–66025, 284, 331, 333, 346, 438
Gov't Code § 66001, 323, 334, 342, 345, 438, 481
Gov't Code § 66001(a), 365
Gov't Code § 66001(b), 333
Gov't Code § 66001(d), 334
Gov't Code § 66001(e), 334
Gov't Code § 66001(g), 345
Gov't Code § 66002, 334
Gov't Code § 66005, 345, 438
Gov't Code § 66005.1, 345
Gov't Code § 66005.1(a), 345
Gov't Code § 66006, 284, 323, 334
Gov't Code § 66006(b), 334
Gov't Code § 66007, 334
Gov't Code § 66007(b)(1), 344
Gov't Code § 66007(b)(2), 344
Gov't Code § 66007(g), 344
Gov't Code § 66013, 555, 556, 559
Gov't Code § 66014, 340, 555, 556, 558, 559
Gov't Code § 66014(a), 555, 586
Gov't Code § 66015, 474
Gov't Code § 66016, 340, 343, 344, 558
Gov't Code § 66016(a), 334, 340, 559
Gov't Code § 66017, 344
Gov't Code § 66017(a), 343
Gov't Code § 66018, 344
Gov't Code § 66020, 118, 282, 283, 330, 334, 335, 435, 524, 554, 555, 556, 557, 559
Gov't Code § 66020(a)(1), 554
Gov't Code § 66020(a)(2), 555
Gov't Code § 66020(b), 557
Gov't Code § 66020(c), 557
Gov't Code § 66020(d), 521

Gov't Code § 66020(d)(1), 334, 554, 555, 556
Gov't Code § 66020(d)(2), 334, 556
Gov't Code § 66020(h), 554, 555
Gov't Code § 66021, 330, 334, 521, 556
Gov't Code § 66022, 340, 517, 554, 555, 557, 558, 559
Gov't Code § 66022(a), 340, 521, 554
Gov't Code § 66022(b), 554, 559
Gov't Code § 66022(c), 558
Gov't Code § 66024, 556
Gov't Code § 66030 et seq., 523
Gov't Code § 66031, 538
Gov't Code § 66031(b), 538
Gov't Code § 66031(d), 538
Gov't Code § 66032, 538
Gov't Code § 66032(d), 538
Gov't Code § 66404(i), 104
Gov't Code § 66410 et seq., 6, 25, 472
Gov't Code §§ 66410–66499.37, 517
Gov't Code §§ 66410–66499.58, 339
Gov't Code § 66411, 71, 72, 105, 107
Gov't Code § 66411.1, 126
Gov't Code § 66411.1(a), 126, 127
Gov't Code § 66412, 472
Gov't Code § 66412(a), 74, 81
Gov't Code § 66412(b), 83
Gov't Code § 66412(c), 83
Gov't Code § 66412(d), 79, 128, 135, 258
Gov't Code § 66412(g), 81
Gov't Code § 66412(h), 82
Gov't Code § 66412(i), 83
Gov't Code § 66412(j), 83
Gov't Code § 66412(k), 83
Gov't Code § 66412(l), 83
Gov't Code § 66412.1, 81
Gov't Code § 66412.2, 80
Gov't Code § 66412.3, 112
Gov't Code § 66412.5, 83
Gov't Code § 66412.6, 73, 137
Gov't Code § 66412.6(a), 137
Gov't Code § 66412.6(b), 137
Gov't Code § 66412.9, 83
Gov't Code § 66413(a), 99
Gov't Code § 66413(b), 99
Gov't Code § 66413.5, 99, 120
Gov't Code § 66413.5(a), 99
Gov't Code § 66413.5(c), 100
Gov't Code § 66413.5(e), 99
Gov't Code § 66413.5(f), 99
Gov't Code §§ 66418–66419, 107
Gov't Code § 66418.2, 77
Gov't Code § 66423, 74
Gov't Code § 66424, 73, 74, 75, 76, 78, 79, 128
Gov't Code § 66424.1, 74
Gov't Code § 66424.2, 81
Gov't Code § 66424.6, 128
Gov't Code § 66424.6(a), 78
Gov't Code § 66424.6(d), 79

Gov't Code §§ 66425-66472.1, 121
Gov't Code § 66426, 77, 82, 84
Gov't Code § 66426.5, 79, 80
Gov't Code § 66427, 82
Gov't Code § 66427.1, 111
Gov't Code § 66427.1(a)(1), 121
Gov't Code § 66427.1(a)(1)(D), 121
Gov't Code § 66427.1(a)(2)(A), 121
Gov't Code § 66427.1(a)(2)(B), 122
Gov't Code § 66427.1(a)(2)(E), 122
Gov't Code § 66427.1(a)(2)(F), 122
Gov't Code § 66427.1(d), 122
Gov't Code § 66427.5, 72, 73
Gov't Code § 66428, 66
Gov't Code § 66428, 95
Gov't Code § 66428(a)(2), 80
Gov't Code § 66428(b), 83, 84
Gov't Code § 66428(c), 84
Gov't Code § 66428.1, 84
Gov't Code § 66429, 118
Gov't Code § 66430, 118
Gov't Code § 66433 et seq., 118
Gov't Code § 66434, 118
Gov't Code § 66434(e), 78
Gov't Code § 66435-66443, 118
Gov't Code § 66436, 118
Gov't Code § 66437, 516
Gov't Code § 66439, 118
Gov't Code § 66439(a), 122
Gov't Code § 66439(c), 122
Gov't Code § 66440, 118
Gov't Code § 66442(a), 118
Gov't Code § 66442(b), 119
Gov't Code § 66442.5, 119
Gov't Code §§ 66444-66450, 127
Gov't Code § 66445(d)(3), 78
Gov't Code § 66445(e), 127
Gov't Code § 66447, 127
Gov't Code § 66451 et seq., 86, 114
Gov't Code § 66451.10, 133, 134, 135
Gov't Code § 66451.10 et seq., 81, 136
Gov't Code § 66451.11, 136
Gov't Code § 66451.13, 135
Gov't Code § 66451.14, 135
Gov't Code § 66451.2, 558
Gov't Code § 66451.3, 128, 136
Gov't Code § 66451.3(a), 126
Gov't Code § 66451.30 et seq., 137
Gov't Code § 66451.301, 135
Gov't Code § 66451.302, 135
Gov't Code § 66451.4, 114
Gov't Code § 66451.7, 84
Gov't Code § 66451.10, 134
Gov't Code § 66451.10, et seq., 136
Gov't Code § 66452, 98
Gov't Code § 66452(c), 98, 283
Gov't Code § 66452.1, 7
Gov't Code § 66452.1(c), 86
Gov't Code § 66452.11, 89, 90, 92
Gov't Code § 66452.11(b), 90

Gov't Code § 66452.11(c), 91
Gov't Code § 66452.12(a), 93
Gov't Code § 66452.13, 90, 92
Gov't Code § 66452.13(b), 90
Gov't Code § 66452.13(c), 91
Gov't Code § 66452.14, 122
Gov't Code § 66452.14(b), 122
Gov't Code § 66452.15(a), 122
Gov't Code § 66452.15(b), 122
Gov't Code § 66452.2(c), 86
Gov't Code § 66452.21, 90, 92
Gov't Code § 66452.21(a), 90
Gov't Code § 66452.21(b), 90
Gov't Code § 66452.21(c), 91
Gov't Code § 66452.21(d), 90, 92
Gov't Code § 66452.22, 89, 90, 92, 111
Gov't Code § 66452.22(a), 90
Gov't Code § 66452.22(b), 90, 92
Gov't Code § 66452.22(c), 91
Gov't Code § 66452.22(d), 89, 91
Gov't Code § 66452.23, 90, 92111
Gov't Code § 66452.23(a), 90
Gov't Code § 66452.23(b), 90
Gov't Code § 66452.23(d), 90, 92
Gov't Code § 66452.24(a), 90
Gov't Code § 66452.24(b), 90, 93
Gov't Code § 66452.24(c), 90
Gov't Code § 66452.3, 87, 492
Gov't Code § 66452.4, 85
Gov't Code § 66452.5(a), 115
Gov't Code § 66452.5(d), 116
Gov't Code § 66452.6, 87, 89, 90
Gov't Code § 66452.6(a), 87, 88, 89
Gov't Code § 66452.6(a)(1), 88, 89, 119
Gov't Code § 66452.6(a)(2), 87
Gov't Code § 66452.6(b), 90, 91, 92
Gov't Code § 66452.6(b)(1), 88, 91
Gov't Code § 66452.6(c), 91, 92
Gov't Code § 66452.6(d), 89, 119
Gov't Code § 66452.6(e), 88, 89, 90, 92
Gov't Code § 66452.6(f), 88, 91
Gov't Code § 66453, 87
Gov't Code § 66454, 99
Gov't Code § 66455, 87
Gov't Code § 66455.1, 87
Gov't Code § 66455.3, 87
Gov't Code § 66455.7, 87
Gov't Code § 66456.1, 88, 119
Gov't Code § 66458, 119
Gov't Code § 66458(b), 120
Gov't Code § 66458(d), 120
Gov't Code § 66459, 493
Gov't Code § 66459(f), 122
Gov't Code § 66462(a), 123
Gov't Code § 66462(c), 123
Gov't Code § 66462.5, 106
Gov't Code § 66462.5(b), 105
Gov't Code § 66463, 127
Gov't Code § 66463(a), 125
Gov't Code § 66463.1, 127

Gov't Code § 66463.5, 89, 90
Gov't Code § 66463.5(c), 89
Gov't Code § 66463.5(e), 91, 92
Gov't Code § 66463.5(g), 95
Gov't Code § 66464(a), 120
Gov't Code § 66464(a),(c), 121
Gov't Code § 66464(b), 121
Gov't Code § 66465, 121
Gov't Code § 66466, 121
Gov't Code § 66466(f), 121
Gov't Code § 66468, 120
Gov't Code § 66469, 127, 128
Gov't Code § 66469(a)-(c), 127
Gov't Code § 66469(d), 127
Gov't Code § 66469(e), 127
Gov't Code § 66469(f), 127, 128
Gov't Code § 66469(g), 127
Gov't Code § 66470, 127, 128
Gov't Code § 66471, 128
Gov't Code § 66472, 128
Gov't Code § 66472.1, 127, 128
Gov't Code § 66472.1(a)(1)(f), 122
Gov't Code § 66473, 114, 120
Gov't Code § 66473.1, 105, 114
Gov't Code § 66473.5, 21, 25, 107, 108, 112, 113, 370, 492
Gov't Code § 66473.7, 101, 102, 278, 453
Gov't Code § 66473.7(b)(1), 102, 457
Gov't Code § 66473.7(o), 520
Gov't Code § 66474, 108, 116, 128
Gov't Code § 66474(e), 100, 109, 110, 114, 339
Gov't Code § 66474.1, 99, 116, 119
Gov't Code § 66474.2, 99, 111, 114, 490
Gov't Code § 66474.2(a), 111
Gov't Code § 66474.2(b), 95
Gov't Code § 66474.2(c), 95
Gov't Code § 66474.4(b), 115
Gov't Code § 65474.5, 18
Gov't Code § 66474.5(a), 115
Gov't Code § 66474.5(a)(1), 115
Gov't Code § 66474.5(a)(2), 115
Gov't Code § 66474.5(a)(3), 115
Gov't Code § 66474.5(a)(4), 115
Gov't Code § 66474.6, 114, 116
Gov't Code § 66474.60(c), 116
Gov't Code § 66474.7, 116
Gov't Code § 66474.9, 106
Gov't Code § 66474.9(a), 106
Gov't Code § 66474.9(b)(1), 106
Gov't Code § 66474.9(b)(2), 106
Gov't Code § 66474.10, 107
Gov't Code § 66475, 103
Gov't Code § 66475.1, 103
Gov't Code § 66475.2, 103
Gov't Code § 66475.3, 106
Gov't Code § 66477, 101, 102, 108, 339
Gov't Code § 66477(a), 112
Gov't Code § 66477(a)(1), 101
Gov't Code § 66477(a)(2), 101

Gov't Code § 66477(a)(3), 101
Gov't Code § 66477(a)(3)(B), 101
Gov't Code § 66477(a)(4), 101
Gov't Code § 66477(a)(5), 101
Gov't Code § 66477(a)(6), 102, 112
Gov't Code § 66477(a)(7), 102
Gov't Code § 66477(a)(8), 102
Gov't Code § 66477(a)(9), 102
Gov't Code § 66477(a)(9)(d), 110
Gov't Code §§ 66477(a)-(e), 112
Gov't Code § 66477(b), 112, 132
Gov't Code § 66477(d), 112
Gov't Code § 66477(e), 102
Gov't Code § 66477.1, 122
Gov't Code § 66477.5, 345
Gov't Code § 66478, 103
Gov't Code § 66478.1 et seq., 105
Gov't Code §§ 66478.1–66478.14, 105
Gov't Code § 66478.2, 105
Gov't Code § 66479(c), 103
Gov't Code § 66479 et seq., 103
Gov't Code § 66480, 103
Gov't Code § 66481, 103
Gov't Code § 66483, 103
Gov't Code § 66483(d), 103
Gov't Code § 66483.1, 103
Gov't Code § 66483.2, 112, 132
Gov't Code § 66484, 104, 344
Gov't Code § 66484.3, 371
Gov't Code § 66484.5, 104
Gov't Code § 66484.7, 104
Gov't Code § 66485 et seq., 104
Gov't Code § 66487, 104
Gov't Code § 66490, 104
Gov't Code § 66491, 104
Gov't Code § 66492, 121
Gov't Code § 66493, 120, 121
Gov't Code § 66493(a)(1), 120
Gov't Code § 66493(a)(2), 120
Gov't Code § 66493(d), 120
Gov't Code § 66494.1, 121
Gov't Code § 66495 et seq., 105
Gov't Code § 66498.1, 95, 97, 283, 284
Gov't Code § 66498.1(b), 95, 98, 99, 285, 490
Gov't Code § 66498.1(c), 95
Gov't Code § 66498.1 et seq., 94, 283
Gov't Code § 66498.2, 99
Gov't Code § 66498.3(a), 99
Gov't Code § 66498.5(b), 99
Gov't Code § 66498.5(c), 99
Gov't Code § 66498.5(d), 99
Gov't Code § 66498.7, 95
Gov't Code § 66498.8, 95
Gov't Code § 66498.8(d), 98
Gov't Code § 66498.9, 95, 129
Gov't Code § 66498.9(b), 96, 97
Gov't Code § 66499, 123
Gov't Code § 66499.1, 124
Gov't Code § 66499.11 et seq., 125, 132

Gov't Code § 66499.16, 132
Gov't Code § 66499.17, 112
Gov't Code § 66499.19, 112
Gov't Code § 66499.20½, 128, 132, 135
Gov't Code § 66499.20¾, 135
Gov't Code § 66499.21 et seq., 131
Gov't Code § 66499.25, 132
Gov't Code § 66499.3, 124, 128, 133
Gov't Code § 66499.3(c), 124
Gov't Code § 66499.3(e), 128
Gov't Code § 66499.3 et seq., 497
Gov't Code § 66499.30, 129, 134
Gov't Code § 66499.30(e), 129
Gov't Code § 66499.31, 78, 130
Gov't Code § 66499.32(a), 129
Gov't Code § 66499.32(b), 129
Gov't Code § 66499.33, 129
Gov't Code § 66499.34, 130, 131, 497
Gov't Code § 66499.35, 130
Gov't Code § 66499.35(a), 130
Gov't Code § 66499.35(b), 130, 131
Gov't Code § 66499.35(f)(1)(e), 131
Gov't Code § 66499.36, 130, 497
Gov't Code § 66499.37, 106, 116, 117, 118, 136, 308, 516, 518, 519, 520, 521, 522, 524, 557
Gov't Code § 66499.4, 124
Gov't Code § 66499.5 et seq., 133
Gov't Code § 66499.50, 133
Gov't Code § 66499.7, 125
Gov't Code § 66499.7(a), 125
Gov't Code § 66499.7(b), 125
Gov't Code § 66499.7(c), 125
Gov't Code § 66499.7(d), 125
Gov't Code § 66499.7(h), 126
Gov't Code § 66499.7(i), 126
Gov't Code § 66499.8, 126
Gov't Code § 66499.9, 126
Gov't Code § 66499.10, 126
Gov't Code § 66584.04(d), 412
Gov't Code § 66600 et seq., 211, 264
Gov't Code § 66604, 265
Gov't Code § 66610, 265
Gov't Code § 66620, 265
Gov't Code § 66646.2, 265
Gov't Code § 87100 et seq., 511

Harbors & Navigation Code

Harbors and Navigation Code §§ 100–107, 105

Health & Safety Code

Health & Safety Code § 1566.3, 5
Health & Safety Code § 1597.40(a), 5
Health & Safety Code § 17021.6, 411
Health & Safety Code § 17951, 558
Health & Safety Code § 17951(e)(2), 470
Health & Safety Code § 17958.1, 80
Health & Safety Code § 17958.1(a), 80
Health & Safety Code § 17958.5, 470

Health & Safety Code § 17958.7, 470
Health & Safety Code § 18007, 80
Health & Safety Code § 18021.7, 411
Health & Safety Code § 18930, 470
Health & Safety Code § 18941.5, 470
Health & Safety Code § 18941.10, 468
Health & Safety Code §§ 18950–18961, 253
Health & Safety Code § 19132.3, 558
Health & Safety Code § 19852, 558
Health & Safety Code § 33000 et seq., 366, 505
Health & Safety Code § 33141, 372
Health & Safety Code § 33365, 372
Health & Safety Code § 33450, 372
Health & Safety Code § 38505(g), 459
Health & Safety Code § 41901, 558
Health & Safety Code § 50052.5, 422
Health & Safety Code § 50079.5, 411, 420, 422
Health & Safety Code § 50093, 411, 420
Health & Safety Code § 50105, 409, 411, 422
Health & Safety Code § 50451, 411
Health & Safety Code § 50452, 411
Health & Safety Code § 50453, 411
Health & Safety Code § 54059(c), 418

Labor Code

Labor Code section 1720, 270
Labor Code § 1720(a)(1), 269
Labor Code § 1720(c), 270
Labor Code § 1720(c)(3), 270
Labor Code § 1771, 269
Labor Code § 1773.5(b), 270
Labor Code § 1773.5(c), 270
Labor Code § 1782(a), 271
Labor Code § 1782(b), 271

Penal Code

Penal Code § 10(b), 379, 380
Penal Code § 19, 495

Public Contract Code

Pub. Cont. Code § 22002, 267

Public Resources Code

Pub. Res. Code § 2177(a), 527
Pub. Res. Code § 2621 et seq., 105
Pub. Res. Code § 2622, 105
Pub. Res. Code § 2623, 105
Pub. Res. Code § 2712, 29
Pub. Res. Code § 2761 et seq., 15
Pub. Res. Code § 3715.5, 19
Pub. Res. Code § 4133, 113
Pub. Res. Code § 4142, 113
Pub. Res. Code § 4144, 113
Pub. Res. Code § 4290, 113
Pub. Res. Code § 4511 et seq., 496
Pub. Res. Code § 5020 et seq., 253
Pub. Res. Code § 5020.1, 253

Pub. Res. Code § 6311.5, 476
Pub. Res. Code § 15125(a), 462
Pub. Res. Code § 15126.2, 475
Pub. Res. Code § 15130(b)(1), 462
Pub. Res. Code §§ 15260-15285, 144
Pub. Res. Code § 15262, 408
Pub. Res. Code §§ 15301-15332, 145
Pub. Res. Code § 15306, 408
Pub. Res. Code § 15364.4, 459
Pub. Res. Code § 21000 et seq., 6, 31, 72, 109, 117, 280, 376, 401
Pub. Res. Code § 21000, 139
Pub. Res. Code §§ 21000-21177, 339
Pub. Res. Code §§ 21000-21178.1, 114
Pub. Res. Code § 21001, 139
Pub. Res. Code § 21002, 172
Pub. Res. Code § 21002, 171
Pub. Res. Code § 21081, 171
Pub. Res. Code § 21002.1, 139, 172
Pub. Res. Code § 21002.1(a), 164
Pub. Res. Code § 21002.1(b), 171
Pub. Res. Code § 21002.1, 152
Pub. Res. Code § 21004, 109
Pub. Res. Code § 21004, 171
Pub. Res. Code § 21060.5, 142
Pub. Res. Code § 21060.5, 462
Pub. Res. Code § 21061, 152
Pub. Res. Code § 21061.0.5, 423
Pub. Res. Code § 21064, 150
Pub. Res. Code § 21064.5, 150, 151
Pub. Res. Code § 21065, 141, 142
Pub. Res. Code § 21068, 34, 109, 110
Pub. Res. Code § 21068.5, 153
Pub. Res. Code § 21071, 423
Pub. Res. Code § 21080, 139, 140, 152
Pub. Res. Code § 21080(a), 140
Pub. Res. Code § 21080(b), 144
Pub. Res. Code § 21080(b)(8), 143, 146
Pub. Res. Code § 21080(c), 147, 150
Pub. Res. Code § 21080(e), 150
Pub. Res. Code §§ 21080.01-21080.03, 144
Pub. Res. Code §§ 21080.05-21080.08, 144
Pub. Res. Code § 21080.1 et seq., 152
Pub. Res. Code § 21080.1, 147
Pub. Res. Code § 21080.1, 98, 145
Pub. Res. Code § 21080.14, 142, 144
Pub. Res. Code § 21080.3, 147
Pub. Res. Code § 21080.4, 153, 176
Pub. Res. Code § 21080.5, 145
Pub. Res. Code §§ 21080.7-21080.33, 144
Pub. Res. Code § 21080.35, 466
Pub. Res. Code § 21081, 166, 172, 481
Pub. Res. Code § 21081.6, 173
Pub. Res. Code § 21081.6(1), 173
Pub. Res. Code § 21081.6(a), 498
Pub. Res. Code § 21081.6(b), 498
Pub. Res. Code § 21082.1, 154
Pub. Res. Code § 21082.1(c)(1), 172
Pub. Res. Code § 21082.1(c)(3), 172
Pub. Res. Code § 21082.2(b), 150

Pub. Res. Code § 21082.2(c), 150
Pub. Res. Code § 21083(b), 155
Pub. Res. Code § 21083.05(a), 462
Pub. Res. Code § 21083.3, 144, 153
Pub. Res. Code § 21083.9(a), 154
Pub. Res. Code § 21084(a), 145
Pub. Res. Code § 21084.1, 159
Pub. Res. Code § 21091(d)(1), 170
Pub. Res. Code §§ 21091-21092, 154
Pub. Res. Code § 21092(b)(3), 154
Pub. Res. Code § 21092(b), 151
Pub. Res. Code § 21092.1, 151
Pub. Res. Code § 21092.2, 148
Pub. Res. Code § 21092.4, 153
Pub. Res. Code § 21092.5, 154
Pub. Res. Code § 21093, 153
Pub. Res. Code § 21094.5, 466
Pub. Res. Code § 21094.5(e), 466
Pub. Res. Code § 21095.5, 466
Pub. Res. Code § 21099, 452
Pub. Res. Code § 21099(b)(1), 159
Pub. Res. Code § 21099(b)(2), 159
Pub. Res. Code § 21099(b)(4), 452
Pub. Res. Code § 21099(d)(1), 159
Pub. Res. Code § 21100, 155
Pub. Res. Code § 21100(b)(3), 164
Pub. Res. Code § 21100(b)(5), 155
Pub. Res. Code § 21100(c), 155
Pub. Res. Code § 21100(e), 163
Pub. Res. Code § 21100.2(a)(1)(B), 177
Pub. Res. Code § 21104, 155
Pub. Res. Code § 21104.2, 150
Pub. Res. Code § 21108, 176
Pub. Res. Code § 21151(c), 172
Pub. Res. Code § 21151.5, 85, 148
Pub. Res. Code § 21151.5(a), 151
Pub. Res. Code § 21151.9, 155, 454, 455
Pub. Res. Code § 21152, 176, 516, 518
Pub. Res. Code § 21152(a), 176, 517
Pub. Res. Code § 21152(c), 170
Pub. Res. Code § 21152(c), 515
Pub. Res. Code § 21153, 152
Pub. Res. Code §§ 21155-21155.3, 465
Pub. Res. Code § 21155, 465
Pub. Res. Code § 21155.1, 465
Pub. Res. Code § 21155.1(a), 465
Pub. Res. Code § 21155.1(b), 465
Pub. Res. Code § 21155.2, 465
Pub. Res. Code § 21156, 152
Pub. Res. Code §§ 21156-21159.9, 36
Pub. Res. Code § 21157.1, 152
Pub. Res. Code § 21157.6, 152
Pub. Res. Code § 21158.5(a), 144
Pub. Res. Code §§ 21159.21-21159.24, 144
Pub. Res. Code § 21159.22, 422
Pub. Res. Code § 21159.23, 422
Pub. Res. Code § 21159.24, 422, 465
Pub. Res. Code § 21159.28, 466
Pub. Res. Code § 21161, 176
Pub. Res. Code § 21166, 145, 162, 174

Pub. Res. Code § 21166(c), 175
Pub. Res. Code § 21166, 157
Pub. Res. Code § 21167, 529
Pub. Res. Code § 21167(a), 176, 521
Pub. Res. Code § 21167(b), 176, 520
Pub. Res. Code § 21167(d), 147, 520
Pub. Res. Code § 21167.1(b), 544
Pub. Res. Code § 21167.3(b), 546
Pub. Res. Code § 21167.4, 519
Pub. Res. Code § 21167.4(a), 543, 548
Pub. Res. Code § 21167.6, 538
Pub. Res. Code § 21167.6(a), 518
Pub. Res. Code § 21167.6(b)(2), 550
Pub. Res. Code § 21167.6(e), 549, 550
Pub. Res. Code § 21167.6(e)(10), 550
Pub. Res. Code § 21167.8(c), 538
Pub. Res. Code § 21167.10(a), 549
Pub. Res. Code § 21167.10(c), 549
Pub. Res. Code § 21168, 552
Pub. Res. Code § 21168.5, 552, 553
Pub. Res. Code § 21168.9, 553
Pub. Res. Code § 21177, 527, 531, 551, 552
Pub. Res. Code § 21177(a), 551, 552
Pub. Res. Code § 21177(b), 549
Pub. Res. Code § 21177(c), 552
Pub. Res. Code § 21177(e), 549
Pub. Res. Code § 21177(f), 551
Pub. Res. Code § 21180, 467
Pub. Res. Code § 21185, 467
Pub. Res. Code § 21186, 467
Pub. Res. Code § 22002, 272
Pub. Res. Code § 25228, 474
Pub. Res. Code § 25402(b), 468
Pub. Res. Code § 25402.1(h)(2), 470
Pub. Res. Code § 25405.5, 474
Pub. Res. Code § 25540.5, 19
Pub. Res. Code § 25740 et seq., 472
Pub. Res. Code § 26500 et seq., 354, 355
Pub. Res. Code § 26507, 355
Pub. Res. Code § 26525, 355
Pub. Res. Code § 26530, 355
Pub. Res. Code § 26531, 355
Pub. Res. Code § 26532, 355
Pub. Res. Code § 26533, 355
Pub. Res. Code § 26534, 355
Pub. Res. Code § 26567, 355
Pub. Res. Code § 26570, 355
Pub. Res. Code § 26581, 355
Pub. Res. Code § 26583, 355
Pub. Res. Code § 26587, 355
Pub. Res. Code § 26591, 355
Pub. Res. Code § 26593, 355
Pub. Res. Code § 26650, 355
Pub. Res. Code § 26654, 355
Pub. Res. Code § 30000 et seq., 29, 79, 258, 274,
Pub. Res. Code § 30001.5, 258
Pub. Res. Code § 30005, 262
Pub. Res. Code § 30005(b), 262
Pub. Res. Code § 30103(a), 260

Pub. Res. Code § 30106, 260
Pub. Res. Code § 30108.5, 261
Pub. Res. Code § 30108.6, 261
Pub. Res. Code § 30200 et seq., 259, 262
Pub. Res. Code § 30210-30214, 263, 262
Pub. Res. Code § 30231, 264
Pub. Res. Code § 30233, 264
Pub. Res. Code § 30233(a), 211
Pub. Res. Code § 30240, 261
Pub. Res. Code §§ 30260-30263, 263
Pub. Res. Code § 30301, 259
Pub. Res. Code § 30312, 259
Pub. Res. Code § 30330, 259, 263
Pub. Res. Code § 30339, 264
Pub. Res. Code § 30340.5, 260
Pub. Res. Code § 30343, 264
Pub. Res. Code § 30344, 264
Pub. Res. Code §§ 30350-30555, 264
Pub. Res. Code § 30400, 263
Pub. Res. Code § 30411(b), 264
Pub. Res. Code § 30412(c), 264
Pub. Res. Code § 30413(d), 264
Pub. Res. Code § 30413(c), 264
Pub. Res. Code § 30500, 261
Pub. Res. Code § 30512, 262
Pub. Res. Code § 30512.2(a), 258
Pub. Res. Code § 30514, 262, 263
Pub. Res. Code § 30515, 263, 264
Pub. Res. Code § 30519(a), 262
Pub. Res. Code § 30519.5, 260, 264
Pub. Res. Code §§ 30530-30534, 263
Pub. Res. Code § 30600, 211, 259
Pub. Res. Code § 30600 et seq., 211
Pub. Res. Code § 30600.5(d), 262
Pub. Res. Code § 30601, 261
Pub. Res. Code § 30603, 261, 262
Pub. Res. Code § 30603(a), 263
Pub. Res. Code § 30603(b), 263
Pub. Res. Code § 30603(c), 263
Pub. Res. Code § 30603.1, 260
Pub. Res. Code § 30604(a), 256, 261
Pub. Res. Code § 30605, 263
Pub. Res. Code §§ 30605-30606, 263
Pub. Res. Code § 30607.1, 264
Pub. Res. Code § 30610(c), 59
Pub. Res. Code § 30610, 260
Pub. Res. Code § 30611, 260
Pub. Res. Code § 30716, 263
Pub. Res. Code § 30801, 263, 520, 522
Pub. Res. Code § 65457(b), 520

Public Utilities Code
Pub. Util. Code §§ 399.11 et seq., 472
Pub. Util. Code § 21670, 26
Pub. Util. Code § 21671.5, 588
Pub. Util. Code § 21675, 26, 29, 36
Pub. Util. Code § 21676, 26
Pub. Util. Code § 21676(b), 26, 43, 44

Revenue & Taxation Code
Rev. & Tax. Code § 99, 396
Rev. & Tax. Code § 99.1, 396
Rev. & Tax. Code § 327.5, 74
Rev. & Tax. Code § 423.4, 258
Rev. & Tax. Code § 2050, 74
Rev. & Tax. Code § 2052, 74
Rev. & Tax. Code § 17274, 497
Rev. & Tax. Code § 24436.5, 497

Streets & Highways Code
Sts. & High. Code § 1160 et seq., 394
Sts. and High. Code §§ 2800-3012, 350
Sts. & High. Code § 22500 et seq., 354

Water Code
Water Code § 354, 455
Water Code § 3400 et seq., 104
Water Code § 9612, 18
Water Code §§ 10608-10608.64, 458
Water Code § 10632, 455
Water Code § 10635, 453, 455
Water Code §§ 10800-10853, 458
Water Code § 10910 et seq., 155
Water Code § 10910, 453, 455
Water Code § 10910(h), 457, 458
Water Code § 10910-10912, 453
Water Code § 10911, 458
Water Code § 10911(b), 155, 457
Water Code § 10911(c), 457, 458, 481
Water Code § 10912, 451
Water Code § 13000 et seq., 183, 205
Water Code § 13050(d), 209
Water Code § 13050(e), 209
Water Code § 13260(1), 209, 210
Water Code § 14877.3, 459
Water Code § 31007, 370

Session Laws
1971 Cal. Stat., ch. 1446, 9
1977 Cal. Stat., ch. 234, § 19, 81
1979 Cal. Stat., ch. 868, 264
1984 Cal. Stat., ch. 1187, § 1, 107
1998 Cal. Stat., ch. 283, § 5, 86, 109, 490
1998 Cal. Stat., ch. 407, 108
2008 Cal. Stat., ch. 728, § 1(a), 460
2008 Cal. Stat., ch. 728, § 1(b), 458.

CALIFORNIA REGULATIONS (INCLUDING CEQA 14 CAL. CODE REGS.)
8 Cal. Code Regs. § 16001(a), 269
14 Cal. Code Regs., Appendix. G, 149
14 Cal. Code Regs. § 670.1, 245
14 Cal. Code Regs. § 720, 210
14 Cal. Code Regs § 13347, 480
14 Cal. Code Regs. §§ 15000-15387, 466
14 Cal. Code Regs. § 15000 et seq., 139

14 Cal. Code Regs. § 15004, 145
14 Cal. Code Regs. § 15040, 343
14 Cal. Code Regs. § 15041, 343
14 Cal. Code Regs. § 15051, 140
14 Cal. Code Regs. § 15051(b), 140
14 Cal. Code Regs. §§ 15060-15061, 139
14 Cal. Code Regs. § 15061(b)(3), 144
14 Cal. Code Regs. § 15061, 139
14 Cal. Code Regs. § 15062, 137, 139, 144, 150
14 Cal. Code Regs. § 15062(a), 147
14 Cal. Code Regs. § 15062(d), 147
14 Cal. Code Regs. §§ 15063-15065, 147
14 Cal. Code Regs. § 15063, 147
14 Cal. Code Regs. § 15064(f)(1), 150
14 Cal. Code Regs. § 15064(f)(4), 150
14 Cal. Code Regs. § 15064.4, 161
14 Cal. Code Regs. § 15064.4(a), 161, 463
14 Cal. Code Regs. § 15064.4(a)(1), 161, 463
14 Cal. Code Regs. § 15064.4(a)(2), 463
14 Cal. Code Regs. § 15064.4(b), 463
14 Cal. Code Regs. § 15064.5(a)(1), 159
14 Cal. Code Regs. § 15064.5(a)(2), 159
14 Cal. Code Regs. § 15064.5(a)(3), 159
14 Cal. Code Regs. § 15064.5(b), 159
14 Cal. Code Regs. § 15064.5(b)(1), 160
14 Cal. Code Regs. § 15064.5(b)(2), 160
14 Cal. Code Regs. § 15064.7, 158
14 Cal. Code Regs. § 15064.7(a), 158
14 Cal. Code Regs. § 15064.7(b), 158
14 Cal. Code Regs. § 15070(b), 150, 151
14 Cal. Code Regs. § 15070(b)(2), 150
14 Cal. Code Regs. § 15070 et seq., 150
14 Cal. Code Regs. § 15071, 151
14 Cal. Code Regs. § 15072(a), 151
14 Cal. Code Regs. § 15073.5, 152
14 Cal. Code Regs. § 15075(a), 151
14 Cal. Code Regs. § 15075(e), 176
14 Cal. Code Regs. §§ 15080-15081.5, 152
14 Cal. Code Regs. § 15082, 153, 176
14 Cal. Code Regs. § 15082(a), 154
14 Cal. Code Regs. § 15082(b), 154
14 Cal. Code Regs. § 15082(c), 154
14 Cal. Code Regs. § 15083, 153
14 Cal. Code Regs. § 15084, 154
14 Cal. Code Regs. § 15085, 176
14 Cal. Code Regs. §§ 15085-15089, 154
14 Cal. Code Regs. § 15088, 170
14 Cal. Code Regs. § 15088(a), 169
14 Cal. Code Regs. § 15088(b), 154
14 Cal. Code Regs. § 15088(c), 169
14 Cal. Code Regs. § 15088(e), 170
14 Cal. Code Regs. § 15088.5(a), 170
14 Cal. Code Regs. § 15088.5(b), 170
14 Cal. Code Regs. § 15089(b), 170
14 Cal. Code Regs. § 15090(a)(1), 172
14 Cal. Code Regs. § 15090(a)(2), 172
14 Cal. Code Regs. § 15090(a)(3), 172
14 Cal. Code Regs. § 15090(b), 172
14 Cal. Code Regs. § 15091, 172

14 Cal. Code Regs. § 15091(d), 498
14 Cal. Code Regs. §§ 15091-15093, 172
14 Cal. Code Regs. §§ 15091-15094, 171
14 Cal. Code Regs. § 15092, 171
14 Cal. Code Regs. § 15093, 172.
14 Cal. Code Regs. § 15094, 170
14 Cal. Code Regs. § 15094(a), 173
14 Cal. Code Regs. § 15094(f), 173
14 Cal. Code Regs. § 15096(d), 106, 407
14 Cal. Code Regs. § 15097(c), 173
14 Cal. Code Regs. § 15105, 154, 177
14 Cal. Code Regs. § 15107, 148
14 Cal. Code Regs. § 15108, 148
14 Cal. Code Regs. § 15109, 148
14 Cal. Code Regs. § 15112(c)(5), 176, 521
14 Cal. Code Regs. § 15122, 154
14 Cal. Code Regs. § 15123, 154
14 Cal. Code Regs. § 15124, 155
14 Cal. Code Regs. § 15125, 155, 156
14 Cal. Code Regs. § 15125(a), 156, 462
14 Cal. Code Regs. § 15125(d), 155
14 Cal. Code Regs. § 15126, 155
14 Cal. Code Regs. § 15126(d), 167
14 Cal. Code Regs. § 15126.2, 155, 475, 476
14 Cal. Code Regs. § 15126.2(d), 155, 169
14 Cal. Code Regs. § 15126.4, 155
14 Cal. Code Regs. § 15126.4(a), 164
14 Cal. Code Regs. § 15126.4(a)(1)(B), 164
14 Cal. Code Regs. § 15126.4(a)(1)(D), 164
14 Cal. Code Regs. § 15126.4(c), 162, 463
14 Cal. Code Regs. § 15126.6, 155, 166, 167
14 Cal. Code Regs. § 15126.6(a), 166
14 Cal. Code Regs. § 15126.6(c), 167
14 Cal. Code Regs. § 15126.6(d), 169
14 Cal. Code Regs. § 15126.6(e), 168
14 Cal. Code Regs. § 15126.6(f), 166
14 Cal. Code Regs. § 15128, 155
14 Cal. Code Regs. § 15129, 155
14 Cal. Code Regs. § 15130, 155
14 Cal. Code Regs. § 15130(b), 163
14 Cal. Code Regs. § 15130(b)(1), 462
14 Cal. Code Regs. § 15130(b)(1)(A), 162, 163
14 Cal. Code Regs. § 15130(b)(1)(B), 163
14 Cal. Code Regs. § 15130(d), 163
14 Cal. Code Regs. § 15132, 154
14 Cal. Code Regs. § 15132(d), 169
14 Cal. Code Regs. § 15152, 153
14 Cal. Code Regs. § 15162, 152
14 Cal. Code Regs. § 15162(a), 174
14 Cal. Code Regs. § 15162(a)(3), 175
14 Cal. Code Regs. § 15162(d), 175
14 Cal. Code Regs. § 15164(a), 175
14 Cal. Code Regs. § 15164(b), 175
14 Cal. Code Regs. § 15164(c), 175
14 Cal. Code Regs. § 15164(d), 175
14 Cal. Code Regs. § 15164(e), 175
14 Cal. Code Regs. § 15168, 152, 154
14 Cal. Code Regs. § 15168(c), 152
14 Cal. Code Regs. § 15168(c)(1), 152
14 Cal. Code Regs. § 15168(c)(2), 152
14 Cal. Code Regs. § 15168(c)(3), 152
14 Cal. Code Regs. § 15183, 153
14 Cal. Code Regs. § 15183(a), 153
14 Cal. Code Regs. § 15183.3, 466
14 Cal. Code Regs. § 15204(c), 169
14 Cal. Code Regs. § 15204(f), 169
14 Cal. Code Regs. § 15250, 145
14 Cal. Code Regs. §§ 15260-15285, 144
14 Cal. Code Regs. § 15262, 408
14 Cal. Code Regs. § 15273(c), 146
14 Cal. Code Regs. § 15300, 145
14 Cal. Code Regs. §§ 15300-15332, 144
14 Cal. Code Regs. § 15300.2, 145, 465
14 Cal. Code Regs. §§ 15301-15332, 145
14 Cal. Code Regs. § 15306, 408
14 Cal. Code Regs. § 15307, 146
14 Cal. Code Regs. § 15308, 146
14 Cal. Code Regs. § 15330(d), 145
14 Cal. Code Regs. § 15352(a), 141
14 Cal. Code Regs. § 15352(b), 141
14 Cal. Code Regs. § 15355, 162
14 Cal. Code Regs. § 15356, 172
14 Cal. Code Regs. § 15357, 140
14 Cal. Code Regs. § 15360, 142
14 Cal. Code Regs. § 15364.4, 459
14 Cal. Code Regs. § 15365, 147
14 Cal. Code Regs. § 15378, 143
14 Cal. Code Regs. § 15378(a), 141, 142
14 Cal. Code Regs. § 15378(b)(4), 376
14 Cal. Code Regs. § 15384(a), 150
14 Cal. Code Regs. § 15385, 153
24 Cal. Code Regs., part 6, 463, 467, 468
24 Cal. Code Regs., part 11, 467, 468
24 Cal. Code Regs. § 6, 467, 468, 470
24 Cal. Code Regs. § 10-106, 470

CALIFORNIA ATTORNEY GENERAL OPINIONS

17 Ops. Cal. Atty. Gen. 79 (1951), 73
39 Ops. Cal. Atty. Gen. 82 (1962), 73
40 Ops. Cal. Atty. Gen. 243 (1962), 67
55 Ops. Cal. Atty. Gen. 414 (1972), 74, 78
56 Ops. Cal. Atty. Gen. 274 (1973), 114
57 Ops. Cal. Atty. Gen. 556 (1974), 76
58 Ops. Cal. Atty. Gen. 21 (1975), 9, 19
58 Ops. Cal. Atty. Gen. 41 (1975), 107, 111
58 Ops. Cal. Atty. Gen. 408 (1975), 76
59 Ops. Cal. Atty. Gen. 129 (1976), 11
59 Ops. Cal. Atty. Gen. 581 (1976), 74
61 Ops. Cal. Atty. Gen. 299 (1978), 71, 74
62 Ops. Cal. Atty. Gen. 136 (1979), 74, 81
62 Ops. Cal. Atty. Gen. 140 (1979), 74, 81
62 Ops. Cal. Atty. Gen. 147 (1979), 74
62 Ops. Cal. Atty. Gen. 175 (1979), 127
62 Ops. Cal. Atty. Gen. 410 (1979), 66, 111
63 Ops. Cal. Atty. Gen. 820 (1980), 484
64 Ops. Cal. Atty. Gen. 328 (1981), 105, 114
64 Ops. Cal. Atty. Gen. 762 (1981), 75
64 Ops. Cal. Atty. Gen. 814 (1981), 74
65 Ops. Cal. Atty. Gen. 63 (1982), 486
66 Ops. Cal. Atty. Gen. 120 (1983), 103
66 Ops. Cal. Atty. Gen. 258 (1983), 27
67 Ops. Cal. Atty. Gen. 75 (1984), 20
68 Ops. Cal. Atty. Gen. 108 (1985), 110
68 Ops. Cal. Atty. Gen. 310 (1985), 65
69 Ops. Cal. Atty. Gen. 300 (1986), 271
70 Ops. Cal. Atty Gen. 231 (1987), 413
71 Ops. Cal. Atty. Gen. 163 (1988), 104
71 Ops. Cal. Atty. Gen. 326 (1988), 116
73 Ops. Cal. Atty. Gen. 78 (1990), 20
73 Ops. Cal. Atty. Gen. 152 (1990), 102, 108, 339
73 Ops. Cal. Atty. Gen. 255 (1990), 382
73 Ops. Cal. Atty. Gen. 338 (1990), 116
74 Ops. Cal. Atty. Gen. 89 (1991), 123
74 Ops. Cal. Atty. Gen. 149 (1991), 130, 134
75 Ops. Cal. Atty. Gen. 98 (1992), 81
75 Ops. Cal. Atty. Gen. 984 (1992), 66
76 Ops. Cal. Atty. Gen. 227 (1994), 277
77 Ops. Cal. Atty. Gen. 94 (1994), 277
77 Ops. Cal. Atty. Gen. 185 (1994), 71, 79
77 Ops. Cal. Atty. Gen. 231 (1994), 79
78 Ops. Cal. Atty. Gen. 31 (1995), 67
78 Ops. Cal. Atty. Gen. 77 (1995), 47, 513
78 Ops. Cal. Atty. Gen. 137 (1995), 247
78 Ops. Cal. Atty. Gen. 158 (1995), 126
80 Ops. Cal. Atty. Gen. 183 (1997), 351
81 Ops. Cal. Atty. Gen. 57 (1998), 43
81 Ops. Cal. Atty. Gen. 104 (1998), 383, 351
81 Ops. Cal. Atty. Gen. 106 (1998), 383, 352
81 Ops. Cal. Atty. Gen. 144 (1998), 130, 134
81 Ops. Cal. Atty. Gen. 166 (1998), 85
81 Ops. Cal. Atty. Gen. 181 (1998), 353
81 Ops. Cal. Atty. Gen. 293 (1998), 102
82 Ops. Cal. Atty. Gen. 35 (1999), 349, 535
82 Ops. Cal. Atty. Gen. 43 (1999), 351
83 Ops. Cal. Atty. Gen. 190 (2000), 68
85 Ops. Cal. Atty. Gen. 21 (2002), 106
86 Ops. Cal. Atty. Gen. 70 (2003), 73, 137
87 Ops. Cal. Atty. Gen. 102 (2004), 26, 36
88 Ops. Cal. Atty. Gen. 172 (2005), 104
89 Ops. Cal. Atty. Gen. 173 (2006), 400
89 Ops. Cal. Atty. Gen. 178 (2006), 7

Index

A

AB 32. *See* Global Warming Solutions Act
AB 1600. *See* Mitigation Fee Act
abandonment, 94, 125, 132, 274-75, 275, 297, 308, 569
abatement/abatement districts, 262, 354-56, 392-93, 569
about the origin of Curtin's as a land use and planning reference, xvii
abutting, boundaries/properties, 27, 87, 569
access, defined, 569
accessory building/structure, 136, 426-27, 569. *See also* second unit
adaptive use/reuse, 241-42, 569
administrative and criminal sanctions, 495-98, 535
administrative mandate proceedings. *See* mandate proceedings
Administrative Procedures Act (Gov't Code § 11340 *et seq.*)
    applicable statutes of limitations, 519-22
    ban on *ex parte* communications, 237
    challenges to agency actions, 212, 243-44
    defined, 569
    judicial review of compliance orders, 190-91
    review of evidence, 480n2
administrative res judicata, 508-09
adult entertainment business, 49-52, 499, 519-20
advisory agency
    allowance for exemptions, 83, 472
    appeals, 90, 115-16
    tentative map approval, 84, 85
advisory election (Elec. Code § 9603), 569
aesthetic regulation/control
    CEQA compliance, 142-43
    design review and, 249-52
    historic preservation, 253-55
    judicial rulings, 151, 175-76
    NIMBY attitudes, 449-51
    police powers, 1-3, 331-32
    preservation of agricultural lands, 255-58
    zoning due process and, 45-46
affordability covenants. *See* covenants, conditions & restrictions
affordable housing. *See* housing; inclusionary housing
agriculture/agricultural lands
    Coastal Act of 1976, 259
    conditional zoning changes, 63-64
    conservation easements, 114-15, 257, 569
    conversion to housing, 82-83, 412, 420-21, 422
    conversion to urban use, 165-66, 313
    in General Plan elements, 16, 19
    growth management and, 448-49
    LAFCO role in, 387-89, 391, 395, 400
    leapfrog development, 53
    Map Act exemptions, 82-83
    preservation by initiative, 366, 370
    Smart Growth and, 449-51
    water issues, 458-59
    wetland conversions, 179, 209-10
    Williamson Act preservation, 255-58, 473, 576
    zoning/leasing for agricultural purposes, 82-83
air pollution control, 85, 394, 448, 451, 460, 463-64, 489
air rights, defined, 569
Airport Land Use Commission (Pub. Util. Code § 2621 *et seq.*), 569
Airport Land Use Plan (ALUP), 26, 36, 43-44, 375-76
alcohol treatment (group care facility), 48, 572

Alquist-Priolo Earthquake Fault Zoning Act (Pub. Res. Code § 2621 *et seq.*), 104-05, 569
ambient air, defined, 569
amendment (zoning/rezoning), defined, 569
American Association of Retired People (AARP), 452-53
amortization, 60, 94, 251, 275, 569
    defined, 569
    enforcement actions, 497
amortization, termination of nonconforming use, 60
annexation
    agricultural preserves, 255-58
    defined, 569
    development agreements and, 278-79
    environmental review, 407-08
    exemptions from initiative process, 372
    farmland security zones, 258
    GHAD approval, 355-56
    LAFCOs and, 387, 389, 392, 394-95, 400-401
    map approval/timing and, 99-100
    mediation, 538
    Prop 218 compliance, 354-56
    property tax sharing, 396 & n9
    statutes of limitations, 519, 521
    zoning unincorporated territory, 61
"Anti-NIMBY" law, 569. *See also* Housing Accountability Act
Anti-Rent Control Act (Costa-Hawkins Act), 439-40
anti-SLAPP (Strategic Lawsuit Against Public Participation) statute, 556-58
anti-sprawl legislation. *See* growth management
appeal/appeals
    adjudicatory proceedings, 478-80, 483, 490-91
    CEQA, 171-73, 552
    coastal development, 262-63
    defined, 569

611

General Plan adoption and
    amendment, 27
housing allocation, 411–12
initiative and referendum process,
    376–79
judgments in mandate cases, 547–48
mandate proceedings, 524–29,
    532–37
Map Act, 115–16
Permit Streamlining Act, 86
permits, 206–07, 250
ripeness doctrine and, 299–308
rules of evidence/procedural errors,
    52
rulings by Courts of appeal, 206–07,
    324, 328, 498
arm's length transactions, 78
Army Corps of Engineers. See U.S. Army
    Corps of Engineers
assessed valuation
    defined, 569
    LAFCO role in determining, 393,
        397, 406, 407
assessment bonds. See bonds/bonding
    approval
Association of Bay Area Governments
    (ABAG), 264
attorney advice, this book is no
    substitute for, xix–xx
attorneys' fees
    anti-SLAPP statute, 560
    citizen suits, 211–12, 242–43
    development projects, 123–26,
        450–51
    housing issues, 418–19, 421, 425–26
    judicial awards, 314–15
    land use litigation, 562–64
    mandate proceedings, 540, 546
Avco rule
    building permits, 339–40
    comparison to development
        agreements, 285
    final map approval, 93–94
    open-ended conditions, 277
    vested rights determinations, 273–77
    vesting tenative maps under, 95–96,
        283

B

Bagley-Keene Open Meeting Law (Gov't
    Code § 11120 et seq.), 569. See also
    Ralph M. Brown Act
Bald and Golden Eagle Protection Act,
    240–41

ballot box planning. See initiative and
    referendum
ballot box zoning, 379
base map, defined, 569
Bay Area Air Quality Management
    District (BAAQMD), 28, 463–64, 505
BCDC. See San Francisco Bay
    Conservation and Development
    Commission
benefit assessment, 337–38, 347–49,
    350–51, 569, 575
bicycle/pedestrian pathways, 103, 325,
    327
biota, defined, 569
blighted area (urban decay), 49, 158,
    258, 569
Board of Zoning Adjustment, 569
bonds/bonding approval
    bond oversight, 570
    defined, 569
    final map approval, 118–19
    general obligation bonds, 569
    LAFCO districts, 406n1
    mandate proceedings, 545–46
    performance bonds as security,
        123–26
    Prop 218, 340–42
    school districts, 340–42
    validation suit defined, 576
Bradley-Burns Uniform Local Sales and
    Use Tax Law (Res. & Tax. Code §
    7200 et seq.), 570
bridges
    LAFCO exemptions, 394
    permits and fees, 104, 198, 344–45
    toll bridges, 370
Brown Act. See Ralph M. Brown Act
brownfield development, 450
buffer zone, defined, 570
building coverage/envelope, 570
building permits. See permits/permitting
    authority
Business and Professions Code,
    enforcement, 498

C

California Air Resources Board (CARB),
    459–60
California Bicycle Coalition, 452–53
California Climate Adaptation Strategy,
    473–74
California Coastal Act of 1976 (Pub. Res.
    Code § 30000 et seq.), 29, 73, 210–12,
    258–59, 274, 281, 419–20, 570
California Coastal Commission

appeals, 262–63
authority and responsibilities, 258–
    59, 263–64
challenges and appeals, 262–63, 478,
    491, 537
climate change issues, 474–76
defined, 570
judicial challenges/rulings, 60, 66,
    260–61, 273–77
judicial review, 263
Local Coastal Programs (LCPs),
    261–62
mapping, judicial rulings, 72, 95
Nollan/Dolan decisions, 295, 309–
    10, 323–29
permit process, 209–10, 210–11
procedural guidance, 211–12
statute of limitations, 520, 522
taking/takings, 297–99
wetlands regulation, 179. See also
    coastal zone; San Francisco Bay
    Conservation and Development
    Commission
California Constitution
    approval of Prop 13, 347–48
    approval of Prop 218, 346–54, 439
    defining initiative and referendum,
        358–59
    establishment of spending limits,
        309–10
    initiative and referendum, 368–70,
        373–74, 377, 380–81
    land use regulation, 2–5
    local police powers, 1–2
    Prop 59 amendment, 485n5
    Prop 218 changes, 370
    same-sex marriage, 499–500
    standards of judicial review, 510–11
    tribal casino gaming, 69n.12
California Department of Fish and
    Wildlife [formerly Fish and Game]
    (DFW), 91, 151, 196, 198, 210, 210–11,
    244–48, 245, 247
California Department of Housing and
    Community Development (HCD), 28–
    29, 411–15, 418–20, 426–27, 427–30
California Endangered Species Act
    [CESA] (Fish & Game Code § 2050-
    2098)
    about the State listing process,
        245–46
    comparison to Federal ESA, 244–45
    comparison to Federal "takings,"
        246–47
    incidental take permits, 247–48
California Energy Action Plan, 471–74

Index

California Environmental Quality Act [CEQA] (Pub. Res. Code § 21000 et seq.)
   about the requirements, 139–40
   CEQA and, 464–66
   climate change, 474–76
   climate guidelines changes, 460–67
   cumulative impact, 145, 151, 156, 162–64, 462, 465, 466
   decision-making flow charts, 148–49
   dedications and fees, 343
   defined, 570
   defined, "environment," 142–43
   defined, "project," 140–41
   EIR deadlines and notices, 176
   EIR recirculation, 170–71
   enforcement of land use law, 497–98
   General Plan requirements, 21–22
   guideline changes, 462–64
   historic preservation, 253
   initial study preparation, 147–50, 573
   judicial challenges, 176–77
   judicial review, 177
   LAFCO compliance, 407–08
   lead agency, 573
   Map Act application to, 71–72
   Map Act requirements, 109–10
   mitigated negative declaration, 144, 147–50, 422, 497, 573
   mitigation monitoring and reporting, 173–74
   negative declaration, 147–50, 150–52
   negative declaration defined, 574
   negative declarations, 174–75
   project approval, 141–42, 171–73
   project approval and findings, 171–73
   project exemptions, 140–41, 144–47
   response to comment and recommendations, 169–70
   Smart Growth, 449–51
   specific plan requirements, 36–37
   supplemental EIRs, 174–75
   sustainable development and, 463–67
   unusual circumstances, 145–47, 465
   use of an addendum, 175. See also environmental impact report
California Integrated Waste Management Board, 84–85
California Natural Resources Agency, 474
California Register of Historic Places, 146–47, 253
California State Government
   local police powers and, 4–6
   local zoning regulation and, 66
   regulation of Indian affairs, 68–70, 372–73
California Supreme Court
   attorneys' fees, 563
   CEQA compliance, 141, 146–47, 151, 156–57
   CEQA decision review, 551–54
   Coastal Commission authority, 259
   dedications and fees, 335–36, 337–38, 555n24, 559
   developer taxation and equal protection, 336–37
   due process and equal protection, 86, 311–14, 498–500
   Ehrlich v. Culver City decision, 330–33
   EIR review, 166–68, 170–71, 176–77
   endangered species rulings, 246–48
   ex parte contact, 487–88
   exemptions for historic preservation, 54
   general plan rulings, 10, 20, 30
   growth management, 448
   housing rulings, 435
   initiative and referendum, 138, 357–58, 366, 369, 371, 375, 377, 379–85
   LAFCO CEQA compliance, 407–08
   land use and water supply planning, 453
   liability of public entities, 564–65
   Livermore test, 41–42
   Map Act rulings, 99–100, 107–08, 132–33
   Mitigation Fee Act, 333–35
   police powers authority, 1–4
   Propositions and taxation, 346–54
   regulation of adult businesses, 49–52
   regulatory takings, 117–18, 291–95, 297–99, 307–07, 320
   review of evidence and local actions, 479–80
   termination of nonconforming use, 60
   vested rights rule (*Avco* rule), 93–94, 273–77
   zoning ordinance challenges, 136–37
capital improvement program
   CEQA compliance, 142
   defined, 570
   development project fees, 345–46
   exactions and fees, 322, 333–34
   planning commission role in, 7
   reconveyance of property, 112
   rent control and, 314–15
   traffic planning and, 451–53
casino gambling. See Native American tribes/issues
caveat, on how to use this book, xix–xx
CDFG. See California Department of Fish and Wildlife
cemeteries, 57, 83, 338–39, 339
census tract, defined, 570
Central Business District, 570
CEQA Guidelines (Cal. Code Reg. § 15000 et seq.). See California Environmental Quality Act
certificate of completion, 402, 405
certificate of compliance, 130–31, 570
certificate of occupancy, 344, 570
charter city
   application of zoning law, 39
   defined, 570
   development project exemptions, 269–71
   General Plan requirements, 22–23
   growth management, 426–27
   housing development permits, 424–25
   Prop 62 requirements, 347–49
   Prop 218 requirements, 248–349
   Subdivision Map Act and, 72–73
   use of initiative and referendum, 359, 363
   variance criteria, 55–56
   zoning law, application of, 42–45. See also city/cities
Childhood Lead Poisoning Act, 347
churches. See religion/religious freedom
circulation element
   about map requirements, 120–23
   about the requirements, 10–11
   components, 13
   testing the adequacy, 141–43
   transportation planning, 400, 451–53. See also General Plan
citizens' rights. See rights of the regulated
city councils
   as used/defined in this book, xx
   composition and authority, 6
   election districts, 570
   filling vacancies, 570
   meeting requirements, 8
   politics and citizen's groups, 109–10
city/cities
   agricultural land preservation, 255–56
   as term used/defined in this book, xx
   contract city [Gonsalves Act], 570
   contracts and bidding, 570–71
   development agreements, 278–79

growth management, 236–38
historic preservation, 253–55
LAFCO role in, 390–91
land annexation and incorporation, 99–100
legal basis for regulation, 1–5
new city exceptions, General Plan, 31–32
ordinances (Gov't Code § 36900 et seq.), 570, 574
politics and citizen's groups, 15–16, 21–22, 26–27
regional infrastructure planning, 397, 400
remainder parcels, 78–79
state legislative preemption over, 5–6
tentative map approval, 85–88
use of initiative and referendum, 363–65
Williamson Act contracts, 255–58
zoning and planning after *Euclid*, 62–65, 75–78
zoning exemptions, 67–68. See also charter city; districts; general law city
civil rights actions/claims
doctrine of administrative res judicata, 508–09
under Section 1983, 311–12
substantitive due process, 314–15. See also Federal Civil Rights Act
Clean Air Act (U.S. Code), 14, 418, 570
Clean Water Act of 1972
about wetlands regulation, 179–80
brief history of the law, 180–81
definition of wetland and other waters, 181–83
enforcement by way of "citizen suits," 211–13
investigations and corrective actions, 213–14
legal standing to sue, 212–13
permit process, 207–08, 266–67
refining jurisdictional boundaries, 186–87
role in ESA consultation, 228–31
violations and penalties, 213–15
Climate Adaptation Strategy (CAS, CalAdapt), 474–76
climate change
CEQA Guidelines, 160–62, 462–64
EIR considerations, 161–62, 175–76
endangered species impacts, 218–20, 232–33
General Plan requirements, 11
Green building movement, 467–71
greenhouse gas emissions, 474–76

regional planning efforts, 264–65
Smart Growth, 449–51
sustainable development and, 447
water supply issues, 453–59. See also California Global Warming Solutions Act
Climate Protection Act of 2008, 460–62. See also SB 375
cluster development, 64
Coastal Act. See California Coastal Act
Coastal Commission. See California Coastal Commission; San Francisco Bay Conservation and Development Commission
coastal zone
defined, 259–60
development permits, 95, 259, 260–61
development projects, 285
housing needs, 15, 415–16
impact mitigation, 171
Local Coastal Programs (LCPs), 261–62
takings challenge, 288
wetland issues, 179
Coastal Zone Management Act of 1972 (U.S. Code), 209–10, 264
Coastal Zone Management (Pub. Res. Code § 30600 et seq.), 197, 210–12, 264–65
code, as used/defined in this book, xx
Code of Federal Regulations, 198
color of state law, 563
common law
Avco rule, 273–77, 283
conflict of interest, 478–79, 510–11
definition of special benefit, 350–51
development projects and, 283
exhaustion doctrine, 524–31, 551–52, 557
fraud and misrepresentation, 492–93
initiative and referendum process, 383
Map Act exemptions, 133
notice and hearing process, 477
police powers, 1–2
vested rights doctrine, 94–97, 273, 283
waiver of time limits, 86, 490–91
common ownership, 135–37, 570
community apartments, 76–77, 81–82, 121–22, 492–93
Community Facilities District. See Mello-Roos Community Facilities Act
Community Redevelopment Law (Health & Safety Code § 33000 et seq.), 372, 570

competitive bidding process, 142, 271–72
"Complete Streets Act," 452–53
comprehensive plan. See General Plan
condemnation
conditional use permits and, 58
defined, 570, 573
easements, 106
economic injury and, 290–95, 299–301
judicial rulings, 432–35
partial taking defined, 574
right-of-way defined, 575
statutes of limitations, 117
substantitive due process, 314–15
takings claims, 303–10, 316–17. See also inverse condemnation
conditional use permit (CUP)
about the use of, 56–58
defined, 570
renewable energy projects, 471–74
conditional zoning/rezoning, 63–64, 570
condominiums
associations, 570
conversions, 109–10, 121–22, 492–93
defined, 570
land dedications, 101–02
Map Act requirements, 76–77
Map Act waivers and exemptions, 81–83
conflict of interest, 479, 510–11, 570. See also Political Reform Act
Congestion Management Program (CMP), 451–53
Connectivity of Streams and Wetlands to Downstream Waters: A Review and Synthesis of Scientific Evidence (EPA, 2013), 186
conservation easement (Civ. Code § 815 et seq.), 76, 114–15, 203–05, 570. See also agriculture/agricultural lands
conservation element
about the requirements, 10–11
components, 15
floods/natural hazards, 465
local resource issues, 424–25. See also General Plan; mineral resources
consistency doctrine, 9–10, 36. See also horizontal consistency; vertical consistency
contract city [Gonsalves Act] (Gov't Code § 51350), 570
Contracting for Preservation: An Overview of State Agricultural District Programs ((Safran, 2004), 255
contracts. See competitive bidding process

contractual covenants. *See* covenants, conditions & restrictions
conventions, used in this book, xx
Corps of Engineers. *See* U.S. Army Corps of Engineers
Cortese List, 84, 489
Cortese-Knox Local Government Reorganization Act of 1985 (Gov't. Code § 56000 *et seq.*), 387–88
Cortese-Knox-Hertzberg Local Government Reorganization Act of 2000 (Gov't. Code § 56000 *et seq.*), 61, 388, 402, 538, 558, 571. *See also* Local Agency Formation Commissions
Costa-Hawkins Act (anti-rent control), 433, 439–40
Council of Government [COG] (Gov't. Code § 6500 *et seq.*), 411–12, 460, 571
county/counties
    as used/defined in this book, xx
    contracts and bidding, 570–71
    county charter, 571
    LAFCO limitations, 393–95
    land annexation and incorporation, 99–100
    new county formation, 571
    officers, 571
    ordinances, adoption of, 571, 574
    politics and citizen's group pressure, 15–16, 21–22
    remainder parcels, 78–79
    zoning and planning after *Euclid*, 62–65, 75–78. *See also* districts
county board of supervisors
    as term used/defined in this book, xx
    housing requirement approval, 370
    map approval, 99
    membership on county LAFCO, 389
    Williamson Act contracts, 256
covenants, conditions & restrictions (CC&Rs), 118, 136–37, 309–10, 440, 445, 571, 575
culvert, defined, 571
cumulative impacts, CEQA, 145, 151, 156, 162–64, 462, 465, 466
cut, defined, 571

D

dams/dikes/levees, 181, 191–92
Davis-Bacon Act (U.S. Code), 269
Davis-Stirling Common Interest Development Act (Civ. Code § 1350 *et seq.*), 571
deadlines. *See* statutes of limitations

decibel (dB), defined, 571
dedications and fees
    about the use of, 319, 337–38
    building permits, 339–40
    CEQA compliance, 343
    constitutionality of impact fees, 329–33
    developer avoidance of, 336–37
    effect of Jarvis Initiatives, 346–54
    financing and maintaining facilities, 345–46, 354–56
    General Plan and, 32–33, 337–39
    habitat conservation plans, 342–43
    imposition of fees, 343–45
    judicial review, 345–46
    land use, 571
    Map Act requirements, 100–107
    payment in lieu of, 571, 574
    police powers, 320
    processing fees, 339–40
    public hearings/waiting period, 344
    reconveyance to subdivider, 345–46
    school district facilities fees, 340–42
    subdivision approval, 338–39
    taxation or fee?, 346–47. *See also* impact and development fees
deed restriction, 108, 425–26, 571
demolition permits, 298, 320, 372, 571
demolition ordinances, 42, 62, 159–60, 260, 266, 309, 342
density, housing
    allowable housing, 571
    bonus laws, 425–28, 450–51, 571
    transfers to another area, 571
    zoning, 571
design review
    city ordinances and, 81
    General Plan and, 14–15
    judicial rulings, 151, 249–52
    zoning ordinances and, 47
detention basin/pond. *See* water issues
developer fee. *See* dedications and fees
Development agreements (Gov't. Code § 65864 *et seq.*)
    Avco rule, 277–83
    consistency with General Plan, 10
    dedications and fees, 337–38
    defined, 571
    design review, 14–15, 47, 81, 249–52
    exemptions, 418
    General Plan as a tool for, 32–33
    impact and development fees, 336–40, 571
    initiative and referendum process, 359, 370
    in-lieu fee option, 432–35
    judicial review, 117–18

judicial rulings, 336–37
    ordinances and zoning, 63
    police powers, 6
    specific plan requirements, 35
    subject to referendum, 359
    tentative map approval, 88, 94, 96
    tentative maps and, 283–84
    timing/phased control, 571, 574
    vested rights and, 93–94, 273
    vesting tentative maps compared to, 284–85
    wetland issues, 214–15
development fees. *See* dedications and fees
development projects
    about use of exactions, 319–20
    addressing privilege vs. right, 320–21
    constitutionality of fees (*Ehrlich* decision), 330–33
    constitutionality of fees (*Koontz* decision), 329–30
    highest and best use, land/property, 275, 290, 572
    Mitigation Fee Act and, 333–36
    nexus requirement, 322–23
    Nollan/Dolan decisions, 323–29
    prevailing wage rates, 269–71
    public bidding procedure, 271–72. *See also* infill development; sustainable development
development rights, 32, 228, 571, 576
    defined, 571
    map approval, 93–94
    takings issues, 288–90, 305–06
District Reorganization Act of 1965 (formerly Gov't. Code § 56000 *et seq.*), 387
districts/special districts (Gov't. Code § 50077), 571, 575. *See also* school districts
Dolan v. City of Tigard. *See Nollan/Dolan* decisions
Douglas, William O., 1
downzoning, 292, 303, 305, 418, 448–49, 571
drainage and sewer facilities
    dedications and fees, 112, 337–38, 345–46, 554–56, 557–59
    development moratorium, 88, 91
    easements, 106
    fees, 103, 112, 132
    growth management, 426–27, 448–49
    housing projects, 422
    permits, 267–68
    Prop 218 and, 351–53
    reimbursement agreements, 104

drug abuse/drug treatment (group care facility), 48, 324, 572
due process and equal protection
	adjudicatory acts and, 316–17
	annexation, 403
	civil rights actions/claims, 311–14
	conditional use permits and, 57
	CWA enforcement, 213–15
	defined, 571
	ex parte contacts, 487–88
	exercise of police powers, 4–5
	"fair hearing" requirements, 511–13
	initiative and referendum process, 368–69
	judicial rulings, 287–95, 321, 336–37, 350–51
	land use law enforcement, 498–500
	mandate proceedings, 537, 544
	rent control ordinances, 314–15
	ripeness and finality issues, 531–32
	Section 1983 tasking issues, 311–14
	subdivision approval and, 96, 115, 129–31
	subdivision map approval and, 85–86
	takings issues, 290–95, 301–02
	zoning ordinances and, 42, 44–45, 48, 58. See also rights of the regulated

E

earthquakes, 17, 105, 355. See also Geologic Hazard Abatement District
easements
	agricultural lands exemptions, 83
	conservation, 76
	conservation easement, 76, 114–15, 203–05, 570
	conveyances of parcels, 79, 80–81
	lot line adjustments, 79–80
	non-exclusive, 73–76
	open space easement, 114–15, 574. See also rights-of-way
effluent. See water issues
Ellis Act (Gov't. Code § 7060-7060.7), 298–99
emergency shelters, 410, 413, 419–21
eminent domain
	defined, 571
	development projects, 203–05
	initiative and referendum process, 385–86
	judicial rulings, 299–300
	Map Act actions, 73, 137
	takings claims, 308–10

takings rulings, 299, 308, 312
emission standards
	CEQA compliance, 143–44, 462–64
	climate change and, 160–62, 232–33, 459–60, 474–76
	defined, 572
	permit requirements, 488–89
	point source defined, 575
	tentative map processing, 85
	transportation policy and, 451–53, 460–62
encroachment, 241–42, 276, 324, 364, 572
Endangered Species Act (ESA)
	about regulatory authority, 179–80, 217–18
	consultation process, 228–36
	designation of "critical habitat," 224–28
	determination of species status, 217–19
	"distinct population segment" listing, 220–21
	emergency listings, 224
	exemptions, 236–37
	habitat conservation plans, 241–42, 342–43
	judicial review and enforcement, 242–44
	procedures for initiating a listing, 222–23
	prohibitions against takings, 237–41
	review and delisting of species, 223–24
	"safe harbor" and conservation agreements, 242
	"significant portion of its range" listing, 221–22
	wetlands permits, 208–09. See also California Endangered Species Act
Energy and Water Development Act of 1992 (U.S. Code), 188
Energy Policy Act of 1992 (U.S. Code), 470
Energy Policy and Conservation Act (U.S. Code), 470
environmental impact report (EIR)
	about the preparation, 152–54
	CEQA compliance, 139–40
	certificate of completion, 402, 405
	content and requirements, 154–69
	deadlines and required notices, 176
	defined, 572
	lead agency decision-making, 149–50
	mitigation monitoring and reporting, 173–74

negative declarations, 147–50, 150–52
	notice of completion, 574
	notice of determination, 151, 173, 176–77, 517, 574
	notice of preparation, 153–54, 156–57, 163, 176–77, 574
	project approval and findings, 171–73
	project changes requiring a SEIR, 174–75
	project changes requiring an addendum, 175–76
	recirculation of the final EIR, 170–71
	review and response to comments, 169–71
	time limits for judicial challenge, 176–77. See also California Environmental Quality Act
environmental impact statement (EIS), 197, 200, 207–08, 225–26, 572. See also National Environmental Policy Act
Environmental Protection Agency (EPA)
	Clean Water Act and, 173–86, 190–91
	CWA Section 404 Guidelines, 200
	endangered species enforcement, 236–38
	enforcement actions, 211–13
	mitigation process, 211–12
	permit process, 192–93, 204–05, 206–08
	pollution control, 181, 228–30, 265–66
	wetlands regulation, 179–80, 183, 201–03
equal protection. See due process and equal protection
estoppel defense/theory, 500–501
ethics training (Gov't. Code § 53234 *et seq.*), 572
ex parte contacts, 487–88
exclusionary zoning, 65, 66, 431–32, 448, 572

F

facilities benefit assessment (FBA). See benefit assessment
Fair Apportionment and Individual Representation (FAIR), 366–67
Fair Employment and Housing Act, 508
"Fair hearing"/"fair trial," 512
Fair Housing Act (U.S. Code), 568

Fair Political Practices Commission, 380, 572
fair share housing plan
    defined, 572
    determination of regional needs, 411-14
    disapproval of projects, 419-21
    housing element, General Plan, 13-14, 410-11
    inclusionary housing, 427-30, 429-31, 436-37
    zoning requirements, 425-26. See also housing
farmland preservation. See Williamson Act
Federal Civil Rights Act (U.S. Code), 564, 566-68. See also civil rights actions/claims
Federal Register, 198
    critical habitat designation, 225-26
    endangered species emergency listing, 224
    endangered species listing, 222-23
Federal Telecommunications Act (U.S. Code), 5-6
Federal Water Pollution Control Act. See Clean Water Act
final subdivision map
    about the requirements, 76-77
    content, preparation and filing, 118-19
    defined, 572
    procedures for approval, 119-20
    recording and validity, 120-23
    security requirements, 123-26
    site plan, 492-93, 575. See also Subdivision Map Act
findings
    adjudicatory acts, 481-83
    defined, 572
    legislative acts, 481
fire protection, 17, 113, 335, 351-52, 572
First Amendment. See U.S. Constitution
Fish and Game Commission. See California Department of Fish and Wildlife
Fish and Wildlife Coordination Act (U.S. Code), 208-09
flood control
    capital facilities fees, 66
    conservation element, General Plan, 15
    Federal consultation process, 228-30, 236-37
    LAFCO exemptions, 394
    map approval/disapproval, 115
    Prop 218 exemptions, 350-51
    takings issues, 310-11
    wetland regulation, 179. See also water issues
flood plain/flood plain maps, 13, 325, 572
floor area/floor area ratio
    building coverage, defined, 570
    design guidelines, 508
    development standards, 425-26
    gross floor area/leasable area, 572
    inclusionary housing requirements, 429-31
    Map Act exemptions, 83
    ratio to lot area, 572
    variance requirements, 55-56
    zoning regulation, 425-26, 555
Food Security Act of 1985 (U.S. Code), 209-10
Forest Practices Act (Pub. Res. Code § 4511 et seq.), 496
forests/forestry
    actions under ESA, 223-24, 228-31, 244
    adoption of regulations, 506
    CWA exemptions, 192-93
    General Plan elements, 15, 19
    growth management measures, 448-49
form-based zoning, 13, 61, 572

G

gambling. See Native American tribes/issues
general law city (Gov't. Code § 36501 et seq.)
    application of ACCO Rule, 6
    application of zoning law, 39
    application to charter cities, 570
    Avco rule, 276
    city councils, 6
    defined, 572
    imposition of taxes, 346-47
    initiative and referendum measures, 359
    planning commissions, 7
    taxation authority, 346-47
    vertical consistency requirements, 23-26. See also city/cities
general obligation bonds. See bonds/bonding approval
General Plan (Gov't Code § 65300 et seq.)
    adoption/amendment procedures, 27-28
    as advisory document for planning, 9
    amendment by initiative, 29
    checklist, 29-31
    city exceptions/exemptions, 31-32
    consistency with Airport Land Use Plan, 26, 43-44
    constitutionality, 10
    dedications and development fees, 32-33
    dedications and fees, 337-39
    defined, 572
    general guidelines, 10-12
    growth management and land use control, 33
    guidelines, 572
    horizontal (internal) consistency, 22-23, 31
    implementation and reporting, 28-29
    initiative and referenda limitations, 368-74, 375-76
    judicial review, 33-34
    legal adequacy, 12-20
    legal inadequacy, implications, 20-22
    mandatory elements, 12-19
    Map Act exemptions, 79-83
    Map Act requirements, 108, 111-15
    optional (permissive) elements, 19
    organization and adoption of elements, 19-20
    Planning Commission role, 7-8
    regulating "design" and "improvement," 107-08
    Subdivision Map Act and, 71-73
    tentative maps, 84-87
    tribal consultation, 576
    vertical consistency, 23-26
    vesting tentative maps, 94-99
    zoning consistency, 42-43
    zoning ordinances, 61-64. See also specific element; specific plan
General Plan Guidelines (OPR, 2003), 10-20, 23, 29, 42
general tax (Gov't. Code § 53720 et seq.)
    defined, 572
    Prop 62 compliance, 347-49
    Prop 218 compliance, 348-51, 355-56
geologic factors, 15-16, 15-17, 105, 310, 458-59, 470
Geologic Hazard Abatement District [GHAD] (Pub. Res. Code § 26500 et seq.), 354-56, 394, 572. See also earthquakes
geothermal projects. See renewable energy

Global Warming Solutions Act of 2006 (AB32), 11, 160-62, 447, 459-60
Gonsalves Act [contract city] (Gov't Code § 51350), 570
grade (degree of slope), building lot, 297-98, 572
grandfathering provisions, Map Act, 71, 133, 134
granny unit. *See* second unit
Green building
  defined, 467
  preemptions over building codes, 469-71
  rating systems, 468-69
  standards, local, 468-69
  standards, state, 467-68. *See also* sustainable development
greenhouse gases
  CEQA and, 462-64
  climate change and, 232-33, 474-76
  implementation of reduction targets, 459-60
  sustainable communities strategy, 460-62
  transportation planning and, 460-62
  water supply planning and, 453-59
  "zero-increase" standards, 161-62
gross leasable area. *See* floor area/floor area ratio
ground coverage, building lot, 572
groundwater
  comparison of SB 610 and SB 221, 453-58
  conditional use permits, 58
  conservation element, General Plan, 15
  defined, 572
  ordinances and fees, 104
  recharge programs, 533
  rulings, 294, 352. *See also* Porter-Cologne Water Quality Control Act
group care facilities, 48, 572
growth management
  anti-sprawl efforts, 15, 387, 388-89, 391, 460
  General Plan as a tool for, 32-33
  housing development and, 426-27
  initiative process, 383-86
  Supreme Court rulings, 10
  sustainable development and, 448-49. *See also* Smart Growth

H

habitat conservation plans, 241-42, 342-43
Hazardous Waste and Substance Statement, 84-85
hazardous waste management, 173
  permit requirements, 488-89
HCD. *See* California Department of Housing and Community Development
hearings process. *See* mandate proceedings
highest and best use, land/property, 275, 290, 572
historic preservation
  CEQA exemptions, 146-47
  exemptions, 53-54, 240-41, 254
  federal statues, 252-53
  local authority, 253-55
  project exemptions, 144-47
  state authority, 253
  state statutes, 253
  zoning challenges, 52-53. *See also* California Register of Historic Places; Mills Act; National Register of Historic Places
home occupation, defined, 572
homeless shelters. *See* emergency shelters
homeowner association, defined, 572
horizontal consistency
  equal protection requirements, 337
  General Plan checklist, 31
  General Plan requirements, 22-23
  initiative and referendum requirements, 371. *See also* vertical consistency
housing
  about the affordability crisis, 409-10
  agricultural labor, 82-83
  building coverage/envelope, 570
  density/density bonus law, 425-28, 450-51, 571
  disapproval of projects, 419-21
  emergency shelters, 410, 413, 419-21
  group care facility, 572
  growth management and, 426-27
  incentives for development, 425-28
  inclusionary zoning, 64-65
  initiative and referendum process, 369
  limitations on initiative use, 379
  low-income housing, 270-71, 317, 324, 426-28, 432-35, 573
  Map Act waivers and exemptions, 81-83
  mobile home park conversions, 72-73
  moderate-income housing defined, 573
  multi-family projects, 424-25
  occupancy permit defined, 574
  regional housing needs allocation (RHNA), 411-12
  Smart Growth, 409-10, 427-30, 449-51
  transitional housing, 413, 419n11, 420-21
  use defined, 576
  water and sewer service, 422. *See also* fair share housing plan; inclusionary housing
Housing Accountability Act ["Anti-NIMBY" legislation] (Gov't Code § 65589.5), 14, 419-21, 449-51, 569
housing element, General Plan
  about requirements, 10-11, 19, 21, 29-31, 120-23, 410
  adoption/amendment, 27-29
  coastal zone requirements, 415-16
  components, 13-15, 410-11
  consistency with other elements, 23, 26, 415
  defined, 572
  identifying barriers/constraints, 414-15
  judicial review, 33-34
  LAFCO considerations, 391, 400, 400-401
  land inventory and site identification, 412-14
  legislative intent and compliance, 410-11
  notifications and reporting, 415
  restrictions, 418-21
  review and certification, 418-20
  sustainable development and, 462
  use of initiative, 379. *See also* General Plan
hydrology. *See* wetlands hydrology

I

immunity
  General plan, safety element, 17
  GHADs and, 356
  governments as "persons," 312
  municipal liability, 567-68
  public employees and entities, 566-67. *See also* liability
impact and development fees

constitutionality of impact fees, 329–33
defined, 571
fire protection, 335
habitat conservation, 342–43
land use regulation and, 2
Mitigation Fee Act and, 481
Nollan/Dolan decisions, 321
school districts, 109–10, 112, 340–42, 344–45, 349
subdivision map approval and, 99
transportation funding, 277
impervious surface, 268–69, 326–27, 572
improved land, distinction from unimproved, 73–74
Improvement Act of 1911 (Pub. Res. Code § 26587), 355–56
Improvement Bond Act of 1915 (Pub. Res. Code § 26587), 355–56
incentive zoning. See zoning/zoning regulation
incentives and concessions
  affordable housing, 425–28
  agricultural land preservation, 255–58
  conservation agreements, 242
  development completion, 296–98
  GHG reduction, 459–60
  growth management, 427–30
  historic preservation, 253–55
  inclusionary housing, 427–30, 436, 439, 440, 442–43
  LAFCO recommendations, 388
  recreational development, 334–36
  rehabilitation loans, 17
  renewable energy, 471–74
inclusionary housing
  about programs for, 427–30
  about the requirements, 429–30
  applicant qualifications, 444
  design standards, 442–43
  exclusionary zoning practices, 66, 432–35, 448, 572
  incentives and concessions, 439
  levels and amount of affordability, 442
  maintaining affordability, 443, 444
  mandatory vs. voluntary programs, 440–41
  post-*Nollan-Dolan* era, 432–35
  pre-*Nollan-Dolan* era, 431–32
  program enactment and application, 435–37
  program review and enforcement, 444–45
  rent control, 439–40

  "safety valve" provisions, 437–39
  sales price limitations, 443
  size and class of development, 441
  timing of project completion, 442
  zoning/zoning regulation, 64–65. See also housing
inclusionary zoning. See zoning/zoning regulation
incorporation/disincorporation, 31–32, 99–100, 278–79
  agricultural land preservation, 255–56
  LAFCO role in, 390–91
Indian Gaming Regulatory Act of 1988 (U.S. Code), 68–70
infill development
  CEQA compliance, 146–47, 424–25, 464–67
  defined, 572
  housing needs, 411–12
  leapfrog development, 53
  Smart Growth, 450–51
  sustainable development, 447
  transportation policy and, 451–53. See also development projects
infrastructure/infrastructure plan
  CEQA compliance, 475
  dedications and fees, 32–33, 165–66
  defined, 573
  developer financing, 354–56
  EIR considerations, 167–68
  EIR requirements, 156–57
  exactions and fees, 322–23
  financing/financing districts, 573
  General Plan elements and, 13, 19
  growth management issues, 448–49
  historic preservation issues, 253
  housing projects, 418, 425–30, 426–27, 439
  LAFCO review, 391–92
  LEDPA considerations, 202–05
  MPO funding, 452
  Smart Growth funding, 449–51. See also property tax
initial study, CEQA
  about preparation/purpose, 147–50
  defined, 573
  EIR considerations, 109–10, 143–44, 152
  EIR flow chart, 148–49
  EIR preparation, 152–54
  exemptions, 145–46
  negative declaration, 150–52
initiative and referendum
  about the origins and use of, 357–58
  ballot box zoning, 48

  CEQA compliance, 359, 366, 376, 384
  CEQA exemptions, 140–41
  conflicting/competing measures, 379–81
  defined, 358–59, 573, 575
  effect of Jarvis Initiatives, 346–54
  exemptions, 358–59
  intent to circulate, notice of, 362
  intent to circulate, publication and posting, 362–63
  legislative actions for initiatives, 365–67
  legislative actions for referenda, 367–68
  limitations on use, 368–74
  limitations on zoning and land use, 379
  petition invalidation, 361, 365, 368–70, 373, 376–80
  petition requirements, 360–61
  petition validation, 364–67, 375, 379
  pre-election challenges, 376–79
  procedural requirements, 359–60, 375–76
  restrictions on campaigning, 382–83
  signatures, gathering, 363–64
  signatures, sufficiency and validity, 364–65
injunctions. See stays and injunctions
Intergovernmental Coordination Act of 1968 (U.S. Code), 65
interim zoning, 63, 573
internal consistency. See horizontal consistency
invalidation actions, 361, 379, 559. See also validation actions
inverse condemnation
  conditional use permit as, 58
  defined, 573
  housing issues, 434
  joined with mandate claims, 537
  power of eminent domain, 312
  statute of limitations, 117
  substantive due process, 314–15
  takings issues, 291, 299–300, 304–05, 308–10. See also condemnation

J

Jarvis Initiatives, 347–54, 358, 368, 523
Joint Exercise of Powers Act (Gov't. Code § 6509), 67
joint powers agreement/agency (Gov't. Code § 6500 *et seq.*), 52, 66–68, 573
just compensation

constitutional requirements, 292, 309-10
dedications of land, 319
defined, 573
Ehrlich v. Culver City, 334-36
eminent domain and, 571
flood control projects, 310-11
principles of nuisance and, 310
state procedures, 306-07, 311-12
takings requiring, 117, 287-90, 303-05, 521
temporary takings claims, 295

K

Knox-Nesbit Act of 1963 (formerly Gov't. Code § 54722 *et seq.*), 387

L

LAFCO. *See* Local Agency Formation Commissions
Land Conservation Act of 1965. *See* Williamson Act
land patents and U.S. Survey maps, 134
Land Sales Full Disclosure Act (U.S. Code), 208-09
land use element, General Plan
  about the requirements, 10-11
  components, 12-13
  economic development and, 299-300
  flooding and natural hazards, 465
  LAFCO role in transportation plan, 400
  map requirements, 120-23
  transportation planning and, 400. *See also* General Plan
land use law
  about city enforcement, 495
  administrative inspection warrants, 496-97
  administrative penalties, 496
  denial of due process, 498-500
  enforcement under Business and Professions Code, 498
  enforcement under CEQA, 497-98
  enforcement under Revenue and Tax Code, 497
  enforcement under Subdivision Map Act, 497
  estoppel defense, 498-500
  misdemeanors and infractions, 495-96

land use litigation
  applicable statutes for common decisions, 518-19
  application of anti-SLAPP statute, 560-62
  awarding attorney's fees, 562-64
  basics and terminology, 503-04
  California Tort Claims Act, 564-65
  deadlines for bringing actions, 516-19
  Federal Civil Rights Act, 566-67
  immunity of public employees and entities, 566-67
  liability and immunity under Section 1983, 567-68
  liability of agencies and officials, 564-66
  Smart Growth, 449-51
  standards applied in reviewing decisions, 509-10
  standards for administrative decisions, 512-14
  standards for combined admin-legislative aspects, 514-15
  standards for decisions that interpret or apply law, 515-16
  standards for legislative decisions, 510-12
  statutes of limitations, 519-22
  "under color of state law," 567. *See also* mandate proceedings
land use litigation, under CEQA
  contents of the record, 549-51
  exhaustion standard and standing rules, 551-52
  procedures for CEQA actions, 548-49
  remedies and corrective actions, 553-54
  standards for judicial review, 552-53
land use litigation, under Mitigation Fee Act
  about the application of, 554-55
  challenges to fees on development projects, 555-57
  challenges to fees on water, sewer, or capacity, 557-60
  remedies and corrective actions, 560
land use regulation
  authority and legal basis, 1-5
  dedications and fees, 339-40
  legislative preemption, 5-6
  state statutory framework, 6
  transitional use defined, 576
  use defined, 576
  wetland issues, 214-15

Landscaping and Lighting Act of 1972 (Sts. & High. Code § 22500 *et seq.*), 354-56, 573
Lanham Act (U.S. Code), 251
lead agency
  authority and jurisdiction, 146-47, 167-69, 213-14, 344
  CEQA compliance, 462-64
  cities as, 19, 490-91
  defined, 140n3, 573
  EIR considerations, 153-54, 161-62, 169-74
  initial study defined, 573
  initial study preparation, 147-53
  LAFCOs as, 407-08
leapfrog development, 53, 448, 460-62
Least Cost Zoning Law, 425-26
legal advice, this book is not a substitute for, xix-xx
legislative preemption, 5-6
Legislature, as used/defined in this book, xx
Leroy F. Greene School Facilities Act (Gov't. Code § 65995), 340-42
"Let the Voters Decide Act of 2000" (Prop 24), 374
liability
  under California Tort Claims Act, 564-66
  under Federal Civil Rights Act, 566-67
  release of security for public works, 125-26
  under Section 1983, 567-68. *See also* immunity; penalties
Local Agency Formation Commissions [LAFCOs] (Govt. Code § 56000 *et seq.*)
  about the purpose of, 387
  brief history of LAFCO law, 387-89
  CEQA compliance, 407-08
  change and reorganization, procedures, 395-97
  change proposals, annexation, 400-401
  change proposals, approval/disapproval, 402-03
  change proposals, boundaries, 397, 400
  change proposals, final action and notification, 405, 407
  change proposals, protest hearing, 404-05, 406
  change proposals, reconsideration hearing, 403-04
  change proposals, regional/county issues, 401, 407

composition, powers and duties, 389–90
defined, 573
jurisdiction and authority, 392–93
jurisdiction exclusions, 393–95
municipal service reviews, 391–92
proceedings and hearings, flow charts, 398–99
spheres of influence plan, 390–91
Local Coastal Programs (LCPs), 261–62
local government. See city/cities; county/counties
Local Regulation of Adult Businesses (Gerard, 2005), 52
Longtin's California Land Use (Longtin), 253
lot line adjustments
    affecting property rights, 128–29
    agricultural land preservation, 258
    CEQA exemptions, 140
    coastal zone development, 260–61
    front/rear/side, 573
    Map Act exemptions, 79–80
    merger/unmerger of parcels, 135–37
    temporary takings claims, 297–98
lot/lots
    coverage, by buildings, 573
    lot of record, 573
    metes and bounds, 573
    minor land division, 573
    net area/net acreage, 574
    nonconformance to requirements, 574
    through/double frontage, 573. See also parcels/parcel map
low-income housing, 270–71, 317, 324, 426–28, 432–35, 573
    inclusionary zoning, 64–65
    initiative and referendum process, 369

M

Majority Protest Act (Sts. & High. Code § 2800-3012), 350–51
mandate proceedings
    about the types of, 504–05
    administrative challenges of administrative decisions, 508–09
    administrative challenges under Section 1094.5, 507–08
    appeals of judgments, 547–48
    evidence outside the record, 539–42
    exhaustion of administrative remedies, 522–31
    identifying the parties, 531–36

issuance of the writ, 546–47
joining causes with a writ claim, 537
mediation, 538
preparing the briefs, 544–45
preparing the record of proceedings, 538–39
ripeness and finality test, 529–30
setting the schedule, 543–44
stays or injunctions pending a final decision, 545–46
summary judgment, 544
time limits, 538
traditional challenges under Section 1085, 505–06. See also land use litigation; statutes of limitations
mandate proceedings, CEQA
    about the procedures, 546–47
    contents of a record, 547–48
    judicial review standards, 550–51
    preparation of the record, 548–49
    presentation of the claim, 549–50
    remedies and actions, 551
mandate proceedings, Mitigation Fee Act
    actions involving development fees, 551–52
    actions involving sewer/water/processing fees, 552
    challenges of development fees, 552–55
    challenges of sewer/water/processing fees, 555–56
    remedies and actions, 555–56
Map Act. See Subdivision Map Act
Marine Protection, Research and Sanctuaries Act of 1972 (U.S. Code), 208–09
master-planned community, 64
McAteer-Patris Act, 210–11, 264
McCarthy Legislation, 107–08
Measure H, 10
medical marijuana, 5
Mello-Roos Community Facilities Act (Gov't Code § 53311 *et seq.*), 354–56, 394, 394–95, 570, 573
    Map Act exemptions, 73
metes and bounds, defined, 573
metropolitan planning organization (MPOs), 452, 460–62
Metropolitan Transportation Commission (MTC), 460–62
Millennial Housing Commission, 409–10
"Million Solar Roofs" law of 2006 (SB1), 474
Mills Act (Gov't. Code § 50280 *et seq.*), 573. See also historic preservation

mineral resources, extraction/regulation, 15, 206–07, 441–42. See also conservation element
ministerial acts/decisions
    building permits as, 339
    CEQA exemptions, 140, 517
    city council, 6
    granting licenses as, 499–500
    initiative and referendum, 364–66
    initiative and referendum rulings, 362
    LAFCO role in, 404
    in mandate proceedings, 504–06, 509 & n8
    mandate proceedings challenges, 540
    zoning administrator authority, 499
ministerial permits, 18, 81, 472, 489
misdemeanors and infractions, 244, 487, 493–94
mitigated negative declaration, 573
mitigation
    CEQA project approval, 171–73
    defined, 573
    EIR considerations, 164–67
    EIR requirements, 154–55
    monitoring program, 573
    wetlands projects, 204–06
Mitigation Fee Act of 1987 (AB 1600)
    about the requirements, 322–23, 333–35
    basis for land use restrictions, 6
    development agreements, 283–84, 330–36
    development fees, 344–45, 481, 519
    in-lieu fee option, 438
    judicial review, 345–46
    legal challenges under, 554–60
    taxation or fee?, 346–47
mixed use development
    affordable housing requirements, 435
    CEQA exemptions, 144–47
    concessions and incentives, 426–27
    defined, 573
    disapproval of projects, 418–20
    environmental analysis, 198–99
    inclusionary housing requirements, 441
    transportation planning, 451–53
    zoning, 64, 573
mobile home/mobile home park
    conditional use permit, 57
    conversions, 5, 83–84
    defined, 573
    density bonuses, 425–27
    Map Act exemptions, 72–73, 81
    Map Act requirements, 76

621

rent control, 294, 306-07, 314-15
moratorium
  defined, 573
  development projects, 90-91, 317, 479, 491-92
  map extensions and stays, 91-92
  ordinance time limits, 5
  project approval, 32, 34, 479, 491-92
  project approval extensions, 32
  takings issues, 288-90, 295-98
  as temporary taking, 63, 288, 295-97
  tentative map time limits, 88
moratorium ordinances, 5, 316-17
multiple use, defined, 573
Municipal Improvement Act of 1913 (Pub. Res. Code § 26587), 355-56
Municipal Reorganization Act of 1977 (formerly Gov't. Code § 35000 et seq.), 387
municipal service reviews, 391-92

N

National Appliance Energy Conservation Act (U.S. Code), 470
National Environmental Policy Act of 1969 (U.S. Code), 65-66, 163, 198-99, 219-20, 574. See also environmental impact statement; Environmental Protection Agency
National Historic Preservation Act of 1966 (U.S. Code), 208-09, 252-55
National Register of Historic Places, 208-09, 252
Native American sites/artifacts, preservation, 142
Native American tribes/issues
  artifacts/site preservation, 11, 16, 28, 31
  casino gambling, 142, 146-47
  General Plan consultation, 576
  mitigation of casino impact, 372
  prohibitions against takings, 240-41
  zoning and protection of religious freedom, 52-54
  zoning regulation, 68-70
Natural Community Conservation Planning Act (Fish & Game Code § 2800 et seq.), 241-42
natural community conservation plans, 241-42, 342-43
navigable waterways, 266
  about regulatory authority, 180-81
  challenges in defining, 181-83
  court interpretations, 183-86

defining Corps jurisdiction, 182-83
  permit requirements, 198
  public access easement, 105
  refining jurisdictional boundaries, 186-87
  regulatory exemptions, 192-93
  state authority, 209-11. See also wetlands
Navigation Dredging Permit (Fish and Game Code § 5653), 210-11
negative declaration, defined, 574
new cities. See city/cities
nexus legislation. See Mitigation Fee Act
NIMBY (Not-In-My-Backyard), 14, 449-51
noise element, 10-11, 16, 18, 20-21. See also General Plan
Nollan/Dolan decisions
  constitutionality of dedications, 323-29
  constitutionality of impact fees, 329-33
  development agreements and, 282
  inclusionary housing before, 431-32
  inclusionary housing following, 432-35
  regulatory takings, 295
nonconformance/nonconforming uses
  enforcement actions, 496-97
  General Plan exemptions, 68
  judicial review, 60
  LAFCO issues, 400
  land uses, 574
  lot/lots, 574
  structures/buildings, 574
  tentative maps, 88
  transportation policy, 452
  zoning ordinances and, 42-43
  zoning/zoning regulation, 58-60
non-navigable waters. See wetlands
notice and hearing process. See mandate proceedings
notice of completion (NOC), 176, 407, 574
notice of determination (NOD), 173, 176-77, 517, 574
notice of preparation (NOP), 153-54, 156-57, 163, 176-77, 574
nuisance abatement/regulation, 58, 262, 276, 288, 310, 496

O

occupancy permit. See permits/permitting authority

Office of Planning and Research (Gov't. Code § 65025 et seq.), 11, 13, 23, 42, 113, 153-54, 392, 408, 415, 462
Office of Planning and Research, State Clearinghouse, 151, 576
off-site improvements
  amortization, 60
  CEQA compliance, 463-64
  dedications and fees, 337-38
  defined, 574
  EIR review, 153-54
  housing projects, 414-15, 427-30
  mitigation, 77, 164-66, 204-06
  private development projects, 269-71
  tentative map approval, 92, 95, 105-06
Oil Spill Prevention and Response Act, 263
"one bite of the apple" rule, 91, 111, 353
open meetings. See Ralph M. Brown Act
open space easement (Gov't. Code § 51070 et seq.), 114-15, 574
open space element, 10-11, 16, 425-26, 570. See also General Plan
ordinances (Gov't Code § 36900 et seq.)
  administrative/criminal sanctions, 495-98
  city/cities, 81
  defined, 574
  groundwater, 104
  historic preservation, 52-53
  moratorium ordinances, 316-17
  rent control ordinances, 314-15
  zoning challenges, 3, 153-54
Outdoor Advertising Act, 5
overlay zone, 16, 64, 254, 429n15, 574

P

parcel tax (special tax), 574
parcels/parcel map
  about the requirements, 76-77
  "plot" defined, 574-75
  preparation and filing, 126-27. See also lot/lots; Subdivision Map Act
parks/parkland dedications. See Quimby Act
partial taking. See taking/takings
payment in lieu of. See dedications and fees
peak-hour traffic, 156, 574
penalties
  enforcement of ESA, 218, 244
  land use regulation, 495-98
  Map Act, 78

violations of CWA, 184–85, 191, 212, 213–15. *See also* liability
performance standards
    CEQA guidelines, 463–64
    defined, 574
    EIR, 164–66
    EPA guidelines, 207–08
    mitigation impacts, 204–06
    Smart Growth, 449–51
    sustainable development, 464–65
Permit Streamlining Act (Gov't. Code § 65920 *et seq.*), 488–92
    defined, 574
    land use regulation, 6
    Map Act application to, 71–72
    site plan defined, 575
    tentative map approval, 85–86, 111–12
    tentative map time limits, 86–87
permits/permitting authority
    coastal zone, 260–62
    dedications and fees, 339–40
    defined, 574
    multi-family housing projects, 424–25
    occupancy permit defined, 574
    renewable energy projects, 471–74
    San Francisco Bay Conservation and Development Commission, 265
    storm water discharges, 266–68
    water issues, 186–87
phased development. *See* Development agreements
planned-unit development (PD/PUD)
    dedications and fees, 338–39
    defined, 574
    permit expiration, 93
    zoning/zoning regulation, 64
The Planner's Guide to Specific Plans (OPR, 2001), 37
Planners Pocket Guide (League of California Cities), 569
Planning Commission
    authority and composition, 7–8
    challenges/appeals of actions, 115–16, 316–17
    defined, 574
    development design review, 249–52
    EIR certification, 151, 172
    General Plan responsibilities, 17–18, 27–28, 273
    granting of variances, 54
    initiative and referendum process, 375–76
    map approval, 96, 106
    meeting requirements, 8
    notice and hearing recommendations, 478–79
    open meeting requirements, 484–87
    permit process, 492–93
    role of planning staff in advising, 8
    tentative map approval, 84, 86, 112–13
    zoning responsibilities, 44–45, 48, 63–64
Planning Director, 116, 574
plat (map), 80, 574
plot. *See* parcel/parcel map
point source pollution, 266, 575
police powers
    basis for land use regulation, 1–4
    dedications and fees, 320
    defined, 575
    initiative and referenda limitations, 368–74
    judicial review, 4–5
    land use regulation, 71
    state legislative preemption of, 5–6
    state statutory framework, 6
Political Reform Act (Gov't. Code § 81000 *et seq.*), 511n9, 572, 575. *See also* conflict of interest
pollution control, 147–50, 228–30, 394, 448, 451, 460, 463–64
Porter-Cologne Water Quality Control Act (Water Code § 13000 *et seq.*), 187, 209–11
ppm (parts per million), 575
prezoning, 61, 400–401, 575. *See also* zoning/zoning regulation
property rights, 86, 128–29, 133, 287, 315. *See also* rights of the regulated
property tax
    allocations defined, 575
    constitutional limitations, 309–10
    GHADs and, 355–56
    issue of double taxation, 336
    LAFCO issues, 396 & n9, 407
    lot line adjustments and, 79
    mapping exemptions/issues, 118–19
    Mills Act defined, 573
    Prop 13 defined, 575
    Prop 13 impacts, 346–54
    secondary units, 426–27
    termination of nonconforming uses, 59–60
    Williamson Act and, 255–58, 258, 473. *See also* infrastructure/infrastructure plan
Proposition 1A [1968] (Cal. Const. Art. XI and Art. XIII), 575
Proposition 13 [1978] (Cal. Const. Art. XIII A), 346–54, 575
Proposition 24 [2000] ("Let the Voters Decide Act"), 374
Proposition 59 (access to public records), 485n5
Proposition 62 [1986] (Gov't. Code § 53720 *et seq.*), 346–54, 575
Proposition 105 [1998] ("Public Right to Know Act"), 374
Proposition 111 [1990], 451–52
Proposition 218 [1996] (Cal. Const. Arts. XIII C & D), 346–54, 575
prostitution, 324
protection of rights. *See* civil rights actions/claims; religion/religious freedom; rights of the regulated
public (open) meetings. *See* Ralph M. Brown Act
public bidding, 142, 271–72
public domain, defined, 575
public hearings
    about police powers and, 4
    administrative actions/findings, 481–83
    Brown Act, 484–87
    CEQA compliance, 247–48
    citizens, protection of rights, 477–79
    defined, 575
    development agreements, 281
    development fees, 344, 348–51
    development projects, 492–93
    due process requirements, 316–17, 490–92
    endangered species, 222–23, 237–38
    General Plan adoption and amendment, 27
    initiative and referendum process, 375–76
    LAFCO actions, 391–92, 395–403
    LAFCO protest/reconsideration, 403–05
    Map Act, 103–04, 116–17, 135–37
    meeting requirements, 8
    ordinances and zoning, 39, 60, 62–64
    permits/permitting authority, 56–57, 197
    review of evidence, 479–80
    rules of evidence/procedural errors, 48–49
    tentative map approval, 85–87
    transportation planning, 452
    Williamson Act preserves, 255–58, 257
    zoning, 44–45, 47–48. *See also* mandate proceedings
public improvements
    bid requirements, 271–72

defined, 575
developer performance bond, 123-26
development fees, 343-45
facilities benefit assessment, 337-39
Map Act standards, 105-06
Mitigation Fee Act and, 330-36, 336-37
tentative map approval, 87-93
Public Records Act, 541, 575
Public Records Act (Gov't. Code § 6250 et seq.), 541, 575
"Public Right to Know Act" (Prop 105), 374
public welfare, concept of
growth management and, 324
police powers, 1
regulatory takings, 292-93
review of agency actions, 501, 505
use of initiative and referendum, 368-74
violations and penalties, 213-15
zoning ordinances and, 40-41
publication requirements (Gov't. Code § 6000 et seq.), 575

Q

quasi-judicial acts/decisions
challenges, 536
city council, 6
Coastal Commission, 258-59
denial of due process, 498-500
differences from legislative decisions, 504-05
due process requirements, 44-45, 46, 512
findings requirements, 481-83
legislative acts compared to, 316-17
mandate proceedings under Section 1094.5, 507-08
variances and permits, 54-55, 64
"Quick List" (Senate Local Government Committee), 569
Quimby Act (Gov't. Code § 66477), 101-02, 338-39, 575

R

Ralph M. Brown Act [Open Meeting Act] (Gov't Code § 54950 et seq.)
about legislative intent, 484-86
appeal process, 86-87
applicability to land use decisions, 520-21
closed session exemptions, 281
defined, 570
deliberative process privilege, 540-41
land use regulation, 6
legislative intent, 485
open meeting requirements, 8, 477, 486-87
procedural errors, 479. See also Bagley-Keene Open Meeting Law
redevelopment. See Community Redevelopment Law
Redevelopment Act, 505
referendum. See initiative and referendum
regional transportation planning. See transportation planning
regulation. See rights of the regulated
Regulatory Guidance Letters (RGLs), 198
regulatory takings. See taking/takings
religion/religious freedom
claims of infringement, 52-54
exemptions from preservation laws, 254
free exercise of, 240-41
historic preservation exemptions, 254
sale of church property, 532
subject to takings, 296n1
zoning and protection of churches, 50
Religious Freedom and Restoration Act of 1993 [RFRA] (U.S. Code), 52
Religious Land Use and Institutionalized Persons Act of 2000 [RLUIPA] (U.S. Code), 52-54
renewable energy
about state goals, 471-72
barriers, effort to lower, 472-74
biofuels, 473
geothermal projects, 19, 472n25, 474
solar energy easements, 106, 258
solar energy projects, 83, 466, 472-74, 575
wind-energy projects, 83, 472-73
Renewable Portfolio Standard (RPS), 471-72
rent control
Costa-Hawkins (anti-rent control) Act, 439-40
housing conversions, 81-82, 276-77
police powers, 2, 3
takings issues, 290-95, 306-07, 314-16
tentative map approval, 94

responsible agency, 148, 407-08, 546, 575
restrictive covenant. See covenants, conditions & restrictions
reuse, defined, 575
Revenue and Taxation Code, enforcement actions, 498
revenue bonds. See bonds/bonding approval
rezoning. See zoning/zoning regulation
rights of the regulated
about property owners and, 477
Brown Act requirements, 484-87
evidence, presentation and review, 479-80
ex parte contacts, 487-88
findings requirements, 481-83
notices and adjudicatory hearings, 477-79
Permit Streamlining Act, 488-92
procedural requirements, 492-93
prosecution of fraud and misrepresentation, 493
separating prosecutorial and adjudicatory functions, 483-84. See also due process and equal protection
rights-of-way, 74, 80, 87, 108, 118, 122-23, 126, 575
riparian lands/habitat, 15, 187, 206-07, 575
Rivers and Harbors Act of 1899, 180-83, 210-11
"run with the land" restrictions, 54-55, 575

S

Sacramento Area Council of Governments, 460-62
Sacramento-San Joaquin Valley, 18, 22, 23, 115, 278-79
zoning ordinances, 43
safety element, General Plan
about map requirements, 120-23
about the requirements, 10-11
components, 16-18
flooding and natural hazards, 465
resources issues, 424-25
testing the adequacy, 141-43. See also General Plan
same-sex marriage, 499-500
San Diego Association of Governments (SANDAG), 460-62
San Francisco Bay Area Rapid Transit District, 66

San Francisco Bay Conservation and Development Commission [BCDC] (Gov't Code § 66600 et seq.), 167-69, 179, 209-10, 210-11, 264-65, 474, 569. See also California Coastal Commission
San Joaquin MPOs, 460-62
San Joaquin Valley Air Pollution Control District (SJVAPCD), 463-64, 554
SB 375 (2008), 15
scenic easements/zoning, 180, 255, 281, 324, 575
school districts
    developer fees, 575
    exemption from local regulations, 67
    facilities fees, 340-42
    site dedications, 103
second unit ["granny unit"] (Gov't. Code § 65852), 80, 422, 425-26, 501, 572, 575. See also accessory building/structure
Section 1983 (42 U.S.C. § 1983), 311-14
Senate Bill 1 (2006), 474
Senate Bill 97 (2007), 462
Senate Bill 221 (2001), 453-58
Senate Bill 375 (2008)
    about passage and authority, 460-62
    affordable housing and, 15, 462
    CEQA and, 464-66
    sustainable communities strategy, 460-62
    traffic model guidelines, 461-62
Senate Bill 610 (2001), 453-58
setback requirements, 425-26, 471-74, 575
sewer facilities. See drainage and sewer facilities
sex-oriented business. See adult entertainment business
site plan, 492-93, 575
Smart Growth
    about sustainability and, 447
    barriers to, 449-50
    housing and, 409-10, 427-30
    incorporation into California law, 449-51
    principles of, 449. See also growth management
Soil Erosion and Sediment Control Plan, 194, 355, 575
soil investigations and reports (Gov't. Code § 66490-91), 104-05, 164-65. See also Geologic Hazard Abatement District
solar energy. See renewable energy
Solar Rights Act of 2000, 473-74

solid waste management, 84-85, 172-73, 183, 374, 575
    permit requirements, 488-89
    specific plan requirements, 35
South Coast Air Quality Management District, 156-57, 463-64
Southern California Association of Governments, 460-62
special assessment. See benefit assessment
special districts. See districts/special districts
special tax
    challenges, 319, 321, 555-56
    defined, 576
    financing public facilities, 354-56
    financing school construction, 340n11
    Jarvis Initiatives impacts, 346-54, 352-54, 373-74
    parcel tax, 574
special use permit. See conditional use permit
specific plan (Gov't. Code § 65300 et seq.)
    about content and requirements, 35-36
    additional guidance for, 37
    adoption/amendment procedures, 36
    consistency with CEQA, 36-37
    defined, 576
    judicial review, 37
    zoning/zoning ordinances, 64. See also General Plan
sphere of influence
    boundary change proposals, 397, 400
    city authority as, 278-79
    defined, 576
    developing a city/district plan, 390-91
    LAFCOs as, 390-91
    "real party in interest," 535-36
spot zoning, 576
State Clearinghouse, 151, 576
State Historical Building Code (SHBC), 253
State Zoning Law (Gov't. Code § 65800 et seq.), 39, 44, 62, 64. See also zoning/zoning regulation
statutes of limitations
    CEQA challenges/exemptions, 147, 173, 408
    challenges of fees, 554-55
    deadlines for bringing actions, 516-18

    development agreements, 278, 284
    EIR challenges, 176-77
    ESA challenges, 242-43
    harmonization with other statutes, 519, 522-24
    mandate proceedings, 508
    map approval, 116-18, 284
    naming parties of interest, 535-36
    zoning challenges, 42-43
statutory rights. See rights of the regulated
stays and injunctions
    endangered species emergency listing, 224
    endangered species requirements, 235-36, 236-37, 243-44
    initiative and referendum, 367, 377
    mandate proceedings, 537, 545-46
    nuisance claims, 310
    permanent vs. mandatory, 548
Sterling Act (Educ. Code § 17620), 334-36, 340-42
stock cooperatives, 71, 76-77, 81-82, 102-03, 110-11, 121-22, 492-93
stormwater. See water issues
Strategic Growth Council, 11
Strategic Lawsuit Against Public Participation Act (anti-SLAPP statute), 556-58
Streambed Alteration Agreement (Fish and Game Code § 1602), 210-11
streets
    arterial, 576
    collector, 576
    dedications, 103
    local, 576
strip zone, defined, 576
Subdivided Lands Act (Bus. & Prof. Code § 11000 et seq.), 72, 78, 576
Subdivision Map Act (Gov't. Code § 66410 et seq.)
    a subdivision, as defined by statute, 73-76
    about the goals/powers, 71-73
    antiquated subdivisions, 133-37
    appeals and judicial review, 115-18
    CEQA requirements, 109-10
    certificate of compliance, 492, 570
    city incorporation, 99-100
    city land annexation, 99-100
    consistency, General Plan, 23-26
    counting parcels, 77-79
    determining map requirements, 73-74
    enforcement, remedies and compliance, 129-31
    exclusions and reversions, 131-32

exemptions and waivers, 79–84
exemptions for solar projects, 472
General Plan requirements, 108
grandfathering provisions, 71, 133, 134
legality, presumption of, 137
map approval, conditions to, 100–112
map approval/denial, grounds for, 112–15
map corrections and amendments, 127–29
merger/unmerger of parcels, 135–37
refunds and reconveyances, 112
security instruments (bonds, deposits, liens), 123–26. See also final subdivision map; parcel map; tentative subdivision map; vesting tentative map
subdivisions
  dedications and fees, 338–39
  defined, 73–76, 576
  final subdivision map, 572
  mobile home park conversions, 72–73
  parcel map, 574
  quartering, 77
  remainder parcels, 78–79
  successive subdivisions, 77–78
Suisun Marsh Preservation Act, 227, 265
summary of updates from previous volumes, xvii
supplemental environmental impact report (SEIR), 174–75
Surface Mining and Reclamation Act [SMARA] (Pub. Res. Code § 2712), 29
Sustainable Communities and Climate Protection Act of 2008 (SB375), 447, 460–62. See also SB 375
sustainable communities strategy, 460–62
sustainable development
  about General Plan requirements, 11
  CEQA compliance, 462–66
  components, 447
  global warming/climate change, 459–60, 462, 474–76
  Green building and, 467–71
  growth management and, 448–49
  housing projects, 462
  reduction of emissions, 460–62
  renewable energy, 471–74
  Smart Growth, 449–51
  transportation policy, 451–53
  water supply planning and conservation, 453–59. See also development projects

T

taking/takings
  compensation, 300–320, 309–10
  conditional use permit (special use permit), 57–58
  defined, 576
  denial of claims, 303–10
  endangered species actions, 237–41
  flood control, 310–11
  incidental take permits, 241–42, 247–48
  judicial rulings, 296–300
  just compensation, 117, 287–90, 292, 295, 319, 334–36
  legislative vs. adjudicatory authority, 316–17
  loss of economic use of property, 288–90
  loss of physical property, 287–88
  loss that goes too far, 290–95
  loss through exactions, 295
  Nollan/Dolan decisions, 323–29
  Section 1983 civil rights actions, 311–14
  segmentation/relevant parcel issue, 302–03
  substantive due process claims, 314–16
  temporary takings, 295–96
temporary restraining orders (TRO), 545–46
tentative map
  about the requirements, 76–77, 84–87
  defined, 576
  initial life span and extensions, 87–93
  time limits, 86–87. See also Subdivision Map Act; vesting tentative map
tolling period/agreements, 88–92, 523–24, 538, 549
Tort Claims Act (Gov't. Code § 810-996.6), 355–56, 564–65
traditional mandate proceedings. See mandate proceedings
transfer of development rights. See development rights
transit facilities. See transportation planning
transitional area, defined, 576
transitional land use, defined, 576
transportation planning
  "Complete Streets" program, 452–53
  Congestion Management Program, 451–53
  facilities dedications and fees, 104
  housing and, 15, 412, 418, 461–62
  LAFCO and, 400
  peak-hour traffic, 156, 574
  sustainable development and, 460–62
  transit facilities, 103, 122–23
  trip generation, 334–36, 344–45, 576
transportation systems management (TSM), 576
tribes/tribal issues. See Native American tribes/issues
turbidity. See water quality

U

Uniform Building Code, 253
unimproved land, distinction from improved land, 73–74
unusual circumstances, CEQA, 145–47, 465
updates from previous volumes, xvii
Urban Agriculture Incentive Zones Act (Gov't Code § 51040 et seq.), 258
urban decay (blighted area), 49, 158, 259, 569
urban growth boundary, 370, 374, 448–49
Urban Land Institute, 449–50
Urban Land Institute Smart Growth Initiative, 449
urban service area/limit line, 400–402, 576
Urban Water Management Plan (UWMP), 453, 458
U.S. Army Corps of Engineers
  definition of wetland and other waters, 181–83, 188–89
  dredging and discharge regulation, 190–93
  joint guidance with EPA, 183–86
  operation under CWA Section 404, 200–206
  operation under EPA Guidelines, 198–99
  permit process, 193–98
  regulatory authority, 180–81
  Regulatory Guidance Letters, 198. See also Clean Water Act
U.S. Constitution
  Commerce Clause, 181–83
  Contracts Clause, 353–54
  First Amendment and zoning regulation, 49–52

Fourteenth Amendment, 313, 336–37
Full Faith and Credit Clause, 306
Property Clause, 65–66
Supremacy Clause, 5–6, 65.66
Takings Clause, 287, 321n.2
U.S. Department of Agriculture (USDA), 209–10
U.S. Government
 applicability of local zoning regulation, 65–66
 endangered species enforcement, 242–44
 enforcement of Clean Water Act, 211–15
 regulation of Indian affairs, 68–70
U.S. Supreme Court
 denial of economic use, 302–03
 denial of just compensation, 305–10
 development rights vs. privilege, 320–21
 due process requirements, 86, 317
 judicial review of police powers, 4–5
 land use regulation, 2–3
 Nollan/Dolan decisions, 323–31
 police powers defined, 1
 regulatory takings, 290–95, 295–96, 320
 ripeness requirement, 311–14
 Supremacy Clause, 5–6
 takings, denial of economic use, 292
 takings, denial of use, 305–06
 termination of nonconforming use, 60
U.S. Survey maps and land patents, 134
use, defined, 576
use permits. *See* permits/permitting authority

V

validation actions, 403, 408, 554–56, 559–60. *See also* invalidation actions
validation suit, 576
variances, 54–56, 576
vertical consistency, v, 23–26, 370–71. *See also* horizontal consistency
vested rights
 Avco rule, 273–77
 comparison of California statutes, 283–84
 defined, 576
 development agreement, 277–83
 legislative vs. adjudicatory authority, 316–17
 map approval, 93–94

standards in land use decisions, 509
 takings vs. due process claims, 315–16
 zoning changes, 112
vesting tentative map
 about the purpose/preparation, 283
 about the requirements, 84–86
 approval, 490
 background and procedures, 94–99
 comparison to development agreements, 284–85
 extensions and expiration, 87–93
 incorporation proceedings, 99–100
 map approval and development rights, 93–94. *See also* tentative map

W

wages/wage rates, 269–71, 368
Wal-Mart
 challenge to city zoning, 3
 challenges to EIR, 153, 158
 exemption from CEQA, 517
warrants, 496–97
water issues
 detention basin defined, 571
 EIR considerations, 160–61
 EIR requirements, 154–55
 groundwater recharge, 104
 impervious surface drainage, 268–69, 326–27, 572
 land use and, 453–59, 458–59
 Map Act approval, 102
 riparian lands defined, 575
 riparian lands/habitat, 15, 187, 206–07
 SB 610 and SB 221 comparison, 453–58
 stormwater, 266–69, 526, 576
 subdivision (Gov't. Code § 66473.7), 102, 278–79. *See also* development projects; flood control; wetlands
water quality
 control and regulation of stormwater, 265–66
 effluent, 196, 207–08, 267, 571
 General Permits for storm water discharges, 266–69
 graywater standards/regulation, 458–59
 point source pollution, 266, 575
 turbidity, 267, 576
water table, 576
wetlands, Federal programs/regulations
 about the role and function, 179–80

brief history of, 180–81
 California response to, 187–88
 challenges of defining, 181–83
 court interpretation, 183–86
 delineation of, 189–91
 dredging and discharge issues, 190–93
 enforcement actions, 211–13
 environmental analysis under CWA Section 404, 200–206
 environmental analysis under NEPA, 198–99
 investigations and corrective actions, 213–14
 land development process and, 214–15
 permit process, 206–09
 permitting process, 193–98
 scientific/technical definitions, 188–89
 violations and penalties, 213–15
wetlands, State programs/regulations
 adaptation to Federal changes, 187–88
 California statutes, 209–12
 definitions, 189–90
wetlands hydrology, 188–89, 189, 233, 268–69, 572
Williamson Act (Gov't. Code § 51200 *et seq.*)
 agricultural lands designation, 82–83
 agricultural lands preservation, 255–58
 contract cancellation, 257–58
 defined, 576
 farmland security zones, 258
 renewable energy projects, 473
wind-energy. *See* renewable energy

Z

zero lot line, 577
zero net energy, 468
"zero trash" water run-off standard, 147–50
"zero-increase" standards, greenhouse gases, 161–62
zoning administrator, 7, 55–58, 499, 506, 517, 520, 529, 534, 538, 577
zoning amendment, 569
zoning/zoning regulation (Gov't. Code § 65800 *et seq.*)
 adoption/amendment, 41, 46–48, 569
 agricultural lands, 82–83

applicability to federal/state lands, 65-66
applicability to Indian lands, 68-70
applicability to local agencies/districts, 66-68
California Supreme Court, 136-37
conditional rezoning, 570
conditional zoning, 63-64
consistency with Airport Land Use Plan, 43-44
consistency with the General Plan, 42-43
dedications and fees, 339-40
defined, 39, 577
downzoning, 292, 303, 305, 418, 448, 571
due process requirements, 44-45, 58
exclusionary restrictions, 65, 66, 431-32, 448, 572
exercise of police powers, 2-5
fiscal zoning, 449-51
form-based zoning, 13, 572
housing density, 571
incentive zoning, 425-26, 572
inclusionary housing, 64-65, 572
initiative and referendum process, 48
interim ordinance zoning, 573
interim urgency ordinance zoning, 61-63
interim zoning, 63, 573
judicial review, 39-41
Map Act application to, 71-72
mixed use, 573
nonconforming uses, 58-60, 574
overlay requirements, 574
permits/permitting authority, 488-92, 570
planned-unit development, 64
prezoning and form-based zoning, 61, 400-401, 575
protection of religious freedom, 52-54
public welfare, relationship to, 41-42
regulation of adult businesses, 49-52
rules of evidence/procedural errors, 48-49
setback, 575
spot zoning, 576
standards, sufficiency/clarity, 45-46
unincorporated territory, 575
variances, 54-56, 576